W9-CBN-290

Choices in Sexuality

Susan L. McCammon
East Carolina University

David Knox
East Carolina University

Caroline Schacht
East Carolina University

WEST PUBLISHING COMPANY

Minneapolis/St. Paul *New York* *Los Angeles* *San Francisco*

Artists: C.H. Wooley & Associates, pp. 196, 213, 215, 216, 226, 229, 549, 556, 583, 797, 800, 802, 808, 838, 887

Sally Krahn, pp. 336, 338, 380–383, 385, 386b, 387a, 431, 544
Carlisle Communications, pp. 30, 244, 390, 397, 505, 517, 616, 626
All chapter opening sketches by Honoria

Copy editor: Marilynn Taylor
Cover & text designer: Roslyn Stendahl, Dapper Design
Compositor: Carlisle Communications
Cover image: © Cathleen Toelke
Index: Schroeder Indexing Services

WEST'S COMMITMENT TO THE ENVIRONMENT
In 1906, West Publishing Company began recycling materials left over from the production of books. This began a tradition of efficient and responsible use of resources. Today, up to 95 percent of our legal books and 70 percent of our college and school texts are printed on recycled, acid-free stock. West also recycles nearly 22 million pounds of scrap paper annually—the equivalent of 181,717 trees. Since the 1960s, West has devised ways to capture and recycle waste inks, solvents, oils, and vapors created in the printing process. We also recycle plastics of all kinds, wood, glass, corrugated cardboard, and batteries, and have eliminated the use of styrofoam book packaging. We at West are proud of the longevity and the scope of our commitment to the environment.

Production, Prepress, Printing and Binding by West Publishing Company.

Printed in the United States of America

00 99 98 97 96 95 94 93 8 7 6 5 4 3 2 1 0

Library of Congress Cataloging-in-Publication Data
McCammon, Susan.
Choices in sexuality / Susan McCammon, David Knox, Caroline Schacht.
p. cm.
Includes index.
ISBN 0-314-0-01267-2 (hard)
1. Sex I. Knox, David, 1943– . II. Schacht, Caroline. III. Title.
HQ21.M4627 1993
306.7—dc20

92-38235
CIP

PHOTOS
6 ©Jeane-Claude LeJuene/Stock Boston **12** ©Sara Krulwich/NYT Pictures **14** ©Len Speier/Brooklyn Image Group **16** ©Christopher Brown/Stock Boston **17** The Bettmann Archive **21** ©Nik Kleinberg/Stock Boston **22** ©Frank Siteman/Stock Boston **28** ©Bob Daemmrich/Stock Boston **31** ©Barbara Alper/Stock Boston **32** ©Herb Snitzer/Stock Boston **41** ©Owen Franken/Stock Boston **43** ©Jim Anderson/Stock Boston **52** The Bettmann Archive **54** ©Culver Pictures **56** Richard Redgrave; R.A. (1804 1888) "The Outcast", diploma work 1851, oil on canvas 31 x 14 in. copyright ©Royal Academy of Arts, London **58** The Museum of Questionable Medical Devices, Minneapolis/St. Paul **60** ©Barbara Alper/Stock Boston **79** The Bettmann Archive **81** ©D. Maybury Lewis/Anthro-Photo **82** UPI/Bettmann **83** ©C. Seghers II/H. Armstrong Roberts **88** ©Torin Boyd **92** ©Puttkamer/Zefa/H. Armstrong Roberts **93** ©Rick Smolan/Stock Boston **103** ©Sarah Blaffer Hrdy/Anthro-Photo **116** ©Barbara Alper/Stock Boston **122** ©Karen Mustian **127** ©Jerry Howard/Stock Boston **132** ©A. Panico/Brooklyn Image Group **133** ©Peter Menzel/Stock Boston **150** UPI/Bettmann **159** ©Frans Lanting/Minden Pictures

To Mike, Andrew, and Reagin
To Lisa and Dave
To Emily, Herb, and Isabelle

Preface

The theme of this text is to encourage you to take charge of your life by making deliberate and informed choices in regard to your sexuality. Sexual decision-making is not completed once you've decided whether or when to have sexual activity with a partner; you will continue to make sexuality-related choices throughout your lifespan. These choices have the potential to enhance your enjoyment in life (as in improving communication with a partner, resolving a sexual dysfunction, or providing meaningful sexuality education for your child), or to challenge your enjoyment of life (as in risking exposure to the virus which causes AIDS).

The text is divided into six parts. Part I, Making Sexual Choices, emphasizes that much of our sexuality is based on choices we make, personal and social values, and cultural norms regarding sexuality. Part II, Background for Sexual Choices, provides us with information about our anatomy, physiological functioning, and sexual response patterns that form the basis for many sexual decisions. A discussion of these topics is preceded by a review of the research and theory that academicians use in predicting and understanding sexual choices and their outcomes. Part III, Contexts of Sexual Choices, begins by exploring gender roles—an aspect of our social and psychological life that both influences and is influenced by our sexuality. Part III is also concerned with the individual, interpersonal, and sexual-orientation contexts of sexuality. The context of life span is also discussed to emphasize that many sexual choices are influenced by where we are in the life cycle. Part IV, Enhancement Choices, emphasizes communication, love, and resolving sexual dysfunctions as mechanisms sometimes associated with enhancing one's sexuality. Part V, Health Choices, looks at health and sex, paraphilias, HIV infection and other sexually transmitted diseases, and abuses of sexuality. Part VI, Reproductive Choices, examines some choices that confront individuals in regard to planning for children, the use of birth control, abortion, and sex education for themselves and their children.

The following unique features of the text have been developed with one goal in mind: to provide you with a basis for making the best possible sexual choices.

Choices

Each chapter concludes with a special section on specific choices that are relevant to the content of that chapter. Examples of the sexual choices examined in this text include: "Is Honesty about Sex Always the Best Policy?" "Deciding about Intercourse in a New Relationship," and "Choosing a Method of Birth Control."

Self-Assessment Inventories

Every chapter includes an inventory or scale for self-assessment on a topic discussed in that chapter. For example, in Chapter 1, we discuss the free will-versus-determinism debate in regard to choices. Following the discussion, we provide a Free Will-Determinism Scale, which lets students assess their own belief about the nature of choices and, in many cases, compare how they scored with others. Similarly, in Chapter 11, Sexual Orientation, we provide an Index of Attitudes toward Homosexuals.

Perspectives

To emphasize the research, theoretical, historical, and public policy concerns of the text, we present a Perspective section in each chapter. In this section, we discuss a topic relevant to the content of the chapter, focusing on research findings, a theoretical perspective, an historical view, and/or policy issues. Examples of Perspectives in this text include "Are Adolescents Competent to Make Independent Choices? (Research and Policy Perspective) in Chapter 1, "Some Not So Helpful 'Advice' from 'Experts' on Masturbation" (Historical Perspective) in Chapter 9, "Alpha and Beta Bias in Gender Theories" (Theoretical Perspective) in Chapter 8, and "Gay and Lesbian Life on Campus" (Policy Perspective) in Chapter 11.

Considerations

Sprinkled throughout the text are short Consideration sections. In these sections, we provide insights, implications, explanations, and applications of material presented in the text.

The following Consideration appears in Chapter 11, Sexual Orientation:

> **CONSIDERATION:** The sexual-orientation image a person projects to the world and the sexual behavior in which the person engages are sometimes different. Of 52 men (participating in a blood donor study group) who labeled themselves as heterosexual, almost a quarter (23%) had sex with both women and men (in the last two years) and 6% had sex exclusively with men. Seventeen percent were celibate. Of 95 men who self-labeled themselves as homosexual, 83% had sex exclusively with men. However, 6% had sex with both men and women, and 11% were celibate (Doll, Petersen, White, Johnson, Ward, & the Blood Donor Study Group, 1992, p. 5).

National Data

Because the study of human sexuality is a social science, we present data throughout the text as reported in various professional publications. When the data are based on national representative samples or when they represent national official statistics, we present them as illustrated from Chapter 12 (see National Data in margin).

NATIONAL DATA: In a national sample of 761 married adults, 98% reported that they had had intercourse with only one person (their spouse) in the last 12 months (Smith, 1991). This percentage is in contrast to a national sample of 205 never-married individuals of whom only 52% reported that they had had only one sexual partner in the last 12 months (Greeley, Michael, & Smith, 1990).

These data suggest that most married people are monogamous most of the time (in contrast to popular media, which often emphasize the infidelity of spouses) and that unmarried people are more likely to be at risk for contracting HIV and other STDs because of a higher number of sexual partners.

Exhibits

The exhibits, presented in each chapter, provide interesting discussions or illustrations relevant to the topic of the respective chapter. For example, in Chapter 9, Individual Sexuality, we discuss "Body Image and Eating Disorders" (Exhibit 9.1). Other exhibits in this text include "The Origins of Mouth Kissing" (Exhibit 10.2), "Psychological Reactions to Genital Herpes" (Exhibit 18.1), "Sex Surrogate Therapy for a Person with Severe Cerebral Palsy" (Exhibit 16.2), and "Date Rape: One Woman's Experience" (Exhibit 19.1).

Acknowledgements

Choices in Sexuality is a result of the work of many people. Peter Marshall, executive editor, provided cutting-edge information in regard to the critical issues in sexuality and how faculty and students want these issues addressed. Jane Bass provided quick turnaround on reviews and kept the project on schedule. Angela Musey secured permissions, and Debra A. Meyer served as production editor in St. Paul.

We would also like to thank Kim Tripp for her typing of several drafts of the manuscript; Judy Holt for managing numerous details in the manuscript, from researching Medline and Psychological Abstracts on various topics to ensuring accurate references; Lee Ann Taggart, Gracie Geohagen, Shartra Syllivant, Philip Cook, and Michelle Kinard for conducting library research on an array of sexuality topics; Shartra Syllivant for help in obtaining permissions; Susan Moran for ensuring the accuracy of quotes from English literature; Mary Elesha–Adams and Suzanne Kellerman for sharing their expertise and resources on sexual health; Bob Sammons for providing recent medical information on the treatment of sexual dysfunction; Jack Turner for his insights in regard to human relationships; Jim Walters for his insights on the social construction of sexuality; Tim Britton for his research on extradyadic sexuality/sexual addiction; Boice Daugherty for his limerick; Pat Dunn for sharing materials; Tom Martoccia and Michael Poteat for bringing articles to our attention; Murray Kolknicker for sharing his resources on men's issues; Carol Thompson for sharing her resources on rape statistics; Jill Williams for sharing her medical resources; Stewart LaNeave for his insights on religion and sexual values; Reba Faison for her identification of NOW information; Bruce Grimes and Geoffery Kaiser for their resources and insights into long-term gay relationships; Pat Guyette and Lynne Mallison (and their staff members) for their invaluable help with interlibrary services; the reference and circulation staff members of Joyner and Health Sciences Libraries, the generous professionals and organizations who gave permission for reproduction of materials; and to our students.

I, Susan McCammon, would also like to thank the excellent professors I've had at Drury College and the University of South Carolina (especially Murray Vincent, EdD, for his course in teaching family life education) who gave me a foundation for teaching, research, and clinical-community practice. My colleagues at East Carolina University in the Departments of Psychology and Women's Studies have been especially supportive and encouraging.

We would like to acknowledge and thank the following reviewers for their valuable critiques and suggestions:

Betty Baker
Southeastern Louisiana University

Betsy Bergen
Kansas State University

Sandra Caron
University of Maine

Robert Castleberry
University of South Carolina—Sumter

Peter Chroman
College of San Mateo

Edwin Cook
University of Alabama—Birmingham

Ann Engin
University of South Carolina

Lee Frank
Community College of Allegheny County

Kathi Kibler
Auburn University

Roberta Ogletree
Southern Illinois University

Shirley Ogletree
Southwest Texas State University

Robert Pollack
University of Georgia

Jack Smolensky
San Jose State University

Gary Steggell
California State University—San Bernardino

Parris Watts
University of Missouri

Susan McCammon
David Knox
Caroline Schacht

Brief Contents

PART I Making Sexual Choices 1

CHAPTER 1 Choices in Sexuality: A First View 3
CHAPTER 2 Values in Sexuality 39
CHAPTER 3 Cultural Variations in Human Sexuality 77

PART II Background for Sexual Choices 111

CHAPTER 4 Research in Human Sexuality 113
CHAPTER 5 Theories of Sexuality 157
CHAPTER 6 Sexual Anatomy and Physiology 189
CHAPTER 7 Sexual Response 223

PART III Contexts of Sexual Choices 263

CHAPTER 8 Gender Roles 265
CHAPTER 9 Individual Sexuality 317
CHAPTER 10 Interpersonal Sexuality 351
CHAPTER 11 Sexual Orientation 395
CHAPTER 12 Sexuality Across the Life Span 443

PART IV Enhancement Choices 475

CHAPTER 13 Communication and Sexuality 477
CHAPTER 14 Love and Sexuality 501
CHAPTER 15 Sexual Dysfunctions and Sex Therapy 531

PART V Health Choices 575

CHAPTER 16 Physical Health and Sexuality 577
CHAPTER 17 Paraphilias and Sexuality 607
CHAPTER 18 HIV Infection and Other STDs 639
CHAPTER 19 Abuses and Commercial Uses of Sexuality 677

PART VI Reproductive Choices 731

CHAPTER 20 Planning Children and Birth Control 733
CHAPTER 21 Pregnancy and Childbirth 781
CHAPTER 22 Abortion and Other Pregnancy Outcomes 831
CHAPTER 23 Sex Education 867

Contents

Preface v

PART I Making Sexual Choices 1

CHAPTER 1
Choices in Sexuality: A First View 3

Free Will and Determinism: A Philosophical Inquiry 4
- **Exhibit 1.1** Alternative Views on Free Will and Determinism 5

The Nature of Sexual Choices 6
- Choices Are Continually Being Made 6
- Not to Decide Is to Decide 6
- Choices Involve Tradeoffs 7
- **Self-Assessment:** Free Will and Determinism Scale 8
- Some Choices Are Dichotomous, Others Are Not 8
- Most Choices Are Revocable, Some Are Not 9
- **Exhibit 1.2** More than 100 Choices in Sexuality 10
- **Research and Policy Perspective:** Are Adolescents Competent to Make Independent Choices? 11
- Choices Are Influenced by Social Context and Cultural Forces 15
- Drug Use Influences Choices 15

Elements of Human Sexuality 16
- Anatomy and Physiology 16
- Sexual Self-Concept 17
- Behavior 18
- Cognitions 19
- Values 19
- Emotions 20
- Relationships 20
- Variability 21

Sexual Myths 22
- Myth 1: Most Americans Are Well-Informed about Sexuality 23
- Myth 2: Good Sex Equals Intercourse and Orgasm 23
- **Exhibit 1.3** What College Students Want to Know about Sex 24
- Myth 3: The Double Standard Is Dead 24
- Myth 4: Sex Therapy for Lack of Orgasm Doesn't Do Any Good 26
- Myth 5: Women Secretly Want to Be Raped 26

Social Changes and Their Effects on Sexuality 26
- Sex in the Media 27
- Birth Control 27
- Divorce 28
- Cohabitation 29
- Changes in the Workplace 29
- Women's Movement and Men's Movement 30
- HIV Infection 32
- Technology 33

Choices 34
- Choose Deliberately or by Default? 34
- Human Sexuality: An Academic, Personal, or Career Search? 34
- Choose Tolerance for the Choices and Life-styles of Others? 34

CHAPTER 2
Values in Sexuality 39

Definitions and Functions of Sexual Values 40
- Self-Identity Function 40
- Mate Selection Function 41

Alternative Sexual Value Perspectives 42
- Absolutism 42
- **Exhibit 2.1** Characteristics of Absolutists 44
- Relativism 44
- Hedonism 45
- Are Sexual Values Changing? 45

Historical Roots of Sexual Values 46
- **Research and Policy Perspective:** Abortion Attitudes Reflect Relativism 46
- Jewish Heritage 49
- Christian Heritage 50
- The Puritans 52
- Asia, the Arab World, and Islam 53
- The Victorians 55
- Scientific Sexual Ideologies 56

Influences Affecting Sexual Values in U.S. Society 59
- Challenges to Traditional Gender Roles 59
- Religious Values in the 1990s 60

Influences of Values and Religion on Sexual Emotions, Attitudes, and Behaviors 62
- Sexual Guilt 62
- **Self-Assessment:** Revised Mosher Guilt Inventory, Sex Guilt Subscale 64

NOTE: Each chapter concludes with Summary, Key Terms, and References.

Exhibit 2.2 How Guilty Would You Feel If. . .? 66
Values and Religious Orientation 67
Sex and the Law 68
Private Rights versus Social Morality 68
Should Such Sex Laws Exist? 68
A Continuum of Sex Offenses and Sex Laws 68
Incidence of Sexual Behavior against the Law 69
Reproductive Issues and the Law 70
Choices 71
Is Honesty Always the Best Policy? 71
Choose to Have Intercourse with a New Partner? 71
Choose to Override Culturally Prestructured Choices? 73

CHAPTER 3
Cultural Variations in Human Sexuality 77
Cross-Cultural Research in Human Sexuality 78
Ethnography and Ethnology 78
Problems in Cross-Cultural Research in Human Sexuality 79
What is "Normal" Sexual Behavior? 80
Definitions of "Normal" Are Based on Various Criteria 80
Definitions of "Normal" Sexual Behavior Vary across Time 82
Ethnocentrism versus Cultural Relativism 83
Cross-Cultural Variations in Sexuality 84
Sexual Intercourse 84
Self-Assessment: Sex Knowledge and Attitude Test, Part 1 85
Premarital Sex 88
Extramarital Sex 89
Incest 90
Menstruation 91
Homosexual Sex 91
Gender Roles 92
Cross-Cultural Perspective: Neither Male nor Female 93
Permissive and Restrictive Cultural Contexts 95
Exhibit 3.1 U.S. Sexuality in Black and White 96
The Mangaians: A Permissive Context 96
The Inhabitants of Inis Beag: A Restrictive Context 96
Some Culture-Specific Sex Practices 97
Female Genital Mutilation 97
Male Genital Mutilation 98
Polygamy 99
Mate Selection: A Cross-Cultural View 100
Patterns of Mate Selection 100
Exhibit 3.2 Male Selection: A Palestinian's Experience 101
Preferred Characteristics in a Mate 102
Sexuality in Nonhuman Primates 103
Social versus Hormonal Influences on Nonhuman Primate Sexual Behavior 104
Importance of Touch among Nonhuman Primates 104
Homosexuality among Nonhuman Primates 104
Mating Patterns among Nonhuman Primates 104
Monogamy and Nonhuman Primate Sexual Behavior 104
Choices 106
Choose to Be Less Ethnocentric? 106
Become More Culturally Relativistic? 106
Choose to Conform to Cultural Sexual Norms? 107

PART II BACKGROUND FOR SEXUAL CHOICES 111

CHAPTER 4
Research in Human Sexuality 113
The Roots of Sexology 114
The Study of Sexuality: An Overview of Approaches 115
The Interdisciplinary Nature of Sexology: Biosexology, Psychosexology, and Sociosexology 115
Cross-sectional and Longitudinal Research 118
Qualitative and Quantitative Research 119
Feminist Approaches to Sexuality Research 120
Sex Research: Initial Procedures and Methods 121
Formulating a Research Question 121
Reviewing the Literature 122
Formulating a Hypothesis and Defining Variables 123
Selecting the Sample: Nonprobability versus Probability Sampling 124
Methods of Data Collection 126
Experiments 126
Surveys 127
Exhibit 4.1 AIDS and HIV Clinical Trials 128
Field Research 131
Case Studies 132
Historical Research 133
Diaries 134
Research Perspective: Ethical Considerations in Sexuality Research with Human Participants 134
Data Analysis 138
Description 138
Correlation 139
Causation 140
Reliability and Validity 141
Self-Assessment: Sex Anxiety Inventory and its Development 143
Exhibit 4.2 Before You Believe the Conclusions of a Sex Research Study 146
Major Sex Studies 146
The Original Kinsey Studies on Sexual Behavior 147
The Kinsey Institute Study on Sexual Values 148
The Kinsey Report on Sexual Knowledge 148
Masters and Johnson's Research on Sexual Response 150
Rubin's Assessment of the Sexual and Gender Revolutions 150

National Surveys of Adolescents 151
Magazine Surveys 151
Choices 152
Choose to Become Informed about Sex Research? 152
Choose to Accept Findings of Sex Research? 152
Choose to Be a Participant in Sex Research? 152
Should Taxpayers Fund Sex Research? 152

CHAPTER 5
Theories of Sexuality 157
Biological Theories 158
Physiological Theories 158
Evolutionary Theories 159
Psychological Theories 160
Psychoanalytic Theories 160
Learning Theories 163
Cognitive/Affective Theories 167
Sociological Theories 168
Symbolic Interaction Theories 168
Theoretical Perspective: Gang Rape at Fraternity Houses: A Social Script View 170
Structural-Functional Theories 171
Conflict Theories 171
Systems Theories 172
Exhibit 5.1 Three Sociological Views on Premenstrual Syndrome 173
Feminist Theories 175
Self-Assessment: Attitude Toward Feminism Scale 176
Liberal Feminism 178
Radical Feminism 178
Socialist Feminism 179
Multicultural Feminism 179
Essentialist Versus Social Constructionist Views of Human Sexuality 180
Theoretical Views on Human Sexuality: An Integrated Approach 181
Exhibit 5.2 An Application of the Integrative Model of Human Sexuality 182
Choices 185
Choose to Be a Parental Model for Affection? 185
Choose to View Desires for Specific Sexual Behaviors as Learned? 185

CHAPTER 6
Sexual Anatomy and Physiology 189
Female External Anatomy 190
Mons Veneris 191
Labia 191
Clitoris 192
Vaginal Opening 193
Urethral Opening 194
Female Internal Anatomy 194
Vagina 194
Pubococcygeus Muscle 198
Uterus 198
Fallopian Tubes 199
Ovaries 199
Menstruation 199
Attitudes toward Menstruation 200
Self-Assessment: Menstrual Attitude Questionnaire (MAQ) 201
Phases of the Menstrual Cycle 202
Problems of the Menstrual Cycle 204
Exhibit 6.1 Premenstrual Syndrome 205
Research and Policy Perspective: Premenstrual Disorder and DSM-111-R Controversy 207
The Female Breasts 209
Male External Anatomy 211
Penis 211
Scrotum 214
Male Internal Anatomy 214
Testes 214
Duct System 215
Seminal Vesicles and Prostate Gland 216
Choices 218
Choose to Have a Breast Implant? 218
Choose to Have a Mammogram? 218
Choose to Have a Pelvic Examination and a Pap Test? 219
Choose to Have a Prostate Rectal Exam? 219
Choose to Do Self-Examinations? 219

CHAPTER 7
Sexual Response 223
Four Aspects of Human Sexual Response 224
Sexual Appetite or Drive 224
Central Arousal 225
Genital Responses 226
Peripheral Arousal 226
Masters and Johnson's Four-Stage Model of Sexual Response 227
Excitement Phase 227
Self-Assessment: Sexual Arousability Inventory (SAI) 231
Plateau Phase 234
Orgasm Phase 235
Exhibit 7.1 College Women's Descriptions of Orgasm 237
Resolution Phase 238
Male and Female Differences in Sexual Response 239
Exhibit 7.2 Multiple Male Orgasm 240

Critiques of Masters and Johnson's Model 241
Alternative Sexual Response Models 242
- Ellis's and Beach's Two-Stage Models 242
- Helen Kaplan's Three-Stage Model 243
- David Reed's Erotic Stimulus Pathway (ESP) Model 243

Hormones and Sexual Response 244
- **Exhibit 7.3** Aphrodisiacs? 246

Drugs and Sexual Response 247
- Drugs for Medication 247
- Drugs for Recreation 248
- **Exhibit 7.4** Anabolic Steroid Use Among Athletes 248
- **Research Perspective:** The Social Psychology of Alcohol Consumption and Sexual Effects 250

Erotica and Sexual Response 255
- Sexual Response to Erotica Exposure 256
- Differences between Women and Men 256

Choices 257
- Choose to Engage in Sexual Behavior with Minimal Desire? 257
- Choose to Minimize Focus on the Orgasm Phase of the Sexual Response Cycle? 257
- Choose to Use Erotic Materials and/or Devices to Enhance Arousal? 258

PART III Contexts of Sexual Choices 263

CHAPTER 8 Gender Roles 265

Terminology 266
- Sex versus Gender 266
- Gender Identity 267
- Gender Roles 267
- Sexual Identity 268
- **Self-Assessment:** Sexual Double Standard Scale 269
- Gender Role Ideology 271

Biological Beginnings 272
- Chromosomes 272
- **Exhibit 8.1** The Sexual Politics of Meat: A Feminist-Vegetarian Theory 273
- Hormones 273
- Chromosomal and Hormonal Abnormalities 275
- Gender Dysphoria and Transsexualism 277

Theories of Gender Role Acquisition 280
- Sociobiological Theory 280
- Identification Theory 283
- Social Learning Theory 284
- Cognitive-Developmental Theory 285
- Gender Schema Theory 286
- **Exhibit 8.2** Critiques of Research on Sex Differences 287
- **Theoretical Perspective:** Alpha and Beta Bias in Gender Theories 288

Agents of Socialization in Gender Role Acquisition 290
- Parents 290
- Peers 291
- Teachers and Educational Curricula and Materials 292
- Religion 293
- Media 294
- Consequences of Traditional Female Socialization 296
- Consequences of Traditional Male Socialization 301
- **Exhibit 8.3** 12 Ways Gender Role Socialization Affects Sexual Choices 304

Beyond Gender Roles: Androgyny and Gender Role Transcendence 304
- Androgyny 305
- **Exhibit 8.4** Androgyny and Sexual Relationships 307
- Gender Role Transcendence 308

Choices 309
- Choose New Relationships: Women Asking Men? 309
- Choose to Seek Egalitarian Relationships? 309
- Choose to Pursue Nontraditional Occupational Roles? 310

CHAPTER 9 Individual Sexuality 317

Intrapersonal Aspects of Sexuality 318
- Self-Concept and Sexual Self-Concept 318
- Body Image 318
- Sexual Guilt 319
- **Exhibit 9.1** Body Image and Eating Disorders: A Feminist View 320
- Erotophobia and Erotophilia 321

Sexual Celibacy 321
- **Self-Assessment:** Sexual Opinion Survey 322
- Voluntary Sexual Celibacy 323
- Involuntary Sexual Celibacy 325

Negative Attitudes Toward Masturbation: Historical Origins 325
- Religion and Masturbation 325
- Medicine and Masturbation 327
- **Historical Perspective:** Some Not-so-helpful "Advice" from "Experts" on Masturbation 328
- Traditional Psychotherapy and Masturbation 331
- Parents and Masturbation 331

Benefits of Masturbation 331
Social and Psychological Correlates of Masturbation 333
Gender, Age, and Cohort 333
Education and Religion 335
Locus of Control 335
Techniques of Masturbation 336
Female Masturbation Techniques 336
Techniques of Male Masturbation 338
Exhibit 9.2 Masturbation and Accidental Death 339
Masturbation in Relationships 339
Research on Masturbation among Spouses 339
Effects of Masturbation on Relationships 340
Sexual Fantasies 340
Functions of Sexual Fantasies 341
Content of Sexual Fantasies 342
Gender Differences in Sexual Fantasies 344
Choices 346
Choose to Masturbate? 346
Choose to Use a Vibrator? 346
Choose to Masturbate with One's Partner? 346
Choose to Share Sexual Fantasies with One's Partner? 346
Choose to Use Masturbation Fantasies to Change Sexual Object Choice? 347

CHAPTER 10
Interpersonal Sexuality 351
Social Construction of Sexuality in Relationships 352
Relationships and Sex Frequency 352
Relationships and Nonmonogamy 353
Dating and Sexuality 354
Functions of Dating 354
Sexual Expectations in Dating 355
Research Perspective: The College Bar Scene: A Happy Hunting Ground? 356
Dating among the Divorced and Widowed 358
Cohabitation and Sexuality 360
Definition, Incidence, and Types of Cohabitating Relationships 360
Exhibit 10.1 Living Together as Preparation for Marriage 361
Sexuality in Cohabitating Relationships 362
Marriage and Sexuality 362
Motivations for Marriage 362
Types of Marriage Relationships 364
Sexuality in Marital Relationships 365
Relationship Quality 366
Comparisons of Types of Partners 366
Extradyadic Sexuality 367
Self-Assessment: Index of Sexual Satisfaction (ISS) 368
Types of Extradyadic Sexual Involvements 369
Motivations and Reasons for Extradyadic Sexual Involvements 371
Sexual Involvements with Co-Workers 374
Managing Sexual Attraction at Work 374
Intimate Relationships at Work: Issues for Employees 375
Interpersonal Noncoital Sexual Behavior 377
Touching 377
Kissing 378
Exhibit 10.2 The Origin of Mouth Kissing 378
Breast Stimulation 379
Penile Stimulation 379
Clitoral Stimulation 381
Other Petting Behaviors 383
Effects of Petting 384
Sexual Intercourse Positions 385
Man-on-Top Position 385
Woman-on-Top Position 385
Side-by-Side Position 386
Rear-Entry Position 386
Sitting Position 387
Standing Position 387
Variations 388
Choices 389
Choose Extradyadic Sex? No 389
Choose Extradyadic Sex? Yes 390
Choose to Become Involved with Someone at Work? 391

CHAPTER 11
Sexual Orientation 395
Homosexuality and Heterosexuality 397
Definition of Homosexuality and Heterosexuality 397
Prevalence of Homosexuality and Heterosexuality 398
Bisexuality 399
Homophobia and Heterosexism 401
Prejudice against Homosexuals 401
Self-Assessment: Index of Attitudes toward Homosexuals 404
Discrimination against Homosexuals 406
Antigay Violence 407
Research and Policy Perspective: Gay and Lesbian Life on Campus 409
The Gay Liberation Movement 411
Exhibit 11.1 Gay and Lesbian Couples Constitute a Family 413
Lesbian-Feminism 413

Theoretical Explanations for Sexual Orientation 414
Biological Explanations 414
Social Learning Explanations 416
Social-Psychological Explanations 417
Psychoanalytic Explanations 417
Developing a Gay Identity 418
Troiden's Four-Stage Process 418
Coming Out 420
Exhibit 11.2 A Lesbian's Letter to Her Parents Disclosing Her Homosexuality 422
Developing a Positive Gay Self-Concept 426
The Role of the Gay Subculture 426
Inside Gay Relationships 427
Gay Male Relationships 427
Gay Female Relationships 430
Sexual Behavior 432
Sexually Transmissible Diseases 433
Choices 435
The Choice of Some Homosexuals: Lover or Parent? 435
The Choice of Some Parents: Accept or Reject a Gay Son or Daughter? 435
Distress About One's Sexual Orientation: Seek Therapy? 436

CHAPTER 12
Sexuality Across the Life Span 443
Sexuality from Infancy through Adolescence 444
Infancy 444
Childhood 445
Adolescence 446
Exhibit 12.1 First Intercourse Experiences 452
Research Perspective: Postponing Sexual Involvement: More Than "Just Say No" 453
Sexuality in Early Adulthood 454
Sexuality among Never-Married Adults 454
Sexuality among the Married 455
Sexuality among the Divorced 456
Sexuality in the Middle Years 457
Definition of Middle Age 457
Women in Middle Age 457
Men in Middle Age 459
Self-Assessment: Aging Sexual Knowledge and Attitudes Scale 460
Sexuality in the Later Years 464
Sexual Interest, Activity, and Ability among the Elderly 465
Exhibit 12.2 Sexuality Among the Widowed 468
Correlation between Past and Present Sexual Behaviors 468
Choices 469
Choose to Have Hormone Replacement Therapy? 469
Sexual Choices among the Elderly 469
Sexual Choices among the Young in Preparation for the Later Years 470

PART IV ENHANCEMENT CHOICES 475

CHAPTER 13
Communication and Sexuality 477
Communication in Relationships 478
Components of Effective Communication 479
Personal Policy Perspective: Sexual Communication: Informed Consent versus Coercion 479
Exhibit 13.1 Sexual Lies Told By College Students 481
Communication: Content versus Process 483
Communication and Intimacy in Relationships 484
Self-Assessment: Sexual Self-Disclosure Scale 486
Basic Communication Skills 490
Maintain Eye Contact 490
Ask Open-Ended Questions 490
Use Reflective Listening 491
Use "I" Statements 492
Resolving Interpersonal Conflict 493
Address Recurring, Disturbing Issues 493
Focus on What You Want (Rather Than What You Don't Want) 494
Find Out the Other Person's Point of View 494
Generate Solutions to the Conflict 494
Sexual Interactions as Communication 497
Choices 498
Choose to Tell One's Partner of Sexual Dissatisfactions? 498
Choose to Talk about One's Sexual Past to One's Partner? 498
Choose to Disclose Attractions to Others to One's Partner? 498

CHAPTER 14
Love and Sexuality 501
The Nature of Love: Ancient and Modern Views 502
Ancient Views of Love 502
Modern Views of Love 504
Romantic versus Realistic Love 506
Self-Assessment: Love Attitudes Scale 508
Infatuation 508
The Feminization of Love 509

The Origins of Love: Theoretical Views 511
Evolutionary Theory 511
Learning Theory 511
Psychosexual Theory 512
Ego-Ideal Theory 513
Ontological Theory 513
Biochemical Associations of Love 514
Exhibit 14.1 Love: A Natural High? 516
Theoretical Perspective: A Dimension for Organizing Theories of Love and Sex 516
Love Relationships 518
Conditions under Which Love Relationships Develop 518
Dilemmas of Love Relationships 519
Love and Health 520
Sexual Jealousy in Relationships 521
Causes of Jealousy 521
Consequences of Jealousy 522
Techniques for Resolving Jealousy 524
Choices 525
Choose to Have Sex with Love? 525
Choose to Have Sex without Love? 525

CHAPTER 15

Sexual Dysfunctions and Sex Therapy 531

Sexual Dysfunctions: Causes and Contributing Factors 533
Biological Factors 533
Sociocultural Factors 534
Theoretical and Research Perspective: Prevention of Male Sexual Dysfunction by Challenging Sexual Myths and Gender Role Stereotypes 534
Intrapsychic Factors 536
Relationship Factors 537
Educational and Cognitive Factors 538
Aging Factors 538
Self-Assessment: How Much Do You Know about Sexuality? 539
Desire-Phase Dysfunctions 540
Hypoactive Sexual Desire 541
Sexual Aversion 543
Arousal-Phase Dysfunctions 544
Female Sexual Arousal Dysfunction 545
Male Erectile Dysfunction 545
Orgasm-Phase Dysfunctions 550
Inhibited Female Orgasm 550
Inhibited Male Orgasm 553
Early Ejaculation 554
Sexual Pain Dysfunctions 556
Dyspareunia 556
Vaginismus 557
Approaches Used in Sex Therapy 558
Psychoanalytic Approach 558
Masters and Johnson's Approach 559
The PLISSIT Model Approach 559
Cognitive Therapy Approach 560
Helen Kaplan's Approach 561
LoPiccolo's Postmodern Approach 561
Surrogate Partner Therapy 562
Alternative Aids Used in Sex Therapy 563
Effectiveness of Sex Therapy 563
Sex Therapy: Professional and Ethical Issues 565
Training Requirements to Become a Sex Therapist 565
Sexual Involvement between Therapist and Client 565
Values in Sex Therapy 566
Choices 567
Choose to Have Individual Therapy or Couple (Conjoint) Therapy? 567
Choose to Have Private Therapy or Group Therapy? 567
Choose to Have a Male-Female Sex Therapy Team or an Individual Therapist? 568

PART V Health Choices 575

CHAPTER 16

Health and Sexuality 577

Myths about Disease, Disability, and Sexuality 578
Psychobiological and Psychosocial Factors in Sexual Health 580
Psychobiological Factors 580
Psychosocial Factors 581
Neurological Disabilities and Sexuality 582
Spinal Cord Injury 583
Stroke 584
Multiple Sclerosis 584
Traumatic Brain Injury 585
Cerebral Palsy 586
Exhibit 16.1 Surrogate Partner Therapy for a Person with Severe Cerebral Palsy 586
Intellectual and Psychological Disturbances and Sexuality 587
Intellectual Disability 587
Psychological Disturbances 589
Cancer and Sexuality 590
Cancer of the Breast and Reproductive System 590
Self-Assessment: Torabi-Seffrin Cancer Attitude Scale 592
Research Perspective: Attitudes Toward Breast and Testicular Self-Exams 596
Other Diseases and Illnesses and Sexuality 599

Arthritis 599
Cardiovascular Disease 599
Diabetes 600
Chronic Obstructive Pulmonary Disease 601
Endometriosis 602
Choices 602
Choose to Exercise? 603
Choose to Take Cognitive Control of One's Life and Sexuality? 603

CHAPTER 17 Paraphilias and Sexuality 607

Paraphilia: Definition and Overview 608
Types of Paraphilias 609
Exhibitionism 609
Frotteurism 612
Pedophilia 612
Voyeurism 614
Fetishism 614
Tranvestic Fetishism 616
Self-Assessment: The Cross-Gender Fetishism Scale 617
Sexual Sadism 618
Sexual Masochism 618
Other Paraphilias 620
Legal versus Illegal Paraphilias 621
Is Rape a Paraphilia? 622
The Origins of Paraphilias: Theoretical Perspectives 622
Psychoanalytic Perspective 622
Feminist Perspective 623
Learning Theory 623
Biological Theory 623
Paraphilia as a Vandalized Lovemap 624
Paraphilia as a Courtship Disorder 624
Treatment of Paraphilias 625
Research Perspective: Methods of Assessment of Sexual Interest in Sex Offenders 625
Decreasing Deviant Sexual Arousal 628
Exhibit 17.1 Medications and Paraphilia Control 629
Increasing Nondeviant Sexual Arousal 631
Teaching Social Skills 631
Changing Faulty Cognitions 632
Resolving Sexual Dysfunctions 632
Treating Alcohol Abuse 632
Exhibit 17.2 The Treatment of Formicophilia 633
Sexual Addiction 633
Characteristics of Sex Addicts 633
Treatment of Sexual Addictions 634
Effectiveness of Treatment Programs 635
Choices 636
Choose to Disregard Social Disapproval of Paraphilias? 636
Choose to Control One's Paraphilia? 636

CHAPTER 18 HIV Infection and Other Sexually Transmissible Diseases 639

Human Immunodeficiency Virus (HIV) Infection 640
Categories and Symptoms 640
Transmission of HIV and High-Risk Behaviors 641
Homosexuals and HIV Infection 642
Heterosexuals and HIV Infection 643
Prevalence of HIV Infection and AIDS 643
Knowledge and Attitudes about HIV and AIDS 644
Tests for HIV Infection 646
Self-Assessment: STD ATTITUDE SCALE 648
Treatment for HIV Infection 649
Genital Herpes 650
Human Papilloma Virus (HPV) 653
Exhibit 18.1 Psychological Reactions to Genital Herpes 654
Chlamydia 655
Gonorrhea 656
Syphilis 657
Other Sexually Transmissible Diseases 660
Nongonococcal Urethritis (NGU) 660
Lymphogranuloma Venereum (LGV) 660
Granuloma Inguinale 660
Chancroid 660
Hepatitis B 661
Vaginitis 661
Pubic Lice 662
Scabies 662
Prevention of Sexually Transmissible Diseases 662
Exhibit 18.2 Condom Communication 665
Perspective: Prevention Models for HIV Transmission 667
Choices 670
Choose to Engage in Low-Risk Behaviors? 670
Choose to Be Tested for HIV? 670
Choose How to Tell a Partner That One Has an STD? 671
Choose to Allocate Government Funds to HIV Infection Research? 671
Choose to Require Health-Care Workers to Be Tested for HIV? 671

CHAPTER 19 Abuses and Commercial Uses of Sexuality 677

Sexual Coercion: Rape and Sexual Assault 678
Prevalence and Incidence Rape 679
Patterns of Rape 682

Exhibit 19.1 Date Rape: One College Student's Experience 683
Theories of Rape 686
Impact of Rape and Sexual Assault 689
Treatment for the Rape Survivor 691
Treatment for the Rape Perpetrator 693
Self-Assessment: Rape Empathy Scale 694
Prevention of Rape 698
Research and Policy Perspective: Rape Prevention on the College Campus 700

Sexual Abuse of Children 702

Incidence and Prevalence of Extrafamilial and Intrafamilial Child Sexual Abuse 703
Theories of Child Sexual Abuse 703
Patterns of Child Sexual Abuse 704
Impact of Child Sexual Abuse 707
Treatment of Sexually Abused Children and Abusers 708
Prevention of Child Sexual Abuse 710

Sexual Harassment in the Workplace 712

Prevalence and Incidence of Sexual Harassment 712
Definition of Sexual Harassment 712
Theories of Sexual Harassment 712
Consequences of Sexual Harassment 713
Responses to Sexual Harassment 713
Prevention of Sexual Harassment 714

Commercial Uses and Abuses of Sexuality 714

Prostitution 714
Pornography 717

Choices 723

Choose to Have Children Testify in Court in Cases of Alleged Child Sexual Abuse? 723
Choose to Confront Sexual Harassment? 723
Choose to Legalize or Decriminalize Prostitution? 724

PART VI Reproductive Choices 731

CHAPTER 20
Planning Children and Birth Control 733

Family Planning: A Worthy Choice 734

Incidence of Unplanned Pregnancy in the United States 734
Personal and Social Benefits of Family Planning 735

Do You Want to Have Children? 735

Social Influences on Deciding to Have Children 736
Motivations for Having Children 737
Difficulties and Stresses Associated with Parenthood 738
The Childfree Alternative 741
How Many Children Do You Want? 741
Factors to Consider in the Timing of Children 743
Self-Assessment: Attitudes Toward Timing for Parenthood Scale 744

History of Birth Control 746
Methods of Birth Control 748

Oral Contraceptives 748
Exhibit 20.1 Norplant: Personal Choice or Social Control? 752
Condom 753
Exhibit 20.2 Male Hormonal Contraceptives 753
Exhibit 20.3 The Female Condom 755
Intrauterine Device (IUD) 755
Diaphragm and Cervical Cap 757
Vaginal Spermicides 758
Vaginal Sponge 759
Coitus Abstentia 760
Periodic Abstinence 761
Coitus Interruptus (withdrawal) 763
Postcoital Contraception 764
Sterilization 764
Research Perspective: Psychological Influences in Contraceptive Use 767

Birth Control Technology and Availability: An International View 772
The Future of Birth Control Technology 774
Choices 775

Choose to Have a Child without a Partner? The Biological Clock Issue 775
Choose to Use Which Method of Contraception? 776

CHAPTER 21
Pregnancy and Childbirth 781

Fertilization and Conception 782

Infertility 784
Causes of Infertility 784
Psychological Reactions to Infertility 785

Reproductive Technology 785

Hormone Therapy 786
Artificial Insemination 786
Artificial Insemination of a Surrogate Mother 788
Ovum Transfer 789
In Vitro Fertilization 789
Self-Assessment: Acceptance of Adoption and Five Alternative Fertilization Techniques 790
Other Reproductive Technologies 791
Public Policy Perspective: Reproductive Technology: Liberating or Enslaving? 792

Pregnancy and Labor 796

Pregnancy Testing 796
Physical Changes during Pregnancy 798
Prenatal Care and Prenatal Testing 798
Psychological Changes during Pregnancy 803
Sex during Pregnancy 804

Exhibit 21.2 The Empathy Belly 804
Labor 805
Childbirth Preparation 809
Dick-Read Method 810
Lamaze Method 810
Bradley Method 812
LeBoyer Birth Experience 812
Cesarean Childbirth 813
The Transition into Parenthood 815
The Transition to Motherhood 817
The Transition to Fatherhood 818
Sex after Childbirth 820
Choices 822
Choose Home or Hospital Birth? 822
Choose to Breast-feed or Bottle-feed the New Infant? 822
Choices Resulting from New ReproductiveTechnologies 823

CHAPTER 22

Abortion and other Pregnancy Outcomes 831
Attitudes Toward Abortion 832
Attitudes of the General Public 832
Self-Assessment: Abortion Attitude Scale 833
Attitudes of College Students 834
Abortion Advocacy Groups: Prolife and Prochoice 834
Exhibit 22.1 Opposition to Abortion: A Feminist View 836
Ethical Issues and Abortion 836
When Does Personhood Begin? 836
Is Abortion Immoral? 837
Exhibit 22.2 Abortion is not (Necessarily) a Sin: A Catholic View 837
Methods of Induced Abortion 838
Suction Curettage and Dilation and Suction 838
Dilation and Evacuation 839
Saline Abortion 839
How Safe Are Surgical and Saline Abortions? 840
Prostaglandins 840
RU-486 840
Menstrual Extraction 841
A Cross-Cultural View of Abortion 842
Abortion in Preliterate Societies 842
International Trends in Abortion 842
Abortion in the United States 843
Incidence of Abortion 843
Who Gets an Abortion and Why? 844
Theoretical Perspective: Gilligan's Study of Abortion Decision Making 846
Availability of Abortion Services 848
Abortion Legislation in the United States 849
Historical Background of Abortion Legislation 849
Roe v. Wade and Rulings Since 1973 850
Psychological Effects of Abortion 853
Other Pregnancy Outcomes 856
Miscarriage and Stillbirth 856
Perinatal Death 857
Adoption 858
Parenting the Baby 859
Choices 861
Multifetal Pregnancies: Choose Selective Termination? 861
Choose Whether to Have an Abortion? Some Guidelines 861

CHAPTER 23

Sex Education 867
Sex Education 868
Components of an Ideal Sex Education Program 869
Goals of Sex Education 871
Self-Assessment: Miller-Fisk Sexual Knowledge Questionnaire (SKQ) 872
Extent of Sex Education 873
Special Audiences for Sex Education 874
Sources of Sex Education 876
Parents 876
Friends 879
School Teachers 879
Family Planning Clinic Personnel 880
Religion 881
Media 881
Pornography 883
Effects of Sex Education 883
Effect on Knowledge 883
Effects on Sexual Behaviors 884
Exhibit 23.1 Why AIDS Risk-Taking Behavior Continues 885
Effects on Attitudes 887
Effects on Contraceptive Usage 887
Effect on Teenage Pregnancy 888
Research Perspective: The Fourth Generation of Sex Education Curricula 889
Choices 892
Choose to Allow Children to Sleep in Their Parents' Bed or to expose Children to Parental Nudity? 892
Choose to Have Parents Participate in Sex Education Programs? 892
What Should the Schools Teach about Sex? 893

Glossary A–1

Appendices A–17
A Sexual Choices Autobiography Outline A–17
B Resources and Organizations A–18

Index A–21

***Opposite page:** Pablo Picasso.* The Love of Jupiter and Semele, *plate opposite page 70 from* Les Metamorphoses d'Ovid, *published Lausanne, Albert Skira, Editeur, 1931. Etching (executed 1930), printed in black, page: 12 13/16 × 10 1/4″. Collection, The Museum of Modern Art, New York. The Louis E. Stern Collection.*

Making Sexual Choices

PART ONE

D*ances With Wolves* was an Academy Award-winning film featuring Kevin Costner in the role of a white man who was befriended by a Lakota Indian tribe in what is now South Dakota during the frontier days of the West (mid- to late 1800s). While the film did not focus on sexual choices, it inadvertently emphasized the major chapter points of Part I: (1) sexual choices permeate life; (2) sexual choices are based on sexual values; and (3) sexual choices differ in reference to the cultural setting.

That sexual choices permeate life (Chapter 1, Choices in Sexuality: A First View) was illustrated in Costner's (referred to by the Indians as "Dances With Wolves") decision to stay as the only soldier in an isolated Army outpost. By his choice, he concomitantly chose a temporary life of celibacy (unmarried, commonly implying no sex partner). Contemporary individuals who choose to marry usually also choose to limit their sexual partners. Throughout our lives, many of our decisions are sexual or have sexual implications.

Sexual values, the subject of Chapter 2, were reflected in Dances With Wolves' decision not to sleep with the Indian woman until he had developed a relationship with her. This value, as we shall see, is gaining increased acceptance in our society.

Finally, that sexual choices vary by culture (the subject of Chapter 3) was illustrated in the fact that the tribe permitted the couple to establish their formal sexual relationship only after an elaborate ceremony. Other examples of how culture influences our sexual choices will be detailed in Chapter 3.

CHAPTER ONE

Choices in Sexuality: A First View

Chapter Outline

Free Will and Determinism: A Philosophical Inquiry
- **Self-Assessment:** Free Will–Determinism Scale

The Nature of Sexual Choices
- Choices Are Continually Being Made
- Not to Decide Is to Decide
- Choices Involve Tradeoffs
- Some Choices Are Dichotomous, Others Are Not
- Most Choices Are Revocable, Some Are Not
- **Research and Policy Perspective:** Are Adolescents Competent to Make Independent Choices?
- Choices Are Influenced by Social Context and Cultural Forces
- Drug Use Influences Choices

Elements of Human Sexuality
- Anatomy and Physiology
- Sexual Self-Concept
- Behavior
- Cognitions
- Values
- Emotions
- Relationships
- Variability

Sexual Myths
- Myth 1: Most Americans Are Well-Informed about Sexuality
- Myth 2: Good Sex Equals Intercourse and Orgasm
- Myth 3: The Double Standard Is Dead
- Myth 4: Sex Therapy for Lack of Orgasm Doesn't Do Any Good
- Myth 5: Women Secretly Want to Be Raped

Social Changes and Their Effects on Sexuality
- Sex in the Media
- Birth Control
- Divorce
- Cohabitation
- Changes in the Workplace
- Women's Movement and Men's Movement
- HIV Infection
- Technology

Choices
- Choose Deliberately or by Default?
- Human Sexuality: An Academic, Personal, or Career Search?
- Choose Tolerance for the Choices and Life-styles of Others?

Is It True?*

1. The root of the word *decide* means to "slay" (as in *homicide* or *suicide*), implying that making a decision involves "slaying" the options one has not chosen.

2. People in the United States spend more money on beauty and fitness aids than they do on social services or education.

3. Men are more concerned about the physical appearance of their female partners than women are concerned about the physical appearance of their male partners.

4. All obese women report being ashamed to be nude with their partners and report unsatisfactory sex lives.

5. Drug use is associated with anonymous sex with numerous partners, not using a condom during intercourse, and contracting human immunodeficiency virus (HIV) and other sexually transmissible diseases (STDs).

*1 = T, 2 = T, 3 = T, 4 = F, 5 = T

We should exercise our right to choose among our sexual options with informed discrimination, and with respect for the basic values of honesty, equality, and responsibility for ourselves and others.

Ira L. Reiss
Harriet M. Reiss

What do the following questions have in common?

Is sex with a new person worth the risk of contracting HIV or other STDs?

Do I bring up the issue of using a condom? When?

Do I tell my partner of my previous sexual experiences (masturbation, casual sex, homosexual encounters, number of sexual partners)?

Do I disclose to my partner that I have fantasies of sex with other people?

Do I tell my partner that I sometimes *feel* sexually abnormal (am sexually apathetic, don't have orgasm, can't sustain an erection, or ejaculate too quickly)?

To decide means that action will follow. If no action occurs, then no true decision has been made.

Irvin Yalom

Each of the above questions involves making sexual choices. Choices are decisions among alternative courses of action. The goal of this text is to emphasize the importance of making deliberate and informed choices in regard to your sexuality and to act on those choices. The alternative is for you to give little thought to such decisions and to let happen whatever may happen. While letting chance take its course is also a choice, you might want to exercise more control over your choices.

In this chapter, we look at the nature of choices, the elements of human sexuality, the myths some of us may have been taught about sexuality, how changes in the twentieth century have affected sexuality, and some initial sexual choices you might consider. We begin by looking at the philosophical notions of free will and determinism and examine the degree to which we have control over our choices.

Free Will and Determinism: A Philosophical Inquiry

A basic assumption of this text is that humans have free will, which may be defined as the capacity to choose for oneself (Windt, 1982). The belief that people have **free will** is also referred to as **libertarianism.** For some individuals, "this belief that people freely choose how they will act is simple common sense, a basic and important working assumption of ordinary life" (Sappington, 1990, p. 19). According to the libertarian belief in free will, heredity and environment influence our choices but do not determine them.

We are not passive victims of life, we do make choices, and we do have the power to change major aspects of our lives as we struggle toward a more authentic existence.

Gerald Corey
Marianne S. Corey

Another and competing assumption of this text is that human behavior is influenced by past and present factors in our heredity and environment. For example, throughout this text, we discuss "causes" of a variety of sexual behaviors and attitudes, including gender-role behavior, inability to experience orgasm, inability to achieve or maintain erection, paraphilias (such as fetishes), homosexuality, jealousy, and the desire to have children. The view that human behavior is caused by past and present factors in our heredity and environment is known as **determinism.** According to determinism, "what we call human choices may reflect our desires and even our central ideals, but . . . every motive, desire, ideal, or idea is simply the result of factors in our heredity and environment" (Hollis, 1985, p. 80).

CONSIDERATION: Libertarians admit that "people are not free to implement all of their choices; they are faced with external constraints that serve as barriers and with personal constraints such as lack of ability" (Sappington, 1990, p. 20). However, libertarians suggest that people are still free to choose how they view and respond to these barriers and constraints. For example, an infertile woman who wants to have a child may consider options such as use of reproductive technologies or adoption. In this case, a determinist would argue that the woman's likelihood of choosing an alternative, and even her desire for a child, are largely determined by cultural norms regarding pronatalism and women's roles, a partner or family's influence, and her access to a child she would be willing to adopt.

For over two thousand years, philosophers and scientists have developed a variety of alternative views on free will and determinism. Some of these views are summarized in Exhibit 1.1.

Freedom is all our joy and all our pain.
Joyce Cary

Definitive answers to the philosophical questions about the nature of human freedom and the degree to which choices are free or determined probably will never be found. As we have seen, there is a range of views pertaining to these issues, only a few of which are discussed here. Psychologist Charles Spezzano (1992) suggested that

> All of us experience ourselves as both active and reactive. We act with will and a sense of purpose, but we also react to what the world presents to us. The critical question is whether we believe that the scale is tipped in the direction of our being in control of our behavior or on the side of external forces determining what we do. (p. 55)

EXHIBIT 1.1 Alternative Views on Free Will and Determinism

Fatalism

Fatalism involves the belief that human destiny is determined by fate or predestination. One form of fatalism is astrology, or the belief that our lives are influenced by the position and movement of the planets and stars. A modern version of fatalism is the belief that much of our lives is determined by chance or accident. Fatalism rejects the notion that people can decide their future through free choice.

Self-Determinism

Self-determinism involves the belief that every human act or choice is caused but that people themselves are causal agents. "Human beings can reflect and deliberate before they act; they can give reasons for what they do and reasons are causes" (Hollis, 1985, p. 88). Self-determinists recognize that our attitudes, desires, and motives may be determined by environmental or biological factors. However, they emphasize that we can evaluate our attitudes, desires, and motives; reformulate our values; and modify our behavior accordingly. Making deliberate choices and being in control of one's life is associated with personal happiness (Myers, 1992).

Passive Self-Determinism

According to passive self-determinism, freedom is the absence of outside coercion. Therefore, "we are free to the degree that in our choices we express our selves—what we are and what we want. We are unfree insofar as circumstances limit our self-expression or other persons force us to do what we do not want to do" (Hollis, 1985, p. 89). In addition, passive self-determinism implies that free choice involves choosing from a set of alternatives; choice is not free when only one option is available.

Active Self-Determinism

According to active self-determinism, freedom involves making choices through reflective thinking and insightful awareness. Active self-determinists believe that

> People are unfree insofar as their behaving and choosing stem from desires, habits, beliefs, or any aspect of themselves or their environment of which they are unconscious, unaware, or lacking in insight. People are free to the degree that their behaving and choosing are guided by insightful awareness of the situation within and outside themselves. People can learn to be free in this sense of the word 'freedom.' (Hollis, 1985, p. 90)

The Self-Assessment: The Free Will-Determinism Scale is designed to assess the direction in which you believe the scale is "tipped" (to use Spezzano's term). Do you tend to believe that you control your choices and behavior? Or do you tend to believe that your behavior and choices are determined by environmental or biological factors?

The Nature of Sexual Choices

This text emphasizes making choices in regard to sexuality and sexual issues. Understanding the nature of choices may provide a foundation for making sexual choices in your life. In the discussion to follow, we examine the nature of choices.

Choices Are Continually Being Made

You will be confronted with numerous sexual choices. (see Exhibit 1.2). Life involves a series of some big decisions and a constant stream of smaller ones. For example, if you choose to become involved in a committed emotional and sexual relationship, you must also choose whether you will be sexually monogamous, how you will handle issues of jealousy, and whether you and your partner will be tested for sexually transmissible diseases.

Happy people believe they choose their destinies.

David G. Myers

It is also important to remember that "deciding does not end either with a decision or with a failure to make one. The individual must re-decide over and over" (Yalom, 1980, p. 331). You may face many sexual choices more than once, including choices about being faithful, how much of your sexual past to reveal, and whether to use a condom.

Not to Decide Is to Decide

It is important to recognize that to not make a decision is a decision. The act of not deciding against something is to decide for something. For example, if you are sexually active and do not decide to use birth control, you have decided to risk

What is not possible is not to choose, but I ought to know that if I do not choose, I am still choosing. (Jean-Paul Sartre)

pregnancy. If you do not decide to confront sexual harassment, you have decided to allow the harassment to continue. If you do not decide to buy, carry, or discuss condoms with a sexual partner, you have decided to risk contracting HIV and/or other STDs. Yalom (1980) observed that "one cannot not decide" (p. 333).

CONSIDERATION: "Indecision is decision" applies not only to individuals but also to social policy. For example, each society must decide what to do about sex education of its youth. The choice is not sex education: yes or no. Sex education takes place all the time. The choice is whether it will be planned or inadvertent; whether it will be conducted in the street or in the home, school, religious, and community settings; and whether it will be left to the media or will be mediated by responsible, skillful, and caring adults (Selverstone, 1989).

Choices Involve Tradeoffs

There really are genuine forks in the road . . .

Pete Dawkins

Choices often involve tradeoffs, or disadvantages as well as advantages. The choice to become involved in an extrapartner or extramarital affair may provide excitement, but it may also result in permanent damage to one's current relationship. The choice to tell your partner that you are unhappy with him or her as a sexual partner may lead to constructive change in your sexual relationship, but it may also result in your partner feeling inadequate. The choice to have an abortion may enable you to avoid the hardship of continuing an unwanted pregnancy, but it may also involve the risk that you will experience feelings of guilt, anxiety, or regret. Likewise, the choice to continue an unwanted pregnancy enables you to avoid the trauma of abortion but may also involve the risk of hardships in parenting or placing the baby for adoption.

CONSIDERATION: Making choices also involves relinquishing the options that are not chosen. "For every yes there must be a no, each decision eliminating or killing other options" (Yalom, 1989, p. 10). The root of the word *decide* means "slay" as in *homicide* or *suicide.* Making decisions, or choices, involves the "slaying" of options that are not chosen.

When faced with decisions that involve tradeoffs, people often experience ambivalence. **Ambivalence** refers to conflicting feelings that produce uncertainty or indecisiveness as to what course of action to take. There are two forms of ambivalence: sequential and simultaneous. In sequential ambivalence, the individual experiences first one wish and then the other. For example, a pregnant woman may vacillate between wanting to have the baby and wanting to terminate the pregnancy. In simultaneous ambivalence, the person experiences two conflicting wishes at the same time. For example, a pregnant woman may, at the same time, feel both the desire to have the baby and the desire to have an abortion.

CONSIDERATION: Ambivalence can produce extreme psychological discomfort, pain, and anxiety. Being in conflict over which decision to make often leads people to seek counseling. One psychotherapist said of his patients, "Almost everyone is wrestling with some decision" (Yalom, 1980, p. 317).

Self Assessment

Free Will-Determinism Scale

The following statements represent opinions by those who believe in free will and those who believe in determinism. Please read each of the statements carefully and then place an X under the statement which most closely corresponds to your opinion on the topic. If your opinion seems to fall somewhere between the statements provided, then mark an X on one of the intermediate spaces.

The following five questions pertain to possible influences on free will. Some people believe that there are few restrictions on free will; others believe in free will, but view it as very delicate; still others deny altogether that free will exists. Please read each item under a given question and then mark the item which most closely corresponds to your opinion.

1. When does free will first manifest itself?

Free will manifests itself at a very early age in most children.		Free will may not exist in infants, but gradually develops during an "age of accountability."		Free will, if it exists at all, is very limited and manifests itself only in mature adults.

2. Are there social conditions which interfere with free will?

Free will, at best, is delicate and probably manifests itself only when we are not the victims of oppressive social conditions.		The exercise of free will is somewhat limited by such social conditions as poverty, unemployment, and class.		Free will is a basic human quality and there are few social conditions which interfere with it.

3. To what extent do physical health problems interfere with free will?

Health is not a factor in free will as long as we are alive.		There are a few physical problems which interfere with free will. For example, some crippling illnesses may interfere.		Free will may be very limited by a great many health problems.

4. Does level of intelligence place restrictions on free will?

Those who are severely retarded may have no free will.		In general, free will and intelligence are unrelated, but low intelligence may place some restrictions on free will.		All people, regardless of their level of intelligence, have free will.

5. Do mental problems place restrictions on free will?

Those who are mentally disturbed still have free will.		Very severe mental disturbances may interfere with free will.		Even mild mental disturbances may interfere with free will.

The following two statements pertain to philosophical problems related to the free will-determinism issue. Please read each item under a given question and then

Continued

Some Choices Are Dichotomous, Others Are Not

Some choices are "either/or." Having intercourse (penile penetration of the vagina), using a condom, or having an abortion are examples of "either/or" sexual choices. There is no continuum of having intercourse, wearing a condom, or having an abortion. Dichotomous choices often result in dichotomous consequences. For example, choosing to have intercourse or not, or choosing to use a condom or not, results in pregnancy or not; there is no such thing as "kind of" pregnant.

Other sexual choices are less dichotomous and occur on a continuum. For example, in deciding to live together, partners often spend increasing amounts of time

Self-Assessment—*Continued*

mark the item that most closely corresponds to your opinion. Remember, if you do not agree with either of the statements, mark one of the intermediate areas.

6. What is the source of human morality?

Behavior must be based on choice or free will in order to be considered moral.	So-called moral behavior is not dependent upon free will. Morality is simply a label used to describe behaviors which are in accord with society's norms.

________ ________ ________

7. Indicate where you stand with respect to the free will-determinism issue.

I believe strongly in free will.	I believe strongly in determinism.

________ ________ ________

Scoring Procedures The five response categories on the Free Will-Determinism (FWD) Scale are scored 1, 3, 5, 7, and 9. However, you must reverse the scoring (assign the values 9, 7, 5, 3, 1) for questions number 1, 3, 5, 6, and 7. A rating of 1 indicates agreement with an answer more consistent with a deterministic viewpoint and 9 indicates an answer more consistent with a libertarian viewpoint. Total your score across the items. The range of possible scores is from 7 (representing extreme deterministic responses on all questions) to 63 (representing extreme libertarian responses on all questions).

Interpreting Your Score It may be helpful in interpreting your score to compare it to those of other college students. Viney, Waldman, and Barchilon (1982) studied 122 introductory psychology students whose scores ranged from 15 (most deterministic) to 59 most libertarian). The students' mean score on the FWD Scale was 38.48 (SD = 8.81). The median score was 38.64. These scores were similar to those collected by Waldman, Viney, Bell, Bennett, and Hess (1983) among 85 male and 56 female introductory psychology students at Colorado State University. Their mean FWD score was 39.63 (SD = 8.33).

Reliability In developing this scale, Viney et al. conducted pilot studies with students in psychology (n = 94)and philosophy (n not reported) courses. The reliability of the scales (coefficient alpha) was .62 for the psychology students and .79 for the philosophy students. In the study population of the 122 introductory psychology students, the coefficient alpha was also rather low (.64). Viney et al. suggested that these results indicate the scale accurately measures an inconsistency in some people's belief in both determinism and free will—that people may see no conflict in answering one question as a determinist and another as a libertarian. Another explanation they offered is that the scale may be more reliable for people who have given considerable thought to the free will-determinism issue (assuming that philosophy majors have done so).

References

Viney, W., Waldman, D. A., & Barchilon, J. (1982). Attitudes toward punishment in relation to beliefs in free will and determinism. *Human Relations, 35,* 939–950.

Waldman, D. A., Viney, W., Bell, P. A., Bennett, J. B., & Hess, S. (1983). Internal and external locus of control in relation to beliefs in free will and determinism. *Psychological Reports, 53,* 631–634.

Source: Used by permission of Plenum Publishing Corp. Viney, Waldman & Barchilon (1982) *Human Relations, 35,* 946-947.

with each other until they gradually define themselves as living together. Similarly, deciding if we are in love with a particular person may not be an either/or issue; rather, we may have gradations of love feelings for that person.

Most Choices Are Revocable, Some Are Not

Most sexual choices are revocable, that is, they can be changed. For example, a person who has chosen to be sexually active with multiple partners can decide to be monogamous or to abstain from sexual relations. Or, individuals who, in the past, have chosen to accept being sexually unsatisfied in their pair-bonded relationship can decide to address the issue with their partner and/or seek sex therapy. In

EXHIBIT 1.2 More Than 100 Choices in Sexuality

Act on Sexual Orientation
- Heterosexual?
- Homosexual?
- Bisexual?

Sexual Life-style
- Committed relationship?
  - Traditional marriage?
  - Egalitarian relationship?
  - Sexually open committed relationship?
- Singlehood?
  - Never married?
  - Separated/divorced?
- Living Together?
  - Convenience?
  - Involved but not committed to marriage?
  - Prelude to marriage?
  - Instead of marriage?
- Group Marriage?
  - Few couples?
  - Numerous couples?
- Commune?
  - Urban?
  - Rural?

Sexual Values
- Absolutism?
- Situation ethics?
- Hedonism?

Emotional Context of Sexual Encounters
- Sex with love?
- Sex without love?
- Sex under the influence of alcohol or drugs?

Communication with New Partner about Sex
- Ask if partner has HIV or other STDs?
- Ask partner's feelings about using a condom?
- Ask partner's feelings about using other contraceptives?
- Discuss previous sexual experiences?
  - Previous partners?
  - Previous STDs?
  - Previous abortions?
  - Previous same-sex experiences?

Communication with Committed Partner about Sex
- Disclose what you like and don't like?
- Ask partner for likes and dislikes?
- Disclose sexual fantasies?
- Disclose homosexual encounters?

Masturbation—Yes or No?
- Use of vibrator?
- Use of erotica?
- Alone or with partner?

Interpersonal Sexual Activities
- Breast stimulation?
- Manual stimulation of genitals?
- Cunnilingus?
- Fellatio?

Coitus
- Before marriage or committed relationship?
- Number of partners (group sex)?
- Extradyadic sexual activity
  - One-night encounter?
    - Friend or stranger?
    - Prostitute?
  - Extended affair?
  - Sexual involvement with a co-worker?
  - Swinging?
- Race relevant?
- Age relevant?

Contraceptives
- Oral contraceptives?
- Condom?
- Norplant?
- Intrauterine device?
- Diaphragm or cervical cap?

Continued

The two biggest mistakes in life are failing to recognize bad choices and failing to correct those choices (if possible) once they have been made.

Marty Zusman

addition, contraceptive technology allows women to choose a form of sterilization (Norplant) that can be revoked (Norplant is discussed in Chapter 20). Even sterilization procedures that are intended to be permanent may sometimes be reversed. In 1992, Roseanne Arnold (star of television series *Roseanne*) underwent surgery to reverse a previous sterilization procedure so she could attempt to become pregnant.

Although most choices can be modified or changed, some cannot. You cannot eliminate the effects of some sexually transmissible diseases or undo an abortion.

A current debate regarding choices and sexuality involves the question of whether adolescents should be allowed to make choices regarding such issues as abortion and birth control. In the research and policy section to follow, we examine research on the issue of adolescent competency in decision making.

Exhibit 1.2 More Than 100 Choices in Sexuality—Continued

- Vaginal spermicides?
- Vaginal sponge?
- Postcoital birth control?
  "Morning-after" pill?
- Periodic abstinence
  Calendar method?
  Basal body temperature (BBT) method?
  Cervical mucus method?
  Hormone-in-urine method?
- Ineffective or no methods
  Withdrawal?
  Douching?

Sterilization
- Vasectomy?
- Tubal ligation?
- Laparoscopy?
- Minilaparotomy?

Infertility
- In-vitro fertilization?
- Artificial insemination by partner?
- Artificial insemination by donor?
- Sperm bank?
- Adoption?
- Contracted motherhood?
- Ovum transfer?

Unwanted Pregnancy
- Abortion?
- Carry pregnancy to term?
- Place baby for adoption?
- Get married?

Childbirth Methods for Desired Pregnancy
- Lamaze method?
- Dick-Read method?
- Bradley method?
- LeBoyer method?

Sex Education for Children
- In the home?
- In the school?
- In the church?

Physical Checkup for
- HIV?
- Other STDs?
- Breast cancer?
- Cervical cancer?
- Prostate cancer?
- Testicular cancer?

Parental Choices Regarding Children's Sexuality
- Allow children to see parents nude?
- Allow children to "play doctor" with peers?
- Give children books about sex?
- Allow children to see adult films?
- Circumcision of male child?

Pornography or Erotica
- Observe by self?
- Observe with partner?
- Allow children to see?

If Erectile Dysfunction
- Decide not important?
- Seek therapy?
- Have surgery—penile implant?
- Inject Papavarine?
- Use vacuum pump device?

If Can't Achieve Orgasm with Desired Frequency
- Decide not important?
- Reduce expectations?
- Seek therapy?
- Masturbate?
- Use vibrator?

If Sexual Problem of Apathy, Ejaculatory Incompetence, Vaginismus, or Dyspareunia
- Decide not a problem?
- Discuss with partner?
- Seek therapy?
- Follow recommended treatment?
- Continue or terminate sexual relationship with partner who has sexual dysfunction?

RESEARCH AND POLICY PERSPECTIVE

Are Adolescents Competent to Make Independent Choices?

In most states, parental consent must be obtained before medical services can be delivered to adolescents (or minors of any age). However, in many states, an exception is made for services related to sensitive health concerns, such as sexuality, substance abuse, and mental health. Health professionals have recognized that minors may be reluctant to seek health care if they are required to tell their parents or obtain parental consent (Greenberger & Connor, 1991).

> States have been especially mindful of a minor's need for privacy in obtaining services related to sexual activity: Almost half permit minors to consent to family planning services; over half authorize minors to consent to pregnancy-related care; and almost all allow minors to consent to treatment for sexually transmissible diseases. (Greenberger & Connor, 1991, p. 34)

Continued

Continued

An adolescent's capacity to independently make decisions regarding abortion has recently been a focus of legislation in many states. Most states have enacted laws requiring parental involvement. Parental consent is required before a minor can obtain an abortion in 26 states, although this is currently enforced in only 10 states. In 12 states parental notification is required, but is currently enforced in 8 states. Connecticut and Wisconsin require counseling, and Maine requires either counseling or consent from a parent or adult relative. The only legislatures which have not restricted minors' access to abortion are the following: Hawaii, Iowa, Kansas, New Hampshire, New Jersey, New York, North Carolina, Oklahoma, Oregon, Texas, Vermont and the District of Columbia (Haffner, 1992)

A Minnesota law that required parental consent for abortion was challenged in 1990 but was upheld by the Supreme Court (*Hodgson v. Minnesota*). The results may influence the enforcement of laws in other states. The Supreme Court allowed the state of Minnesota to require that both parents of a young woman under the age of 18 be notified prior to obtaining an abortion. Limited exceptions were allowed (e.g., if the minor reports sexual or physical abuse by a parent). However, the Court also ruled that a judicial bypass procedure must be available, in which a judge could bypass the parental involvement if the minor were judged sufficiently mature to give her own consent or if it were judged that parental notification was not in her best interests (Greenberger & Connor, 1991).

A number of psychologists who have analyzed the Supreme Court's decisions on regulation of minors' access to abortion argue against one assumption upon which those regulations have been based: "that adolescents are less likely than adults to make sound decisions when they are faced with an unintended pregnancy" (Interdivisional Committee on Adolescent Abortion, 1987, p. 73). A review of child development and psychological research does not reveal evidence for the Court's belief that adolescents lack decision-making skills (Gardner, Scherer, & Tester, 1989; Lewis, 1987; Melton, 1990).

Continued

Adolescents are capable of making wise sexual decisions.

Continued

Lewis (1987) reviewed research and theory in three areas related to adolescent decision-making skills: seeking, evaluating, and adhering to advice; the influence of developmental tasks unique to adolescence; and reasoning skills. Following are examples of the research reviewed by Lewis, as well as more recent studies.

Advice seeking

Lewis (1987) reported several studies affirming that the younger the minor, the more likely she was to involve parents in the abortion decision. Likewise, those with low self-perceived competence and with high conflict regarding the pregnancy decision were more likely to involve their parents. Mothers were reported as a stronger influence than peers or male partners (except for the white teens who planned to keep their baby). Lewis cited general child development research on adolescent conformity to peers, which indicates that peer conformity peeks at early adolescence (age 11 or 12), then declines, while conformity to parents becomes more a function of the relationship between child and parents. Lewis concluded, "Across adolescence youths become increasingly likely to 'own' their decisions, especially about serious matters, and to consider information and opinions from diverse sources" (p. 86).

A recent study at four Minnesota abortion clinics compared minors who used the court bypass option (43%) and those who notified both parents (Blum, Resnick, & Stark, 1990). Five factors were associated with notifying both parents: high perceived maternal support, young age, low socioeconomic status, living with both parents, and infrequent attendance at religious services. The interview results revealed that girls who were not close to their mothers did not turn to them. Fathers were described as being in a catch-22: "If he is absent, he is irrelevant and thus not informed; if he is compassionate and open, his daughter does not want to disappoint him" (p. 160). Many reasons (besides fear of parental disapproval) were given for not notifying parents: absent father, combination of family stresses, family violence, substance abuse by parents, and feeling that one's pregnancy "betrayed" the family.

Issues of adolescent development

While some theorists have hypothesized that grappling with the unique tasks of adolescent development impede rational decision making, Lewis (1987) found no empirical evidence of this. She cited a study of adolescents' responses to hypothetical treatment decisions and found that 14-year-olds seemed to understand and make rational treatment choices as well as 18- and 21-year-olds. A small exception was a limited number of 14-year-olds who replied that they would be less likely to take an antiseizure medication that had a side effect of facial disfiguration. However, their understanding and treatment choices reflected competence.

A more recent study has provided further evidence that adolescents are competent decision makers in abortion decisions (Ambuel & Rappaport, in press). At a women's medical clinic, 75 young women who were seeking a pregnancy test completed an audio taped interview which was scored on four criteria of legal competence. All the adolescents who considered abortion appeared as competent as legal adults. Only the adolescents who were age 15 or younger, and who did not consider abortion appeared less competent. The researchers recommended shifting the focus from trying to identify a particular age as an indicator of competency, to "developing procedures for obtaining consent that promote genuine *informed* consent" (p. 31).

Reasoning skills

Research on problem-solving skills measures the ability to generate multiple solutions to problems and to anticipate potential outcomes. Lewis cited a study revealing that,

Continued

Sexual decisions are often made in reference to one's peer group.

Continued

although high school students generate fewer alternative solutions to hypothetical stories than college students, the high school students were better able to generate potential consequences. However, younger adolescents may not be as able to consider potential risks associated with outcomes, and adolescents are known to engage in risk-taking behaviors. Lewis argued that minors may be as competent as adults in reasoning about decisions, but the social circumstances in which they function may limit their ability to implement their reasoning.

It has been suggested that social science research results should not be overstated in comparing adolescent and adult competence in decision making (Gardner, Scherer, & Tester, 1989). However, as policymakers struggle with the issue of adolescent access to abortion, Lewis's (1987) conclusion may provide helpful information: "At present, psychological research gives no basis for restrictions on minors' privacy in decision making on the ground of competence alone" (p. 87).

References

Ambuel, B. & Rappaport, J. (in press). Developmental trends in adolescents' psychological and legal competence to consent to abortion. *Law and Human Behavior.*

Blum, R. W., Resnick, M. D., & Stark, T. (1990). Factors associated with the use of court bypass by minors to obtain abortions. *Family Planning Perspectives, 22,* 158–160.

Gardner, W., Scherer, D., & Tester, M. (1989). Asserting scientific authority: Cognitive development and adolescent legal rights. *American Psychologist, 44,* 895–902.

Greenberger, M. D., & Connor, K. (1991). Parental notice and consent for abortion: Out of step with family law principles and policies. *Family Planning Perspectives, 23,* 31–35.

Haffner, D. W. (1992). Report card on the states: Sexual rights in America. *SIECUS Report, 20* (3), 1–7.

Interdivisional Committee on Adolescent Abortion (1987). Adolescent abortion: Psychological and legal issues. *American Psychologist, 42,* 73–78.

Lewis, C. C. (1987). Minors' competence to consent to abortion. *American Psychologist, 42,* 84–88.

Melton, G. B. (1990). Knowing what we *do* know: APA and adolescent abortion. *American Psychologist, 45,* 1171–1173.

Choices Are Influenced by Social Context and Cultural Forces

You do not make choices in a vacuum. Sexual choices occur in a social and cultural context that affects those choices (Reiss, 1986). The choices we make are influenced by various social and cultural norms. For example, while some people would prefer to swim in the nude, most U.S. resort communities do not permit nude swimming. Nude beaches are common in Sweden and France, but they are very rare in the United States.

Religion also represents a social context that influences sexual choices and behavior. Religiously devout people are much more likely to express disapproval of premarital sex, abortion, and homosexuality. Individuals who are low in religious devoutness are more likely to express acceptance or approval of such phenomena (Klassen, Williams, & Levitt, 1989, p. 70).

As social beings, we are never free from influence when we make decisions. We cannot separate ourselves from our experiences, our history, or our social environment.

Elissa Rashkin

Gender roles represent another aspect of society that influences our choices in the area of sexual attitudes and behavior. For example, the traditional male gender role that equates masculinity with sexual aggressiveness is viewed as an underlying cause of rape and sexual assault (see Chapter 19). Gender-role socialization may account for numerous differences between women and men regarding sexual attitudes. For example, in a study of 829 college students, only 1.9% of the women agreed with the statement "If a woman is heavily intoxicated, it is OK to have sex with her," whereas 22.6% of the men agreed with that statement (Holcomb, Holcomb, Sondag, & Williams, 1991).

Gender roles may also influence how we feel about the choices we make. For example, some research suggests that women tend to feel more guilty than men about a variety of sexual behaviors (e.g., extradyadic sex) (Knox, Walters, & Walters, 1991).

CONSIDERATION: "I am a part of all that I have met" wrote the famous poet Tennyson in "Ulysses." His statement suggests that who we are and the choices we make are influenced by other people, especially our family and peers.

Sexual choices are also influenced by previous experiences. The person who has been raped by a date may choose to date only in groups. The person who has had a sexually transmissible disease may insist on knowing the sexual history of new partners and on using a condom.

We can use social context to our advantage. If we value making certain choices, we can create certain contexts to influence those choices. For example, if we value commitment and fidelity to an absent partner, placing ourselves in contexts that foster that commitment (dinner with the absent partner's parents) is a choice. On the contrary, choosing to go drinking with friends who are unfaithful to their partners (and who are bar hopping to pick up a sex partner) may be incompatible with the goal to be faithful.

Drug Use Influences Choices

Just as the culture influences choices, so do mind-altering substances. Researchers have demonstrated that individuals who drink heavily, who have moderate to heavy drug use (marijuana, cocaine, etc.), or who use other illicit drugs are more likely to be nonvirgins (Orr, Beiter, & Ingersoll, 1991), to have anonymous sex with numerous partners (Penkower et al., 1991), to not use condoms (Biglan et al., 1990), to have sex with prostitutes (Wilson, Chiroro, Lavelle, & Mutero, 1989), and to be at greater risk for contracting HIV (Penkower et al., 1991). While these studies are correlational and do not imply that drug use is a causal factor, it is commonly known that various drugs, including alcohol and such prescription drugs as Valium and Halcion, affect our moods and emotional states, perceptions, cognitions, and judgments.

The best way to encourage responsibility is to support informed choice and to set a value on conscious decision in all actions.

Mary Catherine Bateson
Richard Goldsby

Interaction and sexual choices sometimes occur in the context of alcohol

In its report to the membership of the Presbyterian Church, the Committee on Human Sexuality (1991) emphasized:

> Among other things, sexual responsibility requires avoiding dependency on alcohol, illicit drugs, and other chemical substances to give us permission to be sexually active, whether we genuinely desire intimacy or not. Sexually responsible persons do not dull their senses or their judgment, but stay in touch with their real feelings. Only when we assume responsibility for our choices can we offer genuine consent, freely and in good faith. Only when we assume responsibility for our choices can we also withhold consent—and respect the right of others to do likewise. (p. 45)

Elements of Human Sexuality

Having looked at the nature of sexual choices, we now focus on several elements of human sexuality.

Anatomy and Physiology

Human sexual anatomy typically refers to the genitals of women and men; physiology refers to the functioning of the genitals and reproductive system. (Both anatomy and physiology are discussed in Chapter 6.) Anatomy also refers to other aspects of our physical body, such as height, weight, face, and shape. How these are regarded assumes major significance in terms of a person's physical appearance and sexual self-concept.

As this photo of a Victorian woman illustrates, one's dress and body image are influenced by the society and time in which one lives.

Sexual Self-Concept

With the shape I'm in, you could donate my body to science fiction.
Rodney Dangerfield

One's sexual self-concept is comprised of one's body image (self-concept in regard to physical attractiveness and desirability) and the perceived ability to satisfy a partner's emotional and sexual needs. Physical appearance is central to how individuals view themselves and others. In a study of 93 white and 65 black people, only 9% reported that physicalaids than they do on social services or education (Rodin, 1992). appearance was not important to them (Porter & Beuf, 1991). The degree to which people in the United States are concerned with physical appearance is reflected in the fact that they spend more money on beauty and fitness

CONSIDERATION: Rodin (1992) suggested that

> Getting in shape has become the new moral imperative—an alluring substitute for altruism and good work, the desire to look good replacing the desire to do good. In this new secular morality, values and ideals of beauty and appearance supplement moral and religious standards. (p. 58)

Women are socialized to be much more concerned with their body images than are men. Women are more stigmatized for being overweight than are men (Fuller & Groce, 1991). In a study of 15 obese women, Fuller and Groce (1991) found that women in their sample reported difficulty getting a date in their teenage years. However, none of the women reported having problems with sexuality once they formed pair-bonded relationships. "They apparently feel no inhibitions in letting spouses or other intimates see their naked bodies and they feel that their sex lives are satisfactory or 'ideal' " (Fuller & Groce, 1991, p. 170).

CONSIDERATION: Some people regard physical attractiveness as a liability. One attractive female medical student lamented that people tended to underestimate her intellect and did not take her ideas seriously because she was physically attractive (author's files). Another liability of being physically attractive is that others may view attractive individuals as less likely to be monogamous. In a study of 128 undergraduate psychology students, attractive men were seen as more likely to seek extramarital affairs (Tucker & O'Grady, 1991).

Physical appearance also plays a role in mate selection. However, physical appearance is less important to women when choosing a mate than to men. Townsend and Levy (1990) observed that, for women, the socioeconomic potential of the male and his willingness to become involved in a committed relationship outweighed the effects of his physical appearance. Men, on the other hand, were more concerned about the physical attractiveness of a potential partner than her socioeconomic potential.

CONSIDERATION: The effects of a person's physical appearance influence many aspects of the individual's life. Persons who have faces and heads that are widely discrepant from the cultural norm are more likely to have negative self-concepts, lower self-esteem, poorer-quality peer and parent relationships, and lower school performance. In contrast, persons who match the cultural ideal of being physically attractive are more likely to feel good about themselves, to have good relationships with others, and to perform well in school. This finding is based on research by Lerner et al. (1991), who studied the effect of physical appearance on the psychosocial functioning of 153 adolescents.

In the courtroom, physical appearance affects the outcome of sexual harassment suits initiated by women. In regard to such suits, one researcher noted that "the chances of obtaining guilty verdicts will be significantly decreased when the accused is a good-looking man and the alleged victim is a not-so-good-looking woman" (Castellow, Wuensch, & Moore, 1990, p. 560).

Behavior

Another element of sexuality is behavior. Table 1.1 summarizes the sexual behaviors reported by 272 university students enrolled in a human sexuality course. These data reflect similar rates of behavior for intercourse and oral sex among women and men but not for masturbation and number of partners.

TABLE 1.1 Sexual Behaviors of University Students Enrolled in a Human Sexuality Course

	Men (N = 79)	Women N = 193)
Intercourse	95.65%	92.75%
Masturbation	86.88%	57.82%
Received Cunnilingus	na	72.48%
Received Fellatio	76.66%	na
Average number of partners	13.71	8.39

Source: Knox, D. & Schacht, C. (1992). Sexual behaviors of university students enrolled in a human sexuality course. *College Student Journal 26,* 38–40. Table 1.1 Used by permission.

Sexual behavior may be the most important of all human activities. It is the process by which the species is reproduced, it is the central behavior around which families are formed, and it is the key component in the emotional lives of individuals.

Tom W. Smith

Previous studies have shown that men report higher rates of intercourse and oral sex than women. In a study of sexual behavior at a large, southern state-supported university over a 20-year period, researchers observed that 79% of the men and 63% of the women reported having experienced intercourse (Robinson, Ziss, Ganza, Katz, & Robinson, 1991). Regarding oral sex, 81% of the men and 74% of the women reported having engaged in this behavior. It should be noted that the participants in the this study were not just students enrolled in human sexuality classes. However, among 172 university students enrolled in three human sexuality courses, similar data were found. Men were more likely to have experienced premarital intercourse than women (86% and 72%, respectively). Regarding cunnilingus, 83% of the men reported having experienced cunnilingus in contrast to 72% of the women (Weis, Rabinowitz, & Ruckstuhl, 1992).

NATIONAL DATA: Based on a national random sample of adults in the United States, 97% report that they have had intercourse since age 18 and that they have had an average of 7.2 partners (Smith, 1991).

Women and men had significantly different rates for masturbation and the number of intercourse partners, as reported by Knox and Schacht (1992). Women were less likely than men to report ever having masturbated (58% versus 87%), and women reported having had fewer sexual partners (8 versus 14). These respondents were primarily middle-class and may not be representative of lower-income individuals. In a study of lower-income inner city women, only 31% reported ever having masturbated (House, Faulk, & Kubovchik, 1990).

The studies above reflect sexual behaviors from relatively small samples. Some national data are available. (See National Data in margin).

Cognitions

Another element inherent in the concept of human sexuality is cognition, or the thoughts and meanings individuals attach to anatomy, behavior, and objects. Cognitions are influenced by cultural definitions. For example, a naked body, kissing, and a dildo have no sexual connotations until they are defined by society as sexual.

Sexual fantasies (discussed in detail in Chapter 9, Individual Sexuality) are one aspect of cognitions in sexuality. In a study of 625 Danish women, 68% of women in their 20s, 48% of women in their 40s, and 50% of women in their 70s reported having sexual fantasies during masturbation (Lunde, Larsen, Fog, & Garde, 1991). Jones and Barlow (1990) observed that women and men were equally as likely to report having had sexual fantasies. Many men and women report positive feelings about their fantasies. Eighty-eight percent of 182 women and 93% of 125 men used the terms *good, happy, excitement, elation,* and *involvement* to describe their sexual fantasies. No respondents selected *disgust* to describe their sexual fantasies (Ellis & Symons, 1990, p. 540).

Everything can be taken from a man but one thing: the last of the human freedoms—to choose one's own attitude in any given set of circumstances, to choose one's own way.

Victor Frankl

While cognitions in the form of positive sexual fantasies may contribute to sexual enjoyment, cognitions may also interfere with healthy sexuality. In Chapter 15 (Sexual Dysfunctions and Sex Therapy), we note how cognitions can cause or contribute to lack of sexual desire, inability to experience orgasm, and other sexual dysfunctions. In Chapter 19 (Abuses and Commercial Uses of Sexuality), we discuss how cognitions (i.e., rape-supportive beliefs) may contribute to the incidence of rape and other forms of sexual harassment and assault.

Values

Sexual behaviors and thoughts do not occur in a vacuum but in the context of a value system. Values are a set of guidelines or principles that provide a basis for determining what is right and wrong, good and bad. Values provide a blueprint for our sexual behavior. In Chapter 2, Values in Sexuality, we examine how values guide choices (a complex process; Crow, Fok, Hartman, & Payne, 1991) in regard to sexual behavior.

TABLE 1.2 The Liberalization of Values Regarding Premarital Sex

Percentage of university students agreeing with the statement: "I feel that premarital sexual intercourse is immoral."

	1965	1985
Women	70%	17%
Men	33%	16%

Note: The intervening years showed a gradual decline in the percentage of students who agreed with the above statement, suggesting a liberalization of sexual values across time at this university.

Source: Adapted from Robinson, I., Ziss, K., Ganza, B., Katz, S. & Robinson, E. (1991). Twenty years of the sexual revolution, 1965-1985: An update. *Journal of Marriage and the Family, 53,*: 216–220. Used by permission.

Over the last two decades, the moral acceptability of some sexual behaviors has increased among some college students. This trend was observed by Robinson et al. (1991), who asked men and women at a large university over a 20-year period to indicate their agreement with the statement, "I feel that premarital sexual intercourse is immoral." The results, which are presented in Table 1.2, suggest a liberalization of sexual values concerning premarital sex.

Today's university students report approval of premarital intercourse if the partners are engaged. In a study of 172 students, 85.6% of the men and 90.3% of the women reported that premarital sex was acceptable for an engaged man. For 81.1% of the men and 89.8% of the women, premarital sex was acceptable for an engaged woman (Weis et al., 1992).

Emotions

As *Homo sapiens,* we experience emotions. Just as we are capable of feeling joy and excitement, we are also capable of feeling hurt, sadness, and anger. Sexual encounters and relationships may trigger each of these feelings. Sometimes we require a certain feeling context (e.g., love and trust) as a prerequisite for a sexual encounter. Townsend and Levy (1990) observed that university women were much more likely to prefer a context of love, affection, and commitment for a sexual encounter than university men. Rubin (1991) observed the same phenomenon in her sample of 1,275 respondents that included teenagers, university students, and older adults.

Free individuals may make unwise decisions in love and marriage . . . but who of those involved in any kind of romantic relationship would give up the freedom to make their own choice, for good or for ill?

Anthony Walsh

CONSIDERATION: One's emotional state affects the choices that one makes. For example, Forgas (1991) noted that "critical decisions and judgments about a relationship or one's partner are more likely to be lenient and positive when a person is in a positive mood state, and more likely to be negative or critical when the judge is in a dysphoric mood" (p. 172).

Relationships

While some aspects of sexuality are individual (masturbation, fantasy, viewing pornography or erotica), much of sexuality occurs in the context of a relationship. Tiefer (1991) observed, ". . . sexuality might be reconceptualized not as a dimension or quality inside one person, but something which only emerges in interaction" (p. 25). Such relationship interaction may be heterosexual or homosexual; marital, premarital, or extramarital; casual or intimate; and long-term or brief. The quality of a

Although heterosexual relationships are more common, sexual decisions also occur in the context of homosexual relationships.

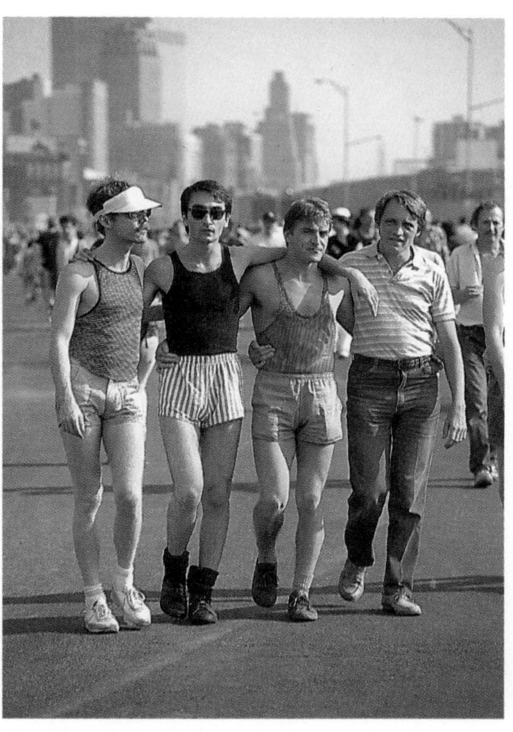

Sexuality is more in the domain of interpersonal relations than in the medical domain of individualized response.
Leonore Tiefer

relationship often determines the quality of the sexual experience within that relationship. A sample of 625 Danish women reported that their best orgasms were "obtained with a partner with whom they had a close, loving relationship and whom they trusted" (Lunde et al., 1991, pp. 114, 115). Marriage remains the relationship of choice for most people in the United States.

Variability

Human sexuality is characterized by variability. Sexual values, behaviors, thoughts, and relationships vary within the same person, between persons, and between cultures. The same person may have multiple sex partners at one age but later may be pair-bonded and monogamous. Two people from the same culture may differ in their backgrounds (low or high exposure to pornography), sexual orientation (heterosexual or homosexual), and sexual expressions (disgust or delight in oral sex).

CONSIDERATION: As you read this text, you will encounter some research studies that you feel do not reflect your own sexual behavior and attitudes. While this may be due, in part, to small samples that are not representative of the larger population, it may also be due to the fact that there is a great variability in sexuality across individuals.

When a cross-cultural perspective is considered, variations in sexuality become even more extensive. For example, while homosexual behavior is viewed as a competing sexual life-style in the United States, in the New Guinea Highlands, it is regarded as a pathway to heterosexuality (Herdt, 1981, 1989). In the Sambia (New Guinea Highlands), preadolescent boys are taught to perform fellatio (oral sex) on older unmarried males and ingest their sperm in order to produce their own sperm in adulthood and thereby be able to impregnate their wives.

CONSIDERATION: The term human sexuality is broad and includes many elements, only some of which we have defined in this chapter. A psychologist and sex educator noted that

> "Sexuality" also includes male and female social roles and social conventions (such as marriage, divorce, and other interpersonal relationships); childrearing; issues of sexual orientation; issues of sex and medicine (such as birth, birth control, abortion, and sexually transmissible diseases); and the manner in which sex and the sexes are portrayed by the media. (Selverstone, 1989, p. 7)

Sexual Myths

One of the benefits of taking a course in human sexuality is that you will become better informed about a number of topics regarding sexuality. In spite of the openness with which our society treats sex in the media, many people are uninformed or misinformed about sexual facts. Inaccurate beliefs, or sexual myths, are widespread in our society. Indeed, one myth is that the U.S. public is generally well-informed about sexuality.

In spite of the plethora of sex books, we are woefully ignorant about our sexuality.

EXHIBIT 1.3 What College Students Want to Know About Sex,—Continued

Can a man's penis be too big for a woman?

Until what age can you still have sex?

How do you know if you are ready to have sex?

Oral and Anal Sex

What is anal sex?

Is it normal to enjoy anal sex?

How safe is anal sex? Is it dangerous?

What is oral sex?

Do men really enjoy giving oral sex, or do they do it just to please their partner?

What do people mean when they talk about body fluids being exchanged during oral sex? Are these fluids harmless if ingested?

Homosexuality

Can homosexuals identify other homosexuals in a crowd?

What causes homosexuality?

When I masturbate, I think of my friend. I don't want to have sex with him or with any other man. Does my masturbation fantasy mean that I'm gay?

Besides oral sex, what do lesbians do in bed?

Pregnancy and Birth Control

Can you become pregnant the first time you have sex with someone?

When is the safest time for a woman to have sex without the worry of pregnancy?

Can you get pregnant from swallowing semen?

Is it possible to get pregnant without actually having sex, and if so, how close can you come?

What is the safest method of birth control?

How soon after conception does a woman know if she is pregnant?

How do you put a condom on?

How long does the penis have to stay in the woman's vagina to let sperm out?

Orgasm and Ejaculation

Is it true that men must have ejaculations fairly regularly for physical reasons?

Why do men reach orgasm after 30 seconds? Is it my fault?

Why do women hold off having an orgasm longer than men?

Is there such a thing as a multiple orgasm?
I think I've had an orgasm, but I'm not sure. How do I know?

How long should a male take to come?

How important are simultaneous orgasms?

Is it true that once you've reached a certain point or have gone so far, a man must ejaculate? Does it hurt?

Relationships and the Other Sex

Is it possible to be in love with two people at once?

How do you know when you're in love?

Can a man who you date rape you?

Source: Adapted from Caron, S. L. & Bertran, R. M. (1988) What college students want to know about sex. *Medical Aspects of Human Sexuality 22,* 18–20, 22–25. Used by permission.

sinful." (A promiscuous person was defined as someone who has casual sex with more than one partner.) The researchers found that a greater percentage of both men and women now consider promiscuity immoral or sinful compared to those of the mid-1970s. But, regardless of the time period, a greater percentage of men and women find the promiscuous woman more immoral or sinful than the promiscuous man (see Table 1.3). Hence, both men and women feel that women who are promiscuous are more immoral or sinful than men who are promiscuous. The researchers conclude, "the double standard, therefore, has not disappeared . . . " (p. 220).

In another study, Holcomb et al. (1991) reported that 17.7% of college men agreed with the statement, "Multiple sex partners are OK for a man, but not for a woman." Only 7.1% of the college women in this study agreed with the same statement. Similarly, 36.6% of 48 university men in contrast to 14.8% of 124 university women agreed with the statement that "premarital sex without affection is acceptable for the male" (Weis et al., 1992). The percentages agreeing that "pre-

TABLE 1.3 The Double Standard Is Not Dead

Over a 20-year period, the composite average percentage of university students agreeing with the following statements:

	% Men	% Women	% Total
Promiscuous male is immoral/sinful	29.8	39.0	34.4
Promiscuous female is immoral/sinful	40.4	54.6	47.5

Source: Robinson, I., Ziss, K., Ganza, B., Katz, S. & Robinson, E. (1991). "Twenty years of the sexual revolution, 1965-1985: An update." *Journal of Marriage and the Family, 53,* 216–220. Used by permission.

marital sex without affection is acceptable for the female" were 27.8 and 13.7, respectively (Weis, et al. 1992). These data consistently suggest the existence of a double standard for men and women.

Myth 4: Sex Therapy for Lack of Orgasm Doesn't Do Any Good

Another common myth in our society is that sex therapy is usually a waste of money. A common complaint of some women is that they are incapable of having an orgasm. Data suggest that sex therapy is helpful for the majority of women. In a survey of 289 sex therapists in the United States, 56% reported that they have successfully treated secondary orgasmic dysfunction cases (Kilmann, Mills, Caid, Bella, Davidson, & Wanlass, 1984). Women with secondary orgasmic dysfunction have been able to have an orgasm in the past but are currently unable to do so. (Orgasmic dysfunction and its treatments are discussed in Chapter 15, Sexual Dysfunctions and Sex Therapy.)

Myth 5: Women Secretly Want to Be Raped

In the last decade, the problem of rape has been publicized through the news media, public awareness campaigns, feminist political agendas, and college campus education programs. Despite this increased public attention, many people have erroneous beliefs about rape. For example, some individuals believe that women secretly want to be raped and that women who are raped enjoy the experience. In a study of 829 college students (Holcomb et al., 1991), 44.7% of men and 20.6% of women agreed with the statement: "Some women ask to be raped and may enjoy it." While some individuals do fantasize about being forced to have sex, in the fantasy, the individual controls what happens and does not suffer physical or emotional trauma (unlike the reality of rape). Rape myths are discussed further in Chapter 19, Abuses and Commercial Uses of Sexuality.

CONSIDERATION: We learn sexual myths through our parents, peers, and the media. Even when we are exposed to facts and perspectives that contradict our beliefs, we are sometimes reluctant to change our inaccurate beliefs. Changing them is not easy, but choosing to question our beliefs and exposing ourselves to other perspectives is a beginning.

Social Changes and Their Effects on Sexuality

During the last century, many social changes have occurred that affect human sexuality. These changes include sex in the media, developments in birth control, increased divorce and cohabitation rates, changes in the workplace, the women's movement and the men's movement, HIV infection, and technology.

Sex in the Media

In contrast to a mere generation ago, sexuality in U.S. society is highly visible in the media. Television talk shows, such as "Donahue," "Geraldo," "Oprah Winfrey" and "Sally Jesse Raphael," regularly feature sexual issues. Abigail Van Buren and Ann Landers answer explicit sexual questions from their readers. Portrayals of sexuality are common in today's television programming and films. Madonna, Prince, and Janet Jackson provide erotic visual images and sexually explicit lyrics on MTV as they perform their music. In addition to television, film, newspapers, magazines, and radio (in 1992, the Supreme Court ruled that late-night radio and television could carry more sexually explicit messages), some T-shirts and bumper stickers carry messages with sexual connotations. Examples include "Sociologists do it in groups," "Elevator operators like to go down," and "Firemen have long hoses."

The media has also become a mechanism for finding an intimate companion. Through personal advertisements, women and men seek both short-term sexual encounters and long-term emotional and sexual relationships. In a study of personal advertisements, Koestner and Wheeler (1988) noted that women were more likely to offer physical attractiveness and to seek professional status, while men tended to offer professional status and to seek physical attractiveness.

Media portrayals and discussions of sexuality and sexual issues have had both positive and negative influences on sexuality. On the positive side, the media have given visibility to women's and gay rights issues. Media attention to HIV infection and other sexually transmittable diseases provides a valuable public service in educating the population about STDs and their prevention. Media reports on date rape and sexual harassment have helped to bring these abuses of sexuality out of the closet and into the arena of public concern. In a 1992 episode of the television program "Beverly Hills, 90210," the value of sexual abstinence among teenagers was emphasized, along with the message that teenagers who are sexually active should use condoms. Colleges and universities, billboards, subways, buses, and other public places often display posters with such messages as "Use condom sense" and "Against her will is against the law."

On the negative side, the media have been criticized for portraying women and men in stereotyped roles, depicting sexuality in violent contexts, and exposing youth to sexually explicit images before they are mature enough to make responsible sexual choices. Women are often portrayed in the media as sexual objects. In a study of magazine advertisements, female models were more likely to be provocatively clad, partially clad, or nude than were male models (Soley & Kurzbard, 1986).

The media may also have a negative impact on our body image—an important component of our sexual self-concept. Rodin (1992) noted,

> Of all the industrial achievements of the 20th century that influence how we feel about our bodies, none has had a more profound effect than the rise of the mass media. Through movies, magazines, and TV, we see beautiful people as often as we see our own family members; the net effect is to make exceptional beauty appear real and attainable. (p. 57)

Birth Control

In 1873, the U.S. Congress passed the Comstock Act, which prohibited the mailing of "obscene" matter, including advertisements for methods of contraception. Anthony Comstock, the author of the bill, was also instrumental in the passage of legislation in New York that made it illegal to give contraceptive information verbally. Over 3,600 offenders were jailed for breaking these contraceptive laws.

Today, in stark contrast to the Comstock era, condoms are advertised and widely available in stores and vending machines throughout the nation. Contraceptive

A new openness about condoms has occurred in our society.

NATIONAL DATA: Methods of birth control available in our society today include sterilization, the pill, the IUD, the diaphragm, and the condom. Sixty percent of all women ages 15 to 44 in the United States use one of these birth control methods (*Statistical Abstract of the United States: 1992,* Table 98).

services for students are also provided by most colleges and universities and some high schools.

If birth control methods are not used or fail to work, an abortion may be legally obtained during the first two trimesters of pregnancy.

CONSIDERATION: Throughout history, women have always attempted to control their fertility; the difference today is that now we have methods that are more effective and safe.

Birth control has had the most dramatic affect on the lives of women. As Kaplan (1990) noted:

> . . . childbirth and childcare are no longer an automatic, "natural," part of woman's life cycle: this centrally affects women's sex and work lives—women may not only be sexual before marriage, but need not have children at all; meanwhile, they can compete with men in the work sphere. (p. 412)

Divorce

Divorce, the legal termination of a valid marriage contract, is a part of the U.S. relationship experience for over 2 million individuals each year (National Center for Health Statistics, 1992). It is estimated that the majority of marriages will end in divorce.

Divorce has an impact on the sexuality of both the divorcing couple and their children. One's marital status is associated with the number of sexual partners one has in a year. In a national sample of adults in the United States, married people reported an average of one partner (actually, 0.96) the preceding 12 months, in contrast to separated individuals, who reported an average of 2.41 sexual partners. When married and separated people were asked to report their number of sexual partners since age 18, they reported 5.72 and 11.75, respectively (Smith, 1991, p. 103).

NATIONAL DATA: Researchers Martin and Bumpass (1989) estimate that "About two-thirds of all first marriages are likely to disrupt" (p. 49). In first marriages, couples are likely to divorce after an average of 11 years; in second marriages, 7 years; in third marriages, 5 years (National Center for Health Statistics, 1990).

Divorce also affects the sexuality of children. Parents who are divorced and dating again often provide different models of sexual behavior for their children than do married couples. While daughters of nondating single mothers are no more likely to be sexually active at an early age than daughters in two-parent families, daughters of dating single mothers are at high risk for becoming sexually active (Peterson, Moore, Furstenberg, & Morgan, 1985, as cited in Strouse & Fabes, 1987). This finding suggests that parental modeling may be more important than parental monitoring (Christopher & Roosa, 1991).

Divorce may also affect the gender-role socialization of children. Divorce results in more children growing up in single-parent homes. It is estimated that by age 17, 70% of all white children and 94% of all black children will spend some time in a single-parent home (Hofferth, 1985). For male children, whose mothers get custody in 90% of the cases, this translates into less exposure to their fathers as male models for sexuality.

Divorce often leads to remarriage. About 20% of all current marriages are remarriages (Giles-Sims & Crosbie-Burnett, 1989). Remarriage, and the presence of a stepparent, may increase a child's risk for being sexually abused. Among women whose principal male parent was a stepfather, about 1 in 6 reported that they had been sexually abused by him before she reached the age of 14. In comparison, 1 in 43 women whose principal male parent was a biological father reported having been sexually abused by him (Russell, 1986).

Cohabitation

NATIONAL DATA: In 1970, there were 523,000 cohabiting couples; in 1980, there were 1,589,000; in 1991, there were over 2,764,000 cohabitating couples (*Statistical Abstract of the United States: 1992,* Table 52).

Cohabitation, also referred to as living together, may be defined as two unrelated people of the opposite sex who share an emotional and sexual relationship in the same residence for four or more nights a week for three consecutive months. The Census Bureau identifies cohabitants with the acronym **POSSLQ** (Persons of Opposite Sex Sharing Living Quarters) and counts the number of such households. In the last few decades, cohabitation has increased dramatically in our society.

The increase in cohabiting couples is associated with increased social acceptance of sex outside of the marital context. Although some people still disapprove of unmarried couples living together, more are accepting of cohabitation today than in previous decades.

CONSIDERATION: Has cohabitation increased because premarital sex has gained social acceptance? Or has premarital sex gained social acceptance because cohabitation has increased? Perhaps this is not an "either/or" question; rather, both interpretations are probably true (see Figure 1.1)

Changes in the Workplace

The number of women in the work force has increased dramatically over the last few decades.

Being in the labor force increases women's financial independence and thus decreases their dependence on sexual/pair-bonded relationships with men. Indeed, employed wives who work 35 or more hours per week are four times as likely to divorce than wives who average less than 20 hours per week (Greenstein, 1990). Increased female labor force participation also contributes to the developing norm of egalitarian gender-role expectations for women and men.

NATIONAL DATA: In 1975, 44.4% of U.S. wives were in the labor force. In 1991, the percentage rose to 88.5. (*Statistical Abstracts of the United States: 1992,* Table 621).

The increase in the number of women in the workplace is accompanied by changes in childbearing and child care. More women are having fewer children and at later ages; this is partly due to the fact that more women than in previous decades are giving

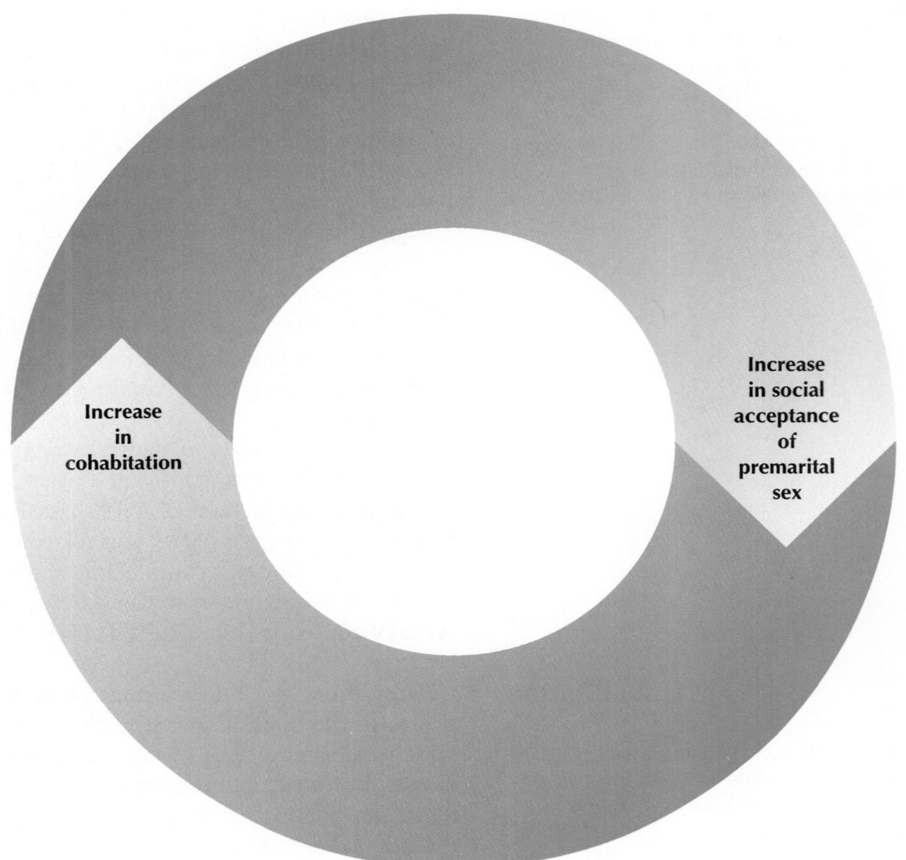

FIGURE 1.1 The Relationship Between Cohabitation and Social Acceptance of Premarital Sex

their careers priority over having children. The increase in women in the workforce has also fostered social concern for such issues as maternity and paternity leave (leave related to pregnancy, childbirth, or adoption), family leave (leave to care for ill or disabled family members), parental or infant care leave (leave to care for an infant), and quality day-care provisions. In response to these concerns, workplaces have begun to provide workers with a variety of parental and family leave options, as well as such services as on-site day care, school-age care, and sick care (for children), and provisions for breastfeeding on site (Ferber & O'Farrell, 1991).

Another effect of the increase in women in the workplace is the added potential for both men and women to have sexual relationships, including extradyadic relationships, with co-workers (sex with co-workers is discussed further in Chapter 10, Interpersonal Sexuality). Finally, more women in the labor force has resulted in increased visibility of the problem of sexual harassment in the workplace (discussed further in Chapter 19, Abuses and Commercial Uses of Sexuality).

Women's Movement and Men's Movement

In the nineteenth century and earlier, few voices protested the inferior and subordinate status of women in our society. The women's movement emerged to fight for equal rights and opportunities for women and against exploitation and sexual harassment. The women's movement also supports the belief that women should have the right to make choices regarding their bodies and reproduction. Specifically, the

Gloria Steinem has played an important role in the women's movement.

women's movement has advocated access to sex education, contraception, and abortion.

The roots of the women's movement can be traced back to the early antislavery movement in the 1800s. The first Women's Rights Convention was held in Seneca Falls, New York, in 1848 (Doyle & Paludi, 1991). However, the modern women's movement did not gather momentum until 1966, when the National Organization for Women (NOW) was created.

CONSIDERATION: While the women's movement has existed for over a hundred years, many women's issues have been addressed only in the last few decades. For example, it wasn't until 1972 that "the social problem of wife abuse first came to the attention of the British public. . . after being 'discovered' by a small group of women working to put the principles of the women's movement into practice" (Dobash & Dobash, 1988, p. 52). In addition, only in recent decades has the women's movement had success in developing crisis services for rape victims and promoting legislative and judicial reforms related to the prosecution of sexual assault crimes.

In addition, the women's movement reflects women's concern for equality in sexual interaction. Increasingly, women are emphasizing their rights and needs as sexual beings. Women in heterosexual relationships want their male partners to know that they have sexual needs and to learn how to satisfy them.

The women's movement has also resulted in women having a stronger sense of self. In a recent study of 600 women age 18 and older, only 6% wished that they were a man; in 1940, 25% of the women sampled wished that they had been born a man (Rubenstein, 1990).

The women's movement has also spawned a new generation of women who are less emotionally dependent on men for their happiness. According to Rubenstein (1990), only 31% of today's women reported that they feel they need a man in their life to be happy. In 1970, 66% of women sampled said that they needed a man in their life to be happy.

While women have long been aware of the oppressiveness of the traditional female role, men are just beginning to form a movement of their own. The men's movement represents men's rebellion against traditional male role expectations. Increasingly, men want greater acceptance of their emotional expression (e.g., crying, feeling hurt), to be free from having sole financial responsibility for women and children, and to have greater equality in court-ordered child custody and visitation arrangements. Another major social development affecting sexuality is the gay rights movement, which is discussed in Chapter 11, Sexual Orientation

HIV Infection

Perhaps the most significant recent social change affecting the sexuality of all people has been the spread of **HIV** (human immunodeficiency virus). This virus oftentimes leads to **AIDS** (Acquired Immune Deficiency Syndrome).

The threat of contracting HIV has put a new fear in sexual relationships. As a result of the HIV epidemic, more people are considering the value of abstinence and monogamy (Stevenson & Stevenson, 1990). In addition, condom use and other "safer sex" practices have gained widespread visibility and acceptance.

For the first time in history, sex is more dangerous than the cigarette afterward.
Jay Leno

However, values do not always translate into behavior. A national sample of U.S. adults revealed that 33% had engaged in relatively risky sexual behavior (sex with multiple partners, sex with less familiar partners, sex with male homosexual partners, and sex without a condom) since they were age 18 (Smith, 1991). Seven percent were currently engaging in such risky behavior (p. 106). In a sample of 91 gay and bisexual men, being caught up in the "heat of passion" was the reason for

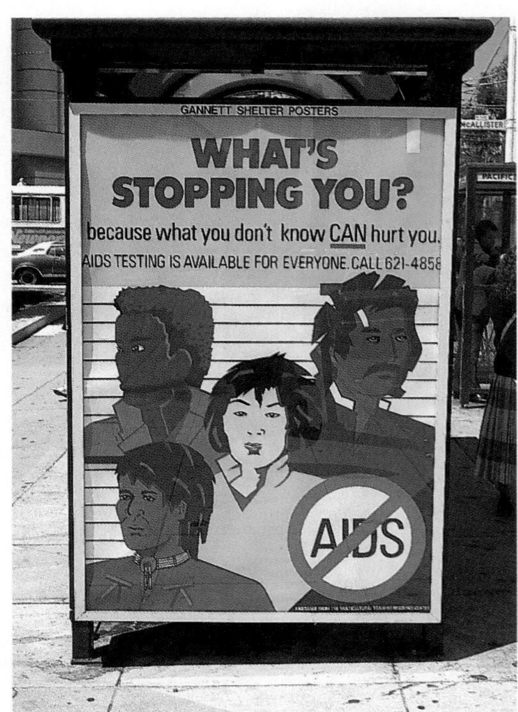

In response to the threat of HIV infection, sex education and AIDS testing are now openly encouraged.

their participation in unsafe sex (Thomas & Hodges, 1991). HIV infection and other sexually transmissible diseases will be discussed in detail in Chapter 18.

Technology

Examples of recent technological advances include artificial insemination, "test tube" fertilizations, penile implants, a woman's condom, subdermal contraceptive implants (e.g., Norplant), and postcoital methods of contraception (e.g., RU-486). Advances in medical technology allow individuals to change their gender (transsexual surgery is discussed further in Chapter 8). The widespread use of videocassette recorders allows individuals to view sexually explicit films in the privacy of their own bedroom. Table 1.4 summarizes some of the social changes in U.S. society and their subsequent effects on choices in sexuality.

TABLE 1.4 Social Changes in U.S. Society and the Effects on Sexuality

Social Change	Effects on Sexuality
Sex in the Media	Perpetuation of gender-role stereotypes. Objectifies women and associates sex with violence. Exposes youth to sexual images before they can make responsible sexual decisions. Negatively affects body image by perpetuating unrealistic appearance ideals. Educates public about women's issues (including sexual harassment and date rape), gay rights issues, and STDs. Provides mechanism (personal ads) for finding sexual companions or mates.
Birth Control, Sterilization, Contraception, Abortion	Love making separated from procreation. Increased sexual freedom for women.
Divorce	Separated individuals have twice as many sexual partners as married people. Increase in female-headed single-parent homes has implications for social and sexual development of children—more children reared in homes without fathers. Divorced parents who are dating serve as models for more casual sexual behavior. The presence of a stepfather increases the risk of a female child being sexually abused.
Cohabitation	Increased societal acceptance of sex between unmarried couples.
Changes in the Workplace	Being in the work force decreases women's economic dependence on men and may influence them to have fewer children at later ages. Increasing pressure on workplaces to provide family benefits (e.g., parental leave and on-site day care) provides more parenting options. More women in workforce also creates more opportunities for sexual relationships among co-workers (including extradyadic relationships) and more sexual harassment.
Women's and Men's Movements	Antipornography campaigns, sexual harassment suits, pro-choice campaigns, equality in the bedroom. Women also have stronger sense of self and are less dependent on a man for personal happiness. Men have begun to rebel against traditional male role expectations and to assert their emotional and nurturing qualities.
HIV Infection	Fear of contracting HIV and other STDs has led to an increased consideration of the value of abstinence, monogamy, and condoms in lowering the risk of infection.
Technology	Artificial insemination and "test tube" fertilization; penile implants and inflatable devices for men with erectile dysfunction. Transsexual surgery allows individuals to change their gender. Videocassette recorders allow individuals to make and to view sexually explicit films in their own home.

CHOICES

We will end each chapter with a section on specific choices in sexuality relevant to the content of the chapter. The choices on which we now focus include deciding to decide, the level of personal involvement you might choose in studying sexuality, and the degree to which you choose to be tolerant of the choices of others in regard to their sexuality.

Choose Deliberately or by Default?

Sometimes we delude ourselves into believing that we can avoid making sexual decisions. We cannot, because not to decide is to decide by default. Some examples follow:

- If we don't make a decision to avoid having sex with a new partner early in the relationship, we have made a decision for such sexual activity to occur.
- If we are sexually active with someone of the opposite sex and do not make a decision to consistently use some effective form of contraception, we have made a decision to allow pregnancy to occur.
- If we have intercourse with a stranger and do not decide to use a condom, we have made a decision to risk contracting HIV and/or other STDs.
- If we don't make a decision to be sexually faithful to our primary sexual partner, we have made a decision to be open to situations and relationships that present the possibility of extradyadic sex.
- If we have a sexual problem (sexual apathy, infrequent orgasm, erectile dysfunction early ejaculation) and do not decide to seek ways to resolve it, we have made a decision to allow the problem to continue.
- If we are frustrated with our partner because we are not being sexually satisfied and we do not tell our partner of the dissatisfaction and what we want, we have made a decision to remain dissatisfied with our partner's way of relating to us sexually.

Throughout the text, we will consider various choices with which we are confronted in our sexuality. It may be helpful for us to keep in mind that we cannot avoid making choices—that not to make a choice is to make one.

Human Sexuality: An Academic, Personal, or Career Search?

Until you receive your final grade for this course, you will be involved in the systematic study of human sexuality. One way to regard this course and this text is as an academic exercise in which you remain aloof from its content. This is a legitimate choice. People take human sexuality courses for a variety of reasons, such as to fulfill a social science requirement, to complete a transcript, or to satisfy their intellectual curiosity.

Another reason for studying human sexuality is to explore your own sexuality and the various choices associated with it. What sexual behaviors you engage in, with whom, in what contexts, with what motivations, with what frequency are all issues of personal choice. A course of this nature lends itself to such personal exploration.

A final alternative is for you to take the course as background for a career as a sex educator, counselor, or therapist. The American Association of Sex Educators, Counselors, and Therapists requires courses in human sexuality for certification. Knowledge about human sexuality is also very important for persons in a variety of occupational fields, including nursing, psychology, and medicine.

Choose Tolerance for the Choices and Life-styles of Others?

Regardless of the choices we make about our own sexuality, we might also make a choice about the rights of others to make choices that are different from ours. Such a perspective recognizes that "there is, in sum, no one right way to be" (Tavris, 1992, p. 333). While you may not choose or agree with any number of specific behaviors and life-styles (e.g., premarital sex, singlehood, abortion, homosexuality), you might consider choosing to be tolerant of others who make such choices or have such life-styles. The alternative of not doing so is to be constantly frustrated because people do not live the way you think they should.

SUMMARY

1. Two underlying assumptions of this text are 1) humans have free will; that is, humans have the capacity to make choices and 2) human behavior is determined or influenced by past (heredity) and present (environmental) factors.
2. In making sexual choices, it may be helpful to keep the following in mind: 1) we are constantly making choices; 2) not making a decision is itself a decision; 3) choices often involve advantages and disadvantages, which is why we may experience ambivalence; 4) some choices are "either/or," other choices are less dichotomous and occur on a continuum; 5) most choices are revocable, some are not; 6) choices are influenced by social context and cultural forces and 7) drug use may influence choices we make.
3. Human sexuality involves one's anatomy, sexual self-concept, behavior, thoughts, values, emotions, and relationships. Human sexuality is also variable in the same individual as well as between individuals and cultures.
4. Many adults, including college students, are uninformed about sexual information.
5. Common sexual myths include: 1) most people are well-informed about sexuality, 2) good sex requires intercourse and orgasm, 3) there is no longer a sexual double standard for women and men, 4) sex therapy does not help women who have difficulty experiencing orgasm, and 5) women secretly want to be raped.
6. The media have both educated the public about sexual harassment, date rape, HIV infection, and "safer sex" practices as well as harmed by contributing to sexual stereotypes and objectification, pairing sexual behavior with violence, and exposing young people to sexual innuendo and images before they are mature enough to make responsible choices.
7. In addition to increased sex in the media, other social changes that have affected sexuality include safer and more effective birth control methods, increased divorce, increased cohabitation and acceptance of nonmarital sex, increased participation of women in the paid work force, the women's movement and the men's movement, and technological advances.
8. A significant social change affecting sexual choices is the increased risk of HIV and other STD infections.
9. Choices in sexuality not only involve one's self but may involve tolerance for the choices of others.

KEY TERMS

free will
libertarianism
determinism
double standard
cohabitation
POSSLQ
HIV
AIDS
ambivalence

REFERENCES

Biglan, A., Metzler, C. W., Wirt, R., Ary, D., Noell, J., Ochs, L., French, C., & Hood, D. (1990). Social and behavioral factors associated with high-risk sexual behavior among adolescents. *Journal of Behavioral Medicine, 13,* 245–261.

Caron, S. L., & Bertran, R. M. (1988, April). What college students want to know about sex. *Medical Aspects of Human Sexuality,* pp. 18–20, 22–25.

Castellow, W. A., Wuensch, K. L., & Moore, C. H., (1990). Effects of physical attractiveness of the plaintiff and defendant in sexual harassment judgments. *Journal of Social Behavior and Personality 5*, 547–562.

Christopher, F. S. & Roosa, M. W. (1991). Factors affecting sexual decisions in the premarital relationships of adolescents and young adults. In K. McKinney & S. Sprecher (Eds.), *Sexuality in close relationships* (pp. 111–113). Hillsdale, NJ: Lawrence Erlbaum Associates.

Committee on Human Sexuality of the General Assembly of the Presbyterian Church (U.S.A.). (1991). *Keeping body and soul together: Sexuality, spirituality, and social justice.* Louisville, KY: Presbyterian Publishing House.

Crow, S. M., Fok. L. Y., Hartman, S. J., & Payne, D. M. (1991). Gender and values: what is the impact on decision making? *Sex Roles, 25,* 255–268.

Denney, N. W., Field, J. K., & Quadagno, D. (1984). Sex differences in sexual needs and desires. *Archives of Sexual Behavior, 13,* 233–245.

Dobash, R. E., & Dobash, R. P. (1988). Research as social action: The struggle for battered women. In K. Yllo, & M. Bograd, (Eds.), *Feminist perspectives on wife abuse* (pp. 51–74). Newbury Park, CA: Sage.

Doyle, J. A., & Paludi, M. A. (1991). *Sex and gender: the human experience* (2nd ed.). Dubuque, IA: Wm. C. Brown.

Ellis, B. J., and Symons, D. (1990). Sex differences in sexual fantasy: An evolutionary psychological approach. *Journal of Sex Research, 27,* 527–555.

Ferber, M. A., & O'Farrell, B., (Eds.), with La Rue Allen (1991). *Work and family: Policies for a changing work force.* Washington, D.C.: National Academy Press.

Forgas, J. P. (1991). Affect and cognition in close relationships. In Garth J. O. Fletcher & Frank D. Fincham (Eds.), *Cognition in close relationships* (pp. 151–174). Hillsdale, NJ: Lawrence Erlbaum Associates.

Fuller, M. L., & Groce, S. B. (1991). Obese women's responses to appearance norms. *Free Inquiry in Creative Sociology, 19(2),* 167–174.

Giles-Sims, J. & Crosbie-Burnett, M. (1989). Stepfamily research: Implications for policy, clinical interventions, and further research. *Family Relations, 38,* 19–23.

Greenstein, T. N. (1990). Marital disruption and the employment of married women. *Journal of Marriage and the Family, 52,* 657–688.

Herdt, G. (1981). *Guardians of the flutes: Idioms of masculinity.* New York: McGraw-Hill.

Herdt, G. (1989, June). Sexuality and masculine development up to middle adolescence among Sambia (Papua New Guinea). Paper presented at the annual meeting of the International Academy of Sex Research. Princeton, NJ.

Hofferth, S. L. (1985, February). Updating childrens' life course. *Journal of Marriage and the Family,* pp. 93–115.

Holcomb, D. R., Holcomb, L. C., Sondag, K. A., & Williams, N. (1991). Attitudes about date rape: Gender differences among college students. *College Student Journal, 25*(4), 434–439.

Hollis, M. (1985). *Invitation to philosophy.* Oxford: Basil Blackwell.

House, W. C., Faulk, A., & Kubovchik, M. (1990). Sexual behavior of inner-city women. *Journal of Sex Education and Therapy, 16,* 172–184.

Jones, J. C., & Barlow, D. H. (1990). Self-reported frequency of sexual urges, fantasies, and masturbatory fantasies in heterosexual males and females. *Archives of Sexual Behavior, 19,* 269–280.

Kaplan, E. A. (1990). Sex, work and motherhood: The impossible triangle. *Journal of Sex Research, 27,* 409–425.

Kilmann, P. R., Mills, K. H., Caid, C., Bella, B., Davidson, E., & Wanlass, R. (1984). The sexual interaction of women with secondary orgasmic dysfunction and their partners. *Archives of Sexual Behavior, 13,* 41–49.

Klassen, A. D., Williams, C. J., & Levitt, E. E. (1989). *Sex and morality in the United States.* Middletown, CN: Wesleyan University Press.

Knox, D., and Schacht, C. (1992). Sexual behaviors of university students enrolled in a human sexuality course. *College Student Journal, 26,* 38–40.

Knox, D., Walters, L. H., & Walters, J. (1991). Sexual guilt among college students. *College Student Journal, 25,* 432-433.

Koestner, R., & Wheeler, L. (1988). Self-presentation in personal advertisements: The influence of implicit notions of attraction and role expectations. *Journal of Social and Personal Relationships, 5*(2), 149–160.

Lerner, R. M., Lerner, J. V., Hess, L. E., Schwab, J., Javonovic, J., Talwar, R., & Kucher, J. S. Physical attractiveness and psychosocial functioning. *Journal of Early Adolescence, 11,* 300–320.

Lunde, I., Larsen, G. K., Fog, E. & Garde K. (1991). Sexual desire, orgasm, and sexual fantasies: A study of 625 danish women born in 1910, 1936, and 1958. *Journal of Sex Education and Therapy, 17,* 111–115.

Martin, T. C., & Bumpass, L. L. (1989). Recent trends in marital disruption. *Demography, 26,* 37–52.

Myers, D. G. (1992). The secrets of happiness. *Psychology Today*, 25, 38–45.

National Center for Health Statistics. (1992). *Births, marriages, divorces, and deaths for January, 1992* (Monthly Vital Statistics Report, vol. 40, no. 11). Hyattsville, MD: Public Health Service.

National Center for Health Statistics. (1990). *Advance report, final divorce statistics, 1987* (Monthly Vital Statistics Report, vol. 38, No. 12 suppl 2). Hyattsville, MD: Public Health Service.

Orr, D. P., Beiter, M., & Ingersoll, G. (1991). Premature sexual activity as an indicator of psychosocial risk. *Pediatrics, 87,* 141–147.

Penkower, L., Dew, M. A., Kingsley, L., Becker, J. T., Satz, P., Schearf, F. W., & Sheridan, K. (1991). Behavioral, health, and psychosocial factors and risk for HIV infection among sexually active homosexual men: The multicenter AIDS cohort study. *American Journal of Public Health, 81,* 194–196.

Porter, J. R., & Beuf, A. H. (1991). Racial variation in reaction to physical stigma: A study of degree of disturbance by vitiligo among black and white patients. *Journal of Health and Social Behavior, 32,* 192–204.

Reinisch, J., & Beasley, R. (1990). *The Kinsey Institute new report on sex.* New York: St. Martin's Press.

Reiss, I. L. (1986). A sociological journey in sexuality. *Journal of Marriage and the Family, 48,* 233–242.

Reiss, I. L., & Reiss, H. M. (1990). *An end to shame—shaping our next sexual revolution.* New York: Prometheus Books.

Robinson, I., Ziss, K., Ganza, B., Katz, S., & Robinson, E. (1991). Twenty years of the sexual revolution, 1965-1985: An update. *Journal of Marriage and the Family, 53,* 216–220.

Rodin, J. (1992, January/February). Body mania. *Psychology Today.* pp. 56–60.

Rubenstein, C. (1990, October). A brave new world. *New Woman,* pp. 158–164.

Rubin, L. B. (1991). *Erotic wars.* New York: Harper Perennial.

Russell, D. E. H. (1986). *The secret trauma: Incest in the lives of girls and women.* New York: Basic Books.

Sappington, A. A. (1990). Recent psychological approaches to the free will versus determinism issue. *Psychological Bulletin, 108*(1), 19–29.

Selverstone, R. (1989, March/April). Where are we now in the sexual revolution? *SEICUS Report,* pp. 7–12.

Smith, T. W. (1991). Adult sexual behavior in 1989: Number of partners, frequency of intercourse and risk of AIDS. *Family Planning Perspectives, 23,* 102–107.

Soley, L. C., & Kurzbard, G. (1986). Sex in advertising: A comparison of 1964 and 1984 magazine advertisements. *Journal of Advertising, 15*(3), 46–54, 64.

Spezzano, C. (1992, January/February). What to do between birth and death: The art of growing up. *Psychology Today,* pp. 54-55, 86-87.

Statistical abstract of the United States: 1992 (112th ed.) (1992). Washington, DC: U.S. Bureau of the Census.

Stevenson, M. R., and Stevenson, D. M. (1990). Beliefs about AIDs among entering college students. *Journal of Sex Education and Therapy, 16,* 201–204.

Strouse, J. S., & Fabes, R. A. (1987). A conceptualization of transition to nonvirginity in adolescent females. *Journal of Adolescent Research, 2,* 331–348.

Tavris, C. (1992). *The mismeasure of woman.* New York: Simon & Schuster.

Thomas, S. B., & Hodges, B. C. (1991). Assessing AIDS knowledge, attitudes, and risk behaviors among black and Hispanic homosexual and bisexual men: Results of a feasibility study. *Journal of Sex Education and Therapy, 17,* 116–124.

Tiefer, L. (1991). Commentary on the status of sex research: Feminism, sexuality, and sexology. *Journal of Psychology and Human Sexuality, 4,* 5–42.

Townsend, J. M., & Levy, G. D. (1990). Effects of potential partners' physical attractiveness and socioeconomic status on sexuality and partner selection. *Archives of Sexual Behavior, 19,* 149–164.

Tucker, M. W., & O'Grady, K. E. (1991). Effects of physical attractiveness, intelligence, age at marriage, and cohabitation on the perception of marital satisfaction. *Journal of Social Psychology, 131,* 253–269.

Weis, D. L., Rabinowitz, B., & Ruckstuhl, M. F. (1992). Individual changes in sexual attitudes and behavior within college-level human sexuality courses. *Journal of Sex Research, 29,* 43–59.

Wilson, D., Chiroro, P., Lavelle, S., & Mutero, C. (1989). Sex worker, client sex behaviour and condom use in Harare, Zimbabwe. *AIDS Care, 1,* 269–280.

Windt, P. Y. (1982). *An introduction to philosophy: Ideas in conflict.* St. Paul: West.

Yalom, I. D. (1989). *Love's executioner and other tales of psychotherapy.* New York: Basic Books.

Yalom, I. D. (1980). *Existential psychotherapy.* New York: Basic Books.

CHAPTER TWO

Values in Sexuality

Chapter Outline

Definitions and Functions of Sexual Values
- Self-Identity Function
- Mate Selection Function

Alternative Sexual Value Perspectives
- Absolutism
- Relativism
- Hedonism
- Are Sexual Values Changing?
- **Research and Policy Perspective:** Abortion Attitudes Reflect Relativism

Historical Roots of Sexual Values
- Jewish Heritage
- Christian Heritage
- The Puritans
- Asia, the Arab World, and Islam
- The Victorians
- Scientific Sexual Ideologies

Influences Affecting Sexual Values in U.S. Society
- Challenges to Traditional Gender Roles
- Religious Values in the 1990s

Influences of Values and Religion on Sexual Emotions, Attitudes, and Behaviors
- Sexual Guilt
- **Self-Assessment:** Revised Mosher Guilt Inventory, Sex Guilt Subscale
- Values and Religious Orientation

Sex and the Law
- Private Rights versus Social Morality
- Should Such Sex Laws Exist?
- A Continuum of Sex Offenses and Sex Laws
- Incidence of Sexual Behavior against the Law
- Reproductive Issues and the Law

Choices
- Is Honesty Always the Best Policy?
- Choose to Have Intercourse with a New Partner?
- Choose to Override Culturally Prestructured Choices?

Is It True?*

1. Women, in contrast to men, are more likely to make sexual value choices on the basis of the consequences for the relationship with their partners.

2. College students have become more approving of a number of sexual issues, such as premarital sex and sex education.

3. The membership of the Presbyterian Church (USA) rejected the report of their Committee on Human Sexuality, which encouraged acceptance of homosexual relationships.

4. Persons are more likely to feel guilt over a sexual behavior if they feel that significant others are likely to find out.

5. In 1990, the U.S. Supreme Court ruled that individuals have a constitutional right to engage in sodomy.

* 1 = T, 2 = T, 3 = T, 4 = T, 5 = F

VIRGIN: Teach your kid it's not a dirty word.

Billboard in Baltimore

The January 26, 1992, CBS "60 Minutes" interview with Democratic presidential candidate Bill and his wife, Hillary, on whether he had an extramarital affair emphasized the importance our society assigns to sexual values. Bill Clinton had been accused by Gennifer Flowers of being her lover for 12 years, which he denied. Writing about the event for *Time* magazine, one journalist asked, "Why is it all right for Bob Kerrey to divorce his wife and invite an actress, Debra Winger, to move into the Nebraska governor's mansion for a time and wrong for Bill Clinton and his wife to stay married and work through their troubles?" (Morrow, 1992, 15).

This chapter is about a core aspect of life, relationships, and sexuality—sexual values. Consider the following situations, which elicit one's sexual values.

> Two people are slow dancing to romantic music at a party. Although they met only two hours ago, they feel a strong attraction to each other. Each is wondering how much sexual intimacy is appropriate when they go back to one of their apartments later that evening. How much sex in a new relationship is appropriate?
>
> A woman has a career that involves her being away from home for extended periods of time. While she loves her spouse, she is lonely, bored and sexually frustrated when she is traveling. She has been asked to dinner by a single colleague in the same corporation in another city. Should she go to dinner and maybe a movie afterward?
>
> While Mary was away for a weekend visiting her parents, her partner with whom she has lived for two years had intercourse with a previous lover. Mary's partner "confessed" and apologized, promising never to be unfaithful again. What should Mary do?

The individuals in each of these situations will make a decision based on their personal value system. In this chapter, we examine the various values that guide sexual behavior and the historical, social, and religious origins of these values. We end by discussing sexual values in regard to honesty in relationships and making decisions about sexual involvement in a new relationship. We begin by looking at the definition and functions of sexual values.

Definition and Functions of Sexual Values

Values are moral guidelines for behavior. **Sexual values** are moral guidelines for sexual behavior. For example, choices about premarital and extramarital intercourse are made on the basis of sexual values. Of 188 university students enrolled in a human sexuality course, 91 percent of the men and 87 percent of the women approved of premarital intercourse; only 3 percent of the men and 3 percent of the women approved of extramarital intercourse (Rubinson & De Rubertis, 1991, p. 35). Sexual values serve an important function in our self-identity and in the selection of a mate.

Self-Identity Function

Our self-identity refers to who we are, that is, how we perceive that others view us and how we view ourselves. Our sexual values are a reflection of how we view ourselves. Persons who value sex without love, sex with casual partners, extramarital sex, and sex with children may have a different view of themselves than those who value sex with love, sex in long-term, committed, monogamous relationships, and sex with consenting adults. The sexual behaviors individuals engage in influence how others view them. Sixty-four percent of 256 university women reported that a woman who has sexual intercourse with "a great many men" is immoral. Thirty-eight percent of 205 university men reported that a man who has intercourse with "a great many women" is immoral (Rubinson & De Rubertis, 1991, p. 219).

Mate Selection Function

If I were the man that you wanted, I would not be the man that I am.
Lyle Lovett

Sexual values are also an important factor in selecting our friends, dating partners, and mates. The value theory of mate selection suggests that individuals with radically dissimilar sexual values are unlikely to consider each other as potential dating or marriage partners (Williams & Jacoby, 1989). Those who value egalitarian gender role relations, monogamous sexual relationships, and abortion rights tend not to select mates who value traditional gender role relationships, extradyadic sexual relationships, and legal restrictions on abortion. For example, one woman from a conservative religious background stated (in the authors' human sexuality class) that she valued virginity. While she felt that this value was not predominant on the university campus, she felt that it was right for her. A man in the class also spoke up in support of virginity. The two of them emphasized their disgust with the casual sex norms that permeate the university. Before the semester was over, they began to date.

In contrast, other individuals in the same class commented that they thought intercourse before marriage was essential and provided important information about the person. One woman said, "I wouldn't want to become involved with anyone who wouldn't have intercourse . . . it would mean that they were too uptight about sex." It is likely that this student will attract and be attracted to others who share her value.

Individuals who discuss and agree on sexual values are more likely to consider each other as potential mates.

CONSIDERATION: Compatible sexual values are an important consideration in mate selection. However, some couples develop and maintain a relationship in spite of differences between their sexual values. For example, a person who values sexual monogamy may become involved with a person who values sex with multiple partners. Couples with conflicting sexual values may consider the following options: changing their values, changing their behavior (while retaining their values), accepting their differences, or ending the relationship.

ALTERNATIVE SEXUAL VALUE PERSPECTIVES

There are at least three sexual values in regard to choices in sexual behavior: absolutism, relativism, and hedonism. Sometimes people change value perspectives across their life span.

Absolutism

There are a lot of advantages to a clear allegiance to traditional morality, including the protection it often offers against sexually transmitted disease, and every discussion of safer sex needs to emphasize the strengths of traditional values and the resilience and depth sometimes achieved in relationships whose exclusivity is unquestioned.

Mary Catherine Bateson
Richard Goldsby

NATIONAL DATA: Based on interviews with over 3,000 adult respondents throughout the United States, researchers at the Kinsey Institute concluded (Klassen, Williams, & Levitt, 1989): "With regard to many forms of sexual expression, our respondents were extremely conservative. A majority disapproved of homosexuality, prostitution, extramarital sex, and most forms of premarital sex. Even masturbation, a near universal behavior among males, was disapproved by 48 percent of our respondents. Furthermore, except for masturbation and for premarital sex between people who are in love, our data suggest that a majority of Americans are 'moral absolutists' in that they see these behaviors as *always* wrong." (p. 17)

Absolutism refers to a belief system that is based on the unconditional power and authority of science, law, tradition, or religion. An absolutist from a religious perspective would make sexual choices on the basis of moral considerations. To make the correct moral choice is to comply with God's will. Such choices also have a supernatural basis, and not to comply is a sin. (The absolutist might also be a legalist and make sexual decisions on the basis of a set of laws).

The official creeds of most Christian and Jewish denominations reflect an absolutist's view of sexual values. According to these creeds, intercourse between a man and a woman has a spiritual meaning and is to be expressed only in marriage; violations (premarital sex, homosexuality, and extramarital sex) are sins against God, self, and community. People who are guided by absolutism in their sexual choices have a clear notion of what is right and wrong.

For example, the official position of the Episcopal Church reflects an absolutist approach. Erdey (1991) identified three organizations within the Episcopal Church whose mission is to maintain traditional sexual values:

1. Episcopal Synod of America. This group rejects movements within the Episcopal Church to accept "fornication, adultery, and homosexuals unions as 'alternative Christian lifestyles' " (p. 14).
2. Episcopalians United. The best-funded of the Episcopal Church's conservative organizations, this group believes that the "modern drift toward the secularization of the faith and practice, doctrine and discipline of the Episcopal Church is destructive of the institution" (p. 14).
3. Prayer Book Society. The main objective of this group is to confront and defeat modern morality. " 'The church absolutely must stand for something (in questions of morality)' says Fr. Shackles, 'It's a pure question of values' " (p. 16).

More widely known than the official positions of the Episcopalian church is that of the Catholic Church (with which 55 million people identify). The Catholic Church rejects premarital sex, adultery, homosexuality, and abortion. It also rejects "safe sex" as a way to combat AIDS ("Bishops' Plan Deplores Abortion, 'Safe' Sex," 1991). The National Conference of Catholic Bishops said, "Instead of promoting the illusion of 'safe sex,' we need to warn our children and society of the dangers of sexual promiscuity . . . " (p. A3).

Traditionally, religion has held an absolutist view of sexual values against premarital, extramarital, and homosexual sex.

Many people in the United States are also absolutist in their sexual values. Although the basis of their absolutism may involve tradition and law, as well as religion, many are certain of their sexual values. Examples of the sexual values displayed by these individuals are found in Table 2.1.

Researchers at the Kinsey Institute also noted that the moral standards of these respondents were reported to be stable over time. "A large majority of our respondents reported that they have always held the same standards" (p. 19). Exhibit 2.1 presents a profile of those likely to hold absolutist sexual values.

A subcategory of absolutism is asceticism, which is reflected in the sexual values of Catholic priests, monks, nuns, and some other celibates. **Asceticism** involves the belief that giving into carnal lust is unnecessary and one must rise above the pursuit

TABLE 2.1 Sexual Values of over 3,000 Adults in the United States

Sexual Behavior	% Regarding the Behavior as Wrong or Almost Always Wrong
Extramarital sex	87%
Premarital sex by an adult woman with a man she loves	52%
Masturbation	48%

Source: Adapted from Klassen, Albert D., Williams, Colin, J. & Levitt, Eugene E. (1989). *Sex and morality in the United States: An empirical enquiry under the auspices of the Kinsey Institute,* (p. 18). Middletown, CT: Wesleyan University Press. Used by permission.

EXHIBIT 2.1 Characteristics of Absolutists

Older

The older a person, the more likely that person is to always disapprove of various sexual behaviors.

Women

Women are more likely to always disapprove of various sexual behaviors than men. Whether the behavior is premarital sex, homosexuality, or extramarital sex, women are more disapproving.

Blacks

Blacks, when compared with whites, are more likely to be absolutist in regard to masturbation.

Married

Those who are married are more likely to always disapprove of sexual behaviors than those who are not married.

of sensual pleasure into a life of self-discipline and self-denial. Accordingly, the spiritual life is viewed as the highest good, and self-denial helps us to achieve it.

Relativism

In contrast to absolutism is **relativism**—a value system that emphasizes that sexual decisions should be made in the context of a particular situation (hence, values are relative). The relativist, also known as the situationist (e.g., **situation ethics**), believes that to make all decisions on the basis of rules is to miss the point of human love. King Edward VIII of England was acting as a relativist when he gave up his throne to marry Wallis Simpson, a divorcee. He did so in the name of love and, at least publicly, said he never regretted his decision.

Whether or not two unmarried people should have intercourse may be viewed differently by absolutists and relativists. Whereas the absolutist would say that it is wrong for unmarried people to have intercourse and right for married people to do so, the relativist would say, "It depends on the situation." For example, suppose a married couple do not love each other and intercourse is an abusive, exploitative act. Also, suppose an unmarried couple love each other and intercourse for them is an expression of mutual concern and respect. A relativist might conclude that, in this particular situation, it is "more right" for the unmarried couple to have intercourse than the married couple.

It is sometimes difficult to make sexual decisions on a case-by-case basis. "I don't know what's right anymore" reflects the uncertainty of a situation ethics view. Once a person decides that mutual love is the context justifying intercourse, how often and how soon is it appropriate for the person to "fall in love"? Can love develop after two hours of conversation? How does one know that love feelings are genuine? The freedom that relativism brings to sexual decision making requires responsibility, maturity, and judgment. In some cases, individuals may deceive themselves into thinking that they are in love so they will not feel guilty about having intercourse with someone. In such a case, it is difficult to know if they are relativists or rationalizing absolutists.

We want to emphasize that many questions which cry out for simple answers are not so simple after all. The very desire for such answers, expressed so frequently, is itself a symptom of complexity—for the "clear answers" given to us by many sincere and dedicated people during our open hearings were themselves many and varied.

Minority Report of the Special Committee on Human Sexuality, prepared for the 203rd General Assembly (1991) of the Presbyterian Church

You've got to stand for something or you'll fall for anything.

Aaron Tippin

CONSIDERATION: Kohlberg (1984) suggested that during early adolescence, decisions are made on the basis of an absolutist perspective in regard to what is considered conventional and traditional (e.g., premarital intercourse is wrong). In late adolescence and into the early 20s, this perspective shifts to relativism (e.g., premarital intercourse is acceptable if the partners decide it is right for them).

Hedonism

Although it is usually—if not always—*desirable* for human beings to have sex relations with those they love rather than with those they do not love, it is by no means *necessary* that they do so.
Albert Ellis

Hedonism suggests that the ultimate value and motivation for human action lie in the pursuit of pleasure and the avoidance of pain. The hedonistic value is reflected in the statement "If it feels good, do it." Hedonism assumes that sexual desire, like hunger and thirst, is an appropriate appetite and its expression is legitimate.

The principle of hedonism has been debated for centuries. In the *Philebus,* Plato presented a debate concerning the proper goal of human existence. One view argues that humans should strive for knowledge, intelligence, and wisdom. Mead (1936) commented that "the greatest things are those for which we sacrifice ourselves and thus realize ourselves" (p. 209).

The opposing view is that pleasure is the only true goal in life. Ellis (1966) noted that in addition to being social, sex is a biological drive and that its biological phases are essentially nonaffectional. He argued that needless guilt arises from insisting that sex occur only in the context of love.

CONSIDERATION: When hedonism is defined as "what's in it for me," rather than "what's in it for us," men may be more prone to hedonism than women. Linn (1991) reviewed the work of Carol Gilligan (Gilligan, Ward, & Taylor, 1988) and suggested that men and women have different perspectives in making sexual decisions. While men look at deciding to have intercourse in a relationship as confirming their masculinity and autonomy, women are more likely to focus on the impact of such a decision on their relationship with their respective partners ("Will he love me afterward?"). Hence, men may be more hedonistic.

Table 2.2 reflects how the absolutist (religious or legal), relativist, and hedonist might make various sexual decisions.

Are Sexual Values Changing?

One way to assess if sexual values are changing is to examine the degree to which relativism, as opposed to absolutism, is being used more often as a basis for making sexual choices (hedonism is used less often as a value framework than relativism or absolutism). In the following Research and Policy Perspective, a shift from absolutism toward relativism on the abortion issue (in the United States) is evident.

Another way to assess changes in sexual values is to identify the degree to which people approve and disapprove of various aspects of sexuality. Smith (1990) com-

TABLE 2.2 Value Perspectives and Sexual Choices

Dilemma	Value Perspective	Sexual Choice
1. Disclose number of sexual partners to new lover.	Religious absolutism	Yes
	Relativism	Yes or No
	Hedonism	No
2. Disclose HIV infection to new lover.	Legal absolutism	Yes
	Relativism	Yes
	Hedonism	No
3. Have extrapartner sex.	Religious absolutism	No
	Relativism	Depends
	Hedonism	Yes

Sexual ethics is a very complicated issue.
Reverend Carter Heyward

pared the data from 13 research organizations (e.g., National Opinion Research Center, Roper, Gallup, Harris, and General Social Survey) over the past 30 years and found that attitudes have remained unchanged, become more liberal (more people approve), or become more conservative (more people disapprove), depending on the issue and the time frame being studied. For example, attitudes toward extramarital sex have been stable (most people disapprove throughout the 30 years); attitudes toward premarital sex, pornography, sex education, and birth control information have become more liberal (more people approve now than earlier); and attitudes toward homosexuality have become more conservative (more people disapprove). However, by the late 1980s, values on all issues were shifting slowly toward increased approval. This trend was true "especially among students" (Smith, 1990, p. 419).

NATIONAL DATA: Seventy-eight percent of the women in contrast to 67 percent of the men said that extramarital sex was "always" wrong (Klassen et al., 1989, p. 25).

Sexual values are continually changing. A team of researchers (Robinson, Ziss, Banza, Katz, & Robinson, 1991) studied the attitudes and behaviors of college students toward premarital intercourse over a 20-year period. They found a "continuing liberalization for both males and females, with the larger shift for females" (p. 216). Specifically, university males approving premarital intercourse increased from 65 percent in 1965 to 79 percent in 1985; the corresponding increases for university females were 28 percent and 63 percent. In another study of university students, 87 percent of the men in 1972 and 91 percent of the men in 1987 approved of premarital intercourse: the corresponding increases for university women at the same university were 80 percent and 87 percent (Rubinson & De Robertis, 1991, p. 35). The findings document a liberalization of premarital sexual values. In another study of 172 university students, over 85% of both women and men approved of premarital sex if the partners were in love (Weis, Rabinowitz, & Ruckstuhl, 1992).

NATIONAL DATA: Regarding extramarital sex, 73% of those who are married regard it as "always" wrong in contrast to 56% of those who are single (Klassen et al., 1989, p. 34).

Historical Roots of Sexual Values

For some individuals, religion serves as a basis for sexual values and decision making. In their study on religion and sexual behavior, Thornton and Camburn (1989) concluded, "Because religious values are the source of moral proscriptions for many individuals, the teachings of the churches are likely to play a role in the formation of individual attitudes, values, and decisions" (p. 642).

RESEARCH AND POLICY PERSPECTIVE

Abortion Attitudes Reflect Relativism

Abortion provides a fascinating focus for study of ethical beliefs, attitudes, and behaviors. Based on public opinion surveys in the United States, the majority of respondents believe that abortion is morally wrong. According to the Los Angeles Times Poll (a national telephone survey of 3,583 adults), 61% of respondents reported they believe abortion is "morally wrong." However, in the same poll, most respondents confirmed that they believe abortion should be legally available ("Majority in Poll," 1989). Seventy-four percent agreed with the statement "I personally feel that abortion is morally wrong, but I also feel that whether or not to have an abortion is a decision that has to be made by every woman for herself."

More recent polls have documented a small but statistically significant shift in the direction of supporting the legality of abortion ("Public Opinion," 1990). In the spring of 1990, two polls revealed a "prochoice" shift in attitudes toward the legality and acceptability of abortion (see Table 1).

Continued

TABLE 1 Opinions regarding the Legality and Acceptability of Abortion

	Percent of Respondents	
	1988	*1990*
Gallup Poll		
Abortion should be legal:		
Under any circumstance	24%	31%
Under no circumstance	17	12
National Opinion Research Center		
Approve of abortion for any reason	36	43

Continued

These data indicate that a minority of respondents are absolutists in their views on abortion. Rather than viewing abortion as always right or always wrong (absolutist position), most people view abortion from a relativistic position. Table 2 contains data from a 1982 poll of women and a 1990 poll of men and women (Henshaw & Martire, 1982; "Public Opinion," 1991). These data suggest that the attitudes of most respondents toward abortion vary according to the circumstances under which the abortion occurs. Over the 1980s, opinions regarding abortion under specific circumstances have become more accepting.

Physicians also seem to have relativistic views regarding performing abortions. A national survey of members of the American College of Obstetricians and Gynecologists was conducted by telephone and questionnaire to investigate attitudes toward various services, including abortion. It was interesting that female obstetrician-gynecologists (ob-gyns) were more supportive of abortions than male ob-gyns (see Table 3). In opinion polls of the general public, there is usually not a significant sex difference or men are slightly more favorable toward abortion (Weisman, Nathanson, Teitelbaum, Chase, & King, 1986).

Moral dilemmas involving reproduction and abortion have become more complex with the development of fetal tissue research and transplant technology. Fetal tissue transplants are being examined as possible cures or treatments for Parkinson's disease, diabetes, leukemia, sickle cell anemia, cancer, Huntington's chorea,

Continued

TABLE 2 Morality of Abortion under Specific Circumstances

	Percent who believe abortion is: "not morally wrong"	"approved of"
Circumstance Surrounding Abortion	*1982*	*1990*
Woman's health is endangered	80%	92%
Woman has been raped	80	85
Fetal defect	75	81
Cannot afford another child		48
Married woman already has large family	48	
Unmarried woman does not want to marry		45
Unwed teenager becomes pregnant	48	

TABLE 3 Percentage of ob-gyns who would have no ethical reservations about performing first-trimester abortions under specific conditions, and mean score on ethical reservations scale,† by gender

Condition	Male (N=567)	Female (N=603)
The life of the mother is endangered by the pregnancy*	86	91
The mother's health is seriously endangered by the pregnancy*	81	89
There is a strong chance of serious genetic defect in the fetus*	79	88
The pregnancy resulted from rape or incest*	74	86
The mother's psychological well-being is seriously endangered by the pregnancy*	57	73
The mother is an unmarried teenager*	51	68
The family is poor and cannot afford more children*	49	66
The mother is married and does not want more children*	45	63
Mean score on ethical reservations scale***	12.17	10.47

*Responses are significantly different, $p<0.05$, according to the t-test.
***The means are significantly different, $p<0.001$, according to the t-test.
†For each condition, respondents were asked to indicate whether they had strong personal ethical reservations about performing an abortion, moderate reservations or no reservations. The mean score was calculated by averaging the scale scores—the sum of reported replies for each respondent. Strong reservations received a score of 3, moderate reservations, a score of 2, and no reservations, a score of 1. Thus, the scores could (and did) range between 8 and 24, with a higher score indicating greater overall ethical reservations about abortion. The modal score was 8.
Used by permission. Carol S. Weisman, Constance A. Nathanson, Martha A. Teitelbaum, Gary A. Chase, and Theodore M. King, "Abortion Attitudes and Performance Among Male and Female Obstetrician-Gynecologists," *Family Planning Perspectives,* volume 18: Number 2 (March/April 1986) p. 69. ©The Alan Guttmacher Institute.

Continued

epilepsy, stroke, and AIDS (Gold & Lehrman, 1989). Currently, there is debate over whether it is morally acceptable for parents to conceive a child explicitly for the purpose of providing needed organs or tissues for another child and whether an abortion is acceptable if the fetal tissue is incompatible. Table 4 summarizes the results of a Time-CNN telephone poll of 1,000 U.S. adults who were asked about the morality of conception and abortion for fetal donation (Morrow, 1991).

Currently in the United States federal funding for research using fetal tissue is prohibited, a ban that is closely tied to abortion considerations. An advisory panel was convened by the National Institutes of Health in 1988 to review the ethical, scientific, and legal implications of research involving the transplantation of human fetal tissue obtained from abortions. Some witnesses contended that because the tissue was obtained from induced abortions, its use was morally tainted and should not be permitted. One argument was that ". . .abortion and fetal tissue research 'cannot be ethically separated, any more than obtaining benefits from stolen goods can be separated from the ethical condemnation of the theft itself' "(p. 10).

Continued

TABLE 4 Moral Acceptability of Conception and Abortion for Fetal Donation

Is it morally acceptable. . .	Yes	No
For parents to conceive a child in order to obtain an organ or tissue to save the life of another of their children?	47%	37%
To use fetal tissue to treat diseases?	36	47
To conceive and intentionally abort a fetus so the tissue can be used to save another life?	18	71
To abort a fetus if the fetal tissue is not compatible for a transplant?	11	78

Continued

The panel concluded that "induced abortion creates a set of morally relevant considerations, but noted further that the possibility of relieving suffering and saving life cannot be a matter of moral indifference to those who shape and guide public policy" (Gold & Lehrman, 1989, p. 10). While the panel endorsed transplantation research as acceptable and recommended lifting the ban on federal funds for such research, the members did recommend that safeguards be established to discourage profiteering or financial incentives for women to obtain abortions. Nevertheless, a moratorium on federal funding of such research remains in place. A diversity of opinions and values regarding abortion will necessitate continued efforts to balance personal morality, respect for the rights of others to exercise their choices, and legal policies.

References

Gold, R.B., & Lehrman, D. (1989). Fetal research under fire: The influence of abortion politics. *Family Planning Perspectives, 21,* 6–11, 38.

Henshaw, S.K., & Martire, G. (1982). Abortion and the public opinion polls: Morality and legality. *Family Planning Perspectives, 14,* 53–60.

Majority in poll backs abortion right. (1989, March 19). *The News and Observer,* Raleigh, NC, p. 1.

Morrow, L. (1991, June 17). When one body can save another. *Time,* pp. 54–58.

Public opinion on abortion shifts (1990). *Family Planning Perspectives, 22,* 197.

Weisman, C.S., Nathanson, C.A., Teitelbaum, M.A., Chase, G.A., & King, T.M. (1986). Abortion attitudes and performance among male and female obstetrician-gynecologists. *Family Planning Perspectives, 18,* 67–73.

Although we live in a pluralistic society in which people have different values, many of the roots of our values are religious. The Jewish and Christian influences have been the most prominent.

Jewish Heritage

Many of our values concerning sexuality can be traced to the laws and customs of Mosaic Judaism. The Old Testament, written between 800 and 200 B.C., reflects the society of the Jewish people at that time and should be viewed in its historical context. The Jews were a small, persecuted group. While they believed in God and that their sexual values were God-given, from a sociological perspective, their goal was to increase their numbers as rapidly as possible and to minimize defections. From this need to solidify their position as a group and a nation, they developed the following sexual norms.

History is particularly important in throwing light on the source of our attitudes about sex because many of the assumptions we make are not necessarily scientific or rational but holdovers of past belief systems that are no longer held by modern society.

Vern Bullough

Marriage Is Good Marriage (to a person of one's faith) was a way to encourage the birth of new members into the Jewish faith and to control their upbringing in this communal faith. Males were permitted to marry at 15; females even younger. Eighteen was considered the maximum age a male could remain single before he would have to explain to the elders of the community why he was still unmarried. Hence, singlehood was regarded as unnatural and immoral. Even widows and widowers were encouraged to remarry as soon as possible. In the case of a widow, her husband's brother could marry her.

Children Are Expected Once married, the couple was expected to "be fruitful and multiply." Sexual intercourse was encouraged. During the first year of marriage, the husband was exempt from military service so he could be with his wife. "When a man hath taken a new wife, he shall not go out to war, neither shall he be charged with any business: but he shall be free at home one year, and shall cheer up his wife which he hath taken" (Deut. 24:5).

Adultery Is Wrong The couple was restricted to having intercourse with each other. The Jewish society did not tolerate adultery. "And the man that committeth adultery with another man's wife, even he that committeth adultery with his neighbor's wife, the adulterer and the adulteress shall surely be put to death" (Lev. 20:10).

Other Sexual Admonitions Homosexuality, bestiality (sex with animals), and masturbation were forbidden as they did not involve marriage or procreation. As in many other societies, incest was prohibited. Indeed, any form of sexual expression outside of heterosexual marriage was regarded as immoral. The absolutist sexual value prevailed (Nelson, 1983). In addition, transvestism was disapproved of because it was a pagan practice and, as such, a threat to the community.

CONSIDERATION: Judaism has had a major impact on our view of sexual values. Our feelings about marriage (more than 90 percent of us marry), children (more than 90 percent of us express a desire to have children), and sex in marriage (most U.S. adults regard infidelity as something to be ashamed of) have been significantly influenced by the ancient Hebrews. But Christianity has also strongly affected our sexual values.

Christian Heritage

While Judaism was based on the teachings of Moses in the Old Testament, Christianity was based on the teachings of Jesus in the New Testament. Since early Christian congregations were geographically scattered, interpretations differed; "there were hundreds of competing groups with different and contradictory doctrines" (Bullough, 1987, p. 52).

Teachings of Jesus Most of Jesus's teachings were about salvation and living positively. He said very little about sex, although in one instance, he equated thoughts about having intercourse with the act itself. "But I say unto you that whosoever looketh on a woman to lust after her hath committed adultery with her already in his heart" (Matt. 5:28).

Teachings of St. Paul After the death of Jesus, his followers continued to preach the message of Christianity. Among these was St. Paul, who added his own interpretations of sexuality. He felt that while marriage was a difficult relationship, it was good and the most desirable context for sex. He felt that premarital intercourse was to be avoided.

The writings of St. Paul should be viewed in their historical context. He and others of his day believed that the return of Christ (the "second coming") was imminent. Sex and marriage were seen as unnecessary uses of a person's time when there was so much to do in preparation for Christ's return (such as recruit new members) and so little time.

CONSIDERATION: St. Paul's ideas about sex reflected the impact of Greco-Roman culture and its Hellenist philosophy, spiritualistic dualism. The body and spirit or mind were seen as being at odds with each other. The body was "temporal, material, corruptible and corrupting," while the spirit was pure and responsible for delivering the body from sin (Nelson, 1983, p. 122). "Sex was particularly bad because it was not only pleasurable but because it might lead to procreation and the imprisonment of other souls" (Bullough, 1987, p. 50).

This preoccupation with the body-spirit dichotomy continues today. "Much sex-negativity in this culture displays this spiritualistic distortion, which generates both fear of and, simultaneously, fixation with sex and the body" (Special Committee on Human Sexuality, 1991, p. 29).

Teachings of St. Augustine Around 386 A.D., at the age of 32, Augustine read the writings of St. Paul. Before this time, he had lived a promiscuous life that included fathering a son outside of marriage, cohabitating with his son's mother while becoming engaged to another woman, and being unfaithful to his fiancée. Frustrated with his inability to control his sexual desires, he converted to Christianity, broke off his engagement, stopped his affairs, and never married.

His own writings, particularly *The City of God,* reflect a very negative view of sex and sexuality. He felt that sexual desires, emotions, and passions, expressed through sexual intercourse, were sinful. While the only justification or purpose for intercourse was procreation, even in marriage, the act itself was tainted with shame. This shame, according to St. Augustine, was a result of the lust Adam and Eve felt for each other, their disobedience to God by engaging in sexual intercourse, and their expulsion from the Garden of Eden.

St. Augustine rose to be a bishop in the Roman Catholic Church, and his views became widespread. The ritual for infant baptism grew out of the belief that children were conceived in an impure act (original sin) and must be cleansed of this sin. This sacrament is still practiced and recognized by many Christian faiths.

CONSIDERATION: Early Christian interpretations of sexuality as evil led to the adoption of a reward-punishment model to control believers. People who controlled their sexual appetites were rewarded by the knowledge that they were like Christ, who was essentially asexual. Those who gave in to their lusts would be punished in Hell's fires after death. However, a way to avoid such threats was to confess one's sins to members of the clergy. Such confession helped the church monitor the sexual behavior of its members and ensure compliance (Bullough, 1987, p. 53).

Other Influential Religious Leaders St. Thomas Aquinas is another important writer whose thinking influenced sexual values in Western culture. A thirteenth-century Roman Catholic, Aquinas specified in *Summa Theologica* that any sexual act

Unlike earlier religious teachers (e.g. St. Paul, St. Augustine), John Calvin believed that sex, particularly in marriage, was a desirable, holy, and honorable experience.

that did not lead specifically to procreation was sinful and against the will of God. Masturbation, bestiality, and homosexuality headed the list. Even sexual caresses were sinful if engaged in solely for pleasure. Also, face-to-face intercourse was the only acceptable position.

NATIONAL DATA: Thirty-four percent of blacks, in contrast to 27 percent of whites. regard masturbation as "always" wrong (Klassen et al., 1989, pp. 32, 31).

Martin Luther and John Calvin, in their break from the Roman Catholic Church, adopted a more positive view of sexuality. According to Luther (who married and had over ten children), marriage was a good and positive relationship and not second to singlehood. He also regarded sexual desires as normal appetites much like hunger and thirst. Calvin, too, saw sex, at least in marriage, as holy, honorable, and desirable. Hence, marital sex was for more than procreation (Carswell, 1969).

The different Christian views of sexuality over time are illustrated in Table 2.3.

The Puritans

The Puritans who settled along the coast of New England in the seventeenth century were radical Protestants who had seceded from the Church of England. We can trace many of our sexual values to their beliefs and social norms. Tannahill (1982) noted that the forcefulness and power of the Puritans in imposing their ways on others and the fact that new immigrants were predominantly Protestant explain why the Puritans influenced several generations of later colonists. In fact, Tannahill suggested, the Puritan ethic has had a disproportionate influence in the history of the United States. "Senators and Congressmen today, struggling (whatever the state of their faith and/or marital relationships) to project an image of dedicated family men, at work, at rest, at church, at play, owe this particular electoral hazard to the early New England settlers who wove the public demonstration of family solidarity into the American ethos" (p. 330).

The Puritans wanted their members to get married and stay married. Religious values (avoiding temptation), social values (being a member of a close-knit community), and economic values (working hard for material reward) helped to emphasize the importance of the marital relationship. The Puritan woman had little

TABLE 2.3 Christian Religious Values Across Time

Year A.D.	Spokesperson	Values
50	St. Paul	Marital sex is moral; unmarried sex is immoral.
375	St. Augustine	Sexual desires and behaviors are sinful.
1200	Thomas Aquinas	Sex is for procreation only.
1500	Martin Luther	Sex is good, honorable, holy.
1930	Lambeth Conferences of Anglican Bishops	Sex is noble and creative; married love is strengthened by intercourse.
1991	Presbyterian Assembly	Sexuality is a good gift from God; the marital covenant between one man and one woman is to be lived out in Christian fidelity.

Sources: Carswell, R.W. (1969). Historical analysis of religion and sex. *Journal of School Health, 39,* 673–684. and *Presbyterians and Human Sexuality 1991.* The 203rd General Assembly (1991). Response to the Report of the Special Committee on Human Sexuality. Office of the General Assembly Presbyterian Church (U.S.A.). Louisville, Ky.

choice of an adult role other than wife and mother. Only in marriage could she achieve status in the community. Men and women were taught that their best chance for survival was to find a spouse to satisfy their needs for clothing, food, companionship, and sex.

The Puritans approved of sex only within marriage. Like Augustine and Aquinas, they viewed sex as a passion to conquer or control and marriage as the only safe place for its expression. Rigid codes of dress helped to discourage sexual thoughts.

Any discussion of sex among the Puritans would not be complete without reference to bundling, also called tarrying. Not unique to the Puritans, bundling was a courtship custom in which the would-be groom slept in the prospective bride's bed in her parents' home. But there were rules to restrict sexual contact. Both partners were fully clothed, and a wooden bar was placed between them. In addition, the young woman might be encased in a long bag up to her armpits, her clothes might be sewn together at strategic points, and her parents might be sleeping in the same room.

The justifications for the bundling were convenience and economics. Aside from meeting at church, bundling was one of the few opportunities a couple had to get together to talk and learn about each other. Since daylight hours were consumed by heavy work demands, night became the time for courtship. But how did the bed become the courtship arena? New England winters were cold. Firewood, oil for lamps, and candles were in short supply. By talking in bed, the young couple could come to know each other without wasting valuable sources of energy.

Although bundling flourished in the middle of the eighteenth century, it provoked a great deal of controversy. "Jonathan Edwards attacked it from the pulpit, and other ministers, who had allowed it to go unnoticed, joined in its suppression" (Calhoun, 1960, p. 71). By about 1800 the custom had virtually disappeared.

Asia, the Arab World, and Islam

Francoeur (1992) noted that in the Bible, sexual pleasure is associated with an original sin—a fall from grace. He suggested that "Americans . . . are increasingly fascinated by more sex-positive images of Eastern Sexual philosophies" (p. 1).

China Instead of prohibiting sexual behaviors that could interfere with fertility, Asian cultures actively encouraged sexual behaviors, not only to promote conception but also to contribute to spiritual growth. Tannahill (1982) noted that

In contrast to today, Puritan courtship couples (mid 18th century) were allowed to sleep together only if they were fully clothed ("bundled up") and if there was a board between them.

Eastern sexual and spirirtal traditions can help Westerners break out of the prevailing reduction of sexuality to genital activity.

Robert T. Francoeur

> Just as the European of early medieval times knew, without quite understanding why, that sex was sinful but occasionally permissible, so his contemporary in China knew, without quite understanding why, that sex was a sacred duty and one that he must perform frequently and conscientiously if he was truly to achieve harmony with the Supreme Path, the Way, *Tao*. (p. 168)

The world's earliest known and most detailed sex manuals were produced by the Chinese (Tannahill, 1982). The manuals, intended for women as well as men, typically included "introductory remarks on the cosmic significance of the sexual encounter" (p. 169), foreplay recommendations, and techniques and positions for intercourse (illustrated for bedside reference). The longer a man prolonged intercourse, the more *yin* essence he would absorb. The woman's yin essence was believed to be in generous supply. However, the man's *yang* essence (semen) was seen as limited and not to be squandered. The man was encouraged to nourish his yin with a number of women. "If in one night he can have intercourse with more than ten women it is best" (p. 172). And to prevent these encounters from being boring, the handbooks listed a variety of positions, "really only 30 basic ones" (p. 175), many of which were poetically named and acrobatically described. Noncoital activities were allowed as long as no precious yang essence was lost. These values persisted until the late seventeenth century, when Chinese sexual attitudes resembled those of the Puritans. Confucianism ultimately triumphed over Taoism.

India Between the third and fifth centuries A.D., the *Kamasutra,* the most famous of the Indian sex manuals, was compiled (Tannahill, 1982). By this time, Hinduism had saturated India and had separated its people by color and class. The doctrine of *Karma* (transmigration of souls) held that through correct behavior one could be reincarnated at a higher level. Sex was one of a Hindu Indian's religious duties—"not one that would put him straight into tune with the infinite, but certainly one of the least taxing and most pleasurable ways of improving the state of his *Karma*" (p. 201).

Buddhism, the second predominant Indian faith, also helped one live the best life possible while fatalistically anticipating relief (nirvana). Tantra, on the other hand, promised relief in a single lifetime. It involved sexual intercourse as part of religious ritual, a hedonist approach.

In Islam, the most male-oriented of the modern religions, a woman is nothing but a vehicle for producing sons, and the male function is, in part, the protection of the women.

Joseph Campbell

Islam The nomads who lived between the Red Sea and the Persian Gulf served as intermediaries in the east-west spice trade. But these disparate parts of the world were not united until the Prophet Muhammad (622 A.D.) began to preach a "composite of Arab, Jewish, and Christian beliefs that came to be known as the religion of Islam" (Tannahill, 1982, p. 230), whose followers were called Muslims. This faith spread throughout Syria, Mesopotamia, Persia, Africa's Mediterranean coast, and Spain. Through Islam, the West absorbed ideas and attitudes classical in origin, as well as from Asia's furthest reaches. "Very curiously indeed, the Arab love song—product of a society that remains today the last bastion of female subservience—was to provide the stimulus that transformed the West's image of woman . . . the "Lady' of the Chivalric ideal" (p. 231).

The Victorians

Another influence that lingers in our society is that of the Victorians. The Victorian era, which took its name from the English queen Alexandria Victoria, who reigned from 1837 to 1901, is popularly viewed as a time of prudery and propriety in sexual behavior. However, there was a great disparity between expressed middle-class morality and actual practices. In his study of this era, Wendell Johnson (1979) wrote:

> What were the Victorians actually doing? One might reply "Just about everything." Free love, adultery, male homosexuality and (in spite of the Queen's disbelief) lesbianism, nymphetism, sadism, and masochism, exhibitionism—the Victorians practiced them all . . . the number of whores per acre in mid-Victorian London and the consumption of pornography . . . would put today's Times Square to shame. (p. 11)

But the official view of sexuality during the Victorian era was that sexual behavior and the discussion of it should be suppressed. Some specific Victorian notions of sexuality are discussed below.

Marital Sexuality Sex was a passion that should be channeled into marriage. Uncontrollable sexual desires were believed to be characteristic only of men. Women were thought to be asexual and nonorgasmic. William Hammond, the surgeon general of the United States Army during the 1860s, wrote that it was doubtful that women experienced the slightest degree of pleasure in even one-tenth of the occasions of sexual intercourse. (Of course, such lack of pleasure may be related to the insensitivity of their husbands, who were not concerned about creating pleasure for their partners during intercourse.)

Prudishness Examples of Victorian prudishness include skirts to the ankle and discreet references to anything sexual. Women were not pregnant, they were "in an interesting way." Ladies delicately nibbled their "bosom of chicken," and librarians shelved books by male and female authors separately.

Female Types There were "good" women and "bad" women in Victorian society. The latter were whores or women who practiced no social graces in expressing their sexuality. Women who were not whores but who did enjoy sexual feelings were in conflict. Some felt degraded, even insane. "If I love sex, I must be like a whore" was an inescapable conclusion. Some women even had clitoridectomies (surgical removal of the clitoris) performed to eliminate the "cause" of their sexual feelings.

This painting illustrates the Victorian attitude toward the "fallen woman" who had allowed herself to be overcome by sexual desire.

Tannahill (1982) traced how the Victorian reincarnation of courtly love, which cast women in the role of untouchable moral guardians, fueled "an explosive increase in prostitution, an epidemic spread of venereal disease, and a morbid taste for masochism" (p. 347). The subsequent attempts of women to "set society to rights" was the foundation of their struggle for suffrage. In the twentieth century, scientific ideologies, discoveries, and their dissemination and the industrial revolution and economic reality presented a challenge to the artificial ideal of the Victorian family. The rise of scientific approaches is described in the following section.

Scientific Sexual Ideologies

Sexual behavior is one form of social behavior. Every society develops an ideology, a way of viewing or interpreting the social behavior of its members. Beyond the religious ideology (the mind must monitor the corrupt body) presented earlier, the scientific ideology began to compete for influence. "Since the turn of this century, there has been a general change in our way of thinking about the world. We are less likely to look to religion to explain the unknown, but are more likely to look to science" (Petras, 1978, pp. 76–77).

Several early-twentieth-century scientists were instrumental in shifting society's ideas about sex from a sacred to a scientific perspective including Richard von Krafft-Ebing, Sigmund Freud, Havelock Ellis, Magnus Hirschfeld, and Hendrick van de Velde. Richard von Krafft-Ebing (1840–1902) was a Viennese psychiatrist and sexologist who focused on the study of abnormal or pathological sexuality. *Psychopathia Sexualis* (1886) contains Krafft-Ebing's case histories of over 200 individuals. He described the most lurid details in Latin, and according to Tannahill (1982, p. 382), the work "soon became the bible of all pornographers who could afford a good Latin dictionary."

Theories developed by the Austrian physician Sigmund Freud (1885–1939) will be described in Chapter 5, Theories of Sexuality. Freud described stages of psychosexual development in terms of the erogenous zones (areas of the body that can bring pleasure). Personality formation was shaped by one's negotiation of predictable developmental crises, such as the Oedipal conflict with its castration anxiety and the Electra complex with its penis envy. Even those who advocate psychoanalytic theory, however, allow that "it is difficult to prove Freudian contentions empirically. Much of the difficulty here lies in the fact that we are dealing in the realm of fantasy and infant fantasy to boot!" (Cameron & Rychlak, 1985, p. 47). Nevertheless, this did not prevent Freud's ideas from being widely disseminated and influential in our thinking about sex roles and sexual expectations.

Havelock Ellis (1859–1939) emphasized that sexual behavior was learned social behavior, that "deviant" sexual behavior was merely that which society labeled as abnormal, and that an enjoyable sex life (a desirable goal) was not something that just happened but had to be achieved. About the sex education of children, Ellis (1931) wrote, "No doubt is any longer possible as to the absolute necessity of taking a deliberate and active part in this sexual initiation, instead of leaving it to chance or to revelation of ignorant and perhaps vicious companions or servants" (p. 43).

The work of Magnus Hirschfeld (1868–1935) is described in Chapter 4, Research in Human Sexuality. Inspite of the importance of his major works on homosexuality and transsexualism, Hirschfeld's writings had not been translated into English until recently. Perhaps this is because the scholarly community felt that he could not be objective, given that he was openly homosexual (and possibly transvestite, inferred from his empathy for transvestites and campaign for acceptance of them). However, his book, *Transvestites,* is considered to be "an outstanding classic that, while often cited, has been rarely read" (Bullough, 1991, p. 13).

Theodore Hendrik van de Velde (1873–1937) was a Dutch gynecologist, who, in 1926, published a guide to sex, *Ideal Marriage,* which became a best-seller. Like Ellis, van de Velde believed that sexual response was not automatic. He prescribed specific sexual techniques whereby his patients—and readers—could translate their emotional commitments into delightful orgasms. He also emphasized that sex is an interpersonal experience, and he considered lack of orgasm and impotence a couple's problem, rather than the wife's or husband's problem.

While a scientific emphasis contributed a valuable approach to understanding sexuality, it is important to recognize that even "objective" observations of scientists are framed and interpreted by cultural and historical context. For example, since the days of Aristotle, semen was emphasized as the essential element in reproduction. Although the ovaries had been discovered by the start of the Christian era, they were seen as an unimportant feminine replica of the testes. Tannahill (1982) quoted a sixteenth-century Spanish anatomist as reluctantly reporting their existence, hoping that "women might not become all the more arrogant for knowing that they also, like men, have testicles" (p. 344).

Following the discovery of the ovum in 1672, there were decades of debate over the relative contributions of the ovum and sperm (first seen under a microscope by Antony van Leeuwenhoeck in 1675). By the mid-1800s, observation of the fusion of a frog ovum and sperm confirmed what botanical study implied, that children derived characteristics as much from their mothers as from their fathers. This information was applied with dire social consequences. Racially mixed marriages were seen as dangerous, especially in anti-Semitic Germany and a conflicted United States grappling with the abolition of slavery. Race mixing would dilute the superior strain, according to prominent zoologist and geneticist C. B. Davenport. In 1929, Davenport published his comparison of white, brown, and black people from Jamaica and concluded that "the browns had a larger number who were 'muddled and wuzzleheaded.' What these engaging terms signify was not made clear, nor was any statistical evidence offered" (Thomas & Sillen, 1972 pp. 109–110). The term "miscegenation" (race mixing) wore the cloak of scientific authenticity but was actually coined by two journalists in an attempt to discredit Abraham Lincoln and antislavery forces by presenting Abolitionists as promoting systematic race mixing.

In addition to being used in acts of deliberate political trickery, science has been used to promote social agendas. LoPiccolo (1983) noted, "Indeed, it would appear that many of the pronouncements on sexuality made by experts (psychiatrists, psychologists, and sexologists) over the years have been little more than translation of cultural biases into pseudoscientific jargon" (p. 51). For example, the dire warnings of the dangers of masturbation, although presented as medical wisdom, were based on moral concerns (see the Historical Perspective in Chapter 9, Some Not-So-Helpful "Advice" from "Experts" on Masturbation). Krafft-Ebing described applying a white-hot iron to the clitoris of young girls brought in by their parents for "treatment" of masturbation.

Freud's work has been especially criticized for his pronouncements regarding the sexuality of women. "A large volume of empirical evidence has been accumulated to indicate that virtually all of Freud's inspired guesses about sexuality were wrong . . . Yet we continue to see couples applying for sex therapy with concerns that reflect this Freudian view of female sexuality" (LoPiccolo, 1983, p. 52). Freud's views of male sexuality, judging that any sexual behavior other than penile penetration of the

THE TIMELY WARNING

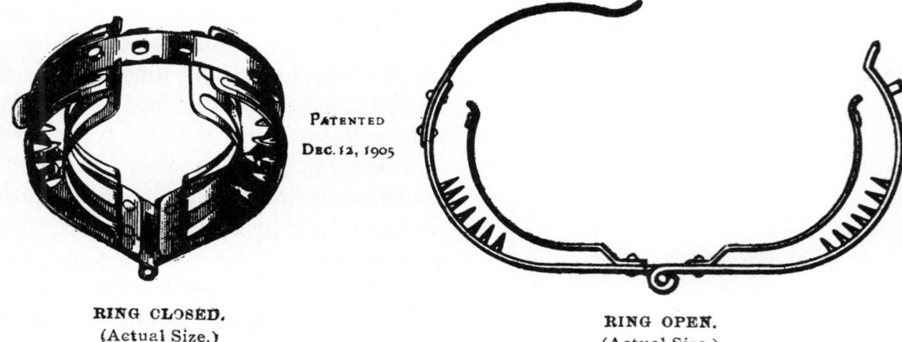

PREVENTS NIGHT EMISSIONS BY AROUSING THE WEARER

NASHVILLE, ARK., Aug. 18, 1905.

"I have had my ring five or six months. I have had just one emission in that time, when my ring was not adjusted tight enough. I am well pleased with it. I think it is just what I need."

PRINCETON, ILL., July 4, 1905.

"I have had a few seminal losses since I finished the treatment, but they are rare. I haven't worn the ring for several months. It was all right while I used it, but the losses finally got so far apart that I quit wearing the ring."

This timely warning device, designed to wake up a man about to have a nocturnal emission, illustrates how the medical profession used its scientific influence to promote a moral agenda against nonprocreative sex.

vagina implied arrested sexual development, were simply reflecting traditional Jewish attitudes, according to sexuality educator Sol Gordon. " 'Infantile,' 'immature,' 'personality defect' is just name calling and the substitution of Freudian pseudoscientific language for the prohibitions of the Talmud" (LoPiccolo, 1983, p. 52).

Nevertheless, early sexology pioneers set a precedent for studying sexuality from the perspective of a more scientific ideology. One historian (Johnson, 1979) offered the analogy that Havelock Ellis was to modern sexual theory what Albert Einstein was to modern physics, in that he offerred a paradigm that has influenced modern sexual theory. These early theorists paved the way for the next quantum leap. The works of Alfred Kinsey and Masters and Johnson (discussed in Chapter 4, Research in Human Sexuality) have added scientific credibility to the study of sexuality and have served as a foundation for further research. Indeed, it was said of Kinsey's research that he did for sex what Columbus did for geography (Ernst & Loth, 1948).

Influences Affecting Sexual Values in U.S. Society

Challenges to Traditional Gender Roles

The social changes of the twentieth century described in the previous chapter as influences on sexual behavior have also affected sexual values. A basic theme of the women's movement has been the equalization of rights and privileges for women and men. In the area of sexual behavior, the movement attacked the double standard that allowed men the privilege of enjoying sex outside marriage without being stigmatized. Traditionally, women were expected to avoid sex before marriage so as to increase their acceptability as a marriage partner and help them to achieve a secure economic future. In this regard, the movement has been successful. A woman's value in the United States is less affected by whether or not she has had intercourse, and women are becoming more economically independent. However, women who have a great many sexual partners are still at greater risk for being stigmatized as promiscuous than are men (Holcomb, Holcomb, Sondag, & Williams, 1991).

The availability of fairly reliable contraceptive methods has also influenced sexual values. According to Money (1988), the technology that allowed a reduction in fear of pregnancy set the stage for a "new ethic of love, sexuality, and eroticism as recreational, and not exclusively procreational" (p. 7). Of 700 students enrolled in a human sexuality class at a large midwestern university, 96% reported that unmarried women should be able to obtain contraceptives. When actual use was questioned, 61% reported to have used a method consistently and another 23% used a method frequently (Rubinson & De Rubertis, 1991, p. 36).

While the women's movement has been the most prominent social movement in the past few years, the gay liberation movement has increased the visibility of alternative sexual norms and life-styles. Carrying banners that read "Out of the closet" and "Better blatant than latent," male homosexuals and lesbians march annually during Gay Pride Week in major cities, including San Francisco and New York, seeking an end to discrimination on the basis of sexual orientation. In addition to public demonstrations, hundreds of homosexual organizations and publications in the United States have helped raise people's consciousness and offered support to their members. We will explore homosexuality and bisexuality in detail in Chapter 11, Sexual Orientations.

We need to reconceptualize intimate relationships in truly mutual terms instead of the dominant/subordinate model of traditional heterosexual marriage.
Pamela W. Darling

The gay liberation movement has increased the visibility of alternative sexual values, orientations, and lifestyles.

Although homosexuals still receive little social support and often encounter hostility from heterosexuals, public awareness of the homosexual's social world, values, and difficulties has encouraged some rethinking of both homosexual and heterosexual values. The result has been a more liberal society that recognizes the existence of alternative sexual norms and behaviors.

Religious Values in the 1990s

What sexual values does religion promote in the contemporary United States? We live in a pluralistic society with numerous religious faiths, denominations, and sects, which have different philosophies about and foundations for sexual values. While conservative Protestant churches and the Roman Catholic Church take the position that intercourse before marriage is wrong, some liberal religious groups, such as the Unitarians, believe there are conditions under which it is morally legitimate for two unmarried people to have intercourse.

CONSIDERATION: Sex-related issues are the concern of many religious groups and denominations that are struggling to balance their doctrines with the actual sexual values and behaviors of their members. An example of such a struggle is that of the Presbyterian Church, as reflected in its human sexuality committee's report to its membership.

The Special Committee on Human Sexuality of the Presbyterian Church (USA) was appointed to review current knowledge regarding human sexuality and its expression, biblical-theological guidance related to these issues, and the implications for the church's role in education, counseling supportive services, and ministry (Special Committee on Human Sexuality, 1991). After three years of work, the committee offered its report, "Keeping Body and Soul Together: Sexuality, Spirituality, and Social Justice," to the governing body for the denomination to use as a study document for a two-year period (Carey, 1991). Although the governing body voted not to accept the report, church and secular news media gave it wide coverage. An estimated 42,000 copies have been sold (Jameson, 1991); it was dubbed a "Presbyterian best-seller" in *Newsweek* (Woodward & Cohen, 1991).

Among the most controversial views were those relating to cohabitation, moral maturity, and homosexuality. Regarding living together, the report said:

> A Christian ethic of sexuality is needed that honors but does not restrict sexual activity to marriage alone, nor blesses all sexual activity within marriage as morally acceptable. (Sexual violence and coercion, within or outside of marriage, are wrong). (p. 38)

Regarding moral maturity:

> Moral maturity requires an acceptance—and a celebration—of a diversity of sexual relations with integrity and moral substance. The value of heterosexual marriage or of celibacy, when each enhances the dignity and well-being of persons, is not in question here. What is questionable is their exclusive claim to moral propriety and legitimacy. (p. 38)

In regard to homosexuality:

> The overwhelming power of God's justice that reaches to all human beings is dawning upon the hearts and consciences of God's people with respect to gays and lesbians. The time has come to embrace more fully the goodness of sexuality, whether it be homosexual or heterosexual. Heterosexuality and homosexuality are both God's good gifts of sexual being. What matters morally and ethically is how we live our lives as faithful people, regardless of our sexual orientation. (p. 103)

On the other hand, in the minority report issued by dissenting members of the committee, the following statement was made.

> It is God's intention that *social* relations be entered by all, but that *sexual* relations be contained within the more specific bond of marriage. Within that bond, protected as they are by promises of fidelity and permanence, sexual relations nourish the unity of the couple, lead to the procreation of children, and provide a most immediate way for a man and a woman to learn what it is to love another as one loves oneself.

The Presbyterians are not the only U.S. denomination addressing issues of sexuality. Others include the Episcopal Church, the Evangelical Lutheran Church in America, and the United Methodist Church (Jameson, 1991). At its 1991 biennial meeting, the American Baptist Church affirmed a statement of concern on "Human Sexuality" and appointed a task force to initiate a study process on local levels to guide members in developing a Christian perspective on sexuality. It also affirmed "A Statement of Concern Addressing Homosexuality and the Church," which encouraged "the repentant homosexual" to begin new relationships; it proclaimed nonacceptance of homosexual life-style, marriage, or ordination (ABC on Sexuality, 1991). Catholicism has been challenged on its sexuality restrictions. Uta Ranke-Heinemann, a feminist theologian, has drawn criticism from the Roman Catholic hierarchy following the U.S. release of her book, *Eunuchs for the Kingdom of Heaven: Women, Sexuality, and the Catholic Church*. In 1990, the book was the best-selling nonfiction title in Germany (Ranke-Heinemann, 1990). In an interview in an Episcopal publication, Faye Wattleton called on churches to support "a woman's right to reproductive choice." She stated, "Religious denominations need to take strong, clear, unambiguous stands on this issue, because women look to their religious institutions for guidance in making these decisions" (Wattleton, 1989).

Historically, black churches in the United States have not played as much of a role for blacks in prohibiting premarital and extramarital sexual behavior as white churches have played for whites (Staples, 1974). This is attributed to the view in many African religions that violations of the group's sexual mores are against individuals, rather than God. Staples observed that in the United States, black churches have focused on meeting expressive needs (releasing tensions from the effects of oppression), rather than on enforcing moral standards for members. While many of the churches have emphasized moral restraint and promoted chastity, they have not adopted the puritanical approach of many of the white churches. (Although in the middle-class and fundamentalist groups, such as Seventh-Day Adventists, Jehovah's Witnesses, and Black Muslims, this is not as true.) The holistic integration of sexuality and life was identified by Eugene (1985) as an important ministry of the black church. "Although the black church has been one of the key supportive institutions for upbuilding family life and values, the need to address issues and attitudes dealing with sexuality, with mutuality in male/female relationships, and with the more recent impact of black feminism has never been greater than today" (p. 122).

Clearly, the churches of the 1990s are wrestling with what their teachings should be on sexual issues. Is their role to call errants to repentance and redemption, or is it to swim in the mainstream so they can help those in distress—or can they do both (Sheler, 1991)?

Although ideas about sexual values differ between religious groups and, to some extent, their leaders, there is general agreement among the major religions in the United States (Protestant, Catholic, and Jewish) on the following sexual issues:

1. Sexual behavior has a spiritual dimension. A person's self-concept and relationship to divinity and to the larger community all affect and are affected by his or her sexual choices, especially when sexual encounters result in pregnancy to parents not committed to care for the offspring.
2. The highest moral approval is attached to sexual intercourse in marriage between a man and a woman. This implies that both premarital and extramarital intercourse are wrong.

CONSIDERATION: Reiss and Reiss (1990) argued for a society of tolerance and endorsed pluralism—the view that all forms of sexuality are acceptable if they are carried out with honesty, equality, and responsibility. They further condemned dogmatism, which dominates education, religion, and politics, and suggested that conservative elements of our society have created the very social problems we deplore—teen pregnancies, births to unmarried parents, and high STD rates among adolescents.

Influences of Values and Religion on Sexual Emotions, Attitudes, and Behaviors

It seems likely that religious or other values influence sexual decision-making and behavior. In the following sections, we review research that looks at the influence of values on sexual emotions, attitudes, and behaviors.

Sexual Guilt

We know that sexual behavior is not always consistent with sexual morals (Mosher & Vonderheide, 1985). **Sex guilt** was defined by Mosher (1966) as a tendency toward self-punishment for violating one's personal sexual standards. Sex guilt may inhibit the disapproved behavior but does not necessarily do so, as it is only one factor involved in making sexual decisions. Donald Mosher, a psychology professor at the University of Connecticut (1966), developed a measure of sex guilt that has been used in many studies. The Sex Guilt subscale of an updated form of his measure, the Revised Mosher Guilt Inventory, is reproduced as the Self-Assessment for this chapter.

Studies using Mosher's earlier measure have found that sex guilt is related to a number of sex-related attitudes and behaviors. These include findings that people with high sex guilt are less likely than people with low sex guilt to engage in sexual behavior or expose themselves to sexual or erotic materials, and enjoy them less when exposed (Gerrard & Gibbons, 1982).

Smith and Walters (1988), in their review of the literature, also found that the higher the sex guilt, the lower:

- the frequency of masturbation;
- the frequency of female orgasm;
- the use of reliable, effective contraception;
- the chance of selecting abortion to end an unwanted pregnancy; and
- the chance of avoiding a premarital pregnancy.

Cado and Leitenberg (1990) found that high sex guilt was associated with sexual dissatisfaction and dysfunction.

One study of undergraduate college students (Gerrard & Gibbons, 1982) investigated the relations between sexual experience, sex guilt, and sexual moral reasoning. Using the Mosher sex guilt measure and a survey that asked about the frequency of six sexual behaviors (masturbation, adultery, unusual sexual practices, reading erotic literature, prostitution, and premarital sex), the researchers replicated the results of earlier studies. They confirmed that men reported more sexual experiences than women and that students with low sex guilt reported more sexual experiences than those with high sex guilt. They randomly selected 35 men and 33 women from the high and low sex guilt scorers to complete a measure of sexual moral reasoning. Their responses to open-ended questions were rated according to the stage of moral reasoning (as outlined by Kohlberg). Gerrard and Gibbons found that sex guilt and moral reasoning were negatively related ($r\ [66] = -0.52$, $p = 0.001$) and that the reasoning seemed to be influenced by level of sexual experience. The level of reasoning was higher for behaviors that the students had experienced. It appeared that sex guilt indirectly retarded sexual moral development "by inhibiting behavior and thereby reducing the conflict and deliberation it produces" (p. 356).

An additional finding highlighted by Gerrard and Gibbons was the response pattern of the high-guilt women. Although the students in this group were the least sophisticated in expressing moral reasoning, their moral *preferences* (endorsement of preferred reasoning) were the highest of any group. Gerrard and Gibbons suggested that this is related to their greater vulnerability to unwanted pregnancies and abortions because, due to their sexual inexperience, their sexual standards are not clearly defined and only loosely related to their behavior. "Thus, one interpretation of the current results is that sexually inexperienced high guilt females hold on to their (relatively unsophisticated) moral standards rather tenuously, and will abandon them readily in favor of a more 'persuasive argument' when it is presented to them" (p. 358). Perhaps, as they gain sexual experience, their moral reasoning will become more sophisticated and consistent with behavior and lead to more pragmatic use of contraception (Gerrard & Gibbons, 1982).

Self Assessment

Revised Mosher Guilt Inventory, Sex-Guilt Subscale

Instructions This subscale consists of 50 items arranged in pairs of responses written by college students in response to sentence completion items, such as "When I have sexual dreams . . .". You are to respond to each item as honestly as you can by rating your response on a 7-point scale from 0, which means "not at all true of (for) me," to 6, which means "extremely true of (for) me." Ratings of 1 to 5 represent ratings of agreement-disagreement that are intermediate between the extreme anchors of "not at all true" and "extremely true" for you. This limited comparison is often useful since people frequently agree with only one item in a pair. In some instances, both or neither item may be true for you, but you will usually be able to distinguish between items in a pair by using different ratings from the 7-point range for each item.

Rate each of the items from 0 to 6 as you keep in mind the value of comparing items within pairs. Please do not omit any items.

	NOT AT ALL						EXTREMELY
"Dirty" jokes in mixed company. . .							
5. do not bother me.	0	1	2	3	4	5	6
6. make me very uncomfortable.	0	1	2	3	4	5	6
Masturbation. . .							
7. is wrong and will ruin you.	0	1	2	3	4	5	6
8. helps one feel eased and relaxed.	0	1	2	3	4	5	6
Sex relations before marriage. . .							
11. should be permitted.	0	1	2	3	4	5	6
12. are wrong and immoral.	0	1	2	3	4	5	6
Sex relations before marriage. . .							
13. ruin many a happy couple.	0	1	2	3	4	5	6
14. are good in my opinion.	0	1	2	3	4	5	6
Unusual sex practices. . .							
15. might be interesting.	0	1	2	3	4	5	6
16. don't interest me.	0	1	2	3	4	5	6
When I have sexual dreams. . .							
17. I sometimes wake up feeling excited.	0	1	2	3	4	5	6
18. I try to forget them.	0	1	2	3	4	5	6
"Dirty" jokes in mixed company. . .							
25. are in bad taste.	0	1	2	3	4	5	6
26. can be funny depending on the company.	0	1	2	3	4	5	6
Petting. . .							
31. I am sorry to say, is becoming an accepted practice.	0	1	2	3	4	5	6
32. is an expression of affection, which is satisfying.	0	1	2	3	4	5	6
Unusual sex practices. . .							
35. are not so unusual.	0	1	2	3	4	5	6
36. don't interest me.	0	1	2	3	4	5	6
Sex. . .							
41. is good and enjoyable.	0	1	2	3	4	5	6
42. should be saved for wedlock and childbearing.	0	1	2	3	4	5	6
"Dirty" jokes in mixed company. . .							
51. are coarse, to say the least.	0	1	2	3	4	5	6
52. are lots of fun.	0	1	2	3	4	5	6
When I have sexual desires. . .							
53. I enjoy them like all healthy humans beings.	0	1	2	3	4	5	6
54. I fight them, for I must have complete control of my body.	0	1	2	3	4	5	6
Unusual sex practices. . .							
61. are unwise and lead only to trouble.	0	1	2	3	4	5	6
62. are all in how you look at it.	0	1	2	3	4	5	6
Unusual sex practices. . .							
63. are OK as long as they're heterosexual.	0	1	2	3	4	5	6
64. usually aren't pleasurable because you have pre-conceived feelings about their being wrong.	0	1	2	3	4	5	6

Self-Assessment—*Continued*

	NOT AT ALL						EXTREMELY
Sex relations before marriage. . .							
67. in my opinion, should not be practiced.	0	1	2	3	4	5	6
68. are practiced too much to be wrong.	0	1	2	3	4	5	6
As a child, sex play. . .							
71. is immature and ridiculous.	0	1	2	3	4	5	6
72. was indulged in.	0	1	2	3	4	5	6
Unusual sex practices. . .							
75. are dangerous to one's health and mental condition.	0	1	2	3	4	5	6
76. are the business of those who carry them out and no one else's.	0	1	2	3	4	5	6
When I have sexual desires. . .							
81. I attempt to repress them.	0	1	2	3	4	5	6
82. they are quite strong.	0	1	2	3	4	5	6
Petting. . .							
83. is not a good practice until after marriage.	0	1	2	3	4	5	6
84. is justified with love.	0	1	2	3	4	5	6
Sex relations before marriage. . .							
87. help people adjust.	0	1	2	3	4	5	6
88. should not be recommended.	0	1	2	3	4	5	6
Masturbation. . .							
93. is wrong and a sin.	0	1	2	3	4	5	6
94. is a normal outlet for sexual desire.	0	1	2	3	4	5	6
Masturbation. . .							
101. is all right.	0	1	2	3	4	5	6
102. is a form of self-destruction.	0	1	2	3	4	5	6
Unusual sex practices. . .							
103. are awful and unthinkable.	0	1	2	3	4	5	6
104. are all right if both partners agree.	0	1	2	3	4	5	6
If I had sex relations, I would feel. . .							
107. all right, I think.	0	1	2	3	4	5	6
108. I was being used, not loved.	0	1	2	3	4	5	6
Masturbation. . .							
111. is all right.	0	1	2	3	4	5	6
112. should not be practiced.	0	1	2	3	4	5	6

Scoring Scores are summed for the subscale (guilty script) by reversing the nonguilty alternatives (underlined item numbers in the following key).

Sex Guilt Sex guilt involves awareness of sexual arousal, the feelings of interest-excitement and enjoyment-joy, and shame due to moral cognitions about sexual behavior. The items for this subscale are: 5, ***6, 7,*** 8, 11, ***12, 13,*** 14, 15, ***16,*** 17, ***18, 25,*** 26, ***31,*** 32, 35, ***36,*** 41, ***42, 51,*** 52, 53, ***54, 61,*** 62, 63, ***64, 67,*** 68, ***71,*** 72, ***75,*** 76, ***81,*** 82, ***83,*** 84, 87, ***88, 93,*** 94, 101, ***102, 103,*** 104, 107, ***108,*** 111, and ***112.***

Higher scores indicate more scripted guilt.

Reliability and Validity The original Mosher Guilt Inventories were developed in the 1960s, with separate forms for men and women. The revised version was developed following an updated item analysis of prior items. Split-half or alpha coefficients of reliability for past versions of the scale have averaged around .90 (Mosher, 1988). Mosher reported that a review of approximately 100 studies by 1977 confirmed the construct validity of the inventory as a measure of guilt as a personality construct. The revised version of the scale was constructed for inclusion in the 1988 volume, *Sexuality-Related Measures* and psychometric data for the new version were not available at the time of its publication.

In the context of a larger study at Texas Tech University, Hendrick and Hendrick asked 105 students to complete this subscale. Using a different scoring system (determining the mean item rating on a 5-point scale) they found that students gave the items a mean rating of 3.59 (*s.d.* =.60) (C. Hendrick, personal communication, July 14, 1992). This indicated that the students tended to rate the items slightly toward the guilty side of the mid-point.

Reference

Mosher, D. L. (1988). Revised Mosher Guilt Inventory. In C. M. Davis, W. L. Yarber, & S. L. Davis (Eds.), *Sexuality-related measures: A compendium. Lake Mills, IA: Graphic. Used by permission.*

Sexual guilt may also be assessed by identifying how guilty a person anticipates feeling after engaging in various sexual behaviors (Knox, Walters, & Walters, 1991). Exhibit 2.2 reflects the average level of guilt on a four-point continuum for various sexual situations reported by 249 undergraduate university students. You might compare your answers with theirs.

The degree of guilt college students predict that they would feel for engaging in various sexual behaviors depends on whether or not someone is likely to find out. Sexual guilt is higher to the degree that discovery by significant others is possible. Women and younger individuals also report being more guilty than men and older individuals (Knox et al., 1991).

Sexual guilt also varies by culture. Japanese, Vietnamese, and Hispanic women are expected to feel more guilty for engaging in extramarital sexual behavior than their husbands for engaging in the same behavior (Mindel, Habenstein, & Wright, 1988). Researchers at Anadolu University in Eskisehir, Turkey, observed that those who engage in sexual behavior in spite of the restrictive culture are likely to experience high proportions of guilt (Erkmen, Dilbaz, Serber, Kaptanoglu, & Tekin, 1990).

EXHIBIT 2.2 How Guilty Would You Feel If. . . ?

How guilty would you feel if . . .	Average score
1. You have intercourse with someone 18 years older than you? Both of you are unmarried.	2.04
2. You decide not to tell the person you are about to marry any information concerning your previous affectional relationships because you believe it will have no bearing on your marriage?	2.18
3. The person you are about to marry learns of a previous sexual affair you had with another person you did not particularly care for prior to your present relationship?	2.29
4. You reveal to an associate that a person who had invited you to dinner was gay and there were to be no other guests?	2.48
5. Your mother discovers that you, at age 16, are having intercourse with a member of the opposite sex?	2.76
6. You concealed from the person you are about to marry that you had earlier contracted and were cured of gonorrhea?	2.88
7. Your parents learn of your sexual relationship with someone of another race and you know they disapprove?	3.03
8. As a student, you are in love with a teacher who is fired because your sexual relationship has been brought to the attention of the instructor's dean?	3.51
9. You are in a committed relationship with a person, yet you had intercourse with someone else?	3.52
10. The person you are about to marry learns that you had a sexual encounter with his or her best friend while he or she was away visiting his or her grandmother?	3.66

1 = No guilt; 2 = Little guilt; 3 = Moderate guilt; 4 = Considerable guilt

Source: Adapted from the original research conducted for "Sexual Guilt among College Students" by D. Knox, L. H. Walters, and J. Walters. (1991). *College Student Journal, 25,* 432–433.

Values and Religious Orientation

Another study that investigated the influence of moral development on sexual decision-making was Juhasz and Sonnenshein-Schneider's (1987) study of 500 teenagers. The 13- to 19-year-olds were asked the extent to which their decisions about sexual intercourse would be influenced by specified factors. Their responses revealed six categories of influence: family establishment and competence, external morality, consequences of childbearing, self-enhancement through sexual intercourse, intimacy considerations regarding sexual intercourse, and consequences of marriage. Predictable gender differences revealed boys' emphasis on sexual enhancement through intercourse and girls' emphasis on intimacy considerations. As boys grew older, the influence of external morality (parents, peers, and religious authorities) declined. However, the more religious adolescents found the opinions of parents, peers, and religious leaders more important. In Kohlberg's schema, these adolescents were mainly functioning in the second level of moral development, which involves pleasing others and maintaining the conventional order.

It is not surprising that researchers have found that religious participation and sexual attitudes and behavior are related. However, a study by Thornton and Camburn (1989) suggested that the influence is more reciprocal than previously viewed. In a longitudinal study of respondents from randomly sampled birth records, interviews were conducted with mothers in 1962, 1966, 1977, and 1980. Their children were also interviewed at age 18 (in 1980). Those who attended church most frequently and who said religion was important to them had more restrictive attitudes and reported less sexual experience. Regression analysis confirmed the usual assumption that religiosity influences sexual attitudes and behavior but also suggested that sexual attitudes and behavior influence religious involvement. Except for fundamentalist Protestant or Baptist affiliation or Jewish identity, mere affiliation with a particular group was a small influence; participation was more important.

> Human beings may use their sexuality in moral or immoral ways and the way in which it is used should be the subject of judgment.
>
> *Mary Calderone, M.D.*

The relation of religious orientation and sexual attitudes has also been studied in adults. Reed and Meyers (1991) surveyed 201 people affiliated with religious institutions in the Sacramento, California, metropolitan area. Respondents completed the Religious Orientation Scale and the Derogatis Sexual Functioning Inventory. Those returning the surveys were typically married, college-educated women, attending Baptist, nondenominational, or Presbyterian churches. The study distinguished between those with intrinsic religious orientation (internalized commitment, as incorporating moral teachings into one's own ethics) and extrinsic orientation (pursuit of religion as a means to particular outcomes, as attending church to socialize). Those with stronger intrinsic orientations were more conservative in their sexual attitudes and expressed a somewhat more positive body image. Those with more extrinsic orientations were more liberal but less satisfied with their sexual relationships.

Family life specialists have identified religious settings as providing an opportunity for comprehensive education for sexual decision-making. Some churches have initiated programs for sexuality education and prevention of premature parenthood. Allen-Meares (1989) challenged the black church to develop educational programs to focus on sexual development from childhood through adolescence. Following a church-based program, Powell and Jorgensen (1985) documented increases in sex knowledge and clarity of personal sexual values, although they found no change in self-esteem. They concluded that the opportunity "to discuss controversial topics in a context of values and moral decision-making" (p. 476) promotes sexual learning and responsible action.

SEX AND THE LAW

One of the ways society's sexual values are evident is through its laws. In this section, we look at the debate over the appropriateness of laws that regulate consenting adult sexual behavior, categories of sexual behavior that are against the law, the incidence of sex offenses among a group of "normal" college undergraduate males, and reproductive issues and the law.

Private Rights versus Social Morality

Debate exists over whether there should be laws to ensure private rights or social morality. For example, should consenting adults be permitted to engage in any sexual behaviors they choose, or should the law define morally acceptable parameters? More specifically, sodomy laws prohibit oral-genital sex and anal-genital sex between individuals. "The Supreme Court has held that there is no federal constitutional right to engage in private, consensual, same-sex sodomy" (Friedman, 1990, p. 126). While sodomy laws are most frequently enforced against gays, currently there are sodomy laws in 25 states and the District of Columbia (NGLTF Policy Institute, 1992).

> "These laws criminalize our private lives and relationships," says Robert Bray of the National Gay and Lesbian Task Force. "And if it isn't 10 toes up and 10 toes down, heterosexuals risk going to jail too." (Sachs, 1990, p. 98)

Should Such Sex Laws Exist?

John Stuart Mill (1859) emphasized the rights of the individual by arguing that the only purpose of government should be to protect its citizens from harm by others. He also advocated

> liberty of taste and pursuits . . . of doing as we like, subject to such consequences as may follow: Without impediment for our fellow creatures so long as what we do does not harm them even though they should think our conduct foolish, perverse, or wrong.

In contrast, Lord Devlin (1965) argued that no private morality should operate outside the concern of criminal law. He felt that the health of a society was defined by its adherence to a binding moral code and recommended that legal definitions of morality be identified and enforced. A modern version of legislating morality was reflected by the Meese Commission Report on pornography (see Chapter 19, Abuses and Commercial Uses of Sexuality). The commission took the position that the protection of society's moral environment is a legitimate purpose of government and recommended more restrictive laws on pornography.

Private citizens also "praise sex laws as an expression of a collective conscience" (Sachs, 1990, p. 98). Rebecca Hagelin of Concerned Women for America, speaking of adultery laws, noted, "If these laws had been enforced with regularity in this country, then a lot more people would think twice about participating in sexually immoral acts" (p. 98).

A Continuum of Sex Offenses and Sex Laws

One of the ways our society has achieved compromise and balance between radically opposing views of private versus public morality has been to regard certain sexual behaviors as on a continuum of offensiveness and to assign relative penalties for engaging in them. For example, child sexual abuse and rape are regarded as severely offensive and are subject to strong sanctions. However, frottage (See Chapter 17,

"Paraphilias and Sexuality") is regarded as being minimally offensive and carries no legal sanction.

MacNamara and Sagarin (1977) identified five categories of sexual acts according to criminal classification:

Category I—Criminal acts that require enforcement to protect society. Rape and child molestation are examples. Individuals who engage in child sexual abuse have been found to have the greatest degree of psychopathological thought disturbance (Kalichman, 1991).

Category II—Sexual acts with potential victimization. Exhibitionism and voyeurism are examples. While these behaviors themselves may not be regarded as morally severe, they may create harm to the victims, who deserve protection.

Category III—Sexual acts midway between those considered morally reprehensible and those creating victims. Prostitution and adultery are examples. Both are said to reflect immorality, and both have the potential to produce victims (the prostitutes in the case of prostitution and the spouse and/or children of the adulterer).

Category IV—Sex acts between consenting adults, including homosexual sexual behavior and behaviors within marriage.

Category V—Behaviors that are nonsexual but are either criminalized or considered to be sex crimes. Abortion, topless dancing, and the sale and distribution of pornography are examples. Dial-a-porn services have also become the concern of the law. The U.S. Supreme Court rejected a challenge to a federal law requiring telephone companies to block access to sex message services unless a customer asks in writing to receive them. The goal is to protect children from sexual telephone messages ("Court deals blow," 1992).

CONSIDERATION: New fears associated with HIV infection have resulted in lawsuits against former lovers. Mark Christian won a judgment of $21.75 million for emotional damages he said resulted from Rock Hudson's (his former lover) lack of disclosure that Hudson had AIDS.

> The imposition of liability is based on one or more of the following legal theories: (a) negligence, (b) deceit, (c) assault and battery, and (d) the intentional infliction of emotional distress. (Friedman, 1990, p. 63)

A litigious society in combination with the prevalence of sexually transmitted diseases has the potential to permanently alter the attitudes and feelings individuals have about new sexual partners.

Incidence of Sexual Behavior against the Law

It is commonly assumed that most people have not committed criminal sexual acts. However, people often engage in sexual activities (or have the desire to do so) and are not apprehended by the law. In a sample of 60 undergraduate college men (who are often used as nonoffender controls in sex research), nearly two-thirds had engaged in some form of sexual misconduct in the past. Over half (52%) had engaged in a sexual offense for which they could be arrested (Templeman & Stinnett, 1991). Some examples included voyeurism (42 percent), frottage (35 percent), obscene phone calls (8 percent), and coercive sex (8 percent) (p. 142). In spite of the relatively high incidence of having engaged in punishable sex offenses, only two of the 60 respondents (3%) had been arrested.

Reproductive Issues and the Law

Aside from individual sexual behavior, the law extends into the area of reproductive choices. The concerns of reproductive law include the following (Cohen & Taub, 1989, p. 4):

1. Time limits on abortion—When is it too late to have an abortion from the states' legal perspective?
2. Prenatal Screening—How is prenatal screening to be used in regard to selective abortion?
3. Fetus as Patient—What are the legal rights of the fetus?
4. Reproductive Hazards in the Workplace—What safeguards are necessary by industry to avoid harming an individual's reproductive system and to maintain reproductive choice?
5. Interference with Reproductive Choice—Violence directed toward abortion clinics and sterilization abuse are among the activities that interfere with reproductive choice.
6. Alternative Methods of Reproductive Choice—What are the appropriate laws on artificial insemination by donor, surrogate pregnancy, and embryo transfer? And who's baby is it that results?
7. AIDS and the Workplace—Davis (1988) emphasized that both medical employees and their clients have a right to work and be treated in an AIDS-free environment.

CHOICES

Three primary choices in regard to values in sexuality include deciding the degree to which one will be open and honest with a partner about one's sexual thoughts and behaviors, deciding whether to engage in sexual behavior with a new partner, and deciding the degree to which one will override cultural influences that prestructure choices.

Is Honesty Always the Best Policy?

How honest should partners be with each other? Does a "we tell each other everything" disclosure policy have more positive consequences than a "selective disclosure" policy? Two researchers (Ryan & Plutzer, 1989) compared wives who had an abortion and who told their husbands with wives who had an abortion and who did not tell their husbands. They found that "the unqualified generalization that notification and discussion promote marital harmony is not valid" (p. 49). In other words, telling the spouse about the abortion was not always a good idea because the relationship sometimes suffered more stress as a result.

One reason for being careful about what is disclosed is that sometimes total honesty may be too brutal and might best be tempered with caring. A situation in which tempered honesty may be the best policy is when you are extremely upset. You may honestly feel and think horrible thoughts about your partner. If you express such thoughts and feelings, they may be difficult to retract later, when you are calm. At such times, it may be best to not be totally honest about your thoughts and feelings. Instead, consider admitting that you are upset and either wait until you are calm to talk about the problem or, if you do talk, refrain from expressing thoughts that are hurtful to your partner.

Though tempering honesty with kindness may be best in some situations, in others, being completely honest may be preferable. While personal values will always dictate what is disclosed to whom in what contexts, many might argue that certain information should not be withheld from the partner: for example, previous marriages and children, a sexual orientation different from what the partner expects, alcohol or drug addiction, having a sexually transmissible disease, and physical disabilities, such as sterility.

Choose to Have Intercourse with a New Partner?

In addition to making choices about honesty, sexual values are also operative in choosing whether to engage in sexual behavior in a new relationship. While not all sexual encounters or relationships involve intercourse, we will focus on intercourse in this section. The following might be considered in making such a decision.

Personal Consequences How do you predict you will feel about yourself after you have intercourse? An increasing number of individuals feel that if they are in love and have considered their decision carefully, the outcome will be positive (the quotes in this section are from students in the authors' classes):

> I believe intercourse before marriage is okay under certain circumstances. I believe that when a person falls in love with another, it is then appropriate. This should be thought about very carefully for a long time, so as not to regret engaging in intercourse. I do not think intercourse should be a one-night thing, a one-week thing, or a one-month thing. You should grow to love and care for the person very much before giving that ultra-special part of you to your partner. These feelings should be felt by both partners; if this is not the case, then you are not in love and you are not "making love."

Those who are not in love and have sex in a casual context sometimes feel badly about the experience:

> I viewed sex as a new toy—something to try as frequently as possible. I did my share of sleeping around, and all it did for me was to give me a total loss of self-respect and a bad reputation. Besides, guys talk. I have heard rumors that I sleep with guys I have never slept with. The first couple of guys I had sex with pressured me, and I regret it. I don't believe in casual sex; it brings more heartache than pleasure. It means so much more when you truly love the partner and you know your love is returned.

However, not all people who have intercourse within the context of a love relationship feel good about it:

> The first time I had intercourse, I was in love and I thought he loved me. But he didn't. He used me, and I have always hated him for it.

Some also report positive consequences for casual sex:

Continued

Continued

> We met one night at a mutual friend's party. We liked each other immediately.
>
> We talked, sipped some wine, and ended up spending the night together. Though we never saw each other again, I have very positive memories of the encounter.

The effect intercourse will have on you personally will be influenced by your personal and religious values and your emotional involvement with your partner. Some people prefer to wait until they are married to have intercourse and feel that this is the best course for future marital stability and happiness. There is often, but not necessarily, a religious basis for this value. Strong personal and religious values against intercourse plus a lack of emotional involvement usually result in guilt and regret following intercourse. In contrast, values that regard intercourse as appropriate within the context of a love relationship are likely to result in feelings of satisfaction and contentment after intercourse.

Partner Consequences Because a basic moral principle is to do no harm to others, it may be important to consider the effect of intercourse on your partner. Whereas intercourse may be a pleasurable experience with positive consequences for you, your partner may react differently. What are your partner's feelings about intercourse and her or his ability to handle the experience? If you suspect your partner will not feel good about it or be able to handle it psychologically, then you might reconsider whether intercourse would be appropriate with this person.

One man reported that after having intercourse with a woman he had just met, he awakened to the sound of her uncontrollable sobbing as she sat on the end of the bed. She was guilty and depressed and regretted the experience. He said, "If I had known how she was going to respond, we wouldn't have had intercourse."

One woman reported that she made a mistake in having intercourse with a friend. "To me," she said, "it was just a friendship and I knew that there was no romantic future. For him, it was different. He fell in love and wanted us to be lovers. It destroyed him when he learned I had no such interest."

Relationship Consequences Does intercourse affect the stability of an unmarried couple's relationship? Apparently not. In a two-year follow-up study of the sexual behavior of 5,000 college sophomores and juniors who had ongoing sexual relationships (Hill, Rubin, & Poplau, 1976), the researchers found that those who had intercourse were no more likely to have broken up than those who had not had intercourse. In another study, less than 2% of 163 respondents said their relationship terminated as a result of their last intercourse. "Remained the same" was the most frequently chosen description of the effect intercourse had on the unmarried relationship (Brigman & Knox, 1992).

What is the effect on a couple's subsequent marital relationship if they have intercourse with each other before they are married? Ard (1990) studied couples who did and did not have intercourse and who subsequently married each other. The most prominent effect (67%) reported by those who had intercourse was "no effect," with about 20% reporting a favorable effect and 13% reporting a negative effect. However, those *not* having intercourse reported that the most prominent effect on their subsequent marriage to each other was no effect (54%), with 39% reporting a favorable effect and 7% reporting an unfavorable effect. Hence, almost twice as many of those who choose not to have intercourse before marriage with their partner reported a positive effect, compared with those who choose to have intercourse with their partner. Women were more likely than men to report favorable effects on the marriage from choosing not to have premarital intercourse (Ard, 1990, p. 36).

Suppose individuals who have intercourse before marriage don't choose to marry each other but end up marrying someone else. What is the effect of having had intercourse on one's subsequent marriage to another person? Kahn and London (1991) examined national data on premarital intercourse and subsequent divorce of all U.S. women age 15 to 44 and found that divorce was more likely among individuals who had had premarital intercourse. The explanation for this correlation suggested by the researchers is that both premarital intercourse and divorce are nontraditional behaviors and that individuals who break traditional norms of intercourse before marriage are also more likely to express their nontraditionalism in regard to divorce.

Contraception Another potential consequence of intercourse is pregnancy. Once a couple decides to have intercourse, a separate decision must be made as to whether intercourse should result in pregnancy. Some couples want children and make a mutual commitment to love and care for their offspring. Other couples do not want children. If the couple wants to avoid pregnancy, they must choose and effectively use a contraceptive method. But many do not. Among black women under age 20, 75% of all births are to unmarried women, compared to 25% of all births to young white women (Staples, 1986). In general, the interval between the first intercourse and the use of a prescription method of birth control is about one year (Zelnik, Koenig, & Kim, 1984). In many cases, the pregnancy was a surprise. One woman recalled:

> It was the first time I had intercourse, so I didn't really think I would get pregnant my first time. But I did. And when I told him I was pregnant, he told me he didn't have any money and couldn't help me pay for the abortion. He really wanted nothing to do with me after that.

HIV and Other Sexually Transmissible Diseases Avoiding HIV infection and other sexually transmissible diseases is an important consideration in deciding

Continued

Continued

whether to have intercourse in a new relationship. The result of increasing numbers of people having more frequent intercourse with more partners has been the rapid spread of the bacteria and viruses responsible for numerous varieties of STDs.

Although popular magazines suggest that there is less anonymous sex among heterosexual persons (Randolph, 1989; Njeri, 1989), there is no conclusive documentation that individuals are actually changing their sexual behavior because of fear of contracting HIV or other STDs. While over half of the sexually active students in one study claimed that they had altered their sexual behavior, there was no relationship between what they said they did and what they actually did. While they said that they had intercourse less often, the actual frequency of their doing so in the past year had not changed (Carroll, 1988).

Although no method is completely safe (Magic Johnson says, "No sex is the safest sex"), a sexually active person can reduce the chances of getting AIDS and other STDs by not having sex with someone who has had multiple sexual partners. Finding such a partner is very difficult because people often lie to each other about sexual matters. Cochran and Mays (1990) noted in a sample of 18- to 25-year-old college students that 34% of the men and 10% of the women who were sexually experienced reported having told a lie in order to have sex. Individuals are particularly likely to lie about their number of previous sexual partners. In a study entitled, " Sexual Lies among University Students," the second most frequently reported lie to their sexual partners reported by the respondents was the number of previous sexual relationships or partners they had had (Knox, Schacht, Holt, & Turner, 1993).

Deciding to have sex in a new relationship is a complex issue. Allgeier (1985) summarized some of the issues individuals might consider before deciding to have intercourse, including: (1) feeling guiltless and comfortable with your present level of involvement; (2) feeling confident that you will not be humiliated and that your reputation will not be hurt; (3) feeling free to choose not to have intercourse, rather than feeling pressure to have intercourse (hence, you do not feel exploited); (4) not using intercourse as an attempt to improve a poor relationship; and (5) not being motivated to have intercourse for inappropriate reasons—to prove love to the other person, to prove that you are desirable, to gain affection, or to rebel against your parents.

Choose to Override Culturally Prestructured Choices?

We have noted throughout this chapter that various sexual norms are culturally induced and influence individuals to make some choices without awareness. Such culturally induced norms include sexism and heterosexism. The woman who chooses to be dependent, the man who encourages such dependence, and the heterosexual couple who assume that heterosexual relationships (as opposed to homosexual relationships) are the only "normal" relationships are responding to cultural influences.

While one's personal values may be similar to those promoted in the culture, an alternative to the acceptance of sexism and heterosexism is to consider choices made on the basis of respect for human dignity and equality.

Summary

1. Sexual values guide sexual choices, reflect one's self-identity, and affect partner choice.
2. Sexual value perspectives include absolutism (there is a correct choice), relativism (all choices are relevant to the context in which they are made), and hedonism (the pursuit of pleasure should be the basis of one's choices). In making sexual choices, there has been a societal drift from absolutism to relativism.
3. Many contemporary sexual values (e.g., masturbation, adultery, and homosexuality are wrong) have their roots in Jewish and Christian religious influences that emphasize sexuality within marriage.
4. The rise of a scientific approach to thinking about sexuality reframed some sexuality attitudes and provided new information. Even "objective" science is influenced by cultural and societal values.

5. Contemporary influences on sexual values include challenges to traditional gender roles. Many religious denominations have begun the 1990s with examinations of sexuality-related issues.
6. Women and younger individuals are more likely to report sexual guilt than men and older individuals. High sex guilt is also associated with less use of reliable, effective contraception, lower sexual satisfaction, and higher reported sexual dysfunction.
7. Religious orientation and participation are related to sexual attitudes and behaviors.
8. There is disagreement about the degree to which laws should constrain personal, private, adult, mutually consenting sexual behavior. There is agreement that laws should exist to protect citizens from abuse and exploitation (e.g., child sexual abuse, rape).
9. "No effect on the relationship" is the most likely outcome for having intercourse in a premarital relationship.
10. Many individuals (men more than women) are prone to lie to their current sexual partner about the previous sexual partners they have had.
11. The sexual behaviors individuals say they engage in and the behaviors they actually engage in are often different.
12. Individuals deciding to have intercourse for the first time in a new relationship might consider doing so only if they have a high comfort level in their current relationship, do not feel pressure to have intercourse, and are not motivated to use intercourse to improve the relationship. Additional considerations include the possible consequences for one's partner, protection from STDs, and the selection of a reliable contraceptive if pregnancy is not desired.

KEY TERMS

sexual values
absolutism
asceticism
relativism
situation ethics
hedonism
sexual guilt

REFERENCES

ABC on Sexuality (July 24, 1991). *The Christian Century,* p. 713.

Allgeier, E. R. (1985, July). Are you ready for sex? Informed consent for sexual intimacy *SIECUS Report,* p. 8–9.

Allen-Meares, P. (1989). Adolescent sexuality and premature parenthood: Role of the black church in prevention. *Journal of Social Work and Human Sexuality, 8,* 133–142.

Ard, B. N. (1990). *The sexual realm in long-term marriages: A longitudinal study following marital partners over twenty years.* San Francisco: Mellen Research University Press.

Bishops' plan deplores abortion, 'safe' sex. (1991, November 15). *The Daily Reflector* Greenville, N.C. p. A3.

Brigman, B., & Knox, D. (1992). University students' motivations to have intercourse. *College Student Journal,* 26, 406–408.

Bullough, V. L. (1987). A historical approach. In J. H. Greer & W. T. O'Donohue (Eds.), *Theories of human sexuality* (pp. 49–63). New York: Plenum Press.

Bullough, V. L. (1991). Introduction. In M. Hirschfeld, (M. A. Lombardi-Nash, Trans.). *Transvestites: The erotic drive to cross dress.* Buffalo: Prometheus Books.

Cado, S., & Leitenberg, H. (1990). Guilt reactions to sexual fantasies during intercourse. *Archives of Sexual Behavior, 19,* 49–63.

Calhoun, A. (1960). *A social history of the american family.* New York: Barnes and Noble.

Cameron, N., & Rychlak, J. F. (1985). *Personality development and psychopathology* (2nd ed.). Boston: Houghton Mifflin.

Carey, J. J. (1991, May 8). Body and soul: Presbyterians on sexuality. *The Christian Century,* pp. 516–520.

Carroll, L. (1988). Concern with AIDS and the sexual behavior of college students. *Journal of Marriage and the Family, 50,* 405–411.

Carswell, R. W. (1969). Historical analysis of religion and sex. *Journal of School Health, 39,* 673–684.

Cochran, S., & Mays, V. (1990). Sex, lies and HIV. *New England Journal of Medicine, 322,* 774–775.

Cohen, S., & Taub, N., (Eds). (1989). *Reproductive laws for the 1990s.* Clifton, NJ: Humana Press.

Court deals blow to "dial-a-porn" industry. (1992, January 28). *The Daily Reflector,* Greenville, N.C., p. A2.

Davis, M. J. (1988). *Lovers, doctors, and the law.* New York: Harper and Row.

Devlin, P. (1965). *The enforcement of morals.* Oxford: Oxford University Press.

Ellis, A. (1966). *Sex without guilt.* New York: Lyle Stuart.

Ellis, H. (1931). *Studies in the psychology of sex: Sex in relation to Society* (Vol. 6). Philadelphia: F. A. Davis. (Original work published in 1910).

Erdey, S. (1991). Who's who among traditionalists. *The Witness, 74,* 14–17.

Erkmen, H., Dilbaz, N., Serber, G., Kaptanoglu, C., & Tekin, D. (1990). Sexual attitudes of Turkish university students. *Journal of Sex Education and Therapy, 16,* 251–261.

Ernst, M. L., & Loth, D. (1948). *American sexual behavior and the Kinsey Report.* New York: Greystone Press.

Eugene, T. M. (1985). While love is unfashionable: ethical implications of black spirituality and sexuality. In B. H. Andolsen, C. E. Gudorf, & M. D. Pellauer (Eds.), *Women's consciousness, women's conscience: A reader in feminist ethics* (pp. 121–141). Minneapolis: Winston Press.

Francoeur, R. T. (1992). Sexuality and spirituality: The relevance of Eastern traditions. *SIECUS Report, 20,* 1–8.

Friedman, S. E. (1990). *Sex law.* Jefferson, NC: McFarland.

Gerrard, M., & Gibbons, F. X. (1982). Sexual experience, sex guilt, and sexual moral reasoning. *Journal of Personality, 50,* 345–359.

Gilligan, C., Ward, V. W. & Taylor, M. (Eds.). (1988). *Mapping the moral domain.* Cambridge: Harvard University Press.

Hill, C. T., Rubin, Z., & Poplau, L. A. (1976). Breakups before marriage: The end of 103 affairs. *Journal of Social Issues, 32,* 147–168.

Holcomb, D. R., Holcomb, L. C., Sondag, K. A., & Williams, N. (1991). Attitudes about date rape: Gender differences among college students. *College Student Journal, 25,* 434–439.

Jameson, V. (1991, July/August). Assembly maintains traditional Presbyterian sexuality policies. *Presbyterian Survey,* pp. 24–25.

Johnson, W. S. (1979). *Living in sin: The Victorian sexual revolution.* Chicago: Nelson-Hall.

Juhasz, A. M., & Sonnenshein-Schneider, A. (1987). Adolescent sexuality: Values, morality and decision making. *Adolescence, 22,* 579–590.

Kahn, J. R., & London, K. A. (1991). Premarital sex and the risk of divorce. *Journal of Marriage and the Family, 53,* 845–855.

Kalichman, S. C. (1991). Psychopathology and personality characteristics of criminal sexual offenders as a function of victim age. *Archives of Sexual Behavior, 20,* 187–195.

Klassen, A. D., Williams, C. J., & Levitt, E. E. (1989). *Sex and morality in the United States: An empirical enquiry under the auspices of the Kinsey Institute.* Middletown, CN: Wesleyan University Press.

Knox, D., Schacht, C., Holt, J., & Turner, J. (1993). Sexual lies among university students. *College Student Journal* (in press).

Knox, D., Walters, L. H., & Walters, J. (1991). Sexual guilt among college students. *College Student Journal, 25,* 432–433.

Kohlberg, L. (1984). *The psychology of moral development: Essays on moral development* (Vol. 2). San Francisco: Harper and Row.

Krafft-Ebing, R. von. (1886; reprinted in 1892). *Psychopathia Sexualis* (C. G. Chaddock, Trans.). Philadelphia: F. A. Davis.

Linn, R. (1991). Sexual and moral development of Israeli female adolescents from city and kibbutz: Perspectives of Kohlberg and Gilligan. *Adolescence, 26,* 59–70.

LoPiccolo, J. (1983). The prevention of sexual problems in men. In G. Albee, S. Gordon, & H. Leitenberg (Eds.), *Promoting sexual responsibility and preventing sexual problems* (pp. 39–65). Hanover: University Press of New England.

MacNamara, D., and Sagarin, E. (1977). *Sex, crime, and the law.* New York: Free Press.

Mead, G. H. (1936). *Movements of thought in the nineteenth century.* Chicago: University of Chicago Press.

Mill, J. S. (1859). *On liberty.* New York: Penguin.

Mindel, C. H., Habenstein, R. W., & Wright, R. Jr. (Eds.). (1988). *Ethnic families in America: Patterns and variations (3rd ed.). New York: Elsevier.*

Money, J. (1988). Commentary: Current status of sex research. *Journal of Psychology and Human Sexuality, 1,* 5–15.

Morrow, L. (1992, February 3). Who cares, anyway? *Time,* p. 15.

Mosher, D. L. (1966). The development and multitrait-multimethod matrix analysis of 3 measures of 3 aspects of guilt. *Journal of Consulting and Clinical Psychology, 30,* 25–29.

Mosher, D. L., & Vonderheide, S. G. (1985). Contributions of sex guilt and masturbation guilt to women's contraceptive attitudes and use. *Journal of Sex Research, 21,* 24–39.

National Gay & Lesbian Task Force Policy Institute (1992, July). "Deviate sexual conduct" law under fire. *Activist Alert,* p. 2.

Nelson, J. B. (1983). Religious dimensions of sexual health. In G. W. Albee, S. Gordon, & H. Leitenberg (Eds.), *Promoting sexual responsibility and preventing sexual problems* (pp. 121–132). Hanover and London: University Press of New England. pp. 121–132.

Njeri, I. (1989, January). A new sexuality. *Essence,* 66–68.

Petras, J. W. (1978). *The social meanings of human sexuality.* Boston: Allyn and Bacon.

Powell, L. H., & Jorgensen, S. R. (1985). Evaluation of a church-based sexuality education program for adolescents. *Family Relations, 34,* 475–482.

Randolph, L. B. (1989, June). The new black sexuality. *Ebony,* 146–150.

Ranke-Heinemann, Uta. (1990, December 17). People. *U.S. News & World Report,* p. 39.

Reed, L. A., & Meyers, L. S. (1991). A structural analysis of religious orientation and its relation to sexual attitudes. *Educational and Psychological Measurement, 51,* 943–952.

Reiss, I. L., with Reiss, H. M. (1990). *An end to shame.* Amherst, NY: Prometheus Books.

Robinson, I., Ziss, K., Banza, B., Katz, S., & Robinson, E. (1991). Twenty years of the sexual revolution, 1965–1985. *Journal of Marriage and the Family, 53,* 216–220.

Rubinson, L., & De Rubertis, L. (1991). Trends in sexual attitudes and behaviors of a college population over a 15-year period. *Journal of Sex Education and Therapy, 17,* 32–42.

Ryan, B., & Plutzer, E. (1989). When married women have abortions: Spousal notification and marital interaction. *Journal of Marriage and the Family, 51,* 41–50.

Sachs, A. (1990, October 1). Handing out scarlet letters. *Time,* p. 98.

Sheler, J. L. (June 10, 1991). The gospel on sex. *U.S. News & World Report,* pp. 59–64.

Smith, R., & Walters, J. (1988). *Sexual Guilt.* Unpublished paper, University of Georgia, Department of Child and Family Development, Athens. Used by permission.

Smith, T. W. (1990). The polls—A report. *Public Opinion Quarterly, 54,* 415–435.

Special Committee on Human Sexuality. (1991). *Part I: Keeping body and soul together: Sexuality, spirituality, and social justice.* General Assembly, Presbyterian Church (USA).

Staples, R. (1974). Black sexuality. In M. S. Calderone (Ed.), *Sexuality and human values* (pp. 62–70). New York: Association Press.

Staples, R. (1986). Black masculinity, hypersexuality, and sexual aggression. In Robert Staples (Ed.), *The black family.* Belmont, CA: Wadsworth Publishing.

Tannahill, R. (1982). *Sex in history.* New York: Stein and Day.

Templeman, T. L., & Stinnett, R. D. (1991). Patterns of sexual arousal and history in a 'normal" sample of young men. *Archives of Sexual Behavior, 20,* 137–150.

Thomas, A., & Sillen, S. (1972). *Racism and psychiatry.* New York: Brunner/Mazel.

Thornton, A., & Camburn, D. (1989). Religious participation and adolescent sexual behavior and attitudes. *Journal of Marriage and the Family, 51,* 641–653.

van de Velde, T. H. (1930). Ideal marriage: Its physiology and technique. New York: Covici-Friede.

Wattleton, F. (1989, June). Planned Parenthood head calls on churches to support choice. *The Witness,* pp. 6–8.

Weis, D. L., Rabinowitz, B., & Ruckstuhl, M. F. (1992). Individual changes in sexual attitudes and behavior within college-level human sexuality courses. *Journal of Sex Research, 29,* 43–59.

Williams, J. D., & Jacoby, A. P. (1989). The effects of premarital heterosexual and homosexual experiences on dating and marriage desirability. *Journal of Marriage and the Family, 51,* 489–497.

Woodward, D. L., & Cohen, A. (1991, May 6). Roll over John Calvin: The Presbyterians rethink the sexual revolution. *Newsweek,* pp. 59–60.

Zelnik, M., Koenig, M.A., & Kim, Y., J. (1984). Sources of prescription contraceptives and subsequent pregnancy among young women. *Family Planning Perspectives, 16,* 6–13.

CHAPTER THREE

Cultural Variations in Human Sexuality

Chapter Outline

Cross-Cultural Research in Human Sexuality
- Ethnography and Ethnology
- Problems in Cross-Cultural Research in Human Sexuality

What is "Normal" Sexual Behavior?
- Definitions of "Normal" Are Based on Various Criteria
- Definitions of "Normal" Sexual Behavior Vary across Time
- Ethnocentrism versus Cultural Relativism
- **Self-Assessment:** Sex Knowledge and Attitude Test, Part I

Cross-Cultural Variations in Sexuality
- Sexual Intercourse
- Premarital Sex
- Extramarital Sex
- Incest
- Menstruation
- Homosexual Sex
- Gender Roles
- **Cross-Cultural Perspective:** Neither Male nor Female

Permissive and Restrictive Cultural Contexts
- The Mangaians: A Permissive Context
- The Inhabitants of Inis Beag: A Restrictive Context

Some Culture-Specific Sex Practices
- Female Genital Mutilation
- Male Genital Mutilation
- Polygamy

Mate Selection: A Cross-Cultural View
- Patterns of Mate Selection
- Preferred Characteristics in a Mate

Sexuality in Nonhuman Primates
- Social versus Hormonal Influences on Nonhuman Primate Sexual Behavior
- Importance of Touch among Nonhuman Primates
- Homosexuality among Nonhuman Primates
- Mating Patterns among Nonhuman Primates
- Monogamy and Nonhuman Primate Sexual Behavior

Choices
- Choose to Be Less Ethnocentric?
- Become More Culturally Relativistic?
- Choose to Conform to Cultural Sexual Norms?

Is It True?*

1. The average age of first intercourse for Japanese men and women is about 21.

2. African-American women report performing fellatio on their partners less often than white women report performing fellatio on their partners.

3. In some societies, intercourse before marriage is punishable by death.

4. The traditional Muslim woman believes that Allah would approve of her having her clitoris cut off so as to reduce her temptation to have sex.

5. Asian couples view sexual expression in basically the same way as Western couples.

* 1=T, 2=T, 3=T, 4=T, 5=F

Each sexual attitude, action, or belief of a person can only be fully and completely understood by an examination of the cultural context in which it occurs.

Linda Schoonover Smith

Suppose that as a 7- to 15-year-old-boy, you learned that fellating older males was necessary in order to develop your own sperm and become capable of fertilizing a woman? Or, suppose that as a preadolescent girl, you learned that one of the ways to show that God (Allah) approved of you was to eagerly submit to having your clitoris cut off? Sambian boys (of New Guinea) and Muslim girls (in some parts of the Middle East) have willingly engaged in fellatio and clitoridectomy (respectively) in response to cultural influences. As these examples illustrate, the cultural context in which a person is reared dictates what sexual behavior the person may engage in and the attitude that person is expected to have toward the behavior.

While human biology is the ultimate basis for our sexual behavior, culture and society are the most important influences on how individuals experience and express their sexuality.

J. Patrick Gray
Linda Wolfe

In this chapter, we examine human sexuality from a cross-cultural perspective. After discussing cross-cultural research in human sexuality, we examine the issue of what is "normal" sexual behavior and review how the same sexual behaviors are viewed differently in different cultures. Our emphasis is to suggest that sexual choices are often influenced by cultural contexts and forces.

Cross-Cultural Research in Human Sexuality

Early studies (pre-1920s) of human sexuality in non-European cultures largely consisted of unsystematic observations and anecdotal reports from a variety of sources, including missionaries, government officials, and travelers. Despite the fact that these early observations were unreliable, they nonetheless suggested that many aspects of human sexuality were shaped by culture.

In the 1920s, anthropologist Bronislaw Malinowski published *Sex and Repression* (1927), which compared psychosexual development in the Trobriand culture with the segment of European society that Freud had studied. In 1929, Malinowski published *Sexual Life of Savages in North-western Melanesia,* which described sexuality in that culture. These two landmark studies led to the development of two types of cross-cultural research in human sexuality—ethnography and ethnology.

Ethnography and Ethnology

Ethnography refers to the descriptive study of cultures or subcultures. Ethnographic studies of sexuality describe the sexual patterns of behavior and beliefs in various cultures or subcultures. Malinowski's *Sexual Life of Savages in North-western Melanesia* (1929) is an ethnographic study.

Ethnographic studies involve collecting data by field observations and organizing the data in published form. Today, ethnographic research is usually carried out by a single researcher or a small team studying a community for an extended period of time.

Ethnology refers to the comparative study of two or more cultures or subcultures. Ethnological studies of sexuality compare the sexual patterns of behavior and beliefs of two or more cultures or subcultures. Malinowski's *Sex and Repression* (1927) is an ethnological study comparing psychosexual development in two cultures.

CONSIDERATION: Ethnological studies are vital to the understanding of human sexuality. Through ethnological studies of human sexuality, "we learn the extent of cultural variation, thus, the limits to which cultures influence the biological potentialities that all human populations inherit" (Davenport, 1987, p. 198).

Problems in Cross-Cultural Research in Human Sexuality

Ethnologists and ethnographers studying human sexuality must contend with several problems. First, researchers must be fluent in the language of the culture they study. In some cases, researchers may use interpreters or translators; however, every language has nuances of meaning that are difficult or impossible to translate.

CONSIDERATION: An accurate description of a culture greatly depends on how well the researcher knows the language of the culture. Heider (1988) reported, "I once heard two people who both claimed linguistic competence give drastically different translations of a phrase shouted at a ceremony" (p. 77).

Another problem in cross-cultural sex research is that researchers often obtain their data from informants. These individuals may be established experts in some area that is related to sexuality or may simply be ordinary members of the culture that the researcher has befriended. The main problem with using informants to study sexuality is that many aspects of sexual behavior are private and informants are only able to give reliable reports of their own experiences. In addition, informants may want to present themselves in a way they feel is socially desirable.

Every culture is actually composed of at least two subcultures, one for men and one for women.

William H. Davenport

Another difficulty in doing cross-cultural research stems from the fact that every culture is composed of different subcultures and subpopulations. In studying the same culture, one ethnographer may focus on people of a particular gender, class, age, or occupation, whereas another ethnographer may focus on a different group. Formulating a description of an entire culture based on the observation of one particular subset of the population is misleading.

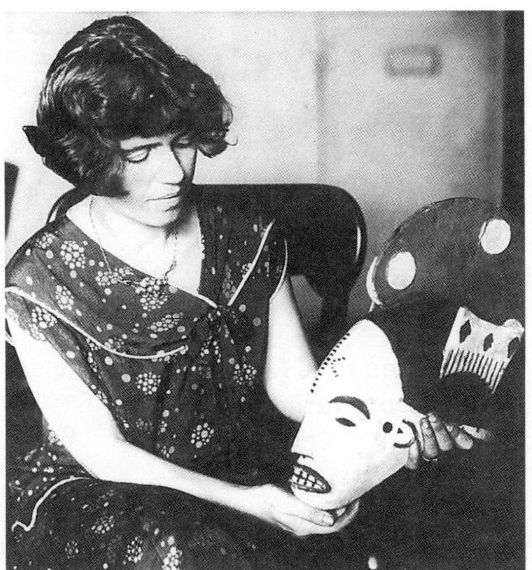

Margaret Mead studied sexuality in various Pacific Island cultures.

CONSIDERATION: Much cross-cultural sex research is gender-biased. Given that most ethnologists and ethnographers are men, we may assume that "they do not or cannot obtain data on women that are comparable to that for males" (Davenport, 1987, p. 200).

Even the Western perspective of the egg and sperm has a gender bias. The egg is described as feminine in that it does not "move" or "journey" but "passively" is "transported," is "swept," or even "drifts" along the fallopian tube. In utter contrast, sperm are small, "streamlined," and invariably active. They "deliver" their genes to the egg, "activate the developmental program of the egg," and have "velocity" that is often remarked upon (Martin, 1991, p. 489).

Lastly, culture is not static but rather changes across time. Therefore, ethnographic or ethnological research that was conducted many years ago may not accurately reflect current cultural practices and beliefs.

In *The Coming of Age in Samoa,* Margaret Mead (1928) described adolescent Samoan females as sexually relaxed, carefree, peaceful, loving, and free of psychological conflict. Derek Freeman, another ethnographer who studied the Samoan culture between 1940 and 1967, reported evidence that contradicted Mead's findings (Freeman, 1983). Contrary to Mead's report, the Samoan adolescent females that Freeman describes are aggressive, impulsive, status-hungry, violent, and sexually hungup. Part of the reason why Freeman's description differed from Mead's is that Mead's study took place in the 1920s, whereas Freeman's study spanned the 1940s through the 1960s, times of significant change (Scheper-Hughs, 1987).

WHAT IS "NORMAL" SEXUAL BEHAVIOR?

We were born into the world without attitudes or values. Our culture taught us its values along with its language through such institutions as the family, school, and church. With no standard of comparison and no knowledge of alternatives, as children we accepted as normal the things our society taught us. For example, if we grew up in the United States, we were likely punished for public nudity and learned that wearing clothes in public was normal. But if we had been born into the Chavantez Indian tribe in Brazil, we would have learned that it is normal to walk around without clothes (Smith, 1979).

Cross-cultural research in human sexuality reveals wide variations in what individuals learn to regard as "normal" sexual behavior. Our concepts of what is normal or abnormal, natural or unnatural, legitimate or illegitimate, appropriate or inappropriate are learned. Normalcy is determined by the value system of the society in which we live. Concepts of sexual normalcy vary according to the criteria being used and the society and historical period in which the sexual behavior occurs.

Definitions of "Normal" Are Based on Various Criteria

In defining what is "normal," various criteria may be used. For example, a specific sexual behavior may be considered "normal" if it is prevalent, considered to be morally correct, and/or is viewed as "natural."

Prevalence One common meaning of the term *normal* refers to its frequency of occurrence. We tend to assume that if most people engage in a behavior, it is normal. Three-fourths of the 600 university students who responded to Rubin's question-

Nudity is "normal" among the children in this Brazilian tribe.

naire reported that they engaged in oral sex (Rubin, 1991). So, we conclude, oral sex, at least among the students in this sample, is relatively normal. Defining *normal* in terms of prevalence implies that sexual behaviors that rarely occur are not normal. Since only a fourth of Rubin's university respondents reported having engaged in group sex, there may be a tendency to assume this sexual behavior is not normal.

Each culture envelops sex with a different environment of ideas, beliefs, values, and regulations, and no two are identical.
William H. Davenport

CONSIDERATION: All sexual behaviors that are prevalent in a population are not necessarily viewed as "normal" by all individuals. For example, some people regard the use of vibrators in sexual play as strange, even though they are widely available in department stores and mail-order catalogs (Blank, 1989).

Morally Correct Sexual behaviors have also been considered normal if they were viewed as morally right. Penile-vaginal intercourse between husband and wife is the only morally correct form of sexual behavior, according to some religions. Homosexuality, masturbation, and oral sex are, therefore, not normal, since they are viewed as immoral (Lawrence, 1989).

Natural Finally, sexual behaviors have been viewed as natural or unnatural depending on whether they resulted in procreation. This view grew out of the early Greek and Roman beliefs that sexual feelings distorted a person's thinking and that the only justifiable sexual passions were those oriented toward procreation. Since masturbation, homosexuality, oral sex, and anal sex do not result in children, they are "unnatural acts" (Francoeur, 1990). Even though sexual behaviors are found in nonhuman primates (e.g., masturbation and homosexual and oral-genital sex have been observed) (Wolfe, 1991), such acts are still viewed by some as "unnatural" and by implication "not normal" in humans.

CONSIDERATION: In view of the societal variations regarding what is labeled as abnormal and normal, Reiss (1986) suggested we use the term *abnormal* only as it refers to an inability to function in any society. For example, a person who enjoys walking around in the nude would be regarded as abnormal on Main Street USA but normal for a member of the Chavantez Indian tribe. In the absence of cognitive or emotional traits that disable a person (for which Reiss does use the term *abnormal),* Reiss uses the term *nonconformist.* The emphasis is then on the society that generates the norms, rather than the person reacting to them.

Definitions of "Normal" Sexual Behavior Vary across Time

Cultures have different views over time of what they consider "normal" sexual behavior. Kissing and intercourse before marriage were viewed differently during the American colonial era than today. For example, kissing in public was considered unacceptable behavior. One historian recorded the event of a Captain Kemble who, returning from a long sea voyage, kissed "his lady" as he stepped on shore. As a result, he "was promptly lodged in the stocks" (Train, 1931, p. 347).

The penalty for premarital intercourse during that era was more severe. Both men and women were expected to come to the marriage bed as virgins. If they did not, it was evidence that they had succumbed to the temptations of the flesh, which marked them as not being among the "chosen." Once discovered, they had to make a public confession following which they may have been subject to fines, lashes, or more.

During the American colonial era, a man might be lodged in the stocks for kissing in public.

> In Hartford, Connecticut, in 1739, not only was Aaron Starke pilloried, whipped, and branded on the cheek for seducing Mary Holt, and ordered to pay ten shillings to her father, but he was ordered to marry her when both should be "fit for the condition." (Turner, 1955, p. 74).

This concern for morality had been imported from England, where there was "no lack of evidence for the litigious nature of the pre-industrial population over sexual matters. In the early seventeenth century, for instance, all sorts of cases were brought to the courts, from the seduction of wives to the incidence of prostitution" (Weeks, 1989, p. 22).

Havelock Ellis (1938) emphasized that the cultural sexual norms in any given historical time period do not furnish a universal standard.

> When we are concerned with an impulse so primitive and fundamental as that of sex we cannot decide what is "natural" and what is "perverse" merely by the standard set up in accordance with shifting fashions of thought, the religious or social customs of one particular age. (p. 101)

CONSIDERATION: Society is so effective in socializing members of each new generation that they sometimes believe that they live in the best of all periods. Professor Gumploviez of the University of Gratz coined the term *acrochronism* to refer to the belief that the time in which one lives is superior to any period that has preceded it (Robinson, 1921). Indeed, both the Victorians and individuals of today may feel acrochronistic about the sexual values of their day.

Ethnocentrism versus Cultural Relativism

Members of every society learn to view the cultural norms of their own social group as appropriate and the norms of other cultures as strange. Judging other cultures according to the standards of one's own culture is called **ethnocentrism.** Most people are ethnocentric in that they assume that their cultural norms are natural, universal, and correct and that the norms of other cultures are strange or wrong. The

It is difficult to view these patterns of dress and ritual without being ethnocentric.

Self-Assessment in this chapter provides a way for you to compare your sexual attitudes to those of people from other cultures.

Any effort to educate and promote healthy sexuality must take into consideration the practices of the culture in which the individual has been socialized.

Barbara Rynerson

CONSIDERATION: A new term developed by Dick Skeen (1991) is **erotocentrism.** He defined this term as "an overriding belief that one's sexual behavior and attitude is superior to all others and that one's own sexuality is the standard by which all others should be judged" (p. ix).

The principle of **cultural relativism** suggests that to understand other cultures, we must view them according to their own standards. Those who adopt the principle of cultural relativism view the beliefs and practices of another culture according to the values and standards of that culture. The Choices section at the end of this chapter further discusses ethnocentrism and cultural relativism.

Cross-Cultural Variations in Sexuality

Sexual norms and practices vary widely in different societies. In this section, we look at cultural variations regarding sexual intercourse, premarital sex, extramarital sex, incest, menstruation, homosexual sex, and gender roles.

Sexual Intercourse

While sexual intercourse is a universal act, it is influenced by culture. Societies have different norms regarding intercourse positions, frequency, and age of first intercourse.

CROSS-CULTURAL DATA: The average Japanese girl experiences menstruation and an attraction to the opposite sex at age 12. However, first dating does not occur until age 17 and first intercourse does not occur until age 21. Among Japanese boys, first ejaculation occurs around age 14, but they do not begin to date until age 18 and have first intercourse at age 21 (Hatano, 1991, p. 14). While the ages of menstruation and ejaculation are similar to those of U.S. youth, the ages of first dating and intercourse are considerably later because of Japanese cultural influences.

Positions In most cultures, the preferred coital position is face to face, with the woman supine (lying on her back). Another frequent position is one in which the partners are lying face to face on one side (Davenport, 1987).

CONSIDERATION: Due to crowded sleeping arrangements in many cultures, couples try to be inconspicuous when they are engaging in sexual intercourse. Hence, the side position for intercourse is favored in many cultures because it is less conspicuous than other positions.

Frequency The frequency of intercourse also varies. Although most couples throughout the world have intercourse between two and five times a week (Gebhard, 1972), the Basongye in the Sasai province of Zaire, even in their 50s and 60s, have intercourse every night (Merriam, 1972). In contrast, a man of the Cayapa Indians of Ecuador may go for several years without having intercourse. Their term for intercourse, *medio trabajo,* means "a little like work."

Age at First Intercourse Similarly, cultural values dictate the age at which individuals are expected to engage in various sexual behaviors (see data in margin).

A major factor affecting the expression of sexual behavior among Japanese youth is the emphasis in the culture on academic preparation.

> The unnecessarily tight pressure of university entrance examinations (admission to which university of what rank) is often considered to be the decisive factor for the whole life of a Japanese; senior high school students are particularly oppressed in their

Self Assessment

Sex Knowledge and Attitude Test, Part I

Please indicate your reaction to each of the following statements on sexual behavior in our culture, using the following alternatives:

A. Strongly agree
B. Agree
C. Uncertain
D. Disagree
E. Strongly disagree

_____ 1. The spread of sex education is causing a rise in premarital intercourse.

_____ 2. Mutual masturbation among boys is often a precursor of homosexual behavior.

_____ 3. Extramarital relations are almost always harmful to a marriage.

_____ 4. Abortion should be permitted whenever desired by the mother.

_____ 5. The possession of contraceptive information is often an incitement to promiscuity.

_____ 6. Relieving tension by masturbation is a healthy practice.

_____ 7. Premarital intercourse is morally undesirable.

_____ 8. Oral-genital sex play is indicative of an excessive desire for physical pleasure.

_____ 9. Parents should stop their children from masturbating.

_____ 10. Women should have coital experience prior to marriage.

_____ 11. Abortion is murder.

_____ 12. Girls should be prohibited from engaging in sexual self-stimulation.

_____ 13. All abortion laws should be repealed.

_____ 14. Strong legal measures should be taken against homosexuals.

_____ 15. Laws requiring a committee of physicians to approve an abortion should be abolished.

_____ 16. Sexual intercourse should occur only between married partners.

_____ 17. The lower-class male has a higher sex drive than others.

_____ 18. Society should offer abortion as an acceptable form of birth control.

_____ 19. Masturbation is generally unhealthy.

_____ 20. A physician has the responsibility to inform the husband or parents of any female [on whom he or she performs an abortion].

_____ 21. Promiscuity is widespread on college campuses today.

_____ 22. Abortions should be disapproved of under all circumstances.

_____ 23. Men should have coital experience prior to marriage.

_____ 24. Boys should be encouraged to masturbate.

_____ 25. Abortions should not be permitted after the twentieth week of pregnancy.

_____ 26. Experiences of seeing family members in the nude arouse undue curiosity in children.

_____ 27. Premarital intercourse between consenting adults should be socially acceptable.

_____ 28. Legal abortions should be restricted to hospitals.

_____ 29. Masturbation among girls is a frequent cause of frigidity.

_____ 30. Lower-class women are typically quite sexually responsive.

_____ 31. Abortion is a greater evil than bringing an unwanted child into the world.

_____ 32. Mutual masturbation in childhood should be prohibited.

_____ 33. Virginity among unmarried girls should be encouraged in our society.

_____ 34. Extramarital sexual relations may result in a strengthening of the marriage relationship of the persons involved.

_____ 35. Masturbation is acceptable when the objective is simply the attainment of sensory enjoyment.

Continued

SKAT - Part I used by permission of Harold Lief. (Item 20 phrasing updated.)

The Sex Knowledge and Attitude Test (SKAT; Lief & Reed, 1972) was developed as a teaching aid for courses on human sexuality, as well as a social science research instrument. It was designed to describe *groups* of students, not to assess the attitudes of individuals *(Preliminary Technical Manual,* undated). Its components include measures of attitudes, knowledge, personal background, and frequencies of sexual behaviors. Part I, Attitudes, is reproduced in this Self-Assessment. Lief and Reed have made the SKAT available to researchers from a number of countries. Comparative data from four countries are presented here. Designed for post-high school use, data are available mainly from medical and nursing students. The SKAT norming sample was composed of 850 medical students from 16 medical schools in the United States.

Scoring The attitude component of the SKAT yields four subscales.

1. ***Heterosexual Relations*** (HR) focuses on attitudes towards pre- and extramarital encounters. High scores indicate an accepting, even encouraging, attitude toward premarital and extramarital relations, while low scores indicate a conservative or disapproving attitude.
2. ***Sex Myths*** (SM) deals with one's acceptance or rejection of mistaken yet commonly held beliefs. High scores indicate rejection and low scores acceptance of the misconceptions.
3. ***Autoeroticism*** (M) addresses attitudes toward masturbation. High scorers view masturbation as a healthy way to relieve tension and obtain pleasure. They believe that parents should not prohibit their children from masturbating. In contrast, low scorers view masturbation as unhealthy and a practice that parents should prohibit.
4. ***Abortion*** (A) focuses on medical, legal, and social judgments on abortion. High scorers view abortion as an acceptable practice that should be permitted whenever the woman desires. Low scores indicate an orientation in which abortion is viewed as a form of murder that should be strictly medically supervised.

To compute your scores, assign the following values: Strongly Agree (A) = 1, Agree (B) = 2, Undecided (C) = 3, Disagree (D) = 4, and Strongly Disagree (E) = 5 for all items except the following, which should be scored in reverse (A = 5, B = 4, C = 3, D = 2, E = 1): 4, 6, 10, 13, 15, 18, 23, 27, 34, and 35.

Then, total the scores for the items in each scale:

HR: 3, 7, 10, 16, 23, 27, 33, 34.
SM: 1, 2, 5, 8, 14, 17, 26, 29, 30.
A: 4, 11, 13, 15, 18, 25, 31.
M: 6, 9, 12, 19, 24, 32, 35.

Interpreting your Score You may wish to compute the average scores for your class and compare them to those of medical students from various countries. In Table 1, data are presented from Chan's (1990) study comparing Chinese medical students with U.S. medical students (from the SKAT validation sample collected in 1972). Chinese students consistently scored more conservatively than the U.S. students. The two groups were more similar in attitudes toward autoeroticism but more dissimilar in attitudes toward premarital and extramarital sex.

Two other studies that reported comparisons of medical students in other countries with those in the United States are described here. Their data were presented as standard scores (not raw scores, as above), so you cannot directly compare your scores. However, you may be interested in comparisons among these groups. Both studies were published in 1982, with Alzate's study using students from Manizales, Colombia; and Moracco and Zeidan's study using students from Beirut, Lebanon. Compared with U.S. students, Colombian students were more conservative toward abortion and more likely to endorse sexual myths.

Comparisons of the Arab and U.S. scores of men and women are presented in Table 2. Moracco and Zeidan (1982) stated that the obvious explanation for

TABLE 1 Comparing SKAT Raw Scores of Chines and U.S. Medical Students

	Chinese students			U.S. students*			
Scale	$\overline{X}$	*SD*	*n*	$\overline{X}$	*SD*	*nz*	*z*
Heterosexual relations	20.34	5.23	83	28.10	6.41	420	11.87
Sexual myths	29.34	4.26	83	34.72	4.62	422	10.37
Abortion	24.45	4.72	83	29.70	6.08	423	8.80
Autoeroticism	22.04	4.03	83	25.65	4.20	424	7.41

*SKAT scores of U.S. students were those reported for the original validation sample.

Source: Chan, D. W. (1990). Sex Knowledge, attitudes, and experience of Chinese medical students in Hong Kong. *Archives of Sexual Behavior, 19,* 73–93. Used by permission of Plenum Press.

Continued

Self-Assessment—*Continued*

the differences in each category is the strong sexual conservatism of Arab cultures, which hold strict sexual codes and taboos. They explained that violating these codes are seen as some of the greatest acts of dishonor in the culture.

Reliability and Validity The reliability of the SKAT has been considered both from the standpoint of responses to individual items and of scale scores (composed of summing item groups). Measures of internal consistency (coefficient alphas) on the four attitudinal scales ranged from 0.68 to 0.86 across two validation samples. This was interpreted as providing evidence of high stability and internal consistency of the attitude scale scores (*Preliminary Technical Manual,* undated).

The standard error of the mean was used as a reliability estimate of the scale means to determine how representative a particular scale mean is of a population. The standard error of scale means for the attitude scales were presented in the SKAT *Preliminary Technical Manual* (undated).

Construct validity of the attitudinal scales was addressed by examining the intercorrelations among the scales, which range from $r = 0.31$ to $.0.59$. Correlations of the four attitude scale scores with other SKAT responses confirm the meaning and interpretation of the scales (Miller & Lief, 1979). For example, liberal (high) HR scores related to a higher number of coital partners $(r = 0.39)$ and rejection of conservative social values $(r = 0.48)$. Greater sexual knowledge scores were related to rejection of sexual myths (higher SM scores) (r = 0.57). Conservative abortion attitudes (low A scores) were associated with Catholicism $(r = 0.34)$. Finally, liberal masturbation attitudes (high M scores) were related to higher reported frequencies of masturbation in high school $(r = 0.23)$.

Further validation of construct validity for the SKAT is revealed in score changes following educational programs. Several studies of sexuality education show SKAT changes measuring an increase in the Knowledge scale score, as well as liberalization of attitudes on the four attitude scores (Miller & Lief, 1979).

References

Alzate, H. (1982). Effect of formal sex education on the sexual knowledge and attitudes of Colombian medical students. *Archives of Sexual Behavior, 11,* 210–214.

Chan, D. W. (1990) Sex knowledge, attitudes, and experience of Chinese medical students in Hong Kong. *Archives of Sexual Behavior, 19,* 73–93.

Lief, H. I., & Reed, D. M. (1972). *The Sex Knowledge and Attitude Test (S.K.A.T.) (2nd ed.).* Available from Harold I. Lief, M.D., Garfield Duncan Building, Suite 503, 700 Spruce Street, Philadelphia, PA 19107.

Miller, W. R., & Lief, H. I. (1979) The sex knowledge and attitude test (SKAT). *Journal of Sex and Marital Therapy, 5,* 282–287.

Moracco, J., & Zeidan, M. (1982). Assessment of sex knowledge and attitude of non-Western medical students. *Psychology: A Journal of Human Behavior, 19,* 13–21.

Preliminary Technical Manual, SKAT (2nd ed.). Philadelphia: University of Pennsylvania School of Medicine, Center for the Study of Sex Education in Medicine.

TABLE 2 **Comparisons of Arab and U.S. Scores on the Four Subscales of the Attitudinal Scale of the SKAT**

		Mean	SD	N	t-value*
Heterosexual Relations	U.S. Males	49.26	10.80	3014	33.87*
	Arab Males	30.84	5.85	133	
	U.S. Females	48.77	11.10	460	16.33*
	Arab Females	26.97	6.79	30	
Sexual Myths	U.S. Males	49.13	10.10		48.65*
	Arab Males	28.21	4.48		
	U.S. Females	52.97	9.40		24.17*
	Arab Females	27.23	5.32		
Autoeroticism	U.S. Males	49.59	9.50		63.44*
	Arab Males	23.02	4.40		
	U.S. Females	49.60	10.00		33.39*
	Arab Females	22.17	3.71		
Abortion	U.S. Males	48.33	10.50		28.44*
	Arab Males	32.58	5.99		
	U.S. Females	48.42	11.20		12.43*
	Arab Females	32.10	6.59		

*$p < .001$

Source: Adapted from Moracco, J., & Zeidan, M. (1982). Assessment of sex knowledge and attitude of non-Western medical students. *Psychology: A Journal of Human Behavior,* 19, 13–21. Used by permission.

The premarital, marital, and extramarital behavior of this couple will be in reference to Japanese norms.

> heterosexual behaviors in lieu of the preparatory studies. Based on the same logic, parents, and perhaps classroom teachers too, are eager to require that the children concentrate only on school works, and therefore they definitely discourage the sexual activity of the children (Hatano, 1991, pp. 12, 13).

Premarital Sex

Premarital sexual behavior may be punished in one society, tolerated in a second, and expected in a third (see Table 3.1). In the Gilbert Islands, virginity until marriage is an exalted sexual value, and violations are not tolerated. Premarital couples who are discovered to have had intercourse before the wedding are put to death. Our society tolerates premarital intercourse, particularly if the partners are "in love." In contrast, the Lepcha people of India believe that intercourse helps young girls to mature. By the age of 12, most Lepcha young women are engaging in regular intercourse.

The Marquesans on Nuku Hiva Island in Eastern Polynesia encourage premarital sexual explorations (homosexual and heterosexual) in both males and females at an early age (10). To ensure proper sexual instruction, boys have their first intercourse with a woman in her 30s or 40s; young girls have intercourse with elder male tribal leaders.

TABLE 3.1 Premarital Sex in Four Cultures

Culture	Norm regarding Premarital Sex
United States	Tolerated
China	Prohibited
India	Prohibited
Pokomo (Kenya, East Africa)	Expected

Source: Robert Bunger, 1992. Department of Sociology and Anthropology, East Carolina University, Greenville, North Carolina. Prepared specifically for this chapter. Used by permission of Dr. Bunger.

A culture can be more usefully defined as the contingencies of reinforcement maintained by the group.

B. F. Skinner

As the girl reaches adolescence, her parents will encourage nocturnal meetings between her and a high-status, well-off male with the hope of establishing ties with him and his family. Marquesan mothers are proud that their daughters have a number of lovers.

In contrast to group approval for premarital intercourse among the Marquesan, the Kenuzi Nubians (a group located along the Nile River in Egypt) strongly impress upon girls the importance of being a virgin when they marry. In addition to the removal of the clitoris and sewing up of the vagina by age four, the penalty levied against a girl for premarital intercourse is to be killed by her nearest relative.

> Where punishment is severe, the woman's actions seem to be regarded as an offense to the men in her family or to her prospective husband. For example, the friends of a young Fijian girl strangled her because of a premarital transgression. They then apologized to her fiancé for her disloyalty to him. The fact that male relatives or friends slay the woman attest to their interest in the maintenance of her sexual integrity. (Frayser, 1985, p. 205)

Most societies communicate disapproval to the woman who has premarital intercourse by shunning her, making it difficult for her to marry (her reputation is ruined), and imposing divorce if it is discovered after marriage that she is not a virgin. A Wolof man (of Gambia) has the right to demand an immediate divorce if his wife is not a virgin when he marries her.

CONSIDERATION: Although we have been discussing consequences of premarital sex to the woman, men also receive negative social sanctions for engaging in premarital sex. In some societies (26% of 51 societies), the man is the only one punished, or he is punished more severely than the woman. For example, a Kafa man of southwestern Ethiopia may be punished for premarital intercourse by having his head or hands cut off (Frayser, 1985, pp. 205–206).

Extramarital Sex

Most societies are less tolerant of extramarital than premarital sex. The former involves not only the couple and their children but also the larger kinship system. In some cases, the entire community is affected. Among the Suku of southwest Zaire, intercourse between the wife of a chief and a man of another tribe could result in the chief going to war against the lover's village.

CROSS-CULTURAL DATA: Extramarital intercourse is ranked after incest as the most strictly prohibited sexual bahavior. Frayser (1985) observed that three-quarters of 58 societies forbade extramarital intercourse for one or both sexes (p. 209).

When extramarital intercourse is permitted, there are limitations. For example, the wife of an Aleut male may have intercourse with a house guest as a symbol of hospitality extended by the husband. Such wife-lending illustrates how tightly extramarital intercourse may be controlled.

Other examples of restricted but approved extramarital intercourse include:

- The Marshallese of the Jaluit Atoll allow a woman to have sexual access to her sister's husband.
- The Comanche male may have intercourse with his brother's wife (but only with the express consent of the brother).
- The Hidatsa allow a man to have intercourse with his wife's sister, but only when his own wife is in the advanced stages of pregnancy. "The woman's parents think it is preferable to offer him another daughter than to risk having him get involved with an unrelated woman" (Frayser, 1985, p. 209).
- The Fijians allow extramarital intercourse after the men have returned to the village with war captives.

CROSS-CULTURAL DATA: Cross-culturally, the double standard seems evident in regard to who is allowed to have extramarital intercourse with whom. In her study of 58 societies, Frayser (1985) reported that she found no society that gave the option to women to have affairs while denying it to men (p. 210).

CONSIDERATION: Sociologists operating from a structure-function perspective emphasize that all norms that exist in a society provide some benefits for the society. Permitting extramarital intercourse may have both economic and political benefits for a tribe or group. Economic benefits are illustrated in the case of the Aweikoma of St. Catarina, Brazil, in that an affair may motivate a man to join his paramour's band and thus increase the number of hunters in the group. Otherwise, men might go elsewhere for meeting their sexual needs. Political benefits also can occur, as illustrated by the Aleut men who lend their wives to guests. Such wife-lending may solidify the friendships of the males.

Individuals who ignore the rules under which extramarital intercourse is to occur are often severely punished. Such severe punishment was observed in 85% of 54 societies (Frayser, 1985, p. 211). Forms of punishment include: lover pays a fine to the woman's husband and brother, lover submits to a public beating by the husband, and wife submits to a private beating by the husband. A Kenuzi husband (in Egypt) can kill his wife if he even suspects her of infidelity.

CONSIDERATION: While in regard to premarital sexuality women are punished more than men for violations, in regard to extramarital sexuality men may receive more severe punishment than women. In a study of 48 societies in which both partners were punished, the punishment for the man was more severe (31% of 48 societies inflicted severe punishment on the man) than for the woman (12.5% of 48 societies inflicted severe punishment on the woman) (Frayser, 1985, p. 214).

Incest

Incest is considered the only nearly universal sexual taboo. While virtually all cultures forbid incest, they differ with regard to how incest is defined and socially sanctioned (Davenport, 1987). In some cultures, certain kinds of cousins are permitted and even encouraged to have sexual relations, but marriage between them is forbidden. In some cultures, the incest taboo is extended to only primary relatives (parents, offspring, siblings), while in other cultures, incest is prohibited among all traceable relatives. The incest taboo may be asymmetrical in that it may apply to one set of cousins (children of same-sex siblings) but not to another set of cousins (children of opposite-sex siblings). In Chinese culture, all persons with the same surname are subjected to the incest taboo, even though millions of Chinese people with the same surname are not related. The Dahomey of West Africa and the Inca of Peru have viewed sex between siblings as natural and desirable, but not between parents and children (Stephens, 1982).

CROSS-CULTURAL DATA: Thirty-one percent, or 9 of 29 societies, impose severe punishment for individuals who violate the incest taboo. Such severe punishments include death, mutilation, sterilization, and expulsion from the community (Frayser, 1985, p. 105).

Social sanctions against those who commit incest range "from ridicule to threats of supernatural punishment to the partners being put to death" (Gray & Wolfe, 1992, p. 645). Frayser (1985) described a variety of sanctions that are applied to those who violate the incest taboo. The Cayapa Indians of Ecuador have been known to suspend violators over a table covered with candles and roast them to death. The ancient Incas also imposed death for violation of the incest taboo.

In some cultures, the sanctions for violating the incest taboo are less severe. Punishment may be as mild as temporary verbal disapproval. For example, the Havasupai Indians of the Grand Canyon merely reprimand offenders verbally. Moderate punishment may involve temporary body damage (e.g., whipping) or ostracism for a limited period of time.

It has been generally assumed that the incest taboo was universal. However, historical records show that in a number of societies, royalty were encouraged to marry (and therefore, be incestuous with) a family member, especially a sibling. Furthermore, "in some societies there are no obvious incest taboos in the sense of rules (and sanctioned rules especially) against it, only a notion that no one would commit incest anyway" (Brown, 1991, p. 119).

CONSIDERATION: It has also been assumed that animals—unlike humans—mate incestuously. Thus, "the human prohibition of incest was a distinctively cultural marker of humanity's separation from the animal world" (Brown, 1991, p. 118). However, "it is now known that incest is rare among animals in the wild" (p. 118).

Brown (1991) noted that the incest taboo is not universal, though it might be a "near-universal." However, incest avoidance may be a universal. Brown (1991) concluded that recent efforts to understand the incest taboo/avoidance lead to "the sobering reflection that an alleged universal that has exercised the anthropological imagination for over 100 years is still not explained to everyone's satisfaction" (p. 128).

Menstruation

Most people in the United States regard menstruation as a normal biological process associated with reproduction. However, the Kimam of southern New Guinea regard menstrual blood as dangerous, polluting, and contagious. The Hill Maria Gond of southeastern India sequester menstruating women in special huts on the outskirts of their settlement so they do not infect others (Frayser, 1985, p. 2). In a study of 30 nonindustrialized societies, 70% regarded the menstrual flow or a menstruating woman as dangerous to others in the community (Frayser, 1985, p. 221).

Homosexual Sex

The majority of nonindustrialized societies permit, indeed encourage, homosexual sex for some of its individuals.

CONSIDERATION: Most of the cross-cultural literature on homosexuality focuses on male homosexual behavior. Most anthropologists have been men, and therefore, little attention has been given to the cross-cultural study of female homosexuality.

Each culture, explicitly and implicitly, specifies a unique configuration of qualities that delineate and color the expressions of sexuality.
William Davenport

Among the Sambia in the Eastern Highlands of Papua New Guinea, boys 7 to 15 years old spend a decade or more in a close homosexual relationship with a male mentor. It is believed that it is necessary for young males to perform fellatio on and ingest the sperm of older men so that the boys will be able to produce sperm when they get older (Herdt, 1991).

Among the people of East Bay, a village in Melanesia, homosexuality is tolerated only in males. Prior to marriage, young men engage in mutual masturbation and anal intercourse. Many married men are bisexual (Shepherd, 1987).

Batak males (in northern Sumatra) engage in homosexual relations before marriage. At puberty, Batak boys leave their parents' home and sleep in a home with 12 to 15 boys. In this group, each boy is initiated into homosexual practices. After marriage, the majority of Batak men cease homosexual activity (Money & Ehrhardt, 1973).

Homosexuality in industrialized nations is more repressed. In Hungary, homosexuality in women or men is punishable by up to five years in prison (Drakulic,

Cultures dictate appropriate gender roles as evidenced by this all-male capture of an anaconda by Suia Indians, Xingu, Brazil.

1990). Homosexuals in the former Soviet Union must keep their sexual orientation hidden for fear of government reprisal.

Gender Roles

While we focus on gender roles in Chapter 8, it is important to emphasize here that gender roles are largely a product of culture. What it means to be a woman or a man depends on the culture.

Gender Roles in Western Samoa Western Samoa is a South Pacific island nation of Polynesians. Mead (1928) observed that cultural influences on gender roles began at birth, when the umbilical cord of the female infant was buried under a mulberry tree to ensure that she would be industrious at household tasks. In contrast, the umbilical cord of the male infant was planted under a taro plant or thrown into the sea so that he would become a good farmer or fisherman. The sexual division in Samoan society dictates that young girls learn to weave, prepare food, do laundry, and organize social events. Young Samoan boys are expected to tend the family farm and become involved in village leadership (Muse, 1991). In addition, female Samoans engage in activities that are close to where they live, while male Samoans are explorative and engage in activities away from the village center.

As women become more educated and more oriented toward reducing the gender asymmetry of their cultures, changes will take place in the defintions and evaluations of male-female relationships.
Harriet P. Lefley

Gender Roles in the Middle East In most cultures of the world, men dominate and control women. In the Middle East, male domination exists to an extreme. A Hindu code reads, "In childhood a woman must be subject to her father; in youth, to her husband; when her husband is dead, to her sons. A woman must never be free of subjugation" (quoted in Doyle & Paludi, 1991, p. 159).

Hindu and Muslim women are expected to cover their heads with veils, which is "but one feature of the mandatory code for a woman's conduct which requires that she behave modestly, restrained in speech, restricted in movement" (Mandelbaum, 1988). Within the household, men and women often sleep in separate rooms, and they sit apart at all social or religious occasions. In the presence of others, a young

This little girl is learning that as an adult in her society she must keep her body covered while in public.

wife must not speak to her husband or look steadily at him. At meals, women eat only after the men have been served. A wife walking with her husband is expected to follow a few steps behind him.

Gender Roles in Sweden The Swedish government has been making efforts toward establishing equality of the sexes since before U.S. women won the right to vote (Scriven, 1984). The government has instituted a family policy that provides benefits to either the mother or the father who stays home with children. By encouraging fathers to participate more in child rearing, the government aims to provide more opportunities for women to pursue other roles. Women hold about a quarter of the seats in the Swedish Parliament. However, few Swedish women are in high-status positions in business, and governmental efforts to reduce gender inequality are weak, compared to the power of tradition.

We have been discussing the gender roles of women and men in different societies. However, some cultures acknowledge a gender role that is neither male nor female. The following Cross-Cultural Perspective discusses the *hijras* of India.

CROSS-CULTURAL PERSPECTIVE

Neither Male Nor Female

Is there a third gender? In some contemporary cultures, members live a social role other than what we identify as male or female. These include the *hijra* of India (Nanda, 1990), the *berdache* of Native Americans (Williams, 1986), and the *xanith* of Oman. John Money (1990) suggested that what these groups have in common, along with occidental male-to-female transsexuals, is gynemimesis (woman-miming). In these groups, some males at some stage in their development act like women. Cultural reactions to these people vary greatly, from tolerance in India to persecution in the Western world (Money, 1990).

Continued

Continued

Serena Nanda, who published an ethnography of the hijras, is a professor of anthropology at John Jay College of Criminal Justice at the City University of New York. Her field work in India on the hijras began in 1981 and continued through 1986. She gathered information through observation of hijras from many parts of India (necessitating translation from several languages), informal open-ended interviews, lengthy personal narratives, and conversations yielding "substantial knowledge of more than 20 hijras" (p. xvi). Nanda said that the hijras she met were eager to tell their stories so that "people everywhere will know we are full human beings" (p. xx). The following descriptions and quotations are taken from her book, *Neither Man Nor Woman: The Hijras of India* (1990).

The hijras (HIJ-ras) are a "religious community of men who dress and act like women and whose culture centers on the worship of Bahuchara Mata, one of the many versions of the Mother Goddess worshipped throughout India" (p. xv). In conjunction with the worship of this goddess, the hijras undergo an emasculation operation in which their penis and testicles are surgically removed. However, no vagina is constructed; their sexual nature is ambiguous. (Actually, not all who identify themselves as hijras submit to this illegal and life-threatening surgery.) The hijra's occupational role is that of a ritual performer after a child's birth and at weddings and temple festivals, although many do not earn their living by performing. The Hindu theme of "creative asceticism" explains the positive role afforded the hijra in Indian society. "Intersexed and impotent, themselves unable to reproduce, hijras can, through emasculation, transconfer blessings of fertility on others" (p. 30). This connection with the powers of generativity explains the relevance of the hijra participation in rituals at times of childbirth or marriage to give blessings of prosperity and fertility. Despite their renunciation of male sexuality and their identification with religious ascetics, many hijras earn a living as prostitutes (having sexual relations with men).

The folk belief about hijras is that they were born hermaphrodites and taken away by the hijra community. However, Nanda found that all the hijras she met said they had voluntarily joined the hijra community, typically as teenagers. Salima was one hijra who described being born as an intersexual.

> My parents felt sad about my birth, but they realized it was their fate to have me born to them. They were looking forward to my birth—I was the eldest child—and they were sad that I was born "neither here nor there." From my childhood I am like this. From my birth, my organ was small. My mother felt, as I grow up, naturally it will grow also. But it didn't, so she tried taking me to doctors and all that. But the doctors said, "No, it won't grow, your child is not a man and not a woman, this is God's gift." (p. 99)

More often, the hijras submit to an emasculation operation conducted by a midwife (*dai ma*) who has no medical training but operates with the power of the Mata. One dai ma confided to Nanda that she had performed 18 operations; she stopped performing them after the Mata appeared in a dream and told her to stop. In spite of the criminalization of and government pronouncements against the procedure, it is still performed in hijra communities. Why is it so important to have the surgery? A hijra called Kamladevi explained:

> See, when you go for a dance, some people may ask, "Are you a hijra or are you a man?" So that way, if you have had the operation you can show them. Only those who have had the operation are real hijras; they are called *nirvan,* nirvan sultans (like a king, that is, a very important person). If you want to be a *pukka* (pure) hijra, you must have the operation. So like when you might go out of station (take a trip) with a group of hijras, and when you are sleeping in the night your clothes may go up, but you need not bother if you have had the operation. Otherwise people will make fun of you and

Continued

Continued

the local rowdies will say, "Oh, this is a man, he has got male organs, he has come to dance with the hijras only for the sake of earning money." For that we lose respect and they will abuse us also. (p. 67)

The number of hijras is estimated at 50,000 nationwide, predominantly living in the cities of northern India. They may live in communal households (sometimes combining Hindu, Muslims, and Christians), alone, or with a husband. Social organization and control are arranged through a hierarchy of gurus (teachers) and *chelas* (disciples).

Nanda identified two points about gender identity and role from her study of the hijras. First, is that the hijra narratives indicate that the Indian culture is one that offers an institutionalized alternative or intermediate gender role other than masculine or feminine. "The hijra role in India and some cross-cultural parallels provoke reflection on our Western belief that there are only two sexes and two genders, each naturally and permanently biologically determined, and each exclusive of the meanings and characteristics of the other" (1990, p. xvii). Nanda raised the possibility that there are alternative genders and provokes consideration of the cultural construction of gender categories and identities.

The second point is that the hijra accounts suggest that gender identity and role may not be fixed and immutable, but rather flexible. Her views represent an "interactionist" perspective on gender identity and role, in which sexual assignment and biological factors converge and are sometimes overridden by subsequent socialization.

References

Money, J. (1990). Foreward. In S. Nanda, *Neither Man Nor Woman: The Hijras of India*. Belmont, CA: Wadsworth.

Nanda, S. (1990). *Neither Man Nor Woman: The Hijras of India*. Belmont, CA: Wadsworth.

Williams, W. (1986). *The Spirit and the Flesh*. Boston: Beacon Press.

While we have focused on the impact of culture on gender roles, culture also influences sexuality within subcultures in the same society. Exhibit 3.1 looks at differences in sexual behaviors of whites and blacks in the United States.

Permissive and Restrictive Cultural Contexts

The attitudes of a culture toward sexuality may be described in terms of the degree to which it is permissive or restrictive. Mangaia, a sexually permissive society, and Inis Beag, a sexually restrictive society, represent two cultural extremes.

CONSIDERATION: While we may consider a culture to be either sexually permissive or sexually restrictive, the distinction is not always clear. For example, a society may be permissive in one aspect of sexual life (e.g., premarital sex) and restrictive in another (e.g., extramarital sex). In the United States, there are so many cultural variations and so much lack of cultural unity that it is difficult to say whether it is a sexually permissive or a restrictive society. For example, some Americans, both gay and heterosexual, are accepting of homosexuality as a legitimate life-style, while others view homosexuality as unacceptable.

EXHIBIT 3.1 U.S. Sexuality in Black and White

Given that white and black cultures in the United States are different, one might assume that there would be differences in the sexual behaviors of whites and blacks. But are there?

Black and White Sexuality Compared

A study by Belcastro (1985) comparing 25 sexual behaviors of 565 white and black unmarried undergraduates revealed only a few differences, some of which are discussed below.

Black men were significantly more likely than white men to have had interracial intercourse (40% versus 13%) and to have never masturbated (44% versus 17%). More frequent interracial intercourse among black men may result from their socializing each other to have sex with a white woman and white men socializing each other to avoid sex with a black woman. Masturbation among black men has traditionally been viewed as an admission of not being able to seduce a woman for intercourse. Black men usually have sexual intercourse with more black women at younger ages than white men do with white women.

When black women were compared to white women, they were found to be significantly less likely to have performed fellatio (48% versus 82%). The infrequent reporting of fellatio by black women is probably largely due to their socialization that fellatio is an unclean and demeaning sexual act. Black women may also feel that the best sex is "natural" (not oral or manual).

Another study comparing black and white sexual values revealed that 34% of blacks compared to 26% of whites felt that masturbation was "always wrong." In addition, 66% of blacks compared to 56% of whites felt that prostitution was "always wrong" (Klassen, Williams, & Levitt, 1989).

In another study by Harrison and Pennell (1989), black adolescent girls are more likely to have children without being married than white adolescent girls due to the greater tolerance for unmarried parenthood in the black community. In addition, black adolescent girls may have higher self-esteem and be less concerned about physical appearance and being popular than white adolescent girls. Such a difference may be a result of black adolescents, particularly those in the lower class, developing confidence in themselves as a result of being pressed into child-care and household responsibilities earlier than white adolescents.

The Mangaians: A Permissive Context

Anthropologist Donald Marshall (1971) studied the sexual patterns of the Mangaians of Mangaia (southern Polynesian Islands) and observed the extreme sexual openness with which its members are reared. Adult Mangaians copulated in the same room with all kin. Their doing so was not regarded as particularly significant since household members (including children) were busy with work or play. Masturbation by both sexes at 7 to 10 years of age was advocated and practiced (Marshall, 1971).

Beyond early exposure to parental intercourse and masturbation, childhood sex play with the same- or opposite-sex individuals was encouraged. Premarital sex was also encouraged, with no stigma for the experienced bride or groom. In marriage, partners were expected to mutually enjoy sex, and orgasm was a goal for both wife and husband. Extramarital sex also was tolerated.

A major theme of sexuality among the Mangaians was active participation on the part of the woman. She was to be sexually active beginning in childhood, to be orgasmic, and to be an active participant. Sexual passivity was viewed as deviant. In addition, affectional feelings usually followed, rather than preceded, sexual behavior with others in adult relationships.

The Inhabitants of Inis Beag: A Repressive Context

In contrast to the sexual openness of the Mangaians is the restrictive society of Ines Beag. John Messenger studied every member (350) of the small agrarian Irish island community (which he named as Inis Beag to protect its identity) from 1958 to 1966 (Davenport, 1977). From birth, members were segregated by sex in the family, church, and school. Men bonded with men and women with women. Marriage was for economic and reproductive reasons only, with women marrying around age 25 and men around age 36. This latter age for men was necessary since they had to own land before they could ask a woman to marry them.

Unlike the Mangaian women who were taught to be assertive and to enjoy sex, women of Inis Beag were taught to be sexually passive and to endure the sexual advances of men. Female orgasm was not in the vocabulary of the islanders, and nudity was avoided. Even though the economic livelihood of the community depended on the men catching fish from canoes, they could not swim because they were embarrassed to be without clothing and thus had never learned. Even bathing was to be done in absolute privacy.

Prepubertal sex play, masturbation, and premarital intercourse were considered sinful. Because sex was rarely discussed, sexual myths permeated the community. Women believed that menopause caused insanity, and men believed that sex debilitated them. Hence, they would avoid sex the night before a strenuous event.

CONSIDERATION: The culture in which a person lives influences the degree to which that person is happy with his or her sexuality. When 166 female students at Anadolu University in Eskisehir, Turkey, were asked to respond yes or no to "All in all, I am satisfied with my sex life," 8.5% responded yes; 24% of 172 male students responded yes (Erkmen, Dilbaz, Serber, Kaptanoglu, & Tekin, 1990). These percentages differ from Eysenck's study of British students, in which 60% of the women and 40% of the men responded yes (Eysenck, 1971). These percentages may reflect the greater restrictiveness of female sexuality in Turkey.

Some Culture-Specific Sex Practices

Beyond being generally permissive or repressive, cultures encourage various patterns of sexual behavior. These variations include female genital mutilation, male genital mutilation, and polygamy.

Female Genital Mutilation

CROSS-CULTURAL DATA: Over 80 million women and female children have been mutilated by genital operations throughout the world. The practice is widespread in Africa, where it occurs in 28 countries (Armstrong, 1991).

Female genital mutilation refers to different things in different cultures. In its mildest form, known to the Muslims as *sunna*, it involves the removal of the prepuce or hood of the clitoris. Because this operation removes skin only, it is sometimes referred to as "female circumcision" and is analogous to male circumcision.

Female genital mutilation more often refers to **clitoridectomy**, a process that involves the removal or excision of the entire glans and shaft of the clitoris and the labia minora, or **infibulation.** In the latter operation, the two sides of the vulva are stitched up to leave only a small opening for the passage of urine and menstrual blood. After marriage, the sealed opening is reopened to permit intercourse and delivery. After childbirth, the woman is often reinfibulated.

Female genital mutilation is usually performed by illiterate elderly midwives without anesthesia or sterile precautions and with such tools as scissors, razor blades, or broken glass (Armstrong, 1991). The operation usually occurs in the girl's home with her relatives assisting. Infection, hemorrhage, and chronic pelvic inflammatory disease occur in about 25% of the cases (Cutner, 1985). In many cases, female genital mutilation occurs a few days after the birth of the girl. In a study of female circumcision in Nigeria, 79% of the respondents had been circumcised as infants but only 6% percent as adults (Odujinrin, Akitoye, & Oyediran, 1989).

The cultural beliefs behind clitoridectomy and infibulation are economic, social, and religious. The virgin bride can inherit from her father, thus making her an economic asset to her husband. By cutting off her clitoris, she would have less sexual desire and be less tempted to have sex before marriage. Furthermore, by sewing her vaginal lips together soon after birth, the bridegroom is supposedly assured of getting a sexually passive woman who has not had intercourse. If she has had no such operation, her virginity might be questioned, which would make her less valuable.

Social and religious justifications account for female circumcision in Muslim cultures. Muslim women are regarded as inferior to men: they cannot divorce their husbands, but their husbands can divorce them; they are restricted from buying and inheriting property; and they are not allowed to have custody of their children in the event of divorce. Female circumcision is merely an expression of the low social status women have in Muslim society. Female circumcision also has a religious basis in the Muslim religion. Allah is believed to approve of female circumcision (Hosken, 1981, p. 419).

Other cultural beliefs include that the "female genitalia are unclean and cutting them away purifies a woman; that the sex drive of an uncircumcised woman is uncontrollable; and that unless the labia of a woman are cut they will grow until they hang down between a woman's knees" (Armstrong, 1991, p. 44).

CONSIDERATION: The World Health Organization and the United Nations Children's Fund have unanimously agreed that all forms of female genital mutilation should be abolished. But since there is no mechanism to resocialize parents to stop mutilating their daughters, the practice probably continues at the same rate (Smith, 1990).

Male Genital Mutilation

The most familiar form of **male genital mutilation** is **circumcision**, which involves the surgical removal of the foreskin, usually during infancy. Circumcision was performed by the Egyptians as early as 4000 B.C. Male circumcision occurs in cultures that share the Judaeo-Christian-Islamic tradition and among the Aborigines of Australia and in sub-Saharan Africa.

There are various reasons why some cultures practice male circumcision, including religious, aesthetic, hygienic, and sociological. To Jewish people, circumcision symbolizes Abraham's covenant with God. In some cultures, male circumcision has a sociological function in that it testifies that "the circumcised individual has undergone rituals and ordeals that establish maturity or it is an enhancement of masculinity" (Davenport, 1987, p. 207). In the United States, male circumcision is practiced primarily for traditional as well as for hygienic reasons. Men who were circumcised feel that circumcision for their sons is desirable, and some people feel that a circumcised penis is easier to clean and therefore inflammation and infection are less likely to occur. (Circumcision is also discussed in Chapter 6.)

Another form of male genital mutilation is **penile supraincision**, which involves making a longitudinal slit through the dorsal of the foreskin. Among the Mangaian youths, this practice occurs around age 13 to denote the onset of adolescence. After having received the proper sexual training (on style, timing, and position) by an older woman from the community, the male is supraincised, which certifies that he is ready for sexual intercourse.

A more drastic form of male genital mutilation that occurs in parts of Australia is **penile subincision**, which involves slitting the ventral side of the penis all the way into the urethra. Only subincised men can participate in sacred rituals during which drops of blood are drawn from inside the exposed urethral canal. The blood from this area is viewed as sacred and is associated with mystical powers.

CONSIDERATION: Bruno Bettelheim (1968) suggested that some forms of male genital mutilation may be a way of symbolically acquiring the creative, reproductive functions of a woman. Because menstrual blood is a periodic reminder of the woman's reproductive power, genital bleeding may signify creative potential. Blood shed from penile mutilation operations, which mimics the menstrual periods of women, may provide men with the feeling that they, too, possess creative reproductive powers.

Another form of male genital mutilation occurs among some of the inland Dayak peoples of Borneo. A few Dayak men voluntarily undergo a transverse perforation of the penis through which a wooden pin is inserted. A small knob is attached to each protruding end of the pin. The Dayak people believe that these knobs increase the woman's sexual pleasure during intercourse. This form of genital mutilation is quite painful and provides "an opportunity to display fortitude, hence it signals something about the courage, virility, and stoicism of those who suffer the operation" (Davenport, 1987, p. 208).

Polygamy

Polygamy is a general term that refers to having several spouses. Polygamy occurs in cultures or subcultures whose norms sanction multiple partners. One form of polygamy is **polygyny**, in which one husband has several wives. "Societies allowing polygyny are by far the commonest" (Brown & Hotra, 1988, p. 154).

CROSS-CULTURAL DATA: Polygyny is permitted in 83% of 862 societies studied by Murdock (1967).

Specific societies that permit polygyny are the Yoruba of Nigeria and the Pokomo of Kenya. The Yolngu tribe of the Aborigines in northern Australia also practice polygyny. Among the Yolngu, a girl between the ages of 12 and 16 is married to a man in his 40s. She is usually the fifth or sixth wife, many of whom are her sisters. The wives receive the sexual affection of their husband as he chooses (Money & Musaph, 1977).

CONSIDERATION: Most people in the United States assume that polygyny exists to satisfy the sexual desires of the man, that the women are treated like slaves, and that jealousy among the wives is common. In most polygynous societies, however, polygyny has a political and economic, rather than sexual, function. Polygyny is a means of providing many male heirs to continue the family line. In addition, with many wives, a greater number of children for domestic and farm labor can be produced. Wives are not treated like slaves, as all household work is evenly distributed among them and each is given her own house or sleeping quarters. Jealousy is minimal because the husband often has a rotation system for conjugal visits that ensures that each wife has equal access to sexual encounters (Smith, 1990).

One subculture in the United States that practices polygyny are some religious fundamentalist groups in Arizona, New Mexico, and Utah, some of which have split off from the Church of Jesus Christ of Latter-day Saints (commonly known as the

Mormon Church). Among these small sects, polygyny serves a religious function in that large earthly families are believed to result in large heavenly families. Notice that polygynous sex is only a means to accomplish another goal (large families) (Embry, 1987).

Buddhist Tibetans foster yet another brand of polygamy, referred to as **polyandry,** in which one wife has several husbands. These husbands, who may be brothers, pool their resources to support one wife. Polyandry is a much rarer form of polygamy than polygyny and is sometimes motivated by the need to keep the population rate down (Crook & Crook, 1988). Several men marrying one wife will have fewer children as a family than one man marrying several women.

Sexual access by Tibetan brothers who are polyandrously linked to one wife is determined by age and maturity, with the eldest brother having the greatest access. This necessarily implies that younger brothers will have less access and are less likely to be the biological fathers of the children born to the wife (Crook & Crook, 1988).

Mate Selection: A Cross-Cultural View

All societies recognize and institutionalize some form of pair-bonded sexual relationships. While mate selection occurs in all societies, patterns of mate selection vary widely. In addition, members of different cultures have different preferences regarding the characteristics they desire in a mate.

Patterns of Mate Selection

Cultural patterns for mate selection vary. In some cultures, arranged marriages predominate; in others, including our own, free choice is the rule. In the following sections, we look at mate selection patterns in a variety of cultures.

The United States and Canada Mate selection in the United States and Canada is considered to be a matter of free choice. Individuals usually choose a mate with whom they have "fallen in love." However, parents have a great deal of informal influence regarding the mate selection of their children (Denmark, Schwartz, & Smith, 1991). For example, since people can marry only those whom they meet, parents can influence these possibilities by deciding what schools their children will attend, in what neighborhoods their children will live, and the friends with whom their children will be allowed to spend the night.

Parents also express approval or disapproval of whom their children choose to date. The result is that North Americans tend to select mates who are similar to themselves with regard to age, race, religion, social class, education, and level of physical attractiveness. Hence, while mate selection in the United States is generally thought to be characterized by free choice, numerous social influences restrict the choice.

Poland Polish men traditionally play an active role in selecting a wife. Women play a passive role; they are expected to wait until a man proposes to them (Grzymala-Moszczynska, 1991). Before World War I, marriages were arranged by parents with the help of a matchmaker. Since then, more and more Polish men and women are selecting their mates independently; however, the traditional arranged marriage still predominates, particularly in rural areas.

In the arranged marriages a dowry is an important consideration in mate selection. The dowry that a wife brought to her new husband's house often included money, household utensils, a featherbed, and pillows. More affluent families gave their daughters land, a house, and a cow. More recently, a woman's profession or university education serves as a replacement for the traditional dowry.

Israel In Israel, once a couple begin to date, they are expected to date for a minimum of several months; casual dating is frowned upon. Dating is viewed as preparation for marriage, and relationships that are not likely to lead to marriage are discouraged. "A girl who dates a boy once or twice and then dates a new boy and switches again is considered flighty even if there has been no sexual relationship" (Safir & Izraeli, 1991). It is not uncommon for couples who formed at age 14 to ultimately marry (although the majority meet during college or military service). Dating couples may participate in family events, but their families do not formally meet until they decide to marry. Although most Israelis select their mates independently, the ultraorthodox religious population still practices matchmaking.

One constraint in the Israeli culture is that kibbutz members virtually never marry a peer member of their own kibbutz with whom they have grown up. This may be because the sibling-like relationship is subject to incest taboos. Marriage partners may be selected from older or younger groups, peers who joined the kibbutz as adults, members of other kibbutzim, or nonmembers.

In Exhibit 3.2, a Palestinian university student describes her experience in finding a mate.

Nigeria Various tribes in Nigeria have different patterns of mate selection. Among some tribes, it is customary to propose marriage to a girl before she is born. In this

EXHIBIT 3.2 Mate Selection: A Palestinian's Experience*

My name is Tahaia Brothers. I am a 19-year-old university student and moved to the United States when I was six. I was socialized as a Palestinian and never touched my husband until we were married.

In America, you date, have sex, and live together before you are married. Palestinian ways are very different—adolescents never date. We are never allowed to be alone with a member of the opposite sex unless we are in our parents' house (with our parents present).

Any physical contact before marriage is strictly prohibited. Sex before marriage is unheard of. If a girl has sex before she is married, her parents disown her. This means that she is thrown out of their house and not allowed to live with, see, or associate with them or other relatives again.

If a man knows that a woman has had sex before marriage, he will not want her. Men require that their brides be pure—this is the way I was until I met my husband. I have known only one man.

My father loves me very much but is very strict. He wants only what is best for me. He selected my husband-to-be and arranged a time I would meet with him in my house. This man (who was a stranger to me) and I talked and decided that we would tell our parents that we wanted to be engaged.

The engagement lasted five months during which time we only saw each other in the presence of my parents. After the wedding (the ceremony and celebration lasted seven hours) we took a short "honeymoon" before coming back to school.

People ask me about love. In my culture, love follows marriage, it does not precede it. I respected my husband before I married him—now I love him. People also ask me if I think about having sex with other men. Never. I am devoted to my husband, he is devoted to me, and that is the way it should be.

We have a "traditional marriage" as you would call it. I cook, clean, and serve my husband. My classmates sometimes laugh when I use the term "serve" but that is the way I was taught. My husband is good to me. He loves me and supports us financially. We are very happy.

* Used by permission of Tahaia Brothers, East Carolina University, Greenville, North Carolina.

case, the father of a young boy arranges with the pregnant wife of a friend that if her baby is a girl, she shall be wed at birth to his son. The boy's father is expected to supply food to the girl's mother until the two children reach marriageable age, which occurs when the girl attains puberty.

China Traditional Chinese marriages are arranged. Some poor Chinese families gave their young daughters away as future daughters-in-law (Yu & Carpenter, 1991). The primary role of the traditional Chinese wife was to bear male children to perpetuate the husband's line of descent. Because Chinese females married young, they could become grandmothers at a relatively young age. However, it was considered a disgrace for the grandmother (even though she may still be fairly young) to bear another child. Therefore, the "young grandmother" no longer engaged in intercourse with her husband. The husband would then select a nonmarital sexual mate referred to as a **concubine** to satisfy his sexual needs.

In China in 1980, a marriage law was passed that abolished the traditional mate selection pattern, which had deprived women of the right to choose their partners.

> This law installed a democratic marriage system that gave women free choice of partners, mandated monogamy, and equal rights for both sexes. It also. . . outlawed bigamy, concubinage, child betrothal. . . and the extraction of money or gifts in connection with marriage. (Yu & Carpenter, 1991, p. 197)

We have sampled just a few cultures to illustrate the cultural variation in mate selection patterns. Next, we consider the differences between individuals in different cultures regarding desired characteristics in a mate.

Preferred Characteristics in a Mate

Buss et al. (1990) looked at preferred mate characteristics in 37 cultures from 33 countries located on 6 continents and 5 islands (N = 9,474). Several differences in mate selection preferences between the various cultures were identified.

The largest effect of culture on mate selection preferences occurred for the variable of chastity, or desiring a mate with no previous experience in sexual intercourse. In some cultures (China, India, Indonesia, Iran, Taiwan, and Palestinian Arab), chastity was viewed as extremely important in a potential mate. In other cultures (Sweden, Finland, Norway, Netherlands, and West Germany), chastity was viewed as irrelevant or unimportant.

In South Africa (Zulu), Estonia, and Colombia, a high value was placed on one's potential mate being a good housekeeper and cook. Relatively low value was placed on housekeeping skills in the United States, Canada, and all Western European samples, with the exception of Spain.

CONSIDERATION: Mate selection preferences differ between women and men in the same culture, as well as between both sexes of different cultures. For example, the cross-cultural study by Buss et al. (1990) revealed that women generally value good earning capacity in a potential mate more than men. Men generally value physical attractiveness and housekeeping and cooking skills more than do women. However, Buss et al. (1990) noted that

> In general, the effects for sex are substantially lower than those for culture. This suggests that there may be more similarity between men and women from the same culture than between men and men or women and women from different cultures. (p. 17)

CROSS-CULTURAL DATA: In a study of 37 cultures, "mutual attraction-love" was rated as the most valued mate characteristic (Buss et al., 1990, p. 45).

Although cross-cultural research reveals that cultures have strong effects on mate selection preferences, Buss et al. noted that there are also strong similarities among cultures and between sexes on the preference ratings of mate characteristics.

CONSIDERATION: The data (see margin) "imply a degree of psychological unity or species-typicality of humans that transcends geographical, racial, political, ethnic, and sexual diversity" (Buss et al., 1990, p. 45).

Sexuality in Nonhuman Primates

Humans belong to the mammalian group referred to as primates. One suborder of primates is anthropoids, which consist of monkeys in South and Central America (known as New World monkeys), monkeys in Africa and Asia (known as Old World monkeys), larger animals such as gibbons and apes (orangutans, gorillas, and chimpanzees), and humans. While a direct link between lower animals and humans cannot be made, our understanding of human sexuality may be enhanced by examining sexuality among our closest evolutionary relatives.

Frayser (1985) summed up the significance of nonhuman primate sexual behavior:

> . . . the line between nonhuman and human primate sexual behavior is a fine one. Human sexuality is part of the primate sexual continuum, not a separate category. (p. 46)

Some of what we know about nonhuman primate sexuality follows.

Monkeys learn to copulate through social observation of other monkeys.

Social versus Hormonal Influences on Nonhuman Primate Sexual Behavior

The prolonged dependency period of young primates on their mother results in learning patterns of social interaction necessary to the offspring's survival. If the infant is deprived of social contact with other animals, it will become antisocial, self-destructive, and withdrawn. Male monkeys reared in isolation rarely, if ever, mate. Female monkeys are also less likely to mate. Those who do are more often indifferent and abusive to their offspring (Harlow & Harlow, 1962, pp. 144, 145).

In her study of Old World monkeys, Wolfe (1991) concluded that, for the most part, sexual behavior is learned in a social context with little hormonal influence.

> Socialization in a stable social unit, sexual rehearsal with both same and opposite sex partners by infants and juveniles, and sexual experience while growing to full adulthood have all come to play important roles in the development and maintenance of sexual behavior among humans, Old World monkeys, and apes. (p. 134)

Importance of Touch among Nonhuman Primates

Monkeys groom each other (e.g., stroke each other's hair, pick off lice). Such grooming may be by mother to child to build social ties or by adults as foreplay or afterplay to copulation. New and Old World adult monkeys engage in grooming behaviors with each other only when the female is in heat. In addition, just before copulation, male apes and monkeys manually stimulate the female's genitalia. Female apes and monkeys are less likely to stimulate the male genitalia (Ford & Beach, 1972, pp. 53, 54).

Homosexuality among Nonhuman Primates

Wolfe (1991) studied female homosexual behavior among free-ranging and captive alloprimates (primates other than humans) and described two females engaging in one or more mounts resembling a heterosexual copulation. While she acknowledged that the label "homosexual" denotes nothing about sexual-object orientation or sexual eroticism, 11 of 180 species evidenced female homosexual behavior. In some cases, female homosexual behavior seemed to be a substitute for heterosexual activities (no males were available). In other cases, the homosexual activity seemed to be a result of female preference. However, among female Japanese Macaque monkeys, she noted that in no case was female homosexual behavior the exclusive mode of sexual expression if the female was in a group composed of adults and peers of both sexes (p. 133).

Mating Patterns among Nonhuman Primates

Just as humans smile at each other alluringly to indicate sexual availability, adult male Japanese Macaque monkeys shake tree branches and make loud guttural vocal sounds as a form of self-advertisement. Once in the presence of a specific female, the male monkey may signal further sexual interest by facing the female with his body hair erect and by moving his ears and eyebrows up and down. The facial, anal, and genital areas of these male monkeys also turn bright red during the mating season, which may function to increase their visibility and attractiveness (Gray & Wolfe, 1992, p. 656).

Monogamy and Nonhuman Primate Sexual Behavior

Monogamy is not unheard of among primates. Researchers suggest that the percentage is between 10 and 18. Wolfe (1991) noted that of 180 species, 10% are monogamous or pair-bonded for life. Hrdy (1981) noted that 18% of primates live in breeding pairs that mutually care for offspring. Monogamy is particularly common among New World primates (Kinzey, 1987).

> Gibbons and siamangs live in stable, lifelong, monogamous families whose members forage and sleep together as a unit. Territories are primarily defended by male-female dueting. (Wolfe, 1991, p. 136)

Man is no more a naked ape than chimpanzees are hairy people, but he is a mammal and a primate, and as such shares certain physical and behavioral characteristics with other members of his class and order.

Frank A. Beach

CONSIDERATION: Do nonhuman primates make choices in regard to their partners? Observations of primate mating behavior suggest that primates do not mate randomly but rather have preferences regarding a mating partner. Primates do not necessarily engage in sexual behavior for reproductive purposes but rather because it is enjoyable in its own right (Frayser, 1985). Both male and female primates have been observed to exhibit strong preferences for mating with a specific primate. Wolfe (1991) observed that some monkeys follow other monkeys around continually as if they had a romantic crush on their object of desire. Female Japanese macaque monkeys may also have a preference for "novel males as mating partners" (p. 132).

As we close this chapter, we reemphasize the enormous influence culture has on human sexual expression. Earlier, we made reference to the "homosexual" behavior (the term is in quotes because the Sambia have no term for homosexual; they acknowledge only that humans are sexual beings) of Sambia seven-year-olds. When these young boys reach their mid-teens, they are expected to stop their sexual contacts with males and to "seek out and find exclusive, habitualized, opposite-sex contacts, with their wives" (Herdt, 1991, p. 8). This movement from one sexual target to another is culturally induced. Of this cultural direction and redirection, Herdt (1991) noted

> What the New Guinea material advises—and that from other cross-cultural and historical periods too—is that sexual function and development are under greater social and cultural regulation, even at the organismic level, than we once believed. (p. 11)

CHOICES

Given that human sexual behavior is influenced by the cultural context, three choices we might consider include becoming less ethnocentric, becoming more culturally relativistic in regard to our view of sexuality, and assessing the degree to which we choose to conform to cultural sexual norms.

Choose to Be Less Ethnocentric?

As noted earlier, ethnocentrism involves the attitude that one's own culture is superior to another. We are being ethnocentric when we believe that monogamy in the United States is a more moral and desirable value than polygyny among the Pokomo in Kenya. Ethnocentrism also involves the belief that one's own way of doing things is normal and natural and that variations are abnormal and against nature. Heterosexuals and homosexuals alike may view their own sexual orientation, beliefs, and practices as normal and the alternative as abnormal. The result of these ethnocentric perspectives is that we divide the world into "us" and "them," with "us" being the desirable group.

An alternative to viewing sexual beliefs and behaviors of others as inferior and as abnormal is to view them as different, without a judgment on the moral correctness or degree of normality. Both monogamy and polygyny, heterosexuality and homosexuality might then be viewed as variations in human sexual expression that are products of different cultural and biosocial influences independent of a value being placed on those behavioral patterns. Were we to look at our own behavioral patterns as others do, we might discover that "we" are "they" to them.

Another area in which our ethnocentrism guides our behavior is in our conception of what constitutes a good sexual experience. Voigt (1991) noted that Western views of sexuality emphasize "sexual performance, sexual satisfaction, or the pursuit of orgasm or pleasure" (p. 216). In contrast, Asian views of sexuality emphasize sexual expression as a "vehicle for spiritual development and personal transformation" (p. 214). Tantric sex, described in Hindu and Buddhist Tantric scriptures, reflects the essence of Asian sexuality. The Sanskrit term *Tantra* means "integration," suggesting full involvement of the natural human drives in the pursuit of a fully realized existence.

While Western couples view specific sexual problems (early ejaculation, lack of orgasm) as something to get rid of, Asian couples focus on their commitment to the transformation of their sexual experience. Orgasm for Westerners is seen as a result of proper stimulation; Asians see it as "a product of deep relaxation and a profound level of contact between partners" (p. 215). One technique in Tantric practice is to be still and motionless during intercourse so as not to have orgasm. "The purpose of avoiding or refraining from orgasm is to intensify the sexual-spiritual energy" (p. 218). Indeed, we as Westerners might profit from questioning our ethnocentrism.

Become More Culturally Relativistic?

Related to becoming less ethnocentric is the idea of choosing to become more culturally relativistic. Such a view attempts to understand cultural norms and practices from the viewpoint of the culture in which they exist.

Group marriage, in which men and women in the group consider themselves married to each other, is a sexual pattern that can be better understood from a culturally relativistic perspective. In the mid-1800s, a group of 175 individuals became known as the Oneida Community (because they settled along the Oneida Creek in New York). A distinguishing characteristic of the Oneidains was the practice of group marriage. According to their leader, John Humphrey Noyes, "It is natural for all men to love all women, and for all women to love all men (Kephart, 1987, p. 68). The group also believed that emotional pair bonding between any two people in the group was not acceptable. Hence, if two people fell in love, they were not allowed to sleep together again (who slept with whom was decided by a "go between" committee).

While the idea of group marriage is foreign to most of us, group marriage becomes more plausible when seen within

Continued

Continued

the context of the Oneida Community and its view of relationship sexuality. Choosing to view sexuality from a cultural relativistic stance does not imply acceptance of another culture's value as one's own. For example, a cultural relativistic view of female genital mutilation (discussed earlier in this chapter) does not mean acceptance of this practice; it merely means that this practice is viewed from the perspective of the cultures that practice it.

Sex therapists may be particularly in need of a culturally relativistic perspective. Therapists without exposure to Portuguese, Mexican, Puerto Rican, and Hispanic cultures may not be aware of the pervasiveness of the double standard. "[W]omen are required to be sexually pure and uncontaminated by eroticism, and sex is something that needs to be repressed; whereas, for men, sexuality is a proof of manhood ("machismo")" (Lavee, 1991, p. 206).

Choose to Conform to Cultural Sexual Norms?

Reiss (1986) emphasized that one of the benefits of knowing that different cultures have different rules regarding sex is that most any form of sexual behavior can be normal or abnormal. Given this truism, he noted that "one can choose to be out of line on this or any issue with the dominant ideological positions" (p. 133). That persons choose to be sexual nonconformists is evident from the number of guests on talk shows such as "Geraldo," "Donahue," "Oprah Winfrey," and "Sally Jesse Raphael." Examples of nonconformity to our culture's sexual norms include people in open marriages and homosexual relationships, as well as those who choose celibate lives. Such choices emphasize the right of people to pursue their own pattern of relationships and sexuality.

Summary

1. Ethnographic and ethnological studies of sexual behavior may be suspect because of differences in language, use of informants, and the existence of subcultures within cultures.
2. The criteria for what is considered "normal" sexual behavior involves prevalence, morality, and "naturalness." Normalcy varies across cultures and time periods.
3. The same sexual behaviors prohibited in one culture are tolerated in another and expected in a third.
4. Members of every society learn to view the cultural norms of their own group as appropriate and the norms of other cultures as strange.
5. Cross-cultural variations in sexuality include variations in behaviors, attitudes, and sanctions related to sexual intercourse, premarital sex, extramarital sex, incest, menstruation, homosexual sex, and gender roles.
6. Extramarital intercourse ranks second to incest as one of the most forbidden sexual behaviors in most societies.
7. Incest is nearly universally tabooed sexual behavior, although cultures vary in their definition of incest.
8. The majority of nonindustrialized societies permit or encourage homosexual behavior for some of their members.
9. Some sex practices that occur in some cultures include female genital mutilation, male genital mutilation, and polygamy. Over 80 million women and female children worldwide have had their genitals mutilated. The practice reflects the inferior status of females in most societies.
10. Patterns of mate selection and preferred characteristics in a mate vary cross-culturally.

11. Human sexuality may be viewed as part of the primate sexual continuum. Hence, our understanding of human sexuality may be enhanced by examining the sexuality of nonhuman primates.
12. Viewing human sexuality from a culturally relativistic view (rather than from an ethnocentric view) involves understanding a culture's sexual norms and practices from the viewpoint of the culture in which they exist.

KEY TERMS

ethnography
ethnology
ethnocentrism
cultural relativism
erotocentrism
female genital mutilation
male genital mutilation
clitoridectomy
infibulation
circumcision
penile supraincision
penile subincision
polygamy
polygyny
polyandry
concubine

REFERENCES

Armstrong, S. (1991). Female circumcision: Fighting a cruel tradition. *New Scientist, 2,* 42–46.

Belcastro, P. A. (1985). Sexual behavior differences between black and white students. *Journal of Sex Research, 21,* 56–67.

Bettelheim, B.(1968). *Symbolic wounds: Puberty rites and the envious male.* New York: Macmillan/Collier Books.

Blank, J. (1989). *Good vibrations: The complete guide to vibrators.* New York: Harmony Books.

Brown, D. E. (1991). *Human Universals.* Philadelphia: Temple University Press.

Brown, D. E., & Hotra, D. (1988). Are prescriptively monogamous societies effectively monogamous? In L. Betzig, M. B. Mulder, & P. Turke (Eds.), *Human reproductive behavior: A Darwinian perspective* (pp. 153–160). Cambridge: Cambridge University Press.

Buss, D. M., Abbott, M., Angleitner, A., Asherian, A., Biaggio, A., Blanco-Villasenor, A., Bruchonschweitzer, M., Ch'U, H., Czapinski, J., Deraad, B., Ekehammar, B., El Lohamy, N., Fioravanti, M., Georgas, J., Gjerde, P., Guttman, R., Hazan, F., Iwawaki S. Janakiramaiah, N., Khosroshani, F., Kreitler, S., Lachenicht, L., Lee, M., Liik, K., Little, B., Mika, S., Moadel-Shahid, M., Moane, G., Montero, M., Mundy-Castle, A. C., Niit, T., Nsenduluka, E., Pienkowski, R., Pirttila-Backman, A., Ponce de Leon, J., Rousseau, J., Runco, M. A., Safir, M., P., Samuels, C., Sanitioso, R., Serpell, R., Smid, N., Spencer, C., Tadinac, M., Todorova, E. N., Troland, K., Van Den Brande, L., Van Heck, G., Van Langenhove, V., and Yang, K. (1990). International preferences in selecting mates. *Journal of Cross-Cultural Psychology, 21,* 5–47.

Cutner, L. P. (1985). Female genital mutilation. *Obstetric Gynecology Survey, 40,* 437–443.

Crook, J. H. & Crook, S. J. (1988). Tibetan polyandry: Problems of adaptation and fitness. In L. Betzig, M. B. Mulder, & P. Turke (Eds.), *Human reproductive behavior: A Darwinian perspective* (pp. 97–114). Cambridge: Cambridge University Press.

Davenport, W. H. (1977). Sex in cross-cultural perspective. In F. A. Beach (Ed.), *Human sexuality in four perspectives* (pp. 115–163). Baltimore: Johns Hopkins University Press.

Davenport, W. H. (1987). An anthropological approach. In J. H. Geer & W. T. O'Donohue (Eds.), *Theories of human sexuality* (pp. 197–236). New York: Plenum Press.

Denmark, F. L., Schwartz, L. & Smith, K. M. (1991). Women in the United States and Canada. In L. L. Adler (Ed.), *Women in cross-cultural perspective* (pp. 1–18). New York: Praeger.

Doyle, J. A. & Paludi, M. A. (1991). *Sex and gender* (2nd ed.). Dubuque, IA: W. C. Brown.

Drakulic, S. (1990, July/August). In their own words: Women of eastern Europe. *Ms.*, pp. 36–47.

Ellis, H. (1938). *Psychologoy of sex.* Garden City, NY: Garden City Books.

Embry, J. L. (1987). *Mormon polygamous families.* Salt Lake City: University of Utah Press.

Erkman, H., Dilbaz, N., Serber, G., Kaptanoglu, C., & Tekin, D. (1990). Sexual attitudes of Turkish university students. *Journal of Sex Education and Therapy, 16,* 251–261.

Eysenck, H. J. (1971). Personality in sexual adjustment. *British Journal of Psychiatry, 118,* 593–603.

Ford, C. S., & Beach, Frank A. (1972; originally published in 1951). *Patterns of sexual behavior.* New York: Harper Colophon Books.

Francoeur, R. T. (1990). New dimensions in human sexuality: The theological challenge. In R. H. Iles (Ed.), *The gospel imperative in the midst of AIDS: Towards a prophetic theology.* Wilton, CT: Morehouse.

Frayser, S. G. (1985). *Varieties of sexual experience.* New Haven: Human Relations Area Files Press.

Freeman, D. (1983). *Margaret Mead and Samoa: The making and unmaking of an anthropological myth.* Cambridge: Harvard University Press.

Gebhard, P. H. (1972). Human sexual behavior: A summary statement. In D. S. Marshall & R. C. Suggs (Eds.), *Human sexual behavior* (pp. 206–217). Englewood Cliffs, NJ: Prentice-Hall.

Gray, J. P., & Wolfe, L. D. (1992). An anthropological look at human sexuality. In W. H. Masters, V. E. Johnson, & R. C. Kolodny (Eds.), *Human sexuality* (4th ed.). La Porte, IN: HarperCollins.

Grzymala-Moszczynska, H. (1991). Women in Poland. In L. L. Adler (Ed.), *Women in cross-cultural perspective* (pp. 54–67). New York: Praeger.

Harlow, H. F., & Harlow, M. (1962). Social deprivation in monkeys. *Scientific American, 207,* 136–146.

Harrison, D. F., & Pennell, R. C. (1989). Contemporary sex roles for adolescents: New options or confusion? *Journal of Social Work and Human Sexuality, 8,* 27–45.

Hatano, Y. (1991). Changes in sexual activities of Japanese youth. *Journal of Sex Education and Therapy, 17,* 1–14.

Heider, K. G. (1988). The Rashomon effect: When ethnographers disagree. *American Anthropologist, 90,* 73–81.

Herdt, G. (1991). Commentary on status of sex research: Cross-cultural implications of sexual development. *Journal of Psychology and Human Sexuality, 4,* 5–12.

Hosken, F. P. (1981). Female genital mutilation in the world today: A global review. *International Journal of Health Services, 11,* 415–430.

Hrdy, S. B. (1981). *The woman that never evolved.* Cambridge: Harvard University Press.

Kephart, W. M. (1987). *Extraordinary groups.* New York: St. Martin's Press.

Kinzey, W. G. (1987). Monogamous primates: A primate model of human mating systems. In W. G. Kinzey (Ed.), *The evolution of human behavior: Primate models* (pp. 105–114). Albany: State University of New York Press.

Klassen, A. D., Williams, C. J., & Levitt, E. E. (1989). *Sex and morality in the United States.* Middletown, CN: Wesleyan University Press.

Lavee, Y. (1991). Western and non-Western human sexuality: Implications for clinical practice. *Journal of Sex and Marital Therapy, 17,* 203–211.

Lawrence, R. J. (1989). *The poisoning of eros: Sexual values in conflict.* New York: Augustine Moore Press.

Malinowski, B. (1927). *Sex and repression in savage society.* New York: Harcourt, Brace.

Malinowski, B. (1929). *Sexual life of savages in north-western Melanesia.* New York: Halcyon House.

Mandelbaum, D. G. (1988). *Women's seclusion and men's honor: Sex roles in north India, Bangladesh and Pakistan.* Tucson: University of Arizona Press.

Marshall, D. S. (1971). Sexual behavior on Mangaia. In D. S. Marshall & R. C. Suggs (Eds.), *Human sexual behavior: Variations in the ethnographic spectrum* (pp. 103–162). New York: Basic Books.

Martin, E. (1991). The egg and the sperm: How science has con-'structed a romance based on stereotypical male-female roles. *Signs: Journal of Women in Culture, 16,* 485–501.

Mead, M. (1928). *Coming of age in Samoa.* Middlesex: Penguin Books.

Merriam, A. P. (1972). Aspects of sexual behavior among the Bala (Basongye). In D. S. Marshall & R. C. Suggs (Eds.), *Human sexual behavior* (pp. 71–102). Englewood Cliffs, NJ: Prentice-Hall.

Money, J., & Ehrhardt, A. A. (1973). *Man and woman, boy and girl.* Baltimore: Johns Hopkins University Press.

Money, J., & Musaph, H. (Eds). (1977). *Handbook of sexology* (pp. 519–540). North Holland: Excerpta Medica.

Murdock, G. P. (1967). *Ethnographic atlas.* Pittsburgh: University of Pittsburgh Press.

Muse, C. J. (1991). Women in western Samoa. In L. L. Adler (Ed.), *Women in cross-cultural perspective* (pp. 221–241). New York: Praeger.

Odujinrin, O. M., Akitoye, C. O., & Oyediran, M. A. (1989). A study on female circumcision in Nigeria. *West African Journal of Medicine, 8,* 183–192.

Reiss, I. L. (1986). *Journey into sexuality: An exploratory voyage.* Englewood Cliffs, NJ: Prentice-Hall.

Robinson, W. J. (1921). *Sexual problems of today.* New York: Truth.

Rubin, L. B. (1991). *Erotic wars: What happened to the sexual revolution.* New York: Harper Perennial.

Safir, M. P., & Izraeli, D. N. (1991). Growing up female: A life-span perspective on women in Israel. In L. L. Adler (Ed.), *Women in cross-cultural perspective* (pp. 79–89). New York: Praeger.

Scheper-Hughes, N. (1987). The Margaret Mead controversy: Culture, biology and anthropological inquiry. In H. Applebaum (Ed.), *Perspectives in cultural anthropology* (pp. 443–460). Albany: State University of New York.

Scriven, J. (1984). Women at work in Sweden. In M. J. Davidson & C. L. Cooper (Eds.), *Working women: An international survey.* (pp. 153–182). New York: Wiley.

Shepherd, G. (1987). Rank, gender, and homosexuality: Mombasa as a key to understanding sexual options. In P. Caplan (Ed.), *The social construction of sexuality.* New York: Tavistock.

Skeen, D. (1991). *Different sexual worlds: Contemporary case studies of sexuality.* Lexington, MA: Lexington Books.

Smith, R. D. (1979). What kind of sex is natural? In V. Bullough (Ed.), *The frontiers of sex research* (pp. 103–112). Buffalo, NY: Prometheus Books.

Smith, L. S. (1990). Human sexuality from a cultural perspective. In C. I. Foegel & D. Lauver (Eds.), *Sexual health promotion* (pp. 87–96). Philadelphia: W. B. Saunders.

Stephens, W. N. (1982). *The family in cross-cultural perspective.* Washington, DC: University Press of America.

Sumner, W. G. (1960; originally published in 1906). *Folkways* New York: New American Library.

Train, A. (1931). *Puritan's progress.* New York: Scribner.

Turner, E. S. (1955). *A history of courtship.* New York: Dutton.

Voigt, H. (1991). Enriching the sexual experience of couples: The Asian traditions and sexual counseling. *Journal of Sex and Marital Therapy, 17,* 214–219.

Weeks, J. (1989). *Sex, politics and society* (2nd ed.). London: Longman.

Wolfe, L. D. (1991). Human evolution and the sexual behavior of female primates. In J. D. Loy & C. B. Peter (Eds.), *Understanding behavior: What primate studies tell us about human behavior* (pp. 122–151). New York: Oxford University Press.

Yu, L. D., & Carpenter, L. (1991). Women in China. In L. L. Adler (Ed.), *Women in cross-cultural perspective* (pp. 189–204). New York: Praaeger.

Opposite page: *Pablo Picasso, Spanish, 1881–1973.* The Lovers, *canvas, 1923, 51¼ × 38¼ in.; National Gallery of Art, Washington, Chester Dale Collection.*

Background for Sexual Choices

PART TWO

Before beginning a rigorous aerobic workout, the individual first does a series of stretches. These are designed to stretch the muscles that will be used in the more strenuous endeavor to follow. Failing to stretch adequately before jogging, lifting weights, or doing aerobics increases the risk of injury.

Similarly, making sexual choices involves a period of preparation. Taking the time for such preparation increases the probability of making wise decisions and decreases the probability of error. For example, in deciding to use a particular condom, adequate background preparation involves identifying the various membranes (latex rubber or animal skin), types (reservoir tip or full rounded end), and spermicides (anti-HIV non-oxynol 9 or others). By acquiring the necessary background information, the individual is more likely to make an informed choice: latex membrane, reservoir tip, and non-oxynol 9 spermicide.

In Part II, Background for Sexual Choices, we examine various research methods used to gather and evaluate data on human sexuality (Chapter 4), become familiar with several theoretical frameworks used to explain human sexuality (Chapter 5), review male and female sexual anatomy and physiology (Chapter 6), and explore various models of human sexual response (Chapter 7). Without a knowledge of this background, we are limited in making various sexual choices.

For example, women and men who are, respectively, considering breast and penile implant surgery are well advised to read the available literature on the consequences of such elective surgery. However, interpreting such reading involves a knowledge of theory, research methods, anatomy and physiology, and patterns of sexual response. Various theoretical perspectives are used to explain why women and men seek implant procedures; various research methods are used to gather data on and evaluate implant procedures; the actual implementation of the procedures involves anatomical and physiological changes; and implants may affect the sexual response patterns of individuals. By taking the time to learn this background information, individuals faced with making such choices are at less risk for making an error than those who elect the procedures with no background for decision making.

CHAPTER FOUR

Research in Human Sexuality

Chapter Outline

The Roots of Sexology

The Study of Sexuality: An Overview of Approaches

- The Interdisciplinary Nature of Sexology: Biosexology, Psychosexology, and Sociosexology
- Cross-sectional and Longitudinal Research
- Qualitative and Quantitative Research
- Feminist Approaches to Sexuality Research

Sex Research: Initial Procedures and Methods

- Formulating a Research Question
- Reviewing the Literature
- Formulating a Hypothesis and Defining Variables
- Selecting the Sample: Nonprobability versus Probability Sampling

Methods of Data Collection

- Experiments
- Surveys
- Field Research
- Case Studies
- Historical Research
- Diaries
- **Research Perspective:** Ethical Considerations in Sexuality Research with Human Participants

Data Analysis

- Description
- Correlation
- Causation
- Reliability and Validity
- **Self-Assessment:** Sex Anxiety Inventory and its Development

Major Sex Studies

- The Original Kinsey Studies on Sexual Behavior
- The Kinsey Institute Study on Sexual Values
- The Kinsey Report on Sexual Knowledge
- Masters and Johnson's Research on Sexual Response
- Rubin's Assessment of the Sexual and Gender Revolutions
- National Surveys of Adolescents
- Magazine Surveys

Choices

- Choose to Become Informed about Sex Research?
- Choose to Accept Findings of Sex Research?
- Choose to Be a Participant in Sex Research?
- Should Taxpayers Fund Sex Research?

Is it True?*

1. The first Institute of Sexology was founded in the 1960s during the sexual revolution.

2. Feminists view traditional sex research as very compatible with the principles of feminism.

3. New laws require all individuals who are known to have HIV or AIDS to participate in clinical research trials designed to test new treatments for HIV and AIDS.

4. Men are more likely than women to participate in sex research.

5. In sex research studies, individuals tend to underreport the degree to which they engage in sexual behavior that places them at high risk for transmitting HIV.

* 1 = F, 2 = F, 3 = F, 4 = T, 5 = T.

Given the growing interest in research on sexuality, the rapid development of appropriate methodologies, the avalanche of empirical data, and the generation of new theoretical formulations, the future of this field is both exciting and an occasion for scientific optimism.

Donn Byrne

People often snicker when someone says, "I am a sex researcher." Professional sex researchers often feel maligned by and concerned about such a reaction. Perhaps your professor has conducted sex research and has been teased by colleagues for doing so. Dr. Donald Mosher, the former president of the Society for the Scientific Study of Sex, emphasized the significance of this concern: "My goal is to make people take our field seriously, so that, when we say we are sexual researchers, people will no longer laugh" (Irvine, 1990, p. 1).

It ain't so much the things we don't know that get us in trouble. It's the things we know that ain't so.

Artemus Ward

While the study of sexuality is a credible and valuable professional endeavor, it is unlikely that you, as a student taking a course in human sexuality, will conduct sex research. However, as a consumer of sex research, it is important that you be informed about what constitutes good research. For example, you are constantly bombarded by the media with advertisements, editorials, and expert opinions that make competing claims, such as the following:

- "High school students should not have access to condoms because it would increase the number of sexually active students" versus "Providing condoms to high school students reduces teenage pregnancy and the spread of HIV and other STDs."
- "People who are known homosexuals should not be hired in the public school because they will molest the children" versus "The notion that homosexual individuals are child molesters is an unfounded stereotype; no individual should be discriminated on the basis of sexual orientation."

Which of the above positions is more credible depends on how the research was conducted. Katzer, Cook, and Crouch (1991) emphasized that "in order to make sensible decisions, viewers, readers, and constituents must be able to evaluate. . . information" (p. 4). In this chapter, we provide basic information about research with a focus on evaluating research. We begin with a brief look at the development of the scientific study of sex.

The Roots of Sexology

The term **sexology** refers to the scientific study of sex. The term was first used by Iwan Bloch, a German physician who published *The Sexual Life of Our Time* (1907), in which he emphasized the need to study the sexual life of the individual from the viewpoint of medicine and the social sciences.

The first sexologists emerged in Europe out of public concerns over prostitution, sexually transmissible diseases, and eugenics (the study of heredity and genetic control). Germany was known as the center of sexology and Berlin became the home of the first sexological institute, the Institute of Sexology. Founded in 1919 by Mangus Hirschfeld, the Institute housed over 20,000 volumes, 35,000 photographs, and an abundance of archival material. Hirschfeld, along with Havelock Ellis (*Studies in the Psychology of Sex*) and Sigmund Freud (*On Sexuality*) have been credited with breaking the "conspiracy of silence" that surrounded the study of sex in the nineteenth century and bringing sex into the open for scientific inquiry and public discussion. Prior to the early 1930s, approximately 80 sex reform organizations, with a total membership of 350,000, exerted a considerable force in German life. These organizations, composed of physicians, laypeople, and various professionals who staffed clinics, provided medical and sexual information as well as counseling (Irvine, 1990, p. 6).

It has taken a potentially fatal sexually transmittted disease (AIDS) to establish the legitimacy of the rigorous scrutiny of human sexuality.

Paul R. Abramson

The early flurry of sexological activity soon ended when Hitler came into power. The Nazis raided the Institute, removed its books and papers, and burned them in the streets. Since most early sexologists were Austrian or German Jews, they were arrested or went into hiding.

Today, there has been a renewal of the professional interest in sexuality within a variety of fields, particularly psychology, medicine, sociology, family studies, and health education. In addition, the study of sexuality is relevant to anthropology, archaeology, history, religion, art, music, and dance (Coleman, 1990). The Society for the Scientific Study of Sex, which advocates an interdisciplinary approach to the study of sexuality, was founded in 1957. This organization has over 1,000 members, 11% from 22 countries outside the United States (Coleman, 1990, p. 474).

The Study of Sexuality: An Overview of Approaches

In this section, we provide an overview of various approaches to the study of sexuality. After discussing disciplinary approaches to sexology (biosexology, psychosexology, and sociosexology), we compare cross-sectional and longitudinal, as well as quantitative and qualitative, research approaches. Finally, we present the feminist approach to the study of sexuality.

The Interdisciplinary Nature of Sexology: Biosexology, Psychosexology, and Sociosexology

The study of sexuality is an interdisciplinary field that incorporates a number of different professions, including biology, psychology, social work, sociology, anthropology, family studies, history, medicine, public health, and education (see Table 4.1). The interdisciplinary nature of sexology is reflected in the various types and applications of sexuality research.

> Sexology ranges from biomedical laboratory work investigating hormonal determinants of sexuality to nude therapy sessions for people seeking better sexual relations. "Multiple orgasms," "gender dysphoria," "ejaculatory incompetence," "sissy boys," "sex reassignment," and "disorders of desire" are among the concepts integral to the discourse of modern sexology. (Irvine, 1990, pp. 8–9)

Much of the research in sexuality originates in the biological or social sciences. Byrne (1986) suggested that the study of sexuality may be divided into three main disciplinary approaches: biosexology, psychosexology, and sociosexology.

Biosexology The study of biological aspects of sexuality is referred to as **biosexology.** This approach includes research that focuses on the role of evolution and genetics in our physical or behavioral sexual traits. Biosexology also includes the study of the physiological and endocrinological aspects of sexual development and sexual response. Another research area within biosexology involves the study of how sexuality is affected by drugs and medications, physical illness and disease, and diet and exercise.

TABLE 4.1 Interdisciplinary Structure of the Society for the Scientific Study of Sex (1985)

Discipline	Percentage of Total Members (N=949)
Anatomy, Physiology, Zoology	.9 %
Anthropology	.6 %
Biology, Biochemistry	.5 %
Counseling and Therapy	3.3 %
Education	7.4 %
Family Studies	1.1 %
Health, Public Health	1.1 %
History	.3 %
Human Sexuality	10.2 %
Medicine and Psychiatry	15.6 %
Nursing	2.2 %
Osteopathy and Chiropractic	.5 %
Psychology	30.2 %
Social Work	6.6 %
Sociology	4.6 %
Theology and Law	.6 %
Multiple Disciplines and Other	14.44%

Source: Adapted from Pollis, Carol A. (1988). An assessment of the impacts of feminism on sexual science. *Journal of Sex Research, 25,* 85–105. Used by permission.

Biosexologists study the effect of exercise on sexual interest and activity.

CONSIDERATION: Technology has played a significant role in the development of biosexology. Through advances in technology, researchers now have sophisticated means of observing and measuring various genetic and physiological components of sexuality. For example, the sexual arousal of both women and men may be measured through the use of technological equipment.

Psychosexology **Psychosexology** involves the study of how psychological processes both influence and are influenced by sexual development and behavior. For example, psychosexologists may be interested in how emotions, such as fear, anger, jealousy, pain, and disgust, affect sexual motivation and performance; they may also be interested in the effects of various sexual and reproductive experiences (e.g., childbirth or rape) on the emotional state of the individual.

Psychosexology also involves the study of how sexual behavior, beliefs, and attitudes are learned. For example, psychosexologists are interested in how people learn attitudes, beliefs, and behaviors related to contraceptive use, paraphilias, sexual communication, masturbation, sexual abstinence, homosexuality, and sexual aggression.

A major benefit of an interdisciplinary approach to human sexuality is that different angles of the same phenomenon (sexuality) are being examined by experts who are adept and trained at studying their own piece of the pie.

Terri Orbuch
John Harvey

The assumption that much sexual behavior is learned implies that it can also be changed. Much research is done to design and evaluate the effectiveness of various educational and therapeutic intervention strategies to change dysfunctional or criminally deviant sexual behavior. In later chapters, you will encounter research that focuses on the effectiveness of various clinical approaches to rehabilitating rapists, resolving sexual dysfunctions, eliminating paraphilic behavior (e.g., exhibitionism), and treating victims of rape and sexual assault. Finally, psychosexology includes research that evaluates educational programs, such as those designed to promote sexual abstinence or condom use.

Sociosexology **Sociosexology** is concerned with the study of how social and cultural forces both influence and are influenced by sexual attitudes, beliefs, and behaviors. As we saw in Chapter 3, research that examines sexuality from a cross-cultural perspective suggests that sexuality is, to a large degree, socially and culturally created. We learn the norms for what is considered appropriate sexual behavior from the culture in which we live. Sociosexology is concerned with describing cultural and subcultural sexual norms and identifying how demographic factors, such as age, socioeconomic status, race, and sex, are associated with variations in sexuality.

Sociosexological research also includes historical studies of sexuality. For example, historical studies have been done on gays and lesbians in the United States (Katz, 1976), the origins of national abortion policy (Mohr, 1978), prostitution in the United States (Rosen, 1982), and childbirth in early modern Europe (Gelis, 1991). Sociosexology is also concerned with how social policy and social institutions (e.g., marriage, religion, economics, law and politics, the health care system, and science) affect and are affected by human sexuality. Sociosexological research findings are often used to evaluate and develop social policies. For example, some sex research may focus on the following issues:

- How effective the U.S. health care system is in preventing and treating cases of HIV infection and AIDS.
- How the gay rights movement has influenced laws regarding homosexuality.
- How religious institutions have affected abortion laws in this country.

- What the effect of nontraditional gender roles is on marital relationships.
- How rape laws affect the reporting of and incidence of marital rape.

Another focus of sociosexological research is the study of how sexual processes affect and are affected by close, intimate relationships. Examples of research with an interpersonal focus include studies that look at the relationship between sexual satisfaction and relationship satisfaction, sexual aggression in relationships, and interpersonal communication about sexuality (Orbuch & Harvey, 1991).

CONSIDERATION: Each of the three general approaches to sex research discussed above (biosexology, psychosexology, and sociosexology) contribute important information to our understanding of human sexuality. Byrne (1986) suggested that these approaches "are complementary rather than in conflict, and together they provide an integrative picture of human sexual functioning" (p. 7).

We have seen how approaches to the study of sexuality may be divided into the three general categories: biosexology, psychosexology, and sociosexology. Another way to categorize sexuality research was proposed by Gebhard (1969), who identified five fields of sex research: (1) clinical/medical (sexual dysfunctions and treatments), (2) legal/forensic (laws governing sexuality), (3) reproductive/population (fertility and contraception), (4) sex education (sexual knowledge and control through teaching), and (5) basic research (variables affecting sexual attitudes and behavior).

CONSIDERATION: Research on human sexuality does more than passively describe sexuality and its interrelationships with biology, psychology, and sociology. Research findings affect our beliefs, attitudes, and behaviors. Research in human sexuality also plays a major role in shaping our social institutions, laws, and policies. Thus, sex research has a major impact on the sexual choices that we make as individuals and as a society.

Cross-Sectional and Longitudinal Research

Cross-sectional research involves collecting data at a single point in time. For example, the U.S. census is a study that aims to describe the nation's population at a given point in time. Cross-sectional research is frequently compared to taking a still photograph: it allows the researcher to see a "picture" of what is being studied or of some aspect of the research topic. Much of the research conducted in human sexuality is cross-sectional. The main advantage of cross-sectional research is that it is usually less costly in terms of both money and time than longitudinal research. The major disadvantage of cross-sectional research is that it does not provide information on how variables change over time.

Longitudinal research involves collecting data across time, often on the same individuals. Longitudinal research allows researchers to look at how the variables under study (e.g., interest in sex and frequency of intercourse) change over time. Thus, longitudinal research is frequently likened to taking a motion picture, rather than a still photograph. The main disadvantage of longitudinal research is that it is time-consuming and expensive.

In sexuality research, longitudinal methods are often used to study sexuality across the lifespan. Hallstrom and Samuelsson (1990) conducted a longitudinal study on how sexual desire changes during middle age. They interviewed 677 middle-aged women and then interviewed the same women six years later. The researchers found that 27% reported a decrease in sexual desire, 10% reported an increase in sexual desire, and the remaining 63% reported no change in their sexual desire over the six-year period.

Ard (1990) also conducted a longitudinal study across a 20-year period on the marriages of 161 couples. He reported surveying various aspects of their marital relationship during the early years, middle years, and last three years of the 20-year period. A progressive decline in the frequency of intercourse was observed:

> Here the couples in this sample report that they had sexual intercourse better than nine times a month during the early period of their marriage, about six times a month during the middle period, and about four to five times per month during the last three years (some twenty years later). (p. 48)

Qualitative and Quantitative Research

Qualitative research focuses on the subjective aspects of human experience and the meanings and interpretations that humans ascribe to their world. The goal of qualitative research is to provide an empathic understanding of the individuals, groups, or other social phenomena being studied. Examples of qualitative research in sexuality include studies designed to understand and explain gay father identity development (Bozett, 1988), the life-style, identity, and norms of prostitutes (Prus & Irini, 1988), and the meaning of menopause for women in their 40s and the effect of these meanings on self-concept (Gergen, 1988).

Because of the detailed and in-depth nature of qualitative research, it is usually conducted on small samples. Thus, qualitative research is sometimes criticized for using samples that may not be representative of the larger population. However, qualitative research provides details and nuances of the research topic that quantitative research is unable to provide.

Quantitative research focuses on numerical quantification of human and social phenomena and statistical analyses of relationships among variables. You will see numerous references to quantitative research in this text: percentages of women who have been raped by a date, statistical analyses of factors related to condom use, average frequency of masturbation among women and men, and demographic factors associated with attitudes toward premarital sex, to name a few examples.

> In science (as in everyday life) things must be believed in order to be seen as well as seen in order to be believed.
> *Walter L. Wallace*

The quantitative approach to studying sexuality allows us to identify and predict patterns of sexuality. One application of quantitative data is in the study of HIV transmission rates. Abramson (1990) noted that detailed quantitative information is needed on different patterns of sexual behavior in order to assess the rate of the spread of HIV and AIDS.

Some researchers have criticized the quantitative approach to research on the basis that quantitative data are often misinterpreted, distorted, irrelevant, or incomplete (Armstrong & Armstrong, 1987). However, many researchers recognize value in both quantitative and qualitative approaches to research (Abramson, 1990; Coleman, 1990; Armstrong & Armstrong, 1987). The benefits of each approach may be achieved through a process called "triangulation" (Nachmias & Nachmias, 1987). "Triangulation" refers to the use of more than one research technique (usually one quantitative and one qualitative) to study a given topic. Combining quantitative and qualitative findings yields a broader understanding of the research topic.

CONSIDERATION: Jayaratne (1981) suggested that quantitative research is more superficial than qualitative research. However, numbers appear more objective and can, therefore, be more effective in changing public opinion. Quantitative research has also played a significant role in legitimizing sex research: "if we couldn't assign it a number, then it wasn't based on data—it wasn't research" (Coleman, 1990, p. 477).

Feminist Approaches to Sexuality Research

While there are different versions of feminist thought (see Chapter 5), "feminism is fundamentally a political movement and a political analysis that aims to understand and change the subordinate situation of women throughout the world" (Tiefer, 1988, p. 16). Sexuality is a primary interest and concern of feminist thinkers, because "sexuality. . . is a prominent locus of women's oppression," (p. 16).

Feminist researchers view much of the traditional research as incompatible with the principles of feminism. A feminist approach to sexuality research rejects many of the principles, assumptions and procedures of traditional science. In this section, we will discuss a few of the feminist criticisms of traditional sexuality research and present alternative feminist research approaches.

Feminism directly confronts the idea that one person or set of people [has] the right to impose definitions of reality on others.
Liz Stanley
Sue Wise

Feminist Criticisms of Traditional Research One major feminist criticism of traditional research is that much of it is sexist (Eichler, 1987). For example, it has been noted that many studies generalize to both sexes, even though only one sex was studied (Tavris, 1992). In studies based on samples composed of only one sex, men are studied more often than women. The overrepresentation of male single-gender studies has resulted in basing many behavioral, attitudinal, and personality norms on the male experience (Ward & Grant, 1985). Women, who may deviate from such male-based norms, are often viewed as "subnormal." In addition, the omission and underrepresentation of women in sexuality studies results in a lack of knowledge about women's sexual concerns. For example, in Chapter 16, we note that most of the research on the sexuality of persons with spinal cord injuries is conducted on men.

Female researchers are also underrepresented in the field of sexuality research. Between 1980 and 1986, 64% of all authors of articles published in the *Journal of Sex Research* were men; only 33% were women (Pollis, 1988).

Another major criticism of traditional research, which is made by many nonfeminists as well as feminists, is that objectivity and neutrality are falsely claimed (Tiefer, 1988; Gergen, 1988; Coleman, 1990). Claims of objectivity and neutrality mask the degree to which social context and personal bias influence what researchers notice and accept as real. They also mask the degree to which sexuality research may be motivated by the personal or political values and agendas of researchers and their sponsors.

Feminists in all disciplines have demonstrated that objectivity has about as much substance as the emperor's new clothes.
Connie Miller

Feminists are also critical of the power imbalance between researchers and research participants and the exploitation of research participants (as well as research assistants, such as secretarial staff and graduate students) to satisfy the personal and professional needs of the researcher. Feminists also reject the assumption that researchers have superior status, compared to research participants.

Feminist Research Approaches Feminist research may be characterized by the following features (McHugh, Koeske, & Frieze, 1986; Harding, 1987; Tiefer, 1988): (a) an emphasis on qualitative research that is based on women's experiences;

(b) the recognition that the researcher's beliefs and biases affect the research question and findings; (c) the commitment to designing research with the aim of eliminating sexism and improving the lives of women; (d) an emphasis on the heterogeneity of human experience and behavior (researchers should study "sexualities," rather than "sexuality"); (e) the recognition that race, class, community, culture, and language play central roles in shaping our sexual attitudes and behaviors; (f) an acknowledgement of the pervasive influence of gender in all aspects of social life, including the practice of science; (g) the conceptualization of gender as a socially created category; and (h) the conceptualization of sexuality as a social construction, rather than as a biological imperative.

CONSIDERATION: McHugh, et al. (1986), distinguished between nonsexist research (also called "sex-fair" research), which does not discriminate against women, and feminist research, which actively works toward the advancement of women. They viewed sex-fair research as one aspect of feminist research.

Despite the fact that feminist scholarship has contributed a significant body of literature to the field of research methods, feminism has had limited impact on mainstream social science. Miller (1991) suggested that "feminists are the primary consumers of other feminists' work, and articles about women or feminism tend to be published in journals devoted to that purpose" (p. 3).

Feminism has also had limited impact on sexuality research. Pollis (1988) noted that from 1980 to 1986, only three out of the 198 articles published in the *Journal of Sex Research* were listed under the key word of *feminism* in the journal's subject index. However, Coleman (1990) suggested that the boundaries of sexuality research are expanding and that scholars in the field of sexuality are increasingly recognizing the value of nontraditional research approaches, including feminist approaches.

Sex Research: Initial Procedures and Methods

Now that we have discussed some general approaches to the study of sexuality, we focus on specific procedures and methods used in research. While these procedures and methods are applied to research in many fields, we focus on how these procedures and methods are applied specifically to sex research. We also note the problems and difficulties that researchers have in using scientific procedures and methods in the study of sexuality.

Formulating a Research Question

A research study usually begins with a question. When the Kinsey Institute decided to explore the issue of homosexuality, the researchers formulated a number of questions they wanted to answer (Klassen, Williams, & Levitt, 1989, p. 293):

> What perceptions and information about homosexuality are held among the public; how widely are they held?
>
> To what extent, and in what ways, is homosexuality seen as a threat to the social order?
>
> How common is the desire for strong negative sanctions against homosexuality?
>
> In what ways are homosexual females viewed differently from males?
>
> What are the correlates of negative views toward homosexuality?

Where do research questions come from? How does a particular researcher come to ask a particular research question? In some cases, researchers have a personal interest in a specific topic because of their own life experience. For example, a researcher who experienced sexual abuse as a child may wish to do research on such questions as "Why do adults sexually abuse children?" and "What are the long-term effects of child sexual abuse?" Other researchers may ask a particular research question because of their concern for certain human or social problems and their desire to improve human life. For example, researchers who are concerned over the spread of HIV may want to do research on such questions as "What are people's beliefs about how HIV is transmitted?" and "What percentage of documented HIV-infected individuals acquired the virus through heterosexual transmission?" Some research questions are also asked in order to test specific theories.

Scientists are human first, and individuals involved in even the most glorious of quests may also be motivated by such mundane factors as greed, desire for fame, and envy of fellow scientists.

Donn Byrne

CONSIDERATION: What types of research questions would you want to ask if you were a sex researcher? How are the research questions you would be interested in related to either your personal life experience or your concern for particular problems?

Numerous journals may be used by the Sexuality Researcher.

Not all research questions stem from the researcher's personal interest, life experience, or humanitarian concerns. Many researchers are hired by government, industry, or other organizations to design and conduct research to investigate questions or topics that are of interest to the organization.

CONSIDERATION: Not all questions that may concern us can be answered through scientific research. Questions involving values, religion, morality, and philosophical issues are often outside the domain of science. For example, scientific research cannot answer the question of whether extradyadic sex is right or wrong or whether abortion is moral or immoral. Scientific research can, however, reveal information that may help us make or evaluate our own moral or value judgments. For example, research can tell us how other segments of the population describe their views on these issues and what social and personal factors are associated with different views on these issues. Research can tell us what the psychological, social, physical, and economic consequences are of allowing versus disallowing abortion. Regarding extradyadic sex, research can investigate people's motives for engaging in extradyadic sexual relations and the consequences of such activity for the individuals and their relationships.

Reviewing the Literature

After a research question is formulated, the researcher reviews the literature to find out what is already known about the topic. Reviewing the literature involves reading articles, books, and research reports related to the topic. Numerous journals publish research on human sexuality, including: *Journal of Sex Research, Archives of Sexual Behavior, Journal of Sex Education and Therapy, Journal of Homosexuality, Family Planning Perspectives, Journal of Sex and Marital Therapy, Journal of Marriage and the Family, Sex Roles, American Psychologist, Child Development, Journal of Personality and Social Psychology, and Journal of the History of Sexuality.*

Reviewing the literature is important for both conducting research and for evaluating research and other information (including classroom lecture material). A literature review enables the researcher to find out whether other researchers have already asked (and perhaps answered) the researcher's question. Reviewing the literature also provides researchers with ideas about how to conduct their research and helps them formulate new research questions. As an evaluation tool, a literature review allows a comparison of research reports (or other sources of information, such as classroom lecture material, expert opinions, political claims, etc.) with other findings on the topic of interest.

Formulating a Hypothesis and Defining Variables

After reviewing the research literature, researchers formulate a **hypothesis**, which is a prediction or guess about how one variable is related to another variable. A **variable** refers to any measurable event, characteristic, or property that varies or is subject to change. For example, a researcher may be interested in how alcohol consumption (variable A) affects sexual desire (variable B). Alcohol consumption and sexual desire are referred to as *variables* because they are events or characteristics that vary.

In research, the variable that the researcher wants to explain is referred to as the **dependent variable.** The variable that is expected to explain change in the dependent variable is known as the **independent variable.** In formulating a hypothesis, the researcher predicts how the independent variable affects the dependent variable. For example, in a study of the effect of alcohol consumption on female orgasmic response, researchers hypothesized that alcohol consumption (independent variable) would result in increased latency to orgasm and decreased intensity of orgasmic contraction (dependent variables) (Malatesta, Pollack, Crotty, & Peacock, 1982). The results of the study supported their hypothesis.

In Table 4.2, the independent and dependent variables of several research hypotheses are identified.

Human behavior and attitudes are complex and influenced by numerous factors. In studying sexuality, researchers often assess the effects of several independent variables on one or more dependent variables. This is because any one variable usually explains only a portion of the variation in the dependent variable. When more independent variables are introduced into a study, more of the variance in the dependent variable may be explained. For example, Jaccard and Dittus (1991) conducted a study on premarital teenage sexual activity in a sample of 210 primarily white, middle-class, suburban families. In their research, Jaccard and Dittus attempted to explain how variation in teenage sexual activity (dependent variable) may be explained by a number of independent variables, including (a) parenting practices used by parents of teenagers, (b) general communication patterns between parents and teenagers, (c) nature and timing of parental discussions with teenagers about sex, and (d) attitudes of parents toward teenage sexual activity, premarital sex,

TABLE 4.2 Independent and Dependent Variables

Hypothesis	Independent Variable	Dependent Variable
Women are sexually harassed more often than men.	Sex (male or female)	Sexual harassment
Couples with a high level of relationship conflict tend to have a low level of sexual satisfaction.	Relationship conflict	Sexual satisfaction
Teenage pregnancy rates are higher among nonwhites than among whites.	Race	Teenage pregnancy rate
The frequency of intercourse decreases as marital duration increases.	Duration of marriage	Frequency of intercourse

and use of birth control by teenagers. (The findings of this research are discussed in Chapter 13).

Once a research hypothesis is formulated, it must be tested. Testing hypotheses usually involves observing and measuring the variables in which the researcher is interested. Some variables, such as sex (female or male), age, duration of marriage, and heart rate, are easy to define and measure. But many of the variables that sex researchers study are not so easy to define and measure. For example, how would you define and measure such variables as "sexual desire," "sexual harassment," "relationship conflict," and "sexual satisfaction"?

One of the difficulties in conducting and interpreting sex research is the lack of consensus on how some variables are defined and measured. In the past, efforts to measure sexual desire have focused on frequency of intercourse, incidence of sexual thoughts or fantasies, and number of sexual contacts (including masturbation). Presently, many researchers use both objective and subjective criteria in measuring sexual desire; that is, sexual desire is defined in terms of both (a) the frequency of all sexual activities engaged in and (b) the person's subjective interest in participating in various sexual activities (Leiblum & Rosen, 1988a). However, Leiblum and Rosen (1988b) noted that research on sexual desire is handicapped by the lack of standardized laboratory measures of sexual desire. They suggested that "there is a pressing need for the development of both physiological and subjective measures of sexual interest" (Leiblum & Rosen, 1988b, p. 457).

CONSIDERATION: Research findings are sometimes reported in newspapers, television news broadcasts, and popular magazines. The next time you hear or see research findings reported in the media, notice whether the report describes how the research variables were defined. If you don't know how the researcher defined the research variables, you will not be able to interpret the findings. For example, if research findings suggest that viewing pornography leads to sexual aggression, you need to know how the researcher defined *pornography* and *sexual aggression* in order to interpret the findings.

Selecting the Sample: Nonprobability versus Probability Sampling

One of the most important parts of doing research involves selecting a sample. A **sample** is a portion of the population. The findings of research are usually based on samples, which are then generalized to a larger population.

In research, the term **population** refers to all of the cases in which the researcher is interested. For example, if the researcher is interested in the attitudes of U.S. college students toward homosexuals, then the population consists of all U.S. college students. Similarly, if the researcher is interested in comparing the types of sexual fantasies that U.S. men and women have, the population would be all U.S. men and women.

A research population does not necessarily consist of people. For example, if a researcher is interested in studying the sexual content of music videos, the research population might consist of all music videos aired on MTV during a given year. The specific nature of the research population depends on the research question.

Ideally, researchers would like to collect data from the entire population. But often the research population is so large that it would be impossible, impractical, time-consuming, and costly to collect data from every unit in the population. Instead of studying the population, researchers usually study a sample selected from the population.

Representative versus Biased Samples

A **representative sample** is one that allows the researcher to make inferences from the sample to the population. If a sample is representative, then it accurately reflects the population from which it was selected. We may assume that research findings based on a representative sample are similar to findings we would obtain if we studied the entire population.

A **biased sample** is a sample that is *not* representative of the population. Research findings that are based on a biased sample are of limited value because they cannot be unequivocally generalized to the larger population.

Nonprobability versus Probability Sampling Methods There are several sampling methods, which may be categorized as either nonprobability sampling or probability sampling. In **nonprobability sampling,** there is no way to determine the probability that each member of the population has of being included in the sample. Hence, there is no way of establishing that a nonprobability sample is representative of the population.

One commonly used nonprobability sampling method is known as **convenience sampling**, which involves selecting members of a sample to whom the researcher has convenient access. For example, many sex research samples consist of college students, simply because professors who conduct research have easy access to students. But research findings based on college students may not reflect the population of young adults who are not in college. Christopher and Roosa (1991) noted that

> Our knowledge of older adolescents' and young adults' sexuality is severely biased by the overuse of college samples. Such samples tend to be composed of white, educated, and middle- and upper-class youths. When sexual expression occurs in a college milieu, it is relatively easy to make romantic contacts. This environment may effect such important influences on sexual expression as perceived peer behavior and social pressures felt by males. (p. 129)

The alternative to nonprobability sampling is **probability sampling**, which allows the researcher to specify the probability that any given member of the population will be included in the sample. A probability sample makes it possible for the researcher to estimate the extent to which the findings based on the sample are similar to the findings that would be obtained if the entire population were studied. Thus, probability samples allow us to determine if the findings based on the sample can be generalized to the population. It is beyond the scope of this chapter to describe the various types of probability samples, which include simple random samples, stratified samples, systematic samples, and cluster samples.

CONSIDERATION: Probability sampling requires the researcher to have a list of every member of the research population from which to select the sample. However, in many sex research studies, there is no available list of members of the research population. For example, a researcher who wishes to study women who have had an abortion, homosexuals, transsexuals, or rape victims cannot obtain a list of all members of the research population because no such lists exist. Therefore, "for special subpopulations, in particular those populations of individuals engaging in deviant, rare, or illegal sexuality, we will be unable to utilize probability sampling" (McKinney, 1986, p. 120). Instead, nonprobability sampling methods, including convenience sampling and other methods not described in this chapter, are often used to study the sexuality of specific subpopulations. The problem with using nonprobability samples is that the findings based on such samples may be different from the findings that would be obtained if the entire "special subpopulation" were studied.

Even when probability sampling procedures are used, a sample may not be representative due to fact that not all members of a sample agree to participate in a sex research study. If participants systematically differ from nonparticipants, the study suffers from what is called **participation bias.** For example, women are generally less likely to participate in sex research. Catania, Gibson, Chitwood, and Coates (1990) explained that in interview studies, women may "feel more vulnerable to sexual exploitation and, therefore, require much more evidence of the credibility of the study and the interviewer before participating in a sex survey" (p. 355).

Another example of participation bias was reported by Hull, Bettinger, Gallaher, Keller, Wilson, and Mertz (1988), who found that men who failed to volunteer for HIV-antibody testing were 5.3 times more likely to be infected with HIV; black and Hispanic nonparticipants were 8.8 times more likely to be infected than black and Hispanic volunteers.

Methods of Data Collection

Doing scientific research involves collecting data. Several methods used in data collection include experiments, surveys, field research, case studies, historical research, and diaries.

Experiments

Experiments involve manipulating some variable (the independent variable) in order to determine the effect it has on some other variable (the dependent variable). In some experiments, there are one or more **experimental groups** that are exposed to the experimental treatment(s) and a **control group** that is not exposed. In other experiments, there may be one or more experimental groups but no control group.

In experimental research, subjects are randomly assigned to either an experimental or a control group. **Randomization** allows the researcher to assume that the experimental group and the control group, or the two or more experimental groups, are theoretically the same in terms of members' characteristics. Thus, randomization allows the researcher to compare the experimental group with the control group (or to compare two or more experimental groups) and conclude that any differences between the two groups are due to the experimental treatment(s).

After the researcher randomly assigns participants to either an experimental or a control group, the researcher measures the dependent variable (e.g., administers a pretest). After the experimental group(s) are exposed to the treatment, another measure of the dependent variable is made (e.g., posttest). If participants have been randomly assigned to the different groups, the researcher may conclude that any posttest difference between the groups is due to the effect of the dependent variable.

CONSIDERATION: In order to do experimental research, researchers must be able to randomly assign subjects to experimental and control groups. However, many of the variables that sex researchers study make it impossible or unethical to assign subjects to the experimental group. For example, suppose a researcher is interested in studying the effect of teenage pregnancy (independent variable) on academic performance (dependent variable). In order to do experimental research, the researcher would have to randomly assign half of the subjects to the experimental group that becomes pregnant! Similarly, a researcher studying the effects of herpes on self-esteem cannot randomly assign subjects to be in the experimental group that contracts herpes.

Some topics in human sexuality may be studied using the experimental method. For example, experimental methods have been used to assess the causes of interpersonal attraction (Harvey, Christensen, & McClintock, 1983); sexual and aggressive responses to erotica and pornography (Donnerstein & Berkowitz, 1981); and perceptions and attributions of rape and rape victims (Shotland & Goodstein, 1983).

Most experimental studies in human sexuality are related to biological or medical research. For example, White, Case, McWhirter, and Mattison (1990) did an experimental study on the effect of aerobic exercise on sexual activity in elderly men. The results showed that the men who exercised (when compared with the controls) reported more frequent sexual behaviors and more satisfying orgasms.

I think clinical trials are important to help make new drugs available and to help science—but most of all to help me.

Ramon Dominquez

The major strength of the experimental method is that it provides information on causal relationships. A primary weakness is that experiments are often conducted on small samples, usually in artificial laboratory settings; thus, the findings may not be generalizable to other people in natural settings.

In Exhibit 4.1, we look at experimental research that is particularly relevant today—the search for effective treatments for AIDS and HIV infection. Experimental research studies on new drugs are known as **clinical trials.**

Surveys

Survey research involves eliciting information from respondents through questions. Three major methods of survey research are face-to-face interviews, mail questionnaires, and telephone surveys.

Face-to-Face Interviews One method of survey research involves gathering information through face-to-face interviews with respondents. During these interviews, trained interviewers ask respondents a series of questions. Alfred C. Kinsey and his colleagues (1948, 1953) conducted the largest interview survey research project on sexuality, interviewing 5,300 men and 5,940 women. Each interview consisted of between 350 and 521 questions (Pomeroy, 1976, p. 39.) More recently, Lillian B. Rubin conducted interviews with 675 individuals in regard to their sexuality in preparation for her book *Erotic Wars* (1991).

My latest survey shows that people don't believe in surveys.

Laurence Peter

Sexual attitudes and opinions are sometimes gathered in face-to-face interviews.

EXHIBIT 4.1 AIDS and HIV Clinical Trials

AIDS and HIV clinical trials are experimental research studies in which new drug treatments for AIDS and HIV infection are tested in volunteers who are HIV infected or who have AIDS (see Chapter 18 for discussion of AIDS and HIV). There are three general types of clinical trials: Phase I, Phase II, and Phase III. Phase I clinical trials are conducted with very small numbers of HIV-infected volunteers who are often very sick and have no other choice of treatment. These trials are designed to determine how the drug is absorbed, metabolized, and excreted; the duration of action; and safe dosage levels, and to look for side effects. Phase I trials, which are completed in about one year, are basically safety studies conducted only after a new drug is tested in the laboratory and animal studies.

Phase II trials, which generally take longer than one year to complete are conducted with larger groups of patients who have AIDS. Phase II trials are studies designed to assess the effectiveness of new drugs and clarify their side effects based on longer use of the drug.

Phase III trials, which may take even longer to complete, are usually conducted on groups of 1,000 to 3,000 patients with AIDS. Phase III trials involve more extensive testing of the effectiveness and side effects of new drugs. These trials are also designed to compare new drugs to a placebo or standard treatment, or compare effects of two or more dosage levels.

Because of the urgency of the need for HIV/AIDS treatment and the lack of effective drugs, Phase I, II, and III clinical trials are often combined to speed up testing. For example, although drug efficacy is usually assessed in Phase II and III trials, Phase I trials may also look at drug efficacy.

Currently, clinical trials are underway to develop treatments that may (a) stop HIV's destruction of the immune system, (b) help rebuild a damaged immune system, and (c) prevent or cure the various opportunistic infections that result from a damaged immune system. In some cases, government or private organizations may pay for clinical trials. Frequently, however, the company that makes the drug being tested pays for the research expenses involved in the clinical trials. The goal of the drug company is to obtain research support for the safety and effectiveness of its drug in order to win Food and Drug Administration (FDA) approval to sell the drug in the United States.

In clinical trials, experimental methods are used, including randomization, double blinding, and placebos. (It is important to note that not all of these methods are used in every clinical trial and not all of these methods are ethical in every situation.)

Randomization

In clinical trials, researchers often compare the effects of one drug on a group of people with the effects of another drug on another group of people. Randomization involves assigning people by chance or lottery to the different treatment groups. As discussed earlier in this chapter, randomization allows the researcher to assume that the two (or more) treatment groups are similar in their characteristics and that any posttest differences between the groups are due to the drugs or treatments being tested. Randomization is ethical when doctors cannot agree or do not know which of the treatments being studied is better. If it is known that a particular treatment is more effective than another, it is unethical to withhold the more effective treatment from any individual in need of treatment.

Double Blinding

Most clinical trial studies use an experimental research method known as "double blinding." In double blind studies, the researcher (and/or medical staff) and the individuals in the treatment groups do not know who is receiving which treatment. (In studies involving a treatment and a control group, the researcher and participants do not know who is in which group—until, of course, after the posttest.) This blinding method helps to ensure that the beliefs or expectations of the researcher or patients do not influence the experimental results. However, some drug treatments have characteristic side effects that "unblind" the treatment. Studies that do not blind the treatment are called "open label" studies.

Placebo

Placebos are usually "sugar pills" that look and taste like the drug being studied. In clinical trials, placebos are the quickest way to determine if the drug being studied produces a clinical response. Placebos may also be used to compare a new treatment with the beneficial effects that sometimes result from the belief that treatment has been given. Placebo trials are only ethical when there is no other effective treatment for the disease or when there is no immediate danger in temporarily withholding treatment. Otherwise, the experimental treatment should be compared to the best treatment currently available.

As of this writing, there is still no treatment that has been shown to cure HIV infection or AIDS. We can only

Continued

EXHIBIT 4.1 AIDS and HIV Clinical Trials—*Continued*

hope that medical researchers will continue to search for safe and effective treatments for HIV-infected individuals and individuals with AIDS. Such research efforts depend on the willingness of such persons to participate in clinical trials. The risks and benefits of participating in clinical trials are summarized in figure 1:

For more information on participating in clinical trials, contact:

1) 1-800-Trials-A (for information about AIDS and HIV clinical trials conducted by the National Institutes of Health).

2) 1-800-638-8480 (The National Library of Medicine provides three on-line AIDS databases: AIDSLINE, AIDSDRUGS, and AIDSTRIALS).

3) 1-800-39 AmFAR (Treatment Information Services of the American Foundation for AIDS Research (AmFAR)).

Source: "What Is an AIDS clinical trial?:" published by the *AIDS clinical trials information service (ACTIS), AIDS-HIV clinical trial handbook.* N.Y.C., N.Y.: American Foundation for AIDS Research, and the Treatment Information Services of the American Foundation for AIDS Research,N.Y.C., N.Y.

FIGURE 1 Risks and Benefits of Participating in HIV and AIDS Clinical Trials

Risks:

– *Experimental drugs may not have any beneficial effects or may even be harmful.*
  – *New drugs may have unanticipated and unpleasant side effects.*
  – *Clinical trials may require a lot of the patient's time and frequent trips to the study site.*

Benefits:

+ *Patients gain access to new treatments not available to the public.*
  + *Experimental drugs are often provided free of charge to participants.*
  + *Patients receive expert medical care at leading health-care facilities.*
  + *Participants have a chance to help others by contributing to medical research.*

Although interviews are often conducted one-on-one, sometimes they are held in a group. An example is a study on women's construction of menopause and their related self-image in which the researcher participated in a group discussion with women about their views of menopause and self-image (Gergen, 1988).

The advantage of personal interviews is that they allow the researcher to clarify questions for the respondent and follow up on answers to particular questions. Also, personal interviews often yield information that is more detailed than that obtained through other survey methods. Zeiss, Davies, Wood, and Tinklenberg (1990) interviewed 55 male patients who had been diagnosed as having Alzheimer's Disease.

> Questions about erectile functioning were specifically asked, along with questions about any inappropriate or disturbing sexual behavior. If difficulty with erections was reported, the year of onset of clear problems was elicited (e.g., the date when problems with erection began occurring consistently, not just on an occasional level). (p. 326)

Another advantage of face-to-face interviews is that they may be conducted with groups of individuals that otherwise may not be accessible. For example, some AIDS-related research attempts to assess the degree to which individuals engage in behavior that places them at high risk for transmitting HIV. Street youth and intravenous drug users are two groups that may not have a telephone or mailing address due to their transient life-style (Catania et al., 1990). These groups may be accessible, however, by locating their hangouts and conducting face-to-face interviews with them.

The most serious disadvantage of interview research is the lack of privacy and anonymity. Respondents cannot hide their identity from the interviewer; therefore, they may feel threatened or embarrassed by being asked questions that relate to such personal and sensitive issues as sexuality. Respondents who are threatened or embarrassed by being asked questions about their sexual behavior may choose not to participate in interview sexuality research. Those who do participate may conceal their true sexual behavior and, instead, give socially desirable answers to the interviewer's questions.

Lastly, face-to-face interviews may involve interviewer bias. Interviewers may unintentionally communicate their own personal biases, which may influence the answers given by respondents. Also, the age, race, and sex of the interviewer may influence respondents' answers to questions. For example, Delamater (1974) found that young adult women reported lower frequencies of sexual behavior to male than to female interviewers.

Another disadvantage of interview research is that it is expensive to conduct. These expenses include paying the interviewers for their time and travel expenses.

Questionnaires Instead of personally interviewing respondents, researchers may construct a questionnaire that may be mailed or given to a sample of respondents. For example, professors doing survey research on samples of college students may give a questionnaire to students in classes. Most large-scale survey research involves mailing a questionnaire to the research sample. A letter, which usually accompanies the questionnaire, explains who is doing the research and what the research is about and attempts to persuade the recipient to take the time to complete and return the questionnaire.

The most important advantage of questionnaire sexuality research is the provision of privacy and anonymity to the research participant. The assurance of privacy and anonymity reduces the degree to which individuals may feel threatened or embarrassed by answering sexual questions and increases the likelihood that they will agree to participate in the research, answer all the question items, and provide answers that are not intentionally inaccurate or distorted. Millstein and Irwin (1983) found, for example, that female adolescents reported vaginal intercourse and masturbation more often on computer-assisted questionnaires (74% and 38%, respectively) than in face-to-face interviews (63% and 25%, respectively).

Another advantage of questionnaires is that they are less costly than personal interviews. The cost of paper and mailing is much less than the cost of hiring interviewers and paying travel expenses involved in personal interviews.

The major disadvantage of a mail questionnaire is that it is difficult to obtain an adequate response rate. Many people do not want to take the time or make the effort to read a questionnaire, answer the questions, and return it. Others may be unable to read and understand the questionnaire.

CONSIDERATION: The typical response rate for a mail questionnaire is between 20% and 40%. In contrast, the response rate for a personal interview is usually about 95% (Nachmias & Nachmias, 1987). (These estimates are not based specifically on sexuality research.)

A study by Hite (1987) has been widely criticized for its low response. Hite mailed 100,000 questionnaires to women to obtain data on women's experiences and attitudes toward love, sex, relationships, and marriage. Only 4.5% of Hite's sample returned a completed questionnaire.

The problem with having a low response rate is that nonrespondents (those people who do not respond) are usually different from those people who do respond. In general, questionnaire nonrespondents are often poorly educated or elderly and may be unable to read or understand the questions (Nachmias & Nachmias, 1987). Because respondents do not constitute a representative sample, the researcher may not be able to generalize the findings to the entire population.

Telephone Survey Another form of survey research involves collecting data through telephone interviews. One benefit of telephone surveys is that they may produce a higher response rate than personal interviews. People who are reluctant to let an interviewer come into their homes may be more willing to talk on the telephone.

The telephone interview is also less time-consuming for interviewers, because they do not have to travel. Telephone interviews are also less expensive to conduct than face-to-face interviews.

NATIONAL DATA: In 1991, 6% of all households in the United States did not have a telephone (*Statistical Abstract of the United States,* 1992, Table 884).

A major disadvantage of telephone surveys is that they cannot sample people who do not have a telephone. People who do not have a phone are more likely to be poor; thus, telephone survey samples may be biased in underrepresenting the poor.

Another weakness of telephone surveys is that they may produce less information than personal interviews, since interviewers cannot describe the respondents' characteristics or environment in detail. In addition, some respondents feel uncomfortable discussing personal or sensitive topics over the phone. Telephone interviews provide more privacy and anonymity than personal interviews but less than mail questionnaires. Individuals may be suspicious of telephone sexual surveys because of the possibility that the interviewer may really be someone making an obscene phone call. However, this problem may be reduced by sending the potential respondents a letter prior to the telephone interview informing them that an interviewer will be calling them and describing the nature and purpose of the research study, as well as who is conducting it.

Field Research

Field research involves studying sexual phenomena in settings in which it naturally occurs. Field research is frequently done in studies of sexual behavior in other cultures. Two types of field research are participant observation and nonparticipant observation. In each case, the researcher observes the phenomenon being studied and records these observations through note taking, audio or videotaping, and/or coding schemes. Interviews are sometimes part of field observation research.

In participant observation research, the researcher participates in the phenomenon being studied. The researcher attempts to attain membership or close attachment to the group that is being studied. Participation as a group member allows the researcher to obtain an insider's perspective of the people and/or behavior being observed. For example, Bartell (1970) conducted participant observation research on "swinging" (a couple having sex with another person or couple). Bartell and his wife contacted swinging couples who had placed ads in the newspaper. To learn about swinging, Bartell and his wife interviewed swinging couples and attended swinging parties.

Other examples of participant observation sexuality research include a study of nude beaches in which the researchers went to nude beaches and observed interaction patterns (Douglas, Rasmussen, & Flanagan, 1977); a study on crowd behavior at a male strip show in which the researchers observed and participated with the crowd (Petersen & Dressel, 1982); and a study on casual, homosexual behavior of

One way to study erotic dancers is to become one and become a participant observer.

men in a public restroom in which the researcher participated in the role of the lookout (Humphreys, 1970).

In nonparticipant observation research, the researcher observes the phenomenon being studied without actively participating in the group or the activity. For example, Masters and Johnson (1966, 1970) observed the sexual functioning of individuals in a laboratory setting. (The research of Masters and Johnson is described later in this chapter.) Prus and Irini (1988) studied prostitution through observations (and interviews) without participating as either prostitutes or customers; similarly, Warren (1974) studied the gay community through observation without participating in the gay life-style.

Participant and nonparticipant observation research may be covert, in which the individuals being studied do not know that they are being studied, or overt, in which the researcher informs the individuals in the study that they are being studied. The disadvantage of overt research is that individuals may alter their behavior if they know that they are being studied; thus, the researcher may not obtain a true picture of the phenomenon being studied. While covert research alleviates this problem, it creates another by violating the individuals' right to know that they are being studied.

Another potential problem with participant and nonparticipant research is that the researcher's observations may be biased. Also, small samples that may not be representative may make such research findings not generalizable.

The main advantage of both participant and nonparticipant research is that they are qualitative approaches and, as such, yield detailed information about the values, rituals, behaviors, symbols, beliefs, and emotions of those being studied. Such qualitative information may complement quantitative data on the research topic and lead to ideas for further research.

Case Studies

A **case study** is a qualitative research approach that involves a descriptive analysis of an individual, group, relationship, or event. Data obtained in a case study may come from in-depth interviews, observations, and analysis of records (e.g., legal, educational, and medical). Case studies are frequently conducted on rare or deviant

Nonparticipant observation involves observing sexual life-styles without participating in them (e.g. heterosexuals observing homosexuals or vice versa).

sexual phenomena because in such cases, obtaining large samples is difficult. Examples of case studies in sexuality research include Bogdan's (1974) study of transsexuals and Money and Ehrhardt's (1972) studies of individuals who were born with an inconsistency between their genetic sex (XX or XY chromosomes) and their anatomical sex (discussed further in Chapter 8). Szasz, McLoughlin, and Warren (1990) conducted a case study on a 31-year-old man who had his penis, scrotum, and testicles cut off in a fight. Their report described the "return to erection, orgasmic, and ejaculation capabilities after penile replantation" (p. 344).

More recently, Skeen (1991) conducted ten case studies of individuals reflecting different aspects of sexuality, including:

By studying many different sexual lifestyles, we begin to understand the way sexual meanings are constructed in our own lives.

Dick Skeen

- a woman's discovery that she is gay
- a Catholic priest's choice to be celibate
- a prostitute and her adjustment to leaving the profession
- a financially successful man's view of how money affected his sexuality
- a rock-and-roll band leader and his sexual encounters
- an incest survivor
- a person with AIDS

The advantage of the case study method is that, as mentioned above, it allows rare cases of sexual phenomena to be investigated. In addition, case studies provide detailed information that often leads to new research questions. The main disadvantage of the case study method is that findings based on a single case are not generalizable.

Historical Research

Historical research involves investigating sexuality and sexual issues through the study of historical documents. Data sources used in conducting historical research include newspapers, magazines, letters, literature (e.g., novels and poetry), diaries, medical texts and popular health manuals, court records, hospital records, prison records, and official (government) statistics on such things as birth rates, arrest and conviction rates, sexually transmittable diseases, and premarital pregnancies. An example of an historical document is Samuel Solomon's *Advice to Both Sexes,* which ran through 66 editions between 1782 and 1817. Advertisements in this small magazine were for "potions for, or to safeguard against, potency, abortion, masturbation, etc." (Weeks, 1989).

One researcher (Davis, 1990) investigated how motherhood has been conceptualized in the popular media and analyzed the articles on parents and parenting reported in the *Nineteenth Century Readers' Guide to Periodical Literature* and the *Readers' Guide to Periodical Literature* for the years 1890 through 1985. By conducting a content analysis on these documents, Davis was able to identify three distinct stages in the way media treated women in the workplace who had families: "working girl," working wife, and working mother.

The farther backward you can look, the farther forward you are likely to see.
Winston Churchill

Historical sexuality research provides information about the changing nature of sexual behavior, norms, social control, and socially constructed meanings of sexuality. Historical sexuality research has also linked sexuality to issues of power and social conflict in U.S. history (Duggan, 1990). In an analysis of sexuality in U.S. life from colonial times to the present, D'Emilio and Freedman (1988) traced changes in sexual themes from a reproductive emphasis in the eighteenth century, to a focus on gender relations in the nineteenth century, to a concern for eroticism in the twentieth century. Historical research led Freedman and D'Emilio (1990) to conclude that "the very term 'sexuality' is a modern construct which originated in the nineteenth century" (p. 483).

Diaries

While diaries may be used in historical research, they are also used to gather qualitative and quantitative data concerning sexual thoughts, feelings, and behaviors as they occur. Reading (1983) assessed sexual behavior and dysfunctions through the use of daily diary cards. One group of research participants recorded their sexual activity in diary cards daily for three months.

CONSIDERATION: Participants in Reading's (1983) study were also interviewed at the end of each month and asked about their sexual activities during the previous month. Participants consistently reported lower levels of sexual activity in the interviews than in their diary reports (e.g., average monthly frequency of sexual intercourse reported in diaries was 19.4; in interviews, the average reported frequency was 14.7). This difference may be due to either recall problems or the lack of anonymity involved in the interview method. In either case, diaries are likely to result in accurate information because they avoid the problems of recall and lack of anonymity.

Before leaving this section on various methods of research, we present a Research Perspective on the ethical considerations to which researchers must adhere in conducting research with human participants.

RESEARCH PERSPECTIVE

Ethical Considerations in Sexuality Research with Human Participants

Social scientists, allied health professionals, and others who conduct research with human participants are responsible for carrying out their research with consideration for the dignity and welfare of the people who participate. Researchers must also be familiar with federal and state regulations, as well as professional standards directing the conduct of research (Nachmias & Nachmias, 1987; American Sociological Association, 1984; Committee for the Protection of Human Participants in Research, 1982). Two general considerations are paramount in planning research with human beings (Committee for the Protection of Human Participants in Research, 1982). First,

Continued

Continued

any potential negative effect to participants must be warranted by the importance of the research. Second, participants' welfare must be protected.

> The fundamental requirements are that the participants have made a fully informed and competent decision to participate and that they emerge from their research experience unharmed—or, at least, that the risks are minimal, understood by the participants, and accepted as reasonable. If possible, participants should enjoy some benefit. In general, after research participation, the participants' feelings about the experience should be such that the participants would willingly take part in further research. (p. 18)

Following is a discussion of how researchers' responsibilities to participants have been addressed in sexuality research.

Fairness and Freedom from Exploitation

Treating participants with fairness and ensuring that they will not be exploited is addressed through providing (a) freedom from coercion to participate, (b) informed consent, and (c) safeguards when deception is necessary.

Freedom from coercion to participate

A participant should have the freedom to decline to participate or to withdraw from participating in research. When the investigator is in a position of authority or influence over a participant, this may require careful consideration (Committee for the Protection of Human Participants in Research, 1982). For example, many studies of sexuality knowledge, attitudes, and behavior are conducted using college students. It would be inappropriate for professors to *require* their students to participate in their research. However, even if participation were optional, some students might feel pressure to participate or might fear their grade would be lower if they did not take advantage of an opportunity for extra credit. To reduce the risk of students' feeling coerced to participate, professors typically provide alternative options for earning extra credit for students who do not choose to serve as research participants. Have you ever had the opportunity to participate in a research study? Did you feel any implicit (or overt) coercion?

Informed Consent

An investigator is required to inform participants "of all aspects of the research that might reasonably be expected to influence willingness to participate" (Committee for the Protection of Human Participants in Research, 1982, p. 32). A study by Bohlen (1980) reviewed published articles by sexual physiology researchers to see if they reported procedures for obtaining informed consent and other aspects of participants' orientation to research involvement. He identified 20 orientation topics (e.g., description of instrument placement, laboratory tour, potential risks and benefits, remuneration, and privacy) and found gaps in many of the reported procedures. He found that more recent articles were more likely to include a discussion of how research participants were oriented to the research study.

Bohlen provided a list of recommendations for orientation of participants as a model for research; he used the recommended procedures in his laboratory at the University of Minnesota Medical School in his investigations of arousal during sexual response. The recommended procedures include a tour of the laboratory; details on how anonymity and privacy during undressing and data collection will be ensured; instructions on how instrumentation works, including a private practice session in which monitoring equipment is hooked up, but data are not collected; ample opportunity to ask questions; and signing of the consent form.

Continued

Continued

A frequently cited example of violation of the principle of informed consent is the participant-observer study of "tearoom trade" (sexual behaviors conducted between strangers in public bathrooms) by Humphreys. He served as a "watchqueen" (lookout), allowing him to observe sexual encounters without revealing his research role. He copied down automobile license numbers of participants, through which he then traced the owners' identities and addresses. A year later, he included these men as participants in an unrelated social health survey that he helped to conduct. In this way, he obtained background and personal information on those who had frequented the "tearooms." In a retrospective discussion of his research, Humphreys (1975) responded to ethical critiques and agreed with the criticism of the part of his research in which he traced the license numbers to interview men in their homes. He recognized that he put these men at risk (they could have been arrested if the records had been retrieved by law enforcement officers). He stated,

> Since then, although I remain convinced that it is ethical to observe interaction in public places and to interview willing and informed respondents, I direct my students to inform research subjects before interviewing them. Were I to repeat the tearoom study, I would spend another year or so in cultivating and expanding the category of willing respondents. . . . (p. 231)

Deception and Debriefing

When it is necessary to disguise the purpose of the research, participants should be given accurate information (debriefing) as soon as possible. For example, in studies on the impact of viewing pornography, Malamuth and Check (1981) employed a research protocol in which participants viewed films as part of the regular campus film program (one film with violent sexual content and one control film). Then, a few days later, in an apparently unrelated questionnaire, their acceptance of interpersonal violence toward women, acceptance of rape myths, and beliefs in adversarial sexual relations were covertly assessed. After the data had been analyzed, the results were described to study participants, and a discussion was held concerning mass media effects and the prevalence of rape myths.

Even when deception is not a part of the research protocol, debriefing may be used to attempt to mediate any harm that might have resulted from participating in the research. For example, in a study of exposure to degrading depictions of women, Linz, Donnerstein, and Penrod (1988) exposed college men to "slasher," "pornographic," and "teen sex" films. Following their participation in the study, the participants viewed a videotape in which one of the researchers explained the purpose of the study. Participants who viewed the R-rated violent movies were told that they could become desensitized to the violence in the movies and that they could be influenced to see the violence more positively by the way it was paired with sexual content. Additionally, Linz et al. (1988, p. 762) reported "subjects were strongly reminded that women do not seek or deserve to be victims of sexual or nonsexual violence." To viewers of the R-rated teen films and the X-rated sex films, it was pointed out that the presentation of women was often solely as sexual objects and that one effect of viewing these films is that viewers begin to believe that the sexual scenes presented are representative of real-life situations.

Malamuth, Donnerstein, and their colleagues have investigated whether such debriefing procedures are effective. Their results have consistently shown that participating in their studies and then receiving a debriefing does result in a reduction of belief in rape myths. In fact, there may even be benefits of participating in their pornography studies; the combination of exposure to violent pornography and debriefing yielded a greater reduction in rape myth belief than the debriefing alone (Linz, Turner, Hesse, & Penrod, 1984)!

Continued

Continued

Protection from Harm

Physical protection of participants

A researcher is obliged to protect participants from harm. For example, Rosen and Beck (1988) emphasized the importance of proper sterilization of genital devices used to measure physiological responses of research participants. In addition, they cautioned that equipment should be grounded and checked regularly for electrical safety to ensure that subjects could not be accidentally shocked.

Psychological protection of participants

Care must also be taken to protect research participants from psychological and emotional harm. Data regarding sexual response yield sensitive information, and care must be taken to ensure confidentiality, so that participants' privacy is respected and they are protected from embarrassment. Exposing participants to sexually arousing materials may cause discomfort to some people. The investigator is obliged to minimize the degree and duration of discomfort, unless there is compelling reason to continue (Committee for the Protection of Human Participants in Research, 1982). The investigator must inform research participants that they may terminate their participation at any point, if they wish. Further, if a participant is inadvertently harmed through research participation, the investigator is responsible to provide for remediation of the harm.

For example, Orbuch and Harvey (1991) pointed out the possibility that studying sexuality within close relationships may actually change or influence the relationships. They gave the example of a study focusing on blame, control, and marital satisfaction. When asked about her complaints about her spouse, a wife might complain about her husband's sensitivity to her sexual desires. If she were to voice dissatisfaction to her husband following her participation in the research, her husband might blame the study or the investigator for stirring up these concerns. This could lead to positive or negative outcomes for the relationship, depending on the couple's communication and problem-solving skills. Therefore, the investigator might want to include only couples with strong relationships that could withstand scrutiny. Or the researcher might use a strategy that would not restrict who could participate, but would warn participants of potential conflict and offer counseling support as needed.

Finally, care must be taken in how research results are reported and publicized. Rosen and Beck (1988) observed that in our society, people are so concerned about sexual "normality" that they are quite susceptible to sexual research findings. People may feel that patterns of masturbation, orgasm, and sexual fantasy that they hear or read about are prescriptions that they must follow in order to conform to current sexual standards. Despite the possibility of misuse, however, sexuality research does help to provide knowledge regarding a most important aspect of our lives. And, to the extent that well trained researchers adhere to ethical and professional standards, being involved in research studies can be a positive experience for participants.

References

American Sociological Association. (1984). *Code of ethics.* Washington, DC: Author.

Bohlen, J. G. (1980). A review of subject orientation in articles on sexual physiology research. *Journal of Sex Research, 16,* 43–58.

Committee for the Protection of Human Participants in Research. (1982). *Ethical principles in the conduct of research with human participants.* Washington, DC: American Psychological Associaton.

Continued

Continued

Humphreys, L. (1975). *Tearoom trade: Impersonal sex in public places* (Enlarged edition with a retrospect on ethical issues). New York: Aldine.

Linz, D. G., Donnerstein, E., & Penrod, S. (1988). Effects of long-term exposure to violent and sexually degrading depictions of women. *Journal of Personality and Social Psychology, 55,* 758–768.

Linz, D., Turner, C. W., Hesse, B. W., & Penrod, S. D. (1984). Bases of liability for injuries produced by media portrayals of violent pornography. In N. M. Malamuth and E. Donnerstein (Eds.), *Pornography and sexual aggression* (pp. 277–304). Orlando: Academic Press.

Malalmuth, N. M., & Check, J. V. P. (1981). The effects of mass media exposure on acceptance of violence against women: A field experiment. *Journal of Research in Personality, 15,* 436–446.

Nachmias, D., & Nachmias, C. (1987). *Research methods in the social sciences* (3rd ed.). New York: St. Martin's Press.

Orbuch, T. L., & Harvey, J. H. (1991). Methodological and conceptual issues in the study of sexuality in close relationships. In K. McKinney and S. Sprecher (Eds.), *Sexuality in close relationships* (pp. 9–24). Hillsdale, NJ: Lawrence Erlbaum.

Rosen, R. C., & Beck, J. G. (1988). *Patterns of sexual arousal: Psychophysiological processes and clinical applications.* New York: Guilford.

Data Analysis

There are three levels of data analysis: description, correlation, and causation. In addition, data analysis may involve assessing reliability and validity.

Description

The goal of many sexuality research studies is to describe sexual processes, behaviors, and attitudes and the people who experience them. Descriptive research may be qualitative or quantitative. Qualitative descriptions are verbal narratives that describe details and nuances of sexual phenomena. Quantitative descriptions of sexuality are numerical representations of sexual phenomena. Quantitative descriptive data analysis may involve computing the following: (a) means (averages), (b) frequencies, (c) mode (the most frequently occurring observation in the data), (d) median (the middle data point; half of the data points are above and half are below the median), and (e) range (a measure of dispersion, comprising the highest and lowest values of a variable in a set of observations).

CONSIDERATION: Descriptive quantitative research findings should be interpreted with caution. For example, research suggests that in regard to motivations for sexual intercourse, men emphasize the desire for sexual pleasure, conquest, and relief of sexual tension more often than women, who emphasize emotional closeness and affection (Townsend & Levy, 1990). Does this mean that women never emphasize sexual pleasure and men never emphasize emotional closeness? Of course not! What these findings mean is that men generally tend to emphasize sexual pleasure and women tend to emphasize emotional closeness. While these generalizations are based on averages, they do not account for the range of variability among women and men. Indeed, some men are more concerned about intimacy than some women, and some women are more interested in sexual pleasure than some men. As you read the research findings in this text, remember that they are generalizations, not absolute truths.

Correlation

Researchers are often interested in the relationships among variables. Remember that a variable is simply a measurable item or characteristic that is subject to change. **Correlation** refers to a relationship among two or more variables. Correlational research may answer such questions as "What is the relationship between sex and attitudes toward masturbation?", "What factors are associated with engaging in high-risk sexual behavior (e.g., failure to use condoms)?", and "What is the relationship between homophobia and religion?"

There is no absolute knowledge, and those who claim it, whether they are scientists or dogmatists, open the door to tragedy.
J. Bronowski

If there is a correlation or relationship between two variables, then a change in one variable is associated with a change in the other variable. A **positive correlation** exists when both variables change in the same direction. For example, in general, the greater the number of sexual partners a person has, the greater the chances are of contracting a sexually transmissible disease. As variable A (number of sexual partners) increases, variable B (chances of contracting an STD) also increases. Therefore, we may say that there is a positive correlation between number of sexual partners and contracting STDs. Similarly, we might say that as the number of sexual partners decreases, the chance of contracting STDs decreases. Notice that in both cases, the variables change in the same direction.

A **negative correlation** exists when two variables change in opposite directions. For example, there is a negative correlation between condom use and contracting STDs. This means that as condom use increases, the chance of contracting STDs decreases.

CONSIDERATION: Students often make the mistake of thinking that if two variables decrease, the correlation is negative. To avoid making this error, remember that in a positive correlation, it does not matter whether the variables increase or decrease, as long as they change in the same direction.

Sometimes the relationship between variables is curvilinear. A **curvilinear correlation** exists when two variables vary in both the same and opposite directions. For example, suppose that if you have one alcoholic beverage, your desire for sex increases. With two drinks, your sexual desire increases more, and three drinks raise your interest even higher. So far, there is a positive correlation between alcohol consumption (variable A) and sexual desire (variable B); as one variable increases, the other also increases. But suppose after four drinks, you start feeling sleepy, dizzy, or nauseous, and your interest in sex decreases. After five drinks, you are either vomiting or semiconscious, and sex is of no interest to you. There is now a negative correlation between alcohol consumption and sexual desire; as alcohol consumption increases, sexual interest decreases. Figure 4.1 illustrates how positive, negative, and curvilinear correlations look when they are plotted on a graph.

A fourth type of correlation is called a spurious correlation. A **spurious correlation** exists when two variables appear to be related but only because they are both related to a third variable. When the third variable is controlled through a statistical method in which a variable is held constant, the apparent relationship between the dependent and independent variables disappears.

For example, some research suggests that the more religiously devout you are, the more likely you are to contract a sexually transmissible disease (Smith & Walters, 1988). How can that be? Is there something about being religiously devout that, in and of itself, leads to STDs? The explanation is that religiously devout unmarried individuals are less likely to plan intercourse, and therefore, when they do have intercourse, they often are not prepared in terms of having a condom with them.

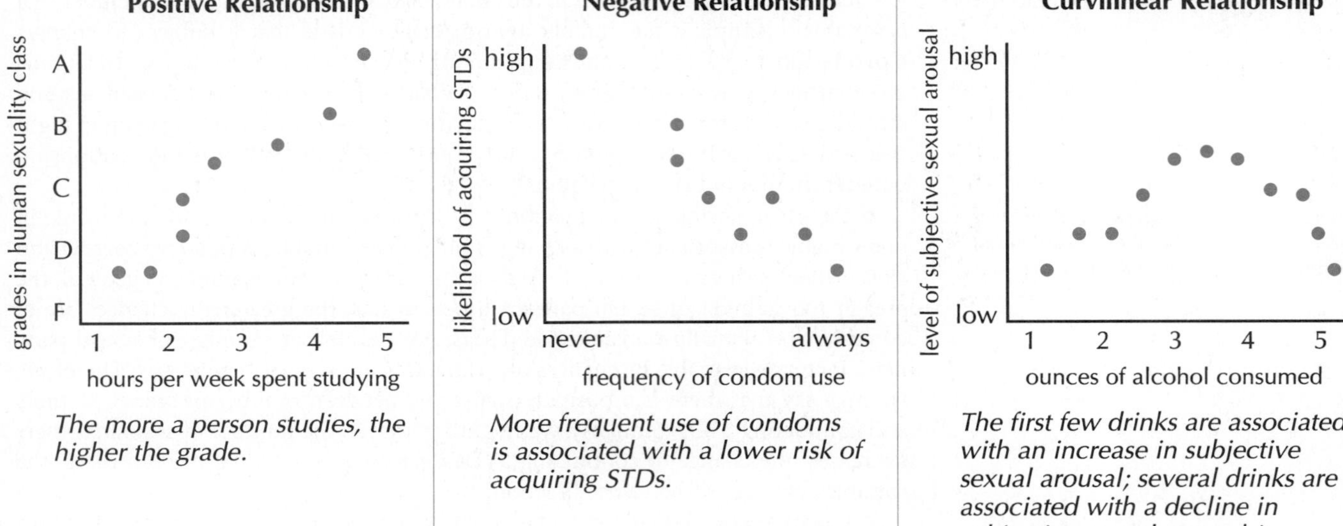

FIGURE 4.1 This figure illustrates how positive, negative, and curvilinear relationships might look on a graph.

Therefore, the correlation between religious devoutness and STDs is spurious. These variables appear to be related only because they are both related to a third variable (in this case, condom use).

Causation

If data analysis reveals that two variables are correlated, we know only that a change in one variable is associated with a change in the other variable. We cannot assume, however, that a change in one variable causes a change in the other variable unless our data collection and analysis are specifically designed to assess causation. The research method that best allows us to assess causal relationships is the experimental method.

> An educated person is one who has learned that information almost always turns out to be at best incomplete and very often false, misleading, fictitious, mendacious—just dead wrong.
>
> *R. Baker*

In order to demonstrate causality, three conditions must be met. First, the research must demonstrate that variable A is correlated with variable B. In other words, a change in variable A must be associated with a change in variable B. Second, the researcher must demonstrate that the observed correlation is nonspurious. A nonspurious correlation is a relationship between two variables that cannot be explained by a third variable. A nonspurious correlation suggests that there is an inherent causal link between the two variables. As we saw earlier, the correlation between religious devoutness and sexually transmissible diseases is spurious because a third variable—condom use—explains the correlation. Third, the researcher must demonstrate that the presumed cause (variable A) occurs or changes prior to the presumed effect (variable B). In other words, the cause must precede the effect.

For example, suppose a researcher finds that there is a negative correlation between marital conflict and frequency of marital intercourse (i.e., as marital conflict increases, frequency of marital intercourse decreases). In order to demonstrate that marital conflict causes the frequency of marital intercourse to decrease, the researcher must show that the marital conflict preceded the decrease in marital intercourse. Otherwise, the researcher cannot be sure whether marital conflict causes a decrease in marital intercourse or a decrease in marital intercourse causes marital conflict.

CONSIDERATION: Establishing causality is extremely difficult in the social sciences. Therefore, much of social science research, including sex research, is descriptive or correlative, rather than causative. However, many people make the mistake of interpreting a correlation as a statement of causation. As you read the correlative research findings cited in this text, remember the following adage: "Correlation DOES NOT equal causation."

Reliability and Validity

An important aspect of data analysis involves assessing reliability and validity. **Reliability** refers to the consistency of a measuring instrument or technique, that is, the degree to which the way in which information is obtained produces the same results if repeated. Measures of reliability are made on scales and indexes (such as those in the Self-Assessment sections of this text), on instruments that measure physiological processes, and on specific information-gathering techniques, such as the survey methods described earlier.

Various statistical methods exist for determining reliability; however, the most frequently used method in sex research is called the "test-retest method" (Lief, Fullard, & Delvin, 1990). The test-retest method involves gathering data on the same group of people twice (usually one or two weeks apart) using a particular instrument or method and then correlating the results. If the results are the same (or highly correlated), the instrument or method is considered reliable.

Test-retest correlations also provide a measure of the stability of self-reported estimates of sexual activities. For example, Kinsey et al. (1948, 1953) reported test-retest data for the adult, heterosexual, college-educated portion of their sample. In general, incidence questions (i.e., "Have you ever performed. . .") on intercourse, same-sex contact, masturbation, petting, and animal contact elicited answers that were highly reliable (0.90-0.95), whereas questions about the frequency of these behaviors produced answers that were much less reliable (0.58-0.67).

Measures that are perfectly reliable may be absolutely useless unless they also have a degree of validity. **Validity** refers to the extent to which a research instrument measures what it intends to measure.

Validity Measures of Scales and Indexes Validity measures are important in research that uses scales or indexes as measuring instruments. Scales and indexes, such as those found in the Self-Assessment sections of this text, are tools designed to measure complex or abstract traits, attitudes, and behavior. Examples included in this text are sex guilt (see Revised Mosher Guilt Inventory in Chapter 2), sexual arousability (see Sexual Arousability Inventory in Chapter 7), sexual satisfaction (see Index of Sexual Satisfaction in Chapter 10), and sexual self-disclosure (see Sexual Self-Disclosure Scale in Chapter 13). Scales and indexes are designed to provide a more valid measure of some attitude, characteristic, or trait than single-item measures. Thus, a score on a scale or index is more likely to reflect the property being measured than is a measure based on a response to one question or item.

CONSIDERATION: A scale or index is similar to an exam that students take to provide a measure of their knowledge. Students would not want their exam grade to be based on their answer to a single test question, since that answer probably does not represent the degree to which the student has learned the class material.

Two types of validity may be assessed to determine if scales and indexes really measure what they say they measure: criterion validity and face validity. Criterion validity involves assessing the correlation between a group of scores obtained on a given scale or index and some external criterion. In other words, criterion validity involves checking a measuring instrument against some outcome or against other previously validated measures. For example, assume a researcher has developed a new sex guilt scale and wishes to assess its validity. The researcher could have a group of individuals complete the newly developed scale along with another sex guilt scale (or index) that has been previously validated. If the scores on both scales are highly correlated, then the new scale has a degree of validity.

Another criterion that could be used to assess the validity of a sex guilt scale might be church attendance. There is a correlation between church attendance and sex guilt (Smith & Walters, 1988). Thus, the validity of a sex guilt scale may be assessed by having a group of individuals complete the scale and also indicate the number of times per month that they go to church. If these variables (scores on sex guilt scale and church attendance) are correlated, the sex guilt scale has a degree of validity.

Face validity refers to the subjective evaluation of the degree to which a measuring instrument is valid. Researchers may use their own subjective evaluation or seek such evaluations from other researchers or specialists in the field. For example, Hetherington and Soeken (1990) asked a panel of nurse-midwives to evaluate the items on a relationship intimacy scale in terms of the degree to which the items reflected intimacy. The main problem with face validity is that there is no objective measure of the validity of the instrument, since face validity is determined entirely through subjective judgments. The following Self-Assessment is a scale designed to measure sexual anxiety. The development of the scale is described, so you can review the researchers' steps in assessing its reliability and validity.

Validity Measures of Self-Report Data. Much of the data obtained through sex research are self-report data, or information that individuals provide through questionnaires or interviews. In sex research, validity may also refer to the degree of the accuracy of self-report data.

While we often assume that self-report data are accurate, they may not be. Individuals may provide inaccurate information about their sexual lives for several reasons. For example, some research participants may attempt to conform with strong cultural machismo values by overreporting the number of lifetime sexual partners. Or, due to embarrassment or fear of disapproval from the interviewer, a research participant in an interview study may intentionally underreport the number of lifetime sexual partners or overreport the use of condoms.

When I was younger I could remember anything—whether it happened or not.
Mark Twain

Respondents may also unintentionally over- or underreport data due to recall difficulty. For example, individuals who have had numerous sexual partners may not be able to accurately recall the exact number they have had. Inaccurate self-reports of sexual behavior may also result from the research participant's lack of understanding of the sexual terminology used by the researcher. For example, Catania, et al. (1990) described a situation in which a woman was asked by a researcher if she had ever performed anal intercourse. The woman said that she had, but when she was asked to describe the behavior, she described rear-entry vaginal intercourse.

Some efforts have been made to validate self-reports of sexual behavior. For example, correlations between partners' reports of how often they have sex over a given time period have been interpreted as validity measures of self-reported sexual

Self Assessment

Sex Anxiety Inventory and its Development

Circle the letter of the alternative that comes closest to describing your feelings.

1. Extramarital sex
   a. is OK if everyone agrees.
   b. can break up families.

2. Sex
   a. can cause as much anxiety as pleasure.
   b. on the whole is good and enjoyable.

3. Masturbation
   a. causes me to worry.
   b. can be a useful substitute.

4. After having sexual thoughts
   a. I feel aroused.
   b. I feel jittery.

5. When I engage in petting
   a. I feel scared at first.
   b. I thoroughly enjoy it.

6. Initiating sexual relationships
   a. is a very stressful experience.
   b. causes me no problem at all.

7. Oral sex
   a. would arouse me.
   b. would terrify me.

8. I feel nervous
   a. about initiating sexual relations
   b. about nothing when it comes to members of the opposite sex.

9. When I meet someone I'm attracted to
   a. I get to know him or her.
   b. I feel nervous.

10. When I was younger
    a. I was looking forward to having sex.
    b. I felt nervous about the idea of sex.

11. When others flirt with me
    a. I don't know what to do.
    b. I flirt back.

12. Group sex
    a. would scare me to death.
    b. might be interesting.

13. If in the future I committed adultery
    a. I would probably get caught.
    b. I wouldn't feel bad about it.

14. I would
    a. feel too nervous to tell a dirty joke in mixed company.
    b. tell a dirty joke if it were funny.

15. Dirty jokes
    a. make me feel uncomfortable.
    b. often make me laugh.

16. When I awake from sexual dreams
    a. I feel pleasant and relaxed.
    b. I feel tense.

17. When I have sexual desires
    a. I worry about what I should do.
    b. I do something to satisfy them.

18. If in the future I committed adultery
    a. it would be nobody's business but my own.
    b. I would worry about my spouse's finding out.

19. Buying a pornographic book
    a. wouldn't bother me.
    b. would make me nervous.

20. Casual sex
    a. is better than no sex at all.
    b. can hurt many people.

21. Extramarital sex
    a. is sometimes necessary.
    b. can damage one's career.

22. Sexual advances
    a. leave me feeling tense.
    b. are welcomed.

23. When I have sexual relations
    a. I feel satisfied.
    b. I worry about being discovered.

24. When talking about sex in mixed company
    a. I feel nervous.
    b. I sometimes get excited.

25. If I were to flirt with someone
    a. I would worry about his or her reaction.
    b. I would enjoy it.

 Janda, L. H. & O'Grady, K. E. (1980). Development of a sex anxiety inventory. *Journal of Consulting and Clinical Psychology, 48,* 169–175.

Note: In the actual scale, these items are interspersed with 15 filler items. Copies of the entire Sex Anxiety Inventory (SAI) are available from the first author, Louis H. Janda, Department of Psychology, Old Dominion University, Norfolk, VA 23508.

Continued

Self-Assessment—*Continued*

Scoring For each item, one alternative indicates a response associated with anxiety and the other, a nonanxiety response. Each anxiety response is scored as one point. The anxiety response is "a" for items 2, 3, 5, 6, 8, 11, 12, 13, 14, 15, 17, 22, 24, and 25. For the remaining items, "b" is the anxiety response. The possible score ranges from 0 to 25.

Interpreting your score The higher one's score, the more sex guilt is indicated. In a study of undergraduate psychology students at Old Dominion University, Janda and O'Grady (1980) found a significant difference between men's and women's scores. The mean score for men was 8.09, with a standard deviation of 5.19. For women, the mean was 11.76, with a standard deviation of 5.31.

Development of the scale To demonstrate how a research scale is developed, we will describe the six sets of procedures used by Janda and O'Grady (1980). The researchers hoped to determine whether it was possible to distinguish between sex guilt (as measured by Mosher, whose Sex Guilt Inventory you took in Chapter 2) and sex anxiety. They defined sex anxiety as "a generalized expectancy for nonspecific external punishment for the violation of, or the anticipation of violating, perceived normative standards of acceptable sexual behavior" (p. 170). While sex guilt reflects people's concern with what they think of themselves, sex anxiety refers more to their concern with what others will think of them. Although the concepts are related, Janda and O'Grady thought their influence could be separately analyzed "and that, used together, they could predict sexual behavior more accurately than either used alone" (p. 170).

1. Item construction, selection, and analysis. The researchers wrote 40 forced-choice items, trying to offer response choices that would be viewed as equally good or bad. These items, along with the Marlowe-Crowne Social Desirability Scale (SDS) and the Sex Guilt subscale of the Mosher Forced Choice Guilt Inventory (MFCGI), were presented to 95 male and 135 female undergraduate psychology students who earned extra credit for participating. Correlations between each SAI item and the SAI total score were calculated. High item-test correlations are interpreted as confirming the internal consistency of the scale, as this shows that each item measures a similar construct to that measured by the total scale. Correlations were also computed between SAI items and the MFCGI Sex Guilt subscale and the SDS.

   An item was selected for the final version of the SAI if it met four criteria: (a) the item-total correlation was statistically significant, (b) the item was more highly correlated to the SAI total than to the Sex Guilt Subscale of the MFCGI, (c) the item was more highly correlated to the SAI total than to the SDS, and (d) the item-total correlation was not significantly different for men and women. Twenty-five items met these criteria and were retained for the final version. Only four of these 25 items were significantly correlated with social desirability, two positively, and two negatively.

   The final SAI version showed a high internal consistency value of 0.86 (using the Kuder-Richardson formula). Men and women did not significantly differ on their item-total correlations. The correlation with the Sex Guilt subscale was 0.67, indicating that the two instruments appear to be measuring similar concepts (these two scales shared about 45% of the variance). The correlation between the SAI and the SDS was low (0.07), indicating little relationship between sexual anxiety and wanting to present a good picture of one's self.

2. Factor analysis of the SAI. To identify the underlying dimensions of the SAI, the interitem correlations of the final version were analyzed through a principal-factor analysis. Three factors were identified. The first "appeared to reflect feelings of discomfort in social situations in which sexuality is implied"; the second seemed to "deal with socially unacceptable forms of sexual behavior"; and the third, with "sexuality experienced in private" (p. 172). Scores for each student on these factors were correlated with sex guilt and the SDS to give information about the factorial validity of the SAI. The researchers interpreted the results as showing that the SAI factors do not overlap very much with sex guilt. Regarding the SAI factors and the SDS, only the third factor seemed to be influenced by social desirability.

3. Test-retest reliability. To determine the test-retest reliability of the SAI, 66 college men and 72 women completed the SAI and then took it again 10 to 14 days later. This confirmed a high level of stability (test-retest reliability) in people's scores ($r = 0.85$ for men and 0.84 for women, $p = 0.001$).

4. Dissimulation. To examine the effects of instruction or motivational set on the SAI, students in one administration were asked to purposely make their responses dissimilar by following different administration instructions. The students (20 men and 20 women) were told to: answer honestly, try to make a favorable impression, or try to make an unfavorable impression. The instructional/motivational variable did make a difference. Both men and women had higher scores in the "fake good" condition than in the "normal" or "fake bad" condition. This suggests that most of the respondents believed that it is socially desirable to be more sexually anxious than they actually were. The women in the "fake bad" condition had lower scores than in the "normal" condition. However, for some of the men, the pattern was reversed;

Continued

Self-Assessment—*Continued*

they scored higher on anxiety when asked to "fake bad" and reported less anxiety when asked to "fake good."

5. Factor analysis of the SAI and the MFCGI Sex Guilt subscale. Another factor analysis, this time of the SAI and Sex Guilt items, was conducted with the responses of 228 of the initial subjects. The SAI and Sex Guilt items did tend to load on different factors, which is another indication they are measuring different constructs.

6. Concurrent validity. Finally, Janda and O'Grady investigated whether the sex anxiety and sex guilt were related to sexual experiences. They administered the Sexual Experiences Inventory to 72 women and 113 men who had not taken any of the measures previously. Through their regression analysis, they found that for the female students, sex anxiety and sex guilt predicted the extent of sexual experiences ($r = 0.72$, $F [2, 69] = 37.29$, $p = 0.001$). For the men, however, only sexual anxiety was helpful in predicting sexual experiences ($r = 0.41$, $f [1,110] = 11.09$, $p = 0.001$). The lower multiple correlation for men, however, may have been influenced by the restricted range of men's sexual experiences scores (more experienced) compared to those of the women. The analyses of the psychometric properties of the SAI and its relationship to related measures indicate that is a sound, valid scale. Janda and O'Grady suggested it may be useful in clinical settings. For example, it might be useful to sex therapists in assessing the relative contributions of sexual anxiety versus sex guilt to sexual dysfunctions and planning treatment accordingly. They also proposed additional research questions that could be investigated using this scale. Are sex guilt and sexual anxiety aroused by the same kinds of situational cues? What are the relationships among the concepts of sexual guilt, sexual anxiety, and moral shame?

The development of a measurement scale of demonstrated reliability and validity is an important contribution to clinical assessment, measurement of therapeutic progress, and research. This is one reason your professional discipline, which you may have entered with more of a goal of "helping" than "researching," requires courses in statistics and psychometrics!

Reference

Janda, L. H. & O'Grady, K. E. (1980). Development of a sex anxiety inventory. *Journal of Consulting and Clinical Psychology, 48,* 169–175.

behavior (Catania et al., 1990). However, this assumes that the couples' self-reports are valid, which may not be the case. Catania et al. (1990) concluded that satisfactory validity measures of self-report data on sexual behavior are lacking.

CONSIDERATION: The spread of HIV and AIDS has spurred a great deal of research investigating the level of high-risk sexual behavior in our society and the specific subpopulations that are more likely to engage in high-risk sexual behavior. Such investigations are essential in estimating the spread of HIV and AIDS, identifying subpopulations to be targeted for intervention, and evaluating programs designed to reduce HIV transmission. Research in this area relies heavily on self-report data on such topics as number of sexual partners, types of sexual activities, and condom use. Yet, how valid are these data?

Do research participants underreport the number of sexual partners? Do people who say they use a condom every time they engage in intercourse really use a condom every time? Catania at al. (1990) asked an important question:

> To what extent does the increased use of condoms reported in the gay community over the past 5 years reflect socially desirable responses in the face of increased social pressure by the gay community to use condoms or actual behavior change? (p. 347).

Because of the difficulties in validating self-reports of number of sexual partners and condom use, we may not be able to answer this question. However, according to Catania et al., (1990), "current estimates of high-risk [for contracting HIV] sexual behavior among adults in the United States are probably underestimates" (p. 343).

EXHIBIT 4.2 Before You Believe the Conclusions of a Sex Research Study. . .

Although sex research may furnish a basis for making choices in sexuality, it is wise to be cautious about research. Some issues to keep in mind in evaluating a sex research study include:

Sample

Is the sample a probability (i.e., representative) sample, or is it a nonprobability sample that is not representative of the population to which it refers? If the sample is not representative, the conclusions are limited only to the specific group of people studied.

Randomization

If the research involves manipulating the research variable to assess its effects on one or more dependent variables, were the research participants randomly assigned to either an experimental or control group? If not, you cannot be sure that any observed changes in the dependent variable are due to the independent variable.

Researcher Bias

Is the researcher biased in the questionnaire or interview or in interpreting the data? Remember that some scholars believe that, because researchers are human, it is impossible for a researcher not to be biased. It may be important, however, to know what the researcher's bias is in order to evaluate that researcher's findings. For example, it may be important to know if a researcher supports or opposes legal abortion in interpreting that researcher's findings on the psychological effects of having an abortion.

Male Bias

Some scholars have observed that some sex research is biased toward male sexual experience as the model for healthy human functioning. For example, since men usually ejaculate each time they have intercourse, a researcher with a male bias might assume that women should experience orgasm each time they have intercourse. Some research may also use only males as research participants, in which case generalizations made to females may be inaccurate.

Self-Presentation Bias

To what degree is the topic of the sex research so personal that respondents might want to distort their answers or deceive the researchers? For example, if the researcher asked questions about the number of sexual partners, did the respondents give a high number out of boasting or a low number out of guilt? If the researcher asked questions about the sexual behavior of the respondents over the last five years, were the respondents able to accurately recall their behavior of five years ago?

Terminology

In survey research, did the researcher use sexual terminology that the respondents understood?

Reliability and Validity

To what degree are the data reliable and valid?

Age of Data

When were the data collected? The Kinsey data that formed the basis for *Human Sexual Behavior in the Human Male* and *Human Sexual Behavior in the Human Female* were collected in the 1940s. The data are old and may no longer reflect current sexual attitudes and behaviors.

In addition to assessing reliability and validity, other aspects of research must be considered in order to interpret research findings. Some of these are detailed in Exhibit 4.2.

MAJOR SEX STUDIES

Although social scientists have the research methods, statistical techniques, and skills to conduct quality sex research, they have encountered considerable resistance to doing so. Byrne (1977) noted that an historical analysis of research on sexual behavior shows that sexuality research began with less taboo concerns, such as animal sexual behavior, sexuality in other cultures, and abnormal sexual behavior. With the publication of the first Kinsey report in 1948:

> the data hit the fan. . . people were reading about themselves and their friends and neighbors with respect to masturbation practices, incidence of premarital intercourse, homosexual episodes, extramarital experiences, average weekly rate of coitus for their age group and so on. (Byrne, 1977, pp. 5-6)

Reinisch and Beasley (1990) commented on the specific reaction to the Kinsey studies:

> Some members of the clergy declared that he [Kinsey] was doing the devil's work. McCarthyism was in full swing by the time the second volume was released, and one Congressman insisted that studying human sexual behavior was paving the way for a Communist takeover of the United States. Kinsey and his research became the subject of a special investigative committee of the House of Representatives. Responding to pressure from Congress, the Rockefeller Foundation withdrew financial support after many years as the major source of Kinsey's funding. (p. xviii)

Although sex researchers today are less often accused of being immoral and communistic or lose their jobs (see Magoun, 1981), they and their research are still held suspect. For example, although the National Academy of Sciences and the Institute of Medicine strongly supported a new national study on sexual behavior that was sponsored by the National Institute on Child Health and Human Development, it was blocked by President Bush's Office of Management and Budget. Some of the conservative opponents of the survey charged that the adult survey represented "the politics of the homosexual movement" (Freiberg, 1990, p. 22).

> Very little information exists about sexual behavior, so a lot of scientists are curious . . . . But if the government is going to be paying for something like this, we have to justify it from a public health standpoint.
> *Rayford Kytle*

Another national survey on teen sexual behavior was blocked by Health and Human Services Secretary Louis Sullivan. The proposed five-year, $18 million government-funded study would have questioned 24,000 junior and senior high school students. However, the "red flag went up because some of the conservative groups and family coalition groups started a campaign to discredit it" (Cabrera, 1991).

In the following pages, we present some of the more important studies on human sexuality. These include classic studies (e.g., Kinsey, Masters and Johnson), and examples of studies on selected populations (adolescents) and studies on selected topics (gender-role issues). The list is not exhaustive, and other research studies will be referred to throughout the text.

The Original Kinsey Studies on Sexual Behavior

Numerous references are made in this text to sexuality studies conducted by Alfred C. Kinsey and his colleagues. These efforts constitute the first comprehensive study of reported sexual behavior. Data were collected through face-to-face interviews with 5,300 men and 5,940 women. Each interview included between 350 and 521 questions (Pomeroy, 1976). The research of Kinsey and his colleagues, which was published in *Sexual Behavior in the Human Male* (1948) and *Sexual Behavior in the Human Female* (1953), investigated such topics as masturbation; petting; premarital, marital, and extramarital intercourse; attitudes toward sexuality; and social patterns affecting sexual patterns.

While no study has duplicated the scope of the Kinsey studies, some reservations should be kept in mind about the data. These concerns include the nonrepresentativeness of the sample, the age of the study, and the reliance on respondents' recall.

Kinsey's sample has been criticized as being nonrepresentative because it consisted of a disproportionate number of college students, urbanites, Protestants, college-educated people, young adults, and people living in Indiana and the northeast. Also, while some blacks were interviewed, only interviews with whites were reported in the Kinsey publications. Regarding the age of the data, earlier we pointed out that the Kinsey studies may be of limited value today since they reflect data collected over 45 years ago. Sexual behavior today is presumably quite different from sexual behavior in the 1940s. Another weakness of the original Kinsey studies was their reliance on the respondents' ability to recall information accurately. The question "How many persons have you had intercourse with?" required respondents to remember events that occurred up to 40 years earlier. Some of the Kinsey data, therefore, is probably flawed due to inaccurate recall; however, Kinsey did check the reliability of the data by reinterviewing some of his respondents. As we noted earlier in the section on reliability, data provided by respondents on the frequencies of various sexual behaviors were found to be much less reliable than data on the incidence questions.

In spite of these concerns, the Kinsey volumes on male and female sexuality are still regarded by most sex researchers as two of the most extensive research studies on sexuality ever published. In the words of Brecher (1969),

> The effect of the Kinsey Reports was to subject human sexuality to sober and rational examination. Helping to remove sex from the realm of mystery, they educated millions of people and profoundly affected their opinions regarding sexuality. (p. 104)

The Kinsey Institute Study on Sexual Values

To provide data on emotional and value aspects of sexuality not obtained in previous Kinsey studies, the Institute for Sex Research at Indiana University conducted a study that was published as *Sex and Morality in the U.S.* (Klassen, Williams, & Levitt, 1989). This study was based on data obtained in 1970 through questionnaires and face-to-face interviews of 3,018 adults who constituted a national representative sample.

> Human sexuality is a domain of knowledge and experience that is not only of scientific, scholarly, and personal human interest, but it also has political, legal, and religious significance in many societies.
>
> *June Reinisch*
> *Ruth Beasley*

The results of the original Kinsey studies, which indicated that a high frequency of sexual behavior was occurring, shocked much of the U.S. public. The subsequent Kinsey study on sexual values revealed that "a majority disapproved of homosexuality, prostitution, extramarital sex, and most forms of premarital sex. Even masturbation, a near-universal behavior among males, was disapproved of by 48% of our respondents" (p. 17). Other findings suggest that younger people tend to be less conservative than their elders and that women tend to be more conservative than men. The more—educated respondents were generally not as conservative as those with less education.

A major limitation of the Kinsey Institute study on sexual values is that it is based on data obtained over 20 years ago. Nevertheless, these data provide a valuable baseline to which more current data can be compared. The data are also valuable because they are based on a national representative sample.

> Indeed, it was the first and, as far as can be ascertained, it remains the only national survey centered wholly on the sexual experiences and the sexual norms of a representative sample of the adult American population. . . the much needed national data base for studying the moral context of sexual conduct (p. xxii)

A further strength is the comprehensiveness of the study. The researchers examined 70 variables and their correlations with the sexual values of the respondents (as measured by the Sexual Morality Scale).

The Kinsey Report on Sexual Knowledge

To provide information about the degree to which U.S. citizens are knowledgeable about sexuality, the Kinsey Institute, in conjunction with the Roper Organization, questioned a national statistically representative sample of 1,974 adults in the fall of 1989. It published its findings in *The Kinsey Institute New Report on Sex* (Reinisch & Beasley, 1990).

The study included face-to-face interviews and a written test of sexual knowledge. Respondents were instructed to "circle one answer after reading each question carefully." There were 18 multiple-choice questions on the test, each question had either three or 12 answers to choose from. The 18 test questions are listed in Table 4.3 (multiple choice answers are not provided in this table).

Reinisch and Beasley reported that 55% of respondents "failed" the test of sexual knowledge, that is, 55% correctly answered only half the questions or fewer. Twenty-seven percent answered ten to 11 questions correctly, 14% answered 12 to 13, and 4% answered 14 to 15 correctly. Less than 1% (0.5%) answered 16 to 18 items correctly.

TABLE 4.3 **The Kinsey Institute/Roper Organization National Sex Knowledge Test***

1. Nowadays, what do you think is the age at which the average or typical American first has sexual intercourse?
2. Out of every ten married American men, how many would you estimate have had an extramarital affair—that is, have been sexually unfaithful to their wives?
3. Out of every ten American women, how many would you estimate have had anal (rectal) intercourse?
4. A person can get AIDS by having anal (rectal) intercourse even if neither partner is infected with the AIDs virus.
5. There are over-the-counter spermicides people can buy at the drugstore that will kill the AIDS virus.
6. Petroleum jelly, Vaseline Intensive Care, baby oil, and Nivea are *not* good lubricants to use with a condom or diaphragm.
7. More than one out of four (25%) of American men have had a sexual experience with another male during either their teen or adult years.
8. It is usually difficult to tell whether people are or are not homosexual just by their appearance or gestures.
9. A woman or teenage girl can get pregnant during her menstrual flow (her "period").
10. A woman or teenage girl can get pregnant even if the man withdraws his penis before he ejaculates (before he "comes").
11. Unless they are having sex, women do not need to have regular gynecological examinations.
12. Teenage boys should examine their testicles ("balls") regularly just as women self-examine their breasts for lumps.
13. Problems with erection are most often started by a physical problem.
14. Almost all erection problems can be successfully treated.
15. Menopause, or change of life as it is often called, does not cause most women to lose interest in having sex.
16. Out of every ten American women, how many would you estimate have masturbated either as children or after they were grown up?
17. What do you think is the length of the average man's erect penis?
18. Most women prefer a sexual partner with a larger-than-average penis.

*Answers (according to Reinisch and Beasely [1990]): 1) 16 to 17 years old; 2) three to four out of ten; 3) three to four out of ten; 4) false; 5) true; 6) true; 7) true; 8) true; 9) true; 10) true; 11) false; 12) true; 13) true; 14) true; 15) true; 16) six to eight out of ten; 17) five to seven inches; 18) false.

Source: Copyright © 1990 by the Kinsey Institute for Research in Sex, Gender, and Reproduction. From the book *The Kinsey Institute New Report on Sex* and reprinted through arrangement with St. Martin's Press, Inc., New York.

Masters and Johnson's Research on Sexual Response

Two of the most widely known names in contemporary sex research are Masters and Johnson. William Masters and Virginia Johnson are co-directors of the Masters and Johnson Institute in St. Louis, Missouri. Their publications *Human Sexual Response* (1966) and *Human Sexual Inadequacy* (1970) were on the nonfiction best-seller list of the *New York Times* within four weeks after their respective releases. The first book was a result of 12 years of research in which 694 participants experienced more than 10,000 orgasms under laboratory conditions. The purpose of conducting this research was to examine the physiological reactions to sexual stimulation. Based on their observations, Masters and Johnson identified four stages of sexual response (see Chapter 7 on sexual response). The sequel focused on the treatment of sexual problems, such as lack of orgasm, erectile dysfunction, and early ejaculation.

Rubin's Assessment of the Sexual and Gender Revolutions

In an attempt to understand the sexual and gender revolutions, Lillian B. Rubin (*Erotic Wars,* 1991), a psychologist and sociologist at Queens College, New York, interviewed 375 teenagers (ages 13 to 17) and 300 adults (ages 18 to 48) about the intimate details of their sexual history and its meaning to them. In addition, she had 600 additional respondents (mostly college students) from eight colleges and universities complete a 13-page questionnaire, giving her a total sample of 1,275 respondents.

Rubin's sample consisted of various social classes (30% working class, 45% middle class, and 25% upper middle class), races (88% white, 5% black, 5% Asian, and 2% Latino), and ages. Religious beliefs ranged from Christian fundamentalism to agnosticism and atheism. However, Rubin's research was directed only toward the heterosexual orientation. References to Rubin's research are found throughout the text.

Virginia Johnson and William Masters

National Surveys of Adolescents

NATIONAL DATA: Three fifths of the 1,800 adolescent males in a national study reported that there was "an almost certain chance" that they would use a condom if they had intercourse with a new partner. Three-fifths of sexually experienced males said that they had used a condom during their last intercourse experience) (Pleck, Sonenstein, & Ku, 1990).

The Institute for Survey Research of Temple University interviewed 1,800 adolescent males in 1988 (Pleck, Sonenstein, & Ku, 1990). The sample is one of the largest representative samples of noninstitutionalized never-married males ages 15 to 19 in the continental United States. A self-administered questionnaire was completed by the respondents. The study was prompted by concerns over the high rate of premarital pregnancy and the spread of AIDS. Results are described in margin data.

Another example of a study focusing on adolescents is Suzanne Ageton's (1983) study on sexual assault. In Ageton's study a nationally representative sample of adolescents (11 to 17 years old at the start of the study) was interviewed every year for a 5-year period. The longitudinal design is important, as it allowed identification of characteristics prior to an adolescent's experiencing or perpetrating sexual abuse.

Magazine Surveys

Questionnaires about sexuality and relationships can commonly be found in such magazines as *Cosmopolitan, Playboy, Redbook,* and *New Woman.* Readers may complete the questionnaire and mail their responses to the magazine editor. The questionnaire responses are compiled and the survey results are published in a subsequent issue of the magazine.

The editors of *New Woman* magazine received completed questionnaires from over 15,000 readers about their respective interpersonal relationships (Schwartz & Jackson, 1989). Sixty-one percent of these respondents reported that they had "excellent" or "very good" marriages. One characteristic of these happy marital relationships was a high frequency of sexual intercourse— 8 to 12 occasions each month.

Cosmopolitan magazine reported findings about divorce based on completed questionnaires from 20,000 of its readers who were divorced or who were considering divorce. Seventy-two percent of the divorced respondents reported that a major reason for their divorce was "sexual incompatibility"; in 90% of the cases, one partner lost passion for the other (Bowe, 1992). Younger women were more likely to have lost passion and less likely to report that their partners lost passion for them; older women reported the reverse.

Magazine editors also hire research organizations to conduct surveys for them. Editors of *New Woman* hired Yankelovich, Clancy, and Shulman in 1990 to conduct a national survey of U.S. households in regard to new gender issues between women and men. Yankelovich et al. telephoned 600 adult women and 601 adult men and asked them a series of questions. A major finding was that the ideal man and woman (according to both men and women) have the same characteristics: they are caring and nurturing (Rubenstein, 1990).

CONSIDERATION: The results of magazine surveys should be viewed with caution because the data are based on biased samples. The responses to the survey questions are provided only by those people who are readers of a particular magazine. We can safely assume that readers of different magazines differ from each other in many ways, including attitudes and behaviors. Furthermore, those readers who complete magazine surveys probably differ from those readers who do not complete the surveys. Therefore, the findings of any particular magazine survey are only generalizable to other readers of that magazine who completed the survey.

CHOICES

We conclude this chapter by identifying some choices that we make regarding sex research. These choices include: Should I become informed about sex research? Should I accept sex research findings? Should I be a participant in sex research? And should taxpayers fund sex research?

Choose to Become Informed about Sex Research?

Some of the sexuality decisions you make might benefit from sex research relevant to the choices with which you are confronted. Rather than rely on an opinion from a friend or a professional, you might seek and obtain information from specific sex research studies relevant to your decision. For example, a woman considering postponing having a child until after her career is established may benefit from reading recent research about the safety of childbearing in later ages. A man who has difficulty creating and maintaining an erection might benefit from reading research concerning the causes and treatments of erectile dysfunction.

Computers in most libraries allow you to do a topical search of the sex research available in regard to the specific choice with which you are confronted. The choice to take the time to become aware of relevant sex research may be an important one.

Choose to Accept Findings of Sex Research?

If you make the choice to become informed about relevant sex research, you have another choice in regard to whether you accept the findings of the sex research you read. In the late 1960s, Congress created a commission to investigate the effects of pornography and obscenity on U.S. citizens. After a review of the literature on pornography and after conducting its own research, the commission concluded that, in general, pornography was not harmful and recommended that "federal, state, and local legislation should not seek to interfere with the right of adults who wish to read, obtain, or view explicit sexual materials" (*Report of the Commission on Obscenity and Pornography,* 1970, 57). After reading the Report, President Richard Nixon promptly rejected both the findings and recommendations of the report.

While Nixon's rejection of scientific sex research may have been politically motivated, he did exercise his choice to do so. You also have a choice to accept, reject, or withhold judgment of the findings of sex research. If you read enough sex research in a particular area, a general direction of findings emerges—alcohol during pregnancy harms the fetus, living together before marriage is not a guaranteed method of ensuring a happy marriage, and condoms with the spermicide nonoxynol-9 help to protect against contracting the AIDS virus. Hence, choosing to accept sex research is an issue of reading the available research and evaluating the studies for yourself on the basis of the cautions presented in this chapter.

Choose to Be a Participant in Sex Research?

As a student at a college or university, you may be asked to complete a questionnaire or participate in an interview as part of a sex research project being conducted by one of your professors. As long as you are informed about the nature and purpose of the study, protected from physical and psychological harm, guaranteed confidentiality and anonymity, and have the option to decide not to particpate without penalty, you might consider doing so. (Reputable researchers will willingly provide the requested information; students should feel free to ask.)

Participating in sex research may be beneficial to you in that it may lead you to process experiences in a productive way. For example, some women who responded to the *Cosmopolitan* survey mentioned earlier said that answering the questionnaire was " 'a cathartic experience' that helped them sort through feelings about their own divorce for the first time" (Bowe, 1992, p. 199).

In addition, the willingness of each person who participates in sexuality research benefits the larger society. The sexual information you share with a researcher (which is later disseminated in professional journals) may, it is hoped, permit all of us to make more informed choices.

Should Taxpayers Fund Sex Research?

While many taxpayers value sex research and are willing to subsidize sexuality research studies, other taxpayers object to sexuality research and feel they should not be required to fund it. Abramson (1990) noted that public resistance to funding sexuality research may stem,

Continued

Continued

in part, from negative feelings surrounding sexuality. "Sexual science invokes a variety of emotional responses (e.g., disgust, shame, guilt, etc.) which directly undermine both the legitimacy and progress of sex research" (Abramson, 1990, p. 150). Even scholars in various academic fields undervalue sexuality as an academic discipline and thus fail to support the funding of sexuality studies. Abramson noted that "the collection of basic data on human sexual functioning has not been a scholarly priority" (p. 156).

However, in order to answer important questions about such issues as the spread of HIV and other STDs, teenage pregnancy, child sexual abuse, pornography, sexual dysfunctions, and the role of sexuality in intimate relationships, we need to support sexuality research. If we fail to do so, "future generations will find it incomprehensible—perhaps unconscionably negligent—that so little effort was marshalled to obtain data on and establish a science of human sexual behavior" (Abramson, 1990, 162).

Summary

1. It is as important to know how to evaluate sex research as it is to know how to conduct it.
2. Research on sexuality is interdisciplinary, including psychology, public health, sociology, biology, social work, family studies, and medicine.
3. Research may be cross-sectional (one point in time), longitudinal (across time), qualitative (involving interpretations of respondent), or quantitative (percentages, frequencies).
4. Feminist researchers have observed a male bias in most sex research and are committed to a more balanced research agenda.
5. Steps involved in conducting research include formulating a research question, reviewing the literature, formulating one or more hypotheses, and defining the variables in the study.
6. Most sex research is conducted on nonprobability samples, which limit the generalizability of the findings.
7. Methods of data collection used in research include experiments, surveys, field research, case studies, historical research, and diaries.
8. Researchers who conduct research with human participants must follow ethical and professional guidelines that protect the participants' welfare.
9. Correlation (two variables are related) is not causation (one variable causes another). Most sex research is correlational.
10. Sex research is more valuable to the degree that it is both reliable (repeated measures yield the same result) and valid (measures what it purports to measure).
11. Alfred C. Kinsey (with his colleagues) is regarded as providing the first large-scale studies on the sexuality of women and men. However, the early Kinsey studies are dated and methodologically limited.
12. Masters and Johnson have provided detailed information about the physiology of human sexual response. Their research has been criticized because of the lack of qualitative information.
13. Magazine surveys are to be regarded as specific to the population of readers who participate in the studies. Most magazine surveys are not generalizeable to the larger population.

KEY TERMS

sexology
biosexology
psychosexology
sociosexology
cross-sectional research
longitudinal research
qualitative research
quantitative research
hypothesis
variable
dependent variable
independent variable
sample
population
representative sample
biased sample
nonprobability sampling
convenience sampling
randomization
probability sampling
participation bias
experiments
experimental groups
field research
control groups
clinical trial
survey
case study
correlation
positive correlation
negative correlation
curvilinear correlation
spurious correlation
reliability
validity

REFERENCES

Abramson, P. R. (1990). Sexual science: Emerging discipline or oxymoron? *Journal of Sex Research, 27,* 147–165.

Ageton, S. S.(1983). *Sexual assault among adolescents.* Lexington, MA: Lexington Books.

Ard, B. N. (1990). *The sexual realm in long-term marriages.* San Francisco: Mellen Research University Press.

Armstrong, P., & Armstrong, H. (1987). Beyond numbers: Problems with quantitative data. In G. H. Nemiroff (Ed.), *Women and men: Interdisciplinary readings on gender* (pp. 54–79). Markham, Ontario: Fitzhenry & Whiteside.

Bartell, D. (1970). Group sex among the mid-Americans. *Journal of Sex Research, 6,* 113–130.

Bogdan, R. (1974). *Being different: The autobiography of Jane Fry.* New York: Wiley.

Bowe, C. (1992, February). Everything we think, feel, and do about divorce. *Cosmopolitan.* pp. 199–203.

Bozett, F. W. (1988). Gay fatherhood. In P. Bronstein and C. P. Cowan (Eds.), *Fatherhood today: Men's changing role in the family* (pp. 214–235). New York: John Wiley.

Brecher, E. M. (1969). *The sex researchers.* Boston: Little, Brown.

Byrne, D. (1977). Social psychology and the study of sexual behavior. *Personality and Social Psychology Bulletin, 3,* 3–30.

Byrne, D. (1986). Introduction: The study of sexual behavior. In D. Byrne and K. Kelley (Eds.), *Alternative approaches to the study of sexual behavior* (pp. 1–12). Hillsdale, NJ: Lawrence Erlbaum Associates.

Cabrera, D. (1991, July 21). Teen sexual behavior survey put on hold. *The Daily Reflector*, Greenville, NC, p. A1.

Catania, J. A., Gibson, D. R., Chitwood, D. D., & Coates, T. J. (1990). Methodological problems in AIDS behavioral research: Influences on measurement error and participation bias in studies of sexual behavior. *Psychological Bulletin, 108,* 339–362.

Christopher, F. S., & Roosa, M. W. (1991). Factors affecting sexual decisions in the premarital relationships of adolescents and young adults. In K. McKinney and S. Sprecher (Eds.), *Sexuality in close relationships* (pp. 111–133). Hillsdale, NJ: Lawrence Earlbaum Associates.

Coleman, E. (1990). Expandng the boundaries of sex research. *Journal of Sex Research, 27,* 473–480.

Davis, R. A. (1990). Working women and the popular print media: A changing view of motherhood. *Free Inquiry in Creative Sociology, 18,* 43–47.

DeLamater, J. (1974). Methodological issues in the study of premarital sexuality. *Sociological Methods and Research, 3,* 30–61.

D'Emilio, J., & Freedman, E. B. (1988). *Intimate matters: A social history of sexuality in America.* New York: Harper and Row.

Donnerstein, E., & Berkowitz, L. (1981). Victim reactions in aggressive erotic films as a factor in violence against women. *Journal of Personality and Social Psychology, 41,* 710–724.

Douglas, J. D., Rasmussen, P. H., & Flanagan, C. A. 1977. *The nude beach.* Beverly Hills: Sage.

Duggan, L. (1990). From instincts to politics: Writing the history of sexuality in the U.S. [Review essay]. *Journal of Sex Research, 27,* 95–109.

Eichler, M. (1987). The relationship between sexist, non-sexist, woman-centered, and feminist research in the social sciences. In G. H. Nemiroff (Ed.), *Women and men: Interdisciplinary readings on gender* (pp. 21–53). Markham, Ontario: Fitzhenry & Whiteside.

Ellis, H. (1936). *Studies in the psychology of sex.* New York: Random House.

Freedman, E. B. & D'Emilio, J. (1990). Problems encountered in writing the history of sexuality: sources, theory and interpretation. *The Journal of Sex Research, 27,* 481–495.

Freiberg, P. (1990, August). Stalled sex surveys elicit APA protest. *APA Monitor,* pp. 22, 23.

Freud, S. (1977). *On sexuality.* Harmondsworth, England: Pelican Freud Library.

Gebhard, P. H. (1969). Human sex behavior research. In M. Diamond (Ed.), *Perspectives in reproduction and sexual behavior* (pp. 391–410). Bloomington: Indiana University Press.

Gelis, J. (1991). *History of childbirth: Fertility, pregnancy and birth in early modern Europe.* R. Morris, (Trans.). Boston: Northeastern University Press.

Gergen, M. M. (1988). Toward a feminist metatheory and methodology in the social sciences. In M. M. Gergen (Ed.), *Feminist thought and the structure of knowledge* (pp. 87–104). New York: New York University Press.

Hallstrom, T., & Samuelsson, S. (1990). Changes in women's sexual desire in middle life: The longitudinal study of women in Gothenberg. *Archives of Sexual Behavior, 19,* 259–268.

Harding, S. (1987). Introduction: Is there a feminist method? In S. Harding (Ed.), *Feminism and methodology: Social science issues* (pp. 1–12). Bloomington: Indiana University Press.

Harvey, J. H., Christensen, A., & McClintock, E. (1983). Research methods. In H. H. Kelley, E. Bersheid, A. Christensen, J. H. Harvey, T. L. Huston, G. Levinger, E. McClintock, L. A. Peplau and D. R. Peterson (Eds.), *Close relationships* (pp. 1–58). San Francisco: Freeman.

Hetherington, S. F., & Soeken, K. L. (1990). Measuring changes in intimacy and sexuality: A self-administered scale. *Journal of Sex Education and Therapy, 16,* 155–163.

Hite, S. (1987). *Women in love: A cultural revolution in progress.* NY: Alfred A. Knopf.

Hull, H., Bettinger, C., Gallaher, M., Keller, N., Wilson, J., & Mertz, G. (1988). Comparison of HIV-antibody prevalence in patients consenting to and declining HIV-antibody testing in an STD clinic. *Journal of the American Medical Association, 260,* 935–938.

Humphreys, L. (1970). *Tearoom trade: Impersonal sex in public places.* Chicago: Aldine.

Irvine, J. M. (1990). *Disorders of desire: Sex and gender in modern American sexology.* Philadelphia: Temple University Press.

Jaccard, J., & Dittus, P. (1991). *Parent-teen communication: Toward the prevention of unintended pregnancies.* New York: Springer-Verlag.

Jayaratne, T. E. (1981). The value of quantitative methodology for feminist research. In G. Bowles and R. Duelli-Klein (Eds.), *Theories of women's studies II* (pp. 140–161). Berkeley: University of California, Women's Studies Department.

Katz, J. N. (1976). *Gay American history: Lesbians and gay men in the U.S.A.* New York: Thomas Crowell.

Katzer, J., Cook, K. H., & Crouch, W. W. (1991). *Evaluating information: A guide for users of social science research* (3rd ed.). New York: McGraw-Hill.

Kinsey, A. C., Pomeroy, W. B., & Martin, C. E. (1948). *Sexual behavior in the human male.* Philadelphia: Saunders.

Kinsey, A. C., Pomeroy, W. B., Martin, C. E., & Gebhard, P. H. (1953). *Sexual behavior in the human female.* Philadelphia: Saunders.

Klassen, A. D., Williams, C. J., & Levitt, E. E. (1989). *Sex and morality in the U.S.* Middletown, CN: Wesleyan University Press.

Leiblum, S. R., & Rosen, R. C. (1988a). Introduction: Changing perspectives on sexual desire. In S. R. Leiblum and R. C. Rosen (Eds.), *Sexual desire disorders* (pp. 1–20). New York: Guilford Press.

Leiblum, S. R., & Rosen, R. C. (1988b). Conclusion: conceptual and clinical overview. In S. R. Leiblum and R. C. Rosen (Eds.), *Sexual desire disorders* (pp. 446–458). New York: Guilford Press.

Lief, H. I., Fullard, W., & Delvin, S. J. (1990). A new measure of adolescent sexuality: SKAT-A. *Journal of Sex Education and Therapy, 16,* 79–91.

Magoun, H. W. (1981). John B. Watson and the study of human sexual behavior. *Journal of Sex Research, 17,* 368–378.

Malatesta, V. J., Pollack, R. H., Crotty, T. D., & Peacock, L. J. (1982). Acute alcohol intoxication and female orgasmic response. *Journal of Sex Research, 18,* 1–17.

Masters, W. H., and Johnson, V. E. (1966). *Human sexual response.* Boston: Little, Brown.

Masters, W. H., and Johnson, V. E. (1970). *Human sexual inadequacy.* Boston: Little, Brown.

McHugh, M. C., Koeske, R. D., & Frieze, I. H. (1986). Issues to consider in conducting nonsexist psychological research. *American Psychologist, 41,* 879–890.

McKinney, K. (1986). The sociological approach to human sexuality. In D. Byrne and K. Kelley (Eds.), *Alternative approaches to the study of sexual behavior* (pp. 103–129). Hillsdale, NJ: Lawrence Erlbaum Associates.

Miller C., with Treitel, C. (1991). *Feminist research methods: An annotated bibliography.* New York: Greenwood Press.

Millstein, S., & Irwin, C. (1983). Acceptability of computer-acquired sexual histories in adolescent girls. *Journal of Pediatrics, 103,* 815–819.

Mohr, J. C. (1978). *Abortion in America: The origins and evolution of national policy, 1800-1900.* New York: Oxford University Press.

Money, J., & Ehrhardt, A. (1972). *Man and woman, boy and girl.* Baltimore: Johns Hopkins.

Nachmias, D., and Nachmias, C. (1987). *Research methods in the social sciences* (3rd ed.). New York: St. Martin's Press.

Orbuch, T. L., & Harvey, J. H. (1991). Methodological and conceptual issues in the study of sexuality in close relationships. In K. McKinney & S. Sprecher (Eds.), *Sexuality in close relationships* (pp. 9–24). Hillsdale, NJ: Lawrence Erlbaum Associates.

Petersen, D. M., & Dressel, P. L. (1982). Equal time for women: Social notes on the male strip show. *Urban Life, 11,* 185–208.

Pleck, J. H., Sonenstein, L., & Ku, L. C. (1990). Contraceptive attitudes and intention to use condoms in sexually experienced and inexperienced adolescent males. *Journal of Family Issues, 11,* 294–312.

Pollis, C. A. (1988). An assessment of the impacts of feminism on sexual science. *Journal of Sex Research, 25,* 85–105.

Pomeroy, W. B. (1976). Kinsey and the Institute. In M. S. Weinberg (Ed.), *Sex Research: Studies from the Kinsey Institute* (pp. 34–59). New York: Oxford University Press.

Prus, R., & Irini, S. (1988). *Hookers, rounders, and desk clerks: The social organization of the hotel community.* Salem, WI: Sheffield.

Reading, A. (1983). A comparison of the accuracy and reactivity of methods of maintaining male sexual behavior. *Journal of Behavioral Assessment, 5,* 11–23.

Reinisch, J. M., & Beasley, R. (1990). *The Kinsey Institute new report on sex: What you must know to be sexually literate.* New York: St. Martin's Press.

Report of the commission on obscenity and pornography. (1970). New York: Bantam Books.

Rosen, R. (1982). *The lost sisterhood: Prostitution in America, 1900-1918.* Baltimore: Johns Hopkins University Press.

Rubenstein, C. (1990, October). The *New Woman* survey. *New Woman,* pp. 158–163.

Rubin, L. B. (1991). *Erotic wars: What happened to the sexual revolution?* New York: Harper Perennial.

Schwartz, P., & Jackson, D. (1989, February). How to have a model marriage. *New Woman,* 66–74.

Shotland, R. L., & Goodstein, L. (1983). Just because she doesn't want to doesn't mean it's rape: An experimentally based causal model of the perception of rape in a dating situation. *Social Psychology Quarterly, 46,* 220–232.

Skeen, D. (1991). *Different sexual worlds: Contemporary case studies of sexuality.* Lexington, MA: Lexington Books.

Smith, R., & Walters, J. (1988). Sexual guilt. Unpublished paper, University of Georgia, Department of Child and Family Development, Athens. Used by permission.

Statistical abstract of the United States: 1990 (110th ed.). (1989). Washington, DC: U.S. Bureau of the Census.

Szasz, G., McLoughlin, M. G., & Warren, R. J. (1990). Return of sexual functioning following penile replant surgery. *Archives of Sexual Behavior, 19,* 343–348.

Tavris, C. (1992). *The Mismeasure of Women.* New York: Simon & Schuster.

Tiefer, L. (1988). A feminist perspective on sexology and sexuality. In M. McCanney Gergen (Ed.), *Feminist thought and the structure of knowledge.* (pp. 16–26). New York: New York University Press.

Townsend, J. M. & Levy, G. D. (1990). Effects of potential partner's physical attractiveness and socioeconomic status on sexuality and partner selection. *Archives of Sexual Behavior, 19,* 149–164.

Ward, K. B., & Grant, L. (1985). The feminist critique and a decade of published research in sociology journals. *Sociological Quarterly, 26,* 139–157.

Warren, C. (1974). *Identity and community in the gay world.* New York: Wiley.

White, J. R., Case, D. A., McWhirter, D., & Mattison, A.M. (1990). Enhanced sexual behavior in exercising men. *Archives of Sexual Behavior, 19,* 193–210.

Weeks, J. (1989). *Sex, politics, and society: The regulation of sexuality since 1800.* New York: Longman.

Zeiss, A. M., Davies, H. D., Wood, M., & Tinklenberg, J. R. (1990). The incidence and correlates of erectile problems in patients with Alzheimer's disease. *Archives of Sexual Behavior, 19,* 325–331.

CHAPTER FIVE

Theories of Sexuality

Chapter Outline

Biological Theories
- Physiological Theories
- Evolutionary Theories

Psychological Theories
- Psychoanalytic Theories
- Learning Theories
- Cognitive/Affective Theories

Sociological Theories
- Symbolic Interaction Theories
- **Theoretical Perspective:** Gang Rape at Fraternity Houses: A Social Script View
- Structural-Functional Theories
- Conflict Theories
- Systems Theories

Feminist Theories
- **Self-Assessment:** Attitude Toward Feminism Scale
- Liberal Feminism
- Radical Feminism
- Socialist Feminism
- Multicultural Feminism

Essentialist Versus Social Constructionist Views of Human Sexuality

Theoretical Views on Human Sexuality: An Integrated Approach

Choices
- Choose to Be a Parental Model for Affection?
- Choose to View Desires for Specific Sexual Behaviors as Learned?

Is It True?*

1. Humans are the only species among whom adult females have permanently enlarged breasts, independent of lactation.

2. Negative reinforcement is another term for punishment.

3. Most theories of sexuality view sexuality in the context of interpersonal relationships.

4. Sexual desire is an example of an aspect of human sexuality that can only be explained by biological theories.

5. Some fraternities have made attempts to teach their members to relate to women in nonexploitative, nonabusive ways.

* 1=T, 2=F, 3=F, 4=F, 5=T

Sexuality is a topic as diverse as any relating to human behavior. One of the exciting aspects of the field is that it can be and, indeed, is viewed from a wide variety of conceptual perspectives.

James H. Greer
William T. O'Donohue

Some common questions about human sexuality are:

Why are men more sexually aggressive than women?

Why is pornography primarily consumed by men?

Why do women (in contrast to men) express greater interest in love and commitment than in lust and genital sex?

Why does our society define homosexuality as deviant?

Why are men in most societies allowed to have a variety of sexual partners?

We can only fully understand our needs and desires when we grasp the social and historical forces, the unconscious motivations, and the personal and collective responses that shape our sexualities.

Jeffrey Weeks

Theories in sexuality provide a way for us to understand and answer such questions about human sexuality. The purpose of this chapter is to provide an overview of the major theoretical approaches to studying sexuality, including biological, psychological, sociological, and feminist approaches. We also discuss essentialist and social constructionist views of sexuality, as well as an approach that integrates various theories of sexuality. We begin with a review of biological theories.

Biological Theories

Biological theories of sexuality include a) physiological theories that focus on the role of physiology in sexuality and b) evolutionary theories that explain sexual behavior on the basis of our evolutionary past.

Physiological Theories

Many aspects of physiological functioning affect and are affected by sexual behavior. Cardiovascular, respiratory, neurological, and endocrinological functioning, as well as genetic factors, are all involved in sexual behaviors and processes. Physiological theories of sexuality attempt to describe and explain how various physiological factors affect and are affected by sexuality. For example, what are the physiological processes involved in sexual desire, arousal, lubrication, erection, and orgasm? How do various drugs and medications affect sexual functioning? How do various hormones influence sexuality? Is the experience of love associated with physiological changes? To what degree can we attribute observed differences between females and males to their different hormonal makeups?

Human sexuality has a biological base. The neurophysiology of sexual arousal, the mechanics of sexual intercourse, and the production and release of gametes appear to be the same in every human society.

John DeLamater

Physiological aspects of sexual functioning are emphasized throughout this text. Therefore, we will not discuss in detail the physiology of sexual functioning here. We do wish to note, however, one major problem in physiological theories of sexuality, especially theories concerning how various hormones influence sexuality.

To a large degree, hormonal theories of human sexuality have been based on animal studies. Yet, generalizing research findings from animals to humans should be done with considerable caution, if at all. Hormonal influence may be greater in

Generalizing research findings from animals to humans must be done with extreme caution.

animals than in humans. The latter are subject to a variety of psychological, social, and cultural factors that influence sexual behavior; therefore, it is far more difficult to demonstrate the effects of variations in hormones in humans than in lower animals.

Evolutionary Theories

Evolutionary theories of sexuality attempt to explain human sexual behavior and sexual anatomy on the basis human evolution. Evolutionary theory is associated with Charles Darwin (although Darwin himself did not use the term *evolution*) who, in 1859, published *Origin of Species*. According to evolutionary theories of sexuality, sexual behaviors and traits evolve through the process of "natural selection." Through natural selection, individuals who have genetic traits that are adaptive for survival are more likely to survive and pass on their genetic traits to their offspring.

Several features of human sexuality and anatomy unique to the human species have been explained using evolutionary theory. These unique features include a) concealed ovulation (i.e., ovulation in humans is not accompanied by external cues) and b) permanent adult female breast enlargement (in other female species, breast enlargement only occurs during lactation) (Gallup, 1986).

Gallup (1986) explained that concealed ovulation evolved to ensure "continuous male provisioning" (p. 28). If our female ancestors exhibited signs of ovulation, then males theoretically would be attentive to them (in terms of providing for their food and other survival needs) only during ovulation. Because males could not detect when ovulation occurred, they were more likely to provide continuous care for the female.

In explaining why adult human females have enlarged breasts, Gallup (1986) noted that several evolutionary theories have been proposed, including: a) enlarged female breasts, which resemble the buttocks, evolved to compensate for the development of bipedalism (i.e., upright posture) and the consequent shift in intercourse positions from rear-entry to face-to-face and b) enlarged breasts evolved as an appendage for infants to hold onto. Another explanation, proposed by Gallup, is that enlarged breasts signal the male that the female has reached sexual maturity and is potentially capable of reproducing.

Evolutionary theories have also attempted to explain social differences between women and men as a product of different reproductive strategies. These theories are discussed in detail in Chapter 8, Gender Roles. In Chapter 14, Love and Sexuality, you will encounter evolutionary theories of love.

CONSIDERATION: Evolutionary theory explains the development of sexual reproduction itself. Some organisms do not require another organism in order to reproduce; this form of reproduction is known as **asexual reproduction.** For example, some worms reproduce by *fragmentation*—a form of asexual reproduction in which a piece or fragment of the parent breaks off and develops into a new organism. Male honeybees are reproduced through another form of asexual reproduction called parthenogenesis, in which a specialized egg cell produced by a female develops directly into a new organism.

According to evolutionary theory, sexual reproduction, that is, the reproduction of organisms through mating of males and females, probably evolved because it introduces greater variablity in the species (Daly & Wilson, 1978). While asexual reproduction most often produces offspring that are identical to the parent, sexual reproduction produces offspring that reflect traits of two distinct parents. Through this variability that results from sexual reproduction, humans are better able to adapt to their changing environment.

In concluding this section on biological theories, we note that while biological theories of sexuality are central to our understanding of sexuality, they are also limited. Robert Padgug (1989) noted:

> Biological sexuality is the necessary precondition for human sexuality. But biological sexuality is only a precondition, a set of potentialities, which is never unmediated by human reality, and which becomes transformed in qualitatively new ways in human society. (p. 19)

Part of the joy of being human often lies in transcending the biological constraints that have, nevertheless, shaped us.
John A. W. Kirsch
James D. Weinrich

Psychological Theories

Psychologists have developed various theories to explain human sexual behavior. These theories include psychoanalytic theories, learning theories, and cognitive/affective theories.

Psychoanalytic Theories

Psychoanalytic theory, which was originally developed by Sigmund Freud (1888–1939), emphasizes the role of the unconscious in our lives. Freud's thinking dominated the early views of the nature of human sexuality and how it influenced a person's life. Freud's ideas about personality structure and personality development are important for understanding his theories of sexuality.

Structure of Personality Freud believed that each person's personality consists of the id, ego, and superego. The **id** refers to instinctive biological drives, such as the need for sex, food, and water. Human sexuality was seen as a biological force that drove individuals toward the satisfaction of needs and desires. The id seeks immediate gratification of the sexual urge. Wanting to suck a nipple or have an ejaculation or orgasm were viewed as natural desires of the person's id.

Another part of the personality, the **ego**, regulates the desires of the id. Whereas the id is self-centered and uninhibited, the ego is that part of the person's personality

Sigmund Freud's emphasis on the influence of sexuality on one's personality continues today.

that inhibits the id in order to conform to social expectations. While the id operates on the "pleasure principle," the ego operates on the "reality principle." The ego ensures that individuals do not attempt to fulfill every need and desire whenever they occur.

The **superego** is the person's conscience, which guides the individual to do what is morally right and good. It is the superego that creates feelings of guilt when the ego fails to inhibit the id and the person engages in socially unacceptable behavior.

CONSIDERATION: Consider a person in your human sexuality class to whom you feel sexually attracted. Freud would say your id is operating to create lustful fantasies in reference to this person. You might like to go up to this person and begin a sexual encounter with him or her. But your ego keeps you in check and prevents you from making a fool of yourself. Your ego reminds you that it is inappropriate to engage in sexual behavior with someone whom you hardly know in a classroom setting. Your superego makes you feel guilty for having such lustful thoughts because you may already be in a committed relationship. Your superego recommends that you abandon such lustful thoughts and focus on your own partner.

Personality Development Freud emphasized that one's personality develops in stages. When we successfully complete one stage, we are able to develop to the next stage. If we fail to successfully complete any given stage, we become fixated, or stuck in that stage. The five basic stages Freud identified were the oral, anal, phallic, latency, and genital stages.

In the **oral stage**, which begins in the womb and lasts about a year and a half, infants derive pleasure from sucking, licking, chewing, and putting objects in their mouth. Infants at this age derive a great deal of pleasure from activity associated with their mouths, and their ids are constantly in search of oral gratification. From a Freudian perspective, an adult who likes only to tongue kiss and to give oral sex may be fixated in the oral stage.

According to Freud, the oral stage is followed by the **anal stage**, which begins about age 1 1/2 and lasts until about age 3. During the anal stage, the infant's pleasures shift from the mouth to the anus, and gratification results from the retention and elimination of both urine and feces. Adults who enjoy giving and getting "golden showers" (urinating during sexual encounters) might, according to Freud, be regarded as fixated in the anal phase.

Freud noted that children between the ages of three to six enter the **phallic stage**, in which they regard their genitals as the primary source of pleasure. During this phallic stage, the id encourages the child to stimulate the genitals, but the superego recognizes society's rules and associates self-stimulation with shame, anxiety, and/or guilt, and the ego inhibits the child from masturbating. This is the stage during which the Oedipal and Electra complexes develop in boys and girls, respectively. These complexes, which attempt to explain gender differences between females and males, are described in Chapter 8, Gender Roles.

The fourth stage of psychosexual development according to Freud is the **latency stage.** This stage lasts from about age six to the onset of puberty and is characterized by the repression of the sexual urges. Children in the latency stage are viewed as being asexual.

The fifth stage, called the **genital stage**, begins at puberty, when adolescents develop mature sexual feelings for opposite-sex members in socially appropriate contexts. According to Freud, adolescents who do not make the transition into the genital stage may be fixated at an earlier stage. Psychoanalysis provides a way to untangle the repressed feelings of a fixation at an earlier stage so that mature sexuality may emerge. Table 5.1 provides an overview of the various stages of psychosexual development.

"Freud, up against the Victorian era, was impressed by the importance of sex in human life" (Wisdom, 1992, p. 17). He proposed that **libido** (the sex drive) was the most important of human instincts. He used this concept to explain not only sexual lust, but also neuroses and extraordinary achievements through his theory that libido had three outlets: normal sex, neurosis, and sublimation. However, even though his libido theory has been described as "a great piece of thinking" (p. 20) and "ingenious" (p. 36), it has been criticized as overemphasizing sexual motivation for behavior.

Some clinicians and theorists initially attracted to psychoanalytic interpretations of human behavior later extended Freud's work (Anna Freud, Erikson, and other ego-analysts). They along with more culturally-oriented writers such as Karen Horney, recognized the importance of childhood personality development, but they believed that social, rather than sexual, factors were dominant in personality formation (Ford & Urban, 1963). They felt that the need to emerge from the helpless controlled state of an infant to that of an independent, autonomous individual was the driving force of the individual. Sex played a minor role in the drive for independence.

Erikson (1950) also acknowledged that individuals progress through a series of stages as they develop, but, unlike Freud, he felt that the stages were psychosocial, not psychosexual. Erikson believed that central developmental tasks did not involve seeking oral, anal, and genital pleasures but rather establishing basic trust with people. Also, Erikson felt that personality formation did not end in adolescence but was a lifelong process (most contemporary psychologists agree).

TABLE 5.1 Freud's Five Stages of Psychosexual Development

Stage	Age	Characteristics
Oral	Womb to 18 months	Pleasures are derived primarily from meeting oral needs of sucking, licking, and chewing. Pleasure principle dominates, and id focuses on meeting pleasure needs.
Anal	1 1/2 to 3 years	Pleasures shift to anal needs and are derived from retention and elimination of urine and feces. Pleasure principle and id are still dominant mechanisms.
Phallic	3 to 6 years	Pleasures shift to stimulation of genitals. Masturbation may be practiced, and ego negotiates with id and superego for social control of sexual impulses. Oedipus and Electra complexes develop during this period.
Latency	6 to puberty	Repression of sexual urges.
Genital	Adolescence	Shift away from immature masturbation to appropriate peer-sex interaction.

Unlike Freud, Karen Horney emphasized the importance of social rather than sexual factors in personality development.

Some of Freud's concepts are also difficult to verify using the standards of scientific objectivity required today. The presence of unconscious processes operative in the Oedipus and Electra complexes are very difficult to assess empirically. Freud's ideas, according to Wisdom (1992, p. 13) "should all be regarded, not as hypotheses, still less as established, but as great seminal ideas like those all the known sciences have sprung from." It should also be noted that Freud was a psychiatrist whose observations were based on people with problems. Hence, his sample of human behavior may have been biased toward psychopathology.

CONSIDERATION: In spite of the many criticisms of Freudian theory, Freud is credited with "discovering" the sexuality of children. He demonstrated that "infantile sexual development had profound consequences for the adult's erotic life and character structure . . ." (Person, 1987, p. 385).

Learning Theories

Learning theories basically view sexual attitudes and behaviors as learned. The major learning theories include operant learning theory, classical conditioning theory, and social learning theory.

Operant Learning Theory

Operant learning theory, largely developed by B. F. Skinner, emphasizes that behavior is a function of the consequences that follow the occurrence of a behavior. Operant learning theory states that the consequences of a behavior influence whether or not that behavior will occur in the future.

Consequences that follow a behavior may increase or decrease the behavior. An increase in a behavior as a result of the consequences that follow is known as **reinforcement.** A decrease in a behavior as a result of the consequences that follow is known as **punishment.** There are two types of reinforcement and punishment: positive and negative. Positive reinforcement and positive punishment involve increasing or decreasing a behavior through adding a stimulus. Negative reinforcement and negative punishment involve increasing or decreasing a behavior through removing a stimulus. Let's look at some examples of how reinforcement and punishment may explain sexuality-related behavior.

1. *Positive reinforcement.* Consider the case of a man who inserts his finger into his partner's vagina while he performs oral sex. His behavior was followed by a stimulus provided by the woman in the form of verbal approval ("I really like it when you do that."). Hearing her comment increased the frequency with which he inserted his finger into her vagina during oral sex. This is an example of positive reinforcement because a behavior (inserting a finger in the vagina during oral sex) increased as a result of adding a stimulus (the woman's verbal approval).
2. *Negative reinforcement.* Suppose a woman who has been raped by a date attends a group therapy session for rape survivors and, as a result, begins to feel less guilty and anxious about her date rape experience. Consequently, the woman decides to attend the group therapy meeting on a weekly basis. This is an example of negative reinforcement because a behavior (attending group therapy sessions) increased as a result of removing a stimulus (guilt and anxiety).
3. *Positive punishment.* A woman tells her partner that she is attracted to someone at work. The partner becomes jealous and reacts by making accusatory remarks. Consequently, the woman no longer discloses attractions to others to her partner. This is an example of positive punishment because a behavior (disclosure of attraction) decreased as a result of adding a stimulus (the partner's accusatory remarks).
4. *Negative punishment.* A gay woman tells her dormmates, with whom she has had a friendly relationship for six months, that she is gay. After her disclosure, the dormmates seem to ignore her; they no longer ask her to go to lunch with them or out on the weekends, and they rarely engage her in friendly conversation. The

B. F. Skinner emphasized that sexual behavior is learned on the basis of its consequences.

gay woman consequently learns to keep her gay identity hidden from casual friends. This is an example of negative punishment because a behavior (disclosure of sexual orientation) decreased as a result of removing a stimulus (friendly interactions with dormmates).

Table 5.2 illustrates the distinctions between positive reinforcement, negative reinforcement, positive punishment, and negative punishment.

In summary, the operant learning view of human sexuality emphasizes that we learn sexual behaviors through the consequences of those behaviors. Behavior is increased or maintained through positive and negative reinforcement and is decreased or eliminated through positive and negative punishment.

Classical Conditioning Theory **Classical conditioning** may be defined as the process whereby a stimulus that is originally not linked with a reflex or response comes to be so linked. Pavlov, a Russian physician of the early 1900s observed that the presence of food caused dogs to salivate. As salivation is a natural reflex to the presence of food, we call food an *unconditioned stimulus*. However, if Pavlov rang a bell and then gave the dogs food, they soon learned that the bell meant that food was forthcoming, and they would salivate to the sound of the bell. Hence, the bell became a *conditioned stimulus* because it had become associated with the food and was now capable of producing the same response as the food (an unconditioned stimulus).

The process of classical conditioning may explain why some individuals develop sexual fetishes. A fetish is a previously neutral stimulus that becomes a conditioned stimulus for erotic feelings. For example, some people have feather, foot, or leather fetishes, and they respond to these stimuli in erotic ways. But there is nothing about a feather that should serve to elicit erotic feelings unless the feather has been associated with erotic feelings in the past.

How could a person become conditioned to view a feather as an erotic stimulus? Perhaps the person may have masturbated and picked up a feather and rubbed it on his or her genitals. Or the person may have observed a stripper in person or on film who used a feather as part of the strip. In either case, the feather would become a conditioned stimulus and would elicit erotic feelings in the same way the masturbation and naked body served as an unconditioned stimulus.

Three other concepts are relevant to the classical conditioning theory of sexuality: extinction, generalization, and discrimination. *Extinction* means that the conditioned stimulus loses its capacity to elicit the previous response. If Pavlov rings a bell but does not follow it with food, the dogs soon learn that the bell is not associated with food, so they stop salivating when they hear it. When two lovers stop sharing romantic dialogue and erotic escapades and begin arguing and having a miserable

TABLE 5.2 Concepts of Operant Learning Theory

Operant Learning Concept	Stimulus	Effect on Behavior
Positive reinforcement	Added	Increases
Negative reinforcement	Removed	Increases
Positive punishment	Added	Decreases
Negative punishment	Removed	Decreases

time together, their stimulus value for each other changes. Loving responses that once resulted from the sight or sound of the partner have become extinguished.

Generalization means that a stimulus similar to a conditioned stimulus may have the same effect as the unconditioned stimulus or the conditioned stimulus. Pavlov's dogs may salivate to a buzzer as well as a bell. Likewise, red-framed glasses on a stranger may elicit similar erotic feelings as the current lover who also wears red-framed glasses.

Discrimination refers to the capability of a person to select out the original conditioned stimuli from stimuli that are similar and respond only to the former. Pavlov taught his dogs not to salivate to the sound of any bell but only to the sound of a specific bell. In reference to human sexuality, people in monogamous relationships choose to discriminate among the people who are sexually available to them and to respond only to their partner in erotic ways.

CONSIDERATION: Mistrust and jealousy are among the most frequently encountered feelings in human relationships. These feelings may result from the perception that the partner is not selective and discriminating in his or her response to people who signal that they are emotionally and/or sexually available.

Social Learning Theory Another learning-based approach to understanding human sexuality is social learning theory, which is largely based on the work of Bandura (1969). While **social learning theory** incorporates concepts of operant learning theory, it emphasizes the process of learning through observation and imitation. Observational learning occurs through observing a model demonstrate attitudes or behavior. For example, we may imitate the sexual attitudes and behaviors that we observe in our parents, peers, and siblings. In addition, images from the media (television, movies, and magazines) provide models of sexual behavior.

Much of one's sexuality is learned through interaction with peers.

Bandura (1977) revised his original version of social learning theory to include cognitive processes. The integration of cognitive theory with social learning theory stems from the recognition that we do not respond passively to models, reinforcers, and punishers in our environment. Rather, we actively filter and interpret environmental influences through our thought processes. Next, we look at cognitive/affective theories, which emphasize the role of thought processes and emotions.

Cognitive/Affective Theories

The importance of cognitions in human life was recognized nearly 2,000 years ago by Epictetus, a philosopher who said, "Man is disturbed not by things but by the view that he takes of them" (quoted in Walen & Roth, 1987, p. 335). A number of theorists have attempted to describe the relationship between cognition and affect (i.e., emotion).

Aaron Beck and Albert Ellis have emphasized that cognition precedes emotion. To Ellis and Beck, emotional distress is largely a product of distressing thoughts that are characterized by "misconception, distortion, exaggeration, and horrific evaluation" (Walen & Roth, 1987, p. 337).

Albert Ellis (1962), founder of rational emotive therapy (RET), provided examples of irrational cognitions. Four core irrational evaluative cognitions and their relevance to sexuality follow:

1. Should statements—reflecting a belief that there are universal rules or "musts." Example: "I must be able to have an orgasm, or I will be abnormal."
2. Need statements—reflecting a belief that one must have certain things in order to live or function happily. Example: "I need to stop masturbating, or I will be unable to develop a happy interpersonal relationship."
3. Human worth statements—reflecting a belief that people can be categorized and rated. Example: "Beautiful people are more desired and have happier lives."
4. "Awfulizing" statements—reflecting a belief that there is a terrible, even catastrophic event occurring in our lives. Example: "I have genital herpes, and no one will ever want to touch me again. I may as well commit suicide."

CONSIDERATION: The goal of rational emotive therapy is to challenge and modify clients' irrational beliefs in order to alleviate negative and distressing emotions. However, many women want men to stop withdrawing emotionally, to stop being so rational, and to express their raw emotions more openly. Thus, it is possible that therapies such as RET are simply perpetuating and reinforcing a method of emotion control already used by a great number of men in Western society. It is interesting to speculate that for every woman who has known the frustration of having a man explain to her why her emotion is neither appropriate nor rational, there is probably a man who has been instructed from his earliest years that he ought not experience any emotions at all. (Fitness & Strongman, 1991, p. 185)

One application of cognitive theory to human sexuality involves the therapist viewing some sexual problems as a result of irrational beliefs (Baucom & Epsten, 1989). Partners who are having sexual problems may benefit by examining their beliefs and assessing the degree to which these contribute to the sexual problem.

For example, the way a couple perceives early ejaculation influences their individual and relationship happiness. One wife said that her husband ejaculated prematurely because he did not really like her and that this was his way of frustrating

By now, it is common knowledge that our most significant sex organ is not located between our legs, but between our ears: the cognitive activity of the brain can quickly either augment or inhibit a sexual response cycle.

Susan Walen
David Roth

her by making sure that she did not have an orgasm. This belief created resentment and unhappiness. As a result of cognitive therapy (which is based on cognitive theory), she changed her thoughts in regard to her husband's early ejaculation. She chose to view her husband's early ejaculation as a learned behavior, rather than as an expression of his presumed negative feelings for her. Together, they used the squeeze technique (discussed in Chapter 15, Sexual Dysfunctions and Sex Therapy) to teach the husband how to delay his ejaculation. Once he was able to delay his ejaculation, the wife's cognitions changed to "he loves me and cares about my being sexually satisfied." These new thoughts (which resulted from a choice on her part to view his early ejaculation as learned) had a positive outcome and increased the couple's happiness.

Grammer (1989) noted that cognitive processes also play a major role in the presentation of one's self during courtship. Women, according to Grammer, emphasize their physical attractiveness and their potential to produce offspring, while men emphasize their economic potential. These traits are deliberately emphasized because of the belief that they are valued by the opposite-sex partner.

While emotions are often viewed as related to cognitions, they are also studied as a separate phenomenon. In a discussion of emotions and sexuality, DeLamater (1991) noted that emotions (such as love, anxiety, and depression) may precede sexual expression. Emotion may also be viewed as a component of sexual expression. Lastly, emotion (such as embarrassment, anxiety or fear, frustration, and satisfaction) may be a consequence of sexual activity.

Sociological Theories

While psychological theories focus on individuals and how they develop personality traits and process information, sociological theories focus on the interaction between individuals, groups, and societies. Sociology emphasizes that much of human behavior is a reflection of the society in which it occurs (DeLamater, 1987) and can be understood in reference to the social context of which it is a part. Social context influences all aspects of human life.

> The social context limits alternatives, restricts decisions, and creates outcomes. The thoughts and behaviors of individuals have more to do with their social relationships, the social context in which they live, and the social organizations of which they are a part, than any inherent personality characteristic(s). (Zusman, 1992, p. 4)

Every society shapes, structures and constrains the development and expression of sexuality in all of its members.

Frank Beach

Various sociological theories focus on different aspects of social contexts and how they influence human behavior. Here, we will discuss three sociological theoretical perspectives: symbolic interaction, structural-functional, and conflict.

Symbolic Interaction Theories

Symbolic interaction theories suggest that human behavior is based on definitions and meanings and that these definitions and meanings are learned through interaction with others. For example, our definitions of what is appropriate and inappropriate sexual behavior are learned through our relationships with others. Sexual self-concept, including body image and perception of one's self as an emotional and sexual partner, is also influenced by interactions with others.

The concept of "social scripts" is an important component of symbolic interaction theory. **Social scripts** are shared interpretations and expected behaviors of a social situation. The social scripts we learn influence how we perceive a situation, the meanings we attribute to it, and the behaviors in which we engage. Much of our sexual behavior is influenced by the social scripts we learn concerning sexuality (Gagnon, 1977; Gagnon & Simon, 1973). Gagnon (1983) observed that ". . . no one will be a satisfactory sexual member of a culture without acquiring at least a partial version of the relevant intrapsychic and interpersonal scripts and cultural scenarios" (p. 40).

Scripts have two dimensions: external and internal. The external dimension refers to shared meanings or sexual understandings of two actors. These shared meanings are conveyed through words and gestures and serve to cue individuals as to the appropriate and expected behaviors.

The internal dimension of sexual scripts refers to physiological changes that occur within the individual as a result of attaching sexual meanings to environmental stimuli. Viewing pornography, watching a love scene, or feeling the touch of a partner's lips may trigger physiological arousal (erection for the man and vaginal lubrication for the woman). These are learned reactions to stimuli in the culture that have been labeled as sexual.

Children are dependent on others for definitions of what is sexual. Young children stroking their genitals are not masturbating in the same sense that a 15-year-old would be. The latter has developed a script about sexual organs and learned ways of producing different sexual feelings and interprets these feelings as sexual. Unlike young children, adults have developed sexual scripts that, like blueprints, specify the whos (persons of similar age, race, social class?), whats (porno movie, whips and chains?), whens (after marriage, how soon after meeting?), wheres (parent's house, car, own apartment?), and whys (intimacy, lust, pregnancy?) for sexual activity.

The content of a social script varies by the culture in which a person lives. It is the culture that gives meaning to behavior. While men who wear women's clothes in U.S. culture are regarded as transvestites (and sometimes transsexuals), in Myanmar (formerly Burma), men dress up like women for religious reasons. By doing so, they confirm that they are married to the spirit god of Manguedon and can function as an intermediary for those seeking good fortune and success (Coleman, 1990). The culture dictates that the behavior has a religious significance only.

This male from India who is dressed up as a female goddess at a festival has learned that this social script is appropriate.

CONSIDERATION: Different cultures designate different stimuli as sexually arousing. Although our society imbues the female breasts with considerable erotic potential, other societies attach no sexual significance to them. In those societies, the sight or touch of a woman's breasts will not produce an erection or physiological response since no sexual meaning is attached to them.

In the following Theoretical Perspective, we look at how the social scripts that some fraternity members learn may contribute to episodes of gang rape. We also note recent efforts by fraternities to change the social scripts that their members learn in regard to sexual behavior toward women.

THEORETICAL PERSPECTIVE

Gang Rape at Fraternity Houses: A Social Script View

In the last decade, media attention has focused the public's eye on the problem of rapes that occur in fraternity houses at U.S. colleges and universities (Freeman, 1990). One estimate suggests that over 90% of all gang rapes on college campuses involve fraternity men (Tash, 1988). While there are various explanations for why some fraternity men participate in gang rape (see Chapter 19), here we focus on the social script theory.

Martin and Hummer (1989) conducted research on fraternities as social contexts that encourage the sexual coercion of women. Their analysis suggested that the social scripts fraternity members learn contribute to sexual coercion of women. Martin and Hummer identified the following social scripts that are promoted in this context:

1. Excessive concern with masculinity. Fraternity members strive to maintain a macho image.

> Valued [fraternity] members display, or are willing to go along with, a narrow conception of masculinity that stresses competition, athleticism, dominance, winning, conflict, wealth, material possessions, willingness to drink alcohol, and sexual prowess vís-a-vís women. (Martin & Hummer, 1989, p. 461)

2. Loyalty, group protection, and secrecy. In an alleged gang rape at Florida State University, all but one of the approximately 150 fraternity brothers were accused by the university and criminal justice officials of lying to protect the fraternity.
3. Alcohol use. Fraternity men are expected to drink alcohol and to use alcohol to obtain sex. At some fraternity parties, women are served alcohol and are then taken advantage of sexually. The woman who was gang raped at Florida State was unconscious during the rape and almost died of alcohol overdose.
4. Fraternities' exploitation of women. Martin and Hummer stated that

> . . . fraternities knowingly, and intentionally, use women for their benefit. Fraternities use women as bait for new members, as servers of brothers' needs, and as sexual prey. (1989, p. 467)

Sexual exploitation of women among fraternity members has been considered normative within the context of some (not all) fraternities, despite the fact that our society regards gang rape as a deviant and criminal act. However, rather than view the fraternity members as deviant, sociologists emphasize the fraternity as a social context that teaches its member deviant social scripts.

In recent years, many fraternities have actively campaigned against sexual exploitation of women and have made significant attempts to change the social scripts that fraternity men learn. For example, the Pi Kappa Phi Foundation distributed a publication entitled "What Is Sexual Abuse?" with the instructions that it be read at the next meeting of its chapters and posted on the chapters' bulletin board. The publication concludes with the following message: "Please take the time to educate your chapter as well as other fraternities on your campus, so the next female abused will not be your sister, your girlfriend, or someone you know."

Pi Kappa Phi has also been recognized for its efforts to bring awareness of the problem of date rape to the country's college campuses. For example, Pi Kappa Phi fraternities around the country have put up posters of Nicolas Poussin's painting *The Rape of the Sabine Women* saying, "Today's Greeks call it date rape." Underneath, in smaller print, it says, "Against her will is against the law."

References

Freeman, P. (1990, December 17). Silent no more. *People,* pp. 94–104.

Martin, P. Y., & Hummer, R. A. (1989). Fraternities and rape on campus. Gender and Society, 3, 457–473. Used by permission.

Tash, G. B. (1988). Date rape. *Emerald of Sigma Pi Fraternity, 75,* pp. 1–2.

The major limitation of social script theory is that it does not explain how or why specific scripts originate. For example, why does a society teach women sexual scripts that differ from those scripts learned by men? Two other sociological theories, structural-functional theory and conflict theory, attempt to answer this question.

Structural-Functional Theories

According to **structural-functional theories**, society is made up of interconnected parts that operate together to achieve social stability. Social behavior may either be functional or dysfunctional. Functional behavior is behavior that contributes to social stability; dysfunctional behavior disrupts social stability. Structural-functional theory assumes that society develops and maintains social roles and norms that contribute to social stability. For example, the different traditional roles that women and men have occupied in the family may be viewed, according to structural-functional theory, as necessary for family stability (Parsons & Bates, 1955).

In a classic and controversial study on prostitution, Kingsley Davis (1937) proposed that prostitution is functional for society.

> Enabling a small number of women to take care of the needs of a large number of men, it [prostitution] is the most convenient sexual outlet for an army, and for the legions of strangers, perverts, and physically repulsive in our midst. It performs a function, apparently, which no other institution fully performs. (p. 754)

The institution of marriage, which is based on the emotional and sexual bonding of individuals, may be viewed as functional for society. For example, marriage provides a structure in which children are born and socialized to be productive members of society. Divorce, that is, the breakup of a marriage, is often considered dysfunctional for society since it disrupts the socialization of children.

The functionalist model views family as essential for reproducing and socializing new members of society (i.e., children). Thus, from a functionalist view, homosexuality has been defined as deviant because it fails to result in families that produce and socialize children.

CONSIDERATION: Jeffrey Weeks (1991) suggested that the functionalist argument against homosexuality is flawed.

> A functionalist model which sees the family as an essential and necessary agent of social control, and with the role of ensuring efficient reproduction, ignores both the constant ineffectiveness of the family in doing so and the immense class variations in family forms. (p. 23)

Structural-functional theory is criticized on the basis that it is tautological, that is, it uses circular reasoning. Specifically, structural-functional theory says that some aspect of society (e.g., gender roles, prostitution, marriage) is the way it is because it is functional. Yet, how do we know if something is functional? According to the theory, we know something is functional if it remains a part of the social system.

Another criticism of structural-functional theory is that it overlooks the role of power in our society. Conflict theories examine how those in power influence society and social behavior.

Conflict Theories

While structural-functional theories view society as comprised of different parts working together, **conflict theories** view society as comprised of different parts competing for power and resources. Conflict theories focus on how social power imbalances between men and women influence sexual norms (including scripts) and behavior. For example, rape and sexual assault may be viewed as an abuse of power that some men engage in as an attempt to intimidate women and remind women of their subordinate role (Brownmiller, 1975; Russell, 1982). Committing violent crime may be one way that otherwise powerless men can "prove" their masculinity (Basow, 1992, p. 322). A conflict view of sexuality emphasizes that sexual aggression against women is an expression of male dominance. "Dominance eroticized defines the imperatives of masculinity, submission eroticized defines femininity" (MacKinnon, 1987, p. 69).

CONSIDERATION: Male dominance has also resulted in a male bias in the language used to describe sexuality. " 'We had sex three times' thus typically means the man entered (penetrated) the woman three times and orgasmed three times" (MacKinnon, 1987, p. 72). Similarly, the term *foreplay* suggests that patterns of noncoital pleasuring behavior are "appetizers," rather than the "main course."

Conflict theories also explain why some aspects of sexuality and sexual behavior are (and are not) defined as deviant. For example, from a conflict theory perspective, prostitution and homosexuality are threats to our capitalistic system; prostitution offers women an alternative source of income, and homosexuality fails to produce potential members of the work force (i.e., children). Thus, prostitution and homosexuality are defined as deviant to dissuade individuals from adopting these lifestyles. Conflict theory also explains why some behaviors are not defined as deviant. For example, being a prostitute is much more socially stigmatized than being a john (customer of a prostitute) and prostitutes are arrested more frequently than johns. This may be explained on the basis of the power imbalance between men and women and the fact that men primarily make and enforce laws. Similarly, until fairly recently, rape in marriage was not viewed as a crime punishable by law. It is primarily men who have made our laws; therefore, marital rape laws have been made to protect men, rather than women. (Marital rape laws have changed significantly to give women more protection; see Chapter 19).

Real equality means never having to say you're premenstrual.

Carol Tavris

From a conflict perspective, Szasz (1980) has criticized the medical profession as labeling certain sexual attitudes and behaviors as forms of illness that require medical treatment that physicians offer for a price. Thus, some sexual "dysfunctions" may be explained as existing because the medical profession has "created" them in order to profit by treating them. In Exhibit 5.1, we describe how premenstrual syndrome may be viewed from three sociological theoretical perspectives: symbolic interaction, structural-functional, and conflict.

Systems Theories

One criticism of many theories of sexuality is that they fail to recognize the interpersonal relationship aspect of sexuality (Tiefer, 1991). McKinney and Sprecher (1991) noted that "researchers in the area of sexuality have traditionally ignored the relationship and examined the *individual's* sexuality" (p. 4). A **systems theory** approach to studying sexuality emphasizes the role of interpersonal and relationship aspects of sexuality.

One application of systems theory in understanding sexuality is in the area of sexual dysfunctions. For example, while a biological view of low sexual desire emphasizes the role of hormones or medications and a psychological view might emphasize negative cognitions and emotions regarding sexual arousal, a systems

EXHIBIT 5.1 Three Sociological Views on Premenstrual Syndrome

During the premenstrual phase of a woman's menstrual cycle, some women experience symptoms that have become known as premenstrual syndrome (PMS). These symptoms include tender breasts, weight gain due to retention of water, food cravings, and emotional symptoms such as depression and irritability. PMS has been explained largely by biological theories; that is, hormonal changes during the premenstrual phase are supposedly responsible for the symptoms associated with premenstrual syndrome (see also Chapter 6, Sexual Anatomy and Physiology).

However, Carol Tavris, a noted social psychologist and writer on women's issues, noted that

> biomedical researchers have taken a set of bodily-changes that are normal to women over the menstrual cycle, packaged them into a "Premenstrual Syndrome," and sold them back to women as a disorder, a problem that needs treatment and attention. (1992, p. 133)

Tavris (1991, 1992) provided sociological explanations for the existence of PMS. Although Tavris did not identify them as such, her explanations of PMS may be viewed according to three sociological theories: symbolic interaction, structure-function, and conflict.

Symbolic Interaction Theory

As you may recall, symbolic interaction theory focuses on how meanings and definitions are learned through interaction with others and how these meanings and definitions influence behavior. Tavris suggested that women learn the idea that once a month, they are "at the mercy of their hormones." Thus, they are likely to attribute any negative moods or experiences during that once-a-month time to premenstrual hormonal changes.

Tavris also described how men are influenced by socially created meanings and definitions of PMS:

> If you give men those same checklists of symptoms (reduced or increased energy, irritability and other negative moods, back pain, sleeplessness, headaches, confusion, etc.), men report having as many "premenstrual symptoms" as women do—when the symptoms aren't called PMS. If the identical checklist is titled "Menstrual Distress Questionnaire," however, men miraculously lose their headaches, food cravings, and insomnia. (1992, p. 148)

Structure-Function Theory

Tavris cited the work of anthropologist Emily Martin at Johns Hopkins University, who examined medical concerns about menstruation in relation to the labor force. Martin noted that during times of job scarcity, studies focused on the debilitating effects of the premenstrual phase on women's job performance. For example, one study published in 1931 (during the Depression) discussed premenstrual women's "ill-considered actions" on the job. At the start of World War II, when men were fighting a war and women were needed in the work force, "studies suddenly found that menstruation and 'premenstrual tension' were not problems for working women or their employers. After the war, the pendulum swung back again" (Tavris, 1991, p. 38). Thus, the conclusion drawn is that "when women's participation in the work force is seen as a threat instead of a necessity, menstruation is called a liability" (p. 38).

This explanation fits structure-function theory in two ways. First, it explains historical variation in conceptions of the premenstrual phase on the basis of what is functional for the society at a given period in history. Second, this view focuses on how a social institution, in this case the economic institution, affects another social pattern (i.e., social definitions of menstruation and the premenstrual phase).

Conflict Theory

Conflict theory explains social patterns on the basis of how they benefit some group in terms of money and/or power. Tavris noted that the growing focus on PMS may stem from the fact that more research money has been granted to researchers studying menstruation as a disease or a physiological abnormality than to researchers studying menstruation as a normal process. In addition, drug companies profit from perpetuating the "myth of PMS."

> Drug companies . . . stand to make a great deal of money if every menstruating woman would take a few pills every month. It's in the drug companies' interest . . . if physicians and the public confuse the small minority of women who have severe premenstrual symptoms with the majority who have normal, undrugworthy cycles. (1991, pp. 36, 38)

While drug companies and physicians profit monetarily from treating so-called PMS, another group profits in terms of maintaining power and status—men. The belief that premenstrual women are subject to irrational behavior, work inefficiency, and emotional irritability supports negative stereotypes about women, which maintains the social power and status imbalance between the sexes. We are led to the conclusion that "how fortunate we are that men are running things!" (p. 36). Given the oppression that women have lived with, perhaps women *should* be angry. As Tavris suggested,

> Maybe the real question is not why some women become irritable before menstruation, but why they aren't angry the *rest* of the month, and why they (and others) are so quick to dismiss their irritations as being mere symptoms of PMS. (1992, p. 156)

TABLE 5.3 Sexuality Observations and Theoretical Explanations

Observations	Theory
1. Men are more sexually aggressive than women.	*Operant Learning* Men have been reinforced for being sexually aggressive. Women have been punished for being sexually aggressive. *Social Script* Our society scripts men to be more aggressive and women to be more passive sexually. Each sex learns through interactions with parents, peers, and partners that this is normative behavior. *Physiological* Men have larger amounts of androgen and women have larger amounts of progesterone, which account for male aggressiveness and female passivity.
2. Pornography is consumed primarily by men.	*Operant Learning* Men derive erotic pleasure (reinforcement) from pornography. *Social Script* Men script each other to regard pornography as desired entertainment. Men swap pornography, which reflects a norm regarding pornography among males. Women rarely discuss pornography with each other. *Evolutionary* Men are biologically wired to become erect in response to visual sexual stimuli.
3. Men in most societies are allowed to have a number of sexual partners.	*Structural-Functional* In many societies, women outnumber men. Polygyny potentially provides a mate for every woman. *Conflict Theory* Social, political, and economic power of men provides the context for men to exploit women sexually by making rules in favor of polygyny. *Evolutionary* Men are biologically wired for variety; women for monogamy. These respective wirings produce reproductive success for the respective sexes.

Continued

perspective views low sexual desire as a product of the interaction between two partners.

> Low sexual desire is a subjective complaint about the absence of sexual feelings, voiced by one or both sexual partners . . . that reflects an imbalance of interactions. Such a complaint . . . can be voiced by a person whose sexual norms and expectations demand a much higher frequency of sexual activity than is provided for by his or her physiological cycle of arousal. Alternatively, the complaint may arise in a couple that fails to synchronize the partners' markedly different individual rhythms. (Verhulst & Heiman, 1988, p. 245)

In Table 5.3, we present different theoretical explanations for various observations about sexuality.

TABLE 5.3 Sexuality Observations and Theoretical Explanations—*continued*

Observations	Theory
4. Women and men tend to report lower levels of sexual desire in their elderly years.	*Social Script* Aging women and men learn social scripts that teach them that elderly persons are not expected to be sexual. *Systems* Elderly persons are often not in a relationship that elicits sexual desire. *Biological* Hormonal changes in the elderly account for decreased or absent sexual desire (physiological). There is no reproductive advantage for elderly women to be sexual; there is minimal reproductive advantage for elderly men to be sexual (evolutionary).
5. Extradyadic relationships, including marital infidelity, are common.	*Operant Learning* Immediate interpersonal reinforcement for extradyadic sex is stronger than delayed punishment for infidelity. *Biological* Humans (especially men) are biologically wired to be sexually receptive to numerous partners. *Structural-Functional* Infidelity reflects the weakening of the family institution. *Systems* Emotional and sexual interactions between couples are failing to meet the needs of one or both partners.

Feminist Theories

A feminist theory of sexuality that seeks to understand women's situation in order to change it, must first identify and criticize the construct "sexuality" *as* a construct that has circumscribed and defined experience as well as theory.
Catherine MacKinnon

Feminist theories have made important contributions to our understanding of human sexuality. Because of the different perspectives reflected in feminist theories, different classifications of feminist theory have been proposed. Next, we outline four categories of feminist theories: liberal feminism, radical feminism, socialist feminism, and multicultural feminism (Travis, 1988; Sapiro, 1990, Basow, 1992).

CONSIDERATION: Advocates of feminist ideas often incorporate the theoretical perspectives, methods, and objectives of more than one type of feminism (Travis, 1988).

Self Assessment

Attitude Toward Feminism Scale

Following are statements on a variety of issues. Left of each statement is a place for indicating how much you agree or disagree. Please respond as you *personally* feel and use the following letter code for your answers:

A - Strongly Agree   B - Agree   C - Disagree   D - Strongly Disagree

______ 1. It is naturally proper for parents to keep a daughter under closer control than a son.

______ 2. A man has the right to insist that his wife accept his view as to what can or cannot be afforded.

______ 3. There should be no distinction made between woman's work and man's work.

______ 4. Women should not be expected to subordinate their careers to home duties to any greater extent than men.

______ 5. There are no natural differences between men and women in sensitivity and emotionality.

______ 6. A wife should make every effort to minimize irritation and inconvenience to her husband.

______ 7. A woman should gracefully accept chivalrous attentions from men.

______ 8. A woman generally needs male protection and guidance.

______ 9. Married women should resist enslavement by domestic obligations.

______ 10. The unmarried mother is more immoral and irresponsible than the unmarried father.

______ 11. Married women should not work if their husbands are able to support them.

______ 12. A husband has the right to expect that his wife will want to bear children.

______ 13. Women should freely compete with men in every sphere of economic activity.

______ 14. There should be a single standard in matters relating to sexual behavior for both men and women.

______ 15. The father and mother should have equal authority and responsibility for discipline and guidance of the children.

______ 16. Regardless of sex, there should be equal pay for equal work.

______ 17. Only the very exceptional woman is qualified to enter politics.

______ 18. Women should be given equal opportunities with men for all vocational and professional training.

______ 19. The husband should be regarded as the legal representative of the family group in all matters of law.

______ 20. Husbands and wives should share in all household tasks if both are employed an equal number of hours outside the home.

______ 21. There is no particular reason why a girl standing in a crowded bus should expect a man to offer her his seat.

______ 22. Wifely submission is an outmoded virtue.

______ 23. The leadership of a community should be largely in the hands of men.

______ 24. Women who seek a career are ignoring a more enriching life of devotion to husband and children.

______ 25. It is ridiculous for a woman to run a locomotive and for a man to darn socks.

______ 26. Greater leniency should be adopted towards women convicted of crime than towards male offenders.

______ 27. Women should take a less active role in courtship than men.

______ 28. Contemporary social problems are crying out for increased participation in their solution by women.

______ 29. There is no good reason why women should take the name of their husbands upon marriage.

______ 30. Men are naturally more aggressive and achievement-oriented than women.

______ 31. The modern wife has no more obligation to keep her figure than her husband to keep down his waist line.

______ 32. It is humiliating for a woman to have to ask her husband for money.

______ 33. There are many words and phrases which are unfit for a woman's lips.

______ 34. Legal restrictions in industry should be the same for both sexes.

______ 35. Women are more likely than men to be devious in obtaining their ends.

______ 36. A woman should not expect to go to the same places or to have quite the same freedom of action as a man.

______ 37. Women are generally too nervous and high-strung to make good surgeons.

______ 38. It is insulting to women to have the "obey" clause in the marriage vows.

______ 39. It is foolish to regard scrubbing floors as more proper for women than mowing the lawn.

______ 40. Women should not submit to sexual slavery in marriage.

______ 41. A woman earning as much as her male date should share equally in the cost of their common recreation.

______ 42. Women should recognize their intellectual limitations as compared with men.

Used by permission of Bernice Lott, Department of Psychology, University of Rhode Island.

Self-Assessment—*Continued*

Scoring Score your answers as follows: A = +2, B = +1, C = −1, D = −2. Since half the items were phrased in a pro-feminist and half in an antifeminist direction, you will need to reverse the scores (+2 becomes −2, etc.) for the following items: 1, 2, 6, 7, 8, 10, 11, 12, 17, 19, 21, 23, 25, 26, 27, 30, 33, 35, 36, 37, and 42. Now sum your scores for all the items. Scores may range from +84 to −84.

Interpreting your score The higher one's score, the higher their agreement with feminist (Lott used the term "women's liberation") statements. You may be interested in comparing your score, or that of your classmates, with those obtained by Lott (1973) from undergraduate students at the University of Rhode Island. The sample was composed of 109 men and 133 women in an introductory psychology class, and 47 additional women who were older and participating in a special Continuing Education for Women (CEW) program. Based on information presented by Lott (1973) the following mean scores were calculated: Men = 13.07, Women = 24.30, and Continuing Education Women = 30.67.

Among the younger students (excluding the CEW students) those scoring in the top and low quarters had the following scores (see Table 1).

More recently, Biaggio, Mohan, and Baldwin (1985) administered Lott's questionnaire to 76 students from a University of Idaho introductory psychology class and 63 community members randomly selected from the local phone directory. Although they did not present the scores of their respondents, they reported they did not find differences between men and women; unlike Lott's students, in Biaggio et al.'s sample, women were not more pro-liberation than men. Biaggio et al. (1985, p. 61) stated, "It seems that some of the tenets of feminism have taken hold and earned broader acceptance. These data also point to an intersex convergence of attitudes, with men's and women's attitudes toward liberation and child rearing being less disparate now than during the period of Lott's study." It would be interesting to determine if there are sex differences in scores from your class.

Was the idea of measuring feminism new to the 1970's? Hardly! In 1936 Kirkpatrick published a scale for measuring attitudes toward feminism. Lott obtained some ideas for items from his scale. Kirkpatrick (1936, p. 421) suggested that scales such as his "may prove to have value in the analysis and prediction of success in marriage as well as in throwing light on problems of sex antagonism and economic competition and culture conflict." He found that his questionnaire distinguished between members of the National Woman's Party and a comparison group of Lutheran pastors.

Reliability and Validity Lott (1973) did not report reliability data for the questionnaire. To test the validity, respondents rated on a 9-point scale "How much do you agree with the dominant positions of the women's liberation movement?" (p. 579). Results were consistent with other findings of her study in that more feminist women were less interested in having and rearing children than more traditional women, with no significant difference for men. In Biaggio et al.'s replication study (1985), the researchers found that anti-liberation women were still more personally interested in child rearing, although they judged child-rearing to require more creativity than in the 1970's.

References

Biaggio, M. K., Mohan, P. J., & Baldwin, C. (1985). Relationships among attitudes toward children, women's liberation, and personality characteristics. *Sex Roles, 12,* 47–62.

Kirkpatrick, C. (1936). The construction of a belief-pattern scale for measuring attitudes toward feminism. *Journal of Social Psychology, 7,* 421–437.

Lott, B. E. (1973). Who wants the children? Some relationships among attitudes toward children, parents, and the liberation of women. *American Psychologist, 28,* 573–582.

TABLE 1 High and Low Proliberation Scores

	Men		Women	
	Mean	*Range*	*Mean*	*Range*
Highest scorers (Proliberation)	39.83	62 to 30	50.53	79 to 41
Lowest scorers (Anti-liberation)	−16.36	−42 to −2	−3.68	−33 to 9

Before reading the following sections, you might want to complete the Self-assessment Attitude Toward Feminism.

Liberal Feminism

Liberal feminist theories view biological differences between women and men as minimal. Apparent biological differences are explained as socially constructed; that is, sex differences are explained by social and environmental factors. (The social constructionist view is discussed later in this chapter). For example, gender inequality is viewed as socially created. According to Chafetz (1988),

> The gender-related status quo is viewed as the product of sociocultural and historical forces which have been created, and are constantly re-created by humans, and therefore can potentially be changed by human agency. (p. 5)

Liberal feminism is characterized by three concerns: a) the sexist division of labor justified on the basis of supposed biological differences between women and men, b) barriers to equal opportunity in education and occupations, and c) limited choices in the expression of self imposed by cultural definitions of masculinity and femininity. In response to this last concern, liberal feminist theories have been developed that propose new conceptions of gender. For example, a variety of instruments and scales have been developed based on the theoretical construct "androgyny," which represents the integration of female and male gender (androgyny is discussed in Chapter 8, Gender Roles).

Radical Feminism

Radical feminism emphasizes essential differences between females and males. According to this essentialist view (essentialist views are discussed later in this chapter), there are core differences between women and men that result in unique features of femaleness and maleness. The essence of femininity is trust, cooperation, and creativity; the essence of masculinity is competition, exploitation, and mistrust. Some radical feminist theories argue that men are awed by women's ability to bear children, causing men to both envy and fear women.

A major concern of radical feminists involves encouraging women to assert ownership of their own bodies so that they can control their reproductive lives and

Pursuing a career provides women the opportunity to escape economic oppression

determine their health care. Radical feminists also encourage women to look to other women as sources of emotional nurturance and as collaborators in social change. Lastly, radical feminists view the nature of power relationships as problematic. Travis (1988) described this concern by suggesting that

> The nature of power relations has been interpreted [by radical feminists] as corrupting to all parties; therefore, it is not adequate to simply replace men with women in positions in power. The *process* of reaching and implementing decisions and allocating resources must be reconstructed. (p. 39)

Socialist Feminism

Socialist feminism views sexism and discrimination against women as the result of how societies are structured economically and reproductively. According to socialist feminist theories, modes of production and reproduction are inextricably intertwined. (Socialist feminist theories overlap with conflict theories discussed earlier).

For example, the discovery of paternity, or the male's role in reproduction, is associated with the transition from group to pair marriage and the nuclear family system. Within the nuclear family system, women became viewed as bearers of children that were considered male property. This led to the development of patriarchy—a system of social organization in which family descent is traced through the male line (e.g., wives and children take the last name of the husband and father). Socialist feminist theory views patriarchy as a major source of the oppression of women.

In the traditional economic structure of social life, men have been associated with the work of production while women have been associated with consumption. As producers, men work in public settings, while women (the consumers) perform household and child-care duties in isolation. These economic roles of men as producers and women as consumers are associated with an "assymmetrical organization of parenting," that is, a socially constructed system of parenting in which women are primarily responsible for child rearing. Thus, according to socialist feminist theories, patriarchy and the nuclear family are major factors in the oppression of women.

Multicultural Feminism

A recent change in feminist theory in the 1980s was a shift toward a **multicultural feminism.** Prior to this shift, feminist theories attempted to validate women's experiences and solidify group identity by focusing on the commonalities among women. This approach, however, failed to recognize the diversity among women of different classes and races.

While all feminist theories view women as an oppressed class, multicultural theories recognize that there are classes within the class of women. For example, lower-income women, African-American women, and Hispanic women experience different forms of oppression that must be addressed. African-American women may face oppression not only due to being a female but also due to racial prejudice and discrimination. Similarly, Hispanic women, lower-income women, and other classes of women experience oppression based on unique aspects of the class of women to which they belong.

In concluding this section on feminist theories, we note that while we have presented one classification system of feminist theories (i.e., liberal, radical, socialist, and multicultural), other classification systems are also found in the literature. Furthermore, the feminist theoretical frameworks we have described are not rigid or fixed categories with clearly delineated boundaries. "The reality of feminist theory and practice is that it is a constant discussion among many perspectives and continues to change over time" (Sapiro, 1990, p. 424).

CONSIDERATION: Chafetz (1988) suggested that the acid test of whether a theory is feminist is whether it can be used to challenge, counteract, or change a status quo that disadvantages or devalues women. In addition, feminist theories have three other defining characteristics: 1) a focus on gender; 2) a view of gender relations as problematic; and 3) a view of gender relations as neither natural nor immutable.

Essentialist Versus Social Constructionist Views of Human Sexuality

Human action can be modified to some extent, but human nature cannot be changed.

Abraham Lincoln

The various theories of sexuality we have discussed in this chapter may be viewed according to whether they represent the essentialist view or the social constructionist view of sexuality. According to the **essentialist view**, sexuality is basically a biological drive or instinct and the female nature and male nature are fundamentally different. The essentialist view of human sexuality is reflected in many of the biological theories of sexuality and some psychological and feminist theories, as well. For example, in *The Evolution of Human Sexuality*, Donald Symons (1979) attempted to demonstrate that there is a female human nature and a male human nature that are distinctly different; thus, differences between women and men are innate, rather than learned. Freud's psychoanalytic theories of sexuality are, to an extent, essentialist in that they describe sexual libido as an innate biological drive. The radical feminist perspective views female qualities as inherently different from male qualities.

According to the **social constructionist view** of sexuality, sexual meanings, sexual identities, and gender relations are socially defined and controlled. This view holds that

> . . . sexuality is not primarily a biological category; it is not an innate, unchanging 'drive' or 'instinct' immune to the shifts that characterize other aspects of society. Instead, as social constructionists maintain, sexual behavior and sexual meanings are subject to the forces of culture. Human beings learn how to express themselves sexually, and the content and outcome of that learning vary widely across cultures and across time. (Freedman & D'Emilio, 1990, p. 485)

The social constructionist view is characteristic of sociological theories of sexuality, particularly symbolic interaction and conflict theories. Most feminist theories also embrace a social constructionist view of sexuality (e.g., Tiefer, 1988). Psychological theories that focus on social learning processes may also be viewed as social constructionist.

CONSIDERATION: Due to the AIDS epidemic, efforts are being made to change the socially constructed concepts of eroticism and masculinity through "safer-sex" advertising and education campaigns (Tiefer, 1991). The goal of such campaigns is to change the definitions of these concepts so they are associated with safer-sex practices (e.g., condom use).

Historical research in sexuality has contributed to the development of social constructionist views. For example, Freedman and D'Emilio (1990) noted that at different times, social constructions of female sexuality have involved images of "Eve, the Temptress" as well as images of women as innately passionless beings.

Throughout history, however, social constructions of male sexuality have consistently viewed men as innately sexually aggressive due to biological factors.

Social constructionist views of homosexuality have largely stemmed from historical research (e.g., McIntosh, 1968; Weeks, 1991). Historical research suggests that the gay identity is a modern, Western concept and that sexual contact between partners of the same gender has not always been understood the same way it is today. This insight has led historians of sexuality to question when and how other sexual identities (such as "heterosexual," "pedophile," and "lesbian") have been socially constructed.

Blumstein and Schwartz (1990) presented a social constructionist view of sexual desire. They noted that sexual desire may not exist as an essential or biological aspect of human sexuality. Rather, our culture creates understandings about how people experience their sexuality and what constitutes or determines sexual desire.

In recent years the concept of "sexual addiction" has been used to refer to excessive sexual desire or a lack of control over erotic impulses. From a social constructionist view, however, "sexual addiction" may be viewed as a stigmatizing label attached to behaviors that diverge from prevailing cultural standards of sexual normalcy. "There is nothing intrinsically pathological in the conduct that is presently labeled as sexual compulsive or addictive, these behaviors have assumed pathological status only because powerful groups are beginning to define them as such" (Levine and Troiden, 1988, p. 360).

CONSIDERATION: Social construction theory is a type of "meta-theory" because it may be used to explain how and why various theories of sexuality have been developed. Specifically, social constructionist theory views other theories of sexuality as socially constructed. Indeed, according to social construction theory, the social constructionist view of sexuality is, itself, socially constructed.

The essentialist and social constructionist views are not necessarily incompatible. For example, Weinrich and Williams (1991) supported an essentialist view of homosexuality in that they suggested that there is an underlying essence or trait that characterizes what we call "homosexuality," despite the existence of historical and cross-cultural variation in homosexual behavior and identities. However, Weinrich and Williams also recognized the positive contributions that the social constructionist movement has made toward our understanding of homosexuality. Weinrich and Williams suggested that "there is a need to go beyond a social constructionist view . . . by emphasizing the interaction of numerous factors in producing human eroticism" (1991, p. 55). In the next section, we discuss the trend toward integrating theories of sexuality. This trend represents an attempt to account for the interaction of the numerous factors that influence sexuality.

Genetic stories tend to omit experience; psychoanalytic stories tend to overlook the environment; . . . social-psychological stories tend to ignore biology; childhood-blame stories leave out current events. We do best, I believe, by adding explanations to our quiver of life stories rather than limiting ourselves to only one.
Carol Tavris

Theoretical Views on Human Sexuality: An Integrated Approach

While many scholars who study human sexuality focus on one theoretical approach, many others recognize that each theoretical approach may contribute to our understanding of sexuality. Consequently, evidence of a trend toward integrating theories of sexuality is emerging in the academic sexuality literature. The need for integrating theoretical views on sexuality was expressed by Abramson (1990): "The growth of

The professional who ignores the contributions of others has a diminished view of sexuality.
James H. Greer
William T. O'Donohue

EXHIBIT 5.2 An Application of the Integrative Model of Human Sexuality

To illustrate the integrative model of human sexuality, Schover and Jensen (1988) presented a hypothetical case example of a diabetic man experiencing erectile difficulty. The following adaptation of their example integrates elements from four theoretical perspectives: psychological, biological (i.e., physiological), systems (i.e., relationship factors), and sociological.

Hypothetical Case Example

Fred was diagnosed with diabetes at age 59 and has been treated with oral medication and a restricted diet for four years. Over the last two years, he gradually lost the ability to become fully erect. Before the sexual problem began, he and his wife, Angie, had intercourse about twice a week. After the erection problems began, Angie asked Fred to stop initiating sex. "You just get frustrated and then take it out on me," she said. "Besides, I don't like getting all excited and then having it go nowhere."

Fred went to his internist to seek help for his erection difficulties. The physician told Fred that diabetic men often become impotent and that, at age 63, Fred should be grateful not to have any more serious health problems.

Discouraged by his physician's response, Fred made an appointment with the sexual dysfunction clinic at a nearby medical school and was surprised by the requirement that Angie come with him. Fred and Angie were interviewed about their marital and sexual relationship by a psychiatry resident. Angie's problems with vaginal dryness and difficulty reaching orgasm were explored. Angie expressed frustration with Fred's habit of sneaking sweet desserts, and Fred complained that Angie never hugged him anymore and slept on the far side of the bed. The couple also talked about their fears that Fred's diabetes would lead to incapacitating side effects.

The psychiatry resident then scheduled Fred to have a complete physical examination, as well as specialized tests of erectile function. These tests showed that Fred had a mild decrease in blood circulation to his penis, but his nocturnal erections were in the normal range for his age.

The suggested treatment plan was to encourage Fred to comply with his diabetic diet and quit smoking and to have Fred and Angie come to 15 weekly sessions of sex therapy. The counseling would focus on improving the couple's communication and helping both partners express affection verbally and nongenitally. The clinicians felt that with a more relaxed and sensual sexual interaction, Fred's erections might become firmer. Quitting smoking might also improve the blood flow to his penis. Fred expressed concern about the expense of the therapy, since his insurance would not pay for couple therapy. The clinic had a sliding fee scale, however, and the staff agreed to limit the treatment to 10 sessions if possible.

Three months later, Fred and Angie were much happier with their relationship. Their sexual routine involved more extensive caressing, often ending in noncoital orgasm for each partner. About half the time, Fred was able to achieve an erection firm enough for satisfying intercourse. Both spouses felt they had met their goals and saw no need for further treatment.

The successful assessment and treatment of Fred's difficulty with erection depended on an integrated approach. In Table 5.4, we summarize the various psychological, physiological, relationship (systems theory), and social factors that were considered in the assessment and treatment of Fred's erection difficulties.

Source: Adapted from Schover, L. R., & Jensen, S. B. (1988). *Sexuality and chronic illness: A comprehensive approach.* New York: Guilford Press. Table taken from p. 12. Used by permission.

Continued

sexual science is undoubtedly dependent upon multidisciplinary collaboration" (p. 161).

> Sexual behavior is ultimately the interactional outcome of three types of forces—biological, psychological, and social.
>
> *Herant Katchadourian*

For example, in her synthesis of biological, psychological, and social aspects of aging female sexuality, psychologist Barbara Sherwin (1991) concluded that "human sexual behavior is multidetermined" (p. 194). Sherwin suggested that sexual desire or libido in aging women is influenced by biological, psychological, and sociocultural factors. Estrogen deficiency is a biological factor that plays an important role in determining sexual response patterns (e.g., pelvic vasocongestion and vaginal lubrication) of aging women. These changes in the sexual response patterns of older

EXHIBIT 5.2 An Application of the Integrative Model of Human Sexuality—*Continued*

TABLE 5.4 The Integrative Model Applied to the Case of Fred

Psychological Factors	Physiological Factors	Relationship Factors	Social Factors
Assessment			
• Poor compliance with diabetic diet • Anxiety about long-term diabetic complications	• Mild pelvic vascular deficit • Heavy smoker • Wife's postmenopausal vaginal atrophy	• Poor communication of affect and sexual preferences • Decrease in expressing affection since sexual problem began • Sexual routine performance-oriented; focus on erections and intercourse • Wife overprotective of husband's health, encouraging him to take passive role	• Primary care physician disapproves of sexuality for older adults • Insurance does not cover couple therapy
Treatment			
• Encourage more active role for Fred in controlling his diet and quitting smoking • Use cognitive behavioral techniques, such as self-monitoring, positive thinking, and self-reinforcement	• Quit smoking • Educate couple on water-based vaginal lubricants; use vaginal estrogen cream if conservative treatment fails	• Communication training • Negotiation on expressing caring more effectively in nonsexual contexts • Sensate focus and enrichment of sexual routine • Give wife insight into husband's need to actively control his health; enlist her support for his efforts in that direction	• With Fred's permission, send assessment report to his physician; follow with phone call to increase physician's knowledge of clinic services • Sliding fee scale; reduce planned sessions from 15 to 10

> To focus on one set of influences while ignoring the other is like trying to calculate the area of a field based on its width but not on its length.
>
> *Gordon G. Gallup, Jr.*

women may, in turn, influence psychological variables, such as subjective arousal and desire. Other influences of sexuality in aging women include the following psychosocial and cultural variables (Sherwin, 1991):

1. Availability of a sexual partner who is interested and capable of engaging in sexual activity (older women are frequently widowed or divorced; if they do have a partner, the partner may not be interested in sex and/or may have erection difficulties).
2. Socioeconomic status and level of education (Sherwin cited three studies on Swedish, U.S., and Belgian peri- and postmenopausal women that found that sexual interest was decreased in lower socioeconomic status groups. This finding

is attributed to the notion that education leads to greater freedom from cultural inhibitions and sexual stereotypes).

3. Cultural views and stereotypes of aging women (in societies in which older women are accorded higher status, postmenopausal sexuality is characterized by more openness and playfulness, compared to U.S. society, which has traditionally devalued older women and stereotyped them as being asexual).

As an academic discipline, human sexual behavior is the "jack of all trades, master of none."

Paul R. Abramson

The trend toward integrating theories of sexuality is also emerging in the field of medicine, which has traditionally focused on biological theories. In Exhibit 5.2, we illustrate the integration of various theoretical orientations in the assessment and treatment of a hypothetical case example of a diabetic man seeking medical treatment for erection difficulties. This illustration was presented by Schover and Jensen (1988) in their book *Sexuality and Chronic Illness*.

CHOICES

The different theories of human sexuality provide frameworks for choices in regard to sexuality.

Choose to Be a Parental Model for Affection?

If you adopt a learning view of human sexuality, you recognize that one of the ways individuals learn to be affectionate is through observing significant others who are affectionate toward each other. If you have parents who hugged and kissed each other in your presence, you have been exposed to a very powerful model in terms of your own potential to be affectionate. On the other hand, if you never observed your parents being affectionate toward each other, you have been exposed to an equally powerful model in terms of being cold and withdrawn in your own relationships.

Rather than repeating the lack of affection you may have observed in your parent's relationship in your own relationships, you might override your parental modeling and cognitively choose to express your affection openly with your partner. Not only might you experience more emotional closeness with your partner as a consequence of being more affectionate, you might also develop a pattern of being affectionate to which your children will be exposed. Providing such a model for them will make it easier for them to be affectionate in their own relationships. Just as your parents were a significant modeling influence on you, you will be a significant modeling influence on your children.

Choose to View Desires for Specific Sexual Behaviors as Learned?

It is not unusual that one partner in a relationship enjoys a particular sexual behavior that the other defines as disgusting. One man wanted his partner to fellate him, but she regarded oral sex as "sick and dirty." Rather than viewing each other's desires and attitudes as abnormal, an alternative is to view these as different desires and attitudes that have been learned. The man may have had an early positive experience with fellatio by a loving partner. To him, fellatio meant love, acceptance, and pleasure. The woman, on the other hand, might have had an entirely different exposure to fellatio. For example, consider this woman's experience:

> When I was seven or so, my stepfather took me hunting with him. This particular time, he took a blanket with us, and when we got deep into the woods, he said that he wanted us to play mamma and daddy. He told me that mamas like to treat their daddy's "thing" like a Popsicle by licking and sucking it, and that's what he wanted me to do. I felt bad doing it and knew that it was wrong when he told me I couldn't tell my mother or he would give me a beating I would never forget. Since then, I have never wanted my mouth to get near a man's penis.

As these respective experiences illustrate, the same principles of learning that explain why one person likes a sexual behavior can explain why another person may abhor it. The man was reinforced for participation in fellatio; the woman was punished. Rather than viewing a partner's preferences as sick and one's own as healthy and natural, one might consider choosing to view both sets of preferences as learned. In addition, partners might consider discussing the previous learning experiences that contributed to their feeling a certain way about a sexual behavior. The choice to view sexual behaviors as learned and the choice to discuss them are two very important choices in one's sexual relationships.

SUMMARY

1. Making informed sexual choices involves a knowledge of the theories of human sexuality. Theories of human sexuality attempt to explain why people think and behave sexually.
2. Theories may be biological (physiological, evolutionary), psychological (psychoanalytic, learning, cognitive), or sociological (symbolic interaction, structural-functional, conflict, systems).
3. Operant learning theory emphasizes that people have sexual thoughts and engage in sexual behavior as a result of the consequences that follow those thoughts and/or behaviors. The principles of positive reinforcement, negative reinforcement, positive punishment, and negative punishment are helpful in explaining how sexual thoughts and behaviors are learned.
4. Classical conditioning theory explains how a stimulus develops the capability of eliciting a specific response. The development of a fetish can be explained through the use of classical conditioning theory.
5. Cognitive theories emphasize the relationship between emotions and cognitions. Theorists such as Ellis and Beck suggest that emotions follow cognitions. Still others emphasize the interactive nature of emotions and cognitions.
6. Gang rape in fraternities may be described in terms of social scripting of deviant behavior that is reinforced in a group context.
7. No one theory dominates the field of human sexuality. Theories that integrate several aspects of biology, psychology, and sociology are the most promising.
8. Feminist theories are gaining increased attention. These include liberal, radical, socialist, and multicultural feminism.
9. Theories of sexuality may be classified as essentialist or social constructionist. The former emphasizes biological influences; the latter stresses social and cultural influences.
10. Knowledge of theories can beu sed to alter one's view of human sexual behavior. Behavior can be viewed as learned, rather than as an innate personality trait.

KEY TERMS

asexual reproduction
id
ego
superego
oral stage
anal stage
phallic stage
latent stage
libido
genital stage
reinforcement
punishment
operant learning theory
classical conditioning
social learning theory
social scripts
symbolic interaction theories
conflict theories
systems theories
structural-functional theories
liberal feminism
radical feminism
socialist feminism
multicultural feminism
essentialist view
social constructionist view

REFERENCES

Abramson, P. R. (1990). Sexual science: emerging discipline or oxymoron? *Journal of Sex Research, 27,* 147–165.

Bandura, A. (1969). *Principles of behavior modification.* New York: Holt, Rinehart & Winston.

Bandura, A. (1977). Self-efficacy: Toward a unifying theory of behavioral change. *Psychological Review, 84,* 191–215.

Basow, S. A. (1992). *Gender stereotypes and roles* (3rd Ed.). Pacific Grove, CA: Brooks/Cole.

Baucom, D. H., & Epsten, N. (1989). *Cognitive-behavioral marital therapy.* New York: Brunner/Mazel.

Blumstein, P., & Schwartz, P. (1990). Intimate relationships and the creation of sexuality. In D. P. McWhirter, S. A. Sanders, and J. M. Reinisch (Eds.). *Homosexuality/heterosexuality: Concepts of sexual orientation* (pp. 307–320). New York: Oxford University Press.

Brownmiller, S. (1975). *Against our will: Women and rape.* New York: Simon and Schuster.

Chafetz, J. S. (1988). *Feminist sociology: An overview of contemporary theories.* Itasca, Il: F. E. Peacock.

Coleman, E. (1990). Expanding the boundaries of sex research. *Journal of Sex Research, 27,* 473–480.

Daly, M., & Wilson, M. (1978). *Sex, evolution, and behavior: Adaptations for reproduction.* North Scituate, MA: Duxbury Press.

Davis, K. (1937). The sociology of prostitution. *American Sociological Review 2,* 774–755.

DeLamater, J. (1987). A sociological approach. In J. H. Greer and W. T. O'Donohue (Eds.), *Theories of human sexuality,* (pp. 237–255). New York: Plenum Press.

DeLamater, J. (1991). Emotions and sexuality. In K. McKinney and S. Sprecher (Eds.), *Sexuality in close relationships* (pp. 49–70). Hillsdale, NJ: Lawrence Erlbaum.

Ellis, A. (1962). *Reason and emotion in psychotherapy.* New York: Lyle Stuart Press.

Erickson, E. H. (1950). *Childhood and society.* New York: W. W. Norton.

Fitness, J., & Strongman, K. (1991). Affect in close relationships. In G. J. O. Fletcher and F. D. Fincham (Eds.), *Cognition in close relationships* (pp. 175–202). Hillsdale, NJ: Lawrence Erlbaum.

Ford, D. H., & Urban, H. B. (1963). *Systems of Psychotherapy: A Comparative Study.* New York: Wiley.

Freedman, E. B., & D'Emilio, John. (1990). Problems encountered in writing the history of sexuality: Sources, theory, and interpretation. *Journal of Sex Research, 27,* 481–495.

Freeman, P. (1990, December 17). Silent no more. *People,* pp. 94–104.

Gagnon, J. H. (1977). *Human sexualities.* Glenview, Il: Scott, Foresman.

Gagnon, J. H. (1983). Modern sexual theory and sexual reform: Emergence, transformation, and criticism. In C. Davis (Ed.), *Challenges in sexual science* (pp. 32–41). Philadelphia: Society for the Scientific Study of Sex.

Gagnon, J. H., & Simon, W. (1973). *Sexual conduct: The social sources of human sexuality.* Chicago: Aldine.

Gallup, G. G., Jr. (1986). Unique features of human sexuality in the context of evolution. In D. Byrnn and K. Kelley (Eds.), *Alternative approaches to the study of human sexuality* (pp. 13–42). Hillsdale, NJ: Lawrence Erlbaum.

Grammer, K. (1989). Human courtship behavior: Biological basis and cognitive processes. In A. E. Rasa, C. Vogel, and E. Voland (Eds.), *Sociobiology of sexual and reproductive strategies* (pp. 147–169). London: Chapman and Hall.

Greer, J. H., & O'Donohue, W. T. (Eds.), *Theories of human sexuality.* New York: Plenum Press.

Levine, M. & Troiden, R. R. (1988). The myth of sexual compulsivity. *The Journal of Sex Research. 25,* 347–363.

MacKinnon, C. A. (1987). A feminist/political approach: Pleasure under patriarchy. In J. E. Greer and W. T. O'Donohue, *Theories of human sexuality* (pp. 65–90). New York: Plenum Press.

Martin, P. Y., & Hummer, R. A. (1989). Fraternities and rape on campus. *Gender and Society, 3,* 457–473.

McIntosh, M. (1968). The homosexual role. *Social Problems, 16,* 182–192.

McKinney, K., & Sprecher, S. (1991). Introduction. In K. McKinney and S. Sprecher (Eds.), *Sexuality in close relationships* (pp. 1–8). Hillsdale, NJ: Lawrence Erlbaum.

Padgug, R. A. (1989). Sexual matters: On conceptualizing sexuality in history. In K. Peiss and C. Simmons (Eds.), *Passion and power: sexuality in history* (pp. 14–31). Philadelphia: Temple University Press.

Parsons, T., & Bales, R. F. (1955). *Family socialization and interaction process.* New York: Free Press.

Person, E. S. (1987). A psychoanalytic approach. In J. H. Greer and W. T. O'Donohue, (Eds.), *Theories of human sexuality* (pp. 385–410). New York: Plenum Press.

Russell, D. (1982). *Rape in marriage.* New York: Macmillan.

Sapiro, V. (1990). *Women in American society* (2nd Ed.). Mountain View, CA: Mayfield.

Schover, L. R., & Jensen, Soren Buus. 1988. *Sexuality and chronic illness: A comprehensive approach.* New York: Guilford Press.

Sherwin, B. B. (1991). The psychoendocrinology of aging and female sexuality. In J. Bancroft, C. M. Davis, and H. J. Ruppel (Eds.), *Annual review of sex research* (Vol. 2, pp. 181–198). Lake Mills, Iowa: The Society for the Scientific Study of Sex.

Symons, D. (1979). *The evolution of human sexuality.* New York: Oxford University Press.

Szasz, T. (1980). *Sex by prescription.* New York: Penguin Books.

Tash, G. B. (1988). Date rape. *Emerald of Sigma Pi Fraternity, 75,* 1–2.

Tavris, C. (1992). *The mismeasure of woman.* New York: Simon & Schuster.

Tavris, C. (1991, November). The myth of PMS. *Redbook,* pp. 36, 38, 40–41.

Tiefer, L. (1988). A feminist perspective on sexology and sexuality. In M.M. Gergen (Ed.), *Feminist thought and the structure of knowledge* (pp. 16–26). New York: New York University Press.

Tiefer, L. (1991). Commentary on the status of sex research: Feminism, sexuality and sexology. *Journal of Psychology and Human Sexuality, 4,* 5–42.

Travis, C. B. (1988). *Women and health psychology: Biomedical issues.* Hillsdale, NJ: Lawrence Erlbaum.

Verhulst, J., & Heiman, J. R. (1988). A systems perspective on sexual desire. In S. R. Leiblum and R. C. Rosen (Eds.), *Sexual desire disorders* (pp. 243–267). New York: Guilford Press.

Walen, S., & Roth, D. (1987). A cognitive approach. In J. H. Greer and W. T. O'Donohue (Eds.), *Theories of human sexuality* (pp. 335–362). New York: Plenum Press.

Weeks, J. (1991). *Against nature: Essays on history, sexuality and identity.* London: Rivers Oram Press.

Weinrich, J. D., & Williams, W. L. (1991). Strange customs, familiar lives: Homosexualities in other cultures. In J. C. Gonsiorek and J. D. Weinrich (Eds.), *Homosexuality: Research implications for public policy* (pp. 44–59). Newbury Park, CA: Sage.

Wisdom, J. O. (1992). *Freud, Women and Society.* New Brunswick: Transaction Publishers.

Zusman, M. E. (1992). *Introduction to sociology: A social context approach.* Unpublished manuscript. Used by permission of Marty Zusman.

CHAPTER SIX

Sexual Anatomy and Physiology

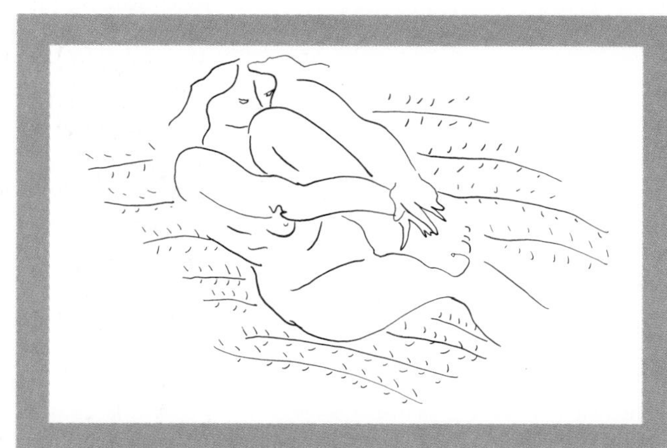

Chapter Outline

Female External Anatomy
- Mons Veneris
- Labia
- Clitoris
- Vaginal Opening
- Urethral Opening

Female Internal Anatomy
- Vagina
- Pubococcygeus Muscle
- Uterus
- Fallopian Tubes
- Ovaries

Menstruation
- Attitudes toward Menstruation
- **Self-Assessment:** Menstrual Attitude Questionnaire (MAQ)
- Phases of the Menstrual Cycle
- Problems of the Menstrual Cycle
- **Research and Policy Perspective:** Premenstrual Disorder and DSM-111-R Controversy

The Female Breasts

Male External Anatomy
- Penis
- Scrotum

Male Internal Anatomy
- Testes
- Duct System
- Seminal Vesicles and Prostate Gland

Choices
- Choose to Have a Breast Implant?
- Choose to Have a Mammogram?
- Choose to Have a Pelvic Examination and a Pap Test?
- Choose to Have a Prostate Rectal Exam?
- Choose to Do Self-Examinations?

Is It True?*

1. Most researchers agree that there is a particular spot, known as the ''G spot'' on the anterior wall of the vagina that, when stimulated, results in erotic feelings in the woman.

2. Some unmarried Japanese women who have had intercourse arrange to have their hymen surgically reconstructed so that they will be accepted as a virgin bride.

3. Being circumcised is associated with having a lower risk of contracting HIV.

4. Due to recent medical advances, there is now agreement on the frequency, nature, cause, and cure for premenstrual syndrome.

5. Men, in addition to women, should give themselves breast exams.

* 1=F, 2=T, 3=T, 4=F, 5=T

Whoever named it necking was a poor judge of anatomy.

Groucho Marx

The United States is currently experiencing a fitness craze (Rodin, 1992). Athletic clubs, body workouts on videotape, and marathons reflect a new interest in exercise and health. Increasingly, people are choosing to be physically fit, which promotes a healthy body for sexual experiences.

Choices in anatomy and physiology include making decisions about skin exposure, physical checkups, and medical intervention. The body is like a car, which must be used with care if it is to last, taken in for periodic checkups, and submitted to certain procedures as indicated. As the ozone layer continues to disappear, the prolonged exposure of unprotected skin to ultraviolet rays will cause premature aging of the skin (wrinkles) and possibly skin cancer. Failure to have periodic medical exams sometimes lets medical problems (e.g., breast or prostate cancer) intensify so that treatment may be too late. Bobby Riggs, the tennis pro, said that he neglected to have a prostate exam in his 50s. By his 60s, it was too late, and one testicle had to be removed.

In the culture in which we live, it is the custom to be least informed upon that subject concerning which every individual should know most—namely, the structure and functions of his/her own body.

Ashley Montague

In this chapter, we discuss the anatomical and physiological aspects of human sexuality. It may be helpful to think of the body as a machine, with **anatomy** referring to the machine's parts and **physiology** referring to how the parts work. Technically, anatomy is the study of body structure; physiology is the study of body functions. Our emphasis in this chapter is on anatomy with some physiological information. We provide a more detailed discussion of the physiology of sexual response in Chapter 7, Sexual Response.

Female External Anatomy

Women keep trying to degenitalize men's focus and teach them that there are only two erogenous zones—the heart and the skin.

Sam Keen

The external female genitalia are collectively known as the **vulva** (VUHL-vuh), a Latin term meaning "covering." The vulva consists of the mons veneris, the labia, the clitoris, and the vaginal and urethral openings (see Figure 6.1). A less preferable term for these structures is **pudendum** (pyoo-DEN-dum), derived from the Latin word *pudendus,* meaning "something to be ashamed of." (This term reflects the ambivalent feelings that some people have toward women's genitalia). Like faces, the female genitalia differ in size, shape, and color, resulting in considerable variability in appearance (see Figure 6.2).

We face a past and a present in which there has never been a *language* allowing us to think about and define women's sexuality.

Lucy Bland

CONSIDERATION: Terms for male genitalia (e.g., penis, testicles) are more commonly known than are terms for female genitalia. Tavris (1992) noted that, "In spite of living in a culture that seems sexually obsessed, many women still do not even accurately name their genitals. At best, little girls are taught that they have a vagina, which becomes the word for everything 'down there,' they rarely learn they also have a vulva and a clitoris." (p. 244)

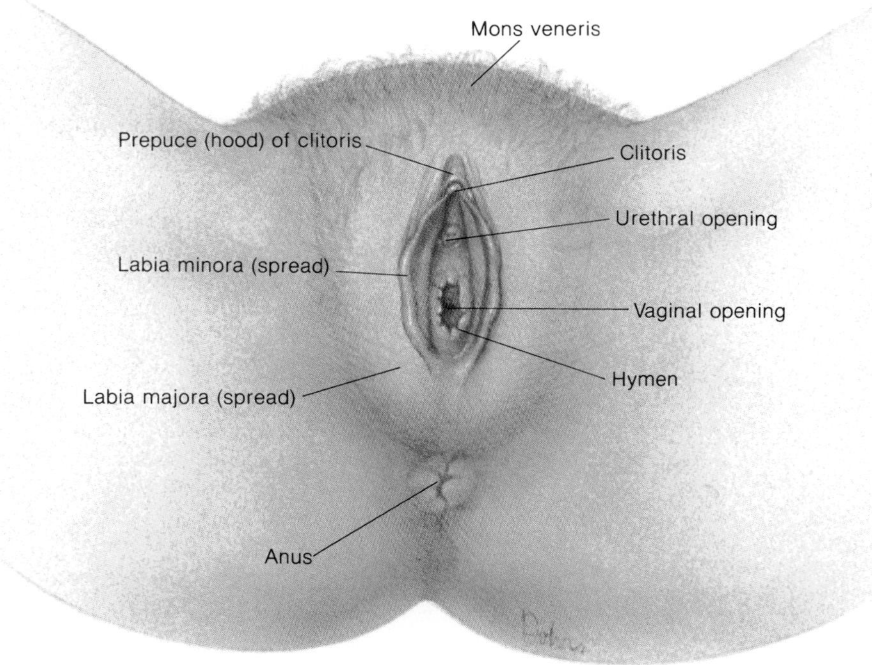

FIGURE 6.1 External Female Genitalia

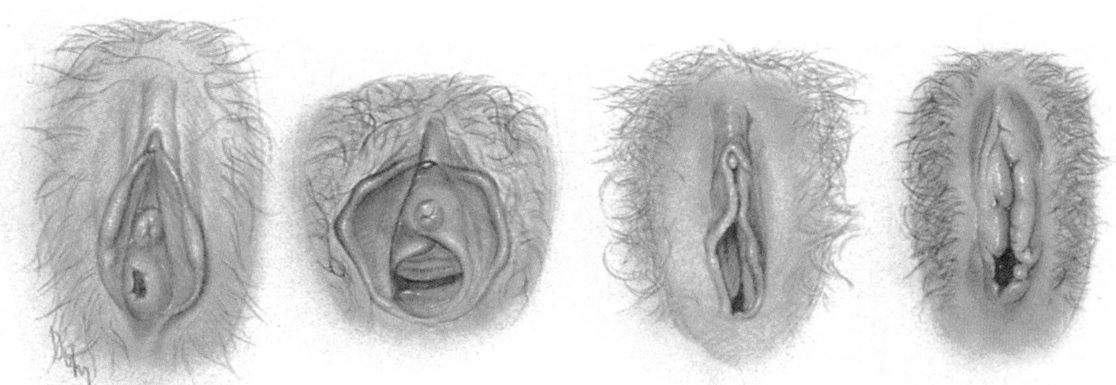

FIGURE 6.2 Variations in the Vulva

Mons Veneris

The soft cushion of fatty tissue overlaying the pubic bone is called the **mons veneris** (mahns vuh-NAIR-ihs), Latin for "mound of Venus," the Roman goddess of love. Also known as the mons pubis, this area becomes covered with hair at puberty. Pubic hair varies in color and texture depending on genetic factors. The mons has numerous nerve endings, and many women find that gentle stimulation of this area is highly pleasurable. In addition, the mons acts as a cushion to protect the pubic region during intercourse. The pubic hair also serves to trap semen secretions that occur during sexual arousal.

Labia

In the sexually unstimulated state, the urethral and vaginal openings are protected by the **labia majora** (LAY-bee-uh muh-JOR-uh), or "major lips"—two elongated folds of fatty tissue that extend from the mons to the **perineum** (pair-uh-NEE-uhm), the area of skin between the opening of the vagina and the anus. Located between the labia majora are two additional hairless folds of skin called the **labia minora** (muh-NOR-uh), "minor lips," which also cover the urethral and vaginal openings and join at the top to form the prepuce or hood of the clitoris. It is not uncommon for the labia minora to protrude beyond the labia majora. In fact, in some societies, such as the Hottentots of Africa, this is considered desirable and the women purposely attempt to elongate their minor lips by pulling on them.

The labia minora, which have numerous nerve endings making them very sensitive to tactile stimulation, also have a rich supply of small blood vessels. During sexual stimulation, the labia minora become engorged with blood, causing them to swell and change in color. With prolonged stimulation, the inner surfaces of the labia minora receive a few drops of fluid from the small Bartholin's (BAR-toh-lihnz) glands, which are located at the base of the minor lips. However, the small amount of fluid does not make a significant contribution to vaginal lubrication, and the function of the glands remains unknown. Unfortunately, the Bartholin's glands are sometimes the site of cystic infection, and any swelling or local irritation should be examined by a physician.

Clitoris

The **clitoris** (KLIHT-uh-ruhs) is the most sensitive area of the female genitalia (see Figure 6.3). It has no direct reproductive function and is apparently the only structure whose sole purpose is to focus sexual sensations and erotic pleasure. The clitoris develops embryologically (see Chapter 8, Gender Roles) from the same tissue as the penis and has as many or more nerve endings as the much larger penis. In a sexually unaroused woman, the only visible part of the clitoris is the glans, which is a small external knob of tissue located just below the clitoral hood. The size of the clitoral glans, which is about one-quarter inch in diameter and one-quarter to one inch in length, is not related to the subjective experience of pleasure. Nor is female responsiveness related to the distance between the vaginal opening and the clitoral glans, as some people mistakenly believe. Hidden from view by the clitoral hood is the shaft of the clitoris, which divides into two much larger structures called crura (CROO-ruh), which are attached to the pubic bone.

The body of the clitoris consists of spongy tissue that fills with blood during sexual arousal, resulting in a doubling or tripling in size. Like the penis, stimulation

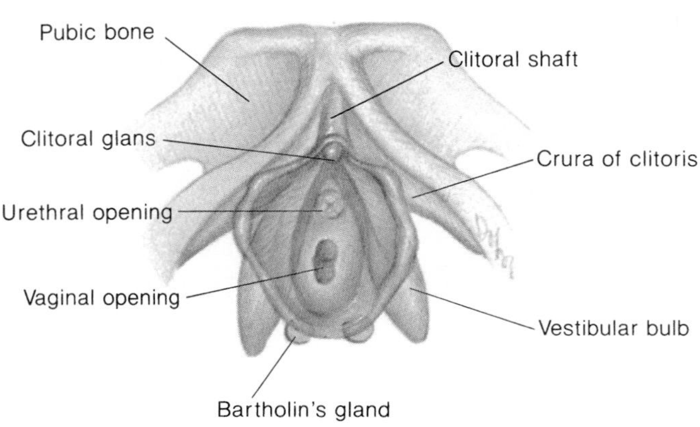

FIGURE 6.3 Anatomy of the Clitoris

of any part of the body may result in erection of the clitoris. With sufficient sexual arousal, however, the glans of the clitoris disappears beneath the clitoral hood. As we discussed in Chapter 3 on cultural variations in human sexuality, surgical removal of the clitoris, or clitoridectomy, is a common ritualized practice in many Middle Eastern and African countries.

Vaginal Opening

The area between the labia minora is called the **vestibule.** This includes the urethral opening and the vaginal opening, or **introitus** (ihn-TROH-ih-tuhs), neither of which is visible unless the labia minora are parted. Like the anus, the vaginal opening is surrounded by a ring of sphincter muscles. Although the vaginal opening can expand to accommodate the passage of a baby at birth, under conditions of tension, these muscles can involuntarily contract, making it difficult to insert an object, including a tampon or penis, into the vagina. On the other hand, women may learn to voluntarily contract these muscles to increase sensation during intercourse (the PC muscle and Kegel exercises will be discussed later). Also contributing to the tightness of fit are the vestibular bulbs, which are located underneath the bulbocavernosus muscles on both sides of the vaginal opening. These swell with blood during sexual arousal and may help the vagina to grip a penis. The vaginal opening has numerous nerve endings and is very sensitive to stimulation.

Human females are typically born with a thin membrane called the **hymen** partially covering the opening to the vagina (see Figure 6.4). It has no known physiological function. The appearance of the hymen varies from a single opening (annular hymen) to two (septate hymen) or more openings (cribiform hymen). In rare instances, the hymen may have no opening (imperforate hymen), but this may be corrected by a simple surgical incision at the time of first menstruation. The opening of the hymen is usually large enough to allow insertion of a finger or tampon.

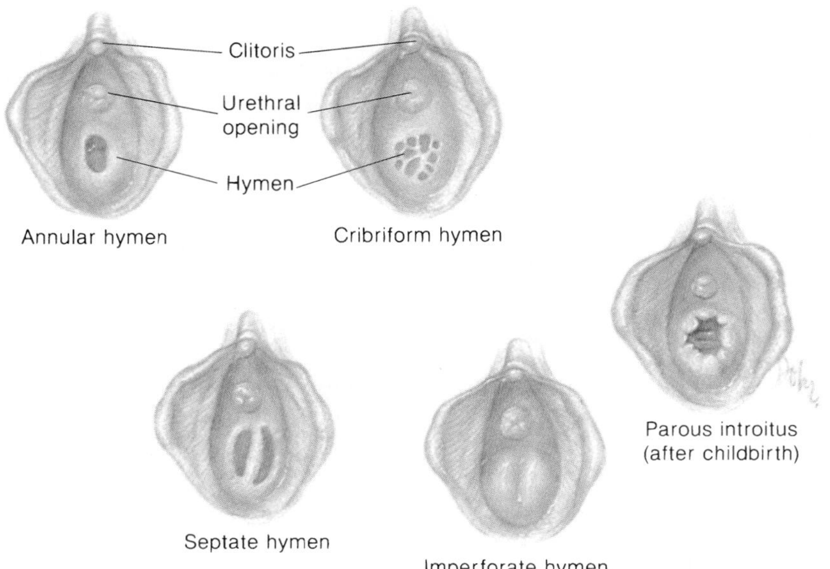

FIGURE 6.4 Variations in the Hymen

CONSIDERATION: Probably no other body part has caused as much grief to so many women as the hymen, which has been regarded throughout history as proof of virginity. A newly wed woman who was thought to be without a hymen was often returned to her parents, disgraced by exile, or even tortured and killed. It has been a common practice in many societies to parade a bloody bedsheet after the wedding night as proof of the bride's virginity. The anxieties caused by the absence of a hymen persist even today; in Japan and other countries, sexually experienced women may have a plastic surgeon reconstruct a hymen before marriage. Yet the hymen is really a poor indicator of virginity. Some women are born without a hymen or with incomplete hymens. In others, the hymen is accidentally ruptured by vigorous physical activity or insertion of a tampon. In some women, the hymen may not tear but only stretch during sexual intercourse. Even most doctors cannot easily determine whether a woman is a virgin.

Urethral Opening

The female's urinary system, (unlike the male's), is not related to the reproductive system; there are separate openings for coitus and urination. Urine passes from the body through the very small urethral opening, which is located below the clitoris and above the vaginal opening. A short tube, the urethra, connects the bladder where urine collects with the urethral opening. Small glands called Skene's glands are located just inside the urethral opening and develop from the same embryonic tissue as the male prostate gland. Some researchers believe that these glands are the source of the fluid some women emit from the urethra during orgasm (other researchers believe the source is the bladder) (Perry & Whipple, 1981).

Because of the shorter length of the female urethra and the close proximity of the anus to the vestibular area, women are more susceptible than men to **cystitis**, a bladder inflammation. The most common symptom is frequent urination accompanied by a burning sensation; there also may be a discharge of blood or pus. A gynecologist should be consulted if a woman experiences any of these symptoms. A common cause of cystitis is the transmission of bacteria that live in the intestines to the urethral opening. After a bowel movement, a woman should avoid wiping herself from the anus toward the vulva, and anal intercourse should never be followed by vaginal intercourse. Vigorous intercourse, particularly in women who have not been sexually active, can also cause irritation of the urethral wall, but this "honeymoon cystitis" is less serious than that caused by bacterial infection.

Female Internal Anatomy

The internal sex organs of the female include the vagina, the uterus, and the paired Fallopian tubes and ovaries (see Figures 6.5 and 6.6).

Vagina

The **vagina** (vuh-JIGH-nuh) is a three- to five-inch-long muscular tube located behind the bladder and in front of the rectum pointing at a 45-degree angle toward the small of the back. In addition to its high elasticity during intercourse, the vagina functions as a passageway for menstrual flow and as the birth canal. The walls of the vagina are normally collapsed. Thus, the vagina is actually a potential space, which can expand by as much as two inches in length and diameter during intercourse.

The walls of the vagina have three layers, the inner layer having a soft, pliable, mucosal surface similar to that of the mouth. Vaginal lubrication begins within seconds after sexual arousal (Kaplan, 1974). The vaginal walls become engorged with

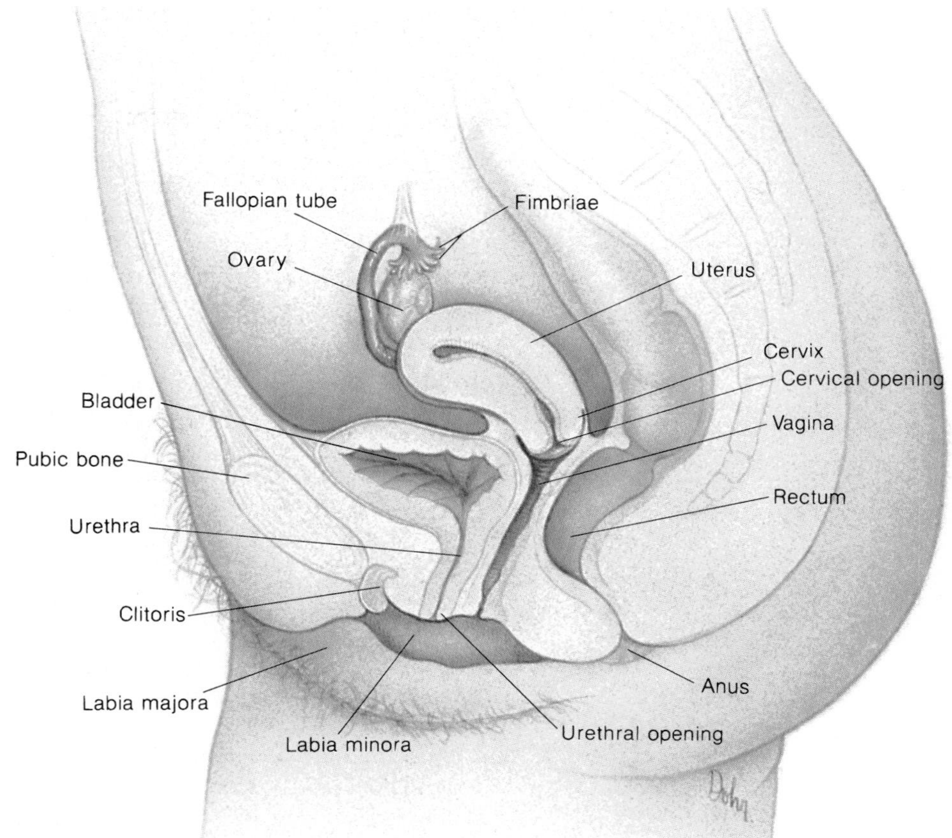

FIGURE 6.5 Internal Female Sexual and Reproductive Organs, Sagittal View

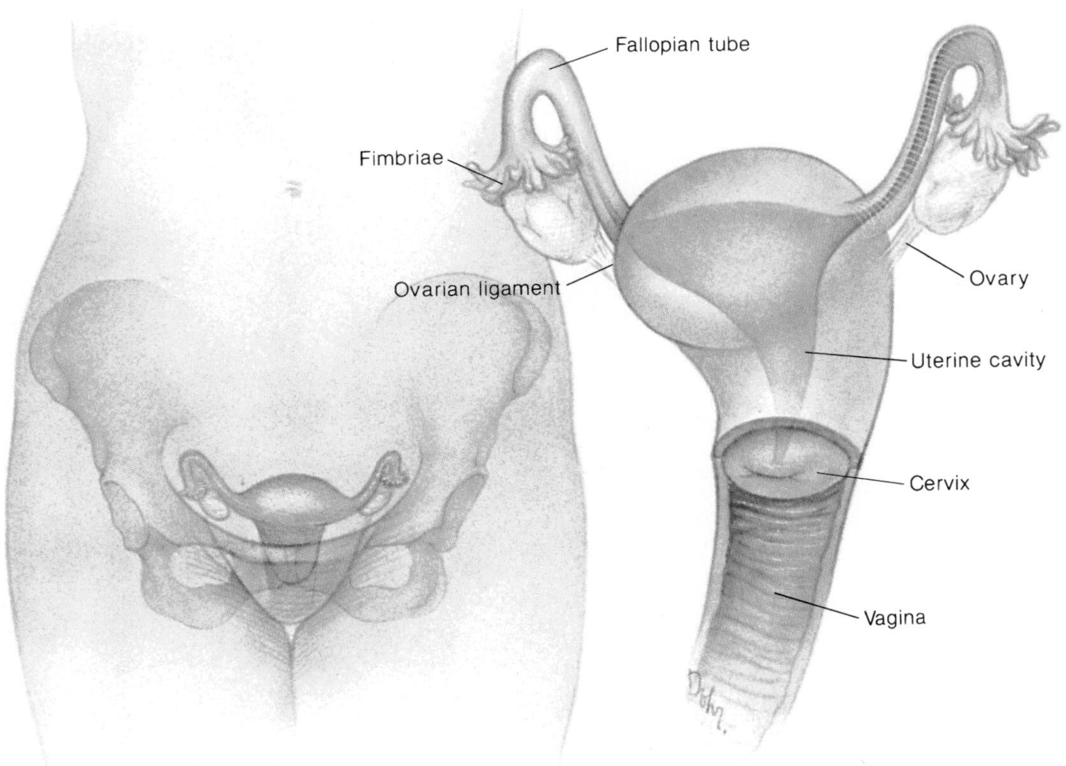

FIGURE 6.6 Internal Female Sexual and Reproductive Organs, Front View

blood, and the consequent pressure causes the mucous lining to secrete drops of fluid. The vaginal walls are very thin before puberty but thicken and become highly vascularized during puberty as a result of increasing hormone levels. Lower levels of female hormones after menopause cause the walls again to become thinner and less richly supplied with blood, decreasing the amount of lubrication during sexual arousal. In some cases, vaginal lubrication may be so impaired after menopause that a lubricant may be required for intercourse.

CONSIDERATION: Some people erroneously believe that the vagina is a dirty part of the body. In fact, the vagina is a self-cleansing organ. The bacteria that are found naturally in the vagina help to destroy other potentially harmful bacteria. In addition, secretions from the vaginal walls help to maintain its normally acidic environment. The use of feminine hygiene sprays, as well as excessive douching, may cause irritation, allergic reactions, and, in some cases, vaginal infection by altering the normal chemical balance of the vagina. Feminine hygiene sprays are characterized in *The New Our Bodies, Ourselves* (Boston Women's Health Book Collective, 1984) as "at best unnecessary and often harmful" (p. 518).

One group of researchers (see Figure 6.7) have reported that some women experience an extremely sensitive area in the front wall of the vagina one to two inches into the vaginal opening. The spot swells during stimulation, and although a woman's initial response may be a perceived need to urinate, continued stimulation generally leads to orgasm (Perry & Whipple, 1981). The area was named the **"Grafenberg Spot"** or "G Spot," for gynecologist Ernest Grafenberg (1950), who first noticed the erotic sensitivity of this area over 40 years ago. Grafenberg (1950) reported a sensitive area along the urethra in the anterior wall of the vagina. How-

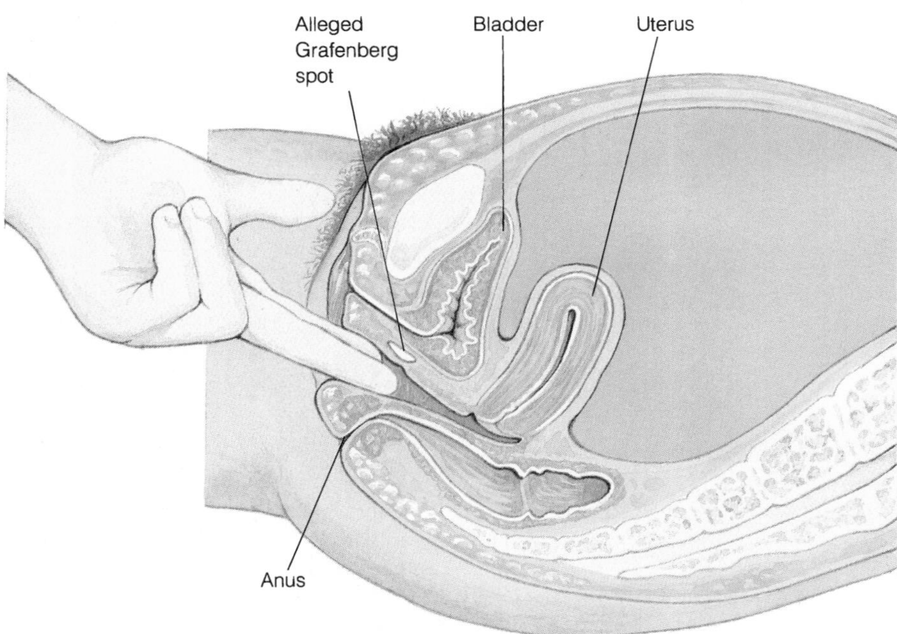

FIGURE 6.7
According to some sexologists, the **Grafenberg spot, or "G spot,"** is found on the upper surface of the front of the vagina.

ever, he also noted that there are many erotogenic areas throughout a woman's body, and stated that all parts of a woman's body are sexually responsive.

In 1982, Ladas, Whipple and Perry popularized the notion of the G spot with their book, *The G Spot and Other Recent Discoveries About Human Sexuality*. In a recent review of the G Spot research, Tavris (1992) criticized the lack of scientific rigor backing the notion of the G Spot. Tavris characterized the professionally published material offered as evidence as consisting of anecdotal accounts, a case study of one woman who demonstrated female ejaculation, Perry and Whipple's sample of women, and one disputing scientific study (which was not included in the G Spot book). In speaking of Perry and Whipple's sample, Tavris criticized that although 400 women were examined, no information was provided about them other than the finding of their G Spots, and no further information was ever published in a scientific journal. More recent studies investigating the G Spot have yielded equivocal results, at best.

In a study of 1,230 professional women who completed a 192-item questionnaire, 66 percent reported "an especially sensitive area in their vagina which, if stimulated, produced pleasurable feelings. Seventy-three percent reported that stimulating this area during arousal produced an orgasm" (Darling, Davidson, & Conway-Welch, 1990, p. 40). Greater psychological satisfaction was also reported by those who were aware of a G Spot in contrast to those who were not aware of such a sensitive area (84% versus 76%) (Darling et al., 1990, p. 43). In another study, 10 of 27 women expelled a whitish opalescent fluid from the urethra after the Grafenberg spot was stimulated. This has been referred to as "female ejaculation" (Zaviacic, Zaviacicova, Holoman, & Molcan, 1988) which we will discuss in Chapter 7 on sexual response.

Other researchers feel that it is a misnomer to refer to the existence of a specific "G Spot."

> The "G spot" does not exist as such, and the potential professional use of this term would be not only incorrect but also misleading. . . .The entire extent of the anterior wall of the vagina (rather than one specific spot), as well as the more deeply situated tissues, including the urinary bladder and urethral region, are extremely sensitive, being richly endowed with nerve endings. (Hock, 1983, p. 166)

In one study, 48 women volunteered to allow one of several physicians to stimulate them digitally to assess the degree to which they felt erotic sensitivity in their vaginas. Of the 48 women, 45 reported erotic sensitivity located, in most cases, on the anterior walls of the vagina; of those, 66.7% either reached orgasm or requested the physician stop stimulation short of orgasm. The researchers concluded that the study supported the idea of erotic sensitivity in the vagina but that it did not support the idea of a particular location (Alzate & Lodoño, 1984).

> The scientific enterprise of reducing sex to its component physiological elements—the goal of much of modern sexology—itself reflects a traditional male vision of genitally focused sexuality. . . .But in sexuality, the whole is greater than the sum of it's parts.
>
> *Carol Tavris*

According to Tavris (1992), the story of the G Spot illustrates the tendency of sexologists to "reduce sexuality to its component muscles, tissues, arteries, nerve endings, and 'magic spots'" (p. 230). While the notion of finding and pushing the right button for physical bliss may be appealing, sexual response is more complicated. "The reason, as Grafenberg himself acknowledged so long ago, is that sex occurs in many places, beginning in the brain and including, but not limited to, various interesting anatomical parts" (p. 241). Winton, a sociologist, observed that the G Spot may be viewed as a biological capacity that has been given meaning through social construction (1989).

Some women fear that an erect penis may be too large for their vagina and cause pain or injury during intercourse; extreme anxiety can cause severe involuntary contractions of the pelvic muscles (called vaginismus), preventing intercourse. However, as we have noted, the vagina expands during sexual arousal and is capable of expanding just enough to accommodate a penis of virtually any diameter. Stories that a couple can become locked together, which are based on observations of dogs during coitus (the penis of a dog expands into a knot), are unfounded. If a penis should prove to be too long for full penetration by the male, which seldom occurs, simple adjustments can be made in the position of intercourse. Most of the so-called problems of vaginal size are caused by psychological factors.

Pubococcygeus Muscle

Also called the PC muscle, the **pubococcygeus muscle** (pu-bo-kok-SIJ-e-us) is one of the pelvic floor muscles that surrounds the vagina, the urethra, and the anus. In order to find her PC muscle, a woman is instructed to voluntarily stop the flow of urine after she has begun to urinate. The muscle that stops the flow is the PC muscle. In a study of 1,172 professional women, 96% reported that they were aware of the existence of the pubococcygeus muscle and could "consciously identify the location of this muscle" (Darling et al., 1990, p. 41).

A woman can strengthen her PC muscle by performing the **Kegel exercises,** named after the physician who devised them. The Kegel exercises involve contracting the PC muscle several times for several sessions per day. Strengthening the PC muscle has been hypothesized as likely to increase the woman's sexual pleasure by increasing the sensitivity of the vaginal area, and may also permit the woman to create more pleasure for her male partner. However, Kaplan (1974) reported that no controlled studies have substantiated that one's perineal muscle tone influences one's experience of orgasm. Kegel exercises are often recommended after childbirth to restore muscle tone to the PC muscle (which is stretched during childbirth), and help prevent involuntary loss of urine.

Uterus

The **uterus** (YOOT-uh-ruhs), or womb, resembles a small, inverted pear. In women who have not given birth, it measures about three inches long and three inches wide at the top. It is here that the fertilized ovum develops into a fetus. No other organ is capable of expanding as much as the uterus does during pregnancy. Held in the pelvic cavity by ligaments, the uterus is generally perpendicular to the vagina. However, in 1 in every 10 women, the uterus tilts backward, which poses no serious problems but may cause discomfort in some positions during intercourse.

The broad rounded part of the uterus is the **fundus,** and the narrower portion, which projects into the vagina, is the **cervix.** The cervix feels like a small slippery bump (like the end of your nose) at the top of the vagina. The opening of the cervix, through which sperm and menstrual flow pass, is normally the size of a pencil lead, but at childbirth, it dilates to about four inches to allow passage of the baby. Secretory glands located in the cervical canal produce mucus that differs in consistency at different stages of the menstrual cycle.

The uterus consists of three layers. The inner layer, the endometrium, where the fertilized ovum normally implants, is rich in blood vessels and glands. It is surrounded by a layer of strong muscles, the myometrium, which contracts during childbirth, aiding delivery. The external cover of the uterus is called the perimetrium. Although the cervix has little sensitivity, pressure on the cervix from a finger or penis can "jostle" the uterus. Following a hysterectomy a woman may notice the loss of this internal sensation (Boston Women's Health Book Collective, 1984, p. 171).

CONSIDERATION: All adult women should have a pelvic exam, including a Pap test, each year. A Pap test is extremely important in the detection of cervical cancer. Cancer of the cervix and uterus is the third most common form of cancer in women; about 2% to 3% of all women develop such cancer. Some women may neglect to get a Pap test because they feel embarrassed or anxious about it or because they think they are too young to worry about getting cancer. For all women over age 20, however, having annual Pap tests may mean the difference between life and death. This choice is detailed in the Choices section at the end of the chapter.

Fallopian Tubes

The **Fallopian tubes** (fuh-LOH-pee-uhn), or oviducts, extend about four inches laterally from either side of the uterus to the ovaries. It is in the Fallopian tubes that fertilization normally occurs. The tubes transport the ovum, or egg, from the ovary to the uterus, but the tubes do not make direct contact with the ovaries.The funnel-shaped ovarian end of the tube, or infundibulum (in-fun-DIB-u-lum), is close to the ovary and has fingerlike projections called fimbria (FIM-bre-ah), which are thought to aid in picking up the egg from the abdominal cavity. However, there are cases in which women who are missing an ovary on one side and a Fallopian tube on the other side have become pregnant, suggesting some sort of chemical attraction of the ovum for the tube.

Passage of the egg through the tube, which takes about three days, is aided by the sweeping motion of hairlike structures, or cilia, on the inside of the tubes. Occasionally, a fertilized egg becomes implanted outside the uterus, called an ectopic pregnancy. The most common type of ectopic pregnancy occurs within a Fallopian tube and poses a serious health threat unless surgically treated.

Tying off the Fallopian tubes, so that egg and sperm cannot meet, is a common type of sterilization procedure in females. The tubes can also be blocked by inflammation, and serious infections can result in permanent scarring and even sterility.

Ovaries

The **ovaries** (OH-vuhr-eez), which are attached by ligaments on both sides of the uterus, are the female gonads corresponding to the testes in the male. These almond-shaped structures have the two functions of producing ova and the female hormones estrogen and progesterone. At birth, the ovaries have about 400,000 immature ova, each contained in a thin capsule to form a follicle. Some of the follicles begin to mature at puberty, but only about 400 mature ova will be released in a woman's lifetime.

MENSTRUATION

Sometime around the age of 12 or 13 in females, a part of the brain called the hypothalamus signals the pituitary gland at the base of the brain to begin releasing **follicle-stimulating hormone** (FSH) into the bloodstream. It is not known what causes the pituitary gland to release FSH at this time, but the hormone stimulates a follicle to develop and release a mature egg from the ovary. If the egg is fertilized, it will normally implant itself in the endometrium of the uterus, which has become thick and engorged with blood vessels in preparation for implantation. If the egg is not fertilized, the thickened tissue of the uterus is shed. This flow of blood, mucus, and dead tissue cells from the uterus is called **menstruation**, and the time of first menstruation is **menarche.** Except during pregnancy, this process will repeat itself at roughly monthly intervals until menopause.

> **CONSIDERATION:** Although the average menstrual cycle is 28 days in length, cycles may vary between 15 and 45 days in different women. However, a few women have cycles so consistent that they can accurately predict the day when menstruation will begin.

Attitudes toward Menstruation

In many societies throughout history, menstruating women were thought to have special powers and to be unclean. They have been blamed for such things as crop failure and dogs going mad. They have also been feared as a source of contamination of their sexual partner. The Bible warns men against having intercourse with a menstruating woman. "And if a woman have an issue, and her issue in her flesh be blood, she shall be put apart seven days; and whoever toucheth her shall be unclean" (Leviticus 15:19). In some societies, menstruating women have been quarantined to prevent contamination.

Some feelings women and men today have about menstruation are illustrated in Table 6.1 (authors' files).

The following Self-Assessment permits you to assess your own attitudes toward menstruation.

TABLE 6.1 Feelings Women and Men Have About Menstruation

What women say . . .	What men say . . .
I'm tired of going through it (cramps, headaches, backaches) every month. I'm also irritable and emotional.	It means my partner isn't pregnant.
It doesn't bother me.	I'm glad I don't have to go through it.
I hate it.	My partner gets edgy.
It is part of being female.	It's a good healthy thing for a woman; it cleans the inner body.
I dread it coming but am always glad it's here.	Women deserve some understanding from the male.
It's a pain and bother.	It's natural.
It's inconvenient.	Not having it is one of the benefits of being a male.
Yucko!	It means my partner won't have sex, so I don't like it.
I get depressed.	
It doesn't change my moods or alter my sex behavior.	
If they take tampons off the market, I'm going to stop having mine. It's already enough of a pain without having to use rags.	
I wish there was a way to turn it off until I am ready to have children.	
I wish men had to go through it.	
It is a curse; sometimes I wonder if being able to have a baby is worth all the trouble.	
It makes me feel good to know that I am a woman and can have a baby.	

Self Assessment

Menstrual Attitude Questionnaire (MAQ)

The following scale measures attitudes and expectations toward menstruation. To complete the MAQ, rate each statement on a 7-point scale (disagree strongly = 1, agree strongly = 7). Men can also complete the questionnaire by substituting the word *women* in items using the first person. For example, instead of "Menstruation is something I just have to put up with," revise the item to read "Menstruation is something women just have to put up with."

Subscale 1

1. A woman's performance in sports is not affected negatively by menstruation.* ________
2. Women are more tired than usual when they are menstruating. ________
3. I expect extra consideration from my friends when I am menstruating. ________
4. The physiological effects of menstruation are normally no greater than other usual fluctuations in physical state.* ________
5. Menstruation can adversely affect my performance in sports. ________
6. I feel as fit during menstruation as I do any other time of the month.* ________
7. I don't allow the fact that I'm menstruating to interfere with my usual activities.* ________
8. Avoiding certain activities during menstruation is often very wise. ________
9. I am more easily upset during my premenstrual or menstrual periods than at other times of the month. ________
10. I don't believe my menstrual period affects how well I do on intellectual tasks.* ________
11. I realize that I cannot expect as much of myself during menstruation, compared to the rest of the month. ________
12. Women just have to accept the fact that they may not perform as well when they are menstruating. ________

Subscale 2

1. Menstruation is something I just have to put up with. ________
2. In some ways, I enjoy my menstrual periods.* ________
3. Men have a real advantage in not having the monthly interruption of a menstrual period. ________
4. I hope it will be possible someday to get a menstrual period over within a few minutes. ________
5. The only thing menstruation is good for is to let me know I'm not pregnant. ________
6. Menstruation provides a way for me to keep in touch with my body.* ________

Subscale 3

1. Menstruation is a reoccurring affirmation of womanhood. ________
2. Menstruation allows women to be more aware of their bodies. ________
3. Menstruation provides a way for me to keep in touch with my body. ________
4. Menstruation is an obvious example of the rhythmicity which pervades all of life. ________
5. The recurrent monthly flow of menstruation is an external indication of a woman's general good health. ________

Subscale 4

1. I can tell my period is approaching because of breast tenderness, backache, cramps, or other physical signs. ________
2. I have learned to anticipate my menstrual period by the mood changes which precede it. ________
3. My own moods are not influenced in any major way by the phase of my menstrual cycle.* ________
4. I am more easily upset during my premenstrual or menstrual periods than at other times of the month. ________
5. Most women show a weight gain just before or during menstruation. ________

Subscale 5

1. Others should not be critical of a woman who is easily upset before or during her menstrual period.* ________
2. Cramps are bothersome only if one pays attention to them. ________
3. A woman who attributes her irritability to her approaching menstrual period is neurotic. ________
4. I barely notice the minor physiological effects of my menstrual periods. ________
5. Women who complain of menstrual distress are just using that as an excuse. ________
6. Premenstrual tension/irritability is all in a woman's head. ________
7. Most women make too much of the minor physiological effects of menstruation. ________

Self-Assessment—*Continued*

Scoring

A mean is computed for each subscale by dividing the sum of items by the number of items in each factor (reversing the scoring of items where necessary). An * indicates items for reverse scoring. (For example, a rating of 1 is changed to 7, 2 is changed to 6, 3 is changed to 5.)

Interpretation

A higher score indicates stronger endorsement of the concept measured by each subscale. Following is a summary of data obtained from four different samples. You may want to compare your scores with these groups.

Psychometric Information

Brooks-Gunn and Ruble (1980) investigated the replicability and internal consistency of the factors. They reported high Cronbach's alpha coefficients ranging from 0.90 to 0.97 for each factor (presented here as subscales) across two samples. There was high congruence between the same factors across the two samples.

Reference

Brooks-Gunn, J. & Ruble, D. N. (1980). The menstrual attitude questionnaire. *Psychosomatic Medicine, 42,* 503–512. © American Psychosomatic Society. Scale items and table used with permission.

TABLE 1 Summary Statistics for the Menstrual Attitude Questionnaire

		Sample		
	College women	*College women*	*College men*	*Adolescent girls*
Factor Scores	**(N=191)**	**(N=154)**	**(N=82)**	**(N=72)**
1. Menstruation as a	(mean) 3.39	3.61	4.45	3.75
debilitating event	(SD) 1.09	0.98	0.73	1.28
2. Menstruation as a bothersome	4.18	4.65	4.13	3.99
event	1.26	1.09	0.93	1.54
3. Menstruation as a natural event	4.64	4.51	4.55	4.62
	1.09	1.04	0.93	0.84
4. Anticipation and prediction of	3.79	4.98	5.04	3.85
the onset of menstruation	1.16	1.11	0.74	1.34
5. Denial of any effect of	2.73	3.17	2.83	3.12
menstruation	0.96	1.05	0.79	1.08

Source: Reprinted by permission of the American Psychosomatic Society (Brooks-Gunn J., & Ruble, D.N., (1980), *Psychosomatic Medicine, 42,* p. 507)

Phases of the Menstrual Cycle

The menstrual cycle can be divided into four phases (see Figure 6.8): preovulatory (also known as the follicular or proliferative phase), ovulatory, postovulatory (also known as the secretory or luteal phase), and menstrual (also called destructive phase). The preovulatory phase begins with the release of FSH from the pituitary, stimulating the growth of a follicle in the ovary. As the follicle grows, it secretes increasing amounts of estrogen, which causes growth of the endometrium of the uterus and an increase in the cervical mucus to provide a hospitable environment for sperm. Estrogen also signals the pituitary to inhibit further releases of FSH and to begin secreting **luteinizing hormone** (LH). When the levels of estrogen reach some critical point, there is a great surge in blood levels of LH followed within 36 hours by ovulation. During ovulation, the follicle moves to the periphery of the ovary and expels the ovum into the abdominal cavity. Ovulation occurs about 14 days before the start of menstruation, regardless of the length of the cycle.

Events occurring between day 1 of menstrual cycle (first day of flow) and day 14 (ovulation):

Pituitary gland releases FSH, LH.

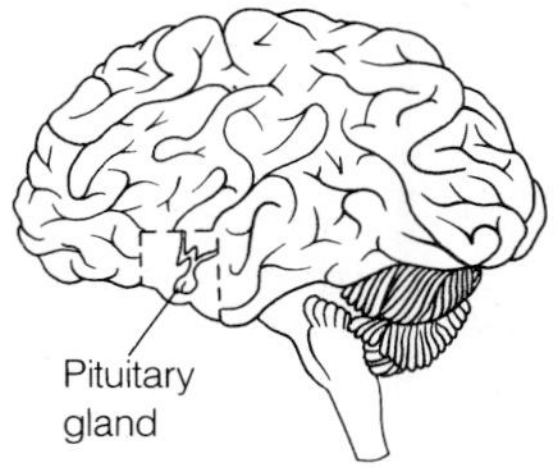

Pituitary gland monitors estrogen levels and reduces FSH and LH production when estrogen level is high enough.

Ovary produces estrogen.

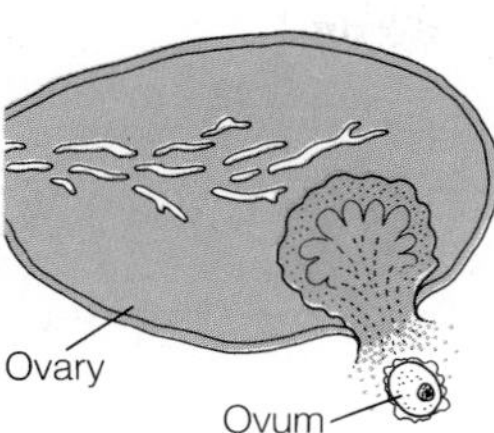

Ovum matures and leaves follicle (ovulation).

Follicle becomes corpus luteum.

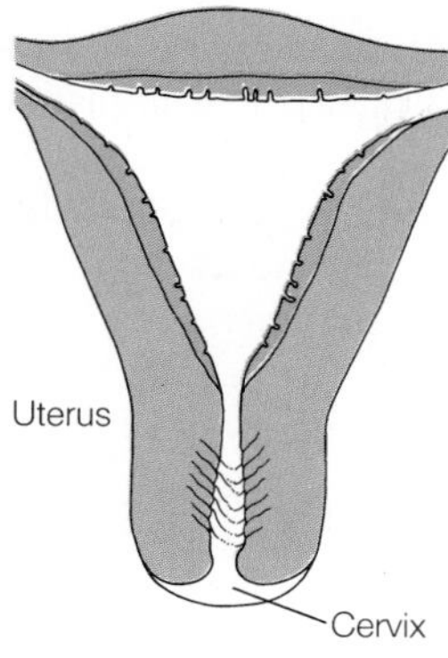

After shedding, endometrium begins to build up.

(a) In the first part of the monthly cycle, an ovarian follicle (an ovum with its surrounding sac of cells) begins to mature. The follicle grows. Ovulation is the bursting of this follicle, which frees the now-ripe ovum.

Events occurring between ovulation and day 1 of next menstrual cycle:

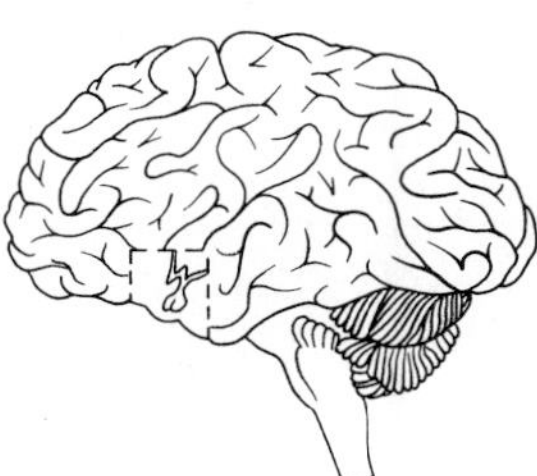

Lower FSH and LH levels.

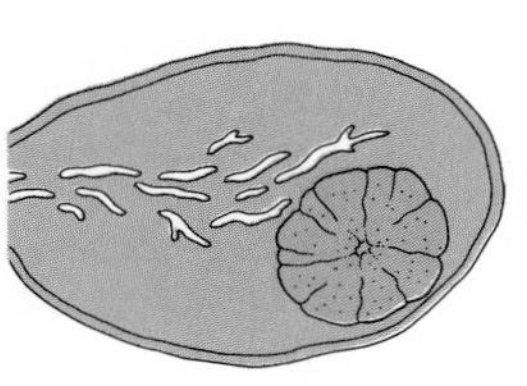

Corpus luteum produces progesterone.

Lower estrogen production.

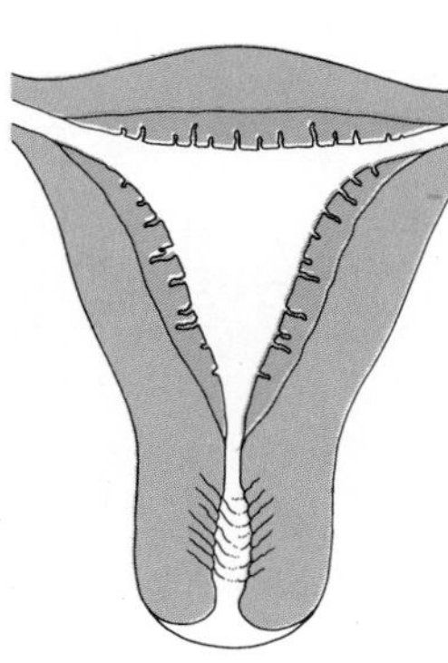

Thickened endometrium is maintained by progesterone.

(b) If fertilized, the ovum settles in the uterus. Simultaneously, the uterus prepares for the ovum by building up its lining (the **endometrium**), storing extra blood and glycogen in it to provide nourishment for the growth of an embryo. Meanwhile, the empty follicular sac develops into the **corpus luteum** ("yellow body"), a sort of remote control device that releases the hormone progesterone that will maintain pregnancy-favoring conditions in the uterus. (It is the corpus luteum for which the pituitary hormone, luteinizing hormone, is named.)

Events occurring on day 1 of next menstrual cycle:

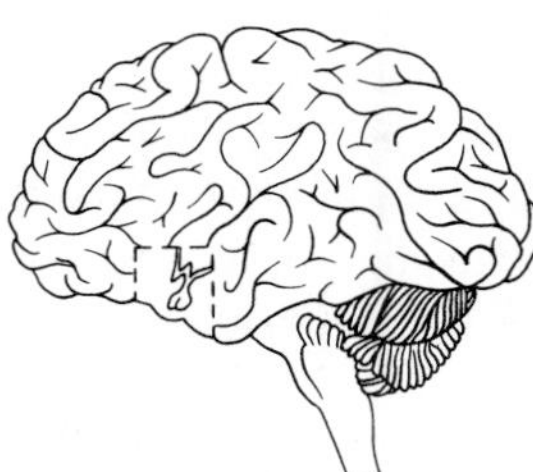

FSH and LH levels begin to rise.

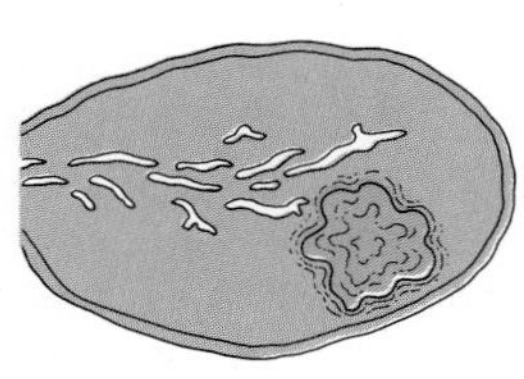

Corpus lutem begins degenerating; progesterone level begins to decline; estrogen level begins to rise.

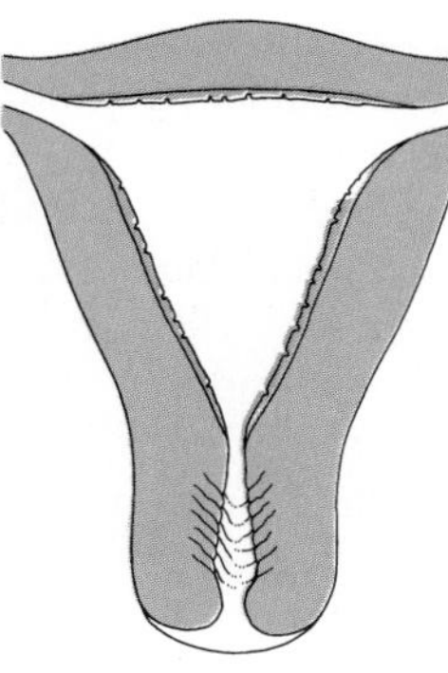

Uterine lining is shed.

(c) If fertilized and implanted, the ovum produces a factor to maintain these conditions and support pregnancy. If the ovum is shed, the conditions for pregnancy cannot be maintained. The corpus luteum withers away, the hormonal climate changes, and the cycle begins again.

FIGURE 6.8 **Physiology of the female reproductive system.**

In the postovulatory phase, the remaining cells of the follicle in the ovary (now called the corpus luteum) secrete estradiol–17B and progesterone. These hormones cause the endometrium to thicken further and build up nutrients. If the egg is fertilized and implants in the uterine wall, the lining of the uterus is maintained during pregnancy by continuous secretion of estradiol-17B and progesterone from the corpus luteum. Steroids secreted by the corpus luteum of pregnancy also initiate the development of the mammary glands and inhibit ovulation by exerting feedback on pituitary gonadotropin secretion.

If fertilization does not occur, the corpus luteum disintegrates, resulting in decreasing levels of the two hormones maintaining the endometrium and in menstruation. Menstruation lasts from three to seven days. With the decrease in estrogen levels, the pituitary again begins to secrete FSH, and the cycle starts over again.

During menstruation, the endometrial matter is sloughed off in small shreds or larger pieces. A smaller amount of blood does not mean, as old folklore suggests, that blood is accumulating elsewhere in the body, later to poison the female.

Problems of the Menstrual Cycle

Although most adolescent girls have regular periods, irregularity, or **oligomenorrhea**, is not unusual; the intervals may range from every three weeks to every six weeks. Some women have periods only once a year. If periods have not stabilized by age 17 or so, a gynecologist should be consulted. Spotting or bleeding between periods also suggests the need for a checkup.

CONSIDERATION: A missed period may or may not indicate pregnancy. Anxiety over work or the relationship with a partner, or the fear of being pregnant can cause a woman to miss her period. Training for competitive athletics may also be a cause.

Amenorrhea is the absence of menstruation for three or more months when the woman is not pregnant, menopausal, or is breast feeding. A pituitary or ovarian tumor or a metabolic disease are possible causes of amenorrhea; hence, a physician should be consulted. Excessive or prolonged menstruation, or **menorrhagia**, may suggest other problems. These include uterine infection and tumors.

Some women experience painful menstruation, or **dysmenorrhea**, symptoms of which can include spasmodic pelvic cramping and bloating, headaches, and backaches. In addition, they may feel tense, irritable, nauseated, and depressed. As the result of the hormone changes, some women retain excess body fluids and experience painful swelling of the breasts (mastalgia) during menstruation. Dysmenorrhea is caused by prostaglandins, chemicals in the menstrual flow that cause spasms of the uterus, and can be relieved by prostaglandin inhibitors. Masters and Johnson (1966) reported that orgasms provided relief from painful menstruation by speeding up the menstrual flow, thus eliminating the prostaglandins. Some women who experience dysmenorrhea report less intense symptoms after taking birth control pills, which contain estrogen and progesterone and disrupt the normal hormonal changes of the menstrual cycle. During ovulation, some women complain of lower abdominal pains, referred to as "mittlelschmerz" (or middle pain).

Painful menstruation can also be caused by endometrial tissue growing outside the uterus, for example, in the Fallopian tube or abdominal cavity, a condition

So I am perfectly happy if all the women in the world wish to say, "I have this thing called Premenstrual Syndrome," as long as they recognize that Harry has "testosterone swings" or "Excessive Testosterone Syndrome." Just give me equality.

Carol Tavris

The cure for PMS may lie in resocialization and societal change, not medicine.

Boston Women's Health Book Collective

known as **endometriosis.** These tissues deteriorate during menstruation, just as the lining of the uterus normally does, and a painful infection can result when the tissue cannot be expelled. Treatment ranges from aspirin to surgery.

Another serious problem is **toxic shock syndrome** (TSS), which has been linked to the use of superabsorbent tampons. The onset of the syndrome is rapid, with high fever, vomiting, diarrhea, abdominal pain, and rapid drop in blood pressure. Once the body is in shock, coma and death can result. The cause is unknown, but the syndrome may be produced by toxins from the bacteria Staphylococcus aureus. One theory suggests that the larger tampons might collect a lot of blood and provide a favorable environment for the bacteria. Women with weak immunity systems are particularly vulnerable. It has been suggested that women who want to continue to use tampons should avoid the superabsorbent variety, change the tampon every few hours, and alternate tampons with pads (see instructions in the package).

A more frequent problem with menstruation is premenstrual syndrome (PMS), described in Exhibit 6.1. Sexual problems associated with PMS include lack of desire, dyspareunia (painful intercourse), lack of arousal and/or lubrication, and difficulty achieving orgasm (Gise, 1991).

EXHIBIT 6.1 Premenstrual Syndrome

Premenstrual syndrome (PMS) refers to the physical and psychological problems some women experience from the time of ovulation to the beginning of, and sometimes during, menstruation. Shaughn-O'Brien (1987) emphasized that knowledge about PMS is plagued by anecdote, opinion, and a mass of uncontrolled therapeutic studies.

There are over 159 symptoms, which may include the following:

Psychological
- Tension
- Depression
- Irritability
- Lethargy
- Altered sex drive
- Excessive energy
- Mood swings
- Suicidal thoughts
- Indecision
- Confusion
- Poor judgment
- Feeling insecure

Neurological
- Migraine
- Epilepsy

Respiratory
- Asthma
- Rhinitis

Dermatological
- Acne
- Herpes

Orthopedic
- Joint pains
- Backaches

Behavioral
- Increased drug use
- Increased alcohol use
- Impulsivity
- Accident prone
- Crying

Physical
- Weight gain (due to increased appetite and water retention)
- Breast tenderness
- Change in metabolism

In a study of 702 women with PMS symptoms, the most frequently reported symptoms were negative affect (crying, irritability, depression, tension, restlessness, wordy quarrel), problems with concentration (decreased efficiency, confusion, avoiding social activity, accidents), pain (headache, cramps, backache, feeling sick), and water retention (weight gain, swelling, change in eating habits) (Van Der Ploeg, 1991).

Almost all women experienced at least one premenstrual symptom. Those experiencing two or three symptoms not severe enough to affect daily functioning were regarded as having premenstrual syndrome. A proposed disorder, as defined by the American Psychiatric Association (see the following Research and Policy Perspective on PMS and the DSM-III-R controversy), involves having five or more symptoms that are severe enough to impair daily functioning. Some people have attributed child abuse, alcoholism, divorce, and suicide to PMS. In Great Britain, PMS has been used successfully as a defense for criminal behavior. A court there ruled that PMS was a factor to consider in the mitigation of punishment, not as an excuse for violent, assaultive criminal behavior (Lewis, 1990). Such a defense has not been tried, but likely will, in the United States.

The following example from the authors' files is of a woman experiencing premenstrual disorder.

Continued

EXHIBIT 6.1 Premenstrual Syndrome—*Continued*

Alice, a 35-year-old housewife and mother, is usually a friendly and productive person, but two weeks out of each month, she is overwhelmed by extreme irritability, tension, and depression.

> It's as if my mind can't keep up with my body. I cook things to put in the freezer, clean, wash windows, work in the yard—anything to keep busy. My mind is saying slow down, but my body won't quit. When I go to bed at night, I'm exhausted. And everything gets on my nerves—the phone ringing, birds singing—everything! My skin feels prickly, my back hurts, and my face feels so tight that it's painful. I scream at my husband over ridiculous things like asking for a clean pair of socks. I hate myself even when I'm doing it, but I have no control. I can't stand being around people, and the only way I can even be civil at parties is to have several drinks.
>
> This lasts for about a week, and then I wake up one morning feeling as if the bottom has dropped out of my life. It's as if something awful is going to happen, but I don't know what it is and I don't know how to stop it. I don't even have the energy to make the beds. Every movement is an effort.
>
> I burst out crying for no reason at crazy times, like when I'm fixing breakfast or grocery shopping. My husband thinks I'm angry with him, and I can't explain what's wrong because I don't know myself. After about four days of fighting off the depression, I just give up, take the phone off the hook, and stay in bed. It's terrifying. I feel panicky, trapped.
>
> Then one morning, I wake up and suddenly feel like myself. The sun is shining, and I like life again.

While the media demonstrate a strong bias in favor of reporting negative menstrual cycle changes (Chrisler & Levy, 1990), less than 5% of women experience premenstrual disorder as described by Alice (Gise, 1991).

Other women experience a milder form of PMS, including different symptoms in varying degrees. Because so many symptoms have been associated with PMS, there is little agreement on whether or when a person is experiencing the phenomenon. In a study (McFarlane, Martin, & Williams, 1988) of the menstrual cycles of 21 women who were "normally cycling" and 21 women who were taking oral contraceptives, the researchers concluded:

> Our results indicate that the women in this study did not actually experience the classic menstrual mood pattern. . . . The evidence regarding their actual moods suggests that the stereotype that most women are victims of their raging hormones is wrong. (p. 216)

Indeed, men in the same study were also asked to keep daily mood and symptom diaries. They also reported great variability in their irritability, energy, and creativity throughout the month (McFarlane et al., 1988).

While PMS is associated with negative symptoms, some women report positive changes associated with their premenstrual period. In a study of 100 women, 66% reported at least one positive premenstrual change in the premenstrual week (Stewart, 1984). Positive changes included increased sexual interest, increased sexual enjoyment, more attractive breasts, more energy, tendency to get things done, and increased creativity.

PMS symptoms may be exacerbated by social influences. For example, in a study of 150 married women, those with careers and primary childrearing responsibility reported the highest PMS distress (Coughlin, 1990). Tavris (1992) observed that both men and women tend to attribute a woman's depression, hostility, or anger during her premenstrual phase to biological explanations like PMS. However, the real problems that "PMS sufferers" have may not be biological or hormonal in nature; the real problems include family conflicts, low pay, long hours, unsupportive partners and "housework blues."

Various social and biological causes of PMS have been suggested. (Refer to Exhibit in Chapter 5, Theories of Sexuality, for a review of sociological theories of PMS.) Some physicians view PMS as an imbalance of hormones and prescribe progesterone. Still others focus on nutrition and exercise. Diet changes that may relieve PMS symptoms include eliminating alcohol, sugar, salt, and caffeine. Eating several small meals every two to four hours is also suggested. Dr. Leslie Hartlye Gise, director of the Premenstrual Syndrome Program at Mount Sinai School of Medicine, recommends group meetings with other women, regular aerobic exercise, and such medications as alphrazolam (Gise, 1991).

The Premenstrual Syndrome Clinic in Reading, Massachusetts, has treated more than 1,000 women. The clinic's approach to therapy is multidimensional, including diet, exercise, vitamins, and progesterone (if necessary). The clinic also assists women in diagnosing PMS and recognizing its impact on their lives. Such diagnosis is facilitated by getting women to chart their physiological and psychological reactions as they progress through their cycles.

RESEARCH AND POLICY PERSPECTIVE

Premenstrual Disorder and DSM-III-R Controversy

Late luteal phase dysphoric disorder (LLPDD) consists of a group of negative symptoms that occur late in the premenstrual phase of a woman's menstrual cycle. These symptoms remit after the onset of menses (or in women who have had a hysterectomy, after the onset of the follicular phase of the cycle). The addition of the LLPDD diagnosis in the *Diagnostic and Statistical Manual of Mental Disorders* (3rd ed., rev. 1987) (DSM-III-R) has been the source of much debate and controversy. Although the diagnosis is relegated to an appendix in the manual, there has been concern that it (along with two other diagnoses in the appendix) is not adequately based on scientific research and is potentially dangerous to women. At its annual meeting in 1986, the American Psychological Association passed a resolution opposing the inclusion of these diagnoses and urging its members not to use them. Nevertheless, the LLPDD diagnosis is being considered for full diagnostic status in the upcoming fourth edition of the DSM.

The diagnostic criteria for LLPDD as they appear in the DSM-III-R (1987, p. 369) are:

Diagnostic criteria for Late Luteal Phase Disorder*

A. In most menstrual cycles during the past year, symptoms in B occurred during the last week of the luteal phase and remitted within a few days after onset of the follicular phase. In menstruating females, these phases correspond to the weeks before, and a few days after, the onset of menses. (In nonmenstruating females who have had a hysterectomy, the timing of luteal and follicular phases may require measurement of circulating reproductive hormones.)

B. At least five of the following symptoms have been present for most of the time during each symptomatic late luteal phase, at least one of the symptoms being either (1), (2), (3), or (4):
   (1) marked affective lability, e.g., feeling suddenly sad, tearful, irritable, or angry
   (2) persistent and marked anger or irritability
   (3) marked anxiety, tension, feelings of being "keyed up," or "on edge"
   (4) markedly depressed mood, feelings of hopelessness, or self-deprecating thoughts
   (5) decreased interest in usual activities, e.g., work, friends, hobbies
   (6) easy fatigability or marked lack of energy
   (7) subjective sense of difficulty in concentrating
   (8) marked change in appetite, overeating, or specific food cravings
   (9) hypersomnia or insomnia
   (10) other physical symptoms, such as breast tenderness or swelling, headaches, joint or muscle pain, a sensation of "bloating," and weight gain

C. The disturbance seriously interferes with work or with usual social activities or relationships with others.

D. The disturbance is not merely an exacerbation of the symptoms of another disorder, such as Major Depression, Panic Disorder, Dysthymia, or a Personality Disorder (although it may be superimposed on any of these disorders).

E. Criteria A, B, C, and D are confirmed by prospective daily self-ratings during at least two symptomatic cycles. (The diagnosis may be made provisionally prior to this confirmation.)

"Premenstrual syndrome" (PMS) is an imprecise term, often used to refer to physical premenstrual symptoms. Controversy among obstetricians and gynecologists

Continued

*Diagnostic criteria for LLPDD reprinted with permission from **Appendix A: Proposed Diagnostic Categories Needing Further Study** of the *Diagnostic and Statistical Manual of Mental Disorders, Third Edition, Revised.* Copyright 1987 American Psychiatric Association.

Continued

regarding PMS was discussed by Reid (1986). The emphasis in the LLPDD diagnosis is on the unpleasant mood states (dysphoria). Many researchers have called for diagnostic criteria that could differentiate between cases involving only physical symptoms, those involving mood disturbance, and cases of other mental health problems being exacerbated premenstrually. Proponents of the LLPDD diagnosisadvocate that its use will a) improve research by providing specific symptom criteria and a method of documenting symptom patterns and b) improve treatment for women with these symptoms (Spitzer, Severino, Williams, & Parry, 1989 & 1990).

Objections to labeling symptoms of the menstrual cycle as a psychopathology (or mental disorder) have been summarized by Alagna and Hamilton (1986) and Hamilton and Gallant (1990 a & b). They suggested that psychopathologizing the menstrual cycle stems from long-standing myths and misconceptions about how menstruation and the menstrual cycle influences the moods and behavior of women and about menacing effects premenstrual and menstruating women have on others. In addition, numerous methodological problems with research on premenstrual symptoms have been documented, revealing deficiencies in sample size and composition, assessment of menstrual phase, and inadequate statistical analysis. Contextual factors have been identified as influencing symptoms, such as seasonal effects, victimization history, and whether one works at home caring for small children. Finally, studies on premenstrual symptoms often rely on self-report data, which may be biased or distorted.

Hamilton and Gallant (1990a) suggested that naming the LLPDD after a phase in the menstrual implies an unproven *causal* effect, where current data confirm only an apparent *correlation* to timing of symptoms. They suggested that diagnosticians use a more neutral label, such as "periodic affective syndrome" or "cyclic dysphoric disorder," that does not imply that the menstrual cycle *causes* the associated symptoms. Spitzer et al. (1989, p. 896) suggested that if the LLPDD diagnosis is included in the DSM-IV, it have a less cumbersome name—"luteal dysphoric disorder." The debate on the LLPDD diagnosis was described by Spitzer et al. as possibly the most controversial issue in the revision of the DSM-III. Heated debate is likely to continue as the developers of the DSM-IV address this dispute.

References

Alagna, S. W., & Hamilton, J. A. (1986 August). Science in the service of mythology: The psychopathologizing of menstruation. Paper presented at the American Psychological Association Annual Convention, Washington, DC.

American Psychiatric Association. (1987). *Diagnostic and statistical manual of mental disorders* (3rd ed., rev.). Washington, DC.: Author.

Hamilton, J. A., & Gallant, S. J. (1990a). Problematic aspects of diagnosing premenstrual phase dysphoria: Recommendations for psychological research and practice. *Professional Psychology, 21,* 60–68.

Hamilton, J. A., & Gallant, S. J. (1990b). Debate on late luteal phase dysphoric disorder. *American Journal of Psychiatry, 147,* 1106.

Reid, R. L. (1986). Premenstrual syndrome: A time for introspection. *American Journal of Obstetrics and Gynecology, 155,* 921–926.

Spitzer, R. L., Severino, S. K., Williams, J. B. W., & Parry, B. L. (1989). Late luteal phase dysphoric disorder and DSM-III-R. *American Journal of Psychiatry, 146,* 892–897.

Spitzer, R. L., Severino, S. K., Williams, J. B., & Parry, B. L. (1990). Dr. Spitzer and associates reply. *American Journal of Psychiatry, 147,* 1106–7.

The Female Breasts

The breasts are not part of the reproductive system but are a secondary sex characteristic like pubic hair. They are considered part of the female's sexual anatomy in most Western societies. The breasts of females develop at puberty in response to increasing levels of estrogen. The hormone has a similar effect if injected in males.

The breast of an adult female consists of 15 to 20 mammary, or milk-producing, glands, each of which is connected to the nipple by a separate duct (see Figure 6.9). The soft consistency and size of the breasts are due to fatty tissue that is loosely packed between the glands. Breasts vary (see Figure 6.10). It is common for one breast to be slightly larger than the other. The nipple is made up of smooth muscle fibers and has numerous nerve endings, making it sensitive to touch. The nipples are kept lubricated during breastfeeding by secretions of oil from the areola (uh-ree-

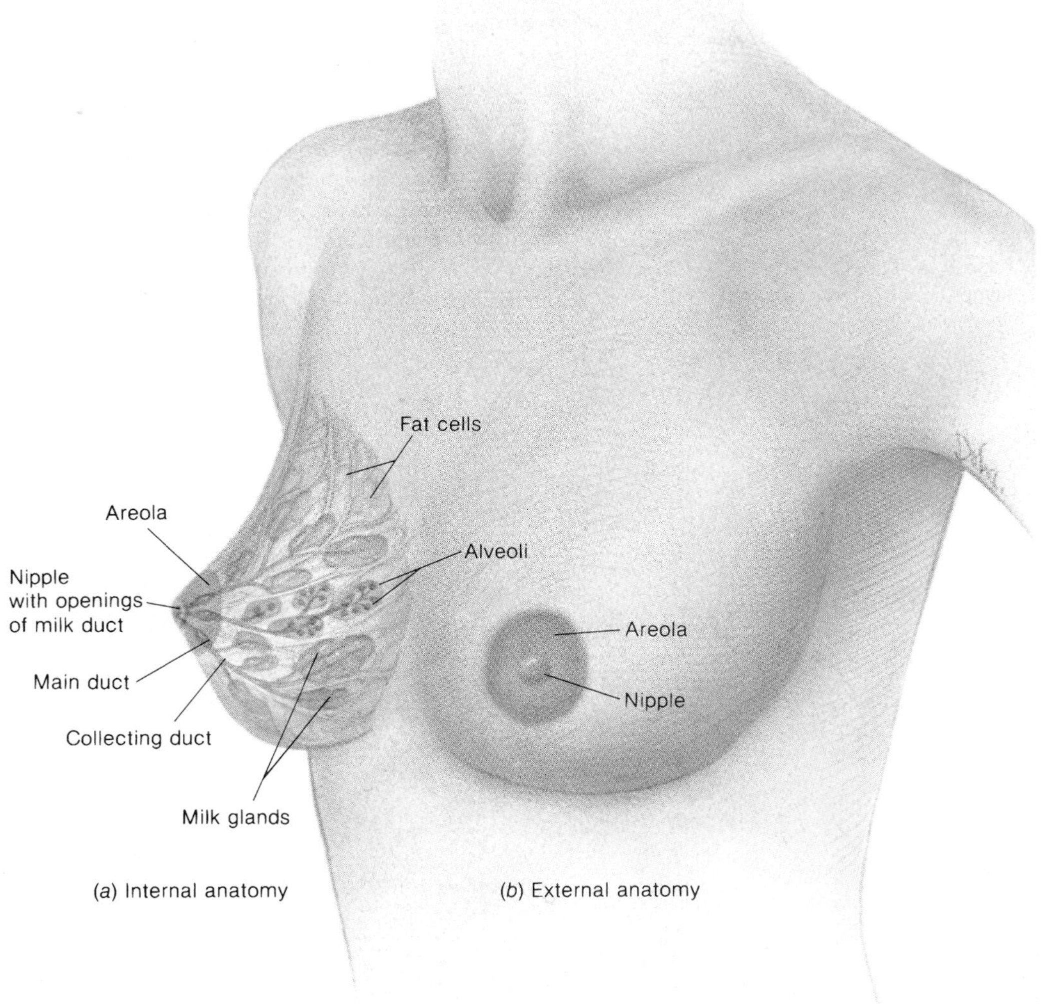

FIGURE 6.9 Internal and External Anatomy of the Female Breast

OH-lah), the darkened area around the nipple. This area becomes permanently darker after pregnancy.

CONSIDERATION: The female breasts have been given considerable public attention. The Metropolitan Museum of Art published a coffee-table edition of Metropolitan Tits, 50 20-inch-by-26-inch color photographs of women's breasts. What is notable about the photos is that the artist "eliminates the woman's head and represents her like a piece of furniture" (Neumaier, 1990, p. 123). The focus is the woman's body as an object devoid of any awareness of the humanness of the person inside the body.

In the United States and many other countries, women's breasts are considered to be highly erotic. There is no relation between the size (or shape) and sensitivity of the breasts. Many women, small- and large-breasted, enjoy having their breasts stimulated, and a few are capable of achieving orgasm from this means of arousal. However, others derive no particular pleasure from breast stimulation.

While some women feel that their breasts are too large and seek breast reduction surgery, others feel their breasts are too small and attempt to enlarge their breasts. However, lotions, mechanical devices, and so-called breast augmentation exercises are not effective, and injection of liquid silicone, which was once popular, has been found to result in medical complications. Whether to seek breast enlargement through breast implant surgery is considered in the Choices section.

Some women have nipples that are inverted, but this is generally not a health problem even for women who wish to nurse. Still other individuals, including males, may have extra nipples, but this also does not pose any health problem. Surgical removal is possible for cosmetic considerations.

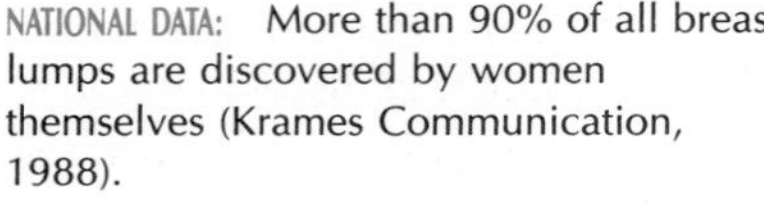

NATIONAL DATA: More than 90% of all breast lumps are discovered by women themselves (Krames Communication, 1988).

The Choices section at the end of the chapter suggests that women should choose to conduct regular breast exams.

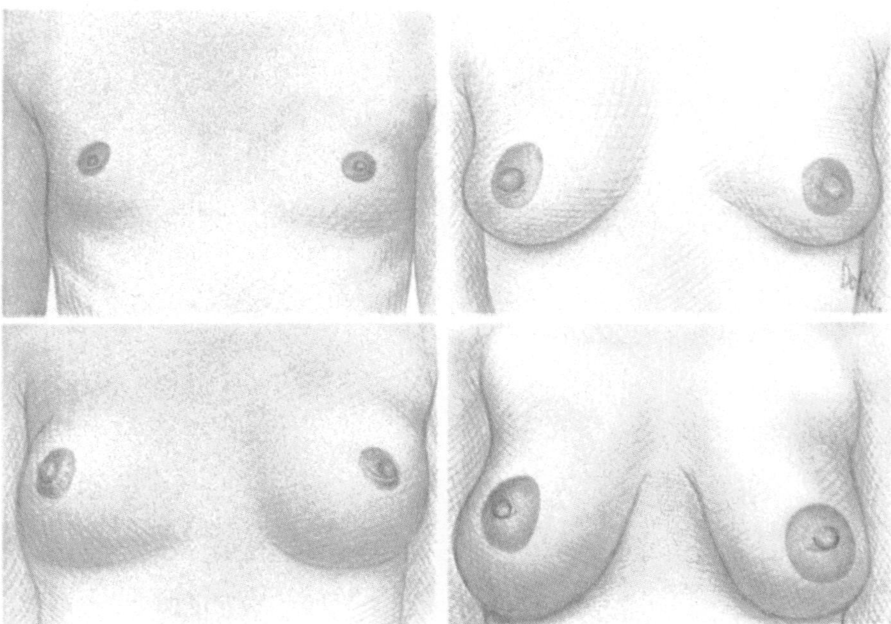

FIGURE 6.10 Variations in the Female Breast

Male External Anatomy

Whereas women find it difficult to view their genitals except by use of a mirror, male genitalia are easily visible. Men also touch and hold their genitals when urinating. Most men, therefore, are very much aware of the appearance of their own penis and scrotum. Like the vulva, male genitalia differ in appearance, and no single example can be labeled "normal" (see Figure 6.11).

Penis

The **penis** (PEE-nihs) is the primary male sexual organ, which, in the unaroused state, is soft and hangs between the legs. When sexually stimulated, the penis enlarges, hardens, and becomes erect, enabling penetration of the vagina. The penis functions not only reproductively (depositing sperm in the female's vagina) but also as a passageway from the bladder to eliminate urine.

When the penis rises to the sky, the brains fall to the ground.

Italian adage

The visible, free-hanging portion of the penis consists of the body, or shaft, and the smooth, rounded **glans** at the tip. Like the glans of the female clitoris, the glans of the penis has numerous nerve endings. The penis is especially sensitive to touch on the raised rim, or **corona**, and on the **frenulum**, the thin strip of skin on the underside, which connects the glans with the body. The body of the penis is not nearly as sensitive as the glans. The urethral opening, or meatus, through which urine is expelled from the body, is normally located at the tip of the glans. Occasionally, the urethral opening is located at the side of the glans, a minor anatomical defect that may prevent depositing the sperm at the cervical opening; this can be surgically corrected.

NATIONAL DATA: Based on a sample of 2,770 men who measured their flaccid and erect penises from base to tip, the shorter the penis, the more it grew. The average short penis grew by 85% or more, to 5.8 inches. Long penises grew only 47%, to 6.5 inches (Jamison & Gebhard, 1988).

Unlike the penises of some other mammalian species, the human penis has no bone. Nor is the penis a muscle that the man can contract to cause erections. In cross-section, the penis can be seen to consist of three parallel cylinders of tissue containing many cavities, two corpora cavernosa (cavernous bodies) and a corpus spongiosum (spongy body) through which the urethra passes (see Figure 6.12). Each is bound in its own fibrous sheath. The spongy body can be felt on the underside when the penis is erect. The penis has numerous blood vessels, and when it is stimulated, the arteries dilate and blood enters faster than it can leave. The cavities of the cavernous and spongy bodies fill with blood, and pressure against the fibrous membranes causes the penis to become erect. Like the clitoris, the penis is attached to the pubic bone by the inner tips of the cavernous bodies, called crura.

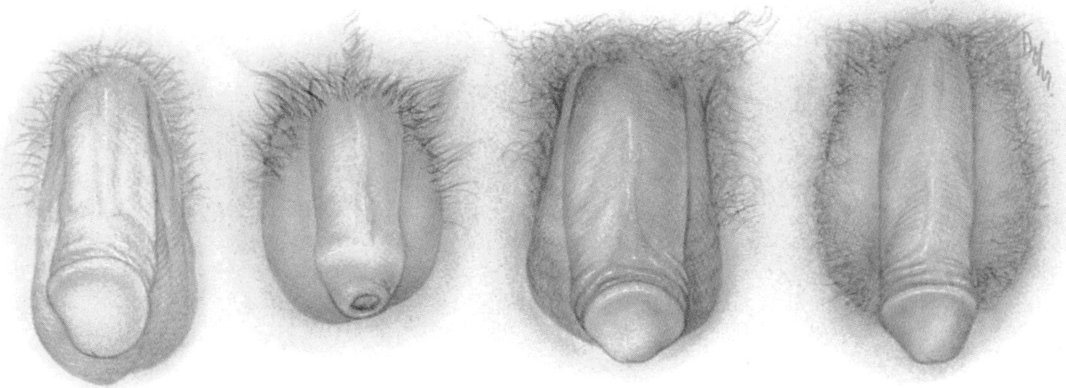

FIGURE 6.11 Variations in External Male Genitalia

FIGURE 6.12 Internal Male Sexual Organs, Sagittal View, Showing Cross Section of Penis

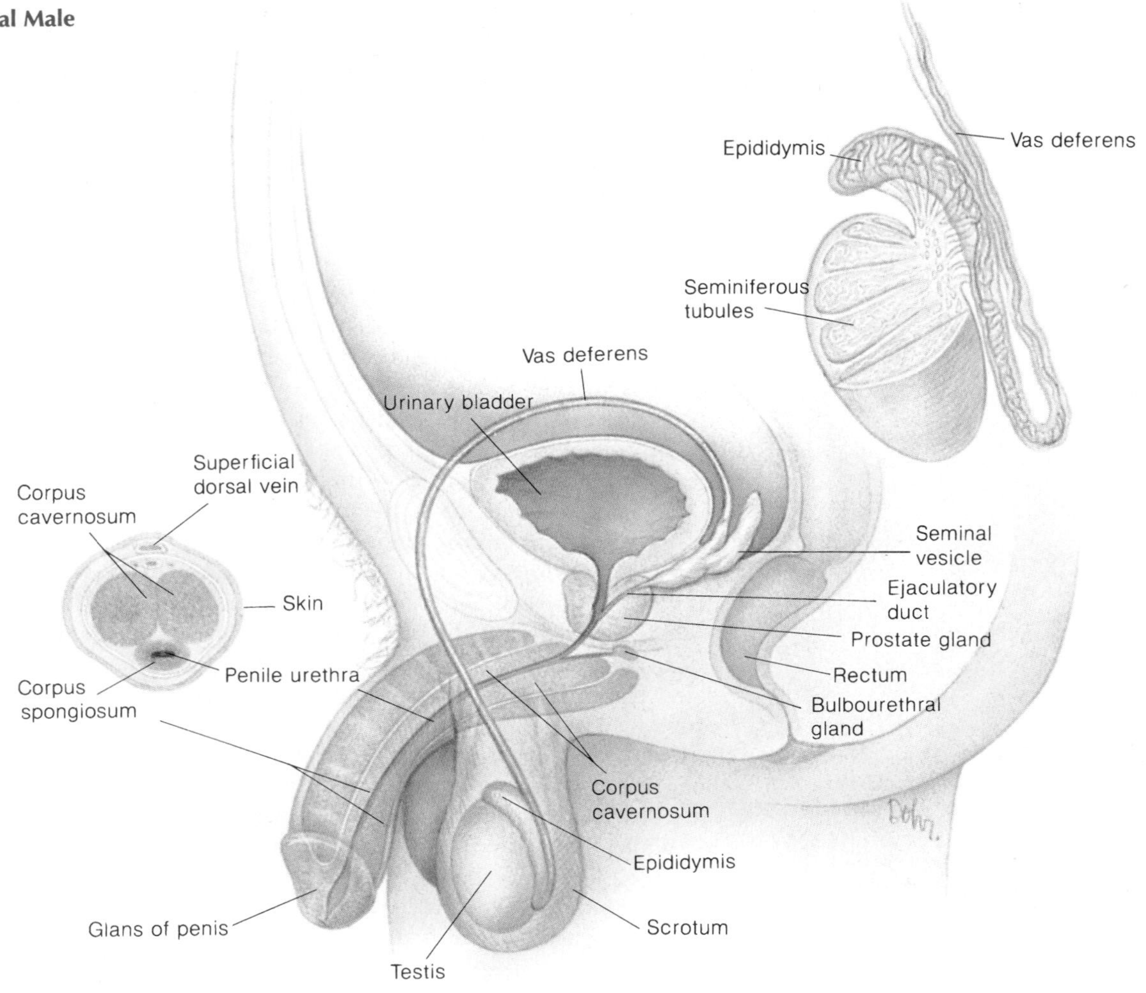

NATIONAL DATA: In Kinsey's study of penis length among white college males, 95.2% reported that their erect penis measured between 5 and 7.75 inches (Gebhard & Johnson, 1979).

The root of the penis is made up of the crura and the inner end of the spongy body, which is expanded to form the bulb. Two muscles surround the root of the penis and aid in ejaculation and urination. Voluntary and involuntary contractions of these muscles result in a slight jerking of the erect penis.

The glans of the penis is actually the expanded front end of the spongy body. The skin of the penis, which is extremely loose to enable expansion during erection, folds over most of the glans. This foreskin, or prepuce, is fixed at the border between the glans and body of the penis. Small glands beneath the foreskin secrete small amounts of oils that have no known physiological function. These oily secretions can become mixed with sweat and bacteria to form smegma, a cheesy substance similar to that which can build up under the clitoral hood in females.

Circumcision, the surgical procedure in which the foreskin of the male is pulled forward and cut off (see Figure 6.13) has been practiced for at least 6,000 years

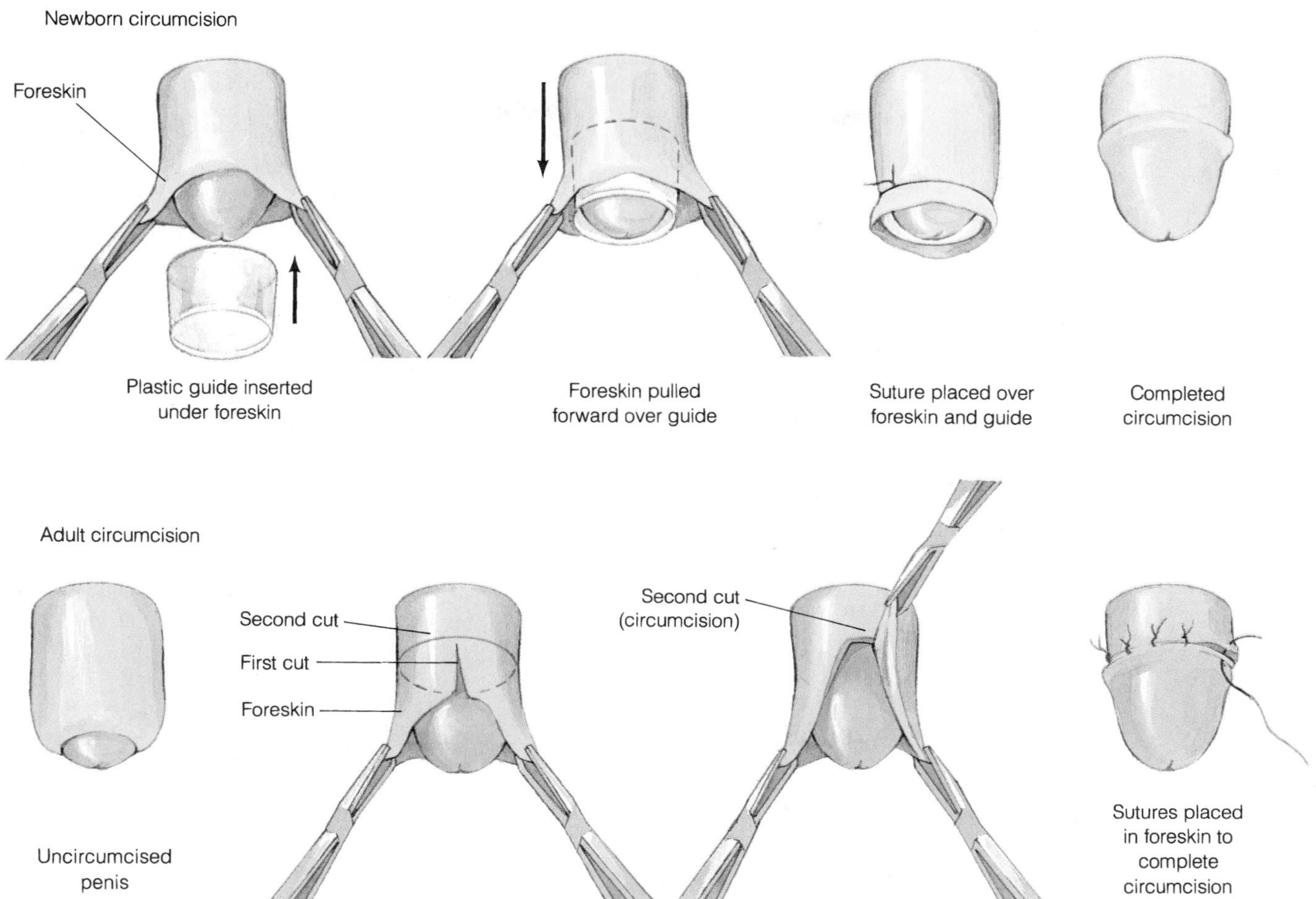

FIGURE 6.13 In **newborn circumcision** a cup placed over the glans penis protects it from injury when a cut is made to remove the foreskin. In **adult circumcision** the foreskin is held with small clamps, then cut. The cut end is sutured.

(Wilkes & Blum, 1990). About 80% of men in the United States have been circumcised. In a study of newborn males at a hospital in New York state, 70% of the whites and 25% of the Hispanics had been circumcised; blacks fell between these extremes (Wilkes & Blum, 1990).

Circumcision is a religious rite for members of the Jewish and Moslem faiths. To Jewish people, circumcision symbolizes the covenant made between God and Abraham. In some societies, circumcision is performed, often very crudely without anesthesia, as a puberty rite to symbolize the passage into manhood. In the United States, the procedure is generally done within the first few days after birth. Among non-Jewish people in the United States, circumcision first became popular during the nineteenth century as a means of preventing masturbation. But research by Masters and Johnson (1966) indicates there is no difference in excitability in men with circumcised and uncircumcised penises.

CONSIDERATION: Should parents choose to have their male infants circumcised? Today, the primary reason for performing circumcision is to ensure proper hygiene and to maintain tradition. The smegma that can build up under the foreskin is a potential breeding ground for infection. But circumcision may be a rather drastic procedure merely to ensure proper hygiene, which, as the Academy of Pediatrics suggests, can just as easily be accomplished by pulling back the foreskin and cleaning the glans during normal bathing. However, being circumcised is associated with having a lower risk of contracting the AIDS virus (Bongaarts, Reining, Way, & Conant, 1989). Regardless of the reason for deciding in favor of circumcision, the surgical procedure is relatively low-risk (Lund, 1990). While the newborn does feel pain, it can be minimized by administering local anesthesia (Masciello, 1990).

Scrotum

The **scrotum** (SCROH-tuhm) is the sac located below the penis that contains the testicles. Beneath the skin is a thin layer of muscle fibers that contract when it is cold, helping to draw the testicles closer to the body. In hot environments, the muscle fibers relax and the testicles are suspended further away from the body. Sweat is produced by the numerous glands in the skin of the scrotum. These responses help to regulate the temperature of the testicles. Sperm can only be produced at a temperature several degrees lower than normal body temperature, and any variation can result in sterility.

Male Internal Anatomy

The male internal organs, often referred to as the male reproductive system, include the testicles where sperm is produced, a duct system to transport the sperm out of the body, and some additional structures that produce the seminal fluid in which the sperm are mixed before ejaculation (see Figure 6.14).

Testes

The paired **testes**, or testicles, are the male gonads and develop from the same embryonic tissue as the female gonads, the ovaries. The translation of the Latin *testes* is "witness." In biblical times, it was the custom when giving witness to hold the testicles of the person to whom one was making an oath (hence "testifying"). The Romans adopted this custom, except that they held their own testes while testifying. In essence, a man's word was literally as good as his testes (Rosen & Beck, 1988, p. 56).

The two oval-shaped testicles are suspended in the scrotum by the spermatic cord and enclosed within a fibrous sheath. The testes are undescended in about 2% of males at birth, a condition called *cryptorchidism,* but in most cases, the testicles descend within a few months. It is normal for the left testicle to hang lower than the right one in right-handed men and the reverse in left-handed men. However, the two testicles should be about the same size, and if one is noticeably larger, a physician should be consulted. The testes are very sensitive to pressure; some men find gentle touching or squeezing of the scrotum to be sexually arousing, while others may wish to avoid this type of stimulation.

The function of the testes, complementary to that of the ovaries, is to produce spermatozoa and male hormones. Billions of sperm are produced each month in the

FIGURE 6.14 Cross section of testicle

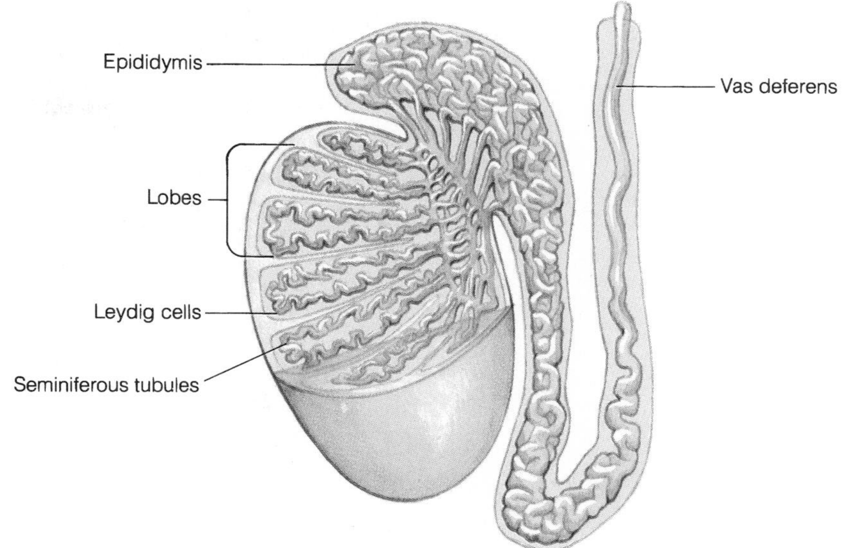

seminiferous tubules, and the male hormone testosterone is produced in the interstitial or Leydig's cells, which are located between the seminiferous tubules.

> **CONSIDERATION:** It is particularly hazardous for an adult man to contract a case of the mumps, a viral infection that often causes swelling of the testicles. The sheath in which the testes are enclosed does not readily expand and the resulting pressure can cause destruction of the seminiferous tubules and sterility.

Duct System

The several hundred seminiferous (sehm-uh-NIHF-er-uhs) tubules come together to form a tube in each testicle called the **epididymis** (ehp-uh-DIHD-uh-miss), the first part of the duct system that transports sperm. The epididymis, which can be felt on the top of each testicle, is a C-shaped, highly convoluted tube, which if uncoiled would measure 20 feet in length. The sperm spend from two to six weeks traveling through the epididymis as they mature; they are reabsorbed by the body if ejaculation does not occur.

The sperm leave the scrotum through the second part of the duct system, the **vas deferens** (vas DEF-uh-renz), or ductus deferens. These 14- to 16-inch-long paired ducts transport the sperm from the epididymis up and over the bladder to the prostate gland, where sperm mix with seminal fluid to form semen (see Figure 6.15).

The final portion of the duct system is about eight inches long and is divided into prostatic, membranous, and penile portions. In the prostatic portion, the previously paired duct system joins together to form the final common pathway. The male urethra transports urine from the bladder, as well as semen. The urethral sphincter muscles surround the membranous portion of the urethra, enabling voluntary control of urination. The penile portion of the urethra runs through the corpus spongiosum, and the urethral opening is at the top of the glans. As in women, transmission of bacteria to the urethral opening can result in inflammation of the urethra and bladder (urethritis). The most common symptoms are frequent urination ac-

FIGURE 6.15 The male reproductive system posterior view.

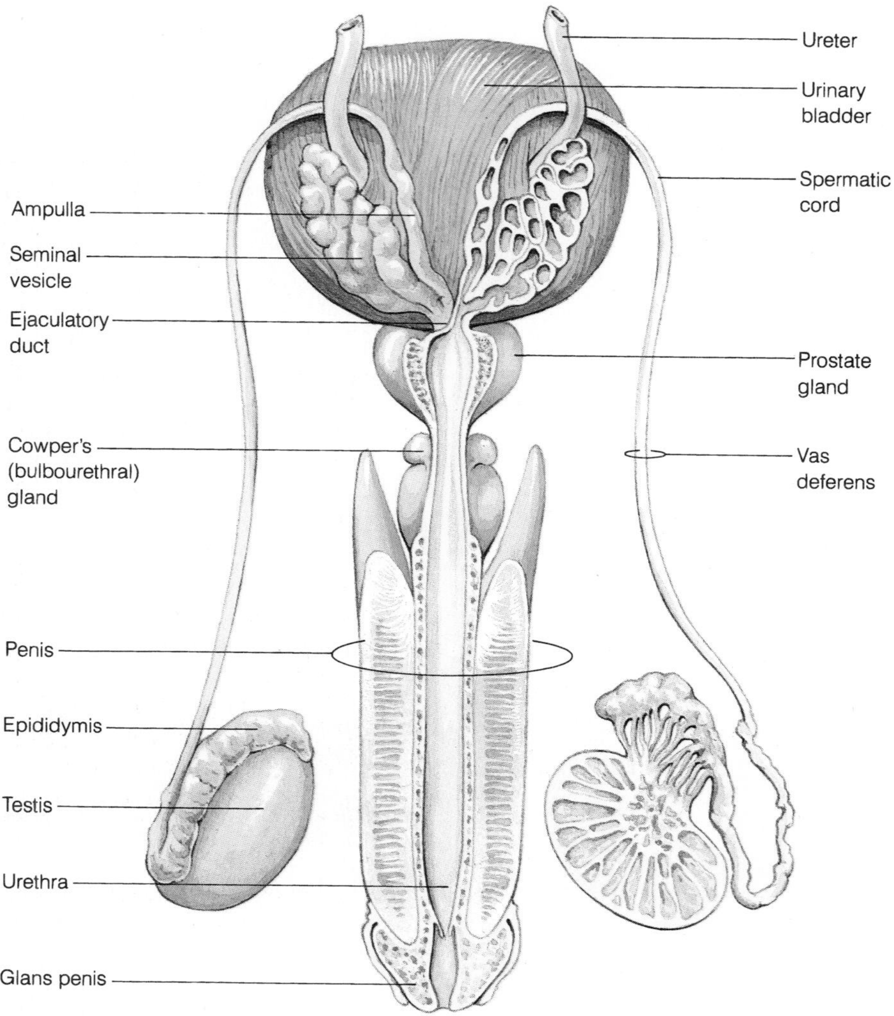

companied by a burning sensation and discharge. The man should consult a health care provider if these symptoms appear.

Seminal Vesicles and Prostate Gland

The **seminal vesicles** resemble two small sacs about two inches in length located behind the bladder. They are mistakenly called vesicles because it was once believed that they were storage areas for semen. The seminal vesicles, however, secrete their own fluids that mix with sperm and fluids from the prostate gland. Substances secreted from the seminal vesicles include fructose and prostaglandins. Sperm that reach the ejaculatory duct as a result of both muscular contractions of the epididymis and vas and the sweeping motion of hairlike cilia on their inner walls are made active by fructose. Prostaglandins induce contractions of the uterus, aiding movement of the sperm within the female.

Much of the seminal fluid comes from the **prostate gland** (see Figure 6.15), a chestnut-sized structure located below the bladder and in front of the rectum. In the prostate, the ejaculatory ducts join the initial portion of the urethra from the bladder to form a single common passageway for urine and semen. The prostate enlarges at puberty as the result of increasing hormone levels. It normally shrinks as men get older, but in some cases, it becomes larger and constricts the urethra, interfering with urination. Surgical removal of the prostate may be required. The prostate is also a common site of infection, resulting in an inflamed condition called prostatitis. Major symptoms are painful ejaculation or defecation. The condition can be treated with antibiotics. Some men develop prostate cancer. Among men, the frequency of prostate cancer is second only to lung cancer, and the risk increases with age. All men should have their prostate checked annually, a procedure in which the physician inserts a finger in the rectum and palpates the prostate to check for any abnormalities. (See the Choices section at the end of this chapter for further information.)

The structures of the prostate give the whitish seminal fluid its characteristic odor. In addition to sugars, prostaglandins, and bases (sperm cannot live in acidic environments), seminal fluid has recently been reported to contain a potent antibiotic, which probably serves to protect both the vagina and male reproductive system from infection. About one teaspoonful of semen, consisting of sperm and seminal fluid from the prostate gland and seminal vesicles, is expelled from the urethra during ejaculation. Although a normal ejaculation contains several hundred million sperm, most of the volume consists of seminal fluid.

A small amount of clear, sticky fluid is also secreted into the urethra before ejaculation by two pea-sized Cowper's, or bulbourethal, glands located below the prostate. This fluid can often be noticed on the tip of the penis during sexual arousal. The quantity of this alkaline fluid is too small to serve as a lubricant, and it probably acts to neutralize the natural acidic environment of the urethra. It may contain stray sperm, however, making withdrawal of the penis from the vagina (before ejaculation) a risky method of birth control.

CHOICES

Individuals are confronted with a number of choices in regard to their anatomy. Whether to have one's breasts reduced or enlarged, whether to have a mammogram and/or a Pap smear, whether to conduct breast and testicle self-exams, and whether to have a prostate rectal exam are issues.

Choose to Have a Breast Implant?

While some women elect to have their breasts reduced in size, more are concerned about breast enlargement. In 1990, 150,000 women had breast augmentation surgery (Tavris, 1992). Done mostly for cosmetic reasons, breast implants involve a surgeon making an incision at the base of the breast(s), placing the implant(s) inside, and sewing the tissue back up. Implants have traditionally been composed of a silicone gel that is inside an outer shell also made of silicone. The "Meme," a silicone implant with a polyurethane coat, has also been used. In view of the recent negative publicity (Seligmann & Church, 1992) about breast implants, should you get a breast implant?

Only with great caution, warns the U.S. Food and Drug Administration. Problems associated with breast implants include deterioration with age, ruptures, and leaking. Some patients develop silicone-associated disease 3 to 12 months after implantation as a consequence of the implants leaking fluid into their immune system. Swollen glands, fevers, chills, sore throat, and joint pains are among the associated problems that require removal of the implants. In addition, there isevidence that the fluid silicone does not permit areas of the breast to be examined in mammography (Beisang, Geise, & Ersek, 1991). In view of these concerns, the FDA recommended that silicone-gel breast implants be made available only to women who would participate in clinical studies to evaluate the safety of the device (Panel recommends restricting silicone breast implants, 1992).

Not all research findings on breast implants are negative. Although cancer has been implicated in breast implants, Van Natta, Thurston, and Moore (1990) reviewed the literature and stated that no clinical evidence of carcinogenesis in humans has been noted in those who had silicone gel breast implants in more than 25 years of use. On the basis of these data, they concluded that silicone-gel breast implants are safe. Nevertheless, Dow Corning, a major manufacturer of the silicone breast implant, has ceased production.

An alternative to silicone is peanut oil, which does not obscure mammography diagnosis. Implants filled with saline solution also are being recommended.

Choose to Have a Mammogram?

About 150,000 women are diagnosed with breast cancer each year, and about 41,000 die from breast cancer annually (Stein, Fox, & Murata, 1991). Since breast cancer is the leading cause of death among women in their early 40s, early detection is essential. Most women who choose to use procedures to detect breast cancer early can be treated and survive. Mammography, an Xray of the breast, is a diagnostic procedure that may confirm the existence of a breast lump. Mammography is the most reliable method for detecting breast cancer while a tumor is very small (before it can be felt). The National Cancer Institute suggests that beginning at age 40, all women should have a mammogram every one or two years. Beginning at age 50, they should have a mammogram each year. Other medical organizations have different opinions about the age at which routine mammographic examinations should begin. There is also some concern about frequent mammograms because of the cancer-causing potential of Xrays.

In a study of 963 women over the age of 35 in three communities in Los Angeles County, 57% of the white women, 52% of the black women, and 29% of the Hispanic women reported that they had had a mammogram. Those least likely to have a mammogram were deterred by the cost ($50 to $150 or more), fear of radiation, and fear of pain (Stein et al., 1991). When making a decision about having a mammogram, individuals should be aware that public health departments may offer mammograms at affordable prices, that the pain is less than that experienced during a pelvic examination, and that radiation exposure is minimal (Stein et al., 1991).

Another diagnostic technique is thermography, which produces a picture of heat variations over the body. The greater heat given off by rapidly multiplying malignant cells will show up on the thermograph.

The most accurate way to find out if a tumor is malignant is to perform a biopsy

Continued

Continued

in which a portion of the lump is removed and analyzed in the laboratory by a pathologist.

> When a biopsy is necessary, a woman has a choice to make. She can have a biopsy and immediate breast removal (mastectomy) if cancer is found. This is a one-step procedure. Or she can choose a two-step procedure. This method involves biopsy on one day; if cancer is found, the treatment usually takes place within a couple of weeks. The two-step procedure is recommended for most women because it offers extra time for:
>
> 1. Additional tests to determine the extent of the disease;
> 2. A second medical opinion;
> 3. Discussion of treatment alternatives;
> 4. Emotional preparation; and
> 5. Domestic and work arrangments for the recovery period. (National Cancer Institute, 1988, pp. 7, 8)

If the analysis reveals that the lump is malignant, one of several surgical procedures may be recommended. A radical mastectomy involves the removal of the whole breast, underlying muscle, and lymph nodes. In a modified radical mastectomy, the breast and lymph nodes are removed but not the muscles. In a partial mastectomy, or lumpectomy, only the lump is removed. Radiation therapy or chemotherapy may be used in combination with surgery. Around 90% of those who have localized breast cancer and are treated with these various methods survive at least five years.

Removal of a breast can be an emotionally traumatic experience. Some women feel they have been mutilated both physically and psychologically. One of their greatest fears is that their partner will cease to love them or view them as attractive. Some women elect to have breast reconstruction surgery.

Choose to Have a Pelvic Examination and a Pap Test?

The death rate for uterine cancer has decreased more than 70% over the last 40 years, mainly due to the Pap test for early detection of cervical cancer (American Cancer Society, 1992). Although vaginal discharge, pain, and bleeding are the typical symptoms, the cancerous cells can be present for 5 to 10 years before being detected. For early detection, sexually active women taking oral contraceptives and women age 20 and over are encouraged to have an annual Pap test in combination with a pelvic examination for abnormalities of the uterus and ovaries.

A Pap test is done by a health-care professional who uses a speculum to open the vagina wide enough to obtain a sample of cells from the cervix. The cells are examined under a microscope; if they look cancerous, a biopsy is performed—a portion of the cervical tissue is removed and examined to confirm the diagnosis.

Cervical cancer in its early stage may be treated by cryotherapy (destroying the abnormal tissue by freezing) or by electrocoagulation (using an electric current to destroy the tissue). The advantage of these procedures is that the cancer can be eliminated without having to remove the uterus. When cervical cancer is in advanced stages, surgery to remove the uterus and cervix may be performed. This is known as hysterectomy. If the ovaries are also removed during hysterectomy, estrogen replacement therapy may be indicated because of the abrupt cessation of the body's ability to produce estrogen. Radiation therapy and chemotherapy also may be used in the treatment of cervical cancer.

The cure rate for cancer of the cervix is about 60%. However, if detected in the earliest stages by a routine Pap smear, the cure rate approaches 100%. Regular Pap tests are advised for all women. Some women seem particularly vulnerable to cervical cancer, including those who have genital herpes, those who have a variety of sexual partners, and those who began having intercourse at an early age. A woman is most likely to get cervical cancer at age 45 and over.

Choose to Have a Prostate Rectal Exam?

Just as women confront choices involving mammograms, Pap tests, and pelvic examinations, men are faced with the decision to have a prostate rectal exam. Over 100,000 new cases of prostate cancer are detected each year, and approximately 30,000 men die from the disease. It is the most common form of cancer for men over the age of 70 (Soloway, 1990). Death can often be avoided by an early diagnosis. Prostate rectal examinations may also detect rectal or colon cancer.

The most common procedure is a digital rectal exam (DRE) in which the health-care professional (physician or physician's assistant) inserts a gloved lubricated finger into the rectal canal and rotates the finger to see if the size of the prostate is normal and to check for any unusual lumps in the rectum. Men often feel embarrassed and uncomfortable when confronted with this procedure, which may influence their decision to avoid it. But the life-saving potential of having a prostate rectal exam may be worth the embarrassment.

A new diagnostic tool for evaluating early localized prostate cancer is transrectal ultrasound. This safe, relatively noninvasive procedure involves the physician inserting an ultrasound probe into the rectal vault that produces an image of the prostate and the vault on a screen.

The American Medical Association recommends such an examination every year after age 30. After age 50, a fecal blood test, a proctoscope examination (a small telescope is inserted into the rectum to assess the presence of abnormalities), and a digital exam are recommended every three to five years. Earlier, we referred to tennis pro Bobby Riggs, who lamented that he had not had a prostate examination sooner.

Choose to Do Self-Examinations?

Individuals can do much to ensure early detection of breast and testicular cancer through self-examinations. Most do not conduct self-examinations, however, be cause of a lack of knowledge, discomfort in examining their own bodies, and anxiety over what they might find (only 20%

Continued

Continued

of breast lumps are cancerous). One choice might be to tell a health-care professional of your desire to conduct self-examinations and to teach you how. This will ensure that you will learn how to conduct the examination properly and make learning how easier since someone shows you. Some individuals, however, will choose to learn how to conduct self-examinations through reading.

Breast Self-Examination The American Medical Association encourages women to give themselves a breast exam once a month (preferably after menstruation) using the following procedure (men may also benefit from giving themselves breast exams):

1. In the shower or bath: Examine your breasts during a bath or shower; hands glide easier over wet skin. Move your fingers, held flat, gently over every part of each breast. Use the right hand to examine the left breast, the left hand for the right breast. Check for any lump, hard knot, or thickening.

2. Before a mirror: Inspect your breasts with your arms at your sides. Next, raise your arms high overhead. Look for any changes in the contour of each breast, a swelling, dimpling of skin, or changes in the nipple. Then, rest your palms on your hips and press down firmly to flex your chest muscles. The left and right breast will not exactly match—few women's do.

3. Lying down: To examine your right breast, put a pillow or folded towel under your right shoulder. Place your right hand behind your head: this distributes the breast tissue more evenly on the chest. With your left hand, fingers flat, press gently in small circular motions around an imaginary clock face. Begin at outermost top of your right breast for 12 o'clock, then move to 1 o'clock, and so on around the circle back to 12. A ridge of firm tissue in the lower curve of each breast is normal. Then move in an inch, toward the nipple, keep circling to examine every part of your breast, including the nipple. This requires at least three more circles. Now slowly repeat this procedure on your left breast with a pillow under your left shoulder and your left hand behind your head. Notice how your breast structure feels.

Finally, squeeze the nipple of each breast gently between thumb and index finger. Any discharge, clear or bloody, should be reported to your doctor immediately.

Testicular Self-Exam Regular examination of the testicles is also important since men can have cancer and not feel pain. Testicular cancer is the most common cancer in men aged 20 to 35 and accounts for 10% of all cancer deaths in this age group. Although the cause is unknown, testicular cancer can be cured if detected and treated early. In a study of 137 introductory psychology students, 41% reported having heard of the testicular self-exam and 21% had actually performed it (Steffen & Gruber, 1991, p. 170). The self-examination procedure involves the following:

1. Stand in front of a mirror. Look for obvious lumps or swelling of the scrotal sac or growth of the breasts.

2. Examine each testicle gently with the fingers of both hands by rolling the testicle between the thumb and the fingers. Feel for any lumps or swelling.

3. Identify the epididymis (the rope-like structure that collects the sperm) on the top and back of each testicle. Don't confuse this structure with an abnormal lump.

4. Repeat exam on the other testicle.

In the Steffen and Gruber (1991) study, college men who performed the self-exam were more likely to feel positively about the experience and to repeat the procedure in the future.

Abnormal lumps are often painless, as small as the size of a pea, and usually located in the front part of the testicle. If you find a lump, contact your doctor or clinic immediately. Remember that not all lumps are cancerous. If the lump is cancerous, treatment usually involves surgical removal of the affected testicle or radiation or chemotherapy.

Summary

1. Choices in anatomy and physiology include making decisions about sun exposure, physical checkups, and medical intervention.
2. Female external anatomy includes the mons veneris, labia, clitoris, vaginal opening, urethral opening, and breasts.
3. Female internal anatomy includes the vagina, pubococcygeus muscle, uterus, Fallopian tubes, and ovaries.
4. There is no specific "G spot"; rather, the entire extent of the anterior wall of the vagina is richly endowed with nerve endings and may respond to erotic sensitivity.

5. The menstrual cycle involves four phases: preovulatory, ovulatory, postovulatory, and menstrual.
6. Only 5% of women report experiencing premenstrual disorder whereby they are almost nonfunctional. Professionals do not agree on the nature, cause, or treatment of PMS.
7. Male external anatomy includes the penis and scrotum.
8. Male internal anatomy includes the testes, duct system, seminal vesicles and prostate gland.
9. Choice in regard to anatomy include whether to have one's breasts reduced or enlarged, whether to have a mammogram and/or Pap smear, whether to conduct breast and testicular self-exams, and whether to have a prostate rectal exam.

KEY TERMS

anatomy
physiology
vulva
pudendum
mons veneris
labia majora
labia minora
perineum
clitoris
vestibule
introitus
hymen
cystitis
vagina
Grafenberg spot (G spot)
pubococcygeus muscle
Kegel exercises
uterus
fundus
cervix
Fallopian tubes
ovaries
follicle-stimulating hormone
menstruation
menarche
luteinizing hormone
oligomenorrhea
amenorrhea
menorrhagia
dysmenorrhea
endometriosis
toxic shock syndrome
premenstrual syndrome
penis
glans
corona
frenulum
circumcision
scrotum
testes
vas deferens
epididymis
seminal vesicles
prostate gland

REFERENCES

Alzate, H., & Lodoño M. L. (1984). Vaginal erotic sensitivity. *Journal of Sex and Marital Therapy, 10,* 49–56.

Beisang, A. A., Geise, R. A., & Ersek, R. A. (1991). Radiolucent prosthetic gel. *Plastic and Reconstructive Surgery, 87,* 885–892.

Bongaarts, J., Reining, P., Way, P., & Conant, F. (1989). The relationship between male circumcision and HIV infection in African populations. *AIDS, 3,* 373–377.

Boston Women's Health Book Collective. (1984). *The New Our Bodies, Ourselves.* New York: Simon & Schuster.

Chrisler, J. C., & Levy, K. B. (1990). The media construct a menstrual monster: A content analysis of PMS articles in the popular press. *Women and Health, 16,* 89–104.

Coughlin, P. (1990). Premenstrual syndrome: How marital satisfaction and role choice affect symptom severity. *Social Work, 35,* 351–355.

Darling, C. A., Davidson, J. K., & Conway-Welch, C. (1990). Female ejaculation: Perceived origins, the Grafenberg spot/area, and sexual responsiveness. *Archives of Sexual Behavior, 19,* 29–47.

Gebhard, P. H., & Johnson, A. B. (1979). *The Kinsey data.* Philadelphia: Saunders

Gise, L. H. (1991). Premenstrual syndrome: Which treatments help? *Medical Aspects of Human Sexuality, 25,* 62–68.

Hock, Z. (1983). The G spot. *Journal of Sex and Marital Therapy, 9,* 166–167.

Jamison, P. L., & Gebhard, P. H. (1988). Penis size increase between flaccid and erect states: An analysis of the Kinsey data. *Journal of Sexuality Research, 24,* 177–183.

Kaplan, H. (1974). *The new sex therapy.* New York: Brunner/Mazel.

Kaplan, H. (1979). *Disorders of sexual desire.* New York: Brunner-Mazel.

Krames Communication. (1988). *Breast lumps: A guide to understanding breast problems and breast surgery.* Daly City, CA: Author.

Ladas, A. K., Whipple, B., & Perry, J. D. (1982). *The G spot and other recent discoveries about human sexuality.* New York: Holt, Rinehart, Winston.

Lewis, J. W. (1990). Premenstrual syndrome as a criminal defense. *Archives of Sexual Behavior, 19,* 425–442.

Lund, M. M. (1990). Perspectives on newborn male circumcision. *Neonatal Network, 9,* 7–12.

Masciello, A. L. (1990). Anesthesia for neonatal circumcision: Local anesthesia is better than dorsal penile nerve block. *Obstetrics and Gynecology, 75,* 834–838.

Masters, W. H., & Johnson, V. E. (1966). *Human sexual response.* Boston: Little, Brown

McFarlane, J., Martin, C. L., & Williams, T. M. (1988). Mood fluctuations: Women versus men and menstrual versus other cycles. *Psychology of Women Quarterly, 12,* 201–228.

National Cancer Institute. (1988). *Breast cancer: We're making progress every day.* U.S. Department of Health and Human Services. Publication No. 88-2409.

Neumaier, D. (1990). Essay: Metropolitan tits. *Journal of Sex Research, 27,* 123–129.

Panel recommends restricting silicone breast implants. (1992). *FDA Consumer,* April, p. 2.

Perry, J. D., & Whipple, B. (1981). Pelvic muscle strength of female ejaculation: Evidence in support of a new theory of orgasm. *Journal of Sex Research, 17,* 22–39.

Rodin, J. (1992, January/February) Body mania. *Psychology Today,* pp. 56–60.

Rosen, R. C., & Beck, J. G. (1988). *Patterns of sexual arousal.* New York: Guilford Press.

Seligmann, J., & Church, V. (1992, March 2). "A vote of no confidence: An FDA panel advises limiting breast implants" *Newsweek,* p. 75.

Shaughn-O'Brien, P. M. (1987). *Premenstrual syndrome.* Oxford: Blackwell Scientific Publications.

Soloway, M. S. (1990). Prostate cancer: Diagnosis, treatment, and implications for sexual function. *Medical Aspects of Human Sexuality, 24,* 23–28.

Steffen, V. J., & Gruber, V. A. (1991). Direct experience with a cancer self-exam: Effects on cognitions and behavior. *Journal of Social Psychology, 131,* 165–177.

Stein, J. A., Fox, S. A., & Murata, P. J. (1991). The influence of ethnicity, socioeconomic status, and psychological barriers on use of mammography. *Journal of Health and Social Behavior, 32,* 101–113.

Stewart, D. E. (1984). Positive changes in the premenstrual period. *Acta-Psychiatrica-Scandinavica, 79,* 400–405.

Tavris, C. (1992). *The mismeasure of women.* New York: Simon and Schuster.

Van Der Ploeg, H. M. (1991). The factor structure of the Menstrual Distress Questionnaire-Dutch. *Psychological Reports, 66,* 707–714.

Van Natta, B. W., Thurston, J. B., & Moore, T. S. (1990). Silicone breast implants—Is there cause for concern? *Indiana Medicine, 83,* 184–185.

Wilkes, M. S., & Blum, S. (1990). Current trends in routine newborn male circumcision in New York State. *New York State Journal of Medicine, 90,* 243–246.

Winton, M. A. (1989). Editorial: The social construction of the G-spot and female ejaculation. *Sex Education and Therapy, 15,* 151–163.

Zaviacic, M., Zaviacicova, A., Holoman, I. K., & Molcan, J. (1988). Female urethral expulsions evoked by local digital stimulation of the G-spot: Differences in the response patterns. *Journal of Sex Research, 24,* 311–318.

CHAPTER SEVEN

Sexual Response

Chapter Outline

Four Aspects of Human Sexual Response
- Sexual Appetite or Drive
- Central Arousal
- Genital Responses
- Peripheral Arousal

Masters and Johnson's Four-Stage Model of Sexual Response
- Excitement Phase
- **Self-Assessment:** Sexual Arousability Inventory (SAI)
- Plateau Phase
- Orgasm Phase
- Resolution Phase
- Male and Female Differences in Sexual Response

Critiques of Masters and Johnson's Model

Alternative Sexual Response Models
- Ellis's and Beach's Two-Stage Models
- Helen Kaplan's Three-Stage Model
- David Reed's Erotic Stimulus Pathway (ESP) Model

Hormones and Sexual Response

Drugs and Sexual Response
- Drugs for Medication
- Drugs for Recreation
- **Research Perspective:** The Social Psychology of Alcohol Consumption and Sexual Effects

Erotica and Sexual Response
- Sexual Response to Erotica Exposure
- Differences between Women and Men

Choices
- Choose to Engage in Sexual Behavior with Minimal Desire?
- Choose to Minimize Focus on the Orgasm Phase of the Sexual Response Cycle?
- Choose to Use Erotic Materials and/or Devices to Enhance Arousal?

Is It True?*

1. It is not unusual for women and men to report having engaged in sexual activity when they were not experiencing sexual desire.

2. The elimination of all sources of androgen in a person's body is associated with the loss of sexual desire.

3. Some men are capable of having an orgasm without ejaculating.

4. Some acne medications can cause vaginal dryness in women, erectile problems in men, and decreased libido in both sexes.

5. The bulk of the evidence suggests that women and men have more differences than similarities in their responses to erotica.

*1 = T, 2 = T, 3 = T, 4 = T, 5 = F

The sexual response, like other emotional reactions, is experienced intuitively, and is elusively difficult for the scholar or scientist to define.

Raymond Rosen
J. Gayle Beck

The film *Manhattan* features Woody Allen at a party listening to two women discuss the nature of their orgasms—clitoral versus vaginal. Finding a pause in their banter, Allen quips, "I have never had a bad orgasm." His statements and those of the two women reflect a general awareness that there is a sexual response system. In this chapter, we examine various models of the sexual response cycle. We also discuss the effects of hormones, drugs, and erotica on sexual response. We close the chapter with an examination of choices we make in reference to the sexual response cycle. We begin with identifying four aspects of most sexual response models.

Four Aspects of Human Sexual Response

Researchers have provided at least three models to describe the sexual response cycle: Masters and Johnson's four-stage model, Ellis's and Beach's two-stage models, and Kaplan's three-stage model. Before we describe each of these models in the next section, in this section, we look at the four essential features of human sexual response (Bancroft, 1983).

Sexual Appetite or Drive

Sexual appetite or drive refers to one's sexual desire. Sexual desire may be defined as "a subjective feeling state that may be triggered by both internal and external cues which may or may not result in overt behavior" (Lieblem & Rosen, 1988). Using this definition, Beck, Bozman, and Qualtrough (1991) identified how often a sample of 144 college students (58 men and 86 women) ages 18 to 54 reported experiencing sexual desire. Over a quarter of the men (25.7%), in contrast to only 3.5% of the women, reported experiencing sexual desire "several times a day" (similar respective percentages were reported for the time frame of "once a day"). Ninety-one percent of the men and 52% of the women reported that they experienced sexual desire "several times a week."

When these respondents were asked how they knew they were experiencing sexual desire, men reported that their index of sexual desire was sexual fantasies, sexual daydreams, and genital arousal. Women reported that they were aware of sexual desire because they had sexual daydreams or became genitally aroused (Beck et al., p. 452).

CONSIDERATION: In addition to reporting how often they experienced sexual desire and their criteria for doing so, the majority of the university respondents in Beck's et al. study (1991) reported that they had engaged in sexual activity without experiencing any desire. Eighty-two percent of the women and 60% of the men reported having done so. In general, the older the respondent, the more likely the person had experienced sexual activity without desire. The primary motivation for engaging in sexual activity without desire was to please the partner. However, consistent with the belief that desire is an important phase of the sexual response cycle, the majority of both women and men reported that sexual desire usually or often preceded sexual activity—either masturbation or sex with a partner.

Central Arousal

I think orgasm is a brain experience.
Joseph Bohlen

Central arousal refers to the brain, central nervous system, and cognitions involved in transmitting and processing sexual stimuli. Research on the brain, central nervous system, and cognitions as they affect sexuality is the most recent component of the sexual response cycle to be studied empirically (Bancroft, 1983; 1989). For central arousal to occur, the brain and central nervous system must be working and properly "connected" (see Chapter 16, Physical Health and Sexuality), and one's cognitions must be focused on incoming sexual stimuli. To illustrate the importance of focused attention, Geer and Fuhr (1976) asked college males to complete complex cognitive tasks (counting and labeling) while listening to erotic audiotapes. They found that the more difficult the cognitive task, the less aroused the subjects became. Emotions, as well as cognitions influence the capacity to become aroused. Wiseman (1985) observed that wives who are angry at their partners found it difficult to become sexually aroused by them. Bancroft (1989) noted, "The whole body is involved in this interplay of psychological and somatic processes" (p. 12).

CONSIDERATION: The importance of the brain in sexual response is illustrated in the fact that when certain areas of the brain of a male monkey are stimulated, he will have an orgasm and ejaculate. "Ejaculation obtained by EBS (electric brain stimulation) may occur before erection is attained and is observed despite the fact that the animal's hands are prevented from manipulating his genitals" (Kaplan, 1974, p. 39).

The human brain may have similar circuits that, when stimulated, induce pleasure, orgasm, and ejaculation. Hence, the brain and its attendant nerve connections are necessary for movement through the various "stages" of the sexual response cycle.

But beyond brain circuits and cognitions, certain chemicals produced by the endocrine glands (see Figure 7.1) must be present to activate the genitals. In men, nitric oxide is necessary to relax the smooth muscles in the corpus cavernosum.

Flirting may result in central arousal.

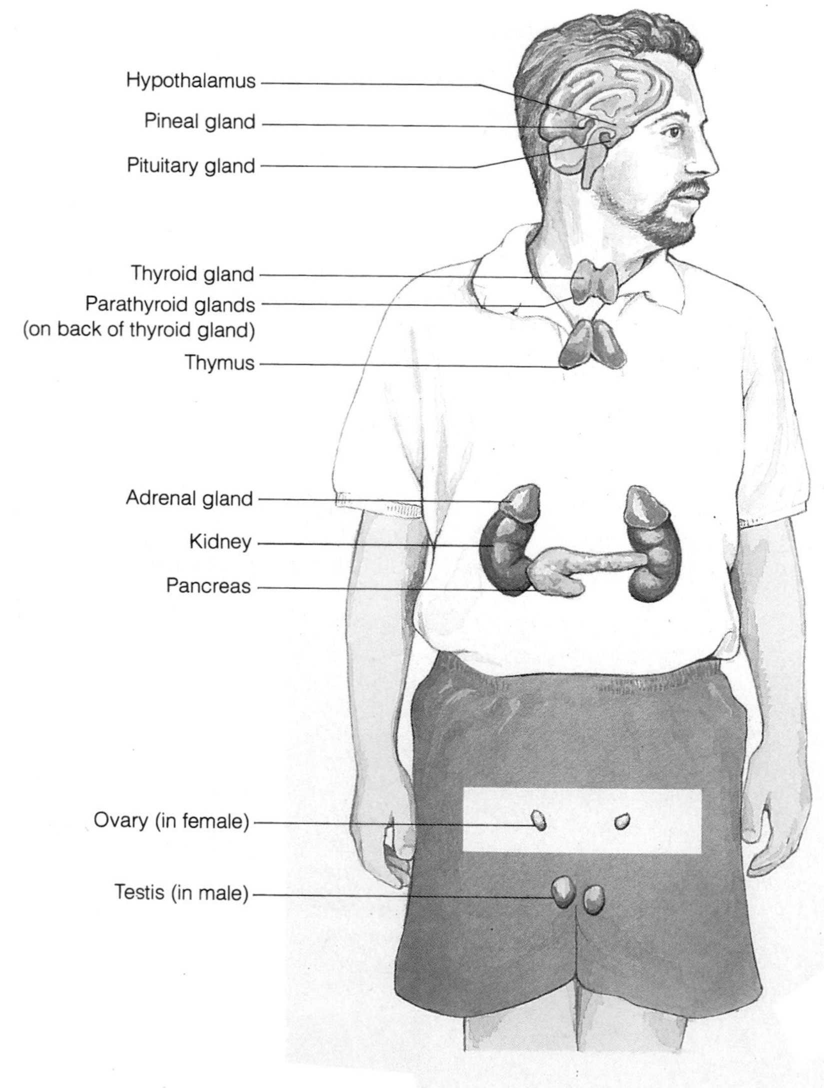

FIGURE 7.1 **Endocrine system**
Endocrine glands produce and release chemical regulators called hormones that affect sexual functioning.

Once these muscles are relaxed, the blood vessels open and blood fills the penis to produce an erection (Rajfer, Aronson, Bush, Dorey, & Ignarro, 1992).

Genital Responses

Genital responses indicative of initial sexual response include vaginal lubrication and penile erection. These and other genital responses (discussed later) are usually associated with sexual response. Genital responses and peripheral arousal have been the most extensively studied aspects of sexual response (Bancroft, 1983).

Peripheral Arousal

Peripheral arousal refers to increased heart rate, blood pressure, breath rate and skin temperature as well as skin color changes and pupillary dilation. These changes occur as a person becomes sexually excited and moves toward and beyond orgasm. How peripheral arousal symptoms change throughout the sexual response cycle will be described as we discuss the various models of the sexual response cycle.

Researchers generally place more confidence in signs of sexual arousal than in their absence, as research participants have been able to suppress and hide their arousal on physiological and self-report measures. When there are discrepancies between genital measures of arousal and self-report, usually people underestimate their level of arousal (Malamuth, Feshback, Fera, & Kunath, 1988).

MASTERS AND JOHNSON'S FOUR-STAGE MODEL OF SEXUAL RESPONSE

A fundamental assumption of any schema in regard to sexual response is that the sexual arousal process follows a predictable sequence of events. Rosen and Beck (1988) noted that "there is lack of consensus among researchers in the field concerning the number of phases to be included in the sexual response cycle, as well as the order and sequencing of such phases" (p. 38). In general, the sexual response cycle is the sequence of possible events that occur when Homo sapiens moves from a state of nonarousal to a state of resolution following orgasm. The adjective *possible* is used since it is recognized that individuals may not experience all stages at any given time (e.g., individuals may become excited but may not have an orgasm).

Various models of the sexual response cycle have been suggested. We begin with the Human Sexual Response Cycle Model (HSRC) provided by Masters and Johnson (1966), since it has been accorded the most professional visibility. The primary stages identified by Masters and Johnson (1966) are those of excitement, plateau, orgasm, and resolution.

Excitement Phase

Figures 7.2 and 7.3 depict the female and male genitals in the quiescent, unaroused state. During the *excitement phase,* individuals become sexually aroused in response to hormonal, sensory, cognitive, and relationship cues. Sensory cues may be olfactory, visual, tactile, and auditory. In effect, a person is turned on by certain scents, visual images, touch, and sounds.

These sensory cues may be real and cognitively labeled as exciting, or imaginary, as in one's fantasy. Specific other people may also provide a cue for sexual excite-

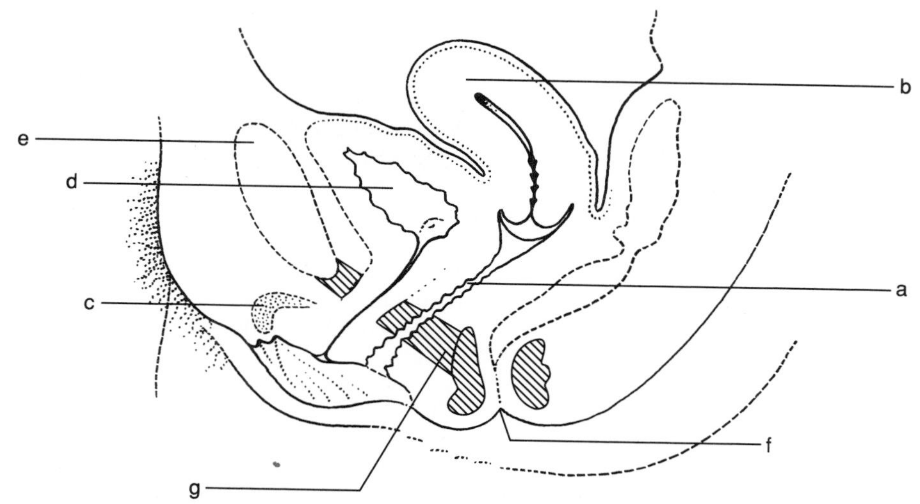

FIGURE 7.2 The female genitals in a quiescent state
The vagina (a) is a dry, collapsed potential space. The uterus (b) is in its normal pelvic position. The clitoris (c) hangs ventrally. (d) represents the urinary bladder, while (e) is the pubic bone and (f) the anus. (g) is a schematic representation of the pubococcygens and bulbocavernosus muscles.

Source: *The New Sex Therapy* by Helen Singer Kaplan. New York: Brunner/Mazel, Publishers, 1974. Copyright by Helen Singer Kaplan, 1974, p. 6. Used by permission.

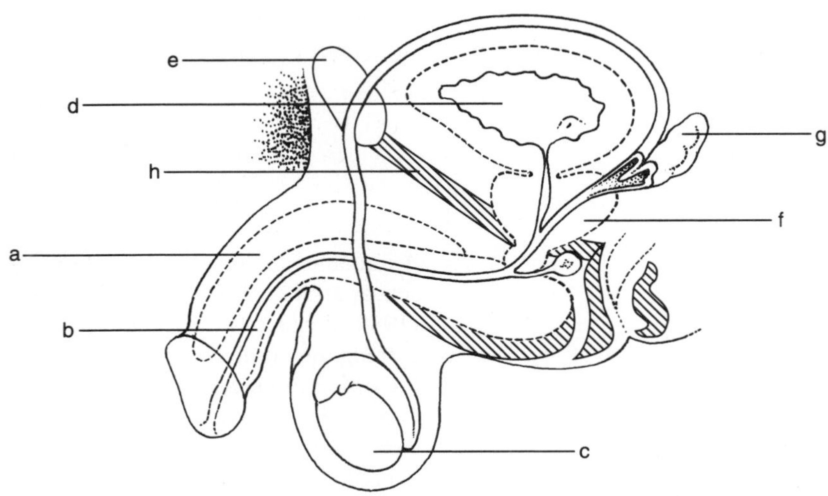

FIGURE 7.3 The male genitals in a quiescent state
The penis is flaccid because there is relatively little blood in the corpora cavernosa (a) and in the corpus spongiosum (b). The testes (c) are in their normal low position during quiescence. (d) represents the urinary bladder and its anatomic relationships to (e) the pubic bone, (f) the prostate and (g) the seminal vesicles. (h) is a schematic representation of the bulbocavernosus and perineal muscles.

Source: *The New Sex Therapy* by Helen Singer Kaplan. New York: Brunner/Mazel, Publishers, 1974. Copyright by Helen Singer Kaplan, 1974, p. 7. Used by permission.

ment. "Some people seem to have a special sexual chemistry, that is, sex is especially passionate (hot) between them" (Moser, 1992, p. 66).

Physiological and Subjective Aspects of Arousal Within 10 to 30 seconds (Bancroft, 1983) of receiving sexual stimuli (olfactory, tactile, visual, or auditory), physiological evidence of arousal occurs. One of the most visible changes due to sexual arousal is genital **vasocongestion**, or increased blood flow to the genital area (Bancroft, 1983). In men, increased blood flow to the penis causes erection—the primary physiological response during the excitement phase of the male sexual response cycle. Erection occurs when blood flows into the penis at a rapid rate while only a small amount of blood flows back. The trapped blood engorges the penis, which is transformed from a soft to a hard state. In young men with normal erections, the amount of blood flow during erection increases 25 to 60 times over baseline levels (Wagner & Green, 1981, p. 29).

CONSIDERATION: As we will note in Chapter 12 on sexuality across the life span, the older the man, the less likely he is to become sexually aroused. This was the finding of Nagayama Hall (1991) in a study of 169 nonpsychotic male sex offenders who noted an inverse relationship between chronological age and sexual arousal.

In women, vasocongestion results in vaginal lubrication and in the external genitals (labia majora, labia minora, and clitoris) becoming engorged (See Figure 7.4). The labia minora may turn a darker color, and the clitoris may expand. During sexual arousal, the upper two-thirds of the vagina expand in width and depth and become lubricated.

CONSIDERATION: Genital arousal and subjective arousal are not always linked. Tavris (1992) noted that many women can be aroused without lubricating, and lubricating is not always a sign of sexual arousal. It can also be a response to nervousness, excitement, or fear. Similarly, a man can have an erection without feeling sexually aroused, as a response to fear, anger, exercise, or waking up. (p. 228)

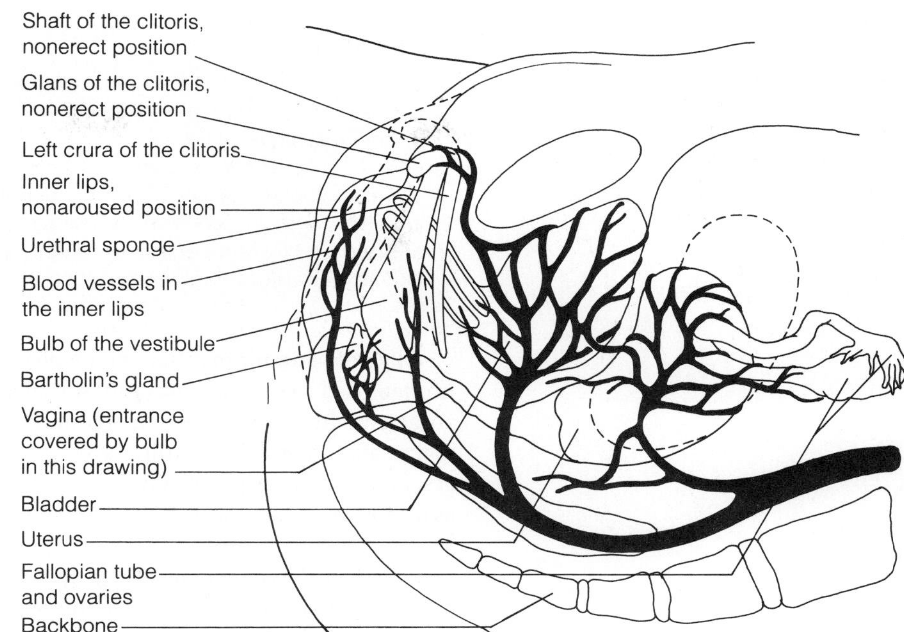

FIGURE 7.4 Internal Genital Change During Sexual Arousal

The dotted lines indicate most of the changes that take place.

- The blood vessels through the whole pelvic area swell, causing "engorgement and creating a feeling of fullness and sexual sensitivity. (The blood vessels in this drawing actually represent only a fraction of what's there.)
- The clitoris (glans, shaft and crura) swells and becomes erect.
- The inner lips swell and change shape.
- The urethral sponge and the bulbs of the vestibule enlarge.
- The vagina balloons upward.
- The uterus shifts position.

In addition to vasocongestion, both women and men experience increases in heart rate, blood pressure, respiration, and overall muscle tension (Masters & Johnson, 1966). However, sexual arousal not only involves physiological but subjective factors.

For some individuals, sexual excitement is dependent on a stable environment with minimal distractions. For example, if a person is aroused and masturbating and someone knocks on the door and calls out, sexual arousal may diminish. Such a disruption in sexual arousal suggests the role of subjective or cognitive factors in sexual arousal. Rosen and Beck (1988) emphasized that "physiological changes alone are not sufficient to account for the range of experiences involved in sexual arousal" (p. 26) and that a "cognitive-subjective criterion for defining sexual response is essential" (p. 29). Indeed, Nagayama Hall (1991) reported that he instructed his subjects to consciously suppress their sexual arousal when listening to erotic tape recordings and that they were able to do so. Mahoney and Strassberg (1991) also reported that 48 adult male volunteers were able to voluntarily suppress their sexual arousal while viewing a sexually explicit videotape and to generate an arousal response while viewing a neutral videotape. Sometimes a person's mood may influence the ability of the person to become aroused. Meisler and Carey (1991) observed that depressed affect was associated with lower male arousal.

CONSIDERATION: There is considerable variation in what constitutes the conditions of arousal for a particular individual. Hoon and Hoon (1977) (reported in Hoon, 1979) contrasted 370 female and 205 male volunteer respondents on 26 items of their Sexual Arousal Inventory and observed the conditions for women and men that were associated with sexual arousal. For women, being touched or kissed on the nipples by a partner, being caressed by his or her eyes, being caressed (other than on the genitals), and reading suggestive or erotic poetry were associated with

Continued

Continued

increased arousal. For men, seeing erotic pictures or slides, seeing a strip show, caressing one's partner (nongenitally), seeing the partner nude, caressing the partner's genitals with one's fingers, being undressed by the partner, and lying in bed with him or her were among the behaviors associated with increased arousal.

In another study of 75 undergraduate males, those who were exposed to classical music (in contrast to heavy-metal rock music) reported being sexually aroused (St. Lawrence & Joyner, 1991). "The relationship between classical music and sexual arousal has been part of folklore for years" (p. 59).

Olfactory stimuli may also be involved in sexual arousal. The term **pheromone** is often used to describe olfactory sexual cues. While pheromones serve as chemical attractants in insects, "there is nothing of comparable specificity or potency in the mammalian world" (Bancroft, 1983, p. 63). Nevertheless, "anecdotal evidence suggests that for some people olfactory cues are extremely important, not only in initial attraction to a sexual partner but also in the maintenance of a stable relationship" (p. 65).

Measures of Sexual Arousal Sexual arousal may be measured both physiologically and subjectively. Penile erection or **tumescence** may be measured by a variety of circumferential, volumetric, and temperature-sensitive devices. One such device involves placing a Davis mercury-in-rubber strain gauge two-thirds of the way down the shaft of the man's penis toward the base. The gauge functions as an elastic variable resistor, so that changes in resistance are recorded when the gauge expands during tumescence (Davis, 1988). The vascular supply of the penis is also assessed by using a small inflatable cuff and manometer (to measure arterial pressure) as well as doppler ultrasound (to assess flow abnormalities within the arteries) (Bancroft, 1989).

> It seems ludicrous that after scientists have been seriously searching for extraterrestrial intelligence for a decade . . . basic research into the physiology of the female vagina on this planet by pioneers such as Levin and Wagner (1976) has just begun.
>
> *Peter W. Hoon*

In women, sexual arousal is physiologically assessed by measuring vaginal vasocongestion. Types of vaginal vasocongestion measuring devices include (Rosen & Beck, 1988, p. 87):

1. Mechanical devices such as the photoplethysmograph that measure tissue changes resulting from genital tumescence.
2. Devices such as thermistor clip and a vaginal infrared probe (Hoon, 1979) that measure vaginal heat dissipation, internal temperature changes, and temperature changes of external genitalia.
3. Filter paper that is used to collect vaginal secretions.

Bancroft (1989) noted that unlike what has been done with men, little use has been made of psychophysiological diagnostic techniques for treating sexual dysfunctions of women.

Measures of subjective arousal often involve researchers interviewing individuals and asking them to self-report their feelings of sexual arousal. The subjects may be asked to respond on a Likert-type rating scale from zero (not aroused) to 10 (extremely aroused) or to complete a multi-item scale assessing various aspects of arousability. The Sexual Arousability Inventory in the following Self-Assessment is an example of a multi-item scale.

Arousal Myths Before leaving this section, we examine some common myths about sexual arousal. First, it is assumed that women are more likely to be sexually aroused in response to romantic rather than explicit sexual content. However, Heiman (1977) found that both women and men were more aroused by explicit sexual content independent of romantic content.

Self Assessment

Sexual Arousability Inventory (SAI)

Instructions The experiences in this inventory may or may not be sexually arousing to you. There are no right or wrong answers. Read each item carefully, and then circle the number which indicates how sexually aroused you feel when you have the described experience, or how sexually aroused you think you would feel if you actually experienced it. *Be sure to answer every item.* If you aren't certain about an item, circle the number that seems about right. The meaning of the numbers is shown on the right.

– 1 adversely affects arousal; unthinkable, repulsive, distracting
0 doesn't affect sexual arousal
1 possibly causes sexual arousal
2 sometimes causes sexual arousal; slightly arousing
3 usually causes sexual arousal; moderately arousing
4 almost always sexually arousing; very arousing
5 always causes sexual arousal; extremely arousing

ANSWER EVERY ITEM.	**How you feel or think you would feel if you were actually involved in this experience**						
*1. When a loved one stimulates your genitals with mouth and tongue	–1	0	1	2	3	4	5
*2. When a loved one fondles your breasts with his/her hands	–1	0	1	2	3	4	5
3. When you see a loved one nude	–1	0	1	2	3	4	5
4. When a loved one caresses you with his/her eyes	–1	0	1	2	3	4	5
*5. When a loved one stimulates your genitals with his/her finger	–1	0	1	2	3	4	5
*6. When you are touched or kissed on the inner thighs by a loved one	–1	0	1	2	3	4	5
7. When you caress a loved one's genitals with your fingers	–1	0	1	2	3	4	5
8. When you read a pornographic or "dirty" story	–1	0	1	2	3	4	5
*9. When a loved one undresses you	–1	0	1	2	3	4	5
*10. When you dance with a loved one	–1	0	1	2	3	4	5
*11. When you have intercourse with a loved one	–1	0	1	2	3	4	5
*12. When a loved one touches or kisses your nipples	–1	0	1	2	3	4	5
13. When you caress a loved one (other than genitals)	–1	0	1	2	3	4	5
*14. When you see pornographic pictures or slides	–1	0	1	2	3	4	5
*15. When you lie in bed with a loved one	–1	0	1	2	3	4	5
*16. When a loved one kisses you passionately	–1	0	1	2	3	4	5
17. When you hear sounds of pleasure during sex	–1	0	1	2	3	4	5
*18. When a loved one kisses you with an exploring tongue	–1	0	1	2	3	4	5
*19. When you read suggestive or pornographic poetry	–1	0	1	2	3	4	5
20. When you see a strip show	–1	0	1	2	3	4	5
21. When you stimulate your partner's genitals with your mouth and tongue	–1	0	1	2	3	4	5
22. When a loved one caresses you (other than genitals)	–1	0	1	2	3	4	5
23. When you see a pornographic movie (stag film)	–1	0	1	2	3	4	5
24. When you undress a loved one	–1	0	1	2	3	4	5
25. When a loved one fondles your breasts with mouth and tongue	–1	0	1	2	3	4	5
*26. When you make love in a new or unusual place	–1	0	1	2	3	4	5
27. When you masturbate	–1	0	1	2	3	4	5
28. When your partner has an orgasm	–1	0	1	2	3	4	5

Continued

Self-Assessment—*Continued*

Scoring The total score on the SAI is computed by (a) adding positive scores, (b) adding negative scores, and (c) subtracting the sum of any negative scores from the sum of positive scores. (The asterisks are not related to scoring; they indicate items on alternative short forms of the measure.) The maximum possible score is 140.

Reliability and validity Although the scale is suitable to administer to men or women (regardless of sexual orientation or marital status), reliability, validity, and interpretive information on men's scores are currently not available. Canadian and U.S. samples of female undergraduate and graduate students, members of womens' groups, and women referred for sex therapy completed the measure (Hoon, Hoon, & Wincze, 1976). Spearman-Brown split-half coefficients were computed for two samples (r = 0.92). The coefficient alpha values for two samples were 0.91 and 0.92. A test-retest reliability coefficient was 0.69.

The SAI scores compared favorably with scores on the Bentler Heterosexual Experience Scale and with self-reported sexual activity. Factor analysis has demonstrated construct validity, but norms for the separate factor scores have not been provided (Hoon, 1979). While mean scores of women seeking therapy for sexual dysfunction fell at the fifth percentile of the measure (Hoon, Hoon, & Wincze, 1976), in a clinical outcome study, scores on the SAI were not reactive to therapy for arousal dysfunction (Wincze, Hoon, & Hoon, 1978).

TABLE 1. Smoothed Cumulative Percentile SAI Norms Based on 285 North American Women

Raw total score	Cumulative percentile
4	1
17	2
25	3
32	4
37	5
48	8
52	10
56	12
60	15
66	20
70	25
73	30
77	35
80	40
83	45
86	50
88	55
91	60
94	65
97	70
99	75
102	80
105	85
107	88
108	90
110	92
113	95
115	96
118	97
121	98
126	99

Interpreting your score As mentioned earlier, only norms for women's scores are currently available. On the following table, you can find your raw total score in the column on the left and then see the percentile on the right at which your score ranks. These norms were obtained from educated, middle- and upper-class North American women. Subsequently obtained percentile norms remained remarkably consistent (Hoon & Chambless, 1988), with a slightly lower average arousability score from a younger sample (averaging 19 years of age), and a slightly higher average score among a somewhat older sample (with an average age of 26).

The scale's authors noted that women who have had more sexual experience tend to have higher scores, indicative of their being more easily aroused by erotic activity (Hoon, Hoon & Wincze, 1976). The cause for this correlation is uncertain, but the researchers speculated that in therapy for female arousal dysfunction, it might be helpful to gradually expand the woman's erotic experiences.

References

Hoon, P. W. (1979). The assessment of sexual arousal in women. In R. M. Hersen and P. M. Miller (Eds.), *Progress in behavior modification* (Vol. 7) (pp. 1–59). New York: Academic Press.Hoon, E. F., & Chambless, D. (1988). Sexual arousability inventory (SAI) and sexual arousability inventory-expanded (SAI-E). In C. M. Davis, W. L. Yarber, and S. L. Davis (Eds.), *Sexuality-Related Measures: A Compendium* (pp. 21–24). Lake Mills, IA: Graphic.

Hoon, E. F., Hoon, P. W., & Wincze, J. P. (1976). An inventory for the measurement of female sexual arousability: The SAI. *Archives of Sexual Behavior, 5,* 291–300. Used by permission of Plenum Publishing.

Wincze, J., Hoon, E., & Hoon, P. (1978). Multiple measure analysis of women experiencing low sexual arousal. *Behaviour Research and Therapy, 16,* 43–49.

A second myth involves the assumption that anxiety inhibits sexual arousal. However, Palace and Gorzalka (1990) conducted an experimental study in which some women viewed an anxiety-provoking three-minute videotape of threatened amputation followed by a three-minute videotape of a nude heterosexual couple engaging in foreplay and intercourse. Other women viewed a three-minute travel film followed by the erotic film. Those women who first watched the amputation video experienced higher levels of sexual arousal than those who watched the travel film first. The authors concluded that "anxiety may enhance sexual arousal through the direct instigation and facilitation of sympathetic activation (e.g., increased blood pressure, heart rate, respiration, and muscle tension) which serves to prepare the person for sexual arousal (vasocongestion)" (p. 410). An alternative interpretation might be that once the women were anxious, they labeled their feeling of anxiety as being that of arousal when they saw the sex videos.

CONSIDERATION: Individuals who have been raped or sexually abused sometimes report that they were sexually aroused during the event(s). They may feel guilt and shame for their having been aroused in these contexts. However, as noted above, sexual arousal may occur in spite of stark terror or severe anxiety. In effect, such arousal may be considered normal.

A third myth involves the assumption that individuals become aroused to socially appropriate stimuli only. However, in a sample of 60 college men (less than 1% of which had ever been arrested), 5% reported being aroused by female children less than 12 years old. Those college men with a high capacity for arousal had also had a number of previous sexual experiences, including frottage, obscene phone calls, and sex with children. The authors commented that "it may be that adolescent males are easily aroused and seek out a variety of sexual experiences . . ." (Templeman & Stinnett, 1991, p. 148). We will examine arousal to inappropriate sexual stimuli in more detail in Chapter 17, Paraphilias and Sexuality.

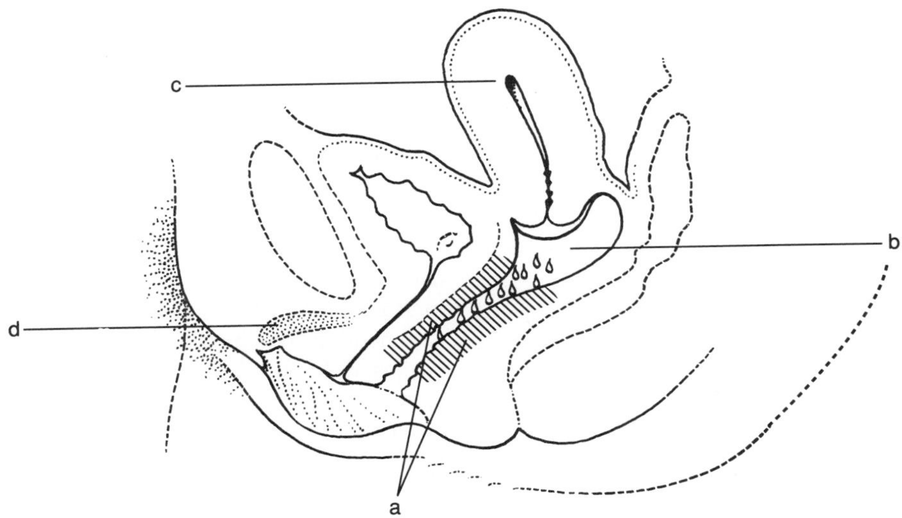

FIGURE 7.5 The female genitals in a highly aroused state (plateau)
The perivaginal tissues engorge and form the "orgasmic platform" (a). The vagina (b) balloons and is covered with transudate. The uterus (c) has risen from the pelvic cavity. Just before orgasm, the clitoris (d) rotates and retracts.

Source: *The New Sex Therapy* by Helen Singer Kaplan. New York: Brunner/Mazel, Publishers, 1974. Copyright by Helen Singer Kaplan, 1974, p. 8. Used by permission

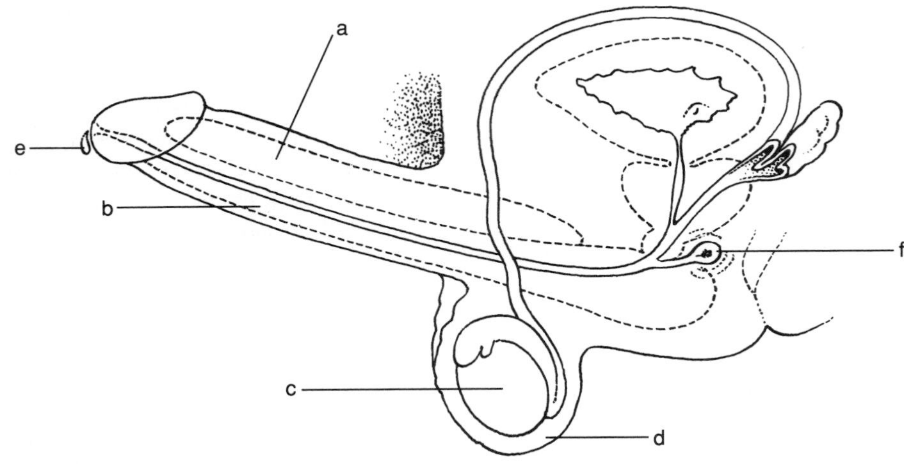

FIGURE 7.6 The male genitals in a highly aroused state (plateau)
The corpora cavernosa (a) and the corpus spongiosum (b) are filled with blood, causing erection of the penis. The testicles (c) are also engorged and increase in size and just before orgasm rise against the perineal floor. The dartos tunic (d) which covers the testes is thickened and contracted. A drop of clear mucoid secretion (e) from Cowper's gland (f) appears at the urethral meatus during intense excitement.

Source: *The New Sex Therapy* by Helen Singer Kaplan. New York: Brunner/Mazel, Publishers, 1974. Copyright by Helen Singer Kaplan, 1974, p. 9. Used by permission.

Plateau Phase

After reaching a high level of sexual arousal, men and women enter the **plateau phase** of the sexual response cycle (see Figures 7.5 and 7.6). In the plateau phase in women (defined primarily by physiological changes), the lower third of the vagina becomes smaller while the upper two-thirds expands (presumably to form a pool to catch the semen). The expansion of the upper two-thirds of the vagina is caused by the engorgement of the uterus and its elevation within the pelvis.

If the sexual contact is through intercourse, the constriction of the lower third (nerve endings are more concentrated here) adds to the stimulation of the penis (Bancroft, 1989). This narrowing of the outer third of the vagina is referred to as the **orgasmic platform.** At the same time, the clitoris withdraws behind a fold of skin known as the clitoral hood, which provides insulation for the extremely sensitive glans of the clitoris. While continuous stimulation of the clitoris is necessary for progress through the plateau stage, direct clitoral stimulation may be painful at this time since the glans has a tremendous concentration of nerve endings in a relatively small area. Even though the clitoris is under the hood, it continues to respond to stimulation as long as the area surrounding the clitoris (for example, the mons) is stimulated.

Male reactions during the plateau phase include a slight increase in the diameter of the penis and considerable increase in the size of the testes (from 50% to 100%). In some men, the head (glans) of the penis turns a deep red-purple color.

Some changes during the plateau phase are common to men and women: muscle contractions and spasms (myotonia), heavy breathing (hyperventilation), heart rate increase (tachycardia), and blood pressure elevation. Also, some women and men experience a "sex flush," which looks like a measles rash on parts of the chest, neck, face, and forehead; it sometimes suggests a high level of sexual excitement or tension.

The cognitive factors contributing to arousal in the previous stages are also important in the maintenance of the plateau phase. The individuals in this stage must continue to define what is happening to them in erotic excitatory terms. Without such labeling, there will be a return to prearousal levels of physiological indicators.

Orgasm Phase

Orgasm is the climax of sexual excitement and is experienced as a release of tension involving intense pleasure. But the orgasmic reflex is not like the simple knee jerk reflex. Rather, according to Paul MacLean, a neuroscientist, "For orgasm, you have to keep feeding in the stimuli . . . it's more like filling a reservoir till you get some water over the dam" (quoted in Gallaher, 1986, p. 54).

Orgasm has three components: a sensory component (stimulus), a cognitive component (interpretation), and a motor component (response). The individual's body receives the sensory (tactile, auditory, visual, olfactory) information, and the brain interprets the signals in positive terms and activates the genitals. While everyone is different and each person's experience of orgasm is different, researchers have provided some information on the various experiences of women and men.

Orgasm is perception. Looking for its nature in physiological changes is like looking for a set of lost keys under the street lamp because that's where the light shines.
Gorm Wagner

Female Orgasm While we will discuss how therapists treat the problem of anorgasmia (inability to have an orgasm) in Chapter 15, for now we discuss orgasm as reported by women who have experienced it. Physiologically, the orgasmic experience for the women involves "simultaneous rhythmic contractions of the uterus, the orgasmic platform (outer third of the vagina), and the rectal sphincter, beginning at 0.8 second intervals and then diminishing in intensity, duration, and regularity" (Kolodny, Masters, & Johnson, 1979, p. 15). In one study, an average of 18 contractions lasting a total of 36 seconds was observed in 11 women (aged 24 to 33) who masturbated to orgasm (Bohlen, Held, Sanderson, & Boyer, 1982).

Sexual response is a total mind and body involvement. Orgasm can be produced with minimal mental stimulation or with minimal physical stimulation.
Virginia Johnson

Various typologies have been suggested for female orgasm:

1. *Clitoral versus vaginal orgasm.* Freud identified a "clitoral" orgasm and a "vaginal" orgasm. **Clitoral orgasm** resulted primarily from manual stimulation of the clitoris, began in adolescence, and was (according to Freud) an "immature" type of orgasm. **Vaginal orgasm** (according to Freud) was a result of intercourse experienced by more "mature" married women. While his model has been heavily criticized by researchers and feminists alike, its influence has continued. Taublieb and Lick (1986) observed that in their sample of 180 men and 186 women, respondents tended to regard penile stimulation as more appropriate and less pathological than manual stimulation to induce orgasm in women. While Masters and Johnson (1966) acknowledged that although a woman's feelings of orgasmic intensity and satisfaction may vary, the physiological response pattern does not vary due to the source or site of stimulation.
2. *Nonterminative versus terminative orgasm.* Fox and Fox (1969), a husband-and-wife team, examined the subjective and physiological characteristics of the orgasms experienced by the wife and described them as being nonterminative or terminative. **Nonterminative orgasms** referred to brief, clitoral orgasms that were not deeply satisfying. **Terminative orgasms,** also labeled as postejaculatory orgasms, referred to longer, more satisfying orgasms resulting from contractions in the vagina and uterus. These descriptions are similar to those provided by Freud for clitoral and vaginal orgasms, respectively.
3. *Vulval, uterine, and blended orgasms.* Singer (1973) described **vulval orgasms** as being similar to clitoral or nonterminative orgasms and characterized by spastic contractions of the outer third of the vagina. **Uterine orgasms** are caused by deep intravaginal stimulation and are similar to terminative orgasms. These orgasms resulted in a deep sense of satisfaction and satiation. **Blended orgasms** are those in which the woman experienced both vulval contractions and deep terminative enjoyment.

Women sometimes discuss the variability of their orgasmic experiences with each other.

People and their responses are unique, not made by cookie cutters.

Virginia Johnson

CONSIDERATION: Our intent in discussing various orgasmic experiences is to make explicit the variability of such experiences and to encourage each person to be comfortable with his or her own unique sexual response. In addition, orgasms originating primarily from clitoral or vaginal stimulation may be regarded as equally enjoyable and satisfying by different women.

Exhibit 7.1 reflects college women's descriptions of orgasm. As has already been noted, the orgasmic experience varies from woman to woman and from time to time in the same woman. The descriptions are not represented here as typical or ideal.

4. *Ejaculatory orgasm.* Some women experience what they define to be an ejaculation at the time of orgasm. Forty percent of 1,172 women reported that they experienced an "ejaculation" at the moment of orgasm. The difference between the ejaculation and vaginal lubrication was that the former came as a spurt and was thinner, more slippery, and more intense than the latter (Darling, Davidson, & Conway-Welch, 1990, p. 38). Ladas, Whipple, and Perry (1982) proposed that the ejaculatory orgasm is in response to direct stimulation of the G Spot discussed in Chapter 6.

   One group of researchers (Addiego et al., 1981) assessed the contents of "female ejaculate" and reported it to be chemically different from urine, hypothesizing that it might originate from tissue similar to a male's prostate. However, subsequent studies have failed to confirm this finding (Alzate & Lodoño, 1984; Goldberg et al., 1983).

   Alzate (1985), examined 27 coitally experienced, paid volunteers (female prostitutes and friends of theirs) to assess vaginal eroticism. Following digital stimulation of the vaginal walls 24 of the women reached orgasm, but none was observed to ejaculate. However, one of the women was emphatic that she often ejaculated at orgasm through coitus or clitoral stimulation and was able to demonstrate ejaculation on two occasions. The orgasmic emission was chemi-

EXHIBIT 7.1 College Women's Descriptions of Orgasm

One woman in a college sexuality course wrote the following account of an orgasmic experience.

> The slow build up begins as soon as he comes into sight—tightness around the outer muscles of my vagina and the wetness of lubrication. As his smell reaches my senses, my vaginal muscles again quiver in recognition of his sexual attractiveness.
>
> Once the touching and kissing begins, the whole area of my vagina pushes outward in slow, rhythmic motions. It feels swollen and sensitive. This pleasure gradually heightens and turns from an outward pushing to an inner craving felt far inside my body. The area of intense sensitivity and extreme constriction is now focused on the inner lips directly around the opening of my vagina. Breathing becomes quicker, and the deep inhaling brings a slow-moving projection of my breasts with larger, erect nipples. My body and thoughts swell with sensual feelings. . .
>
> Just before I orgasm, the inner craving rushes back to a concentrated feeling in my clitoral area, and the muscles around my vaginal opening become even more profoundly tense. This tension is reflected in the rest of my body as my arms and legs stiffen and my fingers press rigidly into my partner's skin as if to ground myself before the explosion.
>
> Then it hits—the vaginal muscles wildly contract—a vibrating sense of extreme pleasure as the tension throbs to relief. It is a sensation which absolutely cannot be expressed words. The pulsating of my vagina is heavy, and the thrill is carried throughout my body with involuntary shaking and thrusting of the pelvis and limbs. . . My head has totally floated away—I can't think and don't want to—I just enjoy! (Authors' files)

Of course, not all women experience such pronounced orgasmic sensations. From sexual autobiographies written by college students from five universities, Segal (1984) offered a wide range of accounts. One woman confided, "Sometimes I would have these tinglings that were real nice but I never exploded like a rocket" (p. 39).

Several women described the types of stimulation that led to orgasm. One said, "I usually come during foreplay through manual or oral stimulation." Another wrote an account of her partner rubbing his erect penis against her genitals.

> The combination of the material of his shorts and the friction of the rubbing was very arousing and I always had an orgasm. I realize that it is partly because I masturbate in that way that helped me reach an orgasm every time. (p. 52)

We have never had this reported by any of the students in our classes, but Segal (1984) quoted one woman who described an orgasm while taking an exam! She reported an excited, tense feeling at the end of the test, and a tight feeling in her vagina. "I decided to punt the last question and to concentrate on squeezing my legs together." She reported feeling a wave of contractions moving up and down her vagina—her first orgasm! She concluded, "I think I must have looked kind of strange smiling up at Dr. John when he asked me to turn in my test! It was a very pleasurable experience, plus I made a B on a hard test." (p. 38)

cally analyzed but was indistinguishable from a sample of the woman's urine. Alzate concluded that most women have zones in the vaginal walls that are responsive to strong tactile stimulation and "some women do expel a fluid through the urethra at orgasm" (p. 535).

Male Orgasm Orgasm in men occurs in two stages. First, there is a buildup of fluid from the prostate, seminal vesicles, and vas deferens in the prostatic urethra (the area behind the base of the penis and above the testes). Once this pool of semen collects, the man enters a stage of ejaculatory inevitability; he knows he is going to ejaculate and cannot control the process. During orgasm, the penile muscles contract two to three times at 0.8-second intervals and propel the ejaculate from the penis. Thereafter, the contractions may continue but at longer intervals. The more time since the last ejaculation, the greater the number of contractions. The average duration of a male orgasm is about 25 seconds (Bohlen, Held, & Sanderson, 1980).

Male orgasms have not been categorized as have female orgasms. This may be due to there being more male than female sexologists with the former having greater interest in the female than the male orgasmic experience. Alternatively, the greater variability of the female experience may account for greater interest. Earlier, we provided college women's descriptions of orgasm. Below are descriptions provided by two men of their respective orgasmic experiences (Authors' files).

> The rough edges melt away—life flows through uninterrupted—every cell is hot. My muscles tingle and the fluid boils in my belly. There is a sensation of fullness and weightlessness—sharing my life, savoring all the juices, all the passion, rising above what's been, creating what is. Naturally, each touch of her fingers on the smoothness of my skin stirs life in my inner being—the feeling swells, it spreads, it concentrates, and when it erupts to join her, all of my life is propelled outward. For an instant, I am breathless, suspended. . . .
>
> Prior to ejaculation, warm sensations begin to build, whether it be through foreplay or actual intercourse itself. The buildup gives a very warm and gentle feeling throughout my body. The buildup wants to explode. When ejaculation occurs, it is like the body is being massaged with the perfect touch from the inside out. There is warmth but there is coolness in the tingling sensations that make the five to seven seconds what it really is . . . outrageous!

Some male orgasms occur in the form of nocturnal emissions, or wet dreams (women may also experience orgasm during REM sleep). Typically, adolescent males begin to experience nocturnal emissions at age 13 to 14 as a response to an erotic dream. The boy wakes up to find his clothes, leg, and bed sheet wet with semen. Unless the boy has been told that wet dreams occur, are normal, and signify the capacity to reproduce, he may think something is wrong with him. Not all boys have nocturnal emissions.

Physiologically, in both men and women, orgasm involves an increase in respiration (sometimes reaching 40 breaths per minute), heart rate (from 110 to 180 beats per minute), and blood pressure (systolic pressure may elevate 30 to 80 millimeters and diastolic pressure, 20 to 40 millimeters).

The orgasm experience is usually one of intense pleasure—some individuals report that their orgasm is so intense that they "can't stand it anymore" (Simpson, 1991, p. 9). However, researchers have found it difficult to "measure the pleasure"—in one study, there was little correlation between what subjects said they experienced and what the monitors reflecting physiological changes showed (Gallaher, 1986).

CONSIDERATION: The psychological and emotional aspects of sexual response are just as important as the physiological changes that occur during sexual functioning. However, "it is easier to measure physiological changes than emotional states, and so physiology tends to become the major indication of whether 'the sexual response cycle' is working or not" (Tavris, 1992, p. 228).

Resolution Phase

After orgasm, the **resolution phase** of the sexual response cycle begins, which involves the body's return to its preexcitement condition. In women, the vagina begins to shorten in both width and length, and the clitoris returns to its normal anatomic position. In men, there is the loss of erection (see Exhibit 7.2 for the exception), and the testes decrease in size and descend into the scrotum. In both women and men, breathing, heart rate, and blood pressure return to normal. A thin layer of perspiration may appear over the entire body.

> The sexual experience is par excellence psychosomatic.
>
> *John Bancroft*

In the resolution phase, individuals may prefer to avoid additional genital stimulation. "My clitoris feels very sensitive—almost burns—and I don't want it touched after I orgasm" characterizes the feelings of some women. Other women say their clitoris tickles when touched after orgasm. Men often want to lie still and avoid stimulation on the head of their penis. When sexual arousal does not result in orgasm, resolution still takes place, but more gradually. Some women and men experience an unpleasant sensation of sexual tension or fullness in the genital area due to prolonged vasocongestion in the absence of orgasm.

The resolution phase is a time that many lovers savor. They relax in physiological and emotional joy. Other lovers feel uneasy during the resolution phase and withdraw from each other. It is an old adage that you can tell more about the nature of a couple's relationship after sex than before.

Male and Female Differences in Sexual Response

Both women and men experience physiological changes during sexual excitement, plateau, and orgasm. In addition, the subjective experience of orgasm for women and men is similar. In one study, 48 descriptions of orgasm were submitted to a panel of judges. Half of the descriptions were written by women, and half were written by men. The judges were unable to accurately identify which descriptions were written by women and which by men (Vance & Wagner, 1976). However, there are differences in patterns of sexual responses sometimes experienced by women and men. A discussion of these differences follows.

Alternative Cycles in Women Masters and Johnson (1966) stated that a woman may experience the sexual response cycle in one of three ways. When there is sufficient and continuous stimulation, the most usual pattern is a progression from excitement through plateau to orgasm to resolution, passing through all phases and returning to none of these stages for a second time. Experientially, the woman gets excited, enjoys a climax, and cuddles in her partner's arms after one orgasm. If she is masturbating, she relaxes and savors the experience.

In another pattern (again, assuming sufficient and continuous stimulation), the woman goes from excitement to plateau to orgasm to another or several orgasms and then to resolution. The interval between orgasms varies; in some cases, it is only a few seconds. In effect, the woman gets excited, climbs through the plateau phase, and bounces from orgasm to orgasm while briefly reaching the plateau phase between orgasms. In a study (Darling, Davidson, & Jennings, 1991) of 805 professional nurses, 48% of the respondents reported that they had experienced "multiple orgasm" at least once (43% did so usually). The number of orgasms reported during a multiorgasmic experience ranged from two to 20. Forty percent reported that each successive orgasm was stronger, 16% said they were weaker, and 9% reported no difference.

Multiorgasmic women were more likely to have begun masturbation and intercourse at an earlier age, to have both given and received oral sex, to have partners who delayed their first orgasm during sexual intercourse until after the woman had had her first orgasm, and to have used sexual fantasies, erotic films, and erotic literature to become aroused and experience orgasm. In addition, they were more likely to experience clitoral stimulation (by either partner or self) during intercourse. "Clitoral stimulation is very important to multiorgasmic women" (Darling et al., 1991, p. 538).

Still another pattern of female sexual response is to move through the sequence of phases of the sexual response cycle but skip the orgasm phase. The woman gets excited, climbs to the plateau phase, but does not have an orgasm. Insufficient stimulation, distraction, or lack of interest in the partner (if one is involved) are among the reasons for not reaching orgasm (other reasons are discussed in Chapter 15, Sexual Dysfunctions and Sex Therapy). The woman moves from the plateau phase directly to the resolution phase.

> An appreciation of male diversity in sexual response would help to dispel the prevalent myth that male sexuality is natural, unlearned, and entirely beyond a man's control.
>
> *Carol Tavris*

Alternative Cycles in Men Men typically progress through the sexual response cycle in a somewhat different pattern. Once sexual excitement begins, there is usually only one pattern—excitement through plateau to orgasm (it is recognized that, for a variety of physiological and psychological reasons, the male may plateau but not have an orgasm). Following orgasm, most men experience a longer **refractory period** than women, during which the person cannot be sexually aroused. During the refractory period, the penis usually becomes flaccid and further stimulation (particularly on the glans of the penis) is not immediately desired. However, some men remain erect after orgasm and desire continued stimulation.

The desire and ability to have another erection and begin stimulation depends upon the man's age, fatigue, and the amount of alcohol or other drugs in his system. In general, the older, exhausted, alcohol-intoxicated individual will be less interested in renewed sexual stimulation than the younger, rested, sober man. The time of the refractory period varies. As noted above, some men maintain an erection after orgasm and skip the refractory period to have another orgasm (see Exhibit 7.2). Although this is rare, it does occur.

Exhibit 7.2 Multiple Male Orgasm

A study by Robbins and Jensen (1978) reported on 13 subjects (ages ranged from 22 to 56) who were capable of inhibiting or controlling their ejaculation while having several orgasms until a final ejaculatory orgasm after which detumescence occurred. In a more recent study, Dunn and Trost (1989) interviewed 21 men who reported that they were capable of having multiple orgasms. The researchers defined multiple orgasms in men as "two or more orgasms with or without ejaculation and without, or with only very limited, detumescence during one and the same sexual encounter" (p. 379). This definition has five important elements:

1. At least two orgasms must occur;
2. Ejaculation does not have to occur;
3. One or more of the orgasms can be combined with ejaculation;
4. Limited detumescence occurs; and
5. The orgasms have to occur in one and the same sexual encounter.

The researchers identified two categories of men who reported multiple orgasms—primary and secondary. Primary multiple-orgasmic men reported experiencing the phenomenon since they began masturbating or during their first partner orgasmic experience. Thirteen of the 21 men in the Dunn and Trost study fell into the primary category.

> . . . One subject reflected that he must have been multiple orgasmic since he began ejaculating at age 12. He recalls enjoying the sensation of the first ejaculation very much. He continued to stimulate himself, because it still felt good, and went on to have another orgasm. He recalled being multiple orgasmic on first intercourse. It never occurred to him to stop after one orgasm and he believed that it was natural to continue. He was surprised at age 23 to learn from his fiancée that her previous lovers had not been multiple orgasmic. (p. 381)

A second category of multiple-orgasmic men referred to as secondary reported having experienced the capacity to have multiple orgasms later in life. The occasion was a surprise. One man who had his first multiple orgasmic experience when he was about 40 reported having a "normal" ejaculatory orgasm during intercourse with his wife. However, he continued thrusting "without losing his erection and after a short while had another orgasm" (p. 381).

Two of the men in the Dunn and Trost research deliberately trained themselves to be multiple orgasmic. Hartman and Fithian (1984), in their book *Any Man Can,* discuss the techniques whereby men can learn to accomplish this phenomenon. These techniques include coming to a sexual peak, stopping, building again to a peak, stopping, and so on, and then deeply relaxing. The sensation of orgasm follows the deep relaxation. Other men used muscle contractions at the point of ejaculatory inevitability. It is as though they were clamping down so as to inhibit or control the ejaculation. Regardless of the technique, some men learn how to separate the orgasm from the ejaculation. In the Dunn and Trost study,

> Most men reported from two to nine orgasms per session. One man has had as many as 16 orgasms during one sexual encounter. Subjects estimated time frames lasting from 15 minutes to more than 2 hours without noticeable detumescence between orgasms. (p. 382)

When the sexual response cycles of women and men are compared, three differences sometimes occur:

1. Whereas men usually climax once, women's responses are more variable. They may have an orgasm once, more than once, or not at all.
2. When the woman does experience more than one climax, she is capable of doing so with only seconds between climaxes. In contrast, the man usually needs a longer refractory period before he is capable of additional orgasms.
3. Orgasm in men is never accompanied by urination, whereas this may occur in women. In a sample of 281 women, 32% reported that they expelled urine during orgasm "occasionally" (Darling et al., 1990, p. 41).

Critiques of Masters and Johnson's Model

Although the Masters and Johnson's model is the most widely presented model of human sexual response, it has been criticized on several counts. First, the idea of a four-stage process has been criticized as an arbitrary and imprecise division that is no improvement over the two-stage model proposed by Havelock Ellis (Tiefer, 1991). For example, a clear distinction between the four-stage model's excitement and plateau phases is not apparent. Robinson (1976) observed, "Clearly what is being described here . . . is not a two-stage process (excitement/plateau), but a continuous progression, or if you prefer a musical metaphor, a gradual crescendo" (p. 129). Psychologist Carole Wade noted that the "stages" of sexual response "are not like the stages of a washing machine. You don't hear a 'click click' when it shifts to a new phase of the cycle" (quoted in Tavris, 1992, p. 226).

A second criticism is that the Masters and Johnson model virtually ignores cognitive-affective states, focusing on objectively measured genital and extragenital bodily changes. According to Tiefer (1991, p. 13) this focus results in a view of sexual functioning and a diagnostic system in which the body "has become a fragmented collection of parts which pop in and out at different points in the performance sequence." The measurement of physiological changes, primarily changes in the genitals, may be taken to represent sexuality, rather than being seen as one component of it. Tiefer (1991) suggested that clinical application of the HSRC model has resulted in a list of genitally focused disorders, which omit sexual difficulties, such as feeling attracted to someone other than one's mate, trouble relaxing, or problems with one's partner being too hasty, not tender, or focusing excessively on orgasm. "The vast spectrum of sexual possibility is narrowed to genital (i.e., reproductive) performance" (p. 16).

A third criticism of the HSRC model is that it was proposed and is disseminated as *the* human sexual response cycle instead of *a* human sexual response cycle (Tiefer, 1991). Because of the bias in subject selection and the assumptions that guided Masters and Johnson's research, the appropriateness of this generalization has been challenged. Tiefer (1991, p. 9) observed that only participants who had experienced masturbatory and coital orgasm were included in the sample. Once in the laboratory, they were given a period of training to boost their confidence in being able to respond "successfully" while their responses were being measured. Other sample biases included the higher than average educational level, socioeconomic backgrounds, and sexual enthusiasm of the participants. "No research was undertaken to investigate 'human' sexual physiology and subjectivity," concluded Tiefer (p. 6), "only to measure the responses of an easily orgasmic sample." She compared these subject selection practices to selecting only international recording artists to study human singing behaviors. Where does that leave those of us who only sing in the shower?

Finally, the HSRC model has been criticized as favoring the sexual interests of men over those of women. Tiefer (1991) suggested that given our culture's emphasis on sexual experience and physical gratification for men and an emotional connection and intimacy for women the HSRC model is slanted toward men's development. She also challenged the bias of Masters and Johnson's goal of studying men's and women's response to "effective sexual stimulation." Tiefer asserted that given the social realities of women (having less power than men due to socioeconomic discrepancies, fear of violence, and society's double standard), "it seems likely that 'effective sexual stimulation' in the laboratory or home is what men prefer" (p. 19). In other words, the context of sexual behaviors must be considered when studying human sexual response.

Alternative Sexual Response Models

While the Masters and Johnson four-stage model of sexual response has received the most professional visibility, there are others. Three of these follow:

Ellis's and Beach's Two-Stage Models

In 1906, Havelock Ellis suggested a two-stage model of human sexual response consisting of tumescence and detumescence. "In tumescence the organism is slowly wound up and force accumulated; in the act of detumescence, the accumulated force is let go, and by its liberation the sperm-bearing instrument is driven home" (vol. 1, p. 142). The tumescence-detumescence model emphasized the buildup and release of sexual energy, and the cycle was applied to both women and men. As noted in the standard sexual response cycle presented earlier, the terms *tumescence* and *detumescence* continue to be used today and refer primarily to genital vasocongestion in men.

Havelock Ellis emphasized a tumescence and detumescence model of sexual response.

In 1956, Beach conducted copulatory studies of rats and suggested "sexual arousal mechanism (SAM)" and "intromission and ejaculatory mechanism (IEM)" as new labels for the Ellis typology. The SAM referred to the time of initial excitement, which resulted in mounting and intromission; IEM described the ejaculatory or orgasmic phase of the cycle. Beach's SAM-IEM model also allowed for the cycle to begin again after a brief refractory period.

Helen Kaplan's Three-Stage Model

In an effort to emphasize the motivational and psychological aspects of the sexual response cycle Helen Kaplan conceptualized a triphasic model consisting of desire, excitement, and orgasm. The desire phase is regarded as "the experience of specific sensations that motivate the individual to initiate or become responsive to sexual stimulation" (Rosen & Beck, 1988, p. 42). Moser (1992) noted that desire "is a conscious, probably hormonally mediated, perception of an interest in sex" (p. 67).

Bozman and Beck (1991) noted that one of the conditions that interferes with the development of sexual desire is anger. They asked 24 male undergraduates (free from psychological and medical problems that interfere with sexual function) to rate their level of sexual desire when they were feeling anxiety, anger, or no particular feelings. They noted that the least sexual desire was associated with conditions of anger.

Once the environmental conditions are right, Kaplan noted, the source of sexual desire is the brain:

> These sensations are produced by the physical activation of a specific neural system in the brain. When this system is active, a person is "horny," he may feel genital sensations, or he may feel vaguely sexy, interested in sex, open to sex, or even just restless. (Kaplan, 1979, p. 10)

Kaplan's excitement and orgasm phases are very similar to those of Masters and Johnson, who focus on vasocongestion and reflex pelvic contractions in the respective phases. The primary criticism of Kaplan's model is in regard to her insistence that desire is a necessary prerequisite for excitement. We have noted earlier that desire is not necessary for arousal and orgasm. Indeed, Garde and Lunde (1980) reported that approximately 33% of a representative sample of 40-year-old Danish women never experienced desire despite "adequate arousal" and orgasm.

David Reed's Erotic Stimulus Pathway (ESP) Model

In an effort to further blend the physiological features of the Masters and Johnson model with the cognitive features of the Kaplan model, psychologist David Reed identified four phases of the sexual response cycle (Stayton, 1992). These include:

1. *Seduction.* The seduction phase has two components: "first, seducing oneself into being interested in another person and second, learning how to seduce the other person into being interested in you" (p. 11).
2. *Sensations.* Occurring at the same time as the excitement and plateau stages of the Masters and Johnson model, this phase emphasizes the importance of touch, vision, hearing, smell, and taste in sexual stimulation and pleasure.
3. *Surrender.* Orgasm occurs in the surrender phase of Reed's model. "For orgasm to take place as a pleasurable experience, one needs let go and give control over to the experience" (p. 11).
4. *Reflection.* During the last phase of Reed's ESP Model of sexual response, a person evaluates the sexual experience that has just occurred (see Figure 7.7 for Reed's model).

> If the immediate reflection is positive; that is, warm, loving, pleasurable, then the desire will be stimulated for the next time. If, on the other hand, the reflection is negative; that is, the person did not like the way s/he experienced his/her response, or is negative about the partner or the situation, then the feedback will act to lower desire for the next time (Stayton, 1992, p. 11).

Hormones and Sexual Response

Hormones are chemical messengers that typically travel from cell to cell via the blood stream. Manley (1990) summarized how little is known about the hormonal influences on human sexual response: "The role of hormones in human sexual behavior is not well understood because not enough is known and what is known is not clear" (p. 338). In regard to what is known, androgen increases sexual desire in both men and women. Indeed, when both men and women are deprived of testosterone (a primary type of androgen), they lose all sexual desire (Kaplan, 1974). Estrogen and progesterone have less specific effects and "may have no specific effect on sexual behavior" (p. 53).

Researchers have attempted to correlate the amount of specific hormones in the bloodstream with sexual behavior in humans. In a study (Heiman, Rowland, Hatch, & Gladue, 1991) of premenopausal women between the ages of 21 and 45, hormone levels of cortisol, prolactin, luteinizing hormone, and testosterone were assessed as the subjects viewed both erotic and neutral videotapes. Few consistent changes in hormone levels and few correlations with behavioral arousal signs were observed. The authors commented on the "complexity and subtlety of endocrine interactions with sexual response" (p. 171). They suggested that compared to that of women, the sexual behavior of men may be more affected by hormonal factors.

Researchers have attempted to study the relative importance of psychosocial factors and hormone levels on sexual behavior. Udry, Talbert, and Morris (1986) noted that in female adolescents, peer group sexual activity (e.g., whether their close friends were sexually active), rather than hormonal levels, was the most reliable

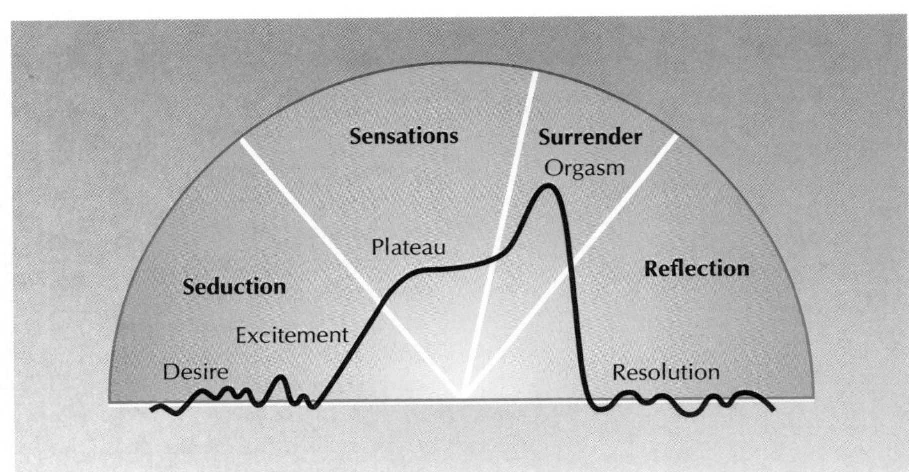

FIGURE 7.7 David M. Reed's Erotic Stimulus Pathway Model

Source: Reproduced with permission from *SIECUS Report,* Vol 20, #4, 1992. Copyright Sex Information and Education Council of the United States, Inc. 130 West 42nd Street, Suite 2500, New York, New York, 10036. Phone # 212-819-9770; Fax # 212-819-9776.

predictor of sexual behavior. Male adolescents, on the other hand, were more likely to be influenced by testosterone levels than by their peer group (Udry, Billy, Morris, Groff, & Raj, 1985).

A study by Slob, Ernste, and van der Werff ten Bosch (1991) attempted to correlate menstrual cycle phase with sexual arousability in women. While the 24 women studied differed from each other in arousability, only 1 in 12 in the luteal phase (the last half of the menstrual cycle), in contrast to 6 in 12 in the follicular phase (the first half, before ovulation, of the menstrual cycle), indicated an increase in the desire to make love. While these data suggest that certain hormones at certain times of the woman's menstrual cycle may trigger certain sexual feelings, the data are not consistent and individual variations are emphasized.

A team of researchers (Bancroft, Sherwin, Alexander, Davidson, & Walker, 1991) examined the relationship between *plasma free testosterone* (FT) (testosterone that is carried by the bloodstream and is free to induce activity, in contrast to testosterone that is bound, site-based, and inert) and the sexual behavior of 55 undergraduate women using oral contraceptives and 53 undergraduate women who were not using oral contraceptives. The researchers found a positive correlation between FT and sexual intercourse among the women using birth control pills. There was no significant correlation between FT and masturbation or sexual fantasy. There was a negative association between FT levels and having a value system that made the women uncomfortable with taking the pill. The researchers concluded that psychosocial factors override hormonal factors: ". . . it is suggested that androgen-behavior relationships in women are easily obscured by psychosocial influences and in this study such influences may have been more powerful among those not using oral contraceptives" (p. 121).

The ultimate aphrodisiac is your own imagination.

Ronni Sandroff

In attempts to manipulate sexual desire and behavior, individuals have attempted to discover aphrodisiacs to boost sexual interest and energy (see Exhibit 7.3).

Some individuals use weight lifting to improve their physique and to increase their sexual interest and energy.

EXHIBIT 7.3 Aphrodisiacs?

The term **aphrodisiac** refers to any substance that increases sexual desire. One of the more prevalent myths of human sexuality is that specific foods have this effect. In reality, no food reliably increases a person's sexual desire. Where sexual interest does increase, it is often a result of a self-fulfilling prophecy. If the person thinks a substance will have a desire-inducing effect, it sometimes does.

Nevertheless, folklore about aphrodisiacs has a long history, from the Chinese belief in the sex-enhancing power of a ground-up rhinoceros horn (the origin of the word *horny*) to beliefs regarding foods and other substances, such as:

Oysters Crabs Tomatoes Eggs Carrots Celery Pepper
Turtle soup Paprika Nutmeg Ginger Saffron
Spanish fly Yohimbine Mandrake

Spanish fly is among the substances most commonly thought of as aphrodisiacs. Also known as Spanish flies, or cantharides, it is the common name for a variety of beetles found in Mediterranean countries, the Near East, and Britain. The beetles are caught, dried, and crushed into a powder that is typically used as a blistering agent by veterinarians. When ingested by humans, it can cause "an intense burning sensation in the mouth and throat, severe abdominal cramps and vomiting, followed by diarrhea and the passing of blood in the urine" (Taberner, 1985, p. 103).

Given this effect, one wonders how Spanish fly has become associated with sexual arousal. Taberner noted:

> In a romantic and less scientific age it was probably very easy and natural to equate the emotional and psychological effects of love and desire with the physical effects of an artificial stimulant. In other words, if love or desire evokes burning, fainting, and distraction, and cantharides produce the same symptoms, then may not cantharides also provoke love and desire? (p. 104)

In addition, Spanish fly may irritate and inflame the entire urinary tract, resulting in a sustained erection (Lieberman, 1988). This effect also helps to account for the presumed sexual effects of cantharides.

Similar beliefs about drugs suggest that sexual desire can be increased chemically. However, "no pharmacologic agent has been demonstrated in well-controlled trials to have reliable aphrodisiac value, although self reports suggest that a variety of drugs may in some cases boost libido" (Young, 1990, p. 122). An example of the latter is Deprenyl (also known as Selegiline), which is used in the treatment of Parkinson's and Alzheimer's diseases (Uitti, Tanner, Rajput, Goetz, Klawans, & Thiessen, 1989; Falsaperla, Monici Preti, & Oliani, 1990). The effect of the drug is to slow the natural aging process of the brain (decrease dopamine and "trace amines" in the brain) and to increase sexual vigor. Some physicians recommend that Deprenyl be used routinely by elderly persons, independent of any Parkinson's diagnosis (Knoll, 1985; 1983). An article in *Longevity* magazine detailed Dr. Knoll's research and labeled the drug as "An Anti-Aging Aphrodisiac" (Kahn, 1990). Other researchers have identified various benefits of Deprenyl, which include improvement in short- and long-term memory, concentration, and verbal fluency (Falsaperla et al., 1990).

Another prescription drug that has been shown to increase sexual desire is bupropion hydrochloride (trade name, Wellbutrin). When 60 women and 60 men who had various sexual dysfunctions (lack of sexual desire, inability to attain orgasm) were randomly assigned to one of two experimental groups (those receiving Wellbutrin and those receiving a placebo), the results were dramatic. Sixty-three percent of those in the Wellbutrin group reported marked increases in sexual interest and improved sexual functioning, compared with only 3% of the placebo group (Crenshaw, Goldberg, & Stern, 1987). According to the authors, the study is the "first demonstration in a well-controlled clinical trial of an improvement in the psychological aspects of sexual dysfunction due to pharmacologic treatment" (p. 239).

Other research has suggested that drinking coffee (with caffeine) has a positive effect on maintaining sexual involvement. Diokno, Brown, and Herzog (1990) observed that at least one cup of coffee per day is significantly associated with a higher prevalence of sexual activity in women (age 60 and over) and with a higher potency rate in men (age 60 and over). Although some substances have been shown to have aphrodisiac effects, Young (1990) emphasized that good mental health, an interesting and interested partner, and continuity of sexual function "form the soundest base for sustained sexual capability" (p. 122).

Drugs and Sexual Response

Drugs affect sexual response in both women and men. While some drugs are designed to enhance sexual response (e.g., papavarine to induce erection will be discussed in Chapter 15 on Sexual Dysfunctions and Sex Therapy), many drugs have a negative effect on sexual response. Drugs may be categorized as those used for medication and those used for recreation.

Drugs for Medication

More than 200 drugs influence sexual performance (either positively or negatively), according to drug manufacturers' official product literature (Lieberman, 1988, p. 2). Individuals are not likely to discuss the negative effects. Only 10% of patients on high blood pressure medication spontaneously reported that they had experienced difficulties with erection. When questioned by their physician, the percentage rose to 26. But when the patients were asked to complete a questionnaire in private, the percentage rose again to 47% (DeLeo & Magni, 1983).

CONSIDERATION: Since patients are usually not informed about the effects of a particular medication on their sexual response, they often take such medications unaware. For example, Accutane (isotretinoin) is widely marketed in the United States as a treatment for severe acne. Yet, this medication has been found to be associated with vaginal dryness in women, erectile problems in men, and decreased interest in sex for women and men (Lieberman, 1988, pp. 147–148).

Various prescription drugs have been reported to have a negative effect on sexual response.

- Antihypertensive medications, designed to lower blood pressure, are associated with erectile dysfunction in men and decreased vaginal lubrication in women. Both men and women may experience loss of sexual interest, delayed orgasm, or inability to attain orgasm (Smith & Talbert, 1986).
- Psychotropic medications (used to improve psychological functioning) may have a negative effect on sexual functioning. Two broad categories of psychotropic medications are antidepressant and antianxiety drugs. Antidepressant drugs (monoamine oxidase inhibitors and tricyclic antidepressants) are associated with a variety of effects on sexual functioning, including erectile dysfunction, inhibited orgasm, retrograde ejaculation, and ejaculatory incompetence (Rogers, 1990). Antidepressants such as trazodone have also been associated with inhibited female orgasm. "Treatment of such a complication is generally managed by discontinuing the offending drug and restarting the patient on another tricyclic" (Jani & Wise, 1988, p. 279). Antianxiety drugs, such as barbiturates and benzodiazepines, have also been associated with depressed sexual interest and orgasmic response (Rogers, 1990).

  Other psychotropic medications that are reported to cause erectile dysfunction include Tofranil, Vivactil, Pertofran, Anafranil, Elavil, Parnate, Actomol, Nadil, Eskalith, Prolixin, and Mellaril. Those reported to impair or delay ejaculation include Librium, Haldol, Stelazine, Mellaril, Elavil, and Tofranil. Drugs that are reported to delay female orgasm include Nardil and imipramine (Segraves, 1981).

- Anabolic steroids, endogenous androgens, and testosterone are used in replacement therapy for men with a deficiency or absence of endogenous testosterone. These agents may also be used in women as adjunctive therapy for inoperable metastatic mammary cancer (Rogers, 1990). Both sexes taking these agents have reported both increases and decreases in sexual desire. The use of anabolic steroids among athletes is discussed in Exhibit 7.4.

Drugs for Recreation

Drugs that are not used for medical purposes under the supervision of a physician are referred to as recreational drugs. Recreational drugs have mixed effects on sexual functioning.

Alcohol Alcohol is the most frequently used recreational drug in our society and on college and university campuses. Alcohol is a central nervous system depressant that has both psychological and physiological effects on sexual response. In a review of research on the physiological effects of alcohol consumption on sexuality, Crowe and George (1989) noted that alcohol consumption in very low doses appears to enhance male sexual responding, as assessed by measurement of penile tumescence. As the level of alcohol consumption increases, a steady decline in sexual responsivity results, as indicated by erectile dysfunction. The point at which there is a significant

EXHIBIT 7.4 Anabolic Steroid Use Among Athletes

A type of drug abuse that is specific to competitive athletes is the use of **anabolic steroids.** Synthetic anabolic steroids are used by some weight lifters, football players, body builders, runners, swimmers, pole vaulters, cyclists, high jumpers, wrestlers, and participants in throwing competitions (shot put, discus, javelin, and hammer). Most athletes who use anabolic steroids obtain them from sources other than medical providers and use them in doses much greater than the recommended levels. The percent of college athletes who reported using anabolic steroids in the mid-1980s ranged from 11% to 20% (men are more likely than women to report such use) (Taylor, 1991, p. 152).

Anabolic steroids, which are hormones that resemble testosterone, have the effect of accelerating tissue growth. Although testosterone is not considered a pure anabolic steroid, its use among athletes has increased due to the difficulty of detecting it through laboratory testing.

Athletes who use anabolic steroids do so because they believe it will increase their strength and muscle mass and enhance their athletic performance. Gymnasts may also use anabolic steroids with the intention of stunting growth. Other reported effects of anabolic steroids include euphoria and a sense of decreased fatigue—more energy and endurance. Some researchers claim that the belief that anabolic steroids increase muscle mass and strength has not been substantiated by research (Hill, Suker, Sachs, & Brigham, 1983).

There are numerous negative side effects of anabolic steroid use. In men, these include gynecomastia (abnormally large breasts), a reduction of the size of the testicles, enlargement of the prostate gland, a lower sperm count, nausea, and diarrhea. In addition, it reduces the body's own production of testosterone and gonadotropins, which results in reduced spermatogenesis. In women, use of anabolic steroids may cause masculinization (excessive hair growth in unwanted areas, such as face and chest, and deepening of the voice), enlargement of the clitoris, and cessation of menstruation. While acne is a common side effect in both sexes, a more serious side effect of anabolic steroid use in both men and women is progressive liver damage. Because of the side effects and the limited beneficial effects of anabolic steroids, the American College of Sports Medicine released the following statement:

> Serious continuing effort should be made to educate male and female athletes, coaches, physical educators, physicians, trainers, and the general public regarding the inconsistent effects of anabolic steroids on improvement of human physical performance and the potential danger of taking certain forms of these substances, especially in large doses for prolonged periods. (Quoted in Hill, Suker, Sachs & Brigham, 1983, p. 271)

linear decrease in sexual response has not been precisely determined. However, Crowe and George (1989) cited an estimate of 0.05 blood alcohol concentration (or about the equivalent of three mixed drinks consumed in one to two hours by a 150-pound person) as the point at which alcohol may interfere with male sexual functioning. Sexual responsivity in women (orgasmic response) seems to be adversely affected by increased alcohol intake.

CONSIDERATION: In Rosen and Beck's (1988) review of alcohol effects on male sexual function, studies were cited that revealed that moderate drinking was related to some impairment of erection ability. However, with high doses of alcohol, significant interference occurred. In contrast to the actual experience, most research participants believed that alcohol improved their sexual performance and persisted in this erroneous belief despite knowledge of their laboratory results. Perhaps most important in mediating alcohol's sexual effect are the individual's expectations. If alcohol is expected to heighten sexual arousal, it will.

Long-term heavy use of alcohol causes damage to the hypothalamus, which results in decreased testosterone levels; "the effects are often irreversible" (Munsat, 1990, p. 596). Sexual effects of long-term alcohol usage in men include erectile dysfunction, lowered sex drive, infertility, and feminization syndrome, the characteristics of which include varying degrees of breast enlargement and testicular atropy (Munsat, 1990; Crowe & George, 1989). In a study of 50 hospitalized alcoholic men, half reported erectile dysfunction (Schiavi, 1990, p. 26). A return to normal sexual functioning has been found in only 50% of the cases after abstinence from alcohol abuse for months or years (Munsat, 1990).

Alcohol abuse also has negative effects on the sexual functioning of women. Munsat (1990) observed that long-term alcohol use in women results in decreased interest in sex and sexual activity, more difficulty in becoming aroused and in having an orgasm, and disturbances in physiological functioning of the reproductive system (menstrual irregularity and infertility).

Wilsnack (1980) identified six possible mechanisms that may help to account for the disruptive effects of chronic alcoholism on sexual function:

1. The acute depressant effects of alcohol on sexual response;
2. The disruption of gonadal hormone metabolism as a result of liver damage;
3. Reduced sexual sensation due to alcohol-induced neuropathy;
4. Organic brain damage causing impairment in both interpersonal and sexual interest;
5. Various health disorders, such as diabetes and hypertension, that are associated with alcoholism; and
6. In chronic alcoholism, major disruption of all aspects of the biopsychosocial system.

Psychologically, low doses of alcohol in both women and men result in increased levels of sexual arousal and disinhibit engaging in sexual behavior. A social learning explanation of the relationship between alcohol and sexuality suggests that people who drink learn to associate alcohol with sexual arousal and behavior. Crowe and George (1989) noted that

> The world is full of associations between alcohol and sex; most of them are positive and few are subtle. Liquor ads feature beautiful women and macho men. James Bond's sexual prowess thrives on vodka martinis and Dom Perignon. Loving wives serve wine at candlelit dinners for two. (p. 382)

Crowe and George (1989) suggested that the disinhibiting property of alcohol on sexuality involves a scapegoating process "in which [sexual] feelings and actions can be blamed on the liquor" (p. 382). This scapegoating function can be used as a proactive disinhibitor or as a retroactive justification for engaging in sexual behavior. Wilson (1981) suggested that sex offenders often exaggerate their degree of intoxication to enhance their legal defense.

Some alcoholic men complain that disulfiram (Antabuse), a medical treatment for alcoholism, causes their erectile dysfunction. But double-blind studies demonstrate higher rates of erectile dysfunction among men on placebo than among men on disulfiram. "Thus, disulfiram seems to provide a convenient alibi for sexual problems but is doubtful as an etiological factor" (Schover & Jensen, 1988, p. 278).

Both women and men may use alcohol as a mechanism to cope with other "feelings of inadequacy, sexual anxiety, mood disorders, and difficulties with interpersonal relationships" (Schiavi, 1990, p. 30). Because alcohol use may be embedded in a web of other concerns, stopping the alcohol abuse may not necessarily translate into a return to positive sexual functioning.

Wiseman (1985) provided further evidence of how the interaction between partners affects perceived sexual satisfaction among alcoholic spouses and among a control group of spouses. First, the presence of an alcoholic spouse does not automatically translate into unsatisfactory sexual relations. Thirty percent of 76 wives of alcoholics reported that they had "no complaints about sexual relations." Almost a fourth (23%) of alcoholic husbands reported satisfactory sexual relations (p. 295). (It should not be overlooked that 70% and 75% of the wives and husbands of alcoholics, respectively, did report a negative effect of alcohol on their sexual relations). Second, wives involved in marriages in which alcohol is not a problem reported a similar level of satisfaction. Twenty-nine percent of 63 such wives reported that sexual relations were satisfying; 62% of husbands in marriages where alcohol was not a problem reported satisfactory sexual relations. Third, when wives of alcoholic spouses were asked to identify the complaints they have about their husbands, 62% said that the husband is noncommunicative, 44% said that he cannot be counted on to be there for family meals, and 34% said that they engaged in little or no joint recreational activities. In contrast, the percentages of wives married to men without a drinking problem who complain about the same issues are 17, 11, and 18, respectively. The importance of this study is that it emphasizes that it is often the way the alcoholic partner treats the spouse (doesn't talk to, doesn't attend family meals, doesn't share recreational time), rather than the fact that the partner drinks, that results in an unsatisfactory sex life.

The psychosocial influences on alcohol's sexual effects are further discussed in the following perspective.

RESEARCH PERSPECTIVE

The Social Psychology of Alcohol Consumption and Sexual Effects

Is alcohol an aphrodisiac? Only in a superficial way, according to Lang's (1985) review of the research on drinking and human sexuality. Based on studies in nonclinical populations, he concluded that alcohol's effects are largely (a) psychological (including one's expectation regarding its effects) and (b) social (the degree to which intoxication is socially allowed as an explanation for sexual behavior). Similarly, Crowe and George (1989, p. 379) referred to the "excuse-giving properties of alcohol" and provided the metaphor of alcohol as "a trumpet against the wall of sexual restraint" (p. 374), invoking the image of one's self-restraint coming tumbling down when alcohol is consumed, as when Joshua's trumpet brought down the walls of Jericho. In summary, consumption of alcohol may lead to

Continued

Continued

increased sexual arousal and/or behavior because a person expects it to (expectancy effect) and/or because people can escape responsibility for their sexual behavior by blaming it on alcohol (alcohol attribution). Following are some examples of studies cited in Lang's and Crowe and George's reviews, along with a description of a more recent study that suggests a possible shift in college students' attitudes toward alcohol.

Many experimental studies on alcohol and sexuality have employed the "balanced placebo" design, in which expectancy of alcohol's effect and the actual alcohol dose can be manipulated. Diluted mixtures of vodka and tonic are typically used (one part vodka to five parts tonic) so that alcohol dose cannot be distinguished by taste. The research participants are distributed among the four groups depicted in Figure 1.

The balanced placebo design was used by Wilson and Lawson (1976a) with male social drinkers. A blood alcohol content (BAC) of 0.04% was reached by the participants who actually received alcohol. The men viewed erotic films while their penile tumescence was recorded. Although actual alcohol content did not affect penile tumescence, beverage expectancy had a significant effect. Greater sexual arousal was measured for men who believed they drank alcohol than for men who believed they drank only tonic water.

When Wilson and Lawson (1976b) replicated the study with female participants, they obtained markedly different results. Expectancy did not affect the women's sexual arousal. However, actual alcohol consumption was related to an increase in self-reported pleasure but a decrease in objectively measured sexual arousal. A study by Malatesta, Pollack, and Crotty (1982) also revealed a pattern among college women of depressed sexual functioning, as measured physiologically, in contrast to higher subjective ratings of sexual pleasure after drinking. Wilson and Lawson hypothesized that in comparison to men, women have less drinking experience, weaker expectancy beliefs, are less likely to recognize and control early signs of sexual excitement, and may feel greater sexual vulnerability while drinking.

Lang, Searles, Lauerman, and Adesso (1980) found that the expectancy effect will not always disinhibit sexual behavior and stated that whether the expectancy effect occurs depends upon how useful it is to a person to use alcohol to explain (or defend) his or her behavior. Using the balanced placebo design, Lang et al. studied the "utility or reinforcement value" of making alcohol attributions. Male social drinkers who scored high, moderate, or low on a sex guilt inventory were equally distributed to the four possible conditions (using vodka and tonic or tonic alone). After viewing slides of erotic photographs, the participants reported their level of sexual arousal. Meanwhile, the investigators unobtrusively measured the amount of time the participants spent looking at each slide. Not surprisingly, higher sexual arousal was reported by those who thought they had received alcohol, whether or not they actually received it. But further analysis revealed that the level of sex guilt

Continued

		Expect Alcohol	
		YES	NO
Receive Alcohol	YES	Active Condition	Antiplacebo
	NO	Placebo	Control

FIGURE 1 Balanced Placebo Design

Continued

mediated the effect. While all participants looked longer at the more sexually explicit slides, this was especially true for the high sex guilt individuals. When the men who scored high on sex guilt believed they had consumed alcohol (alcohol attribution), they were more likely to indulge their interest in the more explicit slides.

Given the likelihood that drinking alcohol influences sexual decision-making and behavior, Crowe and George (1989, p. 384) suggested that one factor that might help promote responsible decision-making would be "to nullify the personal and social excuse-giving qualities of alcohol expectancies." Perhaps this is beginning to occur! Corcoran and Bell (1990) gave narratives to introductory psychology students. The narratives told the story of a pair of college students who went out together to a bar. The narratives varied the account of the man and the woman as drinking soft drinks or as drinking cocktails and getting slightly intoxicated. The research participants were asked to rate the characters on their attractiveness, their level of intoxication, the likelihood of their having sexual contact, and the likelihood of their having sexual intercourse.

Analysis of the results showed that female research participants were slightly more likely to believe that the story's characters would have sexual intercourse when the man in the story had more alcohol to drink. However, male research participants believed that if the female character had any alcohol, sexual intercourse would be significantly less likely to occur. Whether the characters drank alcohol did not affect participants' ratings of attractiveness.

Corcoran and Bell (1990) commented that the men's rating of less likelihood of sexual intercourse when the woman had been drinking does not guarantee that the slightly intoxicated woman is immune from sexual exploitation. In fact, studies of the connection between alcohol use and acquaintance rape suggest that intoxication offers an excuse for sexual aggression and a reason to blame the victim and decreases a victim's ability to resist (Richardson & Hammock, 1991). However, Corcoran and Bell suggested that the connection between alcohol consumption and sexual activity is complex and may be shifting. They concluded that more research is needed to answer such questions as the following:

> . . . is the sexual activity female subjects expect when the male character was drinking desired? forced? Are male college students changing their attitudes about alcohol and sexuality? changing behavior? (p. 10)

References

Corcoran, K. J., & Bell, B. G. (1990). Opposite sex perceptions of the effects of alcohol consumption on subsequent sexual activity in a dating situation. *Psychology: A Journal of Human Behavior, 27,* 7–11.

Crowe, L. C., & George, W. H. (1989). Alcohol and human sexuality: Review and integration. *Psychological Bulletin, 102,* 374–386.

Lang, A. R. (1985). The social psychology of drinking and human sexuality. *Journal of Drug Issues, 15,* 273–289.

Lang, A., Searles, J., Lauerman, R., & Adesso, V. (1980). Expectancy alcohol, and sex guilt as determinants of interest in and reaction to sexual stimuli. *Journal of Abnormal Psychology, 89,* 644–653.

Malatesta, V. J., Pollack, R. H., & Crotty, T. D. (1982). Acute alcohol intoxication and female orgasmic response. *Journal of Sex Research, 18,* 1–17.

Richardson, D. R., & Hammock, G. S. (1991). Alcohol and acquaintance rape. In A. Parrot & L. Bechhofer (Eds.), *Acquaintance rape: The hidden crime* (pp. 83–95). New York: Wiley.

Wilson, G. T., & Lawson, D. M. (1976a). Expectancies, alcohol, and sexual arousal in male social drinkers. *Journal of Abnormal Psychology, 85,* 587–594.

Wilson, G. T., & Lawson, D. M. (1976b). The effects of alcohol on sexual arousal in women. *Journal of Abnormal Psychology, 85,* 489–497.

Centuries after marihuana's effects on libido and sexual performance were first commented on, there is still little reliable information about how marihuana affects human sexuality.

Ernest Abel

Marijuana Marijuana is also used as a recreational drug, but its effects on sexuality are less predictable than alcohol. Although there are numerous self-report studies, "there is a complete absence of direct psychophysiological research comparable to that reported for the effects of alcohol on male and female sexual response" (Rosen & Beck, 1988, p. 312). In one study, researchers found that marijuana in moderate doses enhanced the quality of orgasm for 40% of the women and 68% of the men (Halikas, Weller, & Morse, 1982). In addition, these researchers found that 75% of the men and 90% of the women reported that moderate doses of marijuana increased their sexual pleasure and satisfaction.

CONSIDERATION: Although other studies have reached similar conclusions in regard to the positive effects of marijuana on sexual desire, pleasure, and satisfaction, such studies should be viewed cautiously. Rosen and Beck (1988) identified three methodological problems:

> First, the sampling of such studies tends to be highly selective, typically including a disproportionate number of individuals who have experienced positive effects with the drug. Second, the criteria for drug use or sexual satisfaction are rarely specified. Finally, the frequent marijuana user is also likely to be using alcohol or other drugs, making it difficult if not impossible to attribute sexual effects to marijuana use alone. Moreover, amount of drug used, duration of drug use, quality of drug used, setting in which the drug is used (clinical, social, isolated), and expectations all have an effect on sexual response (p. 312).

Studies that have suggested positive effects of marijuana on sexual response (perhaps due to the relaxation effects of the drug) have indicated that lower rather than higher doses may increase sexual desire. Alternatively, at very high levels of intoxication, some users report "their involvement with their own fantasies and inner experiences distracted from their sexual interaction with a partner" (Rosen & Beck, 1988, p. 313). Other users report that marijuana in large doses often produces sleepiness, lethargy, and dizziness, which interferes with sexual arousal and performance.

Some studies suggest that chronic use of marijuana in men may cause testosterone levels to drop, thereby decreasing sex drive; other studies find no effect on testosterone levels due to marijuana use (Munsat, 1990). Studies also differ on whether marijuana is associated with lowering sperm count. The National Academy of Sciences, Institute of Medicine (1982) reported that while marijuana was associated with reducing sperm production, there was no evidence that marijuana causes sterility.

The effects of marijuana on the female reproductive system are also unpredictable. Some studies suggest that marijuana is associated with shorter menstrual cycles and has been used to reduce menstrual cramps. In lower animals, marijuana has a negative effect on the female reproductive system. However, such a finding may be due to the reduced food and water consumption (malnutrition) that accompanies the use of marijuana in lower animals (Abel, 1985).

Other Recreational Drugs Other recreational drugs that affect sexual arousal and performance include barbiturates, opiate narcotics, amphetamines, cocaine, tobacco, and amyl nitrate. Barbiturates have an effect similar to alcohol in that they blunt anxiety and reduce inhibitions. But because barbiturates are primarily sedatives that depress the central nervous system, higher doses may result in loss of sexual ability. As with most sleeping pills, which contain barbiturates, the desire for sleep replaces the desire for sex.

The effects of marijuana on sexual satisfaction and performance are unpredictable.

Among the opiate narcotics are morphine, heroin, and methadone. Use of these drugs has been associated with decreased sexual interest and ability. DeLeon and Wexler (1973) found in their study of heroin addicts that all subjects reported decreases in intercourse, masturbation, and nocturnal emissions.

Amphetamines, such as pep pills and diet pills, are "uppers" that stimulate the central nervous system. The effect of such drugs is to overcome fatigue and to give a feeling of alertness and energy. Prolonged use of amphetamines may make orgasm difficult for the man, although he may still have an erection. For women, menstrual difficulties have been associated with the use of amphetamines.

Cocaine is a "central nervous system stimulant that increases alertness, elevates mood, and produces euphoria" (Abel, 1985, p. 97). Cocaine became the preferred drug in the mid-1970s to enhance sexual desire. However, published studies of the effect of cocaine on sexual response have been virtually nonexistent (Taberner, 1985); those that do exist are based primarily on self-reports. While small quantities of cocaine have been associated with an increased sense of energy and the ability to control orgasm, "chronic use of the drug may be associated in some users with loss of sexual interest or impotence" (Rosen & Beck, 1988, p. 316).

Tobacco is one of the most widely used drugs in the world. "The main psychological effect of nicotine is stimulation of the brain although smokers often feel relaxed. Heart rate is increased and blood pressure is increased whereas blood flow to the extremities is decreased" (Abel, 1985, p. 205). LoPiccolo (1983, p. 55) observed that reduced penile blood pressure in heavy smokers may be accompanied by erectile problems. "In other words, though the Marlboro man may be macho, he may also be impotent." While some argue that nicotine is an aphrodisiac, others disagree. Abel (1985) concluded that "the evidence that smoking affects male libido is inconclusive" (p. 225).

Amyl nitrate, also known as "snappers" or "poppers," is used by heart patients to prevent heart pain (angina). It is inhaled from a small ampule that is broken open and causes rapid dilation of the arteries that supply various organs of the body with oxygen. The effect on the brain is to induce a feeling of giddiness and euphoria; the effect on the genitals is to produce a sensation of warmth. When inhaled at the

TABLE 7.1 How Some Drugs Affect Sexual Response

Drug	Effect on Sexual Response
Alcohol	Low amounts may increase subjective arousal but do not increase physiological arousal; high amounts suppress physiological arousal.
Marijuana	Setting and partner affect evaluation. Low doses associated with enhanced arousal, pleasure, and satisfaction. Heavy doses associated with becoming introspective and less interactive with partner. Testosterone levels may be reduced. Sperm count may be lowered. Menstrual cycles may be shorter among users, and some report the drug relieves menstrual cramps.
Amphetamines	Increased sexual desire reported at low doses. High doses associated with diminished desire. Orgasm may be enhanced at low doses; high doses may interfere with female orgasm.
Cocaine	Similar to effects of amphetamines.
Narcotics	High doses associated with loss of sexual desire and ability.
Barbiturates	In low doses, may increase desire because of the reduction of inhibitions. In high doses, decreases desire. The need for sleep may replace the need for sex.
Amyl Nitrate	Inhaling at time of orgasm causes enhanced feeling of pleasure. Prolonged use results in nasal irritation, nausea, loss of erection, coughing, and dizziness.
Tobacco	Constricts blood vessels. Heavy smoking may be related to erectile problems. Researchers disagree on the effects on sexual desire.

approach of orgasm, the effect is to enhance and prolong the orgasmic experience. The person feels a "rush," along with an altered state of consciousness, a loss of inhibition, a tingling sensation in the head and body, and a sensation of faintness. Negative side effects of amyl nitrate include nasal irritation, nausea, loss of erection, coughing, and dizziness.

Table 7.1 lists some of the effects various drugs have on sexual response.

Erotica and Sexual Response

We will discuss sexual fantasies in Chapter 9, Individual Sexuality, and erotica and pornography in Chapter 19, Abuses and Commercial Uses of Sexuality. For now, we want to mention that the study of erotica and its effects on sexual response in women and men is an example of a current application of sexual psychophysiological research. Rather than rely on subjective reports of arousal, psychophysiological research measures cardiovascular, respiratory, and electrodermal responses as indices of arousal.

Sexual Response to Erotica Exposure

Based primarily on studies of college students, the findings concerning the short-term effects of erotica exposure are not surprising. "Erotica tends to induce a degree of sexual arousal which is often followed by a temporary increase in sexual activity, either masturbation or sex with the usual partner, and the effect is noticeable for no more than 1 or 2 days" (Bancroft, 1989, p. 268). Researchers have documented that types of sexual activity depicted in erotica may be incorporated into fantasy, although not necessarily into overt behavior (Bancroft, 1989).

One variable that influences the degree of arousal to pornography is the amount of exposure. Zillmann (1989) documented that prolonged exposure reduces excitatory responses. One team of researchers (Kelley & Musialowski, 1986) found sex differences related to habituation. Women tended to habituate to erotic films when the film participants repeated the same sexual activities, whereas men tended to habituate when the same film participants were repeatedly shown.

Differences between Women and Men

Studies disagree on whether erotica has different effects on women and men. While Kinsey, Pomeroy, Martin, and Gebhard (1953) suggested that men had greater "conditionability" to erotic stimuli than women, Jakobovits (1965) noted the greater capacity of female subjects to become aroused by hard-core passages. The bulk of the evidence suggests that there are greater similarities than differences in the way women and men respond to erotica (Rosen & Beck, 1988). One area in which differences have been found is in response to presentations of sexual aggression and/or rape. Schmidt (1975) reported that both men and women reported sexual arousal mixed with strong aversion, to rape films. However, while the women were more likely to express fear of being overpowered, the men felt guilty for being sexually aroused by the aggressive scenes. More recently, Malamuth et al. (1988) detected sex differences in the reported levels of sexual arousal, which varied depending on the degree of force presented in a written passage describing intercourse and prior involvement in a self-disclosing discussion. Women who read the more aggressive version of the passage, if they had previously disclosed their sexual preferences, reported greater sexual and general arousal than women who had not engaged in the discussion. Apparently, participating in the discussion reduced inhibitions, as after the discussions women reported greater sexual arousal than men.

CHOICES

We sometimes assume that the sexual response cycle is one in which we are physiologically carried from phase to phase without the exercise of choice. While there are physiological happenings at each stage of the cycle, we do exercise choice in terms of our entry into the cycle and our focus during it.

Choose to Engage in Sexual Behavior with Minimal Desire?

It is not unusual for individuals to bring to sex therapy the problem of having minimal sexual desire yet wanting such desire and to engage in sexual behavior with one's partner. While we will discuss the problem of lack of sexual desire in detail in Chapter 15, Sexual Dysfunctions and Sex Therapy, here we discuss the question of whether one might choose to engage in sexual behavior in the absence of such desire. Moser (1992) noted that

> People may engage in sex, even frequently, but for reasons other than their own desire (e.g., marital duty, to prove that they can, as a form of self-treatment, to become pregnant, to promote intimacy, to please the partner, for self-esteem, etc.). (p. 66)

Data collected by Beck, Bosman, and Qualtrough (1991) also suggest that, indeed, individuals sometimes engage in sexual behavior even though they may have minimal sexual desire at the time. The researchers observed that 82% of 86 college women and 60% of 58 college men reported this phenomenon and that their primary motivation for doing so was to please the partner.

Aside from pleasing the partner, another potential outcome from choosing to enage in sexual behavior independent of desire is that the individual may discover that desire follows involvement in sexual behavior. Tavris (1992) suggested that "many tired adults, desiring nothing so much as a good night's sleep, find that sexual desire can *follow* arousal when their partners start fondling them fondly under the covers" (p. 226).

Cognitive behavior therapists conceptualize this phenomenon as "acting one's self into a new way of feeling, rather than feeling one's self into a new way of acting." Rather than waiting for the feelings of sexual desire to occur before engaging in sexual behavior, the person "acts as though there is feeling," only to discover that the feelings sometime follow. There is an old French saying that reflects this phenomenon: *L'appetit vient en mangeant,* which translates as "the appetite comes with eating."

The alternative of not choosing to initiate or become involved sexually unless one is in the mood may have negative consequences for the individual and for the partner. Since sexual desire, in some cases, may depend on having had a pleasurable sexual experience, unless one first engages in sexual behavior, desire may never be present. Hence, if one believes that sexual desire must be present for sexual behavior and if desire never occurs; then one may never engage in sexual behavior.

The negative consequence for the partner may be the feeling and perception of rejection. "If my partner loves me, my partner would care about my sexual satisfaction" becomes translated to "My partner doesn't really care about me." These feelings of rejection may have devastating effects on the relationship.

We are not suggesting that individuals who lack sexual desire should routinely initiate sexual behavior with their partners. Individuals should respect their own feelings and preferences and should not feel coerced into engaging in sexual behavior when they do not want to. However, when one is generally comfortable engaging in sexual behavior with a particular person with whom coercion is not an issue, the person may choose to engage in sexual behavior with minimal desire for the potential positive outcomes mentioned above.

Choose to Minimize Focus on the Orgasm Phase of the Sexual Response Cycle?

Butler and Lewis (1976), in their study of sexuality among the elderly, noted a focus on the "second language of sex"—the emotional and communication aspects—rather than on orgasmic pleasure. However, for many individuals in our society, the focus of sex is orgasm. One choice individuals can make is to selectively attend to other aspects of sexual response, rather than drift into the cultural focus on orgasm.

One of Hite's (1981) respondents, a husband, illustrated this focus:

> At sixty-five, I am having the best sex life I have ever had. My wife and I have few inhibitions and try anything we like. I'm usually the aggressor, but she likes to pull me into the bedroom and I don't struggle. We wander around our apartment naked,

Continued

Continued

> bathe together, and love each other's body and mind. Our love has been a developing one. First it was more sexual. Now it is that plus many other things. (p. 860)

Choosing a focus other than orgasm allows the respective partners to define their sexual encounter in positive terms independent of an orgasmic experience. Such a choice has a win-win outcome. Not only do the partners enjoy the benefits of a focus on aspects other than orgasm, each encounter is "successful" since it does not depend on an orgasm.

Choose to Use Erotic Materials and/or Devices to Enhance Arousal?

Some couples use erotic materials (X-rated videos, erotic literature and audiotapes) to enhance arousal, pleasure, and satisfaction. Others use devices, such as handcuffs, silk scarfs, and vibrators, to achieve similar goals. Still others are turned off by erotica and devices and feel that use of these is not necessary. We suggest that choosing to use or not use these materials is acceptable as long as the respective partners agree. Disagreements may be handled through acquiescence, compromise, or a combination of these across time.

Summary

1. Sexual response involves desire (a subjective experience), arousal or excitement (central nervous system, brain), genital response (vaginal lubrication or erection), and peripheral changes (heart rate and breathing increase).
2. Masters and Johnson described the four basic phases of the sexual response cycle as those of excitement, plateau, orgasm, and resolution. Kaplan suggested that desire is an important aspect of sexual response that occurs prior to excitement. Other models include Ellis's and Beach's two-stage models and Reed's Erotic Stimulus Pathway model.
3. The Human Sexual Response Cycle model has been criticized as not being representative of all people, due to subject sample bias, experimenter bias, and lack of attention to cultural context.
4. Olfactory, tactile, visual, auditory, and relationship cues are relevant to progressing through the various stages of the sexual response cycle.
5. Sexual arousal is measured both physiologically (penile tumescence, vaginal vasocongestion) and subjectively (self-report).
6. While people may have similar physiological manifestations in having an orgasm, they report different subjective experiences.
7. Women and men sometimes experience sexual responses differently, with women being both less likely to have an orgasm yet more likely to have multiple orgasms without a refractory period.
8. The role of hormones in human sexual behavior is not well understood. However, when both women and men are deprived of testosterone, they lose all sexual desire. Hormonal levels seem to be more influential in men's sexual functioning than in women's.
9. The presumed arousal effects of alcohol are psychological and social, rather than physiological. Drugs for recreation and medication have various effects on sexual response.
10. Exposure to erotica typically results in sexual arousal in women, as well as men.

KEY TERMS

central arousal
peripheral arousal
vasocongestion
pheromone
tumescence
plateau phase
orgasmic platform
orgasm
clitoral orgasm
vaginal orgasm
nonterminative orgasms
terminative orgasms
vulval orgasms
uterine orgasms
blended orgasms
resolution phase
refractory period
hormones
aphrodisiac
anabolic steroid

REFERENCES

Abel, E. L. (1985). *Psychoactive drugs and sex.* New York: Plenum Press.

Addiego, F., Belzer, E. G., Jr., Comolli, J., Moger, W., Perry, J. D., & Whipple, B. (1981). Female ejaculation: A case study. *Journal of Sex Research, 17,* 13–21.

Alzate, H. (1985). Vaginal eroticism; A replication study. *Archives of Sexual Behavior, 14,* 529–537.

Alzate, H., & Lodoño, M. L. (1984). Vaginal erotic sensitivity. *Journal of Sex and Marital Therapy, 10,* 49–56.

Bancroft, J. H. (1983). *Human sexuality and its problems.* New York: Churchill Livingston.

Bancroft, J. H. (1989). *Human sexuality and its problems* (2nd ed.). New York: Churchill Livingston.

Bancroft, J., Sherwin, B. B., Alexander, G. M., Davidson, D. W., & Walker, A. (1991). Oral contraceptives, androgens, and the sexuality of young women: II. The role of androgens. *Archives of Sexual Behavior, 20,* 121–135.

Beach, F. A. (1956). Characteristics of masculine sex drive. In *Nebraska Symposium on Motivation* (Vol. 4, pp. 1–32). Lincoln: University of Nebraska Press.

Beck, J. G., Bozman, A. W., & Qualtrough, T. (1991). The experience of sexual desire: Psychological correlates in a college sample. *Journal of Sex Research, 28,* 443–456.

Bohlen, J. G., Held, J. P., & Sanderson, M. O. (1980). The male orgasm: Pelvic contractions measured by anal probe. *Archives of Sexual Behavior, 9,* 503–521.

Bohlen, J. G., Held, J. P., Sanderson, M. O., & Boyer, C. M. (1982). Development of a woman's multiple orgasm pattern: A research case report. *Journal of Sex Research, 18,* 130–145.

Bozman, A. W., & Beck, J. G. (1991). Covariation of sexual desire and sexual arousal: The effects of anger and anxiety. *Archives of Sexual Behavior, 20,* 47–60.

Butler, R. N., & Lewis, M. I. (1976). *Sex after sixty.* New York: Harper and Row.

Crenshaw, T., Goldberg, J., & Stern, W. (1987). Pharmacologic modification of psychosexual dysfunction. *Journal of Sex and Marital Therapy, 13,* 239–250.

Crowe, L. C., & George, W. H. (1989). Alcohol and human sexuality: Review and integration. *Psychological Bulletin, 102,* 374–386.

Darling, C. A., Davidson, J. K., & Conway-Welch, C. (1990). Female ejaculation: Perceived origins, the Grafenberg spot/area, and sexual responsiveness. *Archives of Sexual Behavior, 19,* 29–47.

Darling, C. A., Davidson, J. K., Sr., & Jennings, D. A. (1991). The female sexual response revisited: Understanding the multiorgasmic experience in women. *Archives of Sexual Behavior, 20,* 527–540.

Davis, D. M. Inc. (1988). *The D. M. Davis HgPC Penis Gauge (general information sheet).* New York: Author.

DeLeo, D., & Magni, G. (1983). Sexual side effects of antidepressant drugs. *Psychosomatics, 24,* 1076–82.

DeLeon, G., & Wexler, H. K. (1973). Heroin addiction: Its relation to sexual behavior and sexual experience. *Journal of Abnormal Psychology, 81,* 36–38.

Diokno, A. C., Brown, M. B., & Herzog, A. R. (1990). Sexual function in the elderly. *Archives of Internal Medicine, 150,* 197–200.

Dunn, M. E., & Trost, J. E. (1989). Male multiple orgasm. *Archives of Sexual Behavior, 18,* 377–387.

Ellis, H. (1906). *Studies in the psychology of sex* (7 vols.). New York: Random House.

Falsaperla, A., Monici Preti, P. A., & Oliani, C. (1990). Selegiline versus oxiracetam in patients with Alzheimer-type dementia, *Clinical Therapeutics, 12,* 376–384.

Fox, C. A., & Fox, B. A. (1969). Blood pressure and respiratory patterns during human coitus. *Journal of Reproduction and Fertility, 19,* 405–415.

Gallaher, W. (1986, February). The etiology of orgasm. *Discover,* pp. 51–59.

Garde, K., & Lunde, I. (1980). Female sexual behavior: A study in a random sample of 40 year old women. *Maturitas, 2,* 225–240.

Geer, J. H., & Fuhr, R. (1976). Cognitive factors in sexual arousal: The role of distraction. *Journal of Consulting and Clinical Psychology, 44,* 238–243.

Goldberg, D. C., Whipple, B., Fishkin, R. E., Waxman, H., Fink, P. J., & Weisberg, M. (1983). The Grafenberg Spot and female ejaculation: A review of initial hypotheses. *Journal of Sex and Marital Therapy, 9,* 27–37.

Halikas, J., Weller, R., & Morse, C. (1982). Effects of marijuana use on sexual performance. *Journal of Psychoactive Drugs, 14,* 1–2.

Hartmann, W., & Fithian, M. (1984). *Any man can.* New York: St. Martin's Press.

Heiman, J. (1977). A psychophysiological exploration of sexual arousal patterns in females and males. *Psychophysiology, 14,* 266–274.

Heiman, J. R., Rowland, D. L., Hatch, J. P., & Gladue, B. A. (1991). Psychophysiological and endocrine responses to sexual arousal in women. *Archives of Sexual Behavior, 20,* 171–186.

Hill, J. A., Suker, J. R., Sachs, K., & Brigham, C. (1983). The athletic polydrug abuse phenomenon. *American Journal of Sports Medicine, 11,* 269–271.

Hite, S. (1981). *The Hite report on male sexuality.* New York: Alfred Knopf.

Hoon, E. F., & Hoon, P. (1977, September). Differences between males and females on sex arousability inventory items. Paper presented at the Sixth Canadian Sex Research Forum, Calgary.

Hoon, P. W. (1979). The assessment of sexual arousal in women. In M. Hersen, R. M. Eisler, and P. M. Miller (Eds.), *Progress in Behavior Modification* (Vol. 7, pp. 1–61). New York: Academic Press.

Jakobovits, L. A. (1965). Evaluational reactions to erotic literature. *Psychological Reports, 16,* 985–994.

Jani, N. N., & Wise, T. N. (1988). Antidepressants and inhibited female orgasm: A literature review. *Journal of Sex and Marital Therapy, 14,* 279–284.

Kahn, C. (1990, December). An anti-aging aphrodisiac. *Longevity,* pp. 42–48.

Kaplan, H. (1979). *Disorders of sexual desire.* New York: Brunner/Mazel.

Kaplan, J. (1974). *The new sex therapy.* New York: Brunner/Mazel.

Kelly, K., & Musialowski, D. (1986). Repeated exposure to sexually explicit stimuli: Novelty, sex and sexual attitudes. *Archives of Sexual Behavior, 15,* 487–498.

Kinsey, A., Pomeroy, W., Martin, C., & Gebhard, P. (1953). *Sexual behavior in the human female.* Philadelphia: W. B. Saunders.

Knoll, J. (1983). Deprenyl (selegiline): The history of its development and pharmacological action. *Acta Neurologica Scandinavica—Supplementum, 95,* 57–80.

Knoll, J. (1985). The facilitation of dopaminergic activity in the aged brain by Deprenyl: A proposal for a strategy to improve the quality of life in senescence. *Mechanisms of Aging and Development, 30,* 109–122.

Kolodny, R. C., Masters, W. H., & Johnson, V. E. (1979). *Textbook of sexual medicine.* Boston: Little, Brown.

Ladas, A. K., Whipple, B., & Perry, J. D. (1982). *The G spot and other recent discoveries about human sexuality.* New York: Holt, Rinehart and Winston.

Leiblum, S. R., and Rosen, R. C. (1988). Introduction: Changing perspectives on sexual desire. In S. R. Leiblum and R. C. Rosen (Eds.), *Sexual desire disorders* (pp. 1–17). New York: Guilford Press.

Lieberman, M. L. (1988). *The sexual pharmacy.* New York: New American Library.

LoPiccolo, J. (1983). The prevention of sexual problems in men. In G. W. Albee, S. Gordon, & H. Leitenberg (Eds.), *Promoting sexual responsibility and preventing sexual problems* (pp. 39–65). Hanover, N.H.: University Press of New England.

Mahoney, J. M., and Strassberg, D. S. (1991). Voluntary control of male sexual arousal. *Archives of Sexual Behavior, 20,* 1–16.

Malamuth, N.M., Feshback, S., Fera, T., & Kunath, J. (1988). Aggressive cues and sexual arousal to erotica. In G. W. Russell (Ed.), *Violence in intimate relationships* (pp. 239–251). New York: PMA.

Manley, G. (1990). Endocrine disturbances and sexuality. In C. I. Fogel and D. Lauver (Eds.), *Sexual health promotion* (pp. 337–359). Philadelphia: W. B. Saunders.

Masters, W. H., & Johnson, V. E. (1966). *Human sexual response.* Boston: Little, Brown.

Meisler, A. W., & Carey, M. P. (1991). Depressed affect and male sexual arousal. *Archives of Sexual Behavior, 20,* 541–554.

Moser, C. (1992). Lust, lack of desire, and paraphilias: Some thoughts and possible connections. *Journal of Sex and Marital Therapy, 18,* 65–69.

Munsat, E. M. (1990). Mental illness, substance abuse and sexuality. In C. I. Fogel and D. Lauver (Eds.), *Sexual health promotion* (pp. 578–604). Philadelphia: W. B. Saunders.

Nagayama Hall, G. C. (1991). Sexual arousal as a function of physiological and cognitive variables in a sexual offender population. *Archives of Sexual Behavior, 20,* 359–369.

National Academy of Sciences, Institute of Medicine. (1982). *Marijuana and health.* Washington, DC: National Academy Press.

Palace, E. M., & Gorzalka, G. B. (1990). The enhancing effects of anxiety on arousal in sexually dysfunctional and functional women. *Journal of Abnormal Psychology, 99,* 403–411.

Rajfer, J., Aronson, W. J., Bush, P. A., Dorey, F. J., & Ignarro, L. J. (1992). Nitric oxide as a mediator of relaxation of the corpus cavernosum in response to nonadrenergic, noncholinergic neurotransmission. *New England Journal of Medicine, 326,* 90–94.

Robbins, M. B., & Jensen, G. D. (1978). Multiple orgasm in males. *Journal of Sex Research, 14,* 21–26.

Robinson, P. (1976). *The modernization of sex.* New York: Harper and Row.

Rogers, A. (1990). Drugs and disturbed sexual functioning. In C. I. Fogel and D. Lauver (Eds.), *Sexual health promotion.* (pp. 485–497). Philadelphia: W. B. Saunders.

Rosen, R. C., & Beck, J. G. (1988). *Patterns of sexual arousal: Psychophysiological processes and clinical applications.* New York: Guilford Press.

St. Lawrence, J. S., D. J. Joyner. (1991). The effects of sexually violent rock music on males' acceptance of violence against women. *Psychology of Women Quarterly, 15,* 49–63.

Schiavi, R. C. (1990). Chronic alcoholism and male sexual dysfunction. *Journal of Sex and Marital Therapy, 16,* 23–33.

Schmidt, G. (1975). Male-female differences in sexual arousal and behavior during and after exposure to sexually explicit stimuli. *Archives of Sexual Behavior, 4,* 353–366.

Schover, L. R., & Jensen, S. B. (1988). *Sexuality and chronic illness: A comprehensive approach.* New York: Guilford Press.

Segal, J. (1984). *The sex lives of college students.* Wayne, PA: Miles Standish.

Segraves, R. T. (1981). Psychopharmacological agents associated with sexual dysfunction. *Journal of Sex Education and Therapy, 7,* 43–45.

Simpson, W. S. (1991). When orgasm is too intense. *Medical Aspects of Human Sexuality, 25,* 9.

Singer, I. (1973). *The goals of human sexuality.* New York: Norton.

Slob, A. K., Ernste, M., & van der Werff ten Bosch, J. J. (1991). Menstrual cycle phase and sexual arousability in women. *Archives of Sexual Behavior, 20,* 567–577.

Smith, P. J., & Talbert, R. L. (1986). Sexual dysfunction with antihypertensive and antipsychotic agents. *Clinical Pharmacology, 5,* 373–384.

Stayton, W. R. (1992). A theology of sexual pleasure. *SIECUS Report, 20*(4), 9–15.

Taberner, P. V. (1985). *Aphrodisiacs: The science and the myth.* Philadelphia: University of Pennsylvania Press.

Taublieb, A. B., & Lick, J. R. (1986). Female orgasm via penile stimulation: A criterion of adequate sexual functioning? *Journal of Sex and Marital Therapy, 12,* 60–64.

Tavris, C. (1992). *The mismeasure of woman.* New York: Simon & Schuster.

Taylor, W. N. (1991). *Macho medicine: A history of the anabolic steroid epidemic.* Jefferson, NC: McFarland & Company.

Templeman, T. L., & Stinnett, R. D. (1991). Patterns of sexual arousal and history in a "normal" sample of young men. *Archives of Sexual Behavior, 20,* 137–150.

Tiefer, L. (1991). Historical, scientific, clinical, and feminist criticisms of "The Human Sexual Response Cycle" model. In J. Bancroft (Ed.), *Annual review of sex research* (vol. 2, pp. 1–23). Lake Mills, IA: Society for the Scientific Study of Sex.

Udry, J. R., Billy, J. O. G., Morris, N. M., Groff, T. R., & Raj, M. H. (1985). Serum androgenic hormones motivate sexual behavior in adolescent boys. *Fertility and Sterility, 43,* 90–94.

Udry, J. R., Talbert, L. M., & Morris, N. M. (1986). Biosocial foundations for adolescent female sexuality. *Demography, 23,* 217–229.

Uitti, R. J., Tanner, C. M., Rajput, A. H., Goetz, C. G., Klawans, H. L., & Thiessen, B. (1989). Hypersexuality with antiparkinsonian therapy. *Clinical Neuropharmacology, 12,* 375–383.

Vance, E. B., & Wagner, N. N. (1976). Written descriptions of orgasm: A study of sex differences. *Archives of Sexual Behavior, 5,* 87–98.

Wagner, G., & Green, R. (1981). *Impotence: Physiological, psychological, surgical diagnosis and treatment.* New York: Plenum Press.

Wilsnack, S. C. (1980). Alcohol, sexuality and reproductive dysfunction in women. In E. L. Abel (Ed.), *Fetal alcohol syndrome: Vol. 2. human studies (pp. 21–46).* Boca Raton, FL: CRC Press.

Wilson, G. T. (1981). The effects of alcohol on human sexual behavior. *Advances in Substance Abuse, 2,* 1–40.

Wiseman, J. P. (1985). Alcohol, eroticism and sexual performance: A social interactionist perspective. *Journal of Drug Issues, 15,* 291–308.

Young, W. R. (1990). Changes in sexual functioning during the aging process. In F. J. Bianoco and R. Hernandez Serrano (Eds.), *Sexology: An independent field* (pp. 121–128). New York: Elsevier Science.

Zillmann, D. (1989). Effects of prolonged consumption of pornography. In D. Zillmann and J. Bryant (Eds.), *Pornography: research advances and policy considerations* (pp. 121–157). Hillsdale, NJ: Lawrence Erlbaum Associates.

Contexts of Sexual Choices

PART THREE

John Donne wrote in *Meditations* No. 17 (and we quote liberally for clarity and to avoid sexist language*), "No person is an island, entirely of itself—each is a piece of the continent, a part of the mainland." Individuals do not make sexual choices in a vacuum. Rather, these choices are influenced by the context in which they occur. In Part III, we look at some of the various contexts influencing human sexuality.

In Chapter 8, Gender Roles, we examine (while not denying the impact of biological factors) the influence of social factors on the sexual choices of women and men. Indeed, the sexual choices of women and men are often different, and many of these differences evolve from the socialization of women and men into different roles in society.

In Chapter 9, Individual Sexuality, we look at how sexual choices in regard to masturbation are influenced by context. While masturbation usually involves solitary behavior, context still influences choices in this area. For example, how does involvement in a sexual relationship with someone affect the decision to masturbate? Some individuals feel that they "shouldn't have to masturbate" if they have a sexual partner, while others think that masturbatory decisions should be independent of one's interpersonal relationship(s). Sexual fantasies and the choices individuals make in sharing their fantasies are also covered.

In Chapter 10, Interpersonal Sexuality, we examine a range of interpersonal contexts—dating, cohabitation, married, extradyadic, and employment—and how these influence sexual choices. For example, two unattached strangers will consider a different set of variables in making sexual choices than will two married people who meet and fall in love at work.

In Chapter 11, Sexual Orientation, we examine heterosexual, homosexual, and bisexual orientations as contexts that influence sexual choices as well as other aspects of life. For example, prejudice toward homosexuals in our society suggests caution in being open about one's homosexuality or bisexuality. To be open is to risk discrimination against one's self and one's partner.

In Chapter 12, Sexuality across the Life Span, we examine the context of a person's age as it influences sexual choices. Children, adolescents, middle-aged adults, and the elderly all make different sexual decisions.

*Donne's exact words were: "No man is an *Island*, intire of itselfe—every man is a peece of the *Contintent*, part of the maine."

CHAPTER EIGHT

Gender Roles

Chapter Outline

Terminology
- Sex versus Gender
- Gender Identity
- Gender Roles
- Sexual Identity
- **Self-Assessment:** Sexual Double Standard Scale
- Gender Role Ideology

Biological Beginnings
- Chromosomes
- Hormones
- Chromosomal and Hormonal Abnormalities
- Gender Dysphoria and Transsexualism

Theories of Gender Role Acquisition
- Sociobiological Theory
- Identification Theory
- Social Learning Theory
- Cognitive-Developmental Theory
- Gender Schema Theory
- **Theoretical Perspective:** Alpha and Beta Bias in Gender Theories

Agents of Socialization in Gender Role Acquisition
- Parents
- Peers
- Teachers and Educational Curricula and Materials
- Religion
- Media
- Consequences of Traditional Female Socialization
- Consequences of Traditional Male Socialization

Beyond Gender Roles: Androgyny and Gender Role Transcendence
- Androgyny
- Gender Role Transcendence

Choices
- Choose New Relationships: Women Asking Men?
- Choose to Seek Egalitarian Relationships?
- Choose to Pursue Nontraditional Occupational Roles?

Is It True?*

1. Most men today possess the characteristics women say they are looking for in a partner.

2. A male-to-female transsexual (prior to any intervention) has the sex organs of a man and the gender identity of a woman.

3. Researchers agree that androgyny is a gender ideal for both women and men.

4. Single-parent families provide more androgynous role models than traditional two-parent families.

5. Men who view themselves as "androgynous" in their lovemaking report being the most satisfied in their sexual relationship.

* 1 = F, 2 = T, 3 = F, 4 = T, 5 = T

The gender revolution has profoundly changed the way we think about sex and gender.
Lillian Rubin

The skit "It's Pat" has been featured on "Saturday Night Live" throughout the 1991–1993 NBC television season. Pat, the central character, is an androgynous person, and Pat's friends are continually trying to determine Pat's gender. Pat frustrates them by providing ambiguous cues. For example, when speaking of her or his birth, Pat noted that the doctor announced to her or his parents on delivery that "it's a . . . baby!" (rather than "it's a girl" or "it's a boy"). The skit emphasized the important role gender plays in defining a person and the traditional scripts projected on people whose gender is known. If Pat were a woman, her friends would be more likely to expect her to date men, want to marry, and have children. Alternatively, if Pat were a man, his friends would be more likely to expect him to date women, be somewhat reluctant to marry, and be less interested in children.

In this chapter, we are concerned with how gender roles develop and with the consequences of gender role expectations for the sexual decisions of women and men. We end the chapter with some specific sexual and gender choices with which individuals are confronted. First, we define some terms related to the study of gender.

Terminology

Psychologists, health educators, sociologists, sexologists, and sex therapists often have different definitions and connotations for the terms *sex, gender, gender identity, gender role, sexual identity,* and *gender role ideology.* We use these terms in the following ways.

Sex versus Gender

Sex refers to the biological distinction of being female or male. The primary sex characteristics that differentiate women and men include external genitalia (vulva and penis), gonads (ovaries and testes), sex chromosomes (XX and XY), and hormones (estrogen, progesterone, and testosterone). Secondary sex characteristics include the larger breasts of women and the deeper voice and presence of a beard in men.

NATIONAL DATA: In the United States, there are 95.2 adult biological males for every 100 biological females. (*Statistical Abstract of the United States: 1992,* Table 20).

CONSIDERATION: While we commonly think of biological sex as consisting of two dichotomous categories (female and male), current views suggest that biological sex exists on a continuum. This view is supported by the existence of individuals with mixed or ambiguous genitals (hermaphrodites and pseudohermaphrodites, or intersexed individuals, are discussed later in this chapter). Evidence of overlap between the sexes is also found in the fact that some normal males produce fewer "male" hormones (androgens) than some females and some females produce fewer "female" hormones (estrogens) than some males (Morrow, 1991).

Gender refers to the social and psychological characteristics associated with being female (e.g., being gentle and cooperative) and male (e.g., being forceful and competitive). In popular usage, gender is dichotomized as an either/or concept (male or female). However, gender may also be viewed as existing along a continuum of femininity and masculinity (Freimuth & Hornstein, 1982).

An ongoing controversy in the field of gender studies revolves around the issue of gender differences. Are there differences between male and females? To what degree are gender differences innate versus socially determined? We will address these issues later in this chapter.

Gender Identity

Gender identity is the psychological state of viewing one's self as a girl or a boy and later as a woman or a man. Such identity is largely learned and is a reflection of the society's conceptions of femininity and masculinity.

CONSIDERATION: While gender identity is viewed as a psychological concept, some sex researchers suggest that there is a biological component to gender identity. While the effect of sex steroids in the development of gender identity has not been determined, "it would be highly premature to take this as an exclusion of the possibility" (Gooren, 1991).

Transsexuals, whom we will discuss later in this chapter, have the gender identity that is opposite of their biological sex. A transsexual person may have the self-concept of a woman but have the biological makeup of a man (or vice versa).

Gender Roles

All societies have expectations of how boys, girls, women, and men "should" think and behave. For example, traditionally in U.S. culture, men have been expected to be strong, aggressive, and decisive. Traditionally, women have been expected to be weak, passive, and indecisive. These expectations, or stereotypes combine to form gender roles. **Gender roles** then, are the set of social norms that dictate what is socially regarded as appropriate female and male behavior.

Gender identity is the private experience of gender role, and gender role is the public expression of gender identity.
John Money and Anke Ehrhardt

CONSIDERATION: The term *sex roles* is often confused with and used interchangeably with the term *gender roles.* However, while gender roles are socially defined and can be enacted by either sex, **sex roles** are defined by biological constraints and can be enacted by members of only one biological sex. Examples of true sex roles (as opposed to gender roles) include wet nurse, sperm donor, and childbearer (Schur, 1984, p. 10).

Traditional gender role stereotypes are changing. Women, who have traditionally been expected to give top priority to domestic life, are now expected to be more ambitious in seeking a career outside the home. Men, who have traditionally been expected to be aggressive and task-oriented, are now expected to be more caring and nurturing. However, while 84% of 600 adult women said that the ideal man is caring and nurturing, only 52% of 601 adult men said that the ideal woman is ambitious (Rubenstein, 1990, p. 160).

Society's gender roles influence virtually every aspect of our public and private lives. The following are examples of how gender roles might influence the sexual experiences a person has:

1. Women are less likely to masturbate than men. About 70% of adult women report having masturbated, in contrast to over 95% of adult men (Reinisch & Beasley, 1990).
2. Women are more likely to report being motivated to have intercourse to experience emotional intimacy; men are more likely to report being motivated to have

intercourse to experience relief of sexual tension (Brigman & Knox, 1992). While this pattern is true of younger adults, as people age these differences between women and men decrease (Tavris, 1992).

> People change over the years; more women start enjoying sex for physical pleasure and more men start enjoying the emotional closeness.
>
> *Carol Tavris*

3. Women are generally more sexually conservative than men. College men and women were relatively permissive on many questions related to premarital sex (with men scoring more permissive than the women). On attitudes toward extramarital sex, women were moderately conservative, while men were moderately permissive. (Hendrick, Hendrick, Slapion-Foote, & Foote, 1985).
4. Women report having fewer sexual partners than men. Four percent of white women and 6% of black women, in contrast to 11% of white men and 23% of black men, reported having had sexual intercourse with six or more partners (Moore & Peterson, 1989).
5. Women are more likely than men to have positive attitudes about contraception and to use contraceptives more consistently (McKinney, 1990).
6. Women are more likely to be involved in nonvoluntary sex than men. Among youth aged 18 to 22 in the National Survey of Children, 6.3% of white women and 3.2% of black women, in contrast to 0.4% of white men and 1.4% of black men, reported that they had been raped or forced to have sex by age 15 (Moore, Nord, & Peterson, 1989).
7. Women are less likely than men to pay for sex in the form of hiring a prostitute. Similarly, the majority of money spent on pornography is by men (Knox & Daniel, 1986).
8. Women, in general, regard sex as less important than men. In a study of 102 white women and 100 white men ranging in age from 80 to 102, 67% of the women and 82% of the men said that, in the past, the sexual part of their lives was important to them. Regarding the present, 38% of the women and 66% of the men said that the sexual part of their life was important (Bretschneider and McCoy, 1988, p. 113). College men were more likely than women to disagree with the statement that they could live quite well without sex (Hendrick et al., 1985).

Traditional gender role socialization may perpetuate the sexual double standard. To assess your acceptance of the sexual double standard, complete the Self-Assessment on the next page.

Sexual Identity

In the past, sexual identity referred to one's sexual orientation as a homosexual, heterosexual, or bisexual (sexual orientation is discussed in Chapter 11). More recently, a multidimensional approach to sexual identity has been suggested (Suppe, 1985). Based on this multidimensional approach, the term **sexual identity** encompasses the following components:

1. biological sex
2. gender identity
3. gender role
4. sexual orientation, which is comprised of:
   a) physical sexual activity
   b) interpersonal affection
   c) erotic fantasies
   d) cue-response patterns involving physiological response and arousal
   e) self-concept

Self Assessment

Sexual Double Standard Scale

Rank each statement according to the following scale:
A) agree strongly, B) agree mildly, C) disagree mildly,
D) disagree strongly.

	Statement	A	B	C	D
1.	It's worse for a woman to sleep around than it is for a man.	____	____	____	____
2.	It's best for a guy to lose his virginity before he's out of his teens.	____	____	____	____
3.	It's okay for a woman to have more than one sexual relationship at the same time.	____	____	____	____
4.	It is just as important for a man to be a virgin when he marries as it is for a woman.	____	____	____	____
5.	I approve of a 16-year-old girl's having sex just as much as a 16-year-old boy's having sex.	____	____	____	____
6.	I kind of admire a girl who has had sex with a lot of guys.	____	____	____	____
7.	I kind of feel sorry for a 21-year-old woman who is still a virgin.	____	____	____	____
8.	A woman's having casual sex is just as acceptable to me as a man's having casual sex.	____	____	____	____
9.	It's okay for a man to have sex with a woman with whom he is not in love.	____	____	____	____
10.	I kind of admire a guy who has had sex with a lot of girls.	____	____	____	____
11.	A woman who initiates sex is too aggressive.	____	____	____	____
12.	It's okay for a man to have more than one sexual relationship at the same time.	____	____	____	____
13.	I question the character of a woman who has had a lot of sexual partners.	____	____	____	____
14.	I admire a man who is a virgin when he gets married.	____	____	____	____
15.	A man should be more sexually experienced than his wife.	____	____	____	____
16.	A girl who has sex on the first date is "easy."	____	____	____	____
17.	I kind of feel sorry for a 21-year-old man who is still a virgin.	____	____	____	____
18.	I question the character of a guy who has had a lot of sexual partners.	____	____	____	____
19.	Women are naturally more monogamous (inclined to stick with one partner) than are men.	____	____	____	____
20.	A man should be sexually experienced when he gets married.	____	____	____	____
21.	A guy who has sex on the first date is "easy."	____	____	____	____
22.	It's okay for a woman to have sex with a man she is not in love with.	____	____	____	____
23.	A woman should be sexually experienced when she gets married.	____	____	____	____
24.	It's best for a girl to lose her virginity before she's out of her teens.	____	____	____	____
25.	I admire a woman who is a virgin when she gets married.	____	____	____	____
26.	A man who initiates sex is too aggressive.	____	____	____	____

Source: Muehlenhard, C. L., & Quackenbush, D. M. (1988, November). *Can the sexual double standard put women at risk for sexually transmitted disease? The role of the double standard in condom use among women.* Paper presented at the annual meeting of the Society for the Scientific Study of Sex, San Francisco. Used by permission.

Scoring Convert A's to 0's, B's to 1's, C's to 2's, and D's to 3's. Compute the total = #4 + #5 + #8 + (3 − #1) + (3 − #15) + (3 − #19) + (#24 − #2) + (#3 − #12) + (#6 − #10) + (#7 − #17) + (#22 − #9) + (#26 − #11) + (#18 − #13) + (#14 − #25) + (#21 − #16) + (#23 − #20)

Interpreting your score A score of 0 indicates identical sexual standards for women and men. Scores greater than 0 reflect more restrictive standards for women than for men; the highest possible score is 48. Scores less than 0 reflect more restrictive standards for men than for women; the lowest possible score is −30.

Continued

Self-Assessment—*Continued*

In a study of students from Texas A&M University, the men's mean score was 13.15 (*n* = 255) and the women's mean was 11.99 (*n* =461) (Muehlenhard & Quackenbush, 1988). (When used in a research study, the title would not be at the top of the scale!) When asked to rate their partner's acceptance of the sexual double standard, female students rated their partners as more accepting of it than the women rated themselves. In fact, the women believed that men adhere to the double standard even more than the men reported (Muehlenhard & McCoy, 1991).

Reliability and validity Muehlenhard and Quackenbush (cited in Muehlenhard & McCoy, 1991) reported a coefficient alpha of 0.726 for women's reports of their own acceptance of the sexual double standard and 0.817 for their ratings of their partners' beliefs. Correlations of the measure with other variables, (traditional gender roles, erotophobia-erotophilia, self-monitoring) have been in the predicted directions.

In their study of 403 female general psychology students at the University of Kansas, Muehlenhard and McCoy (1991) examined the relationship between women's acceptance of the double standard (and their rating of their partners' acceptance) with the women's willingness to acknowledge their desire for sexual intercourse. The women were asked if they had ever been in the following situation:

> You were with a guy you'd *never* had sexual intercourse with before. He wanted to engage in sexual intercourse and you wanted to also, but for some reason you indicated that you didn't want to, although *you had every intention to and were willing to engage in sexual intercourse.* In other words, you indicated "no" and meant "yes" (p. 451).

They were also presented a scenario in which they had wanted to engage in intercourse and "made it clear to the guy that you wanted to have sexual intercourse" (p. 452) and were asked if they had ever been in that situation. The women completed the Sexual Double Standard Scale (self and inferences about partner), the Attitudes Toward Women Scale, the Sexual Opinion Survey, and the Self-Monitoring Scale. Of these five variables, only the women's beliefs about their partner's acceptance of the double standard predicted whether the women had ever said "no" when they meant "yes" (scripted refusal) or said "yes" and meant "yes" (open acknowledgement). The researchers found that "women who had offered scripted refusals were more likely to believe that their partners accepted the sexual double standard than women who had openly acknowledged their desire for sexual intercourse" (p. 457).

Meuhlenhard and McCoy observed that the sexual double standard puts women in a double bind. If they are open about their sexual desires, they risk being negatively labeled. So, is the safest (for one's reputation) course of action to be reluctant to acknowledge wanting to have sex? Muehlenhard and McCoy suggested that the sexual double standard could be decreased by pointing out its unfairness to both men and women. Men may feel pressured to push for sex whether or not they desire it (and whether or not they have a willing partner).

The majority of women had never engaged in scripted refusal (and those who had, reported doing so infrequently). Muehlenhard and McCoy emphasized that men should always take a "no" at face value. This may be even better advice in view of recent information obtained by Muehlenhard and her colleagues. Although these researchers thought the scenario for scripted refusal was clearly indicating a situation in which the woman wanted to have sex, more recent examples from women asked to describe the situation reflect *ambivalence* about having sex more than *willingness.* The situations which were described often indicated the respondents had misinterpreted the researchers' questions. The number of respondents who engaged in "token resistance" (as evaluated by trained raters)—only 2% to 14% of women and 2% to 10% of men—was much smaller than the 35% indicated in previous studies (Rodgers & Muehlenhard, 1992). Therefore, despite the sexual double standard and stereotypes about women offering token resistance to intercourse, for the vast majority of men and women "no" really does mean "NO!"

References

Muehlenhard, C. L. & McCoy, M. (1991). Double standard/double bind: The sexual double standard and women's communication about sex. *Psychology of Women Quarterly, 15,* 447–461.

Muehlendard, C. L. & Quackenbush, D. M. (1988, November). Can the sexual double standard put women at risk for sexually transmitted disease? The role of the double standard in condom use among women. Presented at the annual meeting of the Society for the Scientific Study of Sex, San Francisco.

Rodgers, C. & Muehlenhard, C. (1992). Token resistance: New perspectives on an old stereotype. Unpublished manuscript.

CONSIDERATION: The multidimensional model of sexual identity suggests that sexual identity is a complex construct. A person's sexual identity is not simply either male or female. Rather, variations and permutations in the various components of sexual identity can result in sexual identities that do not conform to the either/or dichotomy of male and female.

Gender Role Ideology

Gender role ideology refers to what is regarded as the proper role relationships between women and men.

> All human societies consist of men and women who must interact with one another, usually on a daily basis, and who have developed customs embracing prescriptive beliefs about the manner in which men and women are to relate to one another. (Williams & Best, 1990a, p. 87)

To assess the views of 100 university students in each of 14 countries (Canada, England, Finland, Germany, India, Italy, Japan, Malaysia, Netherlands, Nigeria, Pakistan, Singapore, Venezuela, and the United States), Williams and Best (1990b) developed a series of 30 statements reflecting traditional and modern gender role ideological perspectives. Examples of each follow:

Traditional ideology:

The husband should be regarded as the legal representative of the family group in all matters of law.

A man's job is too important for him to get bogged down with household chores.

The first duty of a woman with young children is to her home and family.

Modern ideology:

More day-care centers should be available to free mothers from the constant caring of their children.

Abortion should be permitted at the woman's request.

Marriage should not interfere with a woman's career any more than it does with a man's.

Results showed that in all countries, women support more modern gender role ideologies than men. In some countries, such as the United States, Canada, and England, women were significantly more modern in their gender role ideologies. Indeed, the more highly developed the country, the more modern the gender role ideologies were. In addition, Christian religions were associated with modern gender role ideologies and Muslim religions with traditional ones.

Traditional U.S. gender role ideology has perpetuated male dominance and male bias in almost every sphere of life. Even our language reflects this male bias; for example, the words *man* and *mankind* have traditionally been used to refer to all humans. There has been a growing trend away from using male-biased language. College business writing courses teach students to avoid sexist language. The American Psychological Association includes suggestions for using nonsexist language in its style manual for preparing articles to be submitted for publication. A recent version of *Random House Webster's College Dictionary* has adopted terms that reflect the growing trend away from male-biased or sexist language (Hopkins, 1991) (see Table 8.1).

> Where agriculture is a main means of support there are earth and goddess powers. Where hunting predominates, it's male initiative that empowers the killing of animals.
>
> *Joseph Campbell*

Even the food we eat may reflect a gender role ideology that is based on the premise of male dominance. Exhibit 8.1 discusses the views of Carol Adams, a feminist-vegetarian who maintains that meat eating in U.S. society reflects a male-biased gender role ideology (Adams, 1990).

TABLE 8.1 ***Random House Dictionary*** **Adopts Nonsexist Language**

Dictionary Entry	Rationale
Chairperson	Nonsexist term for chairman
Firefighter	Nonsexist term for fireman
Humankind	Less sexist than *mankind* (although *human* derives from same Latin root as *man: homo*)
Waitron or Wait-person	Gender-neutral term for waiter or waitress
Womyn (pl.)	Avoids perception of sexism in *wo-men*
Herstory	Distinguishes the study of women across time from the generic *history* (although the word comes from the Greek *histor,* which means "learned, knowing")

Biological Beginnings

The distinction between the female and male sexes begins at the moment of fertilization, when the male's sperm and the female's egg unite to form a **zygote.** The sexual development of a zygote is determined by chromosomal and hormonal factors (Bancroft, 1989).

Chromosomes

Chromosomes are threadlike structures located within the nucleus of every cell in a person's body. Each cell contains 23 pairs of chromosomes, a total of 46 chromosomes per cell. Chromosomes contain genes, the basic units of heredity, which not only determine such physical characteristics as eye color, hair color, and body type but also predispositions for such characteristics as baldness, color blindness, and hemophilia.

One of these 23 pairs of chromosomes is referred to as sex chromosomes because they determine whether an individual will be female or male. There are two types of sex chromosomes, called X and Y. Normally, females have two X chromosomes, while males have one X and one Y chromosome.

When the egg and sperm meet in the Fallopian tube, each contains only half the normal number of chromosomes (one from each of the 23 pairs). The union of sperm and egg results in a single cell called a zygote, which has the normal 46 chromosomes. The egg will always have an X chromosome, but the sperm will have either an X or Y chromosome. Since the sex chromosome in the egg is always X (the female chromosome), the sex chromosome in the sperm will determine the sex of a child. If the sperm contains an X chromosome, the match with the female chromosome will be XX, and the child will be genetically female. If the sperm contains a Y chromosome (the male chromosome), the match with the female chromosome will be XY, and the child will be genetically male.

CONSIDERATION: Although an individual's genetic sex is determined at the moment of conception, whether one is anatomically a male or female depends additionally on the influence of hormones. Genes determine anatomical sex only indirectly by influencing hormone production.

EXHIBIT 8.1 The Sexual Politics of Meat: A Feminist-Vegetarian Theory

In her book *The Sexual Politics of Meat,* Carol Adams (1990) suggested that our society's male-oriented gender role ideology is reflected in our diet, which consists of 60% meat and animal products. Our culture teaches us that we should eat animals and that eating meat is good for us. However, Adams suggested that the symbolic meaning of meat eating is "intrinsically patriarchal and male-oriented" (p. 67). By perpetuating meat eating in our society, patriarchal attitudes are also perpetuated. Such attitudes include that "the objectification of other beings [i.e., animals and women] is a necessary part of life, and that violence [i.e., killing animals] can and should be masked" (p. 14).

From an early age, nursery rhymes teach us that meat eating is associated with male behavior. For example, in one popular nursery rhyme, "the king in his counting-house ate four-and-twenty blackbirds baked in a pie" while "the Queen ate bread and honey." Our culture perpetuates the belief that meat eating is necessary for physical strength. "Meat-and-potatoes men are our stereotypical strong and hearty, rough and ready, able males" (p. 34).

Just as meat symbolizes virility and power associated with masculinity, vegetables symbolize passivity, which has traditionally been associated with femininity. Although the original meaning of the word *vegetable* was "to be lively, active" (p. 36), it is currently used to refer to "passivity or dullness of existence, monotonous, inactive . . . To vegetate is to lead a passive existence; just as to be feminine is to lead a passive existence" (p. 36). Adams further explained that

> The word *vegetable* acts as a synonym for women's passivity because women are supposedly like plants. Hegel [a well-known philosopher] makes this clear: "The difference between men and women is like that between animals and plants. Men correspond to animals, while women correspond to plants because their development is more placid." From this viewpoint, both women and plants are seen as less developed and less evolved than men and animals. Consequently, women may eat plants, since each is placid; but active men need animal meat. (p. 37)

The eating of animals constitutes the ultimate form of oppression of animals, which Adams suggested, is linked to the oppression of women. The symbolic association between animals and the oppression of women is conveyed in language that equates women with animals. For example, women are sometimes referred to as bitches, foxes, pussycats, beavers, cows, pieces of meat, bunnies, squirrels, chicks, and old bats. As shown in the following examples, references to female sexuality often include metaphors that liken women to animals:

1. The Hustler was a Cleveland restaurant whose menu presented a woman's buttocks on the cover and proclaimed, "We serve the best meat in town!"
2. A woman is shown being ground up in a meat grinder as *Hustler* magazine proclaims: "Last All Meat Issue."
3. Women's buttocks are stamped as "Choice Cuts" on an album cover.
4. Frank Perdue plays with images of sexual butchering in a poster encouraging chicken consumption: "Are you a breast man or a leg man?" he asks.
5. A popular poster in the butcher shops of the Haymarket section of Boston depicted a woman's body sectioned off as though she were a slaughtered animal, with her separate body parts identified (p. 58).

Just as feminism opposes the exploitation of women, so do some vegetarians oppose the exploitation of animals, which includes killing and eating them. In conclusion, Adams suggested that "vegetarianism covertly challenges a patriarchal society" (p. 17).

Source: Adams, C. (1990). *The sexual politics of meat.* New York: Continuum. Used by permission.

Hormones

Male and female embryos are indistinguishable from one another during the first several weeks of intrauterine life. In both males and females, two primitive gonads and two paired duct systems form about the fifth or sixth week of development. While the reproductive system of the male (epididymis, vas deferens, ejaculatory duct) develops from the Wolffian ducts and the female reproductive system (Fallopian tubes, uterus, vagina) from the Mullerian ducts, both ducts are present in the developing embryo at this stage. (See Figure 8.1)

If the embryo is genetically a male (XY), a chemical substance controlled by the Y chromosome (H-Y antigen) stimulates the primitive gonads to develop into testes.

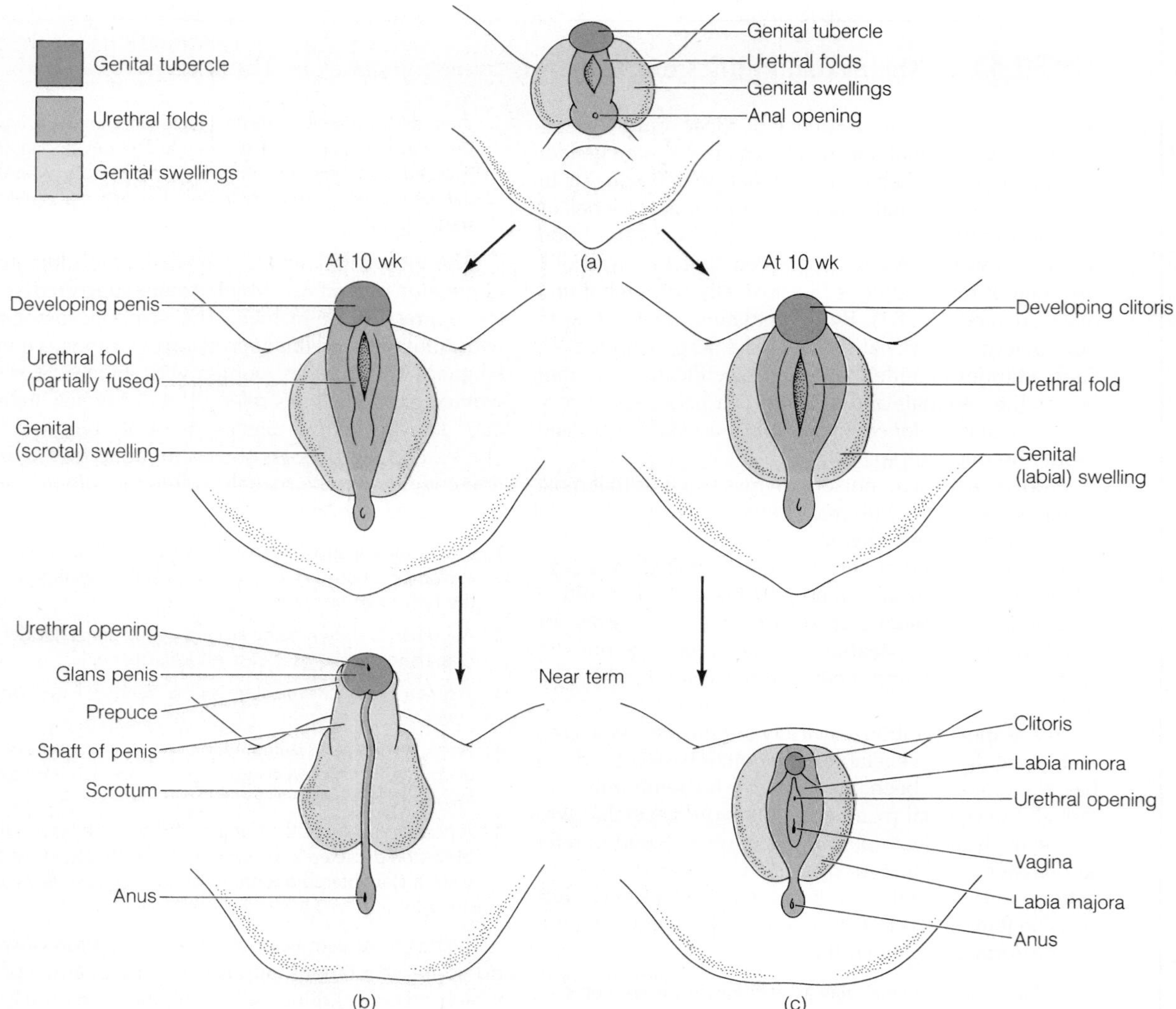

FIGURE 8.1 Sexual Differentiation of External Genitalia (a) Undifferentiated stage (7 wk). (b) Male development. (c) Female development.

The testes, in turn, begin secreting the male hormone testosterone, which stimulates the development of the male reproductive and external sexual organs. The testes also secrete a second substance, called Mullerian duct-inhibiting substance, which causes the potential female ducts to degenerate or become blind tubules. Thus, development of male anatomical structures depends on the presence of male hormones at a critical stage of development (Wilson, George & Griffin, 1981).

The development of a female requires that no additional testosterone be present. Without the controlling substance from the Y chromosome, the primitive gonads will develop into ovaries and the Mullerian duct system into Fallopian tubes, uterus, and vagina; and without testosterone, the Wolffian duct system will degenerate or become blind tubules. Animal studies have shown that if the primitive gonads are removed prior to differentiation into testes or ovaries, the organism will always develop anatomically into a female, regardless of genetic composition.

Although the infant's gonads (testes and ovaries) produce the sex hormones (e.g., testosterone and estrogen), these hormones are regulated by the pituitary gland, which is located at the base of the brain about two inches behind the eyes. The pituitary releases hormones into the blood that determine the amount of testosterone released by the testes and the amounts of estrogen and progesterone released by the ovaries. Production of sex hormones in males is relatively constant, while production of female hormones is cyclic. Does this mean the pituitary glands of males and females are different? In animal studies in which the pituitaries of male organisms have been transplanted into female organisms (and vice versa), the production of sex hormones remains cyclic in females and constant in males. The release of pituitary hormones, as it turns out, is controlled by additional hormones (also called releasing factors) from the hypothalamus, a part of the brain just above the pituitary. It is the hypothalamus that differs in males and females in both the connections between cells and the size of various groups of cells. The presence of testosterone before birth not only stimulates the development of the male reproductive system but also apparently stimulates the development of a male hypothalamus. A female hypothalamus develops in the absence of testosterone.

At puberty, the **hormones** released by the testes and ovaries are necessary for the development of secondary sex characteristics. Higher levels of testosterone account for the growth of facial hair in males and pubic and underarm hair in both males and females. Breast development, on the other hand, results from increasing levels of estrogen.

To summarize, several factors determine the biological sex of an individual:

1. Chromosomes: XX for female; XY for male.
2. Gonads: ovaries for female; testes for male.
3. Hormones: greater proportion of estrogen and progesterone than testosterone in the female; greater proportion of testosterone than estrogen and progesterone in the male.
4. Internal sex organs: Fallopian tubes, uterus, and vagina for female; epididymis, vas deferens, and seminal vesicles for male.
5. External genitals: vulva for female; penis and scrotum for male.

Chromosomal and Hormonal Abnormalities

As we have seen, the normal biological development of males and females requires that chromosomes and hormones be present in exactly the right amount at the right time. Various hormonal and chromosomal abnormalities may result in atypical sexual development of the fetus.

Chromosomal Abnormalities For every sex chromosome from the mother (X), there must be a corresponding sex chromosome from the father (X or Y) for normal sexual development to occur. Abnormalities result when there are too many or too few sex chromosomes. Two of the most common of these abnormalities are Klinefelter's syndrome and Turner's syndrome.

Klinefelter's syndrome occurs in males and results from the presence of an extra X sex chromosome (XXY). Klinefelter's syndrome occurs in 1 out of 500 male births. The result is abnormal testicular development, infertility, low interest in sex (low libido), and, in some cases, mental retardation. Males with an extra X chromosome often experience language deficits, neuromaturational lag, academic difficulties, and psychological distress (Mandoki, Sumner, Hoffman, & Riconda, 1991).

Early identification of Klinefelter's syndrome is crucial to treating many of the developmental, behavioral, and emotional problems associated with the syndrome.

Treatment may include psychiatric treatment, modified educational placement, testosterone supplementation, and corrective surgery in adolescence.

Turner's syndrome occurs in women and results from the absence of an X chromosome (XO). Turner's syndrome occurs in 1 out of 2,500 female births. It is characterized by abnormal ovarian development, failure to menstruate, infertility, and the lack of secondary sexual characteristics (e.g., minimal breast development). In addition, Turner's syndrome results in short stature and a predisposition to heart and kidney defects (Orten, 1990). Treatment for Turner's syndrome includes hormone replacement therapy to develop secondary sexual characteristics and the use of a biosynthetic human growth hormone to promote growth.

Hormonal Abnormalities Too much or too little of the wrong kind of hormones can also cause abnormal sexual development. Two conditions that may result from hormonal abnormalities are hermaphroditism and pseudohermaphroditism.

Hermaphroditism is an extremely rare condition in which individuals are born with both ovarian and testicular tissue. These individuals, called hermaphrodites, may have one ovary and one testicle, feminine breasts, and a vaginal opening beneath the penis. They are generally genetic females (XX), and while their internal reproductive systems are usually mixed and incomplete as well, many hermaphrodites menstruate. Hermaphrodites may be reared as either males or females, depending largely on their appearance.

More common than hermaphroditism is **pseudohermaphroditism,** which refers to a condition in which an individual is born with gonads matching the sex chromosomes but genitals resembling those of the other sex. There are numerous causes of pseudohermaphroditism. Two syndromes that we will discuss here are androgenital syndrome in women and testicular feminization syndrome in men.

You will recall that for the female fetus to develop normally, it must avoid unusually high doses of androgen ("male" hormones). Androgens, however, are produced not only by the testes but also by the adrenal glands. Exposure to high levels of androgen can result from a malfunction of the mother's adrenal glands or from the mother's ingestion of synthetic hormones (e.g., progestin) that have an androgen effect on the fetus (in the 1950s, progestin was often prescribed for pregnant women to prevent premature delivery). Sometimes a genetic defect causes the adrenal glands of the XX fetus to produce excessive amounts of androgens, which results in **androgenital syndrome.** Excessive androgen causes the clitoris to greatly enlarge and the labia majora to fuse together to resemble a scrotum, resulting in genitals that resemble those of a male. Because individuals with this syndrome are genetically female, they are referred to as **female pseudohermaphrodites.** Genetically female infants whose genitals appear to be male are usually reared as males. During adolescence, the male-reared female may notice lack of facial hair growth, failure of the voice to deepen, and enlargement of the breasts. Chromosomal tests would reveal the XX genetic makeup of the individual, at which point it is usually recommended that the individual retain his male gender identity and have surgery to remove female internal organs (ovaries and uterus). In addition, hormone therapy is provided to deepen the voice, produce facial hair growth, and minimize breast growth.

Another hormonal fetal abnormality that results in pseudohermaphroditism, testicular feminization syndrome (TFS), involves the lack of development of male genitals in the body of a person who is genetically male (i.e., has XY chromosomes). In TFS, also known as **androgen-insensitivity syndrome,** the external tissues of the fetus fail to turn into male genitals. Even though normal amounts of androgen are produced, the tissues do not respond to the male hormones, and female external genitals are formed—labia, clitoris, and vaginal opening. The production of Mullerian duct-inhibiting substance is not impaired, so the Fallopian tubes and uterus do not develop and the vagina is quite short. Hence, while the newborn infant has the external genital appearance of a female (and is therefore reared as a female), the infant has testes embedded in the abdomen. These individuals are called **male pseudohermaphrodites.**

Parents are usually unaware of this hormonal abnormality until they realize at midadolescence that their daughter has not menstruated. She cannot since she has no uterus. Surgery can remove the testes and increase the depth of the vagina.

Sometimes infants are born with ambiguous genitals; they are neither clearly male nor female. These infants are called **intersexed infants.** When ambiguous genitals are detected at birth, physicians face the decision of assigning either the male or female gender to the intersexed infant.

As observers of gender we are also its creators.
Rachel Hare-Mustin and Jeanne Marecek

Although recent advances in medical technology have allowed physicians to determine the chromosomal and hormonal sex of intersexed infants, gender assignment is often based on the appearance of the genitals, rather than on the genetic sex of the infant (S. Kessler, 1990). In other words, if the infant's genitals are more similar to those of a female's, then it will be assigned a female gender, regardless of its chromosomal makeup. Specifically, if the infant's penis size is three standard deviations below the mean, then that infant most probably will be reared as a female. This approach suggests that

> chromosomes are less relevant in determining gender than penis size, and that, by implication, "male" is defined not by the genetic condition of having one Y and one X chromosome or by the production of sperm but by the aesthetic condition of having an appropriately sized penis. (Kessler, 1990, p. 12)

CONSIDERATION: S. Kessler (1990) suggested that the practice of gender assignment to infants born with ambiguous genitals reflects a culture than does not accept gender ambiguity as a natural option.

> The belief that gender consists of two exclusive types is maintained and perpetuated by the medical community in the face of incontrovertible physical evidence that this is not mandated by biology. (p. 25)

In a study on gender assignment of intersexed infants, Kessler found that medical professionals base their choice of gender assignment on social and cultural factors, rather than on medical or biological factors. The implication of this is

> that gender identity (of all children, not just those born with ambiguous genitals) is determined primarily by social factors, that the parents and community always construct the child's gender. (p. 17)

Gender Dysphoria and Transsexualism

Some individuals experience **gender dysphoria,** which is a condition in which one's gender identity does not match one's biological sex. These individuals, known as **transsexuals,** have the genetic and anatomical characteristics of one sex but the self-concept of the other. "I am a woman trapped in a man's body" (or the reverse) reflects the feeling of being a transsexual.

> Transsexuals are disgusted with the development of their primary and secondary sexual characteristics, and the penis in males and breasts in females are perceived as the offensive organs, and their removal becomes a preoccupation for transsexual individuals. In addition, these desperately unhappy people seek the anatomical status of the

> opposite gender, and thus the hallmark of this syndrome is the request for change of sex or sex-reassignment surgery (SRS). (Pauly, 1990, p. 3)

At least one in 50,000 individuals over the age of 15 is likely to be a transsexual (Pauly, 1990). The male-female ratio of transsexuals is from 2:1 to 8:1 (American Psychiatric Association, 1987).

CONSIDERATION: Researchers do not agree on the cause of transsexualism. While some point to biological factors (hormonal imbalance at a critical period of development), others emphasize intrafamily dynamics. Still others suggest the influence of societal forces that have rigid expectations in regard to sex roles and homosexuality (Leitenberg, 1983). Most agree that multiple factors are involved—biological predispositions in combination with intrafamily and social forces.

The transsexual does not have the self-concept of a homosexual. Both may be attracted to others of their own biological sex but for different reasons. Whereas a homosexual male is attracted to other males, the transsexual male is attracted to other men because he sees himself as a woman. Likewise, the transsexual woman is attracted to other women because she sees herself as a man. The homosexual's gender identity is consistent with his or her biological sex.

Another important distinction is between transvestite and transsexual. **Transvestites** dress in the clothing of the opposite gender. They experience erotic stimulation from wearing clothing of the opposite sex that is often a prelude to heterosexual sexual activity. But they retain their anatomical sexual orientation and are not interested in sex reassignment surgery (SRS). Hence, a male transvestite has a penis, enjoys dressing up as a woman, but wants to keep his penis. A male transsexual has a penis, but dresses as a woman because he sees himself as a woman, and wants to have his genitals changed so that he can become anatomically female.

This male to female transsexual (Tula) emphasizes the degree to which some individuals can adopt the sexual and gender characteristics of the opposite sex.

Therapy for Transsexuals Transsexuals often seek therapy to relieve their suffering associated with gender dysphoria. Such therapy may include psychotherapy, hormone therapy, and sex reassignment surgery.

Psychotherapy While some gender dysphoric individuals feel that their suffering will only be alleviated by sex reassignment surgery, others benefit from psychotherapy. About 70% of the patients seen at the Case Western Reserve Gender Clinic were able, without surgery, to successfully cope with their gender dysphoria. While some of these might still seek SRS, it is clear that, in some cases, psychotherapy is beneficial and that SRS is not always the answer. Ira Pauly (1990), a specialist in gender dysphoria, recommends exploring all alternatives (e.g., psychotherapy, medication, behavioral/cognitive therapy, electroconvulsive therapy, hypnosis) before irreversible SRS is performed.

Hormone Therapy Hormone therapy is recommended as a prelude to SRS. The goal is to suppress the existing sexual features (e.g., cause the testicles to atrophy in the male-female [M-F] transsexual) and to initiate the development and maintenance of the sexual features belonging to the desired sex (e.g., breast development in the M-F transsexual; facial hair and deepening of voice in the female-male [F-M] transsexual). Estinyl (sometimes in combination with Provera) is given to the M-F transsexual. Depotestosterone is given to the F-M transsexual. Hormone therapy reduces the dissonance between the transsexual's actual body and his or her desired body.

CONSIDERATION: Hormone therapy is not given on demand but only after careful evaluation of the patient by a psychiatrist or psychologist who specializes in the treatment of gender dysphoria. Patients should be advised that some of the hormonally induced changes are irreversible (atrophied testicles in the M-F transsexual and clitoral enlargement in the F-M transsexual).

Sex Reassignment Surgery Physicians are cautious in their identification of patients on whom they perform sex reassignment surgery. Some patients have changed their minds after SRS and sued their physicians for malpractice. Some who seek SRS are psychotic and experiencing an acute episode—they are not in touch with reality. Others are psychopathic and wish to achieve notoriety or financial gain from SRS. They are not sincere in their desire for SRS. In view of these possibilities, physicians are encouraged to consider strict criteria before scheduling a patient for surgery (Pauly, 1990):

1. The patient must be evaluated by two certified and licensed psychiatrists or psychologists who specialize in gender dysphoria and who independently recommend the patient for SRS. Each evaluator should have known the patient for at least six months prior to endorsing the patient's request for SRS.
2. The patient must have demonstrated the discomfort associated with gender dysphoria for a minimum of two years. Parents or others who have known the patient for some time are often interviewed to confirm that the patient has been gender dysphoric for some time. The best candidates for SRS have been gender dysphoric since childhood.
3. The individual should have lived successfully in the opposite gender role for at least one year.

Requiring the patient to pass the test of living in the role of the desired gender (including being hired by an employer) for at least a year forces the patient to confront the uncertainty and anxiety over being able to pass convincingly. Some are unable to do so. Others do so but decide that they no longer wish SRS. Still others pass and are more strongly motivated to seek SRS "feeling much happier than he/she is on the way toward the solution to his/her gender problem" (p. 14).

> The ability to relate socially and develop a support system is also important during this period. And finally, it is essential that the patient be able to cope with less anxiety and depression than before cross-gender living. (p. 15)

Once the decision is made to provide SRS, a urologist, a gynecologist, and a plastic surgeon perform the actual surgery. In the M-F transsexual, the penis, scrotum, and testicles are removed and a functioning vagina is created. If the operation is a success, the transsexual will be able to have intercourse without pain or discomfort (and should be able to have an orgasm as well). Other operations for the M-F transsexual include plastic surgery to increase breast size, soften facial features, and reduce the size of the nose and the Adam's apple. Most transsexuals are pleased with the way they look after the surgeries.

Surgery for the F-M transsexual involves removing the breasts, uterus, ovaries, and vagina. An artificial penis is constructed that will allow the anatomical male to void while standing, engage in sexual intercourse, and have an orgasm. Surgery for the F-M transsexual is less advanced and problems in the

> construction of a cosmetically and functionally satisfactory male-appearing perineum have not yet been alleviated to the point where this is readily available. Until this has

> been accomplished, to the same degree as with the M-F transsexual, it will be difficult to achieve a completely favorable outcome from SRS for female transsexuals. (Pauly, 1990, p. 18)

Nevertheless, patients report positive outcomes from SRS. Based on a study of 651 M-F transsexuals, between 71.4% and 87.8% reported that they were satisfied with sex reassignment surgery. Of 207 F-M transsexuals, between 80.7% and 89.5% reported satisfactory outcomes (Pauly, 1990, p. 19).

Physicians are divided in their opinions of transsexual surgery. While some feel that the procedure should not be done, others feel that the surgery is appropriate if all cautions are heeded. Specifically, SRS surgery should only occur in the context of an extensive evaluation and ongoing therapy and only after the patient has been able to cross-dress successfully for at least a year.

CONSIDERATION: Transsexuals reject their gender role socialization because they do not identify with the gender they are socialized to be. For example, a male transsexual rejects male role socialization because he does not feel he is "really" a male.

Theories of Gender Role Acquisition

Numerous theories attempt to explain why women and men exhibit different characteristics and behaviors. The four main theories about how female and male roles are developed are sociobiological, identification, social learning, and cognitive-developmental.

Sociobiological Theory

Sociobiological explanations of gender roles emphasize that biological differences between men and women account for differences in male and female gender roles. Sociobiologists (or biosociologists) do not view gender role behaviors as acquired, but rather as innate. Consider the following differences between patterns of female and male sexuality:

The question is not whether women are more or less sexual than men. (The answer to that is yes, no, both, and sometimes.) The questions are: What are the conditions that allow women and men to enjoy sex in safety, with self-confidence, and in a spirit of delight? And how do we get there?

Carol Tavris

- Beck, Bozman, and Qualtrough (1991) administered a sexual desire questionnaire to 144 college students and observed that men reported much more frequent sexual desires than women (sexual desire was operationally defined as the desire for sexual intercourse and the occurrence of sexual daydreams). Ninety-one percent of 58 college men reported experiencing sexual desire at least as frequently as several times per week, in contrast to 52% of 86 women. Similarly, 26% of the men reported experiencing sexual desire several times per day, in contrast to 4% of the women (Beck et al., 1991, pp. 448, 449).
- In a national sample of adult sexual behavior in the United States, men reported an average of 12 sexual partners; women reported an average of three sexual partners since age 18 (Smith, 1991).
- Men are more likely to engage in "casual sex," which may be defined as sex that does not involve an emotional relationship component. As evidence, 232 women and 183 men enrolled in introductory-level general education courses were asked the following question:

  > If the opportunity presented itself of having sexual intercourse with an anonymous member of the opposite sex who was as competent a lover as your partner but no more

so, and who was as physically attractive as your partner but no more so, and there was no risk of pregnancy, discovery, or disease, and no chance of forming a more durable relationship do you think you would do so?

Half of the men and 17% of the women in one study reported that they "certainly would" or "probably would" (Symons & Ellis, 1989, p. 136). In another study, 28% of the men and 5% of the women said that their last extramarital encounter was a one-night stand (Spanier & Margolis, 1983).

- Most acts of sexual aggression (e.g., rape and sexual harassment) are perpetrated by men (see Chapter 19, Abuses and Commercial Uses of Sexuality).

Some researchers have attempted to explain differences in the patterns of sexual behavior of women and men (including the patterns described above) on the basis of the different hormonal makeups of women and men. For example, the hormone testosterone, which is usually found in higher levels in males, has been associated with male aggressive behavior. Before puberty, male and female testosterone levels are about the same. At maturity, these levels have increased by a factor of 10 or 20 in males, while they only double in females (Udry, Talbert, & Morris, 1986). Progesterone, a hormone usually found in higher levels in women, has been associated with female nurturing behavior. When female rats are given large doses of testosterone, they become aggressive; similarly, when male rats are given large doses of progesterone, they become nurturers (Arnold, 1980). The same hormonal reversal findings have been found in monkeys (Goy & McEwen, 1980).

CONSIDERATION: Much of the research on hormonal influences on sexual behavior has been conducted on non-primates, due to the constraints on manipulating hormones in humans. As we noted in Chapter 5 (Theories of Sexuality), any generalizations about human behavior made on the basis of animal research should be viewed with caution.

Some research suggests that sexual thoughts and desire may be influenced by physiological factors. One study found that hypogonadal men, whose gonads produce limited amounts of androgen (e.g., testosterone), reported having few to no sexual thoughts (Bancroft, 1984). When they were administered androgen (androgen replacement therapy), they reported rapid increases in the frequency with which they thought about sex within two weeks of receiving the androgen. When the androgen replacement therapy was stopped for a three-week period, the men reported rapid decreases in the frequency with which they thought about sex. This study was a placebo controlled study, which means that the hypogonadal men did not know if they were in the group receiving the androgen or the placebo.

The sexual thoughts of women have also been found to be influenced by androgen. Young, surgically menopausal women (following removal of the ovaries) who received androgen reported increases in desire, arousal, and frequency of sexual fantasies (Sherwin, Gelfand, & Brender, 1985).

Some sociobiologists view differences between women and men as having an evolutionary basis. For example, some research suggests that there may be differences between the female and male brain. These differences are believed to be the basis for frequently cited female superiority in manual dexterity and verbal and communication skills and male superiority in spatial-visual skills (Maccoby & Jacklin, 1974). From an evolutionary perspective, it has been argued that males had to develop spatial-visual skills for hunting and for leading migrations throughout hominid evolution. Females needed to develop language and communication skills in order to care for offspring (Levy, 1972), and manual dexterity was adaptive when women were responsible for gathering food. However, more recent examinations of the cognitive sex-differences research have challenged the notion that men and women are widely divergent in cognitive abilities (Basow, 1992; Tavris, 1992; Tavris & Wade, 1984) and pointed out there are more similarities than differences. When meaningful differences are found, they tend to be among select samples (as in mathematically gifted students and students taking Advanced Placement and Advanced Graduate Record Examinations) (Lubinski & Benbow, 1992). Debate still flourishes between those who emphasize social (Tavris, 1992) versus biological (Lubinski & Benbow, 1992) influences on gender differences in cognitive abilities and preferences.

In mate selection, heterosexual men tend to value women who are youthful and physically attractive, while heterosexual women tend to value men who are economically stable. The pattern of men seeking physically attractive young women and women seeking economically ambitious men was observed in 37 groups of women and men in 33 different societies (Buss, 1989). This pattern is also evident in courtship patterns in the United States (S. Davis, 1990). An evolutionary explanation for this pattern argues that men and women have different biological agendas in terms of reproducing and caring for offspring (Symons & Ellis, 1989; Symons, 1987).

The term "parental investment" refers to any investment by a parent that increases the offspring's chance of surviving and, hence, increases reproductive success. Parental investments require time and energy. Women have a great deal of parental investment in their offspring (nine months' gestation, taking care of dependent offspring) and tend to mate with men who have high status, economic resources, and a willingness "to invest their resources in a given female and her offspring" (Ellis & Symons, 1990, p. 533). Men, on the other hand, focus on the importance of "health and youth" in their selection of a mate because young, healthy women are more likely to produce healthy offspring (Ellis & Symons, 1990, p. 534). Men also "have an aversion to invest in relationships with females who are sexually promiscuous," since men want to ensure that the offspring is their own (Grammer, 1989, p. 149).

The sociobiological explanation for mate selection is extremely controversial. Critics argue that women may show concern for the earning capacity of a potential mate because women have been systematically denied access to similar economic resources and selecting a mate with these resources is one of their remaining options. In addition, it is argued that both women and men, when selecting a mate, think more about their partners as companions than as future parents of their offspring. Finally, the sociobiological perspective fails to acknowledge the degree to which social and psychological factors influence our behavior.

CONSIDERATION: The view that at least some gender role behaviors are biologically based is deeply ingrained in our culture. For example, we tend to think of mothers as naturally equipped and inclined to perform the role of primary child caregiver. Chodorow (1978) argued that the role of child caregiver has been assigned to women, although there is no biological reason why fathers cannot be the primary caregiver or participate in child-rearing activities.

Within the scientific community, much controversy surrounds the issue of biologically based gender differences. Some researchers believe that these presumed differences do not exist or are insignificant (Springer & Deutsch, 1981).

CONSIDERATION: One of the concerns about biologically based gender differences is that these presumed differences are used to justify sexism. For example, data that suggest that males have superior spatial-visual abilities may be used to justify assumptions that women cannot be competent engineers. Even if the presumed biological differences between the sexes exist, these differences may be overcome by learning (Rossi, 1977).

Identification Theory

Freud was one of the first researchers to study gender role acquisition. Freud suggested that children acquire the characteristics and behaviors of their same-sex parent through a process of identification. Boys identify with their fathers, girls identify with their mothers. Freud (1925/1974, 1933/1965) said that children identify with the same-gender parent out of fear. Freud felt this fear could be one of two kinds: fear of loss of love or fear of retaliation. Fear of loss of love, which results in both girls and boys identifying with their mother, is caused by their deep dependence on her for love and nurturance. Fearful that she may withdraw her love, young children try to become like her to please her and to ensure the continuance of her love.

According to Freud, at about age four, the child's identification with the mother begins to change, but in different ways for boys than for girls. Boys experience what Freud called the "**Oedipal complex.**" Based on the legend of the Greek youth Oedipus, who unknowingly killed his father and married his mother, the Oedipal complex involves the young boy's awakening sexual feelings for his mother as he becomes aware he has a penis and his mother does not. He unconsciously feels that if his father knew of the intense love feelings he has for his mother, the father would castrate him (which may be what happened to his mother, because she has no penis). The boy resolves the Oedipal struggle—feeling love for his father but wanting to kill him because he is a competitor for his mother's love—by becoming like his father, by identifying with him. In this way, the boy can keep his penis and take pride in being like his father. According to Freud, the successful resolution of this Oedipal situation marks the beginning of a boy's appropriate gender-role acquisition.

Freud's two greatest mistakes were: (1) the castration-complex and (2) his theory of female sexuality.

J. O. Wisdom

The "**Electra complex**" is based on the Greek myth in which Electra assists her brother in killing their mother and her lover to avenge their father's death. In Freudian terms, the Electra complex refers to unconscious sexual feelings a daughter develops for her father. These feelings develop when three- to six year-old girls become aware that they do not have a penis. Freud believed that girls blame their mothers for cutting off their penis or causing it to be severed and that they develop "penis envy" and wish that they had a penis. To retaliate, girls take their love away from their mothers and begin to focus on their fathers as love objects. Girls feel that they can be fulfilled by being impregnated by their fathers who will give them a baby to substitute for the penis they do not have. To become impregnated by their fathers, girls recognize that they must be more like their mother. So they identify again with the mother.

CONSIDERATION: A modern interpretation of penis envy is that women do not desire to have a penis, but rather they desire the economic and social advantages that men have (Chafetz, 1988).

In *The Reproduction of Mothering,* Nancy Chodorow (1978) used Freudian identification theory as a basis for her theory that gender role specialization occurs in the family because of the "asymmetrical organization of parenting" (p. 49).

> Women, as mothers, produce daughters with mothering capacities and the desire to mother. These capacities and needs are built into and grow out of the mother-daughter relationship itself. By contrast, women as mothers (and men as not-mothers) produce sons whose nurturant capacities and needs have been systematically curtailed and repressed. (p. 7)

In other words, all activities associated with nurturing and child care are identified as female activities because women are the primary caregivers of young children. This one-sidedness (or asymmetry) of nurturing by women increases the likelihood that females, because they identify with their mother, will see their own primary identities and roles as mothers. According to Chodorow, "the social structure produces gendered personalities that reproduce the social structure" (Hare-Mustin & Marecek, 1988).

Chodorow sees the "asymmetrical organization of parenting" as the basis for the continuing unequal social organization of gender. In order to change this social inequality, we must recognize "the need for a fundamental reorganization of parenting, so that primary parenting is shared between men and women" (Chodorow, 1978, p. 215).

Social Learning Theory

Derived from the school of behavioral psychology, social learning theory emphasizes the role of reward and punishment in explaining how a child learns gender role behavior. For example, two young brothers enjoyed playing "lady." Each of them would put on a dress, wear high-heeled shoes, and carry a pocketbook. Their father came home early one day and angrily demanded that they "take those clothes off and never put them on again." "Those things are for women," he said. The boys were punished for playing "lady" but rewarded with their father's approval for playing "cowboys," with plastic guns and "Bang! You're dead!" dialogue.

Reward and punishment alone are not sufficient to account for the way in which children learn gender roles. Direct instruction ("girls wear dresses," "men walk on the outside when walking with a woman") is another way children learn through social interaction with others. In addition, many of society's gender rules are learned through modeling. In modeling, the child observes another's behavior and imitates that behavior. Gender role models include parents, peers, siblings, and characters portrayed in the media.

The impact of modeling on the development of gender-role behavior is controversial. For example, a modeling perspective implies that children will tend to imitate the parent of the same gender, but children are usually reared mainly by women in all cultures. Yet this persistent female model does not seem to interfere with the male's development of the behavior that is considered appropriate for his gender. One explanation suggests that boys learn early that our society generally grants boys and men more status and privileges than to girls and women; therefore, they devalue the feminine and emphasize the masculine aspects of themselves.

Women also do not strictly model their mothers' behavior. Although women who work outside the home usually have mothers who did likewise, their mothers may also be traditional homemakers.

In spite of the controversies over the impact of modeling on the development of gender role behavior, social learning theory has gained widespread support. Much research has contributed to this support. For example, in one study, 26 couples were assigned to a problem-solving, skills-training program after taking the Bem Sex Role Inventory—a test designed to assess the degree to which each person views herself or himself as masculine or feminine. The training consisted of learning how to disclose themselves to each other and to express feelings to each other. After completing the eight-week program, the couples took the Bem Sex Role Inventory again and both the women and the men scored higher on the feminine aspects. Similar changes were not observed in the control group of this experiment. Another study showed that training increased men's empathy (Cleaver, 1987).

Both studies emphasize that self-disclosure and expressing empathy—traits typically associated with women—can be enhanced. These traits are not innate but are acquired through social and cultural exposure to various learning experiences. Another study demonstrated that females display leadership skills similar to those of males when the situational context calls for such behavior (Koberg, 1985). Likewise, men develop empathic skills when it is expedient. Snodgrass (1985) reported that workers learn to read their leader's nonverbal cues better than leaders read followers' cues (regardless of the leader or follower's sex). This suggests that being in the subordinate role, rather than gender per se, is what motivates being sensitive to the behaviors of others. Hence, the experiences a person is exposed to and the cues within a social context dictate the behavior that the individual expresses.

Another illustration of the degree to which gender roles are learned is the fact that spouses in different racial, ethnic, and social class groups reflect a variety of gender role patterns (see Table 8.2). It is recognized that there are wide variations within, as well as between, the various groups.

Cognitive–Developmental Theory

The cognitive-developmental theory of gender role acquisition reflects a blend of biological and social learning views. According to this theory, the biological readiness in terms of cognitive development of the child influences how the child responds to gender cues in the environment (Kohlberg, 1966; 1976).

For example, gender discrimination (the ability to identify social and psychological characteristics associated with being female and male) begins at about age 30 months. At that age, toddlers are able to assign a "boy's toy" to a boy and a "girl's

TABLE 8.2 Multicultural Differences in Gender Roles*

Group	Gender Roles
Whites	Traditional sex roles in lower class. More egalitarian as spouses move up the social class ladder.
African-Americans	Similar to whites in all social classes with greater male domination at all levels. Mother-child bond tends to take precedence over wife-husband relationship.
Native Americans	Women concerned with kinfolk, family, marriage, and sexual relations. Men concerned with employment, money, success, and material matters.
Asian Americans	
Chinese	Mutual sharing of responsibility and authority in decision making, although the wife usually assumes the role of helper, rather than equal partner.
Japanese	Priority given to husband-wife relationship over kinship ties with low instances of male dominance. Still a general tendency to view primary responsibility of males as being concerns outside the home and of females as being tasks inside the home.
Vietnamese	Male dominance; female subordination.
Korean	Men do little household work, while women work outside the home in addition to caring for the home.

*Table developed by Kim Tripp for this text, based on information from Mindel, C. H., Habenstein, R. W., & Wright, R., Jr. (Eds.). (1988). *Ethnic families in America: Patterns and variations* (3rd ed.). New York: Elsevier.

toy" to a girl (Etaugh & Duits, 1990). However, at this age, children do not view gender as a permanent characteristic. Thus, while young children may define people who wear long hair as girls and those who never wear dresses as boys, they also believe they can change their gender by altering their hair or changing clothes.

Not until age six or seven does the child view gender as permanent (Kohlberg, 1966; 1969). In Kohlberg's view, this cognitive understanding is not a result of social learning. Rather, it involves the development of a specific mental ability to grasp the idea that certain basic characteristics of people do not change. Once children learn the concept of gender permanence, they seek to become competent and proper members of their gender group. For example, a child standing on the edge of a school playground may observe one group of children jumping rope while another group is playing football. That child's gender identity as either a girl or a boy connects with the observed gender-appropriate behavior, and she or he joins one of the two groups. Once in the group, the child seeks to develop the behaviors that are socially defined as appropriate for her or his gender.

Some cognitive-developmental theories suggest that the moral development of men and women may be different. Gilligan (1982) observed that many men make judgments on the basis of competing rights and abstract principles, whereas women often make judgments on their assessments of competing responsibilities. Gilligan's point is not only to demonstrate that men and women have different conceptions of morality but that the male conception is regarded as the universal standard by which both men and women are evaluated, and to point out that an alternative moral "voice"—the "care" perspective—is as legitimate as the "rights" perspective. However, while Gilligan's work made an important contribution in calling attention to an ethic of care in moral decision-making, subsequent research has not confirmed that men and women consistently differ in their patterns of moral reasoning (Tavris, 1992).

Gender Schema Theory

Gender schema theory, a more recently developed theory of gender role acquisition, combines aspects of cognitive-developmental theory and social learning theory. The term *schema* refers to a "network of associations that organizes and guides an individual's perception" (Bem, 1983, p. 603). A **gender schema** is a network of associations with the concepts of male and female (or masculinity and femininity) that organizes and guides perception.

Consistent with social learning theory, the male and female associations that comprise the content of gender schemas are learned through interaction with the social environment. The gender schema then influences how an individual processes information by structuring and organizing perception. Gender schema influences how incoming information, including information about the self, is evaluated with regard to gender norms. This aspect of gender schema theory, which emphasizes the role of cognitive frameworks in processing information, reflects cognitive-developmental theory.

Gender schema theory suggests that people follow gender schemas to different degrees and in different ways.

> Some people, for example, organize many of their thoughts, perceptions, and evaluations around concepts of male and female, masculine and feminine. These people, whom we might describe as highly sex typed, rely heavily on gender stereotypes and symbols to understand the social world. They see a wide variety of human characteristics, behavior, roles, and jobs as decidedly masculine or feminine and evaluate themselves and others according to how well they conform to gender norms and stereotypes.

> Other people follow gender schemas less closely or not at all. This does not necessarily mean that they lack what the highly sex-typed person might regard as appropriate masculine or feminine characteristics. Gender may simply not be the central means by which they organize their perceptions of themselves and the social world. Whereas the highly sex-typed person might immediately understand words such as *pink, nurturant, blushing, librarian,* and *curved,* as "feminine," these words might not have any immediate gender connotation to the person with no gender schema. (Sapiro, 1990, p. 88)

The various theories outlined above reflect differing views on whether gender differences are biologically based or are the result of social and cognitive factors. While debate about the source of sex differences continues, another debate centers around the question of to what degree females and males are different and to what degree they are similar. Many feminist critiques emphasize that the differences between males and females are exaggerated and misunderstood. In Exhibit 8.2, we present some critiques of research on sex differences. Following Exhibit 8.2, we discuss Hare-Mustin and Marecek's (1988) notion that gender theories are biased toward either emphasizing or minimizing gender differences. These biases and their consequences are discussed in the Theoretical Perspective: Alpha Bias and Beta Bias in Gender Theories.

EXHIBIT 8.2 Critiques of Research on Sex Differences

A number of critiques of research on gender differences have been made by gender scholars. These critiques include the following:

1. Research findings that describe sex differences often fail to describe the mechanisms by which these differences are produced; in other words, differences are reported without an explanation of the conditions eliciting them (Unger, 1990; Maccoby & Jacklin, 1974). Hence, "gender is seen as the cause of behavior, and description is confused with explanation" (Lott, 1990, p. 70).

   Research that describes sex differences without explaining them implies that differences between females and males are biologically based. However, many gender scholars argue that differences between females and males are due to social differences in female and male roles and status (i.e., power). Based on a review of the meta-analytical literature on gender differences, Alice Eagly (1987) argued that the percentage of variability in social behaviors that is attributable to gender is "generally below 10% and more typically 5%" (1987, p. 115). Hence, according to Eagly, 90% to 95% of the differences in social behaviors of females and males are explained by factors other than gender, including conformity to socially created gender role expectations, situational demands, and gender differences in power.
2. Research that focuses on sex differences overshadows the examination of sex similarities. Unger (1990) commented that "the fact that the sexes are more similar than they are different is not considered noteworthy either by psychology as a discipline or by society as a whole" (p. 104).
3. Research that focuses on between-sex differences (differences between females and males) overlooks the examination of within-sex differences. Variables associated with within-sex differences, such as race, ethnicity, and socioeconomic class, are often ignored in sex difference research.
4. Research studies that find a difference between females and males are more likely to be published than studies that do not find any sex differences (Maccoby & Jacklin, 1974; Kupfersmid, 1988; Tavris, 1992). Hence, the research literature is biased in overrepresenting research in which sex differences are found and underrepresenting research in which no sex differences are found.
5. Much of the research done on sex differences is based on studies of college students, as researchers have convenient access to college students as research participants. Wallston & Grady (1985) noted that choosing college students to study sex differences may inadvertently overrepresent these differences because differences between the sexes are maximized in young adulthood.

   In an analysis of 65 studies on sex differences, Cohn (1991) found that sex differences in ego development and personality traits were greatest among junior and senior high-school students, primarily because girls mature earlier than boys. Cohn also noted that these differences declined significantly among college-age adults and disappeared entirely among older women and men.
6. Research studies that are based on only one sex often report conclusions of differences between the sexes (Maccoby & Jacklin, 1974).

THEORETICAL PERSPECTIVE:

Alpha Bias and Beta Bias in Gender Theories

Lay persons and academicians alike may easily be confused by the contradicting theories that deal with gender differences. There are two competing lines of inquiry into the nature of sex and gender differences that represent what Hare-Mustin and Marecek (1988) refer to as alpha bias and beta bias. **Alpha bias** describes the body of theory and research that *exaggerate* differences between males and females. **Beta bias** describes the body of theory and research that *minimize* differences and stress similarities between females and males.

Alpha bias, or the tendency to emphasize gender differences, is found in research and theories that stress that women and men have distinct natures and qualities. For example, some theorists argue that women are intrinsically emotional, nurturing, and concerned for relationships. Men, on the other hand, are often viewed as inherently rational (as opposed to emotional), aggressive, and task-oriented.

Traditionally, theories about human behavior have been based on observations of males. Such theories represent beta bias, or the tendency to ignore or minimize differences. By using male behavior as a measure of human behavior, such theories ignored differences between men and women.

> The male was the norm against which human behavior was measured, and male experience was assumed to represent all experience. Generalizations about human development based only on the male life course represent a partial view of humanity and overlook the many differences in men's and women's experience. (Hare-Mustin & Marecek, 1988, p. 458)

Hare-Mustin and Marecek (1988) have identified various consequences of alpha bias and beta bias in gender theories. Some of these consequences are described below.

Consequences of Alpha Bias

Alpha bias, which emphasizes differences between females and males, has both positive and negative consequences. On the positive side:

> focusing on differences between women and men . . . has allowed some theorists to assert the worth of certain "feminine" qualities. This has the positive effect of countering the cultural devaluation of women and fostering a valued sense of identity in them. (p. 459)

A negative consequence of alpha bias is that by emphasizing gender differences as dichotomized traits, we overlook the degree to which men and women are similar and share overlapping traits. For example, while achievement or task orientation is typically viewed as a male quality, the job of rearing children (typically regarded as a female predisposition) also involves achievement and task orientation.

Another negative consequence of alpha-biased gender theories is that they mask inequality and conflict between the sexes. For example, rationality is often viewed as a male trait and concern for relationships is often viewed as a female trait. But theories that maintain that these differences are inherent overlook the possibility that these qualities result from social inequalities and power differences. Hare-Mustin and Marecek (1988) illustrated how differences between men and women may be due to their respective positions in the social hierarchy:

> Men's propensity to reason from principles may stem from the fact that the principles were formulated to promote their interests; women's concern with relationships can be understood as the need to please others that arises from a lack of power. (p. 459)

Those in power usually advocate rules, rationality, and control, while those without power emphasize the importance of relationships.

Continued

Continued

> Thus, in husband-wife conflicts, husbands call on rules and logic, whereas wives call on caring. When women are in the dominant position, however, as in parent-child conflicts, they emphasize rules, whereas children appeal for sympathy and understanding. Such a reversal suggests that these differences can be accounted for by an individual's position in the social hierarchy rather than by gender. (p. 459)

Consequences of Beta Bias

Beta bias, which minimizes differences between females and males, also has positive and negative consequences. On the positive side, regarding women and men as equal has led to legislation that has allowed women greater access to educational and occupational opportunities. Thus, beta bias in gender theories has been largely responsible for the improvement in women's status in recent decades.

On the negative side, the argument that there are no differences between women and men draws attention away from the differences in power and resources between men and women and overlooks the special needs of women. For example:

> The failure of the workplace to accommodate women's special needs associated with childbirth represents beta bias, in which male needs and behaviors set the norm. (p. 460)

The following table summarizes the positive and negative consequences of gender theories that emphasize gender differences (alpha bias) and those that minimize gender differences (beta bias).

CONSEQUENCES OF ALPHA AND BETA BIAS IN GENDER THEORIES

Alpha Bias *(theories that emphasize gender differences)*	
Positive Consequences:	Asserts worth of certain "feminine" qualities. Counters cultural devaluation of women, and fosters sense of identity in women.
Negative Consequences:	Overlooks similarities between women and men. Masks social inequality between men and women by claiming that differences between men and women are inherent, rather than due to their unequal positions in the social hierarchy.
Beta Bias *(theories that minimize gender differences)*	
Positive Consequences:	Helps promote legislation that provides women with equal educational and occupational opportunities.
Negative Consequences:	Draws attention away from special needs of women (e.g., parental leave).

Reference

Hare-Mustin, R. T., & Marecek, J. (1988). The meaning of difference: Gender theory, postmodernism and psychology. *American Psychologist, 43,* 455–464. Used by permission.

Agents of Socialization in Gender Role Acquisition

Many gender role scholars believe that the behaviors of females and males are influenced by the interaction of biological and social influences. Basow (1992) concluded:

> It seems likely that some biological predisposition, possibly due to prenatal hormones, interacts with the environment to determine whether the ability itself will be actualized. The environment can either reinforce or discourage such actualization, depending on the behavior's gender-appropriateness in that society. (p. 52)

What is considered "appropriate" gender role behavior is determined by the culture in which one lives. The specific aspects of the environment that socialize individuals into adopting the culture's gender roles are known as agents of socialization, which include parents, peers, teachers and educational curricula/materials, religion, and the media.

Parents

Although parents generally report that they treat their daughters and sons similarly (Antill, 1987), much research suggests the contrary. The following research provides evidence of differential parental treatment in parents' expectations of and reactions to child behavior, toy selection, and household chore assignment.

- Antill (1987) found that most middle-class parents expect their daughters to be more emotional than their sons and expect their sons to be more aggressive and noisy than their daughters.
- A study of the rooms of 120 girls and boys ages two and younger found that girls were provided with more dolls, children's furniture, fictional characters, manipulative toys, and the color pink; boys were provided with more sports equipment, toy vehicles, tools, and the colors blue, red, and white (Pomerleau, Bolduc, Malcuit, & Cossette, 1990).

Little girls sometimes learn how to be feminine from their mothers; boys sometimes learn how to be masculine from their fathers.

- Antill (1987) found that parents (especially fathers) discourage their children (especially their sons) from playing with "other-sex" toys and participating in "other-sex" activities.
- Of 2,238 fathers and mothers, 45% reported that they socialize their children to adopt traditional roles in family settings (Lackey, 1989). Boys and girls tend to be assigned different household chores as early as age five or six (Burns & Homel, 1989; Goodnow, 1988; McHale, Bartko, Crouter, & Perry-Jenkins, 1990). For example, boys are more likely than girls to be assigned maintenance chores, such as mowing lawns and painting, while girls are more likely to be assigned domestic tasks, such as cooking and laundry. Because domestic chores are done daily and maintenance chores are done less frequently, girls spend more time doing household chores than boys.

Patterns of gender stereotypic household chores are more likely to occur in lower-socioeconomic families than in higher-socioeconomic families. When the mother is employed outside the home, it is more likely that both daughters and sons are expected to perform domestic tasks. Single-parent families and employed mothers tend to socialize their daughters to be assertive and independent with fewer traditional gender role attitudes (Kiecolt & Acock, 1988).

CONSIDERATION: What are the effects of assigning gender-typed chores to girls and boys? First, girls learn how to do domestic chores better than boys, and boys learn how to do maintenance work better than girls. In addition, children learn to associate certain types of work with gender, which may influence their future educational and occupational choices. Children who are assigned gender-typed chores may also develop different personal qualities. For example, girls may develop nurturing behaviors because domestic chores (taking care of siblings) may be associated with caring for others. Boys may fail to develop nurturing behaviors because they are assigned chores that focus on caring for things, rather than people. Lastly, "the fact that girls spend more time doing chores than boys also may convey a message about male privilege" (Basow, 1992, p. 131).

Peers

While parents are usually the first socializing agents that influence a child's gender role acquisition, peers become increasingly important during the school years. From preschool through adolescence, children who conform to traditional gender role behavior are more socially acceptable to their peers than children who do not conform to gender stereotypes (Fagot, 1984; Martin, 1989; Martin, 1990).

CONSIDERATION: Peer disapproval for failure to conform to traditional gender stereotypes is reflected in the terms *sissy* and *tomboy.* These terms are used pejoratively to refer to children who exhibit behaviors that are stereotypically associated with the other gender.

The gender role messages from adolescent peers are primarily traditional.

> For adolescent boys, such traits include being tough (through body build or athletic achievement), being cool (not showing emotions, not fearful of danger, staying reasonable under stress), being interested in girls and sex, being good at something, being physically attractive and having an absence of any trait or characteristic that is female or feminine. (Harrison & Pennell, 1989, p. 32)

Female adolescents are under tremendous pressure to be physically attractive, popular, and achievement-oriented. The latter may be traditional (cheerleading) or nontraditional (sports or academics). Adolescent girls are sometimes in great conflict in that high academic success may be viewed as being less than feminine. In a study of 335 adolescents (primarily white and middle- to upper-class), Petersen (1987) found that "those seventh grade girls likely to report poor self-image or depressive symptoms were those who were academically successful" (p. 33). When these girls shifted their focus away from making good grades in the eighth grade, their self-image tended to improve and their depression tended to lift. Petersen and her colleagues found that while there were girls who performed well academically and felt good about themselves, others continued the pattern of trading grades for popularity into their senior year in high school.

CONSIDERATION: Since what is regarded as appropriate gender role behavior is often conflicting and ambiguous, adolescents are often in turmoil, fear, and confusion, which can lead to "retrenchment (clinging to traditional sex roles), rebellion (shedding of anything traditional), or some combination of the two" (Harrison & Pennell, 1989, p. 28). While the 1990s offer each individual an array of sexual and gender role choices, the drawback of having so many choices is confusion and stress.

Teachers and Educational Curricula and Materials

Although parents have the earliest influence and adolescent peers, the most significant influence during the teen years, teachers are another important socialization influence. Research suggests that teachers treat boys and girls differently (Sadker & Sadker, 1990):

> . . . elementary and secondary teachers give far more active teaching attention to boys than girls. They talk to boys more, ask them more lower- and higher-order questions, listen to them more, counsel them more, give them more extended directions, and criticize and reward them more frequently.
>
> This pattern of more active teacher attention directed at male students continues at the postsecondary level . . . In general, women are rarely called on; when female students do participate, their comments are more likely to be interrupted and less likely to be accepted or rewarded. (p. 177)

Female college professors, who comprise about 25% of college professors, have been found to be less biased against female students (Crawford & MacLeod, 1990; Statham, Richardson, & Cook, 1991). The pattern of sex bias in teacher-student interaction prevalent at all levels (elementary, secondary, and postsecondary) of the educational process "may result in lower levels of achievement, career aspiration, and self-esteem for women. Although girls start out ahead of boys in most academic areas, as they progress through school their achievement as measured by standardized tests declines" (Sadker & Sadker, 1990, p. 180).

Gender role stereotypes are also conveyed through educational materials, such as textbooks. In a study of 1,883 stories used in schools, Purcell and Stewart (1990) found that males were more often presented as clever, brave, adventurous, and income-producing, while females were more often presented as passive and as victims. Females were also more likely to be in need of rescue and were depicted in fewer occupational roles compared to males.

Gender stereotyping also occurs in textbooks at the college level. Ferree and Hall (1990) found that women were underrepresented in sociology textbooks. In a study of 27 introduction to psychology and 12 human development textbooks, Peterson and Kroner (1992) found that the representation of the work, theory, and behavior of males significantly exceeded the representation of the work, theory, and behavior of females. Despite the fact that 56% of psychologists and 78% of developmental psychologists receiving Ph.D.s are women, "the picture presented in textbooks is that the majority of persons working in the various domains of psychology are men" (Peterson & Kroner, 1992, p. 31). In addition, females were much more likely to be used in illustrations of various pathologies and to be shown as clients in therapy. Thus, females are still being overrepresented as disordered or dysfunctional, whereas males are more typically portrayed as healthy and competent (p. 31).

Beyond the teachers and textbooks, the curricula and after-school activities of the educational system provide different gender role socialization experiences. Although the Title IX regulation of the 1972 Education Amendments Act prohibits "tracking" students by sex, informal pressures from school systems, parents, and peers results in the tendency for males to take courses in agricultural, technical, trade, and industrial programs and females to take courses in home economics, health, and office skills programs.

Gender role socialization also occurs in sports activities. Boys and men are more likely than girls and women to participate in competitive sports that emphasize traditional male characteristics—winning, aggression, physical strength, courage, adventurousness, and dominance. Research findings suggest that male varsity athletes have more traditional attitudes toward women's roles and more negative attitudes toward nontraditional sex role behaviors than nonathletes (Houseworth, Peplow, & Thirer, 1989). The fact that male athletes are disproportionately involved in cases of rape (O'Sullivan, 1991) also suggests that participation in "masculine" sports is associated with aggression and male dominance over women.

CONSIDERATION: While the participation of women in sports is increasing, women are still excluded from organized ice hockey and football, where their participation is limited to cheerleading. In addition, while funding for female participation in school sports has also increased, the average budget for women's athletics is still much lower than that of men's athletics. For example, in Division I colleges and universities in 1985–1986, expenditures for women's athletic programs were less than one-seventh those for men's (Oberlander, 1989).

Religion

Religion has been criticized as perpetuating gender stereotypes based on traditional patriarchal society. Basow (1992) claimed that "to the extent that a child has any religious instruction, he or she receives further training in the gender stereotypes" (p. 156). For example, the Bible emphasizes the patriarchal nature of the family:

> In Islam, the most male-oriented of the modern religions, a woman is nothing but a vehicle for producing sons, and the male function is, in part, the protection of the women.
>
> *Joseph Campbell*

> But I want you to understand that the head of every man is Christ, the head of every woman is her husband, and the head of Christ is God. (1 Cor. 11:3)
>
> You shall be eager for your husband, and he shall be your master. (Gen. 3:16)

It has also been argued that the Bible does not promote inequality of the sexes. For example, Elizabeth Achtemeier commented, ". . . the Scriptures are a clear proclamation of our freedom and equality in Jesus Christ and our sure guide to abundant and joyful life" (1991, p. 11). While the Bible identifies different roles for women and men, these roles are to be carried out with mutual love, respect, and honor encouraged for both. In regard to the role relationship between women and men:

> Wives be subject to your husband, as to the Lord (Eph. 5:22–24). Husbands, l
> wives, even as Christ also loved the church. (v. 25) (see Col. 3:18–19)
>
> . . . that both male and female are created in the image of God. (Genesis 1:27

While the Bible has been interpreted in both nonsexist and sexist term dominance is indisputable in the hierarchy of religious organizations, where and status have been accorded mostly to men. Until recently, only men cou priests, ministers, and rabbis. Basow (1992) noted that the Catholic church doe have female clergy and men dominate the 19 top positions in the U.S. dioceses. first female cleric in the Protestant religion was ordained in 1970; the first fem rabbi in the Jewish religion in 1972; and the first female Episcopal bishop in 198

Male bias is also reflected in terminology used to refer to God in the Jewish Christian, and Islamic religions. Although God is not a person and therefore has no gender, God is frequently referred to as "He," "Father," "Lord," and "King."

CONSIDERATION: Whereas gender images attached to God have traditionally been masculine, it has been noted that "the character of Jesus is considerably more androgynous. . . . Although Jesus was a male, his unfailing gentleness, humility, simplicity, and nonviolence; his healing qualities and immediately forgiving nature; and his suffering for others were very close to what Western culture considers femininity" (Sapiro, 1990, p. 157).

Some movement has been made toward using gender-neutral terms for God. In 1983, the National Council of Churches published *An Inclusive Language Lectionary* in an effort to revise Bible passages in order to promote nonsexist terminology and eliminate exclusively male metaphors for God. New proposed guidelines include substituting "humanity" for "mankind," "community" for "fellowship," "Creator" for "Father," and "Father and Mother" for God. Jesus is referred to as the "Child" rather than the "Son" of God.

Media

The media—film, magazines, television, newspapers, books, music, and art—both reflect and shape gender roles. Media images of women and men typically conform to traditional gender stereotypes. In addition, women appear less often than men on most television programs. Finally, media portrayals depicting the exploitation, victimization, and sexual objectification of women are common. Consider the following evidence:

- In the fall 1991 television season, all dominant characters on Saturday morning children's programs were male; females played secondary roles, if any (Carter, 1991). This was a marketing decision by television executives based on the finding that boys will only watch shows that feature male characters, while girls will watch shows that feature either female or male characters.
- Most women on prime-time television are young, attractive, and sexy (D. M. Davis, 1990).

> The portrait developed here is of the young, attractive, and sexy female who is more ornamental in many shows than functional. For example, in one episode of Miami Vice, there were 14 speaking characters, all male. There were two female characters with more than three minutes of screen time, but neither spoke. Both were ornamental girlfriends of male episodic characters. (p. 331)

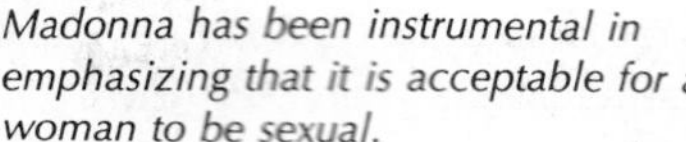

Madonna has been instrumental in emphasizing that it is acceptable for a woman to be sexual.

CONSIDERATION: In a study of prime-time television programming, researchers (Atkin, Moorman, & Lin, 1991) found that the number of series featuring female leads increased through the 1980s. The portrayal of women working in professional or blue-collar jobs also increased during the 1980s. One explanation for the changes in television portrayals of women is that more women have entered management positions in television, such as producer. For example, female producers were behind shows portraying women in assertive or competent roles, including Diane English of "Murphy Brown," Linda Bloodworth of "Designing Women," and Roseanne Arnold of "Roseanne."

- A team of researchers analyzed 160 television commercials shown on Saturday morning television. They observed that about 14% of the commercials related to appearance enhancement and were targeted toward women. In effect, the viewer was told that her attractiveness could be enhanced if she bought the product. The researchers suggested that the higher incidence of eating disorders among women may be influenced by television commercials that portray feminine beauty in terms of thinness (Ogletree, Williams, Raffeld, Mason, & Fricke, 1990).
- Peirce (1990) analyzed the gender role messages of *Seventeen* magazine (1.7 million readership) for the years 1961, 1972, and 1985 and concluded that its ideology for femininity is traditional. *Seventeen* conveys that "a teenage girl, then, should be concerned with her appearance, with finding a man to take care of her, and with learning to take care of a house" (p. 498).
- Mooney and Brabant (1987) conducted a content analysis of six family-oriented Sunday comics (*Blondie, The Born Loser, Dennis the Menace, Hi and Lois, For Better or Worse,* and *Sally Forth*). They concluded that these cartoons communicate the message that "if you are a woman and you want a happy home, do not have a career, and if you are a man, never marry a career woman" (p. 419).

- Top-40 radio stations typically have male disc jockeys, sportscasters, news and weathercasters (Lont, 1990).
- Music videos (such as shown on MTV) typically portray women as sex provocative, emphasizing female sexuality and male aggression.
- Most artists who are considered "great" are men. Artwork done primarily [illegible] women, including needlework, quilting, pottery, and other "crafts," are not considered "high" forms of art (Sapiro, 1990).

In sum, all forms of mass media reflect gender stereotypes. Given that gender role stereotypes are perpetuated by family, peers, education, religion, and mass media, it is no wonder that such stereotypes have continued. Each agent of socialization reinforces gender roles that are learned from other agents of socialization, thereby creating a gender role system that is deeply embedded in our society.

Consequences of Traditional Female Socialization

In this section, we look at some of the consequences of being socialized as a female in our society. Many of these consequences are negative:

> . . . it seems clear that ascribing lower status to women is widely accepted. What has also been revealed through research is that the result of such lower status expectations is often damaging to personal relationships, as well as to professional ones. In the professional realm, women expect and receive lower salaries. . . . on the personal level, gender typed expectations may contribute to experiences of stress, low self-esteem, and dissatisfaction in their roles as spouses, homemakers/workers, mothers, and friends. (Reid & Comas-Diaz, 1990, p. 398)

Other negatives include: less income and education; singlehood more likely; women's value defined in terms of appearance and age; and less marital satisfaction.

NATIONAL DATA: Women earn more than half of all bachelor's (52.5%) and master's (51.9%) degrees. However, women earn only 36.5% of the Ph.D. degrees, 33.0% of M.D. degrees, and 26% of degrees in dentistry (*Statistical Abstract of the United States: 1992,* Table 280).

Less Education and Income: Women earn fewer advanced degrees than men. The strongest explanation for why women earn fewer advanced degrees than men is that women are socialized to choose marriage and motherhood over long-term career preparation (Olson, Frieze, & Detlefsen, 1990). From an early age, women

Increasingly, women such as this professor are pursuing careers rather than jobs.

are exposed to images and models of femininity that stress the importance of family life.

Women who choose to pursue higher education often find that having children, along with the cultural expectation that they (rather than their male partners) take primary responsibility for child care, interferes with academic responsibilities.

CONSIDERATION: Women have also been discriminated against by educational institutions. Such discrimination was often justified on the basis of assumed "scientific" theories, such as those of Edward Clarke, who argued in the 1880s that if women received too much education, the energy that should be going to their wombs would go to their brains instead. Hence, educated women would be too feeble to produce healthy children (Sapiro, 1990).

It wasn't until 1972 that the U.S. government supported equal education for women and took a formal stand against educational discrimination on the basis of sex. Title IX of the Education Amendments Act of 1972 reads, "No person in the United States shall, on the basis of sex, be excluded from participation in, be denied the benefits of, or be subjected to discrimination under any education program or activity receiving federal financial assistance."

Less education is associated with lower income. However, women tend to earn less income than men, even when the level of educational achievement is identical (see Table 8.4).

One factor that contributes to both the educational and salary differentials of women and men is occupational segregation. Most workers are employed in gender-segregated occupations, that is, occupations in which workers are either primarily male or primarily female. Compared to male-dominated occupations, female-dominated occupations tend to require less education, have lower status, and pay lower salaries.

CONSIDERATION: The job of child-care attendant requires more education than the job of dog pound attendant. However, dog pound attendants, who are more likely to be male, earn more than child-care attendants, who are more likely to be female.

Even within the same occupation, women earn less than men. For example, in retail sales, women are more likely to sell less expensive products (such as clothing), while men are more likely to sell more expensive products (such as cars). Thus, male salespeople make more money in commissions and earn more than twice what

TABLE 8.4 **Effect of Education and Sex on Income**

Degree	Median Income	
	Women	*Men*
High school diploma	$18,954	$28,043
College degree	$28,911	$44,554
Five or more years of postsecondary education.	$35,827	$55,831

Source: *Statistical Abstract of the United States: 1992.* (112th, Table 113). (1992). Washington, DC: U.S. Bureau of the Census.

female sales people earn (Blau & Ferber, 1986). Even in high-status occupations, such as medicine, women earn less than men. In 1988, female physicians earned 63% of what male physicians earned (Hilts, 1991). This is because women are overrepresented in lower-status medical occupations, such as general practitioner and pediatrician, while men are more likely than women to have higher-status positions, such as medical administrator and surgeon.

CONSIDERATION: Women who do not pursue higher levels of education or do not pursue higher paying occupations may find themselves economically dependent on their partner or spouse. By choosing to pursue advanced education and well-paying occupations, women create more interpersonal choices and may not be pressured to stay in unsatisfying relationships because they are economically dependent.

NATIONAL DATA: The percentage of women age 75 and older who have never married is 5.5, in contrast to the percentage of men age 75 and older who have never married, which is 3.7 (*Statistical Abstract of the United States: 1991,* Table 51).

Singlehood More Likely Women are somewhat more likely to never marry than men. One explanation for the greater percentage of never-married women is that they have not been socialized to be aggressive in initiating relationships with men. The Choices section at the end of this chapter will discuss this issue in more detail.

Negative Self-Concept More Likely Some researchers have found that women are likely to feel more negatively about themselves than men. In a national study of more than 3,000 students in grades 4 through 10, self-esteem levels of boys decreased only slightly after elementary school; for girls, the drop in self-esteem was more dramatic (American Association of University Women, 1991). For example, the percentage of girls who agreed with the statement "I'm happy the way I am" went from 60% during elementary school to only 37% during middle school and 29% during high school. In a study of college undergraduates in regard to the dimension of self-dislike, women reported significantly higher self-dislike, sense of failure, and self-accusations than men (Oliver & Toner, 1990).

Feminists have observed that women in the United States live in a society that devalues them. "Women's natures, lives and experiences are not taken as seriously, are not valued as much as those of men" (Walker, Kees Martin, & Thomson, 1988, p. 18). As a result, women may not only lack confidence in themselves but feel that whatever successes they have are the result of luck. In a study in which women and men were told that they were incapable of performing a cognitive task, the women were more likely than the men to believe that they were incapable (Wagner, Ford, & Ford, 1986). When women are successful, they were more prone to attribute their success to luck than to their own ability (Heimovics & Herman, 1988).

Disenchantment with being a woman may be related to sexist attitudes toward women. **Sexism** is defined as an attitude, action, or institutional structure that subordinates or discriminates against an individual or group because of their sex. Sexism against women reflects the tradition of male dominance and presumed male superiority in our society. Sexist attitudes exist not only in the United States but also in the Soviet Union, China, India, Japan, and Latin America (Lindsey, 1990).

Not all research demonstrates that women have a more negative self-concept than men. Summarizing their research on the self-concepts of women and men in the United States, Williams and Best (1990a) noted "no evidence of an appreciable difference" (p. 153). They also found that there was no consistency in the self-concepts of women and men in 14 different countries. "In some of the countries the men's perceived self was noticeably more favorable than women's, whereas in others the reverse was found" (p. 152). Another study by Porter and Beuf (1991) found no significant differences in the self-esteem ratings between women and men.

Women's Value Defined in Terms of Appearance and Age The value of a woman is often defined by men in terms of her body and appearance. One hundred men rated various body types and showed a decided preference for women with large breasts and hourglass shapes (Furnham, Hester, & Weir, 1990). Men also emphasize that physical appearance is an important factor in deciding whom to date. In one study, 67% of 143 men, compared to 44% of 50 women, emphasized that physical apearance is an important factor in deciding whom to date (S. Davis, 1990, p. 48).

Rubin (1991) commented on society's preoccupation with youth and beauty:

> A woman who's 40 is already over the hill. Like a fine wine, he gets better with age, but she deteriorates, wilting like a flower left too long in the sun. (p. 152)

Some women feel particularly burdened by the notion that they are valuable only insofar as they are young and pretty. In our youth-oriented society where it is good to be young and bad to be old, women are more victimized by this looks-value connection. In a study of 600 adult women, 97% said that they feel feminine when they are happy about their appearance. Those most happy with their physical appearance were between the ages of 18 and 24; women least happy with their physical appearance were between the ages of 35 and 44 (Rubenstein, 1990).

According to the U.S. cultural definition of feminine beauty, beautiful women are thin women. Consequently, many women strive to achieve a body weight and shape that is unrealistic. It is not surprising that women are more likely than men to have eating disorders. Approximately 90% of all identified bulimic individuals (people who eat large quantities of food and then induce vomiting) are female (Timkom, Striegel-Moore, Silberstein, & Rodin, 1987).

Less Marital Satisfaction In general, wives are less satisfied in their marriages than husbands (Basow, 1992). A major contributing factor is that women experience role overload; they are expected to keep their husbands, children, and employers happy, to keep a clean house, and to keep up the correspondence with her (and his) parents. The result of coping with these unrealistic expectations imposed on women is, when compared to men, more frequent nervous breakdowns, greater psychological anxiety, increased self-blame for not living up to these expectations, and poorer physical health (Bird & Fremont, 1991). Many women develop resentment toward their husbands.

> Dammit, it makes me furious, because when it gets down to the brass tacks of real life, what they (men) really want is a woman who can pay her share of the bills, then turn into some sweet little thing who looks up at them adoringly, cooks wonderful meals, takes care of the kids, and after all that, turns into a sexpot at midnight. (Rubin, 1991, p. 147)

Married women often lack social support, which exacerbates the stress that results from role overload.

> Husbands may feel threatened by their wife's earnings, parents may criticize their daughter or son for putting grandchildren in day care, the workplace may have inflexible hours and job expectations, and society may provide few affordable resources (parental leave, adequate day care) to help manage the load. The outcome, frequently, is a stressed and exhausted woman who feels guilty for not spending enough time with her children. (Basow, 1992, p. 328)

CONSIDERATION: To decrease their frustration, wives might reject the expectation that they be all things to all people, alert their partners to the need for help with housework and child care, and choose to stop doing things that create more frustration than joy (e.g., sending Christmas cards to both sets of relatives).

We have been discussing the negative consequences of being socialized as a female. There are also advantages, which include living longer, having closer bonds with one's children, and having a stronger focus on relationships.

Longer Life Women live longer than men. Women have not always enjoyed the longevity advantage. "Data for Europe indicate that from the Paleolithic through the Middle Ages, women generally had higher mortality than men and only in more recent times has it become common for men to have higher mortality than women" (Waldron, 1990, p. 54). Perhaps one contributor to this change is decreased mortality related to pregnancy and childbirth.

In explaining why women currently live longer than men, social rather than biological factors are more dominant. In industrial societies, women are less often encouraged than men to smoke cigarettes and to drink heavily. The result is that women die less frequently from lung cancer and alcoholism than men. Women are also less likely to work in hazardous occupations. (We will explore this latter notion when we discuss the consequences of male socialization).

Women also are more involved in a network of relationships than men. These relationships are with their parents and same-sex peers. The effect of such relationships on health and mortality is that they provide a sense of meaning and facilitate health-promoting behaviors, such as proper sleep, diet, and exercise and adherence to medical regimens (House, Landis, & Umberson, 1990).

Closer Bond with Children Women tend to be more emotionally bonded with their children. Although the new cultural image of the father is one who engages emotionally with his children, most fathers continue to be content for their wives to take care of their children, with the result that mothers, not fathers, become more bonded with their children. The mother-child bond is particularly strong in African-American, Asian-American, and Hispanic families (Mindel, Habenstein, & Wright, 1988).

I've never been particularly ambitious. I'd like to do good work, but I love to be with my family. They're my first priority.
Susan Sarandon

Stronger Relationship Focus Williams and Best (1990b) collected data from university students in 28 countries (including England, Australia, Nigeria, Japan, and Brazil) and observed that women were more likely to be associated with having certain relationship characteristics than men:

1. Succorance—soliciting sympathy, affection, or emotional support from others.
2. Nurturance—engaging in behavior that extends material or emotional benefits to others.
3. Affiliation—seeking and sustaining numerous personal relationships.

Other research supports the idea that women place more importance on relationships (Hammersla & Frease-McMahan, 1990), have more close friends (Jones, Bloys, & Wood, 1990), and are more cooperative than men (Garza & Borchert, 1990).

In contrast, men were viewed as being more dominant, autonomous, aggressive (Williams & Best, 1990b), and competitive (Garza & Borchert, 1990). These qualities are counter to relationship engagement with others.

CONSIDERATION: Close emotional relationships may provide enormous life satisfaction outcomes for both women and men. Personal interviews with 2,374 adults revealed that satisfaction with family life (rather than work life) is the most important determinant of overall life satisfaction (Carlson & Videka-Sherman, 1990).

Consequences of Traditional Male Socialization

Male role socialization in our society is associated with its own set of consequences. The women's movement has given widespread visibility to the restrictions imposed upon women by the traditional female role. However, there is a growing recognition that the traditional male gender role is also restrictive. Sociologist Edwin Schur stated that:

> There is no denying that the gender system controls men too. Unquestionably, men are limited and restricted through narrow definitions of "masculinity". . . . They too face negative sanctions when they violate gender prescriptions. There is little value in debating which sex suffers or loses more through this kind of control; it is apparent that both do. (1984, p. 12)

As women become more independent, they leave a lot of men struggling with confusion over how to define themselves.
Susan Faludi

In the following sections, we discuss some of the negative and positive consequences of being socialized as a male.

Identity Synonymous with Occupation Ask men who they are, and many will tell you what they do. Society tends to equate a man's identity with his occupational role. Work is the principle means by which men confirm their masculinity and success. African-American and Mexican American men, who are more likely to be unemployed than white men, suffer more emasculation because

Men typically devote more time to their careers than their family and derive their primary source of identity from their work.

of the connection between identity and occupation (Kessler & Neighbors, 1986; Alvarez, 1985).

Our society not only expects men to have a job but also equates masculinity with the income a man generates. In a study of 601 adult men, those who reported feeling "more masculine" than other men earned an average of $35,800. In contrast, men who felt "less masculine" than other men earned an average of $28,300 annually (Rubenstein, 1990).

By the time a man is thirty-five he knows that the images of the right man, the tough man, the true man which he received in high school do not work in life. Such a man is open to new visions of what a man is or could be.

Robert Bly

Expression of Emotions Is Limited When compared to women, men cry less and are less able to express their feelings of depression, anger, fear, and sadness (Snell, Belk, & Hawkins, 1986; Blier & Blier-Wilson, 1989). Men also tend to be less tolerant of or interested in the emotional expression of others. One study found that male English teachers are also less tolerant of emotional writing than female English teachers (Barnes, 1990). Based on the questionnaire responses of over 3,000 women, Hite (1987) found that 76% of women said that the men in their relationships rarely try to draw them out or get them to speak about their thoughts and feelings; 41% said that men sometimes tell them or imply to them that they should not feel what they are feeling or should not express it; 55% reported that men often negate or make fun of the feelings women express.

Shorter Life Men die about seven years earlier than women. Black men are the most vulnerable in that they die about 14 years earlier than white women (*Statistical Abstract of the United States: 1990,* Table 103). Although biological factors may play a role in greater longevity for women than men, traditional gender roles have a significant influence (Harrison, Chin & Ficarrotto, 1992; Strickland, 1988). For example, the traditional male role emphasizes achievement, competition, and suppression of feelings, all of which may produce stress. Not only is stress itself harmful to physical health, it also may lead to compensatory behaviors, such as smoking, alcohol and drug abuse, and dangerous risk taking. In addition, the occupational segregation of the sexes is such that men's jobs tend to be more hazardous than women's jobs (Waldron, 1990, p. 52). For example, men are more likely to be miners than women, and this occupation has the highest rate of mortality.

The degree to which men are socialized to be violent and aggressive is another factor in their shorter life span. For example, in 1989, homocide was the leading cause of death of black males between the ages of 15 and 24. Luckenbill and Doyle (1989) suggested that the high rate of homocide among young, lower-income males is related to the culturally transmitted willingness to settle disputes, especially those perceived as a threat to their masculinity, by using physical force. The poorer health and shorter life span of minority men compared to white men may also be explained by the stress experienced by minority men that results from prejudice, discrimination, and poverty. The frustration and anger that may result from the social and economic disadvantages of minority status may lead to hazardous compensatory behaviors, such as those described in the previous paragraph. In addition, minority men are less likely than white men to have access to adequate health care (Parham & McDavis, 1987).

In sum, the traditional male gender role is hazardous to men's physical health. However, as women have begun to experience many of the same stresses and behaviors as men, their susceptibility to stress-related diseases has increased (Rodin & Ickovics, 1990). For example, since the 1950s, male smoking has declined, while female smoking has increased, resulting in an increased incidence of lung cancer in women.

Early male socialization to be competitive and aggressive may be related to dying earlier than women.

Benefits of Traditional Male Socialization Compared to women, men tend to have a more positive self-concept, have greater confidence in themselves, and enjoy higher incomes and occupational status than women. They also experience less discrimination and sexual harassment than women.

CONSIDERATION: Today's modern heterosexual woman (according to 600 adult women) expects her male partner to be caring and nurturing, open with his thoughts and feelings, and gentle. He is also expected to be ambitious and to help out around the house (Rubenstein, 1990, p. 161). In another study, women described the romantic partner they were looking for as "kind, considerate and honest with a keen sense of humor" (Goodwin, 1990, p. 501).

However, there is a considerable gap between the type of men that heterosexual women want and the type of men available. In interviews with 300 men, Astrachan (1986) concluded in his book *How Men Feel* that no more than 5% to 10% of U.S. men fit the media's description of the enlightened "new age men" that today's modern woman is looking for. Even in the work environment, men are likely to treat male co-workers more favorably than female co-workers (Palmer & Lee, 1990). If the goal is a generation of "new age men," what is needed may be a generation of "new age women" who would rather do without men than be involved with those who treat them as less than equals.

We have been discussing the respective ways in which women and men are socialized in our society. Exhibt 8.3 summarizes 12 implications that traditional gender role socialization has for sexual choices.

Inequality distorts the character and vision of both the oppressors and the oppressed.
Susan Basow

There is a growing recognition that traditional gender stereotypes are restrictive and oppressive to both women and men. The women's movement and the men's movement have contributed to the development of new conceptions of gender roles. Yet, reconstructing gender can only be achieved through massive changes in society.

EXHIBIT 8.3 12 Ways Gender Role Socialization Affects Sexual Choices

Women

1. A woman who is not socialized to pursue advanced education may feel pressure to stay in an unhappy sexual relationship with someone on whom she is economically dependent.
2. Women who are socialized to play a passive role and not initiate relationships are limiting interactions that could develop into valued relationships (sexual and otherwise).
3. Women who are socialized to accept that they are less valuable and important than men are less likely to seek or achieve equalitarian relationships with men.
4. Women who internalize society's standards of beauty and view their worth in terms of their youth and beauty are likely to feel bad about themselves as they age. Their negative self-concept, more than their age, may interfere with their sexual self-concept and relationships.
5. Women who are socialized to accept that they are solely responsible for taking care of their parents, children, and husband are likely to experience role overload. Potentially, this could result in feelings of resentment in their relationships.
6. Women who are socialized to emphasize the importance of relationships in their lives will continue to seek sexual relationships that are emotionally satisfying.

Men

1. Men who are socialized to define themselves in terms of their occupational success and income and less in terms of positive individual qualities (e.g., principled, relationship-focused) leave their self-esteem and masculinity vulnerable should they become unemployed or work in a low-status job.
2. Men who are socialized to restrict their experience and expression of emotions are denied the opportunity to discover the rewards of emotional interpersonal sharing.
3. Men who are socialized to believe that it is not their role to participate in domestic activities (child rearing, food preparation, housecleaning) will not develop competencies in these life skills. Domestic skills are often viewed as desirable qualities by potential partners.
4. Heterosexual men who focus on cultural definitions of female beauty overlook potential partners that might not fit the cultural beauty ideal but who would nevertheless be a good sexual and emotional life companion.
5. Men who are socialized to view women who initiate relationships negatively are restricted in their relationship opportunities.
6. Men who are socialized to be in control of the rhythm and content of sexual encounters may alienate their partners, who may desire equal control in sexual encounters.

Basow (1992) expressed support and optimism for the movement toward changing traditional conceptions of gender:

> Eliminating gender stereotypes and redefining gender in terms of equality does not mean simply liberating women, but liberating men and our society as well. What we have been talking about is allowing people to be more fully human and creating a society that will reflect that humanity. Surely that is a goal worth striving for. (p. 359)

Beyond Gender Roles: Androgyny and Gender Role Transcendence

Imagine a society in which women and men each develop characteristics, life-styles, and values that are independent of gender role stereotypes. Characteristics such as "strong, independent, logical, and aggressive" are no longer associated with "maleness," just as "passive, dependent, emotional, intuitive, and nurturant" are no longer associated with "femaleness." Both sexes are considered equal, and women and men may pursue the same occupational, political, and domestic roles.

The women's movement (or feminist movement) and the men's movement have given increased visibility to the oppressiveness of gender roles in the lives of both men and women. These movements have begun to envision and work toward creating a society that goes beyond gender roles, in the sense of becoming less sex-typed and more egalitarian. Some gender scholars have suggested that persons in such a society would be neither feminine nor masculine but would be described as *androgynous* or a blend of feminine and masculine. Next, we discuss androgyny and the related concept of gender role transcendence.

Androgyny

Prior to the 1970s, feminine and masculine traits were viewed as opposite of each other. However, Sandra Bem (1974; 1975; 1976) found that, on measures of "feminine" and "masculine" traits, individuals could score high on both stereotypically feminine (nurturant-expressive traits) and stereotypically masculine (active-instrumental traits). Bem used the term *androgynous* to describe those individuals who scored high on both active-instrumental traits (such as assertiveness, self-reliance, and independence) and nurturant-expressive traits (such as passivity, compassion, and affection).

Androgyny, then, refers to a blend of traits that are stereotypically associated with masculinity and femininity. Androgyny also implies flexibility of traits; for example, an androgynous individual may be emotional in one situation, logical in another, assertive in another, and so forth.

> Thus, each androgynous individual has the opportunity to develop his or her potential to its fullest, without the restriction that only gender-appropriate behaviors are allowed. (Basow, 1992, p. 326)

Bem devised a fourfold classification system based on individuals' scores on nurturant-expressive and active-instrumental traits. According to Bem's classification system, individuals were either feminine sex-typed, masculine sex-typed, androgynous, or undifferentiated (see Figure 8.2).

According to Figure 8.2, about 40% of college students are traditionally sex-typed in that they describe themselves as having traits that are more characteristic of their sex than of the other sex. About 25% of college students (more women than men) are classified as androgynous. About 23% are undifferentiated (low scores in both sets of traits), and about 12% are classified as cross-sex typed, that is, they describe

As people become more androgynous, occupational roles of men and women blur.

FIGURE 8.2 Bem's Classification System of Sex Typing

Source: Adapted from Bem, S.L. (1981). *Bem Sex-Role Inventory, professional manual.* Palo Alto, CA: Consulting Psychologists Press. Used by permission.

		Masculinity (instrumental-active traits) LOW	Masculinity (instrumental-active traits) HIGH
Femininity (nurturant-expressive traits)	LOW	Undifferentiated 18% females 27% males	Masculine 12% females 42% males
	HIGH	Feminine 39% females 12% males	Androgynous 30% females 20% males

themselves as possessing traits viewed as more characteristic of the other sex than of their own.

The percentages of individuals who could be categorized as androgynous varies as a function of the specific population being studied and the measuring instrument and scoring procedure used. One study of young adult women found that, as measured by the Personal Attributes Questionnaire, black women scored higher in traditional masculine traits than white women (Binion, 1990). About 36% of black women were androgynous, compared to 16% of white women. White women were more likely to be undifferentiated (38%), compared to black women (29%).

CONSIDERATION: While the majority of black women in Binion's (1990) study reported androgynous sexual traits, they also had traditional beliefs about the female role in the family. Research by King and King (1990) also found no or very low associations between self-report measures of gender role attitudes and gender role traits. This suggests that egalitarian attitudes and androgyny are not associated.

In another study, of 145 women in their 30s (both white and black) who completed the Bem Sex-Role Inventory (short form), 28% were androgynous, 31% masculine, 19% feminine, and 22% undifferentiated (Rosenzweig & Dailey, 1991). Hyde, Krajnik, and Skuldt-Niederberger (1991) studied androgyny across the life span using the Bem Sex-Role Inventory and found that both men and women may score higher on nurturant-expressive traits (viewed as feminine traits) as they age.

While some studies have found that androgyny is associated with high self-esteem, social competence, flexibility, and fewer psychological problems, others have found androgyny to be associated with increased work stress, difficulty in directing behavior effectively, and less overall emotional adjustment (Harrison & Pennell, 1989). In Exhibit 8.4, we describe research that suggests that androgynous persons may experience greater satisfaction in their sexual relationships.

While androgyny may be viewed as an alternative to traditional gender roles, gender scholars have noted several problems concerning the concept of androgyny. One concerns the observation that, although androgyny implies equivalence in value of feminine and masculine traits, high scores on active-instrumental traits (which are characteristic of both androgynous and masculine sex-typed individuals) have been shown to be related to high self-esteem, creativity, and psychological adjustment.

EXHIBIT 8.4 Androgyny and Sexual Relationships

To what degree are androgynous characteristics associated with being satisfied in sexual relationships? Rosenzweig and Dailey (1989) asked a stratified random sample of 151 women and 148 men (all in a long-term relationship of about 14 years) to rate on a seven-point scale (Bem Sex-Role Inventory, Short Form) (seven = "most like me") the degree to which 30 characteristics (e.g., gentle, aggressive, sensitive, dominant) described their behavior in a recent typical sexual experience with their partner. Subjects who gave themselves high ratings on such characteristics as "aggressiveness," "dominance," and "forcefulness" were labeled by the researchers as "masculine." Those who rated themselves highly on such characteristics as "gentleness," "tenderness," and "warmth" were labeled as "feminine." Subjects scoring high on both masculine and feminine terms were labeled "androgynous," and those with both low masculine and low feminine scores were labeled "undifferentiated." Of 148 men, 53% were judged as "feminine" during lovemaking and 28% as "androgynous." Twelve percent were rated by the researchers as "undifferentiated" and 9% as "masculine" (Rosenzweig & Dailey, 1989).

These ratings were compared with the degree to which the respondents reported having a high-quality sexual relationship and happiness in their current relationship. Men who were classified as "androgynous" regarded themselves as the most sexually satisfied in their relationships. Androgynous lovemaking behaviors may translate into consideration (brushing teeth and showering before lovemaking), gentleness (whispering soft words of love and slowly carressing his partner all over), and vulnerability (asking how he can please his partner and expressing willingness to follow directives). The result was satisfaction for both self and partner.

Alternatively, those men who were rated as "masculine" in bed reported having the worst sexual relationships. Masculine lovemaking behaviors may translate into controlling each sexual encounter, taking the point of view that the man knows what his partner wants and doesn't need to ask, and regarding sex as a performance where orgasm is the primary goal.

Of 151 women, 44% were rated as "feminine" and 19% were rated as "androgynous" (Rosenzweig & Dailey, 1989). The most satisfied of the 151 women were those who viewed their lovemaking behaviors as both "feminine" and "androgynous." Feminine characteristics include being sexy, exciting, and pleasuring her partner. Androgynous characteristics include initiating sex, assuming the female-superior position, and controlling the rhythm and content of lovemaking.

Men might consider consciously choosing to engage in those behaviors in lovemaking that reflect consideration, gentleness, and vulnerability, while women might consider becoming more aggressive in terms of initiating and controlling sexual encounters. The outcome, as suggested by the Rosenzweig and Dailey (1989) research, may be increased satisfaction for both partners.

Thus, the androgynous "ideal" may really reflect more traditional masculine traits than feminine traits (Hare-Mustin & Marecek, 1988; Morawski, 1987).

I'm very in touch with my feminine side . . . Women don't always want to be manhandled. A lot of times they want to be made love to by a man who can do it softly, like a woman.

Luke Perry

Another major problem with the concept of androgyny is that "androgyny has come to be seen as a combination of the traits of the two sexes rather than as a transcendence of gender categorization itself" (Unger, 1990, p. 112).

> The androgyny model continues to acknowledge and even depend on the conventional concepts of femininity and masculinity. Thus, in spite of its emancipatory promise, the model retains the classic dualism and, hence, the assumption of some real gender difference. (Morawski, 1990, p. 154)

In other words, while androgyny represents a broadening of gender role norms, it still implies two differing sets of gender-related characteristics (i.e., masculine equals active-instrumental; feminine equals expressive-nurturant). One solution to this problem is to simply describe characteristics such as active-instrumental and expressive-nurturant without labeling these traits as "masculine" or "feminine." Another solution is to go beyond the concept of androgyny and focus on gender role transcendence.

Gender Role Transcendence

Earlier in this chapter, we discussed Bem's gender schema theory, which suggests that we develop cognitive schemata that impose a gender-based classification system on the world. Thus, we associate many aspects of our world, including colors, foods, social and occupational roles, and personality traits, with either masculinity or femininity. The concept of **gender role transcendence** involves abandoning gender schema (i.e., becoming "gender aschematic," Bem, 1983), so that personality traits, social and occupational roles, and other aspects of our life become divorced from gender categories.

Androgynous traits may develop from social learning experiences.

One way to transcend gender roles (or become gender aschematic) is to be reared that way, since gender schema develops at an early age. For example, parents can foster nonsex-typed functioning in their children by encouraging emotional expression and independence in both boys and girls. Parents can also deemphasize the importance of gender in children's lives with respect to choosing clothes, toys, colors, and activities.

Eccles (1987) suggested a five-stage development process in achieving gender role transcendence:

Stage 1. Young children, who have not yet learned to differentiate between male and female are gender aschematic.

Stage 2. At ages three to seven, children develop a conception of gender roles in which males and females are seen as distinct and opposite.

Stage 3. At ages seven through 11, gender is viewed as a stable aspect of individuals, though gender is less polarized than in stage 2.

Stage 4. Gender concepts undergo transition. In early adolescence (ages 12 through 14), gender stereotypes are rigid and adolescents feel pressure to conform to such stereotypes. In middle adolescence (ages 15 through 18), adolescents can transcend rigid gender roles if they are exposed to androgynous role models and a relatively egalitarian social environment.

Stage 5. Individuals are able to functionally separate their personal identity from their biological sex. In this stage of gender role transcendence, individual's characteristics and behaviors are not linked to concern for what is gender-appropriate. Rather than view themselves as androgynous (a combination of feminine and masculine traits), individuals who transcend gender role categories do not label traits or behaviors as either "masculine" or "feminine."

The first act of freedom is the willingness to see how we have been enslaved. The system binds us only in the degree that we choose to remain unconscious.

Sam Keen

While many individuals may move toward gender role transcendence as they reach and pass middle age, few individuals reach this stage. As long as gender stereotypes and gender inequalities are ingrained in our social and cultural ideologies and institutions, gender role transcendence will remain an unrealized ideal.

CHOICES

The result of our society becoming less rigid in its gender role expectations for women and men is a new array of choices in gender role behavior. Such choices are becoming increasingly apparent in initiating relationships, seeking egalitarian relationships, and pursuing nontraditional occupational roles.

Choose New Relationships: Women Asking Men?

Traditionally, men have been socialized to be assertive and women to be passive in initiating new relationships. Some women decide that traditional female passivity in regard to initiating relationships is a disadvantage and choose to become more assertive. One woman said:

> I was taught never to call men or to initiate anything with men. 'A real lady,' my mom said, 'waits till the man makes his move.' But I've learned that some men are too shy to risk speaking and if the woman doesn't, nothing happens. I also know that some of my female friends think nothing of calling up a guy to go out with him, and these are the women that end up with the guys.

Heterosexual women may be concerned about what men think about women who initiate relationships. The following are examples of what men in the authors' classes said when they were asked, "How would you feel about a woman asking you to a movie if you had never been with her to an event before?"

> I'd love it. It makes me feel wanted, and I like for a woman to be aggressive.

> I prefer that the woman ask me out. I get tired of having to be the aggressor all the time.

> I'm the traditional type. I'll do the asking.

> Three girls called me up for date last year. I went out with two of them and had a terrific time. I'm now engaged to one of them.

Women who have questioned their socialization and asked men out often feel very good about their choice.

> The boyfriend I have now I asked out over a year ago (he's shy). Things have been going great ever since. He told me about a month ago that if I had never asked him out, he would never have asked me out first because he thought I wasn't interested. I'm glad I let him know that I was.

> I don't have much of a problem asking a guy out. Of course, I wait a little in hopes that he will ask me out first. But if he doesn't, I figure he needs a little push in the right direction—my direction.

Men might also evaluate the consequences of behaving in traditional gender roles and consider allowing women to be assertive without regarding their initiation of interaction in negative ways. By doing so, they increase the chance of more frequent encounters (because women will be reinforced for assertiveness). As noted above, men often express positive feelings about women who initiate interaction.

Choose to Seek Egalitarian Relationships?

Egalitarian relationships are those in which the partners have mutual respect for each other, share the power, and share the work of the relationship. Mutual respect translates into each acknowledging the credibility of the others' thoughts, feelings, and perspectives. Relationships with mutual respect are those in which the power is also shared. Neither partner is dominant but discusses the options and collaborates on a mutual decision with the other.

Partners in egalitarian relationships also share the work of their relationship. Either may cook, clean the house, and return books to the library. For pair-bonded couples, egalitarian relationships provide an opportunity for empathy unknown in traditional relationships. When only the man was employed outside the home and the woman stayed home to take care of the house and children, each partner had a set of experiences that was unknown to the other partner. He might be tired at the end of the day from working at the office; she might be tired from cleaning the house, preparing the food, and taking care of young children. Each was sure that he or she was more tired than the other and regarded his or her own role as the most difficult and the partner's role as "nothing to complain about." Alternatively, when couples decide to share the income getting, food preparation, housecleaning, and child care, each has an experiential understanding of what the other feels.

Research findings suggest that being in a relationship of mutual respect, power, and work sharing is associated with high relationship satisfaction. In one study, of the wives who reported that they had "excellent marriages," 88% reported that they shared the decision making equally with their husbands (Schwartz & Jackson, 1989, p. 72). In another study based on 349 college students, those involved in equitable dating relationships reported more contentment

Continued

Continued

and commitment than those in inequitable dating relationships (Winn, Crawford, & Fischer, 1991).

Choose to Pursue Nontraditional Occupational Roles?

The general trend toward gender role flexibility has implications for occupational role choices. Jobs traditionally occupied by one gender are now open to the other. Men may become nurses and librarians, and women may become construction workers and lawyers. Since the 1960s, occupations have become slightly less segregated on the basis of gender and social acceptance of nontraditional career choices has increased slightly, especially among younger cohorts (Raymond, 1989; Reskin & Roos, 1990).

Choosing nontraditional occupational roles may have benefits for both the individual and for society. On the individual level, women and men can make career choices on the basis of their personal talents and interests, rather than on the basis of arbitrary social restrictions regarding who can and cannot have a particular job or career. Because traditionally male occupations are generally higher paying than traditionally female occupations, women who make nontraditional career choices can gain access to higher-paying and higher-status jobs.

It may be important to note that critical choice points in terms of career possibilities may occur before and during high school. Lubinski and Benbow (1992, p. 65) confirmed that the "number of high school math and science courses is related to entering the math-science pipeline, regardless of gender, and females enroll in fewer math and science courses in high school than males." College course choices are affected by preferences as well as abilities. At Iowa State University, Lubinski and Benbow found that college women enrolled in programs for gifted students were equally divided between courses in math and science and those in English and foreign language. Gifted college men, on the other hand, were "approximately six times more likely to enroll in math and science areas than in English and foreign language" (p. 65).

On the societal level, an increase in nontraditional career choices reduces gender-based occupational segregation, thereby contributing to social equality among women and men. In addition, women and men who enter nontraditional occupations may contribute greatly to the field that they enter. For example, such traditionally male-dominated occupations as politics, science and technology, and medicine have suffered from the relative lack of input from women. Similarly, public school teaching, which is a female-dominated occupation, has provided few male role models for children in school.

Summary

1. Unlike sex, a biological term, gender refers to the social and psychological characteristics associated with being female and male. Both sex and gender may be viewed as existing on a continuum.
2. Gender influences sexual behavior—compared to men, women masturbate less, are more likely to prefer sex in the context of an emotional relationship, are more likely to have fewer sexual partners, and are more likely to be victims of sexual abuse.
3. Determinants of biological sex include chromosomes, hormones, gonads, internal sex organs, and external sex organs.
4. Various hormonal and chromosomal abnormalities may result in atypical sexual development of the fetus.
5. The gender identity of the transsexual is in conflict with his or her biological sex. Attempts to reconcile the discrepant aspects of self may include psychotherapy, hormone therapy, and sex reassignment surgery.
6. Various theories attempt to explain how female and male gender roles develop. These include sociobiological theory, identification theory, social learning theory, cognitive–developmental theory, and gender schema theory. Parents, peers, teachers and educational curricula and materials, religion, and media influence gender role socialization.

7. Both men and women are restricted and limited by traditional gender roles and narrow definitions of masculinity and femininity. Androgyny and gender role transendence are two concepts that attempt to create an alternative to a restrictive gender system. However, androgyny still implies that "masculine" and "feminine" involve different characteristics and gender role transcendence may be an unrealizable ideal.

KEY TERMS

sex
gender
gender identity
gender roles
sex roles
sexual identity
gender role ideology
zygote
chromosomes
hormones
Klinefelter's syndrome
Turner's syndrome
hermaphroditism
pseudohermaphroditism
androgenital syndrome
female pseudohermaphrodites
androgen-insensitivity syndrome
male pseudohermaphrodites
intersexed infants
Oedipal complex
testicular feminization syndrome
Electra complex
alpha bias
beta bias
sexism
gender dysphoria
transsexuals
transvestites
androgyny
gender role transcendence
gender schema

REFERENCES

Achtemeier, E. (1991, March). A critique of the report of the special committee on human sexuality. *News: A Publication of Presbyterians for Renewal,* pp. 1–12.

Adams, C. J. (1990). *The sexual politics of meat: A feminist-vegetarian critical theory.* New York: Continuum.

Alvarez, R. (1985). The psycho-historical and socioeconomic development of the Chicano community in the United States. In R. O. DeLaGarga, F. D. Bean, C. M. Bonjean, R. Romo, and R. Alvarez (Eds.), *The Mexican-American experience* (pp. 32–56). Austin: University of Texas Press.

American Association of University Women. (1991). *Shortchanging girls, shortchanging America.* Washington, DC: Greenberg-Lake Analysis Group.

American Psychiatric Association. (1987). *Diagnostic and Statistical Manual of Mental Disorders* (3rd Ed., Revised). Washington, DC: American Psyciatric Association.

Antill, J. K. (1987). Parents' beliefs and values about sex roles, sex differences, and sexuality: Their sources and implications. In P. Shaver and C. Hendrick (Eds.), *Sex and gender.* (pp. 294–328). Newbury Park, CA: Sage.

Arnold, A. P. (1980, March–April). Sexual differences in the brain. *American Scientist,* pp. 165–173.

Astrachan, A. (1986). *How men feel.* New York: Anchor Press.

Atkin, D. J., Moorman, J., & Lin, C. A. (1991). Ready for prime time: Network series devoted to working women in the 1980s. *Sex Roles, 25,* 677–685.

Bancroft, J. (1984). Hormones and sexual human behavior. *Journal of Sex and Marital Therapy, 10,* 3–27.

Bancroft, J. (1989). *Human sexuality and its problems,* 2nd edition. New York: Churchill Livingstone.

Barnes, L. L. (1990). Gender bias in teachers' written comments. In S. L. Gabriel and I. Smithson, (Eds.), *Gender in the classroom: Power and pedagogy* (pp. 140–154). Chicago: University of Illinois Press.

Basow, S. A. (1992). *Gender: Stereotypes and roles* (3rd ed.). Pacific Grove, CA: Brooks/Cole.

Beck, J. G., Bozman, A. W., & Qualtrough, T. (1991). The experience of sexual desire: Psychological correlates in a college sample. *Journal of Sex Research, 28,* 443–457.

Bem, S. L. (1974). The measurement of psychological androgyny. *Journal of Consulting and Clinical Psychology, 42,* 155–162.

Bem, S. L. (1975). Sex role adaptability: One consequence of psychological androgyny. *Journal of Personality and Social Psychology, 31,* 634–643.

Bem, S. L. (1976). Probing the promise of androgyny. In A. G. Kaplan and J. P. Bean (Eds.), *Beyond sex role stereotypes: Readings toward a psychology of androgyny* (pp. 48–63). Boston: Little, Brown.

Bem, S. L. (1983). Gender schema theory and its implications for child development: Raising gender-aschematic children in a gender schematic society. *Signs, 8,* 596–616.

Bretschneider, J. G., & McCoy, N. L. (1988). Sexual interest and behavior in healthy 80- to 102-year-olds. *Archives of Sexual Behavior, 17,* 109–129.

Binion, V. J. (1990). Psychological androgyny: A black female perspective. *Sex Roles, 22,* 487–507.

Bird, C. E., Fremont, A. M. (1991). Gender, time use, and health. *Journal of Health and Social Behavior, 32,* 114–129.

Blau, F. D., & Ferber, M. A. (1986). *The economics of women, men, and work.* Englewood Cliffs, NJ: Prentice-Hall.

Blier, M. J., & Blier-Wilson, L. A. (1989). Gender differences in self-rated emotional expressiveness. *Sex Roles, 21,* 287–295.

Bly, R. (1990). *Iron John.* Reading, MA: Addison-Wesley.

Brigman, B., & Knox, D. (1992, in press). University students' motivations toward intercourse. *College Student Journal.*

Burns, A., & Homel, R. (1989). Gender division of tasks by parents and their children. *Psychology of Women Quarterly, 13,* 113–125.

Buss, D. M. (1989). Sex differences in human mate preferences: Evolutionary hypotheses tested in 37 cultures. *Behavioral and Brain Sciences, 12,* 1–13.

Carlson, B. E., & Videka-Sherman, L. (1990). An empirical test of androgyny in the middle years: Evidence from a national survey. *Sex Roles, 23,* 305–324.

Carter, B. (1991, May 1). Children's TV, where boys are king. *New York Times,* pp. A1, C18.

Chafetz, J. S. (1988). *Feminist Sociology: An overview of contemporary theories.* Itasca, Illinois: F. E. Peacock Publishers.

Chodorow, N. (1978). *The reproduction of mothering.* Berkeley: University of California Press.

Cleaver, G. (1987). Marriage enrichment by means of a structured communication program. *Family Relations, 36,* 49–54.

Cohn, L. D. (1991). Sex differences in the course of personality development: A meta-analysis. *Psychological Bulletin, 109,* 252–266.

Crawford, M., & MacLeod, M. (1990). Gender in the college classroom: An assessment of the 'chilly climate' for women. *Sex Roles, 23,* 101–122.

Davis, D. M. (1990). Portrayals of women in prime-time network television: Some demographic characteristics. *Sex Roles, 23,* 325–332.

Davis, S. (1990). Men as success objects and women as sex objects: A study of personal advertisements. *Sex Roles, 23,* 43–50.

Eagly, A. H. (1987). *Sex differences in social behavior: A social-role interpretation.* Hillsdale, NJ: Erlbaum.

Eccles, J. S. (1987). Adolescence: Gateway to gender-role transcendence. In B. Carter (Ed.), *Current conceptions of sex roles and sex typing: Theory and research* (pp. 225–241). New York: Praeger.

Ellis, B. J., & Symons, D. (1990). Sex differences in sexual fantasy: An evolutionary psychological approach. *Journal of Sex Research, 27,* 527–556.

Etaugh, C., & Duits, T. (1990). Development of gender discrimination: Role of stereotypic and counterstereotypic gender cues. *Sex Roles, 23,* 215–222.

Fagot, B. I. (1984). Teacher and peer reactions to boys' and girls' play styles. *Sex Roles, 11,* 691–702.

Ferree, M. M., & Hall, E. J. (1990). Visual images of American society: Gender and race in introductory sociology textbooks. *Gender and Society, 4,* 500–533.

Freimuth, M., & Hornstein, G. (1982). A critical examination of the concept of gender. *Sex Roles, 8,* 515–532.

Freud, S. (1965). *New introductory lectures in psychoanalysis* (J. Strachey, Ed. and Trans.). New York: W. W. Norton. (Original work published in 1933).

Freud, S. (1974). Some psychological consequences of an anatomical distinction between the sexes. In J. Strouse, (Ed.), *Women and analysis.* New York: Grossman. (Original work published in 1925).

Furnham, A., Hester, C., & Weir, C. (1990). Sex differences in the preferences for specific female body shapes. *Sex Roles, 22,* 743–754.

Garza, R. T., & Borchert, J. E. (1990). Maintaining social identity in a mixed-gender setting: Minority/majority status and cooperative/competitive feedback. *Sex Roles, 22,* 679–691.

Gilligan, C. (1982). *In a different voice.* Cambridge: Harvard University Press.

Goodnow, J. J. (1988). Children's household work: Its nature and functions. *Psychological Bulletin, 103,* 5–26.

Goodwin, R. (1990). Sex differences among partner preferences: Are the sexes really very similar? *Sex Roles, 23,* 501–514.

Gooren, L. (1991). Body politics: The physical side of gender identity. *Journal of Psychology and Human Sexuality, 4,* 9–17.

Goy, R. W., & McEwen, B. S. (1980). *Sexual differentiation of the brain.* Cambridge: MIT Press.

Grammer, K. (1989). Human courtship behavior: Biological basis and cognitive processes. In A. E. Rasa, C. Vogel, and E. Voland (Eds.), *Sociobiology of sexual and reproductive strategies* (pp. 147–169). London: Chapman and Hall.

Hammersla, J. F., & Frease-McMahan, L. (1990). University students' priorities: Life goals vs. relationships. *Sex Roles, 23,* 1–14.

Hare-Mustin, R. T., & Marecek, J. (1990). On making a difference. In R. T. Hare-Mustin and J. Marecek (Eds.), *Making a difference: Psychology and the construction of gender* (pp. 1–21). New Haven: Yale University Press.

Hare-Mustin, R. T., & Marecek, J. (1988). The meaning of difference: Gender theory, postmodernism, and psychology. *American Psychologist, 43,* 455–464.

Harrison, D. F., & Pennell, R. C. (1989). Contemporary sex roles for adolescents: New options or confusion? *Journal of Social Work and Human Sexuality, 8,* 27–45.

Harrison, J., Chin, J., & Ficarrotto, T. (1992) Warning: Masculinity may be dangerous to your health. In M. S. Kimmel & M. A. Messner (Eds.), *Men's Lives (2nd Ed.)* (pp. 271–285). New York. Macmillan.

Heimovics, R. D., & Herman, R. D. (1988). Gender and the attributes of chief executive responsibility for successful or unsuccessful organizational outcomes. *Sex Roles, 18,* 623–635.

Hendrick, S., Hendrick, C., Slapion-Foote, M. J., & Foote, F. H. (1985). Gender differences in sexual attitudes. *Journal of Personality and Social Psychology, 48,* 1630–1642.

Hilts, P. J. (1991, September 10), Women still lag behind in medicine. *New York Times,* p. C7.

Hite, S. (1987). *The Hite report: Women and love.* New York: Alfred Knopf.

Hopkins, A. (1991, June 24). Defining womyn (and others). *Time,* p. 51.

House, J. S., Landis, K. R., & Umberson, D. (1990). Social relationships and health. In P. Conrad and R. Kern (Eds.), *The sociology of health and illness: Critical perspectives* (3rd ed.) (pp. 85–94). New York: St. Martin's Press.

Houseworth, S., Peplow, K., & Thirer, J. (1989). Influence of sport participation upon sex role orientation of Caucasian males and their attitudes toward women. *Sex Roles, 20,* 317–325.

Hyde, J. S., Krajnik, M., & Skuldt-Niederberger, K. (1991). Androgyny across the life span: A replication and longitudinal followup. *Developmental Psychology, 27,* 516–519.

Jones, D. C., Bloys, N., & Wood, M. (1990). Sex roles and friendship patterns. *Sex Roles, 23,* 133–145.

Keen, S. (1991). *Fire in the belly: On being a man.* New York: Bantam Books.

Kessler, R. C., & Neighbors, H. W. (1986). A new perspective on the relationships among race, social class, and psychological distress. *Journal of Health and Social Behavior, 27,* 107–115.

Kessler, S. J. (1990). The medical construction of gender: Case management of intersexed infants. *Signs: Journal of Women in Culture and Society, 16,* 3–26.

Kiecolt, K. J., & Acock, A. C. (1988). The long-term effects of family structure on gender role attitudes. *Journal of Marriage and the Family, 50,* 709–717.

King, L. A., & King, D. W. (1990). Sex-role egalitarianism and androgyny: Discriminant evidence. *Psychological Reports, 67,* 1129–1130.

Knox, D., & Daniel, H. J., III. (1986). Gender differences in expressions of sexuality: A sociobiological interpretation. *International Journal of Sociology of the Family, 16,* 263–272.

Koberg, C. S. (1985). Sex and situational influences on the use of power: A follow-up study. *Sex Roles, 13,* 625–640.

Kohlberg, L. (1966). A cognitive-developmental analysis of children's sex-role concepts and attitudes. In E. E. Maccoby (Ed.), *The development of sex differences* (pp. 82–172). Stanford, CA: Stanford University Press.

Kohlberg, L. (1969). State and sequence: The cognitive-developmental approach to socialization. In D. A. Goslin (Ed.), *Handbook of socialization theory and research* (pp. 347–480). Chicago: Rand McNally.

Kohlberg, L. (1976). Moral stages and moralization: The cognitive-developmental approach. In T. Lickona (Ed.), *Moral development and behavior* (pp. 31–53). New York: Holt, Rinehart, and Winston.

Kupfersmid, J. (1988). Improving what is published: A model in search of an editor. *American Psychologist, 43,* 635–642.

Lackey, P. N. (1989). Adults' attitudes about assignments of household chores to male and female children. *Sex Roles, 20,* 271–281.

Leitenberg, H. (1983) Transsexuality: The epitome of sexism and homosexual denial. In G. Albee, S. Gordon & H. Leitenberg (Eds.). *Promoting Sexual Responsibility and Preventing Sexual Problems* (pp. 183–219). Hanover, NH: University Press of New England.

Levy, J. (1972). Lateral specialization of the human brain., behavioral manifestations and possible evolutionary basis. In J. A. Kiger (Ed.), *The biology of behavior.* Corvallis: Oregon State University Press.

Lindsey, L. L. (1990). *Gender roles: A sociological perspective.* Englewood Cliffs, NJ: Prentice-Hall.

Lont, C. M. (1990). The roles assigned to females and males in non-music radio programming. *Sex Roles, 22,* 661–668.

Lott, B. (1990). Dual natures or learned behavior: The challenge to feminist psychology. In R. T. Hare-Mustin and J. Marecek (Eds.), *Making a difference: Psychology and the construction of gender* (pp. 65–101). New Haven: Yale University Press.

Lubinski, D. & Benbow, C. P. (1992). Gender differences in abilities and preferences among the gifted: Implications for the math-science pipeline. *Current Directions in Psychological Science, 1,* (2), 61–66.

Luckenbill, D. F., & Doyle, D. P. (1989). Structural position and violence: Developing a cultural explanation. *Criminology, 27,* 419–433.

Maccoby, E. E., & Jacklin, C. N. (1974). *The psychology of sex differences.* Stanford, CA.: Stanford University Press.

Mandoki, M. W., Sumner, G. S., Hoffman, R. P., & Riconda, D. L. (1991). A review of Klinefelter's syndrome in children and adolescents. *Journal of the American Academy of Child and Adolescent Psychiatry, 30,* 167–172.

Martin, C. L. (1989). Children's use of gender-related information in making social judgments. *Developmental Psychology, 25,* 80–88.

Martin, C. L. (1990). Attitudes and expectations about children with nontraditional and traditional gender roles. *Sex Roles, 22,* 151–165.

McHale, S. M., Bartko, W. T., Crouter, A. C., & Perry-Jenkins, M. (1990). Children's housework and psychosocial functioning: The mediating effects of parents' sex-role behaviors and attitudes. *Child Development, 61,* 1413–1426.

McKinney, K. (1990). Gender, sex role, and contraceptive attitudes and behaviors. *Free Inquiry in Creative Sociology, 18,* 191–196.

Mindel, C. H., Habenstein, R. W., & Wright, R., Jr. (Eds.). (1988). *Ethnic families in America: patterns and variations* (3rd ed.). New York: Elsevier.

Mooney, L., & Brabant, S. (1987). Two martinis and a rested woman: 'Liberation' in the Sunday comics. *Sex Roles, 17,* 409–420.

Moore, K., Nord, C. W., & Peterson, J. (1989). Nonvoluntary sexual activity among adolescents. *Family Planning Perspectives, 21,* 110–114.

Moore, K., & Peterson, J. (1989). The consequences of teenage pregnancy: Final report. Washington, DC: Child Trends.

Morawski, J. G. (1987). The troubled quest for masculinity, femininity, and androgyny. In P. Shaver & C. Hendrick (Eds.), *Sex and gender* (pp. 44–69). Newbury Park, CA: Sage.

Morawski, J. G. (1990). Toward the unimagined: Feminism and epistemology in psychology. In R. T. Hare-Mustin & J. Marecek (Eds.), *Making a difference: Psychology and the construction of gender.* (pp. 150–183). New Haven: Yale University Press.

Morrow, F. (1991). *Unleashing our unknown selves: An inquiry into the future of femininity and masculinity.* New York: Praeger.

Oberlander, S. (1989, June 21). Advocates for women's sports say 1988 Civil Rights Act has not brought hoped-for equity with men. *Chronicle of Higher Education,* p. A23.

Ogletree, S. M., Williams, S. W., Raffeld, P., Mason, B., & Fricke, K. (1990). Female attractiveness and eating disorders: Do children's television commercials play a role? *Sex Roles, 22,* 791–797.

Oliver, S. J., & Toner, B. B. (1990). The influence of gender role typing on expression of depressive symptoms. *Sex Roles, 22,* 775–790.

Olson, J. E., Frieze, I. H., & Detlefsen, E. G. (1990). Having it all? Combining work and family in a male and a female profession. *Sex Roles, 23,* 515–534.

Orten, J. L. (1990). Coming up short: The physical, cognitive, and social effects of Turner's syndrome. *Health and Social Work, 15,* 100–106.

O'Sullivan, C. (1991). Acquaintance gang rape on campus. In A. Parrot & L. Bechhofer (Eds.) *Acquaintance Rape: The Hidden Crime* (pp. 140–156). New York: Wiley.

Palmer, H. T., & Lee, J. A. (1990). Female workers' acceptance in traditionally male-dominated blue-collar jobs. *Sex Roles, 22,* 607–626.

Parham, T. A. & McDavis, R. (1987). Black males and endangered species: Who's really pulling the trigger? *Journal of Counseling and Development, 66,* 24–27.

Pauly, I. B. (1990). Gender identity disorders: Evaluation and treatment. *Journal of Sex Education and Therapy, 16,* 2–24.

Peirce, K. (1990). A feminist theoretical perspective on the socialization of teenage girls through *Seventeen* magazine. *Sex Roles, 23,* 491–500.

Petersen, A. C. (1987, September). Those gangly years. *Psychology Today,* pp. 28–34.

Peterson, S. B., & Kroner, T. (1992). Gender biases in textbooks for introductory psychology and human development. *Psychology of Women Quarterly, 16,* 17–36.

Pomerleau, A., Bolduc, D., Malcuit, G., & Cossette, L. (1990). Pink or blue: Environmental stereotypes in the first two years of life. *Sex Roles, 22,* 359–367.

Porter, J. R., & Beuf, A. H. (1991). Racial variation in reaction to physical stigma: A study of degree of disturbance by vitiligo among black and white patients. *Journal of Health and Social Behavior, 32,* 101–113.

Purcell, P., & Stewart, L. (1990). Dick and Jane in 1989. *Sex Roles, 22,* 177–185.

Raymond, C. (1989, October 11). Shift of many traditionally male jobs to women. *Chronicle of Higher Education,* pp. A4, A6.

Reid, P. T., & Comas-Diaz, L. (1990). Gender and ethnicity: Perspectives on dual status. *Sex Roles, 22,* 397–408.

Reinisch, J., & Beasley, R. (1990). *The Kinsey Institute new report on sex.* New York: St. Martin's Press.

Reskin, B. F., & Roos, P. A. (1990). *Job queues, gender queues: Explaining women's inroads into male occupations.* Philadelphia: Temple University Press.

Rodin, J. & Ickovics, J. R. (1990). Women's health: Review and research agenda as we approach the 21st century. *American Psychologist, 45,* 1018–1034.

Rosenzweig, J. M., & Dailey, D. M. (1989). Dyadic adjustment/sexual satisfaction in women and men as a function of psychological sex role self-perception. *Journal of Sex and Marital Therapy, 15,* 42–56.

Rosenzweig, J. M., & Dailey, D. M. (1991). Women's sex roles in their public and private lives. *Journal of Sex Education and Therapy, 17,* 75–85.

Rossi, A. S. (1977). A biosocial perspective on parenting. *Daedalus,* 106, 1–31.

Rubenstein, C. (1990, October). A brave new world. *New Woman,* pp. 158–164.

Rubin, L. B. (1991). *Erotic wars: What happened to the sexual revolution?* New York: Harper Perennial.

Sadker, M., & Sadker, D. (1990). Confronting sexism in the college classroom. In S. L. Gabriel and I. Smithson (Eds.), *Gender in the classroom: Power and pedagogy* (pp. 176–187). Chicago: University of Illinois Press.

Sapiro, V. (1990). *Women in American society* (2nd ed.). Mountain View, CA: Mayfield.

Schur, E. (1984). *Labeling women deviant: Gender, stigma, and social control.* New York: Random House.

Schwartz, P., & Jackson, D. (1989, February). How to have a model marriage. *New Woman,* pp. 66–74.

Sherwin, B. B., Gelfand, M. M., & Brender, W. (1985). Androgen enhances sexual motivation in females: A prospective, crossover study of sex steroid administration in the surgical menopause. *Psychosomatic Medicine, 47,* 339–351.

Smith, T. W. (1991). Adult sexual behavior in 1989: Number of partners, frequency of intercourse and risk of AIDS. *Family Planning Perspectives, 23,* 102–107.

Snell, W. E., Jr., Belk, S. S., & Hawkins, R. C. (1986). The masculine and feminine self-disclosure scale: The politics of masculine and feminine self-presentation. *Sex Roles, 15,* 249–267.

Snodgrass, S. E. (1985). Women's intuition: The effect of subordinate role on interpersonal sensitivity. *Journal of Personality and Social Psychology, 49,* 146–155.

Spanier, G. B., & Margolis, R. L. (1983). Marital separation and extramarital sexual behavior. *Journal of Sex Research, 19,* 23–48.

Springer, S., & Deutsch, G. (1981). *Left brain, right brain.* San Francisco: W. H. Freeman.

Statham, A., Richardson, L., & Cook, J. A. (1991). *Gender and university teaching: A negotiated difference.* Albany: State University of New York Press.

Statistical abstract of the United States: 1992 (112th ed.). (1992). Washington, DC: U.S. Bureau of the Census.

Strickland, B. R. (1988). Sex-related differences in health and illness. *Psychology of Women Quarterly, 12,* 381–399.

Suppe, F. (1985). In defense of a multidimensional approach to sexual identity. *Journal of Homosexuality, 103,* 7–14.

Symons, D. (1987). An evolutionary approach: Can Darwin's view of life shed light on human sexuality? In J. H. Greer and W. T. O'Donohue (Eds.), *Theories of human sexuality* (pp. 91–125). New York: Plenum.

Symons, D., & Ellis, B. (1989). Human male-female differences in sexual desire. In A. E. Rasa, C. Vogel, and E. Voland (Eds.), *Sociobiology of sexual and reproductive strategies* (pp. 131–146). London: Chapman and Hall.

Tavris, C. (1992). *The mismeasure of woman.* New York: Simon & Schuster.

Tavris, C., & Wade, C. (1984). *The longest war: Sex differences in perspective* (2nd ed). San Diego: Harcourt Brace Jovanovich.

Timkom, C., Striegel-Moore, R. H., Silberstein, L. R., & Rodin, J. (1987). Femininity/masculinity and disordered eating in women: How are they related? *International Journal of Eating Disorders, 6,* 701–712.

Udry, R. J., Talbert, L. M., & Morris, N. M. (1986). Biosocial foundations for adolescent female sexuality. *Demography, 23,* 217–227.

Unger, R. K. (1990). Imperfect reflections of reality: Psychology constructs gender. In R. T. Hare-Mustin & J. Marecek (Eds.), *Making a difference: Psychology and the construction of gender* (pp. 102–149). New Haven: Yale University Press.

Wagner, D. G., Ford, R. S., & Ford, T. W. (1986). Can gender differences in equality be reduced? *American Sociological Review, 51,* 47–61.

Waldron, I. (1990). What do we know about the causes of sex differences in mortality? A review of the literature. In P. Conrad and R. Kern (Eds.), *The Sociology of health and illness: Critical perspectives* (3rd ed.) (pp. 45–57). New York: St. Martin's Press.

Walker, A. J., Kees Martin, Sally S., & Thomson, Linda. (1988). Feminist programs for families. *Family Relations, 37,* 17–22.

Wallston, B. S. and Grady, K. E. (1985). Integrating the feminist critique and the crisis in social psychology: Another look at research methods. In V. E. O'Leary, R. K. Unger, and B. S. Wallston (Eds.), *Women, gender and social psychology* (pp. 7–34). Hillsdale, NJ: Lawrence Erlbaum Associates.

Williams, J. E., & Best, D. L. (1990a). *Sex and psyche: Gender and self viewed cross-culturally.* London: Sage.

Williams, J. E., & Best, D. L. (1990b). *Measuring sex stereotypes: A multination study.* London: Sage.

Wilson, J. D., George, F. W., & Griffin, J. E. (1981). The hormonal control of sexual development. *Science, 211,* 1278–1284.

Winn, K. I., Crawford, D. W. & Fischer, J. L. (1991). Equity and commitment in romance versus friendship. *Journal of Social Behavior & Personality, 6,* 301–314.

CHAPTER NINE

Individual Sexuality

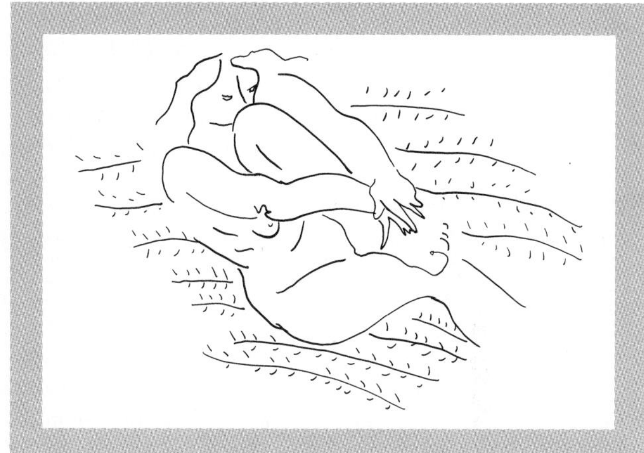

Chapter Outline

Intrapersonal Aspects of Sexuality
- Self-Concept and Sexual Self-Concept
- Body Image
- Sexual Guilt
- Erotophobia and Erotophilia
- **Self-Assessment:** Sexual Opinion Survey

Sexual Celibacy
- Voluntary Sexual Celibacy
- Involuntary Sexual Celibacy

Negative Attitudes Toward Masturbation: Historical Origins
- Religion and Masturbation
- Medicine and Masturbation
- **Historical Perspective:** Some Not-so-helpful "Advice" from "Experts" on Masturbation
- Traditional Psychotherapy and Masturbation
- Parents and Masturbation

Benefits of Masturbation

Social and Psychological Correlates of Masturbation
- Gender, Age, and Cohort
- Education and Religion
- Locus of Control

Techniques of Masturbation
- Female Masturbation Techniques
- Male Masturbation Techniques

Masturbation in Relationships
- Research on Masturbation among Spouses
- Effects of Masturbation on Relationships

Sexual Fantasies
- Functions of Sexual Fantasies
- Content of Sexual Fantasies
- Gender Differences in Sexual Fantasies

Choices
- Choose to Masturbate?
- Choose to Use a Vibrator?
- Choose to Masturbate with One's Partner?
- Choose to Share Sexual Fantasies with One's Partner?
- Choose to Use Masturbation Fantasies to Change Sexual Object Choice?

Is It True?*

1. Physicians, such as Samuel Tissot, have helped to encourage positive attitudes toward masturbation by suggesting that masturbation actually increases body strength and psychological well-being.

2. People whose locus of control is internal are more likely to masturbate than people whose locus of control is external.

3. The sexual fantasies of women (compared to the sexual fantasies of men) reflect a greater degree of emotional involvement in the partners about whom they fantasize.

4. Individuals with less education masturbate more frequently than individuals with a college education.

5. Men are more likely than women to report having fantasized about having sex with a number of partners.

* 1 = F, 2 = T, 3 = T, 4 = F, 5 = T

Masturbation—it's sex with someone I love.

Woody Allen

In one of his stand-up comedy routines Robin Williams mused, "In the '90s, its sex with you and you." His statement emphasizes the individuality of sexual choices in an age of HIV and other STD risks. Individuals not only decide whom to have sex with but also whether to be celibate, to masturbate, and to fantasize about sex. These and other individual choices are influenced by a number of intrapersonal variables, such as self-concept, body image, sexual self-concept, sex guilt, and the propensity to be erotophobic or erotophilic. We begin by exploring these intrapersonal variables.

Intrapersonal Aspects of Sexuality

Intrapersonal variables are those thoughts, feelings, and attitudes occurring inside the individual (as opposed to interpersonal variables, which happen between people). Intrapersonal variables include one's self-concept, body image, sexual self-concept, sex guilt, and the degree to which one is erotophobic or erotophilic.

Self-Concept and Sexual Self-Concept

Self-concept refers to the way individuals view their spiritual and emotional self, intellectual and academic abilities, social competence, and physical attractiveness. An individual who scored 1300 on the SAT, has numerous close friends of both sexes, and is frequently told that she or he is physically appealing will have an entirely different self-concept from one who made 400 on the SAT, failed to pass two grades, is a social isolate, and is laughed at because of a physical characteristic. The former may feel excited and overwhelmed with the number of partners who have expressed an interest in interacting with him or her. The latter may feel depressed and rejected. Franzoi and Shields (1984) suggested that a person's self-concept is related to the degree to which the individual feels physically and sexually attractive.

As noted in Chapter 1, related to self-concept and body image is **sexual self-concept**—the individual's evaluation of his or her own sexual feelings and actions. Sexual self-concept usually improves with age, and the more positive an individual's sexual self-concept, the more likely the individual is to use contraceptives (Winter, 1988).

Body Image

Body image is a specific aspect of self-concept. Pruzinsky and Cash (1990) noted:

> The more we see ourselves as physically attractive and the more we are objectively (i.e., socially) viewed as physically attractive, the more positive our overall self-esteem and the more likely we are to develop higher levels of social competence. Conversely, physical unattractiveness elicits social attitudes and actions that may interfere with the development of social confidence and interpersonal skills. (p. 222)

Our society places great emphasis on physical appearance. We give prizes to the most beautiful people (Miss America, Mr. World) and have derogatory labels for those who are not beautiful (nerd, pig). Most of us are socialized to want to look young, trim, and physically attractive forever. Capitalizing on our need to look more like the cultural ideal, the cosmetic industry sells us the perception of a more attractive self. Its basic product is a younger, sexier appearance, not makeup in a bottle. Some people turn from cosmetics to surgery, including face-lifts and breast enlargements, and hairpieces to improve their physical appearance.

CONSIDERATION: Consistent with the theme of our text, we suggest that individuals who are aware of cultural influences may consider choosing to reevaluate the degree to which physical appearance and clothing are viable indices of the degree to which they or someone else is valuable.

Part of the dissatisfaction women have with their bodies is their reaction to the "new, more demanding cultural and supercultural standards for thinness" (Hesse-Biber, 1989, p. 71). For example, Julia Roberts, a current young female celebrity, is ultrathin. Some evidence suggests that college women are altering their eating patterns so as to attain this cultural ideal of thinness (Hesse-Biber, 1989). Exhibit 9.1 details a feminist view of eating disorders.

Sexual Guilt

In their study of 676 never-married undergraduate women at a midwestern, residential state university, Davidson and Moore (1991) observed that significantly greater guilt was reported by those who masturbated as their only method of sexual activity, in contrast to those who masturbated and had sexual intercourse or who only had sexual intercourse. In another study, Davidson and Darling (1988) reported that sexual guilt interfered with the feelings of sexual satisfaction that women experienced via masturbation.

Sexual guilt may be promoted by religious teachings. One researcher (Gil, 1990) observed that the feelings 160 conservative Christians had about their sexual fantasies included feelings of not being in the best of God's grace, of being guilty, of needing to confess the fantasy, and, in some cases, of being condemned. Ninety-four percent of the respondents reported "substantial or high fantasy guilt" (p. 634).

A woman is socialized to believe that the thinner she is, the more attractive she is.

EXHIBIT 9.1 Body Image and Eating Disorders: A Feminist View

Many of us learn from an early age to be concerned about our body image. We groom ourselves and select clothing to make ourselves feel attractive. But concern for body image can be excessive to the point of endangering one's health. Anorexia nervosa and bulimia nervosa are two eating disorders that are related to excessive concern over one's body image. **Anorexia nervosa** (also called anorexia) involves a conscious struggle to achieve a reduction in body weight by avoiding or eliminating caloric intake. In **bulimia nervosa** (also called bulimia), normal eating patterns are disturbed by gorging and then either vomiting or purging (i.e., taking laxatives). While anorexic individuals appear emaciated, bulimic persons often look normal or may even be overweight.

Anorexia nervosa and bulimia nervosa are regarded as significant problems for adolescents and young adult women—the populations most at risk for these disorders. Within these populations, the prevalence of bulimia nervosa is estimated to be from 3% to 8%; the prevalence of anorexia nervosa is about one half of 1% (Halmi, Schneider, & Cooper, 1989).

Causal explanations for the occurrence of anorexia and bulimia point to both disturbed biological mechanisms and sociocultural forces (Russell & Treasure, 1989). Our concern here involves sociocultural explanations for anorexia and bulimia, particularly how such sociocultural forces might be viewed from a feminist perspective.

First, it is noteworthy that eating disorders are primarily found in women, rather than in men. There are about 10 anorexic women for every one anorexic man. More specifically, anorexia nervosa primarily affects (1) youthful females of the (2) upper classes in (3) developed nations (McHugh, Moran, & Killilea, 1989).

The major sociocultural force cited as being responsible for the occurrence of anorexia and bulimia is the increasing ideal of thinness as a body shape for women. The ideal that a woman can never be too thin, which is promoted by television, movies, magazines, and the fashion industry, has led to the popularization of dieting behavior. Women are constantly reminded that to be beautiful, they must be thin. In occupations where thinness is stressed, such as modeling and dancing, the incidence of eating disorders is increased (McHugh et al., 1989).

From a feminist perspective, anorexia and bulimia may be viewed as manifestations of sexist oppression. In support of this view, Brown (1987) suggested that women are taught the following rules:

1. Small is beautiful. When women are small, they occupy less space, are less visible, and utilize less resources. . . .
2. Weakness of body is valued. Women's physical weakness helps to keep in place patriarchal norms of male dominance of women. . . .
3. Women are forbidden to nurture themselves in a straightforward or ego-syntonic manner. Women are, however, specifically enjoined to attend to the nurturance of others. Because self-nurturance is almost inevitable for human beings, women's self-nurturing behavior should thus be done in ways that induce shame or guilt. . . . (Brown, 1987, p. 297)

Brown suggested that there are stiff penalties imposed on women who break these rules:

> Fat women are stigmatized and shunned, stereotyped as "stupid," "ugly," and "pigs." Assumptions are made about fat women's sexuality, with stereotypes of fat women being fearful of sex and using their fat as protection against intimacy. Fat women are made into a sexual fetish, with those attracted to them defined as perverted. Fat women are discriminated against in a wide range of settings. On the job, in college admissions, and in the availability (or lack thereof) of comfortable, attractive, and affordable clothing. In medical treatment and in psychotherapy, fat women are told that they are bad, wrong, and out of control. (p. 298)

Because patriarchal cultural standards of fat and thin are unstable and vary across time, women are always at risk of violating the rules regarding the ideal body type.

> A woman must thus be constantly fearful and vigilant, guard how she eats, punish herself for rule violation, and fear fat in herself and in other women at all times. (p. 298)

References

Brown, S. (1987). Lesbians, weight, and eating: New analyses and perspectives. In Boston Lesbian Psychologies Collective (Eds.), *Lesbian psychologies* (pp. 294–309). Chicago: University of Illinois Press.

Halmi, K., Schneider, L., & Cooper, S. (1989). Preface. In L. Schneider, S. Cooper, and K. Halmi (Eds.), *The psychobiology of human eating disorders: Preclinical and clinical perspectives* (pp. xi-xii). New York: New York Academy of Sciences.

McHugh, P. R., Moran, T. H., & Killilea, M. (1989). The approaches to the study of human disorders in food ingestion and body weight maintenance. In L. Schneider, S. Cooper, and K. Halmi (Eds.), *The psychobiology of human eating disorders: Preclinical and clinical perspectives* (pp. 1–12). New York: New York Academy of Sciences.

Russell, F. M., & Treasure, J. (1989). The modern history of anorexia nervosa: An interpretation of why the illness has changed. In L. Schneider, S. Cooper, and K. Halmi (Eds.), *The psychobiology of human eating disorders: Preclinical and clinical perspectives* (pp. 13–30). New York: New York Academy of Sciences.

Erotophobia and Erotophilia

Persons with high sex guilt are also likely to score high on erotophobia. **Erotophobia** and **erotophilia** refer to negative and positive emotional reactions to sexual cues. (These concepts may be measured by analyzing reactions to 21 statements on a test called Sexual Opinion Survey, developed in 1977 by Leonard White, Donn Byrne, and William Fisher; see the following Self-Assessment.)

People can be viewed on a continuum from feeling uncomfortable and wanting to avoid sex (erotophobia) to enjoying and wanting to be involved in sex (erotophilia). The erotophobic may feel nauseated by erotic material; the erotophilic may feel aroused by it. The erotophobic may have difficulty talking about contraception; the erotophilic may feel very comfortable doing so. Those who are erotophobic have more fears about sex, high sex guilt, and parents who were strict in their attitudes toward sex (Fisher, Byrne, White, & Kelley, 1988).

CONSIDERATION: Erotophobia may influence the probability that a teenager will get pregnant. Teens who are erotophobic not only feel uncomfortable talking about sex but also anxious about handling contraceptives. Hence, one argument for sex education classes that emphasize reducing erotophobia in regard to contraception is that they may help to cut the number of teenagers (now one in 10) who get pregnant each year (Fisher, Byrne, & White, 1983).

The preceding variables—self-concept, body image, sexual self-concept, sex guilt, and erotophobia or erotophilia—influence the way an individual experiences sexuality. Those with positive self-concepts, body images, and sexual self-concepts, low sex guilt, and high erotophilia are likely to enjoy the sexual aspect of their lives. Those with negative self-concepts, body images, and sexual self-concepts, and high sex guilt and erotophobia are likely to experience some anxiety and discomfort about the sexual aspect of their lives. In the pages to follow, we discuss sexual celibacy, masturbation, and sexual fantasies as other aspects of individual sexuality.

Sexual Celibacy

Early Christian dogma linked marriage with having intercourse and, conversely, being unmarried with not having intercourse. The term for those who chose to remain single and, by implication, not to have intercourse was *celibate*. The condition was known as celibacy, which "imposed no worldly obligations that might interfere with devotion to the Lord" (Tannahill, 1982, p. 139).

NATIONAL DATA: Twenty-two percent of a national sample of U.S. adults reported that they had no sexual partners during the past 12 months (Smith, 1991).

To avoid confusion with the meaning of celibacy that emphasizes being unmarried and the meaning we intend, which is that of sexual abstinence, we use the term *sexual celibacy*. Technically, **sexual celibacy** has two levels. One level involves no sexual behavior with another person but permits the option of masturbation.

Another level of celibacy is engaging in no sexual behavior with others or with one's self. Asexuality is sometimes confused with celibacy. But the asexual has no interest in sex and does not engage in any sexual behaviors—masturbation or partner sexual activity. Asexuality is rare. One percent of 12,000 respondents to a *Psychology Today* survey said that they were asexual (Rubenstein, 1983).

Self Assessment

Revised Sexual Opinion Survey

Please respond to each item as honestly as you can. There are no right or wrong answers. Place an X in the space on the scale that describes your feelings about each statement.

1. I think it would be very entertaining to look at erotica (sexually explicit books, movies, etc.).
   I strongly agree ____:____:____:____:____:____:____ I strongly disagree

2. Erotica (sexually explicit books, movies, etc.) is obviously filthy and people should not try to describe it as anything else.
   I strongly agree ____:____:____:____:____:____:____ I strongly disagree

3. Swimming in the nude with a member of the opposite sex would be an exciting experience.
   I strongly agree ____:____:____:____:____:____:____ I strongly disagree

4. Masturbation can be an exciting experience.
   I strongly agree ____:____:____:____:____:____:____ I strongly disagree

5. If I found out that a close friend of mine was a homosexual it would annoy me.
   I strongly agree ____:____:____:____:____:____:____ I strongly disagree

6. If people thought I was interested in oral sex, I would be embarrassed.
   I strongly agree ____:____:____:____:____:____:____ I strongly disagree

7. Engaging in group sex is an entertaining idea.
   I strongly agree ____:____:____:____:____:____:____ I strongly disagree

8. I personally find that thinking about engaging in sexual intercourse is arousing.
   I strongly agree ____:____:____:____:____:____:____ I strongly disagree

9. Seeing an erotic (sexually explicit) movie would be sexually arousing to me.
   I strongly agree ____:____:____:____:____:____:____ I strongly disagree

10. Thoughts that I may have homosexual tendencies would not worry me at all.
    I strongly agree ____:____:____:____:____:____:____ I strongly disagree

11. The idea of my being physically attracted to members of the same sex is not depressing.
    I strongly agree ____:____:____:____:____:____:____ I strongly disagree

12. Almost all erotic (sexually explicit) material is nauseating.
    I strongly agree ____:____:____:____:____:____:____ I strongly disagree

13. It would be emotionally upsetting to me to see someone exposing himself publicly.
    I strongly agree ____:____:____:____:____:____:____ I strongly disagree

14. Watching a stripper of the opposite sex would not be very exciting.
    I strongly agree ____:____:____:____:____:____:____ I strongly disagree

15. I would not enjoy seeing an erotic (sexually explicit) movie.
    I strongly agree ____:____:____:____:____:____:____ I strongly disagree

16. When I think about seeing pictures showing someone of the same sex as myself masturbating it nauseates me.
    I strongly agree ____:____:____:____:____:____:____ I strongly disagree

17. The thought of engaging in unusual sex practices is highly arousing.
    I strongly agree ____:____:____:____:____:____:____ I strongly disagree

18. Manipulating my genitals would probably be an arousing experience.
    I strongly agree ____:____:____:____:____:____:____ I strongly disagree

19. I do not enjoy daydreaming about sexual matters.
    I strongly agree ____:____:____:____:____:____:____ I strongly disagree

20. I am not curious about explicit erotica (sexually explicit, books, movies, etc.).
    I strongly agree ____:____:____:____:____:____:____ I strongly disagree

21. The thought of having long-term sexual relations with more than one sex partner is not disgusting to me.
    I strongly agree ____:____:____:____:____:____:____ I strongly disagree

Self-Assessment—*Continued*

Scoring

1. Score responses from 1 = I strongly agree to 7 = I strongly disagree.
2. Add scores from Items 2, 5, 6, 12, 13, 14, 15, 16, 19, and 20.
3. Subtract from this total the sum of Items 3, 4, 7, 8, 9, 10, 11, 17, 18, and 21.
4. Add 67 to this quantity.

Interpreting your score The Sexual Opinion Survey (SOS) measures erotophobia/erotophilia, a personality dimension reflecting negative or positive emotional reaction to sexual cues. The possible scores range from 0 (most erotophobic) to 126 (most erotophilic). You may want to compare your score with those of a group of Canadian undergraduate students who completed this revised version of the SOS in a human sexuality course. The mean score of the men was 77.81 (n = 107, SD = 15.16). For women, the mean score was 67.11 (n = 216, SD = 18.59). The difference between the men and the women was statistically significant (t = 0.05) (Fisher, 1988).

Reliability and validity Minor changes in wording were made to update some of the terminology of the SOS. For example, "go-go dancer" has been changed to "stripper," and "pornography" has been changed to "erotica" (defined as sexually explicit books, movies, etc.). Scores on the original and revised versions correlated highly (r = 0.93). Test-retest reliability was found to be acceptable over a two-month span when studied in a group of public school teachers who were preparing to become sexuality educators. For men r (11) = 0.85, p 0.01. For women r (55) = 0.80, p 0.01. Internal consistency, as measured by Cronbach's alpha, is in the 0.85–0.90 range (Fisher, 1988).

SOS results have been shown to be significantly related to self-ratings of emotional response to sexual stimuli and uncorrelated to a measure of social desirability (Fisher, 1988). Research results show erotophobia/erotophilia is related to a broad range of behaviors reflecting avoidance of or approach to sexuality. For example, erotophobic individuals participate in less solitary or heterosexual behavior; have more difficulty learning, talking, or teaching about sexuality; may be less likely to acquire or use contraception; and report briefer, less explicit sexual fantasies (Fisher, 1988). (A discussion of the influence of erotophobia/erotophilia on contraceptive use is included in Chapter 20.) Related personality dimensions include sex guilt, homophobia, traditionalism in gender role, and value orthodoxy (Fisher, 1988).

Reference

Fisher, W. A. (1988). The sexual opinion survey. In C. M. Davis, W. L. Yarber, & S. L. Davis (Eds.), *Sexuality-related measures: A compendium* (pp. 34–38). Lake Mills, Iowa: Graphic Publishing.

CONSIDERATION: Most of us have been asexual to some degree at some time in our lives. We were, to some extent, asexual as children. In the preschool years, most of us engaged in limited sexual behavior and had infrequent or no erotic thoughts. As we moved from childhood into our early adult years, we became increasingly involved in sexual behaviors and thoughts. We are also likely to become less sexual again in our later years (Diokno, Brown, & Herzog, 1990).

Voluntary Sexual Celibacy

Celibacy means more than abstinence; it's living totally for God.

Father Henri Nouwen

A person might choose to be sexually celibate for a number of reasons. Religion is a common one. The official position of the Catholic church remains that priests, nuns, and monks are expected to be celibate (unmarried) so they may have the maximum freedom and energy for the work of the church. Other religious people choose celibacy because they too want to be available to do God's will and work (which may not involve being in an official position of the church). Sexual celibacy may become a life-style through which a person witnesses to the priority of God in his or her life. Still others may regard sexual celibacy as a spiritually pure state and seek to avoid sexual activity as a means to achieve that goal.

Reasons other than religion for choosing to be sexually celibate include previous negative sexual experiences, alternative focus, depression, relationship enhancement, therapy for sexual dysfunctions, therapy for sex addiction, and the desire to avoid pregnancy and/or transmission of sexually transmissable diseases. Regarding previous negative sexual experiences, some women who never orgasm and some men who ejaculate too soon and/or are incapable of creating and maintaining an erection feel inadequate and a failure during sexual encounters. As a result, they avoid relationships with others that involve sexual expectations. Their negative feelings about partner sex may or may not generalize to individual sex. Prior sexual abuse (rape, molestation) may also cause some individuals to choose to refrain from sexual activity.

Involvement in work or other activity is another reason some people elect to be sexually celibate, at least temporarily. They may derive major satisfaction from their work and feel too exhausted or uninterested in sex.

Others choose to be sexually celibate because they are too depressed to choose otherwise. They feel no sexual desire and have no interest whatsoever in sexual or erotic activity or involvement.

Still others choose sexual celibacy because they want to explore relationships without the sexual dimension. They feel that avoiding sex permits the relationship to develop without becoming focused on sex. Based on the data from 1,275 of her respondents, Rubin (1991) noted:

> After years of experience with relationships that never grew beyond the sexual connection, many people now wonder whether it's better to wait until they know each other better, until they have established some basis besides sex for moving ahead. "When you jump into bed like that, I think things get stuck there," explained 35-year-old Brad, a New Jersey salesman. (p. 154)

Individuals may also choose to follow the recommendations of a sex therapist who suggests a period of no partner sex as part of the treatment program for erectile dysfunction. As we will discuss in Chapter 15, Sexual Dysfunctions and Sex Therapy, the inability to create and maintain an erection may be caused by performance anxiety, which is reduced by the directive to refrain from genital sex. Once partners choose to be sexually celibate, the man is no longer anxious about getting an erection and the capability of an erection returns. Indeed, in one study of 61 elderly (average age of 71) men in a nursing home, those without sexual partners reported less emotional stress over sexual issues than those with partners "possibly because of lesser expectations" (Mulligan & Palguta, 1991, p. 203).

One aspect of the treatment program for sex addiction recommended by Patrick Carnes (1983) is sexual abstinence on the premise that one must totally break his or her dependency on sex before getting control of the addiction. Like the alcoholic who must abstain from using alcohol to maintain sobriety, the sex addict must become completely "sex sober" for a period of at least six months.

Some individuals elect to be abstinent so they do not create a pregnancy. Those favoring "natural" methods of contraception abstain from having intercourse during those times when they feel they or their partner are most likely to get pregnant. The term for this type of celibacy is periodic abstinence.

Finally, some men are celibate so as to enhance the chance of impregnating their partners. A team of researchers (Sauer, Zeffer, Buster, & Sokol, 1988) compared the ejaculates of ten fertile donors who were abstinent for increasingly longer periods of time. The longer the donors went between ejaculations, the greater the volume and concentration of the sperm (sperm motility was not affected).

CONSIDERATION: Choosing to be sexually celibate requires a positive view of the decision. Zilbergeld (1978) cautioned:

> Another problem (with celibacy) is the meaning that you and those close to you put on your behavior. You may find yourself wondering if there is something wrong with you, especially when you realize that staying away from sex isn't terribly difficult. And, your friends may wonder along with you. Sex has been so oversold that many people can't even conceive of not having it regularly. So you'll probably have to put up with some questions and astonishment. (p. 154)

Involuntary Sexual Celibacy

While some people may choose to be celibate, others have little choice. Hospitals are notorious for encouraging, or enforcing, sexual celibacy. It is assumed that if you are in the hospital, you should have no sexual experience of any kind. There is no discussion of sexual activity, no privacy for masturbation (the nurse or physician can walk in at any time), and no tolerance of genital contact, even with your partner. Your sexuality is supposed to be nonexistent while you are in the hospital.

Nursing homes also institutionalize sexual celibacy. Added to the hospital atmosphere of a nursing home is the belief that the elderly are sexless. Some nursing homes do not even allow spouses to occupy the same room.

Retirement homes, in which the residents are physically healthy, may also prevent sexual activity. Two-hundred and two residents between the ages of 80 and 102 responded to a 117-item questionnaire about their sexual experiences in retirement homes. Thirty percent reported that living in the home definitely prevented them from engaging in sexual activity at least some of the time (Bretschneider & McCoy, 1988, pp. 14, 15).

NATIONAL DATA: In a national sample of U.S. adults who reported having no sexual partner in the last 12 months, the percentages were as follows: currently married, 9%; never married, separated, and divorced, 20% to 26%; and currently widowed, 86% (Smith, 1991).

The lack of an available partner can also result in nonvoluntary celibacy. This situation is common to many of us at different times in our lives. We may be between relationships, separated, divorced, or widowed. Separation of partners due to military service or prison may also lead to nonvoluntary celibacy.

Negative Attitudes Toward Masturbation: Historical Origins

Masturbation is defined as stimulating one's own body with the goal of experiencing pleasurable sexual sensations. Other terms for masturbation include autoeroticism, self-pleasuring, solo sex, and sex without a partner. Several older, more pejorative terms for masturbation are self-pollution, self-abuse, solitary vice, sin against nature, voluntary pollution, and onanism. The negative connotations associated with these terms are a result of various myths (which we may no longer choose to accept) about masturbation. These myths originated in religion, medicine, and traditional psychotherapy. Parents have also traditionally transmitted a negative view of masturbation to their children.

Table 9.1 lists some of the myths and truths about masturbation.

Religion and Masturbation

While the Jewish and Catholic religions have been most severe in their stand against masturbation, Protestants have not been very positive. Ancient Jews considered masturbation a sin so grave that it deserved the death penalty. Catholics regarded masturbation as a mortal sin that, if not given up, would result in eternal damnation. Although Protestants felt that neither death nor eternal hellfire was an appropriate

TABLE 9.1 Myths and Truths about Masturbation

Myths	Truths
1. Masturbation causes insanity, headaches, epilepsy, acne, blindness, nosebleeds, "masturbator's heart," tenderness of the breasts, warts, nymphomania, undesirable odor, hair on the palms.	1. There is no evidence that masturbation impairs physical or mental health.
2. Masturbation is an abnormal, unnatural behavior.	2. Masturbation is a normal function.
3. Masturbation is immature.	3. Masturbation is an effective way to experience sexual pleasure.
4. Masturbation is practiced mostly by simple-minded people.	4. Many people masturbate throughout their lives. Many sexually active people with available partners masturbate for additional gratification.
5. Masturbation is a substitute for intercourse.	5. Intercourse and masturbation can be viewed as complementary sexual experiences, not necessarily as mutually exclusive.
6. Masturbation is antisocial.	6. Masturbation may be an effective way to learn about your own sexual responses so you can communicate them to a partner.

consequence for masturbation, hell on earth was. The basis for these indictments was that masturbation is nonprocreative sex, and any sexual act that cannot produce offspring is morally wrong. The antidote for this evil behavior was abstinence and prayer (Money, Prakasam, & Joshi, 1991).

In ancient Chinese religion, life was viewed as a balance between the active and passive forces of yin and yang. Sex represented this harmonious balance, the essence of sexual yang was the male's semen and the essence of sexual yin was the woman's vaginal fluids. Female masturbation was virtually ignored, as vaginal fluids (yin) were thought to be inexhaustible. However, semen (yang) was viewed as precious

Catholics have viewed masturbation as a mortal sin that could result in eternal damnation.

and masturbation was regarded as a waste of vital yang essence (Bullough, 1976; Tannahill, 1982).

Medicine and Masturbation

The **semen-conservation doctrine** (from early Ayurvedic teachings in India) held that general good health in both sexes depended on conserving the life-giving power of "vital fluids" (Money et al., 1991, p. 10). These fluids, which include both semen and vaginal fluids, were believed to be important for intelligence and memory and derived from good nutrition. Wastage or depletion of semen (regarded as more important) was discouraged since it might result in loss of resistance to all illnesses and to a decrease in well-being. Agniversa and Susruta are believed to be two of the earliest teachers in India (1500 B.C.) who spoke of the semen-conservation doctrine (Money et al., 1991).

The Western medical community helped reinforce the negative associations of masturbation by bringing "scientific validity" to bear on its description of the hazards of masturbation. In 1758, Samuel Tissot, a Swiss physician, published a book on the diseases produced by "Onanism," in which he implied that the loss of too much semen, whether by intercourse or masturbation, was injurious to the body and would cause debility, disease, and death (Tissot, 1758/1766). Money (1988, p. 163) explained the reasoning behind Tissot's dire pronouncements. Based on his knowledge that semen is no longer produced following castration, Tissot "drew the momentously wrong conclusion" that it is the loss of semen which results in devirilization. "Then, by one more step of logic, he concluded that similar degenerative effects could be prevented by conservation of semen." What Tissot did not recognize, as it had not yet been discovered at that time, was that it is the loss of testosterone, not loss of semen, which causes the devirilizing effects of castration.

CONSIDERATION: Adding to the medical bias against masturbation was John Harvey Kellogg, M.D., who believed, as did the Reverend Sylvester Graham, that masturbation resulted in the loss of fluids that were vital to the body. In 1834, Graham wrote that an ounce of semen was equal to the loss of several ounces of blood. Graham believed that every time a man ejaculated, he ran the risk of contracting a disease of the nervous system. Among his solutions were Graham crackers, which would help prevent the development of carnal lust, which resulted from eating carnivorous flesh (Graham, 1848). Kellogg suggested his own cure—corn flakes. Kellogg's Corn Flakes were originally developed as a food to extinguish sexual desire and curb masturbation desires.

By the mid-nineteenth century, Tissot's theories had made their way into medical textbooks, journals, and books for parents (see the following Historical Perspective, "Some Not So Helpful 'Advice' from 'Experts' on Masturbation"). With no data, physicians added to the list of disorders resulting from masturbation—pimples, hair loss, weak eyes, and suicidal tendencies. However, as belief in these myths declined toward the end of the nineteenth century, they were "quickly replaced by a new set of beliefs that did little to ease the anxiety that most people had about masturbation. The conviction grew that masturbation was a common cause of neurotic disorders and marital sexual problems, a view shared by Freud" (Zilbergeld, 1978, p. 136).

Kinsey and his colleagues contributed the greatest challenge to the existing myths about masturbation through their disclosure that 92% of the men in their sample reported having masturbated (Kinsey, Pomeroy, & Martin, 1948). Yet the researchers

THE VAMPIRE OF YOUTH

THE Corroding Ulcer that is Eating Its Way Slowly Into the Vitals of Thousands of Young Men and Unfitting them for Both the Duties and Pleasures of Life

THE Relentless Vengeance of Youthful Folly or Ignorance. The Searing of the Young Soul with the Hot Coals of Unbridled Passion

THE habit of self-abuse, running riot in a body young and but partly developed, acting over a period of months or years upon a brain or nervous system as soft and susceptible to impressions as potter's clay, must of necessity leave its marks behind....

...Many a bright mind has been wrecked, many a great career blasted, many a happy home broken up by that serpent of ignorance and passion that drags its slimy and repellent lengths through a whole lifetime....

...These delicate parts, like the sensitive film of a photographic plate, are so forcibly impressed at this early age by the "VAMPIRE OF YOUTH," that unless proper measures of relief are taken, a life-time of misery and despair, and sometimes suicide, are the result....

...This disease, when the losses are not promptly checked, invariably ends in complete sexual debility and loss of power, constitutional and nervous weaknesses, spinal trouble, insanity and paralysis.

One of the first local manifestations of this disease is a shrinking or wasting, accompanied by coldness and flabbiness of the parts. In most cases of Spermatorrhea it will be found that the digestive system is deranged, the appetite is poor. There is a loss of fluid, failing memory, hot flashes, (blushing easily), bowels irregular, and general nervousness. The patient's sleep is usually unrefreshing, there is a tired feeling in the morning, coated tongue on account of the derangement of the digestive organs and sluggish liver....

Advertisement denouncing masturbation.

found no evidence of the dire consequences that had been earlier predicted for those who masturbate.

The guilt, fear, anxiety, and repulsion that surrounds masturbation is astounding, especially when one realizes not only how pervasive it is among human beings, but how beneficial, pleasurable, and relaxing an experience it can be.
Lonnie Garfield Barbach

In spite of the documentation that masturbation was not physically, emotionally, or socially debilitating, negative attitudes toward masturbation continued. One explanation is that physicians continued to look upon masturbation negatively and continued to convey this to their patients. Dr. David Reuben, in his best-seller *Everything You Ever Wanted to Know about Sex,* noted that masturbation was okay but that it was less preferable to intercourse and that the practice was mostly enjoyed by "children, the aged, the infirm, and the incarcerated" (Zilbergeld, 1978, p. 138).

HISTORICAL PERSPECTIVE

Some Not-so-Helpful "Advice" from "Experts" on Masturbation

In his article on preventing sexual dysfunction in men, Joseph LoPiccolo (1983) identified factors that have contributed to sexual dysfunction. Among those, he included *iatrogenic factors,* or problems that develop as a result of treatment. He mentioned how some sexual problems have been caused by experts or authorities giving information that has proved inaccurate and harmful. One apt example of misinformation disseminated by "the experts" is the professional "wisdom" regarding masturbation.

In this Perspective, we've drawn from a book published in 1886, written by a physician (Lucien Warner), then revised and enlarged by a member of the medical staff of the New York State Woman's Hospital. The book is titled *Woman's Handbook in Health and Disease: A Popular Treatise on the Functions and Diseases of Woman with the Most Approved Hygienic and Medical Treatment.* In the introductory paragraph of the chapter on "Self-abuse," Dr. Warner was reluctant even to raise the topic of masturbation:

> There is one subject in this connection which we would gladly omit, were it not that the experience of almost every week admonishes us that, in so doing, we should leave a sacred duty unperformed. We need hardly say that we allude to that pernicious habit of

Continued

Continued

self-indulgence of the passions, termed masturbation, or self-abuse. Many have supposed that this practice was almost wholly confined to boys and men; but this, we are pained to say, is far from the truth. (p. 62)

What is the harm in the practice of masturbation? Dr. Warner advised of dire moral and physical effects.

> The greatest evil to girls from the practice of self-abuse, is, we believe, its effects upon their moral natures. Women, as compared with men, have naturally but low sexual feelings; hence, when these feelings are cultivated and forced beyond their normal development by early and unnatural indulgences, there is imminent risk that it may lead to social and moral ruin. We do not mean to say that every girl who practices self-abuse will be likely to become a prostitute, but we do say that when the passions have been thus stimulated, she will be much more likely to yield to temptation, should she fall into the hands of the seducer.
>
> But even if she escapes this depth of iniquity, her moral nature will become perverted and debased. . . . (p. 63)

The physical effects, continued Dr. Warner,

> are sufficient to awaken our serious apprehensions. Among these we may mention partial loss of memory, lassitude, debility, loss of appetite, and sometimes spinal disease, consumption, insanity, or idiocy. Fortunately the habit is not often carried so far as to produce the worst of these evils, yet there are few physicians of extensive practice who have not met with cases which have thus sadly terminated. (pp. 63–64)

Parents are unlikely to be able to prevent their children from masturbating or talking of it. Dr. Warner also warned against pretending the problem does not exist. He offered the following advice to parents:

> The True Course to Pursue
>
> . . . If at any time you have occasion, either from the decline of health, or other cause, to suspect the habit, do not let a day pass, but investigate the matter at once, even though it be several years before the age of puberty.
>
> Usually it is not necessary to speak to children upon this subject until they have arrived at nearly the age of puberty. Then let some judicious person, better the mother if she is qualified for it, talk with them kindly and plainly. A few judicious questions will draw them out upon the subject, and if you find them ignorant, there is no need to be specific in your remarks, but in a general way tell them of the great moral and physical evils which result from any handling or interference with the generative organs. (p. 66)

But what should a parent do if there is evidence that the children are engaging in the "dangerous" practice? Dr. Warner continued,

> If you find them already addicted to the habit do not scold or threaten, but talk to them kindly and seriously, portraying in the strongest light the sin and evil of their conduct. Without appraising them of the fact, see that they are carefully watched. Let some suitable person be with them constantly day and night, for some months until the habit is thoroughly broken up. In the mean time, their moral training should be carefully attended to, and they should be rigidly guarded from any reading or conversation which will excite the passions. (pp. 66–67)

Physicians were not the only "experts" who promulgated information that linked masturbation and guilt. John B. Watson, the father of American behaviorism, wrote about masturbation (with the help of Rosalie Rayner Watson) in his book, *Psychological Care of Infant and Child* (1928). Watson advocated educating children about reproduction and the problem of venereal disease by no later than 11 years of age. He believed this education should also include discussion of masturbation.

Continued

Continued

Watson felt that letting children come to puberty without telling them the facts about masturbation was very cruel. He also abhorred the scare tactics of threatening catastrophic consequences, calling them "little short of criminal." He recognized that masturbation does not produce the physical maladies for which it has been blamed, but he had other grounds for recommending that parents try to inhibit it.

> . . . Nearly all of the enlightened physicians admit that not too frequent masturbation produces no physiological disturbance and no general behavior difficulties if there has been no poor instruction. Straightforward talks every now and then with your son or daughter in which you point out that this act is *not necessary*—that it is a kiddish trick—the sooner broken the better if he or she is ever to be like other grown up men and women is your best procedure. (pp. 176–177)

If masturbation is not physically harmful, why worry about it? Watson feared that if masturbation were practiced too long or frequently, it would make heterosexual adjustment difficult or impossible. He suggested explaining to the intelligent adolescent,

> 'Don't you see that you are doing this so persistently that it takes up your time and energy *for doing and learning the other things* that will help you get along in life?—That it takes up your thoughts (and these for the behaviorist are acts) and gives you no time for organizing your life?—That it makes you unfriendly—makes you withdraw from other people's society? You can't expect to have friends it you have no time or thought for them.' (pp. 177–178)

Watson also suggested a number of ideas for curbing masturbation prior to puberty. He made the following suggestions for wise parents:

> Almost from birth the watchfulness begins. Hygienic care is insisted upon. . . . Clothing should not be tight or too warm. Covers should not be too heavy or too numerous. Their hands should be watched. It is easy to get young children to form the habit of sleeping with their hands outside the covers—this is especially important. Persistent tree climbing, the popular sport of sliding down the banister—and the earlier dangling astride the father's leg—are all forms of activity that must be scrutinized somewhat. Their association with older children should be watched—and this, heaven knows, is the hardest problem of all. A child of 6 or 8 badly brought up associating with your child of 4 can fast make a wreck of your most careful efforts. (pp. 174–175)

But however careful the parents, Watson conceded that masturbation will continue to be used as a sexual outlet. Perhaps the anonymous writer who penned this limerick was right!

> Behaviorists stress excitation,
> Gestaltists, organization.
> But the Freudian credo
> Excites my libido
> And leads me to self-stimulation.

References

LoPiccolo, J. (1983). Preventing sexual dysfunctions in men. In G. Albee, H. Leightenberg & S. Gordon (Eds.), *Promoting sexual responsibility and preventing problems* (pp. 39–62). Hanover, N.H.: New England Press.

Warner, L. C. (1886). *Woman's handbook in health and disease: A popular treatise on the functions and diseases of women with the most approved hygienic and medical treatment.* New York: E. B. Treat.

Watson, J. B. (1928). *Psychological care of infant and child.* New York: W. W. Norton.

Traditional Psychotherapy and Masturbation

In the early twentieth century, psychotherapy joined medicine and religion to convince people of the negative effects of masturbation. Psychotherapists, led by Freud, suggested that masturbation was an infantile form of sexual gratification. People who masturbated "to excess" could fixate on themselves as a sexual object and would not be able to relate to others in a sexually mature way. The message was clear: if you want to be a good sexual partner in marriage, don't masturbate; and if you do masturbate, don't do it too often.

CONSIDERATION: The result of religious, medical, and therapeutic professions denigrating masturbation was devastating. Those who masturbated felt the shame and guilt they were supposed to feel. The burden of these feelings was particularly heavy since there was no one with whom to share the guilt. In the case of a premarital pregnancy, responsibility could be shared. But with masturbation, the "crime" had been committed alone.

Parents and Masturbation

While parents could opt to counter the negative religious, medical, and psychotherapeutic attitudes toward masturbation, they have rarely done so. Rather, their silence on the subject communicates agreement that masturbation is shameful. Rubin (1991) observed:

Masturbation remains the activity that's least likely to be talked about, and even less likely to be named.
Lillian Rubin

> Children who may witness all kinds of emotional expression and sexual innuendo between their parents never see or hear anything that even suggests that this thing they do is something anyone else knows about, let alone engages in. In such a setting, parents don't have to frown upon the masturbatory activities of the child; they have only to avoid noticing and labeling it for it to become suspect. By singling it out with silence, they send a message that the child interprets to mean that this nameless activity is something we don't talk about, one that calls for guilt and concealment. (p. 22)

CONSIDERATION: It may be difficult for parents to choose to be open about the topic of masturbation with their children. Even though they may regard masturbation in positive terms, they may have had no model in their parents to discuss sexual issues, including masturbation. Hence, the choice of being open with one's children about masturbation or any sexual issue may necessitate a choice to seek a context where one might learn to talk with one's children about sex. Such contexts include therapy or sex education courses for parents. Additional options are available in the form of books and pamphlets and programs sponsored by local parent-teacher associations, churches, or family planning agencies.

Benefits of Masturbation

When you ask someone when was the first time she had sex, she usually tells you about the first time she had sex with a partner. But our first sex is with ourselves. That is our base for learning to become erotic human beings, and it is denied to us, shamed out of us early, in childhood.
Ene Riisna

Due to traditional negative attitudes toward masturbation, shame, guilt, and anxiety continue to be common feelings associated with masturbation in our society. But new attitudes are emerging. Although the attitudes of some religious leaders are still negative, most physicians and therapists are clearly positive about masturbation. Masturbation is not only approved but recommended. Specific benefits of masturbation include the following:

1. Self-knowledge. Masturbation can provide immediate feedback about what one enjoys so one may pleasure one's self at a time of one's choosing. Self-knowledge about what turns one on also may benefit one's relationship in that one may

teach one's partner how to provide pleasure. Without such self-knowledge, one may feel incapable of providing pleasure to one's self or teaching a lover to do so.

2. Increased Body Comfort. Barbach (1976) emphasized that masturbation increases an individual's comfort with her or his own body. Such body comfort is associated with less anxiety in interpersonal sexual contexts, which may be related to overall satisfaction. Not all individuals (particularly women) are comfortable when they begin masturbating, but most usually develop such comfort with continued trials.

CONSIDERATION: Masturbation may also increase an individual's physical as well as psychological body comfort. Students in the authors' classes report that they masturbate to relieve tension, to get to sleep, and to help abate menstrual cramps.

NATIONAL DATA: The female respondents in Kinsey's et al. (1953) survey reported that they reached orgasm in 95% or more of their masturbatory attempts. (Men almost always have an orgasm during both masturbation and intercourse).

3. For Women, Orgasm More Likely. Masturbating to orgasm before marriage seems to have a positive effect on having an orgasm during intercourse after marriage. Forty-four percent of the women in Kinsey's et al. (1953) study who had not had an orgasm before marriage failed to have a climax during their first year of marriage. But of those who had experienced orgasm before marriage, only 13% had not had an orgasm during intercourse in their first year of marriage.

   Aware of the link between masturbation and orgasm, therapists often encourage female clients who want to experience an orgasm to learn how to masturbate. LoPiccolo and Lobitz (1972) have developed a treatment program that is designed to help women experience orgasm through masturbation (see Chapter 15 for description of this treatment program).

4. Pressure Taken Off Partner. Inevitably, partners in a relationship will vary in their desire for having sex. During such times, the partner wanting more sex may feel frustrated and the partner wanting less sex may feel guilty for not wanting to be accommodating. Masturbation might provide an alternative of sexual satisfaction for the partner wanting more sex while taking the pressure off the other partner to provide a sexual experience. The result may be less interpersonal stress for both people.

5. No Partner Necessary. In one study (Darling et al., 1991) the most frequently reported reason women gave for masturbating was that a partner was not available (see Table 9.2).

   Choosing to masturbate provides a way to enjoy a sexual experience and/or an orgasm when no partner may be available. Even if a partner is available, the

The good thing about masturbation is that you don't have to get dressed up for it.
Truman Capote

TABLE 9.2 Reasons Given by 709 Female Nurses for Masturbating

Reason	Percent
Preferred sex partner not available	68.8%
No opportunity for sexual intercourse	60.2%
Unable to reach orgasm by sexual intercourse	35.0%
Angry with partner	14.6%
Partner ignores clitoris	14.6%

Source: Darling, C. A., Davidson, J. K., & Cox, R. P. (1991) Female sexual response and the timing of partner orgasm. *Journal of Sex and Marital Therapy,* 17, 3–21. Used by permission.

individual may choose to have a quick release that can be accomplished with no need to interact. Since masturbation does not involve a partner, the risk of contracting HIV and other STDs is also eliminated. As an alternative to heterosexual involvement, masturbation also eliminates risk of unintended pregnancy.

Masturbation is but one option in a menu of choices in a normal, healthy sex life.
Bernie Zilbergeld

6. Unique Experience. Masturbation is a unique sexual experience, different from petting, intercourse, mutual stimulation of the genitals, and other sexual behaviors. As we will note later, many people who have sexual experiences on a regular basis with their respective partners masturbate because they regard masturbation as a unique experience that partner sex cannot duplicate. Indeed, some people masturbate after having partner sex.
7. Extradyadic Entanglements Avoided. When away from their usual partner, some individuals choose to masturbate as a means of relieving sexual tension rather than risk emotional involvement or contracting STDs with another person. Otherwise, the person may feel driven to obtain sexual release that might result in a regrettable interpersonal entanglement or a breech of trust in the primary relationship.
8. Improved Self-Image. Masturbation may also help a woman improve her body image and her perception of herself as a woman. Betty Dodson in her book, *Sex for One: The Joy of Self Love* (1987), emphasized that masturbation is a meditation of self-love. She suggested that people are often confronted with bad body images, shame about body functions, and confusion about sex and pleasure. In contrast, masturbation is—and should be—an intense love affair with one's self.
9. Useful in Treatment of Sexual Offenders. Behavior therapy treatments of sex offenders use masturbation in reconditioning techniques. By shifting the timing and sequence of erotic fantasies and images during masturbation, deviant arousal is weakened and arousal to appropriate stimuli is strengthened (Maletzky, 1991).

CONSIDERATION: In spite of the benefits of masturbation, there are disadvantages. We have already made reference to the enormous guilt sometimes associated with masturbation. Related to such guilt is the feeling that some people have of being abnormal because they fear that they masturbate too frequently. In addition, masturbation to an inappropriate stimulus (e.g., children) may strengthen erotic feelings toward that stimulus. Finally, some partners interpret their lover's masturbation as evidence that they are inadequate and undesirable.

Social and Psychological Correlates of Masturbation

Frequency of masturbation tends to be associated with several factors: gender, age, cohort, education, religion, and locus of control.

Gender, Age, and Cohort

Men are more likely to have masturbated than women. Of the 79 men and 193 women enrolled in a human sexuality class, 87% and 58%, respectively, reported having masturbated (Knox & Schacht, 1992). In Davidson and Moore's (1991) study of 676 undergraduate never-married women, 46% reported that they had masturbated.

CONSIDERATION: Masturbation may begin in infancy. Two researchers (Fleisher & Morrison, 1990) documented five baby girls who evidenced masturbatory posturing (between the ages of three to 14 months) that did not involve rubbing their genitals with their hands. Rather, they would press their genitals against a firm edge or their parents' knee. As a result, they would breathe irregularly, and their faces would flush. While their parents thought that their child was having a seizure or abdominal pain, their physician assured them of the harmless nature of the posturing.

NATIONAL DATA: Of 1,275 respondents, three-fourths of the women and almost all of the men reported having masturbated before their first intercourse experience (Rubin, 1991, p. 20).

The pattern of men masturbating more frequently than women begins in early adolescence. Kinsey and his associates (1948; 1953) observed that 21% of 12-year-old boys masturbated, in contrast to 12% of 12-year-old girls. By age 15, the discrepancy is still evident, with 82% of boys having masturbated and 20% of girls.

The discrepancy is also evident between the sexes in other countries. In a study of over 20,000 Japanese high school and university students, 98% of the boys and 39% of the girls reported having masturbated (Hatano, 1991). In another study, students at Anadolu University, Eskisehir, Turkey, were asked about their masturbatory behavior. Of the 166 female subjects, 11.5% reported that they had masturbated; of the 172 male subjects, 87.2% professed to have done so (Erkmen, Dilbaz, Serber, Kaptanoglu, & Tekin, 1990). In still another study, the discrepancy between women and men was evident, although it was not as large. Seventy percent of 147 Colombian university women, compared to 99% of 144 university men, reported having masturbated (Alzate, 1989).

One of the explanations for why men are more likely than women to have masturbated is greater genital availability. A man's penis is easy to touch or rub; a woman's genitals are more hidden. Most of the over 7,000 men in Hite's (1981) sample reported that they learned about masturbation through self-discovery. Other possible explanations for greater masturbation among men include the desire for release of periodic seminal buildup, traditional male social scripts that emphasize the physical release and pleasure aspects of sexuality rather than the relationship aspect, and the greater social support for sexual expression among males than females. In regard to the latter, traditionally, "good girls" (particularly in adolescence) were not sexual. As women reach their 20s and 30s, they are much more likely to masturbate.

CONSIDERATION: In spite of the high percentage of men who masturbate, some men never choose to masturbate. Kinsey et al. (1948) suggested that a low sex drive, dependency on nocturnal emissions, and the regular availability of a sexual partner may account for this. Another explanation may be that these men have strong religious beliefs against masturbation.

With advancing age, masturbation frequency among men decreases. In a study of 61 men who were in nursing homes (average age of 71.3), only 10% reported that they masturbated. These men also reported that their interest in sex was at a level of 5.4 on a 10-point scale, with 10 being high interest (Mulligan & Palguta, 1991). In Chapter 12, Sexuality across the Life Span, we will note a decrease in all forms of sexual activity, including masturbation, as the person becomes elderly.

Elderly women are less likely to report having ever masturbated than middle-aged women. In a study of 625 Danish women born in three generations (1910,

1936, 1958), the percentages of those who reported ever having masturbated were 38%, 47%, and 81%, respectively (Lunde, Larsen, Fog, & Garde, 1991). These findings suggest that the cohort in which women are born is related to self-reported prevalence of masturbation. As the Lunde et al. (1991) study suggests, contemporary cohorts of women are more likely to report having ever masturbated than earlier cohorts. This may be due to the fact that contemporary cohorts have been reared in a less sexually restrictive society.

CONSIDERATION: Data on the prevalence and frequency of masturbation come from self-reports of masturbation behavior obtained through questionnaires and interviews. Even when anonymity is assured, individuals may distort self-reports of masturbation behavior in a socially-desirable direction. In the Lunde et al. (1991) study, the earlier cohorts of women may have intentionally underreported their masturbation behavior because of the sexually restrictive era in which they grew up.

Education and Religion

The more education a person has, the more often that person is likely to masturbate. Kinsey et al. (1948) noted that college men masturbated twice as often as those who did not go beyond grade school. A similar relationship between education and frequency of masturbation is true of women, but it is less dramatic.

What might account for more educated individuals choosing to masturbate more frequently than less educated people? One explanation suggests that since intercourse begins earlier and is more frequent for those who have less education, masturbation may become viewed as unnecessary if intercourse is available. Also, less education may mean less talk about masturbation. If masturbation is not discussed or read about, then there may be less inclination to practice it.

Taking a college sexuality education course has been shown to influence attitudes toward masturbation. Compared to scores from a survey administered the first day of class, scores from the last day of class revealed a more permissive attitude towards masturbation (Weis, Rabinowitz, & Ruckstuhl, 1992).

Those who attend religious services and who regard themselves as devout are also less likely to choose to masturbate than those who do not attend religious services or who do not regard themselves as devout (Kinsey et al., 1948; 1953). This is not surprising in view of the traditional attitude of religion toward masturbation.

Locus of Control

Psychologists define **locus of control** as the degree to which an individual views outcomes (events and rewards) as depending on his or her own abilities (internal control) or on chance, fate, or other people (external control). For example, if your locus of control were internal and you were at a carnival, you might feel that winning a prize by throwing darts at balloons would be due to your skill and not to luck. But if your locus of control were external, you might feel that no matter how skilled you were, you would not win because forces beyond you would dictate the outcome. In one study (Catania & White, 1982), 30 elderly persons (average age of 68.5) completed a scale that revealed the degree to which they tended to be internally or externally controlled. They also indicated how frequently they masturbated. Results showed that those who felt in control of their lives (internally controlled) had higher masturbatory frequencies than those who felt out of control (externally controlled). The researchers concluded that "internal control in a sexual context may reflect a person's perceptions of self-regulation with regard to his/her body and sexuality" (p. 243).

Techniques of Masturbation

Various masturbatory techniques are used by women and men. Some of these techniques are described in the following sections.

Female Masturbation Techniques

Most women have an orgasm when they masturbate, and most experience an orgasm within five minutes (Kinsey et al., 1953). Those who take longer may deliberately do so to prolong the pleasure they experience during masturbation. Women may use one or more of the following masturbatory techniques.

Lying on Back Many women lie on their back and stimulate the clitoral-vulval area with their hand (see Figure 9.1). In one study (Clifford, 1978), women stated that their most effective masturbatory technique for achieving climax was to lie on their back, use several fingers, and stroke around and on the clitoris. One woman recalled her experience:

> Usually I lie on my back, my legs apart. I almost always have my panties on, as rubbing the clitoris itself directly is just annoying. I use one hand, two fingers together, rubbing up and down in short, quick strokes right over my clitoris. As I get closer to climax, my legs tend to spread apart and my pelvis tilts up more. I don't move around too much, but sometimes during climax I roll from side to side. (Hite, 1977, p. 81)

Stroking the clitoris without sufficient lubrication may be unpleasant. Saliva, vaginal secretions, or commercial lubricants may be used to lubricate the fingers and clitoris during masturbation.

Lying on Stomach Some women prefer to lie on their stomach when masturbating. While they may use their hands to stimulate the clitoral-vulval area, they also may press and thrust the vaginal area against some object—the bed, a pillow, or bedding. One specific technique is for the woman to wad up a blanket into a ball and lie on her stomach on top of it so that it exerts pressure on her vulval area. She then moves her hips in a circular motion until she climaxes.

FIGURE 9.1 Female masturbation.

Thigh Pressure A variation of the preceding masturbatory styles is for the woman to cross her legs and squeeze them together tightly, thereby exerting pressure on her vaginal area. Her clitoris and labia respond to the sensation of muscular tension and pleasurable sexual feelings. Some women stimulate their genitals with their hand at the same time they are exerting thigh pressure.

Water Massage Rather than hand, object, or thigh pressure, some women use water. The woman turns the faucet of the tub or shower to a strong, warm flow. She then lies on her back with her legs up on the wall and her clitoral-vulval area positioned under the rushing water, or she may stand and let the water from the shower stream over her clitoral area. Hose attachments enable a woman to lie in the tub, hold the massage attachment in her hand, and direct the flow of water onto the clitoral area.

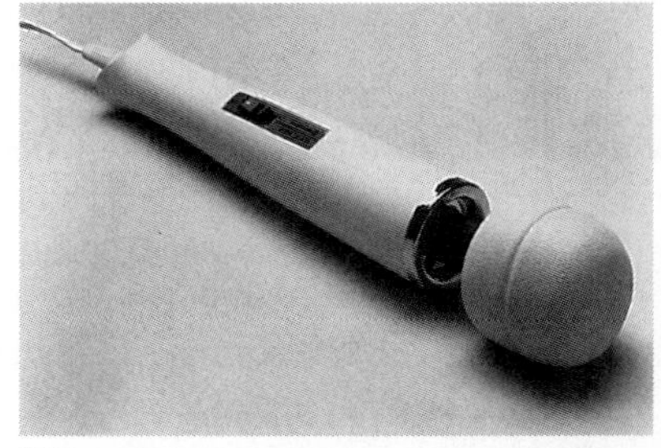

(a)

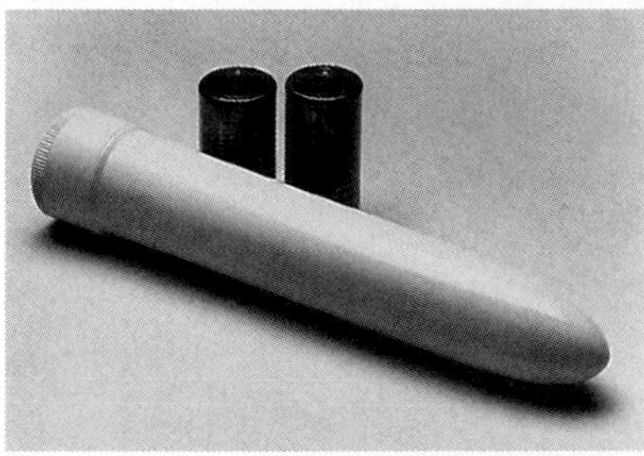

(b)

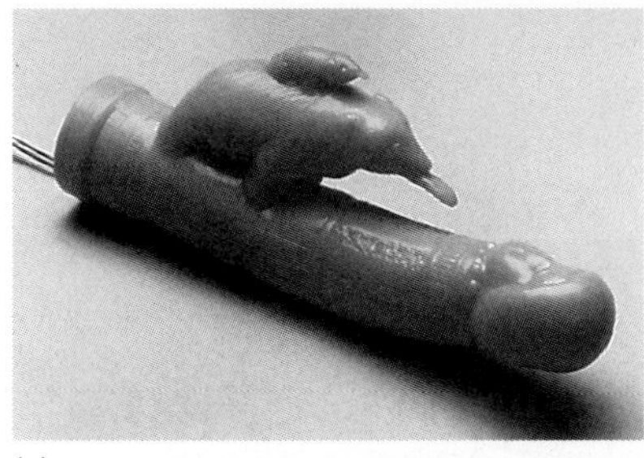

(c)

FIGURE 9.2
Body massagers and vibrators may be used to provide gentle, persistent stimulation; they may be used to help a person relax, as well as to heighten arousal. Here are examples of (a) an electric massager and (b), (c) battery vibrators.

Vibrator Vibrators are gaining increased visibility and acceptance (see Figure 9.2). Indeed, sex therapists sometimes encourage their female clients to use a vibrator to help achieve an orgasm. In their book *Becoming Orgasmic,* (1976) Heiman, LoPiccolo, and LoPiccolo stated:

> Vibrators are wonderful for massaging your body in order to help you relax and to soothe sore muscles. And they can also provide very pleasurable sensations on your genitals. This isn't surprising when you think about it. When you stimulate your genitals with your finger(s), you rub, stroke, and massage. This is what vibrators do at a faster rate, more steadily, and more intensely than most people can achieve with hand stimulation. Some women need this quality of genital stimulation, especially when they are learning to have orgasms. (p. 107)

Although most women do not use a vibrator, those who do seem to enjoy it. While respondents in magazine surveys may not be representative of all women, only 3% of 100,000 women in *Redbook's* survey of married women reported that using the vibrator was not pleasurable (Tavris & Sadd, 1977). If sensations produced by a vibrator are too intense, a towel or piece of clothing may be placed between the vibrator and the vulval region to decrease the intensity.

Vaginal Insertion Hite (1977) reported that it was extremely rare for the women in her sample to masturbate exclusively by inserting fingers or an object into their vagina. Those who did so usually inserted a finger or fingers just inside the vaginal opening to transfer vaginal lubrication to the clitoral area. Rarely did women make deep insertions into their vagina. However, some women enjoy using fingers on one hand to stimulate themselves deep in the vagina while using the other hand to stimulate the clitoris or breasts.

Breast Stimulation Some women derive pleasure from stimulating their breasts. The woman might rub her breasts with her hands or press them against a pillow or some object. In most cases, she stimulates her breasts simultaneously with genital manipulation. Only rarely is breast stimulation sufficient to cause an orgasm.

Anal Stimulation Some women enjoy inserting a finger into their anus while another finger stimulates the clitoris or vagina.

CONSIDERATION: Anal bacteria can cause serious vaginal infections and cystitis (bladder infection), so women should always wash any fingers that have had anal contact before using these fingers to stimulate the vaginal or clitoral areas.

Many women use combinations of these masturbatory techniques. They may begin on their back, then shift to other positions. Although they most often use their hand, they also may use a vibrator or other sexual devices (oils, feathers, objects to insert in vagina). Sexual fantasies frequently accompany masturbation. Sixty percent of the women in one study said they masturbated to a sexual fantasy (Wolfe, 1982). Sexual fantasies are discussed later in this chapter.

Techniques of Male Masturbation

Observations, interviews, and completed questionnaires of nearly 17,000 men reveal how men masturbate (Hite, 1981; Kinsey et al., 1948; Masters & Johnson, 1979; Shanor, 1978) Compared with women, men have a narrow range of masturbatory techniques. Most frequently, the man lies on his back and strokes, rubs, and caresses the shaft and glans of his penis until it becomes hard. Once erection occurs, he increases the pressure and speed of the stroking pattern. He places pressure on the shaft with occasional pressure on the head of the penis (see Figure 9.3). Saliva or a commercial lubricant may be used to lubricate the man's hand and penis. One man described his experience:

> I take my right hand and get a rhythm motion going up and down—moving the loose skin and touching the fringe area around the head. Sometimes I put lotion on my hand to lessen the friction. I start out slowly and go faster and faster. I can feel my penis swell in my hand—then the sperm comes exploding out. (Shanor, 1978, p. 36)

Variations of this technique include putting the penis between the thighs and rubbing them together, using two hands (the other usually stimulates the anus or scrotum), or using an electric vibrator.

FIGURE 9.3 Male masturbation.

EXHIBIT 9.2 Masturbation and Accidental Death

An unusual form of masturbation, referred to as **autoerotic asphyxia syndrome,** involves the man putting a rope or noose around his neck in order to cut off his air supply while masturbating to orgasm (Money, 1986). Some men report that by restricting the air supply, a state of semiconsciousness is achieved that provides a heightened sense of pleasure during masturbation. Men with this proclivity are known as asphyziophiliacs—those who desire a state of oxygen deficiency in order to enhance sexual excitement and orgasm.

Some men accidentally hang themselves while using this technique (Vieira & Da Silva, 1989). The death occurs either as a consequence of consciousness being lost before the man frees himself from the hanging position or failure on the part of the man to provide an adequate escape from the hanging position. There may be as many as 1,000 autoerotic fatalities each year in the United States (Bechtel, Westerfield, & Eddy, 1990).

Autoerotic asphyxia syndrome may be related to a proclivity for other paraphilias and use of sexual paraphernalia (paraphilias are discussed in Chapter 17). In a study of 117 men ages 10–56 who died accidentally during autoerotic asphyxial activities, Blanchard and Hucker (1991) reported that various sexual paraphernalia were found near the deceased men. These included dildos (used for anal stimulation), mirrors (used for self-observation), female clothing (used for cross-dressing), and whips and chains (used for bondage activities).

Masters and Johnson (1979) reported that 20% of men stand when they masturbate. They may stand in the shower or in front of the sink in the bathroom. A few men sit or lie facedown. In the latter position, the penis is stimulated by the friction between the person's abdomen and the bed or whatever he is lying on.

In Exhibit 9.2 we describe a male masturbation technique that is rarely used, but may lead to accidental death.

Masturbation in Relationships

It is assumed that single people masturbate because, among other reasons, they have no regular sexual partner. It is also sometimes assumed that married people and people in on-going relationships do not masturbate because they have a sex partner. But, as we shall see, people with regular sexual partners often choose to have sexual activity with their partners as well as without them.

Research on Masturbation among Spouses

In the *Redbook* study of 100,000 married women, two-thirds said they had masturbated since marriage (Tavris & Sadd, 1977). (You recall from Chapter 4 that magazine surveys are specific to the characteristics of the readers of the magazine; thus in this case, the statistics may not represent all married women). Many women masturbate in bed after their husbands have fallen asleep (Hessellund, 1976). Others masturbate in the bathroom. In one study, 70% of wives reported that their husbands were unaware that their wives masturbated (Gross-Kopf, 1983).

Most wives who masturbate do so because their husbands are away and not available for intercourse. Other wives report masturbating for the unique experience it provides, even though they have intercourse at other times. Still others masturbate to relieve tension and relax. For a smaller percentage of wives, masturbation is used as a substitute for unsatisfactory intercourse with their husbands. These wives say they do not like their husbands, they are averse to intercourse, or they feel rejected by their husbands.

CONSIDERATION: In the Redbook study (Tavris & Sadd, 1977), the more often a wife masturbated, the less likely she regarded sex with her husband as good. For example, of the women who rated their sex lives as very good, only 10% masturbated often, compared to 36% of those who rated their sex lives as very poor. While many of these wives occasionally masturbated for the pleasure of that activity or as a sexual experiment, those who did so often were compensating for bad sex with their husbands, and they didn't find masturbation especially gratifying (p. 95).

Men with sexual partners also masturbate. In a study of 61 elderly men, the frequency of those who masturbated was the same for those who had a sexual partner and those who did not (Mulligan & Palguta, 1991).

In a study of 38 married couples, Hessellund (1976) found a positive correlation between masturbation and intercourse frequency for men, but a negative correlation for women. In other words, the men seemed to use masturbation as a supplement for intercourse, while the women used masturbation as a substitute for intercourse.

Husbands may masturbate because their desired frequency of sex exceeds that of their wives. Some men masturbate because they feel inadequate. An example of the latter is the husband who experiences erection difficulties and would rather masturbate than feel embarrassed. A man may also masturbate if his partner is in the later stages of pregnancy and finds intercourse to be uncomfortable.

Effects of Masturbation on Relationships

Masturbation may have positive effects on a relationship. For some couples, viewing each other masturbate is a "turn on" and adds another dimension to the couple's sex life. Also, differences in desire for sexual interaction can be reduced by the partner with the greater desire masturbating some of the time.

Since women who masturbate are better able to teach their partners how to pleasure them, they may be more satisfied in their relationships. Their partners may also derive satisfaction from being able provide pleasure to the woman. Finally, individuals who masturbate aren't totally dependent on their partners to satisfy them sexually, which can be a freedom for both partners (The Boston Women's Health Book Collective, 1984). The choice of masturbating with one's partner is discussed in the choices section at the end of this chapter.

Masturbation may also have negative consequences for a relationship. Some individuals regard their partner's masturbation as rejection. They may feel that the partner's masturbating symbolizes that they are not a good lover.

Another way masturbation may hurt a couple's relationship is through the guilt it produces. In general, men are more likely to view masturbation positively and women are more likely to view it as wrong, unnatural, or repellent (Hessellund, 1976). In some cases, individuals who have negative feelings about masturbation may unconsciously displace these feelings onto their partners.

Sexual Fantasies

Individuals who masturbate sometimes choose to accompany their masturbation with sexual fantasies. Jones and Barlow (1990) asked 49 men and 47 heterosexual undergraduate women to monitor the frequency with which they employed masturbatory fantasies. While there was no difference in the frequency of sexual fantasies in general, men reported a greater frequency of masturbatory fantasies. This is not surprising in view of the fact that men masturbate more than women.

CONSIDERATION: Sexual fantasies may be regarded as the most common form of sexual experience (Ellis & Symons, 1990). Because they are private and unconstrained, they provide maximum insight into the psychological mechanisms that "underpin sexual feeling, thought and action" (p. 527).

Sexual fantasy may be defined as "a dynamic intrapsychic process which contains imaginal sexual content and is sexually arousing" (Mednick, 1980, p. 684). Critical factors that have been used to define or examine sexual fantasy include (Mednick, 1980):

1. Manifest content—the actual fantasy;
2. Emotional responses—for example, guilt, excitement;
3. Activation of fantasy—internal or external source;
4. Dynamics of action within fantasy—who does what; and
5. Intentionality of the fantasy.

In regard to the latter, is the sexual fantasy unintended in daydreaming or during one's dreams, or is it a deliberate conjuring up of sexual images?

CONSIDERATION: Research on sexual fantasies has focused on whether sexual fantasies are pathogenic or creative, on their use in therapeutic contexts, and on the degree to which sexual aggression and sexual fantasies are related. Results suggest that fantasies reflect considerable creativity, that they are useful in altering what a person finds sexually appealing (e.g., fantasizing to adult sex partners rather than to children), and that there does seem to be a relationship between soon aggressive sexual fantasies and aggressive behavior. This will be discussed further in chapter 17 (paraphilias) and 19 (abuses).

Sexual fantasies, both voluntary and involuntary, serve various functions and involve a variety of content. We will examine both of these aspects of fantasies.

Functions of Sexual Fantasies

A primary function of fantasy is to heighten sexual arousal. In a study of 625 Danish women, sexual fantasies "were most often used to increase sexual desire and to facilitate orgasm (while masturbating)" (Lunde et al., 1991, p. 114). Both women and men are capable of achieving an orgasm through fantasy alone. Eleven percent of the women in Clifford's (1978) study on masturbation reported that they had fantasy-induced orgasms. These most often occurred in a state of semisleep or on waking from a sexual dream.

Erotic fantasies are a strong mental aphrodisiac that triggers sexual arousal.
Domeena Renshaw

It is more rare for men to have an orgasm from fantasy alone. Of the more than 5,000 males in Kinsey's et al. (1948) study, only three or four reported orgasm through fantasy alone. When fantasies are accompanied by masturbation or intercourse, sexual arousal is dramatically increased, as is the chance of orgasm.

Bringing what is not possible in reality within one's cognitive experience is another function of fantasy. Individuals may be desired by the person(s) of their choice who says and does exactly what they want, how they want, when they want, as often as they want. Of the 625 Danish women mentioned above, their main fantasy involved sex with strangers (Lunde et al., 1991).

Fantasy also permits complete control. One can be the perfect lover. The fantasy man is always erect and never ejaculates too soon. The fantasy woman is always desired by her partner, who never comments on her stretch marks. The control aspect of fantasy provides sexual excitement within a safe and secure context.

Fantasy also provides variety. There is no limit to the people, the sexual behaviors, or the level of desired responsiveness of the partners. Also, partners, scenes, and sexual activities can be switched as desired. The limits of fantasy are constrained only by one's imagination.

Fantasy is a pleasure in itself. Unlike actual sexual involvement, either interpersonal or masturbatory, fantasy may provide a preferred uniqueness.

Fantasy may serve as cognitive rehearsal for future sexual experiences. Two individuals who are attracted to each other may, in each other's absence, develop elaborate sexual fantasies about a subsequent encounter. In such fantasies, they may rehearse how they will initiate or respond to a variety of sexual behaviors and topics of conversation.

Fantasies may also serve the purpose of escape. While attending a lecture, driving home, or preparing dinner, individuals may fantasize at will. Several students in the authors' classes wrote that whenever they get bored in class, they switch to a favorite fantasy.

Finally, sexual fantasies provide excitement with safety. There is no embarrassment, no AIDS or other sexually transmissible diseases, and no explanation to another for one's thoughts.

CONSIDERATION: Some of the various purposes (e.g., sexual arousal, variety, control, rehearsal, escape, no AIDS) of fantasy have been commercialized. An array of adult magazines provides pictures and phone numbers of individuals (called fantasy phone mates) who promise "to get you off over the phone" for a fee.

Content of Sexual Fantasies

Table 9.3 details the fantasy content of a group of 78 undergraduate women.

TABLE 9.3 Fantasy Content of 78 Undergraduate Women

Fantasy Activity/Content	Percent Reporting
Strangers	15
Group sex	10
Older partners	8
Famous people	8
Observed	4
Different races	4
Swept away	3

Source: Gold, S. R., Balzano, B. F., & Stamey, R. (1991). Two studies of females' sexual force fantasies. *Journal of Sex Education and Therapy, 17,* 15–26. Used by permission.

Sexual fantasies sometimes involve strangers in unique settings.

Heading the list of the respondents in Gold's study was "strangers." An example of such a fantasy from a woman in the authors' classes follows:

> My best sexual fantasy involves a total stranger. I think it would be fantastic to be going about my routine business or be on a trip somewhere and look across a room, catch the eye of a complete stranger, and having something "click" between us.
>
> I wouldn't want to meet or talk with him then, but run into him a few more times until the attraction was so strong, we knew we couldn't resist each other. I would then like to talk, have dinner, go dancing (all this time the attraction is still escalating), and finally end up in bed at his loft.
>
> Our sexual encounter is fantastic—we totally enjoy and are uninhibited with each other. This would continue for three or four days with the attraction still at a peak and then we would part with no regret (except that our time was up), fond memories, and never see each other again.

Other sexual fantasies reported by over 25% of the female *and* male respondents in Sue's (1979) study on fantasies during intercourse include: oral-genital sex, a former lover, others giving in after first resisting, and others finding the fantasizer irresistible. An example of the latter from a man in the authors' classes follows:

> My fantasy is about washing my clothes at 3 A.M. in an empty laundry room. All of a sudden a beautiful woman walks in and uses the machine next to mine. We exchange small talk when she notices my enlarged member about to bust my zipper. She tells me she can relieve the pressure and bends down and unzips my pants. She then takes out my penis and starts to relieve me. I stop her and then proceed to undress her. We are both naked on top of the two machines as it goes from rinse to spin. As the motor increases, my rhythmic stroking increases, and as the machine tops out, I have a tremendous orgasm.

Friday (1991) analyzed 10,000 letters written by women describing their sexual fantasies. She noted that compared to fantasy narratives collected in the past, these women described fantasies more likely to involve women in the role of pleasure giver, acting assertively, and with other women.

CONSIDERATION: Individuals may fantasize about events that they do not want to actually occur (Gold et al., 1991; Friday, 1980, 1991; Sue, 1979; Wilson, 1978). For example, women who have fantasies of being overpowered and forced to have sexual relations do not want to be raped in reality. Indeed, although 17% of the 79 women in the Gold et al. (1991) study reported having had at least one fantasy with forced sexual activity, they were the most likely to report that they did not want the fantasy to come true.

Why do women fantasize about being raped? One suggestion is that women enjoy the thought of being forced to have sex because this would relieve them of guilt about consenting to sexual relations with someone who is desirable but socially taboo. For example, "conscience would not allow most women to have sex with the husband of their best friend, but how could they be blamed if taken against their will" (Wilson, 1978, p. 52).

Gender Differences in Sexual Fantasies

To assess the degree to which the sexual fantasies of women and men are different, Ellis and Symons (1990) collected data from 182 women and 125 men enrolled in introductory general education courses. Most (86%) were never married and white (74%); Asian (13%), Hispanic (6%), black (4%), and "other" (3%) comprised the rest of the sample.

While some researchers (Rokach, 1990) have found no differences in the sexual fantasies of women and men, Ellis and Symons (1990) found several differences. These are reflected in Table 9.4:

TABLE 9.4 Gender Differences in Sexual Fantasies

Fantasy	Women (*n* = 182)	Men (*n* = 125)
Taking into consideration all of your fantasies, have you fantasized a sexual encounter with over 1,000 different people?	Yes 8%	Yes 32%
Are your sexual fantasies typically about someone with whom you are or have been romantically/sexually involved?	Yes 59%	Yes 28%
During sexual fantasy, do you typically focus on visual images?	Yes 43%	Yes 81%
During sexual fantasy, do you typically focus on emotional feelings?	Yes 57%	Yes 19%
Would any person in your sexual fantasy be acceptable as long as he or she were physically attractive (emotional involvement not relevant)?	Yes 25%	Yes 62%

Source: Adapted from Ellis, B. J., & Symons, D. (1990). Sex differences in sexual fantasy: An evolutionary psychological approach. *Journal of Sex Research, 27,* 527–555. Used by permission.

Ellis and Symons (1990) identified two major differences between women and men in regard to their sexual fantasies:

1. Greater sexual variety in male sexual fantasies. Four times as many men reported they have had sexual fantasies with over 1,000 different partners. Only 8% of women reported such variety. Ellis and Symons (1990) explained this finding on the basis of evolutionary theory that men have limited parental investment and are reproductively successful by impregnating a number of women, not just a few.
2. Greater emotional focus in women's sexual fantasies. Women were twice as likely as men to report being emotionally involved with their sexual fantasy partner. Evolutionary theory emphasizes the need of the female to be concerned about the long-term consequences of her sexual involvement. If a woman has sex with no emotional involvement or commitment, her offspring is at greater risk than if she requires an emotional context for sexual availability. Greater emotional focus of the woman was also illustrated in the fact that women were three times more likely than men to say that they focus on feelings in their sexual fantasies.

As women get older, they tend to become increasingly comfortable with their sexuality, and their imaginations grow more fertile.

Ronni Sandroff

CONSIDERATION: Research on sexual fantasies is largely based on self-report data and is subject to distortion. According to Wilson (1978),

> It is therefore possible that the sex differences [in sexual fantasies] . . . are exaggerated because men are reluctant to appear 'unmanly' and women afraid of seeming 'unfeminine'. Anonymity in data collection is only partial protection against this danger. (p. 51)

Both women and men evaluate the experience of sexual fantasy in positive ways. When asked about the degree to which they enjoyed their sexual fantasies versus repressed them, 89% of the women and 92% of the men reported that they enjoyed the feelings (Ellis & Symons, 1990).

CHOICES

Choices in regard to one's individual sexuality include whether to masturbate, use a vibrator, masturbate in the presence of a partner and share one's fantasies with a partner. Individuals who want to become erotically aroused to a particular stimulus may also decide to use masturbation as a means to help achieve that goal.

Choose to Masturbate?

Earlier we noted that masturbation has a number of benefits, such as gaining knowledge about one's own sexuality, increasing the chance for orgasm, and avoiding extramarital entanglements. Some sex therapists routinely encourage masturbation in those clients who report little interest in sex and who reach orgasm infrequently or not at all (LoPiccolo & Lobitz, 1972).

However, not all therapists agree with this viewpoint. Psychiatrist Thomas Szasz (1980) noted that some clients who feel very uncomfortable about masturbating are, nevertheless, browbeaten into masturbating. In the hope of therapeutic success, therapists induce them into something they do not want to do. Dr. Szasz feels that therapists should recognize that opting not to masturbate is a viable and acceptable choice.

> Masturbation—like any sexual activity uninjurious to others—is a matter of private, personal conduct. It expresses and reflects, as does all behavior, the individual's medical and moral convictions about the nature of human sexuality and its proper role in her or his own life. The fact that a particular act is unpleasant or bad does not make it a disease; nor does the fact that it is pleasant or good make it a treatment. (p. 69)

Choose to Use a Vibrator?

Using a vibrator is also a choice. Such a choice should involve a number of considerations. First, a vibrator should never be used near water since it may produce a deadly shock. Also, some people report a feeling of pain or a sensation that is too intense when the vibrator is placed directly on the clitoris or the head of the penis. To avoid this, the vibrator should not be in direct contact with these areas. A piece of material, such as a thin towel, placed between the clitoris or penis and the vibrator will eliminate these unpleasant sensations.

Virginia Johnson also recommended caution in using the vibrator (Masters & Johnson, 1976). She suggested that if a woman uses intense mechanical stimulation over a long period of time, she may lose her appreciation of the various stages of buildup and may diminish her ultimate joy. In other words, since the vibrator will usually produce an orgasm quickly, it may short-circuit erotic fantasies, slow buildup, and eventual release so that some of the emotional and cognitive aspects of orgasm are lost. Of course, these admonitions are also appropriate to men.

A final caveat to consider in deciding whether to use a vibrator is to be sensitive to a partner's feelings about such use. Some partners encourage the use of a vibrator, but others may be threatened by them. One man said that his fiancee had gotten "hooked" on her vibrator and "I think she prefers it to me." The vibrator should be integrated with caution into an existing sexual relationship.

Choose to Masturbate with One's Partner?

Some partners regard masturbation as a personal and private experience, while others view it as an experience to share (see Figure 1). Regarding the latter, Rubin (1991) noted that couples under 35 were particularly likely to share the experience: "We love to watch each other masturbate; it's a great turn on" (p. 186).

A positive view of masturbating with one's partner is reflected in the following (Boston Women's Health Book Collective, 1984, p. 178):

> When my fiancé asked if he could help me masturbate I thought it was kinky at first. Then I showed him how I do it and he showed me how he does. We watch each other to see what feels good. . . .
>
> My lover rubbed her breasts and clitoris while I made love to her yesterday. After I got over feeling a little inadequate (I should be able to do it all!), I found it was like having another pair of hands to make love to her with. It was a turn-on to both of us.

Choosing to avoid masturbating together should not be interpreted negatively. Rather, one's need for privacy may create discomfort with mutual masturbation and be independent of the positive feelings one has for the partner or the quality of the relationship.

Choose to Share Sexual Fantasies with One's Partner?

Rubin's (1991) under-35-year-old respondents reported that they enjoyed sharing their fantasies. One respondent

Continued

Continued

noted, "It's very exciting to tell our fantasies to each other while we're making love" (p. 186). Other people may be less comfortable. To them, hearing the sexual fantasies of a partner may engender feelings of insecurity, jealousy, and rage—particularly in those cases where the sexual fantasies of a partner involve a previous lover.

In the Davidson and Hoffman (1980) study, about 20% of the respondents reported that their sex partners were aware of their sexual fantasies. Those who disclosed their sexual fantasies to the partners tended to be as satisfied with their current sex life as those who did not. However, more respondents felt that revealing their personal sexual fantasies would have potentially negative (rather than positive) effects on their sex partners. Wilson (1978) suggested that,

> Fantasies may play a constructive role in adding spice to love-making that threatens to become dull. This positive benefit is more likely to be gained if the fantasies are openly shared and discussed with the partner. We should be aware of our own fantasies and what they tell us. We should also recognize those of our partner, so we can take account of them in developing a truly satisfying relationship. (pp. 148–149)

Choose to Use Masturbation Fantasies to Change Sexual Object Choice?

Some individuals have been successful using masturbation fantasies as a means of attaching a positive, pleasurable stimulus value to a previously neutral stimulus. Marquis (1970) detailed the procedure as follows:

> The client is instructed to masturbate to the point where he feels the inevitability of orgasm using whatever fantasy is more arousing. Then he is to switch to the appropriate fantasy. . . . After he has successfully shifted to the appropriate stimulus four or five times (this is arbitrary but seems to work) he is instructed to start moving the introduction of the appropriate fantasy backward in time toward the beginning of masturbation. (p. 266)

For example, a person who is unaroused by a person but would like to be might use whatever fantasy elicits intense sexual arousal and, at the point of orgasm, switch to the partner with whom a sexual attachment is sought. Therapists often hear clients say, "I love my partner and want to be turned on, but I'm not. My partner is just like a bland bowl of lukewarm soup to me." While choosing to use masturbatory fantasies may result in being aroused by the desired object, the procedure does not always work. Of 14 people using this reconditioning procedure, five achieved their goal, four were much improved, three were much improved with treatment continuing, one was slightly improved, and one was not improved (Marquis, 1970, p. 271).

Given that erotic arousal to a particular stimulus may sometimes develop as a consequence of masturbating to that stimulus, it is reasonable to ask, "Is masturbation ever harmful?" Our answer is a qualified "maybe." For example, a man who selects young children as masturbatory fantasies may strengthen a sexual attraction for young children. Deviant sexual fantasy has been hypothesized to desensitize one's inhibitions, as well as to "reinforce positive associations to deviant sexual behaviors" (Lanyon, 1991, p. 38). While not all people act on their sexual fantasies, to encourage the development of some cognitive-arousal linkages may be unwise.

Summary

> The sharing of fantasies requires a great deal of tolerance, understanding, and security in a relationship, and represents the very highest degree of intimacy between sexual partners.
>
> *Glenn Wilson*

1. Sexuality involves both intrapersonal (self-concept, body image, sex guilt) and interpersonal (interactions between individuals) variables.
2. Intrapersonal aspects of sexuality include self-concept and sexual self-concept, body image, sexual guilt, and erotophobia/erotophilia.
3. Erotophobics report fear of sex, high sex guilt, and parents with strict attitudes about sex. Erotophilics have more positive feelings and attitudes toward sex and report less sexual guilt.
4. Celibacy may be both voluntary (for religious or personal reasons) and involuntary (residence in a hospital or nursing or retirement home or no available partner).
5. Masturbation may begin in infancy. Among older adolescents and adults, masturbation is a common sexual behavior, more so for men than for women.
6. Although change is occurring, religious leaders, physicians, therapists, and parents have traditionally taught young people negative attitudes toward masturbation.

7. Masturbation has both advantages (orgasm easier, no partner necessary, extradyadic entanglements avoided) and disadvantages (guilt, potential to develop attraction to inappropriate stimulus, perception by partner that partner is inadequate).
8. Women are more likely to masturbate because their preferred sexual partner is not available; men are more likely to masturbate to relieve sexual tension.
9. There are a variety of masturbation techniques used by women and men.
10. Sexual fantasies are another common form of individual sexual experience. Sexual fantasies serve a variety of functions, including heightening arousal, providing variety and control, and serving as rehearsal for future sexual encounters.

KEY TERMS

sexual self-concept
sex guilt
erotophobia
erotophilia
sexual celibacy
masturbation
autoerotic asphyxia syndrome
semen-conservation doctrine
locus of control
sexual fantasy

REFERENCES

Alzate, H. (1989). Sexual behavior of unmarried Colombian university students: A follow-up. *Archives of Sexual Behavior, 18,* 239–250.

Barbach, L. (1976). *For yourself: The fulfillment of female sexuality.* Garden City, NY: Doubleday.

Bechtel, L. S., Westerfield, R. C., & Eddy, J. M. (1990). Autoerotic fatalities: Implications for health educators. *Health Education, 21,* 38–40.

Blanchard, R., and Hucker, S. J. (1991). Age, transvestism, bondage, and concurrent paraphilic activities in 117 fatal cases of autoerotic asphyxia. *British Journal of Psychiatry, 159,* 371–377.

Boston Women's Health Book Collective. (1984). *The New Our Bodies, Ourselves.* New York: Simon & Schuster, Inc.

Bretschneider, J. G., & McCoy, N. L. (1988). Sexual interest and behavior in healthy 80- to 102-year-olds. *Archives of Sexual Behavior, 17,* 109–129.

Bullough, V. L. (1976). *Sexual variance in society and history.* New York: Wiley.

Carnes, P. (1983). *Out of the shadows: Understanding sexual addiction.* Minneapolis: CompCare Publications.

Catania, J. A., & White, C. B. (1982). Sexuality in an aged sample: Cognitive determinants of masturbation. *Archives of Sexual Behavior, 11,* 237–245.

Clifford, R. E. (1978). Development of masturbation in college women. *Archives of Sexual Behavior, 7,* 559–573.

Darling, C. A., Davidson, J. K., Sr., & Cox, R. P. (1991). Female sexual response and the timing of partner orgasm. *Journal of Sex and Marital Therapy, 17,* 3–21.

Davidson, J. K., & Darling, C. A. (1988). Changing autoerotic attitudes and practices among college females: A two-year follow up study. *Adolescence, 23,* 773–792.

Davidson, J. K., Sr., & Hoffman, L. E. (1980). Sexual fantasies and sexual satisfaction: An empirical analysis of erotic thoughts. Unpublished paper, University of Wisconsin-Eau Claire and University of Notre Dame, Notre Dame, IN. Used with permission.

Davidson, J. K., & Moore, N. B. (1991, November). Masturbation and sexual intercourse among college women: Making choices for sexual fulfillment. Paper presented at the meeting of the Society for the Scientific Study of Sex, New Orleans.

Diokno, A. C., Brown, M. B., & Herzog, A. R. (1990). Sexual function in the elderly. *Archives of Internal Medicine, 150,* 197–200.

Dodson, B. (1987). *Sex for one: The joy of self love.* Glendale, CA: Crown.

Ellis, B. J., & Symons, D. (1990). Sex differences in sexual fantasy: An evolutionary psychological approach. *Journal of Sex Research, 27,* 527–555.

Erkmen, H., Dilbaz, N., Serber, G., Kaptanoglu, C., & Tekin, D. (1990). Sexual attitudes of Turkish university students. *Journal of Sex Education and Therapy, 16,* 251–261.

Fisher, W. A., Byrne, D., White, L. A. (1983). Emotional barriers to contraception. In D. Byrne & W. A. Fisher (Eds.) Adolescents, sex, and contraception (pp. 207–272). Hillsdale, NJ: Lawrence Erlbaum.

Fisher, W. A., Byrne, D., White, L. A., & Kelley, K. (1988). Erotophobia-erotophilia as a dimension of personality. *Journal of Sex Research, 25,* 123–151.

Fleisher, D. R., & Morrison, A. (1990). Masturbation mimicking abdominal pain or seizures in young girls. *Journal of Pediatrics, 116,* 810–811.

Franzoi, S. L., & Shields, S. A. (1984). The body esteem scale: Multidimensional structure and sex differences in a college population. *Journal of Personality Assessment, 48,* 173–178.

Friday, N. (1991). *Women on top: Women's sexual fantasies of power, self-exploration, and insatiable lust.* New York: Simon & Schuster.

Gil, V. E. (1990). Sexual fantasy experiences and guilt among conservative Christians: An exploratory study. *Journal of Sex Research, 27,* 629–638.

Gold, S. R., Balzano, B. F., & Stamey, R. (1991). Two studies of females' sexual force fantasies. *Journal of Sex Education and Therapy, 17,* 15–26.

Graham, S. (1848). *Lecture to young men, on chastity, intended also for the serious consideration of parents and guardians* (10th ed.). Boston: C. H. Price.

Gross-Kopf, D. (1983). *Sex and the married woman.* New York: Wallaby.

Hatano, Y. (1991). Changes in the sexual activities of Japanese youth. *Journal of Sex Education and Therapy, 17,* 1–14.

Heiman, J., LoPiccolo, L., & LoPiccolo, J. (1976). *Becoming orgasmic: A sexual growth program for women.* Englewood Cliffs, NJ: Prentice-Hall.

Hesse-Biber, S. (1989). Eating patterns and disorders in a college population: Are college women's eating problems a new phenomenon? *Sex Roles, 20,* 71–87.

Hessellund, H. (1976). Masturbation and sexual fantasies in married couples. *Archives of Sexual Behavior, 5,* 133–147.

Hite, S. (1977). *The Hite report: A nationwide study of female sexuality.* New York: Dell.

Hite, S. (1981). *The Hite report on male sexuality.* New York: Alfred Knopf.

Jones, J. C., & Barlow, D. H. (1990). Self-reported frequency of sexual urges, fantasies and masturbatory fantasies in heterosexual males and females. *Archives of Sexual Behavior, 19,* 269–280.

Kinsey, A., Pomeroy, W., & Martin, C. (1948). *Sexual behavior in the human male.* Philadelphia: W. B. Saunders.

Kinsey, A., Pomeroy, W., Martin, C., & Gebhard, P. (1953). *Sexual behavior in the human female.* Philadelphia: W. B. Saunders.

Knox, D., & Schacht, C. (1992). Sexual partners of university students enrolled in a human sexuality course. *College Student Journal, 26,* 38–40.

Lanyon, R. I. (1991). Theories of sex offending. In C. R. Hollin & K. Howells (Eds.) *Clinical Approaches to Sex Offenders and Their Victims* (pp. 35–54). New York: Wiley.

LoPiccolo, J., & Lobitz, W. C. (1972). The role of masturbation in the treatment of orgasmic dysfunction. *Archives of Sexual Behavior, 2,* 163–171.

Lunde, I., Larsen, G. K., Fog, E., & Garde, K. (1991). Sexual desire, orgasm, and sexual fantasies: A study of 625 Danish women born in 1910, 1936, and 1958. *Journal of Sex Education and Therapy, 17,* 111–116.

Maletzky, B. M. (1991). *Treating the sexual offender.* Newbury Park: Sage.

Marquis, J. N. (1970). Orgasmic reconditioning: Changing sexual object choice through controlling masturbation fantasies. *Journal of Behavior Therapy and Experimental Psychiatry, 1,* 263–271.

Masters, W. H., & Johnson, V. E. (1976). *The pleasure bond.* New York: Bantam.

Masters, W. H., & Johnson, V. E. (1979, Nov.). Playboy Interview. *Playboy,* p. 87–122.

Mednick, R. A. (1980). Sexual fantasy. In R. Woody (Ed.), *Encyclopedia of clinical assessment* (vol. 2, pp. 684–696). San Francisco: Jossey-Bass.

Money, J. (1986). *Lovemaps: Clinical concepts of sexual/erotic health and pathology paraphilia and gender transpositions in childhood adolescence and maturity.* Buffalo, NY: Prometheus Books.

Money, J., Prakasam, K. S., & Joshi, V. N. (1991). Semen-conservation doctrine from ancient Ayurvedic to modern sexological theory. *American Journal of Psychotherapy, 45,* 9–13.

Mulligan, T., & Palguta, R. F., Jr. (1991). Sexual interest, activity, and satisfaction among male nursing home residents. *Archives of Sexual Behavior, 20,* 199–204.

Pruzinsky, T., & Cash, T. F. (1990). Medical interventions for the enhancement of adolescents' physical appearance: Implications for social competence. In T. P. Gullotta, G. R. Adams, and R. Montemayor (Eds.), *Developing social competency in adolescence* (pp. 220–242). Newbury Park, CA: Sage.

Rokach, A. (1990). Content analysis of sexual fantasies of males and females. *Journal of Psychology, 124,* 427–436.

Rubenstein, C. (1983, July). The modern art of courtly love. *Psychology Today,* pp. 40–49.

Rubin, L. B. (1991). *Erotic wars: What Happened to the Sexual Revolution?* New York: Harper Perennial.

Sauer, M. V., Zeffer, K. B., Buster, J. E., & Sokol, R. Z. (1988). The effect of abstinence on sperm motility in normal men. *American Journal of Obstetrics and Gynecology, 158,* 604–607.

Shanor, K. (1978). *The Shanor study: The sexual sensitivity of the American male.* New York: Dial.

Smith, T. W. (1991). Adult sexual behavior in 1989: Number of partners, frequency of intercourse and risk of AIDS. *Family Planning Perspectives, 23,* 102–107.

Sue, D. (1979). Erotic fantasies of college students during coitus. *Journal of Sex Research, 4,* 299–305.

Szasz, J. T. (1980). *Sex by prescription.* New York: Doubleday.

Tannahill, F. (1982). *Sex in history.* New York: Scarborough Books.

Tavris, C., & Sadd, S. (1977). *The Redbook report on female sexuality.* New York: Delacorte.

Tissot, S. A. (1766). *Onania, or a treatise upon the disorders produced by masturbation* (A. Hume, Trans.). London: J. Pridden. (Original work published 1758).

Vieira, D. N., & Da Silva, A. G. (1989). Accidental hanging during auto-erotic practices. *Acta Medica Protuguesa, 2,* 154–157.

Weis, D. L., Rabinowitz, B., & Ruckstuhl, M. F. (1992). Individual changes in sexual attitudes and behavior within college-level human sexuality courses. *The Journal of Sex Research, 29,* 43–59.

Wilson, G. (1978). *The secrets of sexual fantasy.* London: J. M. Dent & Sons, Ltd.

Winter, L. (1988). The role of sexual self-concept in the use of contraceptives. *Family Planning Perspectives, 20,* 123–127.

Wolfe, L. (1982). *The Cosmo report.* New York: Bantam.

Zilbergeld, B. (1978). *Male sexuality.* Boston: Little, Brown.

CHAPTER TEN

Interpersonal Sexuality

Chapter Outline

Social Construction of Sexuality in Relationships
- Relationships and Sex Frequency
- Relationships and Nonmonogamy

Dating and Sexuality
- Functions of Dating
- Sexual Expectations in Dating
- **Research Perspective:** The College Bar Scene: A Happy Hunting Ground?
- Dating among the Divorced and Widowed

Cohabitation and Sexuality
- Definition, Incidence, and Types of Cohabitating Relationships
- Sexuality in Cohabitating Relationships

Marriage and Sexuality
- Motivations for Marriage
- Types of Marriage Relationships
- Sexuality in Marital Relationships

Relationship Quality
- Comparisons of Types of Partners
- **Self-Assessment:** Index of Sexual Satisfaction (ISS)

Extradyadic Sexuality
- Types of Extradyadic Sexual Involvements
- Motivations and Reasons for Extradyadic Sexual Involvements

Sexual Involvements with Co-Workers
- Managing Sexual Attraction at Work
- Intimate Relationships at Work: Issues for Employees

Interpersonal Noncoital Sexual Behavior
- Touching
- Kissing
- Breast Stimulation
- Penile Stimulation
- Clitoral Stimulation
- Other Petting Behaviors
- Effects of Petting

Sexual Intercourse Positions
- Man-on-Top Position
- Woman-on-Top Position
- Side-by-Side Position
- Rear-Entry Position
- Sitting Position
- Standing Position
- Variations

Choices
- Choose Extradyadic Sex? No
- Choose Extradyadic Sex? Yes
- Choose to Become Involved with Someone at Work?

Is It True?*

1. Married couples have intercourse more frequently than cohabitating couples.

2. Heterosexual wives are more likely to be unfaithful than lesbians in their respective pair-bonded relationships.

3. Couples who live together before marriage are less likely to get divorced than couples who do not live together.

4. Men are more likely than women to have sex with strangers.

5. Extramarital affairs are sometimes reported to have positive consequences for a couple's relationship.

* 1 = F, 2 = F, 3 = F, 4 = T, 5 = T

Sex cannot be contained within a definition of physical pleasure, it cannot be understood as merely itself for it has stood for too long as a symbol of profound connection between human beings.

Elizabeth Janeway

The broken engagement of Julia Roberts and Keifer Sutherland, the marriages of Elizabeth Taylor and Richard Burton, and the legal dispute over the "prenuptual" agreement between Martina Navratilova and her lover emphasize that sexuality is often interpersonal. Aside from masturbation and fantasy, most sexual activity occurs in the context of an interpersonal relationship (McKinney & Sprecher, 1991). While these may involve brief encounters, in this chapter we focus on interpersonal sexuality within the context of relatively enduring relationships. Following a developmental approach, we focus on dating, cohabitating, and marital relationships. We also discuss extramarital sexual encounters and sexual involvements among co-workers. Consistent with the theme of the text, we emphasize that choice is an important element in regard to our interpersonal sexuality.

Intimate relationships shape sexuality.
Philip Blumstein
Pepper Schwartz

According to Kelley and his colleagues (1983), a close interpersonal relationship is characterized by frequent interaction, intense emotionality, pervasiveness of the relationship in the various aspects of the partners' respective lives, and relative durability.

CONSIDERATION: While frequent interaction, intense emotionality, pervasiveness, and relative durability describe most intimate relationships, they do not specify the nature of the relationship. The partners may be friends or lovers; homosexual, heterosexual, or bisexual; legally committed to each other or not; have traditional or nontraditional gender role relations; and interested in varying amounts of sexual interaction. Indeed, the term *relationship* is a general term and can involve a broad range of pairings.

Social Construction of Sexuality in Relationships

The sexual choices an individual makes are influenced by the social processes and cultural expectations regarding various types of interpersonal relationships. Next, we examine how two aspects of sexuality (frequency and nonmonogamy) are influenced by the nature of the relationship (married, cohabitating, homosexual) in which they occur.

Relationships and Sex Frequency

Blumstein and Schwartz (1990) collected data from heterosexual marriages, heterosexual cohabitation relationships, male homosexual couples, and lesbian couples and looked at the frequency of sex in these pair-bonded relationships. Table 10.1 reflects the percentage of couples reporting sex three times a week or more.

According to Blumstein and Schwartz, the declining frequency of sex in all relationships across time is due to habituation, or satiation from repeated exposure to the same stimulus. Partners who are sexually satiated are less interested in having sex with their partners. However, habituation does not occur at the same rate for all couples. For example, male homosexual couples maintain a higher sex frequency

TABLE 10.1 Percentage of Couples Reporting Sex Three Times a Week or More

Years Living Together	Married Couples	Cohabitating Couples	Male Couples	Female Couples
2 or less	45%	61%	67%	33%
2–10	27%	38%	32%	7%
10 or more	18%		11%	1%

Source: Blumstein, P., & Schwartz, P. (1990), Intimate relationships and the creation of sexuality. In D. P. McWhirter, S. A. Sanders, and J. M. Reinish (Eds.), *Homosexuality/heterosexuality: concepts of sexual orientation* (pp. 307–320), p. 315. New York: Oxford University Press. Used by permission.

than lesbian couples. Blumstein and Schwartz explained that society socializes men to be more sexually aggressive and genitally focused than women. Women, in contrast, are more relationship-oriented in their sexuality and are socialized to be more passive and less genitally focused. The result is higher sex frequencies when two men are paired and lower sex frequencies when two women are paired.

The discrepancy between higher sex frequencies among cohabitating couples compared to married couples may, in part, be explained on the basis of power. Women in cohabitating relationships are likely to have less power (if they want marriage), which translates into more passivity regarding sex frequency. Wives, however, may feel more comfortable declining the sexual initiatives of their husband with little risk to his commitment to the relationship. In addition, individuals who live together may differ from married couples in terms of the basis for their relationship. Cohabitating partners may have a greater sexual focus whereas that of marrieds may be more broad-based. Such a sexual basis among cohabitants would translate into higher sexual frequencies.

Relationships and Nonmonogamy

Table 10.2 illustrates the influence of one's relationship on sexual fidelity choices. Norms of fidelity are strongest for spouses, weaker for cohabitants, and the weakest of all for male homosexuals. Again, the type of relationship one is involved in will influence one's sexual choices. A man who moves from a heterosexual marital relationship to a homosexual pair-bonded cohabitating relationship is likely to be less faithful in the latter than in the former.

TABLE 10.2 Percentage of Respondents Reporting at Least One Instance of Nonmonogamy in the Previous Year (Couples Living Together between Two and 10 Years)

Category	Percent	Number of Respondents
Husbands	11%	1,510
Wives	9%	1,510
Male cohabitants	25%	288
Female cohabitants	22%	288
Homosexual males	79%	943
Lesbians	19%	706

Source: Blumstein, P., & Schwartz, P. (1990). Intimate relationships and the creation of sexuality. In D. P. McWhirter, S. A. Sanders, and J. M. Reinish (Eds.), Homosexuality/heterosexuality: Concepts of sexual orientation (pp. 307–320), p. 317. New York: Oxford University Press. Used by permission.

According to Blumstein and Schwartz (1990), homosexual men who are pair bonded and who live together have relatively high rates of nonmonogamy.

For me, the highest level of sexual excitement is in a monogamous relationship.

Warren Beatty

In summarizing their observations, Blumstein and Schwartz (1990) observed,

> This cursory look at sexual expression in intimate relationships is not intended as more than an illustration of the analytic mileage to be gained by conceptualizing sex within the context of social circumstances. Even by looking at relatively crude survey data we can see that sexual behavior is created by relationship expectations and traditions rather than by sexual essences. (p. 318)

We have just looked at how two specific aspects of sexuality (i.e., sex frequency and nonmonogamy) are influenced by the nature of the relationship within which they exist. In the following sections of this chapter, we explore various aspects of sexuality within the social context of dating, cohabitating, marital, extradyadic, and co-worker relationships.

DATING AND SEXUALITY

Individuals often encounter their first interpersonal sexual experiences in dating relationships. Dating is common in adolescence and young adulthood.

Functions of Dating

Because most people regard dating or "getting together" as a natural part of getting to know someone, the other functions of dating are sometimes overlooked. These include:

NATIONAL DATA: In a national sample of 18-year-olds, 97% of the men and 98% of the women reported that they had been on a date (Thornton, 1990, p. 246).

1. Development of Self-Concept. Sociologist Charles Horton Cooley (1902/1964) coined the term "looking-glass self," which refers to the self-concept that results from interactions with others. In dating relationships, we may develop aspects of our self-concept from observing how our dating partner perceives us.

CONSIDERATION: An individual's self-concept is influenced by virtually all of the significant relationships that she or he has, including parents, siblings, and teachers. Dating partners, however, specifically influence our self-concept as intimate and sexual partners.

2. Recreation. Among adolescents, dating provides an opportunity to be with peers (and away from parents) engaging in fun activities. Adults often look to dating to provide a break from the stress of work.

CONSIDERATION: Dating is viewed as an activity engaged in by couples who are not in a marital or cohabitating relationship. However, some married and cohabitating couples go on "dates" or have "date night" with each other. That is, many couples plan and engage in recreational or romantic activities together as a means of ensuring that they spend enjoyable time together to nurture their relationship and escape the daily routines of work, household chores, and child rearing.

3. Companionship, Intimacy, and Sex. Dating provides a context for companionship, intimacy, and sex. Over 70% of a national sample of men and 75% of a national sample of women report having gone steady at least once by age 18. The more steady and involved the relationship, the greater the sexual involvement (Thornton, 1990, p. 246).
4. Socialization. Dating provides the opportunity to develop an array of skills in human relationships, such as conversing, listening, and expressing empathy. Dating also permits an individual to try out different role patterns, such as dominance or submission, and to assess his or her comfort with each.
5. Status, Achievement, and Sorting. Dating is used "partly to achieve, prove, or maintain status" (Rice, 1990, p. 359). Dating can be a means of entry into a prestigious clique. Young people from higher socioeconomic levels date more often than youth from lower levels. While Rice suggested that status-seeking is no longer a major motivation for dating, Basow (1992) noted the persistence of sex role stereotyping in dating, which includes (especially for girls and women) emphasis on attracting a high-status mate.

   "For both sexes, many dating and romantic involvements serve instrumental purposes—peer acceptance and conformity to sex role expectations—and not necessarily emotional ones" (Basow, 1992, p. 213). The pressure many young people feel regarding the need to conform to social expectations pushes them to date. McNaught (1983) described how gay high school and college students "generally faked the [heterosexual] dating ritual and frequently selected a safe companion for the sake of appearances" (p. 142).
6. Mate Selection. Dating may serve to pair two people off for marriage or for a nonmarital long-term committed relationship. Eighty-nine percent of 80 clients at a videodating service said that they were looking for a serious, permanent relationship, rather than a casual one (Woll & Young, 1989, p. 485).

Don't wait until you find someone you can live with; wait until you find someone you can't live without.

Anonymous

Sexual Expectations in Dating

Women and men often have different sexual expectations on dates. In one study (Knox & Wilson, 1983), 227 university women and 107 university men indicated what they felt was appropriate sexual behavior for a specific number of dates. In general, men expected kissing, petting, and intercourse after a fewer number of dates than women. This pattern was particularly evident in regard to intercourse. Almost half (48%) of the men, in contrast to about a quarter (23%) of the women, felt that intercourse was appropriate by the fifth date. When the female students were asked about the discrepancy between what they and their dates expected, 36% reported that "unwanted pressure to engage in sexual behavior" and "sexual misunderstandings" were the primary problems they experienced on dates (Knox & Wilson, 1983).

CONSIDERATION: Sex is often used as a bargaining tool in dating relationships, whereby sex is exchanged for commitment. The unwritten exchange from the woman's perspective is "the more I feel you care about me, the more sex I am willing to have with you." It is said that, traditionally, women give sex to get love and men give love to get sex. Barbach (1982) noted, "Women rarely see sex as being for their own enjoyment; instead they learn that it is a way to get a man" (p. 13).

"The importance attached to sex for men and the double standard attached to sex for women are additional obstacles to be overcome in developing intimate heterosexual relationships" (Basow, 1992, p. 214). Studies continue to document these sexual scripts among college students. For example, in a study of 750 undergraduates, women reported that they preferred a dating partner (and a marriage partner) who had low prior sexual activity. While men preferred a *dating* partner who had had high sexual activity, they wanted a *marriage* partner with low prior sexual activity (Sprecher, McKinney, & Orbuch, 1987). A conventional dating script was identified by Rose and Frieze (1989) in their study of undergraduate psychology students in the midwest. When asked to list activities which would typically be part of a first date the male and female students wrote scripts that portrayed traditional gender roles. The date scripts for women emphasized concern about their appearance, conversation, and controlling sexuality. Scripts for men emphasized planning, paying for and orchestrating the date, as well as initiating physical contact and arranging for the next date. Apparently, cultural norms for the first date have not changed much over the past 30 years!

However, an alternative to formal dating has evolved and is discussed in the following Research Perspective. In this section we describe a two-part research study on the college bar as an informal gathering and coupling forum.

RESEARCH PERSPECTIVE

The College Bar Scene: A Happy Hunting Ground?

In the last two decades dating practices have changed considerably. An informal pattern of "getting together" has partially replaced formal dates. Strouse (1987, p. 375) described the current dating pattern as one in which "young people congregate at mixed-sex places such as parties or bars, meet, and if mutually agreeable, pair off for the evening." Strouse conducted an exploratory study to investigate the function that college bars serve as a context for facilitating heterosexual contacts.

Class Survey

The first group of students surveyed by Strouse were enrolled in an introductory human sexuality class. Questions they were asked included the following:

1. Do you go to the local bars primarily to (1) drink, (2) play games (pool, etc.), (3) socialize with friends, (4) meet a sexual partner, (5) dance, (6) listen to music, (7) relax, (8) not applicable.

Continued

Continued

2. If I want to 'get together' or meet an opposite sex person, I will go to ________, ________, ________ (in order of preference).

Students reported going to bars mainly to socialize with friends (51%). Only 7% reported the motive "to meet a sexual partner." Only 6% reported going primarily to drink. Frequently cited preferred meeting places were settings where alcohol was available. Thirty-five percent preferred a bar and 24% a party or kegger (party with one or more kegs of beer) as their first choice. For their second choice, 32% selected a bar, and 29% chose a party or kegger.

Bar Survey

In addition to administering questionnaires to students in class, Strouse also paid graduate students to disseminate questionnaires to college bar patrons between 9 and 10:30 P.M. The data collectors invited people (avoiding those who were obviously inebriated) to complete a brief questionnaire. Then, about five minutes later, the data collectors returned and collected the paper and placed it in a ballot-like box. Only two people refused to participate. In the survey, respondents were asked to indicate the main reasons they go to bars and why they think others go. Table 1 displays the reasons reported for themselves and for others.

As is evident in the table, there was generally a discrepancy between the respondent's own reported motives and those attributed to others. Most frequently reported was the goal of "seeing friends." Students guessed that others were more likely than they to go for "pickups," "drinking," "get drunk," "fun, relax," "meet person of opposite sex," or to "meet people in general."

Comparing men's responses to women's reveals noticeable differences. Men were more likely to report a motivation of drinking, getting drunk, or sexual interest. Strouse described men as "much more direct, blunt and sexual in their responses

Continued

TABLE 1 Bar Patrons' Expressed Reasons for Why They and Others Go to Bars

	For themselves[a]			For others[b]		
Reason	*Men*	*Women*	*Total*[c]	*Men*	*Women*	*Total*[d]
See friends	21.1	25.2	23.1	26.8	41.9	34.4
Escape boredom	14.8	12.6	13.7	5.5	3.9	4.7
Recreation	7.0	18.1	12.5	1.6	5.4	3.5
Pickups	14.1	.8	7.5	18.9	.8	9.8
Drinking	9.4	4.7	7.1	7.1	8.5	7.8
Get drunk	10.2	2.4	6.3	14.2	6.2	10.2
Fun, relax	9.4	14.2	11.8	11.8	17.8	14.8
Meet person of opposite sex	3.1	5.5	4.3	7.1	3.1	5.1
Meet people in general	.8	2.4	1.6	5.5	9.3	7.4
Other	10.2	14.2	12.2	1.6	3.1	2.3
Total	100.1	100.1	100.1	100.1	100.0	100.0

[a]For answers for themselves, $\chi^2(9, N = 255), = 34.09, p < .0001$.
[b]For answers for others, $\chi^2(9, N = 256) = 38.44, p < .0000$.
[c]Total $N = 255$ (5 missing observations), 128 males and 127 females.
[d]Total $N = 256$ (4 missing observations), 127 males and 129 females.
Published by permission of the *Journal of Sex Research,* a publication of the Society for the Scientific Study of Sex.

Continued

than were the women," as evidenced in the following samples of written responses given by men to indicate their reasons for going to bars.

> Fuck chicks. To find sexual companions (short term). To find a piece of ass! Sex, Sex, Sex. Look for some hole. Get a buzz, hopefully a lay. Sex. To get laid. To meet a neat person of the opposite sex. For some pussy and a little bit of love. (Strouse, 1987, p. 379)

Women, on the other hand, may have had sexual intent but tended to be much less explicit. For example, one woman wrote, "I think the bar is a forum for loosening inhibitions and eliciting new sexual/romantic relationships—generally short-lived."

Conclusions

These college students reported a combination of motivations for going to a pub or bar, including escaping boredom, having fun and relaxing, seeing friends, and possibly meeting a heterosexual partner. Strouse (1987) observed that alcohol consumption clearly acts as a catalyst. As one woman explained, she goes to the bar "to meet people of the opposite sex, to get drunk, thereby creating an easier way to meet people of the opposite sex" (p. 379). Changes in the legal drinking age have probably moved some of this mileu from bars to parties. Still, Strouse concluded, the drinking context and the act of drinking provide a salient milieu for socializing and exploring potential sexual encounters. He suggested that programs designed to reduce problematic use of alcohol by students must take students' motives for drinking into consideration. Such programs, then, must encourage students to use other means for socializing with friends and pursuing sexual encounters and relationships.

Reference

Strouse, J. S. (1987). College bars as social settings for heterosexual contacts. *Journal of Sex Research, 23,* 374–382.

We have been discussing dating relationships among never-married people. Next, we discuss dating "the second time around," that is, among the divorced or widowed.

Dating among the Divorced and Widowed

Over 2 million Americans get divorced each year (National Center for Health Statistics, 1992). Most people who divorce wish to become involved in another relationship (as evidenced by the fact that over three-quarters of the divorced remarry). The "single again" population differs from those dating prior to a first marriage in several ways, including:

1. Age. When divorced men remarry, their average age is around 37; divorced women, 33. When widowed men remarry, their average age is around 63; widowed women, 54. In contrast, when these men and women married for the first time, their average ages were 25 and 23, respectively. Hence, divorced individuals are, on the average, 10 years older when they begin to date again. Widows and widowers are usually at least 30 years older when they begin to date "the second time around" (*Statistical Abstract of the United States: 1992,* Table 130).
2. Number of Available Partners. Since over 60% of the U.S. population is married (*Statistical Abstract of the United States: 1992,* Table 48), most men and women who are dating the second time around find that there are fewer partners from

which to choose than when they were dating prior to a first marriage. Divorced and widowed women, particularly, may have difficulty in finding a partner. Not only are there more women than men in our society, but it is normative for men to date younger women. All the younger women are available to the older men, but all the younger men are not available to the older women. The result is fewer choices of a partner for women.

3. Greater HIV and STD Risk. The older an unmarried person, the greater the likelihood the person has had multiple sexual partners (Thornton, 1990; Knox & Schacht, 1992), which has been associated with increased risk of contracting HIV and other STDs. Therefore, individuals entering the dating market for the second time are advised to be more selective in choosing their sexual partners because the likelihood of those partners having had a higher number of sexual partners is greater. In addition, the divorced are much less likely to be monogamous than married adults (Greeley, Michael, & Smith 1990), so dating an older divorced person may involve even greater risk of contracting an STD.
4. Presence of Children. Over half of those dating again have children from a previous marriage. How these children feel about their parents dating, how the partners feel about each other's children, and how the partners' children feel about each other are complex issues. Deciding whether to have intercourse when one's children are in the house, what the children call the new partner, and how relationship terminations are dealt with are other issues that are familiar to many people dating for the second time.
5. Presence of Ex-spouse. The presence of an ex-spouse who still calls, child support and/or alimony checks to or from an ex-spouse, and the experience and memory of the partner's first marriage all will influence the new dating relationship and sexual choices. For example, if the divorced partner still wants to see the ex-spouse with the possibility of intercourse occurring again, how does this affect the new relationship?
6. Shorter Courtship. Divorced people who are dating again tend to have a shorter courtship period than people who marry for the first time. In a study of 248 individuals who remarried, the median length of courtship was nine months, compared to 17 months the first time around (O'Flaherty & Eells, 1988). A shorter courtship may mean that sexual decisions are confronted more quickly—

Doonesbury BY GARRY TRUDEAU

timing of first intercourse, discussing the use of condoms and/or contraceptives, and discussing when and if the relationship is to be monogamous.

7. Awkwardness of Dating Again. Some divorced and widowed who reenter the dating market comment that they feel awkward about dating again. They are accustomed to being with one person at home every night and feel uncomfortable calling up someone for a date, going out on a date, and being in the role of a date, rather than a spouse. It may be helpful to keep in mind that the feeling is not uncommon and may be a topic to faciliate open communication with a new partner. "I'm not sure how to date anymore," when said to a new partner on a first date, acknowledges the awkwardness of the situation, exposes one's vulnerability, and provides an opportunity for the partner to share similar feelings.
8. Uncertain Sexual Agenda. While a sexual agenda may be unclear among young people who date, what is expected sexually is even less certain among older people. In a study of individuals age 60 to 92 who were divorced or widowed and dating again, Bulcroft & O'Conner-Roden (1986) observed a stronger emphasis on hugging, kissing, and touching, but not always. One 71-year-old widower said of his current dating partner, "You can talk about candlelight dinners and sitting in front of a fireplace, but I still think the most romantic thing I've ever done is to go to bed with her" (p. 68).

Cohabitation and Sexuality

It has become more acceptable in our society to live with someone. They don't have to marry to have some of the things we had to marry to get—a home, respectability, sex.

Phyllis Jackson Stegall

One of the major sexuality changes in our society has been the gradual acceptance of couples who live together before marriage. "The norms that once forbade premarital cohabitation have shifted to a more tolerant position" (White, 1989, p. 544). This new attitude toward living together has increased among people of all ages, races, and social classes. Some view living together as a necessary stage in a developing relationship before making a more permanent or legal commitment. Reasons for choosing to live together include fear of marriage; career or educational commitments; increased tolerance from society, parents, and peers; and the desire for a stable emotional and sexual relationship without legal ties. "Cohabitation outside of marriage is no longer a deviant lifestyle alternative nor a clandestine arrangement apart from the larger context of courtship and marriage" (Spanier, 1989, p. 7).

Definition, Incidence, and Types of Cohabitating Relationships

The terms used to describe live-ins include cohabitants and POSSLQ (people of the opposite sex sharing living quarters), the latter used by the U.S. Bureau of the Census. We define living together as two unrelated adults who live in the same household and have an emotional and sexual relationship.

Cohabitation rates are significantly higher in some European countries. Two-thirds of 4,966 Swedish women reported that they had lived with their first husband prior to marriage (Bennett, Blanc, & Bloom, 1988).

NATIONAL DATA: In a national study of of U.S. adults, 28 percent reported that they were cohabitating (Thomson & Colella, 1992).

The various types of cohabitation arrangements include individuals who are emotionally involved but not ready for marriage, those who are waiting to get married, those who live together for economic reasons (it is cheaper), and those who view living together as a permanent alternative to marriage (such informal unions are common among mainland Puerto Ricans according to Landale and Fennelly, 1992). With the exception of cohabitants in Puerto Rico, where living together is more akin to marriage with children, most cohabitants in the U.S. tend not to have children living with them.

Most individuals who live together have a strong emotional relationship with their partners, but they have not yet made a commitment to marry each other. In traditional terms, they are "going steady," but they have also moved in together.

Other couples are planning to marry each other and are living together until the time is right. Although they may not be officially engaged, they intend to be married and are consciously assessing their compatibility. Exhibit 10.1 addresses the issue of whether living together is an effective way of assessing future marital stability.

EXHIBIT 10.1 Living Together as Preparation for Marriage?

One of the motivations for living together is the opportunity to screen out risky marriages. But do couples who live together before they get married have a greater chance of staying married than couples who do not live together before they get married? The answer is no. Based on a comparison of national samples of couples who did and did not live together before they got married, "the proportion separating or divorcing within 10 years is a third higher among those who lived together before marriage than among those who did not— 36 versus 27 percent" (Bumpass & Sweet, 1989, p. 10). These results are similar to those reported by Balakrishnan and colleagues based on Canadian data (1987) and by Booth and Johnson for the United States (1988). Demaris and Vaninadha (1992) also found higher rates of divorce among those who had lived together before marriage. A Swedish study of 4,966 women found that "dissolution rates of women who cohabit premaritally with their future spouse are, on average, nearly 80 percent higher than the rates of those who do not live together" (Bennett et al., 1988, p. 132). Other researchers have also found lower quality marriages (less happy, more conflict), lower commitment to the institution of marriage (belief that marriage is not a lifetime commitment), and greater perceived likelihood of divorce among couples who had cohabitated (Thomson & Colella, 1992).

Schoen (1992) also found higher divorce risks among first time marrieds who had previously cohabitated but noticed that this phenomenon was largely true of persons who were born before the late forties. Those who were born 1948–52 and 1953–57 who lived together and married did not show a significantly higher divorce risk. Schoen argued that this may be due to the fact that in earlier decades, cohabitation was practiced primarily by persons who were less conventional and stable—characteristics that may be related to relationship instability. In more recent decades, cohabitation has been practiced by a wider range of individuals, not only those who are less conventional and stable. However, the respondents in the DeMaris and Vaninadha (1992) study of cohabitation were from a 1972 high school cohort. This cohort did evidence a greater divorce rate which is contrary to what Schoen (1992) would have predicted.

Divorce rates are high among couples who live together before marriage for various reasons:

1. Weaker commitment to marriage. In the Swedish study mentioned above, the researchers suggested that people who cohabit "may be unsure about, or ideologically opposed to, the institution of marriage itself, but who marry perhaps due to mounting external pressure" (Bennett et al., 1988, p. 134). In other words, cohabitants may have a "weaker commitment to the institution of marriage" (p. 137).
2. False image. Live-ins may still be in courtship with each other in that they may selectively present their best self. After marriage, their real self may emerge and be a shock to the partner. Cohabitants assume that because they are living with their partner that this is the way the partner is and will behave in marriage. This is not necessarily true.
3. Role change. When live-in lovers become spouses, they may find that their roles change. For example, cohabitants who had egalitarian role relationships may drift into traditional gender stereotyped roles after marriage. In addition, once live-ins assume the role of spouse, they may discover that they do not interact in the context of social and legal constraints as they did in a context of relative freedom.
4. Norm breakers. Cohabitants are people who are willing to break social norms and live together before marriage. Once they marry, they may feel less willing to stay married if they are unhappy than unhappily married persons who have no history of unconventional behavior.

These studies suggest that you should not live with a partner before marriage if your sole goal in doing so is to help ensure a happy marriage with that partner. There are no data to support such a causal relationship.

CONSIDERATION: Living together is not limited to young and middle aged couples. Some elderly live together both in and out of nursing homes. As one 63-year-old retiree said, "My girlfriend (age 64) lives just down the hall from me . . . When she spends the night, she usually brings her cordless phone . . . just in case her daughter calls." One 61-year-old woman told us that even though her 68-year-old boyfriend has been spending three or four nights a week at her house for the past year, she has not been able to tell her family. "I hide his shoes when my grandchildren are coming over." (Dychtwald, 1990, p. 221)

Some couples live together as an alternative to marriage. Many of these individuals have been married and do not want to marry again but want a live-in lover relationship. Others are philosophically against marriage or are prohibited from marrying because of their sexual orientation (homosexual).

Sexuality in Cohabitating Relationships

Cohabitants have intercourse more frequently, have more egalitarian sexual relationships, and are less monogamous than marrieds. Regarding more frequent intercourse, there is the cultural notion that sex decreases after marriage. Since the cohabitants are not married, they are not susceptible to the self-fulfilling effects of this cultural expectation. In addition, cohabitants (as compared to marrieds) are more equal in terms of initiating intercourse with each other. In one study, 42% of 646 cohabitants versus 33% of 3,612 spouses had relationships in which the initiation of sexual activity is equal (Blumstein & Schwartz, 1983).

As already noted, cohabitants, when compared to marrieds, also choose to be less monogamous than marrieds. Twenty-five percent of male cohabitants (in contrast to 11% of husbands) reported that they have chosen to have at least one sexual extradyadic relationship in the last year. The corresponding percentages for female cohabitants and wives are 22% and 9% (Blumstein & Schwartz, 1990). The norms of fidelity in marriage may be much more controlling of spouses than the norms of faithfulness in cohabitating relationships. Indeed, cohabitants are twice as likely to report physical abuse in their relationships (Stets & Straus, 1989), and the most likely cause of such violence involves jealousy and sex (Makepeace, 1989).

Marriage and Sexuality

NATIONAL DATA: Of all U.S. men (white, black, Hispanic, and Asian), 96.3% have married by age 75; the percent of all U.S. women marrying by age 75 is 94.5 (*Statistical Abstract of the United States: 1992,* Table 51). Each year, almost 5 million people marry (National Center for Health Statistics, 1992).

Most people eventually marry (see National Date in margin). Most young people have marriage as a goal. In a study of 888 university students, 96% reported an intention to marry. This percentage has remained fairly consistent over a 15-year period at a large midwestern university (Rubinson & De Rubertis, 1991). Reasons people acknowledge for choosing to marry include personal fulfillment, companionship, parenthood, and security.

Motivations for Marriage

Personal Fulfillment We are socialized as children to believe that getting married is what adult women and men do. Even if our parents are divorced, we learn that being married is what they wanted, but it didn't work out. Marriage often becomes a goal to achieve. Achieving that goal is assumed to give us a sense of personal fulfillment.

Companionship Many people marry primarily for companionship—to form a primary-group relationship. Primary groups are characterized by relationships that are intimate, personal, and informal. The family in which you grew up is a primary group.

Although marriage does not ensure it, companionship is the greatest expected benefit of marriage. Companionship is talking about and doing things with someone you love; it is creating a history with someone.

Parenthood Most people want to have children. In a study of 888 university students, 95% reported the intent to have children. This percentage has remained fairly consistent over a 15-year period at a large midwestern university (Rubinson & De Rubertis, 1991). Although some people are willing to have children outside of marriage (in a cohabitating relationship or in no relationship at all), most Americans desire to have children in a marital context. There is a strong presumption in our society that only spouses should have children. The parent role is most frequently attained through marriage.

Security People also marry for the emotional and financial security marriage can provide. However, marriage may no longer be a secure place. Since divorce in the United States can now be obtained by any spouse who wants one, marriage no longer provides the security—financial or otherwise—that it once did. Weitzman (1990) documented that as a consequence of divorce law reform, women's economic status plummets following divorce.

In our culture, most people marry for companionship.

CONSIDERATION: Although individuals may be drawn to marriage for reasons of personal fulfillment, companionship, parenthood, and security on the conscious level, unconscious motivations may also be operating. Individuals reared in a happy family may seek to duplicate this perceived state of warmth, affection, and sharing. Alternatively, individuals reared in an unhappy, abusive family may inadvertently drift into a similar relationship or seek their own marital relationship to improve on what they observed in their parents' marriage.

Types of Marriage Relationships

Two researchers (Cuber & Harroff, 1965) interviewed 211 spouses and identified five types of marriage relationships:

1. **Conflict-habituated.** The spouses have a basic incompatibility and argue frequently. Their relationship is characterized by conflict.
2. **Devitalized.** The spouses don't argue; they are just bored. Their relationship is lifeless and apathetic.
3. **Passive-Congenial.** Whereas the devitalized spouses once shared good times together, the passive-congenial spouses have had a polite and superficial relationship from the beginning. Their interests and energies are directed toward careers and children, not toward each other.
4. **Vital.** The mates share an emotional closeness and enjoy doing things together. Their central satisfactions in life are in their relationship.
5. **Total.** The total relationship is similar to the vital relationship except that it is more multifaceted. The "total" couple schedule their day around each other and anticipate every opportunity to be together.

It is not unusual for couples in courtship to begin with a total relationship and drift into a devitalized or conflict-habituated relationship after several years of marriage. Couples who maintain a vital or total relationship give priority in terms of time and energy to their relationship.

Another way of characterizing marriages is by the degree to which they are traditional versus egalitarian. The extremes of the continuum are presented in Table 10.3.

TABLE 10.3 Traditional and Egalitarian Marriages Compared

Traditional Marriage	Egalitarian Marriage
Emphasis on ritual and roles	Emphasis on companionship
Couples do not live together before marriage	Couples may live together before marriage
Wife takes husband's last name	Wife may keep her birth name
Man dominant; woman submissive	Neither spouse dominant
Rigid roles for husband and wife	Flexible roles for spouses
One income (the husband's)	Two incomes
Husband initiates sex; wife complies	Sex initiated by either spouse
Wife takes care of children	Parents share child rearing
Education important for husband, not for wife	Education equally important for both
Husband's career decides family residence	Family residence decided by career of either spouse

Sexuality in Marital Relationships

Since all marriages are different, it is impossible to identify specific patterns of marital sexual behavior that generalize to all marriages. However, a longitudinal study of 161 marital partners who had been married over 20 years is insightful. These respondents were 26 at the time of their first interview in 1935 and were interviewed again in 1955 (Ard, 1990). Although the sample is not random and represents white, middle-class, educated New England couples, the results reflect what some people report about sex in marriage over time.

NATIONAL DATA: A national random sample of adult spouses (wives and husbands married for varying lengths of time) reported that they had intercourse an average of 67 times during the previous 12 months, or an average of 5.5 times a month (Smith, 1991, p. 103).

Frequency of Intercourse The respondents were asked to indicate how often they had intercourse at three periods in their marriage. The 161 couples who have been married over 20 years reported having intercourse about nine times a month during the first three years of marriage, about six times a month during the middle years, and about four to five times per month during the last three years (Ard, 1990). More recent data indicate similar findings regarding the frequency of marital intercourse (see National Date in margin).

Level of Enjoyment of Sex The spouses in Ard's (1990) study also revealed how they felt about sex throughout their 20 years together. The husbands reporting "great enjoyment" dropped from 85% the first three years of marriage to 70% the last three years of marriage (a significant drop); the wives reporting "great enjoyment" increased from 54% the first three years of marriage to 57% the last three years of marriage (not a significant increase). Hence, husbands had overall greater enjoyment, which decreased across the 20-year span; wives had lower enjoyment than men but increased their level of enjoyment with the passage of time.

The finding that husbands are more satisfied (and wives are less satisfied) with their spouses as lovers is also true of elderly couples. In a study of 102 white women and 100 white men, ages 80 to 102, 64% of the women, in contrast to 82% of the men, reported that they were at least mildly happy with their partners as lovers (Bretschneider & McCoy, 1988, p. 14).

Does anyone really believe that sex doesn't have the potential for contributing immeasurably to the happiness in relationships?

James Walters

Preference for Frequency of Intercourse Related to the greater drop in enjoyment for husbands across time is the slight discrepancy between their preference for frequency of intercourse and that of their wives. Husbands married over 20 years reported that they preferred intercourse 6.5 times per month, in contrast to their wives who reported a preference for five times a month (Ard, 1990).

Orgasm in Wives, Erection Difficulties in Husbands When women were asked about the frequency of orgasm during lovemaking over the last three years, 51% reported "almost always or always;" 19% reported "usually." When men were asked about the frequency of erectile problems, 11% said "always or almost always;" 9% said "usually" (Ard, 1990, p. 55).

The picture that emerges from these respondents is that enjoyment in sexuality in marriage remains for over half of the wives and husbands, the frequency of intercourse declines with the duration of the marriage, and husbands want intercourse somewhat more frequently than wives. Of course, there are considerable variations among couples such that, for some, sexual enjoyment and frequency remain high after years of marriage and wives want intercourse more frequently than their husbands.

Before leaving this section on marital sexuality, we would like to add some general comments on marital sexuality:

1. Marital sex is normative. The most socially approved form of sexual behavior in our society is marital sexuality. Most married couples who are not having sex feel that they should.
2. Some marriages are celibate (Pietropinto, 1987). While it is assumed that being married implies that the spouses have intercourse, this is not always the case. For reasons of health, age, sexual orientation, stress, depression, or conflict, some spouses do not have intercourse with each other. Such lack of intercourse may be short- or long-term and concomittant with limited or extensive affection and/or a range of other sexual behaviors.
3. Some marriages are bisexual. Barry Kohn and Alice Matusow (1980) reported that they married to achieve the traditional monogamous heterosexual marriage. However, as their marriage evolved, they discovered their own and each other's bisexual orientation. While their marriage was one in which both spouses were bisexual, other marriages may include only one bisexual spouse or one homosexual spouse.
4. While gay couples are not allowed to be legally married, many gay couples consider themselves as married. They may have a ceremony to symbolize their union in which vows are spoken and wedding rings are exchanged, and may refer to each other as "my spouse."
5. Most spouses are monogamous in any given year.
6. Rape occurs in marriage. Ten percent of married women in a Boston survey reported that they had been raped by their husbands (Finkelhor & Yllo, 1988). We will discuss marital rape in detail in Chapter 19 on abuses of sexuality.

Relationship Quality

How do partners in various types of relationships rate its level of quality? What factors are associated with a high level of relationship satisfaction? We now address these questions.

Comparisons of Types of Partners

Four types of monogamous couples were surveyed by Kurdek and Schmitt (1986a & b; 1987) to compare partners' ratings of relationship quality and perceived social support. Each couple lived together and had no children living with them. Respondents were obtained through the researchers' personal contacts and through responses following publication of the study's description in three gay/lesbian periodicals. Questionnaires were completed and returned separately by both partners for 44 married, 35 heterosexual cohabitating, 50 gay, and 56 lesbian couples. There was no difference among the four partner groups on psychological adjustment as measured by a symptom checklist.

Relationship quality was measured by scales assessing love for partner, liking for partner, and relationship satisfaction. Cohabitating partners had lower scores for love of partner and relationship satisfaction than any of the other three partner types (Kurdek & Schmitt, 1986b). There were no differences between the gay, lesbian, and heterosexual married partners on these measures of relationship quality. Not surprisingly, married partners reported the most (and cohabitating partners the fewest) barriers to leaving the relationship. Among other differences was the finding that lesbian couples reported more shared decision-making, which is consistent with prior research which suggests that lesbian couples emphasize equality of power in relationships. Gay male partners were the most likely to believe that partners should know each other's thoughts and beliefs without directly communicating them (mind-reading), possibly a result of men's socialization to suppress their expressiveness.

Sex role self-concept (measured by the Bem Sex Role Inventory) was examined for its connection to relationship quality among the four types of couples (Kurdek & Schmitt, 1986a). Regardless of type of couple, couples reporting the highest relationship quality were those in which one or both partners were androgynous or feminine. The lowest relationship quality was reported in couples in which one or both partners were undifferentiated or masculine.

Regarding social support, Kurdek and Schmitt (1986b; 1987) found that married and cohabitating partners perceived greater social support from their families than gay male and lesbian partners. This apparently reflects greater social acceptance of cohabitation without marriage than homosexual partnerships. Kurdek (1988) further investigated perceived social support in gays and lesbians in cohabitating relationships. He found that in these partnerships social support is related to relationship quality and psychological adjustment. The most frequent sources of social support were, in order, friends, partners, family, and coworkers.

Whether individuals are cohabitating or married, heterosexual or homosexual, they have a notion of the degree to which they are sexually satisfied. The following self-assessment provides a way to identify one's level of sexual satisfaction.

Extradyadic Sexuality

So now there's somebody new—
These dreams I been dreaming have all fallen through.

Bonnie Raitt

In dating, cohabitating, and marital relationships, one or both partners may choose to engage in extradyadic relationships, which may be perceived as a threat to the existing relationship. Such a relationship involves spending time with someone else where the perceived motivation is the enjoyment of emotional and relationship interaction. Roscoe, Cavanaugh, and Kennedy (1988) observed that women are more likely than men to regard the partner spending time with another as constituting unfaithfulness. Men, on the other hand, are more likely to regard sexual intercourse with another as the definition of unfaithfulness.

NATIONAL DATA: Ninety-six percent of 672 spouses in a nationally representative sample reported that they were monogamous during the last year (Greeley et al., 1990).

The terms "cheating," "unfaithfulness," and "infidelity" used to describe **extradyadic sexual behavior** reflect societal disapproval of such behavior. Proscriptions against extradyadic sexual activity are not as strong for dating partners and cohabitating partners as they are for marital partners. In a study of college undergraduates, Lieberman (1988) found that about two-thirds of the students expressed that extradyadic sexual intercourse in dating couples were wrong; 80% thought extramarital sex was wrong. In another study, only 3% of 188 university students reported approval of extramarital intercourse (Rubinson & De Rubertis, 1991).

NATIONAL DATA: Only 1.5% of a random sample of married U.S. adults reported that they had had a sexual partner other than their spouse in the past 12 months (Smith, 1991, p. 102).

While extradyadic sexuality may occur among dating and cohabitating partners, we will focus on sexual involvements that married individuals have with someone other than their own spouse. (The consequences of engaging in extradyadic sex are discussed in the Choices section at the end of this chapter.)

Studies differ on the extent of extramarital intercourse (Lawson, 1988; Thompson, 1983; Smith, 1991). In a review of the literature of extramarital intercourse, Thompson concluded that half of all husbands and about the same percentage of wives have intercourse at least once with someone other than the spouse. However, in a longitudinal study of 161 spouses married over 20 years, only 7% of the

Self Assessment

Index of Sexual Satisfaction (ISS)

This questionnaire is designed to measure the degree of satisfaction you have in the sexual relationship with your partner. It is not a test, so there are no right or wrong answers. Answer each item as carefully and accurately as you can by placing a number beside each one as follows:

1	Rarely or none of the time	3	Some of the time
		4	Good part of the time
2	A little of the time	5	Most or all of the time

1. I feel that my partner enjoys our sex life. ________
2. My sex life is very exciting. ________
3. Sex is fun for my partner and me. ________
4. I feel that my partner sees little in me except for the sex I can give. ________
5. I feel that sex is dirty and disgusting. ________
6. My sex life is monotonous. ________
7. When we have sex it is too rushed and hurriedly completed. ________
8. I feel that my sex life is lacking in quality. ________
9. My partner is sexually very exciting. ________
10. I enjoy the sex techniques that my partner likes or uses. ________
11. I feel that my partner wants too much sex from me. ________
12. I think that sex is wonderful. ________
13. My partner dwells on sex too much. ________
14. I try to avoid sexual contact with my partner. ________
15. My partner is too rough or brutal when we have sex. ________
16. My partner is a wonderful sex mate. ________
17. I feel that sex is a normal function of our relationship. ________
18. My partner does not want sex when I do. ________
19. I feel that our sex life really adds a lot to our relationship. ________
20. My partner seems to avoid sexual contact with me. ________
21. It is easy for me to get sexually excited by my partner. ________
22. I feel that my partner is sexually pleased with me. ________
23. My partner is very sensitive to my sexual needs and desires. ________
24. My partner does not satisfy me sexually. ________
25. I feel that my sex life is boring. ________

Scoring Items 1, 2, 3, 9, 10, 12, 16, 17, 19, 21, 22, and 23 must be reverse-scored. (For example, if you answered 5 on the first item, you would change that score to 1.) After these positively worded items have been reverse-scored, if there are no omitted items, the score is computed by summing the item scores and subtracting 25.

Interpretation Scores can range from 0 to 100, with a high score indicative of sexual dissatisfaction. Hudson, Harrison, and Crosscup (1981) suggested that a score of approximately 30 or above is indicative of dissatisfaction in one's sexual relationship. However, they cautioned,

> Actually, no single score for the ISS (or any such scale) should be taken too seriously. . . . In all cases it is important to evaluate the obtained ISS score in relation to all other clinical evidence that is available concerning the presence and severity of difficulties in the sexual component of a dyadic relationship.
> (pp. 166–167)

Psychometric Information Hudson et al. (1981) demonstrated good construct validity for the ISS. The ISS correlated 0.68 with the Index of Marital Satisfaction, 0.47 with the Generalized Contentment Scale, and 0.44 with the Sexual Attitude Scale. The reliability of the scale was examined in three study samples. The average value of Coefficient Alpha for the three samples was 0.916, showing excellent reliability over three separate and heterogenous samples. Two of the samples consisted of adults who were not seeking counseling. Their mean ISS score was 15.2 (SD = 11.28). The third sample was composed of people seeking counseling for personal or relationship problems. The counseling group's mean was 41.5 (SD = 18.13). The test-retest reliability was 0.93 (in an additional sample of graduate students in social work).

Reference

Hudson, W. W., Harrison, D. F., & Crosscup, P. C. (1981). A short-form scale to measure sexual discord in dyadic relationships. *Journal of Sex Research, 17*, 157–174.

Note: This reproduction of the ISS includes the replacement items recommended by the authors following their analysis of the scale's item-total correlations.

husbands and 4% of the wives reported having had an "extramarital love affair" (these occurred during the middle and later years in the marriage) (Ard, 1990, p. 63).

Types of Extradyadic Sexual Involvements

Various types of extradyadic sexual involvements may be distinguished on the basis of 1) the emotional intensity of the sexual involvement (which may be related to the duration of the involvement) and 2) whether or not the involvement is with the consent of both spouses. Next, we discuss some of the types of extradyadic sexual involvements, including "brief encounters," affairs, "open marriages," "swinging" (mate swapping), and group sex.

Brief Encounters We refer to extradyadic sexual involvements that are brief and involve little to no emotional investment as "brief encounters." Although the partners may see each other again, their sexual encounter is a "one-night stand" more often than not. Sexual involvement with prostitutes (male or female) or with women who offer sexual activity in massage parlors may also be viewed as extradyadic sexual involvement of the "brief encounter" variety. Husbands are more likely to have brief encounters than wives. In one study, 28% of the husbands and 5% of the wives who had had an extramarital encounter said that the last encounter was a one-night stand (Spanier & Margolis, 1983).

Love affairs without marriage are not devoid of pleasure—they can be wonderfully fresh and zestful, rather like crisp green lettuce with a sharp dressing. But they need every advantage they can claim to compensate for the inconvenience, insecurity and deception usually implicit in their practice, and for the heartache involved in their dissolution.
Ilka Chase

Affairs **Affairs** refer to "sexual involvement outside a committed intimate relationship without the consent of the partner" (Bringle & Buunk, 1991, p. 135). In contrast to the "brief encounter," affairs involve emotional as well as physical involvement and may be characterized by a longer duration.

CONSIDERATION: Single women may be increasingly willing to have affairs with married men, perhaps partly because they believe single men are scarce, but also because a relationship with a married man requires less commitment and leaves more time for the single woman to devote to her career. Single women may be primarily motivated by the emotional and/or physical attraction to the married man but usually do not envision being married to the man with whom they have an affair. One single woman remarked:

> Where else could I have exactly what I want from a relationship? I have my freedom and my own life separate from him. I have certain wants and he meets those, and on my own terms. (Trotter, 1989, p. 215)

Intense reciprocal emotional feelings characterize most affairs. Such feelings are partly a function of the conditions under which the relationship exists. For example, the time together is very limited. Like Romeo and Juliet who were restricted by their parents, married lovers are restricted by their spouses and other family responsibilities. Such limited access makes the time they spend together very special. In addition, the lover is not associated with the struggles of marriage—bills, child care, housework—and so is viewed in a more romantic setting.

Open Marriages In the book *Open Marriage* (O'Neill & O'Neill, 1972), the authors suggested that for some couples, it is possible to integrate extramarital sex into marriage. **Sexually open marriages** are those in which both spouses have a positive attitude toward extramarital relationships and give each other the freedom to pursue such relationships (Buunk and Van Driel, 1989, p. 99). The concept of "open marriage" may apply to nonmarital committed relationships as well.

When 35 couples in sexually open marriages were compared with 35 married couples who did not have sexually open marriages, the open marriage couples reported greater satisfaction with their marital sexual relationship. The researchers (Wheeler & Kilmann, 1983) commented that for some couples

> . . . engaging in recreational sexual activities with outside partners apparently does not interfere with each member's perception of a positive marital sexual relationship; for these couples, it may be that their marital sexual relationship is enhanced by agreed-on sexual contact with outside partners. This may not be the case for couple members who engage in covert extramarital sexual relationships, often as an "escape" from a dysfunctional marital relationship. (p. 304)

There are various guidelines that couples in sexually open relationships may agree on in order to successfully integrate extradyadic sexual activity into their relationship. Some guidelines identified by Buunk (1980) include:

1. Marriage primacy. Most participants in Buunk's sample emphasized the importance of giving top priority to the marital relationship, showing respect for feelings, being honest, and devoting sufficient time and energy to the spouse.
2. Restricted intensity. About one-third of Buunk's sample agreed to restrict the intensity and degree of extradyadic sexual involvement. One third of the couples had agreed that an extradyadic sexual relationship would be terminated at the request of the partner.
3. Visibility. Many couples in Buunk's sample agreed to keep each other informed about any extradyadic sexual relationships. Some also agreed to restrict such relationships to those persons the partner knew. Others agreed to consult and obtain consent from their spouse before engaging in extradyadic sexual activity.

Swinging Swinging, also referred to as **comarital sex,** is another form of extradyadic sexual involvement in which the partners of one marriage or pair-bonded relationship have sexual relations with the partners of another relationship. Swinging is similar to sexually open relationships in that it involves mutual consent between the partners for extradyadic sexual activity. However, swinging is unique in that it is a more couple-oriented activity. Bringle and Buunk (1991) described swinging as

> extramarital sexual relationships [that] occur with both persons present and only within specified times and settings. The actual sexual contact may be open (occurs in the presence of others) or closed (occurs in separate rooms); in either case, the participants most typically arrive as a couple and depart as a couple. Furthermore, the sexual activity is, to a greater extent than with open marriages, engaged in for its own sake. The philosophy is one of recreational, body-oriented sexuality rather than emotional involvement and personal growth. (p. 148)

CONSIDERATION: Although swinging is viewed as a couple-oriented activity, "it is probably instigated by the male's desire for sexual variety, for the benefit of the male, and the wife serves the function role of creating the opportunity (why else would it be known as 'wife swapping'?" (Bringle & Buunk, 1991, p. 149). It is not surprising then that in a study of ex-swingers, the most common reason that couples discontinued swinging was the wives' dissatisfaction with this form of extradyadic sex (Murstein, Case, & Gunn, 1985).

NATIONAL DATA: In one study of 1,275 U.S. respondents, one-fourth reported that they had experienced group sex (Rubin, 1991, p. 127).

Group Sex While swinging involves couples swapping partners, **group sex** is a sexual encounter involving three or more individuals. Group sex may occur in the context of an ongoing intimate relationship among the participants or among recently acquainted individuals who mutually agree to have group sex. In some cases, a pair-bonded or married couple may invite one or more people to engage in group sex.

Respondents in Rubin's sample reported various reasons for engaging in group sex. Some sought a novel experience, others thought it would be fun, and still others viewed it as the symbol of total sexual freedom. One respondent noted:

> Like I said, it's hard to describe, but there's something about the kind of freedom you feel. You know, sex is a very possessive thing, and when you're having sex with more than one person, no one can possess you or think they're possessing you. Do you know what I mean? (Rubin, 1991, p. 127)

Motivations and Reasons for Extradyadic Sexual Involvements

Partners involved in committed relationships become involved in extradyadic sexual relationships for a number of reasons, including:

Variety, Novelty, and Excitement Extradyadic sexual involvement may be motivated by the desire for variety, novelty, and excitement (Bringle & Buunk, 1991). Sex in long-term committed relationships tends to become routine. Early in a relationship, the partners cannot seem to get enough of each other. But with constant availability, the partners may achieve a level of satiation, and the attractiveness and excitement of sex with the primary partner seems to wane. The *Coolidge effect* is a term used to describe this waning of sexual excitement and the effect of novelty and variety on sexual arousal:

> One day President and Mrs. Coolidge were visiting a government farm. Soon after their arrival, they were taken off on separate tours. When Mrs. Coolidge passed the chicken pens, she paused to ask the man in charge if the rooster copulates more than once each day. "Dozens of times" was the reply. "Please tell that to the President," Mrs. Coolidge requested. When the President passed the pens and was told about the rooster, he asked, "Same hen every time?" "Oh no, Mr. President, a different one each time." The President nodded slowly and then said, "Tell that to Mrs. Coolidge." (Bermant, 1976 pp. 76–77)

CONSIDERATION: The Coolidge effect illustrates the influence of novelty and variety on the copulation behavior of roosters, not humans. Varying levels of sexual novelty and variety may, indeed, be important for achieving sexual satisfaction for many individuals. However, unlike roosters, humans need not have multiple sexual partners in order to experience novelty and variety. Rather, humans may create sexual novelty and variety within a monogamous relationship by having sex in novel places, exploring different intercourse positions, engaging in a variety of noncoital petting behaviors, wearing a variety of erotic clothing, and using sexual fantasies in their sexual encounters.

Data suggest that men are more motivated by the desire for sexual variety than women. Thompson (1984) observed that twice as many men as women have extramarital intercourse for sex only (without an emotional component).

Friendship Extradyadic sexual involvements may develop from friendships. The extramarital involvements of women are more likely to develop out of friendships

The Coolidge effect was named after an incident involving President and Mrs. Coolidge.

than those of men (Atwater, 1979). Friendships that develop into extradyadic sexual relationships often begin in the workplace. Co-workers share the same world eight to 10 hours a day and over a period of time may develop good feelings for each other that eventually lead to a sexual relationship. (Sex among co-workers is discussed later in this chapter).

Relationship Dissatisfaction It is commonly believed that people who have affairs are not happy in their marriage, but this is more likely to be true of wives than of husbands. Men who have affairs often are not dissatisfied with the quality of their marriage or their sexual relationship with their wife (Yablonsky, 1979, p. 15). Rather, men often seek extramarital relationships as an additional experience.

One source of relationship dissatisfaction is an unfulfilling sexual relationship. Some people engage in extradyadic sex because their partner is not interested in sex. Others may go outside the relationship because their partner will not engage in the sexual behaviors they want and enjoy. The unwillingness of the partner to engage in oral sex, anal intercourse, or a variety of sexual positions sometimes results in the other partner looking elsewhere for a more cooperative partner.

Most wives "appear to seek extramarital sex when they experience some deficit—sexual, emotional, or perhaps, economic—in their marriage, or perceive another man as being superior to (not merely different from) their husbands" (Symons, 1979, p. 238). Women who feel trapped in a bad marriage may not want a divorce. "So they turn to an affair or a series of them as a means of treading water, keeping the marriage afloat for the time being until their children grow up or they (the wives) earn a degree, etc." (Schaefer, 1981).

In a study of premarital extradyadic sexual behavior, the most frequently reported justifications for such behavior were, in descending frequency: dissatisfaction with the relationship, boredom, revenge, anger or jealousy, being unsure of the relationship, and variety (Roscoe, Cavanaugh, & Kennedy, 1988).

Revenge Some extradyadic sexual involvements are acts of revenge against one's partner for engaging in extradyadic sexual activity. When partners find out that their mate has had, or is having, an affair, they may be hurt and angry. One response to this hurt and anger is to have an affair to get even with the unfaithful partner. In Hite's (1977) study of over 3,000 women, 7% reported having an affair because their husband had one first.

Desire for Homosexual Relationship Some individuals in heterosexual committed relationships engage in extradyadic sex because they desire a homosexual relationship. As we mention in Chapter 11 on sexual orientation, some gay individuals marry as a way of denying their homosexuality or creating a social pretense that they are heterosexual. These individuals are likely to feel unfulfilled in their marriage and may seek involvement in an extramarital homosexual relationship. Other individuals may marry and then discover later in life that they desire a homosexual relationship. Such individuals may feel that either (1) they have been homosexual or bisexual all along, (2) their sexual orientation has changed from heterosexual to homosexual or bisexual, (3) they are unsure of their sexual orientation and want to explore a homosexual relationship, or (4) they feel predominately heterosexual but wish to experience a homosexual relationship for variety.

Spouses in heterosexual marriages who engage in an extramarital homosexual relationship may or may not be happy with their marital partner. Blumstein and Schwartz (1990) provided an example of a woman

> unhappily married for 23 years but feeling a profound absence of a real "soul mate." She met a woman at her son's college graduation ceremony, and over a long period of time, the two women gradually fell in love and left their husbands. Not only did the respondent's sense of self change but so did her sexual habits and desires. (p. 314)

Aging A frequent motive for intercourse outside of marriage is the desire to re-experience youth. Our society promotes the idea that it is good to be young and bad to be old. Sexual attractiveness is equated with youth, and having an affair may confirm to an older partner that he or she is still sexually desirable. Also, people may try to recapture the love, excitement, adventure, and romance associated with youth by having an affair.

Gordon (1988) interviewed men who had left their wives for a younger woman. These men focused not on the physical youth of their new partners but on their youthful attitude—the openness, innocence, unscarred emotions. They also emphasized the uncritical love they felt from their younger partner. Gordon labeled these men as having "Jennifer Fever"—they had developed a pattern of denying the aging process by seeking a youthful partner to create the illusion that they were not getting older. Gordon suggested the term "Jennifer" because she found that the name of the younger woman was often Jennifer. Gordon further warned that these men would seek another "Jennifer" as the current one aged.

Absence from Partner One factor that predisposes a person to an extradyadic sexual encounter is prolonged separation from the partner. Some individuals whose partners are away on business or military duty report that the loneliness can become unbearable. Some individuals who are away say that it is difficult to be faithful. Partners in "commuter relationships" may also be vulnerable to extradyadic sexual relationships.

CONSIDERATION: The spouse who chooses to have an affair is often judged as being unfaithful to the vows of the marriage, as being deceitful to the partner, and of inflicting enormous pain on the partner (and children). What is often not considered is that when an affair is defined in terms of giving emotional energy, time, and economic resources to something or someone outside the primary relationship, there are other types of "affairs" that are equally as devastating to a relationship. Spouses who choose to devote their lives to their children, careers, parents, friends, or recreational interests may deprive the partner of significant amounts of emotional energy, time, and money and create a context in which the partner may choose to become involved with a person who provides more reinforcement.

Sexual Involvements with Co-Workers

The workplace as a context for sexual interactions achieved nationwide visibility during the Senate confirmation hearings of Supreme Court nominee Clarence Thomas in 1991. Anita Hill, a woman who had worked with Thomas, alleged that he had sexually harassed her. While we will discuss sexual harassment in Chapter 19, in this section we emphasize sexual involvements among co-workers.

Because the number of employed women has increased in recent years and because more women are entering previously male-dominated professions, more men and women are working together than ever before. The workplace has become a major source of intimate interaction as women and men share the physical proximity of working side by side over a long period time and the stimulation of professional challenge. Co-workers often work in close collaboration with each other and may take business trips together. Sexual attraction is common among co-workers because "the workplace is an ideal pre-screener, likely to throw us together with others our own age having similar socio-economic and educational backgrounds, similar sets of values, and similar aspirations" (Eyler & Baridon, 1992, p. 59).

Both married and single women and men may experience sexual attraction for co-workers and may become involved in intimate and/or sexual relationships at work. These attractions may be both heterosexual and homosexual. Twenty-one percent of 706 lesbian couples reported that they met their partner at work ("National Survey Results," 1990).

Managing Sexual Attraction at Work

Being attracted to someone at work can have both positive and negative aspects. On the positive side, being attracted to a co-worker, employer, or employee can provide one with a sense of excitement and enthusiasm for being at work. Increased productivity on the job may result from increased energy and/or an attempt to make a positive impression on the person to whom one is attracted.

One negative aspect of being sexually attracted to someone at work is that such feelings may be distracting to the degree that some individuals are unable to focus on their job. Sexual attraction may also be associated with feelings of tension, fear, or even anger. Such may be the case when individuals feel constrained from acting on their attraction because either they are in a committed relationship or the person to whom they are attracted is in a committed relationship and/or is not interested in a relationship.

Marcy Crary (1988) conducted research on attraction and intimacy in the workplace. She interviewed men and women who worked at financial service companies, consulting groups, mental health clinics, state agencies, hospitals, and universities, among other places. She found that one aspect of managing sexual attraction at work involves the dilemma of whether or not to discuss the attraction to the other person. Crary (1988) suggested that "the difficulty of *not* discussing the attraction is that one can end up with pent-up energy, which can in turn lead to a preoccupation with the attraction . . ." (p. 464). However, some people fear that if they disclose their feelings of attraction to the other person, they must not only deal with their feelings but with the feelings of the other person as well. The other person may also pressure the individual to act on the attraction. One woman consultant said:

> I chose to tell him that I was attracted to him but that for a number of reasons I was not going to act on it. This was in response to his telling me that he found me very attractive. Well, it turned out that in telling him I was attracted to him I had made the situation much worse. He continued to pursue the issue, so much so that it almost felt like sexual harassment. I then chose to back off from working with him because he was making it so difficult. (Crary, 1988, p. 464)

Another potential negative outcome of expressing feelings of attraction to a co-worker is that it may be perceived as sexual harassment. One male bank manager commented:

> It's a litigious society. Others' perceptions rule. I'd rather err on the side of being fearful of others' perceptions than be overly supportive to my women subordinates. (Crary, 1988, p. 465)

> We need to grow comfortable loving one person romantically and deeply valuing another intellectually, artistically, or in a variety of ways that do not diminish our commitment to a primary partner.
>
> *David R. Eyler*
> *Andrea P. Baridon*

Being attracted to someone at work may or may not lead to the development of an intimate relationship. Even so, intimacy among co-wokers does not necessarily involve sex. The following comments describe what some individuals mean by intimacy at work (Crary, 1988, p. 460):

- "It's being able to exchange honest, straightforward, constructive feedback on our work."
- "I can share any or all of the 'backstage' thoughts and feelings that come up for me in this place or in my life outside work."
- "I have the feeling that she is always looking out for me, always ready to help me or make suggestions."

Intimate Relationships at Work: Issues for Employees

In Crary's (1988) study, many of the close relationships described by the individuals interviewed were very positive and important to their personal, social, professional, and physical well-being. However, many difficulties that workers experienced from being in an intimate relationship (whether sexual or nonsexual) with another person at work were also reported. Crary (1988) identified the following basic issues in intimate relationships at work:

1. *Balancing intimacy and work with the same person.* Some people find it difficult to balance the role of lover with their work responsibilities. One financial services employee who had developed a romantic relationship with a female co-worker described the problem of balancing work responsibilities and relationship expectations:

> She walks into my office unannounced, and I don't have the time to be with her. . . . This was interfering with my performance at work. I felt I should spend time with her and I couldn't; she didn't like that. (Crary, 1988, p. 467)

2. *Dealing with outsiders' views of the relationship.* Co-workers in close relationships are subject to being negatively judged by others at work. Other workers may assume that a close relationship is sexual, whether or not it actually is. Other workers also feel that lack of objectivity and unfairness to other workers may result from having too close relationships at work. Some women fear "the classic accusation that associates a woman's rise in an organization with her sexual activity rather than with her competence" (Crary, 1988, p. 468).

   Another concern for those involved in office romances is how management views intimate relationships at work. While some organizations are not concerned about romantic relationships at work, other organizations view such relationships as inappropriate and have formal policies and sanctions against them. One study found that 12.7% of the organizations surveyed have a formal policy against unmarried bosses dating subordinates and 13% have a formal policy against employees marrying each other and continuing to hold their same job. Only 1.2% have a formal policy against unmarried employees living together, and 0.4% have a policy against unmarried co-workers dating each other (Ford & McLaughlin, 1988, p. 452).

   Table 10.4 reflects the results of a study on personnel managers' attitudes toward intimate relationships at work (Ford & McLaughlin, 1988).

3. *Dealing with changes in the relationship.* Over time, all relationships experience various changes, including varying degrees of involvement and commitment. Changes in the relationship may become particularly problematic in the work setting when one partner wants to make changes but the other one does not. For

TABLE 10.4 Personnel Managers' Attitudes toward Intimate Relationships at Work

		Percentage Agreeing
1.	Eventually, an affair between two equal co-workers will turn into a claim of sexual harassment.	9.8
2.	Eventually, an affair between a manager and a subordinate will likely turn into a claim of sexual harassment.	30.3
3.	When co-workers become romantically involved, their job performance suffers.	31.4
4.	Romantically involved co-workers adversely affect other employees' productivity.	38.7
5.	A known office romance has a strong and negative influence on the careers of those involved.	42.8
6.	With so many men and women working together, it is common to see professional interest turn into romantic attraction.	51.4
7.	There is really nothing the organization can do to stop romantic attractions between men and women working together.	69.8
8.	The romantic interests of employees in each other should be of no concern to employers.	38.8
9.	Organizations have a responsibility to avoid placing people in situations which could lead to romantic involvement.	13.1
10.	A company should act to separate co-workers who are found having an affair by transferring or requiring resignation by one.	15.5
11.	It is part of a supervisor's job to recognize and counsel subordinates who are romantically involved.	42.4

Source: Adapted from Ford, R. C., & McLaughlin, F. S. (1988). Should cupid come to the workplace? An ASPA survey. In Fairlee E. Winfield (Ed.), *The work and family sourcebook,* (pp. 449–457). Greenvale, NY: Panel Publishers, Inc. Used by permission.

example, in an intimate but nonsexual relationship, one partner may want to become sexually involved, but the other does not. Or, one partner in an ongoing sexual relationship may want to discontinue having sex or may become disinterested in continuing the relationship. While relationship changes may be problematic in general, in the workplace they may interfere with job security, job performance, and/or the partners' comfort and enjoyment at the workplace.

Interpersonal Noncoital Sexual Behavior

Whether the context is dating, cohabitating, marital, extradyadic, or workplace, partners often choose to engage in an array of interpersonal noncoital sexual behaviors, which include touching, kissing, breast stimulation, penile stimulation, clitoral stimulation, and other petting behaviors. Rothman (1987) chronicled the "invention" of petting in the early nineteenth-century as premarital couples looked for ways to express love and sexual attraction while confining intercourse to marriage.

Getting rid of the notion of foreplay and calling it *all* lovemaking may be difficult for some men to get used to. But it may be a relief to the many men who worry about keeping an erection long enough to satisfy a woman during intercourse.
Boston Women's Health Book Collective

CONSIDERATION: Most people define sex as intercourse. However, intercourse is "a form of lovemaking which is often well suited to men's orgasm and pleasure but is not necessarily well suited to [women's]" (Boston Women's Health Book Collective, 1984, p. 185). One woman commented,

> In high school we had long making-out periods and I had orgasms all the time. When we "graduated" to intercourse, I stopping having them so easily because we stopped doing all the other things. (p. 186)

While non-coital sexual behavior is often referred to as "foreplay," this term suggests that touching, kissing, and stroking, and licking behaviors are merely precursors to the "main act"—intercourse. Thus, we suggest replacing the term "foreplay" with the term "lovemaking."

Touching

Our skin contains about 900,000 sensory receptors (Montagu & Matson, 1979). It is a primary mechanism for experiencing pleasure. Many regard touching as the most significant aspect of sex. The 3,000 women in Hite's (1977) study stated repeatedly that touching, holding, caressing, being close to, lying next to, and pressing bodies together were more important to them than intercourse or orgasms. For many, such physical closeness gives a feeling of emotional closeness that is satisfying whether or not intercourse or orgasm follow. "Long, gentle passionate encounters, with much touching and enthusiasm, give me a feeling of being loved all over and are all I need most of the time," said one woman (p. 556).

Masters and Johnson (1976) echoed the feeling of many women: "It is important to avoid the fundamental error of believing that touch is a means to an end. It is not. Touch is an end in itself. It is a primary form of communication, a silent voice that avoids the pitfall of words while expressing the feelings of the moment" (p. 253).

While women delight in the experience of touching (and often get less touching than they want), they may feel that men do not share their enthusiasm. Most women feel that men engage in foreplay only as a means of priming them for intercourse, and many resent it (some say that while women fake orgasm, men fake foreplay). Their suspicions are mostly accurate. In a study of 7,000 men, the majority said that physical affection should always lead to intercourse and orgasm (Hite, 1981).

Another form of touching is massage. For many individuals, a body massage is more pleasurable than any other form of touching. While many forms of touching are stimulating, massage is relaxing. Being in a state of relaxation, however, can lead to interest in sexual activity. One student commented:

> When I'm finished working all day and taking classes at night, I'm exhausted and usually not interested in sex. But my husband has learned that if he spends twenty minutes massaging me, I feel relaxed, my body feels good, and that's the best time to have sex. (Author's files)

Kissing

Ancient lovers believed a kiss would literally unite their souls, because the spirit was said to be carried in one's breath.
Eve Glicksman

There are different types of kissing. In one style of kissing, the partners gently touch their lips together for a short time with their mouths closed. In another, there is considerable pressure and movement for a prolonged time when the closed mouths meet. In still another, the partners kiss with their mouths open, using gentle or light pressure and variations in movement and time. Kinsey referred to the latter as deep kissing (also known as soul kissing, tongue kissing, or French kissing).

How did the custom of mouth kissing come about? Exhibit 10.2 describes one scientist's ideas concerning the origin of mouth kissing.

Kissing may or may not have emotional or erotic connotations. A good-night kiss may be perfunctory or may symbolize in the mind of each partner the ultimate sense of caring and belonging. It may also mean different things to each partner.

CONSIDERATION: When writing a letter to a loved one, we sometimes write a row of XXXXXXs to represent kisses. This custom stems from the Middle Ages, when so many people were illiterate that a cross (X) was acceptable as a signature on a legal document. The cross (X) stood for "St. Andrew's mark," and people vowed to be honest by writing a cross that represented his sacred name. To pledge their sincere honesty, people would kiss their signature and, in time, the X became associated with the kiss alone (Ackerman, 1990, p. 113).

In our society, kissing is a common experience. Indeed, it is rare that individuals in their 20s have not kissed or been kissed. But, for both men and women, how often this behavior is engaged in varies by educational level, with more education

EXHIBIT 10.2 The Origin of Mouth Kissing

Desmond Morris, a noted zoologist with an interest in the behavior of human animals, suggested that mouth kissing has its origins in mother-infant interactions of early human history.

> In early human societies, before commercial baby-food was invented, mothers weaned their children by chewing up their food and then passing it into the infantile mouth by lip-to-lip contact—which naturally involved a considerable amount of tonguing and mutual mouth-pressure. This almost bird-like system of parental care seems strange and alien to us today, but our species probably practiced it for a million years or more, and adult erotic kissing today is almost certainly a Relic Gesture stemming from these origins . . . . Whether it has been handed down to us from generation to generation . . . or whether we have an inborn predisposition towards it, we cannot say. But, whichever is the case, it looks rather as though, with the deep kissing and tonguing of modern lovers, we are back again at the infantile mouth-feeding stage of the far-distant past . . . . If the young lovers exploring each other's mouths with their tongues feel the ancient comfort of parental mouth-feeding, this may help them to increase their mutual trust and thereby their pair-bonding. (quoted in Ackerman, 1990, p. 112)

Kissing is a frequent behavior among lovers.

associated with more frequent kissing. For example, Kinsey et al. (1948) observed that 88% of men with little education (less than eight years) reported lip kissing on a frequent basis, compared with 98% of those with more education (13 years and over). The less-educated men viewed kissing as "dirty, filthy, and a source of disease," while the college-educated males regarded kissing as erotic play. A more recent study (Pietropinto & Simenauer, 1977) also concluded that educational background is associated with how men view kissing.

Breast Stimulation

Breast stimulation, both manual and oral, was reported by over 95% of female and male students in a study on sexuality at a Colombian university (Alzate, 1989). In our society, the female breasts are charged with erotic potential. A billion-dollar pornographic industry encourages viewing women's breasts in erotic terms. *Playboy, Penthouse,* and an array of other adult magazines feature women with naked breasts in seductive, erotic poses.

Not all women share men's erotic feelings about breasts. Women may or may not manually stimulate their own breasts and often neglect the breasts of their male partners, even though male breasts have the same potential for erotic stimulation as female breasts. For some men, breast stimulation by their partners is particularly important.

Penile Stimulation

Caressing the penis is another form of petting. This may be done by the woman caressing her partner's penis with her hand(s) or with her mouth or rubbing it inside her vaginal lips.

Manual Stimulation Eighty-six percent of university females in one study reported that they had actively manually stimulated their partner's genitals (Alzate,

FIGURE 10.1 Mutual genital stimulation

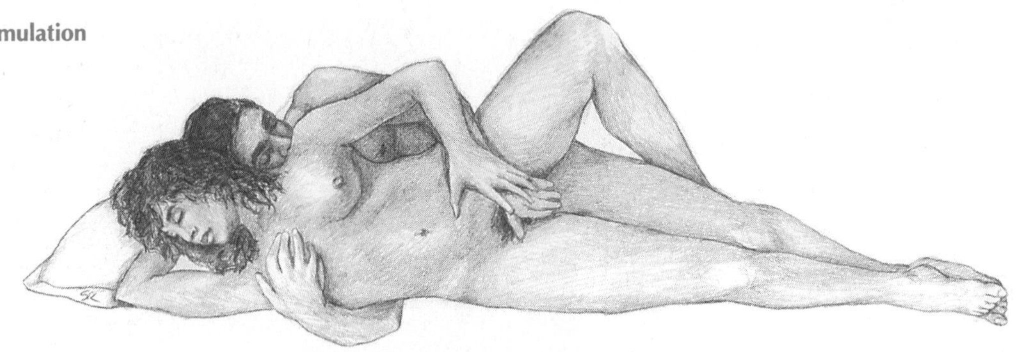

1989). Being in love or feeling strong affection was the condition under which most women report feeling most comfortable engaging in their behavior. Partners may also engage in mutual genital stimulation (see Figure 10.1).

Whether a woman manually caresses her partner's penis is related to whether she has had intercourse. Kinsey et al. (1953/1970) observed that those women who had had intercourse were three times as likely to report manual caressing of the penis. As with other petting behaviors, penile stimulation is influenced by cohort and, to some degree, education. Women in their 20s are much more likely to have stimulated their partner's penis than women in their 40s, and the more educated a woman, the more likely she is to manually stimulate her partner.

Fellatio One of the most intimate forms of petting is **fellatio**, or oral stimulation of the man's genitals by his partner (see Figure 10.2). The term comes from the Latin word *fellare,* meaning "to suck." While fellatio most often involves sucking the penis, fellatio may also include licking the shaft and glans, frenulum, and scrotum. Some partners take only the head of the penis in their mouth while alternating sucking and blowing motions. The partner's hands also may caress the scrotum and perineum during fellatio. Fellatio may be enjoyed as foreplay, afterplay, or as an end in itself. If fellatio results in orgasm, the semen may be swallowed without harm (in the absence of HIV infection) if the partner desires to do so.

CONSIDERATION: A pornographic film entitled *Deep Throat* contributed to the notion that a good fellatio experience involves inserting the penis deep into the throat of the partner. While some partners may enjoy fellatio "*Deep Throat* style," many women and gay men find it unpleasant and/or are unable to take a penis deep into their throat. Because inserting any object into the throat elicits a natural gag reflex, it is unrealistic to expect fellatio to require deep insertion of the penis into the mouth.

Seventy-seven percent of 79 university male students reported that they had been the recipient of fellatio (Knox & Schacht, 1992). Some women regard fellatio as a more intimate form of sexual expression than intercourse, something they only do with a person with whom they are in love. Fellatio may also be the preferred sexual activity in early sexual encounters for women who want to avoid the possibility of pregnancy or who believe in saving intercourse for marriage.

In spite of the reported high incidence of fellatio, it remains a relatively taboo subject for open discussion. Many states statutorily regard fellatio as a "crime against

FIGURE 10.2 Fellatio, the oral stimulation of the man's genitals, may or may not include ejaculation, but can provide a great deal of pleasure to both partners.

nature." "Nature" in this case refers to reproduction and the "crime" is sex that does not produce babies.

People engage in fellatio for a number of reasons. Pleasure is a central one. Next to kissing and hugging, oral sex was reported as the most pleasurable form of petting by more than 4,000 men (Pietropinto & Simenauer, 1977). It is the interpretation of the experience, as well as the physical sensations, that may produce the pleasure. One man said that his partner fellating him meant that she really loved him and enjoyed his body.

Dominance may be another reason for the enjoyment of fellatio. A common theme in pornographic movies is forcing the woman to perform fellatio. In this context, the act implies sexual submission, which may give the male an ego boost. Aware of this motive, some women refuse to fellate their partners. One woman said that her partner viewed her as a prostitute when she fellated him, that she did not like such a perception, and that she had stopped doing so.

Variety is another motive for fellatio. Some lovers complain that penis-in-vagina intercourse is sometimes boring. Fellatio adds another dimension to a couple's sexual relationship. The greater the range of sexual behaviors a couple has to share, the less likely they are to define their sexual relationship as routine and uninteresting.

As noted above, fellatio may also be used as a means of avoiding intercourse. Unmarried couples who feel that intercourse outside marriage is wrong may view oral sex, including fellatio, as an acceptable alternative. Although there may be clear social and religious prohibitions against premarital intercourse, little or nothing is said about oral sex. So any sexual activity that is not intercourse may carry only limited guilt.

Clitoral Stimulation

"Please take me clitorally" is the message most women would like their lovers to act on (Hite, 1977). Again and again, the women in Hite's study, when asked how men made love to them, said their partners spent too little time (sometimes none at all)

Sex is not a soccer game. The use of hands is permitted.

Carole Wade

stimulating their clitoris and that they had to have such stimulation to derive maximum pleasure from the sexual experience. The clitoris may be stimulated by the hand, mouth, or penis.

Manual Stimulation Ninety-six percent of 128 university males reported that they had actively manually stimulated their partner's genitals (Alzate, 1989). Such stimulation may be to ready the woman for intercourse or as an end in itself, and the style of stimulation may vary. Some partners rub the mons veneris area, putting indirect pressure on the clitoris. Others may apply direct clitoral pressure. Still others may insert one or several fingers into the vagina, with gentle or rapid thrusting, at the same time they stimulate the clitoris.

Not all women enjoy the insertion of the man's fingers in their vagina during petting. Some women permit it because their partners want to do it, and often the man wants to do it because he assumes that the woman wants something in her vagina. But the key to sexual pleasure for many women is pressure on and around their clitoris, not necessarily insertion.

Cunnilingus **Cunnilingus** translated from the Latin means "he who licks the vulva." Specifically, cunnilingus involves the stimulation of the clitoris, labia, and vaginal opening of the woman by her partner's tongue and lips (see Figure 10.3). As noted earlier, the clitoris is an extremely sensitive organ. The technique many women enjoy is gentle teasing by the tongue, with stronger, more rhythmic sucking movements when orgasm approaches. While the partner's mouth is caressing and licking the clitoral shaft and glans, some women prefer additional stimulation by finger or vibrator in the vagina or anus.

Three-fourths of the almost 600 college students in Rubin's study (1991) reported that they had engaged in oral sex. The women reported that cunnilingus was one of two ways they were able to have an orgasm (being on top during intercourse was the other way) (p. 121).

To what degree do women enjoy cunnilingus? In a study of women aged 27 to 49 in established sexual relationships, heterosexual cunnilingus was their preferred sexual activity (Kahn, 1983). The moist, warm, mobile tongue on their clitoris or vulva feels very good to most women. Those who find it unpleasant or repulsive often view their vaginal area as dirty and oral sex as obscene and unnatural. One woman said that her partner's mouth was for eating, drinking, speaking, and kissing those he loved—not for using on her genitals.

How do men feel about cunnilingus? In a study of 4,000 men, less than 3% said that cunnilingus was unpleasant or boring (Pietropinto & Simenauer, 1977). Some

FIGURE 10.3

men perform cunnilingus because they want to, rather than because their partners ask them to. Their enjoyment in cunnilingus may spring from doing something forbidden, from their enhanced self-image as a good lover, or from just wanting to please their partner.

Some couples engage in cunnilingus and fellatio simultaneously (see Figure 10.4). The term "69" has been used to identify the respective positions of the couple engaging in mutual oral-genital stimulation. "Sixty-nine" may be enjoyed as a prelude to intercourse or as an end in itself. However, some people find it difficult to be a giver and receiver at the same time.

Clitoral Stimulation via Penis In addition to stimulating the clitoral-vulval area by hand and mouth, some women rub their partner's penis inside their vaginal lips. The penis may be rubbed in a circular motion, up and down the vaginal lips, or directly on the clitoris. Such stimulation may or may not be followed by penetration. As suggested earlier, premarital couples who wish to avoid intercourse for moral reasons may enjoy such stimulation, yet stop short of intercourse to maintain their virginity. This has been referred to as "technical virginity," measured in millimeters!

CONSIDERATION: Although rubbing the penis on or near the clitoris is not the same as intercourse, it can result in the same outcome—pregnancy. If the man ejaculates near the woman's vaginal opening during penis-clitoral stimulation, pregnancy may occur. Even if the man does not ejaculate, his penis may emit a small amount of fluid which probably comes from the Skene's glands (although commonly attributed to the Cowper's gland) (Bancroft, 1989) that contains sperm.

Other Petting Behaviors

Another means of experiencing intense physical stimulation without having intercourse is **genital apposition**, or pressing the genitals close together while clothed or unclothed. The couple lie together, entwine their legs, and "grind." An orgasm may or may not result.

Another form of petting is anal stimulation, which involves manual or oral stimulation ("**rimming**") of the anus and surrounding area. The anal area is particularly sensitive, and some couples routinely stimulate each other there during petting.

Anal intercourse is another alternative to vaginal intercourse. One-third of the almost 600 college students in Rubin's study reported that they had experimented with anal sex (Rubin, 1991, p. 126). Voeller (1991) estimated that more than ten percent of American heterosexual women (about eight million women) and their male consorts regularly engage in anal intercourse (p. 233).

FIGURE 10.4 Simultaneous oral genital stimulation

In *Anal Pleasure and Health* (Morin, 1986), the author detailed the history of the anal taboo and suggested ways for those interested in anal sex to relax, desensitize their fears, and discover potential pleasures.

CONSIDERATION: Couples who engage in anal intercourse should use condoms during anal intercourse as a precaution against contracting HIV and other STDs.

A common risk associated with anal intercourse, as well as with manual or oral stimulation of the women's anus, is cystitis (bladder infection). Cystitis may result from bacteria from the anal region being spread to the urethral opening. Symptoms of cystitis may include a persistent urge to urinate, pain during urination, and fever. Cystitis is treated with antibiotics; if left untreated, a serious kidney infection could develop. Women are much more prone to developing cystitis than men. To avoid cystitis, use a condom. If not, at least clean the anal area before engaging in anal stimulation, urinate immediately after sex, and clean the anal and genital area after sex. Also, once a penis, mouth, or finger has come in contact with the anal area, avoid contact with the vagina and clitoris until the penis, mouth, or finger has been washed thoroughly.

That man hath a tongue, I say, is no man, if with this tongue he cannot win a woman.

William Shakespeare

Fellatio, cunnilingus, manual stimulation, vaginal lip stimulation, genital apposition, and anal stimulation are behavioral forms of petting. But petting may also be verbal. Some lovers stimulate each other by telling sex stories, using sex talk, or sharing fantasies. Still other couples use sexual devices in petting. These include erotic movies, books, sexy underwear, and vibrators. Oils may also be used.

Effects of Petting

Petting usually results in erection for men and vaginal lubrication for women. Lubrication is important in preparing women for comfortable insertion of the penis if intercourse is to follow. But independent of intercourse, petting sometimes results in orgasm. Two-thirds of the single men and half of the single women younger than 25 in Hunt's (1974) study reported that they had petted to orgasm. These orgasms may occur during deep kissing, genital apposition, or manual or oral stimulation.

When prolonged petting does not result in orgasm, people may experience discomfort and frustration as a result of the neuromuscular tensions that have been built up during erotic arousal. Half of the women in Kinsey's et al. (1953/1970) sample reported that they were nervously upset, disturbed in their thinking, and incapable of concentrating on some occasions after prolonged petting. One-quarter reported pains in the groin, the feeling also reported by men who are erotically aroused and who fail to achieve orgasm. Women used physical exercise, masturbation, or intercourse to reduce these feelings of discomfort.

Women who pet to orgasm before marriage report more orgasmic frequency in marriage. Among the women in Kinsey's sample, 90% of those who had experienced an orgasm during premarital petting also reported experiencing a climax during their first year of marriage. Only 35% of those who did not have an orgasm before marriage reported having had a climax the first year of marriage. This correlation suggests that premarital petting may contribute to later enjoyment of marital sex.

Petting provides many women their first orgasmic experience. Whereas most men experience their first orgasm through masturbation, petting is the primary means for numerous women (a quarter of Kinsey's sample). "It is petting rather than the home, classroom, or religious instruction, lectures or books, classes in biology, sociology, or philosophy, or actual coitus, that provides most females with their first real understanding of a heterosexual experience" (Kinsey, 1953/1970, p. 264).

Sexual Intercourse Positions

Individuals have various psychological and physical preferences for a particular intercourse position. There are five basic positions of intercourse. With the exception of rear entry, all of the positions are face to face.

Man-on-Top Position

The man-on-top position is the most frequently used position during intercourse (see Figure 10.5). This position is also referred to as the "missionary position," because the Polynesians observed that the British missionaries had intercourse with the man on top. The woman reclines on her back, bends her knees, and spreads her legs. The man positions himself between her legs, supporting himself on his elbows and knees. The man or woman may guide his penis into her vagina.

This position may be preferred because of the belief that this is the way most people have intercourse and, therefore, it is "normal." In addition, it permits maximum male thrusting and facilitates kissing and caressing. But there are disadvantages to the missionary position. Some women experience pain from the deep penetration. Unless such a woman closes her legs after penetration, she is likely to feel the penis thrusting against her cervix. The man-above position also makes clitoral contact difficult. Although a woman can move her buttocks in circular fashion to achieve some clitoral friction, some women find it almost impossible to achieve clitoral stimulation in this position. However, the woman's clitoris may be stimulated by either the man's or the woman's hand or finger during man-on-top intercourse.

Woman-on-Top Position

An alternative position couples frequently use is the woman on top (see Figure 10.6). She may either lie lengthwise so that her legs are between her partner's or kneel on top with her knees on either side of him. The primary advantage of this position is that it permits maximum freedom of movement for the woman to ensure clitoral stimulation. Many women report that they have an orgasm most often in this position. "I like to be on top," wrote one woman, "because I can better control the amount of friction in the right places." In addition, both partners may have their hands free and either the man or woman may stimulate her clitoris during intercourse.

Some women report drawbacks to the woman-above position. Some feel too shy in this position and do not enjoy "being on display." Others complain that the penis keeps falling out since the woman may lift too high before the downward stroke on the penis. Still others say there is a "lot of work when you're on top" and prefer the more passive role.

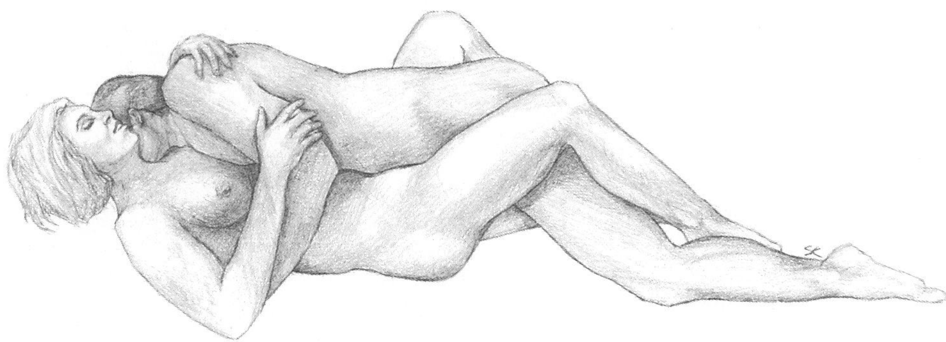

FIGURE 10.5
Man-on-top position

Side-by-Side Position

A relaxing position for both partners is the side-by-side position (see Figure 10.7).The partners lie on their sides, with one leg touching the bed. The top legs are lifted and positioned to accommodate easy entry of the penis. Neither partner bears the strain of "doing all the work," and the partners have relative freedom to move their body as they wish to achieve the desired place of contact and rhythm of movement.

Rear-Entry Position

There are several ways to achieve a rear-entry intercourse position. The woman may lie on her side with her back to her partner (see Figure 10.8). She may also support herself on her knees and hands, (see Figure 10.9) or she may lie on her stomach and tilt her buttocks upward, while the man enters her vagina from behind. In another rear-entry variation, the man may lie on his back and the woman may kneel or squat above him with her back towards her partner.

FIGURE 10.6 Woman-on-top position

FIGURE 10.7 Side-by-side position

Many of the rear-entry intercourse positions permit the man or the woman to manually stimulate her breasts or clitoris or caress her legs and buttocks. Some women are unable to achieve orgasm using the rear-entry position. While some women enjoy the deep penetration that results from rear-entry intercourse, others find it painful. Other disadvantages of rear-entry intercourse include a tendency for the penis to slip out and the loss of face-to-face contact.

Sitting Position

In the sitting position, the man sits on a chair or the edge of the bed with his partner sitting across his thighs (see Figure 10.10). She can lower herself onto his erect penis or insert his penis after she is sitting. She may be facing him, or her back may be turned to him. The face-to-face sitting position involves maximum freedom to stimulate the breasts (manually or orally), to kiss, and to hug.

Standing Position

In the standing position, the woman raises one leg or the man picks her up and places her onto his erect penis. She puts her legs around his waist and her arms around his neck while he is holding her. Both must be well coordinated and in good physical condition for this position.

FIGURE 10.8 Rear entry during pregnancy

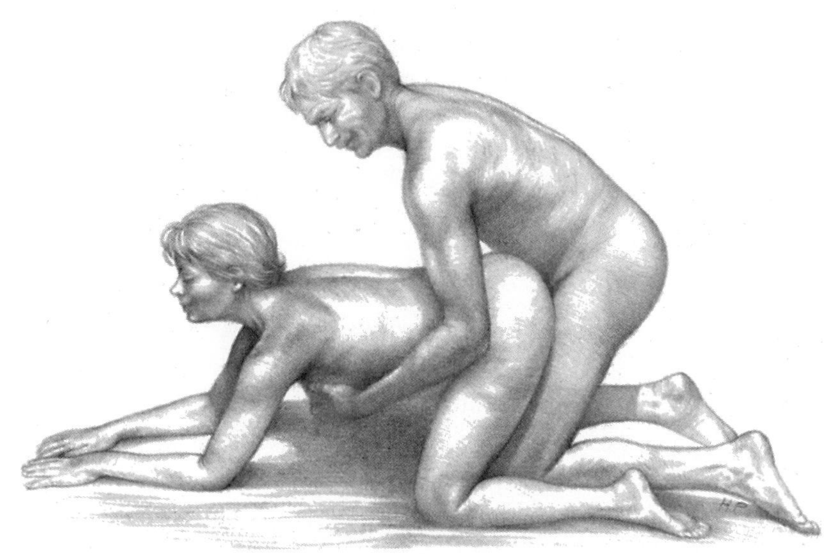

FIGURE 10.9 Rear entry, kneeling

FIGURE 10.10 Sitting position

Another variation of the standing position is for the man to stand while the woman sits or reclines on a raised surface (high bed, table, or chair). The woman's legs are spread and the man inserts his penis into her vagina while standing between her legs.

Variations

There are innumerable variations to the basic positions described above. For example, in the man-above position, the woman's legs may be closed or open, bent or straight, over his shoulders or around his back. The woman may be on her back or raised on her elbows. The partners may face each other or be head to toe. While couples may choose different positions for reasons of variety, pregnancy and health concerns may be other motivations.

CHOICES

Some interpersonal choices with which most people are confronted are whether to become involved in an emotional and/or sexual relationship with someone while simultaneously involved in a "monogamous" relationship with someone else and whether to become involved with someone at work. In this section, we examine these choices.

Choose Extradyadic Sex? No

When 672 spouses were asked if they had been monogamous during the last 12 months, 96% answered affirmatively (Greeley et al., 1990, p. 37). While not all spouses have the opportunity (an available partner) and a context (out of town or away from the spouse) for extradyadic sex, regardless of the reason, the overwhelming majority are faithful in any given year.

Some of those deciding not to have extramarital sex feel that it causes more trouble to themselves and to their partners than it is worth. "I can't say I don't think about having sex with other women, because I do—a lot," said one husband. "But I would feel guilty as hell, and if my wife found out, she would kill me." Spanier and Margolis (1983) found that more women who engaged in extradyadic sex reported guilt feelings than did men (59% versus 34%).

Partners who engage in sex with someone else risk hurting their mate emotionally. Extradyadic intercourse not only involves a breach of intimacy by having sex with someone else, but it also involves deceit. As a result, the partner may develop a deep sense of distrust, which often lingers in the relationship long after the affair is over.

Another reason having an affair hurts the partner and the relationship is that "it represents a regressive transformation from the person considering the couple's joint outcomes to decisions being made on appraisals that are based on individualistic outcomes" (Bringle & Buunk, 1991). In other words, choosing to engage in extradyadic sex is a decision that is based on what the individual wants, not what the couple want.

In addition to guilt, distrust, and emotional pain being potential outcomes of an affair, another danger is the development of a pattern of having affairs. "Once you've had an affair, it's easier the second time," said one spouse. "And the third time, you don't give it a thought." Increasingly, the spouse looks outside the existing relationship for sex and companionship.

Engaging in extradyadic sex may result in the termination of the primary relationship. In a study on how dating partners would cope with learning that their partner had been unfaithful, respondents revealed that they would (in descending order of frequency): terminate the relationship, confront and find out the reason, talk it over, consider terminating the relationship, and work to improve the relationship (Roscoe et al., 1988). Another study found that extramarital affairs played a role in one-third of divorces (Burns, 1984). It is interesting to note that, according to Spanier and Margolis (1983), most people described their own affairs as being a *consequence* of marital problems. However, spouses' affairs were described as being the *cause* of marital problems.

If the partner finds out that the spouse wants a divorce because of an affair, the "adulterer" may also pay an economic price. In some states, adultery is grounds for alimony.

Another potential danger in having extradyadic sex is the potential to contract a sexually transmissible disease. The AIDS epidemic has increased the concern over this possibility. A spouse who engages in extradyadic sex may not only contract a sexually transmissible disease but also may transmit the disease to his or her partner (and potentially their unborn offspring). In some cases, extradyadic sex may be deadly.

Finally, spouses who engage in extradyadic sex relationships risk the possibility of their partner finding out and going into a jealous rage. Jealousy may result in violence and even the death of the unfaithful spouse and/or the lover involved. Another possible tragic outcome of extramarital relationships is that the spouse who has been "cheated on" may become depressed and commit suicide.

Partners who decide to avoid extradyadic encounters might focus on the small choices that lead to a sexual encounter. Since extradyadic sex occurs in certain relationships and structural contexts, the person can choose to avoid these. For example, choosing not to become involved in intimate conversations, not to

Continued

Continued

have lunch with, and not to drink alone in a bar with someone to whom you are attracted decreases the chance that a relationship will develop or that a context will present itself in which a sexual encounter becomes a possibility. The person who chooses to talk intimately with others and have lunch and "happy hour" drinks with them is increasing the chance that an extramarital relationship will develop.

Choose Extradyadic Sex? Yes

A small percentage of spouses who have an affair feel that it has positive consequences for them, their marriage, and/or their partners. Regarding the positive consequences for the person having the affair, one woman whose husband constantly criticized her said of her partner in the extramarital relationship, "He made me feel loved, valued, and worthwhile again." This woman eventually divorced her husband and said that she never regretted moving from an emotionally abusive relationship to one in which she was loved and nurtured.

In a study by Atwater (1982), 60% of women reported that they enjoyed sex more with their extramarital partners than with their husbands. In addition to good sex, other potential positive consequences of engaging in extradyadic sex include personal growth and self-discovery.

For spouses who have an affair and who stay married, the marriage can benefit. Some partners become sensitive to the fact that they have a problem in their marriage. "For us," one spouse said, "the affair helped us to look at our marriage, to know that we were in trouble, and to seek help." Couples need not view the discovery of an affair as the end of their marriage; it can be a new beginning.

A final positive effect of a partner discovering an affair is that the partner may become more sensitive to the needs of the spouse and more motivated to satisfy them. The partner may realize that if the spouse is not satisfied at home, he or she will go elsewhere. One husband said his wife had an affair because he was too busy with his work and did not spendenough time with her. Her affair taught him that she had alternatives—other men who would love her emotionally and sexually. To ensure that he did not lose her, he cut back on his work hours and spent more time with her.

Although an affair is dangerous for most marriages, one researcher (Britton, 1984) interviewed 276 spouses who had had an affair and identified the conditions under which an extramarital encounter is least likely to have negative consequences:

1. The spouse has a solid marriage relationship. The one who has the affair has a strong emotional commitment to the mate. The lover is viewed as short-term only, not as a potential replacement for the mate.
2. The spouse compartmentalizes easily. The one who has the affair can keep the lover and the mate separated in time, place, and

Continued

Attraction...

- Am I aware of being attracted?
- How do I feel about this attraction?
- What do I do about my attraction?
- Do I approach or avoid the person?

If an Intimate Relationship Evolves...

- How do I feel being in this relationship?
- How do I deal with changes in the relationship as they occur?
- How do I balance work roles with relationship expectations?
- How do I deal with other people's views of the relationship?
- Are there formal policies against intimate relationships at my place of employment? Will management disapprove?

Choices about Attraction and Intimacy at Work: Questions to Ask Yourself

Source: Adapted from Crary, Marcy. (1988). Managing attraction and intimacy at work. In Fairlee E. Winfield (Ed.), *The work and family sourcebook* (pp. 459–474). Greenvale, NY: Panel Publishers, Inc. Used by permission.

Continued

thought. Memories of the experiences with the lover are not allowed to blend into the relationship with the spouse so that behavior is adversely affected.

3. The spouse avoids disclosure. Disclosure of extramarital affairs is like a rattlesnake in the relationship; it strikes the spouse and introduces a deadly venom. Few spouses can tolerate the information that their partner had or is having a sexual relationship with someone else.
4. The spouse limits contact with the lover. Frequent contacts with one or more lovers take energy away from the marriage and increase the chance of getting caught.
5. The spouse has extramarital sex for recreation only. Sexual experiences solely for spontaneous recreation do the least damage. Those that are carefully orchestrated for the purpose of emotional involvement take time and energy away from the mate and put the marriage at greater risk.

Choose to Become Involved with Someone at Work?

Earlier, we looked at some of the issues confronting co-workers involved in an intimate relationship. Because intimate relationships usually begin with attraction (not necessarily physical), making choices about whether or not to become involved in an office romance begins with making choices about one's attractions. The diagram (see opposite page) suggests questions one might ask oneself regarding attraction and intimate involvements at work.

Summary

1. Most sexual choices involve another person or persons.
2. The type of relationship a couple is involved in influences sex frequency and nonmonogamy. The longer a couple (married, cohabitating, heterosexual, homosexual) is involved in a relationship, the less frequently they report having sex.
3. Functions of dating include development of self-concept; recreation; companionship, intimacy and sex; socialization; status achievement and sorting; and mate selection. Men expect more sex (kiss, fondling, intercourse) sooner in a dating relationship than women. Dating among the divorced and widowed differs from dating prior to a first marriage. Divorced people report more sexual partners in a given year than married people; thus, their risk for contracting HIV or other STDs may be higher.
4. Cohabitation in our society has increased in recent decades. Couples may cohabit because they are homosexual, fear marriage, have career or educational commitments, aren't ready for marriage, or don't want legal ties. Couples who live together before marriage are more likely to get divorced than couples who do not live together before marriage. This correlation is related to breaking norms—individuals who break norms and live together are more likely to break norms to divorce. Cohabitants tend to have sex more frequently, have more egalitarian sexual relationships, and tend to be less monogamous than married people.
5. Most people eventually marry. Reasons for marriage include personal fulfillment, companionship, parenthood, and security. Husbands tend to be more satisfied (and wives less satisfied) with their spouses as lovers.
6. Research suggests that there are no differences between gay male, lesbian, and heterosexual married partners on measures of relationship quality. Lesbian couples emphasize equality of power in relationships. Married and cohabitating couples receive greater social support from their families than gay male and lesbian partners.

7. Types of extradyadic sexual involvements include brief encounters, affairs, open marriages, swinging, and group sex. Motivations and reasons for extradyadic sexual encounters include variety, novelty and excitement; friendship; relationship dissatisfaction with primary partner; revenge against partner; desire for homosexual relationship; desire to re-experience youthful vitality; and absence from partner.
8. Sexual involvement with co-workers has become more common due to the increase in number of women in the workforce. Managing intimate relationships at work involves balancing work and love roles, dealing with co-workers' perceptions of the relationship, and dealing with changes in the relationship without letting job performance suffer.
9. Non-coital sexual behaviors include touching, kissing, breast stimulation, penile stimulation, clitoral stimulation, and anal stimulation. Sexual intercourse may be performed in a variety of positions. For many individuals, especially women, non-coital sexual behaviors are of as great (if not greater) importance for sexual satisfaction as intercourse.
10. Extradyadic sexual involvement may or may not result in negative outcomes for the individuals involved and for the primary relationship.

KEY TERMS

conflict-habituated relationships
devitalized relationships
passive-congenial relationships
vital relationships
total relationships
extradyadic sexual behavior
affairs
sexually open marriages
comarital sex
group sex
fellatio
cunnilingus
genital apposition
rimming

REFERENCES

Ackerman, D. (1990). *A natural history of the senses.* New York: Random House.

Alzate, H. (1989). Sexual behavior of unmarried Colombian university students: A follow-up. *Archives of Sexual Behavior, 18,* 239–250.

Ard, B. N. (1990). *The sexual realm in long-term marriages: A longitudinal study following marital partners over twenty years.* San Francisco: Mellen Research University Press.

Atwater, L. (1979). Getting involved: Women's transition to first extramarital sex. *Alternative Lifestyles, 2,* 33–68.

Atwater, L. (1982). *The extramarital connection: Sex, intimacy, identity.* New York: Irvington.

Balakrishnan, T. R., Rao, K. V., Lapierre-Adamyck, E., & Krotki, K. J. (1987). A hazard model analysis of the covariates of marriage dissolution in Canada. *Demography, 24,* 395–406.

Bancroft, J. (1989). *Human sexuality and its problems* (2nd Ed.). Edinburgh: Churchill Livingstone.

Basow, S. A. (1992). *Gender stereotypes and roles* (3rd Ed.). Pacific Grove: Brooks/Cole.

Barbach, L. (1982). *For each other: Sharing sexual intimacies.* Garden City, NY: Doubleday/Anchor.

Bennett, N. G., Blanc, A. K., & Bloom, D. E. (1988). Commitment and the modern union: Assessing the link between premarital cohabitation and subsequent marital stability. *American Sociological Review, 53,* 127–139.

Bermant, G. (1976). Sexual behavior: Hard times with the Coolidge effect. In M. H. Siegel and H. P. Zeigler (Eds.), *Psychological research: The inside story* (pp. 76–103). New York: Harper and Row.

Blumstein, P., & Schwartz, P. (1983). *American couples: Money, work, and sex.* New York: William Morrow.

Blumstein, P., & Schwartz, P. (1990). Intimate relationships and the creation of sexuality. In D. P. McWhirter, S. A. Sanders, and J. M. Reinish (Eds.), *Homosexuality/Heterosexuality: Concepts of sexual orientation* (pp. 307–320). New York: Oxford University Press.

Booth, A., & Johnson, D. (1988). Premarital cohabitation and marital success. *Journal of Family Issues, 9,* 255–272.

Bretschneider, J. G., & McCoy, N. L. (1988) Sexual interest and behavior in healthy 18-to 102 year olds. *Archives of Sexual Behavior 17,* 109–129.

Bringle, R. G., & Buunk, B. T. (1991). Extradyadic relationships and sexual jealousy. In K. McKinney and S. Sprecher (Eds.), *Sexuality in close relationships* (pp. 135–152). Hillsdale, NJ: Lawrence Erlbaum Associates.

Britton, T. (1984). Lenoir Community College, Kinston, N.C. Personal communication.

Bulcroft, K., & O'Conner-Roden, M. (1986, June). Never too late. *Psychology Today,* pp. 66–69.

Buunk, B. (1980). Sexually open marriages: Ground rules for countering potential threats to marriage. *Alternative Lifestyles, 3,* 312–328.

Buunk, B. & Van Driel, B. (1989). *Variant lifestyles and relationships.* Newbury Park, CA: Sage.

Bumpass, L., & Sweet, J. (1989). National estimates of cohabitation: Cohort levels and union stability. NSFH Working Paper No. 2, Center for Demography and Ecology, University of Wisconsin-Madison.

Burns, A. (1984). Perceived causes of marriage breakdown and conditions of life. *Journal of Marriage and the Family, 46,* 551–562.

Cooley, C. H. (1964). *Human nature and the social order.* New York: Schocken. (Original work published 1902).

Crary, M. (1988). Managing attraction and intimacy at work. In Fairlee E. Winfield (Ed.), *The work and family sourcebook* (pp. 459–474). Greenvale, NY: Panel.

Cuber, J. F., & Harroff, P. B. (1965). *Sex and the significant Americans.* Baltimore: Penguin Books.

Demaris, A., & K. V. Rao. (1992). Premarital cohabitation and subsequent marital stability in the United States: A reassessment. *Journal of Marriage and the Family,* 54, 178–190.

Dychtwald, K. 1990 *Age wave.* New York: Bantam Books.

Eyler, D. R. & Baridon, A. P. (1992 May/June). Far more than friendship. *Psychology Today,* pp. 58–67.

Finkelhor, D., & Yllo, K. (1988). Rape in marriage. In M. B. Strause (Ed.), *Abuse and victimization across the life span* (pp. 140–152). Baltimore: Johns Hopkins University Press.

Ford, R. C., & McLaughlin, F. S. (1988). Should Cupid come to the workplace? An ASPA survey. In F. E. Winfield (Ed.), *The work and family sourcebook* (pp. 449–457). Greenvale, NY: Panel.

Gordon, B. (1988). *Jennifer fever.* New York: Harper and Row.

Greeley, A. M., Michael, R. T., & Smith, T. W. (1990, July/August). Americans and their sexual partners. *Society,* pp. 36–42.

Hite, S. (1977). *The Hite report: A nationwide study of female sexuality.* New York: Dell.

Hite, S. (1981). *The Hite report on male sexuality.* New York: Alfred Knopf.

Hunt, M. M. (1974). *Sexual behavior in the 1970s.* New York: Dell.

Kahn, S. S. (1983). *The Kahn report on sexual preferences: What the opposite sex likes and dislikes—and why.* New York: St. Martin's Press.

Kelley, H. H., Berscheid, E., Christensen, A., Harvey, J. H., Huston, T. L., Levinger, G., McClintock, E., Peplau, L. A., & Peterson, D. R. (1983). *Close relationships.* New York: W. H. Freeman.

Kinsey, A. C., Pomeroy, W. B., & Martin, C. E. (1948). *Sexual behavior in the human male.* Philadelphia: W. B. Saunders.

Kinsey, A. C., Pomeroy, W. B., Martin, C. E., & Gebhard, P. H. (1970). *Sexual behavior in the human female.* New York: Pocket Books. (Original work published 1953)

Knox, D, & Schacht, C. (1992). Sexual behaviors of university students enrolled in a human sexuality course. *College Student Journal, 26,* 38–40.

Knox, D., & Wilson, K. (1983). Dating problems of university students. *College Student Journal, 17,* 225–228.

Kohn, B., & Matusow, A. (1980). *Barry and Alice: Portrait of a bisexual marriage.* Englewood Cliffs, NJ: Prentice-Hall.

Kurdek, L. A. (1988). Perceived social support in gays and lesbians in cohabitating relationships. *Journal of Personality and Social Psychology, 54,* 504–509.

Kurdek, L. A. & Schmitt, J. P. (1986a). Interaction of sex role self-concept with relationship quality and relationship beliefs in married, heterosexual cohabiting, gay and lesbian couples. *Journal of Personality and Social Psychology, 51,* 365–370.

Kurdek, L. A. & Schmitt, J. P. (1986b). Relationship quality of partners in heterosexual married, heterosexual cohabiting, and gay and lesbian relationships. *Journal of Personality and Social Psychology, 51,* 711–720.

Kurdek, L. A. & Schmitt, J. P. (1987). Perceived emotional support from family and friends in members of homosexual, married, and heterosexual cohabiting couples. *Journal of Homosexuality, 14,* (3/4), 57–68.

Landale, N. S. & Fennelly, K. (1992). Informal unions among mainland Puerto Ricans: Cohabitation or an alternative to legal marriage? *Journal of Marriage and the Family,* 54, 269–280.

Lawson, A. (1988). *Adultery: An analysis of love and betrayal.* New York: Basic Books.

Lieberman, B. (1988). Extrapremarital intercourse: Attitudes toward a neglected sexual behavior. *Journal of Sex Research, 24,* 291–299.

Makepeace, J. (1989). Dating, living together, and courtship violence. In M. A. Pirog-Good and Jan E. Stets (Eds.), *Violence in dating relationships* (pp. 94–107). New York: Greenwood Press.

Masters, W. H. and Johnson, V. E. (1976) *The pleasure bond.* New York: Bantam.

McKinney, K., & Sprecher, S. (1991). Introduction. In K. McKinney and S. Sprecher (Eds.), *Sexuality in close relationships* (pp. 1–8). Hillsdale, NJ: Lawrence Erlbaum Associates.

McNaught, B. R. (1983). Overcoming self-hate through education: Achieving self-love among gay people. In G. Albee, S. Gordon, & H. Leitenberg (Eds.) *Promoting Sexual Responsibility and Preventing Sexual Problems* (pp. 133–145). Hanover, NH: University Press of New England.

Morin, J. (1986). *Anal pleasure and health.* Burlingame, CA: Down There Press.

Montagu, A., & Matson, F. (1979). *The human connection.* New York: McGraw-Hill.

Murstein, B. I., Case, D., & Gunn, S. P. (1985). Personality correlates of ex-swingers. *Lifestyles, 8,* 21–34.

National Center for Health Statistics. (1992). *Births, marriages, divorces, and deaths for October 1991.* (Monthly Vital Statistics Report, vol. 40, no. 10). Hyattsville, Maryland: U.S. Public Health Service.

National Survey Results on Long Lasting Relationships. (1990, May/June). *Partners newsletter for gay and lesbian couples,* p. 1. (S. Bryant and Demian, publishers/editors, Box 9685, Seattle, WA 98109).

O'Flaherty, K. M., & Eells, L. W. (1988). Courtship behavior of the remarried. *Journal of Marriage and the Family, 50,* 499–506.

O'Neill, N., & O'Neill, G. (1972). *Open marriage: A new life style for couples.* New York: Avon Books.

Pietropinto, A. (1987). Sexual abstinence *Medical Aspects of Human Sexuality, 21* (7), 115–118.

Pietropinto, A., & Simenauer, J. (1977). *Beyond the male myth.* New York: Quadrangle.

Rice, F. P. (1990). *The Adolescent* (6th Ed). Boston: Allyn & Bacon.

Roscoe, B., Cavanaugh, L. E., & Kennedy, D. R. (1988). Dating infidelity: Behavior, reasons, and consequences. *Adolescence, 13,* 35–43.

Rose, S. & Frieze, I. H. (1989). Young singles' scripts for a first date. *Gender and Society, 3,* 258–268.

Rothman, E. K. (1987). *Hands and hearts: A history of courtship in America.* Cambridge: Harvard University Press.

Rubin, L. B. (1991). *Erotic wars: What Happened to the Sexual Revolution?* New York: Harper Perennial.

Rubinson, L., & De Rubertis, L. (1991). Trends in sexual attitudes and behaviors of a college population over a 15 year period. *Journal of Sex Education and Therapy, 17,* 32–42.

Schaefer, L. (1981). Women and extramarital affairs. *Sexuality Today, 4,* 3.

Schoen, R., (1992). First unions and the stability of first marriages. *Journal of Marriage and the Family, 54,* 281–284.

Smith, T. W. (1991). Adult sexual behavior in 1989: Number of partners, frequency of intercourse and risk of AIDS. *Family Planning Perspectives, 23,* 102–107.

Spanier, G. B. (1989). Bequeathing family continuity. *Journal of Marriage and the Family, 51,* 3–14.

Spanier, G. B., & Margolis, R. L. (1983). Marital separation and extramarital sexual behavior. *Journal of Sex Research, 19,* 23–48.

Sprecher, S., McKinney, K., & Orbuch, T. L. (1987). Has the double standard disappeared? An experimental test. *Social Psychology Quarterly, 50,* 24–31.

Statistical abstract of the United States: 1992 (112th ed.). (1990). Washington, DC: U.S. Bureau of the Census.

Stets, J. E., & Straus, M. A. (1989). The marriage as a hitting license: A comparison of assaults in dating, cohabiting, and married couples. In M. A. Pirog-Good and Jan E. Stets (Eds.), *Violence in dating relationships* (pp. 33–52). New York: Greenwood Press.

Symons, D. (1979). *The evolution of human sexuality.* New York: Oxford University Press.

Thompson, A. P. (1983). Extramarital sex: A review of the research literature. *Journal of Sex Research, 19,* 1–22.

Thompson, A. P. (1984). Emotional and sexual components of extramarital relations. *Journal of Marriage and the Family, 46,* 35–42.

Thomson, E., & Colella, U., (1992). Cohabitation and marital stability: Quality or commitment? *Journal of Marriage and the Family, 54,* 259–267.

Thornton, A. (1990). The courtship process and adolescent sexuality. *Journal of Family Issues, 11,* 239–273.

Trotter, S. (1989). Single women/married men. *Free Inquiry in Creative Sociology, 17,* 213–217.

Voeller, B. (1991). AIDS and heterosexual anal intercourse. *Archives of Sexual Behavior, 20,* 233–276.

Weitzman, L. J. (1990). Women and children last: The social and economic consequences of divorce law reforms. In S. Ruth (Ed.) *Issues in Feminism: An Introduction to Women's Studies* (pp. 312–335). Mountain View, CA: Mayfield.

Wheeler, J., & Kilmann, P. R. (1983). Comarital sexual behavior: Individual and relationship variables. *Archives of Sexual Behavior, 12,* 295–306.

White, J. W. (1989). Reply to comment by Trussel and Rao: A reanalysis of the data. *Journal of Marriage and the Family, 51,* 540–544.

Woll, S. B., & Young, P. (1989). Looking for Mr. or Ms. Right: Self-presentation in videodating. *Journal of Marriage and the Family, 51,* 483–488.

Yablonsky, L. (1979). *The Extra-sex factor: Why over half of America's married men play around.* New York: Times Books.

CHAPTER ELEVEN

Sexual Orientation

Chapter Outline

Homosexuality and Heterosexuality
- Definition of Homosexuality and Heterosexuality
- Prevalence of Homosexuality and Heterosexuality
- Bisexuality

Homophobia and Heterosexism
- Prejudice against Homosexuals
- **Self-Assessment:** Index of Attitudes toward Homosexuals
- Discrimination against Homosexuals
- Antigay Violence
- **Research and Policy Perspective:** Gay and Lesbian Life on Campus

The Gay Liberation Movement
- Lesbian-Feminism

Theoretical Explanations for Sexual Orientation
- Biological Explanations
- Social Learning Explanations
- Social-Psychological Explanations
- Psychoanalytic Explanations

Developing a Gay Identity
- Troiden's Four-Stage Process
- Coming Out
- Developing a Positive Gay Self-Concept
- The Role of the Gay Subculture

Inside Gay Relationships
- Gay Male Relationships
- Gay Female Relationships
- Sexual Behavior
- Sexually Transmissible Diseases

Choices
- The Choice of Some Homosexuals: Lover or Parent
- The Choice of Some Parents: Accept or Reject a Gay Son or Daughter
- Distress About One's Sexual Orientation: Seek Therapy?

Is It True?*

1. Self-identified heterosexuals, homosexuals, and bisexuals engage in sexual behavior consistent with the labels they attach to themselves. Hence, individuals who say they are heterosexual do not engage in sex with people of the same sex.

2. Compared to heterosexuals, lesbians and gay men who have extradyadic sex are more likely to be open about it with their partners.

3. Because of such intense hostility against homosexuals, most gay people would take a pill to make them heterosexual if such a pill were available.

4. Unlike women in heterosexual relationships, lesbians generally do not experience relationship conflicts over issues of equality of power and division of labor.

5. Compared to people with lower levels of education, people with higher levels of education are less likely to be prejudiced against homosexuals.

*1 = F, 2 = T, 3 = F, 4 = F, 5 = T

There is no such thing as "the" homosexual (or "the" heterosexual, for that matter) and statements of any kind which are made about human beings on the basis of their sexual orientation must always be highly qualified.

Alan Bell
Martin Weinberg

The February 24, 1992, cover of *Newsweek* magazine featured a photo of a blue-eyed baby with the caption, "Is This Child Gay? Born or Bred—The Origins of Homosexuality." The television shows "Beverly Hills, 90210" and "The Golden Girls" have featured episodes about gay relationships. Talk shows such as "Donahue," "Geraldo," and "Oprah Winfrey" regularly feature programs on gay rights and gay marriages. While many individuals regard sexual orientation as a personal and private matter, the topic of homosexuality has become a highly visible issue in our society. Indeed, homosexuality has "come out of the closet."

The theme of this text, choices in sexuality, may imply that one's sexual orientation is a matter of choice. Indeed, the term "sexual preference," which is often used to refer to a person's identification as homosexual, heterosexual, or bisexual, implies voluntary choice. However, Money (1987) argued that homosexuality, bisexuality, and heterosexuality are not a matter of preference, just as handedness and our native language are not determined by our preference.

CONSIDERATION: "Politically, sexual preference is a dangerous term, for it implies that if homosexuals choose their preference, then they can be legally forced, under threat of punishment, to choose to be heterosexual" (Money, 1987, p. 385). While the terms "sexual preference," "sexual orientation," and "sexual status" are often used interchangeably, the latter two terms avoid the implication that homosexuality, heterosexuality, and bisexuality are determined by voluntary choice. Hence, "orientation" is used more often by those who think there is little choice involved, and "preference" is used by those who think choice is important (Weinrich & Williams, 1991, p. 55). We use the term "sexual orientation" as the title of this chapter because we feel that, whether because of biological variables or social forces operative in a heterosexist society, one's choices in sexual orientation are limited. Regarding the social forces operative on the sexual choices of women, Rich (1989) observed, ". . . women's choice of women as passionate comrades, life partners, co-workers, and lovers has been crushed, invalidated, forced into hiding and disguised" (p. 12).

When I realized I was gay I also realized I *did* have a choice, but not between homosexuality and heterosexuality. I could choose to live in the closet, maybe even marry a woman and pretend to be who I'm not, or I could be honest about who I am and live my life openly—no easy thing to do.

Eric Marcus

Regardless of whether one chooses one's sexual orientation, homosexuals do have choices, such as whether, when, and to whom to disclose their sexual orientation, and heterosexuals have a choice to reject or accept homosexual individuals (homosexuals also have the choice to accept or reject heterosexuals) and the antihomosexual views of society. Heterosexuals might also choose to engage in homosexual sex, and vice versa.

In this chapter, we focus on theories and research related to sexual orientation. First, we discuss the difficulties of defining homosexuality and identifying its prevalence in our society (these topics necessarily include a discussion of bisexuality). Next, we discuss the prejudice and discrimination to which gays and bisexuals are subjected and note the reaction in terms of the gay liberation movement. We follow this with an overview of various theories regarding the origin of sexual orientation, a discussion of various aspects of developing a gay identity, and a look at gay relationships. We end the chapter with a discussion of some choices in regard to sexual orientation.

Homosexuality and Heterosexuality

As homosexual issues have become more visible, terms and definitions regarding sexual orientation have been subjected to critical scrutiny.

Definition of Homosexuality and Heterosexuality

We define **homosexuality** or **homoeroticism** as the predominance of cognitive, emotional, and sexual attraction to those of the same sex. The term "gay" is synonymous with the term "homosexual"; it may refer to either males or females who have a same-sex orientation. More often the term "gay men" is used to refer to male homosexuals and the term **"lesbian"** is used to refer to homosexual women (Committee on Lesbian & Gay Concerns, 1991). The term "lesbian" originates from the Greek island of Lesbos, where the ancient poet Sappho taught young women to share the delights of their minds and bodies.

Heterosexuality or **heteroeroticism** refers to a predominance of cognitive, emotional, and sexual attraction to those of the opposite sex. Another term that refers to heterosexual is "straight," from the expression "straight as an arrow," denoting adherence to conventional values and standards of behavior.

The primary distinguishing features of one's **sexual orientation** are one's cognitions (thoughts and fantasies), emotions (feelings), and sexual attractions (desires to touch and enjoy physically). However, other elements may include sexual preference ("I choose a particular orientation"), recurring basis or stability ("My sexual preference is relatively stable"), and self-concept or self-identity ("I regard myself as having a particular orientation"). One's behaviors may also be used to distinguish sexual orientation.

The distinction between homosexuality and heterosexuality is not as clear-cut as it appears. In 1948, Kinsey and his colleagues suggested that sexual orientation may be understood as a continuum (see Figure 11.1).

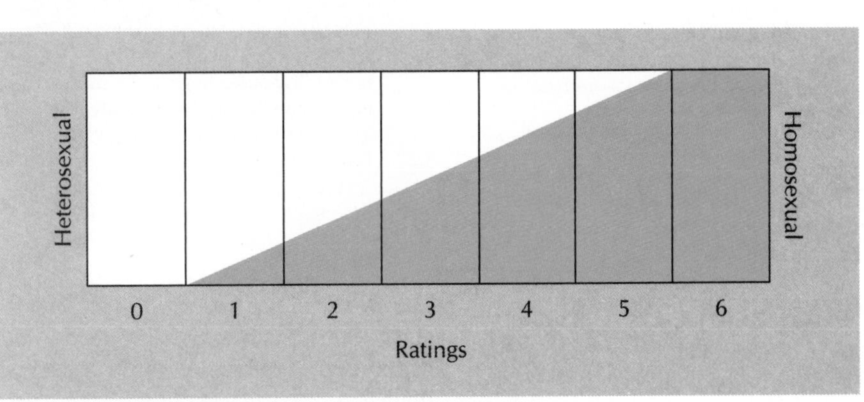

FIGURE 11.1 The Heterosexual-Homosexual Rating Scale

Source: Kinsey, A., Pomeroy, W., Martin, C., & Gebhard, P. (1953). *Sexual behavior in the human female* (p. 470, figure 93). Philadelphia: W. B. Saunders. Reprinted by permission of the Kinsey Institute for Research in Sex, Gender, and Reproduction.

Using this continuum, individuals with ratings of 0 or 1 are entirely or largely heterosexual; 2, 3, or 4 are more bisexual; and 5 or 6 are largely or entirely homosexual. Using this continuum, it becomes clear that few people are entirely heterosexual or homosexual but most have gradations of thoughts, emotions, and behaviors in reference to the opposite and the same sex. The following questions illustrate that "dividing people up into classes such as homosexual or heterosexual . . . ignores evidence suggesting that sexuality exists on a continuum" (Ross, 1987, p. 250). Which of the following individuals would you categorize as homosexual?

> Is it the young person who fantasizes about someone of their same sex in their class or on their school's swimming team? Is it the young person who has had a few sexual experiences with someone of the same sex? Is it the man who is married to a woman for years who occasionally has sex with men? Is it the woman who is married but unhappy with her sexual relationship with her husband and who has very close but non-sexual attachments to other women? What about the person who struggles against but never acts on desires for members of the same sex? What about those who feel an occasional sexual attraction to people of the other sex? (Blumenfeld & Raymond, 1989, p. 84).

NATIONAL DATA: Of 12,000 U.S. men, 46% reported having had varying amounts of sexual activity with both men and women (Kinsey, Pomeroy, & Martin, 1948). Of 8,000 U.S. women, 28% reported having had erotic feelings for other women, 19% had had some sexual contact with other women, and 13% had experienced orgasm with another woman (Kinsey, Pomeroy, Martin & Gebhard, 1953).

In addition to allowing for gradations of sexual orientation, another definitional problem regarding sexual orientation is that "engaging in homosexual sex, or for that matter, heterosexual sex, is not the same as being a homosexual or heterosexual" (Blumenfeld & Raymond, 1989, p. 82). For example, people may engage in heterosexual sex, even though they desire sexual relations with a member of their own sex. Indeed, research supports the conclusion that, "more people have homosexual feelings than engage in homosexual behavior, and more engage in homosexual behavior then develop lasting homosexual identification" (Lever, Kanouse, Rogers, Carson & Hertz, 1992, p. 144).

CONSIDERATION: The sexual orientation a person identifies with and the sexual behavior in which the person engages are sometimes different. Of 52 men who labeled themselves as heterosexual, almost a quarter (23%) had sex with both women and men (in the last two years) and 6% had sex exclusively with men. Seventeen percent were celibate. Of 95 men who labeled themselves as homosexual, 83% had sex exclusively with men. However, 6% had sex with both men and women, and 11% were celibate (Doll, Petersen, White, Johnson, Ward, & the Blood Donor Study Group, 1992, p. 5).

> In another study using 1982 survey data from *Playboy Magazine* (N = 6,982), of those men who reported having prior sexual experiences with both men and women, 69% described themselves as heterosexual, 29% as bisexual, and 2% as homosexual (Lever, Kanouse, Rogers, Carson, & Hertz, 1992). This means that adult bisexual experience does not necessarily result in acquisition of a bisexual self-identity. Most bisexually experienced men (69%) in the study just mentioned labeled themselves as heterosexual. Also, labeling one's self as bisexual does not require having prior bisexual experience. In the study, 18% of those who labeled themselves as bisexual reported no adult homosexual experience whatsoever.

Homosexuality has been a significant part of human sexual activity ever since the dawn of history, primarily because it is an expression of capacities that are basic in the human animal.

Alfred Kinsey, Wardell Pomeroy, and Clyde Martin

Prevalence of Homosexuality and Heterosexuality

Despite the difficulties involved in defining who is and is not homosexual, researchers have attempted to estimate the prevalence of homosexuality in our society. Much of the data are obtained through surveys; samples of individuals complete questionnaires or participate in interviews designed to ascertain their sexual orientation.

NATIONAL DATA: It is estimated that between 5% and 10% of adults in the United States are predominately homosexual. This means that there are between 12.5 and 25 million homosexuals in the United States today (Smith, 1991, Harry, 1990; Whitehead and Nokes, 1990). "If you look at all societies, homosexuality occurs at the same rates with the same kinds of behaviors" (Whitam as quoted in Gelman & Foote, 1992, p. 52).

NATIONAL DATA: Thirty-seven percent of 3,018 respondents believed that they could recognize homosexuals on the basis of their appearance (Klassen, Williams, & Levitt, 1989).

But accurate estimates of the prevalence of homosexuality are difficult to obtain because "societal intolerance [of homosexuality] may cause some survey respondents to conceal histories of same-gender sexual contact (Fay, Turner, Klassen, & Gagnon 1989, p. 338). Nevertheless, some data are available on the percentage of individuals who have had variable amounts of same sex contact (see National Data). Estimates of the percentage of individuals who live an almost exclusive homosexual life-style are much lower (see National Data).

Gay people (as well as heterosexual people) are young and old, single and married, from all educational levels, occupations, income levels, races, and religions, and live in both large and small towns in all countries (Harry, 1990). There is a myth that a homosexual person is instantly recognizable because, it is believed, homosexual men are effeminate and lesbians are masculine (see National Data).

In reality, many heterosexual men have physical and/or behavioral qualities that may be viewed as effeminate, and many gay men have physical and/or behavioral qualities that are viewed as masculine. Similarly, many heterosexual women may be viewed as mannish, while many lesbians have qualities that are viewed as feminine.

Bisexuality

Defining **bisexuality** is also difficult. Kinsey et al. (1948) defined bisexuality as a series of stages between being exclusively heterosexual and exclusively homosexual. A score of zero equals exclusive heterosexuality and a score of six equals exclusive homosexuality. A score between the extremes equates to being bisexual. The Heterosexual-Homosexual Rating Scale (Figure 11.1), developed by Kinsey, suggests that sexual orientation is a bipolar, unidimensional continuum. By using the scale, an individual gains or loses degrees used to describe sexual orientation as he or she moves toward opposite ends of the continuum. Thus, bisexuals are literally seen as both heterosexual and homosexual.

Bisexuality is one of the least understood aspects of sexual orientation. So strong is the tendency to dichotomize sexual orientation that many people simply do not believe it exists.

Margaret Nichols

One problem with the Kinsey definition of bisexuality is that the scale does not account for changes in life situations over time. If a person scores a zero (exclusively heterosexual) at age 23 but has a series of sexual experiences with members of the same sex at age 43, is the person bisexual or homosexual or somewhere in between?

More recently, Berkey, Perelman-Hall, and Kurdek (1990) developed a Multidimensional Sexuality Scale (MSS), which provided six categories of bisexuality rather than an "either you are or you aren't" categorization. These bisexual categories include:

1. Homosexual orientation prior to exclusive heterosexual orientation. The person was gay or lesbian and is now heterosexual.
2. Heterosexual orientation prior to exclusive homosexual orientation. The person was heterosexual but is now gay or lesbian.
3. Predominant homosexual orientation with infrequent heterosexual desires and/or sexual contacts. The person thinks and behaves sexually with members of the same sex most of the time but occasionally thinks and behaves sexually with members of the opposite sex. Of 317 self-identified gay people between the ages of 14 and 23, 23% reported that they were predominately homosexual with some heterosexual interest (Savin-Williams, 1989).
4. Predominant heterosexual orientation with infrequent homosexual desires and/or sexual contacts. The person thinks and behaves sexually with members of the opposite sex most of the time but occasionally thinks and behaves sexually with members of the same sex.
5. Equal orientation toward members of both sexes, where desires for and/or sexual contacts with members of both sexes occur on a fairly regular basis (concurrent

bisexual). Heterosexual and homosexual thoughts and behaviors are interchangeable.

6. Equal orientation toward members of both sexes, where exclusive homosexual orientation is followed by exclusive heterosexual orientation (or vice versa), on an ongoing basis (sequential bisexual).

CONSIDERATION: The value of the MSS scale over the Kinsey scale is that the former allows us to make finer discriminations regarding sexual orientation. Of 15 individuals who scored a three (truly bisexual) on the Kinsey scale, 60% were concurrent bisexuals and 33.3% were sequential bisexuals on the MSS scale. Also, of 40 individuals who identified themselves as exclusively homosexual on the Kinsey scale (scoring six), 27.5% categorized themselves as past heterosexuals but currently homosexual on the MSS scale (Berkey et al., 1990, p. 80).

Fred Klein (1978, 1985) also emphasized that sexual orientation is multifaceted and developed a Sexual Orientation Grid consisting of seven factors. You might ask yourself to what degree you are exclusively heterosexual or homosexual on the basis of your answers to the following questions:

1. Sexual attraction—Who appeals to you as a potential sexual partner?
2. Sexual behavior—Who have you kissed, fondled, and had sex with? With whom would you like to?
3. Sexual fantasies—Who are the objects of your sexual fantasies? Your sexual dreams?
4. Emotional bonds—With whom do you enjoy a close emotional relationship?
5. Social interaction—With whom do you prefer to do things socially?
6. Life-style—Do you spend most of your free time with individuals who see themselves as primarily heterosexuals, homosexuals, or bisexuals?
7. Self-identification—How do you identify yourself on the Kinsey scale and the Multidimensional Sexuality Scale in terms of your sexual orientation?

CONSIDERATION: The various ways in which sexuality are expressed emphasize the fluidity of sexual orientation. While there are those who think and fantasize about, bond, and have sex with only those of their same sex throughout their life, they are, perhaps, rare.

Beyond the definitional problems of bisexuality, other confusions surround the phenomenon. Bisexuality has been described by some as a transition from heterosexuality to homosexuality, as an attempt to deny one's homosexual orientation, as the use of sexual identity to avoid making a commitment to any one person, and as an attempt to be "chic" or "trendy" (Berkey et al., 1990). Whatever the reason, people who use the term to identify their sexual orientation engage in a range of sexual behaviors. In one study of 62 self-labeled bisexual men, 52% had sex with both women and men (in the last two years), 34% had sex exclusively with men, 5% exclusively with women, and 10% were celibate (Doll et al., 1992, p. 6).

CONSIDERATION: Behavior patterns of bisexual men are of special concern to researchers studying the spread of HIV and AIDS because "such men are a potential bridge from the homosexual community to the much larger heterosexual population" (Lever et al., 1992, p. 142).

Homophobia and Heterosexism

Because ours is a predominately heterosexist society, homosexuals (and bisexuals) are victims of prejudice and discrimination. Prejudice refers to negative attitudes, while discrimination refers to behavior that denies individuals or groups equality of treatment.

Prejudice against Homosexuals

Negative attitudes toward homosexuality are reflected in the large percentage of our population that does not approve of or accept homosexuality (see National Data).

NATIONAL DATA: When 3,018 adults, representing a national sample of the U.S. population, were interviewed and asked to express their opinion about "homosexuality with affection," 77.2% of the men and 84.2% of the women said that it was "always" or "almost always" wrong (Klassen et al., 1989, p. 28).

Prejudice against homosexuals extends to those who associate with them. Sigelman, Howell, Cornell, Cutright, and Dewey (1991) found that even voluntary association with a gay person is perceived as having homosexual tendencies one's self or possessing the same stereotypical personality traits that are attributed to gays (e.g., poor mental health). This finding is based on data provided by 116 undergraduates who were asked how they would view those who chose to room with someone gay (voluntary association) versus those who were assigned to a room with a gay person (involuntary association).

The term "**homophobia**" is frequently used to refer to negative attitudes and reactions toward homosexuals (and bisexuals). The term was popularized by psychotherapist George Weinberg (1973), who explored how one develops a gay identity within an antihomosexual culture. Weinberg observed that one of the hazards of any phobia is that not only is the object of fear avoided, but also any acts which are related—even symbolically. "In this case, acts imagined to be conducive to homosexual feelings, or that are reminiscent of homosexual acts, are shunned" (p. 5). Since homosexuality is feared more among men than women, this especially influences men's actions, such as making them reluctant to show affection to other men (or even their sons). Weinberg described homophobia as a prejudice which appears as antagonism directed toward gay men and lesbians. "Inevitably," he said, prejudice against a group of people "leads to a disdain of those people, and to mistreatment of them" (p. 7–8).

More recently, the term homophobia has been criticized, as not all homonegativity reflects a clinical phobia. According to the *Diagnostic and Statistical Manual of Mental Disorders* a phobia involves a compelling desire to avoid the phobic stimuli that arises from a persistent fear or dread. "Invariably the person recognizes that his or her fear is excessive and unreasonable" (American Psychiatric Association, 1987, p. 243). According to these criteria, most individuals who have negative attitudes toward homosexuality are not truly suffering from a phobia (because they do not regard their fear as excessive and unreasonable). In this regard, Haaga (1991) suggested use of the term "antihomosexual prejudice" to describe prejudiced attitudes and discriminatory behavior, with homophobia being one possible cause of antihomosexual prejudice.

Another term that is used to describe prejudice against homosexuality is "**heterosexism.**" This term refers to "an ideological system that denies, denigrates, and stigmatizes any nonheterosexual form of behavior, identity, relationship, or community" (Herek, 1990a, p. 316).

Homosexuality is neither mental illness nor mental depravity. It is simply the way a minority of our population expresses human love and sexuality.

Bryant Welch

In spite of evidence that demonstrates that homosexuals and heterosexuals are similar in personality characteristics, nurturance, and empathy (Whitehead & Nokes, 1990), gay people in the United States are regarded as a "largely unfortunate, minority form by a large percentage of the population" (Weeks, 1989, p. 97). They are called pejorative names ("queer," "dyke," "faggot"), labeled as having negative characteristics ("sick," "dangerous"), and denied equality in social life.

Certain categories of people are more likely to have negative attitudes toward homosexuals. Persons who are older, less educated, widowed, living in the South or Midwest, living in lightly populated rural areas, and Protestant are the most likely to have negative attitudes. In contrast, people who are younger, more educated, never married, living in the West, living in heavily populated urban areas, and Jewish are least likely to have antihomosexual attitudes (Klassen et al., 1989).

NATIONAL DATA: A *Newsweek* poll revealed that 41% of respondents believed that homosexuality is an acceptable alternative lifestyle; 53% do not believe it is an acceptable lifestyle (Wilson, 1992).

In an examination of studies from 1963 to 1983, Kite (1985) found a small effect of sex differences, with men having more negative attitudes than women toward gay men than toward lesbian women. In essence, men in the United States (more than women) have been socialized to be inhibited in experiencing emotional or nonsexual physical closeness with other men. For example,

> Many men refrain from embracing each other, or kissing each other, and women do not. Moreover, men do not as a rule express fondness for each other, or longing for each other's company, as openly as women do. Men tend not to permit themselves to see beauty in the physical forms of other men, or enjoy it; whereas women may openly express admiration for the beauty of other women. Men, even lifetime friends, will not sit as close together on a couch while talking earnestly as women may; . . . . Millions of fathers feel that it would not befit them to kiss their sons affectionately or embrace them, whereas mothers can kiss and embrace their daughters as well as their sons. (Weinberg, 1973, pp. 5–6)

Not all studies suggest that men are more homophobic than women. Klassen et al. (1989) found that men and women (and blacks and whites) have similar attitudes toward homosexuals.

Some conservative religious protesters are adamantly against homosexuals.

CONSIDERATION: The homophobic and heterosexist social climate of our society is often viewed in terms of how it victimizes the gay population. However, heterosexuals too are victimized by homophobia and heterosexism. Due to our antigay social climate, heterosexuals (especially males) are hindered in their own self-expression and intimacy in same-sex relationships. "The threat of victimization [i.e., antigay violence] probably also causes many heterosexuals to conform to gender roles and to restrict their expressions of (nonsexual) physical affection for members of their own sex" (Garnets, Herek, & Levy, 1990, p. 380).

To assess your own feelings toward homosexuality, complete the Index of Attitudes toward Homosexuals questionnaire in the following Self-Assessment.

The Lord is my Shepherd and he knows I'm gay.
Reverend Troy Perry

Religious groups as a whole have tended to view homosexual behavior as a sin. However, religious groups vary in their official and unofficial views on homosexuality and differ in their acceptance of homosexual members. Homosexuality has been described "as a 'fishbone' caught in the [Christian] church's throat that the church can neither eject nor swallow entirely" (Nugent & Gramick, 1989, p. 7). On the one hand, Christian churches have traditionally been associated with love and acceptance and "love's justice requires a single standard for homosexual and heterosexual people alike" (p. 22). In addition, homosexuality may be regarded as "part of the divine plan of creation, that homosexual people are present as a sign of the rich diversity of creation, and that homosexual expression is as natural and good in every way as heterosexuality" (p. 38).

The Roman Catholic Church rejects all homogenital expression and resists any attempt to validate or sanction the homosexual orientation. According to this view, the homosexual condition is regarded as sinful and prohibited by God. Some fundamentalistic churches "have been known to endorse the death penalty for homosexual people, and the 'AIDS as God's punishment' argument is a thinly disguised version of the same" (p. 31). Privately, some priests and ministers are less adamantly against homosexuality and convey a more accepting attitude behind closed doors.

Gay men and lesbians, no less than heterosexuals, are created for lives of joy and passion and intimacy in sexual relationship.
General Assembly Special Committee on Human Sexuality, Presbyterian Church (USA)

In June 1991, a Special Committee on Human Sexuality prepared a report for the larger membership of the Presbyterian Church entitled *Keeping Body and Soul Together: Sexuality, Spirituality, and Social Justice.* Regarding homosexuality, this report concluded that "a majority of our church people are convinced that all homosexual relationships are sinful" (Special Committee on Human Sexuality, p. 62). But the report asserts that

> "It is destructive and inexcusable to condemn, belittle, make fun of, assault, or punish people for being homosexual. . . . No one's sexual orientation should preclude that person from being loved and invited into the fellowship of the church . . . (p. 61)

This report was rejected by the General Assembly of the Presbyterian Church, in part, because of the recommendations by the committee on homosexuality.

We need to reconceptualize intimate relationships in truly mutual terms instead of the dominant/subordinate model of traditional heterosexual marriage.
Pam Darling

Religious groups (in addition to those of the Jewish faith) that are most accepting of homosexuality include Quakers, Unitarians, and the Disciples of Christ. Many Quaker groups, for example, recognize and conduct services for same-sex marriages (also called "celebrations of commitment"), although these marriages are not legally recognized by the state (Grimes, 1991).

Self Assessment

INDEX OF ATTITUDES TOWARD HOMOSEXUALS (IAH)

Name: ______________________________ Today's Date: __________

This questionnaire is designed to measure the way you feel about working or associating with homosexuals. It is not a test, so there are no right or wrong answers. Answer each item as carefully and as accurately as you can by placing a number beside each one as follows.

1 = Strongly Agree
2 = Agree
3 = Neither agree nor disagree
4 = Disagree
5 = Strongly disagree

1. ____ I would feel comfortable working closely with a male homosexual.
2. ____ I would enjoy attending social functions at which homosexuals were present.
3. ____ I would feel uncomfortable if I learned that my neighbor was homosexual.
4. ____ If a member of my sex made a sexual advance toward me I would feel angry.
5. ____ I would feel comfortable knowing that I was attractive to members of my sex.
6. ____ I would feel uncomfortable being seen in a gay bar.
7. ____ I would feel comfortable if a member of my sex made an advance toward me.
8. ____ I would be comfortable if I found myself attracted to a member of my sex.
9. ____ I would feel disappointed if I learned that my child was homosexual.
10. ____ I would feel nervous being in a group of homosexuals.
11. ____ I would feel comfortable knowing that my clergyman was homosexual.
12. ____ I would be upset if I learned that my brother or sister was homosexual.
13. ____ I would feel that I had failed as a parent if I learned that my child was gay.
14. ____ If I saw two men holding hands in public I would feel disgusted.
15. ____ If a member of my sex made an advance toward me I would be offended.
16. ____ I would feel comfortable if I learned that my daughter's teacher was a lesbian.
17. ____ I would feel uncomfortable if I learned that my spouse or partner was attracted to members of his or her sex.
18. ____ I would feel at ease talking with a homosexual person at a party.
19. ____ I would feel uncomfortable if I learned that my boss was homosexual.
20. ____ It would not bother me to walk through a predominantly gay section of town.
21. ____ It would disturb me to find out that my doctor was homosexual.
22. ____ I would feel comfortable if I learned that my best friend of my sex was homosexual.
23. ____ If a member of my sex made an advance toward me I would feel flattered.
24. ____ I would feel uncomfortable knowing that my son's male teacher was homosexual.
25. ____ I would feel comfortable working closely with a female homosexual.

3, 4, 6, 9, 10, 12, 13, 14, 15, 17, 19, 21, 24.

Continued

Self-Assessment—*Continued*

Scoring

To give yourself a score on the IAH, reverse score the items numbered under the copyright in the following way: 1 = 5, 2 = 4, 4 = 2, 5 = 1. For example, if you wrote a 1 for statement number 3 ("I would feel uncomfortable if I learned that my neighbor was homosexual"), change that number to a 5 for scoring purposes. Reverse score the rest of the items in the same way.

Add up the numbers you assigned to each of the items, then subtract 25 from that sum.

Interpreting your score Hudson and Ricketts (1980) suggested that the title "Index of Attitudes Toward Homosexuals" be placed on the scale when it is administered. Another name for the scale, which might influence a respondent's answers if it were at the top, is the Index of Homophobia. Hudson and Ricketts offered the following classifications of scores, although they cautioned against putting too much emphasis on the category labels.

0–25 Nonhomophobic
25–50 Moderately nonhomophobic
50–75 Moderately homophobic
75–100 Strongly homophobic

You may be interested in comparing your score (or those of your class) with those of undergraduate students in psychology classes at a southern state university (Bier, 1990).

Mean Scores on the Index of Homophobia

Subgroup	*n*	*Mean Score*
Introductory Psychology Courses		
Men	324	76.79
Women	379	68.66
Senior Level Psychology Courses		
Men	33	66.94
Women	105	60.29

References

Bier, M. (1990). *A Comparison of the Degree of Racism, Sexism, and Homophobia Between Beginning and Advanced Psychology Students.* Unpublished master's thesis, East Carolina University, Greenville, NC.

Hudson, W. W. & Ricketts, W. A. (1980). A strategy for the measurement of homophobia. *Journal of Homosexuality, 5,* 357–372.

Source: For more information on the IAH contact Walmyr Publishing Company, PO Box 24779, Tempe, AZ 85285-4779. Used by permission.

My lesbianism is an act of Christian charity. All those women out there praying for a man, and I'm giving them my share.
Rita Mae Brown

CONSIDERATION: The homosexual who seeks religious sanctioning must choose between keeping invisible his or her sexual orientation or seeking a religious denomination supportive of homosexuality. Alternatively, individuals may form their own support group and gather enough members so that the religious denomination must reckon with them. Such has been the case for the Jewish homosexuals who formed the World Congress of Gay and Lesbian Jewish Organizations. About 30 groups of Jewish gay men and women throughout the world are devoted to increasing acceptance of homosexuality through community education (Cooper, 1989). Without such a group or supportive network, traditional religion provides little solace for homosexuals. Boswell (1989) concluded, "Especially in modern times, most gays and lesbians in religious life have been terribly alone" (p. 18).

While religion has been prejudicial in regard to homosexuality, societies throughout the world vary in the degree to which they approve or disapprove of homosexuality. *Kathoey* is a word in the Thai culture for a man who enjoys dressing as a woman and having sex with heterosexual men. "It is important to recognize that kathoey are accepted in Thai culture" (Weinrich & Williams, 1991, p. 49.) Among certain Eskimo and North American Indian tribes, *berdache* refers to men who are viewed as having magical powers and who not only may dress as women but have socially approved sex with men (p. 49). However, the Arabic culture of Oman is extremely hostile to homosexuals. "Islam prescribes the death penalty" (p. 51).

Discrimination against Homosexuals

As noted above, prejudice against homosexuals sometimes involves acts against homosexuals. The 1533 Act of Henry VIII in England condemned "buggery" (anal sex) as "against nature" and assigned the death penalty for its commission. In the first third of the nineteenth century in England, more than 50 men were hanged for sodomy. In one year, 1806, there were more executions for sodomy than for murder (Weeks, 1989). Other legal proscriptions for homosexuals have included being lobotomized, castrated, and exterminated (the latter by the Nazis in Germany).

NATIONAL DATA: A *Newsweek* poll revealed that 78% of respondents believed that homosexuals should have equal rights in job opportunities (Wilson, 1992).

Currently, gay individuals are protected from employment discrimination in Massachusetts and Wisconsin and a few dozen municipalities, including New York, San Francisco, and Chicago (Berrill & Herek, 1990a, p. 410). However, many gays are not protected from such discrimination. About 80% of the nation's more than 460 Big Brothers/Big Sister agencies reject openly gay and lesbian volunteers to work with children (Whitehead & Nokes, 1990, p. 90).

Such discrimination is based, in part, on the belief that "homosexuality is deviant and that children, because they are particularly vulnerable to the influence of role models, should not be exposed to adults who are openly homosexual" (p. 90). In addition, many people believe the myth that most homosexuals are child molesters. In fact, child sexual abuse is perpetrated most often by heterosexual males.

Occupational discrimination against gays is perpetuated even by a highly educated segment of our society—physicians. In a survey of 1,000 physicians, 46% said that they would discontinue referring patients to a pediatrician and 43% said they would do so to a psychiatrist who they learned was gay (Martin, 1991).

Occupational discrimination is also present in the defense industry, where lesbian and gay male applicants are routinely denied government security clearances or are subjected to unusually lengthy and intensive investigations. Such discrimination is based on three unfounded assumptions: (1) that gay individuals are more likely than heterosexuals to have psychological disorders, (2) that gay people are more suscep-

The official policy of the U.S. military is against homosexuals, although it may be reconsidered.

tible than heterosexuals to blackmail, and (3) that gay people are less likely than heterosexuals to be trustworthy and respectful of rules and laws (Herek, 1990b).

CONSIDERATION: Rather than being viewed as security risks, Herek (1990b) stated that "gay people actually can be better suited to protecting government security than are many heterosexuals" (p. 1041). This is because the stigmatization of homosexuals forces them to develop skills in managing private information (i.e., their sexual orientation) in order to avoid harassment, discrimination, and violence. Homosexuals, therefore, may be more skilled than heterosexuals in safeguarding secret information.

The legal system also discriminates against gay parents. Gay fathers and lesbian mothers often lose custody of their children because they are viewed as "inappropriate parents." The courts have viewed lesbian mothers as emotionally unstable and have assumed children of lesbians are likely to be emotionally harmed, sexually molested, impaired in gender role development, or to become homosexuals themselves. Falk (1989) concluded that none of these assumptions is supported by theory or research. Gay fathers are discriminated against on the basis of similar unfounded assumptions (DiLapi, 1989; Bozett, 1989).

The fact that individuals define themselves in a significant way through their intimate sexual relationships with others suggests, in a Nation as diverse as ours, that there may be many 'right' ways of conducting those relationships, and that much of the richness of a relationship will come from the freedom an individual has to *choose* the form and nature of these intensely personal bonds.

Supreme Court Justice Harry Blackman

CONSIDERATION: Most researchers recommend that "legal decision makers should focus less or not at all on the sexual orientation of a potential custodian and more on the quality of the relationship between the parent and the child" (Falk, 1989, p. 947.)

Our legal system also prohibits gay people from marrying. Patrick Gill sued the District of Columbia in 1990 for denying him and his lover a marriage license, but the states have steadfastly refused to grant marriage licenses to homosexuals.

In *Bowers v. Hardwick* (1986), the U.S. Supreme Court took a stand against homosexuality when, by a razor-thin majority, it held that the constitutional right to privacy does not extend to "homosexual sodomy" (anal sex). In spite of advice from the American Psychological Association and the American Public Health Association, the Court concluded that laws against sodomy were constitutional.

Antigay Violence

In addition to legal and occupational discrimination, an extreme form of discrimination against homosexuals is violence and victimization. Of all the minority groups that exist in our society, "homosexuals are probably the most frequent victims" of "hate violence" (Finn & McNeil, 1987, p. 2). Various surveys indicate that as many as 92% of lesbians and gay men report that they have been the targets of antigay verbal abuse or threats. As many as 24% reported physical attacks because of their sexual orientation (Herek, 1989).

I have never seen a gay bumper sticker, a fact that may reflect the belief of many gay people that such a sticker would very likely result in vandalism to the car.

Joseph Harry

Berrill and Herek (1990b, p. 269) cited several illustrations of antigay violence (also known as "gay bashing"):

- In 1984, in Bangor, Maine, three teenagers yelling "faggot" and "queer" assaulted a gay man and threw him over a bridge into a river, where he drowned.
- In 1985, in Los Angeles, a man yelling "sick motherfucker" threw a beaker of acid into the face of a lesbian employee of the local Gay and Lesbian Community Services Center.

- In 1988, in Pensacola, Florida, a Christian church with a ministry in the gay community was set afire by an arsonist, causing tens of thousands of dollars in damages. Since the early 1970s, gay community churches have been the targets of arson more than 20 times.

As long as the anti-gay campaigners continue to spread their message of ignorance and hate, our nation will remain a hostile, dangerous and sometimes deadly place for us, our friends and millions of America's gay and lesbian citizens.

Eric Marcus

How is it that our society produces people who go to such violent extremes to express their disapproval of homosexuality? Various reasons help to explain prejudicial attitudes and discriminatory behavior toward homosexuals, including:

1. Homosexual couples generally do not bear children, and societies are reluctant to approve of life-styles that do not result in reproduction of the species. In addition to the need to perpetuate our social existence through reproduction, some societies insist that its members have children so that aging members will have people to care for them. Without such family members, society bears the burden of caring for the elderly. Thailand, for example, regards heterosexual marriage as important because it produces children to care for parents when they are old. Hence, the stigma against gays is not based on any idea of sin or sickness but on the fact that gays are outside the family structure and thus will be left alone and unprovided for in their old age (Jackson, 1989).

   Along the same line of thinking, Weinberg (1973) observed that for some people, the thought of couples who do not plan to have children stirs up a fear of death (due to being confronted with people who plan no vicarious immortality through their offspring). Weinberg explained, "Whether or not the homosexual man or woman has had children in a particular case, the person's very existence becomes a fearful reminder of what life would be without children" (p. 16–17).

NATIONAL DATA: A *Newsweek* poll revealed that 45% of respondents believed that gay rights are a threat to the American family and its values (Wilson, 1992).

2. Our society has traditionally condoned sex only when it occurs in a marital context. Homosexual sex occurs outside the context of marriage.
3. Antigay sentiments also stem from rigid gender roles that dictate that homosexual sex violates what is considered to be socially appropriate gender behavior. In fact, Weinberg (1973) hypothesized that "After years of struggle to achieve a precarious masculine identity, many heterosexual men feel threatened by the sight of homosexuals, who appear to them to be disdainful of the basic requirements of manhood" (p. 13). Weinberg also suggested that gay men and lesbians are thought by some people to have an easier life than people with traditional family responsibilities and may be envied.
4. Religious scripture speaks against sexual acts between people of the same sex. Twice in the Old Testament there are prohibitions against homosexual intercourse. Leviticus 18:22 reads, "You shall not have sexual intercourse with another man, for such is abominable behavior." Leviticus 20:13 reads, "Two men who have sexual intercourse with each other have committed an abomination: they shall be put to death and the fault is theirs alone." However, some theologians have offered reconciliation between homosexuality and the Christian tradition (Boswell, 1980; Scanzoni & Mollenkott, 1978).
5. Since homosexuals have been identified as being at high risk for carrying AIDS, additional prejudice is directed toward them. When 300 university undergraduates were asked their feelings about different illnesses and about heterosexuals and homosexuals, it was clear that both AIDS and homosexuality elicit highly stigmatizing and prejudicial attitudes.

> A patient with AIDS, relative to a patient with another high-mortality illness, was viewed not only as being more deserving and responsible for his disease, but as more deserving to die, more dangerous and deserving to be quarantined, less entitled to

> work, and of less intrinsic worth. . . . Subjects felt that homosexual males, whether they had AIDS or leukemia, were more deserving to die, should more often consider suicide, and would represent less of a loss to society should they die than heterosexual males with the same illnesses. (St. Lawrence, 1990, p. 97)

CONSIDERATION: Berrill (1990) suggested that "AIDS is probably less a cause of anti-gay sentiment than it is a new focus and justification for expressions of pre-existing anti-gay prejudice" (p. 289). In reality, lesbians have less of a chance of contracting HIV than heterosexuals do.

6. Some people may have negative feelings and reactions to homosexuals because they may feel that they themselves may be homosexual, reject this self-image, and unconsciously overcompensate by developing strong negative feelings against homosexuals to "prove" they are not homosexual. The psychological term for this is "reaction formation," which is an unconscious technique used to cope with impulses, feelings, or ideas that are not acceptable to one's self at a conscious level.
7. Homosexuals, like other racial and minority groups, threaten the power of the majority. Fearing loss of power, the majority group may stigmatize homosexuals (and other minority groups) as a way of limiting the power that minority group can attain (Ficarrotto, 1990). Weinberg (1973) suggested that, because they are non-conformists, gay men and lesbians are seen as a threat to society's values and at risk of undermining society.

For too long our society has discriminated against people of varying sexual orientation, which may have been excusable when sexual orientation was not understood, but is not excusable in our time.

Richard Wood

The social climate for homosexuals in our society is, overall, one that fosters prejudice, discrimination, and overt hostility and violence. The following Research and Policy Perspective on "Gay and Lesbian Life on Campus" looks at the social climate for homosexuals in the college environment.

RESEARCH AND POLICY PERSPECTIVE

Gay and Lesbian Life on Campus

What is the campus climate for gay male and lesbian students, faculty, administrators, and staff? Despite changes in U.S. society over the last two decades, history professor John D'Emilio reported, ". . . being openly gay on campus still goes against the grain . . . oppression in its many forms is still alive, and the university is not immune to it" (1990, p. 17).

Studies conducted on university campuses show that a substantial proportion of gay and bisexual members of the academic community have experienced some form of antigay victimization on campus. The following table summarizes the results of surveys conducted at Yale (1986), Pennsylvania State (1988), and Rutgers (1987) universities.

Student groups have been active in the gay liberation movement since the 1960s. More than 400 gay student groups are organized in community colleges and public and private universities. As they have struggled for official recognition and funding, gay student groups have amassed a body of judicial opinion protecting their assembly under First Amendment rights (D'Emilio, 1990). Some campuses granted recognition to gay student groups long ago, such as the University of Maryland. Its Gay and Lesbian Student Union, recognized in 1970, uses student-activity fees to sponsor dances, classes, movies, and counseling services. However, at such campuses as Georgetown University and Southern Methodist University, there have been litigation and hotly contested debates (Bartol, 1990).

Continued

TABLE 1 Percent of Gay Survey Respondents Reporting Antigay Violence on Campus

Type of incident	Yale (a)	Penn (b)	Rutgers (c)
Verbal abuse	65	72	57
Verbal threats	25	25	16
Objects thrown	19	13	11
Chased or followed	25	22	16
Spat upon	3	6	1
Hit, kicked, or beaten	5	4	4
Assault with a weapon	1	1	1
Vandalism or arson	10	16	6
Sexual assault/harassment	12	15	8
Incidents not reported	90	93	88

(a) Yale = Yale Sexual Orientation Survey (N = 166 gay or bisexual members of sample) 43% female and 54% male respondents
(b) Penn = Pennsylvania State University (N = 132) 37% female and 63% male respondents
(c) Rutgers = Rutgers Sexual Orientation Survey (N = 141) 60% female and 40% male respondents
(Table 1 adapted from Herek, 1989.)

Continued

Gay faculty members have also organized. Lesbian and gay caucuses are now part of the professional societies of most social science and humanities disciplines (D'Emilio, 1990). However, most faculty tend not to "come out" until after they attain tenure, if then. Even those who have come out to colleagues may be reluctant to do so with students. One lesbian professor confided to reporters that since she came out three years earlier, all the harassment she experienced was from heterosexual students, not administrators (Bartol, Godchaux & Kizilos, 1984).

The university has been the site of interventions to try to reduce intolerance for gays and reduce homophobia. After they took an undergraduate human sexuality course that included a unit on homosexuality, students whose pretest scores were above the median on homophobia (using the IAH, which you took earlier in this chapter) had lower homophobia scores (Serdahely & Ziemba, 1985). At Earlham College in Richmond, Indiana, a "Teach-In on the Gay/Lesbian Academic" was organized by a student group (Grimes, 1991).

Should the academic community do more to combat the oppression and victimization of gays? D'Emilio (1990) suggested that colleges and universities have the ability and the responsibility to promote gay rights and social acceptance of homosexual people.

> For reasons that I cannot quite fathom, I still expect the academy to embrace higher standards of civility, decency, and justice than the society around it. Having been granted the extraordinary privilege of thinking critically as a way of life, we should be astute enough to recognize when a group of people is being systematically mistreated. We have the intelligence to devise solutions to problems that appear in our community. I expect us also to have the courage to lead rather than follow. (p. 18)

What steps can colleges and universities take to meet this challenge? One researcher who studied antigay discrimination and harassment at Pennsylvania State University recommended the following (D'Augelli, 1989):

Continued

Continued

1. Provide support for victims of harassment and violence through outreach programs staffed by lesbian- and gay-affirming personnel.
2. Provide training of local law enforcement personnel in lesbian and gay issues.
3. Create institutional policies that contain "unequivocal statements that publicly affirm the unacceptability of discrimination based on sexual orientation" (p. 321).
4. Conduct research to document patterns of victimization of lesbians and gays.

Brian McNaught, an articulate speaker and writer, pointed out that commitment to create a campus environment free of homophobic behaviors is not an endorsement of any particular life-style, but rather an endorsement of tolerance of people's diversity. He has developed a discussion guide (McNaught, undated) to help administrators, faculty, staff, and students reflect on and discuss their campus environment. McNaught suggested that like other prejudices, homophobia is best addressed with education—providing accurate information about human sexuality, the experience of being gay, and the toll of persecution.

References

Bartol, B. (1990, May). The fight over gay rights. *Newsweek on Campus,* pp. 4–10.

Bartol, B., Godchaux, E., & Kizilos, P. (1984, May). Escaping the faculty closet. *Newsweek on Campus,* pp. 6–7.

D'Augelli, A. R. (1989). Lesbians' and gay men's experiences of discrimination and harassment in a university community. *American Journal of Community Psychology, 17,* 317–321.

D'Emilio, J. (1990) The campus environment for gay and lesbian life. *Academe, 76*(1), 16–19.

Grimes, B. (1991). Out on campus. *Friends for Lesbian and Gay Concerns Newsletter, 58,* 1–2.

Herek, G. M. (1989). Hate crimes against lesbians and gay men: Issues for research and policy. *American Psychologist, 44,* 948–955.

McNaught, B. (undated). Homophobia on the college campus: A discussion guide. Available from Brian McNaught, 5 St. Louis Avenue, Glouscester, MA 01930.

Serdahely, W. J., & Ziemba, G. J. (1985). Changing homophobic attitudes through college sexuality education. In J. P. DeCecco (Ed.), *Bashers, baiters & bigots: Homophobia in American society* (pp. 109–116). New York: Harrington Park Press.

The Gay Liberation Movement

The gay liberation movement provides a way for both homosexual and heterosexual women and men to band together in the hope of changing public attitudes and policy. Over 60% of gay men in one study reported that they were or had been a member of a homosexual organization (Connell & Kippax, 1990). The National Gay and Lesbian Task Force (NGLTF) (1517 U Street, Washington, DC 20009) is the largest organization representing the movement. Ongoing activities of the NGLTF are summarized in Table 11.1.

NATIONAL DATA: Nationwide, there are 1,580 gay and lesbian organizations, including political, social, activist and student groups.

An earlier organization, specifically for lesbians, was the Daughters of Bilitis (DOB), which published a newsletter *The Ladder* in the 1950s and 1960s. Members of this organization challenged the view that homosexuals were sick and should be cured and offered support for women enjoying a life-style with each other. "By taking risks during a period in which it was clearly dangerous to be lesbian, they increased the possibilities for lesbian organization and acceptance today" (Esterberg, 1990, p. 79).

TABLE 11.1 National Gay and Lesbian Task Force: Ongoing Activities

1.	Media Project	Focuses media attention on gay and lesbian issues.
2.	Violence Project	Documents instances of antigay violence and promotes services for victims of such violence.
3.	Privacy Project	Works to eliminate laws that restrict sexual expression between consenting adults (e.g., antisodomy laws).

While the DOB emerged in San Francisco and served largely white, educated, middle-class women, other local gay and lesbian groups have developed. These provide such services as counseling, referral to STD clinics, and the promotion of civil rights legislation for homosexual people. An example is The Gay and Lesbian Community Action Council in Minneapolis, Minnesota whose programs include advocacy for crime victims, legal advice, a gay and lesbian therapist network, groups for gay and lesbian Native Americans, employee and workplace groups, and community education.

I'm gay, conservative and Republican, and I'm proud to be all three. The Republican, conservative view, based as it is on the inherent rights of the individual over the state, should be the logical political home of gays and lesbians.

Marvin Liebman

One legislative goal shared by many gay and lesbian organizations is to remove criminal penalties for private sexual behavior between consenting adults. With the help of other organizations (the American Law Institute, National Committee for Sexual Civil Liberties), some gains are being made. One victory for gay and lesbian rights involves the new definition of *family* developed by the Supreme Court of New York, which allowed a lover to stay in the apartment he had shared with his partner after his partner (with whom he had had a 10-year relationship) died (see Exhibit 11.1).

Many legal issues concern the gay community. Homosexual people are prohibited from immigrating to the United States, kept out of the military (as was noted earlier), and, in some communities, prohibited from teaching in the public school system. If a teacher's homosexuality becomes public knowledge, the teacher may be dismissed on the grounds of "unprofessional conduct" or "moral turpitude." Gay men and lesbians are taking their dismissals and denials to court. The *McConnel v. Anderson* case dealt with a suit brought by a gay activist who was rejected for employment as a librarian at the University of Minnesota. The U.S. district court held that to reject an applicant for public employment on the grounds of homosexuality, it must be shown that there is an observable and reasonable relationship between efficiency in the job and homosexuality.

Gay political organizations are also concerned with AIDS-related issues. The National Gay and Lesbian Task Force lobbies for greater funding for research and public education on AIDS.

Feminists, whatever their sexual orientation, have to understand that heterosexual privilege is a small and short-term bribe in return for giving up lasting self-discovery and collective power.

Charlotte Bunch

CONSIDERATION: The gay liberation movement has helped to solidify the gay minority and to increase self-confidence and "gay pride" among homosexual individuals. However, the solidification of the gay minority may have negative consequences as well. Dennis Altman suggested that "the more stress that is placed on the idea of a homosexual minority, the more difficult it is to recognize that homosexuality, whether acted out or repressed, is part of everyone's sexuality and has implications for many people other than those who conceptualize themselves as part of the gay minority." (quoted in Garai, 1987, p. 261)

EXHIBIT 11.1 Gay and Lesbian Couples Constitute a Family

Although many homosexual couples live together as married couples, think of themselves as married, and even have weddings or ceremonies celebrating their love and commitment to each other, they are not recognized as legally married by the state. Therefore, homosexual couples are denied benefits that are provided for married couples. For example, partners in homosexual relationships are not allowed to file a joint income tax return, are often denied benefits through one partner's employer-provided family health insurance and retirement plans and Social Security, and are denied leave time to care for a sick partner. Typically, only married couples are eligible to receive these benefits.

However, in the summer of 1989, the New York State Court of Appeals ruled, 4 to 2, that a gay couple who had lived together for 10 years could be considered a family under the city's rent-control regulations ("Homosexual Families," 1989). In effect, the court ruled that male and female homosexual couples may be considered families. At issue was whether a partner in a 10-year homosexual relationship could take over the couple's rent-controlled apartment when the lease-holding member dies. Since state law limits such takeovers to "family members," the partner would have been evicted without the court ruling (Beissert, 1989).

This ruling has enormous implications for how our society views family life. Rather than view family members as partners related by blood, marriage, or adoption, increasingly the courts are choosing to look at the nature of the relationship between the partners. The courts are considering issues such as how long the couple has lived together, whether the partners in the relationship consider themselves a family, and whether the partners are economically interdependent. In effect, families will be defined according to function, rather than by structure. Eight cities (including San Francisco, Berkeley, Santa Cruz, and Seattle) already recognize "domestic partnerships." **Domestic partnerships** are legal relationships that allow the partners to have some of the same benefits that legally married spouses have (e.g., health insurance benefits).

A Minnesota appeals court ruled that Karen Thompson be granted guardianship of her lover, Sharon Kowalski, who was injured in an accident which left her brain damaged and quadriplegic. When Kowalski's father decided he was unable to continue as her guardian, a family friend was named. Thompson's protest and legal challenge resulted in a ruling which affirmed, "Thompson and Sharon are a family of affinity, which ought to be accorded respect" (A victory, 1991).

The broadening of the legal definition of family both reflects and contributes to society's acceptance of nontraditional relationship patterns. As legal status is given to committed relationships, homosexual relationships will carry less social stigma than in the past. Heterosexual couples also benefit from broadened legal definitions of family in that stepchildren, who have been denied health insurance benefits from the stepparent, are more likely to be covered.

Public opinion about gay relationships may be slow to change, however. When 1,000 U.S. adults were asked, "Do you think marriages between homosexual couples should be recognized by the law?," 69% said no. However, when the respondents were asked, "Do you think homosexual couples should be permitted to receive medical and life insurance benefits from a partner's policy?," 54 percent said yes (Isaacson, 1989, p. 102).

Lesbian-Feminism

> . . . Self-loving and independent women are a challenge to the idea that men are superior, an idea that social institutions strengthen and enshrine.
>
> *Charlotte Bunch*

There is a subgroup of lesbians who believe in liberation not only for gays but for women in general. For these women, the lesbian life-style represents a political stand against the traditional oppression and devalued social status of women in our society (Kitzinger, 1987). Such women, whose lesbianism is more a political choice than a sexual orientation, are referred to as lesbian-feminists (or lesbian separatists) (Faderman, 1985). **Lesbian-feminism** refers to lesbianism that is based on the ideological belief that heterosexuality is a political institution that perpetuates male supremacy in our society and is detrimental to women's freedom. Lesbian-feminism defies the traditional power structure of our society by breaking the tradition of female dependence on men and establishing womenkind as independent and self-sufficient.

THEORETICAL EXPLANATIONS FOR SEXUAL ORIENTATION

One of the prevailing questions raised regarding homosexuality is its origin or "cause." Gay people are often irritated by the concern heterosexual people have for finding the "cause" of homosexuality. Since the same question is rarely asked of heterosexuality (there is less emphasis on why individuals are heterosexual since it is assumed that this is normal and in need of no explanation), the concern for homosexual causation implies that something is "wrong" with homosexuality.

> **CONSIDERATION:** The predominant view regarding the development of sexual orientation is both biological and social. While individuals may be biologically predisposed to a particular sexual orientation (an essentialist perspective), their social learning experiences influence their orientation (constructionistic perspective). Any explanation that does not acknowledge the interaction of the biological and social components is incomplete.

Biological Explanations

Biological explanations focus on heredity and hormones.

Heredity Eight-seven percent of 402 parents of homosexuals believed that their children were "born that way" (Robinson, Walters, & Skeen, 1989, p. 69). The explanation that homosexuals are "born that way" reflects the theory that there is a genetic basis for homosexuality. Simon LeVay (1991) suggested such a basis as a result of scanning the brains of 41 cadavers (19 homosexual males, 16 heterosexual men, and 6 heterosexual women). He found that the portion of the brain thought to control sexual activity (the third interstitial nucleus of the anterior hypothalamus known as INAH 3) was half the size in homosexual men as in heterosexual men.

> **CONSIDERATION:** LeVay's research suggested more questions than it answers. While he did document a difference in the brain structures of the hypothalamus, is this the basis for what makes people homosexual or heterosexual? Do the differences occur as a result of heredity or as a result of living a gay life-style? (Social influences may affect brain structure; for example, the brains of people who read Braille after becoming blind increase in size in the area controlling the reading finger.) If the differences occur routinely, when do they occur—prenatally, neonatally, during childhood, puberty, adulthood?

Another study that suggested a hereditary basis for sexual orientation was conducted by Michael Bailey and Richard Pillard (1991), who studied 56 gay men who were twins or had adoptive brothers. The men were recruited through homophile publications, and where possible, the men's relatives were directly interviewed. Of those relatives for whom ratings of sexual orientation could be made, 52% of monozygotic (identical) cotwins, 22% of dizygotic (fraternal) cotwins, and 11% of adoptive brothers were homosexual. These rates were higher than the 9% rate of homosexuality among nontwin biological siblings. This finding of substantial heritability

> provided some support for the view that sexual orientation is influenced by constitutional factors. This contrasts with previous attempts to test psychodynamic and psychosocial theories, which have largely yielded negative findings, and emphasizes the necessity of considering causal factors arising within the individual, and not just his psychosocial environment. (p. 1095)

However, heritability does not guarantee that any trait will be developed. As Bailey and Pillard noted, "That is, given any heritability estimate, there are a variety of possible developmental mechanisms" (p. 1095). Their data are consistent with the possible explanations of sexual orientation as shaped by prenatal brain development or by the development of some physical characteristic which influences how parents treat their offspring.

Earlier twin research by Kallman also found evidence of a genetic link to sexual orientation. He studied twins reared in the same home and found that of 40 identical twins, in 100% of the cases where one sibling was a homosexual, so was the twin (Kallman, 1952). But these twins were not representative of the identical twin population. They were recruited with the aid of psychiatric and penal agencies, and more than half were schizoid, schizophrenic, or alcoholic. It is not known to what degree these factors contributed to their homosexuality, and no valid inference can be drawn unless these factors are eliminated. Bailey and Pillard's (1991) research confirmed that Kallman's 100% concordance rate was too high.

While these results may suggest an inherited predisposition toward homosexuality, they could also be explained by similar learning experiences of the twins. Studies on the origins of homosexuality are inconclusive. One researcher observed that "sexual orientation is the product of multiple influences, of which heredity and genetics may be a part" (Gladue, 1987).

Hormonal Influence There is also some evidence (as well as questions) about the degree to which hormones influence one's sexual orientation. Ellis and Ames (1987) believe that hormonal and neurological factors operating prior to birth (between the second and fifth month of gestation) are the "main determinants of sexual orientation" (p. 235). While these researchers do not deny that environmental factors also play a role, they asserted that "very unusual postnatal experiences would be required to overcome strong predispositions toward either heterosexuality or homosexuality" (p. 235). According to Ellis and Ames, individuals do not learn to be heterosexual or homosexual; rather, they learn how, when, and where their sexual orientation is expressed. In contrast, Doell (1990) observed:

> The most that biology can be shown to determine in humans is a capacity for sexual behavior which each of us can integrate into the experiences of our childhood and adolescence to come to some conclusion as to what is in our own best interest with respect to sexual behavior. (p. 123)

Money (1988) suggested that sexual orientation is programmed into the brain during critical periods of prenatal hormonal influence and early childhood experience. Of the latter, he says that children who are reinforced for opposite-sex behavior continue along that path. Children who are reinforced for same-sex behavior, likewise, develop along this path.

CONSIDERATION: Assuming that there is a biological component to sexual orientation, individuals seem to be aware of it early. In one study comparing the backgrounds of homosexual and heterosexual people, the researchers (Bell, Weinberg, & Hammersmith, 1981) noticed that gay men tended to score higher on "gender nonconformity" than heterosexual men. Specifically, gay men tended to feel sexually different from other boys in childhood and in adolescence, reported being aroused by other males either before or after puberty, and felt sexually indifferent to girls during childhood. Gay women also reported feeling aroused by other girls during childhood and having had homosexual involvements during adolescence.

As noted at the beginning of this section, most researchers view human behavior, including sexual behavior, as influenced by the interaction of biology and the environment. Boxer and Cohler (1989) observed that biological changes in adolescence do not act directly upon behavior "without consideration of the psychosocial and cultural processes that mediate these changes" (p. 334). From this perspective, no single factor is responsible for an individual's sexual orientation. In regard to hormonal theories of homosexuality, Gladue (1987) suggested that "while it is unlikely that hormones *cause* or directly *determine* sexual orientation, they are probably a contributing factor" (p. 143).

Social Learning Explanations

Social learning theory emphasizes that individuals learn their sexual orientation from their parents, peers, culture, and society. Many of these learning experiences occur in childhood. Money (1988) suggested that children who are rewarded for expressing heterosexual scripts (playing house where the assigned roles are "mommy" and "daddy") and punished for same sex behavior (playing doctor with a same-sex peer) are likely to be heterosexual. Likewise, children who are punished for playing heterosexual games and acting out heterosexual scripts may suppress their heterosexual orientation. Without an outlet for heterosexual expression, they drift toward homosexuality. Since homosexual behavior often occurs out of the sight of the parental eye, it goes unpunished and may develop as an alternative to heterosexual expression.

The degree to which early childhood experiences influence one's adult sexual orientation is unknown. However, differences in the childhood behaviorial patterns between homosexuals and heterosexuals have been noted. Green (1987) compared 44 "sissy boys" with a parallel group of "conventionally masculine" boys as the respective groups were growing up. "Sissy boys" liked to dress in girl's clothes, played with Barbie dolls, and avoided sports. Three-fourths of the very effeminate boys in Green's study grew up to be homosexual (Green, 1987). Critics argue that effeminacy is not characteristic of most homoerotic males, so equating the two is unrealistic. To select a group with characteristics that already suggest discomfort with one's gender role is to bias the sample.

CONSIDERATION: Although some childhood and adolescent experiences may predispose a person to homosexuality, no one specific background characteristic seems to cause a person to become homosexual. Some heterosexual males played with dolls and were called sissy by their peers, and some heterosexual

Continued

Continued

women were tomboys. In essence, childhood and adolescent experiences alone account for very little of the variance in explaining how a person becomes a homosexual (Boxer & Cohler, 1989, p. 328). Green (1987) concluded in his study of "sissy boys" that both biological and socialization factors were at work in the development of homosexuality. Bailey and Pillard (1991) found that childhood gender nonconformity does not appear to be related to genetic predisposition for homosexuality.

Social-Psychological Explanations

The development of one's sexual orientation may also be explained through the social-psychological variables of the self-concept and self-fulfilling prophecy. Just as heterosexuals have had social mirrors held up to them that suggest a heterosexual orientation ("You are a pretty girl—the boys will like you" or "You are a fine young man—the girls will be after you"), some homosexuals may have social mirrors reflecting a less heterosexual orientation ("You are a tomboy" or "You are a sissy").

In addition to social mirrors from significant others, an early adolescent homosexual experience may be influential in encouraging a person toward homosexuality if the experience is viewed by the adolescent as "the way I am." Unaware that homosexual contacts in childhood and adolescence are not unusual, children who have sexual experiences with persons of their own sex may see these experiences as evidence of their homosexuality. Once individuals label themselves as homosexuals, they may become locked into a self-fulfilling prophecy whereby their actions and identity conform to the label "homosexual."

Psychoanalytic Explanations

Psychoanalysts suggested that the relationship individuals have with their parents may predispose them toward heterosexuality or homosexuality. While heterosexual men identified closely with their fathers and had more distant relationships with their mothers, homosexual men had close emotional relationships with their mothers and were distant with their fathers (Freud had little to say about the development of sexual orientation of women) (Isay, 1990).

The presumed script for the development of a homosexual male follows: The overprotective mother seeks to establish a binding emotional relationship with her son. But this closeness also elicits strong sexual feelings on the part of the son toward the mother, which are punished by her and blocked by the society through the incest taboo. The son is fearful of expressing sexual feelings for his mother. He generalizes this fear to other women, with the result that they are no longer viewed as potential sexual partners.

The son's distant relationship with his father prevents identification with a male role model. For example, the relationship between playwright Tennessee Williams and his father was one of mutual rejection—the father was contemptuous of his "sissy" son and Williams was hostile to his father because of his father's arrogance.

This theory of male homosexuality is not supported by the scientific community. First, it does not resolve the question: "Is the absent or distant father relationship a result or a cause of the child's homosexuality?" Second, sons with overprotective mothers and rejecting fathers also grow up to be heterosexual, just as those with moderate mothering and warm fathering grow up to be homosexual. Third, two sons growing up in the same type of family may have different sexual orientations. A study of family backgrounds of 979 homosexual and 477 heterosexual people confirmed that parent-child relationships as the "cause" for homosexuality is highly questionable and highly suspect (Bell, Weinberg, & Hammersmith, 1981). The researchers concluded that the relationship individuals have with their parents "cannot be said to predict much about sexual orientation" (p. 62).

What are the implications of one's theoretical stance regarding sexual orientation? Hart (1984) recommended that despite many gay clients' essentialist beliefs, therapists could be helpful by reframing their views toward a more constructionist perspective. He suggested this could help people view themselves in a more flexible way and take more responsibility for their lives. DeCecco (1987, p. 111) cautioned that the premise of psychobiologists is that homosexuals are not *true* "exemplars of their biological sexes." In other words, they are born imperfectly made, "not quite the men and women they ought to be" if development had proceeded normally. On the other hand, research has shown that people who emphasize biological factors are more tolerant of homosexuals. Ernulf, Innala, and Whitam (1989) found that people who believed that gays and lesbians choose or learn to be homosexual hold more negative attitudes toward them than people who believe homosexuality is an inborn trait. It remains to be seen whether the current attention to biological theories will increase acceptance or unwittingly promote intolerance.

Developing a Gay Identity

As we noted earlier, sexual orientation involves not only behaviors, but also emotions, cognitions and self-concept. In this section we focus on the gay self-concept. After describing a four-stage process of gay identity development, we discuss "coming out" and how gays can achieve a positive self-concept and overcome their stigmatized status. Finally, we look at the role of the gay subculture and its importance for gay individuals.

Troiden's Four-Stage Process

Troiden (1989) suggested that developing the self-concept and social identity of a homosexual is a process involving four stages. These four stages include sensitization, identity confusion, identity assumption, and commitment.

Sensitization This stage often begins before puberty and involves the person becoming aware that he or she is different. Lesbians report that they, when compared to their heterosexual friends, were less interested in boys and in traditional girl activities, such as playing house, and more interested in sports. Homosexual men report that they were not sexually interested in girls, were sexually interested in boys, and had less interest in sports than most of their male friends. Although preadolescent children may be sensitized to being "different" from other children, it is typically after puberty that these differences become labeled as indicative of homosexuality.

CONSIDERATION: It should also be kept in mind that the culture determines what behaviors are labeled as homosexual. In the Latin world, same-sex sexual activity may occur without the implication that the person is homosexual (Parker & Carballo, 1990, p. 501).

Identity Confusion As lesbians and gay men continue to experience that they are "different" from their heterosexual counterparts, they become confused about who they are. Typically, lesbians report awareness of feelings of attraction to the same sex between the ages of 14 and 16 and suspicions that they "might" be homosexual beginning at an average age of 18; gay men report awareness of feelings toward the same sex at age 13 and suspicions that they "might" be homosexual at age 17 (Troiden, 1989).

One individual in the middle of such identity confusion recalled:

> You feel that you probably are a homosexual, although you're not definitely sure. You feel distant or cut off from other people. You are beginning to think that it might help to meet other homosexuals but you're not sure whether you really want to or not. You prefer to put on a front of being completely heterosexual. (Cass, 1984, p. 156)

Part of this confusion is that most lesbians and gay men have experienced *both* homosexual and heterosexual arousal and behavior. In one study, only 12% of lesbians and 21% of gay men reported never having a sexual encounter with someone of the opposite sex (Bell et al., 1981). However, engaging in heterosexual sex may not always signify identity confusion among gays. In one study, 12 out of 37 gay male high school seniors (ages 16–18) who identified themselves as gay or bisexual, reported having sex with women. However, "reasons for this were ascribed to loneliness and isolation rather than to confusion over sexual orientation" (Uribe & Harbeck, 1992, p. 22).

Carla Golden (1987) suggested that some women struggle with their sexual identity because they experience their sexuality as fluid and variable. This fluidity and variability make it difficult for these women to identify themselves as a "pure" heterosexual, bisexual, or lesbian.

Golden indicated two remedies for this problem. First, therapists who work with women who are engaged in the process of sexual self-definition should not focus on helping them to adopt a fixed sexuality but rather should facilitate their search for "authenticity." The way a woman feels about her "true" sexual identity may not fit into a neat category, which brings us to the second remedy. Golden suggested that we abandon current social definitions of sexual orientations that artificially restrict our sexual identities. She explained:

> Just as we have protested the constricting definitions of what a real woman is, precisely because it has served to oppress women and to limit the expression of our diverse potentials, so, too, must we be careful in our social construction of sexuality not to construct categories that are so rigid and inflexible that women's self-definitions put them at odds with the social definitions. To do so only limits the expression of the diversities and variabilities in women's sexual identities. (p. 33)

Several mechanisms are used to cope with the feelings of identity confusion:

1. Denial—the individual denies the homosexual thoughts, feelings, and fantasies.
2. Conversion—the person may seek therapy to change homosexual inclinations and "convert" to heterosexuality.
3. Avoidance—the person acknowledges homosexual feelings, regards them as unacceptable, and tries to adopt behaviors similar to a heterosexual (e.g., dating and/or having sex with people of the opposite sex, buying pornography heterosexuals would buy). Reaction formation (discussed earlier in the section on prejudice and discrimination) is an extreme form of avoidance that may involve a person joining causes against homosexuals or becoming involved in "gay bashing." Another form of avoidance involves the use of alcohol and other drugs to dull the anxiety produced by identity confusion.

Identity Assumption Identity assumption refers to the stage in which some people come to define themselves as homosexual. Typically, gay men arrive at homosexual self-definitions between the ages of 19 and 21 as a result of doing what gay men do—interacting with homosexuals in gay bars, parties, parks, YMCAs, and men's rooms. Lesbians arrive at homosexual self-definitions between the ages of 21 and 23 as a result of involvement in an intense love relationship with a woman (Troiden, 1989).

Newly self-identified homosexuals learn strategies for stigma management from other homosexuals. Such strategies include "passing" and group alignment. Passing involves learning how to live a double life: to one's self and intimate others, one is a homosexual; to others (which may include family, employers, and some heterosexual friends), one is a heterosexual.

Group alignment means seeking acceptance in the homosexual community and looking to it for emotional support. Through group alignment, homosexuals are exposed to others who view homosexuality as a legitimate life-style.

Commitment Commitment to homosexuality involves adopting it as a life-style. Internally, this means viewing homosexuality as a legitimate life-style that is "right" for one's self. Externally, this means establishing an emotional and sexual relationship with someone of the same sex and disclosing one's homosexuality to others (coming out will be discussed in the next section). Persons who are committed to a homosexual identity would not change their sexual orientation even if they could. Ninety-five percent of the lesbians and 86% of the gay men in one study claimed they would not take a magic pill, if one existed, that would enable them to be heterosexual (Bell & Weinberg, 1978).

CONSIDERATION: Not all homosexuals go through the above stages in an orderly, predictable fashion. "In many cases, these stages are encountered in consecutive order, but in many instances they are merged, glossed over, bypassed, or realized simultaneously (Troiden, 1989, p. 48).

Coming Out

The term "**coming out**" (a shortened form of "coming out of the closet") refers to "the sequence of events through which individuals recognize their own homosexual [or bisexual] orientation and disclose it to others" (Garnets, Herek, & Levy, 1990). As noted above, coming out helps to solidify commitment to a homosexual identity. Although it is difficult to ascertain the percentage of gays who "stay in the closet," some data suggest that the majority of gay individuals eventually come out. In one study, only 4% of 317 self-identified gays came out to no one (Savin-Williams, 1989, p. 2).

Coming out can refer to acknowledging one's homosexuality to one's self, to one's family of origin (parents, siblings), to one's heterosexual partner or spouse and children, and to friends and employers.

NATIONAL DATA: About 10% of heterosexual teenage boys, in contrast to 35% of teenage homosexual boys, attempt suicide. About 10% of heterosexual teenage girls, in contrast to 20% of homosexual teenage girls, attempt suicide ("Gay Teenagers," 1989).

Coming Out to One's Self To come out to one's self is to be aware that one is gay (or bisexual) and to acknowledge this to one's self. "The first time I thought to myself, 'I am a homosexual,' it stunned me. I was horrified," recalled one homosexual. This initial reaction is typical since the larger heterosexual society holds up social mirrors to the homosexual that reflect disapproval and disdain. Sometimes the disapproval or fear of disapproval leads to suicide attempts (see National Data).

Developing acceptance of one's self is important for one's happiness. Adelman (1990) interviewed 52 self-identified gay men and lesbians and asked them about the importance of coming out to one's self. One respondent said:

> I don't think that anybody, if they cannot accept with good grace whatever they are, can be happy . . . that is important. It's not just important; it's basic. I have fully accepted my homosexuality and embrace it. (p. 22)

Most gays eventually accept themselves and enjoy their lives. Sixty percent of 52 gay women and men in their 60s reported that they were "very satisfied with being gay" (Adelman, 1990, p. 14).

Coming Out to One's Parents and Siblings After coming out to one's self, coming out to one's parents and siblings looms as a major decision.

CONSIDERATION: Before deciding to tell one's family that one is homosexual, it is recommended that the person feel personally secure with his or her homosexuality, have a support group of friends who are also secure and who have experienced coming out to their parents, and have a relatively good relationship with his or her parents. Even if all of these factors exist, however, the reactions of parents are unpredictable (Savin-Williams, 1989).

Deciding to tell or not to tell one's parents is very difficult. Not to do so is to hide one's true self from parents and to feel alienated, afraid, and alone. To tell them is to risk rejection and disapproval. Some parents of homosexuals suspect that their child is gay, even before they are told. Of 402 parents of gay and lesbian children, 26% stated that they suspected their offspring's homosexuality (Robinson et al., 1989, p. 66).

Parents may be told face to face, through an intermediary (sibling, other relative, or counselor), or in a letter. Exhibit 11.2 is a letter written by a 21-year-old lesbian college student disclosing her homosexuality to her parents (authors' files).

CONSIDERATION: Maria offers these suggestions to other gay people who want to tell their parents of their sexual orientation:

1. Avoid speaking from a defensive point of view. Too often gay people are forced to defend their life-style as if it is wrong. If you approach your parents with the view that your homosexuality is a positive aspect of your personality, you will have a better chance of evoking a positive response from them.
2. Avoid talking about your current relationship. Homosexuality is often labeled as a phase, rather than a permanent facet of one's life. Your parents may feel, as mine did, that your current partner is the cause of your life-style. Thus, when your relationship ends (so they hope), so will your homosexuality. Deal with the subject as it affects you as an individual.
3. Try to maintain a constant flow of positive reinforcement toward your parents. Reiterate your love for them as you would like them to do to you.
4. Be confident in your views and outlook on homosexuality. Before you begin to explain your position to anyone else, you must have it clear in your own mind.

EXHIBIT 11.2 A Lesbian's Letter to Her Parents Disclosing Her Homosexuality

Dear Mom and Dad:

I love you very much and would give you the world if I could. You've always given me the best. You've always been there when I needed you. The lessons of love, strength, and wisdom you've taught me are invaluable. Most importantly, you've taught me to take pride and stand up for what I believe. In the past six months I've done some very serious thinking about my goals and outlook on life. It's a tough and unyielding world that caters only to those who do for themselves. Having your help and support seems to make it easier to handle. But I've made a decision that may test your love and support. Mom and Dad, I've decided to live a gay lifestyle.

I'm sure your heads are spinning with confusion and disbelief right now but please try to let me finish. As I said before, I've given this decision much thought. First and foremost, I'd like for you to know that I'm happy. All my life as a sexual being has been spent frustrated in a role I could not fulfill. Emotionally and mentally, I'm relieved. Believe me, this was not an easy decision to make. (What made it easier was having the strength to accept myself). Who I choose to sleep with does not make me more or less of a human being. My need for love and affection is the same as anyone else's; it's just that I fulfill this need in a different way. I'm still the same person I've always been.

It's funny I say I'm still the same person, yet society seems to think I've changed. They seem to think that I don't deserve to be treated as a respectable citizen. Instead, they think I should be treated as a deranged maniac needing constant supervision to prevent me from molesting innocent children. I have the courage and strength to face up to this opposition, but I can't do it alone. Oh, what I would give to have your support!

I realize I've thrown everything at you rather quickly. Please take your time. I don't expect a response. And please don't blame yourselves, for there is no one to blame. Please remember that I'm happy and I felt the need to share my happiness with two people I love with all my heart.

Your loving daughter,
Maria

Parental reactions to the discovery that their child is gay often include shock and anger (Robinson et al., 1989, p. 67). Examples of such reactions reported by three gay people follow (Heron, 1983):

> You can't be gay! You must be mistaken. Go back to school and don't come back home until we say you can. (p. 97)
>
> Dad escorted me to the garage where I was harassed.
>
> "You fucking queer, you goddamn faggot . . . Sissy . . . Do you actually have sex with your lover?" (p. 43)
>
> The one phrase that I'll remember is, "Your mother and I have no further reason to live."
>
> I don't know what the hell we have done to deserve the treatment we are getting. Terry, you were our only hope." (p. 73)

Most of the 52 gay respondents in another study said that their parents rejected them when they learned that they were gay. One 68-year-old man bitterly reported, "My father was very hostile when I told him I was homosexual. I was 21. We didn't have a positive relationship after that" (Adelman, 1990, p. 29).

It may be particularly difficult for gay youth to come out to their families. Among 37 homosexual or bisexual male high school seniors (ages 16–18), only two reported having a positive relationship with their families over the issue of being gay (Uribe & Harbeck, 1992). For the remaining 35 males in this study, coming out to parents resulted in situations that "varied from extreme family disruption to forcible expulsion from home" (p. 22). Over half of the young gay men in this sample lived with either friends, lovers, or in a residential or foster home for gay adolescents. Eight out of 13 lesbian high school seniors in this study told their parents of their sexual orientation. "In each case, their parents told them that it was a passing phase that would go away" (Uribe & Harbeck, 1992, pp. 24–25).

Two explanations may account for parents responding so negatively. One, they suddenly feel that all of the negative stereotypes rampant in our heterosexist society are true of their son or daughter ("my child is a pervert," "child molester," "has AIDS"). Second, some are overwhelmed with a sense of sadness and depression that their child will no longer fulfill their dreams:

> When they learn of the child's homosexuality, they must adjust to the fact that their child is not part of the majority, but is a part of a minority [minorities are persecuted]. Their dreams that their child will have a satisfying traditional marriage, including children, must die. Instead, they must learn to accept a different kind of identity and behavior for their child. It may be that parents experience grief similar to the grief felt by parents whose child has died; they are accepting the "death" of dreams for a heterosexual child and the birth of new dreams and a changed relationship with their homosexual child. (Robinson et al., 1989, p. 59)

Over 60% of the 402 parents of gays said that the adjustment to the knowledge of their offspring's homosexuality involved a five-stage progression of mourning and loss, including shock, denial, guilt, anger, and acceptance. Acceptance was difficult because they were afraid for the child. Seventy-four percent of the parents of gays reported that they were "afraid for their child." Seventy-one percent reported that they were worried that their child might develop AIDS (Robinson et al., 1989, pp. 67, 69).

Parental adjustment to the knowledge that their son or daughter is a homosexual takes time. In the Robinson et al. (1989) study most parents reported that it took them two years to work through their grief and fully accept their child's same-sex orientation. When parents were asked what they would tell other parents who had just learned that their child was gay, some responded (Robinson et al., 1989, p. 74):

> Love her or him, simply love her or him. Respect your child's right and wisdom to make his own choices. Affirm his honesty and courage. Celebrate his sexuality as a gift from God (a 50-year-old mother).
>
> They have gone through so much within themselves, just be there to listen and continue to love them (a 52-year old mother).
>
> Take care, go easy, try to understand (easier said than done) (a 55-year-old father).

Homosexuals usually disclose their sexual orientation to their siblings before they tell their parents. The reactions of siblings influence whether and when parents are told. Sibling reactions are often similar to those of parents. However, unlike parents, siblings do not experience guilt or self-blame (Strommen, 1989).

Coming Out to Heterosexual Partner or Spouse and Children Gay people become involved in heterosexual relationships and marriages for a variety of reasons (Strommen, 1989). These include genuine love for a spouse, wanting to have children, family pressure to marry, help in overcoming homosexuality, and belief that marriage was the only way to achieve a happy adult life. In a probability sample of gay and bisexual men, 42% reported that they were currently married (Harry, 1990). Other researchers estimate that 20% of gay men are married (Strommen, 1989).

Many homosexuals in heterosexual relationships do not disclose their homosexuality to their partners out of fear that their partners will reject them and that there may be legal consequences (getting custody of the children would be jeopardized). The fear of rejection for disclosure is realistic. Of 21 heterosexual women who became aware that their husbands were gay, all went through a painful grief reaction when they learned that their husbands had emotional or sexual, or both, attachments to other men. The suffering was aggravated by feeling deceived or stupid for not having guessed the truth. What made it difficult for them to seek support from family and friends was the fear of encountering social disapproval or ostracism. They were afraid for themselves, their husbands, and their children. At the time of the study, all of the 21 women were still married and living with their husbands, but most felt unsure that the marriage would last. Only three had complete confidence in the future stability of their relationships (Hays & Samuels, 1989, p. 81).

Two of the wives who felt good about the future relationship with their husbands reported having open marriages in which they had extramarital affairs. The other wife reported having "great sex" three to four times per week with her husband. All considered their husbands to be caring and good communicators (Hays & Samuels, 1989).

Some of us think it is good for our kids to have a lesbian mother because they see the options; they do not grow up believing the world to be heterosexual; and they have, right in the family, someone who is willing to be different. The better we can feel about ourselves and our choices, the more we have to share with our kids and each other.

Boston Women's Health Book Collective

Some gay individuals also confront the issue of coming out to their children. About 10% of gay men are fathers (Strommen, 1990). Children who learn of their fathers' homosexuality usually do so without great trauma. Gay fathers report that the reaction of their children is "none" or "tolerant and understanding" (Bozett, 1989). However, daughters tend to be more accepting than sons," although most children feel their father's honesty brings them closer together" (p. 143).

Some children experience embarrassing situations or trauma because of the reactions of other children. Some children are physically or verbally abused, and in one case, a child was subjected to a "mock faggot trial" at school (Hays & Samuels, 1989, p. 96).

Coming Out to Friends and Employers Disclosing one's homosexuality to friends produces reactions that vary from acceptance to termination of the relationship. One friend who could not accept her girlfriend's disclosure of lesbianism said,

> I was shocked and I didn't know how to handle it. It changed how I viewed her—as something awful that I didn't want to be around any longer. I was also ashamed of myself for the way I felt about my friend. But I couldn't change and we didn't see each other again. (Authors' class notes)

CONSIDERATION: Some heterosexuals particularly value and enjoy friendships with homosexuals. Several female heterosexual students in the authors' classes have indicated that it is easier to develop close friendships with gay men because the element of sexual attraction does not get in the way.

In regard to employers, Etringer, Hillerbrand, and Hetherington (1990) found that compared to heterosexual men, gay men are more likely to be anxious about their career choices. This is because homosexuals must consider factors related to their sexual orientation and the implication of its potential public exposure. One study of 52 homosexuals found that those who reported high life satisfaction had "low disclosure at work" of their homosexuality (Adelman, 1990).

Some employment firms have policies forbidding discrimination in hiring or advancement based on affectional or sexual orientation. American Telephone and Telegraph (the nation's largest corporate employer), Bank of America, IBM, the radio and television networks ABC, NBC, and CBS, and McDonald's are examples. Where firms do not protect the right of homosexuals to be employed, sometimes the government does. Such was the case of a homosexual who had been denied the right to reenlist in the Army. In 1990, the Supreme Court let stand a federal appeals court decision requiring the Army to allow Perry Watkins of Seattle to reenlist. Watkins at the time was a 16-year veteran with an excellent service record who had never been denied the right to reenlist (even though the Army knew that he was gay). The 11-judge panel of the 9th U.S. Circuit Court of Appeals had commented the previous year:

> Sgt. Watkins has greatly benefited the Army, and therefore the country, by his military service. In addition, Watkins' homosexuality clearly has not hurt the Army in any way. . . . Equity cries out and demands that the Army be prohibited from refusing to re-enlist Watkins on the basis of his homosexuality. ("High Court Rules for Gay Soldier," 1990)

However, the decision has not changed the military's ban on homosexuals in general. According to the Department of Defense:

> homosexuality is incompatible with military service. The presence in the military environment of persons who engage in homosexual conduct or who, by their statements, demonstrate a propensity to engage in homosexual conduct, seriously impairs the accomplishment of the military mission (Gibbs, 1991, p. 15).

"This prohibition applies not only to those who engage in homosexual behavior but to those who feel that they are inclined toward homosexuality" (Gibbs, 1991, p. 15). The policy toward homosexuals in the military varies by country. While France and Japan admit gays into the armed forces, the former Soviet Union imprisoned any known gay man for up to five years.

CONSIDERATION: Some homosexuals feel that their choice in coming out to their employer is taken away by the act of "outing." This refers to strangers, usually in the media, publicly exposing homosexuals without their consent. "Outing" takes the choice away from homosexuals about whether and to whom they want to disclose their sexual orientation.

In sum, coming out is an important aspect of self-affirmation for gay individuals. But coming out involves difficult choices; gay people must decide if they want to come out, to whom, when, and how. And what will the consequences be of coming out? Brian McNaught (1983) suggested that

> Those persons who have "come out of the closet"—who have affirmed their sexual orientation to themselves and to others—frequently pay an initial price of rejection by some people, but at the same time they report a unique sense of self-determination, worth, and honesty. (pp. 140–141)

CONSIDERATION: Gay men and lesbian women may choose to stay in the "closet" or come out to only trusted family members and friends, and thus avoid or reduce social rejection and discrimination. Mark Freedman, founder of the Association of Gay Psychologists noted that "most gays have been forced to hide behind a mask of heterosexuality in order to survive" (1989, p. 78). While hiding one's gay identity can be distressing, it also has a positive side:

> Gay people in hiding may become quite sophisticated about the masks people wear—about the relationship, that is, between identity and role. This is a useful sensitivity (Freedman, 1989, p. 78).

Developing a Positive Gay Self-Concept

Because of massive societal homophobia and rejection of homosexuals, homosexuals must cope with social rejection to overcome a negative self-concept. The greater the stigmatization of homosexuality and the greater the antihomosexual bias of a country, the greater the negative impact on homosexuals. For example, Ireland and Australia are less accepting of homosexuality than Sweden and Finland. Homosexual youth in Ireland and Australia have more negative self-concepts and are more likely to believe that "being gay is wrong" than homosexual youth in Sweden and Finland (Ross, 1989).

Gay individuals may develop more positive feelings about their sexual identities through a combination of procedures. One is to examine the social basis for the homosexual's negative self-concept. Homosexuals are encouraged to view the negative feelings they have about themselves as resulting from the societal rejection of homosexuals. This rejection is based on prejudice and the perpetuation of negative stereotypes regarding homosexuals.

CONSIDERATION: Heterosexuals are not the only ones to believe the stereotypes regarding gays. In a study of 82 gay males, Jenks and Newman (1991) found that gay men tended to apply stereotypes to other gays, while viewing themselves as not conforming to the stereotypes. The researchers concluded that

> This finding, that gays often view other gays as conforming to the stereotype, would seem to call for not only educating nongays about gays, but also many gays about other gays. (p. 71)

In addition, developing a positive lesbian or gay self-concept is facilitated by labeling one's self as a homosexual and disclosing one's sexual orientation to others (Miranda & Storms, 1989). Gay people are encouraged to establish close relationships with other gay people who feel good about themselves and who can serve as positive models.

> While many minority groups are the target for prejudice . . . and discrimination . . . in our society, few persons face this hostility without the support and acceptance of their family as do many gay, lesbian, and bisexual youth.
>
> *Virginia Uribe*
> *Karen Harbeck*

Family therapy may also be helpful in increasing the self-esteem of gay individuals. In family therapy, the therapist attempts to help the parents alleviate "any guilt they have harbored about producing a homosexual child and free the parents to be less rejecting of this child" (Sultan, Elsner, & Smith, 1987, p. 196). Family therapy may also facilitate supportive communication between parents and their homosexual child.

Developing a positive self-concept may be particularly difficult for gay and bisexual youth. Uribe and Harbeck (1992) observed that among gay and lesbian students who attended a high school in Los Angeles, "low self-esteem, feelings of isolation, alienation, and inadequacy were common" (p. 19). Uribe and Harbeck suggested that,

> it is clear from the information available on suicide rates, drop-out risk, low self-esteem, health risks, substance abuse, and the plethora of other problems often experienced by gay, lesbian, and bisexual adolescents that intervention must occur immediately in every school in this nation (1992, p. 27).

An example of school-based intervention that is correctly being implemented in Los Angeles is PROJECT 10—a counseling and educational program for gay and bisexual youth. PROJECT 10, named after Kinsey's estimate that 10% of the population is homosexual, was also designed to "heighten the school community's acceptance of and sensitivity to gay, lesbian, and bisexual issues" (Uribe & Harbeck, 1992, p. 11).

The Role of the Gay Subculture

The gay subculture plays an important role in the lives of gay women and men. Sociologists use the term "subculture" to refer to the distinctive lifestyles, values, and norms of discrete population segments within a society. The gay subculture provides a supportive network within which gay individuals may affirm their sexual identity,

To function, every social group must have a culture of its own—its own goals, norms, values, and typical ways of doing things.

Henry L. Tischler

develop a positive self-concept, and learn the roles, norms, and values associated with the gay lifestyle.

CONSIDERATION: Subcultures provide a similar function for a variety of groups, including racial, ethnic, religious, occupational, gender, and social class groups. However, Uribe and Harbeck (1992) noted that,

> while most members of minority groups, whether ethnic, national, religious, racial, or gender-related, usually enjoy the support of and enculturation by other family and community members, the homosexual or bisexual young person is usually alone in this process of exploration and identification. (p. 13)

Some gay and lesbian individuals live in communities that have a large gay population. In such communities (e.g. New York City, Key West, Los Angeles and most large cities) the gay subculture provides gay churches, shops, counseling and health services, bars and other meeting places, and gay newspapers that list social activities for the gay community. Gay and lesbian individuals may purchase the *Gayellow Pages*—a national directory that lists all the organizations, publications, and services for gay people in each city in the United States and Canada (McNaught, 1983).

Inside Gay Relationships

Because gays live and conduct their relationships in the context of a predominately heterosexual society, their relationships are somewhat different from traditional heterosexual ones. Next we look at male and female homoerotic relationships and sexual behavior.

Gay Male Relationships

One common stereotype about gay men is that they are sexually promiscuous and do not have long-term committed relationships. However, many gay men do establish long-term committed relationships. In a study of 560 long-term gay male relationships, the average length of a relationship was seven years. Ninety-six percent reported that they were committed to be together "a long time" and 76% reported that they were committed for "life" ("National Survey Results," 1990, p. 1).

Unlike heterosexual couples, homosexual couples receive little social support for continuing long-term relationships. For example, gay couples do not have the institutional support of legal marriage. Family members, who may provide support for heterosexual unions, often do not provide such support to homosexual couples. With a rating of 1 equaling strong support and 7 equaling hostility, the 560 couples in the long-term relationship survey gave their father and mother 2.98 and 3.37 ratings respectively ("National Survey Results," 1990, p. 9).

CONSIDERATION: Being sexually active with numerous partners is often condoned or approved in heterosexual men, yet the same behavior is condemned in homosexual men. "This double standard becomes clear when we consider terms which our culture uses to refer to promiscuous heterosexual men: 'Don Juan,' lady-killer,' or 'stud,' . . . (Blumenfeld & Raymond, 1988, p. 376). In contrast, the term "promiscuous," when applied to gay males, has a negative connotation.

This couple has been in a stable monogamous relationship for 19 years.

Some data suggest that since the AIDS crisis, the number of sexual partners that gay men have has decreased. In 1985, 361 homosexual men reported a median of eight sexual partners; in 1987, the number had dropped to a median of five (median means that half of the men had more and half less than the identified number) (Schechter et al., 1988).

CONSIDERATION: In interpreting data on homosexual relationships, it is important to keep in mind that such data may be biased because of sampling difficulties. For example, research on gay men may be based on samples that are easily accessible, such as those found in gay bars. Gay men who are in committed, long-term relationships are underrepresented in such samples because they, like their heterosexual pair-bonded counterparts, are usually not found in bars, but rather are home with their partners. Therefore, the percentage of gay men in long-term, pair-bonded relationships (such data are not available) may be underestimated.

Gay male relationships are often not monogamous. In their study of 95 gay male couples who had been together more than five years, none of the partners reported that they were sexually exclusive with each other (McWhirter & Mattison, 1984). However, many gay men are interested in establishing and maintaining monogamous, committed relationships. Indeed, an organization (Couples National Network) was formed to support the positive aspects of gay relationships through social, recreational, and educational events. One researcher (Berger, 1990) analyzed the questionnaires of 92 gay male couples who were members of the organization and who were in stable love relationships.

Demographically, the respondents had a median age of 38 and had been together from less than a year to 35 years (average was eight years; median was six years). They were relatively well off, with three-fourths reporting combined incomes of over $40,000.

Many had met their lover in a bar (41%). Ten percent had met at work, 9% at an organization, and 9% at a party. Other meeting places included bookstores, theater lobbies, and church. Over half said that they met their partner by self-introduction.

Since there are no formal social sanctions for newly committed gay relationships (like the engagements and weddings that serve the heterosexual community), moving in together takes on a special significance. While about half of committed lovers do not live together, those who do often move in together soon after meeting. Of these 92 couples, a fourth reported that they moved in together within a month of meeting (p. 38).

Maintaining a relationship in a society which discourages permanence is difficult enough for heterosexuals, but for gay people who generally receive no support for their efforts from family, employers, the church, or the state, the task can seem impossible.

Brian McNaught

What to call each other varied. Most (62%) referred to each other as "lover," 23% as "partner," and 16% as "friend."

CONSIDERATION: What should you call the companion of a homosexual? Berger (1990) suggests that "in the absence of clear consensus, it may be best to ask the individual couple about their preferences" (p. 39).

One way these gay male partners expressed their long-term commitment to each other was through the use of wills, power of attorney, and relationship contracts. Wills ensure that the assets of the partner will be distributed according to his wishes—to the lover, rather than to unaccepting relatives. The power of attorney is a document that permits the lover to make decisions on behalf of his partner if the partner becomes ill or incapacitated. Some gays are very sensitive to this issue, since the gay press has emphasized that "a long term gay lover is often barred from any decision making or even contact with a severely ill partner due to efforts of hostile relatives" (p. 40). With a power of attorney document, the partner is in a legal position to continue to be a part of his lover's life. Half of 92 gay male couples reported that they had a will, 37% had signed a power of attorney, and 14% reported having a relationship contract (Berger, 1990, p. 40). While relationship contracts have no legal validity, they are often functional in specifying the roles for the partners in the relationship.

Acceptance from parents and siblings is also an issue in gay male relationships. Over two-thirds reported that their parents and siblings were polite, friendly, and supportive of their relationship. However, in those cases where the parents were not supportive, there was considerable stress on the gay relationship. The partner felt torn between loyalty to the family and loyalty to the lover (such a choice is examined in the final section of this chapter). Also, partners may clash about the degree to which they should hide their relationship from family members and how much family members should be told. The only other major problem reported by the gay male couples was finances. Apparently, the problem was over issues of partner equality in financial contributions or decision making, rather than stress from insufficient funds.

When couples were asked about the degree to which they had a monogamous or sexually open relationship, 96.4% reported that they were monogamous. Most also acknowledged that the AIDS crisis had had a significant impact on their decision to be sexually exclusive. "Many couples said the crisis had brought them closer together and increased appreciation for their partner" (p. 44). However, 69% of the couples said that they did not use condoms—they either felt that they were safe (because of a negative HIV test) or that they had already been exposed and subsequent exposure would make no difference (Berger, 1990).

CONSIDERATION: Since the AIDS virus has a lengthy incubation period, individuals who are monogamous with each other could be infecting each other because they may have been infected by previous partners. Also, the idea that no additional risk is incurred with continued exposure is fallacious since repeated exposure to a single partner does increase the risk of infection if that partner has had HIV exposure. (See Chapter 18 for further discussion of AIDS.)

Gay Female Relationships

Like many heterosexual women, most gay women value stable, monogamous relationships that are emotionally, as well as sexually, satisfying. Transitory sexual encounters among gay women do occur, but they are the exception, not the rule. Five years was the average length of the relationships of 706 lesbian couples; 18% reported that they had been together 11 or more years. Ninety-one percent reported that they were sexually monogamous ("National Survey Results," 1990).

The majority (57%) of the women in these lesbian relationships noted that they wore a ring to symbolize their commitment to each other. Some (19%) acknowledged their relationship with a ceremony ("National Survey Results," 1990). Most met through friends or at work. Only 4% met at a bar.

Women in our society, gay and straight, are taught that sexual expression should occur in the context of emotional or romantic involvement. Ninety-three percent of 94 gay women in one study said their first homosexual experience was emotional; physical expression came later (Corbett & Morgan, 1983). Hence, for gay women, the formula is love first; for gay men, it is sex first—just as for their heterosexual counterparts.

While gay women's relationships normally last longer than gay men's relationships, long-term relationships (20 years or more) are rare. Of 706 lesbian couples, only 1% had been in relationships lasting over 20 years ("National Survey Results,"

Some lesbian couples choose to rear a child together.

1990). Serial monogamy—one relationship at a time—was the predominant pattern, with almost seven (6.6) being the average number of years in each relationship. When lesbians engage in extradyadic sexual relations, they (like heterosexual women) are likely to have emotional and sexual affairs, rather than just sexual encounters. Nonmonogamy among lesbian couples is also likely to be related to dissatisfaction with the primary relationship. In addition, both lesbians and gay men are more likely than heterosexual couples to be open with their partners about their extradyadic activity (Nichols, 1987).

According to Beverly Burch (1987), intimacy in lesbian relationships may be blocked by conflicts over three major issues: the balance of power, the pulls toward and away from dependency, and the roles involved in nurturing. Burch noted that while heterosexuals must negotiate these three issues, lesbians experience these issues with greater intensity. Burch argued, for example, that "lesbians are often feminists and concerned with women's unequal access to power" (p. 127). Therefore, lesbians are more sensitive to imbalances of power regarding division of labor, money, and recognition, as well as inequalities regarding career success, verbal or physical ability, and racial, social class, and ethnic differences.

The struggle over dependency issues are also unique for lesbian couples.

> A lesbian may strongly value independence, even self-sufficiency, as the way out of the traditional constriction of women's lives. Dependency may be feared because it represents identification with the old sense of heterosexual 'femininity' that she has rejected . . . because she sees its destructiveness to women's, and her own, integrity. (Burch, 1987, pp. 129–130)

Lastly, lesbian relationships frequently involve conflicts over who takes care of whom. Traditionally, women have been expected to be the nurturers, especially of men. In lesbian relationships, women may feel relieved of the burden to be nurturers

FIGURE 11.2 Lesbian lovemaking.

and may hope to be the nurtured one instead. "When both women have that hope and feel freed from the constraints of a caretaking role, there is conflict" (Burch, 1987, p. 131).

Sexual Behavior

The sexual behavior of gays is very similar to that of heterosexuals. Gay people kiss, caress, manually stimulate each other's genitals, orally stimulate each other, and relax after orgasm (see Figure 11.2). But there are some differences in the approach to sexual activity. Masters and Johnson (1979), who observed the sexual behavior of lesbians and gay couples who had lived together for at least a year, were particularly struck by the amount of time, consideration, and care that gay partners took with each other. Each partner apparently knew how the other wanted to be stimulated, and each gave this kind of stimulation to the other. They did not rush to produce an orgasm in their lovers. Rather, they moved slowly from kissing to breast stimulation to genital stroking, holding and caressing each other in loving affection.

The partners also teased each other sexually. Gay men would slowly orchestrate their partner's excitation almost to the point of orgasm but just before ejaculation would stop the stimulation, let the erection subside, and begin again.

Committed partners, both gay men and women, also evidenced variety in their stimulation. When gay men stimulated their partner's penis, their hands were also manipulating the thighs, anus, scrotum, and lower abdomen. Gay women were also inventive in providing pleasure for their partners.

In a study comparing 407 lesbians with 370 heterosexual women (Coleman, Hoon, & Hoon, 1983), lesbians reported having sexual relations more often, more frequent orgasms through masturbation as well as other means of stimulation, more sexual satisfaction, and a greater number of partners. The authors suggested that gender empathy, women's socialization in self-disclosure and communication, and method of orgasm accounted for the more satisfying sex life reported by gay women.

Eighty-seven homosexual men between the ages of 40 and 77 shared their sexual attitudes and behaviors by completing a questionnaire (Pope & Schultz, 1990). All of the respondents reported having a current interest in sex, and 91% reported being "sexually active." Over half (54%) between the ages of 40 and 49 reported having sex once a week; 34%, between the ages of 50 and 59; and 5%, age 60 or over (Pope & Schultz, 1990).

Homosexual men report different levels of sexual satisfaction, depending on whether the question is about emotional or physical satisfaction. The sexual practices homosexual men report that they derive the most emotional satisfaction from include sensuous touching, kissing, and anal intercourse without a condom (59%, 37%, and 36%, respectively). The sexual practices homosexual men report that they derive the most physical satisfaction from include anal intercourse without a condom, oral-genital sex, and sensuous touching (54%, 49%, 27%, respectively) (Connell & Kippax, 1990).

Although gay men are most likely to engage in fellatio, they may also engage in anal intercourse. For this activity, the anal opening and penis are lubricated with saliva or an artificial lubricant, such as KY jelly, and the penis is inserted slowly to keep the anal sphincter relaxed. While the partner receiving the other's penis may experience some discomfort during insertion, it usually dissipates after full penetration. The inserter continues thrusting until he ejaculates; rarely does the partner receiving the penis experience ejaculation unless he masturbates while his partner is thrusting.

CONSIDERATION: A less-known and infrequent sexual activity of gay men is fisting the rectum (also known as brachioprotic eroticism) in which one male inserts his hand and forearm in the anus of a partner. Since there is considerable risk of puncturing the colon, the practice is dangerous.

Sexually Transmissible Diseases

Sexually transmissible diseases are discussed in detail in Chapter 18. However, we wish to note here that HIV infection remains one of the most threatening STDs for male homosexuals and bisexuals. In an effort to document the degree to which homosexuals are at risk, Connell and Kippax (1990) interviewed 535 gay and bisexual men in New South Wales, Australia. When asked what percent had anal intercourse without condoms with a regular partner and with a casual partner, the percentages were 31 and 24, respectively. These percentages suggest that these gay men evidenced greater caution with casual partners. In addition, there is evidence that the use of safer sex practices is increasing, regardless of whom the partner is. When asked if they had ever had anal intercourse without using a condom, 95% of the males responded yes. When asked if they had done so in the last six months, only 48% said yes.

Bisexually experienced men tend to report having more STDs and engage more frequently in high risk behaviors than do men with exclusively heterosexual adult experience, but not as frequently as men with exclusively homosexual experience (Lever et al., 1992). Such high risk behaviors include having multiple sex partners, engaging in anal sex, and having sex with prostitutes.

More recent data on gay men, lesbians, and heterosexuals who frequent bars further emphasized that sexual behavior is changing (Juran, 1991). Based on data

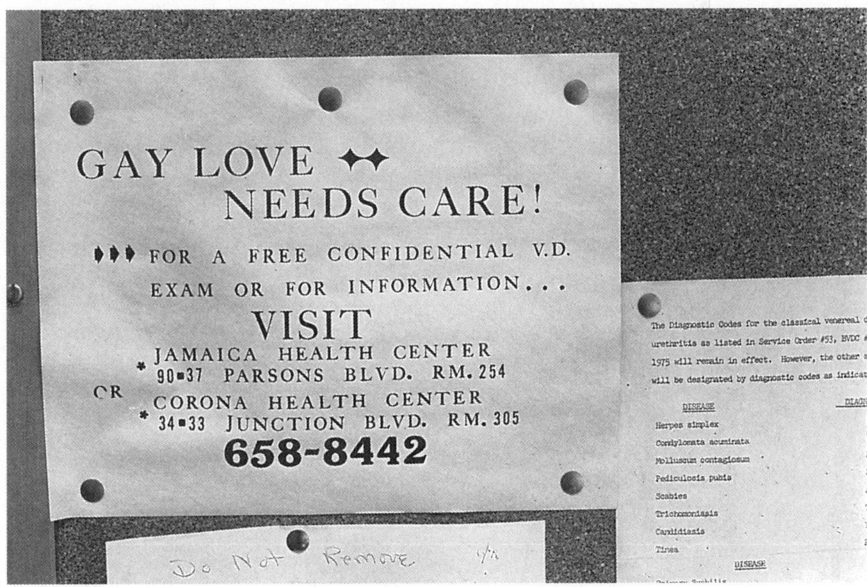

Homosexuals have increased their concern for STDs.

from 71 gay men, 94% reported that they had changed their sexual behavior, with 61% reporting use of condoms in the last two years and a quarter reporting that they no longer engage in casual sex. Of 65 lesbians, one-quarter said that they have less frequent casual sex and one-quarter said they no longer have sex with new men. Heterosexual men and women also reported decreasing casual sexual contacts and increasing condom use (Juran, 1991). These data give support for the belief that some homosexuals and heterosexuals are increasing their use of safer sex practices.

CONSIDERATION: Gay men are becoming more concerned about becoming involved with someone who is a low AIDS risk. Davidson (1991) conducted a content analysis of personals advertisements in *The Village Voice* to assess changes in the language gay men used to refer to their sexuality between 1978 and 1988. Davidson concluded that the gay men, across time, came to refer to themselves in ways that would emphasize their concern for health and safe sex so as to attract a similar partner. Key words and phrases in personals advertisements to connote a stronger health focus included "health conscious," "clean," "monogamy," "exclusive," "HIV negative," and "taking the current situation very seriously" (p. 130).

Unfortunately, however, there is evidence that campaigns to reduce risk factors for HIV exposure have not been uniformly successful in all gay communities. For example, the greater prevalence of IV needle sharing and risky sexual practices within the African-American and Latin communities provides a challenge "to develop prevention programs for Blacks and Latins that are as effective as those that have been mounted for gay white men" (Fullilove, 1988, p. 5). Recently, a study has demonstrated that success in reducing exposure to risk has been observed in large cities, described as AIDS epicenters. However, in smaller cities high rates of risk-taking are still documented. In a study of 487 gay men in Buffalo risk exposure was related to patronizing gay bars, sexual opportunism, and ineffective use of social skills to reduce risk exposure (Ruefli, Yu, & Barton, 1992).

CHOICES

There are numerous choices in sexuality in regard to sexual orientation. Three such choices follow.

The Choice of Some Homosexuals: Lover or Parent

When gays first come out to their parents, it is not unusual that their parents put pressure on them to give up their life-style. Such is the case of Mark, who is a 21-year-old fulltime university student majoring in business. He also works parttime as a waiter at a local restaurant and receives money from his parents to help pay his college expenses. Mark is gay and has made his parents aware of his sexual orientation. They are having a very difficult time adjusting to the fact that their son is homosexual.

Last Thanksgiving, Mark took his lover, Tom, to his grandmother's house for the traditional holiday feast. Although Mark's grandmother is supportive of Mark and his life-style, his parents had asked that he not bring his lover since they are embarrassed by Mark's choice of life-style. They were shocked to find their son and his lover at the Thanksgiving gathering and told him that they would no longer send him money for college, that he was to terminate his "disgusting" relationship with that "fag," and come home to live until he "came to his senses."

Mark's choice—to deny his sexuality and the relationship with Tom or to stand up to his parents—is not unlike that faced by numerous other homosexuals who come out to their parents. In choosing among various courses of action, both positive and negative consequences might be considered. The choice for Mark is not easy. He loves his parents, but he feels committed to the gay life-style and is deeply involved with his lover.

The consequences of doing what his parents want is to maintain their approval and to minimize the conflict in the relationship with them. However, by doing as they demand, Mark not only denies his sexual orientation and lives without his lover but reinforces his parents for making demands on him. Today, they ask him to deny his sexuality; tomorrow they may ask him to get married, have two children, and live next door. At what point, if ever, does Mark decide that *his* choices are more important than *their* choices for him?

Some individuals are tightly bonded with their parents, and no choice is worth damaging that relationship. Other people may find it easier to disengage from their parents and defy their demands.

Mark chose the middle ground. He did not want to lose the approval of his parents nor accede to their demands. He decided to work full-time, take two night classes, and continue the relationship with his lover. He decided that he would no longer subject his parents to his lover. For holiday occasions, he may decide not to go and instead stay with Tom. At other times, he might go alone while Tom visits his parents. The result of Mark's decision was that he became economically independent, kept the relationship with his parents intact, and continued the relationship with his lover.

The Choice of Some Parents: Accept or Reject a Gay Son or Daughter

While young adults are confronted with the decision to tell their parents that they are gay, parents are confronted with deciding to accept or reject the homosexuality of their offspring. It is helpful to keep in mind that, just as homosexuals live in an antihomosexual heterosexual society that encourages a negative self-concept (and are therefore victims of social forces that influence them), parents live in the same society that encourages rejection of homosexuals (and are, therefore, also influenced by negative social forces). If parents want to maintain the relationship with their children, they must decide to override society's antigay bias. One parent said:

> I can't say that I like it. In fact, I am sad that my child is homosexual. But I can't let that come between us and have decided to make it clear that I still love Chris to the fullest.

Some parents are incapable of accepting their child's homosexuality:

> I'm not the kind to put up with such behavior. I told my kid that what he was doing was wrong and that I wouldn't tolerate it. I haven't seen my son in four years. I'm sad about that but I'd be more sad having a faggot in my house.

However, some parents who have rejected their offspring because of their homosexuality have regretted doing so because they missed the relationship with their offspring more than they hated the fact that they were gay. Among the alternatives available to parents include:

1. Outright rejection and attempts to force the child to change.

Continued

Continued

2. Continuing the relationship with the child but denying the child's life-style. "We never talk about it," said one parent, "but he is always welcome here and brings his lovers, too. I'd rather have my son as a homo than have no son at all."
3. Complete acceptance. The child's life-style is openly ackowledged and supported. The parents may be members of an organization for parents and friends of gays (see "Resources" section at end of book). Most parents need time to accept their child's homosexuality, and some benefit from reading the book *Now That You Know; What Every Parent Should Know About Homosexuality* (Fairchild & Hayward, 1979).

Distress About One's Sexual Orientation: Seek Therapy?

As mentioned earlier in this chapter, the *Diagnostic and Statistical Manual of Mental Disorders,* third edition, (DSM-IIIR) no longer classifies homosexuality itself as a mental disorder. As such, homosexuality itself is not a condition that warrants psychological treatment.

Most gay people do not want to be heterosexual. As noted earlier, only a small percentage would take a magic pill to make them heterosexual. However, some gay individuals express persistent and marked distress over their sexual orientation, referred to as **ego-dystonic homosexuality.** This terminology prompted DeCecco (1987) to suggest that gay activists had been successful only in getting homosexuality *re*classified, not *de*classified (as a mental disorder).

Some ego-dystonic homosexuals may seek **conversion therapy,** (for gay persons who have had little or no previous heterosexual experience) or **reversion therapy** (for gays who have previously lived a heterosexual life-style).

Mental health professionals are divided in their opinion about helping homosexuals become heterosexual. Three perspectives follow (Silverstein, 1984):

1. Some therapists maintain that it is immoral to attempt sexual reorientation of gay people under any conditions. These therapists (Davison, 1991) feel that it is unethical to help a gay person live a heterosexual life-style because agreeing to give such help confirms to the gay person that something is wrong with homosexuality. The American Psychological Association's Committee on Lesbian and Gay Concerns is considering a resolution that would ask the association to view attempts by psychologists to reverse the sexual orientation of gay clients as unethical. This position is based on the belief that gay people who seek to change their sexual orientation have been pressured to do so by the society, which is largely antigay.

   Sultan, Elsner, & Smith (1987) suggested that a gay person who is experiencing low self-esteem, but would like to be better adjusted in their homosexual orientation, could seek therapy for help in increasing positive self-regard and mobilizing family and social resources. They stated that therapists are obliged to be aware of resources available in the gay community.
2. Other therapists do not consider homosexuality a mental disorder yet consider reorientation acceptable for those people who find their homosexuality distressing. Aversion techniques designed to extinguish homosexual arousal have been criticized as they "typically involve much physical suffering and have not been found to be successful over an extended period of time" (Sultan et al., 1987, p. 195). Techniques such as those used in the Masters and Johnson program to facilitate heterosexual responsiveness have been effective in terms of increasing ability to interact heterosexually, although not in terms of changing one's basic sexual orientation (Sultan et al., 1987).
3. Although in the minority, some therapists consider homosexuality to be a mental disorder and consider it immoral to withhold reorientation treatment from those who desire it. Diamant (1987) noted that according to an experienced therapist and teacher the DSM-III changes have not necessarily changed the opinions of all therapists.

While many clinicians are reluctant to do research or publish papers that offend gay rights groups, some practitioners have not abandoned their beliefs that homosexuality is a pathology and still provide treatments designed to promote heterosexuality.

In conclusion, Diamant (1987) summarized changes in published discussions of therapy for gays and lesbians. "Reports on aversive type conversion treatments are fewer, and counseling and psychotherapeutic efforts which disdain or minimize or forego emphasis on change to heterosexuality are more common. . . ."

Therapists are "less likely to seize opportunities to convert lesbian women and gay men because they are just that, gay or lesbian." (p. 215).

Summary

1. Sexual orientation may be distinguished by a number of factors, including cognitions, emotions, and sexual attractions as well as one's sexual preference and its stability, self-concept or self-identity, and behaviors. Homosexuality and homoeroticism are terms denoting a predominance of cognitive, emotional, and

sexual attraction to those of the same sex. Heterosexuality and heteroeroticism are terms denoting a predominance of the same factors to those of the opposite sex.

2. It is estimated that between 5–10% of adults in the United States and in other countries are predominately homosexual. However, research shows that more people have homosexual feelings than engage in homosexual behaviors, and more engage in homosexual behavior than develop lasting homosexual identification.
3. Although definitions of bisexuality vary, in general the term refers to a sexual orientation which involves cognitive, emotional, and sexual attraction to both sexes.
4. We live in a heterosexist society where heterosexuality is viewed as the norm and homosexuality is viewed by many as deviant and wrong. Homosexual and bisexual individuals are often victims of prejudice, discrimination, and antigay violence. Homosexuals are also stigmatized and negatively stereotyped. The term homophobia refers to negative attitudes and reactions toward homosexuals (and bisexuals). Prejudice and discrimination against homosexuals may be based on religious values that emphasize procreative sex, intolerance of those who don't conform to sex role norms, and inaccurate beliefs about homosexuals.
5. The gay liberation movement was formed in order to change public attitudes and policies regarding homosexuals. The national Gay and Lesbian Task Force (NGLTF) is the largest organization representing the movement.
6. Several explanations for the origin of sexual orientation have been proposed, including biological explanations, social learning explanations, social-psychological explanations, and psychoanalytic explanations.
7. Developing a gay identity may be viewed as a process (e.g. Troiden's 4-stage process). An important aspect of developing a gay identity is "coming out"—the sequence of events through which individuals recognize their homosexual or bisexual orientation and disclose it to others (family, friends, spouse, children, employer). Given the negative attitudes toward homosexuality in our society, it may be difficult for homosexual and bisexual individuals to develop a positive self-concept. The gay subculture plays an important role in the lives of gay women and men.
8. Unlike heterosexual couples who receive social support for long-term relationships, homosexual couples receive little social support. Lack of social support contributes to difficulty that some homosexual individuals have in maintaining committed relationships.
9. HIV infection remains one of the most threatening STDs for male homosexuals and bisexuals. Some research suggests that gay men are increasing "safer sex" practices to reduce the risk of HIV transmission. However, high risk behaviors are still prevalent within some African-American and Latin communities as well as in some smaller cities.
10. Most gay individuals do not want to be heterosexual. However, some homosexual and bisexual individuals experience distress about their sexual orientation; this is referred to as ego-dystonic homosexuality. Some therapists believe it is appropriate to help homosexuals who are distressed about their sexual orientation to change their sexual orientation (conversion or reversion therapy). However, other therapists believe that ego-dystonic homosexuality is caused by society's antigay attitudes and the social pressure to live a heterosexual life-style. From this perspective, it is unethical for a therapist to help a gay person live a heterosexual life-style because agreeing to do so confirms to the gay person that something is wrong with homosexuality.

KEY TERMS

sexual orientation
homosexuality
heterosexuality
homoeroticism
heteroeroticism
bisexuality
lesbian
lesbian-feminism
homophobia
heterosexism
domestic partnerships
coming out
conversion therapy
reversion therapy
ego-dystonic homosexuality

REFERENCES

Adelman, M. (1990). Stigma, gay lifestyles, and adjustment to aging: A study of later-life gay men and lesbians. *Journal of Homosexuality, 20,* 7–32.

American Psychiatric Association. (1987). *Diagnostic and Statistical Manual of Mental Disorders, Third Edition, Revised.* Washington, DC: Author.

A victory for gay rights. (1991, December 30). *Time,* p. 25.

Bailey, J. M., & Pillard, R. C. (1991). A genetic study of male sexual orientation. *Archives of General Psychiatry, 48,* 1089–1096.

Beissert, W. (1989, July 7). Gay family 'family' too, court rules. *USA Today,* p. 1.

Bell, A. P., & Weinberg, M. S. (1978). *Homosexualities: A study of diversity among men and women.* New York: Simon and Schuster.

Bell, A. P., Weinberg, M. S., & Hammersmith, S. K. (1981). *Sexual preference: Its development in men and women: Statistical appendix.* Bloomington: Indiana University Press.

Berger, R. M. (1990). Men together: Understanding the gay couple. *Journal of Homosexuality, 19,* 31–49.

Berkey, B. R., Perelman-Hall, T., & Kurdek, L. (1990). The Multidimensional Scale of Sexuality. *Journal of Homosexuality, 19,* 67–87.

Berrill, K. T. (1990). Anti-gay violence and victimization in the United States: An overview. *Journal of Interpersonal Violence, 5,* 274–294

Berrill, K. T., Herek, G. M. (1990b). Violence against lesbians and gay men: An introduction. *Journal of Interpersonal Violence, 5,* 269–273.

Berrill, K. T., & Herek, G. M. (1990a). Primary and secondary victimization in anti-gay hate crimes: Official response and public policy. *Journal of Interpersonal Violence, 5,* 401–413.

Blumenfeld, W. J., Raymond, D. (1989). *Looking at gay and lesbian life.* Boston: Beacon Press.

Boswell, J. (1980). *Christianity, social tolerance and homosexuality.* Chicago: University of Chicago Press.

Boswell, J. (1989). Homosexuality and religious life: A historical approach. In J. Gramick (Ed.), *Homosexuality and the priesthood and the religious life* (pp. 3–20). New York: Crossroad.

Boxer, A. M., & Cohler, B. J. (1989). The life course of gay and lesbian youth: An immodest proposal for the study of gay lives. *Journal of Homosexuality, 17,* 315–355.

Bozett, F. W. (1989). Gay fathers: A review of the literature. *Journal of Homosexuality, 18,* 137–162.

Burch, B. (1987). Barriers to intimacy: Conflicts over power, dependency, and nurturing in lesbian relationships. In Boston Lesbian Psychologies Collective (Ed.), *Lesbian psychologies: Explorations and challenges* (pp. 126–141). Chicago: University of Illinois Press.

Cass, V. C. (1984). Homosexual identity formation: Testing a theoretical model. *Journal of Sex Research, 20,* 143–167.

Cohn, B. (1992, Sept. 14). Discrmination: the limits of the law. *Newsweek,* pp. 38–39.

Coleman, E. M., Hoon, P. W., & Hoon, E. F. (1983). Arousability and sexual satisfaction in lesbian and heterosexual women. *Journal of Sex Research, 19,* 58–73.

Committee on Lesbian and Gay Concerns. (1991). Avoiding heterosexual bias in language. *American Psychologist, 46,* 973–974.

Connell, R. W., & Kippax, S. (1990). Sexuality in the AIDS crisis: Patterns of pleasure and practice in an Australian sample of gay and bisexual men. *Journal of Sex Research, 27,* 167–198.

Cooper, A. (1989). No longer invisible: Gay and lesbian Jews build a movement. *Journal of Homosexuality, 18,* 83–94.

Corbett, S. L., & Morgan, K. D. (1983). The process of lesbian identification. *Free Inquiry in Creative Sociology, 11,* 81–83.

Davidson, A. G. (1991). Looking for love in the age of AIDS: The language of gay personals, 1978–1988. *Journal of Sex Research, 28,* 125–137.

Davison, G. C. (1991). Constructionism and morality in therapy for homosexuality. In J. C. Gonsiorek and J. D. Weinrich (Eds.), *Homosexuality: Research implications for public policy* (pp. 137–198). Newbury Park, CA: Sage.

DeCecco, J. P. (1987). Homosexuality's brief recovery: from sickness to health and back again. *The Journal of Sex Research, 23,* 106–129.

Diamant, L. (1987). The therapies. In L. Diamant (Ed.) *Male and female homosexuality: Psychological approaches.* New York: Hemisphere.

DiLapi, E. M. (1989). Lesbian mothers and the motherhood hierarchy. *Journal of Homosexuality, 18,* 101–121.

Doell, R. (1990). Comments on John Money's 1988 *Gay, straight, and in-between: The sexology of erotic orientation. Journal of Homosexuality, 19,* 121–125.

Doll, L. S., Petersen, L. R., White, C. R., Johnson, E. S., Ward, J. W., & the Blood Donor Study Group. (1992). Homosexually and nonhomosexually identified men: A behavioral comparison. *Journal of Sex Research, 29,* 1–14.

Ellis, L., & Ames, M. A. (1987). Neurohormonal functioning and sexual orientation: A theory of homosexuality-heterosexuality. *Psychological Bulletin, 101,* 233–258.

Ernulf, K. E., Innala, S. M., & Whitam, F. L. (1989). Biological explanation, psychological explanation, and tolerance of homosexuals: A cross-national analysis of beliefs and attitudes. *Psychological Reports, 65,* 1003–1010.

Esterberg, K. G. (1990). From illness to action: Conceptions of homosexuality as illness in *The Ladder,* 1956–1965. *Journal of Sex Research, 27,* 65–80.

Etringer, B. D., Hillerbrand, E., & Hetherington, C. (1990). The influence of sexual orientation on career decision-making: A research note. *Journal of Homosexuality, 19,* 103–111.

Faderman, L. (1985). The 'new gay' lesbians. *Journal of Homosexuality, 10,* 85–95.

Fairchild, B., & Hayward, N. (1979). *Now that you know: What every parent should know about homosexuality.* New York: Harcourt Brace Jovanovich.

Falk, P. J. (1989). Lesbian mothers: Psychosocial assumptions in family law. *American Psychologist, 44,* 941–947.

Fay, R. E., Turner, C. F., Klassen, A. D., & Gagnon, J. H. (1989). Prevalence and patterns of same-gender sexual contact among men. *Science, 243,* 338–348.

Ferguson, K. D., & Finkler, D. C. (1978). An involvement and overtness measure for lesbians: Its development and relation to anxiety and social zeitgeist. *Archives of Sexual Behavior, 7,* 211–227.

Ficarrotto, T. J. (1990). Racism, sexism, and erotophobia: Attitudes of heterosexuals toward homosexuals. *Journal of Homosexuality, 19,* 111–116.

Finn, P., & McNeil, T. (1987, October 7). *The response of the criminal justice system to bias crime: An exploratory review.* Contract report submitted to the National Institute of Justice, U.S. Department of Justice.

Freedman, M. (1989). Homosexuals contribute to society. In L. Orr (Ed.), *Sexual values: Opposing viewpoints* (pp. 75–78). San Diego, CA: Greenhaven Press, Inc.

Fullilove, R. E. (1988). Minorities and AIDS: A review of recent publications. *Multicultural Inquiry and Research on AIDS, 2*(1), 3–5.

Garai, J. E. (1987). The humanistic outlook. In L. Diamant (Ed.), *Male and female homosexuality: Psychological approaches* (pp. 261–269). New York: Hemisphere.

Garnets, L., Herek, G. M., & Levy, B. (1990). Violence and victimization of lesbians and gay men: Mental health consequences. *Journal of Interpersonal Violence, 5,* 366–383.

Gay teenagers and suicide. (1989). *Youth Suicide National Report.* (pp. 16–32).

Gelman, D., & Foote, D. (1992, February 24). Born or bred. *Newsweek,* pp. 46–53. Also see Marcia Barinaga's article, "Is Homosexuality Biological?" in *Science, 253,* 956–957, which details LeVay's study.

Gibbs, N. (1991, August 19). Marching out of the closet." *Time,* pp. 14–16.

Gladue, B. A. (1987). Psychobiological contributions. In L. Diamant (Ed.), *Male and female homosexuality: Psychological approaches* (pp. 129–153). New York: Hemisphere.

Golden, C. (1987). Diversity and variability in women's sexual identities. In Boston Lesbian Psychologies Collective (Ed.), *Lesbian psychologies: Explorations and challenges* (pp. 18–34). Chicago: University of Illinois Press.

Green, R. (1987). *The "sissy boy syndrome" and the development of homosexuality.* New Haven: Yale University Press.

Grimes, B. (1991). *Religious Society of Friends: Inclusive minutes on marriage.* Sumneytown, PA: Friends for Lesbian and Gay Concerns.

Haaga, D. A. F. (1991). Homophobia. *Journal of Social Behavior and Personality, 6,* 171–174.

Hart, J. (1984). Therapeutic implications of viewing sexual identity in terms of essentialist and constructionist theories. *Journal of Homosexuality, 9,* 39–51.

Harry, J. (1990). A probability sample of gay males. *Journal of Homosexuality, 19,* 89–104.

Hays, D., & Samuels, A. (1989). Heterosexual women's perceptions of their marriages to bisexual or homosexual men. *Journal of Homosexuality, 19,* 81–100.

Herek, G. M. (1990a). The context of anti-gay violence: Notes on cultural and psychological heterosexism. *Journal of Interpersonal Violence, 5,* 316–333.

Herek, G. M. (1990b). Gay people and government security clearances. *American Psychologist, 45,* 1035–1042.

Herek, G. M. (1989). Hate crimes against lesbians and gay men. *American Psychologist, 44,* 948–955.

Heron, A. (Ed.). (1983). *One teenager in ten.* Boston: Alyson.

High court rules for gay soldier. (1990, November 5). *The Daily Reflector,* Greenville, NC, p. A10.

Homosexual Families and the Law. (1989, July 17). *Newsweek,* p. 48.

Isaacson, W. (1989, November 20). Should gays have marriage rights? *Time,* pp. 101–102.

Isay, R. A. (1990). Psychoanalytic theory and the therapy of gay men. In D. P. McWhirter, S.A. Sanders, J.M. Reinish (Eds.), *Homosexuality/heterosexuality: Concepts of sexual orientation* (pp. 283–303). New York: Oxford University Press.

Jackson, P. A. (1989). *Male homosexuality in Thailand: An interpretation of contemporary Thai sources.* Elmhurst, NY, & Amsterdam: Global Academic.

Jenks, R. J., & Newman, J. H. (1991). Attitudes and perceptions of gay males. *Journal of Psychology and Human Sexuality, 4,* 61–72.

Juran, S. (1991). Sexual behavior changes among heterosexual, lesbian and gay bar patrons as assessed by questionnaire over an 18-month period. *Journal of Psychology and Human Sexuality, 4,* 111–121.

Kallman, F. J. (1952). Comparative twin study in the genetic aspects of male homosexuality. *Journal of Nervous and Mental Disease, 115,* 283–298.

Kinsey, A. C., Pomeroy, W. B., & Martin, C. E. (1948). *Sexual behavior in the human male.* Philadelphia: W. B. Saunders.

Kinsey, A. C., Pomeroy, W. B., Martin, C. E. & Gebhard, P. H. (1953). *Sexual behavior in the human female.* Philadelphia: W. B. Saunders.

Kite, M. E. (1985). Sex differences in attitudes toward homosexuals: A meta-analytic review. In J. P. DeCecco (Ed.), *Bashers, baiters & bigots: Homophobia in American society* (pp. 69–81). New York: Harrington Park Press.

Kitzinger, C. (1987). *The social construction of lesbianism.* Newbury Park, CA: Sage.

Klassen, A. D., Williams, C. J., & Levitt, E. E. (1989). *Sex and morality in the United States.* Middletown, CT: Weselyan University Press.

Klein, F. (1978). *The bisexual option.* New York: Arbor House.

Klein, F. (1985). Sexual orientation: A multi-variable dynamic process. *Journal of Homosexuality, 11,* 35–49.

LeVay, S. (1991). News and comment. *Science, 253,* 956–957.

Lever, J., Kanouse, D. E., Rogers, W. H., Carson, S., & Hertz, R. Behavior patterns and sexual identity of bisexual males. (1992). *The Journal of Sex Research, 29,* 141–167.

Martin, H. P. (1991). The coming-out process for homosexuals. *Hospital and Community Psychiatry, 42,* 158.

Masters, W. H., & Johnson, V. E. (1979). *Homosexuality in perspective.* Boston: Little, Brown.

McNaught, B. (1983). Overcoming self-hate through education. In G. Albee, S. Gordon, & H. Leitenberg (Eds). *Promoting sexual responsibility and preventing sexual problems* (pp. 133–145). Hanover, NH: University Press of New England.

McWhirter, D. P., & Mattison, A. M. (1984). *The male couple: How relationships develop.* Englewood Cliffs, NJ: Prentice-Hall.

Miranda, J., & Storms, M. (1989). Psychological adjustment of lesbians and gay men. *Journal of Counseling and Development, 68,* 41–45.

Money, J. (1988). *Gay, straight, and in-between: The sexology of erotic orientation.* New York: Oxford University Press.

Money, J. (1987). Sin, sickness, or status? Homosexual gender identity and psychoneuroendocrinology. *American Psychologist, 42,* 384–399.

National Survey Results of Gay Couples in Long-Lasting Relationships. (1990, May/June). *Partners: Newsletter for Gay and Lesbian Couples,* pp. 1–16. (Available from Stevie Bryant & Demian, Box 9685, Seattle, WA 98109.)

Nichols, M. (1987). Lesbian sexuality: Issues and developing theory. In Boston Lesbian Psychologies Collective (Ed.), *Lesbian psychologies: Explorations and challenges* (pp. 97–125). Chicago: University of Illinois Press.

Nugent, R., & Gramick, J. (1989). Homosexuality: Protestant, Catholic, and Jewish issues: A fishbone tale. *Journal of Homosexuality, 18,* 7–46.

Parker, R. G., and Carballo, M. (1990). Qualitative research on homosexual and bisexual behavior relevant to HIV/AIDS. *Journal of Sex Research, 27,* 497–525.

Pope, M., & Schulz, R. (1990). Sexual attitudes and behavior in midlife and aging homosexual males. *Journal of Homosexuality, 20,* 169–177.

Rich, A. (1989). Compulsory heterosexuality and lesbian existence. In L. Richardson and V. Taylor (Eds.), *Feminist frontiers II* (pp. 120–141). New York: Random House.

Robinson, B. E., Walters, L. H., & Skeen, P. (1989). Response of parents to learning that their child is homosexual and concern over AIDS: A national study. *Journal of Homosexuality, 18,* 59–80.

Ross, M. W. (1989). Gay youth in four cultures: A comparative study. *Journal of Homosexuality, 17,* 299–314.

Ross, M. W. (1987). A theory of normal homosexuality. In L. Diamant (Ed.), *Male and female homosexuality—psychological approaches* (pp. 237–259). New York: Hemisphere.

Ruefli, T., Yu, O. & Barton, J. (1992). Sexual risktaking in smaller cities: The case of Buffalo, New York. *The Journal of Sex Research, 29,* 95–108.

Savin-Williams, R. C. (1989). Coming out to parents and self-esteem among gay and lesbian youths. *Journal of Homosexuality, 18,* 1–35.

Scanzoni, L. & Mollenkott, V. R. (1978). *Is the Homosexual My Neighbor? Another Christian View.* San Francisco: Harper and Row.

Schecter, M. T., Craib, K. J. P., Willoughby, B., Douglas, B., McLeod, W. A., Maynard, M., Constance, P., & O'Shaughnessy, M. (1988). Patterns of sexual behavior and condom use in a cohort of homosexual men. *American Journal of Public Health, 78,* 1535–1538.

Sigelman, C. K., Howell, J. L., Cornell, D. P., Cutright, J. D., & Dewey, J. C. (1991). Courtesy stigma: The social implications of associating with a gay person. *Journal of Social Psychology, 131,* 45–56.

Silverstein, C. (1984). The ethical and moral implications of sexual classification: A commentary. *Journal of Homosexuality, 9,* 29–38.

Special Committee on Human Sexuality. (1991). *Keeping body and soul together: Sexuality, spirituality, and social justice.* Baltimore: Presbyterian Church (USA).

Smith, T. W. (1991). Adult sexual behavior in 1989: Number of partners, frequency of intercourse and risk of AIDS, *Family Planning Perspectives, 23,* 102–107.

St. Lawrence, J. S., Husfeldt, B. A., Kelly, J. A., Hood, H. V., & Smith, S., Jr. (1990). The stigma of AIDS: Fear of disease and prejudice toward gay men. *Journal of Homosexuality, 19,* 85–101.

Strommen, E. F. (1989). You're a what?: Family member reactions to the disclosure of homosexuality. *Journal of Homosexuality, 18,* 37–58.

Sultan, F. E., Elsner, D. M., & Smith, J. (1987). Ego-dystonic homosexuality and treatment alternatives. In L. Diamant (Ed.), *Male and female homosexuality: Psychological approaches* (pp. 187–197). New York: Hemisphere.

Troiden, R. R. (1989). The formation of homosexual identities. *Journal of Homosexuality, 17,* 43–73.

Uribe, V. & Harbeck, K. M. (1992). Addressing the needs of lesbian, gay, and bisexual youth: The origins of PROJECT 10 and school-based intervention. In K. Harbeck (Ed.)., *Coming out of the classroom closet: Gay and lesbian students, teachers and curricula* (pp. 9–27). New York: The Haworth Press, Inc.

Weeks, J. (1989). *Sex, politics and society* (2nd ed.). New York: Longman.

Weinberg, G. (1973). *Society and the healthy homosexual.* New York: Anchor Books.

Weinrich, J. D. & Williams, W. L. (1991). Strange customs, familiar lives: Homosexualities in other cultures. In J. C. Gonsiorek and J. D. Weinrich (Eds.), *Homosexuality: research implications for public policy* (pp. 44–59). Newbury Park, CA: Sage.

Whitehead, M. M., & Nokes, K. M. (1990). An examination of demographic variables, nurturance, and empathy among homosexual and heterosexual Big Brother/Big Sister volunteers. *Journal of Homosexuality, 19,* 89–101.

Wilson, J. D. (1992, Sept. 14). Gays under fire. *Newsweek,* pp. 35–40.

CHAPTER TWELVE

Sexuality Across the Life Span

Chapter Outline

Sexuality from Infancy through Adolescence
- Infancy
- Childhood
- Adolescence
- **Research Perspective:** Postponing Sexual Involvement: More Than "Just Say 'No' "

Sexuality in Early Adulthood
- Sexuality among Never-Married Adults
- Sexuality among the Married
- Sexuality among the Divorced

Sexuality in the Middle Years
- Definition of Middle Age
- Women in Middle Age
- Men in Middle Age
- **Self-Assessment:** Aging Sexual Knowledge and Attitudes Scale

Sexuality in the Later Years
- Sexual Interest, Activity, and Ability among the Elderly
- Correlation between Past and Present Sexual Behaviors

Choices
- Choose to Have Hormone Replacement Therapy?
- Sexual Choices among the Elderly
- Sexual Choices among the Young in Preparation for the Later Years

Is It True?*

1. Children who play sex games, such as "doctor," are more likely to have numerous sex partners and to have more sexual dysfunctions as adults than children who do not play sex games.

2. Adolescents who have had intercourse feel that the best age for first intercourse is older than the age at which they experienced it.

3. Over 90% of most spouses report that they have been monogamous in the last 12 months.

4. Men aged 90 to 99 report having intercourse once a year.

5. The best insurance for continued sexual activity in later years appears to be frequent sexual activity in the earlier years.

*1 = F, 2 = T, 3 = T, 4 = T, 5 = T

In youth we learn, in age we understand.

Marie Ebner von Eschenbach

Geraldo Rivera (1991) detailed in his book, *Exposing Myself,* numerous sexual exploits with celebrity women. On his own television talk show, Rivera discussed his book as well as the relationship with his third wife, CeeCe. His message to the audience and to his wife was that he was once an adolescent who treated sex as a sport and treated women as objects. He reported incessant infidelity in his previous marriages. But, he said, "I became a man when I made a commitment to myself and to CeeCe (on our wedding day) that I would be faithful to her. I have been faithful to my decision." Other celebrities have reported changes in their sexuality as they moved into adulthood. Robin Williams noted, "Am I going to run around now? No. I am at peace with myself. It's something like, 'God, I don't want to blow this. This is wonderful stuff' " (Krefft, 1992, p. 65).

A person's sexuality varies depending on whether the person is a child, an adolescent, an adult, or a senior citizen. At each stage, his or her sexuality is likely to involve different emotions, motivations, and patterns of expression. In this chapter, we examine sexuality across the life span and look at some of the choices with which we are confronted throughout the life course.

Sexuality from Infancy Through Adolescence

A life cycle view of sexuality must necessarily emphasize early experiences as important influences in subsequent development.

Infancy

Infancy is defined as the first year of life following birth. Just as infants are born with digestive and respiratory systems, they are born with a sexual response system that begins to function very early in life. At birth, a boy is often born with an erection and a girl may "show a vaginal discharge heavy enough to crust over the vaginal opening. This is the infantile equivalent to the lubricating fluid that will eventually be produced whenever she is sexually aroused" (Calderone & Johnson, 1989, p. 16).

In regard to sexuality, lack of bonding and learning to trust in the formative years may translate into an inability to establish an intimate physical and emotional relationship as an adult. In addition, shame, anxiety, depression, denial, isolation, and substance abuse are associated with inadequate trust in the early years (Goff, 1990).

In the wake of frightening reports of child sexual abuse in daycare centers, Finkelhor, Williams, and Burns (1988) attempted to reassure parents that "with a few exceptions, day-care facilities are not inherently high-risk locales for children" (p. 260). To help put the risk of day-care abuse in perspective, they noted that compared to perhaps 1,300 reported cases of day-care abuse in 1985, there were nearly 100,000 children victimized by family members. "The risk of abuse is not sufficient reason to avoid day care in general or to justify parents' withdrawal from the labor force or other important activities that require them to rely on day care" (p. 260). They recommended that parents be involved in their child's day-care facility, show interest in its activities, and be sensitive to their child's reactions.

Consistent with Geraldo and Robin Williams, Magic Johnson noted how his sexual values and behavior have changed across time.

The sexual response system functions even prior to birth, and sexual behavior occurs in infancy. Observers of infants and small children in a nursery reported that at about six to seven months of age boys begin genital play, and girls at 10 or 11 months (Bancroft, 1989). Infants are

> . . . responsive to unconditioned erotic stimuli in the form of genital touch . . . Judging by observation of infantile masturbation, it appears that infants are aroused by such stimulation, they experience positive affective responses (e.g., joy) to this stimulation, and they appear to engage in preparatory sexual behavior (e.g., tugging off diaper) in order to self-stimulate (an overt sexual behavior). (Fisher, 1986, p. 155)

Among boys, obvious masturbation is established at about 15-16 months of age. Girls tend to be more intermittent in genital play and begin to stimulate themselves less directly, such as through rocking or thigh pressure. In boys and girls as young as six months, masturbation to the point of obvious orgasm has been observed (Bancroft, 1989).

Since sexual pleasure is an unconditioned positive stimulus, infants are capable of learning associations via classical conditioning processes. As such, infants may learn to associate sexual pleasure with a particular cloth bunny, hence the beginning of a fetish, or they may learn the positive or negative emotions associated with their bodies. In regard to the latter, parents who slap their infants for touching their own body parts and label such behaviors as "dirty" may teach their children to associate anxiety and guilt with sexuality.

As noted above, it is normal for babies to find pleasure in their bodies. Calderone and Johnson (1989) emphasize that it is an essential part of the baby's growth and development, and Leight (1990) stressed the importance of parents not overreacting.

Childhood

Childhood comprises the time from age one to 12 and involves physical, cognitive, and social development. As the child moves through this period, he or she becomes more physically autonomous, capable of more complex thought processes, and develops increased skill in interacting with others and the environment.

As with infants, children experiment with their own bodies as sources of physical pleasure. The observations of two family members provide examples (Reinisch, 1990):

> My niece's son is 18 months old and has discovered that putting his hand in his diaper and touching his penis is the way to go. (p. 250)

> Our four-year-old daughter has a habit we've never seen in other children. Since she was two, her favorite position when watching TV or playing is to lie on her belly with a cushion between her legs and sway back and forth. (p. 250)

Children are also interested in discovering the bodies of others. This usually begins with siblings or friends and takes place as early as two or three but more often between four and five (Reinisch, 1990). A favorite game played by children is "doctor." The game, which may be played between boys, between girls, or between boys and girls, involves one child assuming the role of the patient and the other the role of the doctor. The patient undresses and the doctor examines the patient both visually and by touching his or her body, including the genitals. Two university students recalled playing doctor as children:

NATIONAL DATA: Kinsey and his associates (1948, 1953) observed that sex play between children is not uncommon: 45% of the women and 57% of the men in their sample reported sexual play experiences with other children by age 12.

> I remember playing doctor when I was really small. There was a girl I knew down the street when I lived in California. She was the only one I knew on the block. All the other kids were weird and she was the only one my parents let me play with. It was in her bedroom. Like I'd be the surgeon and she'd be the patient.

> Doctor was the first sex game that I actually ever played. I was about five. A girl used to come over to my house with her little brother who was about two or so. We just laid there and she explored our genitals. (Markov, 1991, p. 2)

If between children of the same age, the effect of such sex play is negligible. A team of researchers (Leitenberg, Greenwald, & Tarran, 1989) assessed the degree to which 433 college students engaged in preadolescent (prior to age 13) sex play and the effect such sexual experiences had on the incidence of premarital intercourse, age at first intercourse, number of intercourse partners, sexual satisfaction, sexual arousal, and sexual dysfunction. There was no significant association between early sex play and any of the dependent variables studied. In regard to what parents might say when they discover such sex play, Calderone and Johnson (1989) recommended that they might use it as an opportunity to provide information to children. "It is interesting to find out how other people's bodies look, isn't it?" is a phrase parents might initially use to encourage children to talk about what they are curious about (p. 139).

Childhood sexual abuse will be discussed in Chapter 19, Abuses of Sexuality. Here, we will just comment that estimates of child sexual abuse range from 8% to 38% of girls and 3% to 11% of boys (Salter, 1988), depending on research methods, definitions of abuse and the population studied. While abuses are often perpetrated by adults, recent attention has also been paid to adolescents and other children as abusers (Johnson, 1989; Okami, 1992).

Adolescence

Researchers disagree over when **adolescence** begins and ends. Some suggest that it begins at age 12 and ends at age 22. This time is further broken down to refer to different categories of adolescence: early adolescence (12 to 15), middle adolescence (15 to 18), and late adolescence (18 to 22). Other researchers divide adolescence into two major stages:

> The first stretches from the onset of puberty to about ages 14 through 16; psychologically it is characterized by the push for independence from parents and attempts to resolve conflicts between the continuing need for childish dependence and the desire for a separate identity.

The bodies and interests of young children are sometimes asexual in contrast to the budding sexuality of adolescents.

> The second stage is marked by the search for a mature identity, the quest for a mate, and the exploration of different sets of values and of occupational and other life goals. (Chilman, 1989, pp. 3–4)

As these stages suggest, numerous changes occur in adolescence. The most noticeable to the adolescent are the physical changes.

Physical Changes The adolescent's body is undergoing rapid physiological and anatomical change. The very term "puberty" comes from the Latin *pubescere,* which means to be covered with hair. Pubic hair and underarm hair in young girls and pubic hair and facial hair in young boys are evidence that the hypothalamus is triggering the pituitary gland to release gonadotropins into the bloodstream. These are hormones that cause the testes in the male to increase testosterone production and cause the ovaries in the female to increase estrogen production.

Further physical changes in adolescence include the development of **secondary sex characteristics,** such as breasts in the female and a deepened voice in the male. A growth spurt also ensues, with girls preceding boys by about two years. The growth spurt is characterized by girls becoming taller than boys their same age. Genitals of the respective sexes also enlarge—the penis and testes in the male and the labia in the female.

Internally, the prostate gland and seminal vesicles begin to function to make it possible for the young adolescent male to ejaculate (sperm is present in the ejaculate at about age 14). First ejaculation usually occurs around age 13 or 14 but is variable.

Girls are experiencing their own internal changes. The uterus, cervix, and vaginal walls respond to hormone changes to produce the first menstruation, or menarche. This usually occurs between the ages of 12 and 13, but the timing is highly variable. Age of first menstruation and sexual maturity are important because they are associated with earlier dating and coital onset (Phinney, Jensen, Olsen, & Cundick, 1990).

Adolescent males report various reactions to their changing bodies (Bell, 1987). Regarding erections:

> I get a hard-on in drama class almost every time I have to go up onstage. I can never tell if they are laughing at my performance or at my bulging cock. (p. 14)

Regarding first ejaculation:

> I heard everyone talking about coming and jacking off, and at fifteen I hadn't experienced it yet. It was real mysterious to me. I would try and try, masturbating every night, and even though it felt good, it didn't bring results. Finally one night, bang. It happened. (p. 15)

Regarding first wet dream:

> I was about thirteen. I felt like I had this total sexual experience in my dream and I woke up and thought, Wow, did this really happen or not? It blew my mind it felt so real. After a second I realized my pajamas were wet. I sort of knew what it had to be, but still I was a little surprised. (p. 16)

Adolescent females are also responding to the physical changes in their bodies (Bell, 1987).

Regarding pubic hair:

> Me and my friends (age eleven) go swimming at the center every week. In the shower there aren't any doors, so we kind of check each other out. Well, a couple of weeks ago, Amy showed me these hairs that were starting to grow down there, and I thought, Oh my God, that isn't going to happen to me, is it? Then I examined myself closer and I had three hairs there too. Three little dark hairs. (p. 25)

Regarding vaginal awareness

> I figure it's a part of my body, just like any other part, except it's not right out there like your boobs are. Anyway, I sure as hell don't want someone else playing with it if I don't know what it is myself. (p. 26)

Regarding breast development:

> My mom and I are really close, and when I first started getting breasts she took me out to celebrate. It was around my tenth birthday, and I remember feeling very grown-up about it. (p. 21)
>
> When my breasts first started growing I used to wear really supertight shirts—to flatten me. Then I'd wear another shirt over that because I was really self-conscious. I was only in third grade and every other girl in the class was flat as a board. (p. 21)

A team of researchers (Duncan, Ritter, Dornbusch, Gross, & Carlsmith, 1990) reviewed the literature on pubertal timing and body image and found that early maturation in males is associated with being rated as more popular, relaxed, good-natured, and poised. However, data on girls have been inconsistent; some studies show that early maturing girls enjoy greater prestige and self-confidence, while others show that they are more self-conscious and less popular.

Duncan et al. (1990) also studied the effect of weight gain on self-image in adolescence. Females regard it as getting fat, whereas males view it as becoming more muscular. Data on over 5,000 adolescents revealed that 69% of the early maturing girls and only 27% of the late maturers wanted to be thinner. In contrast, most early maturing males (67%) were satisfied with their weight (Duncan et al., 1990).

Psychological Changes Concomitant with physical changes during adolescence are psychological changes. Psychological changes include moving from a state of childish dependence to a state of relative independence, resolving sexual identity issues, and feeling secure that one is normal. The quintessential example of the dilemma adolescents experience as they move from childhood to adulthood is that of an adolescent who had a bottle of blow bubbles and a bottle of perfume on her dresser in her bedroom. Adolescents often want the freedom of adults but still have the dependency of children.

Resolving sexual identity issues means becoming comfortable with one's sexual orientation. While we explored this issue in greater detail in Chapter 11 on sexual orientation, it is important to emphasize here the additional burden homosexual adolescents feel when they discover that they are not part of the heterosexual mainstream (Mercier & Berger, 1989).

Adolescents want to feel that they are normal (Campbell & Campbell, 1990). Part of this quest is to be normal in their sexual thoughts, feelings, and behaviors. Forty percent of 61 undergraduate men reported that they had "concerns about the normalcy of sexual thoughts, feelings, or behaviors" (Metz & Seifert, 1990, p. 82).

CONSIDERATION: While concerns about normalcy are problematic, they are not traumatic. Neither are the teen years when considered as a whole. In a study of 335 young adolescents randomly selected from two suburban school districts, the author concluded, "The vast majority of early teens we studied were trouble-free or had only intermittent problems. Only 15 percent were plagued by trouble and turmoil" (Petersen, 1987, p. 33).

So far, we have discussed the physical and psychological changes (dependence to independence, sexual identity, desire to be normal) adolescents experience. Another significant occurrence during adolescence is the emerging importance of peers over parents in regard to language, dress, drugs, and sexual behavior. Researchers using data from the Carolina Population Center's Adolescent Sexuality Project observed that adolescents were more likely to engage in mildly deviant behavior (premarital intercourse, drinking, smoking, cheating) if their best friend of the same sex did (Rodgers & Rowe, 1990). In addition, peers also become the major source of information about sex during adolescence (Andre, Frevert, & Schuchmann, 1989).

New Sexual Behaviors In addition to the other changes just described, adolescence is a time of sexual unfolding. Sarrel and Sarrel (1979) referred to "unfolding" as a process

> by which a person becomes aware of himself or herself as a sexual being, a male or female, who relates to oneself and others, sexually, in some characteristic ways. When unfolding is successful the person becomes capable of satisfying sexual and psychological intimacy with another (nonfamily) person (or persons). (p. 19)

The first kiss and first intercourse are primary experiences involved in the process of sexual unfolding. Kissing may occur in the context of a "sex game" (Markov, 1991). Such games are socially structured contexts for physical and sexual exploration. An example of a kissing game is spin-the-bottle, which is played by young adolescents at mixed-sex parties. There are three versions:

Adolescence is a time to become aware of one's sexuality and relationships with others.

> In the first version, one member of the group is chosen as "it" and leaves the room. The remaining members gather in a circle and spin the bottle. Whomever the neck of the bottle points to when it stops spinning is to join the other person outside the room and "kiss." In the second version, the spinner is one of the kissing partners and the person the bottle stops spinning on is the other. They both leave the room and "kiss." In the third version, there are two circles, one of boys and one of girls. The bottle is spun twice so as to select the kissing partners. (Markov, 1991, p. 4)

As adolescence continues, mixed-sex group interactions give way to encounters between individuals in dating contexts. By age 16, over 85% of adolescents report having had their first date (Thornton, 1990).

In his probability sample of adolescents, Thornton (1990) observed that the younger individuals were at the time they began to date, the more likely they were to develop steady dating relationships and to have intercourse. Table 12.1 reflects the age at which these adolescents reported having their first intercourse experience. These data reveal that men are more likely to report having intercourse earlier than women.

NATIONAL DATA: Based on data from the National Research Council (1987), by age 20, 83% of males and 74% of females report that they are "sexually active."

CONSIDERATION: The age at which adolescents report having had their first intercourse experience is not the age they feel is the "best" age to have done so. Out of 3,500 junior and high school students, 83% of the sexually experienced adolescents said that the best age for first intercourse is older than the age at which they experienced it (Zabin, Hirsch, Smith, & Hardy, 1984).

CONSIDERATION: Age at first intercourse is associated with the number of subsequent sexual partners and the risk for contracting sexually transmissible diseases. The earlier in life a person has intercourse, the more sexual partners that person is likely to have and the greater the risk for contracting sexually transmissible diseases ("Premarital Sexual Experience," 1991).

TABLE 12.1 Age at First Intercourse

Age at First Intercourse	Male $N = 461$	Female $N = 421$
15 or Younger	21.7%	8.5%
16	15.4	10.7
17	17.0	18.6
18	9.3	15.7
Never	36.7	46.5

Source: Thornton, (1990). The courtship process and adolescent sexuality. *Journal of Family Issues, 11,* 247. Used by permission.

Drug use is associated with earlier first intercourse, and the association is stronger for adolescent girls than boys. The likelihood that a female teenager would have intercourse before age 16 was 3.4 times higher if she was a marijuana user; the likelihood that a male teenager would have intercourse before age 16 was 2.7 times higher if he was a marijuana user. The more frequent the substance abuse, the earlier the sexual activity (Mott & Haurin, 1988). Use of cigarettes and alcohol are also associated with earlier sex (Rosenbaum & Kandel, 1990). While these are correlational data only, they suggest that drug use may create a context for deciding to have intercourse.

One of the risks of adolescent sexual activity is that

> it can become the vehicle for expressing or satisfying emotional and interpersonal needs which have little or nothing to do with sex . . . the teenagers may be looking for affection, trying to bolster self-esteem, ease loneliness, confirm masculinity or femininity, escape boredom, or vent anger. (White & DeBlassie, 1992, p. 189)

Some individuals who are sexually active become interested in information about contraception, HIV, and other STDs.

Sexual activity may provide a "quick fix" for gratifying some uncomfortable feelings, but not satisfy these needs. Despite the claim of some adolescents that sexual activity is an expression of their independence, it may instead be a manifestation of dependence (White & DeBlassie, 1992).

Reactions to first intercourse vary. Weis (1983) studied the emotional reactions to first intercourse among women and found that one-third experienced positive emotions (love, joy), one-third experienced negative emotions (guilt, anxiety), and one-third reported neither positive nor negative reactions. The reactions of this latter group she labeled as the "Peggy Lee Syndrome—Is that all there is?" (One of Peggy Lee's songs, which made the singer famous in the 1950s, was *"Is That All There Is?"*)

CONSIDERATION: Women who reported a positive first intercourse experience also tended to report: 1) extensive prior experience with dating, masturbation, and noncoital sexual behaviors (petting/oral sex), 2) partners who loved them, who were gentle/considerate/patient, 3) permissive sexual attitudes, and 4) having intercourse in a private setting with no fear of discovery or interruption (Weis, 1983).

Linn (1991) observed a basic difference between the way adolescent girls and boys experience intercourse. She studied 100 Israeli adolescents aged 16 and 17. One of the female respondents said:

> I do not know how to explain it, but I am certain that the reason males do not make anything of sexual intercourse is the fact that it does not change their personality. However, I can assure you, at least from my experience, that we are changed after this experience. Maybe because we see it as if we lost something of ourselves. And that is why it is so important to us with whom we have sex and what the quality of our relationship with him is. (p. 66)

Intercourse from a young adolescent boy's perspective was very different. "Their emotional reaction was that of pride, achievement, and satisfaction, or fear of poor performance. In their eyes, girls remained for the most part the object rather than the subject of the relationship" (p. 68).

NATIONAL DATA: About three-fifths of adolescent males in a national survey predicted that they would use a condom the next time they had intercourse (Pleck, Sonenstein, & Ku, 1990). Adolescents most likely to use reliable contraception feel good about themselves and have high expectations for their future educational and occupational success (Chilman, 1989).

Retrospective comments from university students reflect a range of first intercourse experiences (see Exhibit 12.1).

Adolescents who decide to become sexually active face choices regarding condom and contraceptive use (see National Data in margin).

The following Research Perspective emphasizes that helping teenagers to develop skills to handle peer and social pressures for early sexual behavior is more effective than sex education programs teaching them to "just say no." Indeed, in a study of a teenage pregnancy prevention program emphasizing abstinence, the "only change shown by the 191 participants but not in the 129 controls is an increase in precoital

EXHIBIT 12.1 First Intercourse Experiences

Students in the authors' classes were asked to describe their first intercourse experience. Although there was no typical description, elements of pain, fear, anxiety, and awkwardness were evident. Some of the various experiences included the following:

> I was 15 and my partner was 16. I had two fears. The first was my fear of getting her pregnant the first time. The second was of "parking" in dark and desolate areas. Therefore, once we decided to have intercourse, we spent a boring evening waiting for my parents to go to sleep so we could move to the station wagon in the driveway.
>
> After near hyperventilation in an attempt to fog the windows (to prevent others from seeing in), we commenced to prepare for the long-awaited event. In recognition of my first fear, I wore four prophylactics. She, out of fear, was not lubricating well, and needless to say, I couldn't feel anything through four layers of latex.
>
> We were able to climax, which I attribute solely to sheer emotional excitement, yet both of us were later able to admit that the experience was disappointing. We knew it could only get better.

> My first intercourse was actually very nice—both physically and emotionally. I dated the same guy for four years in high school, and it wasn't until my senior year when we actually made love. I was nervous and we did not use any contraception, which doubled my nervousness. Also, for years my mother preached, "Nice girls don't." My philosophy is that nice girls do because they are the ones with the steady boyfriends.

> I had been dating this guy for almost a year when we first made love. The first time was not the best. It was quite painful physically, and I couldn't understand how people could find such enjoyment from sex.

> My first time I really felt nothing. I didn't know what to expect. I didn't feel guilty or sad or happy. I wasn't sorry it happened. I was not forced into the situation, and the guy was not in it just for sex because we are still dating.

> My first intercourse experience was a disaster. Both the girl and I were virgins and had no idea what we were doing. Actually, we really didn't have intercourse the first time; she was so tight that I couldn't get inside of her. We gave up after 15 minutes.

> My first intercourse experience was simply terrible. There was no romance involved. He just came like a bull. He was the worst lover, ever. I was very hurt when he left me, but now I'm glad he did.

> My spouse and I waited until we were married to have intercourse. We felt that it would mean something special for us to wait and we are glad that we did. It was a "spiritual high" for both of us.

sexual activity" (Christopher & Roosa, 1990, p. 68). Good communication with parents has also been found to be associated with delaying intercourse and using contraception (Jaccard & Dittus, 1991; Lewis, 1973).

RESEARCH PERSPECTIVE

Postponing Sexual Involvement: More Than "Just Say No"

Many sex educators believe that young teens would be better off delaying sexual intercourse until they are older. Sol Gordon (1990, p. 5), an internationally known educator, explained his view.

> Sex—70 percent of all high school students will have sex before graduation whether we like it or not and whether they like it or not and even though we don't think teenagers should have sex—they are too young, too vulnerable, and too readily available for exploitation. They don't know that the first experience of sex is often grim. Few teenage girls will experience an orgasm the first time and the typical teenage boy will experience his 'orgasm' three days later when he tells the guys about his sexual encounters.

However, Gordon warned against relying on simplistic and ineffectual slogans, such as "Just Say No." One intervention that was developed with consideration given to the complexity and context of initiating sexual intercourse is "Postponing Sexual Involvement: An Education Series for Young People Age 13-15." It was proposed by Marion Howard, the clinical director of the Teen Services Program at Grady Memorial Hospital in Atlanta. Dr. Howard (1983) explained that this program focuses on helping young people build skills to help them handle peer and social pressures for early sexual behavior. Unlike other sex education curricula, this program does not emphasize facts on reproduction or contraception. Nor is it based upon a decision-making model in which students consider alternatives and evaluate possible solutions (often used for older students, as in this textbook). This program is founded upon the explicit value that students should not have sexual intercourse at a young age; the information, exercises, and skill-building efforts are directed toward helping the participants implement the decision not to have sex at a young age.

Program Description

A large-scale implementation of the "Postponing Sexual Involvement" (PSI) series was launched in 24 Atlanta schools' eighth-grade classrooms with funding from the Ford Foundation. The sessions were led by older teenagers, with one male and one female eleventh-or twelfth-grade student presenting each session. The older students serve as role models to "present factual information, identify pressures, role-play responses to pressures, teach assertiveness skills and discuss problem situations" (Howard & McCabe, 1990, p. 22). These sessions were combined with the original sexuality education curriculum, including information about reproduction, family planning, and sexually transmissible diseases, to yield a 10-session program.

Evaluation Results

An evaluation of the program was completed by including questions about sexual behavior within a larger study of health habits of low-income minority eighth- and ninth-graders. The study was conducted through telephone interviews done at the beginning, middle, and end of eighth grade and at the beginning and end of ninth grade. The students were given verbal codes for answering sensitive questions, so that anyone overhearing the conversation would not understand their answers. In addition, medical records were checked for those students who had been seen in the hospital clinics; these checks validated the reports of the students.

Continued

Continued

As the data indicate, PSI had an especially strong effect on girls who had not initiated sexual activity prior to the eighth grade. The inexperienced girls in schools without the program were 15 times more likely than those with the program to begin having sex that year; inexperienced boys were three times as likely. In addition, the program group had fewer pregnancies. Program students who initiated sex were more likely to use a contraceptive, with 73% crediting what they had learned in school for their contraceptive use. However, program students who had already initiated having sex were no more likely to have abstained in the month prior to the follow-up. Overall, the findings were viewed as promising, as 24% of the PSI participants had begun having sex by the end of the ninth grade, compared to 39% of nonprogram students.

The program developers reported that the orientation, scheduling, and transportation of eleventh-and twelfth-grade leaders was very difficult, but their participation has been critical to capture the interest and acceptance of the younger students. Currently, efforts are underway to develop a program aimed at fifth-and sixth-graders, along with a follow-up program for ninth-and tenth-graders.

References

Gordon, S. (1990). Sexuality education in the 1990s. *Health Education, 21,* 4–5.

Howard, M. (March, 1983). Postponing sexual involvement: A new approach. *Siecus Report,* 5–8.

Howard, M., & McCabe, J. B. (1990). Helping teenagers postpone sexual involvement. *Family Planning Perspectives, 22,* 21–26.

Sexuality In Early Adulthood

A number of theorists who have proposed stage models of lifespan development have identified the early to middle adult years as focusing on intimate partnerships. Erikson (1950) conceptualized the developmental crisis of intimacy versus isolation. In her description of adult passages, Sheehy (1976) named crises from the twenties to the forties: "The urge to merge," "the couple knot, the single spot, the rebound," and "switch-40s and the couple." Bancroft (1989, p. 149) defined "marriage (or the establishment of a stable sexual relationship)" as the fourth basic stage of sexual development. However, people do not necessarily follow the maps of popular stage theories. For example, for young women the intimacy developmental focus may precede the identity crisis (Fischer, 1981)—and there is "no right or only time" (Tavris, 1992, p. 38) to experience developmental milestones. Nevertheless, intimate relationships are important in early adulthood.

NATIONAL DATA: Forty-seven percent of U.S. adult men between the ages of 25 and 29 have never been married. Thirty-two percent of the U.S. adult women of similar age have never been married (*Statistical Abstract of the United States: 1992,* Table 48).

Most individuals (93% of young men and 78% of young women) move into adulthood (age 20 and beyond) as never-marrieds, most (90% of both sexes) eventually marry, over half divorce, and most (particularly women—66% by age 75) become widows. As we noted in the last chapter, not all relationships are heterosexual and/or marriage-focused. Sexuality among adults may also be among homosexuals in committed relationships.

Sexuality among Never-Married Adults

One of the basic decisions during young adulthood is whether to remain single. Whether by structure or choice, a considerable proportion of adults remains single into the late 20s (see National Data).

Most Americans no longer regard getting married as necessarily better than remaining single and do not disapprove of those who eschew marriage.

Arland Thornton
Deborah Freedman

NATIONAL DATA: Of never-married men age 25 to 39 from 1982 to 1986, 24.3% reported that they were "very happy," compared to 13.2% of never-married men from 1972 to 1976. Similarly, of never-married women age 25 to 39 from 1982 to 1986, 24.4% reported that they were "very happy," compared to 13.7% of never-married women from 1972 to 1976 (Glenn & Weaver, 1988, p. 319).

One factor contributing to the delay in getting married is the "desire not to let marriage interfere with education and to obtain some work experience before marriage" (Thornton & Freedman, 1982, p. 297). Another reason some people delay involvement in a committed relationship (sometimes indefinitely) is the freedom to become involved with different sexual partners. The person involved in a committed relationship is expected to answer two basic questions when leaving the home ("Where are you going?" "When will you be back?"), which restricts opportunities to become involved in new sexual relationships. The uncommitted keep their options open and report having a variety of sexual partners. Among 79 never-married men enrolled in a human sexuality class, the average number of sexual partners was 13.71; among 193 never-married women enrolled in a human sexuality class, the average number of sexual partners was 8.39 (Knox & Schacht, 1992).

Regardless of the reason individuals do not marry, an increasing percentage report happiness with the single life-style when compared with those who are married (see National Data in margin).

Sexuality among the Married

In spite of the perceived benefits of singlehood, over 90% of both women and men eventually decide to marry. Five million individuals decide to marry every year (*Statistical Abstract of the United States: 1992*).

While sex among the never married is characterized by its forbiddenness, high frequency, and nonexclusivity, marital sex is more likely to be characterized by its social legitimacy, declining frequency, and monogamy.

Social Legitimacy In our society, marital intercourse is the most legitimate form of sexual behavior. Homosexual, premarital, and extramarital intercourse do not enjoy similar societal approval. It is not only OK to have intercourse when married, it is expected. People assume that married couples make love and that something is wrong if they do not.

Declining Frequency As with intercourse in other situations, marital intercourse declines across time. In a study of 100 well-educated, middle-class couples, 59% of those who had been married less than 10 years reported having intercourse more than once a week. In contrast, 20% of those who had been married 20 years or longer reported having intercourse more than once a week (Frank & Anderson, 1989).

Sex in marriage is like a 7-11 store—there is not much variety but it is available at 3:00 A.M.

Carol Lepher

Reasons for declining frequency are employment, children, and satiation. Regarding the impact of employment, one spouse said:

> Exhaustion is a very big problem. I never thought it could happen. When I'm working and running my business, it is totally absorbing and it takes me a long time to decompress at night, by which time Jerry is usually sound asleep! And I guess Jerry, unlike when we first got married, has a lot of responsibility in his position—so it's work that's taking its toll on our sex life! (Greenblat, 1983, p. 296)

Children also decrease the frequency of intercourse by their presence and by the toll they take on the caregiver's energy. Frank and Anderson (1989) noted, "The never-ending responsibilities and interruptions of child-caring may be a much greater distraction from sexual pleasure than holding a full-time job" (p. 193).

Psychologists use the term "**satiation**" to mean that repeated exposure to a stimulus results in the loss of its ability to reinforce. For example, the first time you listen to a new recording, you derive considerable enjoyable and satisfaction from it.

Today, social conditions favor monogamy. Promiscuity is out, partly because of the threat of AIDS and partly because we're no longer willing to accept the last decades' casual attitudes about sex.
Trudy Cutross

You may play it over and over during the first few days. But after a week or so, listening to the same music is no longer new and does not give you the same level of enjoyment that it first did. So it is with intercourse. The thousandth time that a person has intercourse with the same person is not as new and exciting as the first few times. Although intercourse can remain very satisfying for couples in long-term relationships (Frank & Anderson, 1989), satiation may result in decreased frequency of intercourse.

NATIONAL DATA: In a national sample of 761 married adults, 98% reported that they had had intercourse with only one person (their spouse) in the last 12 months (Smith, 1991). This percentage is in contrast to a national sample of 205 never-married individuals, among whom only 52% reported that they had had only one sexual partner in the last 12 months (Greeley, Michael, & Smith, 1990).

Monogamy "*Hot monogamy*" is a term coined by Helen Kaplan, head of the Human Sexuality Program at the New York Hospital-Cornell Medical Center in Manhattan. "She says nineties couples want the marriages their grandparents and parents had. The emphasis is on stability, children, family togetherness—plus something more: great sex" (Cutross, 1992, p. 63). In any given year, most married people are monogamous (see National Data).

However, during the entire marriage, it is not unusual for a spouse to have intercourse with someone outside the marriage. Thompson (1983) reported that about half of husbands and wives have intercourse at least once with someone other than their spouse during their marriage.

Sexuality among the Divorced

As expected, the sexually active divorced are not as likely to be monogamous as those who are married (see National Data).

NATIONAL DATA: In a national sample of 125 sexually active divorced individuals, 62% reported that they were monogamous in the last 12 months (Greeley et al., 1990).

NATIONAL DATA: Over 2 million people get divorced annually (*National Center for Health Statistics,* 1992).

Some possible motives for sexual interactions among the divorced include:

1. Find and experience sexual passion. In *Cosmopolitan's* survey of over 20,000 of its readers, almost three-fourths (72%) reported that sexual incompatibility was an important reason for their divorcing. The biggest specific sexual problem was loss of sexual passion on the part of one or both spouses. "Younger women were more likely to have lost the flame and less likely to report that their husbands no longer desired them; older women reported the reverse" (Bowe, 1992, p. 200). Among *Cosmopolitan* readers, individuals who divorce may be particularly interested in sex with passion.
2. Repair self-esteem. Sexual activity among the divorced may also be used as a way to repair or reestablish one's self-esteem. Divorce is often a shattering emotional experience. The loss of a lover, the disruption of a daily routine, and the awareness of a new and negative label ("divorced person") all converge on the individual. Questions like "What did I do wrong?" "Am I a failure?" and "Is there anybody out there who will love me again?" may loom in the minds of the divorced. One way (some believe) to feel loved, at least temporarily, is through sex. Being held by another and being told that one is loved provides some evidence that one is desirable. Because divorced people may be particularly vulnerable, they may reach for sex as if it were a lifeboat.
3. Test Sexual Adequacy. The divorced person may have been told by the former spouse that he or she was an inept lover. One man said his wife used to make fun of him because he occasionally lost his erection. Intercourse with a new partner who did not belittle him reassured him of his sexual adequacy, and his erectile dysfunction ceased to be a problem. A woman described how her husband would sneer at her body and say no man would want her because she was so fat. After the divorce, she found men who thought she was attractive and who did not consider her weight to be a problem. Other divorced men and women say that what their spouses did not like, their new partners view as turn-ons. The result is a renewed sense of sexual desirability.

Beyond these motives for sexual interactions, many divorced people simply enjoy the sexual freedom their divorced status offers. Freedom from the guilt that spouses who have extramarital intercourse experience may be a relief: the divorced can have sexual relations with whomever they choose.

CONSIDERATION: A sexual encounter with a divorced person is likely to be different depending on the stage of the sexual adjustment cycle the divorced person is in. If the person has recently divorced, he or she may feel a need for a period of casual sex and be uninterested in any type of relationship commitment. If the person has been divorced for several years, the person is likely to be more interested in an emotional relationship of which sex is a part.

Perceived sexual satisfaction of the divorced person is also influenced by the presence of children, particularly for mothers. Since they are more often in the role of custodial parent, mothers (as compared to fathers) report that their children interfere in their sexual relationships. Mothers also experienced guilt over their involvement with a new partner if it took time away from their children (Darling, Davidson, & Parish, 1989).

Sexuality in the Middle Years

Definition of Middle Age

Middle age is commonly thought of as the years between 40 and 60. The U.S. Census Bureau regards you as middle-aged when you reach 45. Family life specialists define middle age as that time when the last child leaves home and continues until retirement or either spouse dies. Humorist Lawrence Peter (1982) has provided a couple of additional definitions: "Middle age is when you can do just as much as you could ever do—but would rather not" and "Middle age is when work is a lot less fun and fun is a lot more work" (pp. October 9 and May 4). Regardless of how middle age is defined, it is a time of transition for women, men, and their sexuality.

Women in Middle Age

Women in middle age undergo a number of social, sexual, and psychological changes. A major social event for many women in middle age is the departure of their children from the home.

However, family responsibilities do not always decrease during the middle years. For some women family demands increase, and women feel the "dependency squeeze," with pressures from older and younger generations (Boston Women's Health Book Collective, 1984). Adult children may return home out of financial need, or may need assistance with rearing their children. At the same time, the middle years woman may be caring for her (and her partner's) aging parents.

Whereas disengagement from the parental role is the major social event in the life of the middle-aged woman, **menopause** is the primary physical event during this period. Defined as the permanent cessation of menstruation, menopause is caused by the gradual decline of estrogen produced by the ovaries. It occurs around age 50 for most women but may begin earlier or later. Signs that the woman may be nearing menopause include decreased menstrual flow and a less predictable cycle, although sometimes menstruation stops abruptly. After 12 months with no period, the woman is said to be through menopause. During this time, the woman should use some form of contraception. Women with irregular periods may remain at risk of pregnancy up to 24 months following their last menstrual period (Boston Women's Health Book Collective, 1984). Which one she uses (including the pill and the IUD) should not be dictated by her age, since age itself is not considered a contraindication for the use of a hormonal contraceptive or the IUD (Connell, 1991).

The term "**climacteric**" is often used synonymously with menopause. But menopause refers only to the time when the menstrual flow permanently stops, while climacteric refers to the whole process of hormonal change induced by the ovaries, pituitary gland, and hypothalamus. Synonymous with climacteric, the term "perimenopause" refers to the time period between when signs first appear that menopause is approaching until 12 months after the monthly menstrual flow has stopped. The time period that begins 12 months after the last menstrual period is referred to as postmenopause. Table 12.2 identifies the various stages associated with menopause.

Reactions to menopausal hormonal changes may include "hot flashes" in which the woman feels a sudden rush of heat from the waist up. Hot flashes are often accompanied by an increased reddening of the skin surface and a drenching perspiration. They are the sign most commonly associated with menopause. Although the endocrine basis for hot flushes and night sweats is not understood (Bancroft, 1989), they may reflect the body's attempt to respond to the pituitary's signals to produce more estrogen (Boston Women's Health Book Collective, 1984). Their impact may range from mild to serious, disturbing sleep or causing such profuse sweating that a change of clothes is necessary. Other symptoms may include heart palpitations, dizziness, irritability, headaches, backache, and weight gain. Wing, Matthews, Kuller Meilahn, and Plantinga (1991) noted that weight gain is a normal occurrence for women during menopause, which increases their risk of coronary heart disease.

It's disgraceful that in our sophisticated world of medicine, with our phenomenal track record, we still can't answer simple questions about menopause.

Dr. Bernardine Healy
Director, NIH

Many women report other physiological and behavioral changes as a result of the aging process and of decreasing levels of estrogen: (a) a delay in the reaction of the clitoris to direct stimulation, (b) less lubrication during sexual excitement, (c) a less intense orgasm, (d) a smaller vaginal opening, (e) decreased sexual desire, and (f) decreased sexual activity (Sarrel, 1990; Sherwin, 1991b). According to Bancroft (1989), there has not yet been any study of the natural menopause and hormone replacement that explains whether menopausal hormonal changes directly influence sexual desire, orgasmic capacity, or enjoyment. Studies following hysterectomy and oophorectomy (removal of the ovaries) suggest that hormonal changes play a role in a proportion of women. Decreases in both desire and sexual activity may be the result not only of decreasing estrogen levels but also of beliefs that middle-aged women should not be interested in sex and that the woman who is no longer fertile should no longer be sexual (Bachmann, 1991). In addition, decreases in sexual

TABLE 12.2 Stages of Menopause

Premenopause	Reproductive years before menopause
Menopause	Permanenent cessation of menstruation
Perimenopause	Time from first signs of menopause (irregular periods, hot flashes) until 12 months after cessation of menstruation
Climacteric	Synonymous with perimenopause
Postmenopause	Time beginning 12 months after the last menstrual period

desire and activity among middle-aged women are related to lack of a confiding relationship, alcoholism on the part of the spouse, and major depression (Hallstrom & Samuelsson, 1990).

If you get six menopausal women together, you'll find that their doctors are doing six different things. Our joke is that you might as well go to a veterinarian. The scientific data is just not there.
Pat Schroeder
Congresswoman

To minimize the effects of decreasing levels of estrogen, some physicians recommend estrogen replacement therapy (ERT), particularly to control hot flashes during the climacteric. This choice is discussed in detail at the end of this chapter.

Menopause is associated with few psychological changes. Matthews et al. (1990) studied 541 women across two and a half years of menopause and concluded:

> Natural menopause led to few detectable changes in women's psychological characteristics. Natural menopause did not adversely affect Type A behavior, anxiety, anger, total symptoms, depression, public self-consciousness, perceived stress, or job dissatisfaction scores. (p. 349)

Women who expected vasomotor symptoms during menopause to increase did experience an increase in their level of depressive symptoms and angry symptoms (Matthews, 1992). Thus, the self-fulfilling prophesy may be at work.

A cross-cultural look at menopause suggests that a woman's reaction to this phase of her life may be related to the society in which she lives. For example, among Chinese women, fewer menopausal symptoms have been observed. Researchers have suggested this may be due to the fact that older women in China are highly respected, as are older people generally. Griffin (1977) has hypothesized that the magnitude of the symptoms associated with menopause is correlated with the few roles available to the older woman in our society. Researchers Karen Matthews and Nancy Avis have conducted a longitudinal study of 541 women as they progressed through menopause and found that the negative expectations our society has of the menopausal years "may cause at least some of the problems women experience" (Adler, 1991, p. 14).

Men in Middle Age

While traditional women in middle age are adjusting to their children leaving home as well as to hormonal changes associated with menopause, traditional men are adjusting to change or lack of change in their careers. Most men reach the top level of their earning power during middle age (*Statistical Abstract of the United States: 1992,* Table 713), and some find themselves well short of the peak they had hoped to reach.

Physiological changes also accompany middle age in men. The production of testosterone usually begins to decline around age 40 and continues to decrease gradually until age 60, when it levels off. A 20-year-old man usually has 600 to 1,200 nanograms per deciliter (NG/DL) of serum testosterone, whereas a 60-year-old man has 200 to 600 NG/DL (Young, 1990, p. 121). The decline is not inevitable but is related to general health status. The profound hormonal changes and loss of reproductive capacity that occur in women during menopause do not occur in men (Keogh, 1990).

The consequences of lowered testosterone include: (1) more difficulty in getting and maintaining a firm erection, (b) greater ejaculatory control with the possibility of more prolonged erections, (c) less consistency in achieving orgasm, (d) fewer genital spasms during orgasm, (e) a qualitative change from an intense, genitally focused sensation to a more diffused and generalized feeling of pleasure; and (f) an increase in the length of the refractory period, during which time the man is unable to ejaculate or have another erection.

These physiological changes in the middle-aged man, along with psychological changes, have sometimes been referred to as male menopause. During this period,

Self Assessment

Aging Sexual Knowledge and Attitudes Scale

Knowledge Questions Indicate whether you believe each item is true or false or you don't know.

	True	False	Don't Know
1. Sexual activity in aged persons is often dangerous to their health.	_____	_____	_____
2. Males over the age of 65 typically take longer to attain an erection of their penis than do younger males.	_____	_____	_____
3. Males over the age of 65 usually experience a reduction in intensity of orgasm relative to younger males.	_____	_____	_____
4. The firmness of erection in aged males is often less than that of younger persons.	_____	_____	_____
5. The older female (65 + years of age) has reduced vaginal lubrication secretion relative to younger females.	_____	_____	_____
6. The aged female takes longer to achieve adequate vaginal lubrication relative to younger females.	_____	_____	_____
7. The older female may experience painful intercourse due to reduced elasticity of the vagina and reduced vaginal lubrication.	_____	_____	_____
8. Sexuality is typically a life-long need.	_____	_____	_____
9. Sexual behavior in older people (65+) increases the risk of heart attack.	_____	_____	_____
10. Most males over the age of 65 are unable to engage in sexual intercourse.	_____	_____	_____
11. The relatively most sexually active younger people tend to become the relatively most sexually active older people.	_____	_____	_____
12. There is evidence that sexual activity in older persons has beneficial physical effects on the participants.	_____	_____	_____
13. Sexual activity may be psychologically beneficial to older person participants.	_____	_____	_____
14. Most older females are sexually unresponsive.	_____	_____	_____
15. The sex urge typically increases with age in males over 65.	_____	_____	_____
16. Prescription drugs may alter a person's sex drive.	_____	_____	_____
17. Females, after menopause, have a physiologically induced need for sexual activity.	_____	_____	_____
18. Basically, changes with advanced age (65+) in sexuality involve a slowing of response time rather than a reduction of interest in sex.	_____	_____	_____
19. Older males typically experience a reduced need to ejaculate and hence may maintain an erection of the penis for a longer time than younger males.	_____	_____	_____
20. Older males and females cannot act as sex partners as both need younger partners for stimulation.	_____	_____	_____
21. The most common determinant of the frequency of sexual activity in older couples is the interest or lack of interest of the husband in a sexual relationship with his wife.	_____	_____	_____
22. Barbiturates, tranquilizers, and alcohol may lower the sexual arousal levels of aged persons and interfere with sexual responsiveness.	_____	_____	_____

Continued

Self-Assessment—*Continued*

	True	False	Don't Know
23. Sexual disinterest in aged persons may be a reflection of a psychological state of depression.	____	____	____
24. There is a decrease in frequency of sexual activity with older age in males.	____	____	____
25. There is a greater decrease in male sexuality with age than there is in female sexuality.	____	____	____
26. Heavy consumption of cigarettes may diminish sexual desire.	____	____	____
27. An important factor in the maintenance of sexual responsiveness in the aging male is the consistency of sexual activity throughout his life.	____	____	____
28. Fear of the inability to perform sexually may bring about an inability to perform sexually in older males.	____	____	____
29. The ending of sexual activity in old age is most likely and primarily due to social and psychological causes rather than biological and physical causes.	____	____	____
30. Excessive masturbation may bring about an early onset of mental confusion and dementia in the aged.	____	____	____
31. There is an inevitable loss of sexual satisfaction in post-menopausal women.	____	____	____
32. Secondary impotence (or non-physiologically caused) increases in males over the age of 60 relative to younger males.	____	____	____
33. Impotence in aged males may literally be effectively treated and cured in many instances.	____	____	____
34. In the absence of severe physical disability, males and females may maintain sexual interest and activity well into their 80s and 90s.	____	____	____
35. Masturbation in older males and females has beneficial effects on the maintenance of sexual responsiveness.	____	____	____

Attitude Questions (7-point Likert Scale: disagree = 1, agree = 7)

	Disagree 1	2	3	4	Agree 5	6	7
36. Aged people have little interest in sexuality. (Aged = 65+ years of age)	____	____	____	____	____	____	____
37. An aged person who shows sexual interest brings disgrace to himself/herself.	____	____	____	____	____	____	____
38. Institutions, such as nursing homes, ought not to encourage or support sexual activity of any sort in its residents.	____	____	____	____	____	____	____
39. Male and female residents of nursing homes ought to live on separate floors or separate wings of the nursing home.	____	____	____	____	____	____	____
40. Nursing homes have no obligation to provide adequate privacy for residents who desire to be alone, either by themselves or as a couple.	____	____	____	____	____	____	____
41. As one becomes older (say past 65) interest in sexuality inevitably disappears.	____	____	____	____	____	____	____

Continued

Self-Assessment—*Continued*

For items 42, 43, and 44: If a relative of mine, living in a nursing home, was to have a sexual relationship with another resident I would:

	Disagree 1	2	3	4	Agree 5	6	7
42. Complain to the management.	____	____	____	____	____	____	____
43. Move my relative from this institution.	____	____	____	____	____	____	____
44. Stay out of it as it is not my concern.	____	____	____	____	____	____	____
45. If I knew that a particular nursing home permitted and supported sexual activity in residents who desired such, I would not place a relative in that nursing home.	____	____	____	____	____	____	____
46. It is immoral for older persons to engage in recreational sex.	____	____	____	____	____	____	____
47. I would like to know more about the changes in sexual functioning in older years.	____	____	____	____	____	____	____
48. I feel I know all I need to know about sexuality in the aged.	____	____	____	____	____	____	____
49. I would complain to the management if I knew of sexual activity between any residents of a nursing home.	____	____	____	____	____	____	____
50. I would support sex education courses for aged residents of nursing homes.	____	____	____	____	____	____	____
51. I would support sex education courses for staff of nursing homes.	____	____	____	____	____	____	____
52. Masturbation is an acceptable sexual activity for older males.	____	____	____	____	____	____	____
53. Masturbation is an acceptable sexual activity for older females.	____	____	____	____	____	____	____
54. Institutions, such as the nursing home, ought to provide large enough beds for couples who desire to sleep together.	____	____	____	____	____	____	____
55. Staff of nursing homes ought to be trained or educated with regard to sexuality in the aged and/or disabled.	____	____	____	____	____	____	____
56. Residents of nursing homes ought not to engage in sexual activity of any sort.	____	____	____	____	____	____	____
57. Institutions such as nursing homes should provide opportunities for the social interaction of men and women.	____	____	____	____	____	____	____
58. If family members object to a widowed relative engaging in sexual relations with another resident of a nursing home, it is the obligation of the management and staff to make certain that such sexual activity is prevented.	____	____	____	____	____	____	____
59. Institutions, such as nursing homes, should provide privacy such as to allow residents to engage in sexual behavior without fear of intrusion or observation.	____	____	____	____	____	____	____

Continued

Self-Assessment—*Continued*

	Disagree 1	2	3	4	Agree 5	6	7
60. Masturbation is harmful and ought to be avoided.	_____	_____	_____	_____	_____	_____	_____
61. Sexual relations outside the context of marriage are always wrong.	_____	_____	_____	_____	_____	_____	_____

Source Used by permission of Charles B. White, Dept. of Psychology, Trinity University, San Antonio, TX

Scoring Following are scoring instructions for the Aging Sexual Knowledge and Attitudes Scale (ASKAS). To score the Knowledge section, questions 1 through 35, reverse score the true and false for questions 1, 10, 14, 17, 20, 30, and 31. Then assign the following values for all Knowledge items: true = 1, false = 2, and don't know = 3. Total your score. Possible scores range from 35 to 105. The Attitude items, questions 36 through 61, are each scored according to the numerical value you selected, with the exception of questions 44, 47, 48, 50, 51, 52, 53, 54, 55, 57, and 59, in which the scoring is reversed. (For reverse scoring, 1 = 7, 7, = 1, 6 = 2, 2 = 6, 3 = 5, 5 = 3, and 4 is unchanged.) Total your score. Possible scores range from 26 to 182.

Interpreting your Score On the Knowledge portion, a *low* score indicates *high* knowledge. This is because "don't know" is given a value of 3, indicating low knowledge. On the Attitudes portion, a *low* score indicates a more *permissive* attitude. You may wish to compare your scores to those in the table below (from White, 1982). These values are not meant to show what is "normative" but to illustrate the variation in ASKAS scores.

Reliability and Validity The reliability of the ASKAS has been evaluated in several studies and been found to be acceptable. Reliabilities (split-half, alpha, and test-retest) have been higher for the Knowledge items, with reliability coefficients ranging from 0.90 to 0.97. The reliability coefficients for the Attitudes items range from 0.72 to 0.96.

The validity of the ASKAS has been examined in several studies measuring the impact of psychological-educational intervention programs for the groups listed in Table 1. In each of these studies, the educational program resulted in significant knowledge increases and significant attitude change (in a more permissive direction). Factor analysis revealed two factors, with items loading in the expected knowledge or attitude portions of the ASKAS (White, 1982).

References

White, C. B. (1981). Interest, attitudes, knowledge, and sexual history in relation to sexual behavior in the institutionalized aged. *Archives of Sexual Behavior, 11,* 11–21.

White, C. B. (1982). A scale for the assessment of attitudes and knowledge regarding sexuality in the aged. *Archives of Sexual Behavior, 11,* 491–502.

White, C. B. (1988). Aging sexual knowledge and attitudes scale. In C. M. Davis, W. L. Yarber, & S. L. Davis (Eds.), *Sexuality-related measures: A compendium* (pp. 12–15).

White, C. B. & Catania, J. (1981). Sexual education for aged people, people who work with the aged, and families of aged people. *International Journal of Aging and Human Development, 15,* 121–138.

TABLE I Means and Standard Deviations of ASKAS Scores by Group[a]

Group	n	Mean	SD
Nursing home residents[b]	273		
Attitudes		84.56	23.32
Knowledge		65.62	15.09
Community aged[c]	30		
Attitudes		86.40	17.28
Knowledge		73.73	12.52
Families of aged[c]	30		
Attitudes		75.00	22.66
Knowledge		78.00	13.61
Persons who work with aged[c]	30		
Attitudes		76.00	17.60
Knowledge		62.46	12.50
Nursing home staff[c]	163		
Attitudes		61.08	25.79
Knowledge		64.9	17.25

[a]The possible range of ASKAS scores are as follows: Knowledge = 35 – 105; Attitudes = 26-182. All scores reported here are the pre-test scores where both pre-tests and post-tests were administered.
[b]White, 1981.
[c]White and Catania, 1981.

Table Source: White, C. B. (1982). A scale for the assessment of attitudes and knowledge regarding sexuality in the aged. *Archives of Sexual Behavior, 11,* p. 497. Reprinted by permission of Plenum Publishing Corp.

the man may experience nervousness, hot flashes, insomnia, and no interest in sex. But these changes most often occur over a long period of time, and the anxiety and depression some men experience seem to be as much related to their life situation as to hormonal alterations.

One of the aspects of growing old in the United States is exposure to a number of negative stereotypes and myths about aging. Belief in these stereotypes is problematic in that people begin to act as though they are true. The Self-Assessment is designed to assess your level of knowledge in regard to the elderly and your feelings about their sexuality.

Sexuality in the Later Years

NATIONAL DATA: Thirteen percent of all U.S. adults (over 25 million whites and over 2.5 million blacks) are over the age of 65. (*Statistical Abstract of the United States: 1992,* Table 18).

The way a society views the elderly influences the expression of their sexuality. Although our society tends to expect people to reduce their sexual activities as they age, this expectation is not characteristic of all societies. Seventy percent of the societies studied by Winn and Newton (1982) had expectations of continued sexual activities for their aging males. Among the Tiv in Africa, many older men "remain active and 'hot' for many years after they become gray-haired" (p. 288); and among the Taoist sects of China, there are records of men retaining their sexual desires past 100 years of age. Similar reports of continued sexual activity among aging women were found in 84% of societies for which data on this age group were available. The researchers concluded "that cultural as well as biological factors may be key determinants in sexual behavior in the later part of life" (p. 283).

Cultures which provide meaningful roles for their elderly continue to value them.

*For age is opportunity, no less than youth itself; though in another dress.
And as the evening twilight fades away
The sky is filled with stars
Invisible by day.*
Henry Wadsworth Longfellow

CONSIDERATION: Our society has perpetuated the myth that growing old and remaining sexual are incompatible. If we are not aware that this expectation is culturally induced, the self-fulfilling prophecy may take effect; because we believe that we should not be sexual when we are old, we stop being sexual.

Research on 45 single people ages 60 to 92 revealed that, indeed, negative cultural expectations can be overcome. These individuals enjoyed dating, being in love, and expressing themselves sexually. They reported that while their sexuality included intercourse, "the stronger emphasis was on the nuances of sexual behavior such as hugging, kissing, and touching" (Bulcroft & O'Conner-Roden, 1987, p. 267).

Sexual Interest, Activity, and Ability among the Elderly

Data based on 427 male veterans (randomly selected) ages 30 to 99 revealed that sexual interest, activity, and ability were lower among the older men. Sexual interest ranged from a mean of 4.4 (4 being very interested and 5, extremely interested) in men aged 30 to 39 to 2.0 (2 being slightly interested) in men age 90 to 99 (Mulligan

TABLE 12.3 Physiological Sexual Changes in Women in the Later Years

Phases of Sexual Response	Changes in Women
Excitement Phase	Vaginal lubrication takes several minutes or longer, as opposed to 10 to 30 seconds. Both the length and the width of the vagina decrease. Considerable decreased lubrication and vaginal expansion is associated with pain during intercourse. Some women report decreased sexual desire and unusual sensitivity of the clitoris (Sarrel, 1990).
Plateau Phase	Little change occurs as the woman ages. During this phase, the vaginal orgasmic platform is formed and the uterus elevates.
Orgasm Phase	Elderly women continue to experience and enjoy orgasm. Of women aged 60 to 91, almost 70% reported that having an orgasm made for a good sexual experience (Starr & Weiner, 1981). In regard to their frequency of orgasm now as opposed to when they were younger, 65% said "unchanged," 20% "increased," and 14% "decreased."
Resolution Phase	Defined as a return to the preexcitement state, the resolution phase of the sexual response phase happens more quickly in elderly than in younger women. Clitoral retraction and orgasmic platform disappear quickly after orgasm. This is most likely in a result of less pelvic vascogongestion to begin with during the arousal phase.

Source: Adapted from Boskin, W., Graf, G. & Kreisworth, V. (1990). *Health dynamics: Attitudes and behaviors.* St.Paul, MN: West Publishing Co., p. 210. Used by permission.

TABLE 12.4 Physiological Sexual Changes in Men in the Later Years

Phases of Sexual Response	Changes in Men
Excitement Phase	As men age, it takes them longer to get an erection. While the young man may get an erection within 10 seconds, it may take the elderly man several minutes (10 to 30). During this time, he usually needs intense stimulation (manual or oral). Unaware that the greater delay in getting erect is a normal consequence of aging, men who experience this for the first time may panic and have erectile dysfunction.
Plateau Phase	Rigidity of the erection may be less than when the man was younger, and there is usually a longer delay before ejaculation. This latter change is usually regarded as an advantage by both the man and his partner.
Orgasm Phase	Orgasm in the elderly male is usually less intense with fewer contractions and less fluid. However, orgasm remains an enjoyable experience as over 70% of older men in one study reported that having a climax was very important when having a sexual experience (Starr & Weiner, 1981).
Resolution Phase	The elderly man loses his erection rather quickly after ejaculation. In some cases, the erection will be lost while the penis is still in the woman's vagina and she is thrusting to experience her own orgasm. The refractory period is also increased. Whereas the young male needs only a short time after ejaculation to get an erection, the elderly man may need considerably longer.

Source: Adapted from Boskin, W., Graf, G. & Kreisworth, V. (1990). *Health dynamics: Attitudes and behaviors.* St.Paul, MN: West Publishing Co., p. 209. Used by permission.

& Moss, 1991). Note that even while sexual interest was low, it was still present. No respondent reported a total absence of interest.

CONSIDERATION: Cross (1989) emphasized, "All older people are sexual. They are not all sexually active, as is also true of the young, but they all have sexual beliefs, values, memories, and feelings. To deny their sexuality is to exclude a significant part of their lives" (p. 14).

Just as interest was lower among older men, so was intercourse frequency. It dropped from a mean of once per week in 30- to 39-year-olds to once per year in 90- to 99-year-olds (Mulligan & Moss, 1991). Part of the lower rate among the 90- to 99-year-old group may be attributed to the lack of a spouse or sexual partner. Regarding the ability of these elderly men to perform sexually, the frequency, rigidity,

The typical patient over 50 has only a partial degree of biological impairment, which has, however, been escalated into a total sexual disability by a variety of cultural, intrapsychic, and relationship stressors.

Helen Kaplan

and duration of erections decreased dramatically with age. Men 90 to 99 reported a mean of 1.9 in terms of rigidity of erection, with 1 being a flaccid erection never lasting long enough for intercourse and 5 being an extremely rigid erection always lasting long enough for intercourse. (In contrast, men aged 30 to 39 reported a mean rigidity of 4.5). Even though these 90- year-olds achieved an erection, only 21% of them were able to have an orgasm.

Other research supports the view that sexual behavior declines with age. Schiavi, Schreiner-Engle, and Mandeli (1990) observed in their cross-sectional data that of 65 healthy married men aged 45 to 74, those who were 65 to 74 reported less sexual desire (thought about sex less frequently and could comfortably go without sex for longer periods of time), engaged in intercourse less often, masturbated less frequently, and had fewer orgasms than the men aged 45 to 65. The older group also reported lower arousal, fewer erections, and more difficulty becoming aroused. Getting an erection was their most frequently reported sexual problem.

Just because your legs aren't as strong as they were when you were twenty doesn't mean you give up walking or running.

E. Douglas Whitehead

However, the enjoyment of sex reported by these men did not change with age. Their satisfaction with their own sexuality remained substantially the same. In another study of 61 elderly men (average age of 71) both with and without sexual partners, sexual satisfaction was rated at an average of 6.3 on a scale where 1 equaled no satisfaction and 10 equaled extremely high satisfaction (Mulligan & Palguta, 1991).

There have been fewer studies on the sexuality of elderly women (Morley & Kaiser, 1989). However, Bretschneider and McCoy (1988) collected data (using a 117-item questionnaires) from 102 white women and 100 white men ranging in age from 80 to 102 who lived in residential treatment centers in Northern California. Some of the findings follow:

1. Thirty-eight percent of the women, in contrast to 66% of the men, reported that sex was important to them in the present.
2. Thirty percent of the women and 62% of the men reported that they had sexual intercourse sometimes (p. 16).
3. Of those with sexual partners, 64% of the women in contrast to 82% of the men, said that they were at least mildly happy with their partners as lovers (p. 114).
4. Forty percent of the women and 72% of the men reported that they currently masturbated (p. 118).
5. Touching and caressing without sexual intercourse was the most frequently engaged in behavior by women (64%) and men (82%) (p. 119).

These findings suggest declines in sexual enjoyment and frequencies are greater for women in the later years than for men.

Another study emphasized the importance of a partner for the sexual activity of women. Of elderly women age 60 and over, 56% of the married women reported that they were still sexually active. However, of the unmarried women, only 5% reported being sexually active (Diokno, Brown, & Herzog, 1990). Seventy-five percent of the women in the retirement homes studied by Bretschneider and McCoy (1988) reported that they had no regular sexual partner.

Other studies show that while elderly women are less sexually active than they were when they were young, many continue to enjoy a range of sexual practices. Of the women over 70 in Brecher's (1984) study, a third said that they masturbated and 43% provided oral sex for their partners. They also reported manual stimulation, anal stimulation, and use of a vibrator. The stereotype of the elderly being sexless is a myth.

It is a myth that the elderly have no interest in sex.

EXHIBIT 12.2 Sexuality Among the Widowed

A significant proportion of our population eventually becomes widowed. Because men, on the average, die about seven years earlier than women, women are much more likely than men to become widowed. In 1991, 11.8% of adult women were widowed, compared to only 2.7% of adult men. (*Statistical Abstract of the United States: 1992,* Table 48). Their sexual behavior is likely to involve less frequent intercourse because they are older, have no readily available sexual partner, and are subject to the cultural expectation that widows are old and sexless. These cultural expectations do not support sexual expression among the widowed.

Coping with sexuality without a partner is an issue for some widows. When a group of widows (ages 67 to 78) were asked how they coped with their sexual feelings when they had no partner, they responded:

> Only by keeping busy. Keep occupied with various activities and friends.
>
> Do physical exercise. Have many interests, hobbies.
>
> We just have to accept it and interest ourselves in other things.
>
> By turning to music or other arts, painting, dancing is excellent . . . using nurturant qualities, loving pets, the elderly, shut-ins. Reading, hiking . . . lots more. My mind controls my sex desires. (Starr & Weiner, 1981, (pp. 165–167)

Another way that some widows cope with their sexual needs is through masturbation. However, given the generally negative view our society has of masturbation, some widows may not consider this option.

Sadly, because of cultural expectations that elderly widows are sexless, many single and divorced individuals do not view widows as potential sexual partners. Even more devastating, some widowed do not view themselves as being appropriate to their age if they are interested in sex. However, not all feel bound by cultural proscriptions. In a study of 34 sexually active widows, only 71% said that they were monogamous within the last 12 months (Greeley et al., 1990).

Death of a spouse is less likely to affect the sexual activity of widowers than widows. Widowers have more access to sexual partners because of an abundance of widows competing for a small number of men at later ages. At age 75 and over, 25% of men are widowed, in contrast to 66% of women age 75 and over (*Statistical Abstract of the United States: 1992,* Table 48).

In a study of deterrents to sexual activity in the elderly, 400 physicians reported that men were half as likely to be without sexual partners as women (Pietropinto, 1987). Widowed men may also feel more comfortable becoming involved sexually with a new partner than widowed women. When the 400 physicians in Pietropinto's study were asked, "Do widowers or widows usually have more difficulty engaging in sexual relations with a new partner?" 18% felt that widowers had more difficulty, compared to 32% who felt that the widows had more difficulty. Given the greater availability to men of partners and their greater psychological comfort in becoming involved with a new partner, it is not surprising that some widowers are very sexually active (Brecher, 1984).

Correlation between Past and Present Sexual Behaviors

"Use it or lose it" is a popular adage in regard to sexuality. (Don't worry—you can always gain it back!) The phrase is most often used in suggesting to middle-aged people that they remain sexually active during the middle years so as to be able to continue being sexually active in their later years. Researchers Bretschneider and McCoy (1988) tested this adage by asking 100 white men and 102 white women between the ages of 80 and 102 to report their past and present frequencies in regard to masturbation, touching and holding, and sexual intercourse. They observed that there was a substantial and significant correlation between masturbating and touching and holding the partner in the past and continuing these behaviors in the present. However, in regard to intercourse, the frequency of having intercourse in the past did not correlate with the current frequency of intercourse. They concluded that the frequency of intercourse may be more affected by physical and social changes than had previously been thought (p. 127).

CHOICES

A sexuality choice that becomes relevant to the menopausal woman is whether to take supplemental hormones during menopause. After menopause and into the elderly years, a series of other choices are relevant to both men and women. We begin with the decision about hormone replacement therapy.

Choose to Have Hormone Replacement Therapy?

Sometimes referred to as **estrogen replacement therapy, hormone replacement therapy** (HRT) involves the menopausal woman taking prescribed doses of estrogen and progesterone (sedatives and tranquilizers are not effective; Young, Kumar, & Goldzieher, 1990) to replace these hormones, which are no longer being produced by her body. As with any medications that are introduced into the body, the advantages and disadvantages must be carefully weighed in consultation with a physician who knows the details of the woman's medical history (Love, 1991). Some research suggests that estrogen alone is sufficient for improvements in sexual functioning, although women who are postmenopausal due to surgery rather than naturally occurring menopause may benefit from androgen as well (Walling, Andersen, & Johnson, 1990).

Although menopause is a universal experience for most women, how it is experienced is not universal. Physiology, anatomy, social support systems, culture, expectations, and the woman's attitudes (especially her self-image) all influence how easy or difficult the menopausal period is for the woman (McGraw, 1991). Some women report hot flashes, depression, tension, decreased libido, and difficulty sleeping. With decreased estrogen, osteoporosis may develop and subject the woman to greater risk of bone fractures. Without estrogen, the menopausal woman is also at greater risk for a heart attack. While HRT benefits are not the same for all women, women who are involved in HRT report fewer hot flashes, less depression, less tension, increased libido (Sherwin, 1991a), fewer bone fractures (Sarrel, 1990), and fewer heart attacks (Pines et al., 1991). However, researchers disagree on the benefits of HRT. Hunter (1990) concluded that HRT does not have significant effects on mood or sexual behavior over and above placebo effects. Bengtsson (1989) suggested further study before acceptance of the positive benefits of estrogen on reducing heart problems.

A significant concern about using HRT has been its increased risk of endometrial cancer. But combining progestin with estrogen has virtually eliminated this increased risk (Bachmann & Grill, 1988). In addition, women who take HRT and who have not had their uterus removed will have a monthly flow. Some women object to this side effect (Bernard, 1990).

Women for whom HRT is not appropriate are those who have uterine cancer or estrogen-dependent breast cancer because it will accelerate the growth rate of these cancers. Some research suggests that low doses (0.625 milligrams per do or less of conjugated estrogens) do not increase breast cancer risk (Dupont & Page, 1991). Other contraindications for HRT include high blood pressure, gallbladder disease, and liver impairment. From 10 to 20% of postmenopausal women may have significant contraindications for the use of HRT (Young et al., 1990). Women considering HRT are advised to consult their physician, who would also be aware of important family history considerations (breast cancer). Given the absence of contraindications, the benefits seem to outweigh the disadvantages of HRT.

Perhaps more information will be available in the near future when The National Institutes of Health releases the initial results of a 3-year study on the toxicity and short-term risks of HRT, and later when results are available from the 14-year Women's Health Initiative focusing on health concerns of women in the last third of life (Beck, 1992).

While estrogen and progesterone are the hormones typically referred to in regard to HRT, physicians may also prescribe androgens to increase the libido of menopausal women. Bachmann (1992) recommended methyltestosterone, a synthetic androgen, for a 46-year-old woman who wanted to increase her libido. Positive effects are expected to occur within three to five days of the start of treatment.

Sexual Choices among the Elderly

Elderly women and men are confronted with at least four sexual choices.

Breaking Free of Cultural Expectations Because the elderly in our society do not have cultural approval for being sexually active, often they are not. However, it is their choice to be sexually active, and they should feel free to exercise this choice without hesitation. Indeed, main-

Continued

Continued

taining an active sex life in the later years "not only maintains normal function but mitigates many of the involution changes caused by sex steroid deprivation (Young, 1990, p. 121). Indeed, "the loss of sexuality is not an inevitable aspect of aging, and the majority of healthy people remain sexually active on a regular basis until advanced old age" (Kaplan, 1990, p. 185).

On the other hand, the elderly should not view the pro-sex publicity on talk shows, such as "Donahue," "Geraldo," and "Sally Jesse Raphael" (which sometimes feature "sexy seniors"), as an obligation to enjoy an active sex life. Sexuality is a choice, and senior citizens are not excepted from the right to exercise it. Each elderly person should decide what patterns, frequencies, and behaviors he or she feels most comfortable with. There are no right or wrong, normal or abnormal answers. Communicating about their preferences is essential. Such communication includes discussing such sensitive topics as the effect of continence problems on sexuality (Wheeler, 1990).

Relabeling Losses as Transitions In addition to choosing the degree to which they will be sexually active, the elderly can choose how they view the physiological changes (which cannot be corrected or adapted to; see next section) that are occurring in their bodies. Rather than viewing partial erection, erectile changes, lack of vaginal lubrication, or pain during intercourse as sexual losses, the elderly might choose to view these as inevitable transitions. We expect change in all other areas of life and should not be dismayed to discover that the normal process of aging involves changes in one's body (Keogh, 1990).

Adapting as Necessary The elderly might also choose to adapt where necessary. Adaptation does not mean resignation. It may mean finding substitute techniques for sexual expression. For example, for a partial erection, some couples use the "stuffing technique," manually pushing the penis in the vagina. This often stimulates the penis to erection, which can be followed by intercourse. Cross (1989) also noted:

> . . . many men (and sometimes their partners) need to learn that wonderful sex is possible without an erect penis. Tongues, fingers, vibrators, and many other gadgets can make wonderful stimulators and can alleviate performance anxiety. (p. 15)

Another sexual problem, pain during intercourse, was reported by slightly more than 10% of the women in the Starr and Weiner study (1981). Such pain may be caused by decreased vaginal lubrication, a smaller vaginal opening, and friction against the thinner walls of the vagina. A liberal use of KY jelly, a sterile lubricant, is helpful in minimizing the pain. Applied to both the penis and vagina, it helps the penis slide in and out with less friction. Saliva also serves as a good lubricant. It is readily available, free, and the right temperature, and its application is more intimate than something from a tube (Cross, 1989, p. 15).

Other sexual problems, such as erectile failure, may be treated with medications and penile implants (discussed in Chapter 15). The importance of maintaining such functioning was illustrated in a study by Singer, et al. (1991) who asked 50 men aged 45 to 70 whether they would choose surgery or radiotherapy for prostate cancer. The former is associated with decreased ability to have erections (Vereecken, 1989) but with a longer life survival. Sixty-eight percent of the respondents faced with this hypothetical choice were willing to trade some years of their life for continued erectile functions.

Choices in Widowhood Widows sometimes choose to question the belief that lovemaking with a husband is the only appropriate way to experience sex. Such a choice may be significant since most women will outlive their husbands by eight or more years. Elderly women (as well as never-married women) may choose to experience masturbation, lesbianism, or having young lovers. There is no biological limitation on the sexual capacity of elderly females, so their sexual expression may take many forms.

Sexual Choices among the Young in Preparation for the Later Years

William Young noted that "the best insurance for continued sexual activity in later years appears to be frequent sexual activity in the earlier years" (1990, p. 121). Hence, one of the choices men and women in middle age might consider is whether to curtail their sexual activity because doing so may diminish their desires for it as they age.

Summary

1. Sexuality changes across a person's life span, beginning in infancy where the development of trust through a nurturing parent-child bond provides the basis for an intimate emotional and sexual relationship as an adult.
2. Nonexploitive sex play with peers in childhood and adolescence is common and has no negative effects.

3. Adolescent girls are more likely to experience their first intercourse with vulnerability and concerns about its impact on the relationship with their partner; adolescent boys are more likely to experience first intercourse in terms of achievement and conquest.
4. Adolescents who have the interpersonal skills to handle peer and social pressure for early first intercourse are more likely to delay first intercourse than adolescents who simply value abstinence.
5. Sexuality among the divorced is sometimes characterized by passion and by the search for repairing damaged self-esteem and developing a renewed sense of adequacy.
6. Sexuality in middle age is characterized by menopause (with varying effects) in women and a diminution of testosterone in men. The latter is associated with less firm erections.
7. Sexual activity often declines in the later years due to changes in physiology and lack of an available partner. However, such changes are not inevitable.
8. Researchers do not agree on the benefits of hormone replacement therapy for menopausal women. Deciding about HRT should be made in consultation with one's health care provider.
9. Continued sexual activity across one's lifetime is the best predictor of being sexually active in the later years.

KEY TERMS

childhood
adolescence
secondary sex characteristics
satiation
middle age
menopause
menarche
climacteric
hormone replacement therapy (HRT)
estrogen replacement therapy

REFERENCES

Adler, T. (1991, July). Women's expectations are menopause villains. *APA Monitor,* p. 14.

Andre, T., Frevert, R. L., & Schuchmann, D. (1989). From whom have college students learned about sex? *Youth and Society, 20,* 241–268.

Bachmann, C. (1991). Sexual dysfunction in the older woman. *Medical Aspects of Human Sexuality, 25,* 42–45.

Bachmann, G. A. (1992). Using androgens to increase libido. *Medical Aspects of Human Sexuality, 26,* 6.

Bachmann, G., & Grill, J. (1988). Endocrine and metabolic changes of menopause. *Medical Aspects of Human Sexuality, 74,* 81.

Bancroft, J. (1989). *Human sexuality and its problems* (2nd Ed.). Edinburgh: Churchill Livingstone.

Beck, M. (1992, May 25). Menopause. *Newsweek,* pp. 71–79.

Bell, R. (1987). *Changing bodies, changing lives: A book for teens on sex and relationships.* New York: Vintage Books.

Bengtsson, C. (1989). Aspects of hormone replacement therapy in the post-menopause. *Maturitas, 11,* 35–41.

Bernard, (1990). Gynecological conditions and sexuality. In C. I Fogel and D. Lauver (Eds.), *Sexual health promotion* Philadelphia: W. B. Saunders. (pp. 436–458).

Bowe, C. (1992, February). Everything we think, feel, and do about divorce: Facts gleaned from Cosmo's in-depth survey. *Cosmopolitan,* pp. 199–203.

Brecher, E. (1984). *Love, sex, and aging.* Boston: Little, Brown.

Boston Women's Health Book Collective. (1984). *The New Our Bodies, Ourselves.* New York: Simon & Schuster.

Bretschneider, J. G., & McCoy, N. L. (1988). Sexual interest and behavior in healthy 80- to 102-year-olds. *Archives of Sexual Behavior, 17,* 109–128.

Bulcroft, K., & O'Conner-Roden, M. (1987). Never too late. In H. E. Fitzgerald and M. G. Walraven (Eds.), *Human development 87/88* (pp. 267–269). Guilford, CT: Dushkin.

Burton, L. M., & Bengtson, V. L. (1985). Black grandmothers: Issues of timing and continuity of roles. In V. L. Bengtson and J. F. Robertson (Eds.), *Grandparenthood* (pp. 61–80). Beverely Hills, CA: Sage.

Calderone, M. S., & Johnson, E. W. (1989). *The family book about sexuality.* New York: Harper and Row.

Campbell, T. A., & Campbell, D. E. (1990). Considering the adolescent's point of view: A marketing model for sex education. *Journal of Sex Education and Therapy, 16,* 185–194.

Chilman, C. S. (1989). Some major issues regarding adolescent sexuality and childrearing in the United States. *Journal of Social Work and Human Sexuality, 8,* 3–26.

Christopher, F. S., & Roosa, M. W. (1990). An evaluation of an adolescent pregnancy prevention program: Is 'Just Say No' enough? *Family Relations, 39,* 68–72.

Clark, S. D., Zabin, L. S., & Hardy, J. B. (1984). Sex, contraception and parenthood: Experience and attitudes among urban black young men. *Family Planning Perspectives, 16,* 77–82.

Connell, E. B. (1991). Contraceptive options for the woman over 40. *Medical Aspects of Human Sexuality, 25* (4), 20–24.

Cross, R. J. (January/February 1989). What doctors and others need to know: Six rules on human sexuality and aging. *SIECUS Report,* 14–16.

Cutross, T. (1992, February). Hot monogamy. *Redbook,* pp. 62–67+.

Darling, C. A., Davidson, J. K., Sr., & Parish, W. E., Jr. (1989). Single parents: Interaction of parenting and sexual issues. *Journal of Sex and Marital Therapy, 15,* 227–245.

Diokno, A. C., Brown, M. B., Herzog, A. R. (1990). Sexual function in the elderly. *Archives of Internal Medicine, 150,* 197–200.

Duncan, P. D., Ritter, P. L., Dornbusch, S. M., Gross, R. T., & Carlsmith, J. M. (1990). The effects of pubertal timing on body image, school behavior, and deviance. In R. E. Muuss (Ed.), *Adolescent behavior and society* (pp. 51–56). New York: McGraw-Hill.

Dupont, W. D., & Page, D. L. (1991). Menopausal estrogen replacement therapy and breast cancer. *Archives of Internal Medicine, 151,* 67–72.

Falsaperla, A., Monici Preti, P. A., & Oliani, C. (1990). Selegiline versus oxiracetam in patients with Alzheimer-type dementia. *Clinical Therapeutics, 12,* 376–384.

Finkelhor, D., Williams, L. M., & Burns, N. (1988). *Nursery crimes: sexual abuse in day care.* Newbury Park: Sage.

Fischer, J. L. (1981). Transitions in relationship style from adolescence to young adulthood. *Journal of Youth and Adolescence, 10,* 11–24.

Fisher, W. A. (1986). A psychological approach to human sexuality: The sexual behavior sequence. In D. Byrne and K. Kelley (Eds.), *Alternative approaches to the study of sexual behavior* (pp. 131–171). Hillsdale, NJ: Lawrence Erlbaum Associates.

Frank, E., & Anderson, C. (1989). The sexual stages of marriage. In J. M. Henslin (Ed.), *Marriage and family in a changing society* (pp. 190–196). New York: Free Press.

Glenn, N. D., & Weaver, C. N. (1988). The changing relationship of marital status to reported happiness. *Journal of Marriage and the Family, 50,* 317–324.

Goff, J. L. (1990). Sexual confusion among college males. *Adolescence, 25,* 599–614.

Greeley, A. M., Michael, R. T., & Smith, T. W. (1990). Americans and their sexual partners. *Society, 27,* (5), 36–42.

Greenblat, C. S. (1983). The salience of sexuality in the early years of marriage. *Journal of Marriage and the Family, 4,* 289–299.

Griffin, J. A. (1977). Cross-cultural investigation of behavioral changes at menopause. *Social Science Journal, 14,* 49–55.

Hallstrom, T., & Samuelsson, S. (1990). Changes in women's sexual desire in middle life: The longitudinal study of women in Gothenburg. *Archives of Sexual Behavior, 19,* 259–268.

Hunter, M. S. (1990). Emotional well-being, sexual behavior and hormone replacement therapy. *Maturitas, 12,* 299–314.

Jaccard, J., & Dittus, P. (1991). Parent–teen communication: Toward the prevention of unintended pregnancies. New York: Springer–Verlag.

Johnson, T. C. (1989). Female child perpetrators: Children who molest other children. *Child Abuse and Neglect, 13,* 571–585.

Kaiser, F. E. (1991). Sexuality and impotence in aging man. *Clinics in Geriatric Medicine, 7,* 63–72.

Kaplan, H. S. (1990). Sex, intimacy, and the aging process. *Journal of the American Academy of Psychoanalysis, 18,* 185–205.

Keogh, E. J. (1990). The male menopause. *Australian Family Physician, 19,* 833–840.

Kinsey, A. C., Pomeroy, W. & Martin, C. (1948). *Sexual behavior in the human male.* Philadelphia, PA: Saunders.

Kinsey, A. C., Pomeroy, W., Martin, C., & Gebhard, P. (1953). *Sexual Behavior in the Human Female.* Philadelphia, PA: Saunders.

Knox, D., Schacht, C. (1992). Sexual behaviors of university students enrolled in a human sexuality course. *College Student Journal, 26,* 38–40.

Krefft, V. (1992, February). Stars and their steadies. *Redbook,* p. 65.

Leight, L. (1990). *Raising sexually healthy children.* New York: Avon.

Leitenberg, H., Greenwald, E., & Tarran, M. (1989). The relationship between sexual activity among children during preadolescence and/or early adolescence and sexual behavior and sexual adjustment in young adulthood. *Archives of Sexual Behavior, 18,* 299–313.

Lewis, R. A. (1973). Parents and peers: Socialization agents in the coital behavior of young adults. *Journal of Sex Research, 9,* 156–170.

Lieblum, S., & Bachmann, G. (1988). The sexuality of the climacteric woman. In B. Eskin (Ed.), *The menopause: Comprehensive management* (pp. 164–180). New York: Yearbook Medical Publications.

Linn, R. (1991). Sexual and moral development of Israeli female adolescents from city and kibbutz: Perspectives of Kohlberg and Gilligan. *Adolescence, 26,* 59–70.

Love, R. R. (1991). Antiestrogen chemoprevention of breast cancer: Critical issues and research. *Preventive Medicine, 20,* 64–78.

Markov, T. (1991). *Sex games and folklore.* Unpublished manuscript. East Carolina University, Greenville, NC.

Matthews, K. A. (1992, in press). Myths and realities of the menopause. *Psychosomatic Medicine, 54,* 1–9.

Matthews, K. A., Wing R. R., Kuller, L. H., Meilahn, E. N., Kelsey, S. F., Costello, E. J., Caggiula, A. W., (1990). Influences of natural menopause on psychological characteristics and symptoms of middle-aged healthy women. *Journal of Consulting and Clinical Psychology, 58,* 345–351.

McGraw, R. K. (1991). Psychosexual changes associated with the perimenopausal period. *Journal of Nurse-Midwifery, 36,* 17–24.

Mercier, L. R., & Berger, R. M. (1989). Social service needs of lesbian and gay adolescents: Telling it their way. *Journal of Social Work and Human Sexuality, 8,* 75–98.

Metz, M. E., & Seifert, M. H., Jr. (1990). Men's expectations of physicians in sexual health concerns. *Journal of Sex and Marital Therapy, 16,* 79–88.

Morley, J. E., & Kaiser, F. E. (1989). Sexual function with advancing age. *Medical Clinics of North America, 73,* 1483–1495.

Mott, F. L., & Haurin, R. J. (1988). Linkages between sexual activity and alcohol and drug use among American adolescents. *Family Planning Perspectives, 20,* 128–136.

Mulligan, T. & Moss, C. (1991). Sexuality and aging in male veterans: A cross-sectional study of interest, ability, and activity. *Archives of Sexual Behavior, 20,* 17–25.

Mulligan, T., & Palguta, R. F., Jr. (1991). Sexual interest, activity, and satisfaction among male nursing home residents. *Archives of Sexual Behavior, 20,* 199–204.

National Center for Health Statistics. (1992). *Births, marriages, divorces, and deaths for September, 1991. (Monthly Vital Statistics Report,* vol. 40, no. 9).

National Research Council. (1987). *Risking the future: Adolescent sexuality, pregnancy, and childbearing* (Table 2-6). Washington, DC: National Academy Press.

Okami, P. (1992). Child perpetrators of sexual abuse: The emergence of a problematic deviant category. *The Journal of Sex Research, 29,* 109–130.

Peter, L. J. (1982). *Peter's almanac,* New York: Morrow.

Petersen, A. C. (1987, September). Those gangly years. *Psychology Today,* pp. 28–39.

Phinney, V. G., Jensen, L. C., Olsen, J. A., & Cundick, B. (1990). The relationship between early development and psychosexual behaviors in adolescent females. *Adolescence, 25,* 321–332.

Pietropinto, A. (1987). Sex and the elderly. *Medical Aspects of Human Sexuality, 21,* 110–117.

Pines, A., Fisman, E. Z., Levo, Y., Averbuch, M., Lidor, A., Drory, Y., Finkelstein, A., Hetman-Peri, M., Moshknwitz, M., Ben-Ari, E., & Ayalon, D. (1991). The effects of hormone replacement therapy in normal postmenopausal women: Measurements of Doppler-derived parameters of aortic flow. *American Journal of Obstetrics and Gynecology, 164,* 806–812.

Pleck, J. H., Sonenstein, F. L., & Ku L. C. (1990). Contraceptive attitudes and intention to use condoms in sexually experienced and inexperienced adolescent males. *Journal of Family Issues, 11,* 294–312.

Premarital Sexual experience among adolescent women—United States, 1970–1988. (1991, January 4). *Morbidity and Mortality Weekly Report, 39,* 929–932.

Reinisch, J. M., with R. Beasley. (1990). *The Kinsey Institute's new report on sex.* New York: St. Martin's Press.

Rivera, G., (1991). Exposing myself. New York: Bantams.

Rodgers, J. L., & Rowe, D. C. (1990). Adolescent sexual activity and mildly deviant behavior. *Journal of Family Issues, 11,* 274–293.

Rosenbaum, E., & Kandel, D. B. (1990). Early onset of adolescent sexual behavior and drug involvement. *Journal of Marriage and the Family, 52,* 783–798.

Salter, A. C. (1988). *Treating child sex offenders and victims: A practical guide.* Newbury Park: Sage.

Sarrel, L. J., & Sarrel, P. M. (1979). *Sexual unfolding: Sexual development and sex therapies in late adolescence.* Boston: Little, Brown.

Sarrel, P. M. (1990). Sexuality and menopause. *Obstetrics and Gynecology, 75,* (4 Suppl), 26s–30s.

Schiavi, R. C., Schreiner-Engle, P., & Mandeli, J. (1990). Healthy aging and male sexual function. *American Journal of Psychiatry, 147,* 766.

Sheehy, G. (1976). *Passages: Predictable crises of adult life.* New York: Dutton.

Sherwin, B. B. (1991a). The impact of different doses of estrogen and progestin on mood and sexual behavior in postmenopausal women. *Journal of Clinical Endocrinology and Metabolism, 72,* 336–343.

Sherwin, B. B. (1991b). The psychoendrocrinology of aging and female sexuality. In J. Bancroft, C. M. Davis, and H. J. Ruppel (Eds.), *Annual review of sex research* (vol. 2) (pp. 181–198). Lake Mills, IA: Stoles Graphic Services.

Singer, P. A., Tasch, E. S., Stocking, C., Rubin, S., Siegler, M., & Weichselbaum, R. (1991). Sex or survival: Trade-offs between quality and quantity of life. *Journal of Clinical Oncology, 9,* 328–334.

Smith, T. W. (1991). Adult sexual behavior in 1989: Number of partners, frequency of intercourse and risk of AIDS. *Family Planning Perspectives, 23,* 102–107.

Starr, B., & Weiner, M. (1981). *The Starr-Weiner report on sex and sexuality in the mature years.* New York: Stein and Day.

Statistical abstract of the United States: 1992 (112th ed.) (1992). Washington, DC: U.S. Bureau of the Census.

Tavris, C. (1992). *The mismeasure of woman.* New York: Simon & Schuster.

Thompson, A. P. (1983). Extramarital sex: A review of the research literature. *Journal of Sex Research, 19,* 1–22.

Thornton, A. (1990). The courtship process of adolescent sexuality. *Journal of Family Issues, 11,* 239–273.

Thornton, A., & Freedman, D. (1982). Changing attitudes toward marriage and single life. *Family Planning Perspectives, 14,* 297–303.

Vereecken, R. L. (1989). Sexual activity of men presenting with prostatism: Effect of prostatectomy. *European Urology, 16,* 328–332.

Walling, M., Andersen, B. L., & Johnson, S. R. (1990). Hormonal replacement therapy for postmenopausal women: A review of sexual outcomes and related gynecologic effects. *Archives of Sexual Behavior, 19, 119–136.*

Weis, D. L. (1983). Affective reactions of women to their initial experience of coitus. *Journal of Sex Research, 19,* 209–237.

Wheeler, V. (1990). A new kind of loving? The effect of continence problems on sexuality. *Professional Nurse, 5,* 492–496.

White, S. D. & DeBlassie, R. R. (1992). Adolescent sexual behavior. *Adolescence,* 27, 183–191.

Wing, R. R., Matthews, K. A., Kuller, L. H., Meilahn, E. N., & Plantinga, P. L., (1991). Weight gain at the time of menopause. *Archives of Internal Medicine, 151,* 97–102.

Winn, R. L., & Newton, N. (1982). Sexuality in aging: A study of 106 cultures. *Archives of Sexual Behavior, 11,* 283–298.

Young, R. L., Kumar, N. S., & Goldzieher, J. W. (1990). Management of menopause when estrogen cannot be used. *Drugs, 40,* 220–230.

Young, W. R. (1990). Changes in sexual functioning during the aging process. In F. J. Bianoco and R. Hernandez Serrano (Eds.), *Sexology: An independent field* (pp. 121–128). New York: Elsevier Science.

Zabin, L. S., Hirsch, M. B., Smith, E. A., & Hardy, J. B. (1984). Adolescent sexual attitudes and behavior: Are they consistent? *Family Planning Perspectives, 16,* 181–185.

Enhancement Choices

PART FOUR

Two of the positive aspects of viewing sexuality from a choice perspective are the opportunity for enhancement of our sexuality and the fostering of a sense of personal responsibility. In Part IV, we discuss various enhancement choices surrounding communication, love, and sexual dysfunctions. In regard to communication, we can choose to discuss issues, resolve conflict, and express preferences involving what we would like our partner to do sexually. Alternatively, we can decide to avoid issues, adapt to conflict, and accept whatever ways our partner relates to us sexually. Enhancement of sexuality seems to be in favor of the first choice.

In regard to love, our choices include having sex along a continuum of emotional intensity from sex without love to sex with love. Although a case for choosing sex without love can be made, most people prefer to choose to enjoy sex in the context of a stable, enduring emotional relationship.

Finally, Masters and Johnson have conservatively estimated that half of all couples experience some form of sexual dysfunction. Given the probability that we will experience a sexual dysfunction at some time, we have choices in how we seek to resolve it. For example, in the case of erectile dysfunction with an organic cause, the couple may consider penile injection, penile prosthesis, or one of several penile vacuum devices. Each of these choices permits the enhancement of sexuality.

CHAPTER THIRTEEN

Communication and Sexuality

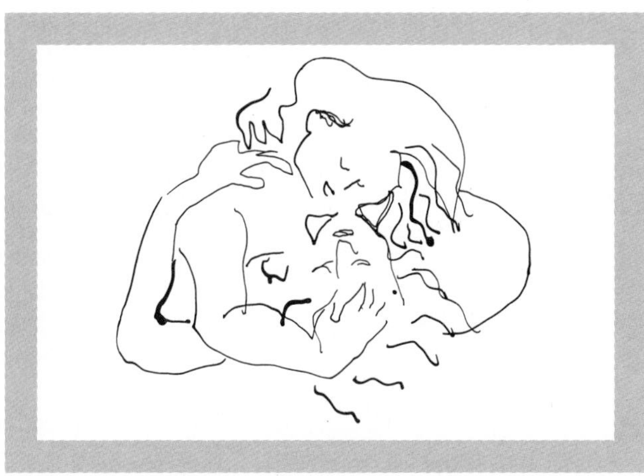

Chapter Outline

Communication in Relationships
- Components of Effective Communication
- **Personal Policy Perspective:** Sexual Communication: Informed Consent versus Coercion
- Communication: Content versus Process
- Communication and Intimacy in Relationships
- **Self-Assessment:** Sexual Self-Disclosure Scale

Basic Communication Skills
- Maintain Eye Contact
- Ask Open-Ended Questions
- Use Reflective Listening
- Use "I" Statements

Resolving Interpersonal Conflict
- Address Recurring, Disturbing Issues
- Focus on What You Want (Rather Than What You Don't Want)
- Find Out the Other Person's Point of View
- Generate Solutions to the Conflict

Sexual Interactions as Communication

Choices
- Choose to Tell One's Partner of Sexual Dissatisfactions?
- Choose to Talk about One's Sexual Past to One's Partner?
- Choose to Disclose Attractions to Others to One's Partner?

Is It True?*

1. Research on college students has revealed that men are more likely than women to lie to someone in order to have sex with that person.

2. Research on deception in close relationships has found that the most frequently reported reason for deception was to avoid hurting the partner.

3. Men and women rely on different nonverbal cues to assess each other's interest in having sex.

4. In order to successfully resolve conflict, one person must "win" while the other person loses.

5. People negotiating sex with a new partner rarely have the information necessary to make an informed decision.

* 1=T, 2=T, 3=T, 4=F, 5=T

Each person's life is lived as a series of conversations.

Deborah Tannen

Mary is involved in an emotional and sexual relationship with Tom. Cunnilingus is the only way she can experience an orgasm, but she is reluctant to talk with Tom about her need. She has a dilemma—if she chooses to tell Tom, she risks his disapproval and his rejecting doing what she asks. If she does not tell Tom of her need, she risks growing resentful and feeling unsatisfied in their sexual relationship.

Bob has drifted into a flirtatious relationship with a woman in his office. He is emotionally and sexually attracted to her. He knows she feels the same. Bob is also in love with Karen and is committed to her emotionally and sexually. Should he tell Karen of his attraction to the woman at work? Should he disclose that he has dreamed about her? How open should he be?

Jane enjoys sexual variety (numerous sex partners). She never gets emotionally involved, is always discrete, and practices safe sex. She is a good mother to her children and loves her husband (with whom she has been married for 11 years). Should she keep this side of her personality hidden or be open with her husband?

As the preceding scenarios illustrate, being open to one's partner about one's sexual dissatisfactions, attraction to others, and sexual wants or desires are examples of how communication interacts with sexuality. In this chapter, we examine communication about sexuality in the context of the larger issue of relationship communication. We also discuss some basic communication skills and strategies for resolving interpersonal conflict and look at sexual interactions as a form of communication. We begin by discussing some general aspects of communication in relationships.

Communication in Relationships

Good sexual communication is associated with the partners having a good relationship in general. In a study of 402 married individuals, satisfaction with sexual communication was significantly and positively associated with marital satisfaction, marital cohesion, and sexual satisfaction (Cupach & Comstock, 1990). Good relationships in general have also been associated with effective communication (Turner, 1991).

Components of Effective Communication

Communication may be defined as the process of exchanging information between two or more individuals. Information may be communicated verbally (spoken or written words) or nonverbally (tone of voice, body language). Effective communication is defined as the exchange of information that is timely, accurate, and precise (Turner, 1991).

Timely Information Timely information is information that is communicated at a time that allows the receiver to make an appropriate response. For example, suppose you have an STD. Choosing to tell a new partner with whom there is the potential

Close, intimate communication is important in creating and maintaining a good relationship.

for sexual involvement very early in the relationship allows the partner to make choices regarding protection against contracting the STD.

Accurate and Honest Information Effective communication in intimate relationships also involves conveying information that is accurate. Simply stated, accurate information is information that is true. If you tell your partner that you have not had intercourse with anyone before, when in fact you have had three sexual partners, you are giving inaccurate information.

CONSIDERATION: In some cases, we may unintentionally provide inaccurate information (for example, when we, ourselves, have been misinformed). When we intentionally convey false information, we are being dishonest. Honesty is a trait that most individuals value in their intimate relationships. In a study of 85 single black professional women, honesty was ranked as the most important quality in a mate (Sparrow, 1991).

In spite of the value of honesty, considerable dishonesty may occur in relationships. Saxe (1991) observed that deception is "a ubiquitous feature of human social interaction" (p. 409). In Exhibit 13.1, we discuss sexual lies reported by college students.

He told me he threw away his old condoms and bought new ones. Well, he lied. He used an old condom. It broke; I became pregnant.

Authors' class notes

In a study on deception in close relationships, researchers found that the most frequently reported specific reason for deception was to avoid hurting the partner (Metts, 1989). This study also revealed that (1) married persons reported more instances of deception by omission and fewer instances of explicit falsification, (2) dating partners reported more reasons for deception focused on protecting their resources and avoiding stress or abuse from the partner, (3) dating partners reported more reasons for deception focused on avoiding relationship trauma or termination, and (4) married persons reported more reasons focused on avoiding threats to the partner's self-esteem.

In Exhibit 13.1, we noted that some sexual lies reported by university students are told for the purpose of coercing another person to engage in sexual behavior. The following Personal Policy Perspective explores the importance of engaging in sexual behavior on the basis of informed consent, rather than coercion.

PERSONAL POLICY PERSPECTIVE

Sexual Communication: Informed Consent versus Coercion

As you will recall from Chapter 4, Research in Human Sexuality, prior to engaging a participant in research, an experimenter must provide the subject with an opportunity to make informed consent to participate. In addition, the participant must be free from coercion and protected from harm, and the balance between the risks and benefits of the research must be considered. Some educators (Allgeier, 1985; Mosher, 1989) have proposed that the same careful decision making and safeguards involved in protecting potential research participants should also be employed to protect potential sexual partners. Mosher lamented:

> . . . initial decisions to engage in sexual intercourse rarely meet either ethically responsible or legal standards of informed consent. People negotiating sexual contacts rarely are given information about the costs and benefits of participating. Even the details of the sexual script to be enacted—who is going to do what sexually to whom, much less exactly how and exactly when—are not explicit. We know few people share information about their histories of sexually-transmitted diseases or negotiate who is going to furnish a condom or be responsible for birth control. (p. 505)

Continued

Continued

Coercion

There is considerable evidence that aside from sexual interactions that are physically forced, many sexual acts are coerced or partners are involved through trickery. Craig, Kalichman, and Follingstad (1989) surveyed college men at a large state university and revealed that 42% of the men admitted to using verbal coercion to obtain intercourse. These men reported having sexual intercourse with a woman "when she didn't really want to by saying things you didn't really mean, making promises, talking her into it, etc." and by use of threats of force if she didn't cooperate (p. 424). A study by Kanin (1985) compared college men who admitted forcing a woman to have intercourse (rapists) with college men who said they had never used force (control group). Not surprisingly, the rapists group more often admitted to using alcohol or marijuana to try to intoxicate a woman so they could have intercourse with her (76%), but 23% of the controls also used this strategy. The rapist group reported falsely professing love (86%), but so did one fourth of the controls (25%).

Women are not the only victims of coercion. A survey of students at a small midwestern university revealed that 16% of college male respondents said they had been forced to have sexual intercourse while on a date. The most frequent method of coercion used by women was verbal pressure, such as pleading, demands, or blackmail (Struckman-Johnson, 1991).

In defining sexual offense, the report of the National Task Force on Juvenile Sexual Offending (National Adolescent Perpetrator Network, 1988) distinguished between consent and mere cooperation or compliance. The task force observed that one might comply with sexual behavior (engage in a sexual behavior without overt resistance, despite opposing beliefs or desire), but that compliance may occur without consent. Consent was defined as including all of the following:

> 1) understanding what is proposed based on age, maturity, developmental level, functioning and experience; 2) knowledge of societal standards for what is being proposed; 3) awareness of potential consequences and alternatives; 4) assumption that agreements or disagreements will be respected equally; 5) voluntary decision; and 6) mentally competent. (p. 8)

Informed Consent in Sexual Relationships

Allgeier (1985, 1986) observed that parents rarely give their adolescents practical guidelines for making sexual decisions and communicating with their potential partners. She suggested (1986) that if we were socialized to ask for and give informed consent in relationships, such problems as unwanted pregnancy, sexually transmissible diseases, assault, sexual exploitation, and guilty feelings would be reduced. In her list of criteria to help determine "Are You Ready For Sex?" (1985) were several criteria which depend upon open communication with a potential partner. In addition to considering motivations for sex (discussed in Chapter 2, Values in Sexuality) the Allgeier criteria included being able to discuss and agree upon the following issues. If pregnancy is not desired, what effective contraceptive method will be used, and how will you handle the details of its use, such as obtaining and paying for it? Considering that contraceptive methods are not 100% effective, have you discussed what you would do if pregnancy occurred? And, finally, have you discussed the potential of contracting or transmitting STDs and agreed on what steps you will take to reduce risk?

Continued

Continued

What is involved in giving and receiving truly informed consent? In considering one's duty to one's partner, Mosher (1989, p. 505) suggested contemplating, "Have I fully informed my partner of all known risks and benefits of being sexual with me to ensure my partner's consent is both informed and voluntary?"

References

Allgeier, E. R. (1985). Are you ready for sex? Informed consent for sexual intimacy. *SIECUS Report, 13,* 8–9.

Allgeier, E. R. (1986). Coercive versus consensual sexual interactions. *G. Stanley Hall Lecture Series, 7,* (pp. 7–63). Washington, DC: American Psychological Association.

Craig, M. E., Kalichman, S. C., & Follingstad, D. R. (1989). Verbal coercive sexual behavior among college students. *Archives of Sexual Behavior, 18,* 421–434.

Kanin, E. J. (1985). Date rapists: Differential sexual socialization and relative deprivation. *Archives of Sexual Behavior, 14,* 219–231.

Mosher, D. L. (1989). Threat to sexual freedom: Moralistic intolerance instills a spiral of silence. *Journal of Sex Research, 26,* 492–509.

National Adolescent Perpetrator Network (1988). Preliminary report from the National Task Force on Juvenile Sexual Offending. *Juvenile and Family Court Journal, 39,* i–66.

Struckman-Johnson, C. (1991). Male victims of acquaintance rape. In A. Parrot & L. Bechhofer (Eds.), *Acquaintance Rape* (pp. 192–213). New York: John Wiley & Sons.

EXHIBIT 13.1 Sexual Lies Told By College Students

It is not uncommon for dishonesty to occur in sexual relationships. Shusterman and Saxe (cited in Saxe, 1991) asked 50 undergraduate students who were involved in relationships whether they had ever lied to their partners. More than 85% reported that they had lied to their partners. Examples of lies that students reported include:

- I kissed another guy at a party and never told my boyfriend.
- I cheated on her with an attractive friend of mine.
- I was sexually involved with a friend of his for about a month.

In the Schusterman and Saxe study, 41% of the lies reported by students involved extradyadic sex. Almost all of the subjects reported that the reason for the deception was to protect their partners or their relationship. For example, students who lied to their partners said that they did so for the following reasons:

- The other guy didn't matter to me at all, so I didn't want to risk the relationship.
- I wouldn't want the hassle of breaking her trust in me.
- I didn't want to hurt him.

Other studies have been conducted in regard to lying in relationships. In one study of 18- to 25-year-old students attending college in California, 34% of men and 10% of women reported having told a lie to someone in order to have sex with that person (Cochran & Mays, 1990). Another study found that lying was one of the strategies that university men use to obtain sexual intimacy (Gray, Lesser, Rebach, Hooks, & Bounds, 1988). In another study, 39% of 252 women reported that they sometimes to always pretended to have an orgasm when they did not (Darling, Davidson, & Cox, 1991).

Men in a sample of undergraduates were asked what they would say if asked by a pretty woman whether they had been tested for HIV and to assume that she would only have sex if they said they had and had tested negative. Twenty-percent of the men reported that they would say that they had had the test and that they had tested negative, even though they hadn't. Only 4% of the women who were asked how they would answer this question from a good-looking man reported that they would tell this lie (Cochran, 1989).

Knox, Schacht, Holt, and Turner (in press) also studied sexual lies among college students. Their data revealed the following sexual lies reported by female and male students:

Continued

EXHIBIT 13.1 Sexual Lies Told By College Students—*Continued*

Sexual Lies Reported by Female College Students

- I have said I wanted to have intercourse with my husband when I really didn't just to make him happy.
- Lied about having an orgasm when I didn't.
- I told him it felt good when it didn't.
- I have said I had a headache when I didn't.
- You're the best lover that I've ever had.
- It's not you, it's me (explaining the reason why she had not reached orgasm).
- I told him that it was O.K. that the lovemaking session wasn't long enough.
- You're the only person I've had sex with.
- No, I don't have any STDs.
- I've never loved anyone as much as I love you.
- I can't have intercourse, I have my period.
- I lied about being with another guy.
- I told my partner that I had sex before, when I really hadn't.
- No, that doesn't hurt.
- I agreed to be on the bottom when I really wanted to be on top.
- I lied about being a virgin when I really wasn't.
- I told my sex partner that I was ready to have intercourse when I was really scared to death.
- I lied about my past boyfriends.

Sexual Lies Reported by Male College Students

- I lied about my name when I slept with a girl.
- I never had sex with another male.
- I don't care about breast size.
- My girlfriend asked me if I ever looked at other girls. I told her no, that my eyes were only for her.
- I'm a virgin.
- I won't tell anyone we had sex.
- It won't be just sex, it will be making love.
- I really do love you.
- I've never loved anyone but you.
- This is my first time.
- I'll pull out in time.
- I haven't been with that many women.
- No, your vagina doesn't smell bad.
- Your weight is fine with me.
- I want to marry you in the future.
- I'm not using you.
- No, I don't have AIDS.

References

Cochran, S. D. (1989). Women and HIV infection: Issues in prevention and behavior change. In V. M. Mays, G. W. Albee, and S. F. Schneider (Eds.), *Primary prevention of AIDS* (pp. 309–327). Newbury Park, CA: Sage.

Cochran, S., & Mays, V. (1990). Sex, lies and HIV. *New England Journal of Medicine, 322,* 774–775.

Darling, C. A., Davidson, J. K., Sr., & Cox, R. P. (1991). Female sexual response and the timing of partner orgasm. *Journal of Sex and Marital Therapy, 17,* 3–21.

Gray, M. D., Lesser, D., Rebach, H., Hooks, B., & Bounds, C., (1988). Sexual aggression and victimization: A local perspective. *Response to the Victimization of Women and Children, 11,* 9–13.

Knox, D., Schacht, D., Holt, J., & Turner, J. (in press). Sex lies among university students. *College Student Journal.*

Saxe, L. (1991). Lying: Thoughts of an applied social psychologist. *American Psychologist, 46,* 409–415.

Precise Information Effective communication implies not only that information be timely, accurate, and honest but also precise. Precise information is that which is clearly expressed with specificity and detail. In relationships, communicating precise information implies revealing *exactly* how you feel and what you want. For example, if there is a particular condom (latex, reservoir tip, with non-oxyonol 9) that you prefer, it is important that you make your wishes known. Otherwise, your partner may select a condom (animal skin, no anti-HIV spermicide agent) that you do not like and will not use.

Being precise about one's emotions may be more difficult than being precise about one's preferred condom. For example, consider a woman whose partner has been invited to a bachelor party at which there will be a stripper. The woman feels that she will be very upset if her partner goes to this party; she may even feel that she does not want to be involved with "the kind of man who goes to those kinds of parties." If she tells her partner that she prefers that he not go to the bachelor party, she is providing accurate information. However, she is not communicating information that is precise; she is not telling her partner exactly how she feels about his going to a bachelor party.

CONSIDERATION: Although the words *accurate* and *precise* are often used interchangeably, there is an important distinction in their meanings. *Accurate* means "true." While *precise* has several meanings (see any dictionary), our usage of the word in this chapter means "clearly expressed." An important implication of this distinction is that information that is accurate is not necessarily precise, and information that is precise is not necessarily accurate.

Communication: Content versus Process

Communication involves both content and process. Content refers to the messages exchanged between individuals. **Process** refers to the way in which the content is delivered, received, and responded to. The flow of communication is the process.

Content in Communication As noted earlier, content may be communicated verbally and nonverbally. Verbal communication involves transmitting the message content through spoken or written words. There are many forms of nonverbal communication, including (Argyle, 1988):

1. facial expression
2. gestures and bodily movements
3. spatial behavior (e.g., how close you stand to a person)
4. gaze and pupil dilation
5. bodily contact
6. nonverbal vocalizations (e.g., sighs, grunts)
7. clothes and other aspects of appearance
8. posture
9. smell

Nonverbal behavior often influences the implied meaning of verbal behavior. For example, assume two individuals are saying good-night at the end of their first date. One says to the other, "I'll call you." Depending on the tone of voice (excitement or sullenness) and body language (looking into the eyes of the person and holding hands with the person or looking down and avoiding hand contact), the implied message will be very different.

Men should talk to each other. Not the proverbial "shop talk," but the deeper feelings about work, about love, about themselves, about their feelings for each other.

P. Garfinkel

Tannen (1990) observed that men and women focus on different content in their respective conversations. To men, communication is meaningful only if it is focused on activities; to women, relationships. To men, talk is information; to women it is interaction.

Every sociolinguistic study of men's and women's conversation, and particularly men in conversation with women, has found that men almost entirely dominate the conversation.

W. Neil Elliot

To men, conversations are negotiations in which they try to "achieve and maintain the upper hand if they can, and protect themselves from others' attempts to put them down and push them around" (p. 25). However, to women, conversations are negotiations for closeness in which they try "to seek and give confirmations and support, and to reach consensus" (p. 25). Their goal is to preserve intimacy and avoid isolation.

Men tend to interpret a woman wearing revealing attire as an indication of her interest in and availability for sexual interaction.

Reiss and Reiss (1990) noted that men and women rely on different nonverbal cues to assess the other's readiness for sex. They noted that a man will look to see if his date had another drink, agreed to go to his apartment, laughed at a dirty joke, and permitted him to touch her breast. Women, on the other hand, will look to see if her date smiled at her in a friendly way, laughed at her jokes, listened to her opinions, and kissed her tenderly. Both will then guess the intentions of the other, and neither will engage in direct, clear communication about the sexual agenda.

Goodchilds and Zellman (1984) found that young women and men tend to have different interpretations of both verbal and nonverbal messages of dating partners. In general, the researchers found that men have a greater tendency than women to attribute sexual meanings to a wide range of behaviors. For example, young men tend to interpret the wearing of certain clothing styles (tight jeans, low-cut top, see-through blouse, and no bra) as indications that the woman wants to have sex. Young women are less certain that a woman wearing these same clothing styles is communicating an interest in sex; "she may simply be trying to keep up with the latest fashion trends" (p. 236).

Kleinke and Taylor (1991) looked at how smiling, eye gazing, and leaning forward affected the subjective evaluations that women and men make of strangers of the opposite sex who engage in or fail to engage in these nonverbal behaviors during interaction. Their study found that men tended to have more favorable evaluations of women who smiled, gazed, and leaned forward during interaction, while women tended to have more favorable evaluations of men who smiled and gazed but did not lean forward. Based on the assumption that gazing, smiling, and leaning forward during interaction are behaviors associated with intimacy, the researchers concluded that "the men in this sample had a somewhat greater tolerance for nonverbal intimacy from an opposite-sex stranger than did women" (p. 452).

Merely looking into someone's eyes does not by itself "mean" sexual interest.
Timothy Perper
David Weis

Process in Communication As discussed earlier, the process of effective communication involves conveying timely, accurate, and precise information. When Mary tells Bob that she is angry with him because he stayed out past 2 A.M., she is giving him specific content about her feelings. Mary's comment to Bob is timely, accurate, and precise. She gave him accurate information (she was angry); she told him in a timely fashion (the next morning, rather than three weeks later in the middle of a heated argument); and she told him precisely what she means by "staying out too late" (past 2 A.M.). Even when the content may be difficult or unpleasant, it is important that the process of effective communication continue.

Communication and Intimacy in Relationships

Communication is an important aspect of intimacy in a relationship. In a study of 15,000 respondents, Brecher (1984) attempted to define those factors associated with enduring happy relationships. He looked at such factors as health, income, education, and religion (and 11 others) and found only one "strongly associated" with marital happiness—the quality of communications between the spouses (Brecher, 1984).

Another researcher (Yandoli, 1989) looked at sources of stress in medical marriages (marriages in which one or more partners are medical doctors). The researcher found that problems in medical marriages are not necessarily associated with the number of hours spent working: satisfaction seemed to be associated with communication and intimacy between partners.

In their extensive study of couples (3,574 married couples, 642 cohabitating couples, 957 gay male couples, and 772 lesbian couples), Blumstein and Schwartz

(1983) emphasized the role of communication. Of one enduring couple, they noted, "The secret of their success? Both agree that it is being able to talk things out" (p. 507).

It is clear that the quality of communication and the quality of relationships are closely related. Cupach and Metts (1991) noted that,

> When communication is incompetent, the quality of the relationships suffers. Of course, causality can manifest itself in the other direction as well; relational problems can trigger disenchantment with one's partner and one's relationship, thereby diminishing the effort devoted to effective communication. (p. 93)

In other words, poor communication can lead to an unsatisfactory relationship *and* an unsatisfactory relationship can lead to poor communication. "In either case, sexual satisfaction and relationship satisfaction are clearly interconnected . . . and both are affected by the ability and willingness of partners to interact effectively with one another" (Cupach & Metts, 1991, p. 93).

Communicating about sex with one's partner is important in maintaining sexual and relationship satisfaction (Banmen & Vogel, 1985; Cupach & Comstock, 1990). Talking about sex allows partners to communicate their sexual needs, desires, and preferences to each other. Through sexual communication (verbal), partners also gain an understanding of the meanings each partner attaches to specific sexual behaviors (Metts & Cupach, 1989).

Talking things out becomes particularly important because of the notion of romantic love in our society. It is assumed by romantics that if a couple is truly in love, their love will enable them to resolve whatever differences they may have. Realists argue that this belief is nonsense and that what is needed is open disclosure about the issues relevant to the partners. Lee (1990) noted that "real talk" is talk about the fundamental contractual relations between the partners—the obligations that make the relationship's future more predictable and thus give it the stability that is essential if the relationship is to survive.

CONSIDERATION: Lee (1990) also warned that open disclosure with each other can "open a can of worms" that may require professional help to resolve. Examples of such disclosures might include involvement in an extradyadic affair or a lie told in courtship about the number of sexual partners. While this chapter emphasizes the importance of open communication, partners might carefully evaluate the consequences of their openness with each other.

The level of intimacy in a couple's relationship at a given point can be described by the eight facets outlined below (Russell, 1990; Waring, 1988). As you will note, four of these eight facets of intimacy relate to communication. The facets related to communication are marked with an asterisk.

*1. Conflict resolution—the ease with which differences of opinion are resolved.
*2. Affection—the degree to which feelings of emotional closeness are expressed by the couple.
3. Cohesion—a feeling of commitment to the relationship.
*4. Sexuality—the degree to which sexual needs are communicated and fulfilled by the partner.
5. Identity—the couple's level of self-confidence and self-esteem.
6. Compatibility—the degree to which the couple is able to work and play together comfortably.

Self Assessment

Sexual Self-Disclosure Scale

Instructions Almost everyone has been in a close, intimate relationship with another person at some point in their life, or else they plan to become involved with someone in the future. People who are involved in a close, intimate relationship have a large variety of things they can discuss with each other. This survey is concerned with the extent to which people are willing to discuss several topics about their close relationships with their intimate partner.

For each of the following topics, indicate how willing you would be to discuss that topic with an intimate partner. Use the following scale:

A = I would *not be willing* to discuss this topic with an intimate partner.
B = I would *be slightly willing* to discuss this topic with an intimate partner.
C = I would *be moderately willing* to discuss this topic with an intimate partner.
D = I would *be mostly willing* to discuss this topic with an intimate partner.
E = I would *be completely willing* to discuss this topic with an intimate partner.

Topics Survey - Part A

	A	B	C	D	E
1. My past sexual experiences.	____	____	____	____	____
2. The kinds of touching that sexually arouse me.	____	____	____	____	____
3. My private sexual fantasies.	____	____	____	____	____
4. The sexual preferences that I have.	____	____	____	____	____
5. The types of sexual behaviors I have engaged in.	____	____	____	____	____
6. The sensations that are sexually exciting to me.	____	____	____	____	____
7. My "juicy" sexual thoughts.	____	____	____	____	____
8. What I would desire in a sexual encounter.	____	____	____	____	____
9. The sexual positions I have tried.	____	____	____	____	____
10. The types of sexual foreplay that feel arousing to me.	____	____	____	____	____
11. The sexual episodes that I daydream about.	____	____	____	____	____
12. The things I enjoy most about sex.	____	____	____	____	____

Topics Survey - Part B

13. What sex in an intimate relationship means to me.	____	____	____	____	____
14. My private beliefs about sexual responsibility.	____	____	____	____	____
15. Times when sex was distressing for me.	____	____	____	____	____
16. The times I have pretended to enjoy sex.	____	____	____	____	____
17. Times when I prefer to refrain from sexual activity.	____	____	____	____	____
18. What it means to me to have sex with my partner.	____	____	____	____	____
19. My own ideas about sexual accountability.	____	____	____	____	____
20. Times when I was pressured to have sex.	____	____	____	____	____
21. The times I have lied about sexual matters.	____	____	____	____	____
22. The times when I might not want to have sex.	____	____	____	____	____
23. What I think and feel about having sex with my partner.	____	____	____	____	____
24. The notion that one is accountable for one's sexual behaviors.	____	____	____	____	____
25. The aspects of sex that bother me.	____	____	____	____	____
26. How I would feel about sexual dishonesty.	____	____	____	____	____
27. My ideas about not having sex unless I want to.	____	____	____	____	____

Continued

Self-Assessment—*Continued*

Topics Survey - Part C

	A	B	C	D	E
28. How I feel about abortions.	______	______	______	______	______
29. My personal views about homosexuals.	______	______	______	______	______
30. My own ideas about why rapes occur.	______	______	______	______	______
31. My personal views about people with AIDS.	______	______	______	______	______
32. What I consider "proper" sexual behavior.	______	______	______	______	______
33. My beliefs about pregnancy prevention.	______	______	______	______	______
34. Opinions I have about homosexual relationships.	______	______	______	______	______
35. What I really feel about rape.	______	______	______	______	______
36. Concerns that I have about the disease AIDS.	______	______	______	______	______
37. The sexual behaviors that I consider appropriate.	______	______	______	______	______
38. How I feel about pregnancy at this time.	______	______	______	______	______
39. My reactions to working with a homosexual.	______	______	______	______	______
40. My reactions to rape.	______	______	______	______	______
41. My feelings about working with someone who has AIDS.	______	______	______	______	______
42. My personal beliefs about sexual morality.	______	______	______	______	______

Topics Survey - Part D

	A	B	C	D	E
43. How *satisfied* I feel about the sexual aspects of my life.	______	______	______	______	______
44. How *guilty* I feel about the sexual aspects of my life.	______	______	______	______	______
45. How *calm* I feel about the sexual aspects of my life.	______	______	______	______	______
46. How *depressed* I feel about the sexual aspects of my life.	______	______	______	______	______
47. How *jealous* I feel about the sexual aspects of my life.	______	______	______	______	______
48. How *apathetic* I feel about the sexual aspects of my life.	______	______	______	______	______
49. How *anxious* I feel about the sexual aspects of my life.	______	______	______	______	______
50. How *happy* I feel about the sexual aspects of my life.	______	______	______	______	______
51. How *angry* I feel about the sexual aspects of my life.	______	______	______	______	______
52. How *afraid* I feel about the sexual aspects of my life.	______	______	______	______	______
53. How *pleased* I feel about the sexual aspects of my life.	______	______	______	______	______
54. How *shameful* I feel about the sexual aspects of my life.	______	______	______	______	______
55. How *serene* I feel about the sexual aspects of my life.	______	______	______	______	______
56. How *sad* I feel about the sexual aspects of my life.	______	______	______	______	______
57. How *possessive* I feel about the sexual aspects of my life (i.e., my partner).	______	______	______	______	______
58. How *indifferent* I feel about the sexual aspects of my life.	______	______	______	______	______
59. How *troubled* I feel about the sexual aspects of my life.	______	______	______	______	______
60. How *cheerful* I feel about the sexual aspects of my life.	______	______	______	______	______
61. How *mad* I feel about the sexual aspects of my life.	______	______	______	______	______
62. How *fearful* I feel about the sexual aspects of my life.	______	______	______	______	______
63. How *delighted* I feel about the sexual aspects of my life.	______	______	______	______	______
64. How *embarrassed* I feel about the sexual aspects of my life.	______	______	______	______	______
65. How *relaxed* I feel about the sexual aspects of my life.	______	______	______	______	______
66. How *unhappy* I feel about the sexual aspects of my life.	______	______	______	______	______
67. How *suspicious* I feel about the sexual aspects of my life.	______	______	______	______	______

Continued

	A	B	C	D	E
65. How *relaxed* I feel about the sexual aspects of my life.	____	____	____	____	____
66. How *unhappy* I feel about the sexual aspects of my life.	____	____	____	____	____
67. How *suspicious* I feel about the sexual aspects of my life.	____	____	____	____	____
68. How *detached* I feel about the sexual aspects of my life.	____	____	____	____	____
69. How *worried* I feel about the sexual aspects of my life.	____	____	____	____	____
70. How *joyful* I feel about the sexual aspects of my life.	____	____	____	____	____
71. How *irritated* I feel about the sexual aspects of my life.	____	____	____	____	____
72. How *frightened* I feel about the sexual aspects of my life.	____	____	____	____	____

Scoring Instructions

The revised Sexual Self-Disclosure Scale (SSDS-R) consists of 24 subscales, each containing three separate items. The 24 subscales are clustered into four topic categories:

(A) Sexual behaviors; (B) sexual values and preferences; (C) sexual attitudes; and (D) sexual affect (feelings and emotions). The labels for each of these clusters (and their subscales) are listed below.

Cluster A:	**(Sexual Behaviors)**
1. Sexual behaviors:	(Items 1, 5, 9)
2. Sexual sensations:	(Items 2, 6, 10)
3. Sexual fantasies:	(Items 3, 7, 11)
4. Sexual preferences:	(Items 4, 8, 12)
Cluster B:	**(Sexual Values & Preferences)**
5. Meaning of sex:	(items 13, 18, 23)
6. Sexual accountability:	(items 14, 19, 24)
7. Distressing sex:	(Items 15, 20, 25)
8. Sexual dishonesty:	(Items 16, 21, 26)
9. Sexual delay preferences:	(Items 17, 22, 27)
Cluster C:	**(Sexual Attitudes)**
10. Abortion and pregnancy:	(Items 28, 33, 38)
11. Homosexuality:	(Items 29, 34, 39)
12. Rape:	(Items 30, 35, 40)
13. AIDS:	(Items 31, 36, 41)
14. Sexual morality:	(Items 32, 37, 42)
Cluster D:	**(Sexual Affect)**
15. Sexual satisfaction:	(Items 43, 53, 63)
16. Sexual guilt:	(Items 44, 54, 64)
17. Sexual calmness:	(Items 45, 55, 65)
18. Sexual depression:	(Items 46, 56, 66)
19. Sexual jealousy	(Items 47, 57, 67)
20. Sexual apathy:	(Items 48, 58, 68)
21. Sexual anxiety:	(Items 49, 59, 69)
22. Sexual happiness:	(Items 50, 60, 70)
23. Sexual anger:	(Items 51, 61, 71)
24. Sexual fear:	(Items 52, 62, 72)

Coding Instructions for Items The items are coded so that A = 0; B = 1; C = 2; D = 3; and E = 4. The three items on each subscale are then summed, so that higher scores correspond to greater willingness to discuss the sexual aspects of one's intimate relationship with an intimate partner.

Reliability The Sexual Self-Disclosure to Intimate Partners is a portion of the Sexual Self-Disclosure Scale Revised (SSDS-R), which was developed by Snell, Belk, Papini & Clark (1989). They administered the scale to 119 male and 116 female students enrolled in undergraduate psychology classes at a midwestern university. The internal consistency of the subscales, determined by calculating Cronbach alpha coefficients, ranged from a low of 0.52 to a high of 0.94 (average was 0.80).

Interpretation Multivariate analyses of variance were conducted to examine sex differences in willingness to self-disclose. The results are summarized in Table 1. You may wish to compare your scores with the mean values reported in this table. As indicated in the table, women reported being more willing than men to discuss their sexual sensations and fantasies with an intimate partner. Men were more willing than women to discuss the meaning of sex, sexual accountability, and sexual delay. Men also reported being more willing to reveal personal information about their attitudes toward abortion and pregnancy, homosexuality, rape, AIDS, and sexual morality. Men and women alike were especially willing to share feelings of sexual satisfaction, calmness, and happiness with an intimate partner. However, they were less willing to discuss sexual feelings of guilt, sadness, and anger.

Continued

Self-Assessment—*Continued*

TABLE 1 Results of the Revised Sexual Self-Disclosure Scale (SSDS-R) for Females and Males

SSDS-R Subscales	Females		Males		Total		F
	Mean	*S.D.*	*Mean*	*S.D.*	*Mean*	*S.D.*	*1,233*
Sexual; Behaviors:							
1. Sexual Behaviors	7.41	2.99	6.78	3.70	7.09	3.38	2.01
2. Sexual Sensations	9.04	2.57	7.96	3.52	8.49	3.13	7.25[b]
3. Sexual Fantasies	6.64	3.19	5.40	6.64	6.01	3.47	7.63[b]
4. Sexual Preferences	9.17	2.58	8.49	2.95	8.83	2.79	3.58
Sexual Values and Preferences:							
5. Meaning of Sex	9.93	2.39	10.77	2.00	10.36	2.24	8.59[c]
6. Sexual Accountability	9.53	2.40	10.34	2.09	9.94	2.28	7.64[c]
7. Distressing Sex	7.75	2.79	8.34	8.05	2.69	2.90	
8. Sexual Dishonesty	6.90	2.28	7.02	2.70	6.96	2.76	<1.00
9. Sexual Delay Preferences	8.28	2.61	9.58	2.35	8.94	2.56	16.03[d]
Sexual Attitudes:							
10. Abortion & Pregnancy	10.63	1.67	11.39	1.31	11.01	1.54	15.06[d]
11. Homosexuality	10.49	2.25	11.21	1.56	10.86	1.96	8.14[c]
12. Rape	10.28	2.28	10.94	1.86	10.61	2.10	6.02[a]
13. AIDS	10.60	1.99	11.31	1.57	10.96	1.82	9.22[c]
14. Sexual Morality	9.63	2.53	10.52	1.87	10.08	2.26	9.47[c]
Sexual Affect:							
15. Sexual Satisfaction	9.25	2.72	9.28	2.90	9.26	2.81	<1.00
16. Sexual Guilt	6.39	3.22	7.13	3.15	6.77	3.20	3.22
17. Sexual Calmness	8.53	2.82	9.00	2.94	8.77	2.89	1.59
18. Sexual Depression	6.69	3.10	7.16	3.55	6.93	3.34	1.16
19. Sexual Jealousy	7.83	2.96	8.07	3.05	7.95	3.00	<1.00
20. Sexual Apathy	6.91	3.10	7.01	3.28	6.96	3.19	<1.00
21. Sexual Anxiety	7.44	3.15	7.83	3.32	7.64	3.24	<1.00
22. Sexual Happiness	9.51	2.59	9.73	2.91	9.62	2.75	<1.00
23. Sexual Anger	6.71	3.21	7.52	3.33	7.12	3.29	3.64
24. Sexual Fear	7.05	3.38	8.34	3.16	7.71	3.33	9.18[c]

Note: Total N = 235; n for females = 116; n for males = 119. Higher scores indicate greater willingness to discuss the topics on the Revised Sexual Self-Disclosure Scale (SSDS-R). [a] $p < .01$; [b] $p < .05$; [c] $p < .005$; [d] $p < .001$. (Snell et al, 1989, p. 335) Used by permission of Juniper Press.

Reference

Snell, W. E., Belk, S. S., Papini, D. R., & Clark, S. (1989). Development and validation of the sexual self-disclosure scale. *Annals of Sex Research, 2,* 307–335.

7. Autonomy—the success to which the couple gains independence from their families of origin and their offspring.

*8. Expressiveness—the degree to which thoughts, beliefs, attitudes, and feelings are shared within the relationship.

The process of communicating revealing personal information to another person is known as **self-disclosure**. According to Waring (1988), "self-disclosure is the single factor which most influences a couple's level of intimacy" (p. 38).

The Self-Assessment,the Sexual Self Disclosure Scale, provides you the opportunity to assess your willingness to discuss sexual topics with an intimate partner. In the sections that follow the scale we discuss factors that influence one's willingness and ability to discuss these issues with a partner.

Basic Communication Skills

Partners can develop a number of basic skills to enhance their sexual communication. These include the following.

Maintain Eye Contact

When talking about sex with your partner, it may be difficult to look at each other. Such difficulty maintaining eye contact may be the result of uncertainty, embarrassment, and anxiety. However, not looking into the partner's eyes can be misinterpreted as lack of interest, defensiveness, or guilt. When interacting with each other, the respective partners might make a deliberate effort to look into each other's eyes as a way of communicating interest in each other.

Maintaining eye contact during communication also allows you to gain information about your partner's feelings and responses to what you are saying. If you are not looking at your partner, you are unable to see the expressions on his or her face, which may communicate important information.

Ask Open-Ended Questions

When your goal is to find out what your partner's thoughts and feelings are about an issue, it is best to use open-ended questions. An **open-ended question** is one that encourages a person to provide an answer that contains a lot of information. A closed-ended question is one that elicits a one-word answer, such as "yes" or "no."

Couples can practice basic communication skills and talk about their sexual relationship in a variety of settings.

The more important and more emotional the content of the question, the more likely you are to ask an oblique question or to go through a third party, like when you tell your child something you want your husband to know.

Mary Key

Closed-ended questions that can be answered with a "yes" or "no" do not provide the opportunity for the partner to express feelings and preferences in detail. Table 13.1 provides examples of closed-ended and open-ended questions. (Note: Some requests for information are not technically questions; e.g., "Tell me how you feel about premarital intercourse" is technically not a question. However, it is considered an open-ended question because it is a request for information.)

CONSIDERATION: Therapists often recommend the "touch and ask rule" to help clients learn each others' sexual preferences. The touch and ask rule suggests that each touch is always accompanied by the open-ended question "How does that feel?" The partner to whom the question is directed then tells the other of its effect on him or her. However, if the person does not like it, he or she is to suggest an alternative. For example, suppose one lover is massaging the genitals of the other and asks, "How does that feel?" If the partner does not like it, he or she might say, "I would like it better if you would . . ." and take the hand of the lover and move it in the desired way. (See also nondemand pleasuring and sensate focus exercises in Chapter 15 on sexual therapy.)

Use Reflective Listening

If we were supposed to talk more than we listen, we would have two mouths and one ear.

Mark Twain

To be a good communicator, one must be a good listener, and to be a good listener, one must use **reflective listening**. Reflective listening involves paraphrasing or restating what the person you are listening to has said to you. Both the content of what the person has said and the feeling(s) that the person is conveying are restated. Because feelings are often conveyed nonverbally, it is important to "listen to" a person's nonverbal messages (tone of voice, facial expression, etc.) and to reflect the feelings that one observes. You may have to ask an open-ended question (e.g., "How does that make you feel?") in order to find out what a person is feeling and be able to reflect back his or her feelings. Reflective listening serves the following functions:

1. Creates the feeling for the speaker that she or he is being listened to and is being understood.
2. Increases the accuracy of the listener's understanding of what the speaker is saying. If a reflective statement does not accurately reflect what the speaker thinks or feels, the speaker can correct the inaccuracy by restating his or her thoughts or feelings.

TABLE 13.1 Open-Ended and Closed-Ended Questions

Open-Ended Questions	Closed-Ended Questions
What do you want me to do to please you sexually?	Do you want me to engage in more foreplay to please you sexually?
How often would you like to have intercourse?	Would you be satisfied if we had intercourse once a week?
How does that feel?	Does that feel good?
What do I do now in our lovemaking that you would prefer that I not do?	Is there anything about our lovemaking that you don't like?
How do you feel about my having and looking at sex magazines?	Is it OK if I look at sex magazines?
What are your feelings about me spending this Saturday night with some of my friends?	Is it OK if I spend this Saturday night with some of my friends?

TABLE 13.2 Judgmental and Nonjudgmental Reflective Responses to: "I'd Like to Spend One Evening Each Week with my Friends"

Nonjudgmental Reflective Statements	Judgmental Statements
"You have a preference for us to be with our respective friends."	"You only think about what *you* want."
"You think it is healthy for us to be with our friends some of the time."	"You value 'us' less than I do."
"You really enjoy your friends and want to spend some time with them."	"You just want a night out so that you can meet someone new."
"You think it is important that we not abandon our friends just because we are involved."	"You just want to get away so you can drink."
"You think that our being apart one night each week will make us even closer."	"You are selfish."

An important quality of reflective statements is that they are nonjudgmental. For example, suppose two lovers are arguing about spending time with their respective friends, and one says, "I'd like to spend one night each week with my friends and not feel guilty about it." The partner may respond by making a statement that is judgmental (critical or evaluative). Judgmental responses serve to punish or criticize someone for what he or she thinks, feels, or wants and often result in frustration and resentment. Table 13.2 describes several examples of judgmental statements and nonjudgmental reflective statements.

CONSIDERATION: Reflective listening is a simple technique, but many individuals find it difficult to incorporate this technique into their communication style. Reflective listening is particularly difficult when the speaker is angry at the listener and has said something hurtful or critical. For example, your partner may say to you: "I'm sick and tired of your being late all the time. The only person you think of is yourself. You are the most inconsiderate person I know." Because you feel attacked and criticized, you may respond by defending yourself ("I am not always late!") or by attacking back ("I guess you were being thoughtful of me when you chose to go to the beach with your friends instead of coming to my graduation"). It might be more difficult to simply reflect back what your partner has said to you: "It sounds like you feel really hurt and angry that I was late tonight. You feel that my being late means that I don't care about you and that it is inconsiderate to be late. It is important to you that I be on time in the future." Reflections can be stated in your conversational style so it doesn't sound like you are using a formula.

Use "I" Statements

"I" statements are ones that focus on the feelings and thoughts of the communicator, without making a judgment on others. Because "I" statements are a clear and nonthreatening way of expressing what you want and how you feel, they are likely to result in a positive change in the listener's behavior. In contrast, "you" statements blame or criticize the listener and often result in increasing negative feelings and actions in the relationship. Table 13.3 describes several "you" statements and suggestions for how they might be changed into "I" statements.

TABLE 13.3 Examples of "You" Statements and "I" Statements

"You" Statements	"I" Statements
You are always forgetting to take your birth control pills. You are so irresponsible.	I feel that it is critically important that you remember to take your birth control pills. I feel upset when you forget to take your birth control pills because I don't want you to get pregnant.
You are so selfish and inconsiderate. You don't think about anybody else's needs except your own. You are a lousy lover.	When you get up from bed after you have your orgasm, I feel angry and frustrated because my sexual needs have not been met. I want you to keep stimulating me orally or with your finger so I can have an orgasm, too.
You said that you would be home two hours ago. You are so undependable and thoughtless.	When you are late, I get upset because I feel like I can't depend on you. It is important to me for you to be on time or call me if you are going to be late.

Resolving Interpersonal Conflict

Every relationship experiences conflict. If left unresolved, conflict may create tension and distance in the relationship with the result that the partners stop talking, stop spending time together, and stop sharing affectionate and sexual interactions. Developing and using conflict resolution skills is critically important for maintaining a good relationship. The following section describes principles of conflict resolution and mechanisms used to resolve interpersonal conflicts.

Address Recurring, Disturbing Issues

If you or your partner is upset about a recurring issue, talking about it may help. Pam was jealous that Mark seemed to spend more time with other people at parties than with her. "When we go someplace together," she blurted out, "he drops me to disappear with someone else for two hours." Her jealousy was also spreading to other areas of their relationship. "When we are walking down the street and he turns his head to look at another woman, I get furious." If Pam and Mark don't discuss her feelings about Mark's behavior, their relationship may deteriorate due to a negative response cycle: he looks at another woman, she gets angry, he gets angry at her getting angry and finds that he is even more attracted to other women, she gets angrier because he escalates his looking at other women, and so on.

To bring the matter up, Pam might say something like "I feel jealous when you spend more time with other women at parties than with me. I need some help in dealing with these feelings." By expressing her concern in this way, she has identified the problem from her perspective and asked her partner's cooperation in handling it.

An argument usually consists of two people each trying to get the last word—first.

Laurence Peter

When discussing difficult relationship issues, it is important to avoid attacking, blaming, or being negative. Such negative emotions reduce the motivation of the partner to talk about an issue and reduce the probability of a positive outcome (Forgatch, 1989).

CONSIDERATION: It is important to use good timing in discussing difficult issues with your partner. In general, it is best to discuss issues or conflicts when 1) you are alone with your partner in private, rather than in public, 2) you and your partner have ample time to talk, and 3) you and your partner are rested and feeling generally good; avoid discussing conflict issues when you and your partner are tired, upset, and/or under unusual stress.

Interpersonal conflict is inevitable but the skills needed to resolve conflict can be learned.

Focus on What You Want (Rather Than What You Don't Want)

Dealing with conflict is more likely to result in resolution if the partners focus on what they want, rather than what they don't want. For example, rather than tell Mark that she doesn't want him to spend so much time with other women at parties, Pam might tell him that she wants him to spend more time with her at parties. Table 13.4 provides more examples of resolving conflict by focusing on "wants" rather than on "don't wants."

Find Out the Other Person's Point of View

We often assume that we know what our partner thinks and why our partner does things. Sometimes we are wrong. Rather than assume how our partner thinks and feels about a particular issue, we might ask our partner open-ended questions in an effort to get him or her to tell us his or her thoughts and feelings about a particular situation. Pam's words to Mark might be, "What is it like for you when we go to parties? How do you feel about my jealousy?"

Once your partner has shared his or her thoughts about an issue with you, it is important for you to summarize your partner's perspective in a nonjudgmental way. After Mark told Pam how he felt about their being at parties together, she summarized his perspective by saying, "You feel that I cling to you more than I should and you would like me to let you wander around without feeling like you're making me angry." (She may not agree with his view, but she knows exactly what it is—and Mark knows that she knows.)

Generate Solutions to the Conflict

There are various issues to keep in mind when searching for solutions to interpersonal conflict. Next, we discuss the importance of focusing on interests, rather than on positions; brainstorming; and looking for "win-win" solutions.

Positions versus Interests and Needs In order to both understand and resolve interpersonal conflict, it is helpful to focus on the interests, rather than on the

TABLE 13.4 Examples of Focusing on "Wants" Rather Than "Don't Wants"

"DON'T WANTS"	"WANTS"
1. I don't want to make love when you are sweaty and dirty.	I would like you to take a shower before we make love.
2. I don't want to see a sex therapist.	I would like us to try to work on our problem by ourselves before we seek help.
3. Don't rub so hard.	Please rub more softly.
4. I don't want you to stay up so late at night.	I would like you to come to bed earlier.
5. I don't want to have sex in the morning before going to work.	I really prefer to have sex in the evening, when we can relax and take our time.

We sleep in separate rooms, we have dinner apart, we take separate vacations—we're doing everything we can to keep our marriage together.
Rodney Dangerfield

positions, of the individuals involved (Fisher & Ury, 1981). In this context, positions refer to statements about what an individual has decided. For example, Pam wants Mark to spend more time with her at parties and less time with other women; that is Pam's position. Let's assume that Mark wants to continue to spend a lot of time with other women at parties; that is Mark's position.

Interests, in this context, refer to the underlying needs and concerns of the individuals involved. Interests represent why a person wants something or takes a particular position. There are many possible interests that underlie any one position. In the example we have been using, Pam's position that Mark should not spend so much time with other women at parties may be based on a number of different needs and concerns, including the following:

1. Between school and work, Pam has little time with Mark. Her need is to spend more time with Mark.
2. Pam feels unattractive. She views Mark's spending time with other women as evidence that he does not find her attractive and prefers the company of more attractive women. Her need is to feel that Mark views her as attractive.
3. Pam admires Mark's ability to converse and be sociable. Pam feels shy and inadequate in social settings. When Mark talks with others at parties, Pam feels alone and anxious. Her need is to feel more secure interacting with others at a party.

By identifying the interests that underlie the positions, one can generate solutions that satisfy the needs and concerns of the individuals involved in the conflict. Below, we outline different possible solutions to Pam and Mark's conflict, depending on what the underlying interest is.

1. Interest: Pam feels the need to spend more time with Mark.
   Solution: Pam and Mark agree to go out alone two times in addition to the amount of social time they already spend together.
2. Interest: Pam needs to feel that Mark finds her attractive.
   Solution: Mark agrees to say something positive about how Pam looks every day.
3. Interest: Pam wants to avoid feeling isolated at parties.
   Solution: Pam agrees to sign up for an assertiveness training workshop. Her goal is to develop social skills so that she is comfortable interacting with others at a party.

Brainstorming The technique of **brainstorming** involves suggesting as many alternatives as possible, without evaluating them. Brainstorming is crucial to conflict resolution because it shifts the partners' focus from criticizing each other's perspective to working together to develop alternative solutions. Alternatives that might be suggested by Pam and Mark include the following:

1. Change cognitions—Pam might change the way she views Mark's interaction with others at parties. Rather than view him as neglecting and rejecting her at parties, she might choose to view his desire to interact with others as evidence that he likes people and that he is socially skilled in interacting with others (both are positive qualities). She might also choose to view his being across the room as an opportunity for her to meet new people or to talk with those she already knows. Finally, she might view his looking at other women as evidence that he has a strong sex drive and remind herself that he is always faithful to her (two more positive qualities).
2. Change behaviors—Mark might spend more time with Pam at parties, reduce the frequency with which he looks at other women, and point out good-looking men for Pam. Alternatively, Pam might begin to encourage Mark to talk with others at parties and initiate conversations with new people herself.
3. Stop going to parties.
4. Stop seeing each other for two weeks.
5. Stop talking about the issue.
6. Break up.

Any solution is an acceptable one as long as the solution is mutually agreed to.

Win-Win Solutions A **win-win solution** is one in which both people involved in a conflict feel satisfied with the agreement or resolution to the conflict. Finding a win-win solution requires that the interests (needs and concerns) of both parties be addressed. Each person should feel that his or her needs are being met through whatever solution they agree on.

Despite our celebration of openness, in the power struggle, it's the person who's most vulnerable, most generous, most committed who loses.

Robert Karen

Some couples view their conflicts in win-lose terms (one person wins; the other one loses), rather than as opportunities for win-win solutions (both people "win"). In one study, 60 spouses (representing 30 marriages) were interviewed about relationship conflicts and their outcomes (Bell, Chafetz, & Horn, 1982). The results showed that husbands "win most conflicts, regardless of the strategies they or their wives employ" (p. 111). Catholic and Mormon husbands were particularly likely to "win" disagreements. However, among couples in which the wife was a member of NOW (National Organization for Women), seven in 10 of the conflicts were "won" by the wife. We suggest that unless both win, both lose because all the "winner" gets is someone waiting to get back at him or her.

CONSIDERATION: If the goal is to develop and/or maintain a satisfying intimate interpersonal relationship, it is imperative to look for win-win solutions to conflicts. Solutions in which one person wins and the other person loses imply that one person is not getting his or her needs met. Consequently, the person who "loses" may develop feelings of resentment, anger, hurt, and hostility toward the "winner" and may even look for ways to "get even." In this way, the "winner" is also a loser. It is important to remember that, in intimate relationships, one "winner" really means that there are two losers.

Evaluate and Select a Solution After generating a number of solutions, each solution should be evaluated and the best one selected. In evaluating solutions to conflicts, it may be helpful to ask the following questions:

1. Does the solution satisfy both individuals? (Is it a win-win solution?)
2. Is the solution specific? Does the solution specify exactly who is to do what, how, and when?
3. Is the solution realistic? Can both partners realistically follow through with what they have agreed to do?
4. Does the solution prevent the problem from recurring in the future?
5. Does the solution specify what is to happen if the problem recurs?

Pam and Mark, for example, selected aspects from several alternatives from which they derived specific actions. They agreed that they would spend 45 minutes of each hour at a party talking and dancing together; Mark would be responsible for initiating and maintaining their time together, and Pam would be responsible for initiating their time away from each other. They also agreed that Pam would say nothing about the time they were apart unless Mark brought it up. They further agreed that it was OK for each of them to look at members of the opposite sex when they were with each other.

Sexual Interaction as Communication

The expression of love is the cement that maintains intimacy in close relationships.
Jack Balswick

Sexual interaction may be viewed as a form of sexual communication. Motivations for sexual activity include expressing love and emotional intimacy; experiencing pleasure and fun; pleasing the partner; enhancing one's ego; and improving one's relationship (Brigman & Knox, 1992). In regard to how sex can communicate a sense of emotional connectedness with one's partner, one of Hite's (1981) respondents said:

> Even more important than orgasm is being able to wrap your arms and legs and whatever else around another human being. It makes you feel less alone, more alive. There's just nothing like it. (p. 342)

Wheeless, Wheeless, and Baus (1984) suggested that one's satisfaction with sexual communication involves four components: satisfaction with communication about sexual behavior, communication about which sexual behaviors are satisfying, willingness to communicate about sex with one's partner, and satisfaction derived from what is communicated by certain sexual behaviors. Communication through sexual interaction is, then, an important aspect of relationship and sexual satisfaction.

Writers on sexuality have paid little attention to the communication of lovers after sexual encounters. Yet one psychiatrist observed that what happens during the time after sexual relations occur "reveals more about the basic relationship between the partners than any other preceding sexual activity. The instinctual, biological, and sensual phases of this sexual process give way to the more social and circumstantial aspects of the engagement" (Crain, 1978, p. 80). Whereas some partners may curl up in each other's arms and relax in silent companionship, others may avoid touching each other and withdraw as soon as possible. Indeed, people engage in a number of different behaviors after sexual encounters. These include talking, holding each other, drifting off to sleep, giggling, crying, eating, drinking, smoking, taking a shower, or leaving the room. Lovers may use some of these activities as a prelude to further sexual activity.

CHOICES

There are numerous choices in regard to communication and sexuality. Should we tell our partner if we are sexually dissatisfied, or explain our sexual past or our attractions to others? A discussion of these choices follows.

Choose to Tell One's Partner of Sexual Dissatisfactions?

It is not uncommon for sexual partners to want their partners to do something they don't do or to stop doing something they do. In a sample of 709 nurses, the researchers asked what the respondents wanted their sexual partners to do to please them. "The three most often desired changes were more foreplay, more frequent intercourse, and a more romantic approach prior to starting sexual intercourse" (Darling, Davidson, & Cox, 1991, p. 15). "More foreplay" referred not only to increased time spent in foreplay but also the desire for a variety of foreplay behaviors, including stimulation of the clitoral and vaginal areas manually and orally. Regardless of the desired preference, making one's partner aware of one's preferences becomes a choice. If one does not express one's sexual preferences and dissatisfactions, the partner may be under the illusion that everything is OK in the sexual relationship. However, if one does express one's preferences and dissatisfactions, one risks the possibility of hurting the partner's feelings or being rejected.

One solution to this dilemma is to decide to tell the partner one's preferences to avoid the buildup of resentment and to express one's preferences in a way that minimizes any potential for hurting the partner or for being rejected. An example follows:

> You know that I love you and enjoy our life together. I know that you feel the same way about me and that you value our relationship. To help ensure that our relationship stays at the level we both want it, I need to make you aware of something in our sex life that I would like for you to consider changing. Also, I am sure that there are things that you want me to change to make things more pleasurable for you. If neither of us says what we want, we might get silently unhappy about it and neither of us wants that.
>
> What I would like for you to do more often is to . . . and what I would like for you to stop doing is to. . . .
>
> So that you don't do all the work of changing, please tell me what you would like for me to do to make our sex life better for you. And tell me what I now do that you want me to stop doing because you don't like it.

Choose to Talk about One's Sexual Past to One's Partner?

Some partners want to know the details of their partner's previous sex life, including how many partners they had sex with and in what contexts. Other partners have no interest in the sexual past of their partners. Either value is appropriate and depends on the nature of the personalities of the individuals involved, the nature of the couple's relationship, and the nature of the event to be disclosed. Items that individuals will need to make a decision about in terms of whether to disclose include one's sexual orientation (if different from what the partner is aware of), present or past sexually transmissible diseases, and any proclivities or preferences the partner might find bizarre (bondage and discipline).

Choose to Disclose Attractions to Others to One's Partner?

If partners stay together for a long time, it is likely that partners will, at some time and at some level, be attracted to someone outside the relationship. Whether such attractions or interests are to be disclosed to the partner may depend on the nature of the personalities of the individuals, the nature of the relationship with the partner, and the nature and extent of the attraction. Some couples decide to share such feelings and have relationships in which the partners are not insecure or defensive about such disclosures. Other couples decide that it is much too painful to disclose or to hear of such interests. Still other couples ignore the issue. No one strategy might be considered best since each may have both positive and negative outcomes for different couples. However, it is important that couples acknowledge that such attractions are likely to occur and to agree on the nature and extent of the desired disclosure.

As we close this chapter, we emphasize that communication is one of the most important elements of a good sexual relationship. Such communication allows the partners to know the respective wants and needs of each other and to provide feedback to each other about how the partners' behavior is being experienced. By choosing to communicate on such crucial issues, the partners provide an opportunity for enhancing their sexual relationship.

Summary

1. Effective communication involves exchanging timely, accurate, and precise information.
2. Several studies have documented that telling sexual lies is not uncommon among sexual or potential sexual partners.
3. Communication content refers to verbal and nonverbal messages. Women and men tend to differ in their interpretations of the verbal and nonverbal messages of dating partners and in communication styles, with men emphasizing information and women emphasizing emotional interaction. Communication process refers to how messages (i.e. content) are exchanged.
4. The quality of communication affects the quality of the relationship between partners. Communicating about sex with one's partner is important in maintaining sexual and relationship satisfaction.
5. Basic communication skills include maintaining eye contact, asking open-ended questions, using reflective listening, and using "I" statements.
6. In resolving interpersonal conflict, it is important to address recurring, disturbing issues; focus on what you want (rather than what you don't want); find out the other person's point of view; and generate "win-win" solutions by brainstorming and by focusing on interests rather than on positions. After generating a number of solutions, each solution should be evaluated and the best one selected.
7. Sexual interaction may be viewed as a form of sexual communication. Motivations for sexual activity with a partner include to express love and emotional intimacy, to experience pleasure and fun, to please the partner, to enhance one's ego, and to improve one's relationship.

KEY TERMS

communication
process
open-ended question
closed-ended questions
reflective listening
brainstorming
win-win solution
self-disclosure

REFERENCES

Argyle, M. (1988). *Bodily communication.* New York: Methuen.

Banmen, J., & Vogel, N. A. (1985). The relationship between marital quality and interpersonal sexual communication. *Family Therapy, 12,* 45–58.

Bell, D. C., Chafetz, J. S., & Horn, L. H. (1982). Marital conflict resolution: A study of strategies and outcomes. *Journal of Family Issues, 3,* 111–132.

Blumstein, P., & Schwartz, P. (1983). *American couples.* New York: William Morrow.

Brecher, E. M. (1984). *Love, sex and aging.* Boston: Little, Brown.

Brigman, B., & Knox, D. (1992). University students' motivations to have intercourse. *College Student Journal, 26,* 406–408.

Cancian, F. M. (1987). *Love in America.* New York: Cambridge University Press.

Cochran, S., & Mays, V. (1990). Sex, lies and HIV. *New England Journal of Medicine, 322,* 774–775.

Crain, I. J. (1978). Afterplay. *Medical Aspects of Human Sexuality, 12,* 72–85.

Cupach, W. R., & Comstock, J. (1990). Satisfaction with sexual communication in marriage: Links to sexual satisfaction and dyadic adjustment. *Journal of Social and Personal Relationships, 7,* 179–186.

Cupach, W. R. & Metts, S. (1991). Sexuality and communication in close relationships. In K. McKinney & S. Sprecher (Eds.), *Sexu-*

ality in close relationships (pp. 93–110). Hillsdale, New Jersey: Lawrence Erlbaum Associates.

Darling, C. A., Davidson, J. K., Sr., & Cox, P. (1991). Female sexual response and the timing of partner orgasm. *Journal of Sex and Marital Therapy, 17,* 3–21.

Fisher, R., & Ury, W. (1981). *Getting to yes: Negotiating agreement without giving in.* Boston: Houghton Mifflin.

Forgatch, M. S. (1989). Patterns and outcome in family problem solving: The disrupting effect of negative emotion. *Journal of Marriage and the Family, 51,* 115–124.

Goodchilds, J. D., & Zellman, G. L. (1984). Adolescent sexual signaling and sexual aggression. In N. M. Malamuth and E. Donnerstein (Eds.), *Pornography and sexual aggression* (pp. 233–243). New York: Academic Press.

Gray, M. D., Lesser, D., Rebach, H., Hooks, B., & Bounds, C. (1988). Sexual aggression and victimization: A local perspective. *Response to the Victimization of Women and Children, 11,* 9–13.

Hite, S. (1981). *The Hite report on male sexuality.* New York: Alfred Knopf.

Kleinke, C. L., & Taylor, C. (1991). Evaluation of opposite-sex person as a function of gazing, smiling, and forward lean. *Journal of Social Psychology, 131,* 451–453.

Lee, J. A. (1990). Can we talk? Can we really talk? Communication as a key factor in the maturing homosexual couple. *Journal of Homosexuality, 20,* 143–155.

Mazur, R. (1973). *The new intimacy.* Boston: Beacon Press.

Metts, S. (1989). An exploratory investigation of deception in close relationships. *Journal of Social and Personal Relationships, 6,* 159–179.

Metts, S. & Cupach, W. R. (1989). The role of communication in human sexuality. In K. McKinney & S. Sprecher (Eds.), *Human sexuality: The societal and interpersonal context* (pp. 139–161). Norwood, New Jersey: Ablex.

Reiss, I. L., & Reiss, H. M. (1990). *An end to shame: Shaping our next sexual revolution.* New York: Prometheus Books.

Russell, L. (1990). Sex and couples therapy: A method of treatment to enhance physical and emotional intimacy. *Journal of Sex and Marital Therapy, 16,* 111–120.

Saxe, L. (1991). Lying: Thoughts of an applied social psychologist. *Americn Psychologist, 46,* 409–415.

Sparrow, K. H. (1991). Factors in mate selection for single black professional women. *Free Inquiry in Creative Sociology, 19,* 103–109.

Tannen, D. (1990). *You just don't understand: Women and men in conversation.* London: Virago Press.

Turner, A. J. (1991). *Communication in relationships.* Paper presented at Thirtieth Annual Family Life Conference on Mediation in Relationships. East Carolina University, Greenville, NC, 1990. (Revised for this text in 1991.) Used by permission of Dr. Turner.

Waring, E. M. (1988). *Enhancing marital intimacy through facilitating cognitive self-disclosure.* New York: Brunner/Mazel.

Wheeless, L. R., Wheeless, V. E., & Baus, R. (1984). Sexual communication, communication satisfaction, and solidarity in the developmental stages of intimate relationships. *Western Journal of Speech Communication, 48,* 217–230.

Yandoli, A. H. (1989). Stress and medical marriages. *Stress-Medicine, 5,* 213–219.

CHAPTER FOURTEEN

Love and Sexuality

Chapter Outline

The Nature of Love: Ancient and Modern Views
- Ancient Views of Love
- Modern Views of Love
- Romantic versus Realistic Love
- **Self-Assessment:** Love Attitudes Scale
- Infatuation
- The Feminization of Love

The Origins of Love: Theoretical Views
- Evolutionary Theory
- Learning Theory
- Psychosexual Theory
- Ego-Ideal Theory
- Ontological Theory
- Biochemical Associations of Love
- **Theoretical Perspective:** A Dimension for Organizing Theories of Love and Sex

Love Relationships
- Conditions under Which Love Relationships Develop
- Dilemmas of Love Relationships
- Love and Health

Sexual Jealousy in Relationships
- Causes of Jealousy
- Consequences of Jealousy
- Techniques for Resolving Jealousy

Choices
- Choose to Have Sex with Love?
- Choose to Have Sex without Love?

Is It True?*

1. Modern social scientists do not consider love to be a serious topic for research.

2. It is possible to be in love with two people at the same time.

3. Research has found that high blood pressure is associated with love deprivation.

4. Studies consistently show that women are more romantic than men.

5. Jealousy may have both negative and positive consequences for individuals and relationships.

* 1 = F, 2 = T, 3 = T, 4 = F, 5 = T

. . .We now have the ability to destroy our universe if we choose not to love. . . . We have an infinite number of choices ahead, but a finite number of endings. They are destruction and death or love and healing. If we choose the path of love we save ourselves and our universe. Let us choose love and life.

Bernie Siegel

Blanche (played by Rue McClanahan) of the once popular television sitcom "Golden Girls" projected an image of being interested in sex under conditions of limited emotional involvement. In contrast, her roommate Rose (played by Betty White) projected an image of being interested in sex only under conditions of emotional involvement. The latter is a favored value among university students. When 172 students in a human sexuality course were asked whether they approved of premarital intercourse when the partners were in love, over 85% of the women and men agreed (Weis, Rabinowitz, & Ruckstuhl, 1992). Other researchers (Ard, 1990; Klassen, Williams, & Levitt, 1989) have reached similar conclusions. In U.S. society, the greater the affection and love in a relationship, the more willing the partners are to have increasing levels of sexual intimacy with each other. In this chapter, we examine both old and new views of love, several theories of love, the similarities and differences between love and sex, love relationships, and the issue of sexual jealousy. In the Choices section, we look at the choices of having sex with and without love. We begin with looking at the nature of love.

The Nature of Love: Ancient and Modern Views

Love is a difficult concept to understand. The refrain of an old song aptly expresses the difficulty of getting a firm grip on the experience of love (O'Brien, 1956):

For love is such a mystery,
  I cannot find it out,
For when I think I'm best resolved,
  I then am most in doubt.

CONSIDERATION: The fact that love is difficult to define and has varied meanings has implications for love relationships. Pedersen (1991) noted that, oftentimes,

> Two people who proclaim that they love each other have not considered that even though they use the same word, each of them attaches very different meanings to it. They may be "in love" and have entirely different behavioral expectations of what that means. (p. 187)

Despite the elusive nature of love, philosophers, theologians, and social scientists have speculated on love throughout human history. Next, we look at some ancient and modern views on the nature of love.

Ancient Views of Love

Many of our present-day notions of love stem from the writings of early Buddhists, Greeks, and Hebrews.

Buddhist Conception of Love The Buddhists conceived of two types of love: an "unfortunate" kind of love (self-love) and a "good" kind of love (creative spiritual attainment). Love that represents creative spiritual attainment was described as "love of detachment," not in the sense of withdrawal from the emotional concerns of others but in the sense of gladly accepting others as they are and not requiring them to be different from their present selves as the price of friendly affection. To a Buddhist, the "best" love was one in which you accept others as they are without requiring them to be like you (Burtt, 1957).

Greek and Hebrew Conceptions of Love Three concepts of love introduced by the Greeks and reflected in the New Testament are: phileo, agape, and eros. **Phileo** refers to love based on friendship; this type of love can exist between family members, friends, and lovers. The city of Philadelphia was named after phileo love. Another variation of phileo love is **philanthropia**, which is the Greek word meaning "love of humankind."

Agape refers to a love based on a concern for the well-being of others. Agape is spiritual, not sexual, in nature. This type of love is altruistic and requires nothing in return.

Eros refers to sexual love. This type of love seeks self-gratification and sexual expression. In Greek mythology, Eros was the god of love and the son of Aphrodite. Plato described "true" eros as sexual love that exists between two men. According to Plato's conception of eros, homosexual sex is the highest form of love because it exists independent of the procreative instinct and free from the bonds of matrimony.

CONSIDERATION: Eros refers to the type of love that we might describe as romantic and passionate. Agape and phileo refer to love that is compassionate, rather than passionate (Walsh, 1991).

In Greek mythology, Eros was the god of love and the son of Aphrodite.

Modern Views of Love

While love has been pondered for centuries, it may be no less mysterious today than it was a thousand years ago. Among the modern-day social scientists who have speculated on the nature of love are Abraham Maslow, John Lee, Zick Rubin, Robert Sternberg, Ellen Berscheid, and Dorothy Tennov. The concept of love seems to lend itself to study by social scientist couples, including Elaine and Arthur Aron, Susan and Clyde Hendrick, Bernice and Albert Lott, and Elaine Hatfield and William Walster.

Maslow: B-Love and D-Love Abraham Maslow believed love was a basic psychological need. The need to love and be loved must be satisfied, according to Maslow, in order for individuals to realize their innate potential for maturity and self-actualization.

Maslow identified two types of love: B-love (love for the *b*eing of another person) and D-love (love based on *d*eficiencies) (1968). **B-love** is "unneeding love" or "unselfish love." B-love is not possessive, and B-lovers are more independent of each other, more autonomous, and less jealous or threatened. B-lovers encourage each other to pursue their goals and grow as individuals.

D-love is "selfish love." D-lovers have deficiencies in their nurturing and have been deprived of love and thus hunger for it desperately. **D-love** seeks gratification, rather than growth. D-lovers are dependent on each other and tend to be jealous and possessive. Love partners are valued for their ability to satisfy an intense hunger for love.

Lee: Love Styles Sociologist Alan Lee (1973, 1988) identified six styles of love: **Eros** (romantic, passionate love), **ludus** (game-playing love), **storge** (friendship, companionate love), **pragma** (logical, pragmatic love), **mania** (possessive, dependent love), and agape (altruistic, selfless love). Lee viewed these styles as different but equally valid ways of loving. Lee also believed it was possible to be simultaneously in one type of relationship with one person (e.g. erotic) and in another type (e.g. storgic) with another person.

A Love Attitudes Scale based on Lee's typology has been developed (T. Lasswell & Lasswell, 1976; C. Hendrick & S. Hendrick, 1986). (Note: The Love Attitudes Scale based on Lee's typology is not the same scale as the Love Attitudes Scale in the Self-Assessment section of this chapter, although they have the same name.) An example of one item measuring each of Lee's six styles of love is presented below.

1. Eros: I feel that my lover and I were meant for each other.
2. Ludus: I enjoy playing the "game of love" with a number of different partners.
3. Storge: Love is really a deep friendship, not a mysterious, mystical emotion.
4. Pragma: It is best to love someone with a similar background.
5. Mania: When I am in love, I have trouble concentrating on anything else.
6. Agape: I would rather suffer myself than let my lover suffer.

CONSIDERATION: Susan Hendrick and Clyde Hendrick, researchers in the area of interpersonal relationships, love, and sex, also lecture on these topics. They noticed that

> Many people find our descriptions of Lee's six love styles highly revelatory; the fact that people can and do love romantically in different ways had not occurred to them

Continued

> ***Continued***
>
> . . . because our common language contains just the word "love," or at best "romantic love" as a communication vehicle for numerous emotions. Once people are able to articulate to themselves concepts such as "erotic love," "ludic love," or "manic love," they can become much more discriminating and sophisticated in their love interactions. Such enhanced understanding of love, should . . . reduce the large number of love mismatches and the resulting miseries of love. (1987, p. 163)

Research using the Love Attitudes Scale based on Lee's typology has shown that women report themselves to be less ludic and more storgic and pragmatic than men (C. Hendrick & S. Hendrick, 1986, 1988; S. Hendrick & C. Hendrick, 1987). Lee's love styles have also been shown to be correlated with sexual attitudes as measured by the Sexual Attitudes Scale. This scale is composed of items measuring the following four factors:

1. Permissiveness (open, casual sexuality)
2. Sexual Practices (responsible, tolerant sexuality)
3. Communion (emotional, idealistic sexuality)
4. Instrumentality (egocentric, biological sexuality)

Across three separate studies involving a total of 1,592 participants, Hendrick and Hendrick (1987) found the following associations: Ludus with Permissiveness and Instrumentality, Eros with Communion and Sexual Practices. In two of the three studies, Mania was associated with Agape.

Rubin: Attachment, Caring, and Intimacy Psychologist Zick Rubin (1973) developed a "love scale" whereby he identified those characteristics of people who defined themselves as being in love. These characteristics included attachment, caring, and intimacy; Rubin defined them as follows:

Attachment: The desire to be with the other person and to feel emotional support from and for the other person.

Caring: A concern for the other person's well-being.

Intimacy: The desire to disclose personal thoughts and feelings through communication with the other person.

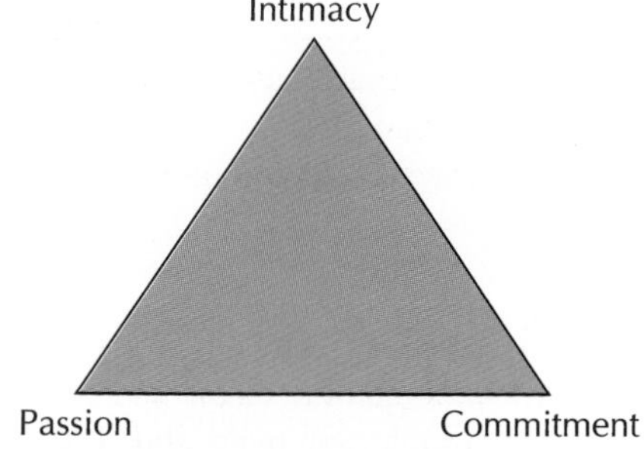

FIGURE 14.1 Triangular Theory of Love

Sternberg: Intimacy, Passion, and Commitment Robert Sternberg (1986) identified several states of love on the basis of the presence or absence of three characteristics: intimacy, passion, and commitment. Sternberg defined these three elements as follows:

Intimacy: Emotional connectedness or bondedness.

Passion: Romantic feelings and physical sexual desire.

Commitment: The desire to maintain the relationship.

These three elements of love may be illustrated by a triangle, as shown in Figure 14.1 Various types of love can be described on the basis of these three elements (see also Table 14.1):

1. **Nonlove:** The absence of all three components of love.
2. **Liking:** Intimacy without passion or commitment.

TABLE 14.1 Sternberg's Eight Types of Love

	Intimacy	Passion	Commitment
1. Nonlove	−	−	−
2. Liking	+	−	−
3. Infatuation	−	+	−
4. Romantic love	+	+	−
5. Companionate love	+	−	+
6. Fatuous love	−	+	+
7. Empty love	−	−	+
8. Consummate love	+	+	+

(Key: + = presence, − = absence)

Source: Sternberg, R. J. (1986). A triangular theory of love. *Psychological Review, 93,* 119-135. Used by permission.

3. **Infatuation:** Passion without intimacy or commitment.
4. **Romantic love:** Intimacy and passion without commitment.
5. **Companionate love:** Intimacy and commitment without passion.
6. **Fatuous love:** Passion and commitment without intimacy.
7. **Empty love:** Commitment without passion or intimacy.
8. **Consummate love:** A combination of intimacy, passion, and commitment.

Romantic versus Realistic Love

Love may also be described as being on a continuum from romantic to realistic. For some people, love is romantic; for others, it is realistic. **Romantic love** is characterized by such beliefs as "love at first sight," "there is only one true love," and "love conquers all." The symptoms of romantic love include drastic mood swings, palpitations of the heart, and intrusive thinking about the partner.

In contrast to romantic love, **realistic love**, or **conjugal love**, tends to be characteristic of people who have been in love with each other for several years. Partners who know all about each other yet still love each other are said to have a realistic view of love. The Love Attitudes Scale (see Self-Assessment) provides a way to assess the degree to which you are romantic or realistic about love.

CONSIDERATION: When you determine your score on the Love Attitudes Scale, be aware that you are merely assessing the degree to which you are a romantic or a realist. Your tendency to be one or the other is not good or bad. Both romantics and realists may be happy, mature people. However, being ultraromantic may be associated with a more difficult adjustment to having children since children involve a great deal of unselfish, nonreciprocal love (Belsky & Rovine, 1990).

Using the Love Attitudes Scale (not the same scale based on Lee's six styles of love), several studies have been conducted to identify demographic characteristics of people who are romantic or realistic. When 100 unmarried male and 100 unmarried female college students completed the inventory, the results revealed that men were more romantic than women and that freshmen were more romantic than seniors (Knox & Sporakowski, 1968). Comparable results were found in a similar study (Knox, 1982) in which 94 was the average score of 97 students; men and freshmen had more romantic scores, and women and seniors had more realistic scores.

A more recent study on the love attitudes of 110 university students also found that men are more romantic and women more pragmatic about love (Dion & Dion, 1991). In this study, researchers found that men tend to play at love and to be less serious and less committed than women. Similarly, in a study of 68 unmarried whites in South Africa, the women scored higher on "conjugal love" than men. Conjugal love was defined as "the belief that love demands serious thought and careful consideration" (Stone & Philbrick, 1991, p. 220). Conjugal love is similar to realistic love as described earlier. Hendrick, Hendrick, Foote, and Slapion-Foote (1984) also found in their study of 800 university students that women were more pragmatic than men in their view of love. Hendrick and Hendrick (1991) suggested that women are more practical in their attitudes toward love than men because of their future possible parental interest with the males they encounter. In effect, the woman must delay her romantic investment until she is secure that the male has an interest in providing for and protecting her offspring.

However, after analyzing the results of a romance survey of slightly less than 12,000 *Psychology Today* readers, one researcher concluded that "more women than men say that romance is important, and men rate their partners as being more romantic" (Rubenstein, 1983, p. 49).

CONSIDERATION: The answer to the question "Who is more romantic, men or women?" depends on how one defines and measures romanticism. If one conceptualizes romanticism as a tendency to fall in love quickly, men are more romantic because they tend to fall in love more quickly than women. But if one conceptualizes romanticism as a tendency to form intense and lasting bonds, women are more romantic (Walsh, 1991).

Arranged marriages are used to prevent the development of romantic love with the "wrong" person.

Self Assessment

Love Attitudes Scale

This scale is designed to assess the degree to which you are romantic or realistic in your attitudes toward love. There are no right or wrong answers.

Directions **After reading each sentence carefully,** circle the number that best represents the degree to which you agree or disagree with the sentence.

1 Strongly agree
2 Mildly agree
3 Undecided
4 Mildly disagree
5 Strongly disagree

	SA	MA	U	MD	SD
1. Love doesn't make sense. It just is.	1	2	3	4	5
2. When you fall "head over heels" in love, it's sure to be the real thing.	1	2	3	4	5
3. To be in love with someone you would like to marry but can't is a tragedy.	1	2	3	4	5
4. When love hits, you know it.	1	2	3	4	5
5. Common interests aren't really important; as long as each of you is truly in love, you will adjust to your differences.	1	2	3	4	5
6. It doesn't matter if you marry after you have known your partner for only a short time as long as you know you are in love.	1	2	3	4	5
7. If you are going to love a person, you will "know" after a short time.	1	2	3	4	5
8. As long as two people love each other, the educational differences they have really do not matter.	1	2	3	4	5
9. You can love someone even though you do not like any of that person's friends.	1	2	3	4	5
10. When you are in love, you are usually in a daze.	1	2	3	4	5
11. Love "at first sight" is often the deepest and most enduring type of love.	1	2	3	4	5
12. When you are in love, it really does not matter what your partner does because you will love him or her anyway.	1	2	3	4	5
13. As long as you really love a person, you will be able to solve the problems you have with the person.	1	2	3	4	5
14. Usually you can really love and be happy with only one or two people in the world.	1	2	3	4	5

Continued

Infatuation

Infatuation is an experience that is related to, and sometimes confused with, love. **Infatuation** comes from the same root word as fatuous, meaning "silly" or "foolish" and refers to a state of passion or attraction that is not based on reason. Liebowitz (1983) differentiated between infatuation and "true" love by suggesting that "true" love is attraction plus attachment and infatuation is attraction minus attachment (p. 191).

Do I love you because you're beautiful? Or are you beautiful because I love you? Are you the sweet invention of a lover's dream or are you really as wonderful as you seem?

Oscar Hammerstein II (from Cinderella)

Infatuation is characterized by the tendency to idealize the love partner. People who are infatuated magnify their lover's positive qualities and overlook or minimize the lover's negative qualities. Being infatuated with someone is like having blinders on that allow you to see only those qualities that you want to see in your partner. The more the partner's actual attributes are distorted, the more difficult the relationship becomes after the blinders are removed. A relationship is more likely to endure if one's idealized image of a love partner does not differ greatly from the partner's actual traits (Money, 1980).

Self-Assessment—*Continued*

	SA	MA	U	MD	SD
15. Regardless of other factors, if you truly love another person, that is a good enough reason to marry that person.	1	2	3	4	5
16. It is necessary to be in love with the one you marry in order to be happy.	1	2	3	4	5
17. Love is more of a feeling than a relationship.	1	2	3	4	5
18. People should not get married unless they are in love.	1	2	3	4	5
19. Most people truly love only once during their lives.	1	2	3	4	5
20. Somewhere there is an ideal mate for most people.	1	2	3	4	5
21. In most cases, you will "know" when you meet the right partner.	1	2	3	4	5
22. Jealousy usually varies directly with love; that is, the more you are in love, the greater your tendency to become jealous will be.	1	2	3	4	5
23. When you are in love, you are motivated by what you feel rather than by what you think.	1	2	3	4	5
24. Love is best described as an exciting rather than a calm thing.	1	2	3	4	5
25. Most divorces probably result from falling out of love rather than failing to adjust.	1	2	3	4	5
26. When you are in love, your judgment is usually not too clear.	1	2	3	4	5
27. Love often comes only once in a lifetime.	1	2	3	4	5
28. Love is often a violent and uncontrollable emotion.	1	2	3	4	5
29. When selecting a marriage partner, differences in social class and religion are of small importance compared with love.	1	2	3	4	5
30. No matter what anyone says, love cannot be understood.	1	2	3	4	5

Scoring Add the numbers you circled. 1 (strongly agree) is the most romantic response, and 5 (strongly disagree) is the most realistic response. The lower your total score (30 is the lowest possible score), the more romantic your attitudes toward love. The higher your total score (150 is the highest possible score), the more realistic your attitudes toward love. A score of 90 places you at the midpoint between being an extreme romantic and an extreme realist. Ninety-four was the average score of 97 students (Knox, 1982).

Source: From Knox, D. (1983). *The love attitudes inventory* (rev. ed.). Saluda, NC: Family Life Publications. Used by permission.

Love is a gross exaggeration of the difference between one person and everybody else.

George Bernard Shaw

CONSIDERATION: Walsh (1991) suggested that some level of idealization is normal and healthy. He pointed out that people often idealize their parents, children, and even countries to varying degrees and that such idealization reflects enthusiasm and optimism toward a love object. Furthermore, "the idealization of the loved one may in fact result in his or her conforming more to the idealized image . . . " (p. 191). Projecting an idealized image of a loved one may create a self-fulfilling prophecy whereby the loved one internalizes the idealized image and acts according to this image.

The Feminization of Love

In Chapter 8, Gender Roles, we discussed the idea that cultural notions of masculinity are associated with instrumental qualities, while cultural notions of femininity are associated with expressive qualities. When we think of love, we commonly think of expressive qualities- those that are associated with our cultural definitions of femininity. For example, "we identify love with emotional expression and talking about feelings, aspects of love that women prefer and in which women tend to be more skilled than men" (Cancian, 1987, p. 69). Love then, has become "feminized" (Cancian, 1987; Tavris, 1992). Indeed, Tavris (1992) suggested that "love is the one domain in which women are thought to excel and to represent the healthy model of normalcy . . . " (p. 248).

Part of the reason that men seem so much less loving than women is that men's behavior is measured with a feminine ruler.

Francesca M. Cancian

One consequence of the feminization of love is that men are not given credit or validation for their instrumental style of loving. "Men tend to have a distinctive style of love that focuses on practical help, shared physical activities, spending time together, and sex" (Cancian, 1987, p. 75). But these qualities and behaviors are not always recognized as expressions of love—hence men are viewed as inferior to women in their ability to love and many heterosexual women feel unsatisfied in their love relationships. Therapist Loren Pedersen (1991) observed,

> A man's expectations of himself as a loving partner may strongly rest on the traditional idea of "providing for," so that he feels he *is* being loving by fulfilling those expectations. He is surprised, as well as hurt, when his partner expresses disappointment in his providence as well as his performance. A man typically counters his wife's accusations that he doesn't love her with reference to all the things he's *done* to make her happy. . . . he bought her a new car . . . he makes a good salary . . . he sends the kids to private school, and so on, but none of these satisfies his wife's sense of what it means to feel loved by him. (p. 188)

In a study of the determinants of marital satisfaction (cited in Cancian, 1987), researchers told a husband to increase his affectionate behavior towards his wife. The husband decided to wash his wife's car "and was surprised when neither his wife nor the researchers accepted that as an 'affectionate' act" (Cancian, 1987, p. 76).

From a wife's point of view,

> It is not enough that he supports us and takes care of us. I appreciate that, but I want him to share things with me. I need for him to tell me his feelings. (Cancian, 1987)

CONSIDERATION: The feminization of love obscures not only the loving aspect of the male provider role, but also the competent, active component of women's love. Cancian explained,

> A major way that women are loving is by actively caring for others and doing physical, productive (but unpaid) work for their families. Nurturing children or a husband consists largely of instrumental acts like preparing meals, washing clothes, or providing care during illness. But because of our focus on the expressive side of love, the work of caring for another person is either ignored or is redefined as expressing feelings. . . . A wife washing her husband's shirt is seen as expressing feelings, while a husband washing his wife's car is seen as doing a job. (p. 79)

As an alternative to a feminized conception of love, Cancian suggested that love be viewed as a combination of expressive ("feminine") and instrumental ("masculine") qualities. Her definition of enduring love between adults is:

> A relationship where a small number of people both (1) express affection, acceptance, and other positive feelings to each other, and (2) provide each other with care and practical assistance. Love also includes (3) commitment—an intention to maintain the affection and the assistance for a long time, despite difficulties; and (4) specialness—giving the loved person priority over others. . . . Enduring sexual love . . . also includes sexual intimacy and physical affection. . . . Finally, the new images of love add the qualities of promoting each other's self-development, and communicating and understanding each other's personal feelings and experiences. (1987, p. 70)

THE ORIGINS OF LOVE: THEORETICAL VIEWS

The development of love, both in individuals and in the human species, may be explained from different theoretical perspectives. Some theoretical views on love follow.

Evolutionary Theory

According to the evolutionary view of the origin of love, love is part of nature's design to achieve reproductive success and to ensure the survival of the human species (Buss, 1988; C. Hendrick & S. Hendrick, 1991; Mellen, 1981). For example, the love of a mother for her child is basic to the survival of the child. Walsh (1991) explained:

> If no one feeds a human infant it will starve; . . . if no one shelters and protects it, it will die. The human infant is at the mercy of the adults of its species far longer than any other newborn. Only a strong biologically based tendency on the part of the mother to care for the infant unconditionally will see it successfully through its period of dependency. The human adult's willingness to invest time and energy in someone else's goals, even at the expense of one's own, is called love—an active concern for the well-being of another. (p. 42)

I know my love must
seem a distant thing to you
For there's so many
that I must give it to
But it'll flow
like a river to the sea
There will be no end to it
Till there's an end to me.

Anne Dodson—
songwriter and singer

Walsh (1991) also explained the evolutionary basis of love between men and women:

> Men and women fall in love today because ancient couples with the propensity to do so stayed bonded together long enough to allow for their offspring to survive and pass on that propensity. Couples who simply copulated and parted were less likely to have any [offspring] of that union survive. Evolution selected love as a way of insuring that men would stick around long enough to assist women to care for the children. (p. 189)

CONSIDERATION: In his book *The Evolution of Love,* anthropologist Sydney Mellen (1981) suggested that if a sense of love, bonding, and attachment between women and men had not evolved about 500,000 years ago, the human species would be extinct today.

Learning Theory

Unlike evolutionary theory, which views the human experience of love as innate, learning theory views love as a set of feelings and cognitions that are learned. These feelings may be learned in infancy. Erikson (1963) suggested that infants must experience love and trust with a parent or parent surrogate and that the absence of initial developmental bonding experiences makes it difficult for the individual to form attachments.

Hazen and Shaver (1987) further noted the various attachment styles that people may develop: secure lovers, avoidant lovers, and anxious-ambivalent lovers. Secure lovers are those who find it easy to become emotionally close, to depend on others, and to allow others to depend on them. Avoidant lovers become uncomfortable as the relationship becomes closer. They find it difficult to trust others or to depend on them. They panic when someone evidences an interest in getting them more committed to the relationship. In contrast, anxious-ambivalent lovers fear that no one will want to become emotionally involved with them. They want to merge completely with the other person, which sometimes scares the other person away.

According to Erikson's theory, early bonding experiences form the foundation for later relationships.

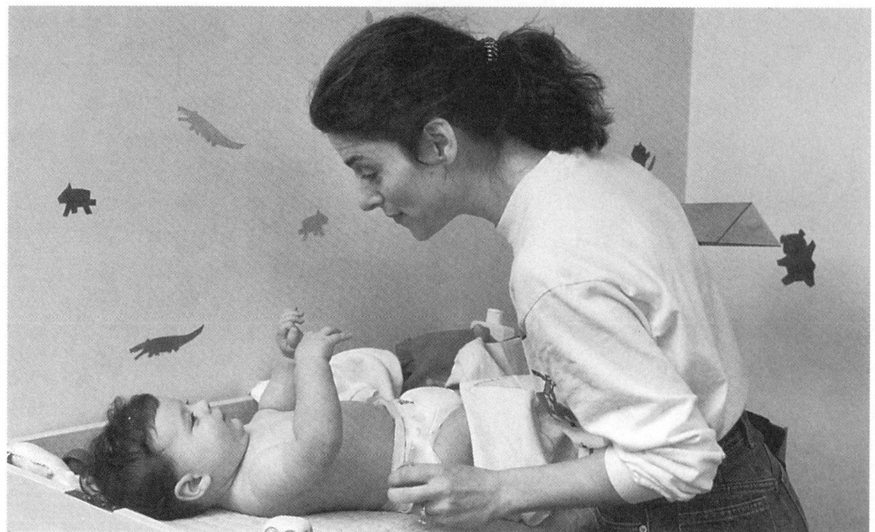

Wayne Bartz and Richard Rasor explained how love feelings are learned through interaction between the partners.

> Love feelings are not "built in" but come from learned social responses, for example, a smile, a touch, a laugh. Most of the things that make us feel good are incorporated into our cultural system of dating and courtship; we treat the other person very courteously, smile a lot, try to be pleasant, avoid saying offensive things, dress to look attractive, use best manners, and perhaps dine on food and enjoy entertainment that takes us beyond our budget. More importantly, all of these pleasurable features appear against a background of escalating physical stimulation or sexual excitement. Indeed, we have a social interaction in which one's dating partner is paired with the widest possible range of pleasurable sensations and activities. (Bartz & Rasor, 1972, p. 36)

"I love you" means "you please me or make me feel good."
B. F. Skinner

Once positive behavior begins in a relationship, it must be reinforced to be maintained. This implies that during a developing relationship, couples have a high frequency of reinforcing each other for desired behaviors. The continuation of love feelings depends on each partner continuing to reinforce the desirable behaviors of the other so these behaviors (and the love feelings they elicit) continue.

Lott and Lott (1961, 1974) examined the development of love feelings as a result of being in a context where one is rewarded. They felt that love for a person develops when one experiences reward in the presence of that person. Sternberg and Beall (1991) noted that "one can become attracted to someone else not because of who he or she is, but because one just happens to experience positive reinforcement in the presence of the person—reinforcement that may have nothing to do with the person to whom one is attracted. Similarly, one can come to view people around whom one is punished as unattractive" (p. 264).

Psychosexual Theory

According to psychosexual theory, love results from blocked biological sexual desires. In the sexually repressive mood of his time, Sigmund Freud (1905/1938) referred to love as "aim-inhibited sex." Love was viewed as a function of the sexual desire a person was not allowed to express because of social restraints. In Freud's era, people would meet, fall in love, get married, and have sex. He felt that the socially required delay from first meeting to having sex resulted in the development of "love feelings." By extrapolation, Freud's theory of love suggests that love dies with marriage (access to the sex object).

Ego-Ideal Theory

Theodore Reik (1949) suggested that love sprang from a state of dissatisfaction with one's self and that love represented a vain urge to reach one's "ego-ideal." He believed that love was a projection of one's ideal image of one's self on another person. For example, suppose you are a shy, passive, dependent person but wished that you were assertive, engaging, and independent. According to Reik's theory, you would probably fall in love with a person who had the qualities you admired but lacked in yourself.

> Tell me whom you love and I will tell you who you are and, more especially, who you want to be.
>
> *Theodore Reik*

Psychologist David Lewis (1985) invited his readers to make a list of their qualities, both favorable and unfavorable. Such a list describes one's "real self." Then he asked the readers to make another list of the qualities that they don't possess but would like to. This list describes the "ideal self." Lewis suggested that many people seek mates who possess the qualities they put in their "ideal self" list. By attaching ourselves to and loving a person who possesses the qualities of our ideal self, we compensate for our inadequacies. We vicariously love our ideal self through loving someone who is a reflection of that ideal self.

Ontological Theory

Ontology is a branch of philosophy that is concerned with being. Love, from an ontological perspective, may be viewed as arising from a lack of wholeness in our being. Such lack of wholeness is implied by the division of humans into males and females. From an ontological perspective, love represents women's desire to be united with their "other half" (i.e., men) and men's desire to be united with their "other half" (i.e., women).

> Love is basically not an emotion but an ontological power, it is the essence of life itself, namely, the dynamic reunion of that which is separated.
>
> *Mahatma Gandhi*

The ontological view of love can be traced to Plato, who, in the *Symposium,* described an ancient myth about a time when humans were physically different from what they are today. Plato's mythical early humans had two organs and appendages for every one we have today, and they reproduced asexually by emission onto the ground, like grasshoppers. Because these mythical humans challenged the power and authority of the gods, Zeus punished them by cutting them in half lengthwise, producing incomplete beings. These incomplete beings longed to reunite with their other half, and whenever the parts encountered each other, they threw their arms around each other and clung together. Their desire to be reunited was so strong that, once together, they would not part even to take care of survival needs. Zeus feared that these human creatures would become extinct and there would be no one left to honor the gods. So he devised a way to assure the survival of the human species: he moved the reproductive organs of humans around to the front so that humans would conceive new life while in each other's embrace.

> It is not the threat of death, illness, hardship, or poverty that crushes that human spirit; it is the fear of being alone and unloved in the universe.
>
> *Anthony Walsh*

The myth of Adam and Eve also suggests an ontological view of love. According to this myth, God created Adam from the dust of the earth. But God believed that "it was not good that man should be alone" so he created Eve from Adam's rib. Adam and Eve were thus two parts that were once whole. While Adam and Eve were separate beings, God dictated that they should reunite into one whole being: "Therefore shall a man . . . cleave unto his wife, and they shall be one flesh."

> Our life without love is like the coconut in which the milk is dried up.
>
> *Henry David Thoreau*

Paul Tillich, a modern Christian theologian, viewed love from an ontological perspective. He stated that love is "the dynamic reunion of that which is separated" (1960, p. 67). Tillich believed that when you seek a marital partner, you are trying to identify that portion of you that was once together but is now separated.

The myth of Adam and Eve suggests an ontological view of love. They represent the dynamic reunion of that which was once separated.

Eric Fromm's (1963) view of love has an ontological slant in that he viewed love as a means of overcoming the "separateness" of an individual and of quelling the anxiety associated with being lonely. Fromm regarded the individual as incomplete without the experience of love.

CONSIDERATION: Both love and sexuality may be viewed from an ontological perspective. Aron and Aron (1991) stated that "sexuality and love are our current means of gaining wholeness through glimpsing and then integrating the otherwise neglected or rejected sides of ourselves" (p. 43).

Table 14.2 presents criticisms of each of the theories discussed above.

Biochemical Associations of Love

A number of biochemical events have been associated with the experience of "falling in love." When our senses of sight, smell, and touch send pleasure messages to the limbic system, the hypothalamus releases a peptide called adrenocorticotrophin, which triggers the release of a hormone (ACTH) from the pituitary gland. The bloodstream carries ACTH to receptors at the adrenal gland, which then releases corticosterone, a substance that increases the metabolism of glucose and results in symptoms associated with love: flushed skin, sweating, and heavy breathing.

Love resides in the brain; it is the organ of love.

Paul Chauchard

In *The Chemistry of Love* (1983), Michael Liebowitz suggested that the experience of romantic love is associated with a naturally occurring amphetamine-like substance called **phenylethylamine (PEA).** When we are in love, our brain produces increased amounts of PEA. One food that contains PEA is

TABLE 14.2 Love Theories and Criticisms

Theory	Criticism
Evolutionary	Assumption that women and children need men for survival is not necessarily true today. Women can have and rear children without men.
Learning	Does not account for 1) why some people will share positive experiences yet will not fall in love and 2) why some people stay in love despite negative behavior.
Psychosexual	Does not account for people who report intense love feelings yet are having sex regularly.
Ego-Ideal	Does not account for the fact that people of similar characteristics fall in love.
Ontological	Does not account for homosexual love. The focus of the ontological view of love is on the reunion of separated heterosexuals.

chocolate, which may explain why some love-deprived individuals crave chocolate. However, the Chocolate Manufacturer's Association disagrees with Liebowitz's theory:

> The PEA content of chocolate is extremely small, especially in comparison with that of some other commonly consumed foods. The standard serving size of three and a half ounces of smoked salami contains 6.7 mg of phenylethylamine; the same size serving of cheddar cheese contains 5.8 mg of phenylethylamine. The standard 1.5-ounce serving of chocolate (the size of the average chocolate bar) contains much less than 1 mg (.21 mg). Obviously, if Dr. Liebowitz's theory were true, people would be eating salami and cheese in far greater amounts than they are today. (quoted in Ackerman, 1990, p. 155)

> Being in love is the closest most of us will come to a true addiction.
>
> *John Money*

Although we don't fully understand the role that biochemical factors play in the experience of love, we can be fairly certain that they do play an important role in producing the physiological arousal that is associated with love. However, physiological arousal alone is not experienced as love unless cognitive processes define such arousal as love. Thus, in order to experience romantic love, the individual must be physiologically aroused and interpret this stirred-up state as love (Schacter, 1964; Hatfield & Walster, 1985).

> Love and sex are inextricably linked, with love as the basis for much of our sexual interaction, and sex as the medium for much of our loving.
>
> *Susan S. Hendrick*
> *Clyde Hendrick*

The biochemical perspective on love suggests that love may be viewed as a "natural high." In Exhibit 14.1, we look at love as a "natural high" that, like some drugs, may be addictive.

> Love is the most important ingredient in lovemaking.
>
> *Helen Kaplan*

Love is often expressed through physical and sexual touching. Physical indices of love relationships have been suggested by researchers. Individuals who are in love are more likely to maintain eye contact with each other (Rubin, 1970), to stand physically close (Byrne, Ervin, & Lamberth, 1970), and to be affectionate with each other in public (Schwartz & Jackson, 1989). What exactly is the relationship between love and sex? In the following theoretical perspective, we explore the possible relationships between love and sex by looking at a dimension for organizing theories of love and sex proposed by Aron and Aron (1991).

EXHIBIT 14.1 Love: A Natural High?

In the previous section, we described various biochemical factors that are associated with the experience of romantic love. These biochemical factors are summarized below:

1) Hypothalamus releases ACTH from the pituitary gland.
2) ACTH stimulates adrenal gland to release corticosterone, which increases metabolism of glucose.
3) Brain produces increased levels of phenylethylamine (PEA), which has a stimulant or amphetamine-like effect.

These biochemical processes are associated with a sense of euphoria and well-being: love makes us feel energized and feel less need for food and sleep. These euphoric feelings are also characteristic of some drug-induced highs. Walsh (1991) said that:

> Stimulant drugs such as cocaine and amphetamine have much the same effect as love—love is a natural high. (p. 188)

Walsh suggested that some people may be driven to take drugs because their lives are lacking in love. Without love, and the natural chemical high associated with love, some people seek to artificially induce euphoria through the use of drugs. Walsh said:

> It is precisely because some people experience so little joy mediated by the brain's own internal chemicals that they resort to artificial chemicals that briefly mimic pleasure, and soon become physically addicted. (p. 188)

The natural chemical high associated with love may also explain why the intensity of passionate love decreases over time. Individuals who regularly use amphetamines or cocaine must take increasing amounts of the drug in order to experience the same effects. This is because their bodies develop a tolerance for the drug, which means that the drug no longer produces its former effects. Similarly, lovers who are high on the "love drug" develop a tolerance for each other over a period of time.

Indeed, love may be addictive (Peele & Brodsky, 1976). It produces a feeling of euphoria that a person learns to enjoy and depend on. Once the person gets accustomed to the euphoria of love, the person needs to be with the partner to feel the heightened sense of contentment and happiness. Withdrawal symptoms—depression, unhappiness, even somatic complaints—may begin when the love relationship is broken. According to Peele and Brodsky, the person suffering from a broken love relationship goes through withdrawal in much the same way as an alcoholic who has given up alcohol.

THEORETICAL PERSPECTIVE:

A Dimension for Organizing Theories of Love and Sex

Arthur Aron and Elaine Aron (1991) suggested that the various views or theories of love and sexuality may be organized along a dimension having two extremes—one arguing that love is really sex and the other arguing that sex is really love. At the midpoint, love and sex are viewed as two independent factors that are equally important. The following diagram describes how various views of love and sex are organized along the dimension proposed by Aron and Aron.

Aron and Aron (1991) suggested that both social science approaches and the general public's approach to sexuality and love fall along a continuum from emphasizing sexuality to emphasizing love. At one end of this continuum (Position A), we find views that sexuality (or natural selection in favor of strategies that perpetuate the species) "causes" love. For example, evolutionary theories of love suggest that love evolved as a mechanism for ensuring the survival of the species. Psychosexual theory, associated with Freud, also suggests that all love relationships are motivated by sexual desire (i.e., the libido). Thus, these theories of love suggest that love is really sex.

At the other end of the continuum (Position E), we find views that love (as some essential quality of the universe or of being human) "causes" sexuality. This end of the continuum also represents theories of love that ignore sexuality. For example, ontological theories of love argue that "Love with a capital 'L' is primary or even the cosmic source of life and therefore of sexuality" (A. Aron & E. Aron, 1991, p. 35).

Continued

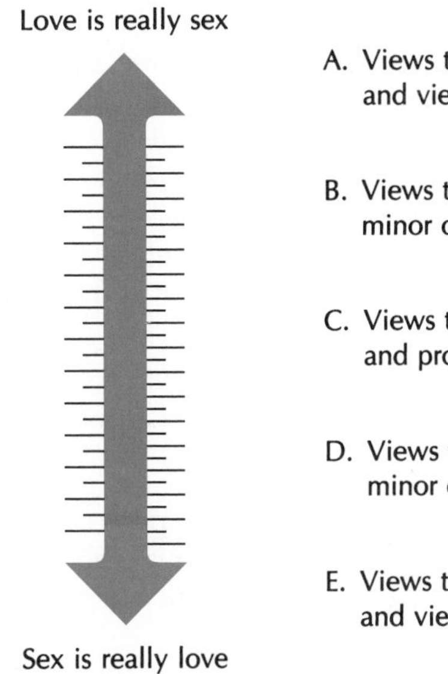

A. Views that consider love as resulting from sexuality and views of sexuality that ignore love

B. Views that emphasize sexuality, considering love a minor or subservient part of sexuality

C. Views that consider love and sexuality as separate and probably equal in importance

D. Views that emphasize love, considering sexuality a minor or subservient part of love

E. Views that consider sexuality as resulting from love and views of love that ignore sexuality

Continued

In addition, Maslow's notion of B-love (for being) implies that sexuality is irrelevant to this higher love.

Position D represents theories of love that emphasize love and view sexuality as a minor part of love. For example, Sternberg's (1986) triangular theory of love views love as having three components: commitment, intimacy, and passion. Sexuality is considered to be an aspect of the third component (passion).

In the middle (Position C), we find views arguing that love and sex are independent or that they cause each other. For example, according to Reik (ego-ideal theory of love), love arises from the desire to realize one's ideal self throughbecoming involved in a relationship with someone who possesses one's ideal traits. This motivation behind love is independent of the sexual drive, although Reik believed the most fulfilling love relationship arose when love and sex went together.

But Aron and Aron suggested that another view of love and sexuality is possible—that there is a spurious relationship between love and sex in that they both may be caused by a third factor. (Although this view is represented on point C, Aron and Aron suggested that this view transcends the continuum.) One such view emphasizes the role of physiological arousal as the basis for both sexuality and love (see the "Biochemical Associations of Love" section). Finally, both sex and love may both be caused by motivation to expand the self or gain wholeness. This view is represented by the ontological theory of love discussed earlier. By having sex and establishing an emotional pair bond with another, the individual feels more "complete."

Adapted from Aron, A., & Aron, E. (1991). Love and sexuality. In K. McKinney and S. Sprecher (Eds.), *Sexuality in close relationships* (pp. 25-48). Hillsdale, NJ: Lawrence Erlbaum Associates. Used by permission.

Love Relationships

Some of the theories of love discussed earlier in this chapter view love as an experience or force that exists independent of any particular interpersonal relationship. However, when most people in our society think of love, they think of it in the context of intimate relationships. Next, we focus on the psychological conditions under which love relationships develop. We also discuss two dilemmas of love: having simultaneous love relationships and being involved in an unfulfilling love relationship. Lastly, we look at the relationship between health and love.

Conditions Under Which Love Relationships Develop

Two psychological conditions associated with the development of healthy love relationships are a positive self-concept and the ability (and willingness) to self-disclose.

Positive Self-Concept A positive self-concept is important for developing healthy love relationships because it enables an individual to feel worthy of being loved. Feeling good about yourself allows you to believe that others are capable of loving you.

In contrast, a negative self-concept has devastating consequences for individuals and the relationships in which they become involved. Individuals who cannot accept themselves tend to reject others. "My daddy always told me I was no good and would never amount to anything," said one man. "I guess I have always believed him, have never liked myself, and can't think of why someone else would either" (Authors' files).

In some cases, a positive self-concept is not a prerequisite for falling in love. People who have a very negative self-concept may fall in love with someone else as a result of feeling deficient (Maslow's D-love). The love they perceive the other person having for them compensates for the deficiency and makes them feel better.

CONSIDERATION: Although it helps to have a positive self-concept at the beginning of a love relationship, sometimes this develops after becoming involved in a love relationship. "I've always felt like an ugly ducking," said one woman. "But once I fell in love with him and he with me, I felt very different. I felt very good about myself then because I knew that I was somebody that someone else loved."

While our focus here has been on how self-esteem affects adult love relationships, it is important to note that love also affects self-esteem. The role that love plays in determining self-esteem is especially important during the formative years. The degree that love is expressed to children strongly affects their feelings of self-worth in later years. One study found that early parental nurturance was the strongest predictor of self-esteem among college students (Buri, Kirchner, & Wash, 1987).

> I love you not only for what you are, but for what I am when I am with you.
> *Roy Croff*

The effect that love has on self-esteem may be different for men and women. Two researchers found that love is approximately 2.8 times more important in determining self-esteem for women than it is for men (Walsh & Balazs, 1990.) The researchers found that women who felt they received little love had a much lower self-esteem than men who felt they received little love. However, women who felt deeply loved had significantly higher self-esteem than men who also felt deeply loved.

Self-Disclosure In addition to feeling good about yourself, it is helpful to disclose your feelings to others if you want to love and be loved. Disclosing yourself is a way of investing yourself in another. Once the other person knows some of the intimate details of your life, you will tend to feel more positively about that person because a part of you is now a part of him or her. Open communication in this sense tends to foster the development of an intense love relationship.

In a study (Rubin, Hill, Peplau, & Dunkel-Schetter, 1980) of 231 couples who defined themselves as "going together," the researchers observed that the more the partners disclosed themselves to each other, the greater their love feelings for each other and the closer they regarded their relationship. As for what they disclosed, 70% of the women and men reported they had disclosed "fully" their feelings about their sexual relationship, and 60% had given full information about their previous sexual experiences. "Even in an area in which one would expect the greatest degree of reserve, 38 percent of the women and 35 percent of the men reported that they had revealed fully to their partners the things about themselves they were most ashamed of" (p. 313).

Dilemmas of Love Relationships

Being in love may create dilemmas. Two such dilemmas are being in love with two people at the same time and being involved in an unfulfilling love relationship.

Simultaneous Loves The lyrics of Mary McGregor's "Torn Between Two Lovers" reflect the dilemma of being in love with two people at the same time:

> Torn between two lovers, feeling like a fool, loving both of you is breaking all the rules.

Such a dilemma is not unusual. It is possible to be involved in several relationships at the same time and to have love feelings for each person.

CONSIDERATION: While our culture frowns on extramarital love, other cultures are more liberal in their acceptance of it. Some cultures view extramarital love as more desirable than marital love. For example, Hindu religious lore describes extramarital love as the purest form of love (Campbell, 1972).

> Sex relieves tension—love causes it.
> *Woody Allen*

Although it is possible to love two or more people at the same time, it is not possible to love them to the same degree (or in exactly the same way) at any particular moment because an individual must make a choice in terms of how to spend his or her time. If you choose to spend time with person X, then you value that person more than others—at least for that moment in time.

Unfulfilled Love Another dilemma of love is being in love with someone who may not fulfill your needs in the relationship or who may have needs that you are unable or unwilling to fulfill. Someone who is considerably different in age, who is an alcoholic, who has radically different values, who criticizes you continually, or who is dishonest with you may be a partner with whom you will experience a great deal of frustration, stress, and disappointment. Nevertheless, you might love and feel emotionally drawn to that person. Most marriage therapists would empathize with your love feelings and suggest that you look at the rewards you derive from being involved in a love relationship with this person. Does it upset your parents? Do you feel this is what you deserve because you are "no good"? Do you feel pity for the person and want to be her or his therapist? These questions imply that your love relationship may be based on motivations that you might want to carefully examine.

CONSIDERATION: Some students in the authors' classes have asked, "Is there a difference between 'loving' and 'being in love'?" A possible answer to this question is as follows: "Loving" involves loving a person; "being in love" involves loving the relationship as well as the person. This implies that we may love a person but not love the relationship we have with that person. Some people going through divorce have indicated that they wanted to divorce not because they did not love their spouse but because they no longer loved the relationship they had with their spouse (Authors' counseling notes). In other words, they still "loved" their spouse, but they were not "in love" (with the relationship).

Love and Health

When children scrape their knee, bang their elbow, or bump their head, their parents often respond by kissing the boo-boo to make it feel better. While not all people believe the adage that "Love heals all wounds," many believe that love has healing properties. This belief also implies that lack of love may be injurious to our health. Indeed, Freud wrote that ". . . in the last resort we must begin to love in order that we may not fall ill . . ." (1924, p. 42).

Expressions of love and affection are the greatest medicines we can give one another.

Anthony Walsh

Considerable research supports the idea that love promotes physical well-being. In *Love, Medicine, and Miracles,* Dr. Bernie Siegel (1986) described some of this research:

- At the Menninger Foundation in Topeka, Kansas, people who are in love, in the romantic sense, have been found to have reduced levels of lactic acid in their blood, making them less tired, and higher levels of endorphins, making them euphoric and less subject to pain. Their white blood cells also responded better when faced with infections, and thus they got fewer colds (p. 182-183).
- In 1982, Harvard psychologists David McClelland and Carol Kirshnit found that even movies about love increase levels of immunoglobulin-A in the saliva, the first line of defense against colds and other viral diseases (p. 183).

While love may enhance physical well-being, love deprivation may jeopardize it. Rene Spitz (1945) conducted a classic study on early love deprivation with institutionalized infants. Spitz was concerned about the unexplained high death rates among infants in a foundling home, despite adequate nutrition, medical care, and hygiene. In contrast, Spitz found less illness and death among infants in a nursery in a penal institution for delinquent girls, even though the level of medical care, hygiene, and nutrition was below that of the foundling home.

Within two years after the start of his study, Spitz observed that 37% of the foundling home children had died, while all of the children in the penal nursery were alive five years later. He concluded that the high death rate among the foundling home infants was due to lack of love. The penal children were cared for by their own mothers, who kissed, held, talked to, played with, and showed affection toward their children. In other words, the penal children were loved. While nurses in the foundling home provided adequate medical and nutritional care to the infants, they had neither the time nor the inclination to develop affectionate bonds with all the babies in their care.

Poets and songwriters have often written about "broken hearts" resulting from the loss of love or a loved one. But physicians and medical researchers have also

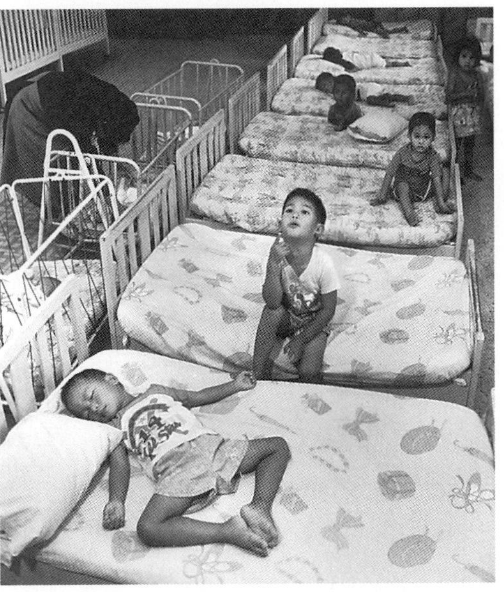

Institutionalized children may suffer from lack of love and attention which has a negative effect on their ability to establish emotional attachments in adulthood.

How can you mend a broken heart?
How can a loser ever win?
Please help me mend my broken heart
and let me live again.

Bee Gees (song lyrics)

explored the effect of terminated love relationships on the heart. In *The Broken Heart: The Medical Consequences of Loneliness* (1977), James Lynch stated: "Growing numbers of physicians now recognize that the health of the human heart depends not only on such factors as genetics, diet, and exercise, but also to a large extent on the social and emotional health of the individual" (p. 13).

Heart disease is often related to high blood pressure. Research by Sisca, Walsh, and Walsh (1985) suggests that high blood pressure is associated with love deprivation. The researchers measured love deprivation in college students by administering two questionnaires that tapped respondents' subjective perceptions of the degree to which they felt loved or unloved. Love deprivation was found to be significantly and positively related to elevated blood pressure levels, that is, the higher the love deprivation, the higher the blood pressure. This effect was independent of age and weight variables.

Sexual Jealousy in Relationships

To demand of love that it be without jealousy is to ask of light that it cast no shadows.

Oscar Hamilton

Sexual jealousy may be defined as any aversive emotional reaction that occurs as the result of a partner's extradyadic relationship that is real, imagined, or considered likely to occur (Bringle & Buunk, 1991, p. 242). Jealousy constitutes "a protective reaction to a perceived threat to a valued relationship or to its quality" (Clanton, 1990, p. 180). Pines (1992) estimated that jealousy is a problem for a third of all couples who seek marital therapy. Jealousy is both a common and a normal reaction to a real or imagined threat to an existing love relationship.

Causes of Jealousy

Jealousy may be caused by external or internal factors.

External Causes External factors refer to behaviors of the partner that suggest:

1 an emotional and/or sexual interest in someone else, or
2 a lack of emotional and/or sexual interest in the primary partner.

Examples of external causes of jealousy include flirting with, spending a lot of time with, or expressing interest in someone else. External causes may also result from spending little time with and expressing little interest in the primary partner.

The term "reactive jealousy" refers to jealousy that is caused by external factors. Reactive jealousy is defined as "the upset that accompanies the revelation of anticipated, current, or past extradyadic sexual behavior by the partner" (Bringle & Buunk, 1991, p. 138).

Jealousy springs more from love of self than from love of another.
La Rochefoucauld (translated from French)

Internal Causes Jealousy may also exist even when there is no external behavior that indicates that the partner is involved or interested in an extradyadic relationship. Internal causes of jealousy refer to characteristics of individuals that predispose them to jealous feelings, independent of their partner's behavior. Examples of internal causes of jealousy include being mistrustful, having low self-esteem, being highly involved in and dependent on the relationship, and having no perceived alternative partners available (Pines, 1992). These internal causes of jealousy are explained below.

1. Mistrust. Individuals who have been deceived or "cheated on" in a previous relationship may learn to be mistrustful in subsequent relationships. Such mistrust may manifest itself in jealousy.
2. Low self-esteem. Individuals who have low self-esteem tend to be jealous because they lack a sense of self-worth and, hence, find it difficult to believe that anyone can value and love them. The fact that a person "cheats" on them confirms that they are worthless. And the fact that they feel worthless, may contribute to their feeling suspicious that someone else is valued more.
3. High degree of relative involvement or dependency. In general, individuals who are more involved in or dependent on the relationship than their partner are prone to jealousy (Bush, Bush, & Jennings, 1988).

CONSIDERATION: The person who is more involved or dependent on the relationship is not only more likely to experience jealousy but may also intentionally induce jealousy in the partner. Such attempts to induce jealousy may involve flirting, exaggerating or discussing an attraction to someone else, and spending time with others. According to White (1980), individuals may try to make their partner jealous in order to test the relationship (e.g., see if the partner still cares) and/or to increase specific rewards (e.g., get more attention or affection). White found that women, especially those who thought they were more involved in the relationship than their partners, were more likely to induce jealousy in a relationship than men.

4. Lack of perceived alternatives. In a study of jealousy among spouses, the most jealous were those who felt that they could not find another partner if their partner became attracted to someone else (Hansen, 1985).

Consequences of Jealousy

Jealousy may have consequences that are both desirable (reinforce one's sense of value, confirm the unacceptability of outside relationships, cause a reevaluation of the relationship, increase communication) and undesirable (increase stress, ignite self-fulfilling prophecy, lead to homicide or suicide). Notice that one has a choice in terms of how one views jealousy.

He that is not jealous is not in love.
St. Augustine

Desirable Outcomes Low levels of jealousy may be functional for a relationship. Not only may jealousy keep the partner aware that he or she is cared for (the implied message is "I love you and don't want to lose you to someone else"), but also the partner may learn that the development of romantic and sexual relationships "on the side" is unacceptable. One wife said:

> When I started spending extra time with this guy at the office, my husband got jealous and told me he thought I was getting in over my head and asked me to cut back on the relationship because it was "tearing him up" and he couldn't stay married to me with these feelings. I felt he really loved me when he told me this and I chose to stop spending time with the guy at work. (Authors' files)

Jealousy may improve a couple's relationship in yet another way. When the partners begin to take each other for granted, involvement of one or both partners outside the relationship can encourage them to reevaluate how important the relationship is and can help recharge it. Bringle & Buunk (1991) summarized the potential desirable outcome of jealousy:

> Suspicious jealousy is not necessarily unhealthy jealousy. When there is a pattern of minor incidents suggesting that the partner might be involved with someone else, vigilance to determine what is happening may be a prudent response that reflects reasonable concern and good strategies to cope with the situation. Furthermore, emotional reactions to these events may forewarn the partner of what will happen if there are serious transgressions and thereby serve the role of *preventing* extradyadic involvements. (p. 137)

CONSIDERATION: Sometimes the reaction to one's partner's jealousy encourages further jealous behavior. Suppose John accuses Mary of being interested in someone else, and Mary denies the accusation and responds by saying "I love you" and by being very affectionate. From a behavioral or social learning perspective, if this pattern continues, Mary will teach John to continue being jealous. When John acts jealous, good things happen to him—Mary showers him with love and physical affection. Inadvertently, Mary may be reinforcing John for exhibiting jealous behavior.

To break the cycle, Mary should tell John of her love for him and be affectionate when he is not exhibiting jealous behavior. When he does act jealous, she might say that she feels badly when he accuses her of something she isn't doing and to please stop. If he does not stop, she might terminate the interaction until John can be around her and not act jealous.

Undesirable Outcomes Shakespeare referred to jealousy as the "green-eyed monster," suggesting that jealousy is a frightening emotion that has undesirable outcomes for individuals and for relationships. Jealousy that stems from low self-esteem may result in the partner withdrawing from the relationship. Walsh (1991) explained:

> An individual with feelings of negative self-worth . . . is continually imagining that no one could really be faithful to such an undeserving soul. If a person feels this way about him or herself, that atmosphere of insecurity, possessiveness, and accusations. . . . makes it more probable that the mate will eventually come to share the self-evaluation and go forth to seek someone more deserving of his or her love. If such an event does occur, it merely seems to vindicate what we've known all along—we're no good. (pp. 240-241)

Jealousy may also create a self-fulfilling prophecy whereby the partner who is accused of having an interest in or being involved with someone else reacts by engaging in the behavior of which he or she is accused. The self-fulfilling prophecy is illustrated by the partner who says, "If I'm going to get accused all the time for something I'm not guilty of, I might as well go ahead and sleep with other people. After all, I get accused of it whether I do or I don't, so I might as well enjoy what I'm being accused of."

In its extreme form, jealousy may have devastating consequences, including murder, suicide, spouse beating, and severe depression. Makepeace (1989) found that violence in steady dating relationships is likely to be precipitated by arguments over jealousy. Violence in cohabitating and marital relationships is also frequently precipitated by jealousy.

CONSIDERATION: Jealousy may serve as an antecedent to sexual behavior (DeLamater, 1991). We have already noted that the "accused" person may seek extradyadic sexual involvement as retaliation against unfair accusations. In addition, the jealous partner may also retaliate against the "accused" by seeking extradyadic sexual involvement. We have also noted that jealousy frequently leads to violence, which may take the form of sexual violence (e.g., rape). On the positive side, jealousy and/or the expression of it may lead to more passionate and consensual sexual activity between the partners.

Techniques for Resolving Jealousy

Clanton and Smith (1986, p. 161) described four basic options individuals may choose when faced with jealousy that becomes problematic.

1. Get out of the relationship.
2. Ignore and/or tolerate the behaviors which are causing the jealousy.
3. Influence your partner to stop or modify the behaviors that are creating jealousy.
4. Work on the internal causes of the jealousy.

Pines (1992) identified several therapeutic techniques used to resolve feelings of jealously, including desensitization, implosion or flooding, and "pretend." Desensitization involves learning to imagine, while being and staying relaxed, scenes in which the partner is with someone else in progressively more intimate encounters. Implosion or flooding involves imagining such scenes to the point that they no longer elicit feelings of anxiety. Use of "pretend" involves the jealous person behaving as though he or she is not jealous. By doing so, the person may be able to view himself or herself as not jealous. This technique is based on the belief that individuals can act themselves into a new way of thinking or feeling more quickly than they can think or feel themselves into a new way of acting.

White and Helbick (1988) reviewed therapeutic strategies for treating jealousy and identified common themes. These included challenging irrational assumptions and beliefs, such as "jealousy implies love," or "I can't stand the thought of my mate being attracted to someone else;" training in communication and negotiation skills; addressing the jealous partner's low self-esteem; and developing new coping behaviors to reduce defensiveness and enhance the relationship. White and Helbick described the two day couples jealousy workshop they have developed, but no treatment outcome research is available.

Sexual jealousy is not an easy emotion with which to cope. A beginning might be for individuals experiencing jealousy to make their partners aware of such feelings and to ask for their help. By doing so, the feelings become visible, which allows the couple to work on them as a unit (thus helping to improve their solidarity as a couple).

CHOICES

Making decisions about the level of emotional intimacy that is appropriate before sexual involvement occurs involves a consideration of sex with and without love.

Choose to Have Sex with Love?

Some individuals are more likely to approve of sex in the context of a love relationship. Twenty-two percent of a national sample of 1,829 sexually experienced adults felt that it is "always wrong" for an adult man who was in love to have intercourse before marriage. Thirty-eight percent felt that it is "always wrong" if the adult man was not in love. Twenty-three percent felt that it is "always wrong" for an adult woman who was in love to have intercourse before marriage; 42% felt that it is "always wrong" for an adult woman who was not in love to have intercourse before marriage (Klassen, Williams, & Levitt, 1989, p. 253).

The following is an example of what a female student said about the importance of an emotional relationship as a context for sexual expression:

> Sex is good and beautiful when both parties want it, but when one person wants sex only, that's bad. I love sex, but I like to feel that the man cares about me. I can't handle the type of sexual relationship where one night I spend the night with him and the next night he spends the night with someone else. I feel like I am being used. There are still a few women around like me who *need* the commitment before sex. (Authors' files)

Hendrick and Hendrick (1983) concluded that

> It is possible to have good sex, even excellent sex without love. However, the *best* sex occurs within the context of love. . . . (p. 131)

Choose to Have Sex without Love?

Other people feel that love is not necessary for sexual expression. Indeed, the theme of the book *Sex without Love* (Vannoy, 1980) is that sex should be enjoyed for its own sake. One person said:

> You choose a lover according to how you wish to be loved, and you choose a sex partner according to how you wish to be laid. There is no guarantee whatever that the person you love and the person whom you find most sexually desirable are one and the same. There are just certain things a lover may not be able to give you, and it may be good sex. (p. 24)

The idea that sex with love is wholesome and sex without love is exploitative may be an untenable position. For example, two strangers can meet, share each other sexually, have a deep mutual admiration for each other's sensuous qualities, and go their separate ways in the morning. Such an encounter is not necessarily an example of sexual exploitation. Rather, it may be an example of two individuals who have a preference for independence and singlehood, rather than permanent emotional involvement and marriage (Vannoy, 1980, p. 26).

Each person in a sexual encounter will undoubtedly experience different degrees of love feelings, and the experience of each may differ across time. One woman in the authors' classes reported that the first time she had intercourse with her future husband was shortly after they had met in a bar. She described their first sexual encounter as "raw naked sex" with no emotional feelings. But they continued to see each other over a period of months, an emotional relationship developed, and "sex took on a love meaning for us."

Sex with love can also drift into sex without love. One man said that he had been deeply in love with his wife but that they had gradually drifted apart. Sex between them was no longer sex with love. Similarly, some women report being in relationships with men who feign love but actually use them for sex. Bepko and Krestan (1991) emphasized the importance of women breaking from these codependent relationships and establishing their own self-love as a secure base for making choices in relationships with others.

Both love and sex can be viewed on a continuum. Love feelings may range from being nonexistent to being intense, and relationships can range from limited sexual interaction to intense interaction. Hence, rarely are sexual encounters with or without love. Rather, they will include varying degrees of emotional involvement. Also, rarely are romantic love relationships with or without sex. Rather, they display varying degrees of sexual expression. Where on the continuum one chooses to be—at what degree of emotional and sexual involvement—will vary from person to person and from time to time.

SUMMARY

1. The word "love" is difficult to define, partly because it is viewed differently by individuals, religions, and societies. Various ancient and modern views of love discussed in this chapter include Buddhist, Greek, and Hebrew conceptions of love, as well as views proposed by Maslow, Lee, Rubin, and Sternberg. These various views differ in their emphasis on the roles that behavior, emotion, and cognition play in love.
2. Love may be viewed along a continuum from romanticism to realism. Love is distinguished from infatuation, which is characterized as attraction without attachment and excessive idealization of one's lover (or desired lover).
3. In our society, love is associated with expressive qualities—those qualities which are emphasized in our cultural notions of femininity. Hence, love in our society is "feminized." The consequences of the feminization of love include (a) men, who tend to have a more instrumental style in their expression of love, are not given credit or validation for their style of love, (b) many heterosexual women are unsatisfied in their love relationships and (c) the instrumental component of women's love is obscured. A conception of love that combines instrumental and expressive qualities is suggested.
4. Various theoretical explanations of love have been proposed. Evolutionary theory suggests that parent/child love developed to ensure the survival of offspring and love between two adults evolved to bond two adults together to provide for, protect, and nurture dependent offspring. Learning theory views love as feelings that result from positive interaction. Love may also result from blocked biological sexual drives (psychosexual theory), finding one's ego ideal (ego-ideal theory), or finding one's other half (ontological theory).
5. The experience of "falling in love" has been associated with a number of biochemical changes. For example, hormonal changes associated with falling in love result in increased metabolism. Love is also associated with a naturally occurring amphetamine-like substance (phenylethylamine) that is produced in the brain. These biochemical changes are associated with a sense of euphoria and well-being. Love, then, may be viewed as a "natural high."
6. Regarding the relationship between love and sex, it has been argued that (a) love is really sex and (b) sex is really love. These two arguments form two ends of a continuum on which theories of love and sex may be organized.
7. Various social and psychological conditions affect the development of love relationships. Healthy love relationships are associated with having a positive self-concept and the ability and willingness to self-disclose.
8. Two dilemmas of love relationships are being in love with two people at the same time and being involved in an unfulfilling love relationship. It is possible to love a person and not love the relationship you have with that person.
9. Considerable research supports the idea that love promotes physical health and well-being.
10. Jealousy may be viewed as having external causes (behaviors of the partner) and/or internal causes (mistrust, dependency, low self-esteem, no perceived alternative partners). Jealousy may have both positive and negative consequences for individuals and relationships.

11. Several techniques for resolving jealousy are described. These include changing irrational beliefs, improving communication and negotiation skills, increasing self-esteem, desensitization and implosion (flooding) techniques, and influencing the partner to stop or modify the behaviors that are creating the jealousy.

KEY TERMS

phileo
philanthropia
agape
eros
B-love
D-love
ludus
storge
pragma
mania
nonlove
liking
infatuation
romantic love
companionate love
fatuous love
empty love
consummate love
realistic love
conjugal love
phenylethylamine (PEA)
sexual jealousy

REFERENCES

Ackerman, D. (1990). *A natural history of the senses.* New York: Random House.

Ard, B. N. (1990). *The sexual realm in long-term marriages.* San Francisco: Mellen Research University Press.

Aron, A., & Aron, E. N. (1991). Love and sexuality. In K. McKinney and S. Sprecher (Eds.), *Sexuality in close relationships* (pp. 25-48). Hillsdale, NJ: Lawrence Erlbaum Associates.

Bartz, W. R., & Rasor, R. A. (1972). Why people fall in and out of romantic love. *Sexual Behavior, 2,* 33-39.

Belsky, J., & Rovine, M. (1990). Patterns of marital change across the transition to parenthood: Pregnancy to three years postpartum. *Journal of Marriage and the Family, 52,* 5-19.

Bepko, C., & Krestan, J. (1991). *Too good for her own good: Searching for self and intimacy in important relationships.* New York: Harper Collins.

Bringle, R. G., & Buunk, B. P. (1991). Extradyadic relationships and sexual jealousy. In K. McKinney and S. Sprecher (Eds.), *Sexuality in close relationships* (pp. 135-154). Hillsdale, NJ: Lawrence Erlbaum Associates.

Buri, J., Kirchner, P., & Wash, J. (1987). Familial correlates of self-esteem in young American adults. *Journal of Social Psychology, 127,* 583-588.

Burtt, E. A. (1957). *A man seeks the divine.* New York: Harper and Brothers.

Bush, C. R., Bush, J. P., & Jennings, J. (1988). Effects of jealousy threats on relationship perceptions and emotions. *Journal of Social and Personal Relationships, 5,* 285-303.

Buss, D. M. (1988). The evolutionary biology of love. In R. J. Sternberg and M. L. Barnes (Eds.), *The psychology of love* pp. 100-118. New Haven, CT: Yale University Press.

Byrne, D. A., Ervin, C., & Lamberth, J. (1970). Continuity between the experimental study of attraction and 'real life' computer dating. *Journal of Personality and Social Psychology, 16,* 157-165.

Campbell, J. (1972). *Myths to live by.* New York: Bantam Books.

Cancian, F. M. 1987. *Love in America: Gender and self-development.* New York: Cambridge University Press.

Clanton, G. & Smith, L. G. (1986). Managing jealousy. In G. Clanton & L. G. Smith (Eds.), *Jealousy* (pp. 161-165). Lanham, MD: University Press of America.

Clanton, G. (1990). Jealousy in American culture, 1945-1985: Reflections from popular culture. In D. D. Franks & E. D. McCarthy (Eds.), *The sociology of emotions: Original essays and research* (pp. 179-193). Greenwich, CT: JAI Press.

Dion, K. K., & Dion, K. L. (1991). Psychological individualism and romantic love. *Journal of Social Behavior and Personality, 6,* 17-33.

Erikson, E. H. (1963). *Childhood and society.* New York: Norton.

Freud, S. (1924). On narcissism. In *Collected papers of Sigmund Freud* (vol. 4). New York: International Psychoanalytic Press.

Freud, S. (1938). Three contributions to the theory of sex. In A. A. Brill (Ed.), *The basic writings of Sigmund Freud.* New York: Random House. (Original work published in 1905)

Fromm, E. (1963). *The art of loving.* New York: Bantam Books.

Grant, V. W. (1976). *Falling in love: The psychology of romantic emotion.* New York: Springer.

Guttentag, M., & Secord, P. F. (1983). *Too many women? The sex ratio question.* Beverly Hills, CA: Sage.

Hansen, G. L. (1985). Perceived threats and marital jealousy. *Social Psychology Quarterly, 48,* 262-268.

Hatfield, E., & Walster, G. W. (1985). *A new look at love.* Lanham, MD: University Press of America.

Hazen, C., & Shaver, P. (1987). Romantic love conceptualized as an attachment process. *Journal of Personality and Social Psychology, 52,* 511-524.

Hendrick, C., & Hendrick, S. S. (1991). Dimensions of love: A sociobiological interpretation. *Journal of Social and Clinical Psychology, 10,* 206-230.

Hendrick, C., & Hendrick, S. (1983). *Liking, loving, & relating.* Montery, CA: Brooks/Cole.

Hendrick, S. S., & Hendrick, C. (1987). Love and sex attitudes: A close relationship. In W. H. Jones & D. Perlman (Eds.), *Advances in Personal Relationships,* Vol I, (pp. 141-169). Greenwich, Connecticut: JAI Press Inc.

Hendrick, C., & Hendrick, S. (1986). A theory and method of love. *Journal of Personality and Social Psychology, 50,* 392-402.

Hendrick, C. & Hendrick, S. S. (1988). Lovers wear rose colored glasses. *Journal of Social and Personal Relationships, 5,* 161-183.

Hendrick, C., Hendrick, S., Foote, F. H., & Slapion-Foote, M. J. (1984). Do men and women love differently? *Journal of Social and Personal Relationships, 1,* 177-195.

Jorgensen, S. R., & Gaudy, J. C. (1980). Self-disclosure and satisfaction in marriage: The relation examined. *Family Relations, 29,* 281-288.

Klassen, A. D., Williams, C. J., & Levitt, E. E. (1989). *Sex and morality in the United States: An empirical enquiry under the auspices of the Kinsey Institute.* Middletown, CT: Wesleyan University Press.

Knox, D. (1970). Conceptions of love at three developmental levels. *Family Life Coordinator, 19,* 151-157.

Knox, D. (1982). What kind of love is yours? Unpublished study, East Carolina University, Department of Sociology, Anthropology, and Economics, Greenville, NC.

Knox, D., & Sporakowski, M. J. (1968). Attitudes of college students toward love. *Journal of Marriage and the Family, 30,* 638-642.

Lasswell, T. E., & Lasswell, M. E. (1976). I love you but I'm not in love with you. *Journal of Marriage and Family Counseling, 38,* 211-224.

Lee, J. A. (1973). *The colors of love: An exploration of the ways of loving.* Don Mills, Ontario: New Press.

Lee, J. A. (1988). Love-styles. In R. Sternberg and M. Barnes (Eds.), *The psychology of love* (pp. 38-67). New Haven: Yale University Press.

Lewis, D. (1985). *In and out of love: The mystery of personal attraction.* London: Methuen.

Liebowitz, M. (1983). *The chemistry of love.* Boston: Little, Brown.

Lott, A. J., & Lott, B. E. (1961). Group cohesiveness, communication level, and conformity. *Journal of Abnormal and Social Psychology, 62,* 408-412.

Lott, A. J., & Lott, B. E. (1974). The role of reward in the formation of positive interpersonal attitudes. In T. L. Huston (Ed.), *Foundations of interpersonal attraction* (pp. 171-189). New York: Academic Press.

Lynch, J. (1977). *The broken heart: The medical consequences of loneliness.* New York: Basic Books.

Makepeace, J. (1989). Dating, living together, and courtship violence. In M. A. Pirog-Good and J. E. Stets (Eds.), Violence in dating relationships. (pp. 94-107). *New York: Greenwood Press.*

Maslow, A. (1968). *Toward a psychology of being.* New York: Van Nostrand.

Masters, W. H., & Johnson, V. E. (1966). *Human sexual response.* Boston: Little, Brown.

Mellen, S. (1981). *The evolution of love.* San Francisco: W. H. Freeman.

Mirchandani, V. K. (1973). Attitudes toward love among blacks. Unpublished master's thesis, East Carolina University, Greenville, NC.

Money, J. (1980). *Love and lovesickness: The science of sex, gender difference, and pair bonding.* Baltimore: Johns Hopkins University Press.

Morgan, D. N. (1964). *Love: Plato, the Bible and Freud.* Englewood Cliffs, NJ: Prentice-Hall.

O'Brien, J. A. (1956). *Happy marriage.* New York: Doubleday.

Pedersen, L. E. (1991). *Dark hearts: The Unconscious forces that shape men's lives.* Boston: Shambhala.

Peele, S., & Brodsky, A. (1976). *Love and addiction.* New York: New American Library.

Pines, A. M. (1992). *Romantic jealousy: Understanding and conquering the shadow of love.* New York: St. Martin's Press.

Reik, T. (1949). *Of love and lust.* New York: Farrar, Straus, and Cudahy.

Rubenstein, C. (1983, July). The modern art of courtly love. *Psychology Today,* pp. 40-49.

Rubin, Z. (1973). *Liking and loving.* New York: Holt, Rinehart & Winston.

Rubin, Z., Hill, C. T., Peplau, L. A., & Dunkel-Schetter, C. (1980). Self-disclosure in dating couples: Sex roles and the ethic of openness. *Journal of Marriage and the Family, 42,* 305-318.

Rubin, Z. (1970). Measurement of romantic love. *Journal of Personality and Social Psychology, 16,* 265-273.

Schacter, S. (1964). The interaction of cognitive and physiological determinants of emotional state. In L. Berkowitz (Ed.), *Advances in experimental social psychology* (pp. 49-80). New York: Academic Press.

Shumante, L. (1990, July). What nurses can't cure, love can. *Nursing,* p. 112.

Schwartz, P., & Jackson, D. (1989, February). How to have a model marriage. *New Woman,* pp. 66-74.

Siegel, B. S. (1986). *Love, medicine, and miracles.* New York: Harper and Row.

Simmons, C. H., Kolke, A. V., & Shimizu, H. (1986). Attitudes toward romantic love among American, German, and Japanese students. *Journal of Social Psychology, 126,* 327-336.

Sisca, S., Walsh, A., & Walsh, P. (1985). Love deprivation and blood pressure levels among a college population: A preliminary investigation. *Psychology, 22,* 63-70.

Spitz, R. A. (1945). Hospitalism: An inquiry into the genesis of psychiatric conditions in early childhood. *Psychoanalytic Studies of the Child* 1: 53-74.

Spitz, R. A. (1945). Hospitalism. In A. Freud et al. (Eds.), *The Psychoanalytic study of the child* (vol. 1) (pp. 52-74). New York: International Universities Press.

Sternberg, R. J. (1986). A triangular theory of love. *Psychological Review, 93,* 119-135.

Sternberg, R. J., & Beall, A. E. (1991). How can we know what love is? An epistemological analysis. In G. J. O. Fletcher and F. D. Fincham (Eds.), *Cognition in close relationships* (pp. 257-278) Hillsdale, NJ: Lawrence Erlbaum Associates.

Stone, C. R., & Philbrick, J. L. (1991). Attitudes toward love among members of a small fundamentalist community in South Africa. *Journal of Social Psychology, 131,* 219-223.

Tavris, C. (1992). *The mismeasure of woman.* New York: Simon & Schuster.

Tillich, P. (1960). *Love, power, and justice.* New York: Oxford University Press.

Vannoy, R. (1980). *Sex without love: A philosophical exploration.* Buffalo, NY: Prometheus Books.

Walsh, A. (1991). *The science of love: Understanding love and its effects on mind and body.* Buffalo, NY: Prometheus Books.

Walsh, A., & Balazs, G. (1990). Love, sex, and self-esteem. *Free Inquiry in Creative Sociology, 18,* 37-42.

Weis, D. L., Rabinowitz, B., & Ruckstuhl, M. F. (1992). Individual changes in sexual attitudes and behavior within college-level human sexuality courses. *Journal of Sex Research, 29,* 43-59.

White, G. L. (1980). Inducing jealousy: A power perspective. *Personality and Social Psychology Bulletin, 6,* 222-227.

White, G. L. & Helbick, T. R. M. (1988). Understanding and treating jealousy. In R. A. Brown & J. R. Field (Eds.). *Treatment of sexual problems in individual and couples therapy* (pp. 245-265). USA: PMA.

CHAPTER FIFTEEN

Sexual Dysfunctions and Sex Therapy

Chapter Outline

Sexual Dysfunctions: Causes and Contributing Factors
- Biological Factors
- Sociocultural Factors
- **Theoretical and Research Perspective:** Prevention of Male Sexual Dysfunction by Challenging Sexual Myths and Gender Role Stereotypes
- Intrapsychic Factors
- Relationship Factors
- Educational and Cognitive Factors
- **Self-Assessment:** How Much Do You Know about Sexuality?
- Aging Factors

Desire-Phase Dysfunctions
- Hypoactive Sexual Desire
- Sexual Aversion

Arousal-Phase Dysfunctions
- Female Sexual Arousal Dysfunction
- Male Erectile Dysfunction

Orgasm-Phase Dysfunctions
- Inhibited Female Orgasm
- Inhibited Male Orgasm
- Early Ejaculation

Sexual Pain Dysfunctions
- Dyspareunia
- Vaginismus

Approaches Used in Sex Therapy
- Psychoanalytic Approach
- Masters and Johnson's Approach
- The PLISSIT Model Approach
- Cognitive Therapy Approach
- Helen Kaplan's Approach
- LoPiccolo's Postmodern Approach
- Surrogate Partner Therapy
- Alternative Aids Used in Sex Therapy
- Effectiveness of Sex Therapy

Sex Therapy: Professional and Ethical Issues
- Training Requirements to Become a Sex Therapist
- Sexual Involvement between Therapist and Client
- Values in Sex Therapy

Choices
- Choose to Have Individual Therapy or Couple (Conjoint) Therapy?
- Choose to Have Private Therapy or Group Therapy?
- Choose to Have a Male-Female Sex Therapy Team or an Individual Therapist?

Is It True?*

1. A man is considered to have erectile dysfunction if he experiences difficulty attaining or maintaining an erection, and this difficulty continues for at least two weeks.

2. Most states require sex therapists to be licensed or certified.

3. Women report that their "favorite part of sexual behavior" is foreplay, rather than sexual intercourse and afterplay.

4. Women involved with men who have difficulty getting and keeping an erection report that they seldom engage in any sexual activity.

5. The person men report that they are most likely to talk to about a sexual problem is their partner, a good friend, and their medical doctor (in that order).

* 1 = F, 2 = F, 3 = T, 4 = T, 5 = T

If *you* need therapy, seek a professional.

James Walters

These musings from one of Hite's (1987) respondents emphasize that sexual intimacy can be one of the most fulfilling aspects of our lives and relationships:

> I usually feel the closest after we make love, because it is an expression of all the wonderful and closest feelings I have toward her. When we make love, I feel as though we are a total entity—I can't tell where she leaves off and where I begin. It seems to be a 'complete' feeling, capturing my emotions, my intellect, and my physical awareness. (p. 219)

While sexual satisfaction is not the only factor that affects our satisfaction in sexually intimate relationships, it is an important element. In other chapters in this text, we discuss various problems that may affect both sexual satisfaction and overall relationship satisfaction (e.g., jealousy in Chapter 14, extradyadic sexual involvements in Chapter 10, poor sexual communication in Chapter 13, health problems related to disease and disability in Chapter 16, and sexually transmissible diseases in Chapter 18). In this chapter, we focus on a set of sexual problems referred to as "sexual dysfunctions."

A **sexual dysfunction** is an impairment or difficulty that affects sexual functioning or produces sexual pain. As you may recall from Chapter 7, Sexual Response, some models of the sexual response cycle include the desire, arousal (or excitement), plateau, orgasm, and resolution phases. Sexual dysfunctions may occur in any of these phases and usually involve a disturbance in both the subjective sense of pleasure or desire and the objective physiological aspects of sexual functioning (American Psychiatric Association [APA], 1987). We begin this chapter by describing factors that may cause or contribute to sexual dysfunction. Then, we discuss the various types of sexual dysfunctions associated with the desire, arousal, and orgasm phases, as well as sexual dysfunctions associated with pain during sexual activity (see Table 15.1).

This organization follows the categorization system of DSMIII-R, as that provides the diagnostic categories typically used in the United States. Tiefer (1991, p. 13) criticized that the "enshrinement" of the HSRC (human sexual response cycle) model "as the centerpiece of sexual dysfunction nomenclature" results in a view of sexuality as the mechanical performance of disjointed body parts. Physical processes within the genitals are emphasized more than overall satisfaction with sexual functioning.

TABLE 15.1 Types of Sexual Dysfunctions in Women and Men

Aspects of sexuality affected	Sexual Dysfunction	
	Women	*Men*
Sexual Desire	Hypoactive sexual desire Sexual aversion	Hypoactive sexual desire Sexual aversion
Arousal	Female sexual arousal dysfunction	Erectile dysfunction
Orgasm	Inhibited female orgasm	Inhibited male orgasm Early ejaculation
Sexual Pain	Dyspareunia Vaginismus	Dyspareunia

An Editor's note in Tiefer's article remarked that this is "a very American viewpoint" (p. 13). The Editor observed that in the most recent version of the International Classification of Diseases (ICD 10) the sexual dysfunction section does not rely on the HSRC, and offers lack of sexual enjoyment as a main heading.

As we discuss each type of sexual dysfunction, we describe its nature, causes, and various treatment alternatives. In the second half of this chapter, we take a broad look at various treatment modalities and the field of sex therapy.

Sexual Dysfunctions: Causes and Contributing Factors

As illustrated in Table 15.1, sexual dysfunctions may be classified as a dysfunction in a sexual response phase or as a sexual pain dysfunction. Two additional dimensions of classification are the time of onset of a sexual dysfunction and the situations in which it occurs (Masters & Johnson, 1970). Regarding timing, a **primary dysfunction** is one that a person has always experienced. A **secondary dysfunction** is one that a person is currently experiencing, after a period of satisfactory sexual functioning. For example, one sexual dysfunction that we will discuss later is hypoactive sexual desire which refers to a lack of sexual desire. A woman who has always experienced a lack of sexual desire has a primary dysfunction. In contrast, a woman who has experienced sexual desire but is not currently experiencing such desire has a secondary dysfunction.

Masters and Johnson (1970) suggested the term **situational dysfunction** be used to describe a problem that occurs in one context or setting and not in another and **total dysfunction** for a problem that occurs in all contexts or settings. For example, a man who is unable to become erect with his wife but who can become erect with his lover has a situational problem, as does a woman who is unable to experience orgasm with one partner but can with another partner. A "total" problem (also known as a "global" or "generalized" problem) is one that occurs in all sexual situations.

A sexual dysfunction may also be classified according to whether it is caused primarily by biological (or organic) or psychosocial factors (i.e., sociocultural, intrapsychic, relationship, or cognitive and educational factors). Next, we describe various biological and psychosocial factors that cause or contribute to sexual dysfunctions.

> In approaching sexual problems, we would begin with the common concerns that people have with sex: feelings of insecurity, unattractiveness, anger, and fear; fatigue, overwork, and conflicting pressures; inability to relax; uncertainties about birth control; and living with three children under the age of five.
>
> *Carol Tavris*

CONSIDERATION: In most cases, sexual dysfunctions are caused by more than one factor (Goldman, 1992; Hawton, 1985).

> In addition, factors are often contributory rather than causal. Each by itself may not ensure the development of a sexual problem, but a problem may result from a complex interaction of factors. (Hawton, 1985, p. 56)

Biological Factors

In the first half of the twentieth century, sexual dysfunctions were viewed largely as symptoms of personality disorders. Today, the role of biological factors in sexual functioning is more fully understood than it was in the past; hence, it is recognized that biological factors are often a major or contributing factor in sexual dysfunctions. Here, we will identify some of the biological or physical factors that cause or contribute to sexual dysfunction (see also Chapter 16, Health and Sexuality).

One common physical cause of sexual dysfunction in our fast-paced society is fatigue. For many people, the persistent demands of career, school, children, and domestic tasks leave little physical energy for sexual activity. Fatigue may affect the sexual desire and arousal phases of the sexual response cycle in both women and men.

Sexual dysfunction may also result from physical illness, disease, or disability and/or its treatment (e.g. surgery, medication, chemotherapy). A physical condition or treatment may directly interfere with physiological or anatomical mechanisms involved in sexual desire, arousal, or orgasm (e.g., diabetes, arthritis, pituitary tumors, vascular disease).

Alcohol, marijuana, barbiturates, and amphetamines, as well as numerous medications used to treat various diseases and illnesses, may also cause or contribute to sexual dysfunction (see also Chapters 7 and 16 for discussion of how drugs affect sexual functioning). Finally, sexual dysfunction may result from a combination of biological and psychosocial factors. For example, a woman may experience lack of sexual desire because she is chronically fatigued (biological factor) from holding a full-time job while taking care of children, a husband, and a house. Compounding her fatigue is resentment (psychosocial factor) toward her husband for not supporting her career and sharing the work of child-rearing and housecleaning.

Sociocultural Factors

In addition to physical or biological factors, sociocultural factors may also cause or contribute to sexual dysfunction. These include restrictive upbringing and religious training. For example, in some families, parents may openly express negative attitudes toward sexuality by teaching their children that "sex is dirty." Some children and adolescents are punished by their parents for engaging in masturbation or other sexual exploration. In many families, sex is never discussed with the children. Children who learn that sex is a taboo subject may come to regard sex as somehow wrong or shameful.

The church has frightened people off their sexuality. I still have a problem as a result of growing up in Catholic Ireland, brought up to believe that sex is something dirty. As a consequence I have a real hard time having sex with someone I like.

Sinéad O'Conner

Some religions teach that sex is only for procreation and that sexual pleasure is evil. Such negative attitudes toward sex that are learned in childhood may interfere with a person's ability to experience sexual desire, arousal, and orgasm as an adult.

Another sociocultural factor that may contribute to sexual dysfunction is society's traditional gender role system. Traditionally, gender role expectations have taught women to be sexually passive and to not enjoy sex, while they have taught men to initiate sexual activity and be in control of sexual interactions. The Theoretical and Research Perspective that follows discusses how sexual dysfunctions in men may result from traditional male gender role expectations and suggests that male sexual dysfunctions may be prevented by challenging male gender role stereotypes.

THEORETICAL AND RESEARCH PERSPECTIVE

Prevention of Male Sexual Dysfunction by Challenging Sexual Myths and Gender Role Stereotypes

Are U.S. gender role stereotypes and myths interfering with sexual functioning? LoPiccolo (1983, p. 45) noted the contradictory and confusing gender role model that women in our society are expected to follow—they are expected to be beautiful, sexy, and seductive, while at the same time chaste and, prior to marriage, virginal. Men, on the other hand, are given a straightforward message. The male role emphasizes "achievement, power, skill, competitiveness, strength, endurance, aggression, and success, while devaluing vulnerability, emotional expressiveness, dependency, and affiliation." While it is unambivalent, several of its directives may set men up for sexual dysfunctions and interfere with optimal sexual relationships. Applying these characteristics to sexual functioning results in the following problems.

The male gender role sets up men to believe that their only sex problem is that they can't get enough sex. It predisposes them to measure their worth in terms of their sexual conquests. This demanding, "always on" role does not allow for a man

Continued

Continued

to be tired or not feel like having sex. It suggests that men should attempt sex whether or not they are sexually or emotionally attracted to their partner. LoPiccolo observed that not surprisingly, in these situations, arousal, pleasure, and erection are often missing.

Another problem is the expectation of expertise and sexual experience. LoPiccolo identified three negative effects of this assumption. First, it perpetuates sexual ignorance. If men are sexual experts, then they are not allowed to attend classes, buy books, or confess that they could benefit from learning more in this area. (Notice the sex ratio of your class. If you attend a coed school, is the enrollment in this sexuality class predominantly female?) Second, an expert doesn't need to communicate with his partner, as he assumes he knows what pleases his partner. Discomfort with discussing sex with one's partner may be a result of reluctance to be in a "learner" role. Third, when a sexual problem arises, men often find it difficult to seek help through talking about the problem or through therapy.

In addition, a man must function flawlessly, his sexual competence measured through erection, ejaculation, and bringing his partner to orgasm(s). Little wonder that given this kind of pressure, dysfunctions might result. LoPiccolo concluded that if we could redefine the male role in our culture, this would be a method of primary prevention of sexual dysfunctions. While it is difficult to change general cultural values, we can change how we related to each other as adults.

One way to begin to make changes was proposed by therapist Bernie Zilbergeld (1978). He suggested examining the models and myths of sexuality that we have been taught and replacing the harmful ones with more appropriate knowledge. In his book, *Male Sexuality,* he attempted to dispell the "Fantasy Model of Sex." For example, he pointed out the fallacies in the way the penis is presented in popular media.

> Not only are fantasyland penises much larger than life, they also behave peculiarly. They are forever 'pulsating,' 'throbbing,' and leaping about. The mere sight or touch of a woman is sufficient to set the penis jumping, and whenever a man's fly is unzipped, his penis leaps out. From Harold Robbin's *The Inheritors:* '. . . she pulled open the buttons on his trousers. He sprang swollen into her hand . . .'. Nowhere does a penis merely mosey out for a look at what's happening. (p. 24)

The problem with this fantasy model is that real men, with real penises, compare themselves to unrealistic descriptions and find they do not measure up. "Instead of asking whether the model is physiologically feasible, personally satisfying, or enhancing of ourselves and our relationships, we ask what is wrong with us for not being able to meet its standards. And that is precisely why this model is too destructive" (Zilbergeld, 1978, p. 31). Can you separate fact from fantasy? Complete the Self-Assessment measure for this chapter.

Is there empirical support for the idea that traditional male gender role adherence is related to sexual dysfunction? The connection was examined in a study of college students from a large state university in the Southwest (Spencer & Zeiss, 1987). Students completed a short form of the Bem Sex-Role Inventory, which categorized their sex-role orientation. They also completed an assessment of sexual problems and concerns in three areas: pressure to perform, concerns related to establishing relationships, and specific dysfunctions. For masculine-typed men, sexual pressure from a partner was more closely associated with sexual dysfunction than for nonmasculine sex-typed men. However, men categorized as androgynous did not report less sexual dysfunction or concern than other men. The relationship between sex-role orientation and sexual satisfaction was not studied, however, and the researchers recommended that a longitudinal study be done to investigate the interaction of sex-role orientation, sexual difficulties, and satisfaction.

Continued

Continued

References

LoPiccolo, J. (1983). The prevention of sexual problems in men. In G. W. Albee, S. Gordon, & H. Leitenberg (Eds.), *Promoting sexual responsibility and preventing sexual problems* (pp. 39–65). Hanover, NH: University Press of New England.

Spencer, S. L., & Zeiss, A. M. (1987). Sex roles and sexual dysfunction in college students. *Journal of Sex Research, 23* 338–347.

Zilbergeld, B. (1978). *Male sexuality: A guide to sexual fulfillment.* Boston: Little, Brown.

Intrapsychic Factors

Intrapsychic factors that may cause or contribute to sexual dysfunction include:

> The pressure on individuals to be sexually interested, responsive, and enthusiastic within a committed relationship is at an all-time high in our society.
>
> *Sandra R. Leiblum*
> *Raymond C. Rosen*

1. Anxiety. In a review of research studies comparing sexually dysfunctional and sexually functional individuals, Norton and Jehn (1984) found that anxiety is common among those with sexual dysfunctions. Anxiety may be aroused by thoughts and fears about one's sexual performance and ability to please the partner. Anxiety may also result from fear of intimacy, concern about the partner's commitment to the relationship, fear of rejection, uncertainty about the partner's intentions or sexual expectations, and about how to initiate physical intimacy. Anxiety may also be related to childhood guilt about sexual thoughts, feelings, and behavior (Kaplan, 1979).

   Anxiety may either facilitate or inhibit sexual arousal (Barlow, 1986). Beggs, Calhoun, and Wolchik (1987) found that sexual arousal in women increased as a result of being exposed to both sexually pleasurable and anxiety-arousing narratives (although the increases associated with pleasurable narratives were greater). Anxiety often plays a role in nonorganic cases of erectile dysfunction. In men with erection difficulties, anxiety may distract attention away from the erotic sensations and cognitions that contribute to sexual arousal (Beck & Barlow, 1986).

   One specific type of anxiety related to sexual dysfunction is known as **performance anxiety**, which refers to an excessive concern with adequate sexual performance.

   > [Performance] anxiety is usually self-imposed, and expectations or standards of performance are often based on something the individual has heard, seen, or read, such as exaggerated accounts of what constitutes sexual adequacy from peers and in fiction, magazine articles, and movies. (Goldman, 1992, p. 309)

   Thus, anxiety results from the self-imposed sense of obligation to perform sexually: men may feel obligated to achieve and maintain erection on demand; women may feel obligated to achieve orgasm during intercourse. While performance anxiety is usually self-imposed, it may also result from pressure from one's sexual partner to perform sexually. Anxiety about one's sexual performance is associated with a behavior that Masters and Johnson (1970) call "spectatoring." **Spectatoring** refers to the act of focusing one's attention on the sexual performance of one's self and one's partner during sexual interaction. Being a "spectator" of sexual performance not only interferes with one's experience of sexual pleasure, it also interferes with sexual performance. When Masters and Johnson (1970) observed how individuals behave during sexual intercourse, they reported a tendency for sexually dysfunctional couples to act as spectators by mentally observing their own and their partners' sexual performance. For example, the man would focus on whether he was having an erection, how complete it was, and whether it would last. He might also watch to see whether his partner was having an orgasm.

2. Fear. Impairment in the desire, arousal, or orgasm phases of sexual response may result from fear of unwanted pregnancy or STDs, intimacy or commitment, physical pain, displeasing a partner, or losing self-control during sexual arousal or orgasm.
3. Guilt. Guilt, which may be related to the enjoyment of sexual activity, choice of sexual partner, or participation in "forbidden" or "sinful" sexual activity, may also interfere with sexual functioning.
4. Depression and Low Self-Esteem. Sexual dysfunction may result from depression, which is known to suppress the sexual drive (LoPiccolo & Friedman, 1988). Related to depression is low self-esteem, which may cause an individual to feel unworthy of being loved or of experiencing pleasure.
5. Conflict Concerning One's Sexual Orientation. Because of the social stigma associated with being homosexual, some gay men and lesbians experience internal conflict about their sexual orientation. Some may deny their homosexuality and seek heterosexual relationships, only to find that sexual activity with other-sex individuals doesn't feel right for them. Internal conflict about being homosexual or the attempt to deny their homosexuality through seeking heterosexual relationships may interfere with sexual response in homosexual individuals.
6. Sexual Abuse. Therapists are increasingly paying attention to the effect of sexual victimization (Wyatt, 1991). Wyatt reviewed studies which examined the impact of childhood and adult sexual abuse on adolescent and adult sexual functioning. Women with sexual abuse histories were more likely than those with no known abuse to have less satisfaction with sex, inhibited desire, sexual aversion, and inhibited orgasm. In one of Wyatt's studies she documented that African-American and White-American women are particularly likely to avoid participating in the type of sexual act that was previously forced upon them when they were abused. While some survivors have been found to be restricted in sexually interacting with a consenting partner, others have been described as having higher frequencies of sexual activity and number of partners.

   Men with histories of sexual abuse have also been documented as experiencing sexual problems. In their report of eleven men who were molested by women, Sarrel and Masters (1982) described sexual consequences of low desire, inability to achieve or maintain an erection, and ejaculation problems. Some men, although certainly not all, who have been sexually abused are more likely to victimize others. Finally, abuse may also lead to sexual identity confusion (Wyatt, 1991).

Relationship Factors

Sexual dysfunction and relationship conflict seldom exist in isolation of each other. One psychiatrist reported that 75% of couples he saw for marital counseling also had significant sexual complaints. Conversely, 70% of couples who sought treatment specifically for sexual dysfunction had significant marital complaints (Sager, 1974).

In some cases, sexual difficulties may cause or contribute to problems in a relationship. In other cases, however, sexual difficulties are symptoms of problems in the relationship. Some relationship factors that may cause or contribute to sexual dysfunctions include anger and resentment, lack of trust, lack of affection, power struggles in the relationship, and lack of communication with the partner about sex (Goldman, 1992; Hawton, 1985).

Educational and Cognitive Factors

What a person learns and believes about sex may be related to sexual difficulties. Consider the following examples:

- A woman in her 50s believes the myth that women her age should not be interested in sex.
- A man in his 50s believes the myth that men his age are unable to achieve an erection that is satisfactory for intercourse.
- A heterosexual couple believe that the only appropriate way for a woman to have an orgasm is through sexual intercourse.
- A person believes that it is wrong to have sexual fantasies during lovemaking.

It ain't so much the things we don't know that get us in trouble. It's the things we know that ain't so.

Artemus Ward

These are just a few examples of beliefs or myths that may interfere with sexual desire, arousal, or orgasm. Inadequate sex education can contribute to belief in such myths. Inadequate sex education can also contribute to ignorance of sexual anatomy and physiology, which may also be related to sexual difficulties. For example, a woman who does not know where her clitoris is (or that it even exists) may have difficulty experiencing orgasm. The following Self-Assessment is designed to assess one's knowledge about sexuality.

Aging Factors

Aging (also see Chapter 12, Sexuality across the Life Span) is associated with a decline in sexual desire, arousability, and orgasm frequency and intensity (Bancroft, 1989). Biological changes due to aging include decreased lubrication in women and decreased capacity for erections in men. In both women and men, aging is associated with a tendency for the speed and intensity of the various vasocongestive responses to sexual stimulation to be reduced (Masters & Johnson, 1966).

However, Hawton (1985) noted that "an individual's reactions to these [biological] changes will be the main determinants of whether sexual dysfunction develops" (p. 66). For example, a postmenopausal woman may lose her interest in sex because she feels embarrassed by her lack of vaginal lubrication. Similarly, a middle-aged man may develop erection difficulties after becoming concerned about the fact that he requires more stimulation than he used to in order to attain and keep an erection.

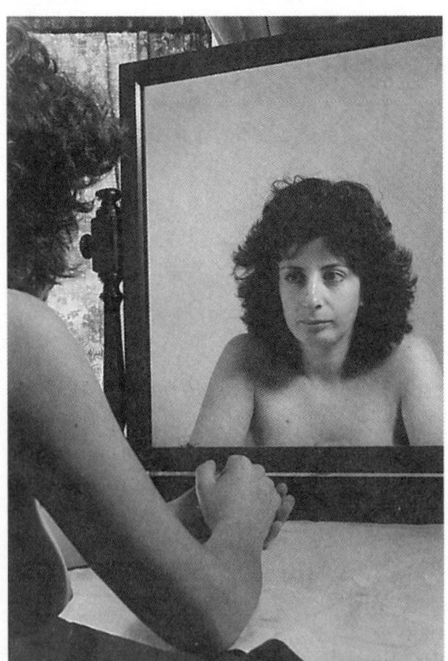

Negative thoughts and feelings about one's partner often have a negative effect on sexual interest and functioning.

Hawton (1985) suggested that several factors contribute to the association between aging and the development of sexual dysfunction. These include:

1. Physical changes, such as wrinkled skin, weight gain, and impaired mobility may contribute to loss of attractiveness or to a person's sense of unattractiveness. Low self-esteem and impaired body image, which may decrease a person's interest in sexual interactions, are *not* the direct result of aging. Rather, low self-esteem and impaired body image result from sociocultural definitions of attractiveness that emphasize youth. Aging persons may also receive negative messages from their partners about their attractiveness (relationship factor), which contribute to their low self-esteem and lack of sexual interest.

Self Assessment

How Much Do You Know about Sexuality?

Take this true-false test to assess how much you know about sexuality.

T F 1. Sexual expression is purely natural, not a function of learning.

T F 2. Foreplay is for the woman; intercourse is for the man.

T F 3. Once a couple establishes a good sexual relationship, they don't need to set aside time for intimacy together.

T F 4. If you love each other and communicate, everything will go fine sexually.

T F 5. Sex and love are two sides of the same coin.

T F 6. Technique is more important than intimacy in achieving a satisfying sexual relationship.

T F 7. Casual sex is more exciting than intimate sex.

T F 8. If you have a good sexual relationship, you will have a fulfilling experience each time you have sex.

T F 9. After age 25 your sex drive dramatically decreases, and most people stop being sexual by 65.

T F 10. It is primarily the man's role to initiate sex.

T F 11. If one or both partners become aroused, intercourse must follow or there will be frustration.

T F 12. Men are more sexual than women.

T F 13. Having a "G" spot and multiple orgasms is a sign you are a sexually liberated woman.

T F 14. Since men don't have spontaneous erections after age 50, they are less able to have intercourse.

T F 15. When you lose sexual desire, the best remedy is to seek another partner.

T F 16. The most common female sexual problem is pain during intercourse.

T F 17. The most common male sexual problem is not having enough sex.

T F 18. Penis size is crucial for female sexual satisfaction.

T F 19. Oral/genital sex is an exciting but perverse sexual behavior.

T F 20. Simultaneous orgasms provide the most erotic pleasure.

T F 21. Married people do not masturbate.

T F 22. Using sexual fantasies during intercourse indicates dissatisfaction with your partner.

T F 23. Clitoral orgasms are superior to vaginal orgasms.

T F 24. Male-on-top is the most natural position for intercourse.

T F 25. People of today are doing much better sexually than the previous generation.

Scoring and Interpretation Add the number of *trues* you checked. This is the number of sex myths you believe. What you took was a sex-myth test, so all the answers are false. Don't be surprised if you believed several of these myths; the average person thinks nine of these statements are true. Even among college students taking a human sexual-behavior course, the average number of myths believed is seven (McCarthy & McCarthy, 1984)! (Used by permission. Carroll & Graf Publishers.)

Reference

McCarthy, B., & McCarthy, E. (1984). *Sexual awareness: Enhancing sexual pleasure.* New York: Carroll & Graf.

2. Physical illnesses and psychiatric disorders that are likely to impair sexual function become more common in older age. These include cardiovascular disease, arthritis, cancer, depression, anxiety, and dementia. Medications used to treat these illnesses may also interfere with sexual functioning.
3. As noted earlier, some sexual myths (educational and cognitive factors) may contribute to sexual dysfunction. These myths include: (a) older people are not

interested in sex; (b) sex should cease when procreation is no longer possible; and (c) the ability to become sexually aroused usually ceases after middle age, and if it does not, this is abnormal.

Up to this point, we have referred to sexual dysfunctions as impairments or difficulties that affect the desire, arousal, or orgasm phase of sexual response or that produce sexual pain. Next, we look more closely at the specific types of sexual dysfunctions and how they may be treated.

CONSIDERATION: How common are sexual dysfunctions? As we discuss each type of sexual dysfunction, we present data on the prevalence of the dysfunction. As you read prevalence figures on each type of sexual dysfunction, keep the following in mind:

1. Samples used in prevalence studies of sexual dysfunction are rarely gathered randomly; hence, they are probably not representative of the population.
2. Standard criteria have not been used to assess the presence of a sexual dysfunction. One reason sexual dysfunction prevalence rates differ widely is because different studies do not use the same definitions of sexual dysfunction or criteria to assess sexual dysfunction.
3. Prevalence rates based on clinical samples (i.e., persons seeking treatment for a sexual problem) do not accurately reflect prevalence rates in the general population. For example, prevalence rates based on clinical samples suggest that erectile dysfunction is more common than early ejaculation. However, in the general population, early ejaculation is actually more common than erectile dysfunction. Clinical samples show a higher prevalence rate of erectile dysfunction because men are more likely to seek treatment for erectile dysfunction than for early ejaculation.
4. The mainstream literature on sexual dysfunctions reflects the assumption that heterosexual sex and relationships are the norm. For example, difficulties with anal sex are not defined or discussed in mainstream literature, even though they are a common presenting problem among gay men in sex therapy. Also slighted in the literature on sexual dysfunction are discussions of problems especially experienced by lesbians such as aversion to cunnilingus (Nichols, 1989).

Desire-Phase Dysfunctions

Helen Kaplan (1974) emphasized the important role that sexual desire plays in sexual response. Desire-phase sexual dysfunctions came to the attention of sex therapists in 1977, when Kaplan (1977) and Lief (1977) independently suggested that desire disorders are a common type of sexual problem.

The *Diagnostic and Statistical Manual of Mental Disorders* (DSM-III-R), published by the American Psychiatric Association, classifies two types of desire-phase dysfunctions: hypoactive sexual desire and sexual aversion. Some sex therapists consider sexual addiction (also known as "hyperactive sexual desire") to be a desire-phase dysfunction. DSM-III-R lists sexual addiction under the category of "Other Sexual Disorders". In this text, we discuss sexual addiction in Chapter

17, Paraphilias and Sexuality. Next, we discuss the nature, causes, and treatment of desire-phase dysfunctions, beginning with hypoactive sexual desire.

Hypoactive Sexual Desire

The term **hypoactive sexual desire** refers to a low interest in sexual fantasies or sexual activities. More specifically, hypoactive sexual desire is defined as follows:

> Persistently or recurrently deficient or absent sexual fantasies and desire for sexual activity. The judgment of deficiency or absence is made by the clinician, taking into account factors that affect sexual functioning, such as age, sex, and the context of the person's life. (APA, 1987, p. 293)

Other terms that are used to refer to a low interest in sex include "inhibited sexual desire," "low sexual desire," and "impaired sexual interest." Like other sexual dysfunctions, hypoactive sexual desire may be primary, secondary, situational, or total.

Both women and men may experience hypoactive sexual desire. One estimate suggested that about 20% of the total adult population in Europe and the United States has low sexual desire (APA, 1987). Female-male differences in regard to the prevalence of hypoactive sexual desire are controversial; some researchers (Schover & Jensen, 1988) have suggested that the problem is more common in women, others (Segraves & Segraves, 1990) have suggested that more men than women may have this problem, and still others (Leiblum & Rosen, 1988b) have suggested that hypoactive sexual desire occurs in equal numbers of women and men.

In discussing sexual problems reported by lesbians, Nichols (1988) observed that the most frequently reported sexual concern among lesbians is low desire. She stated that lesbians do not report "pervasive, across-the-board problems. Rather, their problems seem confined to one specific type: sexual desire *within committed relationships*" (p. 394). The women report general satisfaction when they do have sexual interactions, but often the low desire has been present in previous relationships as well. Coleman and Reece (1988) noted that in their therapy practices low sexual desire, especially sexual desire discrepancy, is the most prevalent sexual problem of gay men. Nichols (1989, p. 290) suggested that "sex therapists must learn to deal with a new case of inhibited sexual desire in gay men: depression resulting from grief over the loss of their age mates, multiple bereavements, fears of their own mortality, and seeing a whole generation of their peers wiped out by AIDS."

Assessing whether or not someone has hypoactive sexual desire is problematic. First, there are no clear criteria for determining "abnormal" levels of sexual desire. Two people can vary greatly in the degree to which they experience sexual interest or desire, and each may feel comfortable with their level of sexual desire. Furthermore, sexual desire in couples predictably decreases over time; in general, the longer a couple have been together, the less sexual desire they report (Carroll & Bagley, 1990). Leiblum and Rosen (1988a) suggested that "there is a real danger of pathologizing normal variations in sexual interest and of unnecessarily stigmatizing the individuals so labeled" (p. 9).

In addition, it is not uncommon for partners to differ in their desire for frequency of sexual activity. When a desire discrepancy occurs, it is often the person who desires less frequent sexual activity who is labeled as having a "problem" (i.e., low sexual desire); rarely is the partner who desires more frequent sexual activity labeled as having "hyperactive sexual desire."

Causes and Contributing Factors Hypoactive sexual desire may be caused by one or more of a variety of factors, including restrictive upbringing; relationship dissatisfaction (e.g., anger or resentment toward one's partner); nonacceptance of one's sexual orientation; having learned a passive sexual role; sexual abuse; and physical factors, such as stress, illness, drugs, and fatigue. In addition, abnormal hormonal states have been shown to be associated with low sexual desire. For example, androgen deficiency is associated with low sexual desire in men (hormonal effects on women's libido are not clearly understood) (Segraves, 1988).

Hypoactive sexual desire may also result from difficulties in other phases of the sexual response cycle. For example, men who have difficulty achieving or maintaining erection or women who have difficulty experiencing orgasm may suppress their sexual desire as a way of coping with their dysfunction.

Treatment Treatment of hypoactive sexual desire varies, depending on the underlying cause(s) of the problem. Some of the ways in which lack of sexual desire may be treated include:

1. Increase Relationship Satisfaction. When relationship problems are identified as the main cause of lack of sexual desire, couple therapy may be helpful if the partners are not able to improve their relationship on their own. Increasing relationship satisfaction may be especially important to women who experience a lack of sexual desire: "Female partners are both more aware of and less willing to tolerate relationship distress . . . consequently . . . desire in women is more readily disrupted by relationship factors" (Leiblum & Rosen, 1988b, p. 449).
2. Identify and Implement Conditions for Satisfying Sex. Bass (1985) suggested that many people who believe they have a low sexual drive have mislabeled the problem. In many cases, the "real" problem (according to Bass) is not that the person has low sexual desire but rather that the person has not identified or implemented the conditions under which he or she experiences satisfactory sex.

The stress of work and parenting may contribute to hypoactive sexual desire.

Bass tells his clients who believe that they have a low sex drive that "just as their desire to eat is only temporarily diminished when confronted with certain unappetizing foods, so too their sexual desire is only temporarily inhibited through their failure to identify and implement their requirements for enjoyable sex" (p. 62).

In such cases, treatment of a lack of interest in sex consists of making sex more "appetizing" by identifying and implementing those exact conditions that, for each client, constitute satisfying sex. This may involve the therapist and the client's partner giving the client permission to engage in certain sexual activities, such as masturbation, oral sex, fantasizing, different positions, or viewing erotica or pornography. In some cases, the client may need encouragement to ask his or her partner to make a behavioral change to make sexual activity more appealing. For example, one client who complained of low sexual desire reported that he did not like the smell and taste of cigarettes on his partner when they kissed. His partner agreed to brush her teeth before sexual activity, which "cured" the client's lack of sexual desire (Author's files).

3. Practice "Sensate Focus." Sensate focus is a series of exercises developed by Masters and Johnson that may be used in treating various sexual dysfunctions. Sensate focus (see Figure 15.1) may also be used by couples who are not experiencing sexual dysfunction but want to enhance their sexual relationship.

   In doing the **sensate focus** exercises, the couple (in the privacy of their bedroom) remove their clothing and take turns touching, feeling, caressing, and exploring each other in ways intended to provide sensual pleasure. In the first phase of sensate focus, genital touching is not allowed. The person being touched should indicate if he or she finds a particular touching behavior unpleasant, at which point the partner will stop or change what is being done.

   During the second phase of sensate focus, the person being touched is instructed to give positive as well as negative feedback; that is, to indicate what is enjoyable and what is unpleasant. During the third phase, genital touching can be included, without the intention of producing orgasm. The goal of progressing through the three phases of sensate focus is to help the couple reestablish positive and pleasurable sensations, promote trust and communication, and reduce anxiety related to sexual performance.

4. Reeducation. Reeducation involves the person being open to examining the thoughts, feelings, and attitudes she or he was taught as a child and reevaluating them. The goal is to redefine sexual activity so that it is viewed as a positive, desirable, healthy, and pleasurable experience.

5. Other Treatments. Other treatments for a lack of sexual desire include rest and relaxation, psychotherapy focusing on trauma resolution, hormone treatment, and changing medications (if possible) in cases where medication interferes with sexual desire. In addition, sex therapists often recommend that people who are troubled by a low level of sexual desire engage in masturbation as a means of developing positive sexual feelings. Therapists also recommend the use of sexual fantasies. Women who do not have sexual fantasies or who report feeling guilty about having them report higher levels of sexual dissatisfaction (Cado & Leitenberg, 1990).

Sexual Aversion

Another desire-phase dysfunction is **sexual aversion** (also known as "sexual phobia" and "sexual panic disorder"), which is defined as "persistent or recurrent extreme aversion to, and avoidance of, all or almost all, genital sexual contact with

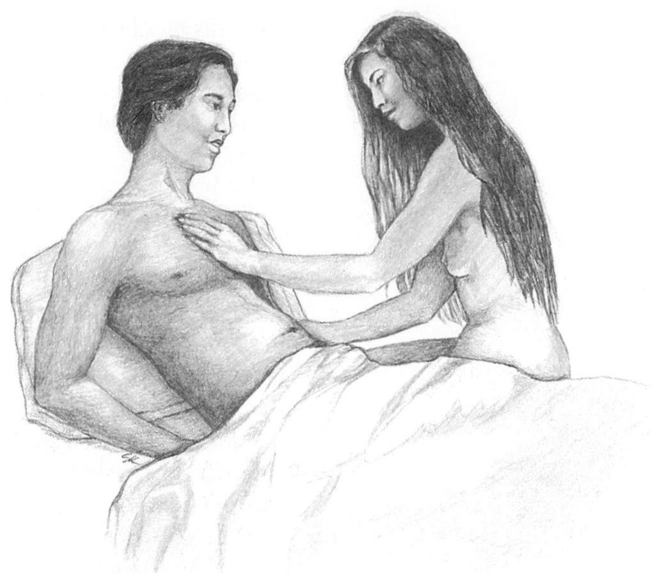

FIGURE 15.1 Sensate focus.

a sexual partner" (APA, 1987, p. 293). Whereas individuals who experience hypoactive sexual desire are often neutral or indifferent toward sexual interactions, sexual aversion may involve disgust, physical illness, and/or high levels of anxiety when the individual is thinking about or confronted with sexual situations. For example, panic reactions to sexual encounters may involve nausea, heart palpitations, and heavy perspiration. Women are more likely to experience sexual aversion than men (Schover & LoPiccolo, 1982).

Causes and Contributing Factors The immediate cause of sexual aversion is an intense fear of sex. Such fear may result from negative sexual attitudes acquired in childhood or from sexual trauma, such as rape or incest. Some cases of sexual aversion may be caused by fear of intimacy, intrapsychic conflicts, or hostility toward the other sex.

Treatment Treatment for sexual aversion involves providing insight into the possible ways in which the negative attitudes toward sexual activity developed, increasing the communication skills of the partners, and sensate focus. Understanding the origins of the sexual aversion may enable the individual to view change as possible. Through communication with the partner and sensate focus exercises, the individual may learn to associate more positive feelings with sexual behavior. Cognitive restructuring, stress innoculation training, systematic desensitization, and other fear reduction tactics may be helpful.

Arousal-Phase Dysfunctions

Some individuals who experience desire for sexual activity have difficulty experiencing sexual arousal. As you may recall from Chapter 7, Sexual Response, the arousal phase of sexual response involves numerous physiological changes, including vaginal lubrication, nipple erection, and genital vasocongestion. Problems of sexual arousal are characterized by failure of the physiological responses that normally occur during this phase and/or by a lack of pleasurable sensations usually associated with sexual arousal. The DSM-III-R (APA, 1987) classifies two types of arousal phase dysfunctions: "female sexual arousal disorder" and "male erectile disorder."

CONSIDERATION: The terms "frigid" and "impotent" have been commonly used to refer to women who are sexually unresponsive and men who have difficulty achieving or maintaining an erection. Because being labeled as "frigid" or "impotent" has negative connotations, sex therapists avoid using these terms and instead use more neutral terms with their clients, such as "arousal difficulties" or "erectile difficulties."

Female Sexual Arousal Dysfunction

Female sexual arousal dysfunction (also known as "impaired sexual arousal" and "general sexual dysfunction") is defined as one or both of the following (APA, 1987, p. 294):

> (1) persistent or recurrent partial or complete failure to attain or maintain the lubrication-swelling response of sexual excitement until completion of the sexual activity.
>
> (2) persistent or recurrent lack of a subjective sense of sexual excitement and pleasure in a female during sexual activity.

Like other sexual dysfunctions, female sexual arousal dysfunction may be primary, secondary, situational, or total. In a review of five small surveys on the incidence of sexual dysfunctions, the rate of low arousal in women ranged from 10% to 50% (Schover & Jensen, 1988).

Causes and Contributing Factors Factors that may cause sexual arousal difficulties are similar to the factors associated with hypoactive sexual desire. Thus, relationship dissatisfaction, restrictive upbringing, and nonacceptance of one's sexual orientation are possible factors associated with arousal difficulties.

Female sexual arousal dysfunction may also result from estrogen deficiency; the most common cause of estrogen deficiency is menopause. Other biological factors that may be related to lack of sexual arousal in women include neurogenic disorders (e.g., multiple sclerosis) and some drugs (e.g., antihistamines and antihypertensives). Strong emotions, such as fear and anger, and stress may also interfere with the autonomic reflex that controls genital vasocongestion (Kaplan, 1974; 1983).

Treatment Treatment of women who have difficulty experiencing sexual arousal is similar to treatment for hypoactive sexual desire. Thus, treatment may involve some combination of the following: increase relationship satisfaction, sensate focus, reeducation, rest and relaxation, hormone treatment, masturbation or fantasy, and medication change. In addition, the problem may not be the woman's inability to become aroused but her partner's not providing the kind of stimulation required for arousal to occur. Goldsmith (1988) noted that "an insensitive partner, whose sexual arousal techniques are too rough or too fast, is thought to contribute greatly to a woman's lack of ability to become aroused" (p. 21). When this is the case, the woman may benefit from identifying and implementing conditions for satisfying sex (the same treatment Bass, 1985, suggested for hypoactive sexual desire, discussed above.)

Male Erectile Dysfunction

Male erectile dysfunction is defined as one or both of the following (APA, 1987, p. 294):

1) persistent or recurrent partial or complete failure in the male to attain or maintain erection until completion of the sexual activity
2) persistent or recurrent lack of a subjective sense of sexual excitement and pleasure in a male during sexual activity.

> The erection is considered by almost all men as the star performer in the drama of sex and we all know what happens to a show when the star performer doesn't make an appearance.
>
> *Bernie Zilbergeld*

Like other sexual dysfunctions, erectile dysfunction may be primary, secondary, situational, or total. Occasional, isolated episodes of the inability to attain or maintain an erection are not considered dysfunctional; these are regarded as normal occurrences. In order to be classified as erectile dysfunction, the erection difficulty should last continuously for a period of at least three months (Sonda, Mazo, & Chancellor, 1990).

One estimate suggests that about 8% of young adult men have erection difficulties (APA, 1987, p. 292). A review of five small survey studies on the incidence of sexual dysfunctions revealed that the rate of erectile dysfunction in men ranged between 0% and 27% (Schover & Jensen, 1988). Erectile dysfunction is a common complaint among men seeking sex therapy. In a study of 374 men with sexual dysfunctions, the majority (69%) had a primary diagnosis of male erectile dysfunction. The average age of the men with erectile dysfunction was 54, with the average duration of the complaint being five years. About 20% of these men also reported having a low sex drive (inhibited sexual desire) (Segraves & Segraves, 1990).

Causes and Contributing Factors It has been estimated that in at least 50% (and up to 80%) of the men who complain of erectile dysfunction, the primary cause of the erection difficulty is biological (Carroll & Bagley, 1990; Sohn & Sikora, 1991). There are numerous biological causes of erectile dysfunction, including fatigue and stress, diabetes, antihypertensive medication, and narcotics. Chronic alcohol abuse may also result in erectile dysfunction (Schiavi, 1990). Neurological disease, such as multiple sclerosis or other illnesses and injuries that impair the lower spinal cord, endocrinological disease that results in androgen deficiency, vascular disease, and some prostatic surgical procedures may also cause erectile dysfunction.

Psychosocial factors that are associated with erectile dysfunction include fear (e.g., of unwanted pregnancy, intimacy, or STDs), guilt, relationship dissatisfaction, and history of sexual abuse. For example, the man who is having an extradyadic sexual relationship may feel guilty. This guilt may lead to difficulty in achieving or maintaining an erection in sexual interaction with the primary partner and/or an extradyadic partner. A man may also feel guilty if he does not love his partner yet says he does to persuade the partner to have sexual relations. In addition, a man with a sexually transmissible disease may feel guilty about having sex with someone. Finally, religious or parental teachings that sex is dirty or sinful may produce guilt associated with sex that can lead to erection difficulties.

Anxiety also inhibits the man's ability to create and maintain an erection. One source of anxiety is "performance pressure," which may be self-imposed or imposed by a partner. In self-imposed performance anxiety, the man constantly "checks" (mentally or visually) to see that he is erect. Such self-monitoring creates anxiety since the man fears that he may not be erect.

Partner-imposed performance pressure involves the partner communicating to the man that he must get and stay erect to be regarded as a good lover. Such pressure usually increases the man's anxiety, thus ensuring no erection. Whether self- or partner-imposed, the anxiety associated with performance pressure results in a vicious cycle—anxiety, erectile difficulty, embarrassment, followed by anxiety, erectile difficulty, and so on.

Performance anxiety may also be related to alcohol use. After consuming more than a few drinks, the man may initiate sex but may become anxious after failing to achieve an erection (too much alcohol will interfere with erection). Although alcohol may be responsible for his initial "failure," his erection difficulties continue because of his anxiety.

CONSIDERATION: Some men are not accustomed to satisfying their partners in any other way (cuddling, cunnilingus, digital stimulation) than through the use of an erect penis. Most of the women in one study (86%) who had male partners with erectile dysfunction reported that their partners never engaged in any sexual activities other than intercourse (Carroll & Bagley, 1990). However, when these women were asked, "What is your favorite part of sexual behavior?," 60% said "foreplay" and 3% said "afterplay"; only 37% said "sexual intercourse" was their favorite part of sexual interactions.

In order to aid in determining whether erection difficulties are due primarily to biological or psychosocial causes, the man's nocturnal penile tumescence is measured. Nocturnal penile tumescence (NPT) refers to the degree of erection that occurs during sleep and may be measured by various methods, including the Snap Gauge Band or the Poten Test (Carroll, Baltish, & Bagley, 1990). In 1970 Karacan proposed that when NPT is present, the erectile dysfunction is probably caused by psychosocial factors. In those cases in which there is little or no erection during sleep, the dysfunction was believed to be caused by biological factors. However, as researchers and clinicians have gained more experience in measuring and interpreting NPT, they have recognized that its use in diagnosing erectile problems is much more complicated than they originally understood (Bancroft, 1989). For example, Bancroft described the "pelvic steal" syndrome, in which erection progresses normally until coital activities begin. With increased movement and muscular activity, the gluteal muscles "steal" blood from arteries in the penis. "We cannot therefore *exclude* psychogenic causation on the basis of abnormal NPT. The presence of a *normal* NPT is more suggestive of psychogenesis, but occasionally this can also be misleading . . ." (p. 434).

CONSIDERATION: Because erectile dysfunction may be a symptom of a serious illness or disease, men who experience recurrent erectile difficulties should be examined by a health care provider.

Treatment Treatment of erectile dysfunction (like treatment of other sexual dysfunctions) depends on the cause(s) of the problem. When erection difficulties are caused by psychosocial factors, treatment may include improving the relationship and removing the man's fear, guilt, or anxiety (e.g., performance pressure) about sexual activity. These goals may be accomplished through couple counseling, reeducation, and sensate focus exercises. A sex therapist might instruct the man and his partner to not engage in intercourse, so as to remove the pressure to attain or maintain an erection. During this period, the man is encouraged to pleasure his partner in ways that do not require him to have an erection. Once the man is relieved of the pressure to perform and learns alternative ways to satisfy his partner, his erection difficulties (if due to psychosocial factors) sometimes disappear.

However, as Joseph LoPiccolo, one of the major scholars in sex therapy observed (1992), the success of sensate focus depends upon the patient or client's not being aware of the underlying paradox. But, with the widespread discussion of modern sex therapy procedures in television talk shows, books, magazine and newspaper articles the premise is widely known. LoPiccolo noted, "it is a rare patient today who is unaware that the therapeutic effect of sensate focus lies in reduction of performance pressure" (p. 189). If the man is aware that the sensate focus procedure is designed to eliminate performance anxiety, and thus facilitates erection, then he may be anxiously anticipating the erection. LoPiccolo referred to this as "metaperformance anxiety," or higher order anxiety "about why eliminating performance anxiety does not lead to erection during sensate focus body massage" (p. 189).

Instead of prescribing sensate focus, LoPiccolo emphasized paying attention to the couple's sexual behavior patterns. More direct physical stimulation of the penis may be helpful to increase the man's arousal. He also emphasized that a woman's sexual pleasure is not dependent upon her partner's erection. "If the patient can be reassured that his partner finds their lovemaking highly pleasurable, and that she is sexually fulfilled by the orgasms he gives her through manual and oral stimulation, his performance anxiety will be greatly reduced" (p. 190). Couples sometimes need support and encouragement in re-examining their sexual attitudes, especially if their sexual socialization taught that only genital-to-genital stimulation is appropriate.

Another reason that sensate focus may not be sufficient for restoring erectile functioning is that for one-third to two-thirds of men with erectile dysfunction, organic factors contribute to impairment (LoPiccolo, 1992). Treatment for erectile dysfunction related to biological factors may include rest and relaxation, modification of medication or alcohol or drug use, or hormone treatment. Surgical occlusion of venous drainage leakage may also be an effective treatment for some men with erectile difficulty (Bancroft, 1989).This surgery seems to work best for men under 60 who are not diabetic and do not have neurological disorders. The success rate may be as low as 50%, and according to early studies only 40% of men maintained improvement one year after surgery (Penile Implants, 1992).

Another option for treating biologically caused erectile dysfunction is a penile prosthesis (or penile implant). Two types of penile prostheses are described below (Findlay & Podolsky, 1992; Hammond & Middleton, 1984):

1. *Semirigid rod.* A pair of flexible silicone rods, with central cores of braided stainless steel wire, are implanted in the penis. This results in a permanent semirigid erection which may be bent down or positioned at an angle suitable for intercourse. The disadvantage of this type of implant is that the erection is permanent; the advantages are that it is a simple implant procedure, has a low risk of infection, and is less expensive than other types of implants.
2. *Inflatable cylinders.* One type of inflatable prosthesis consists of paired inflatable cylinders placed in the shaft of the penis, a fluid reservoir placed in the abdomen, and a pump implanted in the scrotum. The pump has an inflate and deflate mechanism that allows the erection to be controlled. Another inflatable model is self-contained, with the cylinders implanted in the shaft, and the pump implanted in the base of the penis. However, the installation of the inflatable models is more difficult and expensive, with greater risk of infection and malfunction.

While more recently developed models generate fewer complaints than older models, malfunctions and injuries must usually be corrected surgically. In 1991, over 12,000 Medicare recipients obtained penile implants. Alan Bennett, a urological surgeon who had studied the Medicare statistics over the past five years reported that these devices fail about 20% of the time, usually in the first few years following implantation (Findlay & Podolsky, 1992). Investigative reporters Findlay and Podolsky cautioned, "if the public was troubled by silicone breast implants, it should also be concerned about penile implants. The absolute numbers of problems are of the same magnitude, and their relative incidence is greater." (p. 65) By 1993 the Food and Drug Administration is expected to scrutinize the safety and effectiveness of these devices.

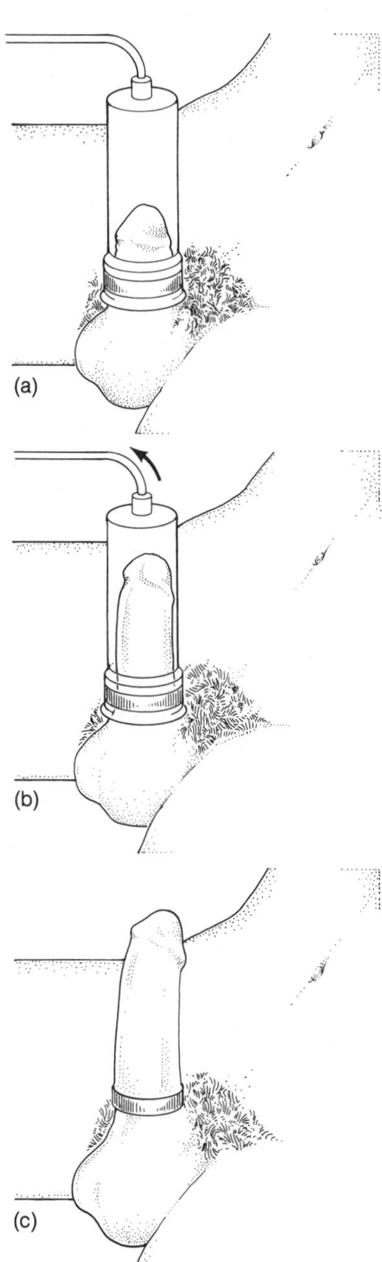

FIGURE 15.2 Vacuum device.
(a) The vacuum chamber is placed over the penis. (b) Activating the pump draws blood into the penis, enlarging it. (c) The tension band is placed at the base of the penis to retain the erection.

How satisfied are individuals who receive penile implants? In a study of 27 men and their partners, the majority of patients (72%) and their partners (65%) would recommend penile implants for men with erectile dysfunction (McCarthy & McMillan, 1990).

Another treatment alternative for erectile dysfunction is "injection therapy," whereby the patient injects premixed solutions of papaverine or prostaglandin E combined with phentolamine into the corpora cavernosa of the penis via a syringe. The injection results in a firm erection five to ten minutes after the injection that lasts 30 to 40 minutes (Kaplan, 1990). In a study of 42 men who used papaverine hydrochloride and phentolamine mesylate, the quality of erections, sexual satisfaction, and frequency of intercourse were all improved (Althof et al., 1991). Disadvantages of injection therapy include discomfort and bruising associated with self-injections; side effects such as sustained or recurring erections, fibrotic nodules, and abnormal liver function values; and lack of research data on long-term effects of injection therapy (Althof et al., 1989; Althof et al., 1991). The most dangerous side effect is **priapism**, a painful erection that will not subside. Penile injections should be performed no more than two times per week, and only when 24-hour medical services are available (Penile Implants, 1992).

Oral drug treatment has also been used for erectile dysfunction. In a study of 215 men with erectile dysfunction, one-third reported improved sexual functioning while taking the drug yohimbine (Sonda, Mazo, & Chancellor, 1990). The Ginkgo biloba extract, which is derived from the Ginkgo tree, grown in Korea, Japan, and France, has also been shown to improve penile vascular flow rates after six months of use (Sohn & Sikora, 1991). However, another study showed no significant increase in erection with use of yohimbine (Morales, Condra, Owen, Fenemore, & Surridge, 1988).

CONSIDERATION: Cultures differ in terms of how they treat sexual dysfunctions. In China, men with erectile dysfunction are regarded as "suffering from deficiency of Yang elements in the kidney" and are treated with a drinking solution prepared with water and several chemicals designed to benefit kidney function. They may also be given acupuncture therapy (Shikai, 1990, p. 198).

An alternative to penile prostheses, injections, and various medications for the treatment of erectile dysfunction is the use of a vacuum device, which produces an erection that lasts for 30 minutes. Vacuum devices contain a chamber large enough to fit over the erect penis, a pump, connector tubing, and tension rings.

> When the pump is activated, negative pressure is created within the system, which pulls blood into the penis to produce either erectile augmentation or an erection-like state. After adequate tumescence is achieved, the tension band is guided from the chamber to the base of the penis to produce entrapment of blood. (Witherington, 1991, p. 73)

In a survey of over 2,000 users of the Erectaid System (a vacuum pump available from Osbon Medical System, P. O. Drawer 1408, Augusta, Georgia 30903-9990), the average age of the user was 65 and the average length of time using the device was less than one year. Prior to using the device, 74% had either no erection or a poor quality erection that made penetration impossible. With the device, 92% could achieve an erection adequate for intercourse; 78% had intercourse at least every two weeks (Witherington, 1991).

Another study examined the results of 36 men, average age of 59, who had used a vacuum device for 12 months. Eighty-seven percent of the men reported that the device produced erections sufficient for satisfactory intercourse. Improvements included "erections of better quality, increased partner arousal, and increased frequency of orgasm and sexual satisfaction for men and women" (Turner, et al., 1991, p. 81). Other researchers have found similar levels of erection, individual, and partner satisfaction associated with use of a vacuum device for treatment of erectile dysfunction (Villeneuve, Corcos, & Carmell, 1991).

Disadvantages include possible bruising from rapid pumping and ejaculation interference from the constrictive band. Users are warned not to keep the band in place longer than 30 minutes or to fall asleep while still wearing it (Penile Implants, 1992).

There is one additional caution regarding the use of mechanical or surgical methods of treating erectile dysfunctions. While these methods can greatly benefit men with organic impairments, an overemphasis on them can be harmful. McCarthy (1992) warned that medicalizing sex problems colludes with some men's denial of how their attitudes and experiences contribute to dysfunction. "The male expects a return to easy, automatic, autonomous erections that he can only get through medical interventions. This allows him to bypass psychological and relationship issues" (p. 27). This may reinforce traditional masculine scripts. Such scripts suggest that having "easy autonomous erections" that can be medically or mechanically gained is preferred over needing to "adopt pleasuring techniques, request partner stimulation and emotional support, and deal with variability of sexual response" (p. 27). McCarthy emphasized the importance of helping couples cognitively frame erotic activities in terms of "sex and pleasure" rather than "sex and performance" (p. 24). He concluded, "The prescription for satisfying sex is an intimate relationship, nondemand pleasuring, and multiple stimulation" (p. 34).

Orgasm-Phase Dysfunctions

Orgasm-phase dysfunctions include inhibited orgasm and early ejaculation.

Inhibited Female Orgasm

Inhibited female orgasm, also known as "anorgasmia," "orgasmic dysfunction," and "orgastic dysfunction," is defined as:

> persistent or recurrent delay in, or absence of, orgasm in a female following a normal sexual excitement phase during sexual activity that the clinician judges to be adequate in focus, intensity, and duration. (APA, 1987, p. 294)

Difficulty achieving orgasm may be a primary, secondary, situational, or total dysfunction. Situational orgasmic difficulties, in which the woman is able to experience orgasm under some circumstances but not others, are the most common. Many women are able to experience orgasm during manual or oral clitoral stimulation but are unable to experience orgasm during intercourse (i.e., in the absence of manual or oral stimulation). For most women, "this represents a normal variation of the female sexual response and does not justify the diagnosis of Inhibited Female Orgasm" (APA, 1987, p. 294). However, many couples view the woman's inability or difficulty reaching orgasm during intercourse as a problem for which they may seek help.

Difficulties achieving orgasm are a common complaint among women (Kaplan, 1974). Orgasm difficulties are estimated to occur in about 30% of U.S. women (APA, 1987, p. 292). In a review of five small survey studies of the incidence of sexual dysfunctions, Schover & Jensen (1988) reported that the incidence of situational orgasm difficulties in women ranged from 18% to 33%; the incidence of total orgasm difficulties in women ranged from 4% to 15%.

Causes and Contributing Factors Biological factors associated with orgasmic dysfunction may be related to fatigue, stress, alcohol, and some medications, such as antidepressants and antihypertensives. Diseases or tumors that affect the neurological system, diabetes, and radical pelvic surgery (e.g., for cancer) may also impair a woman's ability to experience orgasm.

Psychosocial factors associated with orgasmic dysfunction are similar to the causes of a lack of sexual desire. Causes of orgasm difficulties in women include restrictive upbringing and having learned a passive female sexual role. Guilt, fear of intimacy, fear of losing control, ambivalence about commitment, and "spectatoring" may also interfere with the ability to experience orgasm. Other women may not have an orgasm because of their belief in the myth that "women are not supposed to enjoy sex."

Relationship factors, such as anger and lack of trust, may also produce orgasmic dysfunction. For some women, a lack of information may result in orgasmic difficulties; for example, some women do not know that clitoral stimulation is important for orgasm to occur. Some women may not have an orgasm with their partner because they do not tell their partner what sexual stimulation they want because of shame and insecurity (Kelly, Strassberg, & Kircher, 1990). Women are more likely to experience orgasm with their partner if their partner is aware of what gives them sexual pleasure (Kilmann et al., 1984; Kelly et al. 1990).

CONSIDERATION: A woman who does not experience orgasm because of a lack of sufficient stimulation is not considered to have a sexual dysfunction. In one study, 64% of the women who did not experience orgasm during sexual intercourse said that the primary reason was the lack of noncoital clitoral stimulation. The type of stimulation most effective in inducing orgasm was manual and oral stimulation and manipulation of the clitoral and vaginal area (Darling, Davidson, & Cox, 1991).

In another study of about 1,000 wives, two-fifths reported climaxing after one to 10 minutes of noncoital genital stimulation. When such stimulation lasted 21 minutes or more, three-fifths reported an orgasm almost every time (Brewer, 1981). Similarly, the longer her husband's penis stayed erect and inside her, the greater the wife's chance of having an orgasm during intercourse. If penetration was one minute, one-fourth reported orgasm; between one and 11 minutes, one-half reported climax. If penetration lasted more than 15 minutes, two-thirds reported climax.

As far as the ability to satisfy their mates goes, "nice guys finish last."
Anthony Walsh

Treatment Because the causes for primary and secondary orgasm difficulties vary, the treatment must be tailored to the particular woman. Treatment may include rest and relaxation and a change of medication or limiting alcohol consumption prior to sexual activity. Sensate focus exercises may help a woman explore her sexual feelings and increase her comfort with her partner. Treatment may also involve improving relationship satisfaction and teaching the woman or the couple how to communicate their sexual needs.

Masturbation is a widely used treatment for women with orgasm difficulties. LoPiccolo & Lobitz (1972) developed a nine-step program of masturbation for women with orgasm difficulties. The rationale behind such therapy is that masturbation is the technique that is most likely to produce orgasm. Masturbation gives the individual complete control of the stimulation, provides direct feedback to the woman of the type of stimulation she enjoys, and eliminates the distraction of a partner. Kinsey, Pomeroy, Martin, and Gebhard (1953) reported that the average woman reached orgasm in 95% or more of her masturbatory attempts. In addition the intense orgasm produced by masturbation leads to increased vascularity in the vagina, labia, and clitoris, which enhances the potential for future orgasms. The nine-step masturbation program developed by LoPiccolo and Lobitz (1972) is outlined below:

Step 1: The woman increases her self-awareness by examining her nude body. Using a hand mirror, the woman examines her genitals closely and identifies the various areas (e.g., clitoris, labia majora and minora) with the aid of pictures or photographs.

Step 2: The woman explores the various parts of her genitals through touching herself, without any attempt to arouse herself.

Step 3: Through touching herself, the woman locates sensitive areas that produce feelings of pleasure.

Step 4: The woman focuses on manual stimulation of the areas that produce pleasure and explores various techniques of clitoral stimulation (e.g., variations in stroking and pressure and the use of lubricant jelly to enhance pleasure and prevent soreness).

Step 5: If orgasm doesn't occur in Step 4, the woman may increase the intensity and duration of her masturbation (30 to 45 minutes). She may also use erotic fantasies, pictures, or reading material to increase arousal.

If you use the electric vibrator near water, you will come and go at the same time.
Louise Sammons

Step 6: If orgasm is not reached in Step 5, the woman may try masturbating using a vibrator.

Step 7: Once a woman is able to achieve orgasm through masturbation, she may want to experience orgasm through stimulation by her partner. The first step in this process involves the woman masturbating with her partner observing her. (If this is difficult for the woman, she may masturbate with her partner present next to her with the lights off. Then as her comfort increases, she may progress to having the lights on. A dimmer switch can be installed to provide control over the amount of light in the room).

Step 8: After the woman develops comfort reaching orgasm with her partner present, the partner stimulates the woman's genitals in a way similar to how the woman stimulates herself (manually or with a vibrator). It is important for the woman to give her partner instructions and feedback about what gives her pleasure. For example, she may tell her partner "a little harder," "a little slower," "a little more to the right," and "that's good." She may also take her partner's finger and place it directly where she wants stimulation.

Step 9: If the woman wants to reach orgasm during heterosexual intercourse, her partner stimulates her genitals (manually or with a vibrator) during intercourse. This is best achieved in intercourse positions that allow the man easy access to the woman's genitals: the woman sitting on top of the man, side-by-side, or rear entry positions. The man may either continue to stimulate his partner's genitals until she reaches orgasm, or the couple can use the "bridge method":

> The couple enjoy foreplay until the woman is aroused. Then the man penetrates, either in the female superior position or one of the variations of the side-to-side position. Then, with the penis contained, the man (or the woman) stimulates the woman's clitoris. When she nears orgasm, clitoral stimulation ceases at her signal, and the couple commence thrusting actively to bring about her orgasm. (Kaplan, 1974, p. 138)

Learning to masturbate to orgasm may be accomplished without the assistance of a sex therapist. Two popular books written to help women achieve orgasm are: *Becoming Orgasmic: A Sexual Growth Program for Women* (Heiman, LoPiccolo, & LoPiccolo, 1976) and *For Yourself: The Fulfillment of Female Sexuality* (Barbach, 1975). Both of these books are based on teaching the woman to masturbate through the "one step at a time" approach described above.

Inhibited Male Orgasm

Difficulty experiencing orgasm also occurs in men. **Inhibited male orgasm** (also known as "retarded ejaculation" and "inhibited ejaculation") is defined as:

> Persistent or recurrent delay in, or absence of, orgasm in a male following a normal sexual excitement phase during sexual activity that the clinician, taking into account the person's age, judges to be adequate in focus, intensity, and duration. (APA, 1987, p. 295)

Like other sexual dysfunctions, inhibited male orgasm may be primary, secondary, situational, or total. In most cases of inhibited male orgasm, the man is unable to reach orgasm during sexual intercourse but is able to reach orgasm through other means, such as masturbation. Orgasm difficulties are much less common in men than they are in women. A review of five small survey studies on the incidence of sexual dysfunctions revealed that the rate of orgasm difficulties in men ranged from 0% to 4%. Of 374 men with sexual disorders, only 5% were categorized as having a problem with achieving orgasm (Segraves & Segraves, 1990).

Causes and Contributing Factors Several medications may interfere with ejaculation, including some hormone-based medications, tranquilizers, barbiturates, antidepressants, and antihypertensives (Hawton, 1985). Injury or disease that impairs the neurological system may also interfere with orgasm in the male.

Most cases of inhibited male orgasm are believed to be caused by psychosocial factors (Goldman, 1992; Kaplan, 1974; Weinstein & Rosen, 1988). Psychosocial causes of inhibited male orgasm include anxiety, fear, "spectatoring," negative attitudes toward sexuality, and conflict or power struggles in the relationship. For example, traumatic experiences or embarrassing ones, such as being discovered by parents while masturbating, can lead to fear, anxiety, and punishment associated with impending orgasm. Thus, the sensation of impending orgasm can become conditioned to produce the response of fear and anxiety, which inhibits orgasm (Kaplan, 1974). Some men are obsessed with trying to become aroused and pleasing their partners, which may lead to anxiety and "spectatoring," which inhibits the ejaculatory reflex (Shaw, 1990). Fear of pregnancy and guilt may also interfere with a man's ability to orgasm and ejaculate. Learning negative messages about genitals or sexual activities from one's parents or religious training may also lead to ejaculation difficulties. Regarding relationship power struggles, a man's inability to achieve orgasm may be conceptualized as "an expression of the penis's refusal to be commanded interpersonally" (Shaw, 1990, p. 160).

Just as with many women, some men are unable to orgasm because of a lack of sufficient stimulation. Some heterosexual men may have developed a pattern of masturbation that involves vigorous stimulation; then they are unable to obtain sufficient stimulation from the vagina during coitus (Bancroft, 1989).

Treatment Treatment for inhibited male orgasm may involve changing medications. More frequently, treatment focuses on the psychosocial origins of retarded ejaculation and may consist of exploring the negative attitudes and cognitions that interfere with ejaculation and reeducating to change such negative attitudes.

Treatment may also involve sensate focus exercises, which allow the couple to experience physical intimacy without putting pressure on the man to perform sexually. Eventually the man's partner helps him ejaculate through oral or manual stimulation. Research on treating inhibited orgasm has mainly focused on men in heterosexual relationships. After they are confident that he can be brought to orgasm orally or manually, the partner stimulates him to a high level of sexual excitement and, at the moment of orgasm, inserts his penis into her vagina so that he ejaculates inside her. After several sessions, the woman gradually reduces the amount of time she orally or manually manipulates her partner and increases the amount of time she stimulates him with her vagina (Masters & Johnson, 1970). Alternatively, the goal in treating inhibited male orgasm may be to enjoy sexual activities with a partner without the expectation that ejaculation must occur inside the vagina (Leiblum & Rosen, 1989).

Early Ejaculation

Early ejaculation, also known as "rapid ejaculation" or "premature ejaculation" is defined as "persistent or recurrent ejaculation with minimal sexual stimulation or before, upon, or shortly after penetration and before the person wishes it" (APA, 1987, p. 295). McCarthy (1989) recommended use of the term "early ejaculation" as it is less pejorative. Early ejaculation is the most common sexual dysfunction in men (see Table 15.2). One estimate suggests that 30% of the adult male population has early ejaculation (APA, 1987, p. 292). In a review of five small survey studies on the prevalence of sexual dysfunctions, the rate of early ejaculation ranged from 7% to 41% (Schover & Jensen, 1988).

TABLE 15.2 Percentage of 61 University Men Reporting Various Sexual Problems

Dysfunction	Percent Reporting
Early ejaculation	65%
Inhibited sexual desire	39%
Erectile dysfunction	27%
Inhibited male orgasm	10%
Dyspareunia (painful intercourse)	8%

Source: Metz, M. E., & Seifert, M. H., Jr. (1990). Men's expectations of physicians in sexual health concerns. *Journal of Sex and Marital Therapy, 16,* 82. Used by permission.

Assessing early ejaculation is difficult, because most men report ejaculating too quickly on occasion. One researcher reported that the average duration of intercourse before ejaculation in men is two minutes (Hong, 1984). However, whether a man ejaculates too soon is a matter of definition, depending on his and his partner's desires. Some partners define a rapid ejaculation in positive terms. One woman said she felt pleased that her partner was so excited by her that he "couldn't control himself." Another said, "The sooner he ejaculates, the sooner it's over with, and the sooner the better." Other women prefer that their partner delay ejaculation. Thirty-one percent of 709 female nurses reported that their partners ejaculated before they had an orgasm and 23% wanted their partners to delay their ejaculation (Darling et al., 1991). Some women regard a pattern of early ejaculation as indicative of selfishness in their partners. This feeling can lead to resentment and anger.

Causes and Contributing Factors Early ejaculation is rarely caused by biological factors. However, a biological explanation of early ejaculation suggested by Assalian (1991) is that some men have a hypersensitive sympathetic system, which leads to rapid ejaculation. Kaplan (1974, 1983) suggested that early ejaculation is the result of the absence of voluntary control over the ejaculatory reflex.

Psychosocial factors associated with early ejaculation include learning experiences, anxiety, and conflict or power struggles between the man and his partner. Some examples of learning experiences include prostitutes who rush their clients and the use of withdrawal before ejaculation as a birth control method so that ejaculation outside the vagina is trained (Masters & Johnson, 1970). In addition, some men with early ejaculation report that their early masturbation and intercourse experiences were hurried. They felt pressure to ejaculate as soon as they could. One example is the male adolescent who had to masturbate quickly before his parents could discover what he was doing. Another example is that of a teenage male having sex in the back seat of a car or on the couch in the living room when the parents might arrive home at any moment. The learning theory explanation of premature ejaculation has been challenged on the basis that there is no difference in the learning history of men who ejaculate early and men who are able to delay ejaculation. Most men report early ejaculation in their first intercourse experiences (McCarthy, 1989).

While anxiety may inhibit sexual arousal, it may also heighten arousal (Bancroft, 1989). Thus, if a man is anxious about ejaculating early, this anxiety may heighten his arousal and produce the very event he is anxious about—early ejaculation.

Treatment Treatment of early ejaculation may involve exploring relationship factors that may underly the man's lack of ejaculatory control. If anxiety about his early ejaculation is a contributing factor, sensate focus exercises and pleasing his partner through oral or manual sexual stimulation may remove the pressure to delay ejaculation.

Another procedure used for treating early ejaculation is the **squeeze technique,** (see Figure 15.3) developed by Masters and Johnson. The partner stimulates the man's penis manually until he signals that he feels the urge to ejaculate. At his signal, the partner places a thumb on the underside of his penis and squeezes hard for three to four seconds. The man will lose his urge to ejaculate. After 30 seconds, the partner resumes stimulation, applying the squeeze technique again when the man signals. The important rule to remember is that the partner should apply the squeeze technique whenever the man gives the slightest hint of readiness to ejaculate, but

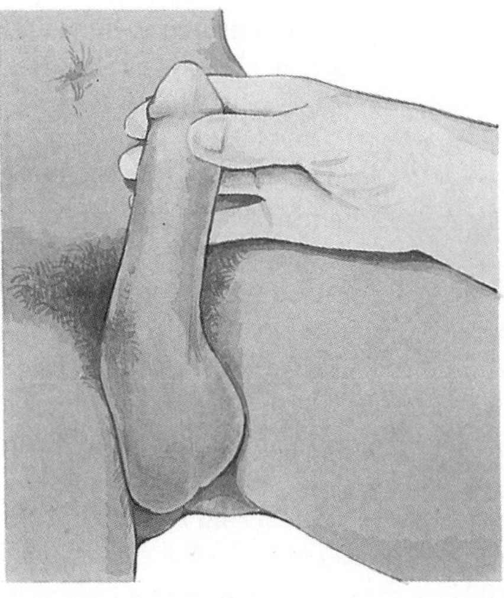
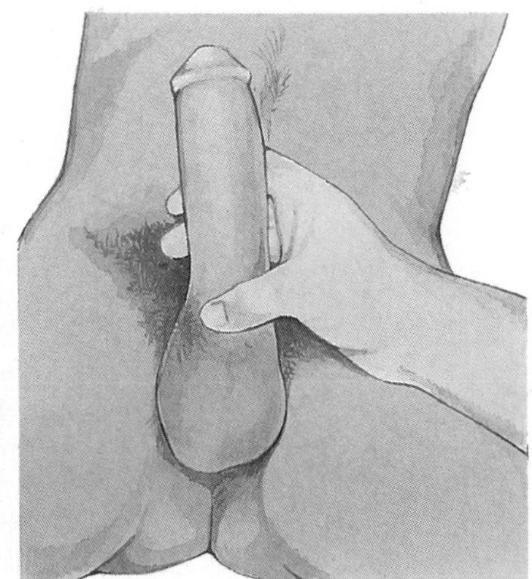

FIGURE 15.3 Squeeze technique.
In using the squeeze technique, the man or his partner applies firm pressure for several seconds below the glans or at the base of the penis (front and back, not sides).

should release the squeeze if the man's ejaculation has begun. (The squeeze technique can also be used by the man during masturbation to teach himself to delay his ejaculation). The basilar squeeze technique may also be employed (see Figure 15.3).

Another technique used to delay ejaculation is known as the "pause technique," also referred to as the "stop-start technique." This technique involves the man stopping penile stimulation (or signaling his partner to stop stimulation) at the point that he begins to feel the urge to ejaculate. After the preejaculatory sensations subside, stimulation resumes. This process may be repeated as often as desired by the partners. McCarthy (1989) reported that the stop-start technique is easier to teach and is more acceptable to couples than the squeeze technique.

Another method for increasing ejaculatory control is for the man to ejaculate often. In general, the greater the number of ejaculations a man has in one 24-hour period, the longer he will be able to control subsequent ejaculation. In addition, McCarthy (1989) suggested that instead of masturbating rapidly to orgasm, a man might attempt masturbation in "a slower, more sensual, whole-body, and pleasure-oriented way." (p. 146).

Medications have also been used to help men control ejaculation. In a study of five men who took clomipramine, all "reported significant delays and heightened control of ejaculation with a small nighttime dose" (Assalian, 1988). Since ejaculation is dependent on the sympathetic component of the autonomic nervous system, clomipramines' effectiveness results from its ability to inhibit receptors in this area. Minor side effects include sleepiness, a dry mouth, and a tendency toward constipation.

Sexual Pain Dysfunctions

Two types of sexual pain dysfunctions are dyspareunia and vaginismus. Next, we look at the nature, causes, and treatment of these sexual dysfunctions.

Dyspareunia

Dyspareunia refers to "recurrent or persistent genital pain in either a male or a female before, during, or after sexual intercourse" (APA, 1987, p. 295). Dyspareunia is more common in women than in men. In a review of five small survey studies on the prevalence of sexual dysfunctions, the rate of dyspareunia in women ranged from 8% to 21%; in men, the rate ranged from 0% to 6% (Schover & Jensen, 1988).

Causes and Contributing Factors Dyspareunia in women may be caused by biological factors, such as vaginal or pelvic infections or inflammations, vaginitis, and allergic reactions to such substances as deodorant, douches, and contraceptive devices. In rare cases, the woman with dyspareunia is allergic to her partner's semen (Hawton, 1985). Coital pain may also result from tender scarring following an episiotomy, which is a surgical slit sometimes made in the perineal area to ease the childbirth process (Bancroft, 1989). Dyspareunia may also be caused by a lack of lubrication, a rigid hymen, or an improperly positioned uterus or ovary. In men, dyspareunia may be caused by inflammations of or lesions on the penis (often caused by herpes), Peyronie's disease (which causes a bending in the penis during erection), and urethritis (Kaplan, 1983). Because dyspareunia is often a symptom of a medical problem, a health care provider should be consulted.

CONSIDERATION: Of 58 female patients who complained of "burning, tight, or focused" pain during intercourse and contacted a physician, 61% were told that the problem was psychological. Another physician, however, discovered that the dyspareunia was caused by a rigid hymen, and coital pain was relieved or improved in 90% of the cases following surgery (Brashear & Munsick, 1991).

Dyspareunia may also be caused by psychosocial factors, including guilt, anxiety, or unresolved feelings about a previous trauma, such as rape or childhood molestation. Religious and parental prohibitions against sexual activity and relationship conflicts may also result in dyspareunia. Lazarus (1989) suggested that in 50% of cases unsatisfactory or unhappy relationships contribute to dyspareunia. The pain may be caused by attempting sexual activity without desire or arousal.

Treatment Dyspareunia that is caused by biological factors may be treated by evaluating the medical condition that is causing the coital pain. If medical or surgical procedures cannot resolve the pain, the person with dyspareunia may try different intercourse positions or other sexual activities that provide pleasure with no or minimal pain.

When dyspareunia is caused by psychosocial factors, treatment may involve reeducation to replace negative attitudes toward sexual activity with positive ones. Individual therapy may help the person resolve feelings of guilt or anxiety associated with sexual activity. Couple therapy may be indicated to resolve relationship conflicts. Sensate focus exercises may help the individual relax and enjoy sexual contact.

Vaginismus

Vaginismus refers to "recurrent or persistent involuntary spasm of the musculature of the outer third of the vagina that interferes with coitus" (APA, 1987, p. 295). Vaginismus is classified as a "sexual pain dysfunction" because the involuntary spasm of the vagina causes the woman to experience pain if she were to attempt sexual intercourse. Although vaginismus is considered to be rather rare, Leiblum, Pervin, and Campbell (1989) speculated that it exists far more than is statistically reported.

Vaginismus may be primary or secondary (Shortle & Jewelewicz, 1986). Primary vaginismus means that the vaginal muscles have always constricted to prevent penetration of any object, including tampons. Secondary vaginismus, the more usual variety, suggests that the vagina has permitted penetration in the past but currently constricts when penetration is imminent.

Causes and Contributing Factors In women who experience dyspareunia (which may be caused by biological or psychosocial factors), vaginismus may be a protective response to prevent pain. In other words, if a woman anticipates coital pain, she may involuntarily constrict her vagina to prevent painful intercourse.

Vaginismus may also be related to such psychosocial factors as restrictive parental and religious upbringing in which the woman learns to view intercourse as dirty and shameful. Other psychosocial factors include rape, incest, and childhood molestation.

Treatment Treatment for vaginismus should begin with a gynecological examination to determine if an organic or physical problem is producing the vaginismus. If the origin is psychological, the treatment may involve teaching the woman relaxation techniques. When relaxation is achieved, the woman is instructed to introduce her index finger into her vagina. The use of lubricants, such as K-Y jelly, may be helpful. After the woman is able to insert one finger into her vagina, she is instructed to introduce two fingers into the vagina, and this exercise is repeated until she feels relaxed enough to contain the penis. Some therapists use graduated dilators. Once the woman learns that she is capable of vaginal containment of the penis, she is usually able to have intercourse without difficulty. Therapy focusing on the woman's cognitions and perceptions about sex and sexuality with her particular partner may precede and/or accompany the finger exercises.

Approaches Used in Sex Therapy

As people become more aware of their sexual choices and as rapid social, cultural, and economic changes cause more conflicts and anxieties, there will be an even greater need for counseling services that address sexuality.

Efrem Rosen
Estelle Weinstein

In the previous section, we discussed how the various sexual dysfunctions may be treated. In this section, we examine the various approaches to sex therapy from which these treatment techniques have developed, the various aides used in sex therapy, and the effectiveness of sex therapy.

Psychoanalytic Approach

Focusing on The Oedipal problems of a man who has developed erectile failure at age 60, after a lifetime of adequate functioning, has not been found to be a productive approach.

Joseph LoPiccolo

Before 1970, most of the treatment of sexual dysfunctions was conducted by psychoanalytically trained psychiatrists who viewed sexual dysfunctions as symptoms of deeply rooted psychological disturbances originating from childhood experiences. Through dream analysis and free association (i.e., saying whatever came into the patient's mind), the therapist using the psychoanalytic approach helped patients to relive childhood experiences in order to achieve insight into the causes of their sexual dysfunction. For example, exploring the childhood of a man with erectile dysfunction might reveal that he harbored unconscious hostility toward his domineering mother. Rather than acknowledge and resolve such feelings of hostility, the man may displace them by generalizing his hostility to all women, including his partner. By being unable to achieve or maintain an erection, the man is able to frustrate his partner, thereby expressing his unconscious hostility toward his domineering mother and all women. Similarly, vaginismus has been viewed by psychoanalysts as resulting from "penis envy" and a concomitant unconscious hatred of men. In other cases, sexual dysfunctions may be related to traumatic childhood sexual experiences, such as rape and incest, that the client has repressed. In exploring the client's childhood, these experiences may be brought to the client's conscious awareness where they may be theoretically resolved. Such exploration took years, was very expensive, and in general, failed to assist clients in achieving their goals.

Masters and Johnson's Approach

Masters and Johnson's approach to sex therapy represented a significant departure from the psychoanalytic approach and a major advance in the treatment of sexual dysfunctions. At the Masters and Johnson Institute in St. Louis, couples go through an intensive two-week sex therapy program. Treatment begins with assessment procedures, including a physical examination and interviews with therapists who take medical and personal histories. On the third day, the therapists meet with the couple to discuss their assessment of the nature, extent, and origin of the sexual problem, to recommend treatment procedures, and to answer any questions. All couples receiving treatment at the Masters and Johnson Institute are instructed to engage in sensate focus exercises (described earlier in this chapter).

The essential elements of the Masters and Johnson approach to resolving sexual dysfunctions are summarized below (Weinstein & Rosen, 1988; Strean, 1983):

1. Both partners in a marital or coupled unit are expected to participate in sex therapy.
2. A male and a female sex therapist provide the treatment for heterosexual couples; in this way, each patient has a same-sex role model.
3. Sexual dysfunctions are conceptualized as having been learned. Hence, much of sex therapy is devoted to sex education and information.
4. Performance anxiety, fear of failure, and excessive need to please the partner are regarded as underlying causes of sexual problems and are addressed in therapy.
5. Communication between the partners is regarded as critical to a good sexual relationship. Hence, enhancing communication between the sexual partners becomes a goal.
6. The specific resolution of a sexual dysfunction involves behavioral change that is accomplished through the assignment of progressive tasks and behavioral prescriptions.

The PLISSIT Model Approach

A helpful approach for treating sexual problems and dysfunctions is the **PLISSIT model** (Annon, 1976). The PLISSIT model outlines four treatment levels: permission, limited information, specific suggestions, and intensive therapy. The **permission** level of the PLISSIT model involves encouraging clients to discuss their sexual problems. The therapist may also assure clients that (in many cases) their thoughts, feelings, behaviors, and concerns are "normal," common, and understandable. The second level of the PLISSIT model involves giving the client **limited information**, such as educating the client about sexual response, sexual anatomy, or the effects of medications or alcohol on sexual functioning. This level of intervention also involves dispelling sexual myths. The third level of intervention involves **specific suggestions.** Examples of specific suggestions include instructing couples on how to do sensate focus exercises, instructing women on masturbation techniques, and instructing men and their partners on how to cope with premature ejaculation (e.g., squeeze technique). The fourth level of treatment involves **intensive therapy.** This level of intervention is used when the other three have not alleviated the sexual dysfunction or problem. Intensive therapy may consist of any of the other sex therapy approaches described in this chapter, such as Masters and Johnson's approach (or a variation of it) or Kaplan's approach.

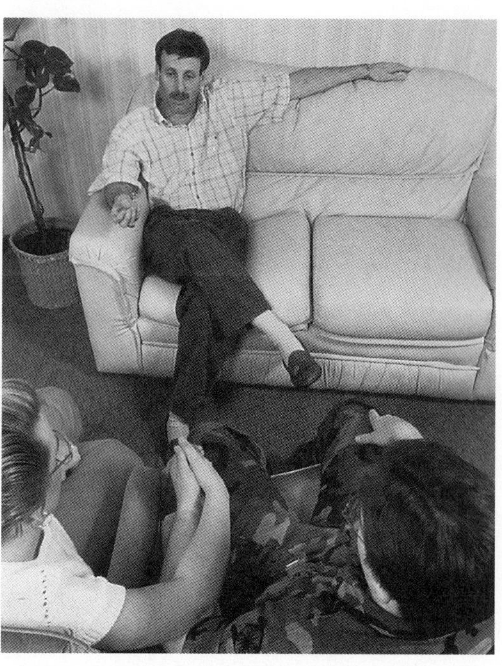

Most sex therapists emphasize the importance of seeing the partners together.

Cognitive Therapy Approach

Cognitive therapy emphasizes that negative thoughts and attitudes about sex interfere with sexual interest, pleasure, and performance. **Cognitive sex therapy** consists of exploring more positive ways of viewing sex and sexuality. For example, a person who has no interest in sex may believe that sex is shameful and sinful and that "good people" regard sex as disgusting. A sex therapist using a cognitive approach might encourage this person to examine the negative consequences of such thoughts and ask the person to consider a different vein of "self-talk." By consciously replacing the old, negative thoughts about sex with positive thoughts like "sex is great, an experience to share, and a fantastic feeling," sexual desire would have a better cognitive context in which to develop. Similarly, a sex therapist may help a couple who think masturbation is sinful and selfish to regard it as a means of discovering self-pleasure so as to enhance their sexual relationship.

Negative cognitions may also interfere with personal, partner, and relationship functioning. Firestone (1990) described thoughts as "voices" and suggested that negative voices may interfere with relationship and sexual satisfaction. For example, one woman reported self-depreciating statements, such as "Why should he [husband] be attracted to me? I'm getting fat; I'm not as young as I used to be." She also tended to have thoughts about her husband, such as "He's so critical of me. He doesn't feel anything for me. He's so insensitive." Both types of negative cognitions (toward self and partner) lead to diminished feelings of sexual attraction and foster the withholding of affectionate and sexual behaviors. The therapeutic process involves each partner in a relationship identifying the negative "voices" they experience, releasing the anger and sadness associated with the voices, developing insight into the origins of the thoughts, and opening up direct communication with their partner.

Negative attitudes and cognitions about sex often result from sexual trauma, such as rape and incest. One way to change these negative attitudes and cognitions is for the therapist to teach the individual to be a survivor, rather than a victim. In addition, the therapist can suggest that "living well is the best revenge" against the person who perpetrated the trauma. Adopting these cognitions may enable the traumatized individual to begin to view sex in more positive terms (McCarthy, 1990; 1992).

Helen Kaplan's Approach

Helen Kaplan (1974) of Cornell Medical Center combined elements of the psychoanalytic, cognitive, and learning approaches (Masters and Johnson) to develop her own approach. Helen Kaplan's approach does not have a rigid two-week format or assume that therapy will continue indefinitely. Her goal is to assist the partners in achieving their sexual goals in as short a time as possible. Sessions are usually held once or twice a week (with an occasional phone call during the week) while the partners continue to live at home. Although participation of both partners is seen as a crucial ingredient for successful sex therapy, Kaplan does not require that sexual partners participate equally in the therapy program. For example, in the case of inhibited female orgasm, Kaplan may spend most of her time working with the woman in individual sessions.

Like Masters and Johnson, Kaplan assigns behavioral "homework" tasks that are designed to help the individual or couple overcome a sexual dysfunction. However, Kaplan suggests that some individuals may not respond to behavioral interventions when the source of the sexual dysfunction is rooted in unconscious intrapsychic conflicts, deep-seated personality traits, or interpersonal dynamics. Thus, an important part of Kaplan's approach to sex therapy is insight therapy, through which the presumed deeper roots of sexual dysfunction are uncovered.

Kaplan also notes that sex therapy clients often resist treatment and that therapists must be aware of such resistance and help clients overcome it. In sex therapy, "resistance" refers to the client's unconscious opposition to or lack of cooperation in treatment. Resistance may involve clients doing something to interfere with the resolution of their sexual problem. Examples of resistance include "forgetting" therapy appointments, "not finding time" to complete homework assignments, doing homework assignments incorrectly, or antagonizing the partner. Kaplan (1974) observed:

> Resistance is a critical therapeutic issue in all but the simplest cases and must be managed effectively for therapy to succeed. The paradoxical tendency of patients to resist "getting well" was first described by Freud in the early days of psychoanalysis, and it is now known that resistance occurs to all kinds of psychological treatments, including sex therapy. (p. 197)

In order for sex therapy to be effective, Kaplan said the sex therapist must diffuse any resistance on the part of the client. Diffusing resistance may be accomplished by confronting the client directly, exploring unconscious conflicts, or making use of dream material.

LoPiccolo's Postmodern Approach

Building on the contributions of Masters and Johnson's system of modern sex therapy, and drawing from cognitive-behavioral therapy and systems theory, Joseph LoPiccolo (1992) offered a three-part theory he dubbed "postmodern." While his comments focused on erectile failure, the three theoretical elements he described are applicable to understanding other categories of sexual dysfunction as well.

1. *Systems theory.* LoPiccolo recommended that in assessing sexual dysfunction, the therapist should carefully examine the effect of the dysfunction on the relationship between the partners. While sexual problems may cause distress, they may also serve a purpose. Unlike Kaplan's approach, in which "resistance" is exam-

ined when standard therapies haven't worked, in LoPiccolo's framework the therapist begins in the first session to prevent resistance. Clients may be asked to anticipate any possible negative effects on their marital relationship if the husband were to regain erectile functioning. "For example, might a husband feel more powerful and revert to a more authoritarian role with the wife if he became 'potent' again? Might the wife find his sexual needs burdensome if the husband regained erectile function?" (p. 178)

Ideally, if the systemic value of the problem is discovered during the initial assessment, therapy can immediately begin to meet the needs that the erectile failure serves. LoPiccolo identified a number of frequently occurring systemic issues, including the following: not feeling attracted to one's partner, being unable to combine feelings of love and sexual desire, discrepancies in the extent of "personal space" needed by the partners, and general unhappiness in the marriage.

2. *Integrated (physiological and psychological) planning.* As discussed earlier in this chapter, it is often not useful, and may be harmful, to classify people's dysfunctions as organic *or* psychogenic. As noted, *both* organic and psychogenic factors are operating. LoPiccolo suggested that even when organic etiology is clearly established, a thorough psychological evaluation is also indicated.
3. *Sexual behavior patterns.* Finally, as discussed in a number of the previous sections on treatment of specific dysfunctions, it is important to examine the specific sexual behaviors of the couple. Are the behaviors used to cue sexual desire and arousal adequate? Does the couple need to reconsider the methods, sites, or philosphies of stimulation?

Surrogate Partner Therapy

About one in three U.S. adults is single, a group that includes the never-married, separated, divorced, and widowed. Sexually dysfunctional individuals without partners may have limited opportunities for practicing sex therapy techniques (e.g., sensate focus). To overcome this problem, some therapists recommend a surrogate partner. **Surrogate partner therapy** involves a person with sexual difficulties becoming sexually involved with a trained individual (other than the primary therapist) for therapeutic purposes. The surrogate partner and the client perform the exercises recommended by the sex therapist. Although most surrogate partners are women, some are men.

Surrogate partner therapy is rarely used. In a survey of 289 members of the American Association of Sex Educators, Counselors, and Therapists (**AASECT**), surrogate partner therapy was the least frequent type of treatment used. In a 12-month period, only 1.8% of clients seen by sex therapists in this survey were treated using surrogate partner therapy (Kilmann, Boland, Norton, Davidson, & Caid, 1986). The hazy legal status of surrogate therapy was noted by Reynolds (1992), who reported that it is not available at university-based sex therapy centers. While surrogate therapy may be effective, its availability is very limited.

Because sex surrogates may be viewed as "therapists," surrogacy partner therapy raises ethical concerns about sexual contact between patient and therapist. Despite the controversial status of surrogacy partner therapy, Bancroft (1989) suggested that "there may be some individuals whose sexual lives will be genuinely enhanced by such experience and who may be difficult to help in other ways" (p. 519). (See Exhibit 16.1 in Chapter 16 for a description of surrogate partner therapy with a client with cerebral palsy.) The professionalism of surrogacy partner therapy is reflected in an organization called the International Professional Surrogates Association (IPSA).

Alternative Aids Used in Sex Therapy

Therapists may use one or more aids in their therapy program. Earlier in this chapter, we already discussed the use of vibrators for women who have difficulty experiencing orgasm. Other aids used by sex therapists include films, and drugs.

Films and Audiotapes Some sex therapists show their clients films or videotapes. While clients are often confused by a verbal description of the squeeze technique, sensate focus, or alternative intercourse positions, there is no misunderstanding when they see two people demonstrate. A film on coital positioning, for example, may show a couple in a series of coital positions: scissors, spoon, male superior, rear entry, and female superior positions. Unlike X-rated pornographic films, films used by sex therapists show couples sharing sexual experiences in the context of a caring relationship. *Three Daughters,* a film produced by Candida Royalle of Femme Distribution, Inc., was presented at the Annual Invitational Film Festival at the national convention of ASSECT. The film was noteworthy because, while sexually explicit, it promoted positive role models.

However, many commercially available sexually explicit films focus on genital or exploitative sex rather than relationship sex in a caring context. Offit (1990) suggested that films emphasizing genital sex may not be helpful, as couples in sex therapy often need to emphasize "love play" rather than "sex play."

The use of audio tape material is another beneficial adjunct in treatment. Reynolds (1992) described using an audio cassette tape program, which he used in the context of group or individual therapy. The program was designed to treat heterosexual men experiencing erectile dysfunction, early ejaculation, limited sexual experience, or sexual relationship anxiety. Each tape included a presentation by Reynolds or a discussion with one of his clients, roleplay exercises to enhance communication and relationship skills, and a homework assignment. Participants found it helpful to hear other clients on the tapes speak of their struggles and progress.

Drugs Since most sex therapy is not conducted by physicians or in a medical setting (Masters and Johnson and Helen Kaplan are exceptions), the use of drugs in sex therapy is minimal. But sometimes drugs have been used successfully in the treatment of sexual dysfunctions—testosterone for low sex interest, clomipramine for early ejaculation, and papavarine or prostaglandin E combined with phentolamine for erectile dysfunction.

Effectiveness of Sex Therapy

The largest series of sex therapy cases for which effectiveness has been reported is that of Masters and Johnson (1970). Masters and Johnson did not report success rates for their sex therapy; rather, they reported a "failure" rate of 20% for the 1,872 cases they treated at their institute from 1959 through 1977 (Kolodny, 1981). This reported average "failure" rate of 20% is often misinterpreted to mean that the "success" rate was 80%. However, the "failure" category included cases that were actually "improved" (to a greater or lesser degree) as well as cases that showed no improvement whatsoever (Kolodny, 1981).

In 1979 Kaplan estimated the overall average percentage of sex therapy cases that are successfully resolved is about 66%. In a number of treatment outcome studies in the 1980s, with followup periods of three months to three years, researchers have documented clients' increased satisfaction with their sexual relationship, although symptom remission and satisfaction in marital relationships were more variable (De Amicis, Goldberg, LoPiccolo, Friedman, & Davies, 1984 & 1985). Kilmann et al. (1986) surveyed randomly selected sex therapists who were members of AASECT. In their reports of therapy outcomes, "highest success rates (client satisfaction with sexual functioning) were for premature ejaculation (62%), secondary orgasmic dysfunction (56%), and desire discrepancies (53%). Primary erectile dysfunctions had the lowest success rate (25%)." (p. 116)

Reports of sex therapy effectiveness are highly varied for several reasons. First, the degree to which sex therapy is effective in resolving sexual problems depends on the problem being treated. Some problems are easier to treat than others. In general, secondary problems are easier to treat than primary problems, and situational problems are easier to treat than total (or global) problems. Early ejaculation and vaginismus are more likely to respond quickly to therapeutic intervention. Problems of sexual desire may be the most difficult to treat (Schover & LoPiccolo, 1982; Kilmann et al., 1986). Erectile dysfunction, inability to achieve orgasm, and hypoactive sexual desire require more time.

LoPiccolo (1992) identified several factors that influence the effectiveness of sex therapy. For example, LoPiccolo suggested that sex therapy is less likely to be effective under the following conditions:

1. Either the patient or his/her partner is unwilling to reconsider how cognitive, behavioral, or systemic factors are contributing to the maintenance of the sexual dysfunction.
2. The patient has a sexual deviation in which he or she is aroused by an inappropriate sexual object (such as children) or has a paraphilia (see Chapter 17).
3. The patient's religious beliefs are interfering with sexual performance. (LoPiccolo suggested that "these cases are best referred to a pastoral counselor, who may have some credibility in changing or at least helping the patient re-examine these beliefs" (p. 187).
4. The patient has severe clinical depression. However, mild to moderate depression due to sexual and relationship issues may respond well to sex therapy.

Sex therapy effectiveness rates may vary because of the methodological problems in determining such rates. For example, who should decide whether treatment has failed or succeeded—the client or the therapist?. What criteria should be used in determining success or failure? What if the client is successful in resolving sexual dysfunctions but is not successful in resolving related nonsexual issues, such as marital conflict, negative body image, and low self-esteem? What if the client is successful in resolving these related nonsexual issues but is still sexually dysfunctional? What criteria will be used to measure success and failure? Different answers to these questions will yield different results regarding reported success rates of sex therapy.

Finally, sex therapy effectiveness rates based on current studies are likely to be lower than effectiveness rates based on older studies because of differences in the severity of the dysfunctions treated. Newcomb and Bentler (1988) suggested that in previous decades, a higher percentage of people with sexual difficulties lacked information about sexuality. In many cases, sexual difficulties were caused by "ignorance, naivete, and misunderstanding." However, people today are more likely to be informed about matters related to sexuality (through self-help books, sex education, the media, and other educational materials available to the public). Thus, compared to sex therapy clients in previous decades, the sex therapy client today often suffers from more than simple lack of sexual information. As Newcomb and Bentler (1988) explained, "People presenting now with sexual problems typically have more basic knowledge of sexual functioning and behavior than previously, and thus arrive with more complex and severe sexual disturbances . . ." (p. 127).

CONSIDERATION: Dr. Thomas Szasz (1980), a noted psychiatrist, expressed skepticism about the role of sex therapists and the effectiveness of sex therapy:

> Promising to teach people how to play the sex game well, sexologists seduce them into believing that they can teach them how to play it safely—which, of course, no one can do. Why? Because the dangerousness of human sexuality lies in the fact that sexual acts are so very personal. Behaving sexually toward another person is risky business because doing so is profoundly self-revealing and because the needs of the participants are constantly changing and are rarely fully complementary. There is simply no way to avoid this. (p. 3)

Sex Therapy: Professional and Ethical Issues

The field of sex therapy is so new and its practitioners are so diverse that many professional and ethical issues have not been resolved. In this section, we present a variety of professional and ethical issues that are of concern to both sex therapists and the public they serve.

Training Requirements to Become a Sex Therapist

With rare exception, there are no laws preventing a person from advertising that she or he is a sex therapist. Anyone can legally open an office in most communities and offer sex therapy. Academic degrees, therapy experience under supervision, and exposure to other aspects of formal training in human sexuality are not legally required to market one's self as a sex therapist. California is the only state that exercises some legal restraint on sex therapy. To be licensed in California as a physician, psychologist, social worker, or marriage, family, or child counselor, a person must have had training in human sexuality.

To help upgrade the skills of those providing sex therapy, the American Association of Sex Educators, Counselors, and Therapists offers a certificate of Certified Sex Therapist to applicants who have a minimum of a master's degree in a clinical field (e.g., psychology, social work, nursing, marriage therapy), have conducted sex therapy under supervision for a minimum of 100 hours, and have attended a two-day workshop on human sexuality (sponsored by AASECT) to sort out their own attitudes and values about human sexuality. AASECT (1985) guidelines indicate that the therapist should have a basic understanding of sexual and reproductive anatomy and physiology, sexual development (biological and psychological), interpersonal relationships, gender-related issues, marital and family dynamics, sociocultural factors in sexual values and behavior, medical issues affecting sexuality (including pregnancy, STDs, drugs, illness and disability, contraception, and fertility), sex research, sexual abuse, and personality theories.

The therapists certified by AASECT are expected to conduct their practice in a manner that reflects the organization's Code of Ethics for Sex Therapists. Beyond being knowledgeable about treating sexual dysfunctions, empathic, and trained in communication and counseling skills, the certified sex therapist is expected to refrain from engaging in sexual activity with clients.

Sexual Involvement between Therapist and Client

The general professional consensus is that it is unethical for therapists (including psychologists, psychiatrists, marriage and family therapists, and sex therapists) to become sexually involved with their clients. Brown and Sollod (1988) explained that "the therapist holds a highly influential position of trust and parent-like authority with clients. Overt sexual activity with the client violates this trust and misuses the authority." (p. 397)

Despite the prohibitions against therapists becoming sexually involved with clients, 5% to 13% of physicians and psychologists reported that they had had sexual relations with their patients during treatment (Edelwich & Brodsky, 1982). In a review of studies, between 5% to 10% of male therapists and 1% to 2% of female therapists admitted to having had sex with a patient (Pope, Keith-Spiegel, & Tabachnick, 1986). The American Psychiatric Association has expelled or suspended 113 members in the last ten years, mostly for sexual misconduct (Beck, Springen, & Foote, 1992).

Women who have been sexually involved with their therapists experience anger and distrust (Pope et al., 1986). Depression may also result. The family of Paul Lozano, a former Harvard medical student, alleges that he committed suicide because of his terminated emotional and sexual relationship with his psychiatrist, Dr. Margaret Bean-Bayog. She admited that her therapy with him was "somewhat unconventional" but "categorically denies" having had sex with him (Adler & Rosenberg, 1992, pp. 56–57).

Professional guidelines that prohibit therapist-patient sexual involvement are clear. However, as the following section illustrates, other professional issues in sex therapy are not so clearly resolved.

Values in Sex Therapy

Values—those of the sex therapist and the client—play an important role in sex therapy. The following two examples illustrate the importance of values in sex therapy.

The Value of Egalitarian Relationships Sex therapists generally value relationship egalitarianism (equal power and decision making between partners in a relationship) (LoPiccolo, 1978). In cases in which an imbalance in relationship power contributes to sexual dysfunction, it is the therapist's responsibility to encourage the partners to become more egalitarian as part of the treatment for the sexual dysfunction. However, Brown and Sollod (1988) cautioned sex therapists to be careful in addressing relationship equality issues that they personally believe are destructive but that do not necessarily affect the sexual dysfunction. Brown and Sollod recommended that the therapist allow the couple to decide if a particular aspect of their relationship (e.g., inequality in decision making) affects their sexual relationship.

Masturbation as Therapy Sex therapists view masturbation as a healthy activity and recommend masturbation as a treatment for women who have difficulty experiencing orgasm. Yet, it is not uncommon for sex therapy clients to feel that masturbation is wrong and should not be part of their treatment. In this case, should the therapist accept the client's negative views of masturbation? Or should the therapist try to change the client's views? When clients reject masturbation as a treatment for their sexual dysfunction, Brown and Sollod (1988) suggested that the therapist say, "We have considerable evidence that masturbation is helpful in learning to reach orgasm. However, in cases such as yours, where you have a strong moral objection to it, we don't have good evidence on whether it is helpful or not" (p. 392). The therapist may also assess the degree to which the woman values experiencing orgasm and is motivated to achieve that goal. If she does not value achieving orgasm highly, it may not be worth it for her to compromise her moral objections to masturbation. If, however, she is greatly concerned about her inability to achieve orgasm, it may be worth the compromise. In either case, the therapist should allow the client the right to make either decision without disapproval from the therapist.

CHOICES

It is not surprising that some people have difficulty talking about sexual problems. Fifty-six percent of 61 university men reported that "it is stressful for me to talk to anyone about my sexual concerns" (Metz & Seifert, 1990, p. 83). Those they were most likely to talk to were their partner or spouse (84%) or a good friend (65%). However, 69% reported that they would be willing to talk with a sex therapist, 61% to a psychologist, and 53% to a family or mental health counselor (p. 83). While the decision to talk to a professional at all is the primary one faced by those with a sexual problem, other decisions also need to be made. These include whether to seek individual or couple (**conjoint**) therapy, to be seen alone or in a group, and to be seen by a female-male team or an individual therapist. An examination of each of these choices follows.

Choose to Have Individual Therapy or Couple (Conjoint) Therapy?

Should a person experiencing a sexual problem who decides to seek therapy go alone (individual therapy) or with his or her partner (couple or conjoint therapy)? It depends. Some people prefer to go alone. One woman said:

> If I ask him to go to therapy with me, he'll think I'm more emotionally involved than I am. And since I don't want to encourage him, I'll just work out my problems without him. (Authors' files.)

Other reasons a person might see a sex therapist alone are if no partner is available, if the partner won't go, or if the person feels more comfortable discussing sex in the partner's absence. In addition, individual therapy might be the best treatment approach when the roots of the sexual conflicts are unconscious, when resistance to therapy is great, and when there is a high level of mistrust in the couple relationship (Strean, 1983).

However, there are also several reasons individuals seeking sex therapy might want their partner to become involved in the therapy, including: to work on the problem with someone, to share the experience, to prevent one partner from being identified as the "one with the problem," to explore relationship factors that may be contributing to the sexual problem, and to address the difficulties of the partner in dealing with the sexual problem. When 356 college students were asked to rate the acceptability and credibility of various marital therapy formats (conjoint, concurrent, group, and individual), the conjoint treatment format (the therapist sees both partners together at the same time) was consistently rated as most acceptable and credible. When asked to choose between the four therapy formats, significantly more research participants chose the conjoint format as the most preferred type of therapy (Wilson, Flammang, & Dehle, 1992). However, a study of 80 college women's ratings of sex therapy formats, showed that including the identified patient's partner in therapy did not influence acceptability ratings (Wilson & Wilson, 1991).

In a study of sexually nonresponsive women, researchers found that sex therapy for the woman alone was as effective as treating the couple in conjoint therapy (Whitehead, Mathews, & Ramage, 1987). However, the researchers also stated that conjoint therapy was "the treatment of choice" in that it had a more positive outcome for the woman's anxiety and for her perception of her partner (p. 204).

Another treatment alternative is to combine individual therapy with conjoint therapy. For example, one or both partners may receive individual therapy and, either concurrently or subsequently, also receive conjoint therapy. If partners are anxious or uncomfortable about sharing their feelings and concerns with each other, "a one-to-one relationship with the therapist should probably be considered initially, so that each spouse can receive enough protection and understanding while communicating with the therapist to eventually develop the strength to share problems with the mate" (Strean, 1983, p. 208).

Choose to Have Private Therapy or Group Therapy?

Once the decision to pursue therapy (with or without a partner) is made, another choice is whether to see the therapist in private or in groups with other people who are experiencing similar problems. While 80 women who were

Continued

Continued

asked their preferences clearly preferred individual therapy (Wilson & Wilson, 1991), each treatment modality has advantages and disadvantages.

Although being seen privately helps to ensure that the therapy will be tailored to fit the specific needs of the client, the cost is considerably higher for private therapy than for therapy in a group. Private therapy may cost $100 or more an hour; therapy in a group of five members may cost $20 or less for the same amount of time.

Another advantage of group therapy is that being surrounded by others who have similar problems helps to reduce the client's feeling of isolation—that he or she is "the only one." One woman who had difficulty achieving orgasm said, "When I heard the other women discuss their difficulty with climaxing, I knew I wasn't abnormal" (Author's notes). The empathy of a group of peers can be extremely effective in helping a person feel less isolated.

A group setting also furnishes the opportunity to try new behaviors. For example, some sexual problems may be part of a larger problem, such as the lack of social skills to attract and maintain a partner. Fear of rejection can perpetuate being alone. But group members, with the help of their therapist, can practice making requests of each other and getting turned down. Such an exercise helps to develop the social skill of approaching others while learning to cope with rejection. Practicing with other group members is safe and gives a person the necessary confidence to approach someone outside the group.

Group therapy has at least three disadvantages. The first is the possibility that not enough time will be spent on the individual's own problem. The second is the risk to the relationship with the partner, who may not be involved in the group. In one study of women in group therapy for lack of orgasm, one in four reported a negative effect on their partner (Barbach & Flaherty, 1980). Finally, some people are reluctant to try group therapy. In Wilson and Wilson's (1991) study of college women's ratings of therapy formats, the students rated the individual format as more credible and acceptable than the group format.

What is the comparative effectiveness of couples being treated in a group or in private therapy? In one study, when group-couple therapy for early ejaculation and orgasmic dysfunction was compared with therapy for the same problems treated in private, there were no differences in outcome. Both treatment patterns were effective. Men reported satisfaction with their ability to prolong intercourse, and women reported satisfaction with their orgasmic ability (Golden, Price, Heinrich, & Lobitz, 1978). Other researchers have found similar results: couples in groups are as successful in achieving their goals as couples in private therapy (Duddle & Ingram, 1980). But group therapy for individuals may not be as effective as therapy with a partner in private or in a couples' group. However, most individuals in group sex therapy without a partner do benefit from the experience.

These studies suggest that couples can be treated effectively in either a private or a group setting. The selection of a therapy setting is therefore a matter of preference and perhaps a matter of affordability. As with individual and conjoint therapy, private and group therapy can be combined.

Choose to Have a Male-Female Sex Therapy Team or an Individual Therapist?

For heterosexual couples, is it best to see one therapist or a male-female sex therapy team? Masters and Johnson recommend the latter for couple therapy, suggesting that the male client can better relate to a male therapist and a female client can better relate to a female therapist. A dual sex team also provides a model for appropriate male-female interaction.

Although many sex therapists have adopted the dual sex team approach, there is no evidence that such a team is more effective than individual male or female therapists (Clement & Schmidt, 1983; LoPiccolo, Heiman, Hogan, & Roberts, 1985). In addition, therapy with a dual sex therapy team is likely to be more expensive than therapy with an individual therapist. Rather than how many therapists of what sex are in the therapy setting, the quality of the therapy seems to be the important variable.

Summary

1. Sexual dysfunctions involve disturbances in both subjective (pleasure) and objective (physiological changes) aspects of sexual functioning. Sexual dysfunctions may be classified as desire-phase, arousal-phase, orgasm-phase, and sexual pain dysfunctions.
2. Sexual dysfunctions in the first half of the twentieth century were viewed as symptoms of personality disorders. Today, sexual dysfunctions are viewed as

being caused by one or more of the following factors: biological (e.g., hormone deficiency, drugs, illness, fatigue), sociocultural (e.g., gender roles, restrictive parental or religious upbringing), intrapsychic (e.g., anxiety, guilt, prior sexual trauma) relationship (relationship dissatisfaction, mistrust, anger), educational and cognitive (sexual ignorance or misinformation, belief in sexual myths), and aging factors. Sometimes a sexual difficulty may be mislabeled as a "dysfunction" when the real problem is not with the person's sexual functioning but rather that the person does not receive adequate sexual stimulation to produce the sexual response.

3. Estimates on the prevalence of sexual dysfunctions vary because research studies are often based on small, nonrepresentative samples and researchers use different criteria in assessing whether an individual has a particular sexual dysfunction.
4. Various approaches to sex therapy include the psychoanalytic (emphasizing resolving unconscious conflicts), Masters and Johnson's (emphasizing the relationship and behavioral change), the PLISSIT model (outlining four levels of progressively involved intervention), cognitive therapy (emphasizing changing thoughts and attitudes), Helen Kaplan's (combining psychoanalytic, behavioral, and cognitive approaches), LoPiccolo's postmodern approach, and surrogacy partner therapy (utilizing a surrogate partner for single clients).
5. Sex therapists may use various aids in treating persons with sexual difficulties, including films and audio tapes (to demonstrate sexual exercises, activities, or positions), and drugs (to treat low sexual desire, erectile dysfunction, and early ejaculation).
6. The effectiveness of sex therapy depends on the person, nature of the sexual problem, the treatment approach used, and the criteria used to assess effectiveness.
7. The American Association of Sex Educators, Counselors, and Therapists (AASECT) certifies sex therapists who meet its certification guidelines. Most states, however, (the exception is California) do not require individuals be certified or licensed to practice sex therapy.
8. Sexual involvement between therapists and patients is considered to be professionally unethical and potentially damaging to patients.
9. Values—those of the sex therapist and the client—play an important role in sex therapy. When therapists and clients differ in their values (e.g., regarding egalitarianism or masturbation), therapists must balance two competing responsibilities: to help their clients resolve their sexual dysfunction and to respect their clients' rights to have values that differ from theirs.
10. Individuals seeking sex therapy may choose individual or conjoint (couple) therapy, private or group therapy, a male-female sex therapy team or an individual therapist. Each of these forms of therapy has advantages and disadvantages. The deciding factors in choosing may be affordability (individual therapy and male-female therapy teams are more expensive) and personal preference.

KEY TERMS

sexual dysfunction
primary dysfunction
secondary dysfunction
situational dysfunction
total dysfunction
performance anxiety
hypoactive sexual desire
sensate focus
sexual aversion
spectatoring
female sexual arousal dysfunction
male erectile dysfunction
priapism
inhibited female orgasm
inhibited male orgasm

cont'd.

early ejaculation
squeeze technique
dyspareunia
vaginismus
surrogate partner therapy
ASSECT
conjoint therapy

REFERENCES

AASECT (American Association of Sex Educators, Counselors and Therapists). (1985, July). *Requirements for sex counselor certification.* Washington, DC: Author.

Adler, J., & Rosenberg, D. (1992, April 13). Dr. Bean and her little boy. *Newsweek,* pp. 56–57.

Althof, S. E., Turner, L. A., Levine, S. B., Risen, C. B., Bodner, D., Kursh, E. D., & Resnick, M. I. (1991). Sexual, psychological, and marital impact of self-injection of papaverine and phentolamine: A long-term prospective study. *Journal of Sex and Marital Therapy, 17,* 101–112.

Althof, S. E., Turner, L. A., Levine, S. D., Risen, C., Kursh, E., Bodner, D., & Resnick, M. (1989). Why do so many people drop out of auto-injection therapy for impotence? *Journal of Sex and Marital Therapy, 15,* 121–129.

American Psychiatric Association. (1987). *Diagnostic and statistical manual of mental disorders* (3rd ed., rev.). Washington, DC: Author.

Annon, J. (1976). The PLISSIT Model. *Journal of Sex Education and Therapy, 2,* 1–15.

Assalian, P. (1988). Clomipramine in the treatment of premature ejaculation. *Journal of Sex Research, 24,* 213–215.

Assalian, P. (1991, November). *Premature ejaculation: Is it really psychogenic?* Paper presented at the annual meeting of the Society for the Scientific Study of Sex, New Orleans. Used by permission. Write to author at Department of Psychiatry, Montreal General Hospital, 1650 Cedar Avenue, Montreal, Quebec, Canada H3G 1A4.

Bancroft, J. (1989). *Human sexuality and its problems* (2nd ed.). New York: Churchill Livingstone.

Barbach, L. (1975). *For yourself: The fulfillment of female sexuality.* New York: Doubleday.

Barbach, L., & Flaherty, M., (1980). Group treatment of situationally orgasmic women. *Journal of Sex and Marital Therapy, 6,* 19–29.

Barlow, D. H. (1986). Causes of sexual dysfunction: The role of anxiety and cognitive interference. *Journal of Consulting and Clinical Psychology, 54,* 140–148.

Bass, B. A. (1985). The myth of low sexual desire: A cognitive behavioral approach to treatment. *Journal of Sex Education and Therapy, 11,* 61–64.

Beck, J. G., & Barlow, D. H. (1986). The effects of anxiety and attentional focus on sexual responding. II: Cognitive and affective patterns in erectile dysfunction. *Behavior Research and Therapy, 24,* 19–26.

Beck, M., Springen, K., & Foote, D. (1992, April 13). Sex and psychotherapy. *Newsweek,* pp. 56–57.

Beggs, V. E., Calhoun, K. S., & Wolchik, S. A. (1987). Sexual anxiety and female sexual arousal: A comparison of arousal during sexual anxiety stimuli and sexual pleasure stimuli. *Archives of Sexual Behavior, 16,* 311–319.

Bozman, A. W., & Beck, J. G. (1991). Covariation of sexual desire and sexual arousal: The effects of anger and anxiety. *Archives of Sexual Behavior, 20,* 47–60.

Brashear, D. B., & Munsick, R. A. (1991). Hymenal dyspareunia. *Journal of Sex Education and Therapy, 19,* 27–31.

Brewer, J. S. (1981). Duration of intromission and female orgasm rates. *Medical Aspects of Human Sexuality, 15,* 70–71.

Brown, R. A., & Sollod, R. (1988). Ethical and professional issues in sex therapy. In Robert A. Brown and Joan R. Field (Eds.), *Treatment of sexual problems in individual and couples therapy* (pp. 387–408). New York: PMA.

Cado, S., & Leitenberg, H. (1990). Guilt reactions to sexual fantasies during intercourse. *Archives of Sexual Behavior, 19,* 49–63.

Carroll, J. L., & Bagley, D. H. (1990). Evaluation of sexual satisfaction in partners of men experiencing erectile failure. *Journal of Sex and Marital Therapy, 16,* 70–78.

Carroll, J. L., Baltish, M. H., & Bagley, D. H. (1990). The use of Poten Test in the multidisciplinary evaluation of impotence: Is it a reliable measure? *Journal of Sex and Marital Therapy, 16,* 181–187.

Clement, U., & Schmidt, G. (1983). The outcome of couple therapy for sexual dysfunctions using three different formats. *Journal of Sex and Marital Therapy, 9,* 67–78.

Coleman, E. M., Hoon, P. W., & Hoon, E. F. (1983). Arousability and sexual satisfaction in lesbian and heterosexual women. *Journal of Sex Research, 19,* 58–73.

Coleman, E. & Reece, R. (1988). Treating low sexual desire among gay men. In S. R. Leiblum & R. C. Rosen (Eds.) *Sexual Desire Disorders* (pp. 413–445). New York: Guilford.

Darling, C. A., Davidson, J. K. Sr., & Cox, R. P. (1991). Female sexual response and the timing of partner orgasm. *Journal of Sex and Marital Therapy, 17,* 3–21.

DeAmicis, L. A., Goldberg, D. C., LoPiccolo, J., Friedman, J., & Davies, L. (1984). Three-year follow-up of couples evaluated for sexual dysfunction. *Journal of Sex & Marital Therapy,* 10, 215–228.

DeAmicis, L. A., Goldberg, D. C., LoPiccolo, J., Friedman, J., & Davies, L. (1985). Clinical follow-up of couples treated for sexual dysfunction. *Archives of Sexual Behavior, 14,* 467–489.

Dow, M. G. (1981). Retarded ejaculation as a function of nonaversive conditioning and discrimination: A hypothesis. *Journal of Sex and Marital Therapy, 7,* 49.

Duddle, C. M., & Ingram, A. (1980). Treating sexual dysfunction in couple's groups. In R. Forleo & W. Pasini (Eds.), *Medical sexology* (pp. 598–605). Amsterdam: Elsevier.

Edelwich, J., & Brodsky, A. (1982). *Sexual dilemmas for the helping professional.* New York: Brunner/Mazel.

Findlay, S. & Podolsky, D. (1992, Aug. 24). Danger: Implants. *U.S. News & World Report,* pp. 62–66.

Firestone, R. W. (1990). Voices during sex: Application of voice therapy to sexuality. *Journal of Sex and Marital Therapy, 16,* 258–277.

Golden, J. S., Price, S., Heinrich, A. G., & Lobitz, W. C. (1978). Group versus couple treatment of sexual dysfunctions. *Archives of Sexual Behavior, 7,* 593–602.

Goldman, H. H. (1992). *Review of general psychiatry* (3rd ed.). Norwalk, CT: Appelton & Lange.

Goldsmith, L. (1988). Treatment of sexual dysfunction. In E. Weinstein & E. Rosen (Eds.), *Sexuality counseling: Issues and implications* (pp. 16–34). Pacific Grove, CA: Brooks/Cole.

Gorowitz. S. (1980). Remarks. In W. H. Masters, V. E. Johnson, & R. C. Kolodny (Eds.), *Ethical issues in sex therapy and research* (vol. 2) (pp. 11–15). Boston: Little, Brown.

Hammond, D. C., & Middleton, R. G. (1984). Penile prostheses. *Medical Aspects of Human Sexuality, 18,* 204–208.

Hawton, K. (1985). *Sex therapy; A practical guide.* Oxford: Oxford University Press.

Heiman, J., LoPiccolo, L., & LoPiccolo, J. (1976). *Becoming orgasmic: A sexual growth program for women.* Englewood Cliffs, NJ: Prentice-Hall.

Hite, Shere. (1987). *The Hite report: Women and love.* New York: Alfred A. Knopf.

Hock, Z., Safir, M. P., Shepher, J., & Peras, J. Y. (1980). An interdisciplinary approach to the study of sexual dysfunction in couples: Preliminary findings. In R. Forleo & W. Pasini (Eds.), *Medical sexology* (pp. 553–558). Amsterdam: Elsevier.

Holden, G. (1976). Sex therapy: Making it as a science and an industry. In A. Kilbride (Ed.), *Focus: Human sexuality* (pp. 98–101). Guilford, CT: Pushkin

Hong, L. K. (1984). Survival of the fastest: On the origin of premature ejaculation. *Journal of Sexual Research, 20,* 109–122.

Kaplan, H. S. (1974). The classification of the female sexual dysfunctions. *Journal of Sex and Marital Therapy, 2,* 124–138.

Kaplan, H. S. (1977). Hypoactive sexual desire. *Journal of Sex and Marital Therapy, 3,* 3–9.

Kaplan, H. S. (1979). *Disorders of sexual desire.* New York: Simon & Schuster.

Kaplan, H. S. (1983). *The evaluation of sexual disorders.* New York: Brunner/Mazel.

Kaplan, H. S. (1990). The combined use of sex therapy and intrapenile injections in the treatment of impotence. *Journal of Sex and Marital Therapy, 16,* 195–207.

Kelly, M. P., Strassberg, D. S., & Kircher, J. R. (1990). Attitudinal and experiential correlates of anorgasmia. *Archives of Sexual Behavior, 19,* 165–177.

Kilmann, P. R., Boland, J. P., Norton, S. P., Davidson, E. & Caid, C. (1986). Perspectives of sex therapy outcome: A survey of AASECT providers. *Journal of Sex and Marital Therapy, 12,* 116–138.

Kilmann, P. R., Mills, K. H., Caid, C., Bella, B., Davidson, E., & Wanlass, R. (1984). The sexual interaction of women with secondary orgasmic dysfunction and their partners. *Archives of Sexual Behavior, 13,* 41–49.

Kinsey, A. C., Pomeroy, W. B., Martin, C. E., & Gebhard, P. H. (1953). *Sexual behavior in the human female.* Philadelphia: W. B. Saunders.

Kolodny, R. C. (1981). Evaluating sex therapy: Process and outcome at the Masters and Johnson Institute. *Journal of Sex Research, 17,* 301–318.

Kolodny, R. C., Masters, W. H., & Johnson, V. E. (1979). *Textbook of sexual medicine.* Boston: Little, Brown.

Lazarus, A.A. (1989). Dyspareunia: A multimodal psychotherapeutic perspective. In S.R. Leiblum & R.C. Rosen (Eds.), *Principles and Practice of sex therapy 2nd edition, Update for the 1990s* (pp. 89–112). New York: The Guilford Press.

Leiblum, S.R., Pervin, L.A., & Campbell, E.H. (1989). The treatment of vaginismus: Success and failure. In S.R. Leiblum & R.C. Rosen (Eds.), *Principles and Practice of sex therapy 2nd edition, Update for the 1990s* (pp. 113–138). New York: The Guilford Press.

Leiblum, S. R., & Rosen, R. C. (1988a). Introduction: Changing perspectives on sexual desire. In S. R. Leiblum & R. C. Rosen (Eds.), *Sexual desire disorders* (pp. 1–17). New York: Guilford Press.

Leiblum, S. R., & Rosen, R. C. (1988b). Conclusion: Conceptual and clinical overview. In S. R. Leiblum & R. C. Rosen (Eds.), *Sexual desire disorders* (pp. 446–458). New York: Guilford Press.

Leiblum, S. R., & Rosen, R. C. (1989). Couples therapy for erectile disorders: Conceptual and clinical considerations. *Journal of Sex and Marital Therapy, 17,* 147–159.

Lief, H. I. (1977). Inhibited sexual desire. *Medical Aspects of Human Sexuality, 11,* (7), 94–95.

LoPiccolo, J. (1978). Direct treatment of sexual dysfunction. In J. LoPiccolo & L. LoPiccolo (Eds.), *Handbook of Sex Therapy* (pp. 1–17). New York: Plenum.

LoPiccolo, J. (1992). Postmodern sex therapy for erectile failure. In R.C. Rosen & S.R. Leiblum (Eds.), *Erectile disorders: Assessment and treatment* (pp. 171–197). New York: The Guilford Press.

LoPiccolo, J., & Friedman, J. M. (1988). Broad-spectrum treatment of low sexual desire. In S. R. Leiblum & R. C. Rosen (Eds.), *Sexual desire disorders* (pp. 107–144). New York: Guilford Press.

LoPiccolo, J., Heiman, J. R., Hogan, D. R., & Roberts, C. W. (1985). Effectiveness of single therapists versus cotherapy teams in sex therapy. *Journal of Consulting and Clinical Psychology, 53,* 287–294.

LoPiccolo, J., & Lobitz, C. (1972). The role of masturbation in the treatment of orgasmic dysfunction. *Archives of Sexual Behavior, 2,* 163–171.

Masters, W. H., & Johnson, V. E. (1966). *Human sexual response.* Boston: Little, Brown.

Masters, W. H., & Johnson, V. E. (1970). *Human sexual inadequacy.* Boston: Little, Brown.

Masters, W. H., & Johnson, V. E. (1979, November). Playboy Interview: Masters and Johnson. *Playboy,* p. 87.

McCarthy, B.W. (1989). Cognitive-behavioral strategies in the treatment of early ejaculation. In S.R. Leiblum & R.C. Rosen (Eds.), *Principles and Practice of sex therapy 2nd edition, Update for the 1990s* (pp. 141–167). New York: The Guilford Press.

McCarthy, B. W. (1990). Treating sexual dysfunction associated with prior sexual trauma. *Journal of Sex and Marital Therapy, 16,* 142–146.

McCarthy, B. W. (1992). Sexual trauma: The pendulum has swung too far. *Journal of Sex Education and Therapy, 18,* 1–10.

McCarthy, J., & McMillan, S. (1990). Patient/Partner satisfaction with penile implant surgery. *Journal of Sex Education and Therapy, 16,* 25–37.

Metz, M. E., & Seifert, M. H., Jr. (1990). Men's expectations of physicians in sexual health concerns. *Journal of Sex and Marital Therapy, 16,* 79–88.

Morales, A., Condra, M.S., Owen, J.E., Fenemore, J., & Surridge, D.M. (1988). Oral and transcutaneous pharmacologic agents in the treatment of impotence, *Urologic Clinics of North America, 15,* 87–93.

Newcomb, M. D., & Bentler, P. M. (1988). Behavioral and psychological assessment of sexual dysfunction: An overview. In R. A. Brown & J. R. Field (Eds.), *Treatment of sexual problems in individual and couples therapy,* (pp. 127–166). New York: PMA.

Nichols, M. (1987). Doing sex therapy with lesbians: Bending a heterosexual paradigm to fit a gay life-style. In Boston Lesbian Psychologies Collective (Ed.), *Lesbian Psychologies: Explorations and Challenges* (pp. 242–260). Chicago: University of Illinois Press.

Nichols, M. (1988). Low sexual desire in lesbian couples. In S. R. Leiblum & R. C. Rosen (Eds.) *Sexual Desire Disorders* (pp. 387–412). New York: Guilford.

Nichols, M. (1989). Sex therapy with lesbians, gay men, and bisexuals. In S.R. Leiblum & R.C. Rosen (Eds.), Principles and practice of sex therapy 2nd edition, Update for the 1990s (pp. 269–297). New York: The Guilford Press.

Norton, G. R., & Jehn, D. (1984). The role of anxiety in sexual dysfunctions: A review. *Archives of Sexual Behavior, 13,* 165–183.

Offit, A. K. (1990). Sexually explicit movies may impede sexual intimacy. *Contemporary Sexuality, 24,* 2–5.

Penile Implants: A Look at Alternatives. (1992, Aug. 24). *U.S. News & World Report,* 67.

Pope, K. S., Keith-Spiegel, P., & Tabachnick, B. G. (1986). Sexual attraction to clients: The human therapist and the (sometimes) inhuman training system. *American Psychologist, 41,* 147–158.

Rajfer, J., Rosciszewski, A., & Mehringer, M. (1988). Prevalence of corporeal venous leakage in impotent men. *Journal of Urology, 140,* 69–71.

Reynolds, B. (1991). Psychological treatment of erectile dysfunction in men without partners: Outcome results and a new direction. *Journal of Sex and Marital Therapy, 17,* 136–146.

Reynolds, B. (1992). An audio tape adjunct in the treatment of sexual dysfunction in men without partners. *Journal of Sex Education and Therapy, 18,* 35–41.

Sager, C. J. (1974). Sexual dysfunctions and marital discord. In H. S. Kaplan (Ed.), *The new sex therapy* (pp. 501–518) New York: Brunner/Mazel.

Sarrel, P. M., & Masters, W. H. (1982). Sexual molestation of men by women. *Archives of Sexual Behavior, 11,* 117–130.

Schiavi, R. C. (1990). Chronic alcoholism and male sexual dysfunction. *Journal of Sex and Marital Therapy, 16,* 23–33.

Schover, L. R., & Jensen, S. B. (1988). *Sexuality and chronic illness: A comprehensive approach.* New York: Guilford Press.

Schover, L. R., & LoPiccolo, J. (1982). Treatment effectiveness for dysfunctions of sexual desire. *Journal of Sex and Marital Therapy, 8,* 179–197.

Segraves, R. T. (1988). Hormones and libido. In S. R. Leiblum & R. C. Rosen (Eds.), *Sexual desire disorders* (pp. 271–312). New York: Guilford Press.

Segraves, R. T., & Segraves, K. B. (1990). Categorical and multi-axial diagnosis of male erectile disorder. *Journal of Sex and Marital Therapy, 16,* 208–213.

Shaw, J. (1990). Play therapy with the sexual workhorse: Successful treatment with twelve cases of inhibited ejaculation. *Journal of Sex and Marital Therapy, 16,* 159–164.

Shikai, X. (1990). Treatment of impotence in traditional Chinese medicine. *Journal of Sex Education and Therapy, 16,* 198–200.

Shortle, B., & Jewelewicz, R. (1986). Psychogenic vaginismus. *Medical Aspects of Human Sexuality, 20,* 82–87.

Sidi, A. A., Cameron, J. S., Duffy, L. M., & Lauge, P. H. (1986). Intracavernous drug-induced erections in the management of male dysfunction: Experience with 100 patients. *Journal of Urology, 135,* 704–706.

Sohn, M., & Sikora, R. (1991). *Ginkgo biloba* extract in the therapy of erectile dysfunction. *Journal of Sex Education and Therapy, 17,* 53–61.

Sonda, L. P., Mazo, R., & Chancellor, M. B. (1990). The role of yohimbine for the treatment of erectile impotence. *Journal of Sex and Marital Therapy, 16,* 15–21.

Strean, H. S. (1983). *Sexual dimension: A guide for the mental health practitioner.* New York: Free Press.

Szasz, T. (1980). *Sex by prescription.* New York: Doubleday.

Talmadge, L. D., & Talmadge, W. C. (1986). Relational sexuality: An understanding of low sexual desire. *Journal of Sex and Marital Therapy, 12,* 3–21.

Tiefer, L. (1991). Historical, scientific, clinical, and feminist criticisms of "The Human Sexual Response Cycle" Model. In J. Bancroft, C. M. Davis, & H. J. Ruppel, Jr. (Eds.). *Annual Review of Sex Research, Vol.* 2 (pp. 1–23). Lake Mills, IA: Graphic.

Turner, L. A., Althof, S. E., Levine, S. B., Bodner, D. R., Kursh, E. D., & Resnick, M. I. (1991). External vacuum devices in the treatment of erectile dysfunction: A one-year study of sexual and psychosocial impact. *Journal of Sex and Marital Therapy, 17,* 81–93.

Villeneuve, R., Corcos, J., & Carmell, M. (1991). Assisted erection follow-up with couples. *Journal of Sex and Marital Therapy, 17,* 94–100.

Warshaw, R. (1988). *I never called it rape: The MS. report on recognizing, fighting, and surviving date and acquaintance rape.* New York: Harper & Row.

Weinstein, E., & Rosen, E. (1988). Introduction: Sexuality counseling. In E. Weinstein & E. Rosen (Eds.), *Sexuality counseling: Issues and implications* (pp. 1–15). Pacific Grove, CA: Brooks/Cole.

Whitehead, A., Mathews, A., & Ramage, M. (1987). The treatment of sexually unresponsive women: A comparative evaluation. *Behavior Research and Therapy, 25,* 195–205.

Wilson, G. L., Flammang, M. R., & Dehle, C. M. (1992). Therapeutic formats in the resolution of relationship dysfunction: An acceptability investigation. *Journal of Sex and Marital Therapy, 18,* 20–33.

Wilson, G. L., & Wilson, L. J. (1991). Treatment acceptability of alternative sex therapies: A comparative analysis. *Journal of Sex and Marital Therapy, 17,* 35–44.

Witherington, R. (1991). Vacuum devices for the impotent. *Journal of Sex and Marital Therapy, 17,* 69–80.

Wyatt, G. E. (1991). Child sexual abuse and its effects on sexual functioning. In J. Bancroft, C. M. Davis, & H. J. Ruppel, Jr. (Eds.). *Annual Review of Sex Research, Vol.* 2 (pp. 249–266). Lake Mills, IA: Graphic.

Zilbergeld, B., & Evans, M. (1980, August). The inadequacy of Masters and Johnson. *Psychology Today,* pp. 29–43.

Health Choices

PART FIVE

The United States is currently incredibly health conscious. Aerobic exercise, low-fat diets, and nonsmoking areas in public places testify to the importance U.S. citizens attach to health. In addition to general health concerns, individuals in our society are also concerned with healthy sexuality. In Part V, we examine four aspects of health as they relate to sexuality.

Health and sexuality is the focus of Chapter 16. While the importance of good physical and mental health is well established, the devastating impact of disease, disability, and mental disorders on sexuality are less well-known. Choices in reference to maintaining good health and adjusting to disease or disability are our concerns in Chapter 16.

Paraphilias and sexuality is the focus of Chapter 17. While most individuals have culturally approved object choices for the expression of their sexuality, some develop sexual attractions to stimuli regarded as not only unusual but illegal. While we discuss what paraphilias are, how they develop, and how they are treated, we emphasize the individual and social choices we make in the expression of, attitude toward, and treatment of paraphilias. In regard to the latter, the question is asked, is castration an acceptable social response to child sexual abuse?

Avoiding HIV infection and other STDs (the subjects of Chapter 18) has become a personal and national health priority. The U.S. surgeon general has delivered a public address on the seriousness of HIV infection, condoms are being distributed without parental consent in some public school systems, and a cultural emphasis on responsible sexual choices has been renewed. Our focus is on the choices in both the prevention and treatment of HIV infection and other STDs.

Part V closes with Chapter 19 on abuses and commercial uses of sexuality. Abuses include rape, child sexual abuse, and sexual harassment; commercial uses involve prostitution and pornography. In regard to each topic, we emphasize both individual and social choices.

CHAPTER SIXTEEN

Health and Sexuality

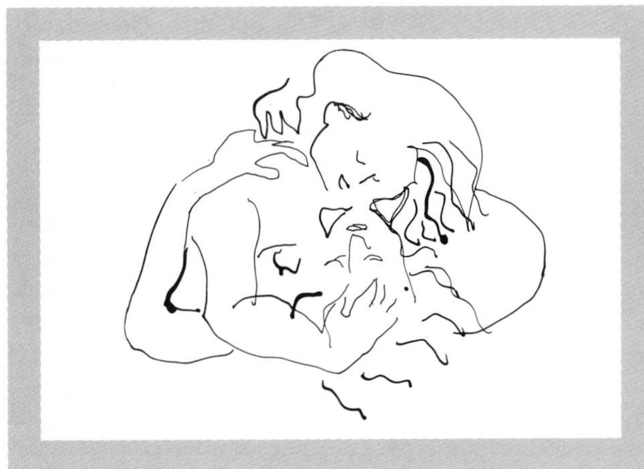

Chapter Outline

Myths about Disease, Disability, and Sexuality

Psychobiological and Psychosocial Factors in Sexual Health

- Psychobiological Factors
- Psychosocial Factors

Neurological Disabilities and Sexuality

- Spinal Cord Injury
- Stroke
- Multiple Sclerosis
- Traumatic Brain Injury
- Cerebral Palsy

Intellectual and Psychological Disturbances and Sexuality

- Intellectual Disability
- Psychological Disturbances

Cancer and Sexuality

- **Self-Assessment:** Torabi-Seffrin Cancer Attitude Scale
- Cancer of the Breast and Reproductive System
- **Research Perspective:** Attitudes Toward Breast and Testicular Self-Exams

Other Diseases and Illnesses and Sexuality

- Arthritis
- Cardiovascular Disease
- Diabetes
- Chronic Obstructive Pulmonary Disease
- Endometriosis

Choices

- Choose to Exercise?
- Choose to Take Cognitive Control of One's Life and Sexuality?

Is It True?*

1. Erectile dysfunction due to diabetes usually disappears when "normal" blood sugars are restored.

2. Diabetes usually has a profound negative effect on the sex drive of the person who has it.

3. Most individuals who have a heart attack should be very careful not to exert themselves in sexual intercourse because they are likely to instigate another heart attack.

4. Individuals whose spinal cords have been severed may still feel pleasure in their genitals by experiencing sensations in their arms and reassigning the feelings to their genitals.

5. Data suggest that intellectually disabled individuals are more sexually active than those closer to normal intelligence.

* 1=F, 2=F, 3=F, 4=T, 5=F

Sexual health is the integration of the somatic, emotional, intellectual and social aspects of sexual beings in ways that are positively enriching and that enhance personality, communication and love.

World Health Organization

Phrases partners say to each other—"I've got a headache," "I'm too tired," and "I'm not feeling well"—all imply a connection between health and choosing to engage in sexual behavior. Ones' physical and psychological health are inextricably tied to one's sexuality.

The World Health Organization estimates that 10% percent of the people in the world (500 million people) are physically or cognitively disabled (Muti & Custo, 1990). One family out of three has a person with a disability. When individuals are born with a disability or develop one later in life, they and/or their families must contend with many concerns—medical care, finances, social stigma, and quality of life. Illness, disease, and disability may negatively interfere with the quality of life in relationships and sexuality. Unfortunately, the sexuality of these individuals has been traditionally ignored by health-care professionals. Recently, however, the sexuality concerns of individuals with disease or disability have received increasing recognition. More and more choices for enhancing sexuality are now available to such individuals.

Sexuality is a health issue.

Theodore Cole

Myths about Disease, Disability, and Sexuality

Individuals with disease or disability are often stereotyped as asexual beings. However, in the words of Cole and Cole (1983), "Desire does not stop when a disability occurs. . . . Physical disability is not synonymous with sexual inadequacy and sexual enjoyment is not exclusively linked to functional movement" (p. 304). Dr. Thomas-Robert H. Ames (1991), who has worked with the blind, deaf, and paralyzed, shared his view about the myth that individuals with disabilities are asexual:

My physical condition was never an insurmountable problem. In order even to get involved with me in the first place, the women had to reject my physical body as being the real me, they had to look past it.

Rick Creech

> I have never met a nonsexual client—but I have known numerous men and women who believed that they had no right to their sexuality and others who thought that their lives were over. When freed of these harmful myths, these people blossomed and another door opened for them. (p. 122)

Someone who challenges the idea that people with physical impairments are asexual is Rick Creech. Rick was born with athetoid cerebral palsy and has no oral speech or muscular control of his arms or legs. However, he refuses the label of "disabled;" he communicates by using an augmented communication device that has speech output, and goes almost anywhere he wants in his wheelchair. While he was a graduate student in Speech, Language, and Auditory Pathology, he published a book, in which he commented on his sexuality.

> I am a sexual person. If that shocks you, well, hold on to your seats, you are in for some more shocks . . . Without going into details, I shall say that I have had four or five romances, been engaged three times, and I married my last girlfriend . . . I met my wife, Yolanda, one morning in my apartment in Richmond. The agency had sent her to get me up, bathe, and feed me breakfast . . . Yolanda says that the only thing she saw when she walked into my room were my blue eyes following her everywhere. Thank God for

> blue eyes! . . . When I met Yolanda, she had a boyfriend, old Georgey, and she thought she was very happy with George. He never knew what happened.
>
> None of the boyfriends of girls I went with could believe that I had taken their girls away from them. Of course, I didn't exactly inform them of my intentions, though I wasn't secretive about it. Really, these men could not believe that I could be any competition, which made things easier for me. And I must admit to taking pleasure in taking these wise guys' girls.
>
> A challenged person can compete with a physically able person. How you treat a lover, whether you build the person up or tear the person down, whether your lover can find love and trust and gentleness in you—these are the areas in which the challenged person need not be limited. It does take a special woman or man to recognize that these qualities are more important in a relationship than physical beauty and strength or the opinions of others. There are special women and men in the world; we have to keep our hearts opened to them and the possibility of love even though it is dangerous to have open hearts in the world today. (Creech, 1992, pp. 30–33. Used by permission.)

In addition to the myth that individuals with disease or disability are asexual, other common myths about health and sexuality include the following (Schover & Jensen, 1988, pp. 74–75):

- Sex saps one's strength and thus is harmful to anyone not in the best of health.
- Too much sex is unhealthy and causes illness.
- Having sex weakens the potency of medical treatments, such as medication or radiation therapy.
- Strokes and heart attacks are very common during sexual intercourse.
- Diabetic men always develop erection problems.
- Cancer is contagious through sexual activity.
- Psychiatric patients are oversexed.

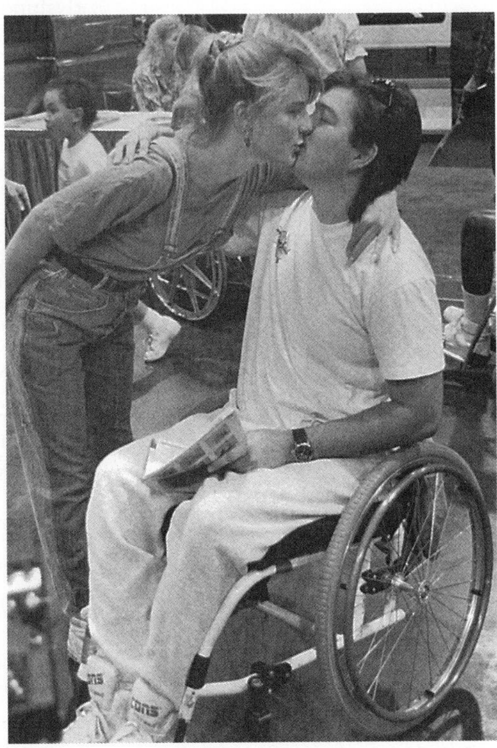

It is a myth that individuals in wheelchairs are asexual.

CONSIDERATION: Sometimes health professionals recommend the use of sexual aids that have been developed specifically for those with traumatic or congenital disability. The Xandria Collection Gold Edition Catalogue (available from the Xandria Collection, Dept. AX0592, P.O. Box 31039, San Francisco, CA 94131) details an array of such aids. Sexual aids for the physically disabled may also be obtained from Rehabtech Inc. (P.O. Box 448, Dobbs Ferry, NY 10522).

Psychobiological and Psychosocial Factors in Sexual Health

The impact of disease and disability on an individual's sexuality involves more than a physical or biological dimension (Schover & Jensen, 1988). Psychobiological and psychosocial factors are also important aspects of sexuality that are affected by disease and disability. Psychobiological factors include pain, fatigue, and depression. Psychosocial factors include self-concept, body image, role function and effects on relationships.

In general, the effects of illness on psychobiological and psychosocial factors are greater with illnesses that are chronic, rather than acute. The degree of chronicity will influence the extent of the disability and the extent of the coping, adaptation, and choices required to adjust to the disability (Nankervis, 1989).

Because of the long-term nature of chronic illness, it may be necessary for chronically ill persons to develop new definitions of sexuality and adopt new forms of sexual expression. For example, Alzheimer's disease in men often involves erectile dysfunction in its later stages (Zeiss, Davies, Wood, & Tinklenberg, 1990). Similarly, epilepsy has been associated with low levels of sexual interest and activity. Both the epileptic individuals and their partners are affected by this chronic condition. In this chapter, we will focus on chronic rather than acute illness.

CONSIDERATION: The effects of illness or disability on sexuality depend not only on the nature of the illness or disability but also on when the illness or disability occurs in the person's life span (congenital condition, childhood, adolescence, or adulthood) (Cole & Cole, 1983).

Psychobiological Factors

Pain "Chronic pain is a health problem of surprisingly large dimensions" (Schover & Jensen, 1988, p. 256). Three common sources of pain are arthritis, migraine headaches, and back problems. The experience of physical pain can have a profound effect on sexuality and sexual functioning. Pain, as well as some medications that are used to control pain, may decrease a person's sexual desire and disrupt the sexual response cycle, resulting in no arousal and no orgasm.

As we shall discuss later in the chapter, there are various approaches to minimizing the degree to which pain interferes with sexual functioning. For example, patients are encouraged to select sexual positions that minimize pain, engage in sexual behavior when their pain is minimal (e.g., in the morning or after taking pain medication), and take warm baths before having sex. Patients with back pain may be encouraged to consider therapeutic message and/or chiropractic medicine as possible solutions.

Fatigue In addition to pain, chronic illness and disease are often accompanied by fatigue. Persons with fatigue feel exhausted, weak, and depleted of energy. Fatigue can cause a marked decrease in sexual interest and functioning.

Fatigue may result from the effects of an illness or disease on the various body organs, as well as from the drugs or other therapy used to treat an illness. Fatigue may also result from the emotional and psychological stress that accompanies chronic illness. Chronically ill persons spend a great deal of emotional energy coming to accept their illness.

CONSIDERATION: The partner of an ill or disabled person may also experience stress as a result of living in an altered relationship. Such stress may affect the sexuality of this partner. For example, researchers (Litz, Zeiss, & Davies, 1990) observed that a male partner of an Alzheimer's patient reported that the stress of coping with his partner increased his erectile dysfunction.

When fatigue interferes with sexual functioning, several interventions may be helpful. First, the fatigued person should engage in sexual behavior at a time when he or she feels most rested and has the most energy. Second, the person may use different positions for sexual activity that are less demanding. Third, counseling may help a person work through the conflicts of accepting the permanent nature of chronic illness in an effort to reduce psychological fatigue.

Depression Persons with chronic illnesses are at a high risk for developing reactive depression (Miller, 1983). For example, about 70% of persons in the advanced stages of multiple sclerosis develop strong reactive depression (Bezkor & Canedo, 1987a).

Reactive depression, the most common form of depression, is brought on by the reaction to the illness and the losses caused by the illness. Depression has been identified as a major cause of inhibited sexual desire and absence of sexual desire (Rosen & Leiblum, 1987). Depression is also associated with "paralysis of the will, low self-evaluation, negative expectations, distortion of body image, dejected mood, reduction in gratification and loss of emotional attachments" (Bezkor & Canedo, 1987b, p. 149).

Chronically ill persons who suffer from depression may benefit from assistance in working through their feelings of grief and loss associated with their illness. Such assistance may be obtained through professional counseling and supportive interpersonal relationships.

Psychosocial Factors

Three psychosocial factors that are affected by disease and disability are self-concept, body image, and role function (Carter, 1990). These factors are frequently overlooked in discussions of how illness affects sexuality.

Self-Concept Self-concept refers to the attitudes, feelings, and perceptions individuals have of themselves. We develop our self-concept through our interactions with others. Persons with chronic illness or disability often develop a negative self-concept, which may interfere with their sexuality. A negative self-concept may create feelings of inadequacy as a sexual partner.

Body Image **Body image** refers to attitudes toward one's own body and perceptions of how one looks to others. Persons with disabilities and/or disease may view themselves as physically flawed and sexually unattractive. Other aspects of illness and disability that may contribute to a negative body image include loss of control over bodily functions (e.g., urination) and the use of cold, hard, metallic appliances. In addition, disability may result in loss of mobility, lack of exercise, and consequent weight gain.

Given the cultural emphasis on the physical appearance of women, women with disease or disability may be particularly prone to developing a negative body image. One man described his wife's reaction to having an artificial arm:

> My wife's first response to the accident was not to express concern about her ability to pick up pencils, but to worry if she would still be able to go on a beach in a bikini. Three weeks after the accident, appearance and disguise are her main concerns. (Thomas, 1982, p. 45)

Role Function Some illnesses and disabilities result in role changes for the individual. Such changes may occur in a variety of social roles, including that of lover or spouse, parent, wage earner, and homemaker. For example, a lover or spouse may be abandoned by his or her partner following an illness or disabling injury. Or, the role of an ill or disabled lover or spouse may change in that he or she becomes partially or totally dependent on the care of the partner. Parents who become ill or disabled may no longer be able to fulfill the role of providing care to their offspring. Indeed, some illnesses and disabilities may prohibit individuals from having children, thereby barring them from the role of parent altogether. Such parental role restrictions may affect women more than men, as women are traditionally socialized to value the role of parent more than men are. Lastly, disease and disability may interfere with one's occupational role and with one's ability to generate income. One woman who had developed multiple sclerosis in her 20s said:

> You feel yourself insecure as a woman, as well as you're insecure as a mother. You feel the dependence of it all, for somebody who is used to independence. I'd started earning and being a big shot. Then suddenly, never mind being a mother and a big shot, you're physically dependent as well. It takes a lot to survive that. (Quoted in Lonsdale, 1990, p. 67)

In some cases, a disabling disease or injury may have positive effects on a person's role function. In a 1985 study of women who had spinal cord injury, Bonwich found that many of these women experienced increased self-esteem as a result of having mastered new roles. In addition, many of these women felt that their disability liberated them from the constraints of traditional feminine gender role stereotypes (reported in Lonsdale, 1990).

Neurological Disabilities

Neurological disabilities affect the central nervous system—the "switchboard" of the sexual system. Examples of such disabilities include spinal cord injury, stroke, and multiple sclerosis. They may directly affect the brain, as in traumatic brain injury and cerebral palsy.

Spinal Cord Injury

People are sexual beings whether they have spinal cord injuries or are unimpaired.

Meredith Drench

About 8,000 individuals in the United States suffer spinal cord injuries each year. The majority are between the ages of 15 and 24, and 82% of the injured are male (Page et al., 1987).

Spinal cord injuries can have profound effects on sexual identity, self-image, role function, and interpersonal relationships (Drench, 1992). The effect of a spinal cord injury on a person's sex life depends on the extent and location of the injury and the etiology or cause of the injury (e.g., trauma, infection, or secondary to multiple sclerosis). Depending on these factors, the spinal cord-injured person may regain varying degrees of his or her functioning abilities within approximately two years of the injury. In general, the lower on the spinal cord the injury occurs, the greater the damage to sexual functioning. However, whether the cord was severed completely or partially and whether the person has any sensation or movement are also relevant variables.

In cases of traumatic injury, if the spinal cord is completely severed, the person will not have genital sensation. But if portions of the spinal cord remain intact, sexual sensation—and functioning—can return. In one study of spinal cord-injured men (Page et al., 1987), 95% of the respondents reported that they had some sexual contacts since their injury.

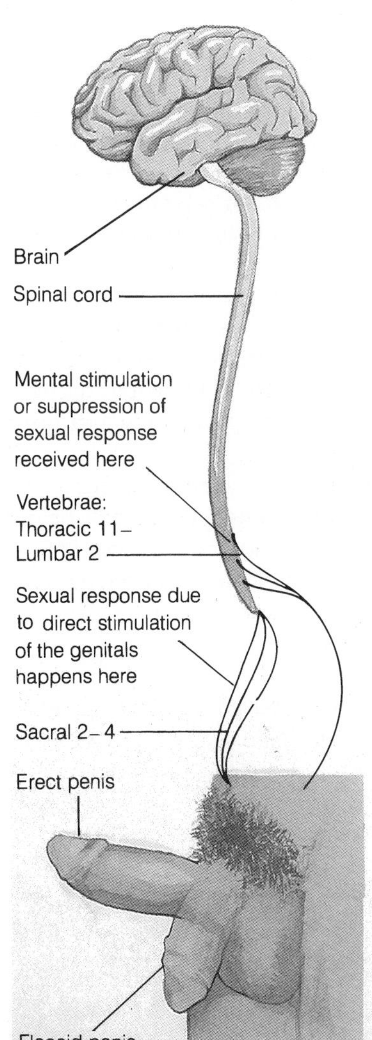

FIGURE 16.1 The Spinal Cord and Sexual Response
The spinal cord is intimately involved in sexual response. Different portions of the spine transmit sensory and mental stimulation.

To what extent may the spinal cord-injured person regain sexual functioning? Are erection, intercourse, orgasm, and ejaculation possible? If only the upper part of the spinal cord has been partially severed, the man may have an erection with sufficient direct stimulation. Schover and Jensen (1988) reported that about 80% of men with cervical or thoracic spine injury above T12 (below the neck to midback) can obtain an erection from tactile stimulation to the penis, but the tumescence is often fleeting because psychic arousal from the brain cannot provide continuing stimulation (p. 93) (see Figure 16.1).

Intercourse may take place with the partner sitting down on the erect penis of the spinal cord-injured man. This is usually preceded by a lot of direct stimulation to ensure an erect penis. But intercourse is possible without an erect penis. Some couples use the "stuffing technique," in which the partners push the soft penis into the woman's vagina. The woman with strong vaginal muscles can contract them around the penis to hold it inside her. An inflatable penile prosthesis implant (see Chapter 15, Sexual Dysfunctions and Sex Therapy) is an alternative for some spinal cord-injured men.

Orgasm is possible in some spinal cord-injury cases. In the Page et al. (1987) study, 61% of the respondents reported that they had had an orgasm since the injury.

While orgasm may occur from direct stimulation of the genitals, it may also occur as a consequence of the person focusing on physical sensations that can be felt in other areas of the body, such as from stroking the arm, and mentally reassigning these sensations to the genitals. The man may also ejaculate, but the aftereffects of orgasm and ejaculation are unpredictable. Although some men report pleasure, sexual excitation, and warm sensations, others report muscular spasticity or a headache.

We have been discussing spinal cord injuries as they affect men. The effects on women are similar in that complete severence of the spinal cord results in no feeling in the genital area. Where the injury is less complete, sensations at various levels are experienced, including orgasm. The woman also may be able to transfer feelings from body parts not affected by the injury.

CONSIDERATION: Spinal cord-injured people will rarely be able to function as they did before their injury. But they may still experience a satisfactory sex life. Indeed, some say their sex lives improve after the injury since they were able to tune in to the sensual aspects of the rest of their bodies. Still other spinal cord-injured people say that they derive immense enjoyment from satisfying their partners by manual, oral, or mechanical (electric vibrator) stimulation and that this enjoyment is a major source of their own sexual satisfaction. All of the spinal cord-injured respondents in the Page et al. (1987) study reported that they were willing to provide oral-genital stimulation of their partner's genitals.

Some men and women who are spinal cord-injured become concerned about their ability to have children. However,

> with new techniques such as electro-ejaculation and electrovibration [mechanical procedures that assist ejaculation] the tide is turning in favor of fatherhood. Women generally have normal vaginal deliveries. Gynecologists must be aware of the complications that are unique to this population . . . a female with a spinal cord injury at or above T10 may not realize when she is going into labor, therefore close monitoring is generally recommended. (Zasler, 1991, p. 28)

Stroke

Strokes are cerebral malfunctions that are also referred to as cerebrovascular accidents. In most cases, a stroke results in some form of paralysis to certain parts of the body. In regard to sexuality, stroke victims report erectile dysfunction, decreased sexual interest, fatigue, bowel and/or bladder incontinence, and decreased frequency of vaginal intercourse.

The effects of a stroke on sexuality partly depend on the location of the cerebral malfunction (i.e., right versus left hemisphere of the brain). In a study of male right-handed stroke patients, half reported reduced sexual interest and 86% reported difficulty getting and maintaining an erection. Right hemispheric stroke patients had significantly higher reduction in sexual interest, compared to left hemispheric stroke patients (Agarwal & Jain, 1989).

Sexual concerns in stroke victims are not specific to the changes in sexual functioning. A study by Burgener and Logan (1989) revealed that sexuality after a stroke is affected by changes in role function due to increased dependency of the afflicted partner. In addition, stroke victims often become depressed over their condition and fear another stroke if they have intercourse. These psychological concerns may be more debilitating than any organic deficit caused by the stroke (Zasler, 1991).

Multiple Sclerosis

Multiple sclerosis (MS) is a progressive disease that attacks the central nervous system. About 60 in 100,000 residents of the United States have been diagnosed as having MS. It usually occurs between the ages of 20 and 40, but cases of individuals over 50 have been documented.

Sexual dysfunction is not uncommon in individuals with MS. Bezkor and Canedo (1987a) reported that 56% of the women and 75% of the men with MS report experiencing sexual dysfunctions. In a more recent study of 65 patients with MS, 55% reported changes in their sexual functioning after the onset of the disease (Stenager, Stenager, & Jensen, 1990). The patients in this study ranged in age from 25 to 55 and had the disease for an average of 8.5 years. All of the patients had sexual partners both before and after the diagnosis of MS.

How individuals (such as Richard Pryor, shown here with family members) choose to view the limitations of a disease such as MS is one of the most important aspects of how the disease affects their sexuality.

> It was registered whether the patient was as sexually active as before the onset of the disease, or if the patient was less active than before or perhaps inactive. If the patient was less active, the reason for this was discussed. Men would complain of erectile dysfunction, premature ejaculation, changed sensation in the penis, reduced sexual desire and orgasmic dysfunction. The females complained of changed sensation in the genital region, reduced vaginal lubrication, and reduced sexual desire. Both sexes also complained of sexual problems due to paresis (partial paralysis), spasticity, and incontinence. (p. 264)

In spite of the problems reported by both women and men in the Stenager et al. (1990) study, only a few regarded the problems as serious. The authors conjectured that of the numerous problems associated with MS (cognitive impairment, limb spasticity, the threat of infertility), loss of sexual function may seem relatively insignificant.

In addition, the MS subjects rarely complained about their partner's reaction to their changed sexuality. Hence, it appears that it is not the presence of a physical disability but the perception of it that is significant. How individuals choose to view their own physical condition or that of their partner may be the most important aspect to consider in how diseases affect sexuality.

Traumatic Brain Injury

Traumatic brain injuries may result from various accidents, including being involved in a car or motorcycle accident, falling from a ladder, or falling down steps. As a result of traumatic head injury, both psychological and biological processes are altered that affect sexual functioning. In a sample of 21 male patients who had experienced traumatic brain injury, negative changes in their sexual behavior involved sex drive, erectile function, and frequency of intercourse. Psychological symptoms included depression, reduced self-esteem, perceived decline in personal sex appeal, and decreased self-confidence (Kreutzer and Zasler, 1989; Zasler, 1991).

Deviant behavior has also been observed following head injury. In one study, deviant behavior, as defined by the inappropriate touching of the opposite sex and initiation of exhibitionism, was observed in brain-injured patients (Zencius, Wesolowski, Burke, & Hough, 1990).

Cerebral Palsy

Cerebral palsy refers to a disability resulting from damage to the motor centers of the developing brain. Brain injury can result from illness in the mother during pregnancy (e.g., German measles) or from hypoxia (lack of oxygen) during birth, which causes brain cells to die. In the young child, infections and head injuries may also cause cerebral palsy.

The symptoms of cerebral palsy vary according to the area and degree of brain injury but generally include muscular incoordination and speech disturbances. Mental retardation, learning disability, and problems with sight and hearing may also occur. Cerebral palsy affects approximately 5% of U.S. babies.

Adolescents with cerebral palsy have difficulty establishing a positive body image, as they often face social isolation or rejection by their peers. Adults with cerebral palsy often require counseling and equipment to aid in masturbation, intercourse, and conception (Shea, 1990).

Exhibit 16.1 describes how a man with severe cerebral palsy benefited from surrogate partner sex therapy.

EXHIBIT 16.1 Surrogate Partner Therapy for a Person with Severe Cerebral Palsy

Robert Joseph (1991) is a human sexuality specialist who detailed his work with a 25-year-old man, Michael, with severe cerebral palsy who had dysarthric speech and whose arms and legs were in constant motion. Michael's verbal IQ score was 78 on the Wechsler Adult Intelligence Scale, and he was regarded as functioning within the borderline intelligence range.

Michael was frustrated because he had never had a sexual partner. His opportunities to meet people were limited because he could not drive himself to social functions. He had been rejected by those who had met him, which negatively affected his self-confidence, happiness, and self-esteem.

After months of trying to relieve his sexual frustration through masturbation, Michael's unhappiness worsened. His friends had thought of fixing him up with a prostitute, but this plan was abandoned in favor of a surrogate partner who had a special interest in working with persons with disabilities. The surrogate partner had a master's degree in rehabilitative counseling and had done a one-year intensive internship in surrogacy training in California. Michael's therapist Robert Joseph described Michael's experience with Amy, his surrogate partner:

> [Michael and Amy] started talking about each other's day. After a few minutes of friendly conversation Amy asked about his sexual experience. Michael told her that he masturbates often but had never been with another person. Amy asked if he was comfortable enough to get undressed. She then wheeled him into the bedroom and helped him on the bed. She slowly undressed him and then herself. Amy caressed his chest and told him how sexy and attractive his body was. They fondled each other and licked each other's skin. Amy showed Michael how to touch her skin and helped guide his hands. They engaged in foreplay for over thirty minutes. When Michael was thoroughly aroused, Amy from the on-top position inserted his penis into her vagina. They rocked slowly back and forth together. Michael had an orgasm. He told me his movement had never been so calm. . . . Michael was proud and expressed how he felt like an adult for the first time in his life. . . . Michael's life was forever changed. (Joseph, 1991, p. 158)

After this occasion, Michael became intent on developing a sexual relationship with someone that he cared about.

Source: Joseph, R. (1991). A case analysis in human sexuality: Counseling to a man with severe cerebral palsy. *Sexuality and Disability, 9,* 149–159. Used by permission.

Intellectual and Psychological Disturbances and Sexuality

Cognitive and psychological functioning influence one's sexual experiences and decision-making. In this section we examine intellectual disability and sexual functioning, emphasizing the need for acknowledging the sexual feelings of intellectually disabled people and becoming sensitive to issues especially relevant to their sexual behavior. We also review how sexuality is affected in several categories of psychological disturbances, as well as how a history of sexual abuse may significantly increase one's vulnerability to specific psychological diagnoses.

Intellectual Disability

Intellectual disability, commonly referred to as mental retardation, refers to "significantly subaverage general intellectual functioning existing concurrently with deficits in adaptive behavior, and manifested during the developmental period" (Grossman, 1983, p. 11). Approximately 3% of the U.S. population is intellectually disabled (Shea, 1990). In general, intellectual disability may result in limitations in the following areas: self-care, receptive and expressive language, learning, mobility, self-direction, capacity for independent living, and economic self-sufficiency. The extent of these limitations vary according to the severity of the retardation (mild, moderate, or severe or profound).

Individuals with intellectual disability often have limited knowledge about sexuality. They may be ignorant about normal sexual development and their own sexual capabilities either because they have not been taught or because they are limited in their comprehension of such information.

A young teenager, described as a slow learner, began menstruating. She had not been taught about menstruation as a normal growth change, and interpreting it as some form of punishment, she buried her soiled underwear (Blum, 1983).

> If this young woman had had an informed, approachable friend or relative she could have consulted, she could have enjoyed the feelings associated with the knowledge of becoming a woman, an adult like other people she looked up to, and having more in common with the rest of the human race. (p. 289)

Blum suggested that teaching methods for slow learners are essentially the same as for other groups, with more repetition, consistent use of simple words, and periodic review. For teaching guidelines to distinguish appropriate sexual behavior, she recommended teaching a simple rule—"private parts of the body are for private places; public parts of the body are for public places" (p. 294).

Intellectually disabled individuals may spend some time living in institutions, such as medical hospitals, state facilities for the mentally retarded, residential schools, or group homes. In such settings are multiple caregivers who may have different and conflicting views of sexuality. For example, some caregivers may ignore masturbation, some may punish it, and some may encourage it as a healthy outlet for sexual feelings (Shea, 1990). This makes it very difficult for institutionalized individuals to develop a clear understanding of social norms and of their own needs for sexual expression. Another problem in institutional settings, especially those with public restrooms and dormitories, may be finding a private place for appropriate touching (Blum, 1983).

Another concern regarding individuals with intellectual disabilities is their vulnerability to being sexually abused and exploited. From 80% to 95% of persons with intellectual disabilities are victims of sexual abuse sometime in their lives—a much higher incidence than in the general population—with over 90% of the perpetrators in caregiving roles (Kempton & Kahn, 1991). Sex by exploiting individuals with those who are intellectually disabled is considered to be sexual abuse because the cognitively disabled often do not meet the legal criteria for consent: knowledge of what they are doing, intelligence to assess the risks and benefits, and voluntariness of choice (Stavis, 1991). Blum (1983) described educational techniques and curricula designed to reduce victimization risk.

The sexuality of individuals with intellectual disabilities is a complex issue involving individual, medical, and societal values and ethics. (Abramson, Parker, & Weisberg, 1988). One social dilemma surrounding the sexuality of the intellectually disabled involves the question of whether they should be allowed to procreate or should be sterilized.

In general, while our society has accorded the physically disabled the right to procreate, procreation for the intellectually disabled has, in some cases, been strictly forbidden (Giami, 1987). One of the consequences of sterilizing intellectually disabled individuals is that it "leads to further depression of their self-image, and makes them feel less worthy of deriving any pleasure from sexual expression" (Andron & Ventura, 1987, pp. 33–34).

CONSIDERATION: One intellectually disabled person spoke to a group of professionals on the issue of whether she and others similarly intellectually disabled should be allowed to have children:

> Perhaps some of us would like to have a baby, but we should wait until we can give it the things it must have—a home, clothes, food—and we are able to teach it what it should know and take care of it when it is sick. But we don't want professionals to tell us that we can't have a baby because we are retarded, because we don't think they do such a good job either! (Kempton & Kahn, 1991, p. 111)

Another social controversy concerns the use of antilibidinal drugs to control the sexual behaviors of the intellectually disabled. The use of antilibidinal drugs is based on the perceived threat to society. In some cases, sexual behavior of the mentally retarded violates social norms and brings them into contact with the law. Such inappropriate sexual behavior includes touching others without their consent, public masturbation, and exhibitionism. In most cases, these behaviors can be managed by counseling and using behavior modification techniques. However,there are a small number of men with mental retardation and aberrant sexual behaviors who benefit from using an antilibidinal drug. (Clarke, 1989).

Although data are limited, what are available suggest that intellectually disabled people are less sexually active than those closer to normal intelligence, with higher degrees of impairment related to lower sexual activity (Bancroft, 1989). But many people, including parents and professionals, assume that intellectually disabled people lack sexual control, and expect sexual offenses from men and promiscuity in women. Bancroft observed,

> To some extent these assumptions become self-fulfilling prophecies because with segregating the mentally handicapped, separating the sexes and giving them no opportunity to learn appropriate sexual expression, they are more likely to manifest their sexuality inappropriately . . . (p. 618)

Balanced sexuality programs that address more than the genitals and sexual acts, and focus on "the privileges and responsibilities of adulthood," may be accepted by parents and communities (Blum, 1983, p. 291).

Psychological Disturbances

The influence of psychological disturbances on sexuality is complex and interactive. For example, depression can affect one's interest in sexual activity and one's capacity to engage in sexual activity and enjoy sexual pleasure (Lustman & Clouse, 1990). However, the lack of sexual activity can create depression, and a reciprocal cycle is set in motion. Woods (1981) observed that "there is no consistent relationship between any specific psychiatric illness and disordered sexuality" (p. 200). Hence, intervention requires a detailed knowledge of the patient's background (development of sexual attitudes and values) and a physical examination to rule out organic pathology. Probably the greatest attention to psychological disturbances affecting sexuality has focused on affective disorders, such as unipolar and bipolor depressive disorders.

Depression often effects sexual desire. Compared to people not diagnosed as depressed, depressed people more often report loss of sexual interest (Mathew & Weinman, 1982). One study found that a person's first depressive episode almost always preceded or occured simultaneously with loss of desire. In their study of men and women with low sexual desire, Schreiner-Engel and Schiavi (1986) found that among those who were not depressed when assessment was done, there was significant history of depression.

Bipolar disorder, also known as manic-depression, is characterized by alternating periods of severe depression and extreme emotional excitement and activity. During manic periods, some individuals may direct their excessive excitement and activity into increased and often indiscriminate sexual activity. During the manic phase, the individual may masturbate in public, initiate extramarital affairs, and act seductively. In a small percentage of individuals with bipolar illness, decreased sexual interest may occur.

Bancroft (1989) offered several hypotheses to explain the connection between sexual interest and depression. In general, people are more likely to be sexually active when they feel well. It is not surprising that negative cognitions and low self-esteem would be related to a low sense of sexual worth. In addition, there are a number of biochemical theories; a change in cerebral amine function may connect sexuality with mood. Side-effects of drug treatment for depression may decrease desire. Depression may also be related to relationship problems; disturbances in the sexual aspect of the relationship may be a cause or an effect of the relationship discord.

Investigators have noted that women are nearly twice as likely as men to experience unipolar depression (depressed affect and mood). Cutler and Nolen-Hoeksema (1991) investigated the hypothesis that this sex difference may be influenced by the high rate of sexual abuse girls experience in childhood. Not only are girls and women at greater risk of being sexually victimized, girls and boys may react differently to sexual abuse. Severity and duration of abuse is a factor: girls seem to experience more serious types of abuse than boys. While Cutler and Nolen-Hoeksema acknowledged that child sexual abuse is not the only contributor to the sex differences in depression, they suggested that it is a very significant factor.

Other investigators have studied the relationship between abuse history and diagnosis of mental disorders. Carmen, Rieker, and Mills (1984) examined the records of 188 men and women who were hospitalized in psychiatric treatment settings. Half of the patients had affective disorders, and the other half had diagnoses which included psychoses, personality disorders, adjustment reactions, and substance abuse. Eighty of the 188 patients (43%) had documented histories of physical or sexual abuse, or both. Female patients were more likely to have been abused, mostly by family members. After retrospectively studying 40 patients with multiple personality disorder, Putnam discovered that 80% had experienced severe abuse during childhood (Abused Child, 1982).

A connection between sexual assault history and certain types of mental health problems has also been found in adults who were not selected on the basis of seeking psychotherapy or psychiatric hospitalization. Burnam et al. (1988) analyzed interview data from a study of over 3,000 randomly selected adults in the two Los Angeles communities. They compared lifetime diagnoses of nine major mental disorders and the respondent's reports of whether they had ever been sexually assaulted.

> Sexual assault predicted later onset of major depressive episodes, substance use disorders (alcohol and drug abuse or dependence), and anxiety disorders (phobia, panic disorder, and obsessive-compulsive disorder) but was not related to later onset of mania, schizophrenic disorders or antisocial personality. (p. 843)

While further research is needed to learn more about the cause of the relationship, it is clear that experiencing sexual assault does increase one's risk of experiencing emotional and psychological problems. As Carmen et al. (1984) said, "From our perspective, a major focus of treatment must be to help victims become survivors" (p. 383).

Another psychological disturbance that affects sexuality is schizophrenia. This psychotic disorder affects behavior and thought processes so severely that it would be surprising if sexual behavior were not affected (Bancroft, 1989). The following examples of sexual effects are from Bancroft's review. The development of schizophrenia, with its onset most likely in young adulthood, is bound to influence social and relationship development. Sexual desire does not seem to be influenced as much by schizophrenia as by other psychological diagnoses, but sexual dysfunctions such as anorgasmia were noted in a study of schizophrenic women. The hallucinations and delusions of schizophrenics often have sexual content, including hallucinations involving genitalia, delusions of genital change, and of sex change. Since sexual hallucinations are often gustatory or olfactory in content, a temporal lobe disorder may be involved (Connolly & Gittelson, 1971). Finally, phenothiazine (antipsychotic drug) treatment may inhibit sexual interest and functioning (Smith & Talbert, 1986).

Cancer and Sexuality

NATIONAL DATA: Of every five deaths in the U.S. one is from cancer (American Cancer Society, 1992).

Until recently, survival rates for patients with cancer were so low that cancer was not thought of as a chronic illness (Schover & Jensen, 1988, p. 216). The American Cancer Society (1992) now predicts that 1 in 3 of Americans will have cancer in their lifetimes. The five-year survival rate for all cancers is 51%. The following Self-Assessment provides a way to evaluate your attitude toward cancer.

Cancer of the Breast and Reproductive System

Cancer of the breast and the reproductive system often has a direct influence on the sexuality of the individuals and couples involved.

Breast Cancer Cancer of the breast is the most common form of cancer in women, accounting for over 30% of all female cancers. One of every 9 U.S. women will develop breast cancer during her lifetime (American Cancer Society, 1992). For women 40 to 44 years of age, breast cancer is the most common cause of death. Only about 1% of breast cancers occur in men (Katchadourian, 1990).

The most important factor that determines a woman's chance of surviving breast cancer is early detection. Of the numerous medical screening technologies for detecting breast cancer, mammography is preferred by many physicians (Travis, 1988, p. 239). A **mammography** involves taking an X ray of the breast to look for growths that may be cancerous. Many physicians recommend that women between the ages of 35 and 39 get a mammogram as a baseline for future comparisons. Women ages 40 to 49 with no other signs of breast cancer should have a mammogram every one to two years; women ages 50 and above should have one each year (American Cancer Society, 1992).

Health professionals may not agree on the age at which women should have regular mammograms (Travis, 1988). However, they do agree that all women should conduct regular breast self-examination (BSE) in order to detect any early signs of cancer (see Choices section in Chapter 6).

CONSIDERATION: Some women may not do BSE because they either do not know how or they are afraid that they will discover cancer. However, 80% of breast tumors are benign (Travis, 1988).

For the woman with breast cancer, a number of treatments are available. Kaplan (1992) noted:

NATIONAL DATA: While there is a 51% five-year average survival rate for all types of cancers, the five–year survival rates for breast, cervical, uterine, prostate, and testicular cancers are 77%, 66%, 83%, 74%, and 93%, respectively (American Cancer Society, 1992).

> The treatments for operable cancer of the breast include mastectomy or lumpectomy along with radiation and axillary lymph node resection. In addition to the surgical removal of a tumor, there is now a growing trend for oncologists to recommend adjuvant therapy in the form of postsurgical courses of radiation, chemotherapy and/or long-term administration of tamoxifen (Norvadex), a drug with anti-estrogen effects. (p. 4)

Mastectomy, removal of breast(s), may be **radical** (the whole breast along with underlying muscle and lymph nodes), **modified radical** (breast and lymph nodes but not muscles are removed), or **partial** (also referred to as lumpectomy; only the cancerous lump is removed). The most difficult aspect of such surgery is the effect on the woman's self-esteem and body image and the relationship with her partner. In regard to her concern that her partner will be put off by her breastless body, Kaplan (1992) observed:

> Happily, such concerns are largely unfounded. The great majority of husbands and lovers, provided of course that they were attracted to their partners prior to surgery, and that she continues to be sexually responsive, do not lose sexual interest nor do they develop potency problems. In most cases, men 'tune out' their partner's missing breast(s), and focus instead on the pleasurable erotic stimulation of love making. However, some women develop a pattern of sexual avoidance because they anticipate rejection, and this can become destructive to themselves and to their relationships. (p. 5)

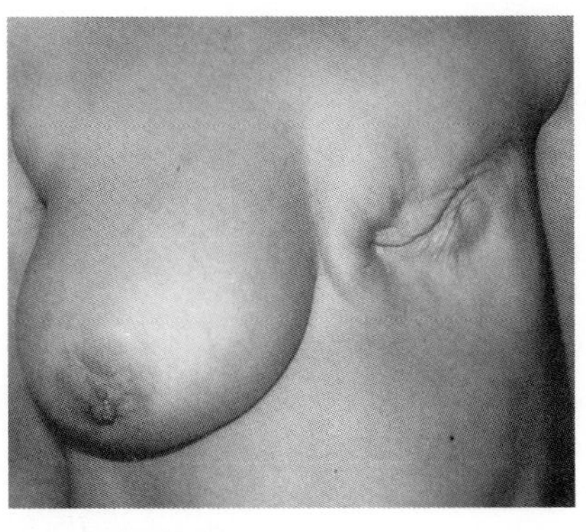

Radical mastectomy

Uterine Cancer. There are two major types of uterine cancer—cancer of the cervix and cancer of the endometrium (lining of the uterus). Cervical cancer is the second most common type of cancer in women. Although vaginal discharge, pain, and bleeding are the typical symptoms, the cancerous cells can be present for five to 10 years before being detected. Factors associated with increased risk for developing

Self Assessment

Torabi-Seffrin Cancer Attitude Scale

This questionnaire has been developed to measure people's attitudes toward cancer prevention. Please read each statement carefully. Record your immediate reaction to the statement by marking how well you agree or disagree with the idea according to the following scale:

SA = Strongly agree
A = Agree
U = Undecided
D = Disagree
SD = Strongly disagree

	SA	A	U	D	SD
1. I would enjoy talking with a cancer patient.	______	______	______	______	______
2. I feel sorry for cancer patients.	______	______	______	______	______
3. I hate to smoke because of its cancer causing effects.	______	______	______	______	______
4. If one feels healthy, [he or she] does not need a physical checkup.	______	______	______	______	______
5. I enjoy smoking regardless of the consequences.	______	______	______	______	______
6. The idea of breast examination by a physician is embarrassing.	______	______	______	______	______
7. It is enjoyable having sexual intercourse with multiple partners.	______	______	______	______	______
8. Colorectal cancer is an embarrassing disease.	______	______	______	______	______
9. I feel sorry for those people who have skin cancer.	______	______	______	______	______
10. Young people do not have to be worried about prostate cancer.	______	______	______	______	______
11. Cancer is a mysterious disease.	______	______	______	______	______
12. Cancer is the worst disease known to mankind.	______	______	______	______	______
13. I think cancer is not a preventable disease.	______	______	______	______	______
14. Breast self-examination is a waste of time.	______	______	______	______	______
15. Because of the carcinogenic (cancer-causing) effect of tobacco, its public use should be prohibited by law.	______	______	______	______	______
16. Breast cancer is exclusively a woman's problem.	______	______	______	______	______
17. I believe that uterine cancer is a rare type of cancer.	______	______	______	______	______
18. It is difficult for me to talk about colorectal cancer.	______	______	______	______	______
19. I believe that skin cancer is a deadly form of cancer.	______	______	______	______	______
20. The rectal exam is not an acceptable technique for checking the prostate gland.	______	______	______	______	______
21. I would rather not hear about cancer.	______	______	______	______	______
22. In order to avoid cancer, I would do almost anything to protect myself.	______	______	______	______	______
23. I prefer to work in a healthy environment, even if it means taking a lower salary.	______	______	______	______	______

Continued

Self-Assessment—*Continued*

24. I intend to see my physician anytime I observe any unusual changes or when suspicious symptoms appear. ____ ____ ____ ____ ____
25. I intend to stay away from smoking cigarettes for the rest of my life. ____ ____ ____ ____ ____
26. I intend to do breast self-examination once a month. ____ ____ ____ ____ ____
27. I would encourage my friends to have a regular Pap test. ____ ____ ____ ____ ____
28. For purposes of preventing colorectal cancer, I intend to encourage my family to have a diet high in fiber. ____ ____ ____ ____ ____
29. I intend to do whatever I can to protect myself against skin cancer. ____ ____ ____ ____ ____
30. I intend to encourage my close friends to be concerned about their prostate gland. ____ ____ ____ ____ ____

Scoring The Torabi-Seffrin Cancer Attitude Scale (TSCAS) includes three components: feelings, beliefs, and intention to act. The "feeling" component consists of items 1 through 10; "belief" component items are 11 through 20; and "intention to act" component items are 21 through 30.

To obtain a subscale score or a total scale score, sum the assigned numerical values for the alternatives you chose. Score the response for items 2, 4 through 14, and 16 through 21 using these values: Strongly agree = 1; Agree = 2; Undecided = 3; Disagree = 4; Strongly disagree = 5. To score all other items, reverse the order of values assigned to the alternatives, that is, 5, 4, 3, 2, 1, for Strongly agree to Strongly disagree. Higher scores indicate a more positive attitude toward cancer and cancer prevention.

Reliability and Validity The TSCAS was administered to 1,040 college undergraduates at five large universities in the United States. Reliability coefficients, as measured by Cronbach Alpha, for the total scale and subscales ranged from 0.94 to 0.78. Of the 30 items, at least 27 discriminated between healthy and risk taker groups. Table 1 summarizes the mean total scale and the subscale scores of healthy and risk taker student groups. You may wish to compare your scores to these means and see which group your scores most resemble.

Reference

Torabi, M. R., & Seffrin, J. R. (1986). A three component cancer attitude scale. *Journal of School Health, 56.* (5), 170–174. Used by permission.

TABLE 1 Difference in Mean Total Scale and the Three Subscales Scores of the Healthy and Risk Taker Groups

Scale and Subscales	Group	# of Cases	Mean	Standard Deviation	t-value	Significant level
Total	Healthy	127	104.53	10.25	7.27	.001
	Risk Taker	33	90.06	9.94		
Feeling	Healthy	127	36.29	5.01	6.87	.001
	Risk Taker	33	30.94	3.67		
Belief	Healthy	127	29.64	.30	2.23	.027
	Risk Taker	33	28.15	.60		
Intention to Act	Healthy	127	38.60	6.20	6.28	.001
	Risk Taker	33	30.97	6.27		

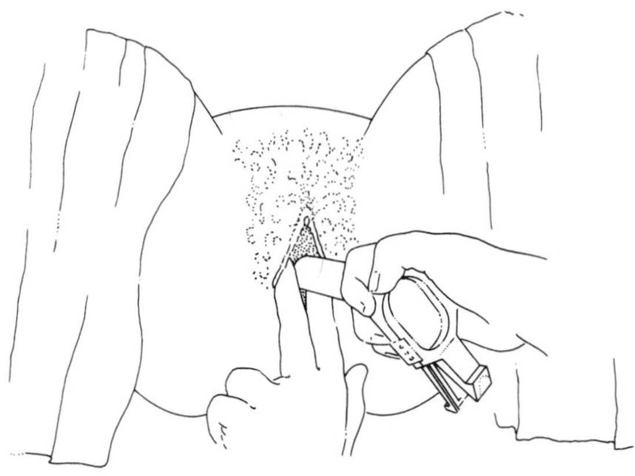

Speculum Examination

Preparation
Usually with the aid of the nurse, your body is draped with a sheet and your feet are placed in stirrups. After routinely examining the breasts, abdomen and groin, your physician inspects the outer genitals. Because good light is important, a lamp may be used during this inspection. Generally, the examiners will place an arm or elbow on your leg or thigh before touching the outer genitals. This is to avoid startling you—in which case your genital muscles might involuntarily contract and interfere with the examination.

Inserting the Speculum
A speculum is an instrument which enlarges the vaginal opening and spreads the vaginal walls so that your physician can "see what is going on" inside the vagina. Your doctor will carefully insert the speculum into the vaginal entrance with one hand, while using the other hand to gently spread the labia. The type or size of the speculum depends on whether the patient is a virgin, has had children or is post-menopausal. To avoid discomfort, the speculum is inserted slowly and at an angle. But if you feel any distress—which is extremely rare—your doctor will adjust the speculum to make you feel more comfortable.

FIGURE 16.2 **Pelvic Examination and Pap Test**

Source: "Reprinted Through the Courtesy of Lederle Laboratories Division, American Cyanamid Company. SERVICE TO LIFE is a Registered Trademark of American Cyanamid Company."

cervical cancer include young age at time of initial sexual intercourse, having multiple sexual partners, cigarette smoking, and low socioeconomic status (American Cancer Society, 1992). Some types of human papilloma virus, a sexually transmitted virus that causes genital warts (see Chapter 18), has also been associated with cervical cancer (Katchadourian, 1990, p. 109).

Endometrial cancer is less common than cervical cancer. It primarily affects women over 50. Risk factors include history of infertility, failure to ovulate, prolonged estrogen therapy, and obesity (American Cancer Society, 1992).

About 10% of all hysterectomies are performed as treatment for cervical or endometrial cancer (Travis, 1988, p. 171). The best detection method for cervical and endometrial cancer is the Pap smear test. Women 20 years of age and older should have a Pap smear test done annually (see Figure 16.2). The Pap test is only partially effective in detecting endometrial cancer; women at high risk should have an endometrial tissue sample evaluated at menopause (American Cancer Society, 1992).

Prostate Cancer Cancer of the prostate is the second most common form of cancer in men after skin cancer. About one of every 11 U.S. men will develop prostate cancer (American Cancer Society, 1992). The chance of getting prostate cancer increases with age; the typical prostatic cancer patient is 65 or older. Symptoms include difficulty in urinating, frequent urinating, painful urination, and blood in the urine. These symptoms are due to the growth of a tumor that disrupts the

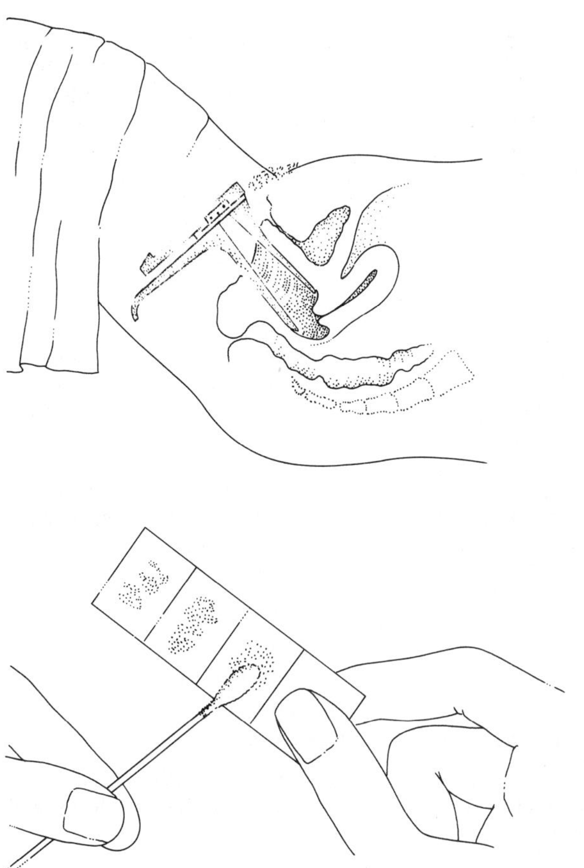

FIGURE 16.2 *Concluded*

Inspecting the Cervix

As it is gradually rotated, the speculum can be opened to expose the cervix—the "neck" of the lower uterus that connects it with the vagina. Again, this is done with very little discomfort to the patient. By manipulating the speculum, the doctor obtains a clear view of the cervix and can examine it for cysts, tears or other abnormalities.

The Pap Smear

Named for its developer, Dr. George N. Papanicolau, the Pap test is a simple procedure which detects pre cancerous cells. In other words, the Pap test can warn of cancer even before clinical signs of disease are apparent.

You've probably been instructed not to use douches, vaginal creams or medications for at least 48 hours prior to your pelvic exam. This is important because these substances can distort the appearance of the cells to be studied in the Pap smear.

While the cervix is still exposed by the speculum, cells are taken from the cervix and vagina with a scraper or cotton-tipped applicator. The cells are then smeared on a glass slide and sent to a laboratory for analysis.

With the speculum still in place, your physician may also take appropriate smears to determine the presence or absence of vaginal infection.

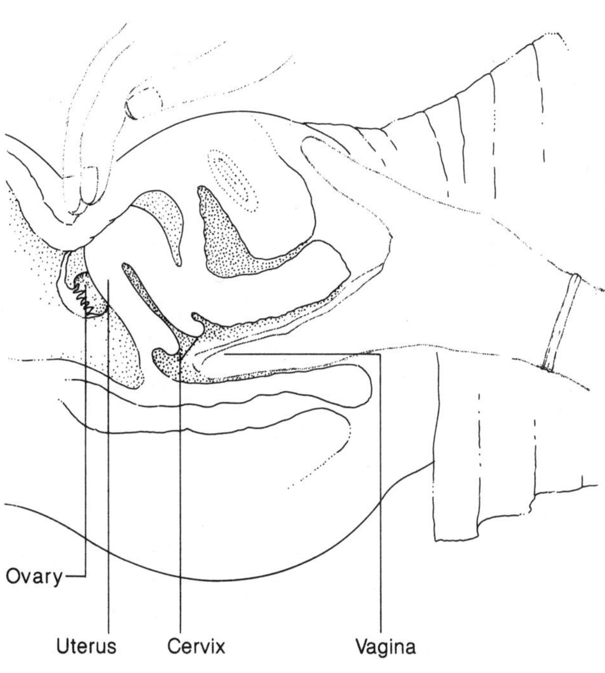

Digital Examination

After gradually withdrawing the speculum, the examiner will carry out the digital examination. This is just what it sounds like: an examination with the fingers or "digits." It is also a "bimanual" examination because both hands are used—one internally and one externally on the abdomen.

Wearing a glove, your physician inserts the index and/or middle finger of one hand into the vagina. In this way, the cervix can be palpated or "felt" for consistency, shape and position. The cervix may be moved from side to side to determine if it is tender to the touch. And the upper vagina is explored for masses, tenderness or distortion.

During the digital exam, your physician will also examine the uterus and ovaries. While the finger (or fingers) within the vagina elevate the cervix and uterus, the other hand is gently placed on the abdomen. By "grasping" the upper portion of the uterus between the vaginal fingers and the abdominal hand, the examiner can determine its size, its mobility and the presence or absence of tenderness. The ovaries also can often be located and felt.

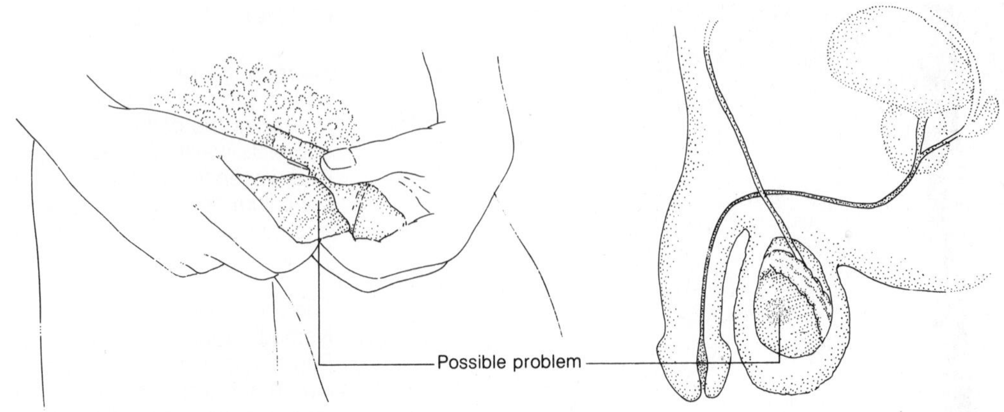

FIGURE 16.3 Testicular self-examination. Roll each testicle between the thumb and fingers; the testicles should feel smooth, except for the normal raised organ located on the back of each. Report any hard lump, enlargement, or contour changes to your health care provider.

normal functioning of the surrounding structures. Some older men may also experience a nonmalignant enlargement of the prostate. This should be treated if it interferes with urination.

Over half of prostate cancers are found during routine digital examinations, before the man has any symptoms (Sackett, 1990). Men over age 40 should have a prostate examination yearly. The effects of prostate cancer on sexual functioning are influenced more by the particular treatment regimen than by the disease itself (Sackett, 1990). Treatment options include a **radical prostatectomy** (removal of the prostate), radiation therapy, hormonal therapy, and orchiectomy (removal of one or both testes). Removal of the testes is a way to reduce testosterone to control tumor growth. These treatments may lead to erectile dysfunction, low sexual desire, ejaculatory incompetence, and/or retrograde ejaculation (Schover & Jensen, 1988).

Testicular Cancer Testicular cancer accounts for less than 1% of cancer in men between the ages of 25 and 34 (Sackett, 1990). The Testicular Self-Exam in Figure 16.3 is recommended to detect testicular cancer at an early stage. The following Research Perspective discusses attitudes toward the testicular and breast self-exams.

RESEARCH PERSPECTIVE

Attitudes Toward Breast and Testicular Self-Exams

What influences people to choose to perform breast or testicular self-examinations? According to the American Cancer Society, current estimates predict that one of every 9 women will develop breast cancer (1992). Despite the fact that women who regularly perform breast self-examination (BSE) are likely to detect breast cancers at an earlier stage and have greater cancer survival rates than women who do not do the BSE, less than 30% of U.S. women (Wyper, 1990) regularly do this examination. Likewise, although testicular cancer, one of the most curable cancers, is a leading cause of death in men age 15 to 44, only 22% of college men had examined their testicles at least once in their lifetime, and just 8% reported practicing testicular self-examination (TSE) once a month (Neef, Scutchfield, Elder, & Bender, 1991).Health-care educators and providers have attempted to identify characteristics related to knowledge and practice of these self-examination techniques.

Continued

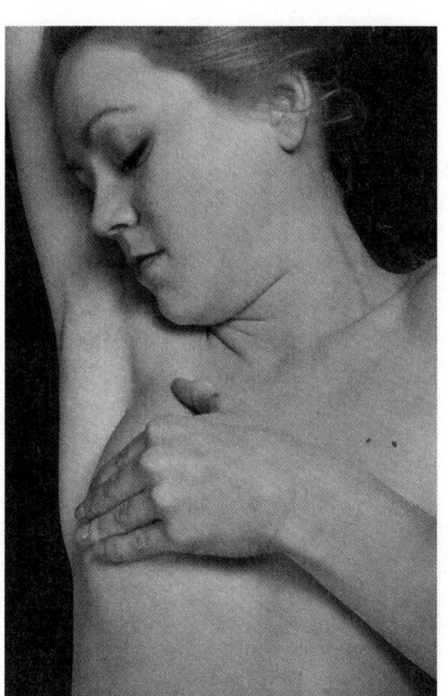

Early detection of breast cancer is enhanced by the woman conducting regular self breast exams.

Continued

Breast Self-Examination

Virtually all women (96% to 99%) are aware of BSE (Alcoe, Wallace, & Beck, 1990), yet despite 25 years of public education, most women do not perform it monthly, as recommended, and from 12% to 31% report not doing so at all (Lierman, Kasprzyk, & Benoliel, 1991). Many researchers have reported that age is a factor; even though older women are at greater risk of breast cancer, they are less likely to perform BSE or have their breasts examined by a health-care provider (Lierman et al., 1991). Attempts to explain preventive health behaviors such as BSE have largely relied on social psychology's research on attitude and attitude change. Three theoretical models have provided the foundation for studying how one's attitudes may predict the behavior of practicing BSE: Becker and Rosenstock's health belief model, Fishbein and Ajzen's theory of reasoned action, and the self-efficacy component of Bandura's social learning theory (Champion, 1990).

Health Belief Model The health belief model proposes that readiness to conduct a preventive health action is based upon the following beliefs: (a) one is personally *susceptible* to the condition, (b) the condition would have at least moderately *severe* impact on some aspect of one's life, (c) taking the recommended action would be *efficacious* in reducing its severity, and (d) it would be worth overcoming *barriers* to action (such as cost, pain, embarrassment). Studies applying this model to BSE have found the concepts of benefits and barriers to be the most useful, with barriers explaining from 12% to 27% of the variance in frequency of examination (Champion, 1990; Wyper, 1990). That is, women who perceive more barriers to performing BSE (such as worrying about cancer, embarrassment, lack of time, unpleasantness, and trouble remembering) are the least likely to engage in it (Champion, 1991).

Self-Efficacy Recently, some researchers have added the concept of self-efficacy, or confidence in being able to detect a breast lump. In Bandura's social learning theory, those who are confident in their ability to execute a behavior are hypothesized to bemore proficient in performing it. This connection has been found in research on BSE, with several studies documenting that confidence is related to proficiency and frequency (Champion, 1990).

Theory of Reasoned Action The theory of reasoned action, recently revised and referred to as the theory of planned behavior (Murphy & Brubaker, 1990), suggests that the best predictor of one's behavior is one's *intention* to perform the behavior. Intention is a function of (a) attitudinal (evaluation of outcomes of participating in a behavior) and (b) normative factors (whether people who are important to one want or expect one to perform the behavior). Studies using this model to predict BSE have found the attitudinal variables to be more important than the social norm component, but one's health-care provider and friends and family were influential (Lierman et al., 1991).

Testicular Self-Examination

Men are likely to be uninformed about TSE. Only two of every 100 men surveyed in New Orleans and Rochester, New York, reported conducting the TSE monthly with

Continued

Continued

the proper method and timing (Sheley, Kinchen, Morgan, & Gordon, 1991). Studies on university campuses have found that 49% to 75% of respondents had never heard of TSE and testicular cancer (Neef et al., 1991). In their study of male students at San Diego State University, Neef et al. (1991) found that men were more likely to practice TSE if they had heard of TSE and testicular cancer (and were familiar with risk factors), knew that monthly TSE practice is recommended, and had been instructed in its use. Those who used TSE seemed prevention-oriented, in that they were more likely than nonusers to exercise, not smoke, and use seat belts. Older students and seniors were more likely to practice TSE. A self-efficacy variable seemed to be operating, since those who reported a belief in personal control over the development of cancer were more likely to use TSE.

An educational program based on the theory of reasoned action was implemented with high school boys (Murphy & Brubaker, 1990). Participants in the theory-based program were more likely than boys in the control group to believe that TSE would help identify testicular cancer before it spread and disagreed more strongly that performing TSE would take too much time. They also believed more strongly that their physicians and parents would want them to do the exam.

Friman and Finney (1990) suggested that perhaps the most effective method for increasing knowledge of TSE is through college and high school curricula and primary medical-care providers. They urged vigorous health education efforts directed toward preventing "lives and potential productive years of life from being lost to a curable disease" (p. 451). As researchers learn more about perceived barriers, normative influences, and health-related attitudes toward the use of BSE and TSE, perhaps more effective educational programs can be developed.

References

Alcoe, S. Y., Wallace, D. G., Beck, B. M. (1990). Ten years later: An update of the case for teaching breast self-examination. *Canadian Journal of Public Health, 81*. 447–449.

Champion, V. L. (1990). Breast self-examination in women 35 and older: A prospective study. *Journal of Behavioral Medicine, 13,* 523–538.

Champion, V. L. (1991). The relationship of selected variables to breast cancer detection behaviors in women 35 and older. *Oncology Nursing Forum, 18,* 733–739.

Friman, P. C., & Finney, J. W. (1990). Health education for testicular cancer. *Health Education Quarterly, 17,* 443–453.

Lierman, L. M. Kasprzyk, D., & Benoliel, J. Q. (1991). Understanding adherence to breast self-examination in older women. *Western Journal of Nursing Research, 13,* 46–66.

Murphy, W. G., & Brubaker, R. G. (1990). Effects of a brief theory-based intervention on the practice of testicular self-examination by high school males. *Journal of School Health, 60,* 459–462.

Neef, N., Scutchfield, F. D., Elder, J., & Bender, S. J. (1991). Testicular self-examination by young men: An analysis of characteristics associated with practice. *Journal of American College Health, 39,* 187–190.

Sheley, J. F., Kinchen, E. W., Morgan, D. H., & Gordon, D. F. (1991). Limited impact of testicular self-examination promotion. *Journal of Community Health, 16,* 117–124.

Wyper, M. A. (1990). Breast self-examination and the health belief model: Variations on a theme. *Research in Nursing & Health, 13,* 421–428.

Males with a undescended testicle have a higher chance of developing testicular cancer. Surgery to bring an undescended testicle down into the scrotal sac is recommended before age five or six to preserve fertility in the testicle and to prevent malignancy from occurring later in life.

Treatment for testicular cancer may involve surgical removal of one or both testicles (**orchiectomy**). If a man has one healthy testicle, testosterone levels will remain normal. Sexual dysfunction following orchiectomy can result from anxiety about masculinity or poor body image (Schover & Jensen, 1988). Testicular prostheses made of silicone can be surgically implanted to restore the appearance and sensation of testicles.

Penile Cancer Cancer of the penis is rare, occurring in one of every 100,000 adult males; most are usually over the age of 50. The symptom is often a painless growth or ulcer on the glans penis. Uncircumcised males who have a foreskin that will not retract are at greater risk for penile cancer (Sackett, 1990).

Men with penile cancer are likely to delay consulting a physician. "Embarrassment, fear of cancer, and fear of castration often prevent a man from seeking treatment until the disease is far advanced; it is not uncommon for the man to feel that the lesion is a result of masturbation or a punishment by God for past misdeeds" (Sackett, 1990, p. 428).

Treatment for the lesion is penile amputation. However, only about one quarter of the actual length of the penis is amputated and the man is capable of having an orgasm and ejaculating after penectomy. In many cases, a shorter penis is viewed as an improvement from the "unsightly, foul-smelling lesion often present prior to treatment" (Sackett, 1990, p. 428).

CONSIDERATION: The physical affects of cancer may not influence the sexual satisfaction of a cancer patient as much as the quality of the person's intimate relationship. A team of researchers (Weijmar Schultz, Van de Wiel, Bouma, Janssens, & Littlewood, 1990) studied sexual satisfaction levels of 10 couples (the woman in these couples had cancer of the vulva) for two years. The researchers concluded that satisfaction with sexual interaction in a relationship appears to be more a function of the intimate aspects of the relationship than the physiological changes the body of one person may undergo as a consequence of cancer. They emphasized the need to focus on the relationship between the partners when one of them is to be treated for cancer, rather than on the physical changes to follow.

Other Diseases and Illnesses and Sexuality

Aside from cancer, numerous other diseases affect an individual's sexuality. Next, we look briefly at arthritis, cardiovascular disease, diabetes, chronic obstructive pulmonary disease, and their affects on sexuality.

Arthritis

NATIONAL DATA: Almost 31 million Americans suffer from arthritis (*Statistical Abstract of the United States: 1992,* Table 195).

Arthritis is the painful swelling of joints that results in muscle weakness, limited mobility, and, in some cases, deformity. Arthritis usually begins in midlife and affects more women than men (four to one).

The joints most often affected by arthritis include the wrist, elbow, shoulder, hip, knee, and ankle. Pain is the predominant symptom, but feeling stiff, fatigued, and weak are common. Individuals also report feeling depressed by the constant pain and embarrassed or shameful because of their altered body image (Palmeri & Wise, 1988). Some men with arthritis complain of erectile dysfunction (Blake, Maisiak, Koplan, Alarcon, & Brown, 1988). Both sexes report that the arthritis affects their sexual mobility, which may inhibit orgasmic enjoyment (Palmeri & Wise, 1988).

Cardiovascular Disease

The various forms of cardiovascular conditions affecting sexuality include hypertension, coronary artery disease, myocardial infarction, and coronary artery bypass surgery.

Hypertension (commonly known as high blood pressure) has been associated with less penile rigidity (Hirschkowitz, Karacan, Gurakar, & Williams, 1989). Many medications used to treat hypertension have been linked to erectile dysfunction and decreased sexual desire (Burke, 1990).

NATIONAL DATA: Over 63 million Americans have one or more forms of heart or blood vessel disease; almost one in four adults has hypertension, and over 2 million have rheumatic heart disease (American Heart Association, 1988).

CONSIDERATION: Burke (1990) suggested that because blood pressure increases during sexual activity, sexually active patients should be counseled about the importance of controlling their hypertension. Such control may be achieved through cessation of smoking (if the individual smokes), weight loss (if the individual is overweight), and/or hypertension medication. However, Burke (1990) noted that many men do not take their high blood pressure medication because of its negative effect (loss of ability to have and maintain an erection) on their sexuality.

Follow-up studies of male heart attack victims demonstrate that about 10% report erectile problems and about two-thirds report a decreased frequency of intercourse. Female heart attack victims also report a decreased frequency of intercourse following a myocardial infarction (MI) (Burke, 1990).

The reduction in frequency of intercourse is most often a function of fear that sexual activity will precipitate another heart attack, initiate angina (tightness in chest, neck, or arm), or cause death. These fears are "based on misconceptions and lack of information regarding the cardiovascular demands of sexual activity" (Burke, 1990, p. 360). While intercourse and orgasm does increase the respiratory rate (from 16 to 60 per minute), the heart rate (from 65 to 170 beats per minute); and blood pressure (120/80 to 220/110), these changes are not sufficient to induce a heart attack. In general, Burke concluded that "the physiological cost of sexual

Aerobic exercise three times per week for twenty minutes helps prevent high blood pressure and cardiovascular disease.

activity is modest for middle-aged, long-married men with chronic heart disease" (p. 362).

Patients may also become depressed due to the feeling that they will become dependent on their partner and will no longer be able to engage in a wide range of activities. Similarly, patients may lose their interest in sex because they may feel that they are no longer sexually adequate. Health-care practitioners have underestimated the sexual concerns of the cardiac patient. Satterfield (1983) suggested that sexual rehabilitation should be incorporated into cardiac rehabilitation programs.

Diabetes

Many diseases of the endocrine system affect sexual functioning, but the most common is diabetes mellitus. **Diabetes mellitus** is a chronic disease in which the pancreas fails to produce sufficient insulin, which is necessary for metabolizing carbohydrates. The symptoms of diabetes include excess sugar in the blood and urine, excessive thirst, hunger, and urination, and weakness. These symptoms may be controlled through injections of insulin.

NATIONAL DATA: Almost 6.5 million individuals in the United States have chronic diabetes. Almost 9% of those over the age of 65 have diabetes (*Statistical Abstract of the United States: 1992,* Table 195).

Much more is known about the effect of diabetes on male sexual functioning than on female sexual functioning (Manley, 1990). In diabetic men, erectile dysfunction may be first symptom of having diabetes that they experience. Studies suggest that the prevalence of erectile dysfunction among diabetic men is 30% to 60% (Manley, 1990). Diabetic men may notice a progressive softening of the penis over a period of six months or longer, eventually leading to inability to perform vaginal penetration. Erectile dysfunction in diabetic men may be caused by both physiological and psychosocial factors (Forsberg et al. 1989). Physiologically, there is damage to the autonomic nerves that is irreversible, even with the restoration of "normal" blood sugars via insulin (Zasler, 1991). Psychosocial factors include anxiety and depression resulting from the perceived disability and difficulty in functioning.

Diabetic men with erectile dysfunction who have the goal of being in control of their erections have three treatment alternatives: "externally applied vacuum devices, which induce passive tumescence under the negative pressure of a vacuum; intracorporeal injections of vasoactive agents; and semirigid or inflatable implants" (Nankervis, 1989, p. 549). In Chapter 15 on sexual dysfunctions, we discussed these as vacuum pumps, papavarine injections, and penile implants.

Ejaculatory disturbances may also occur in diabetic men. These include retrograde ejaculation, the absence of ejaculation, and/or early ejaculation. Studies differ over whether the libido of the diabetic man is negatively affected. In some cases, there is a decrease in libido that follows several episodes of "failure" due to erectile dysfunction (Fairburn et al., 1982).

Research on the effects of diabetes on female sexual functioning has yielded inconsistent results. Since previous studies (Jensen, 1981; Unsain, Goodwin, & Schuster, 1982) disagreed on whether the incidence of sexual dysfunctions (e.g., low sexual desire, less vaginal lubrication, decreased orgasmic capacity) in diabetic women differed from nondiabetic women, a team of researchers (Slob, Radder, & Van Der Werff Ten Bosch, 1990) developed a study to provide recent data on the issue. They compared 24 women with diabetes mellitus (type I) with nondiabetic women in regard to sexual arousal to erotic video material. No differences were observed. In addition, reported sexual activity and the prevalence of major sexual or urogenital problems were not significantly different between the two groups (Slob et al., 1990).

Diabetic women do complain of vaginitis and vaginal dryness. The former is remedied by controlling blood sugar and taking measures to prevent yeast infections; the latter by using water-soluble lubricants and allowing more time for vaginal lubrication to occur.

Chronic Obstructive Pulmonary Disease

Chronic obstructive pulmonary disease (COPD) is a collective term for diseases that affect the flow of air into the body. The three most common subtypes of COPD are asthma, bronchitis, and emphysema. Persons with COPD may experience fatigue, decreased sexual desire, difficulty in achieving and maintaining erection, and a general decrease in sexual activity (Stockdale-Woolley, 1990).

NATIONAL DATA: Almost 12 million cases of bronchitis and 12 million cases of asthma are seen by physicians annually (*Statistical Abstract of the United States: 1992,* Table 195).

The effects of COPD on sexuality are due to a combination of physical, psychological, and social variables. Physically, COPD patients report feeling easily fatigued and irritated by the frequent wheezing and coughing. Psychologically, they often fear that sexual activity will further deplete their energy reserves and will create a new round of coughing.

Socially, COPD patients may experience other changes: "shortness of breath and limited energy reserves force activity restriction, decreased socialization and recreation, and early retirement or disability" (Stockdale-Woolley, 1990, p. 373). In a study of COPD in women, Sexton and Munro (1988) noted that primary complaints included shortness of breath, fatigue, loneliness, depression, and restricted activity. Men were primarily affected by the loss of their wage earner role and the necessity to assume a more dependent role. These changes in social roles may decrease self-esteem and sexual desire.

CONSIDERATION: Many COPD patients engage in unhealthy behaviors, such as smoking and excessive alcohol consumption, which exacerbate their condition. In such cases, "the spouse's frustration with the patient's self-destructive behavior may create further distance in the marital relationship" (Schover & Jensen, 1988, p. 252).

Endometriosis

Endometrial tissue lines the uterus. **Endometriosis** is the presence of this tissue in locations other than the uterus, such as the ovaries or pelvis. Pain is the primary symptom and results from this misplaced uterine tissue expanding and contracting during the menstrual cycle. Other symptoms include inflammation, scarring, adhesions, and cysts. Infertility often results from endometriosis because of its scarring of the ovaries.

Endometriosis most often occurs during the childbearing years. It is confirmed by surgical removal of suspected tissue, which is examined under the microscope. Treatment, which does not cure the disease, involves surgical removal of the tissue and/or hormonal therapy. One such hormone is danazol, which may relieve the pain of endometriosis but may cause weight gain, vaginal spotting, and a decrease in sexual desire (Bernhard, 1990).

CHOICES

The choice of whether to exercise regularly affects not only one's general physical health and well–being, but also one's body image, sexual self–concept, and sexual satisfaction. In "Choose to Exercise?" we describe a research study that supports the idea that exercise has positive effects on our sexuality.

In the last "Choices" in this section, we note that while individuals do not choose to be ill or disabled, they may choose how to view their physical condition and it's effects on their sexuality. We suggest ways in which individuals coping with illness or disability may view their situation in more positive terms.

Choose to Exercise?

Choosing to adopt a life-style that includes regular aerobic exercise has benefits for one's sexuality. A team of researchers (White, McWhirter, & Mattison, 1990) compared the sex lives of 78 sedentary but healthy men (mean age of 48) who participated in a group aerobic workout for 60 minutes 3.5 days a week with 17 men (mean age of 44) who walked at a moderate pace an average of 4.1 days a week. Participants kept a diary on exercise, diet, smoking, and sexuality the first and last month of a nine-month program. Results showed that those men in the aerobic exercise group reported higher frequencies of various intimate activities and reliability of sexual functioning (erection) and more satisfying orgasms compared to those men in the walking group. Indeed, the more the men improved in their respective health profiles, the greater the benefits in their reported sexuality.

Butt (1990) noted that one's overall well-being is enhanced by exercise and that sexual activity itself is a valuable form of exercise. He noted, however, that health educators rarely emphasize the benefits of exercise on sexuality.

Choose to Take Cognitive Control of One's Life and Sexuality?

Spinal cord injuries, multiple sclerosis, and cancer are physically debilitating illnesses over which we have little control. Choosing to get the best medical treatment and advice available and choosing to follow these recommendations are choices that will help us to minimize the negative impact of such illnesses on our sexuality. Beyond what is possible medically, we might choose to reframe our situation and to view changes in our sexuality in positive rather than negative terms.

Individuals with disabilities often view a disability as something to get rid of:

> Because they are in pain, the preferred treatment, as initially seen through their eyes, is eradication. Trying to "get rid of" problems is actually an ineffective approach to life's challenges since the real issue is not what is happening but how we relate to what is happening. (Hulnick & Hulnick, 1989, p. 167)

Questions the researchers recommended we might consider in coping with a disability include (p. 167):

1. How can we use this situation to our advancement?
2. What can we learn from our disability?
3. What might we do that might result in a more uplifting experience for everyone involved?
4. How can we relate to ourselves in a more loving way?

Viewing one's situation in positive terms is a choice. For example, spinal cord-injured individuals who can no longer function as they did prior to their accident may choose to focus on the enjoyments derived from touch, caressing, and emotional closeness. Without such an accident, such a focus may not have occurred to the individual and no movement in that area would have been achieved. Similarly, the heart attack victim, after experiencing a close encounter with death, may have a renewed value for the relationship with the partner with whom he or she is involved. Choosing to focus on what is gained rather than what has been lost may provide a different outcome for the way one feels about a physical disability.

Summary

1. Myths about disease, disability and sexuality include a) ill or disabled individuals are asexual, b) sex saps one's strength and is therefore harmful to those who have poor health, and c) too much sex is unhealthy and causes illness.
2. Illness, disease, and disability are associated with various psychobiological and psychosocial factors that affect sexuality and sexual functioning. Psychobiological factors include pain, fatigue, and depression. Psychosocial factors include self-concept, body image, role function, and effects on relationships.
3. Neurological disabilities that affect sexuality and sexual functioning include spinal cord injury, stroke, multiple sclerosis, traumatic brain injury, and cerebral palsy.
4. Individuals with intellectual disability often have limited knowledge about sexuality either because they have not been taught or because they are limited in their comprehension of such information.
5. Psychological disturbances, including unipolar and bipolar depression and schizophrenia may interfere with sexual desire, ability to experience orgasm, and the development and maintenance of close interpersonal relationships. Prior history of sexual abuse has been associated with specific types of subsequent mental illness (e.g. depression, substance use disorders, and anxiety disorders).
6. Cancer and it's treatment (surgery, chemotherapy, radiation treatment) has various negative effects on a person's sexuality and sexual functioning. Some forms of cancer (e.g. breast and testicular) may be detected early through self-examination procedures.
7. Other diseases and illnesses that affect sexuality and sexual functioning include arthritis, cardiovascular disease, diabetes, chronic obstructive pulmonary disease, and endometriosis.
8. A variety of interventions may be helpful in overcoming sexual difficulties associated with illness, disease, and disability. For example, individuals and couples experiencing such difficulties may experiment with various sexual positions and behaviors to assess what works best for them, focus on a variety of sensual and intimate forms of touch and communication (e.g. sensate focus exercises), change medications that interfere with sexual functioning, use pain medications or other techniques (e.g. warm baths) for pain relief before engaging in sexual activity, use various sexual aids and devices (e.g. penile prosthesis; surrogate partner therapy), and engage in sexual behavior at optimal times (e.g. in morning when energy level is highest).
9. Regular aerobic exercise has positive effects on one's sexuality and sexual functioning.

KEY TERMS

body image
strokes
intellectual disability
mammography
radical mastectomy
modified radical mastectomy
partial mastectomy
radical prostatectomy
orchiectomy
arthritis
diabetes mellitus
chronic obstructive pulmonary disease
endometriosis

REFERENCES

Abramson, P. R., Parker, T., & Weisberg, S. R. (1988). Sexual expression of mentally retarded people: Educational and legal implications. *American Journal of Mental Retardation, 93,* 328–334.

Abused child, multiple personality tied. (1982, September). *Clinical Psychiatry News,* p. 2.

Agarwal, A., & Jain, D. C. (1989). Male sexual dysfunction after a stroke. *Journal of the Association of Physicians of India, 37,* 505–507.

American Cancer Society. (1992). *Cancer facts and figures—1992.* Atlanta, Ga.

American Heart Association. (1988). *Heart facts.* Dallas: AHA.

Ames, T-R. H. (1991). Guidelines for providing sexuality-related services to severely and profoundly retarded individuals: The challenge for the nineteen-nineties. *Sexuality and Disability, 9,* 113–122.

Andron, L., & Ventura, J. (1987). Sexual dysfunction in couples with learning handicaps. *Sexuality and Disability, 8,* 25–35.

Bancroft, J. (1989). *Human sexuality and its problems (2nd Ed.).* Edinburgh: Churchill Livingstone.

Bernhard, L. (1990). Gynecological conditions and sexuality. In C. I. Fogel and D. Lauver (Eds.), *Sexual health promotion* (pp. 436–458). Philadelphia: W. B. Saunders.

Bezkor, M. F., & Canedo, A. (1987a). Physiological and psychological factors influencing sexual dysfunction in multiple sclerosis: Part I. *Sexuality and Disability, 8,* 143–146.

Bezkor, M. F. & Canedo, A. (1987b). Physiological and psychological factors influencing sexual dysfunction in multiple sclerosis: Part II, emotionality and sexuality in persons with multiple sclerosis. *Sexuality and Disability, 8,* 147–151.

Blake, D. J., Maisiak, R., Koplan, A., Alarcon, G. S., & Brown, S. (1988). Sexual dysfunction among patients with arthritis. *Clinical Rheumatology, 7,* 5–60.

Blum, G. J. (1983). Self-esteem and knowledge: Primary requisites to prevent victimization. In G. W. Albee, S. Gordon, & H. Leitenberg (Eds). *Promoting Sexual Responsibility and Preventing Sexual Problems* (pp. 276–296). Hanover, NH: University Press of New England.

Bretschneider, J. G., & McCoy, N. L. (1988). Sexual interest and behavior in healthy 80- to 102-year-olds. *Archives of Sexual Behavior, 17,* 109–129.

Burgener, S., & Logan, G. (1989). Sexuality concerns of the post-stroke patient. *Rehabilitation Nursing, 14,* 178–181.

Burke, L. E. (1990). Cardiovascular disturbances and sexuality. In C. I. Fogel and D. Lauver (Eds.), *Sexual health promotion* (pp. 360–374). Philadelphia: W. B. Saunders.

Burnam, M.A., Stein, J. A., Golding, J. M., Siegel, J. M., Sorenson, S. B., Forsythe, A. B. & Telles, C. A. (1988). Sexual assault and mental disorders in a community population. *Journal of Consulting and Clinical Psychology, 56,* 843–850.

Butt, D. S. (1990). The sexual response as exercise: A brief review and theoretical proposal. *Sports Medicine, 9,* 330–343.

Carmen, E. H., Rieker, P. P., & Mills, T. (1984). Victims of violence and psychiatric illness. *American Journal of Psychiatry, 141,* 378–383.

Carter, M. (1990). Illness, chronic disease, and sexuality. In C. I. Fogel and D. Lauver (Eds.), *Sexual health promotion* (pp. 305–312). Philadelphia: W. B. Saunders.

Clarke, D. J. (1989). Antilibidinal drugs and mental retardation: A review. *Medicine, Science and the Law, 29,* 136–146.

Cole, S., & Cole, T. M. (1983). Disability and intimacy: The importance of sexual health. In G. Albee, S. Gordon, & H. Leitenberg (Eds.), *Promoting sexual responsibility and preventing sexual problems* (pp. 297–305). Hanover, England: University Press.

Connolly, F. H. & Gittelson, N. L. (1971). The relationship between delusions of sexual change and olfactory and gustatory hallucinations in schizophrenia. *British Journal of Psychiatry,* 119, 443–444.

Creech, R. (1992). *Reflections from a unicorn.* Greenville, NC: RC Publishing.

Cutler, S. E. and Nolen-Hoeksema, S. (1991). Accounting for sex differences in depression through female victimization: Childhood sexual abuse. *Sex Roles, 24,* 425–438.

Drench, M. E. (1992). Impact of altered sexuality and sexual function in spinal cord injury: A review. *Sexuality and Disability, 10,* 3–14.

Elesha-Adams, M. & Welch, M. (1991, November). *Counseling patients with chronic disease about sexuality.* Paper presented at annual meeting of the Society for the Scientific Study of Sex, New Orleans.

Fairburn, C. G., Wu, F. C., McCulloch, D. K., Borsey, D. Q., Ewing, D. J., Clarke, B. F., & Bancroft, J. H. (1982). The clinical features of diabetic impotence: A preliminary study. *British Journal of Psychiatry, 140,* 447–452.

Giami, A. (1987). Coping with the sexuality of the disabled: A comparison of the physically disabled and the mentally retarded. *International Journal of Rehabilitation Research, 10,* 41–48.

Grossman, H. G. (Ed.). (1983). *Classification in mental retardation.* Washington, DC: American Association on Mental Deficiency.

Hirshkowitz, M., Karacan, I., Gurakar, A., & Williams, R. L. (1989). Hypertension, erectile dysfunction, and occult sleep apnea. *Sleep, 12,* 223–232.

Hulnick, M. R., & Hulnick, H. R., (1989). Life's challenges: Curse or opportunity? Counseling families of persons with disabilities. *Journal of Counseling and Development, 68,* 16–176.

Jensen, S. B. (1981). Diabetic sexual dysfunction: A comparative study of 160 insulin treated diabetic men and women and an age-matched control group. *Archives of Sexual Behavior, 10* 493–504.

Joseph, R. (1991). A case analysis in human sexuality: Counseling to a man with severe cerebral palsy. *Sexuality and Disability, 9,* 149–159.

Kaplan, H. S. (1992). A neglected issue: The sexual side effects of current treatments for breast cancer. *Journal of Sex and Marital Therapy, 18,* 3–19.

Katchadourian, H. A. (1990). *The biological aspects of human sexuality,* (4th ed.). Fort Worth, TX: Holt, Rinehart & Winston.

Kempton, W., & Kahn, E. (1991). Sexuality and people with intellectual disabilities: Historical perspective. *Sexuality and Disability, 9,* 93–111.

Kreutzer, J. S., & Zasler, N. D. (1989). Psychosexual consequences of traumatic brain injury: Methodology and preliminary findings. *Brain Injury, 3,* 177–186.

Litz, B. T., Zeiss, A. M., Davies, H. D. (1990). Sexual concerns of male spouses of female Alzheimer's disease patients. *Gerontologist, 30,* 113–116.

Lonsdale, S. (1990). *Women and disability: The experience of physical disability among women.* New York: St. Martin's Press.

Lustman, P. J., & Clouse, R. E. (1990). Relationship of psychiatric illness to impotence in men with diabetes. *Diabetes Care, 13,* 893–895.

Manley, G. (1990). Endocrine disturbances and sexuality. In C. I. Fogel & D. R. Lauver, (Eds.), *Sexual health promotion* (pp. 337–359). Philadelphia: W. B. Saunders.

Mathew, R. J. & Weinman, M. L. (1982). Sexual dysfunction in depression. *Archives of Sexual Behavior, 11* 323–328.

Miller, J. F. (1983). *Coping with chronic illness: Overcoming powerlessness.* Philadelphia: F. A. Davis.

Muti, G., & Custo, G. M. (1990). Psycho-handicap and sexuality. In F. J. Bianco & R. Hernandez (Eds.), *Sexology: An independent field* (pp. 315–325). Amsterdam: Elsevier.

Nankervis, A. (1989). Sexual function in chronic disease. *Medical Journal of Australia, 151,* 548–549.

Page, R. C., Cheng, H. P., Pate, T. C., Mathus, B., Pryor, D., & Ko, J. C. (1987). The perceptions of spinal cord injured persons toward sex. *Sexuality and Disability, 8,* 112–132.

Palmeri, B. A., & Wise, T. N. (1988). Sexual dysfunction in the medically ill. In R. A. Brown and J. R. Field (Eds.), *Treatment of sexual problems in individual and couple therapy* (pp. 81–98). Baltimore: PMA.

Rosen, R. C., & Leiblum, S. R. (1987). Current approaches to the evaluation of sexual desire disorders. *Journal of Sex Research, 23,* 141–162.

Sackett, C. (1990). Genitourinary conditions and sexuality. In C. I. Fogel and D. R. Lauver (Eds.), *Sexual health promotion* (pp. 407–435). Philadelphia: W. B. Saunders.

Satterfield, S. B. (1983). Sexual rehabilitation of the cardiac patient. In G. Albee, S. Gordon, & H. Leitenberg (Eds.), *Promoting sexual responsibility and preventing sexual problems,* (pp. 306–312). Hanover, England: University Press.

Schover, L. R., & Jensen, S. B. (1988). *Sexuality and chronic illness: A comprehensive approach.* New York: Guilford Press.

Schreiner-Engel, P. & Schiavi, R. C. (1986). Lifetime psychopathology in individuals with low sexual desire. *Journal of Nervous and Mental Diseases, 174,* 646–651.

Sexton, D. L., Munro, B. H. (1988). Living with a chronic illness: The experience of women with chronic obstructive pulmonary disease. *Western Journal of Nursing Research, 10,* 26–44.

Shea, V. (1990). Developmental disability and sexuality. In C. I. Fogel and D. R. Lauver (Eds.), *Sexual health promotion* (pp. 569–577). Philadelphia; W. B. Saunders.

Slob, A. K., Radder, J. K., & Van Der Werff Ten Bosch, J. J. (1990). Sexuality and psychophysiological functioning in women with diabetes mellitus. *Journal of Sex and Marital Therapy, 16,* 59–69.

Smith, P. J., & Talbert, R. L. (1986). Sexual dysfunction with antihypertensive and antipsychotic agents. *Clinical Pharmacology, 5,* 373–384.

Statistical abstract of the United States: 1992 (112th ed.) (1992). Washington, DC: U.S. Bureau of the Census.

Stavis, P. F. (1991). Harmonizing the right to sexual expression and the right to protection from harm for persons with mental disability. *Sexuality and Disability, 9,* 131–141.

Stenager, E., Stenager, E. N., & Jensen, K. (1990). Multiple sclerosis: Sexual dysfunctions. *Journal of Sex Education and Therapy, 16,* 262–269.

Stockdale-Woolley, R. (1990). Respiratory disturbances and sexuality. In C. I. Fogel and D. R. Lauver (Eds.), *Sexual health promotion* (pp. 372–383). Philadelphia: W. B. Saunders.

Thomas, D. J. (1982). *The experience of handicap.* New York: Methuen.

Travis, C. B. (1988). *Women and health psychology: Biomedical issues.* Hillsdale, NJ: Lawrence Erlbaum Associates.

Unsain, I. C., Goodwin, M. H., & Schuster, E. A. (1982). Diabetes and sexual functioning. *Nursing Clinical North America, 17,* 387–393.

Weijmar Schultz, W. C., Van de Wiel, H. B., Bouma, J., Janssens, J., & Littlewood, J. (1990). Psychosexual functioning after the treatment of cancer of the vulva. A longitudinal study. *Cancer, 66,* 402–407.

White, J. R., McWhirter, D., & Mattison, A. M. (1990). Enhanced sexual behavior in exercising men. *Archives of Sexual Behavior, 19,* 193–209.

Woods, S. M. (1981). Sexuality and mental disorders. In H. Lief (Ed.), *Sexual problems in medical practice* (pp. 199–210). Chicago: American Medical Association.

Zasler, N. D. (1991). Sexuality in neurologic disability: An overview. *Sexuality and Disability, 9,* 11–27.

Zeiss, A. M., Davies, H. D., Wood, M., & Tinklenberg, J. R. (1990). The incidence and correlates of erectile problems in patients with Alzheimer's disease. *Archives of Sexual Behavior, 19,* 325–331.

Zencius, A., Wesolowski, M. D., Burke, W. H., & Hough, S. (1990). Managing hypersexual disorders in brain-injured clients. *Brain Injury, 4,* 175–181.

CHAPTER SEVENTEEN

Paraphilias and Sexuality

Chapter Outline

Paraphilia: Definition and Overview
- Types of Paraphilias
- Exhibitionism
- Frotteurism
- Pedophilia
- Voyeurism
- Fetishism
- Transvestic Fetishism
- **Self-Assessment:** The Cross-Gender Fetishism Scale
- Sexual Sadism
- Sexual Masochism
- Other Paraphilias
- Legal versus Illegal Paraphilias
- Is Rape a Paraphilia?

The Origins of Paraphilias: Theoretical Perspectives
- Psychoanalytic Perspective
- Feminist Perspective
- Learning Theory
- Biological Theory
- Paraphilia as a Vandalized Lovemap
- Paraphilia as a Courtship Disorder

Treatment of Coercive Paraphilias
- **RESEARCH PERSPECTIVE:** Methods of Assessment of Sexual Interest in Sex Offenders
- Decreasing Deviant Sexual Arousal
- Increasing Nondeviant Sexual Arousal
- Teaching Social Skills
- Changing Faulty Cognitions
- Resolving Sexual Dysfunctions
- Treating Alcohol Abuse

Sexual Addiction
- Characteristics of Sex Addicts
- Treatment of Sexual Addictions
- Effectiveness of Treatment Programs

Choices
- Choose to Disregard Social Disapproval of Paraphilias?
- Choose to Control One's Paraphilia?

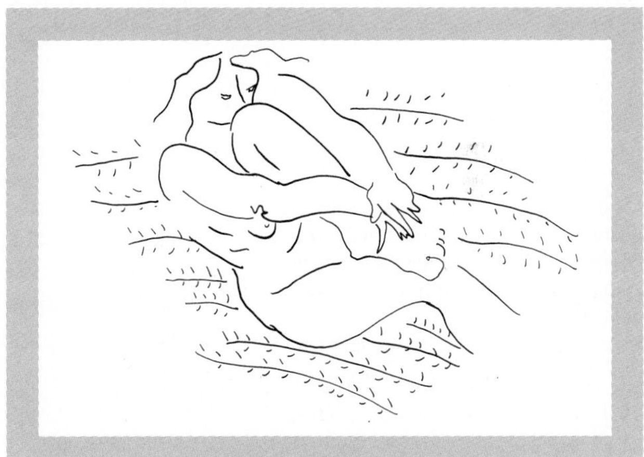

Is It True?*

1. Men are more likely to be paraphilic than women.
2. Pedophiles are much more likely to be heterosexual than homosexual.
3. Some theorists regard rape as a paraphilia.
4. Exhibitionists are harmless; they do not commit "hands-on" offenses.
5. All societies prohibit sexual behavior between adults and children.

* 1 = T, 2 = T, 3 = T, 4 = F, 5 = F

There is no absolute criterion by which to distinguish paraphilic behavior from normal behavior.

Ratnin Dewaraja

In the spring of 1992, the Little Rascals Day Care Center in Edenton, North Carolina, became the focus of national attention when the media revealed that it was the site of alleged sexual abuse of children. Robert F. Kelly, operator of the center, was convicted of 99 counts of sex abuse involving over 20 children. His trial and conviction provided nationwide visibility to an unusual expression of sexuality—pedophilia. In this chapter, we are concerned not just with pedophilia but with a wider range of sexual behavior that our society considers unusual or deviant. Such behavior is often referred to as paraphilic behavior.

Paraphilia: Definition and Overview

The advent of more and more psychiatric pigeonholes, some critics feel, reflects a broader trend toward turning any behavior that departs from the ideal into a medical condition.

Erica E. Goode

A **paraphilia** is an overdependence on a culturally unacceptable or unusual stimulus for sexual arousal and satisfaction. The term "paraphilia" is derived from the words *para,* meaning deviation, and *philia,* meaning attracted. Hence, the paraphiliac is attracted to a stimulus that is regarded by the society in which the person lives as deviant. Paraphilic fantasies usually focus on aggression—images of exhibitionism, obscene phone calling, and frotteurism are rehearsals of partner victimization (Levine, Risen, & Althof, 1990). Other characteristics of the paraphiliac are sexual dysfunction (lack of desire, arousal, or orgasm) if the paraphilia stimulus is not present and a seeming inability to develop an intense emotional connection with others (Levine et al., 1990).

Ultimately, it is the difficulty our culture has in dealing with sexuality that is responsible for the development of psychosexual disorders.

Eli Coleman

The Diagnostic and Statistical Manual of Mental Disorders (American Psychiatric Association, 1987), also known as the DSM-III-R, developed and published by the American Psychiatric Association (APA), defined paraphilias as "characterized by arousal in response to sexual objects or situations that are not part of normative arousal activity patterns and that in varying degrees may interfere with the capacity for reciprocal, affectionate sexual activity" (p. 279). Paraphilias involve recurrent intense sexual urges and sexually arousing fantasies related to one of three elements:

1. nonhuman objects (e.g., fetishism)
2. the suffering or humiliation of oneself or one's partner (not just simulated) (e.g., sadism, masochism),
3. children or nonconsenting adults (e.g., exhibitionism, voyeurism, frotteurism, pedophilia)

The paraphiliac has urges and thoughts, for example, of sex with children, and may *act* on these urges and thoughts. The frequency of such acts may be "always," in the sense that paraphilic fantasies or stimuli are always necessary for erotic arousal and included in sexual activity. In this sense, the paraphilia is experienced as a compulsion that interferes with work and relationships, and the person may feel out of control (Levine et al., 1990). In other cases, the person may feel in control of the paraphilic impulses most of the time and lose control only during periods of stress.

In addition to the compulsive quality of paraphilias, it is not unusual for a person to express more than one paraphilia. According to Abel and Rouleau (1990):

NATIONAL DATA: People who have paraphilias have an average of three to four paraphilias. Except for sexual masochism, the sex ratio is estimated to be 20 males to each female (APA, 1987).

> As an initial paraphilia fades, a second paraphilia begins, accelerates in frequency, and may overtake the initial paraphilia as the most common deviant sexual behavior. In this fashion, some sex offenders have as many as 10 categories of paraphilic interest throughout their lifetime. (p. 14)

CONSIDERATION: Paraphiliacs differ in the way they view their paraphilia. While some feel that the only problem with paraphilia is the negative reaction of others to their behavior, others feel "extreme guilt, shame, and depression at having to engage in an unusual sexual activity that is socially unacceptable or that they regard as immoral" (APA, 1987, p. 281).

NATIONAL DATA: Half of the people with paraphilia who are seen clinically are married (APA, 1987).

The social and sexual relationships of the paraphiliac may suffer if the partner becomes aware of the paraphilia. For example, the partner may regard pedophilia as unacceptable and disengage from the paraphiliac, who is viewed as "abnormal." Similarly, the relationship may end if the partner is asked to participate in the paraphilia (e.g., the partner is asked to be the recipient of the sexual sadist's paraphilia or to dress the partner up in wet diapers [autonepiophilia]).

On the other hand, some sexually variant behaviors, referred to by Comfort (1987) as "off-diagonal behaviors," are practiced by couples with the goal of enhancing physical excitement and mutual pleasuring. Comfort suggested that these behaviors are a part of mature sexual expression when they are "playful, non-dangerous, not anti-social, and reinforcing to both parties." However, intervention is definitely needed "if a behavior is compulsive, limiting, stereotyped, anti-social or associated with deviant nonsexual behavior" (p. 8).

Types of Paraphilias

In this section, we discuss eight major types of paraphilias identified in the DSM-III-R and briefly identify a variety of others. We also discuss legal and illegal paraphilias and consider the question of whether or not rape is a paraphilia.

Table 17.1 identifies and describes eight types of paraphilias. The major emphasis in diagnosis of these paraphilias should be on recurrent, intense urges and fantasies; acting on the urges is secondary and need not necessarily be present.

Exhibitionism

Exhibitionism involves an intense, recurrent sexual urge (over a period of at least six months), often accompanied by sexually arousing fantasies, to expose one's genitals to a stranger. The essential quality of being an exhibitionist is the compelling urge (not necessarily the act) to exhibit one's genitals. The urge to exhibit appears to manifest itself most in persons in late adolescence and the early 20s. Few arrests are made among those over 40 (APA, 1987). The urge to exhibit may be as strong for older people, but they may have gained more control over acting on the urges.

TABLE 17.1 The Eight Major Paraphilias

Paraphilia	Description
Exhibitionism	Exposing one's genitals to a stranger or having a recurrent urge to do so.
Frotteurism	Touching or rubbing a nonconsenting person in a sexual manner or having a recurrent urge to do so.
Pedophilia	Engaging in sexual behavior with a child or having a recurrent urge to do so.
Voyeurism	Watching a person who is either nude, undressing, or engaging in sexual behavior and is unaware that someone is watching or having a recurrent urge to do so.
Fetishism	Becoming sexually aroused by actual or fantasized objects (e.g., leather, lingerie, or shoes).
Transvestic fetishism	Becoming sexually aroused by dressing in the clothes of the opposite sex.
Sexual sadism	Becoming sexually aroused by actual or fantasized infliction of pain, humiliation, or physical constraint on another.
Sexual masochism	Becoming sexually aroused by actual or fantasized inflicted pain, humiliation, or physical constraint by another.

Exhibitionism is virtually never diagnosed in women. The DSM-III-R (APA, 1987) criterion specifies sexual arousal to fantasies or exposing one's genitals to an unsuspecting stranger. Therefore nude dancers and topless waitresses would typically not meet the criterion. A single case of a female exhibitionist was reported by Grob (1985). After gaining the attention of passing truck drivers or occupants of low flying airplanes she would undress and experience a spontaneous orgasm when her genitals were exposed.

Money (1986) provided an example of the extent to which the male exhibitionist feels driven to expose himself:

> When the urge does come, it comes so strong that you really want to do it. It just blocks off everything that makes sense . . . everything else that could maybe stop you. . . . You want to do it so bad. . . . I was driving, and the urge just came out from nowhere to do it. . . . I must have passed up about ten or fifteen places where I could have done it, trying not to do it. . . . But it just kept tingling with me. Stop here! Stop there! Stop Here! Go ahead! You can do it! And the feeling that I had inside was one like, if I didn't do it, I'd be missing out on something very, very great. It just kept on going. I ended up driving halfway to Annapolis, trying not to do it, just passing up places. And it got so strong, I just had to do it. I just had to get out and do it. (p. 35)

The exhibitionist exposes his genitals to women or children he does not know for several reasons. Sexual excitement is a primary one. Hearing a woman yell and watching her horrified face is sexually stimulating for some exhibitionists. Once sexually excited, he may masturbate to orgasm.

Exhibitionism is sometimes regarded as a "victimless" crime.

Another reason is the desire to shock women. Exhibiting himself may be a way of directing anger and hostility toward women. Although the woman he exposes himself to has not injured him, other women may have belittled him (or he has perceived it that way); or he has recently been unable to get and maintain an erection, blames his lack of erection on women, and exposes himself as a way of getting back at them.

Some exhibitionists expose themselves as a way of relieving stress. When the stress reaches a peak, the man exhibits himself, masturbates, and relieves the stress. Still other exhibitionists expose themselves with a "sexually arousing fantasy that the person observing him will become sexually aroused" (APA, p. 282).

DeFazio and Cunningham (1987) described exhibitionism in a 32-year-old spinal cord-injured male with complete sensory and motor deficits below the waist. Despite being unable to obtain feedback physiologically, maintain an erection, or have an ejaculation, his exhibitionism persisted. The researchers suggested that exhibitionism provided the man with a sense of masculinity and sexual adequacy.

Some people have referred to exhibitionism, public masturbation, and voyeurism as "victimless crimes;" however, these behaviors can cause harm because victims may be traumatized. Furthermore, in a small minority of offenders, Maletzky (1991) noted that these offenses can predispose the offender toward more aggressive acts, such as pedophilia and frotteurism. The DSM-III-R (APA, 1987) noted that while a pedophile may expose himself as a precursor to sexual activity with a child, an exhibitionist is not usually physically dangerous to the victim.

CONSIDERATION: If confronted by an exhibitionist we suggest that a victim remain calm and try not to appear shocked or alarmed. However, we recommend leaving the situation and immediately making a report to the local law enforcement agency (police, sheriff, or campus security).

The primary goal of the telephonicophiliac, obscene phone caller, is to become aroused by the activity of the phone call and to shock the stranger.

It may be helpful to law enforcement agencies to obtain reports of "minor" offenses of exhibitionism and voyeurism. One reason is that while sex offenders have a preferred method of offending, if access to that method is unavailable or blocked, they may engage in a less preferred method. Langevin, Paitich, and Russon (1985) reported that all of the voyeurs referred to their sex offender clinic had also committed other sexual offenses. Langevin and Lang (1987) cited two studies of exhibitionists in which "20% of them had committed one or more violent assaults in the past" (p. 213). Information provided in reports to law enforcement agencies may provide information helpful in investigating other crimes.

A variation of the exhibitionist is the obscene phone caller, also known as a **telephonicophiliac.** This person is aroused by and derives satisfaction from using obscene language on the telephone with a stranger. The caller is most often a man who, like the exhibitionist, rarely confronts his victim.

Since the person who is called is usually selected at random from the phone book, single women might consider an unlisted number or using only their first and middle initials in the listing. The best response to an obscene caller is to gently hang up the phone (slamming it down may be interpreted by the caller as having "shocked" the victim). Doing so may eventually result in extinction of the calling behavior. If the phone calls persist, contact the phone company and request help through their annoyance call center. You may also report obscene and harassing calls to your local law enforcement agency.

Frotteurism

Recurring, intense, sexual urges (for at least six months) accompanied by arousing fantasies that involve touching or rubbing, often with the genitals against a non-consenting person is known as **frotteurism** (fro-TUR-izm). **Toucheurism** involves actively using one's hands on the victim. While the person may be distressed over the overwhelming urge to touch or rub against another, he may also act on those fantasies. The person usually chooses a crowded place for the activity. He presses against the sexually desired person while saying, "Excuse me," then moves to another part of the crowd and presses against someone else. This behavior, known as frottage, usually goes unnoticed. But the feelings aroused by pressing against another may be used in a masturbatory fantasy later.

The frotteur may also fantasize about having an exclusive and caring relationship with the person he touches or rubs. "However, he recognizes that in order to avoid possible prosecution, he must escape detection after touching his victim. The victim may not initially protest the frottage because she cannot imagine that such a provocative sexual act would be committed in such a public place" (APA, 1987, p. 283). Langevin and Lang (1987) cautioned that toucherism may be associated with sexually aggressive behavior. When done in lonely or isolated places it may have been a prelude to an attempted rape which was thwarted by the offender's fear or inexperience, or by unexpected resistance from the victim.

Pedophilia

Pedophilia in our society is popularly regarded as "any kind of sexual behavior between an adult and a legally underage person" (Feierman, 1990, p. 3). Pedophilia is characterized by "recurrent, intense, sexual urges and sexually arousing fantasies, of at least six months' duration, involving sexual activity with a prepubescent child" (APA, 1987, p. 284). The pedophile has either acted on these urges or is very much distressed by them. To be diagnosed as having pedophilia, an individual must be at least 16 years old and at least five years older than the child. The child target must be 13 years old or younger (APA, 1987). Attraction to girls is about twice as common as attraction to boys (APA, 1987, p. 284). Many people with pedophilia are sexually aroused by both young girls and young boys.

CONSIDERATION: Whether or not sex between children and adults is considered acceptable varies across societies and historical time periods. Bullough (1990) observed that "what appears obvious from a historical overview is that adult/child and adult/adolescent sexual behavior has had different meanings at different historical times" (p. 70). For example, during the eighteenth and nineteenth centuries in England, a child of 12 could consent to sexual behavior with a middle-aged adult. Even children under 12 "could be seduced with near impunity in privacy" (p. 74).

In addition to the term "pedophilia," a number of other terms have developed to describe adult sexual behavior with children. These include "cross-generational sex," "adult/child sexual interactions," "incest," "man/child association," and "father/daughter sexual abuse" (Bullough, 1990). A wide range of behaviors may also be included in the definition of pedophilia. On one end of the continuum are such activities as undressing the child, looking at the nude body of a child, exposing oneself to the child, masturbating in the presence of the child, and fondling the child. Alternatively, the other end of the continuum includes such behaviors as performing fellatio or cunnilingus on the child, penetrating the child's vagina, mouth, or anus with one's finger, foreign object, or penis, and using various levels of force to do so.

The pedophile often develops a series of rationalizations for engaging in sexual activity with children. These include "it is educational for the child," "the child receives pleasure from these activities," and the child is "sexually provocative" and instigated the activities (APA, 1987, p. 284). Kalichman (1991) observed considerable psychopathology among pedophiles in contrast to sex offenders with adolescent victims.

NATIONAL DATA: In a national survey of adults, 27% of the women and 16% of the men reported that they had been victims of child sexual abuse (Finkelhor, Hotaling, Lewis, & Smith, 1990).

Pedophiles may use a range of strategies for getting into a social context where children are available. Such strategies include becoming a day-care worker or scout leader, marrying a woman with a young child, or abducting children from strangers.

The pedophile is most often an adult male (Fontaine, 1990) who is a relative or family friend of the child. The ratio of heterosexual to homosexual pedophiles is approximately 11 to one (Moser, 1992). Typically, the adult heterosexual male is a family friend visiting the parents of the child. The pedophile may excuse himself as though to go to the bathroom and then sneak into the bedroom of the child for sexual contact; or he may pretend that he is putting the child to bed or saying goodnight when he is actually using the occasion to rub the child's genitals.

CONSIDERATION: Sociologist Edwin Schur (1988) emphasized that traditional male gender role socialization may perpetuate child sexual abuse. Schur suggested that "our culture promotes sexual victimization of children when it encourages males to believe that they have over-powering sexual needs that must be met by whatever means available" (p. 173). Schur said that this belief, and the association of sexual conquest with masculinity, enables men to think of using children for their own sexual gratification. The implication here is that one way to discourage child sexual abuse is to change our traditional notions of masculinity and male sexuality.

Sometimes an adolescent is the object of the pedophile's urges (referred to as **hebephilia**). Sexual behavior between an adult and an adolescent is called ephebosexual behavior. The following illustrates such behavior from the viewpoint of a student.

> Our family was having a family gathering with all the relatives for Thanksgiving. It was held in the back yard of my aunt's. I had to go inside the house to get something and while I was inside one of my uncles came in. At that time we were pretty close and so, at first, I didn't think anything of the following events.
>
> My uncle came into the kitchen where I was alone and hugged and kissed me. I kissed him back. Then he kissed me again and because we were close, I didn't think anything about the second kiss. I then moved into the walk-in pantry and my uncle followed me and wanted to hug and kiss me again.
>
> I then realized this was no longer a "friendly kiss." I tried to move from the pantry and he blocked me. I tried not to act scared, even though I was. Trying to dodge him, he moved quickly and knocked a glass jar off the shelf. He told me to get paper towels to clean up the mess. Then my cousin came in the kitchen so I asked her to help with the broken jar and made an excuse to get outside. That was all that happened. To this day, I get chills when I have to be around my uncle, but I'm always careful not to be alone in his presence.
>
> I never told anyone of this event. He is my mother's favorite and closest brother and at the time I decided not to hurt her. (Author's files)

Voyeurism

Voyeurism involves recurrent, intense urges to look at unsuspecting people who are naked, undressing, or engaging in sexual behavior. These urges usually involve sexually arousing fantasies. In order to be diagnosed as having voyeurism, the person must have had these urges for at least six months and either acted on or been distressed by them (APA, 1987). The person who looks at magazines with nude photos or who watches erotic films is not necessarily classified as having voyeurism because the people posing in the magazines and films know that they are being watched. However, a voyeur may look at nude people in magazines or in movies and fantasize that they do not know they are being looked at.

Most voyeurs spend a lot of time planning to peep and will risk a great deal to do so. The voyeur regards climbing over fences, hiding in bushes, and shivering in the cold as worth the trouble. Peeping is the condition of sexual excitement, which most often results in ejaculation through masturbation either during the peeping or later. The voyeur's targets are usually female strangers. Although some voyeurs are married, they may not derive excitement from watching their wives or any familiar woman undress.

Voyeurism is usually regarded as a male disorder, typically occurring among young men. However, Hurlbert (1992) presented what he believed to be the first reported case study of an adult female voyeurist. The 26-year-old woman he described had a psychological diagnosis of schizoid personality disorder; she was very withdrawn and isolated from social contact. She felt sexual feelings and experienced orgasm only when self-stimulating during voyeuristic activities and fantasies. She felt humiliated and remorseful over her sexual activities, yet dropped out of treatment, resigned to continue her life as a "loner."

Fetishism

Fetishism involves a pattern, of at least six month's duration, of deriving sexual arousal or sexual gratification from actual or fantasized inanimate objects. A diagnosis of fetishism requires that the person has either acted on such urges or has been disturbed by them.

Sometimes a preference for sexual attire may become a prerequisite for becoming aroused. In such case, the clothes may become a fetish.

Gebhard (1976) suggested that fetishes are a "graded phenomenon."

> At one end of the range is slight preference; next is strong preference; next is the point where the fetish item is a necessity to sexual activity; and at the terminal end of the range the fetish item substitutes for a living sexual partner. . . . Statistical normality ends and fetishism begins somewhere at the level of strong preference. (pp. 157–158)

Once a fetish begins at the slight preference level, it may progress in its intensity. Figure 17.1 illustrates how a fetish may progress from being a preference to being a necessity to being a symbolic substitute for a sexual partner.

CONSIDERATION: Gebhard (1976) suggested that fetishism is an illustration of what philosopher Alfred North Whitehead called "the fallacy of misplaced concreteness": the symbol is given all the power and reality of the actual thing and the person responds to the symbol just as he or she would to the thing (p. 161). The powerful symbolic component of fetishes may account for the fact that fetishism is virtually nonexistent in preliterate cultures. Rather, "fetishism seems largely confined to literate people taught to be imaginative and to make extensive use of symbolism in verbal and written communication and hence in their thought processes" (Gebhard, 1976, p. 162).

Fetishes may be divided into two types: media and form (Gebhard, 1976). "A media fetish is one wherein the substance rather than the form of the object is the important aspect" (p. 159). For example, a person with a leather fetish responds to leather as an erotic stimulus whether the leather is in the form of a glove, shoe, or coat. "A form fetish is one wherein the form of the object is more important than the material of which it is constituted" (p. 159). For example, a person with a shoe fetish responds to shoes as an erotic stimulus no matter whether the shoes are made of plastic, leather, or cloth. The most common form fetish objects are clothing items,

FIGURE 17.1 Stages in the Progression of Fetishism

Source: Based on Gebhard, P. H. (1976). Fetishism and sadomasochism. In M. S. Weinberg (Ed.), Sex research: Studies from the Kinsey Institute. New York: Oxford University Press.

STAGE ONE: Preference	STAGE TWO: Necessity	STAGE THREE: Symbolic Substitute
A man dates only women who wear high-heeled red shoes.	A man cannot become aroused and achieve an erection unless his partner is wearing high-heeled red shoes.	A man habitually achieves orgasm by holding or touching high-heeled red shoes during masterbation.

including panties, stockings, lingerie, high-heeled shoes, and boots. Common media fetishes include leather, satin, and latex. Fetishes may also include sounds (a particular song, the clicking of a train on the tracks) and scents (perfume, incense).

Sometimes a paraphilia involves both scents and texture, as in **autonepiophilia** (deriving sexual arousal or gratification from wearing wet diapers). One man explained:

> I've had a fetish for wearing wet diapers and latex rubber panties, since being a bedwetter as a boy. . . . Over the years I have been in seven adult diaper clubs and correspond with some 250 to 300 men, who love diapers, too . . . Marriage was unhappy for me. I could not permit myself to enjoy wearing wet diapers at home, except for a short time when I would fake loss of bladder control. (Money, 1988, p. 142)

Transvestic Fetishism

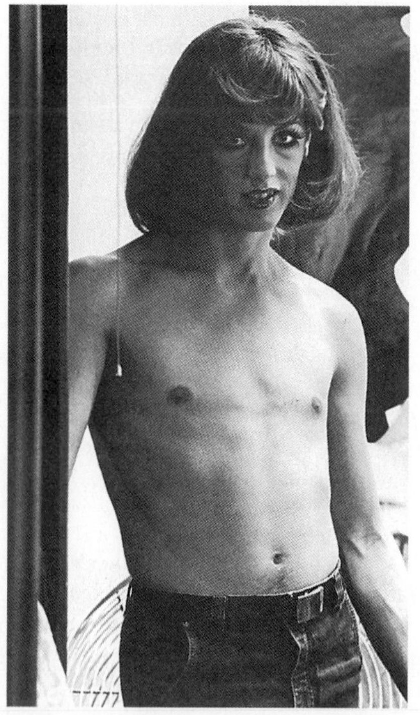

Transvestites, also known as cross dressers, like to wear makeup and wigs so as to look like a woman.

Transvestic fetishism involves recurrent, intense, sexual urges and sexually arousing fantasies, of at least six months' duration, involving cross-dressing (i.e., a man dressing in women's clothes). The person has acted on these urges or is distressed by them (APA, 1987). (See the following Self-Assessment: Cross-Gender Fetishism Scale.)

Transvestic fetishism is diagnosed only in heterosexual men. Women rarely cross-dress because it is common for women to wear clothes similar to what men wear (hence, the forbiddenness of dressing in the clothes of a man is less likely to be sexually provocative). Men who cross-dress because they feel that they are really women trapped in a man's body are not diagnosed as transvestites but rather as transsexuals (transsexuals are discussed in Chapter 8, Gender Roles). Female impersonators are not usually regarded as having transvestic fetishism because they are not sexually aroused by cross-dressing.

Transvestites, also known as cross-dressers, usually own a set of women's clothing that they wear when alone. Some cross-dressers also wear makeup and/or wigs. While cross-dressed, the transvestite usually masturbates and may imagine other men being attracted to him as a woman in his female attire.

Reasons for cross-dressing may be emotional ("I like to dress as a woman to express the feminine aspect of myself"), erotic ("I get sexually excited from wearing a woman's clothes"), or social-psychological ("I like to be somebody else"). Most often the motives are mixed.

The cause of transvestism is unclear, but it is common for a transvestite male to recall dressing up as a girl when he was a child (Bullough, Bullough, & Smith, 1983). He may have been forced to do so, perhaps as punishment or to satisfy his mother's desire. One transvestite in one of the authors' human sexuality class recalled, "Mom always wanted a girl, so she dressed me up to be the girl she never had." Or he may have sought the experience. Another man said, "I began putting on my mother's clothes when I was about 12. The first time I did it, I got very excited.

Self Assessment

The Cross-Gender Fetishism Scale

The following questions ask about your experiences in dressing or making up as the opposite sex. These questions are meant to include experiences you may have had during puberty or early adolescence as well as more recent experiences.

Please circle one and only one answer to each question. If you are not sure of the meaning of a question, you may ask the person giving the questionnaire to explain it to you. There is no time limit for answering these questions.

1. Have you ever felt sexually aroused when putting on women's underwear, stockings, or a nightgown?
   a. Yes (1.0)
   b. No (0)
   c. Have never put on any of these (0)
2. Have you ever felt sexually aroused when putting on women's shoes or boots?
   a. Yes (1.0)
   b. No (0)
   c. Have never put on either of these (0)
3. Have you ever felt sexually aroused when putting on women's jewelry or outer garments (blouse, skirt, dress, etc.)?
   a. Yes (1.0)
   b. No (0)
   c. Have never put on any of these (0)
4. Have you ever felt sexually aroused when putting on women's perfume or makeup, or when shaving your legs?
   a. Yes (1.0)
   b. No (0)
   c. Have never done any of these (0)
5. Have you ever masturbated while thinking of yourself putting on (or wearing) women's underwear, stockings, or a nightgown?
   a. Yes (1.0)
   b. No (0)
6. Have you ever masturbated while thinking of yourself putting on (or wearing) women's shoes or boots?
   a. Yes (1.0)
   b. No (0)
7. Have you ever masturbated while thinking of yourself putting on (or wearing) women's jewelry or outer garments?
   a. Yes (1.0)
   b. No (0)
8. Have you ever masturbated while thinking of yourself putting on (or wearing) women's perfume or makeup, or while thinking of yourself shaving your legs (or having shaved legs)?
   a. Yes (1.0)
   b. No (0)
9. Has there ever been a period in your life of one year (or longer) during which you always or usually felt sexually aroused when putting on female underwear or clothing?
   a. Yes (1.0)
   b. No (0)
   c. Have never put on female underwear or clothing (0)
10. Has there even been a period in your life of one year (or longer) during which you always or usually masturbated if you put on female underwear or clothing?
   a. Yes (1.0)
   b. No (0)
   c. Have never put on female underwear or clothing (0)
11. Have you ever put on women's clothes or makeup for the main purpose of becoming sexually excited and masturbating?
   a. Yes (1.0)
   b. No (0)

Scoring The Cross-Gender Fetishism Scale (CGFS) measures the erotic arousal value (for men) of dressing in women's clothes, putting on perfume and makeup, and shaving the legs. In 1982, Freund, Steiner, and Chan coined the term "cross-gender fetishism" to characterize fetishistic activity that is combined with fantasies of being a woman and carried out with objects symbolic of femininity. This term is roughly equivalent to transvestism.

In the copy of the scale above, following each response option is the scoring weight for that response, either a 1 or a 0. The total is computed by simply adding the scores on the 11 items. Higher scores indicate a more extensive history of cross-gender fetishism. Note that positive endorsement of items doesn't indicate current arousal by cross-gender fantasy but rather acknowledgement of some history of the fantasy.

Reliability and Validity Using scoring weights empirically derived from his sample, Blanchard (1985) found an alpha reliability coefficient of 0.95. He found a strong association between scores on the CGFS and categorization of erotic partner preference of patients in a gender clinic.

References

Blanchard, R. (1985). Research methods for the typological study of gender disorders in males. In B. W. Steiner (Ed.), *Gender dysphoria: Development, research, management* (pp. 227–257). New York: Plenum.

Blanchard, R. (1988). Cross-Gender Fetishism Scale. In C. M. Davis, W. L. Yarber, & S. L. Davis (Eds.), *Sexuality-related measures: A compendium* (pp. 268–270). Lake Mills, IA: Graphic. Used by permission.

Freund, K., Steiner, B. W., & Chan, S. (1982). Two types of cross-gender identity. *Archives of Sexual Behavior, II,* 49–63.

When I looked into the mirror I felt as if I was transformed into a woman, and I was in ecstasy. I would do it every week thereafter, when my mother was out" (Talamini, 1981, p. 72). Other transvestites point to no specific incident that led to their cross-dressing.

When a man first identifies himself as a transvestite, he may feel a sense of shame and disgust. With time, however, the pleasure and satisfaction associated with the deviance outweighs the negative attitudes society has about his behavior. He begins to rationalize his behavior and to feel good about it: "A lot of men would like to express the feminine aspect of themselves but they're afraid to do it" is one such rationalization.

Other men explain their behavior by attributing it to their heredity. They view transvestism as a biological compulsion: "I can't help the way I am." Some transvestites even feel that the stars and planets are astrologically responsible for their destiny (Talamini, 1981).

Sexual Sadism

Sexual sadism and sexual masochism are two sides of the same coin, in that they both involve associating psychological or physical suffering and humiliation with sexual arousal and/or pleasure. **Sexual sadism** is characterized by recurrent, intense, sexual urges and sexually arousing fantasies, of at least six months' duration, involving acts that hurt or humiliate the sexual partner. In some cases, the sadist will have acted on these urges; more often, the sadist will not have acted on these urges but, in either case, will be distressed by them.

The cries and suffering of the sexual partner are the source of sexual excitement for the sadist. Such suffering may be by consenting masochistic partners or by those who are forced to participate. Sadistic acts or fantasies may involve dominance, (e.g., forcing the victim to crawl), restraint or bondage (e.g., tying the victim to a chair), spanking, whipping, beating, burning, shocking (with electricity), cutting, strangling, mutilating, or killing. However, in some cases, the pain may be only symbolic, as when the sadist "whips" someone with a feather.

Sexual Masochism

Sexual masochism is characterized by recurrent, intense, sexual urges and sexually arousing fantasies, of at least six months' duration, in which sexual arousal or gratification is obtained through enacting scripts that involve suffering pain. Such pain may be physical or psychological and may involve being humiliated, beaten, bound, cut, bitten, spanked, choked, pricked, or shocked. While pain may actually be experienced, the diagnosis of the paraphilia may involve only intense, recurrent urges and fantasies for at least six months. The person may have these fantasies while masturbating or while having sexual relations.

Gebhard (1976) emphasized that it is not the pain per se that is sexually exciting to the masochist but rather the enactment of the script that involves pain. In common masochistic scripts, "the masochist must allegedly have done something meriting punishment, there must be threats and suspense before the punishment is meted out. . . . Some masochists dislike the pain while it is being inflicted, but obtain gratification by anticipation of the pain or by thinking about it after it has ceased" (pp. 163–164).

The sadist and the masochist may use each other to act out their sexual scripts. A favorite pattern is bondage and discipline (B and D), where the sadist ties up (bondage) and whips (discipline) the masochist. Often, the sadist will act out a scene by telling the masochist of a series of the latter's wrongdoings and the punishment to follow while the masochist screams for mercy. Both delight in the activity.

These chains and locks are used by the sadist to tie up (put in bondage) and whip (discipline) the masochist.

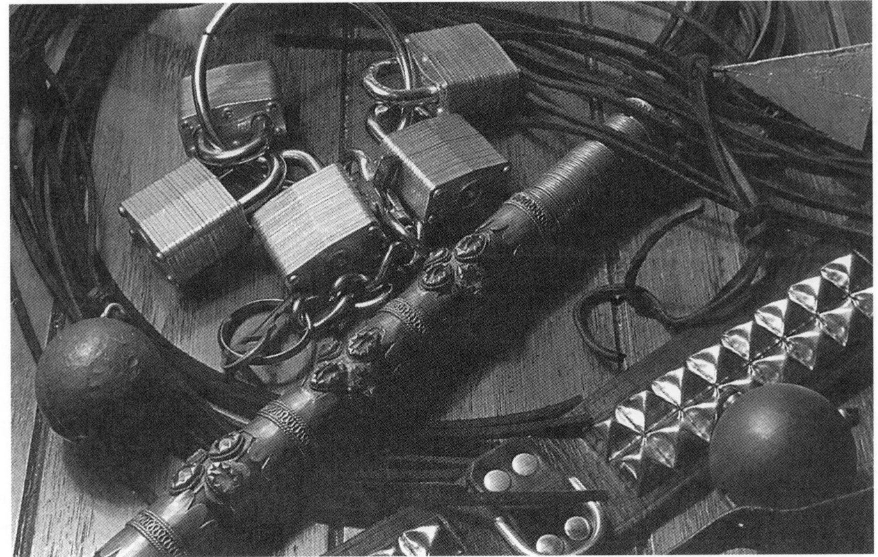

Some large cities have "clubs" that specialize in sadomasochism (S and M). The Chateau in the West Hollywood section of Los Angeles is an example. The "staff" consists of 13 women—six dominants (sadists), three submissives (masochists), and four "switch-hitters." (Weinberg, Williams, & Moser [1984] noted that the majority of those who enjoy S and M are equally comfortable in either role). Equipment includes a wide range of racks, cages, chains, wooden crosses, and whipping posts. The price is a dollar a minute (each treatment is 40 minutes), and more than 1,000 customers have been served by being bound, gagged, stretched, and beaten. Similar clubs are located in San Francisco, Miami, and Dallas.

Some partners exhibit mild forms of S and M in their relationship as illustrated in the following example.

> I like to be tied up and blindfolded. I can't tell what my partner is doing but, on occasion, he has used candles and dripped the hot wax on my body and my breasts. I like it when he orders me around and dominates me. It's not S and M but a step towards it. I, too, tie my boyfriend up and do as I want with him while he is totally submissive. I don't want whips and severe pain, even though we have used handcuffs and ropes; we love each other and know it's fun, and we're not trying to hurt each other. (Authors' files)

A less severe form of S and M involves mild spanking in which one partner will playfully spank the buttocks of the partner. The spanking is not regarded as painful by the giver or receiver. Weinberg et al. (1984) noted that the majority of S and M participants are of the mild variety for whom S and M is "simply a form of sexual excitement which they voluntarily and mutually choose to explore" (p. 388).

In conducting research for his popular counselling book, Alex Comfort (1987) studied what he referred to as "so-called 'bondage' or the playing of 'restraint games.' " He found that it occurred with surprising frequency, not only in fantasy, but also in couples' activities. While he said "the 'bondage' routine is a definite situational fetish for some individuals and a strong preference for others (of both sexes)," a high number of his informants "seemed to be incorporating it into a varied sexual repertoire as one more resource" (p. 13). While this type of "bondage" could be enacted in a sadomasochistic way, he found that couples used it more as a sexual technique, a kind of foreplay, rather than as a compulsive fantasy or activity.

TABLE 17.2 Relative Percentages of Paraphilic Behaviors Among Paraphilias

Paraphilic Behavior	Relative Percentage
Exhibitionism	24.6%
Frotteurism	18.0%
Pedophilia (nonincest)	14.0%
Voyeurism	10.0%
Transvestic fetishism	7.1%
Sexual masochism	6.6%
Fetishism	2.4%
Sexual sadism	1.3%

Source: Abel, G. G., Becker, J. V., Mittelman, M. S., Cunningham-Rathner, J., Rouleau, J. L., & Murphy, W. D. (1987). Self-reported sex crimes of non-incarcerated paraphiliacs. *Journal of Interpersonal Violence, 2,* 3–25. Used by permission.

Gebhard (1976) suggested that "sadomasochism is embedded in our culture since our culture operates on the basis of dominance-submission relationships, and aggression is socially valued" (p. 163). The cultural context for sadomasochism is especially salient to gender relationships: "the male is supposed to be dominant and aggressive sexually and the female reluctant or submissive. Violence and sex are commingled to make a profitable package to sell through mass media" (Gebhard, 1976, p. 163). Comfort (1987) noted that not only is sadomasochistic expression reinforced by U. S. society, but the balance between sexual arousal and aggression is made more precarious by the high degree of "non-sexual, free-floating anger and dominance" (p. 5). But this explanation of sadomasochism is incomplete, since most men are similarly socialized yet relatively few engage in paraphilic sadistic behavior.

The development of masochistic behavior is easier to explain. Some masochists report having experienced sexual pleasure while being punished as children; for example, the person who was spanked on a parent's knee may have become sexually excited by having his or her genitals rubbed on the parent's knee. These experiences became linked in the child's mind.

CONSIDERATION: In psychoanalytic literature, as well as in the larger culture, there is the notion that women are inherently masochistic. This notion underlies the belief that abused women stay with their abusers because they enjoy the abuse. In an article entitled "The Myth of Women's Masochism," Caplan (1984) observed that the notion that women are inherently masochistic is unfounded and does women a "profound disservice."

Some paraphilic behaviors occur more frequently than others. A team of researchers (Abel et al., 1987) looked at the relative percentages of various paraphilic behaviors reported by a sample of nonincarcerated paraphiliacs. The relative percentages of the total number of completed paraphilic acts reported by Abel et al. (1987) are listed in Table 17.2.

Other Paraphilias

Although we have discussed the major paraphilias presented in DSM III-R, many others have been identified. John Money (1986), catalogued 40 or so. Examples of the varieties of paraphilias are presented in Table 17.3.

TABLE 17.3 Other Paraphilias

Paraphilia	Definition
Apotomnophilia	Becoming sexually aroused by the thought of becoming an amputee.
Acrotomophilia	Deriving sexual arousal or gratification from engaging in sex with an amputee.
Asphyxiophilia	Cutting off one's air supply to enhance orgasm.
Autonepiophilia	Deriving sexual arousal or gratification from wearing wet diapers.
Coprophilia	Using feces for sexual arousal either by watching another defecate or by defecating on someone.
Ephebophilia	Engaging in sexual behavior with an adolescent or having a recurrent urge to do so.
Erotophonophilia	Lust murder in which the partner is killed as a means of atoning for sex with the individual.
Formicophilia	Becoming sexually aroused by ants, bugs, or other small, crawling creatures.
Gerontophilia	Becoming sexually aroused by elderly individuals.
Klismaphilia	Becoming sexually aroused by receiving an enema.
Narratophilia	Listening to "dirty talk" as a means of becoming sexually aroused. Phone sex companies depend on people with this paraphilia for their income.
Necrophilia	Deriving sexual arousal or gratification from sexual activity with a dead person (or person acting the role of a corpse).
Nepiophilia	Becoming sexually aroused by babies.
Olfactophilia	Becoming sexually aroused by certain scents.
Partialism	Deriving sexual arousal or gratification from a specific nongenital body part (e.g., foot).
Pictophilia	Becoming sexually aroused in reference to sexy photographs.
Raptophilia	Becoming sexually aroused by surprise attack and violent assault.
Somnophilia	Fondling a person who is sleeping so as to become sexually aroused. The person is often a stranger.
Telephonicophilia	Becoming sexually aroused by calling a stranger on the phone and either talking about sex or making sexual sounds (breathing heavily).
Urophilia	Using urine for sexual arousal either by watching someone urinate or by urinating on someone.
Zoophilia	Becoming aroused by sexual contact with animals. Commonly known as bestiality.

Legal versus Illegal Paraphilias

The definitions of paraphilias presented in this chapter, which are based on the DSM-III-R developed by the American Psychiatric Association (1987), do not necessarily meet legal or other nonmedical criteria for what constitutes mental disease, mental disorder, or mental disability (APA, 1987, p. xxix). Paraphilias are legal or illegal depending on the degree to which the rights of others are affected. Formicophilia, olfactophilia, and klismaphilia do not infringe on the rights of others and are of little concern to the law. Voyeurism, exhibitionism, and pedophilia are examples of paraphilias that interfere with the rights of others and carry legal penalties. Voyeurism and exhibitionism are clinical terms; in the legal system the criminal acts may be referred to as secret peeping and indecent exposure. They are usually regarded as misdemeanors and punishable by a fine (repeated offenses may involve mandatory outpatient treatment at a mental health facility). Pedophilic acts are punishable by imprisonment. Legal charges may range from taking indecent liberties with a minor, to sodomy or rape. The majority of apprehended sex offenders are arrested for acts of exhibitionism, pedophilia, and voyeurism (APA, 1987).

CONSIDERATION: Laws regulating sexual behavior vary from state to state. Some states regard exhibitionism as a misdemeanor, while others classify it as a felony. The penalty ranges from a fine to a prison term. If the exhibitionist is drunk or mentally retarded, police officers tend to regard his self-exposure differently from those who compulsively expose themselves and repeatedly are picked up for exhibitionism.

Is Rape a Paraphilia?

There is professional disagreement over whether rape should be classified as a paraphilia. Abel and Rouleau (1990) argued that rape is a paraphilia on the basis of clinical interviews with rapists who report compulsive urges and fantasies to commit rape, feeling guilty afterwards, and repeating the behavior. Persons with paraphilias characteristically experience compulsive urges and fantasies and guilt and also repeat the paraphilic behavior. In addition, the age of onset for interest in rape and the age of onset for other paraphilias is similar. Over half of rapists report developing their interest in rape by age 21, the age by which other paraphilias often develop.

The DSM-III-R (APA, 1987) does not list rape as a specific paraphilic disorder. Perhaps psychiatrists do not classify rape as a paraphilia because it is more violent and sexually aggressive than other paraphilias (except some expressions of sadomasochism). In addition, society may be reluctant to accept rape as a paraphilia because paraphilias are associated with less punishment than rape.

The Origins of Paraphilias: Theoretical Perspectives

Various theoretical perspectives offer explanations for why paraphilias exist or why particular individuals develop paraphilias. Next, we look for clues to the origins of paraphilias within the theoretical frameworks of psychoanalysis, feminism, learning theory, and biological theory. We also explore the origins of paraphilias using Money's (1986) theoretical construct of "vandalized lovemap" and Freund's (1990) concept of "courtship disorder."

Psychoanalytic Perspective

From a psychoanalytic perspective, paraphilias may be viewed as symptoms of unresolved subconscious conflicts. For example, an exhibitionist may frighten unsuspecting women by exposing himself to them as a way of rebelling against them. Such rebellion may stem from having had a domineering mother or an unresolved Oedipal complex (see Chapter 8, Gender Roles), which has left the exhibitionist unable to engage in heterosexual intercourse. The urge to exhibit himself may be a subconscious symbolic substitute that compensates for the inability to have sexual relations with women.

Kline (1987) reviewed psychoanalytic conceptualizations of paraphilias and empirical research designed to test these theories. He concluded that while the evidence was not sufficient to refute Freudian theories, it also did not offer objective support. He lamented that since psychoanalytic theories "have reached a low ebb" (p. 173) it is unlikely that high quality research will put them to a scientific test.

Feminist Perspective

Paraphilias such as pedophilia and sexual sadism are, from a feminist perspective, expressions of aggression, not sexuality. The pedophile, sadist, and rapist express control and dominance through their paraphilic fantasies and behaviors.

The feminist perspective explains why there are many more male paraphiliacs than female paraphiliacs: Our culture has perpetuated traditional gender roles that emphasize male dominance, sexual aggression, and control.

Learning Theory

Learning theorists emphasize that paraphilias are learned by means of both classical and operant conditioning. In 1966, Rachman demonstrated how a fetish can be learned through classical conditioning. Using an experimental design, Rachman paired women's boots with erotic slides of nude women. As a result, the subjects began to experience erotic arousal to the sight of the boots alone.

Scarf, panty, and red high-heeled shoe fetishes may be a result of classical conditioning. The person may have experienced sexual pleasure when in the presence of these objects, learned to associate these objects with the pleasure, and developed a preference for these objects during sex.

Operant conditioning may also account for the development of some paraphilias. For example, the exhibitionist may be reinforced by the startled response of a woman and seek conditions under which she will exhibit a startled response (exposing his penis). By exposing his penis, she yells, and he is reinforced and wants to repeat the behavior with a new stranger.

Similarly, paraphilias may result from negative reinforcement. Negative reinforcement is defined as the strengthening of a behavior associated with the removal of something aversive. A paraphilia may be established since the associated behaviors remove feelings of anxiety, sadness, loneliness, and anger. Hence, when the exhibitionist exhibits to a victim, he feels a temporary reprieve from feelings of anxiety, which are replaced by feelings of excitement.

Levine et al. (1990) noted that paraphiliacs may be viewed as having "generally poor adaptive functioning" to the stresses of life. For some individuals then, a paraphilia is a retreat to a private world—their erotic hideaway (p. 101).

Biological Theory

Having individuals with different modes of thought and behavior offers a plasticity that promotes the evolutionary possibilities and survival of that species.

Raymond E. Goodman

The degree to which biological variables are responsible for the development of paraphilias is controversial. Just as heterosexuality, homosexuality, and bisexuality may be based on biological predispositions, so may paraphilic tendencies. Some people may be biologically "wired" to respond erotically to atypical stimuli. Moser (1992) contended that paraphilias are strong sexual responses to an individualized specific set of uncommon or inappropriate objects or potential partners and that these "lust" responses are "a basic aspect of sexual identity, set early in life, unchangeable by common sex therapy techniques and are not learned in a classical sense" (p. 66). While he did not define the mechanisms for these presumably innate predilections, other investigators have proposed there are neurochemical interactions during embryo development which influence cerebral organization (Flor-Henry, 1987).

Paraphilia as a Vandalized Lovemap

> In the confusion of so much complexity, it is not surprising that today's scientific knowledge of how the sexual brain develops and maintains its governance of sexuality and eroticism is still very preliminary, and subject to continual revision.
>
> *John Money*

John Money (1986; 1988) used the term "**lovemap**" to describe a mental representation, or template, which develops within the first few years of life. "It depicts your idealized lover and what, as a pair, you do together in the idealized, romantic, erotic, and sexualized relationship" (p. xvi). In other words, it establishes, or at least influences, the type of sexual partner and activities that will arouse you. Given the standard developmental hormones introduced into the developing fetus at the appropriate time and the traditional heterosexual socialization, people tend to be emotionally and sexually attracted to the other sex. "Normophilic lovemaps" are lovemaps that are consistent with what is culturally defined as appropriate. Lovemaps that involve deviations from what is generally considered as normal and acceptable are known as paraphilias. "On the street they are termed kinky or bizarre sex" (Money, 1988, p. 127). Paraphilic individuals are compulsively responsive to and dependent on personally and socially unacceptable stimuli for sexual arousal and orgasm.

The critical years in the development of the lovemap are between ages five and eight. "Major erotosexual traumas during this period may disrupt the consolidation of the lovemap that would otherwise be taking place" (Money, 1986, p. 19). Money provided examples of the social experiences that "vandalize" or disrupt traditional sexual-erotic development socialization and showed how these disruptions may contribute to the development of pedophilia.

Pedophiliacs may have been involved in a relationship with an older male and learned to repeat the age-discrepant sexual experience with a younger boy. "In adolescence and adulthood, they remain sexuoerotically boyish, and are paraphilically attracted only to juveniles of the same age as their own when they became a pedophile's partner" (Money, 1986, p. 21). Oftentimes, the experience itself will not be enough to trigger a pedophiliac lovemap. But in combination with a traumatic experience, such as grief over a loved one's death, the male may become particularly vulnerable. Hence, the feeling of having lost a significant other and of enjoying sexual pleasure in an age-discrepant context may bond one to that context for reasons related to emotional insecurity and physical pleasure. Freund, Watson, and Dickey (1990) found that pedophiles were significantly more likely to have been sexually abused as children than individuals who were not charged with a sexual offense against children.

Paraphilia as a Courtship Disorder

Some paraphilias may also be conceptualized as expressions of a common "underlying" disorder (Freund, 1990). The disorder in this case is a distortion of "normal" courtship, which is assumed to consist of a series of four phases in which progressively more intimate expressions of sexual behavior occur. In this theoretical approach each paraphilia omits most stages of courtship, or enacts them only in a superficial way. For example, "The rapist short-circuits all stages and immediately attempts intercourse" (Langevin & Lang, 1987, p. 203). The four courtship phases and examples of paraphilic distortions are presented in Table 17.4.

Another byproduct of the courtship disorder is that the paraphiliac may have difficulty loving a person because of his preoccupation with the paraphilic object. The deficient ability to love and the inability to progress through the courtship sequence makes it difficult to have a conventional sexual relationship (Levine et al., 1990).

TABLE 17.4 Courtship Phases and Paraphilic Distortions

Courtship Phase	Paraphilia
1. Location and first appraisal of a suitable partner	Voyeurism
2. Pretactile interaction, (e.g., looking, smiling, posturing, and talking to a prospective partner)	Exhibitionism
3. Tactile interaction	Frotteurism
4. Genital union	Raptophilia (forced sexual behavior)

Source: Freund, K. (1990). Courtship disorder. In W. L. Marshall, R. Laws, & H. E. Barbaree (Eds.), *Handbook of sexual assault* (pp. 195–206). New York: Plenum Press. Used by permission.

Treatment of Coercive Paraphilias

It may be discouraging to tell clients that we do not know how or why the development of their lust cues went awry, or how to correct this now. Nevertheless, it may save thousands of dollars in therapy and great amounts of grief and self-doubts.
Charles Moser

The behavioral expression of some of the paraphilias discussed in this chapter (exhibitionism, pedophilia, voyeurism) interferes with the rights of others. When people engaging in such behaviors come to the attention of the law, they are often required to enter a treatment program. In addition, some individuals with paraphilias voluntarily seek treatment before they are caught.

Usually the first step in a sex offender treatment program is a thorough assessment. This involves collecting information regarding the offense of record, as well as a sexual and social history. The therapist usually gathers the law enforcement report, victim statement, presentence investigation, and summaries of previous placements and treatment. Interviews with the client and relevant other people are conducted, and psychological testing may be done. In addition, sexual interest is assessed. The following Research Perspective examines the methods used in clinical and research settings for assessing sexual interest.

RESEARCH PERSPECTIVE

Methods of Assessment of Sexual Interest in Sex Offenders

Two developments in the past 20 years have advanced our understanding of sex offenders: theory development regarding the role of arousal and sexual interest and the development of assessment measures designed for this population (Murphy, Haynes, & Worley, 1991). Most of the research on sex offenders has focused on child sex offenders and rapists of women. Following is a description of the physiological and self-report measures employed in the sex offender research, as well as some discussion of their use.

Physiological Measures

Two physiological measures used to assess sexual interests of sex offenders are penile plethysmography and polygraph testing.

Penile Plethysmograph One of the ways to physiologically measure male sexual arousal to various sexual stimuli is to present the stimuli and measure the resulting degree of penile erection. Murphy et al. (1991, p. 79) credited "Zuckerman's (1972) seminal review" with establishing direct measure of penile tumescence (erection) as the most sensitive assessment of male sexual arousal. (Do you think the pun was

Continued

Continued

intended?) Such assessment involves stimulus material to be presented to the subject, a sensor to measure variations in the size of the penis, and a system for recording (Murphy et al., 1991). The stimulus material typically consists of videotapes, slides, or audiotapes of sexual partners or acts. Either the circumference of the penis or its volume may be measured. The penile plethysmograph consists of a band (transducer) made of mercury and rubber or metal that is placed around the penis to measure changes in its circumference. Not as widely available is a volumetric device, consisting of a cylinder over the penis, that allows measurement of the air displaced when the penis size changes.

Prior to the evaluation session, the researcher or therapist prepares the equipment and sets up the stimuli. Salter (1988) reported that slides are considered the weakest and videotapes the most arousing stimuli. Sometimes both are used, with slides used to assess the age and gender of the preferred object (used most often with child molesters) and audiotapes to determine the degree of force that is arousing (also used with child molesters and rapists). In a room alone, the offender places the transducer on his penis, making sure that his clothes do not touch it. The device is connected to a recording system in another room, which charts variations in penile tumescence. Directions are given via microphone from another room, allowing the offender as much privacy as possible. Safeguards ensure that the offender is attending to the stimulus presented and is not tampering with the plethysmograph.

Results are graphed continuously on chart paper, and penile circumference can be displayed on digital monitors. To present data in a standardized fashion (since circumference varies among men and across time), the results are usually in terms of percent of full erection. Figure 1 shows arousal data from a 39-year-old pedophile presented by Murphy et al. (1991, p. 81). This man reported he was attracted to young boys and revealed that he had molested nearly 30 young boys. These data summarize his responses to two-minute audiotapes portraying various levels of aggression in sexual activity between an adult man and eight- to 12-year-old boys, in contrast to his response to adults.

Research has replicated the finding that pedophile subjects can be distinguished from nonpedophile subjects on the basis of erection measures. Differentiating rapists

Continued

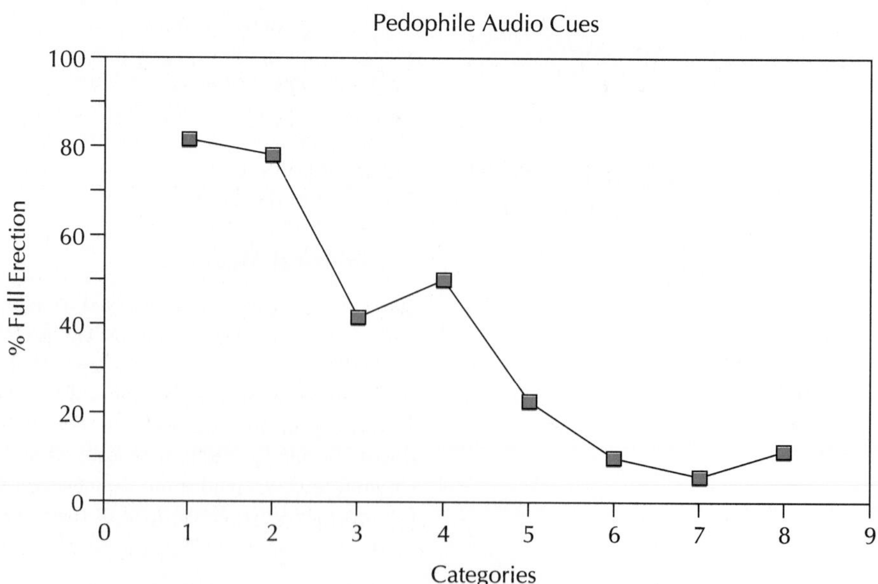

FIGURE 1 Sexual responding of a subject to audiotapes describing sexual interactions with children varying in level of aggression. Categories: 1 = Child Initiates; 2 = Child Mutual; 3 = Verbal Coercion; 4 = Physical Coercion; 5 = Sadism; 6 = Assault; 7 = Adult Female Mutual; 8 = Adult Male Mutual

Continued

from nonrapists, although consistent in early studies, has recently been more difficult, possibly due to differences in the stimulus materials used (Murphy et al., 1991). Plethysmograph results have also been helpful in determining interest in sexual sadism, identifying child molesters inclined toward child rape, separating recidivists from nonrecidivists, and measuring response to treatment (Salter, 1988).

However, important limitations must be noted in terms of accuracy of results and in how results are used. Arousal is not always acted upon, so measurement of deviant arousal does not prove that an individual has ever acted upon that arousal. Further, many offenders have been found to be heterogenous in their sexual interest, so not all offenders have similar (or even deviant) arousal patterns. It is not appropriate, therefore, for these data to be used as proof that a crime was or was not committed. Erection data also should not be the sole basis for making parole, probation, or other release decisions for convicted offenders (Murphy et al., 1991).

Polygraph Testing Borrowed from the justice system, the polygraph (often referred to as a lie detector) has recently been applied to the evaluation of child molesters. Uses include corroboration and challenge of self-reports of sexual interest and verification of results of phallometric testing (Lalumiere & Quinsey, 1991a). Although no studies currently validate the usefulness of the polygraph during other physiologicalevaluation, it could be employed in detecting attempts to control erection response and fake responses to sexual stimuli. It could also be used in asking subjects whether their measured responses are consistent with their true preferences. As with plethysmography, the validity of polygraph results has not been established for suspected rather than committed crimes. Concerns regarding civil rights of offenders preclude the use of polygraph results as the basis for conviction on legal charges. Lalumiere and Quinsey have identified a pressing need for research on reliability, validity, and value of using the polygraph with child molesters (1991b).

Self-Report Measures

Some attention has been given to devising self-report methods for assessing sexual interest patterns, and existing measures were described by Murphy et al. (1991). In addition, at least three structured instruments have been developed.

Clinical interview Most frequently used is probably the clinical interview. Respondents are often asked to tell about their history of sexual experiences, types and frequency of activities, number of consenting and coerced partners, and types and frequencies of sexual fantasies (especially during masturbation).

Card Sort Technique The Abel and Becker card sort uses brief descriptions of sexual behaviors that are rated according to their attractiveness to the respondent (Murphy et al., 1991). The respondent sorts the cards into seven piles, ranging from most to least attractive. Behaviors presented include pedophilia, rape, sadism, exhibitionism, voyeurism, and frottage. One study with pedophilic subjects found that card sort responses correlated from 0.42 to 0.56 with physiological measures of arousal to slide stimuli. The card sort results accurately classified 38 of 42 pedophilic subjects; physiological measures correctly classified 43 of 48 subjects. However, the classification effectiveness with groups other than pedophiles is unknown (Murphy et al., 1991).

Multiphasic Sex Inventory Developed by Nichols and Molinder (1984), the Multiphasic Sex Inventory is a paper-and pencil self-report measure. Respondents report behaviors, as well as sex knowledge and offense-related cognitions. The scales

Continued

Continued

for child molestation and rape are the most psychometrically developed, while little data are available for scales addressing other paraphilias (exhibitionism, fetishism, obscene calling, voyeurism, bondage and discipline, sadomasochism). Sample items quoted by Murphy et al. (1991, p. 87) include, "I have been attracted to boys sexually" and "I have reached orgasm while molesting a child." Murphy et al. cautioned that while research suggests the scales are reliable, their validity has not yet been determined. In a step in this direction, one study has found that the test does distinguish college students from known offenders.

Clarke Sexual History Questionnaire The Clarke Sexual History Questionnaire is another pencil-and-paper measure of sexual behaviors. It includes objects of sexual attraction, as well as behavior toward those objects. Masturbation fantasies and desires to act on behaviors are also assessed. Comparative data have been collected on a number of samples, including individuals with deviance histories and heterosexual groups. The test appears to have good reliability and validity and complements physiological assessment for research and clinical uses (Murphy et al., 1991).

In summary, while there is need for refinement and further research using measures of sexual arousal, promising methods of assessing sexual interest (at least of those who admit to paraphilic interests) are available.

References

Lalumiere, M. L., & Quinsey, V. L. (1991a). Polygraph testing of child molesters: Are we ready? Part one. *Violence Update, 1,* 3, 9, 11.

Lalumiere, M. L., & Quinsey, V. L. (1991b). Polygraph testing of child molesters: Are we ready? Part two. *Violence Update, 1,* 6–7.

Murphy, W. D., Haynes, M. R., & Worley, P. J. (1991). Assessment of adult sexual interest. In C. R. Hollin & K. Howells (Eds.), *Clinical approaches to sex offenders and their victims.* (pp. 77–92). New York: John Wiley & Sons.

Nichols, H. R., & Molinder, I. (1984). *Multiphasic sex inventory manual.* (Available from authors, 437 Bowes Drive, Tacoma, WA 98466.)

Salter, A. C. (1988). *Treating child sex offenders and victims.* Newbury Park, CA: Sage.

There are several treatment approaches for individuals with paraphilias. Generally, treatment goals involve decreasing deviant sexual arousal, increasing nondeviant sexual arousal, teaching social skills, changing faulty cognitions, resolving sexual dysfunctions, and/or managing alcohol abuse.

Decreasing Deviant Sexual Arousal

Effective treatment of a paraphilia involves decreasing the deviant sexual arousal response, or the response to what the society regards as nonsexual stimuli. The therapeutic goal is for the person to no longer require the paraphilic target stimulus as a preferred or necessary condition of sexual arousal. Treatment that focuses on decreasing deviant sexual arousal may involve medications, aversive conditioning, covert sensitization, and/or masturbatory satiation.

Medications The use of medications is addressed in Exhibit 17.1, Medications and Paraphilia Control.

Aversive Conditioning Aversive conditioning involves pairing an aversive or unpleasant stimulus with the paraphilic stimulus in order to decrease the deviant sexual arousal and reduce the probability of engaging in the paraphilic behavior. One example of aversive stimulus is electrical shock. For the heterosexual male

EXHIBIT 17.1 Medications and Paraphilia Control

Hormone therapy and tranquilizers have been used to treat some individuals with paraphilic behavior. The use of medications to control paraphilic urges and behavior is a complex and controversial issue.

Hormone Therapy for Paraphilic Sex Offenders?

Depo-Provera (medroxyprogesterone acetate, or MPA) is a synthetic progestinic hormone that lowers the blood level of testosterone and seems to have a direct pharmacologic effect on brain pathways that mediate sexual behavior. In some cases, Depo-Provera removes the paraphilic preoccupation, "thereby leaving the man more comfortable and able to imagine and act on his sexual interest in his partner without dysfunction" (Levine et al., 1990, p. 99). In other cases, Depo-Provera results in "a complete shutdown of eroticism" (p. 99). While controversial, Depo-Provera has been used to treat exhibitionists, pedophiles, voyeurs, and rapists.

John Money and Richard Bennett (1981) treated 20 adult men with a history of sex-offending behaviors since adolescence with Depo-Provera, or MPA, in doses ranging from 100 milligrams to 600 milligrams per week for periods of three months to more than five years. Counseling was also an important part of their program and helped to encourage socially appropriate pair-bonded relationships.

Money and Bennett are still evaluating the effectiveness of their treatment program. The 20 men under study have been followed for one to 13 years. The specific effects of hormone and counseling therapy have been obscured by patients leaving the program; varying times between hormonal injections; compliance (keeping appointments, staying in therapy); use of alcohol, "street" drugs, and prescription antiepileptic drugs; and, as noted, the establishment of a pair-bondedness with an erotosexual partner. However, "for some patients it proved to be the only form of treatment that induced a long-term remission of symptoms and kept them off a treadmill of imprisonment" (p. 132).

Moser (1992) emphasized that antiandrogen therapy (e.g., for pedophiles) is an effective form of treatment in that it will "stop the man from reacting to his lust cues" (p. 68). Moreover, "these men [hormonal treatment of women is rare] report that they still have some capability and interest in conventional sex behavior (consensual acts with an adult partner)" (p. 68).

Tranquilizers for Paraphilic Sex Offenders?

Mellaril (thioridazine), a major tranquilizer used primarily in the treatment of psychosis, is also sometimes used with sex offenders. Mellaril reduces the probability of erection and, in some cases, sexual desire. But when the sexual desire wanes, it does so not just in reference to the deviant stimulus but to nondeviant stimuli as well. Hence, establishing sexual urges to culturally appropriate stimuli becomes problematic.

In addition to producing decreased sexual desire, erectile dysfunction, and retarded ejaculation, a possible long-term side effect of tranquilizers is tardive dyskinesia (twitching of the face muscles). Mellaril may only be prescribed when the patient has given informed consent. As with Depo-Provera, Mellaril is used in conjunction with some form of counseling.

---

pedophile, shock aversion therapy is carried out by having the patient look at a series of slides of children and adult women flashed on a wall in the therapist's office. After each picture of a child appears, the therapist administers an aversive electric shock so that the patient associates pain with the visual stimulus of the child. At the moment the shock is turned off, the therapist changes the slide to that of an adult woman. In this way, the patient associates relief from pain (and, consequently, a more pleasant feeling) with the visual stimulus of the adult woman.

The therapist might also use emetic drugs, which induce vomiting or noxious odors. Since it is believed that a fetish results from learning to associate a particular object with sexual pleasure, the stimulus object may be reconditioned by associating an unpleasant experience with it. For example, the person might be given emetic drugs to induce vomiting when in the presence of the fetish object. Eleven case studies have reported successful results with this type of therapy, but, the reviewers said, "the results are only suggestive due to the uncontrolled nature of the research" (Kilmann et al., 1982, p. 212).

In using shame aversion therapy to decrease deviant sexual arousal for exhibitionism, the therapist might ask the exhibitionist to exhibit himself to someone while an audience observes. Being aware that others are watching him, the exhibitionist often feels guilty, ashamed, and anxious. The goal of associating these feelings with exhibitionism is to decrease or eliminate the paraphilic behavior.

Covert Sensitization Covert sensitization involves using negative thoughts as a way of developing negative feelings associated with a deviant sexual stimulus. For example, a therapist may induce negative thoughts by saying the following to the patient:

> I want you to imagine going into the bedroom of your 7-year-old niece when her parents are in another part of the house. As you open the door, you see her asleep in her bed. But as you approach the bed, you begin to feel very nauseous and feel that you are going to throw up. You vomit and feel the particles in your mouth and the stench in your nostrils. You also think that if you act on your urges and are discovered, you will be shamed out of the family.

This scenario is designed to associate negative feelings and thoughts with acting on a sexual urge to touch a child in order to reduce the probability that the patient will engage in this behavior.

Masturbatory Satiation According to Abel, Becker, and Skinner (1985), the most effective intervention to reduce deviant sexual arousal is masturbatory satiation (p. 118). Masturbatory satiation involves instructing paraphilic individuals to fantasize about their paraphilic urges during the postorgasmic phase of masturbation.

> The patient is instructed to masturbate to ejaculation as rapidly as possible using nondeviant fantasies, or to masturbate until the usual latency to ejaculation period plus two minutes has passed. Once the patient has ejaculated or the latency period has been exceeded, the patient immediately switches to the use of deviant fantasy, using the most erotic deviant material possible, and continues to masturbate for a total masturbatory time of 1 hour. (p. 118)

Masturbatory satiation has several advantages. First, it is "exceedingly effective" (Abel et al., 1985, p. 119). Second, it provides a powerful pairing of low physiological arousal with the deviant fantasy. Three, it is cost-effective. For every hour of time with the therapist, the patient can have five hours of masturbatory satiation.

Perkins (1991) noted there are limitations, and possibly dangers, of using aversion therapy with those who not only have deviant sexual interests, but also hostility and negative self-images in relating to other people. Aversive conditioning is a controversial therapeutic technique, and in some states (e.g., South Carolina) it is against the law. Money (1986) pointed out "some critics claim that paraphilic sex offenders lose their power of informed consent and will sign for any form of treatment in order to escape arrest or imprisonment" (p. xviii).

CONSIDERATION: In 1981 Becker and Abel observed that many researchers and therapists have tolerated the use of aversive techniques as a necessary evil, in the hope that positive approaches would replace the negative ones in the future. However, Maletzky (1991) stated, "A review of the literature in this area, however, indicates that this promise is as yet unfulfilled, although it appears to be a valid and obtainable goal" (p. 71).

Increasing Nondeviant Sexual Arousal

In treating individuals with paraphilias, it is important not only to decrease deviant sexual arousal but also to increase nondeviant sexual arousal. Thus, treatment of paraphilias also involves increasing the level of sexual arousal the individual has in reference to culturally appropriate sexual stimuli. For example, the therapist would try to increase the sexual urges of a pedophile to the stimulus of a consenting adult partner. The mechanisms for increasing nondeviant sexual arousal include masturbatory conditioning, exposure, and systematic conditioning.

Masturbatory Conditioning Masturbatory conditioning involves associating the pleasure of orgasm with a nondeviant stimulus. In this way, the previously nonarousing nondeviant stimulus becomes a stimulus for arousal. The therapist instructs the paraphilic client to fantasize about the paraphilic urge or behavior while masturbating. Then, as tension mounts and pleasure increases, the paraphilic is instructed to switch fantasies from the deviant stimulus (e.g., child) to a nondeviant stimulus (e.g., consenting adult).

Exposure Exposure involves introducing the individual to the nondeviant stimulus for increasingly longer periods of time during which there is the opportunity to develop positive associations. For example, if the exhibitionist feels uncomfortable in the presence of adult women, the therapist might assign the patient to attend social functions with a male friend and to stand increasingly closer to women at these social functions. Such exposure helps to reduce the fear and anxiety associated with women and facilitates a greater willingness to engage in social interaction with women.

Systematic Desensitization Where the patient feels extreme anxiety in the presence of the nondeviant stimulus, systematic desensitization may be employed to reduce such anxiety. In systematic desensitization, the patient imagines a series of scenes that involve the nondeviant sexual stimulus (e.g., adult female), then ranks these scenes according to the level of anxiety or discomfort they produce. Then, while the patient is relaxed (the therapist will have taught the patient how to relax using a progressive relaxation procedure), the therapist will present the various scenes from lowest to highest anxiety to the patient. Being relaxed while fantasizing about the various encounters with women reduces the fear and anxiety associated with women. To ensure generalization, the therapist will ask the patient to increase the level of real-life exposure to adult women using the exposure technique described in the previous section.

Teaching Social Skills

Earlier in this chapter, we discussed courtship disorder (Freund, 1990) as an underlying problem in the development of some paraphilias. We also noted that involvement in a relationship can be conceptualized according to a number of phases, such as looking at a potential partner, talking with a new person, and negotiating physical intimacy. Individuals with paraphilias often

> lack skills to establish communication, initiate conversation, maintain the flow of conversation, learn about the interests of others, share intimacies about one's own life with others, empathize with others, and ask for a change in another person's behavior. (Abel et al., 1985, p. 108)

Treatment of paraphilias often involves teaching the paraphilic social skills so the person will be better able to initiate and maintain a social relationship that might lead to a closer bonding with an adult partner. Social skill training often takes place in a group therapy setting where group members may practice basic communication and interaction skills with each other.

CONSIDERATION: Although increasing nondeviant sexual arousal and providing social skills for interaction with socially appropriate people are admirable therapeutic goals, their accomplishment does not ensure that the paraphiliac (e.g., pedophile) will not reoffend. To the contrary, Moser (1992) noted:

> Surprisingly, in my clinical experience, many of the offenders who established a consensual adult-adult sexual relationship were those that reoffended. With hindsight, it appears that this goal is a variation of the colloquial "cure" for homosexuality (for lesbianism, good sex with a "real" man; for male homosexuality, a bottle of whiskey and a kindhearted prostitute). It is important to note that lesbians often report that they enjoyed sex with men, just as the sex offender often reports that he enjoys consensual sex with an adult partner. The sex lacked the lust component, which led these people to seek out partners that exhibit the lust cues that they crave. The implication is that enjoyable sex is not a substitute for hot or passionate sex with the appropriate lust cues. (p. 69)

Changing Faulty Cognitions

Some paraphilic behaviors are justified and maintained on the basis of faulty cognitions. For example, the exhibitionist may think that women are really turned on by the sight of a naked penis and need this experience to get sexually excited. The pedophile may think that children profit from sexual experiences with adults as a form of sex education. The rapist may think that women really enjoy being forced to have sex.

Correcting these cognitive distortions often occurs in the context of group therapy. Group members challenge the irrational beliefs of each other, as well as acknowledge their own irrational beliefs. New beliefs are substituted for irrational beliefs: Women are disgusted by exhibitionists, children are harmed by adult sexual exploitation, and women abhor the thought that they enjoy being raped.

Resolving Sexual Dysfunctions

Some paraphilias are continued because of sexual dysfunctions that prevent the paraphilic individual from engaging in sexual behavior in a pair-bonded relationship. For example, the exhibitionist and voyeur may feel unable to engage in sex with a partner due to erectile dysfunction. They may also suffer early ejaculation or retarded ejaculation and want to avoid exposure of these dysfunctions in a relationship. Unless these sexual dysfunctions are treated, the paraphilic individual may continue to feel sexually inadequate and perceive no alternative for sexual gratification other than engaging in paraphilic behavior.

Treating Alcohol Abuse

Some pedophiles, exhibitionists, voyeurs, and rapists report that the use of alcohol lowers their inhibitions and increases the probability that they will engage in paraphilic behavior. Particularly in the case of sex aggressives, disulfiram is used to eliminate the use of alcohol. Also known as antabuse, disulfiram taken in pill form remains in the person's system for three to five days. If alcohol is consumed during this period, severe tachycardia (rapid heart rate), anxiety, nausea, and vomiting will result.

We have discussed the various treatment strategies for treating coercive paraphilias. Exhibit 17.2 illustrates treatment of a noncoercive atypical sexual interest. Although formicophilia is an unusual sexual variation, the following case study gives examples of treatment interventions which could be used with other non-aggressive paraphilias as well.

EXHIBIT 17.2 The Treatment of Formicophilia

Formicophilia is a paraphilia in which "sexuoerotic arousal and orgasm are dependent on the sensation produced by small creatures like snails, frogs, ants or other insects creeping, crawling, nibbling on the body, especially the genitalia, perianal area, or nipples" (Dewaraja, 1987, p. 594). This paraphilia is not dangerous to the patient or to others. Here we describe how one therapist chose to treat an individual with formicophilia (Dewaraja, 1987). The therapist who was presented with this case decided not to treat the paraphilia itself but to focus on the patient's feelings of guilt and depression and lack of social skills.

The patient felt guilty about his formicophilia, depressed about his inability to stop himself, and inadequate because he could not talk to women or interact with them. The therapist asked the patient to keep records on the frequency with which he used ants and other small creatures during masturbation, the frequency of masturbation during which he used heterosexual imagery, the frequency of coitus, and the frequency of heterosexual interactions. These data would provide a baseline to permit the therapist to evaluate the effectiveness of the treatment program.

The treatment plan focused on reducing the patient's guilt for his formicophilia. Although the therapist initially asked the patient to stop his formicophilia, the therapist dropped the request and encouraged the patient not to be too concerned about his paraphilia. Thus, the therapist deliberately avoided using aversive conditioning and covert sensitization in the treatment program.

The therapist used masturbatory conditioning to increase the patient's arousal to nondeviant sexual stimuli. The patient was encouraged to develop heterosexual imagery and to masturbate to heterosexual imagery and pictures. The goal was not only to reduce his guilt about his paraphilia but also to substitute heterosexual imagery and fantasy in the place of the paraphilic imagery and fantasy.

The patient was also encouraged to interact with women. Social skills training was conducted during 12 two-hour sessions in which the therapist would model appropriate gazing, posturing, smiling, and nodding and have the patient do likewise. In addition, a female staff member was brought into the session to allow the patient to practice using newly learned social skills.

Results of the therapy, at one year follow-up, showed that the patient had reduced his formicophilia behavior from three to four times a week to once or twice a week, had increased his masturbating to heterosexual images from zero times a week to three times a week, and had increased his heterosexual social interactions from zero times a week to three times a week.

The therapist emphasized that elimination of a paraphilia may not always be an appropriate goal. Rather, eliminating the feelings of guilt, depression, and inadequacy in reference to the absence of social skills may be more desirable.

Source: Dewaraja, R. (1987). Formicophilia, an unusual paraphilia, treated with counseling and behavior therapy. *American Journal of Psychotherapy, 41,* 593–597. Used by permission.

SEXUAL ADDICTION

Is addiction a label we stick on behaviors we disapprove of?

Eli Coleman

The term "alcohol or drug addiction" is used to refer to the condition in which alcohol or drugs negatively affect health, relationships, and/or work. Similarly, **sexual addiction** refers to the condition in which sexual thoughts and/or behavior negatively affect health, relationships, and/or work. Professionals disagree on the degree to which "sexual addiction" is a valid term. Some professionals suggest that the terms "sexual control," "sexual compulsivity," and "sexual impulsivity" are more appropriate than the term "sexual addiction" (Coleman, 1990). Levine and Troiden (1988) emphasized that all such terms are stigmatizing labels attached to behaviors that diverge from prevailing erotic standards. They are "value judgements parading as therapeutic diagnoses" (p. 360). Nevertheless, Blanchard (1990) claimed that "the concept of sexual addiction is accepted generally by the specialists—and increasingly by the lay public" (p. 45).

NATIONAL DATA: It is estimated that between 3% and 6% of Americans suffer from sexual addiction (Carnes, 1991).

Characteristics of Sex Addiction

All addictions are characterized by denial, loss of control, and pathological prioritization. Sex addicts typically deny that they have a problem, in spite of the difficulties their sexuality causes for their health, relationships, and work. Sex addicts cannot control their sexual addiction, although they believe that they can choose to stop problematic sexual behaviors at any time. Sex addicts also give sex priority to such an excessive degree that it is considered pathological. According to Schneider (1990), for sexual addicts,

> Sex serves functions other than procreation, recreation, and affirmation of the relationship. Sex and the rituals surrounding it become the most important aspects of the addicts' life, for which they are willing to risk job, family and health. (p. 38)

The specific behaviors that sexual addicts engage in have been identified by Naditch and Barton (1990). These behaviors, in order of highest to lowest frequency, are presented below:

- thinking about sex obsessively
- masturbating excessively
- feeling depressed, hopeless, and unworthy following a sexual experience
- needing to be sexual to feel good about one's self
- fantasizing about past or future sexual experiences
- denying the consequences of their sexual addiction
- sexualizing people who are not sexually explicit
- looking at sexually explicit printed material
- neglecting responsibilities and commitments

Sexual behavior with others may also involve extradyadic affairs, frequenting massage parlors, and use of prostitutes.

Individuals who may be classified as sex addicts frequently have other addictions. Seventy-seven percent of the sex addicts in 88 marriages reported that they had other addictions: 39% had chemical addictions (drug abuse), 32% had food addictions (eating disorders), 38% had work addictions (workaholics), and 13% had money addictions (compulsive spending) (Schneider, 1990).

Further characteristics of sex addicts were reported by Blanchard (1990), who studied 109 imprisoned male sex offenders at Wyoming State Penitentiary. She classified 39% of these offenders as sexual addicts and noted several common themes in their backgrounds: depression, low self-esteem, and extensive involvement with pornography.

In his survey of over 600 recovering sexual addicts, Carnes discovered that 83% had been sexually abused as children (cited in Schneider, 1990). When a parent or other caregiver or family member sexually abuses a child, that child may come to believe that sexual behavior is a form of nurturing. Thus, some sex addicts may feel driven to have sex in order to feel nurtured.

Treatment of Sexual Addictions

The most prevalent treatment for sexual addiction is involvement in a self-help group therapy program. There are over 2,000 sexual addiction programs throughout the United States, including such groups as Sex and Love Addicts Anonymous in Boston, Sex Addicts Anonymous groups in Minneapolis, and Sexaholics Anonymous groups in Simi Valley, California. All of these groups are modeled after the 12-step program used by Alcoholics Anonymous. These steps include participants' recognition of their addiction, acknowledgement that they are powerless and need help in overcoming it, and commitment to monitoring their behavior one day at a time. The recovery process involves "the learning of healthy ways to meet needs while avoiding destructive behaviors" (Carnes, 1990, p. 2). The goal of therapy for the sex addict is the attainment of healthy sexuality within the boundaries of a committed relationship (Turner, 1990).

Another aspect of the 12-step program is abstinence. Addicts are encouraged to be celibate in both self and partner sex for a period from six to 12 weeks to prove that they can survive without sex, to learn to be intimate with others without having sex, and to relieve the stress associated with feelings of shame and lack of self-worth in ways other than having sex.

Joseph LoPiccolo (1989) suggested that requiring the sex addict to be abstinent is unrealistic. LoPiccolo suggested that sex is a biological drive that needs an opportunity for release—at least through masturbation. Sex addicts who don't meet this biological need may feel even more self-effacement and drop out of the recovery program altogether.

Ideally, the spouse or partner of the addict attends a group similar to Al-Anon, the self-help group therapy program for family members of alcoholics. Such partners, sometimes labeled as co-addicts (individuals who are addicted to the addict and develop many of the same personality traits), often contribute to the addiction of their partners. Two of the ways they foster the addiction is by shielding the partner from natural consequences (helping to cover up sexual molestation to avoid legal consequences) and supporting the denial of the addiction. In addition, these partners may benefit from help with their own problems, such as feeling blame for the sex addict's behavior. For example, a woman may feel that her partner's addiction to a series of extramarital affairs is the result of her inadequacies as a sexual partner.

CONSIDERATION: One side effect of involvement in therapy for sex addiction is the acknowledgement that relationship issues are more significant than sexual issues. When 138 spouses dealing with sexual addiction were asked to rate the most significant problem in their relationship, only 7% of the men and 5% of the women rated sex as the most important. "Most couples viewed the rebuilding of trust and intimacy as their most significant problem" (Schneider, 1990, p. 38).

Effectiveness of Treatment Programs

Outcome studies on the treatment of sexual addiction using the 12-step program are encouraging. In a follow-up of 216 former patients of the Golden Valley Health Center's Sexual Dependency Unit, 90% reported that their main problem was either "improved" or "greatly improved," and 84% reported that their relationships had "improved" or "greatly improved" since discharge. Furthermore, patients showed no declining levels of change in sexually dependent behavior for up to 24 months after discharge (Naditch & Barton).

Not all professionals agree that the 12-step program is the treatment of choice for sexual addiction. The 12-step program assumes that

> sexual addiction creates a spiritual disease and that recovery involves a program of spiritual recovery. Because this is an inappropriate application of the addiction model, there are dangerous consequences for individuals seeking help for compulsive sexual behaviors. (Coleman, 1990, p. 13)

As an alternative, Coleman recommended that out-of-control sexual behaviors be viewed using the framework of the obsessive-compulsive model, which permits greater flexibility in diagnosis and treatment. Rather than being viewed as a spiritual disease, compulsive sexual behaviors are viewed as driven by attempts to reduce anxiety, rather than by sexual desire. Treatment then focuses on the alleviation of anxiety.

CHOICES

While society makes the decision to label some paraphilias as dangerous and illegal, the individual can choose to either accept or disregard society's negative labeling of the paraphilias. Another choice is to exercise deliberate cognitive control over the expression of one's paraphilias.

Choose to Disregard Social Disapproval of Paraphilias?

Persons with a paraphilia normally do not seek treatment. As Dewaraja (1987) noted:

> In most instances, the paraphile undertakes treatment at the insistance of society, for example, in exchange for a reduced prison term. When he voluntarily seeks treatment, it is done to escape shame, resulting from social censure. (p. 593)

While some paraphilias are illegal and harmful to one's self (asphyxiation) or other people (pedophilia, erotophonophilia), other paraphilias may be viewed as not worthy of the guilt, depression, and social disapproval they engender. Examples of such paraphilias include acrotomophilia (amputee partner), autonepipophilia (wearing wet diapers), and formicophilia. The latter was discussed in Exhibit 17.2, where it was emphasized that the paraphilic might focus on developing social skills and reducing negative feelings, rather than terminating the paraphilia.

Individuals with paraphilias that are not harmful to themselves or others might choose to disregard society's negative label of their behavior. Such a choice in combination with a positive view of themselves may have productive consequences for them with no negative consequences for society. Comfort (1987) stated that among therapists,

> Most of us now ask, at the practical level, not 'is this behaviour normal?' but rather 'what does this behaviour signify for this client? Is it reinforcing or handicapping?' and, of course, 'is the behaviour socially tolerable?' (p. 1)

Choose to Control One's Paraphilia?

Therapists disagree about the degree to which persons with paraphilias can control the behavioral expression of their paraphilia. While some feel that the pedophile, exhibitionist, and voyeur are uncontrollably and compulsively driven to express their paraphilia (and will not be able to change these "lust" cues—Moser, 1992), others suggest that they exercise conscious control over their paraphilic behavior.

Pedophilia, exhibitionism, and voyeurism may be conceptualized as requiring a series of choices leading up to the paraphilic behavior. For example, a pedophile who fondles a young male in the park on a summer afternoon is engaging in a terminal target behavior that was preceded by a number of choices leading to that behavior. These choices may have included: 1) taking off from work, 2) looking at child pornography, 3) drinking alcohol, 4) going to the playground, 5) buying candy, 6) sitting on the bench where a young boy was also sitting, 7) talking to the boy, 8) offering the boy some candy, and so on. At any of these eight choice points, the pedophile may have chosen to engage in a behavior that was incompatible with child molestation. Each of these behaviors, when taken alone, is a relatively easier choice—the person might choose to stay at work, look at alternative magazines, and so forth.

Similarly, the exhibitionist who exposes himself in the library to a stranger may aternatively have chosen to masturbate to ejaculation at home, to avoid alcohol, and to go with a friend to a movie. Finally, the voyeur might choose to schedule time with others when he is particularly vulnerable to "peeping," to avoid walking on another person's property (where peeping often occurs), and to select alternative behaviors, such as going to a movie during prime "peeping time."

In addition to consciously exercising to choose behaviors to control one's paraphilia, it is also possible to control one's level of arousal. Nagayama Hall (1991) studied 169 inpatient adult male sex offenders in terms of their sexual arousal. While listening to erotic tapes, 84% were able to inhibit being sexually aroused as a result of sheer conscious control. The investigator simply asked them to "stop yourself from being sexually aroused" (p. 363), and all but 16% were able to do so.

In addition to making deliberate choices that are incompatible with the expression of paraphilic behaviors, the person who is concerned about his paraphilia may choose to seek therapy to address such issues as self-esteem, guilt, anxiety, sexual dysfunctions, and lack of social skills. By confronting these issues and ensuring that they do not contribute to unwanted behavior, the paraphiliac is taking deliberate control of his sexual expression.

Summary

1. Paraphilias are an overdependence on a culturally unacceptable (e.g., children) or unusual stimulus (e.g., leather) for sexual arousal and satisfaction.
2. Most people who have a paraphilia have an average of three to four.
3. Paraphilias may become the major sexual activity in a person's life and may interfere with the person's capacity for reciprocal, affectionate sexual interactions.
4. In exhibitionism sexual gratification comes from exposing (or fantasizing exposing) one's genitals to be seen, and presumably admired, by an unsuspecting stranger. Exhibitionists are not usually violent, but exhibitionistic acts should be reported to a law enforcement agency.
5. Pedophiles develop various thinking errors or rationalizations (it is educational, pleasurable, desired) to continue the behavior.
6. Fetishes often begin as a preference (e.g., sex with a partner in red high-heeled shoes) and progress to a symbolic substitute for a partner (shoes only).
7. Masochists derive more from the enactment of a script that involves pain than from the infliction of pain itself.
8. Paraphilias are illegal to the degree that they interfere with the rights of others.
9. The theoretical explanations for paraphilias include psychoanalytic (unconscious processes), feminist (control, power, aggression), learning (classical/operant paradigms), biological (innate), and lovemap (e.g., biological predisposition plus unusual learning experiences) perspectives.
10. Treatment of paraphilias involves decreasing deviant sexual arousal, increasing nondeviant sexual arousal, developing interpersonal social skills, changing faulty cognitions, resolving sexual dysfunctions, and treating alcohol and drug abuse.
11. Sexual addiction is most often treated in self-help groups following the model of Alcoholics Anonymous.

KEY TERMS

paraphilia
exhibitionism
telephonicophilia
frotteurism
toucheurism
autonepiophilia
pedophilia
hebephilia
voyeurism
fetishism
transvestic fetishism
sexual sadism
sexual masochism
lovemap
formicophilia
sexual addiction

REFERENCES

Abel, G. G., Becker, J. V. Mittelman, M. S., Cunningham–Rathner, J., Rouleau, J. L., & Murphy, W. D. (1987). Self–reported sex crimes of non–carcerated paraphiliacs. *Journal of Interpersonal Violence, 2,* 3–25.

Abel, G. G., & Rouleau, J. L. (1990). The nature and extent of sexual assault. In W. L. Marshall, D. R. Laws, and H. E. Barbaree (Eds.), *Handbook of sexual assault* (pp. 9–21). New York: Plenum Press.

Abel, G. G., Becker, J. V., & Skinner, L. J. (1985). Behavioral approaches to treatment of the violent sex offender. In L. H. Roth (Ed.), *Clinical treatment of the violent person* (pp. 100–123). Rockville, MD: National Institute of Mental Health.

Abel, G. G., Becker, J. V., Cunningham-Rathner, J., Mittelman, M. S., & Rouleau, J. L. (1988). Multiple paraphilic diagnoses among sex offenders. *Bulletin of the American Academy of Psychiatry and the Law, 16,* 153–168.

American Psychiatric Association. (1987). *Diagnostic and statistical manual of mental disorders* (3rd ed., rev.). Washington, DC: APA.

Blanchard, G. T. (1990). Differential diagnosis of sex offenders: Distinguishing characteristics of the sex addict. *American Journal of Preventive Psychiatry and Neurology,* 2, 45–47.

Bullough, V. L. (1990). History in adult human sexual behavior with children and adolescents in Western societies. In J. R. Feierman (Ed.) (pp. 69–90). *Pedophilia.* New York: Springer-Verlag.

Bullough, V., Bullough, B. & Smith R., (1983). A comparative study of male transvestites, male to female transsexuals, and male homosexuals. *Journal of Sex Research, 19,* 238–257.

Caplan, P. J. (1984). The myth of women's masochism. *American Psychologist, 39,* 130–139.

Carnes, P. J. (1990). Sexual addiction: Progress, criticism, challenges. *American Journal of Preventive Psychiatry and Neurology, 2,* 1–8.

Carnes, P. J. (1991). *Contrary to love: Helping the sexual addict.* Minneapolis: Comprehensive Care.

Coleman, E. J. (1990). The obsessive-compulsive model for describing compulsive sexual behavior. *American Journal of Preventive Psychiatry and Neurology, 2,* 9–14.

Comfort, A. (1987) Deviation and variation. In G. D. Wilson (Ed.). *Variant sexuality: Research and theory* (pp. 1–20). Baltimore: Johns Hopkins University Press.

DeFazio, A., & Cunningham, K. A. (1987). A paraphilia in a spinal-cord-injured patient: A case report. *Sexuality and Disability, 8,* 247–254.

Dewaraja, R. (1987). Formicophilia, an unusual paraphilia, treated with counseling and behavior therapy. *American Journal of Psychotherapy, 41,* 593–597.

Feierman, J. R. (1990). *Pedophilia: Biosocial dimensions.* New York: Springer-Verlag.

Finkelhor, D., Hotaling, G., Lewis, I. A., & Smith, C. (1990). Sexual abuse in a national survey of adult men and women: Prevalence, characteristics, and risk factors. *Child Abuse and Neglect, 14,* 19–28.

Flor-Henry, P. (1987). Cerebral aspects of sexual deviation. In G. D. Wilson (Ed.). *Variant sexuality: Research and theory* (pp. 49–83). Baltimore: Johns Hopkins University Press.

Fontaine, J. L. (1990). *Child sexual abuse.* Cambridge, MA: Polity Press.

Freund, K. (1990). Courtship disorder. In W. L. Marshall, D. R. Laws, & H. E. Barbaree (Eds.), *Handbook of sexual assault* (pp. 195–206). New York: Plenum Press.

Freund, K., & Watson, R. J. (1992). The proportions of heterosexual and homosexual pedophiles among sex offenders against children: An exploratory study. *Journal of Sex and Marital Therapy, 18,* 34–43.

Freund, K., Watson, R. & Dickey, R. (1990). Does sexual abuse in childhood cause pedophilia? *Archives of Sexual Behavior, 19,* 557-568.

Gebhard, P. H. (1976). Fetishism and sadomasochism. In M. S. Weinberg (Ed.), *Sex research: Studies from the Kinsey Institute* (pp. 156–166). New York: Oxford University Press.

Grob, C. S. (1985). Single case study, female exhibitionism. *Journal of Nervous and Mental Disease, 173,* 253–256.

Hurlbert, D. F. (1992). Voyeurism in an adult female with schizoid personality: A case report. *Journal of Sex Education and Therapy, 18,* 17–21.

Kalichman, S. C. (1991). Psychopathology and personality characteristics of criminal sexual offenders as a function of victim age. *Archives of Sexual Behavior, 20,* 187–195.

Kilmann, P. R., Sabalis, R. F., Gearing, M. L., Bukstel, L. H., & Scovern, A. W. (1982). The treatment of sexual paraphilias: A review of the outcome research. *Journal of Sex Research, 18,* 193–252.

Kline, P. (1987). Sexual deviation: Psychoanalytic research and theory. In G. D. Wilson (Ed.). *Variant Sexuality: Research and Theory* (pp. 150–175). Baltimore: Johns Hopkins University Press.

Langevin, R. & Lang, R. A. (1987). The courtship disorders. In G. D. Wilson (Ed.). *Variant sexuality: Research and theory* (pp. 202–228). Baltimore: Johns Hopkins University Press.

Langevin, R., Paitich, D. P. & Russon, A. E. (1985). Voyeurism: Does it predict sexual aggression or violence in general? In R. Langevin (Ed.), *Erotic preference, gender identity, and aggression in men* (pp. 77–98). Hillsdale, NY: Erlbaum.

Levine, M. P. & Troiden, R. R. (1988). The myth of sexual compulsivity. *The Journal of Sex Research, 25,* 347–363.

Levine, S. B., Risen, C. B., & Althof, S. E. (1990). Essay on the diagnosis and nature of paraphilia. *Journal of Sex and Marital Therapy, 16,* 89–102.

LoPiccolo, J. (1989, November 7). The reunification of sexual and marital therapy. Paper presented at the annual meeting of the National Council on Family Relations, New Orleans.

Maletzky, B. M. (1991). *Treating the sexual offender.* Newbury Park: Sage.

Money, J. & Bennett, R. G. (1981) Postadolescent paraphilic sex offenders: Antiandiogenic and counseling therapy follow-up. *International Journal of Mental Health, 10,* 122–133.

Money, J. (1986). *Lovemaps: Clinical concepts of sexual/erotic health and pathology, paraphilia, and gender transposition in childhood, adolescence, and maturity.* New York: Irvington.

Money, J. (1988). *Gay, straight, and in-between.* New York: Oxford University Press.

Moser, C. (1992). Lust, lack of desire, and paraphilias: Some thoughts and possible connections. *Journal of Sex and Marital Therapy, 18,* 65–69.

Naditch, M. P. & Barton, S. N. (1990). Outcomes survey of an inpatient sexual dependence program. *American Journal of Preventive Psychiatry and Neurology, 2,* 27–32.

Nagayama Hall, G. C. (1991). Sexual arousal as a function of physiological and cognitive variables in a sexual offender population. *Archives of Sexual Behavior, 20,* 359–369.

Perkins, D. (1991). Clinical work with sex offenders in secure settings. In C. R. Hollin & K. Howells (Eds.), *Clinical approaches to sex offenders and their victims* (pp. 151–177). New York: Wiley.

Rachman, S. (1966). Sexual fetishism: An experimental analogue. *Psychological Record, 16,* 293–296.

Schneider, J. P. (1990). Sexual problems in married couples recovering from sexual addiction and coaddiction. *American Journal of Preventive Psychiatry and Neurology, 2,* 33–38.

Schur, E. M. (1988). *The Americanization of sex.* Philadelphia: Temple University Press.

Talamini, J. T. (1981). Transvestism: Expression of a second self. *Free Inquiry in Creative Sociology, 9,* 72–74.

Turner, M. (1990). Long-term outpatient group psychotherapy as a modality for treating sexual addiction. *American Journal of Preventive Psychiatry and Neurology, 2,* 23–26.

Weinberg, M., Williams, C., & Moser, C. (1984). The social constraints of sadomasochism. *Social Problems, 31,* 379–389.

CHAPTER EIGHTEEN

HIV Infection and Other Sexually Transmissible Diseases

Chapter Outline

Human Immunodeficiency Virus (HIV) Infection
- Categories and Symptoms
- Transmission of HIV and High-Risk Behaviors
- Homosexuals and HIV Infection
- Heterosexuals and HIV Infection
- Prevalence of HIV Infection and AIDS
- Knowledge and Attitudes about HIV and AIDS
- **Self-Assessment:** STD ATTITUDE SCALE
- Tests for HIV Infection
- Treatment for HIV and Opportunistic Infections

Genital Herpes

Human Papilloma Virus (HPV)

Chlamydia

Gonorrhea

Syphilis

Other Sexually Transmissible Diseases
- Nongonococcal Urethritis (NGU)
- Lymphogranuloma Venereum (LGV)
- Granuloma Inguinale
- Chancroid
- Hepatitis B
- Vaginitis
- Pubic Lice
- Scabies

Prevention of Sexually Transmissible Diseases
- **Research Perspective:** Prevention Models for HIV Transmission

Choices
- Choose to Engage in Low-Risk Behaviors?
- Choose to Be Tested for HIV?
- Choose How to Tell a Partner That One Has an STD?
- Choose to Allocate Government Funds to HIV Infection Research?
- Choose to Require Health-Care Workers to Be Tested for HIV?

Is It True?*

1. STDs such as chlamydia and gonorrhea account for many cases of infertility.

2. Lesbians are more likely to become HIV-infected by having sex with other women than with men.

3. Homosexual men are more likely to use a condom with a casual partner than with a steady partner.

4. Uncircumcised men are at greater risk for HIV infection than circumcised men.

5. Chlamydia is one of the few STDs in which the symptoms appear on the external part of the body and are easy to recognize.

* 1 = T, 2 = F, 3 = T, 4 = T, 5 = F

Safer sex involves choice and planning ahead and a reasonable level of sobriety, lovemaking following from a thoughtful and unfuddled choice of a partner—the kind one would still be glad of by daylight.

Mary Catherine Bateson
Richard Goldsby

I only want what any other girl wants.
Tall, dark, handsome and disease free.
New York City woman

A stunned and disbelieving public marked the point at which HIV came out of the closet the day they heard these words: "Sometimes people are a little naive and they think it can't happen to them. Sometimes we think only gay people can get it. And here I am saying that it can happen to anybody. Even me, Magic Johnson" (Boeck, 1991, p. A-1).

No longer would the public assume that AIDS was a "gay disease," if a popular figure like Magic Johnson could become infected with HIV, then anyone could become infected with the virus. In this chapter, we are concerned with the choices we make that affect our risk of contracting and transmitting HIV infection and other sexually transmissible diseases (STDs), including genital herpes, genital warts, chlamydia, gonorrhea, and syphilis.

Human Immunodeficiency Virus (HIV) Infection

The retroviruses which cause immune dysfunction that leads to AIDS are the human immunodeficiency virus Type 1 and Type 2 (HIV 1, HIV 2). HIV 1 was the first to be recognized. It was originally called by such names as human T-cell lymphotropic virus type III (HTLV-III) (Phair & Chadwick, 1992). **HIV** attacks the white blood cells (T-lymphocytes) in human blood, impairing the immune system and a person's ability to fight other diseases. Of all the diseases that may be transmitted sexually, HIV infection is the most life-threatening. "Presently, the mortality rate (the proportion of deaths) of people with AIDS is practically 100%" (Cox, 1992, p. 21).

Categories and Symptoms

The Centers for Disease Control (CDC) (the official U.S. government public health bureau responsible for tracking disease, whose offices are in Atlanta, Georgia) have identified four categories of HIV infection. The fourth category represents people who have AIDS. Relatively few people who are infected with HIV have AIDS.

Category 1 Category 1 is comprised of people who have been infected with HIV and have developed antibodies against it. Most people in Category 1 either have no symptoms or exhibit flu-like symptoms—fever, muscular aches and pains, and fatigue. These symptoms, if they occur, surface between two and six weeks after infection. Antibodies may appear in the blood in two months, but they may take between six months and one year before they reach detectable levels. Before the antibodies are detectable, HIV-infected individuals will test negative for HIV, so they are "silent carriers" of HIV. Although persons with Category 1 HIV do not have AIDS and may never get it, they are infectious and able to transmit the virus to others (through sex, blood donation, sharing needles, gestation, childbirth and breast feeding).

Category 2 Persons in Category 2 show the presence of HIV antibodies in their blood and may also show a slight decrease in T-4 cells. This suggests that the immune system is under attack, although at this stage, the person still does not have any significant clinical symptoms and may not be aware of having the HIV virus.

Category 3 Persons in Category 3, formerly considered to have AIDS-related complex (**ARC**), show signs of illness. The lymph nodes of the body become swollen and can be felt as small lumps in the armpits, neck, and groin, constituting lymphadenopathy syndrome (LAS). Other symptoms in Category 3 HIV include persistent fever, diarrhea, night sweats, weight loss, fatigue, yeast infections of the mouth and vagina, and reactivation of the chicken-pox virus, causing a painful skin condition called "shingles." These symptoms are usually not life-threatening, unless diarrhea and weight loss are severe. However, persons in Category 3 have a serious risk of progressing to Category 4.

Category 4 Persons in Category 4 are considered to have **AIDS** (**acquired immunodeficiency syndrome**). Their bodies are vulnerable to **opportunistic infections,** which would be resisted if the immune system were not damaged. The two most common diseases associated with AIDS are a form of cancer called Kaposi's sarcoma (KS) and pneumocystis carinii pneumonia (PCP), a rare form of pneumonia. Seventy percent of all HIV deaths result from PCP. In Category 4, HIV may invade the brain and nervous system, producing symptoms of neurological impairment and/or psychiatric illness. However, the cognitive abilities of category 4 HIV-infected individuals are frequently not impaired (Sinforiani et al., 1991).

CONSIDERATION: It may take ten years or longer after a person is infected with HIV before any Category 4 symptoms develop. The progression of HIV infection and susceptibility to diseases such as KS and PCP may be influenced by psychosocial factors, such as stress, social support, depression, life satisfaction, and hopelessness (Coates, Temoshok, & Mandel, 1984).

Transmission of HIV and High-Risk Behaviors

Some students have a hard time understanding that the consequences of one unprotected sexual encounter may not be reversible.

American College Health Association

The human immunodeficiency virus may be transmitted one of five ways:

1. Sexual Contact. HIV is found in several body fluids of infected individuals, including blood, semen, and possibly vaginal secretions. During sexual contact with an infected individual, the virus enters a person's blood stream through the rectum, vagina, penis (a person with an uncircumcised penis is at greater risk because more of the partner's fluids are retained), and possibly the mouth during oral sex. Inserting the penis, fingers, or other objects into the rectum or vagina may produce small tears in the lining of the rectum or vagina. Although these small tears may not be visible or may not produce visible bleeding, they provide an opening through which HIV can enter directly into the bloodstream.
2. Intravenous Drug Use. Drug users who are infected with HIV transmit the virus to other drug users with whom they share needles, syringes, and other drug-related implements. An HIV-infected intravenous drug user leaves HIV-contaminated blood in the needle or syringe. The virus is passed on to the next user of the dirty needle and syringe. In one study of 553 intravenous drug users in Vienna, 30% were found to have HIV-1 antibodies in their blood (Loimer, Presslich, Hollerer, & Werner, 1990). In the Yunnan province of China, 80% of all HIV-infected males (N = 327) are intravenous drug users (Gil, 1991).
3. Blood transfusions. HIV may be transmitted through receiving HIV-infected donor blood or blood products. Currently, all blood donors are screened, and blood is not accepted from high-risk individuals. In addition, blood that is accepted from

An HIV infected intravenous drug user leaves HIV contaminated blood in the needle or syringe and the virus is passed on to the next user of the same needle.

donors is tested for the presence of HIV antibody. However, prior to 1985, donor blood was not screened for HIV. Individuals (including hemophiliacs) who received blood or blood products prior to 1985 may have been infected with HIV. Arthur Ashe, the Wimbledon tennis champion, developed AIDS as a result of a blood transfusion he received before blood was routinely screened for HIV.

4. Mother-Child Transmission of HIV. A pregnant woman infected with HIV may transmit the virus through the placenta to her unborn child. These babies will initially test positive for HIV as a consequence of having the antibodies from the mother's bloodstream. However, not all of these babies will develop AIDS. Although it is rare, HIV transmission through breastfeeding has also been documented (Phair & Chadwick, 1992).
5. Organ or Tissue Transplants and Donor Semen. Lastly, receiving transplant organs and tissues, as well as semen for artificial insemination, may involve a risk of contracting HIV if the donors were not HIV-tested. Such testing is essential, and recipients should insist on knowing the HIV status of the organ, tissue, or semen donor.

CONSIDERATION: HIV is not transmitted through casual contact, such as shaking hands, hugging, crying, coughing, or sneezing. You cannot contract HIV from swimming pools, toilet seats, doorknobs, or telephones or from eating food that is cooked, handled, or served by persons who are HIV-infected. You also cannot contract HIV from sharing bed linens, towels, or eating utensils. Lastly, you cannot get HIV from animals or insects or from donating blood (Koop, 1986).

Homosexuals and HIV Infection

In the U.S. HIV infection was first seen among homosexual and bisexual men having multiple sex partners, which remains the predominant mode of infection (see National Data). For U.S. women diagnosed with AIDS, the predominant modes of infection are injected drugs (50%) and heterosexual contact (35%) (CDC, 1992).

Hence, while homosexual males are at great risk, lesbians are at virtually zero risk from female-to-female contact.

NATIONAL DATA: Sixty-seven percent of all U.S. males diagnosed as having AIDS are men who have sex with men (Centers for Disease Control, 1992).

Research indicates that substantial proportions of men in the gay community continue to engage in sexual practices that are considered high risk for HIV transmission, specifically receptive or insertive anal intercourse without a latex condom. About one-third of 205 gay and bisexual men reported having anal intercourse without a condom, and over 75% reported that they were not monogamous (Meyer-Bahlburg et al., 1991). In a study of 487 gay men in Buffalo, New York, 94% reported having had unprotected anal intercourse with a man (Ruefli, Yu, & Barton, 1992).

Gay men who are involved in steady relationships are also more likely to have anal intercourse without a condom than gay men who report casual encounters. Research on 746 gay and bisexual men in New York City (Martin, Dean, Garcia, & Hall, 1989) suggested that "gay men involved in a primary relationship engaged in higher risk sexual behavior more frequently than gay men who were single" (p. 290).

Number of partners is also associated with higher risk for HIV infection. Gay and bisexual men who test HIV positive report having had more sexual partners than gay and bisexual men who test HIV negative. Of 119 HIV-positive men, the median number of male partners was 308. Of 83 HIV-negative men, the median number of male partners was 143 (Meyer-Bahlburg et al., 1991). In the study by Martin et al. (1989), the researchers reported that "sexual activity has decreased dramatically while efforts aimed at reducing the risk of all types of disease transmission during sex have been incorporated into most gay men's sexual habits" (p. 289). For example, in 1981, approximately 8% of the men in Martin et al.'s study reported sexual contact with a single partner; in 1987, almost 19% reported having had sex with a single partner. The majority of gay men still reported multiple partners in 1981 (90%) and 1987 (75%).

Heterosexuals and HIV Infection

Although only 8% of HIV infection cases in the U.S. have been officially attributed to heterosexual transmission, this rate is increasing. In fact, HIV-infection cases attributed to heterosexual transmission are growing faster than any other category of HIV cases. In 1981, 0.5% of reported adult AIDS cases were caused by heterosexual transmission. By 1992, this percentage had risen to 4% for men and 35% for women (CDC, 1992). Although Fumento (1990) denied that there is an epidemic of "hetero-sexual AIDS" in the United States, recent data suggest the contrary. According to the World Health Organization, by the year 2000, up to 90% of all HIV infections in the world will have been contracted through heterosexual transmission (Aral & Holmes, 1991).

In third world countries, AIDS is primarily a heterosexual disease.
Richard L. Rumley, MD

Some heterosexually transmitted HIV infections may occur in women as a result of their male partner engaging in hidden bisexual activity. However, the majority of heterosexually transmitted HIV cases among women seems to be due to sexual contact with intravenous drug users infected with HIV as a result of sharing injection equipment (CDC, 1992).

Prevalence of HIV Infection and AIDS

CONSIDERATION: In the late spring of 1992, the Centers for Disease Control decided to include in their statistics of those who have AIDS any person who tested positive for HIV, even though that person may have no classic symptoms of AIDS (Magic Johnson is an example). Such a change in definition increased the number of individuals identified as having AIDS by 20 to 25%. More important, it would allow those so diagnosed to qualify for disability payments.

NATIONAL DATA: The CDC estimated that currently in the U.S. one adult man in 100, and one adult woman in 600, are HIV positive (National Commission on Acquired Immune Deficiency Syndrome, 1991).

As of June 1992, 230,179 AIDS cases had been diagnosed in the United States (CDC, 1992). In 1991, over 29,000 died in the U.S. from AIDS (CDC, 1992). Worldwide at least 12.9 million people were estimated to be HIV infected in early 1992 (Goldsmith, 1992). This means that someone in the world is infected with the HIV virus every 15 to 20 seconds. Dr. Michael Merson of the World Health Organization reported to the International Congress on AIDS in July, 1992, that one million of those infected have contracted the virus within just the past six months. He gravely cautioned, "This is just the beginning of the AIDS era and there is no shortcut in sight" (Painter, 1992, p. 1).

NATIONAL DATA: Eighty-nine percent of all diagnosed AIDS cases in the United States have been male, compared to 11% female (CDC, 1992).

AIDS is not distributed equally among women and men. Although women are less likely than men to be infected with HIV, the proportion of infected women is increasing. While women make up 25% of the total infected adults in 1990, by early 1992 they make up 40% (Goldsmith, 1992).

HIV infection is not equally distributed among racial and ethnic groups either. Of those who have been diagnosed (in the United States) as having AIDS, 53% are white, 30% are black, 17% are Hispanic, and less than 1% are Asian/Pacific Islander and American Indian or Alaska Native (CDC, 1992). However, the risk of AIDS in blacks and Hispanics is almost three times as great as that in whites (Selik, Castro, & Papaioanou, 1988). The chance of heterosexual transmission of HIV is approximately 10 times greater for blacks and four times greater for Hispanics than for whites (Aral & Holmes, 1991). Urban minority populations, prostitutes, and those who exchange sex for drugs are regarded as the primary groups among which HIV infection is increasing at epidemic rates (Aral & Holmes, 1991).

CONSIDERATION: "Risk group" is a term that implies that a certain demographic trait determines who will become infected with HIV. Kerr (1990) noted, however,

> It is not the group one belongs to, but the behaviors one practices that puts them at risk for HIV infection. The concept of high-risk groups has led many persons to falsely believe that they are not susceptible to HIV infection since they do not fall into one of these "groups." (p. 431)

Indeed, through September 30, 1987, 2,059 patients identified as having AIDS were not initially identified as having any risk factors (Castro et al., 1988). We emphasize that people make choices that affect their risk of contracting HIV and that it is these choices, rather than one's group affiliation, that influence HIV transmission.

Knowledge and Attitudes about HIV and AIDS

Studies on the knowledge that people have about HIV and AIDS have yielded different results. In a study of 268 college students (101 men, 167 women), representing whites (164), blacks (22), and Hispanics (82), the average student knew slightly more than half of the 20 AIDS information items presented by the researchers (Negy & Webber, 1991). There was no difference in the knowledge between whites and blacks, and both had more knowledge than Hispanics. The researchers attributed the lag in knowledge by Hispanics to the fact that most HIV-infection education is written and spoken in English. Other research by Stevenson and Stevenson (1990) (based on a sample of 2,461 entering college students) revealed that while the students understood the risk of having multiple sexual partners and the value of abstinence and condoms, they did not understand exactly how HIV was transmitted.

Still another study assessed levels of knowledge, attitudes, and perceived susceptibility to AIDS among 226 freshman college students at a southeastern university (Adame, Taylor-Nicholson, Wang, & Abbas, 1991). Researchers found that subjects were generally knowledgeable about AIDS (see Table 18.1).

Seventy percent of the college students at the University of West Florida in Pensacola who took an AIDS attitudes questionnaire agreed with the statement, "The fear of AIDS/HIV makes me more conscious of my social life" (Biasco & Taylor, 1991, p. 398). Research has shown that male students report being more fearful of HIV infection than female students. "The AIDS epidemic represents more of a threat to males than females because thus far, most AIDS victims have been males" (Stevenson & Stevenson, 1990, p. 44).

In spite of the fear people may have about HIV infection, most (including those who engage in high-risk behavior) view their becoming infected as a very low probability event. Such denial was illustrated in a study of 222 men and women ages 18 to 25. Three researchers (Hansen, Hahn, & Wolkenstein, 1990) observed:

> Those who reported having had multiple sex partners in the past year and who did not consistently use condoms, as well as individuals who remained abstinent and engaged in no risk behaviors at all, saw their own chances of getting AIDS to be the same: roughly one in a million. Others who engage in risky sex practices, however, are seen as being at risk—they are seen as having a one chance in 150 (among females) or one chance in 900 (among males) of getting AIDS. (p. 626)

TABLE 18.1 Percentage of Correct Student Responses to AIDS Knowledge Items

Survey Items	Correct Response	% Students
AIDS is a medical condition in which your body cannot fight off diseases.	True	96.0%
AIDS is caused by a virus.	True	91.1%
If you kiss someone with AIDS, you can get AIDS.	False	83.3%
If you touch someone with AIDS, you can get AIDS.	False	96.0%
Anybody can get AIDS.	True	92.9%
AIDS can be spread by using someone's personal belongings like a comb or hairbrush.	False	72.5%
The cause of AIDS is unknown.	False	61.3%
Having sex with someone who has AIDS is one way of getting it.	True	99.6%
If a pregnant woman has AIDS, there is a chance it may harm her unborn baby.	True	94.2%
Most people who get AIDS usually die from the disease.	True	88.9%
Using a condom during sex can lower the risk of getting AIDS.	True	99.1%
AIDS can be cured if treated early.	False	87.6%

Source: Adapted from Adame, D. D., Taylor-Nicholson, M. E., Wang, M., & Abbas, M. A. (1991). Southern college freshman students: A survey of knowledge, attitudes, and beliefs about AIDS. *Journal of Sex Education and Therapy, 17,* 196–206. Used by permission.

In the Adame et al. (1991) study of freshman college students, 72.4% of the subjects indicated that they were afraid of getting AIDS. However, 54.7% thought that they were less likely than most people to contract the disease. The researchers concluded that, in spite of these students' considerable knowledge about AIDS, "they still do not appear to be as concerned about contracting AIDS as perhaps they ought to be (p. 205). These studies emphasize that AIDS education strategies must deal with the issue of denial, as well as with information about how HIV infection is transmitted and how to decrease the risk of contracting HIV.

When a friend tells you he or she has AIDS, the appropriate first reaction is an embrace, not a shudder.

Mary Catherine Bateson
Richard Goldsby

One factor associated with the belief that one is invulnerable to contracting HIV is the belief that a person who has HIV is easy to spot. In a study of 2,461 undergraduate students, 56% felt that they could tell if a person was infected with HIV (Stevenson & Stevenson, 1990).

Some people have negative attitudes toward people with HIV infection. Table 18.2 reveals the results of a national telephone survey of a random sample of 960 individuals conducted by Herek and Glunt (1991).

The following Self-Assessment allows you to assess your attitude toward HIV and STDs in general.

Tests for HIV Infection

One test for HIV, ELISA (enzyme-linked immunosorbent assay), assesses the presence of antibodies to HIV in the bloodstream of a person who has been exposed to HIV as early as two weeks to three months earlier. The test is inexpensive (it costs two dollars) and serves as a basic screening device. A blood sample is taken from the person's arm and tested in the laboratory. This test does not confirm that the person has or will develop AIDS. Hence, the test is not an "AIDS test" but an HIV antibody test.

CONSIDERATION: It can take as long as three years before the HIV infection is evident in a blood test (Chase, 1989) and 10 years from the time of initial infection until the onset of AIDS (CDC, 1989).

One factor associated with the belief that one is invulnerable to contracting HIV is the belief that a person who has HIV is easy to spot. Which of these people may have HIV? Can you tell?

TABLE 18.2 Attitudes Toward AIDS

Aids Issue	Percent Agreement
People with AIDS are a serious risk to the rest of society.	51.6%
People with AIDS should be separated to protect the public health.	19.5%
People with AIDS have only themselves to blame.	19 %
People with AIDS are getting what they deserve.	11 %

Source: Adapted from Herek, G. M., & Glunt, E. K. (1991). AIDS-related attitudes in the United States: A preliminary conceptualization. *Journal of Sex Research, 28,* 99–123, p. 109. Used by permission.

Those testing positive after being administered the ELISA test two times will be given a second type of test (Western blot) for more definitive screening. (The Western blot is considerably more expensive, costing around $40, than the ELISA test). If the result of the Western blot test is positive, the person has been exposed to HIV and is infected. If the result is negative, it is probable that the person does not have HIV. However, in some cases, the result of the Western blot test is neither positive nor negative. One alternative is to wait a month and then repeat the test (to give time for the antibodies to build up).

Hello, Helen. I really like you. Can I have some blood and urine for a test?
Robin Williams

Alternatively, instead of repeating the Western blot test, the person's blood may be tested with the VAL-I.D. PCR (polymerase chain reaction). This is a recently developed test that can detect the HIV virus itself and does not depend on the presence of antibodies to HIV. Hence, it can be used at the earliest stage of HIV and is reliable in as short a time as six weeks after exposure to HIV. It is recommended that newborns be tested with the VAL-I.D. PCR if their mother has been infected with HIV.

A urine test that screens for HIV antibodies has also been developed. Research on its use with 530 people at alcohol treatment centers compared the results of blood and urine screening, and revealed nearly identical results. While the urine test is easier and less expensive to perform, the researchers cautioned that given the widespread use of urine drug screening in the U.S., it could be used by groups who would discriminate against those who test positive (Clinical Studies, 1992).

Once it is determined that a person is HIV-infected, the Centers for Disease Control encourage the practice of "partner identification" (also called "contact tracing"). Persons with HIV identify the person(s) with whom they have had sexual contact. These persons are contacted by a public health official, counseled, and appraised of the availability of the antibody test. In one study, 51 HIV-infected patients identified 135 opposite-sex partners, 34 of whom were tested to yield seven HIV-infected individuals (Rutherford et al., 1991). The researchers noted that the low yield was a function of the long incubation period of HIV and mobility of the population.

How does knowledge that one has HIV affect one's suicide potential and subsequent behavior change? Regarding suicide, Murzuk et al. (1988) observed that men aged 20 to 59 who were diagnosed as having AIDS were 36 times more likely to commit suicide than men aged 20 to 59 who had not been diagnosed as having AIDS. When compared to the general population, men with AIDS were 66 more times as likely to commit suicide. Regarding a subsequent change in sexual behavior, Jacobsen, Perry, and Hirsch (1990) observed that individuals who test positive for HIV reduce their high-risk sexual behaviors; individuals who test negative are less

Self Assessment

STD Attitude Scale

Directions Please read each statement carefully: *STD* means sexually transmitted diseases, once called venereal diseases. Record your first reaction by marking an "X" through the letter which best describes how much you agree or disagree with the idea.

Use This Key:
SA = Strongly agree; A = Agree; U = Undecided; D = Disagree; SD = Strongly disagree.
Remember: STD means sexually transmitted diseases, such as gonorrhea, syphilis, genital herpes, and AIDS.

	(Mark "X" through letter)				
1. How one uses his/her sexuality has nothing to do with STD.	SA	A	U	D	SD
2. It is easy to use the prevention methods that reduce one's chances of getting an STD.	SA	A	U	D	SD
3. Responsible sex is one of the best ways of reducing the risk of STD.	SA	A	U	D	SD
4. Getting early medical care is the main key to preventing harmful effects of STD.	SA	A	U	D	SD
5. Choosing the right sex partner is important in reducing the risk of getting an STD.	SA	A	U	D	SD
6. A high rate of STD should be a concern for all people.	SA	A	U	D	SD
7. People with an STD have a duty to get their sex partners to medical care.	SA	A	U	D	SD
8. The best way to get a sex partner to STD treatment is to take him/her to the doctor with you.	SA	A	U	D	SD
9. Changing one's sex habits is necessary once the presence of an STD is known.	SA	A	U	D	SD
10. I would dislike having to follow the medical steps for treating an STD.	SA	A	U	D	SD
11. If I were sexually active, I would feel uneasy doing things before and after sex to prevent getting an STD.	SA	A	U	D	SD
12. If I were sexually active, it would be insulting if a sex partner suggested we use a condom to avoid STD.	SA	A	U	D	SD
13. I dislike talking about STD with my peers.	SA	A	U	D	SD
14. I would be uncertain about going to the doctor unless I was sure I really had an STD.	SA	A	U	D	SD
15. I would feel that I should take my sex partner with me to a clinic if I thought I had an STD.	SA	A	U	D	SD
16. It would be embarrassing to discuss STD with one's partner if one were sexually active.	SA	A	U	D	SD
17. If I were to have sex, the chance of getting an STD makes me uneasy about having sex with more than one person.	SA	A	U	D	SD
18. I like the idea of sexual abstinence (not having sex) as the best way of avoiding STD.	SA	A	U	D	SD
19. If I had an STD, I would cooperate with public health persons to find the sources of STD.	SA	A	U	D	SD

Continued

Self-Assessment—*Continued*

(Mark "X" through letter)

20. If I had an STD, I would avoid exposing others while I was being treated. SA A U D SD
21. I would have regular STD checkups if I were having sex with more than one partner. SA A U D SD
22. I intend to look for STD signs before deciding to have sex with anyone. SA A U D SD
23. I will limit my sex activity to just one partner because of the chances I might get an STD. SA A U D SD
24. I will avoid sex contact anytime I think there is even a slight chance of getting an STD. SA A U D SD
25. The chance of getting an STD would not stop me from having sex. SA A U D SD
26. If I had a chance, I would support community efforts toward controlling STD. SA A U D SD
27. I would be willing to work with others to make people aware of STD problems in my town. SA A U D SD

Scoring Calculate total points for each subscale and total scale, using the point values below.

For items 1, 10–14, 16, 25: Strongly agree = 5 points; Agree = 4 points; Undecided = 3 points; Disagree = 2 points; and Strongly disagree = 1 point.

For items 2–9, 15, 17–24, 26, 27: Strongly agree = 1 point; Agree = 2 points; Undecided = 3 points; Disagree = 4 points; and Strongly disagree = 5 points.

Total scale: items 1–27
Belief Subscale: items 1–9
Feeling Subscale: items 10–18
Intention to Act Subscale: items 19–27

Interpretation

High score predisposes one toward *high*-risk STD behavior.

Low score predisposes one toward *low*-risk STD behavior.

Yarber, Torabi and Veenker (1989) developed the STD Attitudes Scale by administering three experimental forms of 45 items each. Respondents were 2,980 students in six secondary school districts in the Midwest and East. Based on statistical analysis, the scale was reduced to the final 27 items. Reliability coefficients for the entire scale and the three subscales ranged from .48 to .73. The developers reported evidence of construct validity in that the scale was sensitive to positive attitude changes resulting from STD education.

Reference

Yarber, W. L., Torabi, M. R., & Veenker, C. H. (1989). Development of a three-component STD attitude scale. *Journal of Sex Education and Therapy, 15,* 36–49. Used by permission.

likely to do so. Indeed, those who test negative report a sense of relief and a reduction in anxiety and distress (Jacobsen et al., 1990).

Treatment for HIV and Opportunistic Infections

A number of drugs have been developed and are currently undergoing clinical trials for treating HIV infection, as well as the subsequent opportunistic infections. The *AIDS/HIV Treatment Directory*, published quarterly by the American Foundation for AIDS Research, summarizes recent treatment developments (Abrams & Grieco, 1991). In this section we profile a small sample of current treatments.

One drug that is useful in treating some people infected with the AIDS virus is azidothymidine (AZT).

> Pierre Ludington, a former San Francisco schoolteacher who tested positive, remains healthy and without symptoms after two years of taking AZT (plus a drug called acyclovir) in a research project. "I felt that if it weren't toxic to me, I'd be a fool not to take it . . . . Two years later, I haven't had so much as a cold. It's important for people to know AZT isn't toxic to everyone." (Chase, 1989, p. 10)

Another drug marketed as Videx that has also been given Food and Drug Administration (FDA) approval is dideoxyinosine (**ddI**). In limited trials, the drug seems to be as effective as AZT in slowing the growth of HIV. However, there are side effects, such as painful neuritis and pancreatitis. "Currently, trials alternating AZT and ddI are underway in an attempt to get maximum benefits with minimal negative side effects" (Cox, 1992, p. ix). The drug is still considered experimental and is not a cure.

Still another drug that is being developed to treat HIV is ddC, known as Hivid, and is to be used in combination with AZT. All three drugs (AZT, ddI, and ddC) work by blocking replication of the AIDS virus within the cells that are the targets of the virus. Full FDA approval had not been granted by late 1992. The FDA has warned against purchasing ddC through buyers' clubs (black market shops), as their pills may contain either no ddC or up to twice the recommended dosage. It is safer for one's physician to request the drug directly from its manufacturer, Hoffman–LaRoche, which offers the drug at no charge to patients who meet medical criteria (The AIDS File, 1992).

Pentamidine is also helpful in treating PCP (pneumocystis carinii pneumonia), the pneumonia associated with AIDS. When pentamidine is inhaled directly into the lungs, it is dramatically effective in preventing the pneumonia. While pentamidine prevents the PCP parasite from growing, another drug called "566" directly attacks the parasite that causes PCP and kills it.

Given the availability of various drugs, "it is important to change our conception that everyone dies from AIDS" (Thompson, 1989, p. 52). Physicians are now beginning to think of AIDS as analogous to diabetes. There is no cure, but it can be managed in some cases. The ultimate medical answer rests in the identification of a vaccine to eliminate the threat of HIV. Approximately nine HIV vaccines have already been developed, but none has been tested on humans to find out if it will protect against HIV. "At this time, it appears as if it will be 2005 before we know if a vaccine against AIDS will be possible" (Cox, 1992, p. ix).

In the following sections, we consider other sexually transmissible diseases. The relationship of HIV infection to other STDs is being given increased attention by researchers:

> HIV infection leads to altered manifestations of other STDs and thereby probably promotes their spread. Genital and anorectal herpes ulcers normally heal within one to three weeks, but they may persist for months as highly infectious ulcers in persons with HIV infection. (Aral & Holmes, 1991, p. 66)

Genital Herpes

NATIONAL DATA: At least one in six U.S. adults, or 26 million people, are infected with genital herpes (Johnson et al., 1989).

Herpes refers to more than 50 viruses related by size, shape, internal composition, and structure. One such herpes is genital herpes. Whereas the disease has been known for at least 2,000 years, media attention to **genital herpes** is relatively new. Also known as **herpes simplex virus type 2** (**HSV-2**), genital herpes is a viral infection that may be transmitted during sexual contact. Pregnant women infected with herpes may also transmit the virus to their newborn infants, causing brain damage or death. A cesarean section delivery can reduce the risk to a newborn whose mother has an outbreak.

Another type of herpes, **herpes simplex virus type 1 (HSV-1)**, also known as labial or lip herpes, often originates in the mouth. Herpes simplex virus type 1 is commonly recognized as cold sores on the lips. The Type I and Type II viruses are quite similar, and either type can infect the genitals or the mouth. (Herpes Resource Center, 1991).

Symptoms of genital herpes occur in the form of a cluster of small, painful blisters or sores at the point of infection, most often on the penis or around the anus in men. In women, blisters usually appear around the vagina but may also develop inside the vagina, on the cervix, and sometimes on the anus. However, several studies suggest that the majority of persons who acquire HSV-2 develop asymptomatic infections (Jones & Mertz, 1986). Most people who have herpes do not experience symptoms and are not aware that they are infected. Asymptomatic acquisition is documented in research studies by detecting antibodies to HSV in a person who was previously antibody-negative.

The first symptoms of genital herpes may appear a couple of days to three weeks after exposure. These symptoms may include an itching or burning sensation during urination, followed by headache, fever, aches, swollen glands, and—in women—vaginal discharge. The symptoms worsen over about 10 days, during which there is inflammation and a skin eruption, followed by the appearance of painful sores, which soon break open and become extremely painful during genital contact or when touched. The acute illness may last from three to six weeks, and the clinical manifestations are greater in women than in men (Becker & Nahmias, 1985).

As with syphilis, the symptoms of genital herpes subside (the sores dry up, scab over, and disappear); and the infected person feels good again. But the virus settles in the nerve cells in the spinal column and may cause repeated outbreaks of the symptoms in about one-third of those infected. Based on data from 32 women and 32 men suffering from severe cases of genital herpes, there were no sex differences in the frequency of repeated outbreaks. Women and men are equally likely to experience recurrent outbreaks (Silver, Auerbach, Vishniavsky, & Kaplowitz, 1986).

Stress, menstruation, sunburn, fatigue, and the presence of other infections seem to be related to the reappearance of the virus. Although such recurrences are usually milder and of shorter duration than the initial outbreak, the resurfacing of the virus

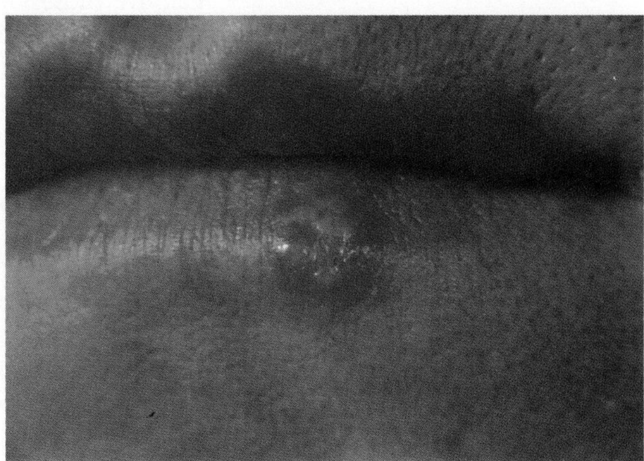

Herpes simplex lesion of the lower lip

may occur throughout the person's life. "It's not knowing when the thing is going to come back that's the bad part about herpes," said one person with herpes (Authors' files).

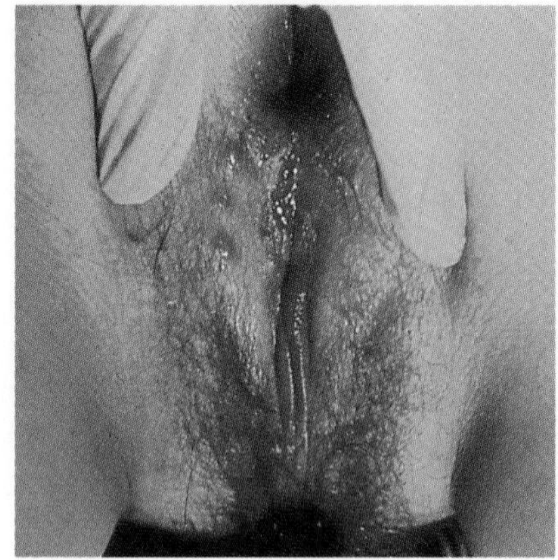

CONSIDERATION: In the past, many medical and sex education personnel have stated that transmission of herpes could be completely avoided simply by avoiding sexual contact when lesions were present. However, the herpes virus is contagious not only during the time that a person has visible sores but also when the infected person experiences itching, burning, or tingling sensations prior to an outbreak (prodome phase). In addition "studies suggest that transmission [of herpes] occurs from individuals who do not have signs or symptoms of HSV and that a significant proportion of transmission occurs from individuals who are not even aware that they have the virus" (Jones & Mertz, 1986, p. 4). Using a latex condom reduces the risk of transmitting or acquiring herpes; however, the virus may permeate the condom.

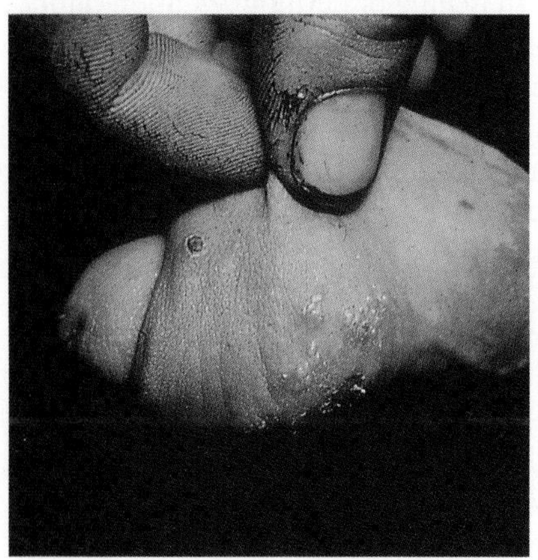

Symptoms of genital herpes occur in the form of a cluster of small painful blisters or sores at the point of infection.

Although undergraduates are generally knowledgeable about herpes, they have gaps in their knowledge. In a study of 351 students who presented themselves to the health service at the University of Virginia, over half thought that a cesarean section was required of women who had herpes, 25% thought that all people with genital herpes had recurrences, and over 30% thought that genital herpes causes cancer (all of these statements are not true) (Hillard, Kitchell, Turner, Keeling, & Shank, 1984).

A virus culture and serodiagnosis (diagnosis of blood) offer the most accurate ways to identify if a person is infected with genital herpes ("New era," 1991). At the time of this writing, there is no cure for herpes. Because it is a virus, it does not respond to antibiotics, as do syphilis and gonorrhea. A few procedures that help to relieve the symptoms and promote healing of the sores include consulting a physician to look for and treat any other genital infections near the herpes sores, keeping the sores clean and dry, taking hot sitz baths three times a day, and wearing loose-fitting cotton underwear to enhance air circulation. Proper nutrition, adequate sleep and exercise, and avoiding physical or mental stress are also associated with reducing recurrences.

Acyclovir, marketed as Zovirax, is an ointment that can be applied directly on the herpes sores, helping to relieve pain, speed healing, and reduce the amount of time that live viruses are present in the sores. For the first outbreak of genital herpes, physicians recommend topical applications to the external genital lesions every four to six hours for five to seven days, or until the lesions have crusted (Becker & Nahmias, 1985).

A more effective tablet form of acyclovir that significantly reduces the rate of recurring episodes of genital herpes is also available. Daily oral acyclovir reduced the number of genital herpes recurrences by 92%, compared with baseline, in the third year of treatment in 525 patients who received such therapy for three years. A similar reduction in outbreaks (89%) occurred for those who received episodic acyclovir treatment for acute infections in the first year before switching to continuous therapy in the second and third years (Kaplowitz et al., 1991). Once acyclovir is stopped, the herpetic recurrences resume. Acyclovir seems to make the symptoms of first-episode genital herpes more manageable, but it is less effective during subsequent outbreaks.

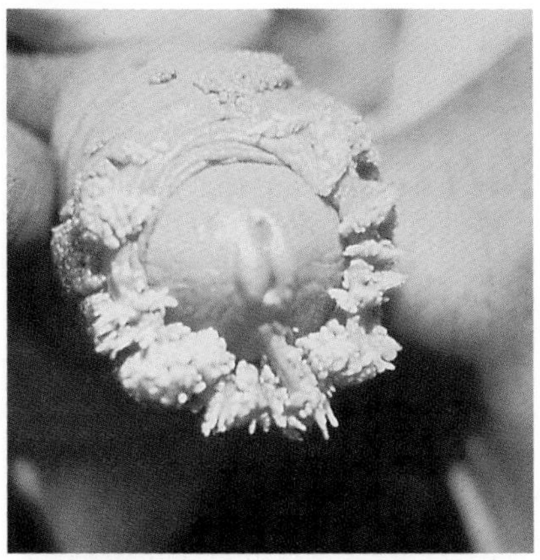

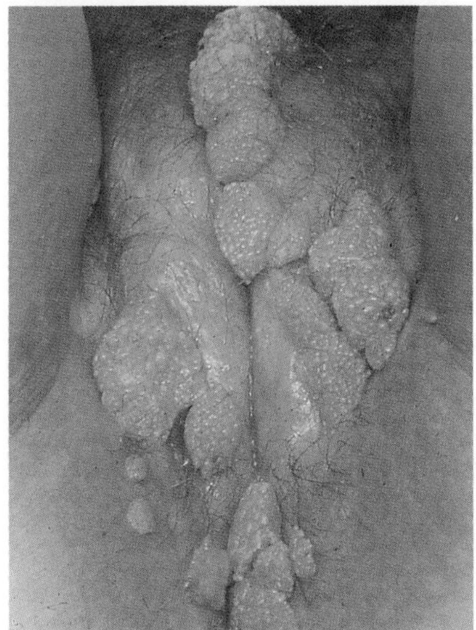

Human papilloma virus infection or HPV on the penis of the male and on the vagina and rectum of the female.

Immu Vir, an alternative to acyclovir, is used primarily by persons who have frequent outbreaks of genital herpes (once a month or more). This ointment is designed to reduce pain, healing time, and number of outbreaks. The drug has no known side effects.

Coping with having any type of STD is difficult. Because there is no cure for herpes, it may be particularly difficult for herpes-infected individuals to cope with the disease. Exhibit 18.1 discusses psychological responses to genital herpes.

Human Papilloma Virus (HPV)

There are more than 60 types of **human papilloma virus (HPV)**. More than a dozen of these types can cause warts (called **genital warts** or **condyloma**), or more subtle signs of infection in the genital tract. The virus infects the skin's top layers and can remain inactive for months or years before any obvious signs of infection appear. Often warts appear within three to six months. However, some types of HPV produce no visible warts. Sometimes referred to as "subclinical infection" or "flat warts" this may involve two categories of infection. One is "microscopic warts" which can be seen through a magnifying lens. The other, "clinically undetectable HPV," cannot be seen at all, but can be detected with special laboratory tests (HPV in Perspective, 1991). Any sexual partner(s) of an infected individual should have a prompt medical examination.

HPV can be transmitted through vaginal or rectal intercourse and through fellatio and cunnilingus. In women, genital warts most commonly develop on the vulva, in the vagina, or on the cervix. They may also appear on or near the anus. In men, the warts appear most often on the penis but may appear on the scrotum, anus, or within the rectum.

Currently scientists are studying the factors that increase a person's vulnerability to cancers of the anogenital tract. Vulvar cancer is associated with having a history of HPV (Brinton et al., 1990). While infection with certain types of HPV may be an important factor, many researchers believe that cervical cancer may result from several combined factors. These include smoking, use of oral contraceptives, history of multiple sexual partners, and a dietary deficiency in folic acid (Risk Factors, 1992). There is also evidence that some types of HPV may increase the risk of anal cancer (HPV and Anal Cancer, 1992), and may infect the lining of the eye (Can the Eyes Have It?, 1992).

It is more important to know what kind of person has the disease than what kind of disease the person has.

Elliot Luby

Because of the different expressions of the virus, it is difficult to obtain an accurate estimate of its prevalence (Horn et al., 1991). In a study of 467 women presenting themselves to a university health service for a routine gynecologic exam, 46% had evidence of cervical or vulvar human papillomavirus infections (Bauer et al., 1991).

NATIONAL DATA: About 500,000 new cases of genital warts are reported annually. According to Aral and Holmes (1991), "At the moment, genital and anal HPV infections appear to be the most prevalent STDS in the U.S. and a large proportion of sexually active adults seem to be infected" (p. 66).

Health care providers disagree regarding the efficacy of treating HPV when there are no detectable warts. However, when the warts can be seen, either by visual inspection or by colposcope, providers do typically advise treatment. There are a number of treatment options. Choosing among them depends upon the number of warts and their location, availability of equipment, training of health care providers, and the preferences of the patient. Most of the treatments are at least moderately effective, but many are quite expensive. They range from topical application of chemicals to laser surgery. Table 18.3 offers information regarding the advantages and disadvantages of the various treatment methods.

Treatment of warts destroys infected cells, but not all of them, as HPV is present in a wider area of skin than just the precise wart location. "The troublesome news, then, is that with any of these treatments—no matter how good the health care

EXHIBIT 18.1 Psychological Reactions to Genital Herpes

Individuals who become aware that they have genital herpes typically go through several psychological stages. Many of these are similar to those experienced in reference to other life crises, such as the death of a loved one, divorce, or separation. Luby (1981) identified the basic stages and reactions as follows:

1. Shock, denial and emotional numbing. "I never thought it would happen to me" is the overwhelming initial reaction. Such feelings are immediately followed by frantically searching for a cure or for reassurance that the disease can be managed.
2. Withdrawal. The person feels unable to cope with the knowledge of having contracted an incurable chronic disease and withdraws from or limits interactions with others.

> "It's hard enough to find someone who is special, who you are attracted to and want to spend time with," said one participant in a HELP (a self-help group of individuals who have genital herpes) group discussion. "But when herpes has to be talked about at the beginning of every new relationship, it makes an already-difficult situation ten times worse." (Hill, 1987, p. 1)

A woman with herpes said:

> I have been very conscientious about not passing the virus on to others. I have gone through months that I would talk to men—but not date them. Or, I would date them, but disappear before things got serious. (Silver et al., 1986, p. 169)

3. Anger. Overwhelmed with the flood of emotions, herpes-infected individuals feel angry at both the person who infected them and the physician who appears helpless to eliminate the disease.
4. Fear. Herpes victims begin to fear how herpes will affect their life in terms of the durability of interpersonal relationships, sexual gratifications, and future children. Questions such as how to tell others of the contagion occur, and fear may reach such a level that it interferes with sexual functioning (e.g., erectile functioning).
5. Leper effect. As individuals begin to see themselves as herpes sufferers, they feel ugly, shameful, contaminated, or even dangerous. To combat these feelings, some become experts on herpes (known as "herpes graduate students"). Others become "celibate, even religiously moralistically anti-sexual" (Luby, 1981, p. 3).
6. Depression. Continued thoughts of hopelessness and helplessness may occur. Because herpes-infected individuals do not know when there will be an outbreak and cannot control the reaction of their partner(s) to such outbreaks, a feeling of "learned helplessness" develops (Silver et al., 1986). In some cases, the frustration may reach a level of a deep suicidal depression.
7. Decomposition. If the depression continues, the feelings may reactivate underlying psychopathology "and disorganize already inadequate coping strategies" Luby, (p. 3).

The psychological reactions that individuals have to herpes affect both their resistance to recurrent outbreaks and their level of coping with the disease (Luby, 1981). In their study of 66 subjects who had genital herpes, Silver et al. (1986) noted that those most likely to have repeated outbreaks tend "to view their fate as being beyond their control and who tend to use emotion-focused, avoidant, wishful thinking as a way of attempting to deal with the stress associated with their situation" (p. 170). Hence, coping mechanisms that were associated with repeated outbreaks were wishful thinking ("If only I had . . .") and a view that one's life was externally controlled (Silver et al., 1986).

Manne and Sandler (1984) also studied the psychological reactions and coping mechanisms of 152 individuals who had contracted genital herpes. Individuals who engaged in characterological self-blame experienced the most difficult adjustment to herpes. The researchers noted the importance of learning how to think more positively. Rather than focus on such thoughts as "Herpes means I'm a loose or promiscuous person," the individual might substitute a rational thought, such as "Having herpes means nothing about my personality. It may be embarrassing, but it does not mean I am a shameful person." Or rather than say to one's self, "Since I have herpes, I will be rejected," an alternative thought is "I fear I'll be rejected—I really don't know that I will be."

Silver et al. (1986) noted the effectiveness of similar strategies in coping with genital herpes.

> Based on the present findings, cognitive-behavioral approaches which would teach and reinforce active, problem-focused coping strategies (e.g., positive coping self-statements, active coping imagery, assertive training) seem to have the most promise for this population. (p. 170)

In addition to these coping skills, herpes patients who seem to cope most adaptively are typically older and married and have considerable information about the disease. They have also been open with their partners and have sexual relations only when there are no lesions (Manne & Sandler, 1984).

Self-help groups and social support from others are particularly helpful for some herpes sufferers in that they remove the feeling of being isolated and being the only one forced to cope with herpes. The Herpes Resource Center, or HELP, is a nationwide resource for patients with herpes of over 10,000 members. It publishes a quarterly newsletter, *The Helper* (P.O. Box 13827, Research Triangle Park, NC 27709) that features information about the management of herpes and provides a listing of local self-help groups.

TABLE 18.3 Therapies Currently Recommended for the Treatment of Genital Warts

Therapy	Clearance Rate	Recurrence Rate	Pain	Cost	No. of Doctor Visits	Anesthesia Required	Can Be Used During Pregnancy?
Podophyllin	22-77%	11-74%	Mild to Moderate	$183	3	No	No
Podofilox	45[1]-50[2]%	21[2]-33[1]%	Mild[1]	Not available	Not available	No	No
Trichloroacetic Acid (TCA)	81%	36%	Moderate	$183	3	No	Yes
Cryotherapy	63-88%	21-40%	Moderate. Some side effects	$285	3	No	Yes
Surgery	93%	29%	Moderate	Not available	1	Yes, local	Yes
Electrodessication	94%	22%	Moderate	$340	2	Yes, local	Yes
Interferon	19-62%	21-25%	Moderate. Some side effects	$1,500	9-18	No	No
Laser	31-94%	3-95%	Moderate to severe	$2,650	1	Yes, local or general	Yes

[1]Karl R. Beutner, et al. Patient applied Podofilox for Treatment of Genital Warts. *The Lancet,* April 15, 1989: 831–834.
[2]David A. Baker, et al. Topical Podofilox for the Treatment of Condylomata Acuminata in Women. *Obstetrics & Gynecology,* Vol. 76, No. 4, October 1990.

Source: Unless otherwise noted, all information has been adapted from "Management of Genital Infection Caused by Human Papillomavirus," published in *Reviews of Infectious Diseases,* Vol. 12, 1990, by Stephen J. Kraus and Katherine M. Stone. Reprinted from the *HPV News* (1992, Spring), by permission of the American Social Health Association.

provider—it's possible that the patient will later have one or more recurrences in which new warts develop" (HPV in Perspective, 1991, p. 5). However, in the vast majority of cases the infection is mild and manageable.

Since the possibility of recurrences cannot be eliminated, patients are advised to schedule followup visits with their health care provider, check themselves regularly for obvious warts, and talk with their sexual partner(s) about what precautions they will take to reduce the risk of transmitting the infection. To reduce recurrences, protecting one's immune system (not smoking tobacco or marijuana, or using other drugs) is recommended. "Investing the time to put HPV in perspective, communicating about the problem with intimate friends, and making general health a priority—all these are steps that can help the patient with genital HPV cut the problem down to size" (HPV in Perspective, 1991, p. 7).

Chlamydia

Chlamydia has been described as the "silent disease." It refers to one of two types of infection: (1) chlamydia trachomatis, which may cause infections in the genitals, eyes, and lungs of humans, and (2) chlamydia psittici, which primarily infects birds. In this discussion, we will focus on chlamydia trachomatis, or the CT variety.

Some health officials believe that chlamydia is the most common sexually transmissible disease. Worldwide, it is estimated that 300 million people contract sexually transmitted chlamydial infections each year (Sammons, 1991). When the eye infec-

NATIONAL DATA: Four million cases of chlamydia are detected annually in the United States. Sexually active teenagers have the highest incidence (Stein, 1991).

tion, chlamydial trachoma, is considered, over 500 million cases are contracted yearly. At least 2 million of the 200 million who contract chlamydia trachoma each year are permanently blinded by the infection; most of these people live in Asia and Africa. The rate of blindness due to chlamydial infections in the United States is much lower, due to climate and the medication readily available to control the infection. Other possible consequences of chlamydia include sterility, a form of infant pneumonia, and premature birth (Aral & Holmes, 1991).

CT is easily transmitted from person to person via sexual contact. The microorganisms are most often found in the urethra of the man, the cervix, uterus, and Fallopian tubes of the woman, and in the rectums of either men or women. In addition to direct contact, CT infections *can* occur indirectly by contact with, as examples, a towel, or a hot tub in which bacteria are present.

Genital-to-eye transmission of the bacteria can also occur. If a person with a genital CT infection rubs his or her eye or the eye of a partner after touching infected genitals, the bacteria can be transferred to the eye, and vice versa. Finally, infants can get CT as they pass through the cervix of their infected mothers during delivery.

CT rarely shows obvious symptoms, which accounts for its being known as "the silent disease." About one in four infected men and at least half of all infected women experience no initial symptoms (Cowley & Hager, 1991). The CDC estimates that 50% to 70% of chlamydial infections in women are asymptomic (Althaus, 1991). Women and men who are infected with CT usually do not know that they have the disease. The result is that they infect new partners unknowingly, who infect others unknowingly—unendingly.

Although CT often exhibits no symptoms, symptoms do occur in some cases. In men, the symptoms include pus from the penis, a sore on the penis, a sore testis, or a bloody stool. In women, symptoms include low back pain, pelvic pain, a boil on the vaginal lip, or a bloody discharge. Symptoms in either sex include a sore on the tongue, a sore on the finger, pain during urination, or the sensation of needing to urinate frequently. Even in the absence of such symptoms, a person who has had sex with an individual who has multiple sex partners should consult a physician. The presence of chlamydia can be determined by a laboratory test. Chlamydia is usually treated with tetracycline, except with pregnant women, who should take a substitute for tetracycline.

Although delay in treatment can be devastating, CT is curable if it is diagnosed and treated before the bacteria have had a chance to flourish. CT has often been overlooked as a cause of genital infections, because, until recently, laboratory tests were not sensitive and accurate enough to detect the presence of CT bacteria. Failure to treat chlamydia may result in **pelvic inflammatory disease (PID)** and infertility. Indeed, most cases of PID are caused by chlamydia, or gonorrhea, and persons with PID are seven to 10 times more likely to experience an ectopic pregnancy. PID probably accounts for the majority of tubal infertility cases (Althaus, 1991).

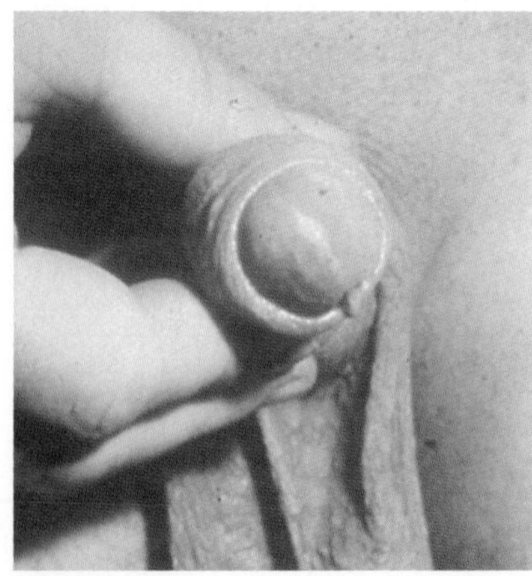

Gonorrhea drip

Gonorrhea

Also known as "the clap," "the whites," "morning drop," and "the drip," **gonorrhea** is a bacterial infection that is sexually transmissible. Individuals most often contract gonorrhea through having sexual contact with someone who is carrying gonococcus bacteria. Gonococci cannot live long outside the human body. Even though these bacteria can be cultured from a toilet seat, there have not been any documented cases of gonorrhea transmission except through intimate physical contact (Murphy, 1992). These bacteria thrive in warm, moist cavities, including the urinary tract, cervix, rectum, mouth, and throat. A pregnant woman may also transmit gonorrhea to her infant at birth, causing eye infection. Many medical experts recommend gonorrhea testing for all pregnant women and antibiotic eyedrops for all newborns.

NATIONAL DATA: While rates of gonorrhea have declined among white men and white women to less than 100,000 cases each year, rates among black men near 300,000 cases each year. Among black women, there are about 200,000 cases each year (Schwebke, 1991a).

Although some infected men show no signs, 80% exhibit symptoms between three and eight days after exposure. They begin to discharge a thick, white pus from the penis and to feel pain or discomfort during urination. They may also have swollen lymph glands in the groin. Women are more likely to show no signs (70% to 80% have no symptoms) of the infection, but when they do, the symptoms are sometimes a discharge from the vagina along with a burning sensation. More often, a woman becomes aware of gonorrhea only after she feels extreme discomfort, which is a result of the untreated infection traveling up into her uterus and Fallopian tubes. Salpingitis (inflammation of the Fallopian tube) occurs in 10–20% of infected women and may cause infertility or ectopic pregnancy (Murphy, 1992).

Undetected and untreated gonorrhea is dangerous. Not only does the infected person pass this disease on to the next partner, but other undesirable consequences may also result. The bacteria may affect the brain, joints, and reproductive systems. Both men and woman may develop meningitis (inflammation of the tissues surrounding the brain and spinal column), arthritis, and sterility. In men, the urethra may become blocked, necessitating frequent visits to a physician to clear the passage for urination. Infected women may have spontaneous abortions and premature or stillborn infants.

A physician can detect gonorrhea by analyzing penile or cervical discharge under a microscope. A major problem with new cases of gonorrhea is the emergence of new strains of the bacteria that are resistant to penicillin (Aral & Holmes, 1991). Because of high rates of resistance to penicillins and tetracyclines, the current recommended treatment for gonorrhea is ceftriaxone (Murphy, 1992).

SYPHILIS

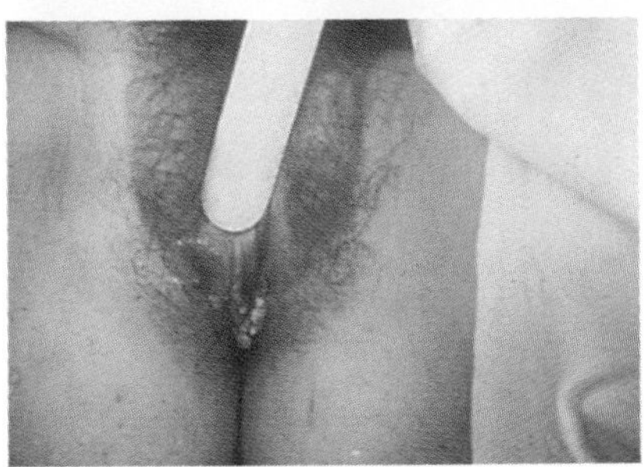

The chancre of primary stage syphilis neither hurts nor itches and if left untreated, will disappear in three to five weeks. (However, the syphilis may still cause damage.)

Syphilis is caused by bacteria that may be transmitted through sexual contact with an infected individual. Syphilis may also be transmitted from an infected pregnant woman to her unborn baby.

Although syphilis is less prevalent than gonorrhea, its effects are more devastating and include mental illness, blindness, heart disease—even death. The spirochete bacteria enter the body through mucous membranes that line various body openings. With your tongue, feel the inside of your cheek. This is a layer of mucous membrane—the substance in which spirochetes thrive. Similar membranes are in the vagina and urethra of the penis. If you kiss or have genital contact with someone harboring these bacteria, they can be absorbed into your mucous membranes and cause syphilitic infection. Syphilis progresses through at least three or four stages.

In stage one (primary-stage syphilis), a small sore or chancre will appear at the site of the infection between 10 and 90 days after exposure. The chancre, which shows on the tip of the man's penis, in the labia or cervix of the woman, or in either partner's mouth or rectum, neither hurts nor itches, and, if left untreated, will disappear in three to five weeks. This disappearance leads infected people to believe that they are cured—one of the tricky aspects of syphilis. In reality, the disease is still present and doing great harm, even though there are no visible signs.

During the second stage (secondary-stage syphilis), beginning from two to 12 weeks after the chancre has disappeared, other signs of syphilis appear in the form of a rash all over the body or just on the hands or feet. Welts and sores may also

NATIONAL DATA: The incidence of syphilis rose 16% from 1985 to 1989, or 11.4 to 18.4 cases per 100,000 (Schwebke, 1991b). Most of the increase occurred among inner-city ethnic groups of low socioeconomic status. Particularly vulnerable are infants of mothers with syphilis (Schwebke, 1991b).

occur, as well as fever, headaches, sore throat, and hair loss. Syphilis has been called "the great imitator" because it mimics so many other diseases (for example, infectious mononucleosis, cancer, and psoriasis). Whatever the symptoms, they too will disappear without treatment. The person may again be tricked into believing that nothing is wrong.

Following the secondary stage is the latency stage, during which there are no symptoms and the person is not infectious. However, the spirochetes are still in the body and can attack any organ at any time.

Tertiary syphilis—the third stage—may cause serious disability or even death. Heart disease, blindness, brain damage, loss of bowel and bladder control, difficulty in walking, and erectile dysfunction may result. Only about half of untreated cases of syphilis reach the final or tertiary stage.

Early detection and treatment is essential. Blood tests and examination of material from the infected site can help to verify the existence of syphilis. But such tests are not always accurate. Blood tests reveal the presence of antibodies, not spirochetes, and it sometimes takes three months before the body produces detectable antibodies. Sometimes there is no chancre anywhere on the person's body.

Treatment for syphilis is similar to that for gonorrhea. Penicillin or other antibiotics (for those allergic to penicillin) are effective. Infected persons treated in the early stages can be completely cured with no ill effects. If the syphilis has progressed into the later stages, any damage that has been done cannot be repaired.

Table 18.4 reviews some of the more common STDs.

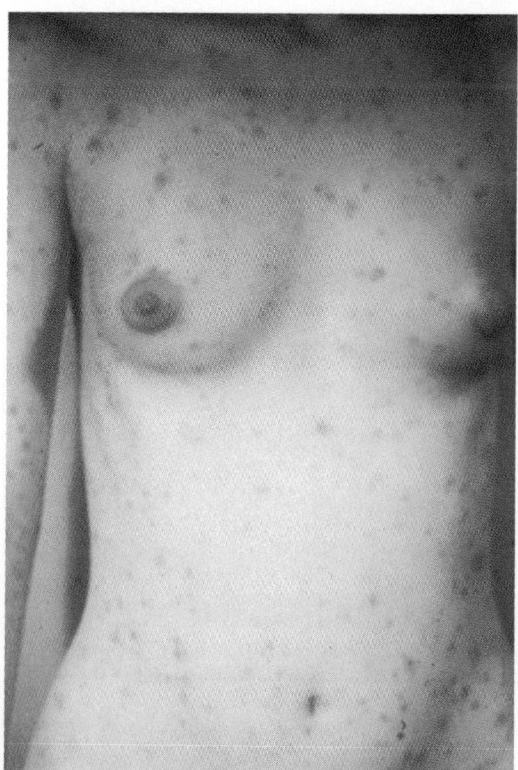

Rash of secondary syphilis

TABLE 18.4 HIV Infection and Other Sexually Transmissible Diseases

STD	Symptoms	Treatment	Complications
Acquired immunodeficiency syndrome (AIDS)	Most people who are infected with the human immunodeficiency virus (HIV), show no signs or symptoms until their condition progresses to full blown AIDS. Symptoms of AIDS include: • persistent cough • fever • weight loss • night sweats • skin rashes • diarrhea	There is presently no cure or vaccine to prevent the AIDS virus. Treatments are available to inhibit HIV growth and to fight opportunistic infections.	Fifty percent of individuals who develop the AIDS virus die within the first 2 years; 80 percent die within the first 3 years.
Chlamydia (a unique species of bacteria that causes one of the most widespread STDs in the United States)	Many individuals who are infected show no signs or symptoms of chlamydial infections. Symptoms include: • pain or burning upon urination • discharge from genital area • low-grade fever • lower abdominal pain • frequent need to urinate	Antibiotics.	If untreated can cause: • arthritis • sterility • permanent damage to the reproductive organs • ectopic pregnancy
Genital herpes (an STD caused by the herpes simplex virus, or HSV).	Skin around genital area becomes red and sensitive. Painful blisters and bumps may appear. Other symptoms include: • swollen glands • headaches • muscle aches • fever	There is presently no cure or vaccine to prevent genital herpes. The drug acyclovir has been used to reduce frequency and duration of genital herpes outbreaks.	Women with genital herpes may be at an increased risk for cervical cancer.
Genital warts (warts or growths that are caused by viruses called human papilloma virus, or HPV, and spread primarily through sexual contact).	Small to large warts or bump-like growths on the genital area. May be pink or red and appear in clusters or alone. There may be no visible warts.	Treatment depends on the size and location of the warts. Podophyllin or surgical methods are commonly used.	Women with HPV may be at an increased risk for cervical cancer.
Gonorrhea (an STD caused by a bacterial pathogen and spread through sexual contact).	Many individuals who are infected show no signs or symptoms. Symptoms include: • discharge from the penis or vagina • burning upon urination • urge to urinate frequently • low-grade fever • fatigue	Antibiotics.	If untreated can cause: • permanent damage to the reproductive organs and/or urinary tract • pelvic inflammatory disease • possible sterility
Syphilis (caused by a bacterium that attacks the nervous and cardiovascular systems and spread through sexual contact).	In the primary stages, a hard, painless chancre or sore will usually appear, then disappear in a few weeks. The secondary stage is characterized by a skin rash and flu-like symptoms.	Antibiotics.	If untreated can cause: • damage to the cardiovascular system • damage to the nervous system • blindness • death

Source: Developed for this text by Suzanne Kellerman, M.A., Health Education Manager, Beaufort County Hospital, Washington, N.C. Used by permission of Suzanne Kellerman.

Other Sexually Transmissible Diseases

Nongonococcal Urethritis (NGU)

Nongonococcal urethritis, (NGU) thought to be caused by microorganisms chlamydia and mycoplasma, affects both men and women. NGU causes penile discharge, which is thinner than that of gonorrhea, and causes burning and pain during urination. Infected women may show no symptoms or may have a slight discharge and discomfort when urinating. NGU is suspected when microscopic examination of the penile discharge does not show gonococcus bacteria or when a culture of the discharge from either gender does not grow it.

Once identified, NGU is treated with tetracyclines or other antibiotics. If left untreated, NGU may be as dangerous as gonorrhea, causing serious problems in both the female and male reproductive tracts. Symptoms may disappear, but the person will remain contagious and at risk for internal damage.

Lymphogranuloma Venereum (LGV)

Lymphogranuloma venereum (LGV) is prevalent in South America, the West Indies, Africa, and Southeast Asia. In the United States, there are less than 400 cases of LGV reported each year. Many of these cases occur in military personnel, travelers, and immigrants.

Symptoms of LGV include fever, chills, headaches, nausea, vomiting, and pain in the abdomen. In addition, sores that drip pus appear on the site of infection (genitalia, mouth, rectum). As with many other genital sores, they are eliminated with antibiotics, such as tetracycline.

Granuloma Inguinale

Granuloma inguinale (GI) is usually found in dark-skinned individuals and is prevalent in Vietnam, Indonesia, Africa, southern New Guinea, and southern India. In the United States, there are fewer than 100 cases of GI reported each year (Smith, Lauver, & Gray, 1990). However, military personnel and individuals traveling to these regions should be aware of the potential for infection if sexual contact is considered.

GI is characterized by a painless papule (pimple) that appears one to 12 weeks after infection. The papule ulcerates and becomes a lesion. Other lesions form and spread around the genital area and may infect the rectum and abdominal wall. Tetracycline and streptomycin are the antibiotics of choice.

Chancroid

Also known as "soft chancre," **chancroid** is transmitted through sexual contact with either the chancroid ulcer or discharge from infected local lymph glands. Two to five days after inoculation, a small papule forms at the site of contact. This lesion develops into an ulcer that exudes pus, bleeds easily, and is very painful. Local lymph glands enlarge, become inflamed, and may drip pus. The difference between a chancroid and a chancre is that the former is soft and painful. While between one and 10 ulcers may develop in men, women are usually asymptomatic (Smith et al., 1990).

NATIONAL DATA: The total number of chancroid cases reported in the United States rose from 665 in 1985 to 4,714 in 1989 (Aral & Holmes, 1991, 64).

Chancroid is most common in tropical countries. In the United States, chancroid is predominantly seen among immigrants or travelers to developing countries. Although chancroid had been rare since World War II, the incidence of infection has begun to increase.

> This increase could have profound public health consequences because chancroid may facilitate HIV transmission. Worse still, the bacterium that causes chancroid has developed resistance to many antimicrobial drugs. In persons who have been exposed to HIV, chancroid often fails to respond to some therapies that are otherwise highly effective. Thus, HIV infection may help the spread of a bacterial STD that in turn helps to spread HIV (Aral & Holmes, 1991, p. 64).

Chancroid is treated with erythromycin or ceftriaxone. Condoms will prevent chancroid transmission in the early stage of the disease.

Hepatitis B

Hepatitis is an inflammatory disease of the liver. When caused by the **hepatitis B virus (HBV)**, it is most often acquired through sexual contact or blood transfusions.

The symptoms of hepatitis B infection, which take two to six months to appear, include skin rash, muscle and joint pain, fatigue, loss of appetite, nausea and vomiting, headache, fever, dark urine, jaundice, and liver enlargement and tenderness (Smith et al., 1990). Hepatitis is diagnosed by special blood tests. There is no treatment for curing hepatitis B; people usually recover naturally and develop immunity to future infection. Some people, however, develop cirrhosis of the liver or liver cancer.

NATIONAL DATA: Hepatitis B infects about 300,000 Americans every year, causing 5,000 deaths (Cowley & Hager, 1991).

There is a vaccine that prevents hepatitis B infection. This vaccine is recommended for high-risk groups, including partners of known carriers, medical personnel, and people in urban areas where rates of HBV are high.

Some diseases of the sex organs may or may not be transmitted through sexual contact. These include the various forms of vaginitis, pubic lice, and scabies.

Vaginitis

Various types of **vaginitis** include trichomoniasis, candidiasis, and nonspecific vaginitis. The primary symptom of vaginitis is vaginal discharge, often accompanied by itching and burning during urination, which results from acidic urine touching an irritated vulva and vaginal opening. Most women get vaginitis at some time in their lives, and many do not develop it from sexual contact.

Vaginal infection may be caused by bacteria from the rectum being transferred to the vagina. This can result from improper hygiene or from anal intercourse or manipulation combined with vaginal intercourse or manipulation. Vaginal infection may also result from foreign objects, such as tampons, diaphragms, and condoms, which are left in the vagina. Lesbians can transmit vaginal infections between partners by mixing vaginal discharge through direct vulva-to-vulva contact or hand-to-vulva contact.

Trichomoniasis

Although some infected women show no symptoms, **trichomoniasis** is usually characterized by a foul-smelling, thin, frothy discharge that may be green, yellow, gray, or white and causes an irritating rash in the vulva. The inner thighs may also become irritated if the discharge is allowed to come in contact with the skin. Left untreated, the irritation continues and causes pain during intercourse. The woman may also infect her male partner, who may experience irritation and pain during intercourse.

Diagnosis is made by examining mucus from the vagina or penis under a microscope. Since trichomoniasis may occur with syphilis or gonorrhea, a specific diagnosis is essential. Antibiotics, such as metronidazole (Flagyl), are usually effective in treating trichomoniasis. Because the man may harbor trichomonas organisms without symptoms, both the woman and her sexual partner should be treated.

Candidiasis

Candidiasis, also known as monilia and fungus, is a yeast infection caused by candida albicans. Candidiasis tends to occur in women during pregnancy, when they are on oral contraceptives, or when they have poor resistance to disease. Symptoms of candidiasis include vaginal irritation, itching, thick cottage cheese-like discharge, and pain during intercourse. Treatment involves antifungal suppositories or creams to be inserted into the vagina. Antibiotics are not effective because candida are not bacteria.

Men may also develop candidiasis from sexual contact. Irritation and redness on the head of the penis, external itching, and painful, burning sensations are the typical symptoms. Locally applied antifungal creams are the best antidote. Oral sex may transmit candida from the mouth into the vagina or from the vagina into the throat.

Nonspecific Vaginitis Sometimes no cause can be found for vaginitis, even though there is itching, pain, and vaginal discharge. When trichomoniasis, candidiasis, and gonorrhea have been ruled out, the diagnosis becomes "**nonspecific vaginitis.**" In some cases, it will disappear only to reappear with complications. Many cases of vaginitis not caused by candida organisms or trichomonas bacteria are believed to be caused by other bacteria. New microscopic and culture methods of diagnosis are being developed. Treatment with antibiotics, especially metronidazole (Flagyl), are effective.

CONSIDERATION: To help prevent vaginitis, women should be taught from the time they are small children to wipe themselves from the front to the back after elimination. Wearing cotton underpants, avoiding nylon underwear and pantyhose, may be helpful since nylon retains moisture and heat which encourage bacterial growth (Boston Women's Health Book Collective, 1984).

Pubic Lice

Pubic lice, also called "crabs," attach themselves to the base of coarse pubic hair and suck blood from the victim. Their biting the skin to release the blood causes severe itching. Pubic lice are caught from an infected person, often through sexual contact, and also may be transmitted by contact with toilet seats, clothing, and bedding that harbor the creatures. Applications of gamma benzene hexachloride, sold under the brand name of Kwell, will kill the lice within 24 hours.

Scabies

Scabies results from a parasite, sarcoptes scabiei, that penetrates the skin and lays eggs. The larvae of these eggs burrow tunnels under the skin, which causes intense itching. Although genitals are a prime target for the mites, the groin, buttocks, breasts, and knees may also be infested with them. Since the itching is intense, scabies sufferers tend to scratch the affected area, which may result in bleeding and spreading the scabies. Treatment includes applying gamma benzene hexachloride (Kwell) or crotamiton (Eurax) and a thorough cleaning of self, clothing, and bedding.

Prevention of Sexually Transmissible Diseases

Preventing STDs represents a difficult but crucial challenge to societies and individuals. As we have already seen, STDs are a threat to psychological and physical health.

CONSIDERATION: Earlier, we emphasized that the acquisition and transmission of STDs are usually the result of behavioral choices we make. However, infants who acquire STDs from their infected mothers have not made any behavior choices: they are victims of the behavioral choices of others. STDs are associated with adverse pregnancy outcomes (syphilitic, HIV-infected, stillborn, or low-birth weight babies). One-third of infants born to HIV-positive mothers face illness or death during their first year (Blanche et al., 1989; Ryder et al., 1989).

The economic costs associated with STDs are staggering. For example, the total estimated cost of PID (associated with chlamydia) and its consequences alone were more than $4.2 billion in 1990. In addition, inpatient hospital costs of a low-birth weight baby are $9,072, compared to $678 for a baby weighing more than 2,500 grams (Althaus, 1991).

Some claim that "the strategy of prevention of HIV transmission through education and the modification of behaviors is clearly the most hopeful approach to the prevention of AIDS" (Albee, 1989, p. 19). While the effect of education programs continues to be debated and will be discussed in Chapter 23, Sex Education, there is unanimous agreement that the best way to avoid getting a sexually transmissible disease is to avoid sexual contact or to have sexual contact only with partners who are not infected (Aral, Soskoline, Joesoef, & O'Reilly, 1991). This means not engaging in sexual behavior where infection is a possibility or restricting your sexual contacts to those who limit their relationships to one person. The person most likely to get a sexually transmissible disease has sexual relations with a number of partners or with a partner who has a variety of partners and does not use a condom.

Recent data suggest that having numerous sexual partners is not unusual. Nine hundred and fourteen heterosexual persons (mean age of 26 for men and 24 for women) who requested care at STD clinics in South Carolina completed a questionnaire about their number of sexual contacts. Women reported an average of 11 lifetime partners and three sexual partners over the preceding year, while men reported 59 lifetime partners and eight sexual partners over the preceding year (Aral et al., 1991).

Seventy-five percent of the women reported eight or fewer lifetime partners, and the remaining 25% reported nine to 100 lifetime partners. Seventy-five percent of the men reported 40 or fewer lifetime partners, and the remaining 25% reported 45 to 1,000 lifetime partners (Aral et al., 1991). Tanfer and Schoorl (1992) suggested that in their study of 1,314 never-married women, "the number of reported sexual partners is an underestimate of the actual number" (p. 48). They also noted that the earlier a woman had her first intercourse experience, the greater the number of sexual partners (and hence the higher the risk of contracting an STD).

In another study of students (ages 13 to 18) in grades nine through 12 in six cities (Chicago, Los Angeles, New Orleans, New York, San Francisco, and Seattle) and in eight states (California, Kentucky, Michigan, New Jersey, New York, Ohio, Pennsylvania, and Washington) plus the District of Columbia, those reporting having had three or more sex partners ranged from 15.1% to 42.6%. Male and older students were more likely to report a larger number of sexual partners than female and younger students (Kolbe et al., 1988).

Even if you are in a mutually monogamous relationship, you may be at risk for acquiring or transmitting an STD. This is because health officials suggest that when you have sex with someone, you are having sex (in a sense) with everyone that person has had sexual contact with in the last 10 years.

CONSIDERATION: Partners may believe that they are in a mutually monogamous relationship when they may not be. It is not uncommon for partners in "monogamous" relationships to have extradyadic sexual encounters that are not revealed to the primary partner. Partners may also lie about how many sexual partners they have had and whether or not they have been tested for STDs. In a study of southern California college students, nearly half of the men and two-fifths of the women said they would lie about how many other people they had slept with. Twenty percent of the men reported they would lie about having been tested for HIV (reported in Adler et al., 1991).

Figure 18.1 illustrates the continuum of sexual behaviors that provide the greatest to the least risk for contracting STDs. This continuum assumes that a condom is not being used.

In addition to restricting sexual contacts, putting on a latex condom containing nonoxynol-9 before the penis touches the partner's body will make it difficult for sexually transmissible diseases, including genital herpes, to pass from one person to another. Natural membrane condoms *do not* block the transmission of STDs. Condoms should be used for vaginal, anal, and oral sex and should never be reused. If a man is receiving oral sex, he should a wear condom. If a woman is receiving oral sex, she should wear a **"dental dam,"** which is a flat latex device that is held over the vaginal area, preventing direct contact between the woman's genital area and her partner's mouth. An article in the *HPV News* noted that "some people use household plastic wrap as a physical barrier to prevent the spread of STDs" (Protecting your partner/relationship, 1992).

In one study, lubricated condoms were ruptured to determine the effect of the lubricant on HIV. Lubricants containing **nonoxynol-9** inhibited HIV more than did those that did not contain nonoxynol-9 (Reitmaijer, Krebs, Feorino, & Judson, 1988). It is recommended that condom users choose brands that are lubricated with nonoxynol-9 in order to receive some level of protection in the event of condom breakage. If foams, creams, or jellies are used for contraception, it is recommended that those containing nonoxynol-9 be selected. Spermicides in the vagina have been shown to reduce the risks of women getting gonorrhea and chlamydia, although their effect on HPV is unknown (Protecting your partner/relationship, 1992).

After genital or anal contact with a latex condom, it is important to withdraw the penis while it is erect so as to prevent fluid leaking from the base of the condom into the partner's genital area. Condom users should choose brands that have an adhesive strip at the base that prevents the condom from slipping off prematurely. In addi-

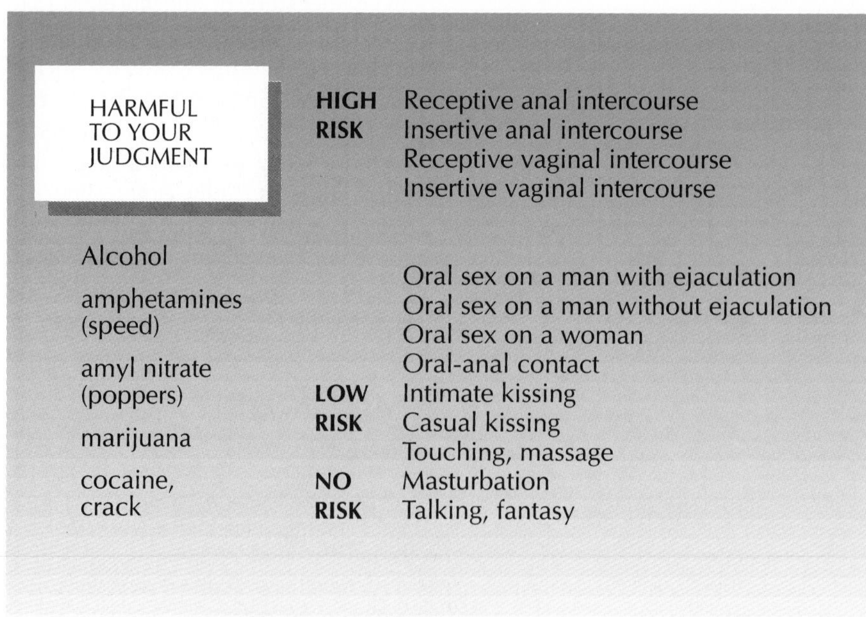

FIGURE 18.1 High to Low Risk Behaviors for Contracting STDs

Source: American College Health Association. Used by permission.

tion, it is also a good idea for the partners to wash their genital area and hands with soap and hot water before and after sexual contact.

Some evidence suggests that individuals are changing their sexual behaviors to reduce their risk of contracting an STD. In a study of 448 men and 404 women, a significant percentage of those who were aware of the ways to prevent HIV infection reported that they had reduced their risk (had fewer partners, increased condom use, and, among men, decreased prostitute contact) (Wilson, Lavelle, Greenspan, & Wilson, 1991). Another study found that between 1975 and 1989, college women in the United States did not change their sexual behavior in terms of number of sexual partners or the frequency with which they engaged in high-risk sexual behaviors. However, the percentage of college women who reported using condoms increased from 6% in 1975 to 25% in 1989 (DeBuono, Zinner, Daamen, & McCormack, 1990).

Researchers have identified that those most likely to use condoms have fewer sexual partners, are comfortable purchasing condoms, are comfortable discussing condoms with their sexual partners, have considerable knowledge about HIV and STDs, and believe that condoms do not interfere with sexual pleasure (MacDonald et al., 1990). Other research suggests that knowledge alone is not associated with changing one's sexual behaviors. In a study of 563 college students, in spite of their negative perceptions of contracting genital herpes, relatively few changed their behaviors to avoid infection. More than half (58%) noted that they neither talked about the disease nor found out if their partner had herpes. In addition, more than half (54%) reported that they had not restricted the number of casual sexual partners to avoid infection (Mirotznik, 1991).

Bandura (1989) emphasized several components that must be present if individuals are to be effective in altering their high-risk sexual behaviors. These include information, self-protective skills, and social supports. Individuals must be aware of the profound threat of AIDS, be sensitized to the need to change sexual behaviors, and be taught what high-risk behaviors must be eliminated.

High risk takers often lack the social skills for safe sex (Ruefli, Yu, & Barton, 1992). Through modeling, individuals can learn what to say and what to do in social contexts to protect themselves. This may involve watching others in a group setting or on a videotape illustrate how they talk with their sexual partners about HIV infection, get tested, and use condoms. Exhibit 18.2 offers suggestions for "condom communication." After observing how one might go about engaging partners in a dialogue to reduce high-risk sexual behavior, the individuals need an opportunity to practice such verbal behaviors. Group settings where individuals can learn to practice their verbal skills on each other in simulated situations are often effective.

EXHIBIT 18.2 Condom Communication

If Your Partner Says . . .	*You Can Say . . .*
I don't have a condom.	Let's get one or satisfy each other in other ways.
I don't have AIDS or any STD.	We can both be infected and not know it.
One time without a condom won't hurt anything.	One time could be enough.
If you insist that I wear a condom it means you think I'm a sleaze.	No it doesn't. It means I care about both of us.
I take the pill; you don't need a condom.	The pill doesn't protect us from getting infections.

Individuals need to be socialized to be supportive of each other to reduce HIV and other STD exposure. Men, particularly, need to be supportive of their partner's desire to use condoms. In the absence of such support, women need to encourage their partners about the importance of condom use. As Bandura noted, such encouragement is not easy:

> It is difficult for women to press the issue in the face of emotional and economic dependence, coercive threat, and subcultural prescription of compliant roles for them. Women who are enmeshed in relationships of imbalanced power need to be taught how to negotiate protected sex nonconfrontationally. At the broader societal level, attitudes and social norms must be altered to increase men's sense of responsibility for the consequences of their sexuality. (p. 137)

In some societies this may be an especially challenging goal. Dr. Jonathan Mann of the Harvard AIDS Institute observed that where the spread of AIDS is most catastrophic—among heterosexuals in Africa and other poverty-stricken areas of the world—women are powerless to get their husbands to use condoms (Health is a right, 1992).

Social support from peers is important for encouraging condom use. Maticka-Tyndale (1991) reported an example of peer support for condom use: a group of friends passed around a box of condoms on a bus transporting them to their skiing weekend accommodations. Some groups are not able to find peer support for condom use. For example, many poor Hispanic communities regard the use of condoms as both "immoral and contrary to the principles of machismo" (Adler et al., 1991, p. 55).

> Alex Vasquez, a 29-year-old Houston homosexual man with AIDS, still has arguments with family members who believe that he's committing a mortal sin by using condoms (p. 55).

CONSIDERATION: Some male teenagers actually boast about acquiring a sexually transmissible disease: "it's proof they've been sexually active, a pathetic badge of manhood" (Adler et al., 1991, p. 55).

Aral and Holmes (1991) noted that "certain policies must be implemented if the U.S. is to control STDs in general and to prevent a heterosexual HIV epidemic in the urban underclass" (p. 62). These policies involve a massive all-out effort at every level of society from improving birth control services to shortening the wait for treatment in STD clinics (p. 69).

CONSIDERATION: In China, the Law of Preventing Infectious Diseases of the People's Republic of China was passed in 1989 by the People's Congress. This law requires that foreigners coming to stay in China for more than one year, as well as expatriate Chinese returning to China, must have proof of being HIV- and AIDS-free. This law also provides for criminal prosecution of anyone who, knowingly infected, transmits the virus to another person (Gil, 1991).

Drunk sex is not safe sex.
Richard Keeling

Some public school systems, such as those in Chicago and New York City, offer free condoms to high school students. The New York City program is the first that doesn't require parental permission. Other school systems throughout the country are considering similar programs offering condoms, counseling, and instruction to high school students. Such programs are criticized on the grounds that "giving kids condoms might seem to sanction their sexual activity—or even encourage promiscuity" (Seligmann, Beachy, Gordon, McCormick, & Starr, 1991, p. 61). However, one school official responded to this argument by saying, "This is not a matter of morality, it is a matter of life and death" (p. 61).

Social support programs are also needed for intravenous (IV) drug users. One method of lowering the HIV-infection risk among IV drug users in Vienna is making alternative "nonneedle drugs" available:

> Poppy heads (sold in florist shops to make dried bouquets) are extracted by boiling, and this "opium tea" is drunk whenever heroin is hard to obtain. However, this tea causes all the signs and symptoms of opiate addiction if it is consumed exclusively. Its use, however, is not related to risk-laden practices. Heroin users can legally buy poppy heads in shops or directly from farms for a reasonable price; thus, there is little use for needle sharing in critical situations. (Loimer et al., 1990, p. 248)

Some people are pessimistic about society's ability to prevent the spread of STDs through efforts to educate individuals.

> People have risked marriages, jobs, inheritances and death by wanting to go to bed with someone they liked—can we really expect to conquer passion with the threat of genital warts? Backed up with a subway poster? (Adler et al., 1991, p. 56)

On the optimistic side, however, Adler et al. (1991) pointed out that it took nearly three decades for social attitudes toward smoking to change. And they add:

> A similar shift is occurring with respect to heavy drinking and even drugs. And it will happen with sex; it has to happen. People want to live. (p. 56)

RESEARCH PERSPECTIVE

Prevention Models for HIV Transmission

"AIDS prevention represents a truly monumental challenge" (Marin & Marin, 1988). Programs for preventing the transmission of HIV infection will be most effective if they are based on issues relevant to promoting behavior change. They must go beyond merely frightening people with the seriousness and scope of AIDS. Usually, first-generation public health education programs lean heavily on fear messages, but as Coates, Temoshok, and Mandel (1984, p. 1312) noted, relying on "warn and scare" tactics can result in denial as a psychological defense, as well as desensitization to the message. Coates et al. recommended research on the psychosocial determinants of behavior and behavior change. They offered the example of the unsuccessful fear-based smoking prevention efforts of the 1960s and 1970s, in contrast to the more successful programs of the 1980s based on a social influence model.

"The AIDS epidemic," agreed Fishbein and Middlestadt (1989, p. 109),

> . . . is much too serious to allow interventions to be based upon some communicator's untested and all too often incorrect intuitions about the factors that will influence the performance or nonperformance of a given behavior in a given population.

Research should be conducted, prior to writing curricula and designing programs, on which factors and issues are relevant for a particular target group. Marin and Marin (1988) observed that campaigns must be carefully targeted to each ethnic or cultural subgroup, or the messages are quite likely to fail. In their study of black, Latin, and white adolescents in San Francisco schools, DiClemente, Boyer and Morales (1988) found that AIDS education had not been uniformly effective across

Continued

Continued

ethnic groups. Black youth, and Latin youth to an even greater extent, were more likely than white youth to have many misconceptions about AIDS. "The challenge," concluded Fullilove (1988, p. 5), "is to develop prevention programs for blacks and Latins that are as effective as those that have been mounted for gay white men."

Carrier and Bolton (1991, p. 49) lamented the limited usefulness of data on human sexual behavior for developing HIV prevention programs. Most of the data have been gathered from samples of "middle-class Anglo 'gay identified' men" through surveys focusing on a small set of sexual behaviors. To point out the inappropriateness of generalizing from this group, Carrier and Bolton discussed the field research findings on men's homosexual behavior that confirmed that patterns of behavior differ cross-culturally. Greek epidemiologists studying in the Middle East and eastern Mediterranean reported a clearer separation of sexual roles among men participating in homosexual encounters than in Anglo gay communities. Likewise, Magaña and Carrier (1991) reported differences between Mexican, Mexican-American, and Anglo men. The Mexican men, especially those less acculturated to the United States, reported more definitive preferences for playing penetrating or receptive roles in anal intercourse. However, while some of the men were involved in bisexual behavior (taking the "active" or masculine role), they considered themselves to be heterosexual. This information may be critically important in assessing the risk of HIV transmission (as receptive anal intercourse has been identified as the highest-risk sexual practice) and developing prevention messages.

Marin and Marin (1988) conducted a two-step investigation into the subjective culture among Hispanics. The first step involved open-ended interviews with Hispanics and white non-Hispanics. The interviews focused on the respondents' preoccupations and ideas regarding sexual relations and drug use. Alternative ways of preventing HIV transmission (ranging from abstinence to monogamy to "safer" sex) were discussed. The researchers noted, "Few AIDS prevention campaigns have promoted monogamy, yet our interviewees mentioned many advantages of monogamy and disadvantages of promiscuity. . . . . Hispanics were generally less likely to mention negative aspects of monogamy" (pp. 5–6). Attitudes toward condoms and spermicides revealed that health education efforts need to emphasize the benefits of their use, while overcoming numerous perceived disadvantages. The second step involved the development of closed-ended items for larger-scale survey research, based on the information highlighted in the interviews.

Anthropologists have observed that in designing HIV intervention and education programs, it is also important to understand how the social and economic conditions of a society influence the sexual choices made by its members (Carrier & Bolton, 1991). The dismal economic situation of Zaire was identified by Schoepf and her colleagues as contributing to the feminization of poverty and subsequently to the spread of HIV infection. Very low-paying agricultural jobs are the main employment opportunity for women, so selling sexual services may generate a survival income.Schoepf reported that low-income prostitutes earn about 50 cents in U.S. currency for each of their 500 to 1,000 sexual encounters per year and often suffer from untreated STDs. They are less informed than other groups of women about safer sex practices. Cultural factors that may also promote HIV infection include the preference of Central African men for intercourse in a dry vagina (conducive to genital lacerations due to the women's use of drying preparations) and beliefs about the value of regular sexual intercourse and the deposit of semen into the vagina (seen as important to "ripen" a pregnancy, as well as to make a woman healthy and fertile). Clearly, a culturally sensitive understanding of sexual beliefs and behaviors is essential in deciphering HIV transmission patterns and developing effective prevention programs.

Continued

Continued

The theory of reasoned action (explained in the Research Perspective on breast and testicular self-examinations in Chapter 16) was proposed by Fishbein and Middlestadt (1989) as a helpful framework for structuring programs for prevention of HIV transmission. They suggested that a sample of 30 to 60 members of a population could provide invaluable information about the salient attitudinal and normative beliefs for that group. This information could then be used in constructing a questionnaire to identify the factors relevant to participants' intentions to perform specified preventive behaviors.

An example of a study using this theoretical model to identify salient beliefs within a specific population was one that assessed 14- to 19-year-old English-speaking adolescents attending adolescent health care clinics in San Francisco (Klitsch, 1990). Five beliefs predicted the young women's intentions to use a condom in the coming year: condoms allow spontaneous sex, are easy to use, are popular with peers, require self-control on the partner's part, and are clean. Intention to use condoms was negatively associated with the belief that condoms are inconvenient. Among the male respondents, four beliefs predicted intention to use condoms: condoms allow spontaneity, are easy to use, are popular with peers, and make the male partner responsible for contraception. Believing that condom use is painful or uncomfortable was negatively associated with intention to use them. It is noteworthy that considerations regarding STD prevention were not significantly associated with the intention to use condoms in this group of adolescents. Short-term social considerations were apparently more important than health considerations. Perhaps interventions to promote condom use among adolescents would be more successful if they focused on convenience and social considerations!

The most hopeful approach to preventing HIV transmission is through education and modification of risk behaviors. Reaching specific groups and influencing them to modify their behavior, especially those for whom our current strategies have not been adequate, is a formidable challenge, but this is the urgent task of the behavioral sciences (May, Albee, & Schneider, 1989).

References

Carrier, J., & Bolton, R. (1991). Anthropological perspectives on sexuality and HIV prevention. In J. Bancroft (Ed.), *Annual review of sex research* (vol. 2) (pp. 49–75). Lake Mills, IA: Society for the Scientific Study of Sex.

Coates, T. J., Temoshok, L., & Mandel, J. (1984). Psychosocial research is essential to understanding and treating AIDS. *American Psychologist, 39,* 1309–1314.

DiClemente, R. J., Boyer, C. B., & Morales, E. (1988). Minorities and AIDS: Knowledge, attitudes, and misconceptions among Black and Latino adolescents. *American Journal of Public Health, 78,* 55–57.

Fishbein, M., & Middlestadt, S. E. (1989). Using the theory of reasoned action as a framework for understanding and changing AIDS-related behaviors. In V. M. Mays, G. W. Albee, & S. F. Schneider (Eds.), *Primary prevention of AIDS: Psychological approaches,* (pp. 93–110). Newbury Park, CA: Sage.

Fullilove, R. E. (1988). Minorities and AIDS: A review of recent publications. *Multicultural Inquiry and Research on AIDS, 2,* 3–5.

Klitsch, M. (1990). Teenagers' condom use affected by peer factors, not by health concerns. *Family Planning Perspectives, 22,* 95.

Magaña, J. R., & Carrier, J. M. (1991). Mexican and Mexican-American male sexual behavior and spread of AIDS in California. *Journal of Sex Research, 28,* 425–441.

Marin, B. V., & Marin, G. (1988). Attitudes toward AIDS prevention strategies. *Multicultural inquiry and research on AIDS, 2,* 5–6.

May, V. M., Albee, G. W., & Schneider, S. F. (1989). *Primary prevention of AIDS: Psychological approaches.* Newbury Park, CA: Sage.

CHOICES

Choices in regard to HIV infection and other STDs are both individual and societal. As individuals, we choose whether to engage in behavior that eliminates or minimizes our potential for infection, whether to seek HIV testing, and, if infected, how to tell a partner that we are infected. As a society, we must make decisions regarding the allocation of public funds for HIV and AIDS research and whether to require health-care workers to be tested for HIV and to inform their patients of their HIV status.

Choose to Engage in Low-Risk Behaviors?

In their book *Thinking AIDS,* Bateson and Goldsby (1988) emphasized that

> the logic of the disease and the uncertainty in which we live make it imperative that every individual should act on the possibility that others around them are infected with AIDS—and on the parallel possibility that they themselves carry the virus and have the obligation to protect others. (p. 102)

They went on to note that the "first decision that presents itself to every individual living in this new world is to behave in such a way as to neither contract nor transmit AIDS" (p. 103). Table 1 summarizes how HIV infection may occur and what choices must be made.

However, as important as latex condoms are in reducing risk of STD transmission, they do not offer a complete solution. For example, HPV may be present on areas not covered by a condom, such as on the scrotum. "Don't get us wrong. Condoms are great," according to the *HPV News.*

> But the protection question is not a simple matter. Your answer may depend on whether you are a man or a woman, the sex of your partner, whether you are in a long-term relationship or not, the type of sex you have, and whether the condom covers the entire area. (Protecting Your Partner/Relationship, 1992, p. 6)
>
> A decision to have safer sex might be seen as an opportunity to experience better and more imaginative sex . . . Certainly it means more caring and conscious sex. In the process of discovering alternatives to penetration, there are new skills to be learned, including talking about sex with a partner and the cultivation of fantasy (Bateson & Goldsby, 1988, p. 109).

Choose to Be Tested for HIV?

There are decided benefits from early medical detection of HIV. These include taking medications to reduce the growth of HIV and preventing the development of some life-threatening conditions. An example of the latter is pneumonia, which is more likely to develop when one's immune system has weakened.

HIV counselors recommend that individuals who answer yes to any of the following questions should definitely seek testing:

- If you are a man, have you had sex with other men?
- Have you had sex with someone you know or suspect was infected with HIV?
- Have you had an STD?
- Have you shared needles or syringes to inject drugs or steroids?
- Have you received a blood transfusion or blood products between 1978 and 1985?
- Have you had sex with someone who would answer yes to any of these questions?

Additionally, counselors suggest that if you have had sex with someone whose sexual risk history you do not know or if you have had numerous sexual partners, your risk of HIV infection is increased, and testing should be seriously considered. Finally, if you are a woman in any of the above risk categories or if you plan to become pregnant, testing is important. HIV-infected women have a one-in-three chance of infecting their baby

Continued

TABLE 18.5 Choices to Make to Avoid HIV Infection

To avoid HIV infection, avoid exposure to an infected person's:	To avoid getting these fluids from an infected person, avoid these behaviors:
• blood	• oral sex
• semen	• anal sex
• preseminal fluids	• vaginal intercourse
• vaginal fluids	• Or use a latex condom with
• breast milk	non-oxynol 9 or a dental dam.

Continued

during pregnancy or delivery (Department of Health and Human Services, 1991).

Choose How to Tell a Partner That One Has an STD?

A primary concern of individuals with genital herpes is "worry over transmitting herpes to a sexual partner" (Silver et al., 1986, p. 167). Individuals who have herpes noted the following about telling a partner of the STD (Hill, 1987):

> There are several reasons why I tell my partners early on in the relationship. One is that if I didn't I would feel as if I was depriving them of their right to choose to continue the relationship. Another is that I want to minimize the time I have to worry about telling a girlfriend. The longer we wait to tell potential partners, the more we set ourselves up for disappointment. If we're rejected early on, we haven't had a chance to really develop any affection for the other person, so it's easy to let go. (p.3)
>
> *****
>
> I tell women that I have herpes as soon as I think I might want to spend more time with them . . . usually after the first or second date. I always tell the woman when I think she can handle the news. I'm careful not to bring it up when we've been drinking heavily or are sexually excited, or stressed out about other things. (p. 3)
>
> *****
>
> "If someone rejects me because of herpes, I genuinely feel I've weeded that person out" (Hill, 1987, p. 5).
>
> *****
>
> I decided to use herpes as a yardstick by which to measure whether a man's affections were real or not for me and as a yardstick as to his strength and maturity in helping me to manage and live with the disease. Any man who could not deal with it, I did not and do not want to deal with. (Silver et al., 1986, p. 170)

Assuming that the decision has been made to tell the partner of an STD or to bring up the subject, what are some ways to do so? Davis and Scott (1988) suggested some possibilities in terms of specifically what to say:

- "I'd like to share with you some of my sexual history. Last year I contracted . . ."
- "I've recently been tested for STDs. I'm afraid I can't make any promises about my health until I get the results . . ."
- "I've had some problems in the past with genital warts. I don't think I've got them now, but just to be safe let's use a condom . . ."
- "I've got an appointment with a doctor at the health clinic. Why don't you come with me and we'll get checked out together?" (p. 12)

It may be important legally to choose to tell your partner of the possibility that you have an STD. In over half the states, transmission of a communicable disease, including many STDs, is considered a crime. Penalties depend on whether the crime is regarded as a felony (which may involve a five-year prison term) or a misdemeanor (which may involve a fine of $100) (Davis & Scott, 1988).

Choose to Allocate Government Funds to HIV Infection Research?

The failure of the United States to take the AIDS threat seriously and to act quickly in the early 1980s is one of the great tragedies of our era. Analyzing this failure, Shilts (1987) observed:

> From 1980, when the first isolated gay men began falling ill from strange and exotic ailments, nearly five years passed before all of these institutions—medicine, public health, the federal and private scientific research establishments, the mass media, and the gay community's leadership—mobilized the way they should in a time of threat. The story of these first five years of AIDS in America is a drama of national failure, played out against a backdrop of needless death. (p. xxii)

In a national phone survey of 960 individuals, 70% reported that the government should "spend more money for research on AIDS even if it means raising taxes" (Herek & Glunt, 1991, p. 109). In addition, 69% of the respondents believed that the government should pay for programs to teach people how to have "safe sex" (p. 109). When asked if the government should give away condoms to stop the spread of AIDS, 47% agreed.

Choose to Require Health-Care Workers to Be Tested for HIV?

In 1991, Kimberly Bergalis appeared before U.S. Senate hearings on whether to require healthcare providers to disclose their HIV status to patients. She had been infected with HIV by her dentist, Dr. David Acer (he subsequently died).

> I never used IV drugs, never slept with anyone and never had a blood transfusion. I blame Dr. Acer and every single one of you bastards; anyone that knew Dr. Acer was infected and had full-blown AIDS and stood by not doing a damn thing about it. You are all just as guilty as he was . . . . (Bergalis, 1991, p. 52)

In a letter she wrote to *Newsweek,* she ended by saying:

> P.S. If laws are not formed to provide protection, then my suffering and death was in vain . . . I'm dying guys. Goodbye. (p. 52)

Bergalis died in December 1991.

A Gallup Poll suggests that adults in the United States are overwhelmingly in favor of surgeons (95%), all physicians (94%), dentists (94%), and all healthcare workers (90%) being required to disclose to their patients that they are HIV-infected ("Disclosure of HIV Status," 1991).

Many healthcare providers do not think that they should be tested for HIV, arguing that even if they were infected, the risk of transmitting the infection to a patient is very low. Hagen et al. (1988) estimated that the risk of a patient being infected by a surgeon with HIV is between one to 450,000 and one to 300 million. Dr. Richard Duff, a physician with HIV, treated hundreds of patients. His justification for doing so was that he did not conduct "invasive medical procedures." But patients feel that, for their protection, they have a right to know if their healthcare provider has HIV.

Healthcare workers, in turn, are also concerned about becoming infected by patients with HIV. Surgeons have higher risks for becoming HIV-infected from patients than vice versa.

Summary

1. HIV infection, rather than AIDS, is the preferred term since the former focuses on the full course of HIV infection, rather than concentrating on the later stages of the disease.
2. It may take 10 years or longer after a person is infected with HIV before any symptoms of AIDS develop.
3. It is estimated that by the year 2000, up to 90% of all HIV infections in the world will be transmitted through heterosexual transmission. Most (89%) diagnosed cases have been among male (90%), white (54%), black (28%), and Hispanic (16%) populations.
4. Denial—"it won't happen to me"—is the primary reason most people view their becoming infected with HIV to be a low-probability event.
5. Psychosocial reactions to contracting genital herpes include shock, withdrawal from others, anger, fear, feeling like a leper, depression, and decomposition. Psychological reactions affect resistance to recurrent outbreaks and the level of coping.
6. Chlamydia, one of the most frequently occurring STDs, can be cured with antibiotics. Women often experience "silent infection," in which they experience no initial symptoms. Untreated it can result in pelvic inflammatory disease and ectopic pregnancy for women, and infertility in men and women.
7. Human papilloma virus (HPV) may result in visible warts, but infection can also be present when there are no observable warts. A range of treatment methods is available to remove warts, but the continued presence of the virus may lead to recurrences.
8. Gonorrhea may have severe health consequences if untreated, but when identified and treated with effective antibiotics it can be cured.
9. Although syphilis is not as prevalent as gonorrhea or chlamydia, there is currently much concern over the fact that its transmission in the U.S. is increasing, especially in inner-city, low income populations. When detected and treated early, it can be cured.
10. Coping with STD infection may challenge one's self-image and relationships. Coping strategies include obtaining accurate information, good communication with an informed health care provider, enlisting social support, and taking good care of one's general health.
11. When you have sex with someone, you are being exposed to that person's sexual partners for the last 10 years.
12. Regular use of condoms is associated with knowledge, learning how to talk with a sexual partner about condoms, and receiving social support from the partner.
13. While U.S. adults are overwhelmingly in favor of requiring surgeons, physicians, dentists, and health-care workers to disclose if they are HIV-infected, most of these groups oppose such a requirement.

KEY TERMS

human immunodeficiency virus (HIV)
ARC
AIDS (acquired immunodeficiency syndrome)
AZT
ddI
genital herpes
herpes simplex virus type 2 (HSV-2)
herpes simplex virus type 1 (HSV-1)
acyclovir
Immu Vir
condyloma

chlamydia
pelvic inflammatory disease (PID)
gonorrhea
syphilis
nongonococcal urethritis (NGU)
lymphogranuloma venereum (LGV)
human papilloma virus (HPV)
genital warts
granuloma inguinale (GI)
chancroid
hepatitis B virus (HBV)
vaginitis
trichomoniasis
candidiasis
nonspecific vaginitis
pubic lice
scabies
dental dam
nonoxynol-9

REFERENCES

Abrams, D., & Grieco, M. (Eds.). (1991). *AIDS/HIV Treatment Directory, 5* (2).

Adame, D. D., Taylor-Nicholson, M. E., Wang, M., & Abbas, M. A. (1991). Southern college freshman students: A survey of knowledge, attitudes, and beliefs about AIDS. *Journal of Sex Education and Therapy, 17,* 196–206.

Adler, J., Wright, L., McCormick, J., Annin, P., Cohen, A., Talbot, M., Hager, M., & Yoffe, E. (1991, December 9). Safer sex. *Newsweek,* pp. 52–56.

Albee, G. W. (1989). Primary prevention in public health: Problems and challenges of behavior change as prevention. In V. M. Mays, G. W. Albee, & S. F. Schneider (Eds.), *Primary prevention of AIDS: Psychological approaches* (pp. 17–22). Newbury Park, CA: Sage.

Althaus, F. A. (1991). An ounce of prevention . . . STDs and women's health. *Family Planning Perspectives, 23,* 173–177.

American Cancer Society. (1992). *Cancer facts & figures—1992.* Author.

Aral, S. O., & Holmes, K. K. (1991). Sexually transmitted diseases in the AIDS era. *Scientific American, 264,* 62–69.

Aral, S. O., Soskoline, V., Joesoef, R. M., & O'Reilly, K. R. (1991). Sex partner recruitment as risk factor for STD: Clustering of risky modes. *Sexually Transmitted Diseases, 18,* 10–17.

Bandura, A. (1989). Perceived self-efficacy in the exercise of control over AIDS infection. In V. M. Mays, G. W. Albee, & S. F. Schneider (Eds.), *Primary prevention of AIDS: Psychological approaches* (pp. 128–141). Newbury Park, CA: Sage.

Bateson, M. C., & Goldsby, R. (1988). *Thinking AIDS.* Reading, MA: Addison-Wesley.

Bauer, H. M., Ting, Y., Greer, C. E., Chambers, J. C., Tashiro, C. J., Chimera, J., Reingold, A., & Manos, M. M. (1991). Genital human papillommavirus infection in female university students as determined by a PCR-based method. *Journal of the American Medical Association, 265,* 472–477.

Becker, T. M., & Nahmias, A. J. (1985). Genital herpes—yesterday today, tomorrow. *Annual Review of Medicine, 36,* 185–193.

Bergalis, K. (1991, July 1). I blame every one of you bastards. *Newsweek,* p. 52.

Biasco, F., & Taylor, R. (1991). College students' attitudes toward AIDS. *College Student Journal, 25,* 398–400.

Blanche, S., Rouziouz, C., Mosiato, M. G., Verber, F., Mayaux, M., Jacomet, C., Tricoire, J., Deville, A., Vial, M., Firtion, G., deCrepy, A., Donard, D., Robin, M., Courpotin, C., Ciraru-Vigneron, N., leDeist, F., Griscelli, C., & the HIV Infection in Newborns French Collaborative Study Group. (1989). A prospective study of infants born to women seropositive for human immunodeficiency virus type 1. *New England Journal of Medicine, 320,* 1643–1648.

Boeck, G. (1991, November 8–10). HIV forces Magic to retire. *USA Today,* p. A-1.

Boston Women's Health Book Collective (1984). *The New Our Bodies, Ourselves.* New York: Simon & Schuster.

Brinton, L. A., Nasca, P. C., Mallin, K., Baptiste, M. S., Wilbanks, G. D., & Richart, R. M. (1990). Case-control study of cancer of the vulva. *Obstetrics and Gynecology, 75,* 859–866.

Campbell, J. M. (1986, March). Sexual guidelines for persons with AIDS and at risk for AIDS. *Human Sexuality,* 100–103.

Can the eyes have it? (1992, Spring). *HPV News,* 2(2), p. 11.

Castro, K. G., Lifson, A. R., White, C. R., Bush, T. J., Chamberland, M. E., Lekatsas, A. M., & Jaffe, H. W. (1988). Investigations of AIDS patients with no previously identified risk factors. *Journal of the American Medical Association, 259,* 1338–1342.

Centers for Disease Control (1988), *Semen banking, organ and tissue transplantation, and HIV antibody testing. Morbidity and Mortality Weekly Report, 37,* (4).

Centers for Disease Control. (1989). *AIDS and human immunodeficiency virus infection in the United States, 1988 update Morbidity and Mortality Weekly Report, 38,* (supp. s-4).

Centers for Disease Control. (1992, July). *HIV/AIDS surveillance report.* U.S. Dept. of Health and Human Services.

Chase, M. (1989, June 13). Many who risk AIDS now weigh carefully whether to be tested. *Wall Street Journal,* pp. 1.

Clinical studies presented at international AIDS meeting. (1992, Aug. 24/31). *American Medical News,* p. 33.

Coates, T. J., Temoshok, L. & Mandel, J. (1984). Psychosocial research is essential to understanding and treating AIDS. *American Psychologist, 39,* 1309–1314.

Cowley, G., & Hager, M. (1991, December 9). Sleeping with the enemy. *Newsweek,* pp. 58–59.

Cox, F. D. (1992). *The AIDS booklet* (2nd ed.). Dubuque, IA: William C. Brown.

Davis, M., & Scott, R. S. (1988). *Lovers, doctors and the law.* New York: Harper and Row.

DeBuono, B. A., Zinner, S. H., Daamen, M., & McCormack, W. M. (1990). Sexual behavior of college women in 1975, 1986, and 1989. *New England Journal of Medicine, 322,* 821–825.

Department of Health and Human Services. (1991). *Voluntary HIV counseling and testing.* Washington, DC: U.S. Government Printing Office.

Disclosure of HIV Status to patients. *Newsweek* Poll. (1991, July 1). *Newsweek,* p. 51.

Dolin, R., Graham, B. S., Greenberg, S. B., Tacket, C. O., Belshe, R. B., Midthun, K., Clements, M. L., Gorse, G. J., Hongan, B. W., Atman, R. L., Karzon, D. T., Bownez, W., Fernie, B. F., Montefiori, D. C., Stablein, D. M., Smith, G. E., Koff, W. C., & the NIAID AIDS Vaccine Clinical Trials Network. (1991). The safety and immunogenicity of a human immunodeficiency virus type 1 (HIV-1) recombinant gp 160 candidate vaccine in humans. *Annals of Internal Medicine, 114,* 119–127.

Fumento, M. (1990). *The myth of heterosexual AIDS.* New York: Basic Books.

Gil, V. E. (1991). An ethnography of HIV/AIDS and sexuality in the People's Republic of China. *Journal of Sex Research, 28,* pp. 521–537.

Goldsmith, M. F. (1992). 'Critical moment' at hand in HIV/AIDS pandemic, new global strategy to arrest its spread proposed. *Journal of the American Medical Association, 268,* 445–446.

Hagen, M. D., Meyer, K. B., & Pauker, S. G. (1988). Routine preoperative screening for HIV: Does the risk to the surgeon outweigh the risk to the patient? *Journal of the American Medical Association, 259,* 1357–1359.

Hansen, W. B., Hahn, G. L., & Wolkenstein, B. H. (1990). Perceived personal immunity: Beliefs about susceptibility to AIDS. *Journal of Sex Research, 27,* 622–628.

Health is a right, AIDS expert says. (1992, July 20). The News and Observer, Raleigh, NC, p. 1A.

Herek, G. M., & Glunt, E. K. (1991). AIDS-related attitudes in the United States: A preliminary conceptualization. *Journal of Sex Research, 28,* 99–123.

Herpes Resource Center (1991). Understanding herpes. Research Triangle Park, NC: American Social Health Association. (Available from P.O. Box 13827, Research Triangle Park, NC, 27709).

Hill, T. (1987, Summer). Herpes and relationships. *The Helper, 9*(2), pp. 1, 3–5.

Hillard, J. R., Kitchell, C. L., Turner, U. G., III, Keeling, R. P., & Shank, R. F. (1984). Knowledge and attitudes of university health service clients about genital herpes: Implications for patient education and counseling. *Journal of American College Health, 33,* 112–117.

Horn, J. E., McQuillan, G. M., Shah, K. V., Gupta, P., Daniel, R. W., Ray, P. A., Quinn, T. C., & Hook, E. W., III. (1991). Genital human papillomavirus infections in patients attending an inner-city STD clinic. *Sexually Transmitted Diseases, 18,* 183–187.

HPV and anal cancer (1992, Summer). *HPV News,* 2(2), p. 11.

HPV in perspective (1991, Winter). *HPV News, 1*(1), pp. 1, 4–7.

HPV Support program (1991, Winter). *HPV News, 1*(1), p. 8.

Jacobsen, P. B., Perry S. W., & Hirsch, D. A. (1990). Behavioral and psychological responses to HIV antibody testing. *Journal of Consulting and Clinical Psychology, 58,* 31–37.

Johnson, R. E., Nahmias, A. J., Mager, L. S., Lee, F. K., Brooks, C. A., & Snowden, C. B. (1989). A seroepidemiologic survey of the prevalence of herpes simplex virus type 2 infection in the United States. *New England Journal of Medicine, 321,* 7–12.

Jones, C., & Mertz, G. (1986). Asymptomatic transmission of genital herpes. *The Helper,* Fall, 1–5.

Kaplowitz, L. G., Baker, D., Gelb, L., Blythe, J., Hale, R., Frost, P., Crumpacker, C., Rabinovich, S., Peacock, J. E., Herndon, J., Davis, G., & the Acyclovir Study Group. (1991). Prolonged continuous acyclovir treatment of normal adults with frequently recurring genital herpes simplex virus infection. *Journal of the American Medical Association, 265,* 747–751.

Kerr, D. L. (1990). "AIDS SPEAK": Sensitive and accurate communication and the HIV epidemic. *Journal of School Health, 60,* 431–432.

Kolbe, L., Jones, J., Nelson, G., Daily, L., Duncan, C., Kann, L., Lawrence, A., Broyles, B., & Poehler, D. (1988). School health education to prevent the spread of AIDS: An overview of a national program. *Hygiene, 7,* 10–30.

Koop, C. E. (1986). *Surgeon general's report on acquired immune deficiency syndrome.* Washington, DC: U.S. Department of Health and Human Services.

Loimer, N., Presslich, O., Hollerer, E., & Werner, E. (1990). Sexual behavior and prevalence of HIV-1 infection among intravenous drug users in Vienna, 1986–1989. *Journal of Sex Education and Therapy, 16,* 242–250.

Luby, E. (1981). Psychological responses to genital herpes. *The Helper, 3,* 1–3.

MacDonald, N. E., Wells, G. A., Fisher, W. A., Warren, W. K., King, M. A., Doherty, J. A., & Bowie, W. R. (1990). High risk STD/HIV behavior among college students. *Journal of the American Medical Association, 263,* 3155–3159.

Manne, S., & Sandler I. (1984). Coping and adjustment to genital herpes. *Journal of Behavioral Medicine, 7,* 391–408.

Martin, J. L., Dean, L., Garcia, M., & Hall, W. (1989). The impact of AIDS on a gay community: Changes in sexual behavior, substance use, and mental health. *American Journal of Community Psychology, 17,* 269–293.

Maticka-Tyndale, E. (1991). Sexual scripts and AIDS prevention variations in adherence to safer-sex guidelines by heterosexual adolescents. *Journal of Sex Research, 28,* 45–66.

Meyer-Bahlburg, H. F. L., Exner, T. M., Lorenz, G., Gruen, R. S., Gorman, J. M., & Ehrhart, A. A. (1991). Sexual risk behavior, sexual functioning, and HIV-disease progression in gay men. *Journal of Sex Research, 28,* 3–27.

Mirotznik, J. (1991). Genital herpes: A survey of the attitudes, knowledge, and reported behaviors of college students at risk for infection. *Journal of Psychology and Human Sexuality, 4,* 73–99.

Murphy, R. L. (1992). Sexually transmitted diseases. In S. T. Shulman, J. P. Phair, & H. M. Sommers (Eds.) *The biological and clinical basis of infectious diseases* (4th Ed.) (pp. 238–268). Philadelphia: W. B. Saunders.

Murzuk, P. M., Tierney, H., Tardiff, K., Gross, E. M., Morgan, E. B., Hse, M. A. & Mann, J. J. (1988). Increased risk of suicide in persons with AIDS. *Journal of the American Medical Association, 259,* 1333–1337.

National Commission on Acquired Immune Deficiency Syndrome (1991). *America living with AIDS.* Washington DC: U.S. Government Printing Office.

Negy, C., & Webber, A. W. (1991). Knowledge and fear of AIDS: A comparison study between white, black, and Hispanic college students. *Journal of Sex Education and Therapy, 17,* 42–45.

New era in HSV diagnosis? (1991, Spring). *The Helper, 13*(1), pp. 1, 6–7. (Available from P.O. Box 13827, Research Triangle Park, NC 27709.)

Painter, K. (1992, July 21). Half of new HIV cases found in women. *USA Today,* p. 1.

Palca, J. (1991). The sobering geography of AIDS. *Science, 252,* 372–373.

Phair, J. P., & Chadwick, E. G. (1992). Human immunodeficiency virus infection and AIDS. In S. T. Shulman, J. P. Phair, & H. M. Sommers (Eds.), *The biological & clinical basis of infectious diseases* (4th Ed.) (pp. 380–393). Philadelphia: W. B. Saunders.

Protecting your partner/relationship. (1992, Summer). *HPV News, 2*(2), p. 6.

Reitmeijer, C., Krebs, J., Feorino, P., & Judson, F. (1988). Condoms as physical and chemical barriers against human immunodeficiency virus. *Journal of the American Medical Association, 259,* 1851–1853.

Risk factors for cervical cancer. (1992). *HPV News, 2*(2), p. 10.

Ruefli, T., Yu, O., & Barton, J. (1992). Sexual risk taking in smaller cities: The case of Buffalo, New York. *The Journal of Sex Research, 29,* 95–108.

Rutherford, G. W., Woo, J. M., Neal, D. P., Rauch, K. J., Geoghegan, C., McKinney, K. C., McGee, J., & Lemp, G. F. (1991). Partner notification and the control of human immunodeficiency virus infection: Two years of experience in San Francisco. *Sexually Transmitted Diseases, 18,* 107–110.

Ryder, R. W., Nsa, W., Hassig, S. E., Behets, F., Rayfield, M., Ekungola, B., Nelson, A. M., Mulenda, U., Francis, H., Mwandgalirwa, K., Davachi, F., Rogers, M., Nzilambi, N., Grenberg, A., Mann, J., Quinn, T. C., Piot, P., & Curran, J. W. (1989). Perinatal transmission of the human immunodeficiency virus type 1 to infants of seropositive women in Zaire. *New England Journal of Medicine, 320,* 1637–1642.

Sammons, R. (1991). *Chlamydia.* Unpublished manuscript. Used by permission of Dr. Sammons.

Schwebke, J. R. (1991a). Gonorrhea in the '90s. *Medical Aspects of Human Sexuality, 29,* 42–46.

Schwebke, J. R. (1991b). Syphilis in the '90s. *Medical Aspects of Human Sexuality, 29,* 44–49.

Seligmann, J., Beachy, L., Gordon, J., McCormick, J., & Starr, M. (1991, December 9). Condoms in the classroom. *Newsweek,* p. 61.

Selik, R. M., Castro, K. G., & Papaioanou, M. (1988). Racial/ethnic differences in the risk of AIDS in the United States. *American Journal of Public Health, 78,* 1539–1545.

Shilts, R. (1987). *And the band played on.* New York: St. Martin's Press.

Silver, P. S., Auerbach, S. M., Vishniavsky, N., Kaplowitz, L. G. (1986). Psychological factors in recurrent genital herpes infection: Stress, coping style, social support, emotional dysfunction, and symptom recurrence. *Journal of Psychosomatic Research, 30,* 163–171.

Sinforiani, E., Mauri, M., Bono, G., Muratori, S., Alessi, E., & Minoli, L. (1991). Cognitive abnormalities and disease progression in a selected population of asymptomatic HIV-positive subjects. *AIDS, 5,* 1117–1119.

Smith, L. S., Lauver, D., & Gray, P. A. (1990). Sexually transmitted diseases. In C. I. Fogel and D. Lauver (Eds.), *Sexual health promotion* (pp. 459–484). Philadelphia: W.B. Saunders.

Stein, A. P. (1991). The chlamydia epidemic: Teenagers at risk. *Medical Aspects of Human Sexuality, 29,* 26–33.

Stevenson, M. R., & Stevenson, D. M. (1990). Beliefs about AIDS among entering college students. *Journal of Sex Education and Therapy, 16,* 201–204.

Tanfer, K., & Schoorl, J. J. (1992). Premarital sexual careers and partner change. *Archives of Sexual Behavior, 21,* 45–65.

The AIDS file. (1992, July/August). *Health,* p. 18.

Thompson, D. (1989, June 19). Longer life for AIDS patients. *Time,* p. 52.

Wilson, D., Lavelle, S., Greenspan, R., & Wilson, C. (1991). Psychological predictors of HIV-preventive behavior among Zimbabwean students. *Journal of Social Psychology, 13,* 293–295.

CHAPTER NINETEEN

Abuses and Commercial Uses of Sexuality

Chapter Outline

Sexual Coercion: Rape and Sexual Assault
- Prevalence and Incidence of Rape
- Patterns of Rape
- Theories of Rape
- Impact of Rape and Sexual Assault
- Treatment for the Rape Survivor
- **Self-Assessment:** Rape Empathy Scale
- Treatment for the Rape Perpetrator
- Prevention of Rape
- **Research and Policy Perspective:** Rape Prevention on the College Campus

Sexual Abuse of Children
- Incidence and Prevalence of Extrafamilial and Intrafamilial Child Sexual Abuse
- Theories of Child Sexual Abuse
- Patterns of Child Sexual Abuse
- Impact of Child Sexual Abuse
- Treatment of Sexually Abused Children and Abusers
- Prevention of Child Sexual Abuse

Sexual Harassment in the Workplace
- Prevalence and Incidence of Sexual Harassment
- Definition of Sexual Harassment
- Theories of Sexual Harassment
- Consequences of Sexual Harassment
- Responses to Sexual Harassment
- Prevention of Sexual Harassment

Commercial Uses and Abuses of Sexuality
- Prostitution
- Pornography

Choices
- Choose to Have Children Testify in Court in Cases of Alleged Child Sexual Abuse?
- Choose to Confront Sexual Harassment?
- Choose to Legalize or Decriminalize Prostitution?

Is It True?*

1. There are more rapes by acquaintances than by strangers.
2. Pornography and erotica are basically the same concept.
3. Men, not just women, must take responsibility for stopping rape.
4. Most victims of child sexual abuse are abused by a relative.
5. Group therapy can be important for sexually abused children since it helps to relieve a sense of isolation.

* 1=T, 2=F, 3=T, 4=F, 5=T

I felt as though I did not have a choice.

Anita F. Hill on her charge of sexual harassment against Judge Clarence Thomas, Supreme Court nominee

The rape trials of Mike Tyson (convicted and sentenced to 10 years in prison for the rape of Desiree Washington) and William Kennedy Smith (acquitted of the charge that he raped a woman in Palm Beach, Florida), the public disclosures of incest by Roseanne Barr Arnold and LaToya Jackson, and the sexual harassment allegations by Anita Hill at the Senate confirmation hearings of Supreme Court nominee Judge Clarence Thomas emphasized some of the ways sexuality is or may be abused. Sexual abuse may be conceptualized as being on a continuum from such devastating abuses as rape, incest, and sexual harassment to commercial uses of sex, such as prostitution and pornography. Other abuses of sexuality include the abuse of sexuality by a therapist who has sex with her or his patients (over 2,000 cases are on record; Beck, Springen, & Foote, 1992) and by a caretaker of disabled individuals (e.g., intellectually or mobility impaired) (Sobsey & Doe, 1991; Crossmaker, 1991).

Sexual Coercion: Rape and Sexual Assault

Sexual coercion involves depriving a person of free choice and forcing (actual or threatened) that person to engage in sexual acts against the person's will. Although accounts of rape and sexual assault have been recorded throughout history (Zillmann, 1984), it is only in the last couple of decades that social scientists, medical and mental-health professionals, and politicians have acknowledged the prevalence and seriousness of sexually coercive acts. The turning point that ended our society's mass silence about rape and sexual assault may have been the publication of Susan Brownmiller's *Against Our Will* (1975), which featured a feminist theory of rape (discussed later in this chapter).

One of the difficulties in studying rape and sexual assault is that these terms are variously defined in legal codes and research literature. Criminal law distinguishes between forcible rape and statutory rape. Forcible rape includes three elements: vaginal penetration, force or threat of force, and nonconsent of the victim. Statutory rape involves sexual intercourse without use of force with a person below the legal age of consent. Marital rape, a new concept now recognized in all but two states, is forcible rape by one's spouse.

The ways in which individual women and men define rape also vary. Some women report that they experienced some event that meets the behavioral definition of rape, even though they do not call what they experienced rape. Similarly, some men may have engaged in behavior that was coercive but do not define themselves as having committed rape. Hence, what actually happens and the label for it may be very different.

CONSIDERATION: Because legal definitions of **rape** are varied and restrictive, it has been suggested that social scientists use the terms "forced sex" or "sexual assault," instead of the term "rape" (Finkelhor & Yllo, 1988; Crawford & Galdi-

Continued

Continued

kas, 1986). Instead of asking if a person has been raped, researchers should ask more general questions like "Have you ever been forced to have sex?" (Kelly, 1988). In this text, we use the term "rape" as synonymous with "forced sex" or "sexual assault." We apply the term "rape" to acts of sex (or attempted sex) in which one party is nonconsenting, regardless of the age and sex of the offender and victim and whether or not the act meets criteria for what legally constitutes rape.

Prevalence and Incidence of Rape

Data concerning the prevalence and incidence of rape are available from three sources: 1) official statistics, based on reports of rape made to the police, 2) victimization surveys in which respondents are asked to indicate if they have been victims of various types of sexual coercion, and 3) self-report offender surveys in which respondents are asked to indicate if they have engaged in forced sex with a nonconsenting person.

NATIONAL DATA: According to the FBI, in 1989, 39.1 female rapes (completed or attempted) per 100,000 people were reported to the police (U.S. Dept. of Justice, 1991, Table 3.108).

Official Statistics Official rape statistics are compiled by the Federal Bureau of Investigation (FBI) and published annually in the Uniform Crime Reports. These statistics are based on citizen reports of completed and attempted rape made to police. The FBI's annual Uniform Crime Reports do not include statistics for male rape victims because, according to the FBI's definition, victims of rape are always female.

Official statistics are not good indicators of the prevalence and incidence of rape because many rapes are not reported to the police. Koss, Gidycz and Wisniewski (1987) estimated that for every rape that is reported, three to 10 are committed but not reported. According to the National Crime Survey, of all attempted or completed rapes between 1973 and 1987, 53% were reported to the police (Harlow, 1991). Tables 19.1 and 19.2 indicate the various reasons that victims of completed or attempted rape chose to report or not report the rape to the police. The percentages do not add up to 100% because the respondents often indicated more than one reason.

CONSIDERATION: According to the National Crime Survey, a rape victim is more likely to report the rape to the police if: 1) the rape was completed, rather than just attempted; 2) the offender was a stranger, rather than someone known to the victim; 3) the offender had a weapon; 4) the victim was physically injured; and 5) the victim was between the ages of 12 and 15 (Harlow, 1991).

TABLE 19.1 Reasons Female Rape Victims Reported the Crime to Police

Reasons for Reporting to the Police	% of Rape Victims Who Reported Rape
To keep the incident from happening again	60%
To punish the offender	47%
To stop the incident from happening again	31%
To fulfill a victim's duty	18%
To get help after the incident	15%
Because there was evidence or proof	8%
Because it was a crime	5%
Other	20%

Source: Based on Harlow, C. W. (1991). *Female victims of violent crime.* NCJ-126826. (Data from National Crime Survey, 1979–1987). Washington, DC: U.S. Department of Justice.

TABLE 19.2 Reasons Female Rape Victims Did Not Report the Crime to Police

Reasons for Not Reporting to Police	% of Rape Victims Who Did Not Report Rape
Private or personal matter or took care of it herself	26%
Afraid of reprisal by the offender or his family	17%
Police would be inefficient, ineffective, or insensitive	16%
Lack of proof or no way to find the offender	12%
Reported it to someone else	10%
Police wouldn't think it important enough	7%
Did not think it important enough	5%
Offender was unsuccessful	5%
Others (embarrassed, feeling of being partly responsible, wanting to get event over with, fear of questions, fear of publicity)	33%

Source: Based on Harlow, C. W. (1991). *Female victims of violent crimes.* NCJ-126826. (Data based on National Crime Survey, 1979–1987).

I'm terrified that victims everywhere will not report because of what's happened to me.

Patty Bowman
(Alleged rape victim of William Kennedy Smith, who was acquitted)

NATIONAL DATA: According to the NCS, each year there are 1.6 rapes per 1,000 women age 12 or older, meaning that one out of every 600 women is a rape victim each year (Harlow, 1991).

Victimization Surveys Because many rapes are not reported to the police, a more accurate source of data concerning the prevalence and incidence of rape is victimization surveys. In these surveys, respondents are asked questions about a range of coercive sexual experiences that may meet the legal criteria for rape, although the victims may or may not label the experience as rape. A primary source of rape victimization data is collected through the National Crime Survey (NCS), which is based on a nationally representative sample of the U.S. population (See National Data).

However, the NCS questionnaire design and training of interviewers has been criticized as leading to a marked underestimate of rape. The interview protocol has asked general questions about being beaten, knifed, shot at, or attacked with a weapon; there were no direct questions about sexual activity or rape (Russell, 1984). Currently, the NCS questions and interviewer training are under revision, so more complete data may become available from future studies.

Unlike the National Crime Survey, other rape victimization surveys focus exclusively on the college population. In a nationwide survey of more than 6,100 women in four-year colleges, 25% reported being victims of rape or attempted rape (Koss, 1988). In a national representative sample of 3,187 women enrolled in 32 academic institutions, 28% reported experiencing (since age 14) an act that met the criteria for a legal definition of rape (Koss, Gidycz, & Wisniewski, 1987).

Some rape victimization surveys focus on specific communities. In 1978, Russell surveyed 930 women in San Francisco and found that 44% of the respondents reported at least one completed or attempted rape; only 8% of the rapes and attempted rapes were reported to the police (Russell, 1984). Data from the Russell survey predict a 26% probability that a woman in San Francisco will be the victim of a completed rape in her lifetime and a 46% probability that she will become a victim of rape or attempted rape (Russell, 1984).

Men are also raped. Men may be forced by another man (the more common) or woman to engage in oral sex, anal sex, or vaginal intercourse. Based on the National

Crime Survey, in 1989, about one per 1,000 men were victims of rape or attempted rape (U.S. Dept. of Justice, 1991, Table 3.10).

Struckman-Johnson (1991) noted that while estimates of male rape and sexual assault victimization are not nearly as high as comparable rates for women, "the rates for men are sufficiently high to show that sexual assault is a real problem affecting the health and welfare of American males" (p. 198). She presented new data from Sorenson and colleagues who conducted representative sampling of white and Hispanic residents of Los Angeles. The men at highest risk of sexual assault were white, college-educated, ages 18 to 39; 16% reported they were sexually assaulted. Surveys of college men revealed high rates (12% to 83%) of engaging in unwanted sex as a result of partner pressure, peer pressure, intoxication, and physical coercion.

One male college student reported the following account of being raped by a woman:

> Of all crimes, rape is one of the most inhuman, despicable acts of violence and human invasion. I experienced such an incident. At the time, I had a girlfriend and was not interested in anyone else. One night we had an argument and I went to a friend's house to relax and calm down. She had two roommates, one of which had made advances at other times which I rejected.
>
> I drank a lot of wine and eased out of reality into sleep. I was awakened by strange (but familiar) feelings in my lower body. I realized that I had been stripped, aroused, and mounted. I then freaked out, snapped sober, and got the hell out of the house.
>
> That was about eight months ago during which I have had to deal with feelings of insecurity and lack of worth. I never told my girlfriend (out of fear she wouldn't understand and think it was a poor confession for cheating) but had myself checked for STDs before I had sexual contact with her.
>
> I'm still dealing with this. I told only two of my friends. One said that it was rape and that I should get help; the other told me that I was lucky and should have stayed to let her finish. I can't figure out the latter reaction; I am too sensitive for that mode of thought. (Author's files)

Self-Report Offender Surveys In a national representative sample of 2,972 men enrolled in 32 academic institutions, 8% of the men reported perpetrating an act that met a legal definition of rape (Koss, Gidycz, & Wisniewski, 1987). In another study of 303 male college students and 286 male prisoners between the ages of 17 and 25, 45% of the college students and 62% of the prisoners admitted having done the equivalent of rape (Frank, 1991).

CONSIDERATION: Studies differ in their estimates of the prevalence and incidence of rape, in part because they involve different samples. In addition, differences in rape estimates are due to major differences in the criteria used to identify rape (Ellis, 1989, p. 4).

They may also differ widely in methodology (personal interview versus questionnaire). The Russell study (1984) was carefully designed to obtain more accurate information than previous studies about the incidence and prevalence of sexual assault of girls and women. Detailed in-person interviews (average length of one hour and 20 minutes) were conducted in private by carefully trained female interviewers. The race and ethnicity of the respondent and interviewer were matched. The random sample of households was drawn by a public opinion polling organization. Although only San Francisco residents were interviewed, the rate of reported rapes there is similar to other large cities such as Los Angeles, Boston, Cleveland, and Dallas.

Patterns of Rape

As noted earlier, women are more likely to be raped than men. Based on National Crime Survey data, other patterns associated with attempted and completed rape include the following (Harlow, 1991):

- Most rapes (about two-thirds) occur at night.
- The most frequent place where rapes occur is at the victim's home (35%); 20% occur on the street; 15% occur at or near a friend's home.
- Black women are significantly more likely to be raped than white women.
- Women age 16 to 24 are three times more likely to be raped than other women.
- Women who live in a central-city area are more likely to be raped than women who live in a suburban or nonmetropolitan area.
- Women who live alone are more likely to be raped than those who live with others.
- Unemployed women are three times and students are one and one-half times more likely to be raped than women overall.
- Rapists and their victims are likely to be of the same race, especially if the rapist and victim know each other.
- Most rape offenders (about 80%) are age 21 or older. Whereas only about 20% of single-offender rapes are committed by persons age 20 or under, about 30% of multiple offender rapes (i.e., gang rapes) are committed by persons age 20 and under.

Next, we look at other patterns of rape, including rape by a stranger, rape by an acquaintance (including date rape), gang rape, and rape by a marital partner.

NATIONAL DATA: Fifteen percent of 489 rape victims in a national sample reported that they were attacked by a stranger (Koss, Dinero, Seibel, & Cox, 1988).

Rape by a Stranger Rape in which the offender does not know the victim is often called **predatory rape** or **classic rape.**

Stranger rapes are more likely to involve weapons (usually guns or knives) than nonstranger rapes. Based on NCS data, 30% of stranger rapes involve a weapon, compared to 15% of nonstranger rapes (overall, one-fourth of all rapes involve a weapon) (Harlow, 1991).

Rapes by strangers are also more likely to be taken seriously by police, courts, and jurors than rapes by aquaintances (Russell, 1990). It follows that most persons convicted of rape are persons who raped a stranger, rather than someone they know.

NATIONAL DATA: In a national sample of 489 rape victims, 85% knew their rapist (Koss et al., 1988).

Rape by an Acquaintance The majority of rapes are committed by someone the victim knows. The following percentages reflect the relationship of the rapist to the victim in the Koss et al. (1988) study: boyfriend or lover (35%); friend, co-worker, or neighbor (29%); casual date (25%); husband (11%).

Acquaintance rape may be defined as "nonconsensual sex between adults who know each other" (Bechhofer & Parrot, 1991, p. 12). One type of acquaintance rape common to college and university students is **date rape,** which refers to nonconsensual sex between people who are dating or on a date. In a random sample of sorority women at Purdue University, 63% reported that since attending college they had experienced a man attempting to force sexual intercourse (get on top of the woman, attempt to insert penis) against their will; 95% of the women reported that they knew their attackers (Copenhaver & Grauerholz, 1991).

CONSIDERATION: While the term "acquaintance" is relatively easy to define, the concepts of "consent" and "nonconsent" are not always clear and unambiguous. Bechhofer and Parrot (1991) suggested that giving consent in a sexual situation involves saying yes and not saying no. In addition, "consent must be obtained on every separate occasion and cannot be assumed from previous interactions" (p. 13). Bechhofer and Parrot (1991) noted that

> most people do not give true consent in their sexual interactions. However, a situation is rape only if the person not consenting does not want to have sex. (p. 13)

In contrast to rape by a stranger, rape by an acquaintance is usually not planned. Bechhofer and Parrot (1991) noted:

> He plans the evening with the intent of sex, but if the date does not progress as planned and his date does not comply, he becomes angry and takes what he feels is his right—sex. Afterward, the victim feels raped, while the assailant believes that he has done nothing wrong. He may even ask the woman out on another date.

However, some date rapes are planned. Exhibit 19.1 describes such an experience as recalled by a woman who was raped by her boyfriend on a date.

Date rapes may often occur in the context of alcohol or drugs. In the study by Copenhaver and Grauerholz (1991), 79% of the women reported that they had been drinking or taking drugs prior to the date rape; 71% reported that the offenders had been drinking or taking drugs. Such alcohol or drug use may not only reduce female inhibitions for sexual involvement, it may increase male sexual aggression and/or provide an excuse for aggression. Parrot (1991) emphasized that "enforcing alcohol prohibition on campus is crucial to reducing the incidence of acquaintance rape" (p. 371).

EXHIBIT 19.1 Date Rape: One College Student's Experience

Last spring, I met this guy and a relationship started which was great. One year later, he raped me. The term was almost over and we would not be able to spend much time together during the summer. Therefore, we planned to go out to eat and spend some time together.

After dinner we drove to a park. I did not mind or suspect anything for we had done this many times. Then he asked me into the back seat. I got into the back seat with him because I trusted him and he said he wanted to be close to me as we talked. He began talking. He told me that he was tired of always pleasing me and not getting a reward. Therefore, he was going to "make love to me" whether I wanted to or not. I thought he was joking, so I asked him to stop playing. He told me he was serious, and after looking at him closely, I knew he was serious. I began to plead with him not to have sex with me. He did not listen. He began to tear my clothes off and confine me so that I could not move. All this time I was fighting him. At one time, I managed to open the door, but he threw me back into the seat, hit me, then he got on me and raped me. After he was satisfied, he stopped, told me to get dressed and stop crying. He said he was sorry it had to happen that way.

He brought me back to the dorm and expected me to kiss him good night. He didn't think he had done anything wrong. Before this happened, I loved this man very much, but afterward I felt great hatred for him.

My life has not been the same since that night. I do not trust men as I once did, nor do I feel completely comfortable when I'm with my present boyfriend. He wants to know why I back off when he tries to be intimate with me. However, right now I can't tell him, as he knows the guy who raped me (Authors' files).

Alcohol consumption often precedes acquaintance rape.

Gang Rapes **Gang rape** is that which involves more than one perpetrator. (Some researchers conceptualize gang rape as involving three or more offenders and exclude rapes with two offenders). Although more than one rapist is more likely to be present in stranger rapes than in acquaintance rapes (Harlow, 1991), some gang rapes are committed by acquaintances.

Chris O'Sullivan (1991) studied acquaintance gang rapes on campus; the mean number of male participants in the cases she studied was five. O'Sullivan noted that men who would not rape alone may become rapists in the company of their sexually aggressive buddies. She also noted that athletes and fraternity men were more likely to be sexually aggressive and explained that, in gang rapes, there is often one leader of a closely knit group (athletic team, fraternity, or dormmates) who instigates the rape. The other group members follow the leader. Participation in gang rape may be motivated by the quest for recreation, adventure, and acceptance by and camaraderie among the group members.

Three social-psychological factors help explain why group members who individually would not commit rape would do so in a group context. First, the group context allows members to diffuse responsibility for the gang rape by blaming others in the group. Second, a group context may produce a state of deindividuation, or "loss of self-awareness, including awareness of one's beliefs, attitudes, and self-standards" (O'Sullivan, 1991, p. 148). Lastly, in a group setting, modeling of aggression occurs. Not only does watching group members rape a woman convey to other group members that this behavior is considered appropriate and fun, it also demonstrates techniques of how to force someone to have sex.

NATIONAL DATA: Between 1978 and 1985, 210 husbands were arrested for raping their wives (National Clearinghouse on Date and Marital Rape, 1991).

Marital Rape Husbands who rape their wives often abuse them in other ways—verbally and physically. Rape is one part of a pattern of violence.

In Russell's 1990 study of female San Francisco residents, 14% of married women revealed having been sexually assaulted by their husbands. Ten percent of married women in a Boston survey reported that they had been raped by their husbands (Finkelhor & Yllo, 1988). Such rapes may have included not only intercourse but

The solution to the problem of wife rape starts with breaking silence about it.
Diana Russell

also other types of sexual activities in which the wife did not want to engage, most often fellatio and anal intercourse. The various types of marital rape identified by the researchers included battering rape, non battering rape, and obsessive rape (Finkelhor & Yllo, 1988).

Battering marital rape occurs in the context of a regular pattern of verbal and physical abuse. The husbands yell at their wives, call them names, slap, shove, and beat them. These husbands are angry, belligerent, and frequent alcohol abusers. An example follows:

> One afternoon she came home from school, changed into a housecoat, and started toward the bathroom. He got up from the couch where he had been lying, grabbed her, and pushed her down on the floor. With her face pressed into a pillow and his hand clamped over her mouth, he proceeded to have anal intercourse with her. She screamed and struggled to no avail. Her injuries were painful and extensive. She had a torn muscle in her rectum, so that for three months she had to go to the bathroom standing up. (pp. 144–145)

Nonbattering marital rape often occurs in response to a long-standing conflict or disagreement about sex. The violence is not generalized to the rest of the relationship but is specific to the sexual conflict. An example follows:

> Their love making on this occasion started out pleasantly enough, but he tried to get her to have anal intercourse with him. She refused. He persisted. She kicked and pushed him away. Still, he persisted. They ended up having vaginal intercourse. The force he used was mostly that of his weight on top of her. At 220 pounds, he weighs twice as much as she. "It was horrible," she said. She was sick to her stomach afterward. She cried and felt angry and disgusted. He showed little guilt. "He felt like he'd won something." (p. 145)

Obsessive marital rape may also be categorized as bizarre. The woman is used as a sex object to satisfy an atypical need of the husband. An example follows:

> "I was really his masturbating machine," one woman recalled. He was very rough sexually and would hold a pillow over her face to stifle her screams. He would also tie her up and insert objects into her vagina and take pictures, which he shared with his friends. The interviewee later discovered a file card in her husband's desk which sickened her. On the card, he had written a list of dates—dates that corresponded to the forced sex episodes of the past months. Next to each was a complicated coding system which seemed to indicate the type of sex act and a ranking of how much he enjoyed it. (p. 146)

As of 1991, 18 states and the District of Columbia had no restrictions on prosecuting marital or cohabitating rape as a crime (National Clearinghouse on Marital and Date Rape, 1991). In the other states husbands can be prosecuted for raping their wives in some circumstances, but not others. For example, in some states rape imposed by force is insufficient unless additional degrees of violence were used, such as kidnapping or threat with a weapon (Russell, 1991). As of this writing it is only in North Carolina and Oklahoma that husbands cannot be prosecuted for rape unless the couple is living apart, is legally separated, or has filed for divorce or an order of protection. Historically, the penalties for rape were based on property right laws designed to protect a man's property (wife or daughter) from forcible rape by other men; a husband "taking" his own property was not considered rape (Russell, 1990).

Wives are extremely reluctant to press charges. Those who do are, in effect, challenging a large segment of society that still tends to view sex as the right of men in a pair-bonded relationship with a woman. In essence, "the marriage license is a raping license" (Finkelhor & Yllo, 1988, p. 150). However, when women do seek prosecution of raping husbands, the conviction rate is high—88% in cases where the victim's report to the police resulted in arrest (Russell, 1991). Russell (1991) suggested that this high conviction rate is probably due to the fact that "wives who charge their husbands with rape have often been subjected to particularly brutal and/or deviant experiences" (p. 136).

Theories of Rape

Various theories have been suggested in an attempt to explain why rape occurs. Some of these follow.

Evolutionary and Biological Theories of Rape Evolutionary and biological theories explain rape on the basis of anatomy, biologically based drives, and natural selection for reproductive success. It is possible for men to have a penile erection when intercourse is not desired; hence, it is possible for women to rape men. However, the biological difference between women and men is such that the woman's vagina is always in state of being "rapable," whereas the man's penis is not. (This statement is true only if the definition of rape that is used involves vaginal penetration).

More important than the biological difference between the penis and the vagina, however, is "another, more critical biological difference between the sexes: the superior physical strength of most men over most women" (Russell, 1984, p. 112). Men are generally bigger, heavier, and stronger than women and are thus physically able to overpower women.

CONSIDERATION: In addition to the biologically based differences between men and women resulting in greater physical strength in men, cultural factors restrict women's development of physical strength as well as their ability to use it. Women are less often encouraged to participate in strength-building sports and activities to the same extent that men are. In addition, cultural dress norms interfere with women's ability to use their physical abilities to protect themselves from potential rapists; women wearing high-heeled shoes and a tight skirt or dress are considerably restricted in their ability to either fight or run from an attacker. (Of course, not all women who are raped are similarly attired).

Some biological theories of rape suggest that rape results from a strong biological sex drive in men. This strong sex drive is explained in part by the high level of androgens and other sex hormones to which the male brain is exposed (Ellis, 1989).

Evolutionary (or sociobiological) theory explains that males have a strong sex drive because natural selection favors males who copulate with numerous females. Males achieve reproductive success through copulating with as many females as possible; females achieve reproductive success through limiting their copulation behavior to males who are committed to help care for the female and her offspring.

While rape is made possible by both men's biological capacity to rape and their greater physical strength, this doesn't explain why some men want to rape women or why they do so (Russell, 1984). Similarly, the idea that men have a strong sex drive does not explain why *some* men rape and others do not.

Psychopathological Theory of Rape According to psychopathological theories of rape, rapists are viewed as having a mental disorder. Many laypeople and some mental health professionals view rapists as being mentally sick or from the "lunatic fringe" of society (Scully & Marolla, 1985a; Rada, 1978).

Nicholas Groth (1979) developed a typology of rapes, each of which is based on some form of emotional or intrapsychic problem. Groth's typology includes the following: 1) anger rape, which results from the rapist's extreme anger; rape is viewed as the ultimate expression of anger toward another person; 2) power rape, which is motivated by the rapist's desire to sexually possess his victim; this need to possess is often based on the rapist's insecurity regarding his masculinity; and 3) sadistic rape, which involves elements of sexuality and aggression; in sadistic rape, the offender derives sexual pleasure from inflicting intense pain and humiliation on his victim (usually a stranger).

One of the problems with psychopathologicial theories of rape is that, with few exceptions, they stem from studies of incarcerated rapists only. Rada (1978) admitted that "many rapists do not show marked deviation on standard psychological testing" (p. 131). Russell (1984) argued that "there is no denying that some rapists are mentally ill; the psychopathological model only becomes objectionable when it is used to apply to all or most rapists, as is done so often" (p. 148).

Feminist Theory of Rape Feminist theories of rape emphasize that rape is a behavior that is influenced by the social inequality between women and men.

> Basically, the feminist theory considers rape to be the result of long and deep-rooted social traditions in which males have dominated nearly all important political and economic activities . . . . Rape is the result of a male's decision to behave toward women in a possessive, dominating, and demeaning manner. (Ellis, 1989, p. 10)

According to feminist theory, rape is primarily an act of aggression and violence, not an act of sex. Men who rape women are viewed as using sexuality to establish or maintain dominance and control of women; sexual gratification is not considered a prime motive (Groth, 1979; Brownmiller, 1975).

Support for the view that rape is essentially a male response associated with social inequality between the sexes is provided by data that suggest that the incidence and prevalence of rape in various societies varies by the degree of equality between women and men in those societies. In one study of 95 societies (Sanday, 1981), rape was either absent or rare in almost half (47%) of the cases. In these societies, for example, among the Ashanti of West Africa, women tend to have equal status with men. "In 'rape free' societies women are treated with considerable respect, and prestige is attached to female reproductive and productive roles" (p. 16).

Societies in which women are viewed as inferior to men tend to be more rape-prone. Women in rape-prone societies are also viewed as property, implying that men may take them by violent means. Research that supports the feminist theory of rape is also provided by Frank (1991), who found that self-reported rapists placed greater emphasis on power and dominance in their relationships with women.

One of the strengths of the feminist view on rape is that it asserts that women should not be blamed for their victimization. Regarding a weakness of this view on rape, Ellis (1989) suggested that "the feminist theory seems to considerably underestimate the degree to which rape is sexually motivated . . ." (p. 31). While domination and power may be primary motivations in predatory rape, sex may be a primary motivation in most date rapes (Kanin, 1957).

Social Learning Theory of Rape The social learning theory of rape views rape as "behavior that males learn through the acquisition of social attitudes favorable to rape, and through the imitation of depictions of sexuality interlinked with aggression" (Ellis, 1989, p. 16). According to Ellis (1989), men learn aggressive behavior toward women, including rape behavior, through four interrelated processes: the sex-violence linkage effect, the modeling effect, the desensitization effect, and the "rape myth" effect.

1. The sex-violence linkage effect refers to the association of sexuality and violence. For example, many slasher and horror films, some pornography, and even some music videos depict sex and violence together, thus causing the viewer to form a link or association between sex and violence.
2. The modeling effect involves imitating rape scenes and other acts of violence toward women that are seen in real life and in the mass media (e.g., films). Frank (1991) also observed that having sexually aggressive friends is associated with self-reported rape.
3. The desensitization effect involves becoming desensitized to the pain, fear, and humiliation of sexual aggression through repeated exposure to sexual aggression.
4. The "rape myth" effect refers to the perpetuation of prejudicial, stereotyped, or false beliefs about rape, rape victims, or rapists (Burt, 1980, 1991). Frank (1991) observed that belief in rape myths, also called "rape-supportive attitudes" and "rape-tolerant attitudes," is associated with self-reported rapes.

Burt (1991) suggested that rape myths, which are learned from family, friends, and mass media, "are the mechanism that people use to justify dismissing an incident of sexual assault from the category of 'real' rape" (p. 27). Belief in rape myths may also predispose rape victims to blame themselves for the rape. Research suggests that the rape myth effect, that is, belief in rape myths, both facilitates the act of rape and serves as a subsequent justification for engaging in rape behavior (Check & Malamuth, 1981; Scully, 1990). Scales measuring rape myths and related attitudes predicted college students' reactions to a fictional rape, a report of an actual rape, and men's predictions of their own likelihood of raping (Check & Malamuth, 1985).

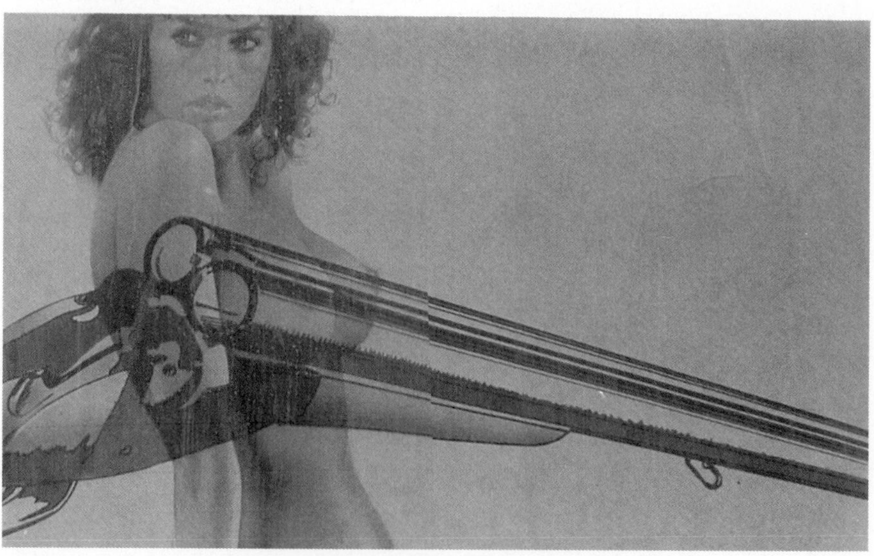

The association of sex and violence in the media may cause the viewer to link the two and become more accepting of rape.

More recent studies confirm these findings. In Frank's study (1991) of university men and prison inmates rape-supportive attitudes was the strongest predictor of raping. He found that such attitudes have a "single core" that centers on the notion that "it is 'OK' to force sex on certain kinds of women who 'deserve it' or in certain kinds of situations," such as when "he has spent alot of money on her, or if she has a 'loose' reputation" (p. 11).

In a study of 829 college undergraduate students at a large midwestern university, researchers found that men were more likely than women to endorse rape-tolerant attitudes (Holcomb, Holcomb, Sondag, & Williams, 1991). Blumberg and Lester (1991) also found that men were more likely to believe in rape myths than women. Table 19.3 presents the percentages of men and women in the Holcomb et al. (1991) study who endorsed various rape-tolerant statements. (Twelve of the 20 statements used in the Holcomb et al. study are presented in Table 19.3).

Impact of Rape and Sexual Assault

Rape is a traumatic experience. The most devastating aspect of rape is not genital contact but the victim's sense of cognitive and emotional violation. The woman who felt that her environment was safe and predictable, that other people were trustworthy, and that she was competent and autonomous is transformed into someone who is fearful of her surroundings, suspicious of other people, and lacks confidence in her ability to control her life.

Sexual Trauma "Sexual trauma" (which includes not only rape but also sexual assault and child sexual abuse) is the term for the acute disorganization a person feels after being raped (Roth & Lebowitz, 1988). Based on interviews with women who had been sexually abused, Roth and Lebowitz (1988) observed the following reactions of rape victims: helplessness and vulnerability, intense anger and rage, and self-blame.

TABLE 19.3 Percentage of College Men and Women Agreeing with Rape-Tolerant Statements

Item	Men (N=407)	Women (N=422)
1. A man sees sex as an achievement or notch in his belt.	47.9	67.8*
2. Rape really only occurs when a man has a weapon.	2.5	1.2
3. Deep down, a woman likes to be whistled at on the street.	54.8	38.9*
4. If a woman is heavily intoxicated, it is OK to have sex with her.	22.6	1.9*
5. Women frequently cry false rape.	28.3	19.0*
6. In a woman, submissiveness equals femininity.	25.8	14.2*
7. In a man, aggressiveness equals masculinity.	32.4	30.3
8. A prostitute cannot be raped.	81.6	93.8*
9. Some women ask to be raped and may enjoy it.	44.7	20.6*
10. Any woman could prevent rape if she wanted to.	27.3	16.6*
11. Rape is often provoked by the victim.	30.5	14.7*
12. If a woman says "no" to having sex, she means "maybe" or even "yes."	36.9	21.1*

* indicates a statistically significant gender difference.

Source: Holcomb, D. R., Holcomb, L. C., Sondag, K. A., & Williams, N. (1991). Attitudes about date rape: gender differences among college students. *College Student Journal, 25,* 434–439. Used by permission.

CONSIDERATION: In a study of rape crisis centers, the most common response of rape victims was blaming themselves for the rape. Such blaming allows the victims to maintain a belief in control, which results in the feeling that they may be able to avoid future rape. Otherwise, the victims feel that they are helpless and vulnerable (Janoff-Bulman, 1979).

Rape Trauma Syndrome Burgess and Holmstrom (1974) defined **rape trauma syndrome** as "the acute phase and long term reorganization process that occurs as a result of forcible rape or attempted forcible rape" (p. 982). On the basis of interviews with rape victims, Burgess and Holmstrom observed the following victim responses:

1. Acute phase. The acute phase manifested itself in one of two styles: the expressed style, in which the woman exhibited feelings of fear, anger, and anxiety through crying, sobbing, and restlessness over the trauma she experienced, and the controlled style, in which "feelings were masked or hidden and a calm, composed, or subdued affect was seen" (p. 982). No style was predominant: an equal number of women expressed both.

   The acute phase also involved various somatic complaints, such as soreness and bruising from the physical attack, tension headaches, stomach pains, and rectal bleeding in those cases where the woman had been forced to have anal sex.
2. Long-term reorganization phase. About half (48%) of the women who had been raped moved to another community. Many also changed their phone numbers or got an unlisted number. Other long-term issues with which the victims had to deal included nightmares, sexual dysfunctions, (Becker, Skinner, Abel, & Cichon, 1986), inability to trust (Carmen, Rieker & Mills, 1984), and phobias associated with the rape. For example, some women developed fear of being alone, of being in the dark, or of seeing or touching a man's penis (Veronen & Kilpatrick, 1983).

Rape and incest seem to be events which can be expected to violate central aspects of being and functioning, such that they will tend to leave psychological scars.
Susan Roth
Leslie Lebowitz

Posttraumatic Stress Disorder A more recent framework in which to assess the nature and degree of impact rape has on the individual is posttraumatic stress disorder (PTSD) (Burge, 1988). According to the American Psychiatric Association's (1987) *Diagnostic and Statistical Manual of Mental Disorders* (DSM-III-R), "the essential feature of this disorder is the development of characteristic symptoms following a psychologically distressing event that is outside the range of usual human experience . . . and is usually experienced with intense fear, terror, and helplessness" (p. 247). Rape is only one trauma that may produce PTSD; other traumas that are associated with PTSD include military combat, natural and accidental disasters, and nonsexual crimes. A diagnosis of PTSD is based on the following criteria (APA, 1987, p. 250):

1. The traumatic event is persistently reexperienced through recollections or dreams of the event, flashbacks, or hallucinations.
2. Persistent avoidance of stimuli associated with the trauma. This may involve efforts to avoid thoughts, feelings, or activities associated with the trauma, a restricted range of affect (e.g., inability to have love feelings), feelings of detachment or estrangement from others, and inability to recall aspects of the trauma (psychogenic amnesia).

CONSIDERATION: In a study of 60 women who were victims of sexual violence, almost 60% of the women who had been raped and 62% of the women who had been incestuously abused forgot their experience for a period of time (Kelly, 1988).

3. Persistent symptoms of increased arousal (not present before the trauma), including difficulty sleeping, irritability or outbursts of anger, and difficulty concentrating.
4. Symptoms must last at least one month.

Eighty-six percent of 29 rape victims showed a range of PTSD patterns that suggested moderate to severe stress (Burge, 1988). In a national sample of rape survivors, 35% met diagnostic criteria for PTSD; 14% among survivors of attempted rape (Kilpatrick et al., 1989, cited in Calhoun & Atkeson, 1991). A more recent study (Rothbaum, Foa, Riggs, Murdock, & Walsh, 1992) confirmed that PTSD is a prominent, although not universal, response following rape. Upon assessing women within the first two weeks following rape 94% had symptoms which met diagnostic criteria for PTSD; at three months after the rape PTSD persisted for 47%.

Burnam et al. (1988) observed that rape victims were at "increased risk for later onset of major depression, substance use disorders, and three anxiety disorders (phobià, panic disorder, and obsessive compulsive disorder)" (p. 848). Specifically, they estimated that being raped increases two to four times the risk for having a subsequent first episode of these disorders. Those particularly vulnerable had been assaulted in childhood.

Waigandt, Wallace, Phelps, and Miller (1990) studied the impact of rape on the physical health of victims two or more years after the assault and concluded that many rape victims suffer from not only long-lasting psychological difficulties but from long-term physical disturbances such as painful menstrual periods accompanied by hot flashes or weakness that forced them to lie down (Waigandt et al., 1990).

CONSIDERATION: The rape victim's partner also experiences reactions to the rape. "Not only must the partner cope with the victim's psychological distress and emotional needs, but he must also deal with his own reactions to the assault" (Calhoun & Atkeson, 1991, p. 117). Partner reactions include shock, rage, self-blame, concern for the victim, and emotional distress.

McEvoy and Brookings (1984) observed that one of the first reactions of the woman's partner is to seek revenge against the rapist. They advise that the person should refrain from contacting the rapist, if the identity of the rapist is known. Their recommendations include (pp. 9–10):

1. Provide a gentle context for the woman to discuss her feelings when she is ready. While you may be angry, her feelings should be primary.
2. Do not require that the woman discuss her feelings or the event immediately. Let her do so when she wants to.
3. Avoid suggesting that the woman is responsible for or cooperated in the rape. "Why didn't you scream and run?" not only induces guilt but may create resentment in the woman toward the partner.
4. Encourage the woman to make her own decisions. Do not take charge of the situation and make decisions, such as whether to press charges, whether to tell family, and whether to tell friends. Having control over one's life and making decisions are important in adjusting to a rape.
5. Communicate that she is not alone, that you are there for her and that you love and support her.

Treatment for the Rape Survivor

Not all rape victims experience symptoms of trauma. Some need only "common sense counseling and advice on coping with unfamiliar matters such as police counseling, compensation claims and trial procedures . . . deeper psychological

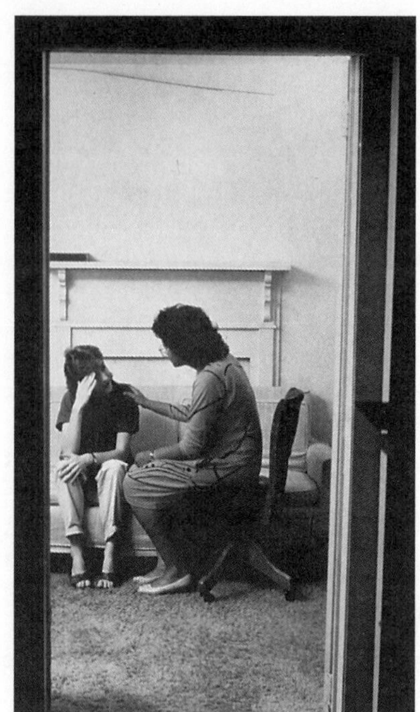

The primary goals of crisis counseling include establishing a therapeutic relationship, encouraging emotional expression, and providing information about reporting rape to the police.

probing is neither indicted nor desired" (West, 1991, p. 61). These individuals, while shaken, are able to bounce back. More often, treatment for the rape experience involves both crisis counseling and long-term therapy.

Crisis Counseling Crisis counseling may last from a few days to two or three months after the assault. The primary goals of crisis counseling include establishing a therapeutic relationship, encouraging emotional expression, and providing information about reporting rape to the police and symptoms the victim may experience. The therapist may also promote adjustment of immediate role responsibilities, which may take the form of encouraging the person to take time off from work or elicit the support of others to provide a period for processing the rape experience.

Crisis counselors also discuss with the victim the importance of seeing a physician to take care of medical needs (care for physical injuries, testing for STDs and pregnancy) as well as to document the rape if the victim decides to take legal action. The latter is often a difficult choice for most rape victims as it makes their rape experience public and exposes them to questioning and interrogation by strangers.

Long-term Therapy Sixty-three percent of 92 rape victims in the Burgess and Holmstrom (1979) sample required more than "a few months" to recover from their rape experience. Veronen and Kilpatrick (1983) found that rape victims had higher levels of fear and anxiety a year after the rape than individuals who had not been raped.

CONSIDERATION: In a study of 87 female victims of rape and incest, about half of the women felt completely or nearly completely recovered at the time they participated in the study (Katz, 1991). The researcher concluded that "although rape may have lifelong effects, it is also possible to feel recovered from it" (p. 265). Indeed, some therapists focus on ways survivors can "emerge from their recovery as stronger, more self-confident individuals" (Burt & Katz, 1987, p. 79).

Rape often has long-term consequences for which long-term therapy is often indicated. The treatment modalities used to help the rape victim adjust include the following (Becker & Kaplan, 1991; Calhoun & Atkeson, 1991; Roth, Dye, & Lebowitz, 1988; Veronen & Kilpatrick, 1983):

1. Systematic desensitization. For the woman overwhelmed with specific fear, systematic desensitization allows her to overcome anxiety and be relaxed while alone or with a man.
2. Flooding and implosion. An alternative to systematic desensitization, this procedure involves extended exposure to the upsetting thoughts and situations "until habituation occurs and the cues no longer elicit anxiety" (Calhoun & Atkeson, 1991, p. 66). Systematic desensitization and implosion are usually effective in reducing the frequency of nightmares and flashbacks.
3. Writing about the trauma. For clients who are not comfortable talking about their experience, writing often provides therapeutic gains by encouraging them to confront the experience.
4. Stress inoculation training. This technique provides rape victims with a systematic way of framing their rape experience, learning how to relax through deep-muscle relaxation procedures and breathing control, and using covert modeling.

The latter involves the rape survivor visualizing a rape encounter and successfully confronting the event.

5. Cognitive therapy. This involves recognizing and eliminating dysfunctional thoughts. Cognitive therapy emphasizes reframing the rape experience from one of great horror to one in which the person has benefited—by learning to be more cautious, to recognize one's vulnerability, and to appreciate the safety of one's close relationships. Cognitive therapy also encourages the person to increase the frequency of positive self-statements so as to enhance self-esteem. For example, persons who have been raped are encouraged to view themselves as survivors, rather than as victims.
6. Sex therapy. Sexual dysfunctions may occur subsequent to a rape experience. Anxiety responses, lack of trust, fear and avoidance of sexual context, and inability to have an orgasm or feel sexual arousal or pleasure are possible outcomes of being raped. A number of sex therapy techniques may be used to remediate these sexual dysfunctions, including systematic desensitization, sensate focus, and graduated assignments (shaping). Initially, all expectations of intercourse are eliminated.
7. Assertiveness training. Rape victims often fear being assaulted again. Through assertiveness training, "victims learn to distinguish passive, assertive, and aggressive behavior, so that they more accurately interpret the behavior of others and gain more control in their interactions" (Calhoun & Atkeson, 1991, p. 74). In addition, victims learn that they have a right to be assertive and to have their needs respected.
8. Group treatment. Providing therapy to rape survivors in a group context (sometimes called a "support group") allows them to share their experience with others who have had similar experiences. Group treatment is one of the more frequently used modalities in reducing a sense of isolation and alienation. "The common bond allowed for the identification of common issues, the sharing of coping methods, and the attainment of insight" (Roth et al., 1988, p. 85). Therapy techniques for treating fear, anxiety, and depression can also be used in a group setting.
9. Conjoint therapy. Conjoint, or couple, therapy helps the rape survivor and his or her partner discuss the impact of the rape on each other and on their relationship.

CONSIDERATION: Roth et al. (1988) observed that treatment for sexual assault was a difficult and painful process for victims and that initially there was a worsening of symptoms. However, sexual assault survivors receiving treatment seem "to value the process of trauma resolution enough to withstand what was perceived as necessary pain" (p. 91).

Before leaving this section, you might want to take the Rape Empathy Scale in the following Self-Assessment to assess the degree to which you have empathy for the rape victim. The scale also helps to assess your empathy for the rapist, whom we discuss in the following section.

Treatment for the Rape Perpetrator

One way to reduce the incidence of repeat rape and sexual assaults is to treat the offender. According to the U.S. Department of Justice, most institutional treatment programs for sex offenders have found that about 15% to 20% of treated offenders will commit a sex offense within three years of release; about 60% of those who have not received treatment will commit another sex offense (Interagency Council on Sex Offender Treatment, 1991).

Self Assessment

Rape Empathy Scale

This is a questionnaire designed to find out how different people feel about certain aspects of a rape situation. For the purpose of this questionnaire, rape is defined as an act in which one adult person (a male) compels another adult person (a female) to submit to penile-vaginal sexual intercourse against her will.

Each question consists of a pair of alternative statements lettered a or b. Please select the one statement of each pair which you more strongly *believe* to be the case as far as you are concerned. Be sure to select the one you actually *believe* to be more true rather than the one you think you should choose or the one you would like to be true. This is a measure of personal belief; thus, there are *no right or wrong answers.* Once you have decided which statement you more strongly believe to be the case, write the letter of the statement that indicates how strongly you prefer one statement over the alternative statement.

1 = strongly prefer statement (a) over statement (b)
2 = moderately prefer statement (a) over statement (b)
3 = slightly prefer statement (a) over statement (b)
4 = prefer both statements equally or can't decide between them
5 = slightly prefer statement (b) over statement (a)
6 = moderately prefer statement (b) over statement (a)
7 = strongly prefer statement (b) over statement (a)

For example, if you strongly prefer statement (b) over statement (a), you would circle the number 7 on your answer sheet for that pair of statements.

In some rare instances, you may discover that you genuinely prefer both statements or neither one. In such cases, and only in such cases, you may indicate a neutral position by circling the number 4.

1. ____ **a)** I feel that the situation in which a man compels a woman to submit to sexual intercourse against her will is an unjustifiable act under any circumstances.

b) I feel that the situation in which a man compels a woman to submit to sexual intercourse against her will is a justifiable act under certain circumstances.

2. ____ **a)** In deciding the matter of guilt or innocence in a rape case, it is more important to know about the past sexual activity of the alleged rape victim than the past sexual activity of the alleged rapist.

b) It is more important to know about the past sexual activity of the alleged rapist than the past sexual activity of the alleged rape victim in deciding the matter of guilt or innocence in a rape case.

3. ____ **a)** In general, I feel that rape is an act that is provoked by the rape victim.

b) In general, I feel that rape is an act that is not provoked by the rape victim.

4. ____ **a)** I would find it easier to imagine how a rapist might feel during an actual rape than how a rape victim might feel.

b) I would find it easier to imagine how a rape victim might feel during an actual rape than how a rapist might feel.

5. ____ **a)** Under certain circumstances, I can understand why a man would use force to obtain sexual relations with a woman.

b) I cannot understand why a man would use force to obtain sexual relations with a woman under any circumstances.

6. ____ **a)** In a court of law, I feel that the rapist must be held accountable for his behavior during the rape.

b) In a court of law, I feel that the rape victim must be held accountable for her behavior during the rape.

7. ____ **a)** When a woman dresses in a sexually attractive way, she must be willing to accept the consequences of her behavior, whatever they are, since she is signaling her interest in having sexual relations.

b) A woman has the right to dress in a sexually attractive way whether she is really interested in having sexual relations or not.

8. ____ **a)** I would find it easier to empathize with the shame and humiliation a rapist might feel during a trial for rape than with the feelings a rape victim might have during the trial.

Continued

Self-Assessment—*Continued*

b) I would find it easier to empathize with the shame and humiliation a rape victim might feel during a trial to prove rape than with the feelings a rapist might have during the trial.

9. _____ **a)** If a man rapes a sexually active woman, he would probably be justified in his actions by the fact that she chooses to have sexual relations with other men.

b) If a man rapes a sexually active woman, his actions would not be justified by the fact that she chooses to have sexual relations with other men.

10. _____ **a)** I believe that all women secretly want to be raped.

b) I don't believe that any women secretly want to be raped.

11. _____ **a)** In deciding whether a rape has occurred or not, the burden of proof should rest with the woman, who must prove that a rape has actually occurred.

b) In deciding whether a rape has occurred or not, the burden of proof should rest with the man, who must prove that a rape has not actually occurred.

12. _____ **a)** I believe that it is impossible for a rape victim to enjoy being raped.

b) I believe that it is possible for a rape victim to enjoy the experience of being raped, whether she admits it or not.

13. _____ **a)** I can really empathize with the helplessness a rapist might feel during a rape, since he's at the mercy of forces beyond his control.

b) I can really empathize with the helplessness a victim might feel during a rape if all of her attempts to resist the rape have failed.

14. _____ **a)** After a rape has occurred, I think the woman would suffer more emotional torment in dealing with the police than the man would.

b) After a rape has occurred, I think the man would suffer more emotional torment in dealing with the police than the woman would.

15. _____ **a)** I feel it is impossible for a man to rape a woman unless she is willing.

b) I feel it is possible for a man to rape a woman against her will.

16. _____ **a)** If a rape trial were publicized in the press, I feel the rape victim would suffer more emotional trauma from the publicity than the rapist.

b) If a rape trial were publicized in the press, I feel the rapist would suffer more emotional trauma from the publicity than the rape victim.

17. _____ **a)** Once a couple has had sexual intercourse, then that issue is resolved and it is no longer possible for that man to rape that woman.

b) Even if a couple has had sexual intercourse before, if the man forces the woman to have sexual intercourse with him against her will, this should be considered rape.

18. _____ **a)** I can understand a wife's humiliation and anger if her husband forced her to have sexual relations with him.

b) A husband has every right to determine when sexual relations with his wife occur, even if it means forcing her to have sex with him.

19. _____ **a)** If I were a member of the jury in a rape trial, I would probably be more likely to believe the woman's testimony than the man's, since it takes a lot of courage on the woman's part to accuse the man of rape.

b) If I were a member of the jury in a rape trial, I would probably be more likely to believe the man's testimony than the woman's since rape is a charge that is difficult to defend against, even if the man is innocent.

Scoring and Interpretation Responses are scored so that an item score of 1 indicates strong empathy for the rapist and 7 indicates strong empathy for the rape victim (Deitz, Blackwell, Daley, & Bentley, 1982). Therefore, reverse the scores (change 1, 2, and 3 to 7, 6, and 5) for the following items: 1, 6, 12, 14, 16, 18, and 19. Then sum the scores.

In Table 1, mean scores for men and women from three studies are presented, so that you may compare your score to those obtained from other students and community members.

Continued

Self-Assessment—*Continued*

TABLE 1 Rape Empathy Scale Mean Scores

Study population	Women	Men
Deitz, et al. (1982)		
Group 1 (Colorado State University undergraduates)	108.86	98.25
Group 2 (Colorado State University undergraduates)	111.71	100.25
Group 3 (Eligible jurors in county)	112.60	101.91
Borden, Karr, & Caldwell-Colbert (1988)		
Group 1 (small midwest state university undergraduates)	107.88	100.36
Group 2 (small midwest state university undergraduates)	112.04	98.56
Weir & Wrightsman (1990)		
Undergraduates	113.97	102.72

Reliability and Validity Deitz et al. (1982) reported that respondents were fairly consistent in answering the items within the scale (coefficient alpha for their juror group as 0.89 and 0.84 for the students), with essentially no difference between men and women's reliability scores. The relation between respondents' endorsement of individual items and their total score (item-total correlations) ranged from 0.33 to 0.75 for the juror group and from 0.18 to 0.52 for the student group. Cross-validation was performed on separate juror and student samples.

References

Borden, L. A., Karr, S. K., & Caldwell-Colbert, A. T. (1988). Effects of a university rape prevention program on attitudes and empathy toward rape. *Journal of College Student Development, 29,* 132–136.

Deitz, S. R., Blackwell, K. T., Daley, P. C., & Bentley, B. J. (1982). Measurement of empathy toward rape victims and rapists. *Journal of Personality and Social Psychology, 43,* 372–384.

Weir, J. A., & Wrightsman, L. S. (1990). The determinants of mock jurors' verdicts in a rape case. *Journal of Applied Social Psychology, 20,* 901–919.

The majority of sex offenders never receive treatment because in most cases, the rapist is neither caught nor convicted. Most often, he is not caught because the rape is not reported. Only 2% of those in Copenhaver and Grauerholz's study (1991) who had been raped or had experienced an attempted rape reported the experience to the police. Among the rapes that are reported and where the alleged rapist is apprehended, few cases come to trial. Of nearly 1,000 rapes that were reported to the Denver police, less than 5% of the accused were brought to trial and even fewer were convicted (Sheppard, Giacinti, & Tjaden, 1976).

In *Against Our Will,* Susan Brownmiller (1975) said that men rape because they can get away with it. Rapists often escape conviction with the help of an attorney who contends that the rape complaint is "unfounded" and requests that the police stop prosecution procedures. A rape complaint may be labeled "unfounded" if the case is seen as weak, for example, if the victim was intoxicated at the time, delayed reporting the alleged attack, refused to submit to a medical examination, or had a previous relationship with the rapist and if there is a lack of physical evidence to document that the rape occurred.

CONSIDERATION: Sex offenders rarely seek treatment prior to any involvement with legal authorities and on their own volition. Most sex offenders in treatment are required to be there by legal authorities, and many therapists in outpatient programs refuse to take voluntary clients.

In group therapy, peer pressure is used to encourage the offender to abandon his denial, to admit that he has a problem, and to be motivated to change his behavior.

The timing of therapy is important. Unless therapy occurs when the offender is facing a court hearing or as a condition of probation, the perpetrator usually denies the existence of a problem and has little motivation for treatment. Experienced clinicians typically request a court order before beginning treatment or recommend a period of inpatient treatment (Salter, 1988; Saunders & Awad, 1988). This has proved to be important in keeping offenders in treatment, due to their denial and minimization of their offenses. It also helps reduce the "two-week cure." "Thank you, doc. That was great. I learned a lot. No, I don't think I need therapy any more. Well, I'll never do that again. So long." (Salter, 1988, p. 87). When well-meaning people allow offenders to seek voluntary therapy instead of reporting the offender to legal authorities there is no leverage to maintain participation in treatment or to protect the safety of the community (Salter, 1988).

Multiple modalities are used in the treatment of sex offenders. Such modalities include (Saunders & Awad, 1988; Interagency Council on Sex Offender Treatment, 1991; Perkins, 1991):

1. Group therapy. In group therapy, peer pressure is used as a means of forcing the offender to abandon his denial, to accept his problem, and to be motivated to change.
2. Reducing rape interests. Techniques and medications for reducing deniant arousal interests (such as rape) were discussed in Chapter 17—Paraphilias and Sexuality.
3. Increasing arousal to appropriate stimuli. This involves orgasmic reconditioning (by having the man masturbate to socially appropriate stimuli) to increase arousal to such stimuli. Social skills training may also be used to provide the perpetrator with the opportunity for emotional, social, and sexual involvement with a partner in a consenting relationship.
4. Cognitive restructuring. Sex offenders often have rape supportive beliefs and attitudes (also called "thinking errors"). Cognitive restructuring involves changing such errors in thinking.

5. Victim empathy. Sex offenders may be required to either write an account of the rape or sexual assault from the point of view of the victim or play the role of the victim in a role-play of the rape or sexual assault. These activities are designed to develop empathy for victims of sexual assault.
6. Additional therapeutic modalities. Other treatment modalities used in sex offender treatment programs include relaxation and stress management, communication skills training, impulse control, sex education, gender-role stereotyping awareness, values clarification, and dealing with the offender's own past sexual and/or physical abuse.
7. After-treatment care. Some sex offender programs have an after-care component designed to assist the client once he is released from treatment. After-treatment care may include assisting the client in gaining further education or in securing employment.

One special focus in treating sex offenders is the development of programs to identify and treat juvenile perpetrators. In 1982 there were only about 20 specialized programs identified in the United States, but by 1988 there were 520. The growth in these programs reflects recognition of the finding that as many as 60% to 80% of adult offenders began offending during adolescence. Reports reveal that 50% of molested boys and 15% to 20% of sexually abused girls were offended by adolescents (The National Adolescent Perpetrator Network, 1988).

In general, the goals for sex offenders in treatment include the following (Interagency Council on Sex Offender Treatment, 1991, p. 26):

- To accept total responsibility for the crime
- To build empathy for victims and other people
- To identify and understand how he or she exploits others
- To learn how to control and eliminate inappropriate impulses
- To develop socially acceptable ways of interacting with others

Prevention of Rape

Effective rape prevention must address the multiple and overlapping causes. In their three-tier approach to rape prevention Rozee et al. (1991) recommended intervention at three levels: societal responsibility, individual awareness to avoid high-risk situations, and self-protection when confronted by an assailant.

Societal Responsibility Several groups of professionals were asked to evaluate which strategies would reduce rape. The option most frequently endorsed by social service personnel was to use educational strategies to encourage a new way of perceiving women in our society (Feldman-Summers & Palmer, 1980). This would be compatible with educating people to reduce acceptance of rape supportive beliefs and interpersonal violence.

CONSIDERATION: Researchers suggest that effective rape prevention efforts should target men, as well as women (Holcomb et al., 1991; Rozee et al., 1991). Rozee et al. suggested,

> Men must begin to protest rape as actively as women do by setting a nonaccepting standard for other men; by refusing to engage in rape jokes or victim-blaming and discouraging other men from doing so; and by joining with women in making the social and institutional changes that will eliminate rape. (pp. 350–351).

Continued

Continued

In a study (Holcomb et al., 1991) of 407 college men, 44.7% agreed that "Some women ask to be raped and may enjoy it" (p. 437). Over a third (36.9%) agreed that "If a woman says 'no' to having sex, she means 'maybe' or even 'yes' " (p. 437). As noted above, over a fifth believed (22.6%) that "If a woman is heavily intoxicated, it is OK to have sex with her" (p. 436). Unless these inaccurate beliefs are corrected, rape-tolerant attitudes may result in rape-tolerant behavior (Holcomb et al., 1991).

Preventing rape involves men making new choices in regard to how they view having sex with a woman. In a random sample of U.S. adults (conducted for *Time* magazine), almost one-fifth (17%) of the men said that it is not "rape" when a man has sex with a woman who has passed out after drinking too much alcohol (Gibbs, 1991). Even when alcohol is not involved, most men (59%) in the random sample felt that the use of emotional pressure to get a woman to have sex does not constitute rape. What is needed is respect for the preferences of another and the value that sexual aggression is wrong. Taking "no" for an answer is both important and necessary.

Given that some men will not choose to be respectful, the woman must make careful choices in regard to how she goes about preventing rape. Some of these choices include the following.

For a woman to survive unraped, particularly in an urban setting, she must learn basic mistrust.
Pauline Bart and Pat O'Brien

Avoidance of High Risk Situations One way to prevent a rape is to avoid situations in which it is likely to occur. Although most rapes (85%) are acquaintance rapes, those by strangers can be reduced by minimizing the time the woman is out alone at night. The choice for many women is how mobile they want to be versus how much they want to reduce their rape exposure. Hitchhiking and picking up hitchhikers should be avoided. Opening the door to strangers is also dangerous. If a stranger comes to a woman's door and asks to use the phone to call an ambulance, she should not let him in but offer to call the ambulance for him.

Avoiding the abuse of alcohol may also be associated with preventing rape. In a study of 407 male college students, over one-fifth (22.6%) agreed that "If a woman is heavily intoxicated, it is OK to have sex with her" (Holcomb et al., 1991, p. 436).

Rozee et al. (1991) noted that most women perform dozens of rape preventive behaviors every day. "But women tend to be torn between what they must do for their safety and what they want to do in order to enjoy a certain quality of life." While locking their doors doesn't challenge quality of life, "many balk, understandably, at treating friends as potential threats. Women must therefore find ways of protecting themselves without having to isolate themselves" (p. 342).

Self Protection During Confrontation When a woman is actually confronted with being raped, what might she do? There are several alternatives, none of which is foolproof but all of which work some of the time.

Trying to talk the rapist out of his plan is one alternative. There are a number of different strategies:

1. "Get the hell away from me." (attack)
2. "You don't really want to do this. Let's be friends and talk." (interpersonal liaison)
3. "My boyfriend will be here any moment." (distraction)
4. "Please don't. I've got AIDS." (disease, illness)

5. "I'll kill myself if you do this; I won't be able to live with myself." (self-punitiveness)
6. "I'm going to be married Saturday. I've never had sex before. Please don't do this to me." (virginity)
7. "It's wrong to do this. You'll go to hell if you do this." (moral appeal)

A woman who screams, kicks, and bites may, indeed, discourage a rapist since the encounter may be more trouble than he anticipated. But her screaming may also frighten him and cause him to knock her unconscious to stop her from screaming. (However, he may also hurt her if he rapes her, so avoiding physical injury may not be possible; Bart & O'Brien, 1985). Quinsey and Upfold (1985) found that resistance of any kind on the part of the victim was associated with an incompleted attack. Bart and O'Brien (1985) noted that both words and physical resistance seemed to be the most effective in thwarting a rape. Sixty-four percent of the sorority women in Copenhaver and Grauerholz's (1991) study also reported that reasoning and pleading was the mechanism they used for extricating themselves from being raped; 48% physically struggled.

Strategies to avoid rape depend on the situation. Rozee et al. (1991) suggested that avoiding and resisting rape

> requires each individual to choose methods that will be consistent with her own life-style and values rather than to adopt some standard set of safety measures. Each individual is faced with making choices that will maximize her resources for both avoidance and resistance. (p. 349)

The following Research and Policy Perspective examines rape prevention on college campuses.

RESEARCH AND POLICY PERSPECTIVE

Rape Prevention on the College Campus

While the topics of rape and its prevention have received heightened attention over the last few years, they are hardly new. Kirkpatrick and Kanin (1957) documented the self-reported incidence of university women's experiences of feeling offended by male sexual aggression. The offensive experiences included forceful attempts at intercourse (revealed by 20.9% of respondents) and forceful attempts involving violence (revealed by 6.2%). Offended women's reluctance to report incidents to authorities was noted. An educational implication of their study, said Kirkpatrick and Kanin, "is that college girls should be trained in *informed* self-reliance . . . parents, peer groups and formal agencies should operate so as to avoid stigmatization" (p. 58). Colleges and universities are still struggling to implement the goals of enhancing skills in preventing assaults and improving institutional response to reported assaults. They have even farther to go in changing the conditions that cause and maintain rape. Following is a framework for approaching rape prevention on the college campus and comments on research on attempts to reduce rape.

The concepts of tertiary, secondary, and primary prevention were applied to rape prevention by Roark (1987). We list tertiary prevention first, because it is the type most widely undertaken in our communities. Tertiary prevention is designed "to limit the damage of violence that has taken place through direct services to individuals who have been victimized" (p. 368). In this category, Roark included remediation attempts and direct services to victims, such as crisis intervention, medical care, posttrauma counseling, judicial procedures, and support for the survivor and parents. (See Sorenson & Brown, 1990, for a discussion of crisis intervention.) Student perpetrators may also be held accountable through university judicial procedures and counseling. Encouraging reporting of sexual aggression is recommended. Parrot

Continued

Continued

(1991a) summarized recommendations for university procedures for dealing with acquaintance rape. Finally, a campus violence resource center can be important for symbolic and actual value in organizing and publicizing campus prevention services.

"Secondary prevention is targeted at a problem already in existence and is intended to minimize the consequences for affected individuals" (Roark, 1987, p. 369). Promoting awareness of the problem and counteracting denial is a goal, and education is the primary vehicle for accomplishing it. Existing academic courses can be used, as well as specially developed courses in such fields as psychology, sociology, health, criminology, and women's studies. The use of networking to share campus resources to promote sexual assault awareness was described by Byington and McCammon (1988).

However, it is important that educational interventions be evaluated to determine their effectiveness. One study (Borden, Carr & Caldwell-Colbert, 1988) revealed that a popular and frequently requested rape awareness program failed to demonstrate attitude change as measured by the Attitudes Toward Rape Questionnaire and the Rape Empathy Scale (the Self-Assessment measure for this chapter). The researchers concluded that a lecture-based program is insufficient for much attitude change and recommended more dynamic, interactive programs.

Preliminary research on the effectiveness of an experiential program for men shows that such a program does alter participants' attitudes toward rape (Lee, 1987). Members of the Rape Prevention Education Project, developed by the Mid-Missouri Men's Resource Group, lead two-hour workshops for teenage and adult men. They meet in dormitory lounges and student centers, as well as classrooms. The four-part workshop includes a didactic presentation on myths and facts about rape, with time allowed for questions. Then an experiential empathy exercise is conducted in which a man reads a detailed personal narrative of being raped, and participants are guided through discussion to feel, even if briefly, the rape survivor's distress. A guided fantasy follows in which participants imagine their roommate coercing his date to have sex against her will. The discussion of that exercise and of the entire workshop concludes the program. One session of the workshop was evaluated to measure its effects on 24 undergraduate men. Scores on the Attitudes Toward Rape measure following the workshop revealed significant changes from pretest scores.

Another avenue for secondary prevention is the development and enforcement of clear university policies on rape, assault, harassment, and hazing. Parrot recommended that the institution's policy regarding acquaintance rape be disseminated during new-student orientation (Parrot, 1991b). She also recommended special attention be given to alcohol problems on campus, as well as training for university faculty and staff.

Primary prevention refers to "actions that take place before the onset of a problem. A major aim of primary prevention is stopping dangerous situations fromoccurring" (Roark, 1987, p. 369). This focus includes attention to the physical environment to provide adequate lighting, accessible parking and telephones, and escort services.

Another primary prevention focus is that of skill building to reduce personal vulnerability to becoming either a victim or perpetrator of sexual assault. Existing skill-building programs on campus can be expanded to include an antiviolence focus, and new programs can be added. Roark's list of topics relevant to skills helpful in reducing victimization and victimizing include the following:

> . . . assertiveness training, leadership workshops, self-esteem-building, values development, sexual decision-making, anger management, conflict resolution, stress management, relationship enhancement, self-defense training, loss resolution, rape prevention, human relations training, alcohol education, counteraction of abuse backgrounds, and social skills training. (p. 370)

Continued

Continued

In a list of strategies to prevent assault from ever occurring, Fischhoff (1992) included several ideas that could be applied in collegiate settings and that extend beyond them. Increasing people's perception that rapists are likely to be punished and providing psychological rehabilitation for rapists were recommended to reduce the propensity to rape. He also suggested altering societal beliefs and attitudes that promote rape, such as the attitude that sex is a commodity. Media depictions of rape could portray it as a violent crime. Likewise, Rozee, Bateman, and Gilmore (1991) emphasized the need to challenge society's devaluing of women and our socialization of men who grow up with notions of sexual entitlement and acceptance of interpersonal violence.

An example of a comprehensive prevention program is Alternatives to Fear (ATF) in Seattle, Washington (Harvey, 1985). ATF was begun in 1971 as a karate course affiliated with the University of Washington. Now an independent organization, it influences programs nationally through its educational and preventive efforts. Institutions of higher education, with their powerful resources and influence, can work to cultivate communities that attach a social stigma to violence and are nonexploitive. In doing so, the ramifications will extend far beyond the collegiate experience (Roark, 1987).

References

Borden, L. A., Karr, S. A., & Caldwell-Colbert, A. T. (1988). Effects of a university rape prevention program on attitudes and empathy toward rape. *Journal of College Student Development, 29,* 132–136.

Byington, D. B., & McCammon, S. L. (1988). Networking as an approach to advocacy: A campus sexual assault awareness program. *Response to the Victimization of Women and Children, 11,* 11–13.

Fischhoff, B. (1992). Giving advice: Decision theory perspectives on sexual assault. *American Psychologist, 47,* 577–588.

Harvey, M. R. (1985). *Exemplary rape crisis programs.* Rockville, MD: National Institute of Mental Health.

Kirkpatrick, C., & Kanin, E. (1957). Male sex aggression on a university campus. *American Sociological Review, 22,* 52–58.

Lee, L. A. (1987). Rape prevention: Experiential training for men. *Journal of Counseling and Development, 66,* 100–101.

Parrot, A. (1991a). Recommendations for college policies and procedures to deal with acquaintance rape. In A. Parrot & L. Bechhofer (Eds.), *Acquaintance rape: The hidden crime* (pp. 368–380). New York: Wiley.

Parrot, A. (1991b). Institutional response: How can acquaintance rape be prevented? In A. Parrot & L. Bechhofer (Eds.), *Acquaintance rape: The hidden crime* (pp. 355–367). New York: Wiley.

Roark, M. L. (1987). Preventing violence on college campuses. *Journal of Counseling and Development, 65,* 367–371.

Rozee, P. D., Bateman, P., & Gilmore, T. (1991). The personal perspective of acquaintance rape prevention: A three-tier approach. In A. Parrot & L. Bechhofer (Eds.), *Acquaintance rape: The hidden crime* (pp. 337–354). New York: Wiley.

Sorenson, B. B., & Brown, V. B. (1990). Interpersonal violence and crisis intervention on the college campus. In H. L. Pruett & V. B. Brown (Eds.), *Crisis intervention and prevention: New directions for student services, 49,* 57–66.

Sexual Abuse of Children

Sexual abuse of children occurs in both extrafamilial and intrafamilial contexts. **Extrafamilial child sexual abuse** may be defined as:

> One or more unwanted sexual experiences with persons unrelated by blood or marriage, ranging from attempted petting (touching of breasts or genitals or attempts at

> such touching) to rape, before the victim turned 14 years, and completed or attempted forcible rape experiences from the ages of 14 to 17 years (inclusive). (Russell, 1984, p. 180)

"I was abused in every way, including sexually, by relatives."
Roseanne Barr Arnold

Intrafamilial child sexual abuse Also referred to as incestuous child abuse, may be defined as:

> Any kind of exploitive sexual contact or attempted sexual contact, that occurred between relatives, no matter how distant the relationship before the victim turned 18 years old. (Russell, 1984, p. 181)

Incidence and Prevalence of Extrafamilial and Intrafamilial Child Sexual Abuse

Herman (1981) reviewed five studies that had been conducted over a 30-year period that provided information from over 5,000 women in regard to their experience with extrafamilial and intrafamilial child sexual abuse.

> One-fifth to one-third of all women reported that they had had some sort of childhood sexual encounter with an adult male. Between four and twelve percent of all women reported a sexual experience with a relative, and one woman in a hundred reported a sexual experience with her father or stepfather. (p. 12)

NATIONAL DATA: In a national survey of adults concerning childhood sexual abuse, 27% of the women reported being victims (Finkelhor, Hotaling, Lewis, & Smith, 1990). This percentage refers to both extra- and intrafamilial contexts.

Russell (1984) conducted interviews with 930 randomly selected women in San-Francisco in 1978. Thirty-one percent reported extrafamilial sex abuse by age 18; 16% reported intrafamilial sex abuse (p. 183). On the basis of these data, we conclude that between a quarter and a third of U.S. women have been victims of sexual abuse in childhood.

A significant number of men also report having been sexually abused as children. In a study of 796 college students, Finkelhor (1979) found that 8.6% of the male students reported that they had been sexually victimized as boys.

Theories of Child Sexual Abuse

Russell (1984) reviewed a number of theories as to why childhood sexual abuse occurs.

Freudian Theory Freudian theory maintains that humans are naturally capable of sexual arousal from a variety of stimuli, including children. For most people, cultural taboos and socialization act to repress sexual interest that adults have in children.

Social Learning Theory Social learning theory suggests that adults learn to regard children as sexual objects. Such learning may result from being exposed to child pornography or from being inadvertently sexually stimulated by a child. For example, the grandfather who bounces his grandchild on his lap could have an erection while doing so and learn to associate sexual feelings with the child. Or a brother hugging his sister may discover that her body feels good against his.

Male Sex Role Socialization Finkelhor pointed out that men are socialized to be sexually aroused by sexual activities independent of the interpersonal context. Hence, some men find it easier to disregard that the sex they are enjoying is with a child. In addition, men are socialized to be attracted to partners who are "smaller, younger, and less powerful than themselves" (Russell, 1984). Finally, fathers are socialized to be the controlling parent in families and use their power advantage to take what they want sexually from the children in the home.

History of Childhood Sexual Abuse Some fathers who sexually abuse their children were sexually abused themselves. Repeating the experience of their own victimization is said to be an expression of trying to control or master the hurt (Araji & Finkelhor, 1986). By being the aggressive parent, they are in control of what is happening (unlike the feeling of helplessness they experienced as a child).

Childhood Sexual Experiences Engaging in preadolescent sex play with younger children may be associated with subsequent sexual activity with children in adulthood. It is believed that such sex play in one's youth may weaken age and sex distinctions in adult life so that the man associates sex with children.

Patterns of Child Sexual Abuse

Next we look at patterns of child sexual abuse, including the stages of victimization and various relationships between the victim and the offender.

Stages of Victimization Child sexual abuse often develops through a set of predictable stages. Twenty-three child victims of sexual abuse revealed the stages that were involved in their victimization (Berliner & Conte, 1990):

1. Sexualization of the relationship. This stage took place gradually and began with the adults engaging in normal affectional contact or typical physical activities, such as bathing or wrestling. Gradually, these behaviors became more sexual.
2. Justification of the sexual contact. The victims were encouraged to perceive that the contact was not really sexual or to regard the sexual contact as appropriate.
3. Maintenance of the child's cooperation. In order to continue the sexual molestation with the child's cooperation, the adults threatened or intimidated the child. Other adults exploited the child's need to feel loved, valued, and cared for by an adult.

Father-Daughter Incest Incest, particularly parent-child incest, is an abuse of power and authority. The child is not in a position to consent to a sex act instigated by an adult. Almost 5% (4.5%) of 930 women in Russell's sample (1984) reported that they had been the victim of incestuous abuse by their biological or adoptive father. Stepfathers were more likely to be abusers than biological fathers. In the survey "17 percent, or 1 out of approximately every 6 women who had a stepfather as a principal figure in her childhood years, was sexually abused by him" (p. 251). For biological fathers the figures were much lower—"2 percent or 1 out of approximately every 40 women."

In another study of 535 pregnant and parenting individuals, 66% reported having experienced molestation; 14% of the perpetrators were the father, 21% the stepfather, and 9% the mother's boyfriend (Boyer, Fine, & Killpack, 1991).

The experience of a woman who, as a child, was forced to have sexual relations with her father is described below:

> I was around 6 years old when I was sexually abused by my father. He was not drinking at that time; therefore, he had a clear mind as to what he was doing. On looking back, it seemed so well planned. For some reason, my father wanted me to go with him to the woods behind our house to help him saw wood for the night. I went without any question. Once we got there, he looked around for a place to sit and wanted me to sit down with him. In doing so, he said, "Susan, I want you to do something for daddy." I said, "What's that, daddy?" He went on to explain that "I want you to lie down, and we are going to play mamma and daddy." Being a child, I said "okay," thinking it was going to be fun. I don't know what happened next because I can't remember if there was pain or whatever. I was threatened not to tell, and remembering how he beat my mother, I didn't want the same treatment. It happened approximately two other times.

> I remember not liking this at all. Since I couldn't tell mama, I came to the conclusion it was wrong and I was not going to let it happen again.
>
> But what could I do? Until age 18, I was constantly on the run, hiding from him when I had to stay home alone with him, staying out of his way so he wouldn't touch me by hiding in the corn fields all day long, under the house, in the barns, and so on, until my mother got home, then getting punished by her for not doing the chores she had assigned to me that day. It was a miserable life growing up in that environment. (Authors' files)

Factors contributing to father-daughter incest include extreme paternal dominance (the daughter learns to be obedient to her father), maternal disability (the mother ceases to function as an emotional and sexual partner for the husband), and imposition of the mothering role on the oldest daughter (she becomes responsible for housework and child care). An added consequence of the oldest daughter taking over the role of the mother is her belief that she is responsible for keeping the family together. This implies not only doing what the father wants but keeping it a secret since she or her father will be expelled from the family for disclosure (Herman, 1981).

My father was a handsome, intelligent man. He served as president of the Denver Area Boy Scout Council and helped establish Denver's Cleo Wallace Village for Handicapped Children. But there was another—secret—side to him. From the time I was 5 until I was 18 and moved away to college, my father sexually violated me.

Marilyn Van Derbur
Former Miss America

CONSIDERATION: Although some fathers may force themselves on their daughters (as in the example of the six-year-old girl described above), incest may begin by affectionate cuddling between father and daughter. The father's motives may be sexual; his daughter's are typically nonsexual. Indeed, the daughter is often unaware of any sexual connotations of her behavior; her motive is to feel acceptance and love from her father. Ambivalent feelings often result:

> My daddy never touched me unless he wanted to have me play with his genitals. I didn't like touching him there, but he was affectionate to me and told me how pretty I was. I was really mixed up about the whole thing. (Authors' files)

Because of her ambivalence, the daughter may continue to participate in sexual activity with her father. Not only may she derive attention and affection from the relationship, but she may also develop a sense of power over her father. As she grows older, she may even demand gifts in exchange for her silence.

CONSIDERATION: What does the mother do when she finds out her husband has been molesting their daughter? In a study of 43 mothers whose daughters were sexually abused by their fathers, 56% sided with their daughters and rejected their mates, 9% denied the incest and took no action, and 35% sided with their mates at the expense of their daughters (Myer, 1985). The latter could have occurred because they believed their daughter was lying, they did not want to threaten the marriage, or they wanted to drive the daughter out of the family.

Mother-Son Incest Incest between mothers and sons occurs less frequently than father-daughter incest (Marvasti, 1986). It rarely includes intercourse but is usually confined to various stimulating behaviors. The mother may continue to bathe her son long after he is capable of caring for himself, during which time she stimulates him sexually. Later, she may stimulate her son to ejaculation. The mother may also sleep with her son. Although no specific sexual contact may occur, she may sleep in the nude; this behavior is provocative as well as stimulating. Marvasti (1986) reported the following case history:

> A white female in her mid-twenties with a past history of sexual victimization by her father was divorced and had a two-year-old son. She admitted to touching her son's penis, while masturbating herself. (p. 67)

Sibling Incest One of the most common and least visible forms of incest occurs between siblings. Siblings are peers. Their incest may seem natural to them, and they may wonder why there is a taboo against it. In a survey of 796 undergraduates at six New England colleges and universities, 15% of the women and 10% of the men reported some type of sexual experience (usually fondling and touching of the genitals) involving a sibling (Finkelhor, 1980). These experiences are often consensual sex play in childhood, which did not involve exploitation. For this reason, it is commonly believed that sibling incest may be a nontraumatic event if it occurs under certain conditions: the siblings are young and of similar age, there is trust and no betrayal between them, the sexual behaviors are a result of natural curiosity and experimentation, and the children are not traumatized by disapproving adults who discover the activity (Forward & Buck, 1978). However, Canavan, Meyer, and Higgs (1992) noted that these conditions are sometimes not met and that sibling incest can be "a significant interpersonal boundary violation with potentially devastating long-term effects" (p. 136). They presented four case histories of sibling incest victims and emphasized that the victims felt powerless, angry, depressed, and anxious. Anne, one of the victims, described how her brother

> would usually offer her some kind of bribe (such as candy) to have sex and then threaten to tell mother how bad she had been if she refused. Anne believed that she, rather than her brother, would be punished for all that went on. Therefore, she never told; the secret persisted. Sexual intercourse occurred on a fairly regular basis until Anne became old enough to spend most of her free time outside the home. (p. 135)

In analyzing the effects of sibling incest, Canavan et al. (1992) commented:

> Such sexual experience creates an alternate path in sexual development; it is an atypical form of sexual expression which deviates from accepted norms. Individuals with this experience—whether male or female, 'perpetrator' or 'victim'—cannot discuss it with friends, family, or others. Children who experience incest learn that sexual expression can occur within the family. Both partners experience isolation, secrecy, shame, anger, and poor communication. (p. 141)

Other Relatives In Russell's study (1984) 60% of incestuous child abuse occurred outside the nuclear family. Abuse by uncles was slightly more prevalent than abuse by fathers. Nearly 5% of the 930 women reported abuse by an uncle, and 4.5% reported paternal abuse. Other familial perpetrators included first cousins (reported by 3% of respondents), brothers (2%), other relatives (2%), grandfathers (1%), in-laws (1%), and sisters and mothers (less than 0.5%).

Extrafamilial Abuse Although we have considered child sexual abuse within the family context, other forms of child sexual abuse include sexual abuse by adults in day-care contexts, sexual abuse by caretakers in institutional settings, sexual abuse by same- or opposite-sex peers, and sexual abuse by strangers.

In Russell's study (1984) the perpetrators of extrafamilial child sexual abuse were as follows: 42% acquaintances; 41% friends (of the family, of the respondent, dates, boyfriends); 15% strangers.

When the cases of incestuous and extrafamilial child sexual abuse were combined it was apparent that the majority of the offenders were *not* relatives: 60% known but unrelated to victims; 29% relatives; 11% total strangers.

When seriousness of offenses was considered, abusers outside the family were more likely to engage in the most serious types of abuse. When Russell examined reported abuse histories for women of varying ages she found that incestuous sexual abuse increased over the years 1916 to 1961, but extrafamilial abuse did not significantly increase or decrease.

Impact of Child Sexual Abuse

Child sexual abuse has serious, negative long-term consequences (Beitchman et al., 1992). The impact of father-daughter incest includes low self-esteem, difficulty in intimate relationships, and repeated victimization (Herman, 1981). Low self-esteem results from repeatedly engaging in behavior society labels as bad. Difficulty in intimate relationships results from the generalization of negative feelings from the incestuous relationship to other relationships, and repeated victimization results from a feeling of entrapment and accommodation: the child feels trapped by her father's control and her only alternative is to accommodate to the situation.

CONSIDERATION: The age at which a child experiences sex abuse is relevant to the effects of the experience. Children who experience sex abuse between the ages of seven and 13, when they are old enough to be aware of cultural taboos, experience the highest incidence of psychopathology (Browne & Finkelhor, 1986). In addition, those women who had suffered forceful, prolonged, or highly intrusive sexual abuse (penetration) or who had been abused by their fathers or stepfathers were the most likely to report long-lasting negative effects of incest (Herman, Russell, & Trocki, 1986; Beitchman et al., 1992).

Two researchers (Morrow & Sorell, 1989) studied adolescent girls who had been sexually abused and observed that the most devastating effects occurred when the sexual behavior was intercourse. Not only are sexually abused girls more likely to have a teenage pregnancy (Boyer et al., 1991), they are likely to have lower self-esteem, higher levels of depression, and greater numbers of antisocial (e.g., running away from home, illegal drug use) and self-injurious (e.g., attempted suicide) behaviors. "This finding supports the contention that sexual intercourse in a tabooed incestuous relationship, which is likely to involve the loss of virginity, is viewed as extremely negative by adolescent incest victims" (p. 683).

Gale, Thompson, and Thomas (1988) observed that sexual abuse is often accompanied by anxiety, depression, and inappropriate sexual behavior (aggressive sexual behavior, such as fellatio, insertion of objects into the rectum, and attempted forcible intercourse with other children). Fear, guilt, shame, sleep disturbances, eating disorders, and adolescent pregnancy have also been associated with child sexual abuse (Browne & Finkelhor, 1986). Adolescents who are sexually abused are more likely to make bad grades, be truant, run away from home, and marry early (Browne & Finkelhor, 1986).

Case studies of eight adult men who were molested as children by their nonpsychotic mothers revealed several problems the men had as adults. These problems included difficulty establishing intimate relationships with significant others (100%), depression (88%), and substance abuse (63%) (Krug, 1989). Elliott and Briere (1992), in their review of the literature, observed that abused males develop negative self-perceptions, anxiety disorders, sleep and eating disturbances, and gastrointestinal problems. They further noted an increased incidence of sexual dysfunctions in the form of decreased sexual desire, early ejaculation, and/or anorgasmia.

Boys who are sexually abused by men (including relatives) also tend to develop concerns about their sexual identities for years afterwards. Myers (1989) described a man who had been victimized as a child and developed a "profound and unrelenting homophobia way out of proportion to social norms and adopted hypermasculine behavior in his community including a 'tough guy image,' excessive drinking, frequent fighting and brawls, and aggressive behavior toward women" (p. 213).

Both women and men who were sexually abused as children experience a set of symptoms that fit the diagnosis of posttraumatic stress disorder. (Edwards, 1989). Sexually abused children also experience sleep disturbances, depression, and anxiety (Goodwin, 1988), as well as adult sexual fantasies with a theme of being under someone's control (Gold, 1991).

Summit (1983) identified a child sexual abuse accommodation syndrome that characterizes what children experience as victims of incest. Children are threatened into secrecy and feel entrapped and helpless with no other choice other than to accomodate to the situation. Disclosure of the incest is delayed and often disbelieved by the non–offending parent. Being disbelieved by the mother and feeling the extreme impending disorganization of the family, the child usually retracts the allegations of abuse. Hence, in the case of father-daughter incest, "unless there is immediate support for the child and immediate intervention to force responsibility on the father, the girl will follow the normal course and retract her complaint" (p. 82). It is usually only when men are in treatment do they concede that the child told the truth (p. 190).

Long-term consequences of child sexual abuse are associated with various negative outcomes for adults. These include the following (Jackson, Calhoun, Amick, Madever, & Habif, 1990; Browne & Finkelhor, 1986): depression, low self-esteem, distorted body image, suicide attempts, sleep disturbances, eating disorders, substance abuse, sexual guilt, martial problems, a greater number of sexual partners, and abuse of their own children. When 344 male pedophiles were compared with men who had not been similarly convicted, the pedophiles were almost twice as likely to have been victims of child sexual abuse (Freund, Watson, & Dickey, 1990).

Whether brother-sister incest is a problem for siblings depends on a number of factors. If the siblings are young (four to eight), of the same age, have an isolated sexual episode, engage only in exploratory, nonintercourse behavior, and both consent to the behavior, there may be little to no harm. However, as we have noted, a change in any of these factors increases the chance that sibling incest may have negative consequences for the individual (depression) and her or his subsequent relationships (unsatisfying sexual relationships) (Canavan et al., 1992).

Treatment of Sexually Abused Children and Abusers

In this section, we follow a family from the time a child tells someone of the abuse until the time the family completes treatment. Father-daughter sexual abuse is the type most frequently reported to professionals; abuse by fathers and father substitutes constituted 62% of *reported* cases (Finkelhor, 1986). Therefore, we will follow the case of a girl who tells a school nurse or counselor that she is being sexually molested by her father. The counselor calls the designated child protection agency to report the suspected abuse. The child protection agency will probably involve the local law enforcement agency and an officer may be sent to obtain an initial statement from the girl. If the community has an interdisciplinary child abuse investigation team this reduces the number of times the child must be interviewed. If the investigation suggests there is sufficient evidence to warrant an arrest and referral to the district attorney for prosecution, the father is arrested and placed in jail or released on his own recognizance. Ideally, he is not allowed to make contact with the daughter or to return to the home until legal disposition of the case is completed and progress in therapy has been made.

Incest is viewed as a family problem in terms of assessment and intervention (McCarthy, 1990). Counseling begins immediately; the individuals are first seen alone and then as a family. The focus of the counseling is to open channels of communication between all family members and develop or reestablish trust between the husband and the wife. Another aspect of the program involves the confrontation between the father and the daughter in which the father apologizes and takes full responsibility for the sexual abuse (Herman, 1981).

Depending on the circumstances and the recommendation of the social worker, the father might face criminal proceedings. If he is convicted (usually for child molestation or statutory rape), a pre-sentencing evaluation may be completed in order to assess whether incarceration and/or treatment are indicated. He may be sent to prison or receive a suspended sentence if he agrees to participate in a treatment program of individual, group, and family counseling. Treatment is usually prescribed to last anywhere from 18 months to five years (Ballard, Williams, Horton, & Johnson, 1990).

CONSIDERATION: In discussing the emphasis on family therapy used in treating incestuous fathers, Finkelhor (1986) noted that some family analyses have exaggerated the role of family dynamics, especially the contribution of the mother to the child's abuse. Finkelhor recommended not limiting attention to the matrix of family dynamics. He observed that many incestuous abusers "have characteristics of pedophiles and other sex offenders who have a rather autonomous proclivity to abuse" (p. 56). Finkelhor cited data from a unique study in which abusers were given absolute confidentiality; 45% of incestuous abusers of girls were sexually involved with children outside their family. These findings suggest deviant arousal patterns which could not be adequately treated without individual and group work with the offender.

A resolution model for treating incest suggested by Orenchuk–Tomiuk, Matthey, and Christensen (1990) is described in Table 19.4.

Bass and Davis (1988) in their book *The Courage to Heal* noted that a basic step in healing from sex abuse is to have compassion for one's previous choices. "Even if you didn't make the wisest, healthiest choices, you took the options you saw at the time. And now you're making better choices. Focus on that" (p. 174). Lew (1990), in *Victims No Longer,* emphasized the importance of forgiving one's self:

> Without question, this is the most important need of all. As long as you continue to accept blame for what happened to you—as long as you buy any part of the lies that you have been told—the abuse is continuing. Although having been abused does not call for forgiveness of others, it is necessary for you to "forgive yourself." (p. 258)

Finally, help for sex abuse victims is available nationwide through Childhelp USA (1-800-422-4453).

TABLE 19.4 A Resolution Model for Treating Incest

Child

Beginning Stage

- feels totally responsible for the sex abuse and the stress to self and family
- exhibits denial, anxiety, and posttraumatic stress

Resolution Stage

- no longer feels responsible for the sex abuse
- accepts the fact that he or she was victimized
- most symptoms have subsided

Nonoffending Parent

Beginning Stage

- refuses to accept that sex abuse has occurred
- blames the child for the disclosure of the sex abuse
- refuses to be an ally for the child
- protects the offending parent

Resolution Stage

- accepts the fact that sex abuse occurred
- reinforces the child for disclosure
- becomes an ally for the child
- agrees to have the offending parent prosecuted

Offending Parent

Beginning Stage

- refuses to accept responsibility for the sex abuse
- does not view the child as a victim
- will not agree to treatment
- continues physical and verbal abuse

Resolution Stage

- accepts responsibility for the sex abuse
- accepts that the child was victimized
- agrees to treatment
- stops physical, verbal, and emotional abuse

Source: Adapted from Orenchuk-Tomiuk, N., Matthey, G., & Christensen, C. P. (1990). The resolution model: A comprehensive treatment framework in sexual abuse. *Child Welfare, 69,* 417–431. Used by permission.

Prevention of Child Sexual Abuse

Incest and sexual abuse of children are best prevented through using a number of measures (Daro, 1991). These include information on sex abuse and healthy sexuality provided for both teachers and children in the public schools at regular intervals, parenting classes to foster bonding between parents and children, and public awareness campaigns.

From a larger societal preventive perspective, Edwin Schur (1988) emphasized that traditional male gender role socialization may perpetuate child sexual abuse. Schur suggested that "our culture promotes sexual victimization of women and children when it encourages males to believe that they have over-powering sexual needs that must be met by whatever means available" (p. 173). Schur said that this belief, and the association of sexual conquest with masculinity, enables men

It is important for parents to show affection for their children in nonsexual ways.

to think of using women and children for their own sexual gratification. The implication here is that one way to discourage child sexual abuse is to change traditional notions of masculinity and male sexuality so that men take responsibility for their sexual behavior and respect the sexuality of women and children.

The Committee for Children (P.O. Box 15190, Wedgewood Station, Seattle, WA 98115; 206-322-5050) is an organization that helps children acquire specific knowledge and skills to protect themselves from sexual abuse. Through various presentations in the elementary schools, children are taught how to differentiate between appropriate and inappropriate touching by adults or siblings, to understand that it is OK to feel uncomfortable if they do not like the way someone else is touching them, to say "no" in potentially exploitative situations, and to tell other adults if the offending behavior occurs.

> Child abuse cases are serious and complex in nature and prosecution is neither the only solution nor a panacea. It does, however, recognize that children are as entitled to protection under the law as adults, and that offenders—whether parents, other caretakers, or strangers—are accountable for their behavior.
>
> *James Peters*
> *Janet Dinsmore*
> *Patricia Toth*

CONSIDERATION: In spite of the worthwhile goals of this and other preventive programs, Reppucci and Haugaard (1989) questioned whether preschool children are capable of conceptualizing sex abuse, discriminating what is and isn't abuse, and being assertive where indicated. Indeed, there is no evidence to date that programs have accomplished the goal of preventing child sexual abuse (Tharinger et al., 1988). Furthermore, prevention programs may have unwanted negative side effects, such as making children feel uncomfortable with nonsexual contact (e.g., tickling) with their parents and teaching them that "sexuality is essentially secretive, negative, and even dangerous" (p. 629).

One aspect of prevention programs that may be inadvertently effective is the increased fear perpetrators may have that children will tell on them if they engage in sexual behavior with them (Reppucci & Haugaard, 1989). However, some men also report that fear of being accused of child sexual abuse prevents them from engaging in nonsexual physical affection with children.

Sexual Harassment in the Workplace

Sexual harassment is another form of sex abuse. As noted earlier, sexual harassment became a nationwide issue with the charge made by Anita F. Hill that Clarence Thomas, Supreme Court nominee, sexually harassed her when she worked in his office. While some critics feared the hearings would make women afraid to come forward with reports of harassment, others hailed them as "a nationwide consciousness–raising session" (Smolowe, 1992, p. 56). In this section, we look at sexual harassment in the workplace, including academic settings.

Prevalence and Incidence of Sexual Harassment

Sexual harassment studies have also been conducted at various colleges and universities (Mazer & Percival, 1989; Allen & Okawa, 1987; Glaser & Thorpe, 1986). Depending on how strict the definition of sexual harassment is, between 12% and 90% of students report having experienced sexual harassment. But what is sexual harassment?

Definition of Sexual Harassment

Sexual harassment is difficult to define. Its meanings range from telling a sexual joke to date rape (Bremer, Moore, & Bildersee, 1991; Mazer & Percival, 1989). (Anita Hill, in her charge of sexual harassment, said that Judge Thomas, who vehemently denied the charges, described his sexual interests and detailed scenes from pornographic movies to her.)

NATIONAL DATA: Forty-two percent of women in a national survey conducted by the U.S. Merit Systems Protection Board (1988) reported that they had been the target of sexual harassment during the previous 24 months. In another study, a telephone poll of 1,300 members of the 250,000-member National Association for Female Executives revealed that 53% had been sexually harassed or knew someone who had been (National Association for Female Executives, 1991).

CONSIDERATION: The definitions individuals use for sexual harassment are sometimes different from the definitions used by researchers who study sexual harassment. For example, it has been demonstrated that 8% of the female students and 6% of the male students in one study felt that they had been sexually harassed, whereas researchers judged 28% of the female students and 12% of the male students to have been sexually harassed using research definitions of harassment (Roscoe, Goodwin, Repp, & Rose, 1987).

Women are more likely to label various categories of behavior as sexual harassment (Bremer et al., 1991; Gutek, 1985; Rossi & Weber–Burdin, 1983). In addition, women with low self-esteem and egalitarian sex role orientations are much more likely to regard behaviors as sexually harassing than women with high self-esteem and traditional sex role orientations (Malovich & Stake, 1990). Finally, sexual harassment is more likely to be viewed as serious if the advances are physical and "accompanied by threats of invoking sanctions in the event of noncompliance" (Rossi & Weber-Burdin, 1983, p. 157).

In this text, we define **sexual harassment** as unwanted sexual comments or behaviors which affect one's performance at work or at school. The behaviors must be defined by the harassee as unwanted in the sense of feeling coerced into such sexual situations (York, 1989).

Theories of Sexual Harassment

One of the most frequently mentioned causes of sexual harassment in the workplace is sex role spillover (Gutek, 1985). This occurs when gender-based expectations about behavior are carried over from other domains into the workplace. For example, sex role spillover occurs when a female employee is expected to be more nurturant than a male employee in the same position or a female employee is expected to be a sex object.

Finally, sexual harassment may be viewed as an expression of men keeping women in a subordinate economic position by requiring that they play by men's rules or forfeit advancement. For example, the woman who does not laugh at or tell sex jokes may suddenly discover that she is no longer needed as an employee (Russell, 1984).

CONSIDERATION: It is assumed that most sexual harassment results from those in positions of authority over the individual. However, in a study of 618 students, faculty, administrators, and support staff, the respondents reported more sexual harassment from peers than from bosses (Bremer et al., 1991).

Consequences of Sexual Harassment

Individuals experiencing sexual harassment complain of depression, loss of weight, sleep disturbances, mood changes, decreased concentration, fear, and physical illness (Hamilton, Alagna, King, & Lloyd, 1987). Sexual harassment also results in employees having lower work satisfaction (Kissman, 1990), resigning, asking for transfers, and having less commitment to the organization for which they work. Ten percent of the female employees and 1% of the male employees in the Gutek (1985) study reported that they quit their job because they were sexually harassed; 5% and 0.2%, respectively, asked for a transfer.

Saroja (1990) looked at how female postgraduate students were affected by being sexually harassed by male students. Saroja found that students who were sexually harassed were more likely to make lower grades in their internship and to drop out of school. Allen and Okawa (1987) studied the impact of sexual harassment at the University of Illinois and identified the following specific effects on students:

- 74% avoided the person doing the harassing
- 56% experienced strong emotions
- 20% reported negative feelings about self
- 19% had impaired academic performance
- 14% altered their academic or career plans
- 4% developed physical problems or symptoms

Responses to Sexual Harassment

As noted above, the most frequent response to sexual harassment is to avoid the person doing the harassing. Maypole (1986) noted that women choose to delay or diffuse the conflict as their primary response. Few report the harasser to a higher authority, and even fewer (2% to 3%) file a formal complaint (Riger, 1991). Women who report sexual harassment tend to have a feminist ideology, regard the specific behavior as very offensive, and consider its frequency intolerable (Brooks & Perot, 1991). Although the Equal Employment Opportunity Commission logged a 50% increase in harassment complaints over the previous year, few of those complaints were actually filed as cases. However, there is a growing sentiment that workplace harassment should not be tolerated, as evidenced by the Pentagon's rebuke of Navy investigators for not taking seriously women's reports of abuse during the Tailhook Convention (Smolowe, 1992).

CONSIDERATION: Anita Hill gave the following reason for not charging Clarence Thomas with sexual harassment several years before she did so in the Senate confirmation hearings: "I was aware . . . that telling at any point in my career could adversely affect my future career. And I did not want, early on, to burn all the bridges to the EEOC [Equal Employment Opportunity Commission]" (Boo, 1991, p. 46).

Prevention of Sexual Harassment

How can sexual harassment in the workplace and academic settings be eliminated if it stems from pervasive gender role inequality that is ingrained in our society? Gutek (1985) suggested that "the workplace may be a more manageable area for change than society at large" (p. 18). Specifically, Gutek recommended that non-sexist managerial role models are more effective than rules and regulations regarding sexual harassment. "Managers who will not tolerate or condone obscene remarks, sexual propositions, and the like can substantially reduce the amount of sexual harassment in the workplace" (p. 171).

Riger (1991) emphasized that the key to reducing sexual harassment is equal opportunity for women. Women who work in environments in which they are not treated as equals not only suffer more harassment but also fear reprisal if they cry foul. How a person may respond to being sexually harassed is addressed in the Choices section at the end of the chapter.

Individuals disagree over what constitutes sexual harassment.

Commercial Uses and Abuses of Sexuality

As noted at the beginning of this chapter, sex abuse may be viewed on a continuum from rape and child sexual abuse to prostitution and pornography. The latter represent more controversial and less direct forms of sex abuse. While some argue that both using sex to sell and selling sex are legitimate ways of generating income, others argue that these commercial enterprises have the capacity to trap, demean, exploit, and abuse those who become involved in them. Are commercial uses of sex a means of sexual and expressive freedom or profiteering which traffics in human beings?

> The swimsuit issue of *Sports Illustrated* pretends to be about swimwear and travel. In fact, it is a commercially successful form of voyeurism.
>
> *Marty Klein*

CONSIDERATION: Although we will focus on the commercial uses of sexuality in regard to prostitution and pornography, a more pervasive example of sex and money is in advertising. That sex sells is indisputable. Our attention is regularly grabbed by references to sex as a means to sell products. Seminudity is used to attract our attention in magazine ads, billboards, movies, and television. Indeed, the annual swimsuit issue of *Sports Illustrated* has one purpose only—to boost sales.

Next we discuss prostitution and pornography. While these are clearly commercial uses of sexuality, there is controversy regarding the degree to which they represent abuses of sexuality.

Prostitution

> When a guy goes to a hooker, he's not paying her for sex, he's paying her to leave.
>
> *Unknown*

Prostitution is the exchange of sexual services for money. Although we will discuss male prostitution later in this chapter, most prostitutes are women who primarily provide oral sex and intercourse to men for money.

While most people would agree that rape, child sexual abuse, and sexual harassment are abuses of sexuality, opinion is divided on prostitution. Proponents of the prostitution-as-abuse perspective state that prostitutes are physically and morally exploited. Prostitutes are viewed as having limited economic and social alternatives and would escape the profession if provided the opportunity. Anthony (1992) observed that prostitution only contributes to the dehumanization, debasement, and humiliation of women.

In opposition, many prostitutes say that their occupation is simply a way of earning an income and argue that they are abused by the courts and the police who harass them. COYOTE, an acronym for Call Off Your Old Tired Ethics, was formed in San Francisco by an ex-prostitute, Margo St. James. COYOTE has promoted the idea of a prostitutes' union to change the public image of prostitutes and the moral and legal discrimination to which they are subjected. Sexual liberals also emphasize that prostitution is and should be a career choice for women (Anthony, 1992).

CONSIDERATION: The image of prostitution has not always been negative. During the nineteenth and early twentieth centuries, many young working-class women in both Britain and the United States moved in and out of prostitution without being stigmatized or segregated from the rest of society (Rosen, 1982).

Prostitution helps people acquire money, power, and pleasure that would otherwise be unattainable.

Sevgi Aral
King Holmes

As a psychotherapist who works with what I call "sex industry survivors," I can confirm that prostitution is hardly a "choice." All of these women are incest and molestation victims who fought to transform their childhood powerlessness into power, independence, and control.

Rita Belton

Becoming a Prostitute Unlike setting out to be a schoolteacher or physician, few women grow up with the goal of becoming a prostitute. Rather, they become economically destitute, drift into the role, and discover that they have few alternatives. Several factors, when combined, may contribute to becoming a prostitute.

Childhood Sexual Abuse and Rape Women who have been sexually abused as children have an increased risk for becoming involved in prostitution (Simmons & Whitbeck, 1991). Various factors may be involved in this association—limited emotional attachments, limited adult supervision, and the development of a negative self-concept. Regarding the latter, being a victim of childhood sex abuse or rape often creates feelings of shame, guilt, and negative feelings about one's self. Such feelings may lead to "disruptive, rebellious behavior," including prostitution (James, 1978).

Early Sexual Activity The average age of first intercourse for the 30 prostitutes in one study was 13.5 (Davis, 1978). This is about three years earlier than is usual for a random sample of women (Zelnik & Shah, 1983).

Lack of Family Ties High rates of divorce, separation, desertion, and alcoholism also seem to characterize the background of prostitutes. Many report having been brought up in foster homes or shuffled from home to home. Strong parental relationships seem to be lacking. The girl often views home as a place to escape from. Being a runaway is strongly associated with being a prostitute. The mean age at which the women in the James (1978) study left home permanently was 16.25 years (p. 193).

Peer Influence Escaping from home means going somewhere, usually with friends. These friends are also escaping from an unhappy home environment, have dropped out of school, and have no job and no source of income. One woman explained that her boyfriend encouraged her to turn her first trick.

> I was on the run . . . I didn't get up until 3 P.M. I was staying with my boyfriend. He was planning to set me up [for prostitution] . . . it was kind of like prearranged for me. Crazy! We were staying in a hotel with lots of pimps, prostitutes and faggots living there. The first time was at the World's Series. I was dressed like a normal teenager. (James, 1978, p. 204)

I am a prostitute . . . I have never been raped, sexually abused, or physically abused as a child. I choose to prostitute because I like the money and the work.

Gabrielle

Quick Money After the first experience, sometimes just for fun, to please her boyfriend, or because "everyone else is doing it," the woman continues to turn tricks, and the connection between the behavior and the money is made. Sex for fun becomes sex for quick money. Since no other job is available to the woman in which she can earn so much so quickly, she finds it easy to continue.

Drug Addiction Some individuals develop an expensive drug dependence and trade sex for drugs. Others learn that prostitution is a way to earn quick money that can be used to buy drugs. Sometimes a cycle develops whereby the person has sex for money to buy drugs, which keeps inhibitions and self-esteem low so as to continue prostitution to earn more money to buy more drugs.

The Pimp Connection A **pimp** finds men for a prostitute, pays off the police, provides companionship for the woman, and, in general, looks after her. In exchange, he demands that she turn over the majority of her earnings to him each night. A relationship with a pimp is usually a sign that the woman has "arrived" at being a prostitute. The boyfriend referred to by the prostitutes is often a pimp who has several women working for him. Pimps' techniques for getting their women to hustle tricks vary. Some feign love for them; others beat them when they fail to meet their quotas. The woman stays with the pimp partly because she is lonely and he is the one stable figure in her environment. The "johns" come and go, but the pimp is there. He is not only her manager and protector, but her lover and companion. In some cases, he may be her husband and the father of her children.

Most prostitutes are trapped in a life-style that is dangerous and unrewarding. One prostitute said:

> It is degrading . . . you develop a total hatred for yourself for being so low, filthy, and dirty. You're like a slave, but like most slaves you don't know how to get out. The horror of opening your eyes and finding someone on top of you . . . it's hard to forget the faces and the smells. Especially the smells . . . . The only thing to do is not feel anything and pretend you don't care. By now I don't think I'm even pretending. I don't think I care about anything. (Silbert, 1989, p. 221)

I always say that being a comedian is like being a hooker. It's humiliating and degrading, but it only lasts 20 minutes and you get $100.

Jay Leno

Customers of Prostitutes In a study of men who went to massage parlors, the researchers reported that the typical customer was 35 to 40 years old, temporarily separated from his spouse or female companion, and away from home (Bryant & Palmer, 1977). They were businessmen or traveling salesmen and clearly middle class.

Men who seek a prostitute may do so for a number of reasons, including the desire for a new experience, curiosity about what a sexual experience with a pros-

Life is treacherous for these two runaways living under a freeway in Hollywood, California. Prostitution is regarded as abuse because sometimes individuals, such as the boy holding the sign in this picture, have no choice.

titute is like, the desire for a sexual companion who will engage in sexual behavior that the client's usual sexual partner is unwilling to do, and as an antidote to boredom. Still other men cannot attract a woman because of their age, looks, deformity, or lack of social skills.

CONSIDERATION: The fact that most men who hire prostitutes are not charged with illegal behavior suggests that women as prostitutes are discriminated against by law enforcement agencies. James (1978) noted that 30% of most women in jail are there because of prostitution statute violations. However, men in jail for participation in "illegal" prostitution are virtually nonexistent.

Male Prostitutes Although the term "prostitute" is most often thought of as referring to women, some men also provide sex for money.

Male prostitutes serving male customers are sometimes known as **hustlers.** They frequent gay bars and homosexual baths and walk the streets in large cities searching for business. Others may be a "kept boy" (supported by a wealthy man) or a "call boy" (similar to a call girl) or work in a homosexual brothel disguised as a massage parlor. Other male prostitutes may be cross-dressers and operate next to female prostitutes or young boys involved in sex rings controlled by pimps.

Gigolos are male prostitutes for women. They are usually attractive young men who serve as companions, escorts, or sex partners to the women who hire them. They operate out of escort agencies, dance studios, and massage parlors. Some gigolos are "kept men" (put on full salary) by wealthy middle-aged and upper-class women.

Male prostitutes report backgrounds similar to those of female prostitutes. They report

> troubled family histories. They describe a great deal of parental fighting, drinking, and emotional abuse or neglect. Their relationships with their families are poor, and they describe themselves, as did the women, as isolated among their peers . . . . Over three-quarters of the males involved in hustling reported that they were victims of juvenile sexual abuse. Half of these were involved in incest (Silbert, 1989, p. 222).

Two researchers (Pleak & Meyer-Bahlburg, 1990) interviewed 50 male prostitutes (aged from 14 to 27) in Manhattan. The average number of lifetime partners was 604 (one respondent reported 1,057 encounters). The sexual behaviors during these encounters included masturbation (86%), fellatio (71%), and anal intercourse (17%). With fellatio, the prostitute fellated the client in 22% of the cases. With anal intercourse, the prostitute was the recipient in 96% of the cases (Pleak & Meyer-Bahlburg, 1990).

The use of the condom was more widespread than the researchers had anticipated. When fellating a customer, 60% of the prostitutes reported using a condom. When receiving anal sex from a customer, 85% reported requiring their partner to use a condom.

Pornography

Pornography comes from the Greek words *porne* ("prostitute") and *grapheim* ("to write") and originally meant "stories of prostitutes." Steinem (1983) commented that the term "pornography" "is about an imbalance of male-female power that allows and even requires sex to be used as a form of aggression" (p. 222). In contrast, Steinem emphasized that **erotica** comes from the Greek word *eros* for sexual desire or passionate love and "contains the idea of love, positive choice, and the yearning for a particular person" (p. 222).

What turns me on is erotic: what turns you on is pornographic.

R. Shea

> The problem is that there is so little erotica. Women have rarely been free enough to pursue erotic pleasure in our own lives, much less to create it in the world of film, magazines, art, books, television, and popular culture—all the areas of communication we rarely control. Very few male authors and filmmakers have been able to escape society's message of what a man should do, much less to imagine their way into the identity of a woman. Some women and men are trying to portray equal and erotic sex, but it is still not a part of popular culture. (p. 222)

My boyfriend said, "I buy *Playboy* to read the articles" so I said, "I go to the mall to listen to the music."

Rita Rudner

The written word is only one form of pornography. Others include any photograph, music, or video that is primarily sexually explicit and designed to arouse or excite a person sexually. Regarding adult videos, researchers Ritts and Engbretson (1991) assessed the degree to which 44 male and 76 female college students had chosen to experience an adult video and how they felt about such videos being legally available for rental. Ninety-five percent of the men and 70% of the women reported that they had chosen to view adult or X-rated videos available in adult bookstores. Almost three-fourths of the men (73%) and half (52%) of the women felt that they should be available for rental. More women than men thought that such viewing was immoral (31% versus 23%).

CONSIDERATION: For individuals who choose to be selective in their adult video viewing, Robert Rimmer (1991) has summarized the plots and highlighted special features of over 1,200 "adult" films produced between 1986 and 1991. Other films made earlier but only recently available on videotape are also featured. In addition, Femme Distribution Inc. is a feminist company specializing in X-rated videos featuring safer sex between equal lovers with mutual interest.

Legal Definition of Obscenity While some people in our society enjoy looking at pictures of nude bodies and sexually explicit scenes, others regard them as offensive and obscene. In order for a group of citizens to close down an adult bookstore or movie theater, they must prove that the materials sold are obscene. There are three criteria for obscenity. First, the dominant theme of the material must appeal to a prurient (literally, "to itch") interest in sex. Such interest implies that the material is sexually arousing in a lewd way. Second, the material must be patently offensive to the community. In general, a community can dictate what its standards are regarding the sale, display, and distribution of sexual materials.

CONSIDERATION: Communities are sometimes quick to ban X-rated videos even though violence is emphasized in only 10% of the cases. However, these same communities allow such films as *Sleepwalkers* (a Stephen King film) to play without notice. This 1992 R-rated film contains incest (between a 17-year-old and his voluptuous mother), attempted date rape, violence against and murder of the 17-year-old's homeroom teacher, violence against and murder of a police officer who stopped the 17-year-old for speeding, and the senseless trapping and killing of numerous cats. Indeed, 90% of R- and GP-rated films contain violence. If communities are uncomfortable with violence, they might consider choosing to question the widespread availability of most R- and PG-rated films, which have violent content, rather than emphasize the violence that less often occurs in pornography.

The third criterion for obscenity is that the sexual material must have no redeeming social value. If the material can be viewed as entertaining or educational (e.g., helps couples communicate), a case can be made for its social value, and a small degree of social value can outweigh prurience and offensiveness. The Better Sex Video Series (telephone 800-232-6612) is an example of videos with explicit sexual content that would likely be viewed as having "socially redeeming value."

CONSIDERATION: Money (1988) noted that pornography has earned its socially redeeming value in its use by gays in what has become known as "jack-off" or "jerk-off clubs." "At club meetings, members were free to socialize in conventional ways, as well as to assemble in a designated area where they could watch videotapes of gay men explicitly engaged in sex, while simultaneously watching one another engaging in hand practice (masturbation), solo or in pairs" (p. 182). As an extension to the larger population, he suggested:

> It would be technologically feasible to have a safe-sex, AIDS-avoidance channel on every television set. Its programming would keep viewers updated on AIDS information and instruction .... The prime attraction of the channel for each target audience would be . . . to enable viewers of either sex to become virtuosos of hand practice, either solo or with a lover, but with no exchange of body fluids" (p. 182).

Studies of Pornography and U.S. Government Policy Recommendations The U.S. government has been involved in several studies of pornography.

U.S. Commission on Obscenity and Pornography To gain more perspective on the pornography issue, President Lyndon Johnson appointed in 1967 a Commission on Obscenity and Pornography to study the effects of sexually explicit materials. The commission recommended that all federal, state, and local legislation prohibiting the sale, exhibition, and distribution of sexual material to adults be repealed. The commission could find no evidence that explicit sexual material played a significant role in causing individual or social harm. On the contrary, it found that erotic materials were sought as entertainment and information and that exposure to such materials seemed to enhance sexual communication. More important, the commission felt that adult obscenity laws impinge on the right of free speech and

Sexually explicit adult videos are a billion dollar business.

communication and that the government should not try to legislate individual moral behavior. In spite of the commission's findings, the U.S. Senate and President Richard Nixon rejected the commission's recommendations.

Meese Commission on Pornography To update what was known about pornography, President Ronald Reagan called for the development of a new commission on pornography in 1985. In response, Attorney General Edwin Meese appointed an 11-member commission.

CONSIDERATION: Critics of the Meese commission argued that it was biased against pornography. Of the 11 members, six had "a clear antipornography bias" (Lynn, 1986, p. 1). Among these was Dr. James Dobson, the president of *Focus on the Family,* a conservative publication. In addition, of the 208 witnesses asked to testify at the commission, 77% advocated tighter controls over sexually explicit material (p. 3).

The Meese commission concluded that pornography is harmful to both individuals and society and called for more stringent law enforcement regulation. Linz, Donnerstein, and Penrod (1987) reviewed the same data considered by the Meese commission and found several "findings and recommendations incongruent with available research data" (p. 946). For example, the commission stated that substantial exposure to images that depict women in subordinate roles, women existing solely for the satisfaction of others, and women engaging in sexual behavior that most people would consider humiliating would lead to the following: (a) individuals would view rape as less serious, (b) rape victims would be seen as more responsible for their plight, and (c) men would be more likely to say that they would force women to engage in sexual practices. Examining the same data used by the commission, Linz, Donnerstein, and Penrod (1987) concluded, "we can find no consistent evidence for these specific conclusions" (p. 951).

Pornography is not about sex.
Gloria Steinem

The Meese commission also concluded that there is a causal relationship between exposure to sexually violent pornography and increased sexual aggression against women. Linz et al. (1987) noted that it is the violence in films and not the sexual content of films that is more related to aggression. As evidence, they noted that exposure to films showing aggression against women that were devoid of explicit sex produced more aggression against women than sexually explicit films that contained no violence or coercion (Linz, Donnerstein, & Penrod, 1985).

In his review of experimental studies conducted since the 1970 pornography commission Linz (1989) examined effects of exposure to sexually explicit materials on attitudes and perceptions about rape. He found that studies consistently showed exposure to violent (slasher) films results in less sensitivity toward rape victims.

> Most consistently, in long-term and short-term studies, negative effects (e.g., lessened sensitivity toward rape victims, greater acceptance of force in sexual encounters) emerge when subjects are exposed to portrayals of overt violence against women or when sex is fused with aggression. This is particularly the case with the so-called "slasher" films. Every study that has included a "slasher" condition has found antisocial effects resulting from exposure to these films. (p. 74)

While the Meese commission recommended legal curbing of the availability of pornography in general because of its presumed sexual aggression against women, Linz et al. (1987) recommended "educational programs that enable viewers to make wiser choices about the media to which they expose themselves" (p. 952). Such choices would involve less exposure to violent images, both sexual and nonsexual.

CONSIDERATION: The general theme of the Meese commission's report was that pornography is harmful to those exposed to it. A study published after the Meese commission's report supports its position. Zillmann and Bryant (1988) exposed 160 male and female students and nonstudents to videotapes featuring common, nonviolent pornography or innocuous content. Exposure was one hour a week for six consecutive weeks. The researchers reported that while exposure to pornography had no influence on the self-assessment of happiness and satisfaction outside the sexual realm, it strongly affected the self-assessment of the sexual experience. Subjects who had been exposed to pornography reported less satisfaction with their intimate partners' affection, physical appearance, and sexual performance. They also assigned more importance to sex without emotional involvement.

Surgeon General's Workshop on Pornography and Public Health U.S. Surgeon General C. Everett Koop asked Henry Hudson, the chair of the Meese commission, to be allowed to provide input to the commission on the issue of pornography. After being given approval, Koop convened a workshop of 19 specialists in the area of pornography in Arlington, Virginia, in the summer of 1986. As a result of the papers presented and the discussions, Koop (1987) observed that the participants reached a number of conclusions including the following:

1. Prolonged exposure to pornography results in people believing that less common sexual practices are more common than they are.
2. Pornography depicting sexual aggression as pleasurable to the victim increases the acceptance of the use of coercion in sexual relations.
3. Such acceptance may increase the chance of engaging in sexual aggression.
4. In laboratory studies measuring short-term effects, exposure to violent pornography increases punitive behavior toward women. In regard to this latter conclusion, Linz et al. (1987) noted, "What is conspicuously absent from the Surgeon General's summary is an endorsement of the view that exposure to sexually violent material leads to aggressive or assaultive behavior outside the confines of the laboratory" (p. 950).
5. Another conclusion of the Surgeon General's Workshop on Pornography was that "children and adolescents who participate in the production of pornography experience adverse, enduring effects" (p. 945). We now look at child pornography.

Child Pornography Pornography is an abuse of sexuality when those who become involved lack free choice. Such lack of free choice is particularly the case in juvenile or child pornography, one of the gravest forms of pornographic abuse. (In an attempt to prevent such exploitation of children by adults, Congress has passed legislation providing a maximum penalty of 15 years in prison and a fine of $15,000 for trafficking in child pornography.)

Also known as "kiddie porn," "child porn," and "chicken porn," juvenile and child pornography consists mainly of photos and films depicting children masturbating, performing fellatio, and having intercourse with adults.

Functions of Child Pornography Lanning and Burgess (1989) identified several functions of child pornography:

1. Sexual arousal and gratification of pedophiles. Were it not for the market created by pedophiles, child pornography would not exist. "They use child pornography the same way other people use adult pornography—to feed sexual fantasies" (p. 241).
2. Seduce children into posing. By showing children that other children appear on film and in books, children are lead to believe that the behavior is acceptable to their peers and that they can have fun participating in the activity.
3. Blackmail. Once a child allows himself or herself to be photographed, the evidence can be used to ensure silence. "Children are most afraid of pictures being shown to their friends" and the pedophile will use the threat as necessary (p. 241).
4. Medium of exchange. Pedophiles exchange photographs of children for phone numbers and photos of other children. "The younger the child and the more bizarre the acts, the greater the value of the pornography" (p. 241).
5. Profit. Individuals involved in the production and sale of child pornography may be primarily motivated by profit.

Effects on the Children Involved in Pornography Mimi Silbert (1989), president of Delancey Street (a self-help residential treatment center for various problems, including sexual abuse) provided data on 100 men and women who, as juveniles, were involved in making pornography (hard-core sex films, videos, and magazines). The median age at the time of their pornographic exploitation was 14; the ages ranged from six to 21.

Of the effects, Silbert (1989) commented, "Short and long term negative effects were apparent in terms of physical, behavioral, attitudinal, and emotional impact on the subjects" (p. 226). During the time they were being exploited, the victims reported being anxious, fearful, withdrawn, moody, and isolated. Many were clinically depressed, lost their appetite, and developed difficulty sleeping.

Other long-term effects include the development of "extremely negative self-concepts, sustained shame and anxiety, deep despair, inability to feel, hopelessness, and psychological paralysis" (Silbert, 1989, p. 229). One of the victims said:

> . . . I just don't think I can touch any girl. I don't even mean sex. I mean I can't love anyone good. I'm like an animal. Why would she want to have anything to do with me? (p. 229)

CHOICES

Among the choices in regard to sex abuse and the commercial uses of sex are deciding whether to encourage children to testify in court in child sex abuse cases, whether to confront sexual harassment, and whether to legalize or decriminalize prostitution.

Choose to Have Children Testify in Court in Cases of Alleged Child Sexual Abuse?

Robert Kelly was the owner and operator of the Little Rascals Day Care Center in Edenton, North Carolina. In the spring of 1992, he was found guilty on 99 counts of sexual abuse of the children in his center. Parents anguished over whether to subject their children to testifying in court, to cross-examination, and to the disruption of their schedules for the six-month trial. After the verdict was read, they sighed with relief that the man who had sexually abused their children had not been allowed to escape with impunity.

In a study by Burgess, Hartman, Kelley, Grant, & Gray (1990), parents whose children testified in trials against defendants charged with committing sexual abuse in day-care centers were compared with parents whose children were also alleged to have been sexually abused but who decided not to encourage their children to testify. The parents' motivation for encouraging their child to testify was "to create safety for their child as well as other children. Safety was defined in terms of the child feeling safe to know the perpetrator was 'locked up' and that the child would be believed and protected during testifying" (Burgess et al., 1990, p. 402). When parents who encouraged their children to testify were asked if they had made the right decision, 70% said "yes."

However, for some parents, the cost of their decision was high. Parents whose children testified presented higher symptoms of psychological distress than parents whose children did not testify. Such distress involved decreased income (legal expenses, time in court), job changes, alcohol or drug abuse, and separation or divorce (Burgess et al., 1990).

Peters, Dinsmore, & Toth (1989) emphasized the importance of prosecuting alleged child sexual abuse perpetuated by family members. Although the argument for not prosecuting is to "keep the family together," there are a number of reasons to pursue prosecution vigorously:

1. Criminal prosecution clearly establishes that children are innocent victims and that the perpetrators are solely responsible for their wrongful behavior.
2. Successful prosecutions educate the public and provide community visibility for the unacceptability of child sex abuse.
3. The court can order offenders into treatment programs to modify their deviant sexual interests.
4. Criminal prosecution gives offenders a criminal record that will follow them from state to state.

Peters et al. (1989) also noted that "in the great majority of cases that are criminally prosecuted, children do not have to testify at trial" (p. 657). But if they do, the benefits may far outweigh the discomfort for the children or the family.

Choose to Confront Sexual Harassment?

Aside from deciding to ignore sexual harassment, there are at least three choices available to the person who is a victim of sexual harassment—verbal, written, and institutional/legal. The verbal choice is to tell the person what behavior he or she is engaging in that you do not like and to ask the person to stop. Direct confrontation (as well as avoiding the person in the future) were successful methods of dealing with sexual harassment as reported by female professors who were sexually harassed by male students (Grauerholz, 1989).

If direct confrontation is not successful in terminating the harassment behav-

Continued

Continued

iors, a written statement of the concerns you expressed verbally is the next level of intervention. Such a letter details your perceptions of sexual harassment behaviors (with the dates of occurrence) and your account of the consequences (personal distress, depression, sleeplessness, and consideration of asking for a transfer or quitting). The letter should end with a statement of what you would like to happen in the future, for example, "I ask that our future interaction be formal and professional."

The letter should be sent immediately after it becomes clear that the person did not take seriously the verbal requests for change. If the desired behavior is not forthcoming, the letter can be used as evidence of intent to alert the offending person of the sexual harassment problem. Such use may be internal in the sense of inside the organization or external in terms of a formal complaint to the Equal Employment Opportunity Commission.

When 142 male and 100 female upper-division undergraduate students and 44 employed women were asked how they would react to being sexually harassed, ignoring or doing nothing, directly verbally confronting, and writing an internal report accounted for 60% of the overallr eactions (Terpstra & Baker, 1989). If ignoring or avoiding the harasser is not effective in resolving the problem, the choice not to pursue verbal, written, or legal redress is to risk continuation of the sexual harassment.

Many work settings and academic institutions have written sexual harassment policies and grievance procedures specifically designed to handle complaints. Large public schools are more likely to have sexual harassment grievance procedures than private schools (54% versus 38%) (Robertson, Dyer, & Campbell, 1988). One of the choices you may make is to become informed about the policies and options for handling a grievance at your school or work site. In the University of Illinois at Urbana-Champaign study (Allen & Okawa, 1987) 19% of sexually harassed women did not know that sexual harassment is prohibited by campus policy. Only 7% of respondents correctly identified the university offices designated to help with sexual harassment. A study to evaluate awareness of the sexual harassment policy at Lewis and Clark College (Carlson & Tibbets, 1988) found that 83% of the undergraduates had not read the policy.

In academic settings usually a written complaint must be obtained to initiate a formal grievance mechanism. Institutional responses to complaints range from giving advice to the complainant, helping the complainant confront the offender in person or through a third party, to an official investigation and hearing. A verbal warning by a supervisor is the most frequent type of sanction imposed; dismissal or forced resignation of an offender are rare. Informal solutions are most often used, and when appropriate, students may be helped to switch classes, change members on a dissertation committee, or get a tuition refund without enduring a lengthy formal grievance procedure (Robertson et al., 1988).

One consideration in choosing to file a complaint is the possibility of countercharges being filed by the alleged offender. For example, at one school a man accused of rape filed a defamation of character charge against his accuser (Hughes & Sandler, undated).

Finally, you may wish to consider legal remedies. Sexual harassment may be litigated as unlawful sex discrimination, as a recoverable civil wrong, or as a crime. The Women's Legal Defense Fund offers an informative pamphlet, "Legal Remedies for Sexual Harassment." (The address is 2000 P Street, NW, Suite 400, Washington, DC 20036.)

Choose to Legalize or Decriminalize Prostitution?

Whether prostitution should be legalized or decriminalized is an unresolved choice among researchers, law enforcement officials, politicians, and prostitutes (Rio, 1991).

Arguments for the legalization of prostitution in the United States are that it would permit the taxation of the billions of currently untaxed dollars spent on prostitution, help control and regulate the criminal activity associated with prostitution, prevent teenage prostitution, and eliminate abuse by pimps and clients since prostitutes could report such abuse. Furthermore, since prostitution is common way that HIV is transmitted, legalization would permit greater control.

Prostitution has been legalized in some districts in Nevada and in West Germany. In West Germany, the women work in large dormitories and are checked regularly by a physician for sexually transmissible diseases. Clients make their selection by observing the available women on closed-circuit TV monitors. "These bordellos have been successful in creating a safe and healthy environment both for prostitutes and clients" (Rio, 1991, p. 214).

There is a negative side to legalization. In Nevada, legal prostitutes cannot choose their customers but must service whomever comes in the door. They also feel that the law interferes with their private lives. For example, they can go to town only during certain hours and cannot appear in the company of a client in a restaurant. The stigmatization of the profession through fingerprinting and registration makes it difficult for prostitutes to leave prostitution and enter another profession.

One researcher (James, 1976) observed that although reducing the abuses of prostitution can begin by a change in our laws, it is also dependent on equality in social and economic relationships. "It is critical that males reject the attitude that sex is purchasable and that society provide women with viable alternatives. Both the clientele and the occupation are dependent upon existing, economic, social, and sexual values in our society" (p. 122).

SUMMARY

1. Information about the prevalence and incidence of rape and sexual assault is obtained through official statistics of rapes reported to the police, victimization surveys, and self-report offender surveys. One estimate suggests that for every rape that is reported, three to ten are committed but not reported. Studies differ in their estimates of the prevalence and incidence of rape, in part, because they involve different samples, use different criteria to identify rape, and use different research methods.
2. Patterns of rape include the following: a) women age 16 to 24 are more likely to be raped than other women; and b) most rapes occur at night and in the victim's home. A rape perpetrator may be a stranger, an acquaintance (including a dating partner), or a cohabitating or marital partner. Rapes may be committed by individuals or gangs. The majority of rapes are committed by someone the victim knows.
3. Theories that attempt to explain why rape occurs include evolutionary and biological theories, psychopathological theory, feminist theory, and social learning theory.
4. Rape victims may experience a variety of reactions, including helplessness and vulnerability, rage, depression, self-blame, sexual dysfunctions, nightmares, flashbacks, and the inability to trust. The terms "rape trauma syndrome" and "post traumatic stress disorder" have been used to describe the acute and persistent presence of these reactions and symptoms of the traumatic experience of rape. In addition, victims of rape may be physically injured during the rape and may experience permanent physical and emotional damage from such injury.
5. Treatment for the rape survivor may involve crisis counseling and long-term therapy. A variety of treatment modalities used to help rape victims are outlined in the chapter. Treatment modalities for rape perpetrators are also described in the chapter. The majority of sex offenders never receive treatment because a) the rape or sexual assault is not reported, b) the rapist is not caught, or c) the rapist is not convicted.
6. Rape prevention may be achieved by intervention at three levels: a) societal responsibility (educate people to reduce acceptance of rape supportive beliefs and interpersonal violence), b) avoidance of high-risk situations and c) self-protection during confrontation by a (potential) rapist.
7. Sexual abuse of children occurs in both intrafamilial and extrafamilial contexts. Various theories that attempt to explain why child sexual abuse occurs are reviewed in the chapter.

   Child sexual abuse develops in stages—sexualization of the relationship, justification of the sexual contact, and maintenance of the child's cooperation. A child may be sexually abused by a parent or stepparent, sibling, uncle or aunt, grandparent, or cousin. A child may also be sexually abused by an acquaintance, friend, or stranger.

   Child sexual abuse may have serious, negative long-term consequences for the victim, including low self-esteem, difficulty in intimate relationships, depression, antisocial and self-injurious behavior (such as substance abuse), anxiety, fear, guilt, shame, sleep disturbances, eating disorders, and sexual dysfunctions as adults. Treatments for sexually abused children and abusers are described in the chapter.

8. Sexual harassment in the workplace and in academic settings is another form of sexual abuse. Individuals and researchers define sexual harassment in a variety of ways. Various theories that attempt to explain why sexual harassment occurs are described in the chapter.

   Victims of sexual harassment may experience a variety of reactions, including depression, decreased concentration, fear, lower work satisfaction, anger and other strong emotions, and impaired academic performance. The victim may confront the offender by direct confrontation, writing a letter asking the harassing behavior to stop, or initiating a formal grievance.
9. Commercial uses of sexuality include stripping, sex in advertising and media, prostitution, and pornography. There is controversy over the degree to which these commercial uses of sexuality also represent abuses of sexuality.
10. Children who testify in court in child sexual abuse cases help to prevent subsequent abuse.

KEY TERMS

sexual coercion
rape
predatory rape
classic rape
acquaintance rape
date rape
gang rape
battering marital rape
nonbattering marital rape
obsessive marital rape
rape trauma syndrome
extrafamilial child sexual abuse
intrafamilial child sexual abuse
sexual harassment
prostitution
pimp
gigolo
pornography
erotica

REFERENCES

Abrahamsen, D. (1960). *The psychology of crime.* New York: Columbia University Press.

Allen, D., & Okawa, J. B. (1987). A counseling center looks at sexual harassment. *Journal of the National Association for Women, Deans, Administrators and Counselors, 51,* 9–16.

American Psychiatric Association. (1987). *Diagnostic and statistical manual of mental disorders* (3rd ed., rev.). Washington, DC: APA.

Anthony, J. (1992). Prostitution as choice. *Ms., 2,* 86–88.

Araji, S. & Finkelhor, D. (1986). Abusers: A review of the research. In D. Finkelhor (Ed). *A sourcebook on child sexual abuse* (pp. 89–118). Newbury Park, CA: Sage.

Ballard, D. T., Williams, D., Horton, A. T., & Johnson, B. L. (1990). Offender identification and current use of community resources. In A. L. Horton, B. L. Johnson, L. M. Roundy, & D. Williams (Eds.) *The incest perpetrator: A family member no one wants to treat* (pp. 150–163). Newbury Park, CA: Sage.

Bart, P. B., & O'Brien, P. H. (1985). *Stopping rape.* Oxford: Pergamon Press.

Bass, E., & Davis, L. (1988). *The courage to heal.* New York: Harper and Row.

Bechhofer, L., & Parrot, A. (1991). What is acquaintance rape? In A. Parrot & L. Bechhofer (Eds.), *Acquaintance rape: The hidden crime* (pp. 9–25). New York: John Wiley & Sons.

Beck, M., Springen, K., & Foote, D. (1992, April 13). Sex and psychotherapy. *Newsweek,* pp. 53–57.

Becker, J. V. & Kaplan, M. S. (1991). Rape victims: Issues, theories, and treatment. In J. Bancroft, C. M. Davis, & H. J. Ruppel, Jr. (Eds.). *Annual Review of Sex Research,* Vol. 2, pp. 267–292. Lake Mills, IA: The Society for the Scientific Study of Sex.

Becker, J. V., Skinner, L. J., Abel, G. G., & Cichon, J. (1986). Level of postassault sexual functioning in rape and incest victims. *Archives of Sexual Abuse, 15,* 37–49.

Beitchman, J. H., Zucker, K. J., Hood, J. E., daCosta, G. A., Akman, D., & Cassavia, E. (1992). A review of the long-term effects of child sexual abuse. *Child Abuse and Neglect, 16,* 101–119.

Berliner, L., & Ernst, E. (1984). Group work with preadolescent sexual assault victims. In I. R. Stuart & J. G. Greer (Eds.), *Victims of sexual aggression: Treatment of children, women, and men* (pp. 105–124). New York: Van Nostrand Reinhold.

Berliner, L. & Conte, J. R. (1990). The process of victimization: The victims' perspective. *Child Abuse and Neglect,* 14, 29–40.

Blumberg, M. L., & Lester, D. (1991). High school and college students' attitudes toward rape. *Adolescence, 26,* 727–729.

Boo, K. (1991, December). "The organization woman: The real reason Anita Hill stayed silent" *Washington Monthly,* pp. 44–50.

Boyer, D., Fine, D., & Killpack, S. (1991, Summer). Sexual abuse and teen pregnancy. *The Network,* pp. 1–2.

Bremer, B. A., Moore, C. T., & Bildersee, E. F. (1991). Do you have to call it 'sexual harassment' to feel harassed? *College Student Journal, 26,* 258–268.

Brooks, L., & Perot, A. R. (1991). Reporting sexual harassment: Exploring a predictive model. *Psychology of Women Quarterly, 15,* 31–47.

Browne, A., & Finkelhor, D. (1986). Initial and long-term effects: A review of the research. In D. Finkelhor (Ed.), *A sourcebook on child sexual abuse* (pp. 143–179). Newbury Park, CA: Sage.

Brownmiller, S. (1975). *Against our will: Men, women, and rape.* New York: Simon & Schuster.

Burge, S. K. (1988). Post-traumatic stress disorder in victims of rape. *Journal of Traumatic Stress, 1,* 193–210.

Burgess, A. W., & Holmstrom, L. L. (1974). Rape trauma syndrome. *American Journal of Psychiatry, 131,* 981–986.

Burgess, A. W., Hartman, C. R., Kelley, S. J., Grant, C. A., & Gray, E. B. (1990). Parental response to child sexual abuse trials involving day care settings. *Journal of Traumatic Stress, 3,* 395–405.

Burnam, M. A., Stein, J. A., Golding, J. M., Siegel, J. M., Sorenson, S. B., Forsythe, A. B., & Telles, C. A. (1988). Sexual assault and mental disorders in a community population. *Journal of Consulting and Clinical Psychology, 56,* 843–850.

Burt, M. R. (1980). Cultural myths and supports for rape. *Journal of Personality and Social Psychology, 38,* 217–230.

Burt, M. R. (1991). Rape myths and acquaintance rape. In A. Parrot & L. Bechhofer (Eds.), *Acquaintance rape: The hidden crime* (pp. 26–40. New York: John Wiley & Sons.

Burt, M. R., & Katz, B. L. (1987). Dimensions of recovery from rape: Focus on growth outcomes. *Journal of Interpersonal Violence, 2,* 57–81.

Calhoun, K. S., & Atkeson, B. M. (1991). *Treatment of rape victims: Facilitating psychosocial adjustment.* New York: Pergamon Press.

Canavan, M. M., Meyer, W. J., III, & Higgs, D. C. (1992). The female experience of sibling incest. *Journal of Marital and Family Therapy, 18,* 129–142.

Carlson, H. M. & Tibbetts, K. E. (1988). Sexual harassment policies: Who reads them? Who needs them? *The Community Psychologist, 21*(2), 17–18.

Carmen, E. H., Rieker, P. P., & Mills, T. (1984). Victims of violence and psychiatric illness. *American Journal of Psychiatry, 141,* 15–20.

Check, J. V. P., & Malamuth, N. M. (1981). Feminism and rape in the 1980's: Recent research findings. In P. Caplan, C. Larson, & L. Cammaert (Eds.), *Psychology changing for women.* Montreal: Eden Press Women's Publications.

Check, J. V. P. & Malamuth, N. (1985). An empirical assessment of some feminist hypotheses about rape. *International Journal of Women's Studies, 8,* 414–433.

Copenhaver, S., & Grauerholz, E. (1991). Sexual victimization among sorority women: Exploring the link between sexual violence and institutional practices. *Sex Roles, 24,* 31–41.

Crawford, C., & Galdikas, B. M. F. (1986). Rape in nonhuman animals: An evolutionary perspective. *Canadian Psychology, 27,* 215–230.

Crossmaker, M. (1991). Behind locked doors—Institutional sexual abuse. *Sexuality and Disability, 9,* 201–219.

Cutler, S. E., & Nolen-Hocksema, S. (1991). Accounting for sex differences in depression through female victimization: Childhood sexual abuse. *Sex Roles, 24,* 425–438.

Daro, D. (1991). Prevention programs. In C. R. Hollin & K. Howell (Eds.), *Clinical approaches to sex offenders and their victims* (pp. 285–313). New York: John Wiley & Sons.

Davis, N. (1978). Prostitution: identity, career, and legal-economic enterprise. In J. M. Henslin & E. Sagrin (Eds.), *The sociology of sex* (rev. ed.) (pp. 195–222). New York: Schocken Books.

Edwards, P. (1989). Assessment of symptoms in adult survivors of incest: A factor analytic study of the responses to childhood incest questionnaire. *Child Abuse and Neglect, 13,* 101–110.

Elliott, D. M., & Briere, J. (1992). The sexually abused boy: Problems in manhood. *Medical Aspects of Human Sexuality, 26,* 68–71.

Ellis, L. (1989). *Theories of rape: Inquiries into the causes of sexual aggression.* New York: Hemisphere Publishing.

Feldman-Summers, S. & Palmer, G. C. (1980). Rape as viewed by judges, prosecutors, and police officers. *Criminal Justice and Behavior, 7,* 19–40.

Finkelhor, D. (1979). *Sexually victimized children.* New York: Free Press.

Finkelhor, D. (1980). Sex among siblings: A survey on prevalence, variety and effects. *Archives of Sexual Behavior, 9,* 171–194.

Finkelhor, D. (1986). Sexual abuse: Beyond the family systems approach. In T. S. Trepper & M. J. Barrett (Eds.). *Treating incest: A multiple systems perspective* pp. 53–65. New York: Haworth.

Finkelhor, D., & Yllo, K. (1988). Rape in marriage. In M. B. Straus (Ed.), *Abuse and victimization across the life span* (pp. 140–152). Baltimore: Johns Hopkins University Press.

Finkelhor, D., Hotaling, G., Lewis, I. A., & Smith, C. (1990). Sexual abuse in a national survey of adult men and women: Prevalence, characteristics, and risk factors. *Child Abuse and Neglect, 14,* 19–28.

Forward, S., & Buck, C. (1978). *Betrayal of innocence: Incest and its devastation.* Los Angeles: J. P. Tarcher.

Frank, J. G. (1991, August 16). *Risk factors for rape: Empirical confirmation and preventive implications.* Poster session presented at the 99th annual convention of the American Psychological Association, San Francisco.

Freund, K., Watson, R., & Dickey, R. (1990). Does sexual abuse in childhood cause pedophilia: An exploratory study. *Archives of Sexual Behavior, 19,* 557–568.

Gale, J., Thompson, R. J., & Thomas, M. (1988). Sexual abuse in young children: Its clinical presentation and characteristic patterns. *Child Abuse and Neglect, 12,* 163–170.

Gibbs, N. (1991, June 3). When is it rape? *Time,* pp. 48–55.

Glaser, R. D., & Thorpe, J. S. (1986). Unethical intimacy: A survey of sexual contact and advances between psychology educators and female graduate students. *American Psychologist, 41,* 43–51.

Gold, S. R. (1991). History of child sexual abuse and adult sexual fantasies. *Violence and Victims, 6,* 75–82.

Goodwin, J. (1988). Post-traumatic symptoms in abused children. *Journal of Traumatic Stress, 1,* 475–488.

Grant, L. (1991). Why men want to do it their way. *New Statesman and Society, 4,* 30–32.

Grauerholz, E. (1989). Sexual harassment of women professors by students: Exploring the dynamics of power, authority, and gender in a university setting. *Sex Roles, 21,* 11–12.

Groth, A. N. (1979). *Men who rape: The psychology of the offender.* New York: Plenum Press.

Gutek, B. A. (1985). *Sex and the workplace.* San Francisco: Jossey-Bass.

Hamilton, J. A., Alagna, S. W., King, L. S., & Lloyd, C. (1987). The emotional consequences of gender-based abuse in the workplace: New counseling programs for sex discrimination. *Women and Therapy, 6,* 155–182.

Harlow, C. W. (1991). *Female victims of violent crime.* NCJ-126826. Washington, DC: U.S. Department of Justice.

Herman, J. (1981). Father-daughter incest. *Professional Psychology, 12,* 76–91.

Herman, J., Russell, D., & Trocki, K. (1986). Long-term effects of incestuous abuse in childhood. *American Journal of Psychiatry, 143,* 1293–1296.

Holcomb, D. R., Holcomb, L. C., Sondag, K. A., & Williams, N. (1991). Attitudes about date rape: Gender differences among college students. *College Student Journal, 25,* 434–439.

Hughes, J. O. & Sandler, B. (undated). Peer harassment: Hassles for Women on Campus. Washington DC: Project on the Status and Education of Women, Association of American Colleges.

Interagency Council on Sex Offender Treatment. (1991). *Treatment brings control: Breaking the cycle.* Austin, TX: Author.

Jackson, J. L., Calhoun, K. S., Amick, A. E., Maddever, H. M., & Habif, V. L. (1990). Young adult women who report childhood intrafamilial sexual abuse: Subsequent adjustment. *Archives of Sexual Behavior, 19,* 211–221.

James, J. (1976). Prostitution: arguments for change. In S. Gordon & R. W. Libby (Eds.), *Sexuality today and tomorrow* (pp. 110–123). North Scituate, MA: Duxbury.

James, J. (1978). The prostitute as victim. In J. R. Chapman and M. Gates (Eds.), *Women's Policy Studies: vol. 3, The victimization of women.* Beverly Hills, CA: Sage Publications.

Janoff-Bulman, R. (1979). Characterological versus behavioral self-blame: Inquiries into depression and rape. *Journal of Personality and Social Psychology, 37,* 1798–1809.

Kanin, E. J. (1957). Male aggression in dating-courtship relations. *American Journal of Sociology, 63,* 197–204.

Katz, B. L. (1991). The psychological impact of stranger versus non-stranger rape on victim's recovery. In A. Parrot & L. Bechhofer (Eds.), *Acquaintance rape: The hidden crime* (pp. 251–269). New York: John Wiley & Sons.

Kelly, L. (1988). How women define their experiences of violence. In K. Yllo & M. Bograd (Eds.), *Feminist perspectives on wife abuse* (pp. 114–132). Newbury Park, CA: Sage.

Kissman, K. (1990). Women in blue-collar occupations: An exploration of constraints and facilitators. *Journal of Sociology and Social Welfare, 17,* 139–149.

Koop, C. E. (1987). Report of the Surgeon General's Workshop on Pornography and Public Health. *American Psychologist, 42,* 944–945.

Koss, M. P. (1988). Hidden rape: Incidence, prevalence, and descriptive characteristics of sexual aggression and victimization in a national sample of college students. In A. W. Burgess (Ed.), *Sexual assault* (vol. 2) (pp. 1–25). New York: Garland.

Koss, M. P., Gidycz, C. A., & Wisniewski, N. (1987). The scope of rape: Incidence and prevalence of sexual aggression and victimization in a national sample of higher education students. *Journal of Counsulting and Clinical Psychology, 55,* 162–170.

Koss, M. P., Dinero, T. E., Seibel, C. A., & Cox, S. L. (1988). Stranger and acquaintance rape. *Psychology of Women Quarterly, 12,* 1–24.

Krug, R. S. (1989). Adult male report of childhood sexual abuse by mothers: Case descriptions, motivations, and long-term consequences. *Child Abuse and Neglect, 13,* 111–119.

Lanning, K. V., & Burgess, A. W. (1989). Child pornography and sex rings. In D. Zillmann & J. Bryant (Eds.), *Pornography: Research advances and policy considerations* (pp. 235–255). Hillsdale, NJ: Lawrence Erlbaum Associates.

Lew, M. (1990). *Victims no longer: Men recovering from incest and other sexual child abuse.* New York: Harper and Row.

Linz, D. (1989). Exposure to sexually explicit materials and attitudes toward rape: A comparison of study results. *The Journal of Sex Research, 26,* 50–84.

Linz, D. G., Donnerstein, E., & Penrod, S. (1985). Effects of long-term exposure to violent and sexually degrading depictions of women. *Journal of Personality and Social Psychology, 55,* 758–768.

Linz, D., Donnerstein, E., & Penrod, S. (1987). The findings and recommendations of the Attorney General's Commission on Pornography: Do the psychological 'facts' fit the political fury? *American Psychologist, 42,* 946–953.

Lynn, B. W. (1986). The new pornography commission: Slouching toward censorship. *SIECUS Report, 14,* 1–6.

Malovich, N. J., & Stake, J. E. (1990). Sexual harassment on campus: Individual differences in attitudes and beliefs. *Psychology of Women Quarterly, 14,* 63–81.

Marvasti, J. (1986). Incestuous mothers. *American Journal of Forensic Psychiatry, 8,* 63–69.

Maypole, D. E. (1986). Sexual harassment of social workers at work: Injustice within? *Social Work, 31,* 29–34.

Mazer, D. B., & Percival, E. F. (1989). Student's experiences of sexual harassment at a small university. *Sex Roles, 20,* 1–22.

McCarthy, B. W. (1990). Treatment of incest families: A cognitive-behavioral model. *Journal of Sex Education and Therapy, 16,* 101–114.

McEvoy, A. W., & Brookings, J. B. (1984). *If she is raped: A book for husbands, fathers, and male friends.* Holmes Beach, FL: Learning Publications.

Money, J. (1988). The ethics of pornography in the era of AIDS. *Journal of Sex and Marital Therapy, 14,* 177–183.

Morrow, R. B., & Sorrell, G. T. (1989). Factors affecting self-esteem, depression, and negative behaviors in sexually abused female adolescents. *Journal of Marriage and the Family, 51,* 677–686.

Muehlenhard, C. L., & Hollabaugh, L. C. (1988). Do women sometimes say no when they mean yes? The prevalence and correlates of women's token resistance to sex. *Journal of Personality and Social Psychology, 54,* 872–879.

Myer, M. H. (1985). A new look at mothers of incest victims. *Journal of Social Work and Human Sexuality, 3,* 47–58.

Myers, M. F. (1989). Men sexually assaulted as adults and sexually abused as boys. *Archives of Sexual Behavior, 18,* 203–215.

The National Adolescent Perpetrator Network (1988). Preliminary report from The National Task Force on Juvenile Sexual Offending. *Juvenile and Family Court Journal, 39*(2), 1–67.

National Association for Female Executives, (1991, October 16). *Sex harassment poll.* ABC "Good Morning America."

National Clearinghouse on Marital and Date Rape. (1991). Berkeley, CA.

Orenchuk-Tomiuk, N., Matthey, G., & Christensen, C. P. (1990). The resolution model: A comprehensive treatment framework in sexual abuse. *Child Welfare, 69,* 417–431.

O'Sullivan, C. S. (1991). Acquaintance gang rape on campus. In A. Parrot & L. Bechhofer (Eds.), *Acquaintance rape: The hidden crime* (pp. 140–156). New York: John Wiley & Sons.

Parrot, A. (1991). Recommendations for college policies and procedures to deal with acquaintance rape. In A. Parrot & L. Bechhofer (Eds.), *Acquaintance rape* (pp. 368–380). New York: John Wiley & Sons.

Perkins, D. (1991). Clinical work with sex offenders in secure settings. In C. R. Hollin & K. Howells (Eds.), *Clinical approaches to sex offenders and their victims* (pp. 151–171). New York: John Wiley & Sons.

Peters, J. M., Dinsmore, J., & Toth, P. (1989). Why prosecute child abuse? *South Dakota Law Review, 34,* 649–659.

Pleak, R. R., & Meyer-Bahlburg, H. F. L. (1990). Sexual behavior and AIDS knowledge of young male prostitutes in Manhattan. *Journal of Sex Research, 27,* 557–587.

Quinsey, V. L., & Upfold, D. (1985). Rape completion and victim injury as a function of female resistance strategy. *Canadian Journal of Behavioral Science, 17,* 40–49.

Rada, R. (1978). *Clinical aspects of rape.* New York: Stein and Day.

Reppucci, N. D., & Haugaard, J. J. (1989). Prevention of child sexual abuse. *American Psychologist, 44,* 1266–1275.

Riger, S. (1991). Gender dilemmas in sexual harassment policies and procedures. *American Psychologist, 46,* 497–505.

Rio, L. M. (1991). Psychological and sociological research and the decriminalization or legalization of prostitution. *Archives of Sexual Behavior, 20,* 205–218.

Rimmer, R. H. (1991). *The X-rated videotape guide II.* Buffalo, NY: Prometheus Books.

Ritts, V., & Engbretson, R. O. (1991). College students attitudes toward adult materials and the legal rental of adult videos. *College Student Journal, 25,* 440–450.

Robertson, C., Dyer, C. E., & Campbell, D. (1988). Campus harassment: Sexual harassment policies and procedures at institutions of higher learning. *Signs: Journal of Women in Culture and Society, 13,* 792–812.

Roscoe, B., Goodwin, M. P., Repp, S. E., & Rose, M. (1987). Sexual harassment of university students and student employees: Findings and implications. *College Student Journal, 21,* 254–273.

Rosen, R. (1982). *The lost sisterhood: Prostitution in America 1900–1918.* Baltimore: Johns Hopkins University Press.

Rossi, P. H., & Weber-Burdin, E. (1983). Sexual harassment on the campus. *Social Science Research, 12,* 131–158.

Roth, S., Dye, E., & Lebowitz, L. (1988). Group therapy for sexual assault victims. *Psychotherapy, 25,* 82–93.

Roth, S., & Lebowitz, L. (1988). The experience of sexual trauma. *Journal of Traumatic Stress, 1,* 79–107.

Rothbaum, B. O., Foa, E. B., Riggs, D. S., Murdock, T., & Walsh, W. (1992). A prospective examination of post-traumatic stress disorder in rape victims. *Journal of Traumatic Stress, 5,* 455–475.

Rozee, P. D., Bateman, P., & Gilmore, T. (1991). A personal perspective of acquaintance rape prevention: A three-tier approach. In A. Parrot & L. Bechhofer (Eds.), *Acquaintance rape: The hidden crime* (pp. 337–354). New York: John Wiley & Sons.

Russell, D. E. H. (1984). *Sexual exploitation: Rape, child sexual abuse and workplace harassment.* Beverly Hills, CA: Sage.

Russell, D. E. H. (1990). *Rape in marriage.* Bloomington: Indiana University Press.

Russell, D. E. H. (1991). Wife rape. In A. Parrot & L. Bechhofer (Eds.), *Acquaintance rape: The hidden crime* (pp. 129–139). New York: John Wiley & Sons.

Salter, A. (1988). *Treating child sex offenders and victims: A practical guide*. Newbury Park, CA: Sage.

Sanday, P. R. (1981). The socio-cultural context of rape: A cross-cultural study. *Journal of Social Issues, 37*, 5–27.

Saroja, K. (1990). A study of counseling needs of female postgraduate students of the University of Agricultural Sciences: A case study approach. *Indian Journal of Behaviour, 14*, 28–32.

Saunders, E. B., & Awad, G. A. (1988). Assessment, management, and treatment planning for male adolescent sexual offenders. *American Journal of Orthopsychiatry, 58*, 571–579.

Schur, E. (1988). *The Americanization of sex*. Philadelphia: Temple University Press.

Scully, D. (1990). *Understanding sexual violence: A study of convicted rapists*. Boston: Unwin Hyman.

Scully, D., & Marolla, J. (1985a). Rape and psychiatric vocabulary of motive: Alternative perspectives. In A. W. Burgess (Ed.), *Rape and sexual assault: A research handbook* (pp. 294–312). New York: Garland.

Scully, D., & Marolla, J. (1985b). "Riding the Bull at Gilley's": Convicted rapists describe the reward of rape. *Social Problems, 32*, 251–263.

Sheppard, D. I., Giacinti, T., & Tjaden, C. (1976). Rape reduction: A citywide program. In M. J. Walker & S. L. Brodsky (Eds.), *Sexual assault* (pp. 169–173). Lexington, MA: Lexington Books.

Silbert, M. H. (1989). The effects on juveniles of being used for pornography and prostitution. In D. Zillmann & J. Bryant (Eds.), *Pornography: Research advances and policy considerations* (pp. 215–234). Hillsdale, NJ: Lawrence Erlbaum Associates.

Simmons, R. L., Whitbeck, L. B. (1991). Sexual abuse as a precursor to prostitution and victimization among adolescent and adult homeless women. *Journal of Family Issues, 12*, 361–379.

Smolowe, J. (1992, October 19). Anita Hill's legacy. *Time*, pp. 56–57.

Sobsey, D., & Doe, T. (1991). Patterns of sexual abuse and assault. *Sexuality and Disability, 9*, 243–259.

Steinem, G. (1983). *Outrageous acts and everyday rebellions*. New York: Holt, Rinehart, and Winston.

Struckman-Johnson, C. (1991). Male victims of acquaintance rape. In A. Parrot & L. Bechhofer (Eds.), *Acquaintance rape: The hidden crime* (pp. 192–214). New York: John Wiley & Sons.

Summit, R. C. (1983). The child sexual abuse accommodation syndrome. *Child Abuse and Neglect, 7*, 177–192.

Terpstra, D. E., & Baker, D. D. (1989). The identification and classification of reactions to sexual harassment. *Journal of Organizational Behavior, 10*, 1–14.

Tharinger, D. J., Krivacska, J. J., Laye-McDonough, M., Jamison, L., Vincent, G. G., & Hedlund, A. D. (1988). Prevention of child sexual abuse: An analysis of issues, educational programs, and research findings. *School Psychology Review, 17*, 614–634.

United Nations. (1959). *Study on traffic in persons and prostitutions*. New York: Author.

U.S. Department of Justice. (1991). *Sourcebook of criminal justice, statistics, 1990*. Washington, DC: U.S. Government Printing Office.

U.S. Merit Systems Protection Board. (1988). *Sexual harassment in the federal government: An update*. Washington, DC: U.S. Government Printing Office.

Veronen, L. J., & Kilpatrick, D. G. (1983). Stress management for rape victims. In D. Meichenbaum & M. E. Janemko (Eds.), *Stress reduction and prevention* (pp. 341–374). New York: Plenum Press.

Waigandt, A., Wallace, D. L., Phelps, L., & Miller, D. A. (1990). The impact of sexual assault on physical health status. *Journal of Traumatic Stress, 3*, 93–102.

West, D. J. (1991). The effects of sex offenses. In C. R. Hollin & K. Howells (Eds.), *Clinical approaches to sex offenders and their victims* (pp. 55–73). New York: John Wiley & Sons.

York, K. M. (1989). Defining sexual harassment in workplaces: A policy-capturing approach. *Academy of Management Journal, 32*, 830–850.

Zelnik, M., & Shah, F. K. (1983). First intercourse among young Americans. *Family Planning Perspectives, 15*, 64–70.

Zillmann, D. (1984). *Connections Between Sex and Aggression*. Hillsdale, NJ: Lawrence Erlbaum Associates.

Zillmann, D., & Bryant, J. (1988). Pornography's impact on sexual satisfaction. *Communication, 18*, 438–453.

Opposite Page: *Pablo Picasso, Spanish, 1881–1973,* Mother and Child, *oil on canvas, 1921, 143.5 × 162.6 cm; Gift of Maymar Corporation, Mrs. Maurice L. Rothschild, Mr. and Mrs. Chauncey McCormick; Mary and Leigh Block Charitable Fund; Ada Turnbull Hertle Endowment; through prior gift of Mr. and Mrs. Edwin E. Hokin, 1954. 270*

Reproductive Choices

Over 90% of all Americans choose to have children. Even those who do not consciously decide to have children may become unintentionally pregnant. In Part VI, we address sexuality issues as they relate to reproductive choices.

In Chapter 20, Planning Children and Birth Control, we emphasize the numerous choices regarding whether to have children, how many, and the consequences of various family-size choices. We also emphasize the social and personal benefits of family planning and look at methods of birth control throughout history, from an international perspective, and in the future. Information that is important in making contraceptive choices is presented, such as effectiveness, side effects, contraindications, and method of use.

The focus of Chapter 21 is pregnancy and childbirth. While 85% of U.S. couples have little difficulty getting pregnant, those who are infertile (as well as people without partners) have a range of alternatives, including artificial insemination, artificial insemination of a surrogate, and in vitro fertilization. Other pregnancy-related choices include prenatal testing and care and childbirth preparation methods.

Chapter 22, Abortion and Other Pregnancy Outcomes, focuses on methods of abortion; ethical, legal, and social issues related to abortion and the psychological effects of abortion. Miscarriage and adoption are also discussed.

In our concluding Chapter 23, we focus on sex education. We conclude that sex education is an incredibly complex issue (involving questions of who should teach what to whom at what ages) but one worthy of our individual and social concern. Without sex education, we reduce the probability of positive outcomes for our sexual choices.

CHAPTER TWENTY

Planning Children and Birth Control

Chapter Outline

Family Planning: A Worthy Choice
- Incidence of Unplanned Pregnancy in the United States
- Personal and Social Benefits of Family Planning

Do You Want to Have Children?
- Social Influences on Deciding to Have Children
- Motivations for Having Children
- Difficulties and Stresses Associated with Parenthood
- The Childfree Alternative
- How Many Children Do You Want?
- Factors to Consider in the Timing of Children
- **Self-Assessment:** Attitudes Toward Timing of Parenthood Scale

History of Birth Control

Methods of Birth Control
- Oral Contraceptives
- Condom
- Intrauterine Device (IUD)
- Diaphragm and Cervical Cap
- Vaginal Spermicides
- Vaginal Sponge
- Coitus Abstentia
- Periodic Abstinence
- Coitus Interruptus (withdrawal)
- Postcoital Contraception
- Sterilization
- **Research Perspective:** Psychological Influences in Contraceptive Use

Birth Control Technology and Availability: An International View

The Future of Birth Control Technology

Choices
- Choose to Have a Child without a Partner? The Biological Clock Issue
- Choose to Use Which Method of Contraception?

Is It True?*

1. In early Egyptian civilization, a paste made of crocodile dung was inserted into a woman's vagina as a means of contraception.

2. For nonsmoking women under age 35, the health problems associated with oral contraceptives outweigh their health benefits.

3. A federal law states that all married individuals who want to be sterilized must obtain written consent from their spouse.

4. Men are choosing to be sterilized at almost twice the rate that they were ten years ago.

5. In 1991, women were more likely to have an unfavorable attitude about IUDs than about any other contraceptive method.

* 1 = T, 2 = F, 3 = F, 4 = F, 5 = T

This choice is probably our most important task as sexually responsible individuals.

John Bancroft, speaking of the reproductive consequence of sex

For most people, family size can now be decided by choice, not chance.

Nafis Sadik

Judith Cohen (1985) noted that parenthood as a "choice" is a relative novelty. Until recently in this country—and still in most of the world—parenthood has been a normal and expected part of the life cycle. To ensure that the lifetime role of parent is one that occurs by choice, the planning of children becomes important. Successful family planning means having the number of children you want when you want to have them. Although this seems to be a sensible and practical approach to parenthood, many women and couples leave the number and spacing of their children to chance. Of 535 pregnant and parenting individuals (in eight counties in Washington state) age 21 and under, almost a quarter (23%) reported that they did not intend to get pregnant (Boyer, 1991).

After a brief look at the incidence of unplanned pregnancy in the United States and the benefits of family planning, we emphasize four basic choices related to family planning: Do you want to have children? If so, how many children do you want, and when do you want to have them? What form(s) of birth control will you use to ensure the family size that you want? We also look at birth control from a historical and international perspective. Finally, we discuss birth control methods that may be available in the United States in the future.

Family Planning: A Worthy Choice

NATIONAL DATA: Every year, there are 3.3 million unplanned pregnancies in the United States (Koop, 1989).

The large number of unintended pregnancies, both in the United States and throughout the world, suggests that family planning is not widespread. The benefits of family planning, however, suggest that family planning may not only be a worthy choice but a necessary choice for the survival of the human species.

Incidence of Unplanned Pregnancy in the United States

While some unintended pregnancies result in miscarriage or abortion (see Chapter 22), many result in births. In 1988, the proportion of births in the previous five years that were unwanted at conception rose to 10%, a 2% increase from 1982 (Williams, 1991). In another study, 12% of pregnant women between the ages of 20 and 29 reported that they did not want their baby at the time they became aware that they were pregnant (Travis, 1988).

The increase in unwanted childbearing is most evident among women living below the poverty level. Between 1982 and 1988, the proportion of unwanted births among women in poverty rose by almost 75% (Williams, 1991).

Groups may shout "anti-this" and "liberate that," but it is the individual who experiences the heartbreaks and joys of their birth-control decisions or indecision.

Philip A. Belcastro

Teenagers also have a larger number of unplanned pregnancies—only about 16% of teenage pregnancies are intentional (Hatcher et al., 1990). Almost a third (32%) of all unintended pregnancies involve teenagers. About three-quarters of unintended teenage pregnancies occur to those who do not use contraception (Hatcher, et al., 1990). This suggests that most unintended teenage pregnancies could be avoided if contraception were used.

Personal and Social Benefits of Family Planning

Family planning has benefits for the mother, the father, and the child. Having several children at short intervals increases the chances of premature birth, infectious disease, and death for the mother or the baby (Travis, 1988). "Maternal and infant deaths are closely correlated with pregnancies that are too early, too late, too many and too close. Thus . . . family planning has the potential for preventing many needless deaths" (United Nations Population Fund, 1991, p. 57).

Both parents may also benefit from family planning by pacing the financial demands of parenthood. For example, through planning the spacing of their children, couples may avoid having two children in day care or college at the same time.

Some parents are happy with an unintended pregnancy. One mother of an eight-year-old daughter commented:

> Being unmarried and still in college, getting pregnant was the last thing I wanted. But once I got over the shock and decided to continue the pregnancy, I was thrilled about being pregnant. Now, I sometimes refer to my wonderful daughter as "the best mistake I ever made!" If I hadn't become pregnant unintentionally, I probably would never have had a child. I'm glad I did. (Authors' files)

While an unintentional pregnancy may turn out to be a positive experience, it may also lead to an abortion (which may be emotionally and financially stressful) or result in children who are unwanted, resented, and poorly cared for by their parent(s). In addition, unintended pregnancy may lead to relationship conflicts in that the pregnant woman, her partner, and their respective families may each want different outcomes. For example, the partner may want to continue the pregnancy, while the woman may not. In addition, one set of parents may want their unmarried pregnant daughter to place her baby for adoption, while the partner's parents may want their son to marry his pregnant girlfriend and have the child.

> Increasingly, governmental and societal consensus is emerging in regard to the right of all individuals to seek to improve the quality of their lives for themselves and their children through family planning.
>
> *United Nations Population Fund*

The benefits of family planning extend beyond parents and their children. Family planning may be not only beneficial but necessary for the survival of the human race and the planet Earth. The world's population has exceeded 5.25 billion. Every day, an additional 220,000 people are added to the world's population. By the year 2025, it is estimated that the planet will be inhabited by 8.5 billion people (Urzua, 1992). It is estimated that at least half of the world's population lives in poverty (Travis, 1988). Yet, birth rates in many countries continue to be high; women in several developing countries typically give birth to six or more children. Family planning is essential to halting the continuing expansion of the world population and the consequent drain on limited social and environmental resources. Without control of population growth, the world faces increased food shortages, unchecked urban growth, environmental damage (including water, soil, and air pollution), depletion of planetary resources, and destruction of the ozone layer. Population growth is also outpacing the provision of needed health, educational, and housing services (United Nations Population Fund, 1991). Sadik (1992) suggested that "Population may be the key to all the issues that will shape the future: economic growth; environmental security; and the health and well–being of countries, communities, and families." (p. 134)

Do You Want to Have Children?

In a study of 700 undergraduate students, 95% reported that they wanted to have children (Rubinson & De Rubertis, 1991). In this section, we examine the social influences that affect our decision to have children. We also look at motivations for having children and some of the potential difficulties and stresses associated with parenthood.

Social Influences on Deciding to Have Children

The United States has a tradition of **pronatalism**—it encourages childbearing among married women. Social influences that encourage childbearing include family and friends, religion, and government.

NATIONAL DATA: Over 90% of U.S. women ages 18 to 34 expect to have children (*Statistical Abstract of the United States: 1992,* Table 97).

Some parents attempt to influence their adult children to have children. Typical comments from parents include: "When will I become a grandparent?" "Don't you want a son to carry on the family name?" Even if our parents do not attempt to influence us in regard to having children, they serve as role models for our having children by their having had children.

Siblings may also be an influence on our decision to have children. One woman commented, "I have six brothers and sisters and I'm the only one who has not had a child; I feel like I am missing out on something" (Authors' files). Likewise, friends may affect our decision to have children. The woman quoted above also commented, "All my friends are having children; it must be the thing to do."

Religion may be another powerful influence on our decision to have children. For example, Catholics have traditionally been taught that having children is the basic purpose of marriage and that the use of contraception constitutes interference with God's plan. Judaism also has a strong family orientation.

The tax structures developed by our federal and state governments support parenthood. Married couples without children pay higher taxes than couples with children, although the reduction in taxes is not large enough to be a primary inducement to have children.

In other countries, the government may encourage or discourage childbearing in various ways. In the 1930s, as a mark of status for women contributing to the

The United States is a pronatalistic society. It encourages married couples to have children.

so-called Aryan race, Adolf Hitler bestowed the German Mother's Cross on Nazi Germany's most fertile mothers—a gold cross for eight or more children, a silver cross for six or seven, and a bronze cross for four or five. Faced with crippling overpopulation, China offers incentives to couples who have only one child; they are given a "one-child glory certificate," which entitles them to priority housing, better salaries, a supplementary pension, and free medical care for the child.

Despite the tradition of pronatalism in the United States, contemporary values that discourage childbearing and support birth control are also evident. Michaels (1988) suggested that the U.S. tradition of pronatalism has weakened. "The decline in pronatalist values has led to a situation in which those who do not want to have children can make this choice without the fear of extreme social criticism or ostracism" (p. 23).

Motivations for Having Children

In their book *Parents in Contemporary America,* researchers LeMasters and DeFrain (1989) wrote that "rearing children is probably the hardest and most thankless job in the world" (p. 21). Yet most Americans express a desire to have this experience. Next, we discuss some of the motivations for having children.

Love and Companionship In a study of 610 married couples, researchers found that children are viewed as important sources of love and affection (Neal, Groat, & Wicks, 1989). Other researchers have also found that women and men view children as providing a) the opportunity to establish a close affiliative relationship with another human being (Campbell, Townes, & Beach, 1982), b) primary group ties and affection (Hoffman, Thornton, & Manis, 1978), and c) someone who needs you (Michaels, 1988).

I think one of the things that has made Chelsea's life bearable as an only child is that we have done so many things together. I have driven her to school every day since kindergarten, unless I was away. The morning is our time.

Hillary Clinton

CONSIDERATION: Some people feel that having children is one way to avoid loneliness in old age. However, Cohen (1985) suggested that "the loneliest people are those who presumed that their children would forestall a lonely future and who have been disappointed in that hope" (p. 93).

Family Relationships Many young married couples view children as necessary for "having a real family life" (Neal et al., 1989). Parents may value the relationships that form between their child and other family members, such as the child's grandparents, aunts, uncles, and cousins. Children are also sometimes viewed as a way to strengthen the bond between a couple (Michaels, 1988). Some women may want to become pregnant as a means of pressuring their partner to get married. In a sample of 242 first-time mothers ages 15–42 who were interviewed one year after giving birth, 12% reported that marriage had resulted as a consequence of the baby's birth (Mercer, 1986). When a couple are experiencing relationship problems, they may feel that having a child will bind them more together and save their marriage (Dorman & Klein, 1984).

Attainment of Adult Status Having a child is one way of attaining adult status and identity.

> The responsibility for new life is expected to elicit mature and conscientious behavior. A new identity emerges; one is now Mother, which is more than just a name. This identity implies a whole new and lasting set of duties, commitments, and values, not the least of which is a new sense of being important, of being truly necessary to another person. (Williams, 1987, p. 307)

Parenthood allows its actors to develop and express a warm, caring, selfless side of themselves, which may go underdiscovered or untapped in other adult roles and settings.

Toni C. Antonucci
Karen Mikus

Personal Fulfillment Some adults view having children as "part of being a man or a woman" (Michaels, 1988, p. 47) and thus necessary for the fulfillment of the feminine or masculine role. Parents report feelings of creativity, accomplishment, and competence from the experience of parenthood. Parents also derive a sense of accomplishment from the accomplishments of their children. Parenthood provides mothers and fathers with an important identity, as well as a sense of power. "Children are also seen as a chance to have an effect on the world, particularly by persons who are otherwise powerless" (Williams, 1987, p. 308).

Some people try to achieve immortality through their offspring or their works. I prefer to achieve immortality by not dying.
Woody Allen

Children may also provide parents with a sense of immortality or expansion of the self. Children represent "a bridge to the future by which one's physical and psychological characteristics can continue beyond the evanescent self" (Williams, 1987, p. 307). Some parents derive gratification from the idea that they will be remembered by their children after the parent dies (Michaels, 1988).

You start to recognize the child in yourself, the child in everybody.
Annie Lennox
(speaking of her motherhood experience)

Recapturing Youth Another motivation for wanting children is that they may provide a mechanism for parents to recapture their own childhood and youth. This may be especially true for men and women who have positive childhood memories (Williams, 1987). One way in which having children helps adults to capture their youth is through play. Children may provide an excuse for adults to play and express the child in themselves that society assumes they have outgrown.

A decision about parenthood can never be entirely rational—even with all the facts in the world . . . the process of reviewing factual information will not necessarily recognize or deal with the powerful but unrecognized feelings that can influence such a personal choice.
Judith Blackfield Cohen

Unconscious Motivations. Reasons for wanting to have a child may exist outside an individual's awareness. For example, Michaels (1988, p. 58) cited two examples from his clinical experience:

- A woman in her twenties wanted a baby chiefly to compete with her sister, who was pregnant.
- A woman in her thirties wanted a baby in order to gain acceptance by her parents, who had rejected her during her adolescence and college years.

Difficulties and Stresses Associated with Parenthood

Every parent knows that parenthood involves difficulties as well as joys. Some of the difficulties and stresses associated with parenthood include the following.

Financial Cost A primary negative aspect of parenthood is the financial costs involved in rearing a child.

CONSIDERATION: The economic value of children varies greatly across societies and historical time periods. In rural, developing countries (and in early U.S. history), children have been viewed as economic assets, in that they have provided valuable work to help sustain their families. In rural societies, adult children have also played a primary role in the care of their elderly parents. However, the role of children has changed in the United States and in other countries with child labor laws and compulsory education. In these countries, children generally represent an economic liability, rather than an economic asset.

Demographers estimate that couples will spend $5,774 on their baby the first year (Cutler, 1990). Up to age 18 (college expenses not included), one child costs an average of $133,000. When couples have more than one child, they spend less on each child (Crispell, 1989). In addition to increased expenses, having a child may mean a decrease in income. Many women, and in some cases men, either stop

A baby costs $474 a month. How much do you have in your pocket?
Poster

working or change from a full-time job to a part-time job in order to stay home and care for young children. Parents who send their children to day care spend an average of $53 per child per week (Cutler, 1990).

Increased Role Demands Another aspect of parenthood involves increased role demands for both parents, but especially for the parent who takes primary responsibility for child care. Some parents enjoy the work involved in the parental role, as reflected in the comments of one mother:

> If your vision of parenthood includes only the rosiest images, the life you plan may have little relation to the life you will live.
> *Judith Blackfield Cohen*

> There is nothing I would rather do than have a baby to take care of. Now that my children are in school, they need me less. I miss breast-feeding, rocking them to sleep, and giving them baths. To me, it wasn't work, it was joy. (Author's files)

Many parents, however, feel burdened by parenting, at least some of the time. One mother, a college student, remarked:

> I don't know how I got through those first three years of parenthood. Every night I was awakened by a crying baby who needed to be fed or changed or rocked back to sleep. During the day, the only time I had to myself was when my daughter was taking a nap; I used that time to study. In the evening, I worked part-time at a restaurant. I was always exhausted. I don't regret it, but once is enough for me. (Authors' files)

> The most effective contraception for parents is to spend an hour with their children before going to bed.
> *Roseanne Barr Arnold*

Life-style Changes Becoming a parent often involves changes in life-style (Neal et al., 1989). Daily living routines often become focused around the needs of the children. Living arrangements may change to provide space for another person in the household. Some parents change their work schedules to allow them to be home more. Food shopping and menus change to accommodate the appetites of children. A major life-style change is the loss of freedom of activity and flexibility in one's personal schedule that comes with parenting. When Hoffman asked a sample of U.S. married couples "What are the disadvantages or bad things about having children . . . ?," the most frequent answer was "loss of freedom." The second most frequent answer was "financial costs" (cited in Michaels, 1988, pp. 34–35).

Worry and Grief Parenthood involves worry or concern about the well-being of one's children (Mercer, 1986., Williams, 1987). Even before the birth of a child, parents worry about whether or not the child will be born "normal" and healthy (Affonso & Mayberry, 1989). Concern over the health and well-being of children continues even when the children are grown and living independently.

> Children are a great comfort in your old age—and they help you reach it faster, too.
> *Lionel Kauffman*

Parenthood may also involve grief. Having a child with congenital or acquired defects, illness, or injury may be extremely difficult for the parents to deal with emotionally. (Children with special needs also involve increased role demands on parents and increased financial cost.) Parents whose child dies often continue to grieve to some degree throughout their lives. Even when parents are spared such tragic events, they may experience grief or disappointment regarding their child's grades in school, behavior toward others, involvement in illegal activities, and life-style values and choices in regard to religion, occupation, and sexuality.

Negative Behaviors of Children One study found that the most frequently reported type of stress experienced by mothers of young children was due to their child's negative behavior (Brailey, 1989). Such behaviors included disobeying instructions or refusing to comply with the mother's wishes, demanding excessive attention, fighting or arguing with siblings, and causing damage to household property.

The transition to parenthood holds the potential for drawing parents into more separate worlds at a time when they dreamed of making a world together.
Philip A. Cowan
Carolyn Pape Cowan

Effect on Marital Relationship Research results are inconsistent regarding the effect of having children on marital happiness. In one study of 75 fathers and 115 mothers, Harriman (1986) observed that if marital satisfaction was high prior to the birth of a baby, the baby's birth was associated with increased marital satisfaction. Conversely, if marital satisfaction was low prior to having children, the birth of a baby was associated with decreased marital satisfaction.

Marks (1989) observed that the birth of a baby to a married couple results in more separation of activities between the spouses; the wife tends to participate more in child care, while the husband tends to participate more in income-producing activities. Separation of activities means spending less time together and having fewer things in common. Some (but not all) couples view spending less time together as a problem in their relationship.

In interviews with 242 first-time mothers one year postpartum, one-fourth reported that having a child had negative effects on the mate relationship (Mercer, 1986). Negative effects included strained relationship, increased arguments, less time together, less privacy, and less depth in their interactions with their mates.

Cowan & Cowan (1988) found that during the 2-year period from late pregnancy to 18 months postpartum, more than 90% of the parents in their study reported an increase in conflict and disagreement. The number one issue leading to conflict was division of labor in the family. However, satisfaction with role arrangements was related not to equity and fairness in the actual division, but rather to whether and how family tasks were discussed. "Neither partner liked to be nagged about doing a task or criticized for the style in which the task was done, and both felt badly when their contributions to the family were unrecognized or unacknowledged" (Cowan & Cowan, 1988, p. 131).

CONSIDERATION: Some parents in the Cowan & Cowan study reported that positive changes in communication occurred after their child was born. "Many couples noted that, with more issues to disagree about and less time available, they had become more efficient and effective problem solvers. As one mother reported with amusement, 'We simply don't have all week to spend on a disagreement any more!' " (Cowan & Cowan, 1988, p. 131)

Parenting is a human right—a reproductive right of all women and men, regardless of their sexual orientation.
Cheri Pies

MacDermid, Huston, and McHale (1990) compared couples with and without children and found that both groups reported declines in love feelings, marital satisfaction, doing things together, and frequency of positive interactions. Their findings suggest that it may be the passage of time, rather than the presence of a child, that results in decreased marital satisfaction.

Parenting Concerns of Gay and Lesbian Individuals and Couples In addition to the aforementioned stresses and difficulties associated with having children, gay men and lesbians face additional parenting concerns (Kenney & Tash, 1992; Pies, 1987; Rivera, 1987; Weston, 1991). Some gay men and lesbians have children from a prior heterosexual relationship. Other gay men who want to be parents must decide whether to adopt or find a woman who is willing to have a child through sexual relations or artificial insemination (these and other reproductive technologies are discussed in Chapter 21). Lesbians may conceive their own child, but must decide whether to have sexual relations with a man or be artificially inseminated with sperm from a known or unknown donor.

Some gay and lesbian parents must also decide what (and when) to tell their child about his or her conception and life-style differences. They are often concerned about how the child can explain the parents' life-style to classmates and friends. Other concerns faced by some gay and lesbian parents relate to legal issues of (1) custody and visitation if the couple terminate their relationship and (2) guardianship if the biological parent dies.

The Child-free Alternative

Some couples who do not have children are not child-free by choice. Between 15% and 20% of U.S. couples are unable to have children and feel relegated to a life of involuntary childlessness (infertility will be discussed in Chapter 21). A smaller percentage of couples decide to be child-free. They may put off having children ("we'll wait till we're out of school . . . until we get a house . . . until our careers are established . . . until we have more money"), become satisfied with their child-free life-style, and decide to continue it. However, those who remain voluntarily child-free are in the minority. Whites are most likely to consider marriage without children. Blacks, Native Americans, and Mexican-Americans are more likely to be family-oriented and to consider children an important part of marital life (Mindel, Habenstein, & Wright, 1988). Women who wanted to remain childfree tended to explain their choice on the basis of their age and the stress and worry associated with rearing children. Men were more likely to emphasize the financial demands (Seccombe, 1991).

NATIONAL DATA: Based on a national sample of married adults of childbearing age who did not have children, 19% of the wives and 13% of the husbands reported that they do not intend to have children (Seccombe, 1991).

How do couples who don't have children feel about their decision later in life? In a study comparing couples in their 70s who did and did not have children, Rempel (1985) concluded:

> . . . today's childless elderly have levels of well-being that match and sometimes exceed those of elderly parents . . . . It is erroneous to assume that the elderly have children who can and will look after them. We have learned from this examination that family is not necessarily the crucial element in determining high-quality life in old age. (pp. 346–347)

How Many Children Do You Want?

If you decide to have children, how many do you want? The number of children a couple choose to have is influenced by the society in which the couple lives. As noted earlier, in China, the one-child family is actively encouraged and has resulted in a drop in the country's birth rate. In the United States, most parents have more than one child.

NATIONAL DATA: Twelve percent of U.S. wives aged 18 to 34 expect to have one child (*Statistical Abstract of the United States: 1990*, Table 98).

One Child As with the decision to have no children, deciding to have only one child has become more common and socially acceptable in recent decades. In a 10-year period (1978 to 1988), the number of women 40 to 44 years with only one child doubled (Dreyfous, 1991). However, the two-child norm in the United States still exerts considerable social pressure on some parents who have one child to have another. It is not uncommon for parents of a single child to complain that family and friends frequently ask when they are going to have their next child.

Only children are often stereotyped as being spoiled, selfish, and lonely. However, there are many benefits to being an only child. Data suggest that only children are often very happy, bright, successful, and socially skilled (Falbo & Polit-O'Harra, 1985; Newman, 1990).

Two Children The most preferred family size in the United States is two children. Couples may choose to have two children, for several reasons (Dreyfous, 1991;

Knox & Wilson, 1978). Some couples feel that a family isn't complete without two children, and they want their first-born child to have a sibling and companion. Parents may have two children with the hope of having a child of each sex. Many mothers want a second child because they enjoyed their first child and wanted to repeat the experience. Others want to avoid having an only child because of the negative stereotypes associated with only children. Or, parents may not want to "put all their eggs in one basket." For example, some parents fear that if they only have one child and that child dies or turns out to be disappointing, they will not have another opportunity to enjoy parenting.

NATIONAL DATA: Fifty percent of U.S. wives aged 18 to 34 expect to have two children (*Statistical Abstract of the United States: 1990,* Table 98).

How does having two children differ from having one? One of the major differences between first-time and second-time parenthood is that second-time parents are not taking on a whole new role, and to this extent the psychological impact may be less dramatic (Goldberg & Michaels, 1988, p. 345). In addition, couples with one child have already experienced the shift from being a couple to being a family.

Some mothers who had two children reported that having a second child increased their level of stress and exhaustion (Knox & Wilson, 1978). Having a second child means not only meeting the needs of an additional child but also dealing with the sometimes conflictual interactions between the two siblings. Mothers in this study also reported that their marriages were more negatively affected by their second child than by their first.

NATIONAL DATA: Twenty-five percent of U.S. wives aged 18 to 34 expect to have three children (*Statistical Abstract of the United States: 1990,* Table 98).

Three Children Some individuals may want three children because they enjoy children and feel that "three is better than two." In some instances, a couple who have two children of the same sex want to try one more time to have a child of the opposite sex.

Having a third child creates a "middle child." This child may be neglected, because parents of three children may focus more on "the baby" and the firstborn than on the child in between. However, an advantage to being a middle child is the chance to experience being both a younger and an older sibling.

NATIONAL DATA: Thirteen percent of all second- and higher-order births occurred within 18 months of the mother's previous live birth, 27% within two years, and 51% within three years (National Center for Health Statistics, 1991).

Four or More Children Men are more likely to want four or more children than women. Blacks and Mexican Americans are more likely than whites to want larger families (Mindel et al., 1988). Larger families have complex interactional patterns and different values. The addition of each subsequent child dramatically increases the possible relationships in the family. For example, in the one-child family, four interpersonal relationships are possible: mother-father, mother-child, father-child, and father-mother-child. In a family of four, 11 relationships are possible; in a family of five, 26; and in a family of six, 57.

CONSIDERATION: When people think about and plan for the size family they want, they rarely take into consideration the possibility of divorce or widowhood. In deciding how many children you want (if you want any at all), consider the following questions: How would you care for the child(ren) if you become widowed? How would you care for the child(ren) if you became divorced and either had primary custody of the child(ren) or had to make child support payments?

When divorced or widowed people with young children remarry, they often find themselves in families that are larger than what they had originally planned. For example, a woman with two children who marries a man with three children suddenly has five children in her family unit. Given the high rate of divorce (50%) and remarriage (80%), it is not unrealistic to consider these issues when thinking about the number of children you want to have.

NATIONAL DATA: Nine percent of U.S. wives aged 18 to 34 expect to have four or more children (*Statistical Abstract of the United States: 1990,* Table 98).

Factors to Consider in the Timing of Children

The issue of whether and when to have children is no longer a biological given or an unavoidable cultural demand, but a matter of true individual choice.

Gerald Y. Michaels

If you want one or more children, when is the best time to have them? In the Self-Assessment you may assess your attitudes toward the timing of parenthood. Next we examine some issues related to timing the birth of children.

Mother's Age The age at which a woman becomes pregnant or gives birth may affect the health of both the woman and her child. In developing countries, women under the age of 15 are five to seven times more likely to die during pregnancy or childbirth than are women ages 20 to 24. Women ages 15 to 19 and women over age 35 also face substantially higher risks than those in the 20 to 24 age group (United Nations Population Fund, 1991).

Babies born to mothers younger than 16 are much more likely to die in their first month of life. Likewise, babies born to women older than 40 are more likely to die in infancy (United Nations Population Fund, 1991). The chance of the infant having a chromosomal abnormality is 1% if the woman is in her early 20s, 2% at ages 35 to 39, 3% at 40, and 10% at 45 (Seashore, 1980). (See Chapter 21 for discussion of antenatal screening for chromosomal abnormalities).

Over the last few decades, the percentage of mothers who had their first child at age 30 or older has increased. The percentage of U.S. women giving birth to their first child at age 30 or above increased from 4% in 1970 to 16% in 1987 (Sapiro, 1990). Several reasons exist for the trend toward giving birth at older ages (Sapiro, 1990; Travis, 1988):

1. Wider availability of contraception and abortion make such choices possible.
2. Changing health-care technology and medical views have raised the age at which pregnancy is considered relatively dangerous.

Due to career interests, health care technology and delay at age of marriage, women are deciding to get pregnant at increasingly older ages.

Self Assessment

Attitudes Toward Timing of Parenthood Scale (ATOP)

Directions Circle the response option which most closely represents your feelings. The options are strongly agree (SA), agree (A), undecided (U), disagree (D), and strongly disagree (SD).

	SD	D	U	A	SA
1. The best time to begin having children is usually within the first two years of marriage.	1	2	3	4	5
2. It is important for a young couple to enjoy their social life first and to have children later in the marriage.	1	2	3	4	5
3. A marriage relationship is strengthened if children are born in the early years of marriage.	1	2	3	4	5
4. Women are generally happier if they have children early in the marriage.	1	2	3	4	5
5. Men are generally tied closer to the marriage when there are children in the home.	1	2	3	4	5
6. Most young married women lack self-fulfillment until they have a child.	1	2	3	4	5
7. Young couples who do not have children are usually unable to do so.	1	2	3	4	5
8. Married couples who have mature love for each other will be eager to have a child as soon as possible.	1	2	3	4	5
9. Couples who do not have children cannot share in the major interests of their friends who are parents, and are therefore left out of most social circles.	1	2	3	4	5
10. Children enjoy their parents more when the parents are nearer their own age; therefore, parents should have children while they are still young.	1	2	3	4	5
11. In general, research indicates that the majority of couples approaching parenthood for the first time have had little or no previous child care experience beyond sporadic babysitting, a course in child psychology, or occasional care of younger siblings. Considering your own background preparation for parenthood, would you judge that you are well prepared for the parenting experience?	1	2	3	4	5

Items 1–10 are from the Attitudes Toward Timing of Parenthood Scale (Maxwell & Montgomery, 1969). Item 11 was an additional item constructed to determine perceived degree of preparation for parenthood.

Source: Knaub, P. K., Eversoll, D. B., & Voss, J. H. (1983). Is parenthood a desirable adult role? An assessment of attitudes held by contemporary women. *Sex Roles, 9,* 358. Used by permission.

Scoring Response options favoring early parenthood receive the highest score (5 points), and those that favor delayed parenthood receive the lowest score (1 point). The range of possible scores is from 10 to 50. Item number 2 is reverse scored, so if you chose option 4, change it to 2 (or vice versa); if you chose option 5, change it to 1 (or vice versa). Then sum the value of the options you selected for all items to compute your total score.

Reliability and validity No reliability information was provided. The scales's developers, Maxwell and Montgomery (1969), reported that in an item analysis, each of the original 10-scale items discriminated significantly between upper- and lower-quartile groups. In their study of 96 married women, consistent attitudes and behavior were found; those who waited longer before having their first child scored lower on the ATOP.

Interpreting your score Maxwell and Montgomery (1969) found that factors that were related to lower scores (favoring delay of parenting) were the following: higher age of respondent, higher education level and socioeconomic status, and having fewer

Continued

Self-Assessment—*Continued*

children. Studies in the decade following publication of this measure revealed that women in the late 1970s and early 1980s were more likely than Maxwell and Montgomery's original sample to favor delayed parenthood (Knaub, Eversoll, & Voss, 1981, 1983). In the 1983 study of 213 female students at a large midwestern university (Knaub, Eversoll, & Voss, 1983), the mean total score (on items 1 through 10) on the ATOP was 21.

Researchers using this measure typically present the percentage of respondents who agree and disagree with each item. Following is a table that summarizes the responses of 213 female students at a large midwestern university (Knaub, Eversoll, & Voss, 1983) and 76 male students from colleges in four states (Eversoll, Voss, & Knaub, 1983). Percentages for the response options "strongly agree" and "agree" are combined, as are the percentages for "disagree" and "strongly disagree."

ATOP Items by Percent of Respondents Agreeing and Disagreeing (*Refer to questions at the beginning of this assessment*)

	Women			Men		
	Agree	*Disagree*	*Undecided*	*Agree*	*Disagree*	*Undecided*
Question 1	7.5	86.8	5.7	6.6	84.1	9.2
Question 2	78.8	10.8	11.3	76.0	11.8	13.2
Question 3	6.6	76.9	16.5	10.5	68.5	21.0
Question 4	5.2	72.7	22.1	5.3	58.0	36.5
Question 5	34.9	44.8	20.3	21.1	56.6	22.4
Question 6	8.9	81.7	9.4	7.9	72.4	19.7
Question 7	2.8	93.9	2.8	2.6	88.2	9.2
Question 8	4.3	84.4	11.3	9.2	81.6	9.2
Question 9	14.6	77.8	7.5	15.8	78.9	5.3
Question 10	15.6	71.2	13.2	19.8	64.5	15.8
Question 11	34.7	53.1	12.2			

References

Eversoll, D. B., Voss, J. H., & Knaub, P. K. (1983). Attitudes of college females toward parenthood timing. *Journal of Home Economics, 75,* 25–29.

Knaub, P. K., Eversoll, D. B., & Voss, J. H. (1981). Student attitudes toward parenthood: Implications for curricula in the 1980's. *Journal of Home Economics, 73,* 34–37.

Knaub, P. K., Eversoll, D. B., & Voss, J. H. (1983). Is parenthood a desirable adult role? An assessment of attitudes held by contemporary women. *Sex Roles, 9,* 355–362.

Maxwell, J. W., & Montgomery, J. E. (1969). Societal pressure toward early parenthood. *Family Coordinator, 18,* 340–344.

3. Women's education levels have increased, and women are pursuing careers in unprecedented numbers, thus making childbearing at a later age desirable.
4. In our youth-oriented culture, some women may view having a child as a means of revitalization and denial of the aging process.
5. Cohen (1985) suggested that

> For many people in their thirties, what they call delaying parenthood is really delaying making a clear personal decision about parenthood . . . . More and more people in their twenties and thirties who have no children are unwilling either to declare themselves permanently childless or to make a decision to go ahead and have children. They may be evasive, uncertain, or ambivalent about the choice, but, in any case, delay is easier for them than decision. (pp. 7, 16)

Father's Age The father's age is also a consideration in deciding when to have the first child. Down's syndrome is associated with increased paternal as well as maternal age. Other abnormalities that may be related to the age of the father include achonodroplasis (a type of dwarfism), Marfan syndrome (height, vision, and heart abnormalities), Apert syndrome (facial and limb deformities), and fibro-dysplasis ossificans progressiva (bony growths). Such congenital defects are rare (2% of all births).

Number of Years in a Stable Relationship While some single women choose to become a parent (see the Choices section on having a child without a partner), most planned births occur in the context of a marriage or stable relationship. Some couples are ambivalent about how long it is best to be in a stable relationship before having a baby. The average length of time between marriage and the first birth is two years (Bloom & Bennett, 1986).

One viewpoint suggests that newlyweds need time to adjust to each other as spouses before becoming parents. If the marriage is dissolved before that point, at least there will not be problems of child custody, child-support payments, and single-parent status. However, if couples wait several years to have a baby, they may become so content with their child-free life-style that parenthood is an unwelcome change. In a study of more than 5,000 parents, Marini (1980) found that marital satisfaction was not affected by the length of time the parents waited before having children.

History of Birth Control

Throughout history, fertility has been worshipped by many religions and recognized as being necessary for the continuation of the human race. Men and women have been told to "be fruitful and multiply." However,

> Coexisting in the past and in the present with the desire to realize fertility potential is the opposing desire to limit or control it, to make it contingent upon individual choice rather than biological chance. (Williams, 1987, p. 269).

Methods of contraception have been traced back to the paleolithic era (10,000 B.C.), when women are believed to have used plant drugs as contraceptives. Some primitive peoples who have survived into the modern world have used plants, some of which, when tested on laboratory animals, have shown contraceptive properties. For example, the Navajo ingested a tea of ragleaf bahia; the Shoshoni of Nevada drank an infusion of stoneseed roots; and the Hopis consumed a powder made from the dried root of the jack-in-the-pulpit (Tannahill, 1982).

According to Tannahill, throughout history, the "simplest and most obvious method of keeping the population down was infanticide" (1982, p. 31). Infanticide was a common practice in Europe, India, and China until the nineteenth century. A common way of committing infanticide was to leave an infant exposed to the elements and without nourishment.

In most cases of infanticide, it is usually the female infant who is the victim. Tannahill (1982) suggested that the female infant is usually the target of infanticide "not for male chauvinist reasons, but because she was herself a child-producer of the future, a threat not only in her person but in her progeny to the food supply" (p. 32).

In contrast to Tannahill's assertions, Riddle and Estes (1992) stated that the evidence of widespread infanticide is largely circumstantial and is controversial. They described the development of oral contraceptives made from plant secretions by ancient medical experts.

Other methods of birth control were described in records from early civilizations. An Egyptian papyrus dated 1850 B.C. described inserting substances such as honey, sodium carbonate, and a paste made of crocodile dung into the vagina to prevent pregnancy. Elephant dung was also used in the Islamic world as late as the thirteenth century (Tannahill, 1982). Although the "discovery" of sperm did not occur until the end of the seventeenth century, inserting such substances into the vagina might have retarded the motility of sperm or had a spermicidal effect. Between the sixteenth century B.C. and the nineteenth century A.D., other substances, such as lint or wool tampons soaked in herbs and wine, were also inserted into the woman's vagina to prevent pregnancy (Williams, 1987).

In the fourth century B.C., Aristotle recommended that women prevent pregnancy by applying a blend of olive oil, cedar oil, lead ointment, or frankincense to "that part of the womb in which the seed falls" (Tannahill, 1982, p. 97). Some early Roman contraceptive techniques included inserting pepper into the mouth of the uterus and creating aversion to sexual intercourse by rubbing a woman's loins with blood taken from the ticks on a wild black bull. Soranus, a second-century Greek gynecologist who practiced in Rome, advised that

> the woman ought, in the moment during coitus when the man ejaculates his seminal fluid, to hold her breath, draw her body back a little so that the semen cannot penetrate into the mouth of the uterus, then immediately get up and sit down with bent knees, and in this position provoke sneezes. (quoted in Tannahill, 1982, p. 129)

In seventh-century China, a method of **coitus obstructus** was used to divert seminal fluid (it was thought) from the penis into the bladder, from which it would later be flushed away during urination. Coitus obstructus was described in a book called *Important Matters of the Jade Chamber* ("jade chamber" was one of several Chinese synonyms for the penis):

> When, during the sexual act, the man feels he is about to ejaculate, he should quickly and firmly, using the fore and middle fingers of the left hand, put pressure on the spot between scrotum and anus, simultaneously inhaling deeply and gnashing his teeth scores of times, without holding his breath. (quoted in Tannahill, 1982, p. 171)

In the sixteenth century, a penile sheath or condom was first described by a physician named Fallopius (whose interest in female anatomy resulted in the name Fallopian tubes). Fallopius described a linen condom that was used to prevent syphilis. By the early eighteenth century, condoms made of gut (intestine) were available (Williams, 1987). Condoms were not mass marketed, however, until the 1870s.

CONSIDERATION: Condoms were first used as a mechanism to protect men from syphilis infection. Williams (1987) noted however, that Casanova partly attributed his fame as a great lover to "his considerate use of it [the condom] to avoid pregnancy for his partner" (p. 280). Casanova is also recognized for using both a gold ball in the vagina to block the passage of sperm and a hollowed-out half of a lemon placed over the cervix.

Margaret Sanger, founder of Planned Parenthood, preparing to give a presentation at the Ford Town Hall in Boston. Adhesive tape is to seal her lips in protest of being warned not to preach birth control while in Boston.

Commercial devices to cover the cervix began to appear during the 1870s. One such device, called the "womb veil," consisted of a rubber cap on a flexible ring that was inserted into the vagina and placed over the cervix (Williams, 1987).

Another method of birth control practiced throughout history and into the present is abstinence. **Coitus interruptus** (withdrawal of the penis from the vagina before ejaculation) also has been a common practice throughout history. In addition, homosexual sex and nonprocreative heterosexual sex (oral, anal, and manual stimulation) have been practiced as methods of birth control.

It has been suggested that "historically, the strongest opposition to birth control has been from religious doctrine and authority" (Travis, 1988, p. 95). Some individuals also took as their mission to stop the use of birth control devices. One such person was Anthony Comstock, who at the turn of the nineteenth century, formed the New York Society for the Suppression of Vice. Comstock was an inspector for the Post Office Department, which allowed him to enforce the Comstock Law (1873) that prohibited the mailing of lewd or obscene material, including anything that mentioned reproductive physiology or birth control. But others opposed such repression. Margaret Sanger, the founder of Planned Parenthood, is known as one of the first advocates of birth control. During the early 1900s, Sanger opposed the Comstock Law and advocated birth control through public lectures and demonstrations. She was arrested and sentenced to jail for opening a birth control clinic.

In 1936, the Supreme Court ruled that there should be an exception to the Comstock Law for physicians. This ruling (*United States v. One Package*) resulted from the arrest of Dr. Hannah Stone for bringing with her on her return from Europe a package of diaphragms. This ruling allowed physicians to dispense birth control information and devices, but only to married people. The access of birth control devices to unmarried individuals wasn't affirmed until 1972 (*Eisenstadt v. Baird,* 405 U.S. 438). Minors were not granted access to contraceptives until 1977 (Travis, 1988).

Methods of Birth Control

Most U.S. women aged 15 to 44 use some form of birth control. The percentage of women using birth control rose from 55.7% in 1982 to 60.3% in 1988 (Mosher, 1990, p. 200). Most methods of birth control have one of three purposes: to prevent the sperm from fertilizing the egg, to prevent the fertilized egg from implanting itself in the uterus, or to terminate implantation. In this section, we discuss the various methods of birth control available in the United States.

Oral Contraceptives

Oral contraceptives (or birth control pills) consist of hormones that prevent pregnancy by inhibiting the release of mature eggs from the ovaries. In the United States, the birth control pill is the most commonly used method of all the nonsurgical forms of contraception.

NATIONAL DATA: In 1988, 30.7% of U.S. women aged 15 to 44 who used contraceptives used the pill (Mosher, 1990).

Recently published data on contraceptive failure rates are available from the 1988 National Survey of Family Growth (NSFG). These data, corrected for the underreporting of abortion, revealed that contraceptive failure remains a serious problem in the U.S. The pill was the most effective reversible contraceptive method for which data were available. During their first year of pill use, 8% of women experienced an unintended pregnancy (Jones & Forrest, 1992).

CONSIDERATION: Actual effectiveness rates for various contraceptive methods are lower than theoretical effectiveness rates. Theoretical effectiveness rates refer to the maximum degree of effectiveness and are based on the assumption that the method of contraception is used consistently and in the correct manner. Actual effectiveness rates are based on the percentage of women using a particular method of contraception who, within one year, do not become pregnant. Actual effectiveness rates are lower than theoretical rates because contraceptive methods are not always used correctly and/or consistently. Some effectiveness studies report results in terms of failures, or conceptions that occurred when the woman reported she had been using a method.

Although there are more than 40 brands available in North America, there are basically two types of birth control pills—the combination pill and the minipill. The combination pill contains the hormones estrogen and progesterone (also known as progestin), which act to prevent ovulation and implantation. The estrogen inhibits the release of the follicle-stimulating hormone (FSH) from the pituitary gland. Normally, follicles mature to become eggs, but without the release of FSH, follicles will not develop into eggs. Thus, estrogen blocks the release of FSH (follicle-stimulating hormone), which prevents the follicle from maturing into an egg.

The progesterone inhibits the release of luteinizing hormone (LH) from the pituitary gland, which during a normal cycle would cause the mature ovum to move to the periphery of the follicle and the follicle to rupture (ovulation). Hence, because of progesterone, there is no ovulation. In this case, the progestin blocks the LH, which would have caused ovulation.

Progesterone also causes the cervical mucus to become thick and acidic, thereby creating a hostile environment for the sperm. So even if an egg were to mature and ovulation were to occur, the progesterone would ward off or destroy the sperm. Another function of progesterone is to make the lining of the uterus unsuitable for implantation.

The combination pill is taken for 21 days, during the first three weeks of the menstrual cycle. During the fourth week, the woman stops taking the pill, resulting in a lower hormone level. Three or four days after the last pill is taken, menstruation occurs, and the 28-day cycle begins again. To eliminate the problem of remembering when to begin taking the pill every month, some physicians prescribe a low-dose combination pill for the first 21 days and a placebo (sugar pill) or an iron pill for the next seven days. In this way, the woman takes a pill every day.

The second type of oral contraceptive, the minipill, contains the same progesterone found in the combination pill, but in much lower doses. The minipill contains no estrogen. Like the progesterone in the combination pill, the progesterone in the minipill provides a hostile environment for sperm and inhibits implantation of a fertilized egg in the uterus. In general, the minipill is somewhat less effective than other types of birth control pills and has been associated with a higher incidence of irregular bleeding.

Other forms of hormone-based contraceptives are used primarily in other countries. The "once-a-month" pill, which contains a long-acting estrogen given in combination with a short-acting progestogen, has been used in China and Mexico. "Paper pills," which were developed in China, are hormone-based contraceptives in the form of a paper-thin wafer resembling a postage stamp. A wafer is dissolved under the woman's tongue daily (Travis, 1988).

Patient education regarding the timing and consistency of pill use and methods of STD prevention is important in prescribing "the pill."

Hormone-based contraceptives should be taken only when prescribed by a physician who has detailed information about the woman's medical history. Contraindications—reasons for not prescribing birth control pills or other hormone-based contraceptives—include hypertension, impaired liver function, known or suspected tumors that are estrogen-dependent, undiagnosed abnormal genital bleeding, pregnancy at the time of the examination, and a history of poor blood circulation. The major complications associated with taking oral contraceptives are blood clots and high blood pressure. Also, the risk of heart attack is increased in women over age 30, particularly those who smoke or have other risk factors. Women over 40 should generally use other forms of contraception, because the side effects of contraceptive pills increase with the age of the user.

Although the long-term negative consequences of taking birth control pills are still the subject of research, short-term negative effects are experienced by 25% of all women who use them. Some undesirable side effects associated with oral contraceptives include the following (Hatcher et al., 1990):

1. missed periods or spotting between periods;
2. breast fullness or tenderness;
3. mood changes, including depression;
4. weight change (gain or loss);
5. chloasma (darkening of skin pigment);
6. decreased vaginal lubrication and sex drive (although some pill users report an increase in enjoyment of sex because the fear of pregnancy is removed);
7. headaches, which may be accompanied by nausea, vomiting, and vision problems (severe headache may be a warning sign of an impending stroke and should be evaluated by a physician);
8. eye problems (on rare occasions, oral contraceptives may cause inflammation of the optic nerve with loss of vision, double vision, or swelling or pain in one or both eyes);

9. chlamydia and gonorrhea infection (in one study, women using the pill had a 73% higher rate of chlamydia and a 70% higher rate of gonorrhea than did nonusers (Witwer, 1989). Hatcher et al. (1990) explained that pills can cause a condition called "cervical ectropion," in which the cervical surface becomes covered with mucus-secreting cells. Cervical ectropion increases vulnerability to chlamydia trachomatis infection;
10. benign liver tumors (in rare cases, oral contraceptives may cause liver tumors, which may cause rupture of the capsule of the liver, extensive bleeding, and even death);
11. circulatory diseases, including hypertension, thrombosis, stroke, pulmonary embolism, and heart attack. Increased risk of cardiovascular side effects of pill use is associated with women over 35 who smoke, have hypertension or other heart or vascular diseases, have a high cholesterol level, or who have a family history of diabetes or heart attack.

CONSIDERATION: According to a Gallup poll (1985), 76% of a representative national sample of women surveyed believe that pill use involves substantial health risks. Although many studies have shown that childbirth involves a greater risk of death than does pill use (Ory, 1983), 58% of the women in the Gallup poll (who had an opinion) think that pill use for women under age 35 is more dangerous than childbirth; 23% believe that the two involve the same amount of risk. What this means is that many people believe the myth that oral contraceptives are more dangerous than pregnancy. In fact, the pill saves many more lives than it costs.

Jacqueline Darroch Forrest, a researcher at the Alan Guttmacher Institute in New York, noted that half of unintended pregnancies in the United States occur among the 10% of women at risk who do not use birth control. Some of these women do not use birth control because of the cost or inconvenience involved, but the most common reason they give is that they're worried about the side effects or the health effects (Painter, 1991).

There are also several noncontraceptive health benefits of taking oral contraceptives, which include (Hatcher et al., 1990):

1. relief of menstrual and premenstrual discomfort (for some women);
2. protection against acute pelvic inflammatory disease (PID);
3. protection against ovarian and endometrial cancer and ovarian cysts;
4. protection against benign breast cysts and noncancerous breast tumors; and
5. protection against ectopic pregnancy (a significant cause of maternal mortality throughout the world).

Another form of hormonal birth control is **Norplant** (see Exhibit 20.1).

Oral contraceptives and other hormonal contraceptives, such as Norplant, are designed for use by women. In recent years, researchers have developed hormonal contraceptives that are designed to be used by men (see Exhibit 20.2).

CONSIDERATION: When this chapter was reviewed prior to publication, one of our reviewers commented that it seems ironic that the reasons given for why men don't have a male pill involve things women have had to tolerate for years—trouble, discomfort, risks!

EXHIBIT 20.1 Norplant: Personal Choice or Social Control?

In December 1990, the FDA approved the use of Norplant, a long-acting reversible hormonal contraceptive consisting of six thin flexible silicone capsules (36 millimeters in length) implanted under the skin of the upper arm (see Figure 20.1). Tested by over 55,000 women in 46 countries, Norplant provides a continuous low dosage of levonorgestrel, resulting in protection against pregnancy for up to five years. A new system, Norplant-2, consists of only two capsules (44 millimeters in length) and is effective for about three years (Shoupe & Mishell, 1989).

Once implanted, the woman need no longer remember to take a pill. With an effectiveness rate of more than 99%, Norplant is one of the most effective contraceptives available. Other advantages of the Norplant include: 1) it is easily reversible with implant removal, 2) it contains no estrogen, so it does not produce estrogen-related side effects, 3) it may decrease menstrual discomfort and ovulatory pain, and 4) it may reduce the risk of endometrial cancer (Hatcher et al., 1990).

Disadvantages of Norplant include: 1) the implants are slightly visible, 2) the initial expense is higher than for short-term methods (however, the surgical procedure costs about $750, which is the price of about five years' worth of birth control pills), 3) discontinuation of the method requires minor surgery, and 4) users may experience changes in menstruation (e.g., prolonged bleeding, spotting between periods, or no bleeding at all).

Some women are advised not to use hormonal contraceptive implants. Contraindications for Norplant use include acute liver disease, jaundice, unexplained vaginal bleeding, and a history of blood clots, heart attack, heart disease, or stroke (Hatcher et al., 1990).

Although the availability of hormonal contraceptive implants, such as the Norplant, allows the woman to make a semipermanent but reversible choice, critics argue that Norplant may be used as a mechanism to prohibit some women from having children or as an incentive to prevent poor women from having children.

For example, legislation has been considered that would enact a plan to offer money to welfare-dependent mothers who receive Norplant. In Kansas, a plan to offer a $500 bonus to welfare-dependent mothers who receive a Norplant implant did not pass the legislature. However, in Louisiana, Representative David Duke's bill to give $100 a year to welfare recipients who practice birth control—including Norplant—passed the House and is being considered in a Senate committee ("Union County," 1991, p. 6B).

In California, a judge granted probation to a convicted child abuser only on the condition that she have a Norplant implant for three years. "Distressed by her fear of a longer prison sentence, the woman agreed to submit to state control over her body" (Planned Parenthood Federation of America, 1991, p. 8). While Norplant may be viewed as a new contraceptive choice for all women, it has "come to be promoted as a new kind of control over the poorest and most vulnerable" (p. 8). Robert Blank (1990) explained:

> Given the current negative attitude of the public toward those on welfare, the increased emphasis on the population problem, the scarcity of public funds for welfare programs, and the emerging focus on the competency of parents, it would not be surprising if the availability of reversible sterilization [such as Norplant] gave impetus to pressures for widespread use of incentives (or coercion) to encourage (or force) sterilization of the poor, retarded, and those otherwise deemed 'unfit.' (p. 130)

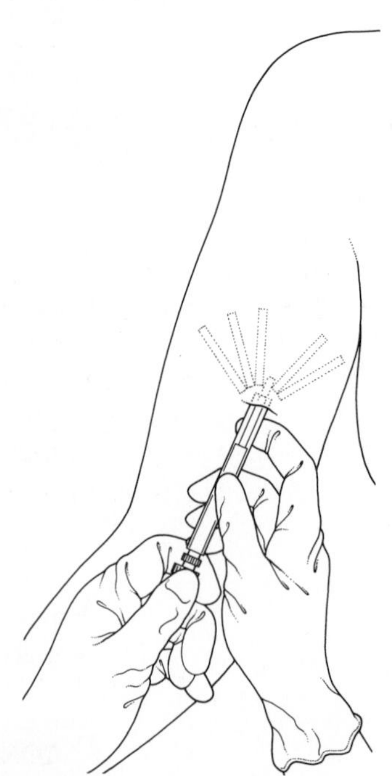

FIGURE 20.1 Norplant injectables

EXHIBIT 20.2 Male Hormonal Contraceptives

Presently, hormonal contraceptives, including the birth control pill and Norplant, are used by women; there are no viable chemical alternatives available for men. However, some research on a hormonal male contraceptive has begun at the University of Washington. Known as testosterone enanthate, or TE, a 200-milligram shot is administered once a week with the effect of lowering sperm production. However, there are drawbacks. It takes months of taking TE before the man becomes infertile (some never do) and months after the injections stop for fertility to be restored. Some men complain of the need to take a weekly shot and report weight gain and acne.

Other hormonal male contraceptives being considered and their drawbacks include those listed in the table below (Bromwich & Parsons, 1990):

Given that these male contraceptive drugs involve unreliability, loss of libido, and uncertain irreversibility, it is unlikely that men will be interested in taking them. In addition, men are unlikely to be willing to take a "pill a day" (too identified with the female pill) or a shot a week (too much trouble and discomfort) for contraceptive purposes. Rather, they would prefer a no-hassle, long-lasting chemical contraceptive that is either injected or implanted and that is reversible. However, drug companies, which are driven by profit, have little motivation to make a long-lasting male contraceptive that does not generate a significant return on their research investment, as does the female pill (taken daily). In addition, if a man were to have a heart attack that was blamed on the male pill, the product would be feared and demand would cease. All of these factors suggest a long wait (at least 10 years) before a male hormonal contraceptive is available to the U.S. public (Prendergast, 1990).

Contraceptive Drug	Effect	Drawback
Depo-Provera	Decreases sperm production	Loss of libido; some sperm still viable
Danazol	Decreases sperm production	Loss of libido
Cyproterone	Decreases sperm production	Loss of libido
Gossypol	Decreases sperm production	Effects not always reversible; affects potassium levels

Condom

NATIONAL DATA: In 1988, 14.6% of U.S. women aged 15 to 44 who used contraception reported that their partner(s) used a condom as their method of birth control (Mosher, 1990).

Also referred to as a "rubber," "safe," or "prophylactic," the **condom** is a thin sheath, usually made of synthetic latex material or lamb intestine, which is rolled over and down the shaft of the erect penis before intercourse (Figure 20.2). When the man ejaculates, the sperm are caught inside the condom.

Like any contraceptive, the condom is effective only when used correctly and consistently. It should be placed on the penis before the penis comes into contact with the vaginal area to avoid any seminal leakage into the vagina. Condoms should also be used during anal intercourse as a protective measure against transmission of HIV (see Chapter 18). Natural skin condoms should not be used because they do not protect against the transmission of some sexually transmissible diseases. Very small viruses, such as HIV, are able to pass through the membranes of natural skin condoms. Latex condoms with reservoir tips are preferable, as they are less likely to break. Finally, the penis should be withdrawn from the vagina (or anus) soon after ejaculation. If the penis is not withdrawn and the erection subsides, semen may leak from the base of the condom into the vaginal lips (or anus). When withdrawing the penis from the vagina or anus, the man should hold on to the condom so it does not slip off.

Condoms are most effective when used in conjunction with a spermicide. In addition to furnishing extra contraceptive protection, spermicides also provide lubrication, which permits easy entrance of the condom-covered penis into the vagina. If no spermicide is used and the condom is not of the prelubricated variety, K-Y jelly, a sterile lubricant, may

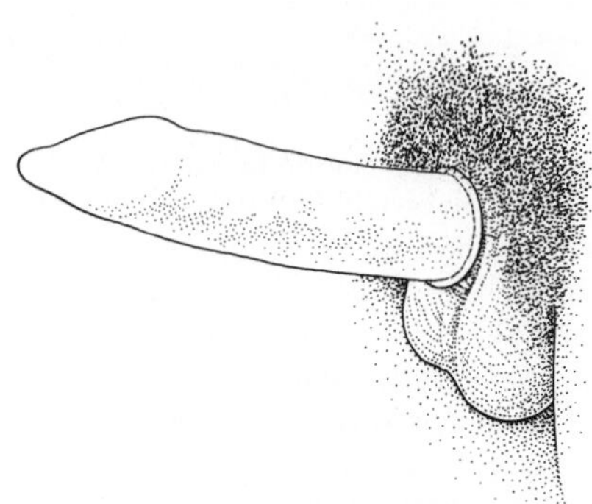

FIGURE 20.2 Condom on penis

be used. Vaseline or other kinds of petroleum jelly should not be used because they increase the risk of vaginal infection and may weaken the condom, causing it to break.

The effectiveness of condoms varies between 64% and 97% (Willis, 1985). The 1988 NSFG data indicated a failure rate of 15% (Jones & Forrest, 1992). The most common contraceptive error made by condom users is failure to use the condom (Hatcher et al., 1990). When used properly during each intercourse and in combination with a spermicide that the woman inserts in her vagina, the effectiveness of the condom is highest.

Condom slippage and breakage rates were studied at the Emory University Family Planning Program in Atlanta, Georgia (Trussell, Warner & Hatcher, 1992). Seventy heterosexual couples were given standard (Trojan-Enz) and experimental (Pleasure Plus) condoms. Of the 405 condoms which were used 8% either broke during intercourse or withdrawal, or slipped off during intercourse. Of the remaining condoms, 7% slipped off during withdrawal. When condoms slipped off during withdrawal it was often related to the use of additional lubricant, such as petroleum jelly or massage oil, which some couples used despite warnings that oil causes deterioration of rubber! The researchers concluded that the slippage rate during withdrawal indicates a considerable level of imperfect use, and is a reminder that better client education is needed. They also observed "If they are accurate, these rates indicate a sobering level of exposure to the risks of pregnancy and of infection with HIV or other STDs, even among those who consistently use condoms." (Trussell et al., 1992, p. 22)

CONSIDERATION: Trussell et al. (1992) lamented that although we are 10 years into the AIDS epidemic we know so little about the efficacy of condoms during use. "One wonders why research on condom efficacy in use has not been accorded higher priority" (p. 23) in funding for AIDS research. They suggested that further study of condom breakage and slippage rates could be done with little expense and would yield valuable information.

The condom plays an important role in reducing the transmission of sexually transmissible diseases. With the spread of HIV infection in our society (see Chapter 18, HIV Infection and Other STDs), it is especially important for sexually active individuals to use condoms (particularly condoms with nonoxynol-9, which has been demonstrated in laboratory tests to kill the AIDS virus). Yet, only about half of sexually active males in a national survey of adolescents reported using a condom the last time they had intercourse (Sonenstein, Pleck, & Ku, 1989).

Some men say they do not like to use a condom because it decreases sensation. However, others say that having their partner put the condom on their penis is an erotic experience and that the condom actually enhances pleasurable feelings during intercourse.

In addition to affording protection from sexually transmissible diseases, condoms offer several other noncontraceptive benefits, including (Hatcher et al., 1990, pp. 170–171):

1 their use encourages male participation in contraception and protection from infection;
2 they are relatively inexpensive and very accessible. Their use does not require an examination, prescription, or fitting. They may be obtained from drug stores, vending machines, gas stations, mail order services, student health centers, or family planning clinics;
3 men who have difficulty maintaining an erection may find that the rim of the condom may have a slight tourniquet effect, helping to maintain an erection; and

4 postcoital discharge of semen from the vagina, which some women find messy and annoying, is avoided.

Two potential problems associated with condom use are that some men and women are allergic to the rubber in condoms and some men are unable to maintain an erection when a condom is used.

While the term "condom" usually refers to a male contraceptive, two types of female condoms are described in Exhibit 20.3.

Intrauterine Device (IUD)

NATIONAL DATA: In 1988, 2% of U.S. women aged 15 to 44 who used contraception used an IUD (Mosher, 1990).

The **intrauterine device**, or IUD, is a small object that is inserted by a physician into the woman's uterus through the vagina and cervix. (see Figure 20.4). The actual effectiveness rate of the IUD is estimated to be between 95% and 96% (Willis, 1985). Although 60 million women use the IUD worldwide (40 million in China alone), use of the IUD in the United States is minimal. In the 1970s, as many as 10% of U.S. women using contraception used the IUD. Due to problems (infertility, ectopic pregnancy, miscarriage, and maternal death) associated with the Dalkon Shield IUD and subsequent lawsuits against the manufacturer by women who were damaged by the device, many brands of IUDs were removed from the market. In 1991, women were more likely to have an unfavorable attitude about IUDs than about any other method of contraception (Forrest, 1992).

Two types of IUDs available in the United States include the Progestasert and the Copper T (Hatcher et al., 1990, pp. 361–362). The Progestasert releases progesterone directly into the uterus and must be replaced every year by the physician. The Progestasert has the effect of reducing menstrual flow, which reduces the risk of anemia. The newer

EXHIBIT 20.3 The Female Condom

The **female condom** resembles a man's condom except that it fits in the woman's vagina (see Figure 20.3) to protect her from pregnancy, HIV infection, and other STDs (Wolinsky, 1988). The vaginal condom is a large, lubricated, polyurethane adaptation of the male version. It is about seven inches long and has flexible rings at both ends. It is inserted like a diaphragm with the inner ring fitting behind the pubic bone against the cervix; the outer ring remains outside the body and encircles the labial area. Like the male version, the condom is not reusable. This new female condom was put on the market in Switzerland in February 1992 and is expected to be available in France, Britain, and perhaps the United States (under the brand name Reality) by the end of 1992 (Nullis, 1992).

The vaginal condom is very tough and does not tear like latex male condoms, but it is trickier to use. The actual effectiveness rate of the vaginal condom is expected to be 94% to 95% because some women will not follow the instructions properly (Nullis, 1992). A major advantage of the female condom is that, like the male counterpart, it protects against transmission of the HIV virus and other STDs. Women and men who have used the vaginal condom are generally satisfied with the device (Gregersen & Gregersen, 1990; Nullis, 1992).

Another type of female condom, which is being tested by International Prophylactic, Inc., consists of a latex condom that may be worn as a G-string by the woman (Hatcher et al., 1990, p. 160). The crotch of the G-string contains a condom pouch, which is rolled up compactly. When the penis enters the vagina, it pushes the condom pouch up into the vagina.

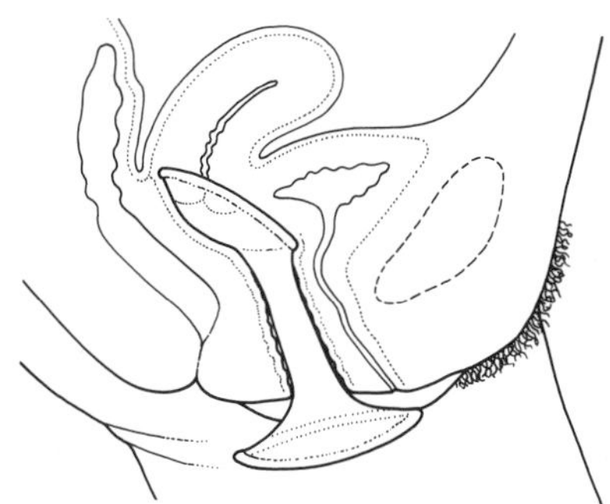

FIGURE 20.3: Female condom

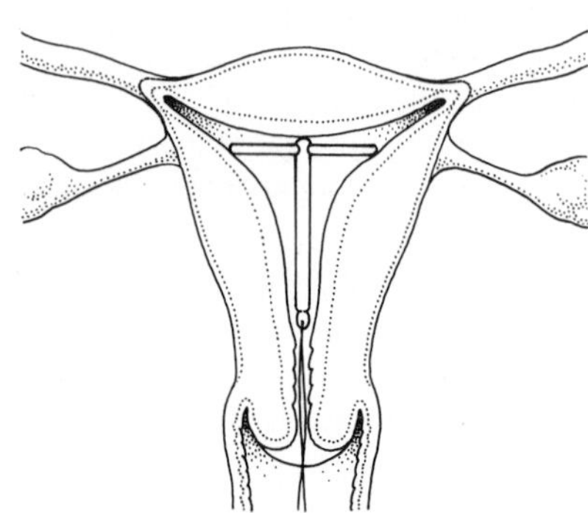

FIGURE 20.4 A T-shaped Intrauterine Device (IUD)

Copper T (T-380A) is approved for four years of use. The Copper T is thought to prevent pregnancy by altering the functioning of the enzymes involved in implantation. Preliminary studies show that it has a failure rate as low as the pill (Thomas, 1988).

One theory suggests that the IUD works by preventing implantation of the fertilized egg in the uterine wall. The exact chemistry is unknown, but one possibility is that the IUD stimulates the entry of white blood cells into the uterus, which attack and destroy "invading cells"—in this case, the fertilized egg. Implantation may also be prevented by the IUD mechanically dislodging the egg from the uterine wall. Because it is possible that the IUD prevents a fertilized egg from developing into a fetus, some view the IUD as a form of abortion. However, some evidence suggests that copper IUDs do not interfere with the development of the fertilized egg but rather prevent fertilization from occurring (Croxatto, 1992).

Several disadvantages and health risks are associated with the use of an IUD, including (Belcastro, 1986; Hatcher et al., 1990; United Nations Population Fund, 1991):

- IUD users are about twice as likely to develop pelvic inflammatory disease (PID), which can result in infertility and even death.
- There is a 1% to 2% chance that pregnancy will occur while the IUD is in place. This can cause medical complications and requires immediate medical attention. If the IUD fails and the woman chooses to have the child, there is an increased risk of a miscarriage.
- About 3% to 5% of IUD users who become pregnant have an ectopic pregnancy (also known as a tubal pregnancy); among nonusers, the rate of ectopic pregnancy is 0.8%. An ectopic pregnancy occurs when the developing zygote grows inside the woman's oviduct, instead of the uterus. This can destroy the oviduct and can result in maternal death.
- Insertions of the IUD may puncture the uterus; incidence of this happening ranges from one in 350 to one in 2,500. Insertion may also result in damage to the bowel, bladder, or cervix.
- Some IUD users experience backaches, anemia, cramping, and spotting. About 15% of users will have their IUD removed because of bleeding or spotting.
- Between 2% and 20% of IUD users will expel the IUD in the first year of use. Expulsion occurs when the uterus rejects the IUD and pushes it out. The woman may not be aware of losing her IUD. The IUD is not recommended for women who have not had a child, as they are more likely to experience expulsion.

About one-third of IUD-related pregnancies are attributable to undetected expulsions. Women who do get pregnant while using the IUD must make a decision about whether to leave it in or remove it. There is a 50% chance of miscarriage if the IUD is left in and a 25% chance of miscarriage if the IUD is taken out. In most cases, the IUD is removed.

CONSIDERATION: Between 1971 and 1974, 2.2 million women were fitted with an IUD called the Dalkon Shield (Perry & Dawson, 1985). Although it was promoted as "the safest and most satisfying form of contraception," the Dalkon Shield was defective and dangerous. At least 20 women have died from it and more than 12,000 women have filed damage suits for complications including pain and severe bleeding, punctured uterus, unplanned pregnancy, miscarriage, and infertility. The tragedy of the Dalkon Shield is attributed not only to the greed and irresponsibility of the A.H. Robins Company, the maker of the IUD, but also to the fact that the FDA did not regulate contraceptive devices until 1976.

The Dalkon Shield was technically flawed and carried a higher PID risk than other IUDs. Petitti (1992) compared it to diethylstilbestrol (DES) during pregnancy, which has also caused much harm. However, she noted that the risk of using an IUD other than the Dalkon Shield may be acceptable, given today's contraceptive alternatives. Petitti cited data from the Women's Health Study, funded by the National Institutes of Child Health and Human Development, which reported that use of IUDs other than the Dalkon Shield slightly increase the risk of PID by a factor of 1.6. She suggested the serious risk of pelvic infection among IUD users might be lowered by "careful selection of users, meticulousness in insertion of the device and close monitoring for early signs of infection" (Petitti, 1992, p. 35). For example, most practitioners today do not recommend the IUD for women who intend to bear children in the future. Petitti recommended we move on to develop safe IUDs and determine safe ways of using them.

Researchers continue to develop new types of IUDs in an attempt to reduce negative side effects. For example, an IUD currently undergoing clinical trials is the Flexigard Intrauterine Copper Contraceptive (ICC) (Wildemeersch, 1992). Advantages of the ICC are that it is better tolerated by the uterus (spontaneous expulsions are virtually nonexistent), and it is effective for more than five years of use.

Diaphragm and Cervical Cap

NATIONAL DATA: In 1988, 5.7% of U.S. women aged 15 to 44 who used contraception used the diaphragm as their method of birth control (Mosher, 1990).

The **diaphragm** is a shallow rubber dome attached to a flexible, circular steel spring. Varying in diameter from two to four inches, the diaphragm covers the cervix and prevents sperm from moving beyond the vagina into the uterus. This device should always be used with a spermicidal jelly or cream. The diaphragm failure rate in the 1988 NSFG study was 22% (Jones & Forrest, 1992).

To obtain a diaphragm, the woman must have an internal pelvic examination by a physician or nurse practitioner who will select the appropriate size diaphragm and show the woman how to insert it. She will be told to apply one teaspoonful of spermicidal cream or jelly on the inside of the diaphragm and around the rim and to insert it into the vagina (Figure 20.5) no more than two hours before intercourse. The diaphragm must be left in place for six to eight hours after intercourse to permit any lingering sperm to be killed by the spermicidal cream.

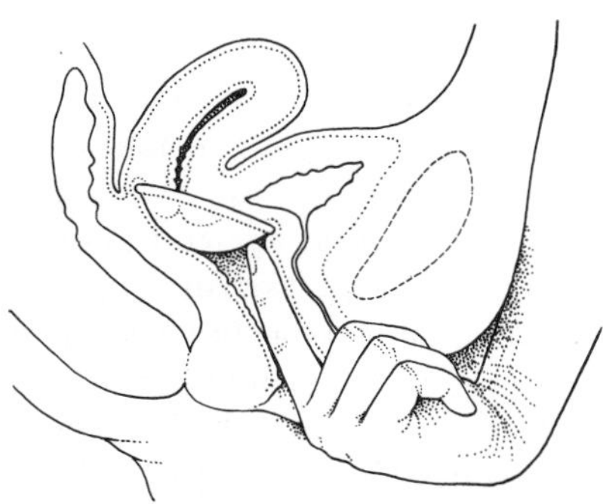

FIGURE 20.5 Diaphragm with spermicide

After the birth of a child, a miscarriage, abdominal surgery, or the gain or loss of ten pounds, a woman who uses a diaphragm should consult her physician or health practitioner to ensure a continued good fit. In any case, the diaphragm should be checked every two years for fit.

There are several advantages and noncontraceptive benefits of using the diaphragm, which include (Hatcher et al., 1990):

- The diaphragm affords *some* protection against sexually transmissible diseases, PID, and cervical dysplasia and/or cancer.
- A diaphragm is well-suited for women who have sex intermittently; they only use the diaphragm when they need it (unlike pills, which are taken daily).
- A diaphragm does not interfere with the woman's hormonal system.

On the negative side, the diaphragm is associated with increased risk for urinary tract infection and may be associated with toxic shock syndrome (Hatcher et al., 1990, pp. 211, 213). Some women feel the use of the diaphragm with the spermicidal gel is messy and a nuisance. For some, the gel may produce an allergic reaction. If the diaphragm is inadvertently left in the vagina for an extended period of time, a foul odor and vaginal discharge may result. Furthermore, some partners feel that the gel makes oral-genital contact less enjoyable.

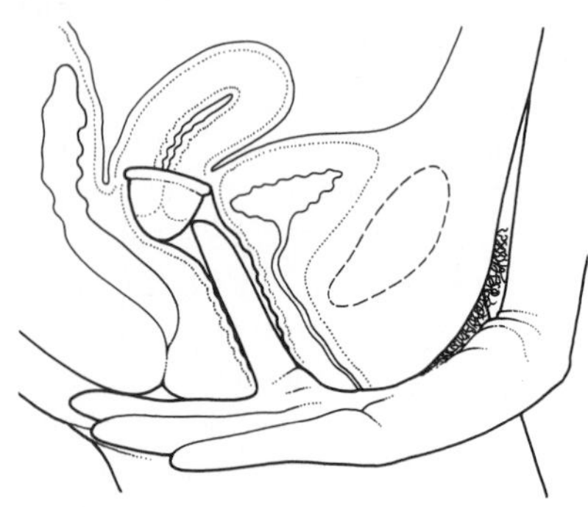

FIGURE 20.6 Cervical cap

While there are no absolute contraindications to diaphragm use, the following conditions may suggest that the diaphragm is not the best contraceptive choice (Hatcher et al., 1990, pp. 210–211):

1 allergy to spermicide, rubber, latex, or polyrethane;
2 abnormalities in vaginal anatomy that interfere with satisfactory fit of diaphragm;
3 inability to learn correct insertion technique;
4 history of toxic shock syndrome or urinary tract infection; and
5 childbirth within the past six weeks, recent miscarriage or abortion, or vaginal bleeding from any cause, including menstruation.

The **cervical cap** is a thimble-shaped contraceptive device made of such material as rubber or polyethylene that fits tightly over the cervix and is held in place by suction (see Figure 20.6). Like the diaphragm, the cervical cap, which is used in conjunction with spermicidal cream or jelly, prevents sperm from entering the uterus. Cervical caps have been widely available in Europe for some time and were approved for marketing in the United States in 1988. The cervical cap cannot be used during menstruation since the suction cannot be maintained. The effectiveness, problems, and risks, and advantages of the cervical cap are similar to those of the diaphragm.

Vaginal Spermicides

NATIONAL DATA: In 1988, 1.1% of U.S. women aged 15 to 44 who used contraception used spermicidal foam as their method of birth control (Mosher, 1990).

A **spermicide** is a chemical that kills sperm. Vaginal spermicides come in several forms, including foam, cream, jelly, and suppository. In the United States, the active agent in most spermicides is **nonoxynol-9**, which has been shown to kill many organisms that cause sexually transmissible diseases (including HIV). Creams and gels are intended for use with a diaphragm. Suppositories are intended for use alone or with a condom. Foam is marketed for use alone but can also be used with a diaphragm or condom (Hatcher et al., 1990, p. 181).

The failure rate of vaginal spermicides (used alone) in preventing pregnancy was 25% in the 1988 NSFG study (Jones & Forrest, 1992). However, using a condom with a spermicide results in a highly effective contraceptive. Kestelman and Trussell (1991) noted:

> When spermicides, which have a first-year failure probability of 21 percent among typical users, are coupled with the condom, which has a first-year failure rate during typical use of 12 percent, the overall first-year probability of failure among typical users would be only 2.5 percent. (p. 226)

Spermicides must be applied (see Figure 20.7) before the penis penetrates the vagina (appropriate applicators are included in the product package) no more than 20 minutes before intercourse. While foam is effective immediately, suppositories, creams, or jellies require a few minutes to allow the product to melt and spread inside the vagina (package instructions describe the exact time required). Each time intercourse is repeated, more spermicide must be applied. Spermicide must be left in place for at least six to eight hours after intercourse; douching or rinsing the vagina should not be done during this period.

One advantage of using spermicides is that they are available without a prescription or medical examination. They also do not manipulate the woman's hormonal system, and they have few side effects. A major noncontraceptive benefit of some spermicides is that they offer some protection against the transmission of sexually transmissible diseases, including HIV.

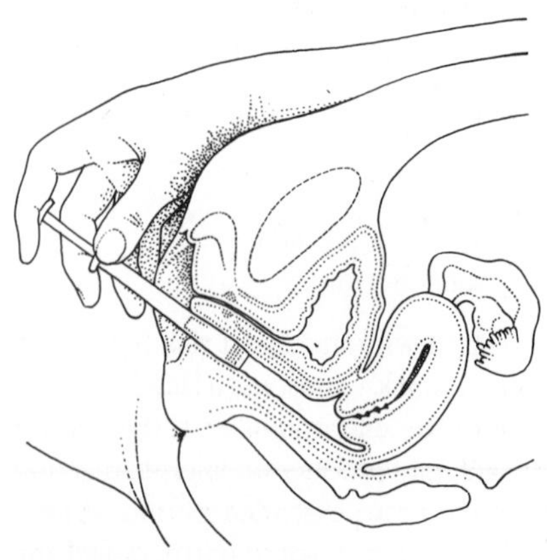

FIGURE 20.7 Spermicide being inserted.

The most common problem associated with spermicides is temporary skin irritation of the vulva or penis caused by sensitivity or allergy to the spermicide.

(Spermicides should not be used if either partner has an allergic reaction.) Some people regard using spermicides as messy. Lastly, the unpleasant taste of spermicides may interfere with the enjoyment of oral-genital contact.

CONSIDERATION: Contraceptive foams, such as Delfen and Emko, should not be confused with vaginal deodorants, such as Summer's Eve. Vaginal deodorants have no contraceptive value. Spermicidal foams should also not be confused with spermicidal gels that are used in conjunction with a diaphragm. These gels should never be used alone because they do not adhere to the cervix as well as foam.

NATIONAL DATA: In 1988, 2.2% of U.S. women aged 15 to 44 who used contraception used either douching, spermicidal jelly or cream alone, vaginal sponge, or other methods (Mosher, 1990).

While some women believe that douching is an effective form of contraception, it is not. **Douching** refers to rinsing or cleansing the vaginal canal. After intercourse, the woman fills a syringe with water or a spermicidal agent and flushes (so she assumes) the sperm from her vagina. But in some cases, the fluid will actually force sperm up through the cervix. In other cases, a large number of sperm may already have passed through the cervix to the uterus, so that the douche may do little good.

In effect, a douche does little to deter conception and may encourage it. In addition, douching is associated with an increased risk for PID and ectopic pregnancy (Hatcher et al., 1990, p. 63).

Vaginal Sponge

The **vaginal sponge** (see Figure 20.8) is two inches in diameter and one and a quarter inches thick and contains spermicide that is activated when the sponge is immersed in water before insertion into the vagina. The woman must wait at least six hours after intercourse before removing the sponge, after which it is discarded. To remove the sponge, the woman reaches into her vagina, grabs a small loop that is attached to the sponge and pulls it out. Like condoms and spermicides, the sponge is available in drugstores without a prescription.

The brand name for the sponge is Today. The sponge prevents fertilization by three modes of contraceptive action: 1) the sponge releases spermicide, which kills sperm on contact, 2) the sponge traps and absorbs sperm, and 3) the sponge blocks the cervix to prevent the sperm from entering (Vorhauer, Rose, McClure, & North, 1984). The actual effectiveness rate of the vaginal sponge was estimated to be between 80% and 87% (Willis, 1985), which was confirmed in the data gathered in the 1988 NSFG reporting a failure rate of 15% (Jones & Forrest, 1992).

A major advantage of the sponge is that it allows for spontaneity in lovemaking. It can be inserted early in the day, may be worn for up to 24 hours, and may be used for more than one act of intercourse without requiring additional applications of spermicide. The vaginal sponge is also relatively inexpensive, does not require the woman to obtain a medical examination or prescription, and does not affect the woman's hormones. Like the diaphragm, the sponge offers some protection against STDs and PID and is well-suited for women who have sex intermittently.

Potential negative side effects of the sponge are similar to those discussed earlier for the diaphragm (allergic reaction, foul odor and discharge if left in the vagina too long, increased risk for urinary tract infection and toxic shock syndrome). The sponge may also increase the incidence of vaginal yeast infections. In addition, use of the sponge may result in vaginal dryness, as the sponge absorbs vaginal lubrication. Some women may have difficulty removing the sponge (Hatcher et al., 1990). During intercourse, some men feel the sponge inside their partners, which may create an unpleasant sensation.

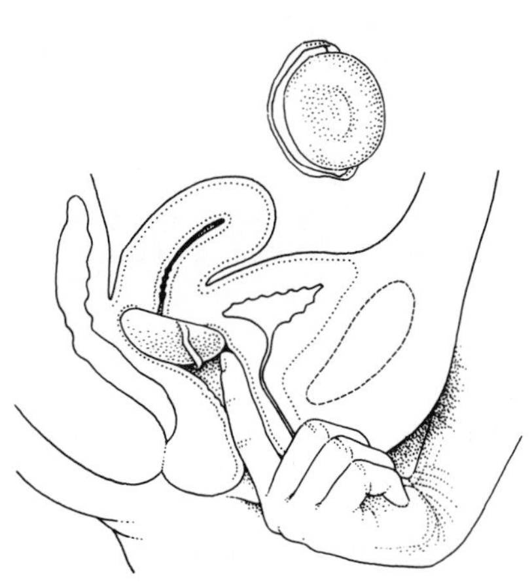

FIGURE 20.8 Contraceptive sponge

Use of the vaginal sponge is contraindicated when 1) the woman or partner has an allergic reaction to the sponge or the spermicide in it, 2) the woman's vaginal anatomy is abnormal, preventing a satisfactory fit of the sponge, 3) the woman is unable to learn the correct insertion technique or is unable to remove the sponge, 4) the woman has a history of toxic shock syndrome, and 5) the woman has given birth in the past six weeks, has had a recent miscarriage or abortion, or is menstruating (Hatcher et al., 1990, pp. 210–211).

CONSIDERATION: Cases of toxic shock syndrome have been reported by women who used the sponge during their menstrual period. A method of contraception other than the sponge should be used during the menstrual period (Greenberg, Bruess, & Sands, 1986).

Coitus Abstentia

Coitus abstentia (also referred to as **abstention**) involves refraining from penile-vaginal intercourse. Individuals may choose to abstain from engaging in sexual intercourse for many reasons. In addition to preventing an unwanted pregnancy or being morally opposed to nonmarital intercourse, other reasons for abstaining from sexual intercourse include (Hatcher et al., 1990, pp. 156–157:

- avoiding sexually transmissible diseases
- post-operative pain or tenderness, such as from episiotomy or vasectomy
- pelvic, vaginal, or urinary tract infection
- dyspareunia or other pelvic pain
- undiagnosed postcoital bleeding
- late third trimester of pregnancy, postpartum, or postabortion

Abstention is a natural method of birth control that requires only the decision to abstain and discipline on the part of the individual or partners. Coitus abstentia is theoretically 100% effective. However, if couples engage in other sexual behaviors (such as rubbing the head of the penis between the vaginal lips) that result in male ejaculation or leakage of preejaculatory fluid, sperm may be deposited in the vagina and pregnancy may result.

An advantage of abstention for noncoital partners is that "it may openly label their relationship as temporarily or permanently noncoital, thereby avoiding misinterpretations of sexual feelings or actions" (Belcastro, 1986, p. 76). The couple may engage in sex play while realizing that their sex play is not a prelude to intercourse. Another advantage of abstention is that it may highlight the nonsexual aspects of the couple's relationship. In addition, modes of sexual expression other than intercourse may be explored by the couple practicing abstention.

CONSIDERATION: Hatcher et al. (1990) noted that "although abstinence has become associated with saying 'no,' viewed from another perspective, abstinence can mean saying 'yes' to a number of other sexual activities" (p. 156).

Hatcher et al. (1990) recommended that individuals who choose to abstain from sexual intercourse consider the following to help achieve their goal (pp. 157–158):

1. Avoid contexts that may encourage sexual interaction (for example, avoid being alone with a date in a bedroom, avoid alcohol consumption while on a date or with a partner).

2. Decide in advance what sexual activities you are willing to engage in and discuss these with your partner.
3. If you say "no," say it like you mean it. Make it clear to your partner that you do not want to have intercourse. Leave if you feel that your wishes are not being respected.
4. If you suspect you will be pressured, either don't go out with the person or double date; keep trusted friends nearby.
5. Maintain relationships with other men and women (so that you will not become dependent on one relationship in which you may be pressured to have intercourse).
6. Learn about available birth control methods should you choose to engage in intercourse. Have a back-up method accessible.
7. Learn what postcoital methods are available should you have unprotected intercourse.

Periodic Abstinence

Also referred to as "natural family planning" and "fertility awareness," **periodic abstinence** involves refraining from sexual intercourse during the period of time each month that the woman is thought to be fertile. Women who use periodic abstinence must know their time of ovulation and avoid intercourse just before, during, and immediately after that time. Calculating the fertile period involves three assumptions (Hatcher et al. 1990, p. 340): 1) ovulation occurs on day 14 (plus or minus two days) *before the onset of the next menstrual period,* 2) sperm remain viable for two to three days, and 3) the ovum survives for 24 hours.

NATIONAL DATA: In 1988, 2.3% of U.S. women aged 15 to 44 who used contraception used periodic abstinence as their method of birth control (Mosher, 1990).

The effectiveness of periodic abstinence in preventing pregnancy is highly variable and estimated to be between 53% and 86% (Willis, 1985). Periodic abstinence is used by couples who do not wish to practice other family planning methods for religious or personal reasons. Couples using periodic abstinence as a method of contraception must accept the greater possibility of unplanned pregnancy.

There are four ways of predicting the time period during which the woman is fertile: the calendar method, the basal body temperature method, the cervical mucus method, and the hormone-in-urine method. These methods may not only be used to avoid pregnancy, they may also be used to facilitate conception if the woman wants to become pregnant. We provide only basic instructions here for using periodic abstinence as a method of contraception. Individuals considering this method should consult with a trained health practitioner for more detailed instruction.

Calendar Method The calendar method is the oldest and most widely practiced method of avoiding pregnancy through periodic abstinence (Hatcher et al., 1990, p. 340). The calendar method allows women to calculate the onset and duration of their fertile period. When using the calendar method to predict when the egg is ready to be fertilized, the woman keeps a record of the length of her menstrual cycles for eight months. The menstrual cycle is counted from day one of the menstrual period through the last day before the onset of the next period. She then calculates her fertile period by substracting 18 days from the length of her shortest cycle and 11 days from the length of her longest cycle. The resulting figures indicate the range of her fertility period (Hatcher et al., 1990, pp. 340–341). It is during this time that the woman must abstain from intercourse if pregnancy is not desired.

For example, suppose that during an eight-month period, a woman had cycle lengths of 26, 32, 27, 30, 28, 27, 28, and 29 days. Subtracting 18 from her shortest cycle (26) and 11 from her longest cycle (32), she knows the days that the egg is likely to be in the Fallopian tubes. To avoid getting pregnant, she must avoid intercourse on days 8 through 21 of her cycle.

CONSIDERATION: The calendar method of predicting the "safe" period may be unreliable for two reasons. First, the next month the woman may ovulate at a different time from any of the previous eight months. Second, sperm life varies; they may live long enough to meet the next egg in the Fallopian tubes.

Basal Body Temperature (BBT) Method This method is based on determining the time of ovulation by measuring temperature changes that occur in the woman's body shortly after ovulation. The basal body temperature is the temperature of the body at rest on waking in the morning. To establish her BBT, the woman must take her temperature before she gets out of bed for three months. Shortly before, during, or right after ovulation, the woman's BBT usually rises about 0.4 to 0.8 degrees Fahrenheit (Hatcher et al., 1990, p. 344). Some women notice a temperature drop about 12 to 24 hours before it begins to rise after ovulation. Intercourse must be avoided from the time the woman's temperature drops until her temperature has remained elevated for three consecutive days. Intercourse may be resumed on the night of the third day after the BBT has risen and remained elevated for three consecutive days.

Cervical Mucus Method The cervical mucus method, also known as the ovulation method and the Billings method of periodic abstinence, is based on observations of changes in the cervical mucus during the woman's monthly cycle. The woman may observe her cervical mucus by wiping herself with her finger or toilet paper. In assessing the mucus she focuses primarily on the texture (its qualities of elasticity, wetness, or tackiness), and secondarily on its color and quantity (Trussell & Grummer-Strawn, 1990).

The woman should abstain from intercourse during her menstrual period, as the mucus is obscured by menstrual blood and cannot be observed and ovulation can occur during menstruation. Also, women with short cycles may be fecund (fertile) during the last days of bleeding (Trussell & Grummer-Strawn, 1990).

After menstruation ceases, intercourse is permitted on days during the time that there is no mucus present or thick mucus is present in small amounts. Intercourse should be avoided just prior to, during, and immediately after ovulation if pregnancy is not desired. Before ovulation, mucus is cloudy, yellow or white, and sticky. During ovulation, cervical mucus is thin, clear, slippery, and stretchy and resembles raw egg white. This phase is known as the "peak symptom." During ovulation, some women experience ovulatory pain referred to as "mittelschmerz." Such pain may include feelings of heaviness, abdominal swelling, rectal pain or discomfort, and lower abdominal pain or discomfort on either side. Mittelschmerz is useful for identifying ovulation but not for predicting it. Intercourse may resume four days after the disappearance of the "peak symptom" and continue until the next menses. During this time, cervical mucus may be either clear and watery or cloudy and sticky. There may be no mucus noticed at all during this period (Hatcher et al., 1990, pp. 344–345). The woman using this method should also abstain from intercourse during periods of stress, as stress can affect the quality of mucus. For a woman who has a typical cycle of 29 days, intercourse would be permissible on about 12 nights (Trussell & Grummer-Strawn, 1990).

Advantages of the cervical mucus method include 1) it requires the woman to become familiar with her reproductive system, and 2) it can give early warning about some STDs (which can affect cervical mucus). However, the cervical mucus method requires the woman to distinguish between mucus and semen, spermicidal agents, lubrication, and infectious discharges. Also, the woman must not douche because she will wash away what she is trying to observe.

An accidental pregnancy is most likely if any of the three most serious rules is violated: no intercourse during mucus days, during the three days after the peak day, or during periods of stress. Breaking one of these rules increased pregnancy risk by almost 30%. Trussell and Grummer-Strawn (1990) reported pregnancy rates from a World Health Organization clinical trial of the ovulation method. Pregnancy probability during the first year was only 3% with perfect use of the method. However, with imperfect use it was 86%. They summarized, "Thus, if used perfectly, the ovulation method is very effective. However, it is extremely unforgiving of imperfect use" (p. 65).

Hormone-in-Urine Method A hormone is released into the bloodstream of the ovulating female 12 to 24 hours prior to ovulation. Women can purchase over-the-counter tests, such as First Response and Ovutime, that are designed to ascertain if they have ovulated.

CONSIDERATION: Some of the periodic abstinence methods are very effective, however, they are not ideal for all couples. Trussell and Grummer-Strawn (1990) found that couples with a poor attitude toward the rules are likely to take risks in implementing the method. Those who got away with risk-taking were likely to take risks again. To use the ovulation method a couple must be willing to abstain for nearly half of each menstrual cycle. Josef Roetzer, the pioneer of the sympto-thermal method of periodic abstinence emphasized that " 'natural conception regulation' is not contraception, but a way of life" (Trussell & Grummer-Strawn, 1990, p. 75).

Coitus Interruptus (Withdrawal)

Coitus interruptus, more commonly known as **withdrawal**, is the practice of the man withdrawing his penis from the vagina before he ejaculates. The actual effectiveness rate of withdrawal in preventing pregnancy is estimated to be about 85%. In other words, about 15% of women who use withdrawal as their method of contraception become pregnant in the first year (Kost, Forrest, & Harlap, 1991). While withdrawal is not generally advised as a method of effective contraception, some regard it as "a considerably better method than no method at all" (Hatcher et al., 1990, p. 353).

NATIONAL DATA: In 1988, 2.2% of U.S. women aged 15 to 44 who used contraception used withdrawal as their method of birth control (Mosher, 1990).

The advantages of coitus interruptus are 1) it requires no devices or chemicals, and 2) it is always available. The disadvantages of withdrawal include 1) it does not provide protection against STDs, 2) it may interrupt the sexual response cycle and diminish the pleasure for the couple, and 3) it is less effective than some other methods.

Withdrawal is not a reliable form of contraception for two reasons. First, a man may emit a small amount of preejaculatory fluid (which is stored in the prostate or penile urethra) that may contain sperm. This fluid contains more sperm after the man has recently ejaculated; one drop may contain millions of sperm (Hatcher et al., 1990). In addition, the man may lack the self-control to withdraw his penis before ejaculation, or he may delay his withdrawal too long and inadvertently ejaculate some semen near the vaginal opening of his partner. Sperm deposited here can live in the moist vaginal lips and make their way up the vagina to the uterus.

Postcoital Contraception

Postcoital contraception, refers to various types of "morning-after" pills that may be used after unprotected intercourse occurs during the woman's fertile time of the month. Hatcher et al. (1990) suggested that postcoital methods of contraception "should be reserved for emergency situations only . . . when unprotected intercourse occurred unexpectedly and when medication can be given within 72 hours of exposure" (p. 423).

While various types of morning-after pills have been developed, the treatment of choice is a combined birth control pill that is marketed as Ovral. When used as postcoital contraception, two Ovral pills are taken within 72 hours (preferably between 12 and 24 hours) of coitus, and two more pills are taken 12 hours later. Estimates of the effectiveness of Ovral in preventing continued pregnancy range between 90% and 99% (Hatcher et al., 1990, p. 424). An older treatment of high-dose oral estrogens, known as DES (diethylstibestrol), is no longer recommended due to the high rate of birth defects in women whose pregnancy continued despite treatment with DES.

A newer drug, RU-486, has no significant side effects and can end a pregnancy in 95% of the cases if taken with prostaglandin within seven weeks of conception. This drug is not available in the United States. RU-486 is discussed in greater detail in Chapter 22, Abortion and Other Pregnancy Outcomes.

CONSIDERATION: Postcoital methods of contraception are a controversial issue; some people regard them as a form of abortion, while others regard them as a means of reducing the need for abortion. Although the FDA has not approved postcoital methods of contraception, some physicians in the United States have provided postcoital methods to rape victims (Hatcher et al., 1990, pp. 423–424).

Sterilization

Unlike the temporary and reversible methods of contraception just discussed, **sterilization** is a permanent surgical procedure that prevents reproduction. Sterilization, which was once stigmatized as an extreme and undesirable method of birth control, is gaining social acceptance. It may be a contraceptive method of choice when the woman should not have more children for health reasons or when individuals are certain about their desire to have no more children or to remain childless. Most couples complete their intended childbearing in their late 20s or early 30s, leaving more than 15 years of continued risk of unwanted pregnancy. Due to the risk of pill use at older ages and the lower reliability of alternative birth control methods, sterilization has become the most popular method of contraception among married women who have completed their families. Sterilization has become the most widely used method of family planning in the world for both developed and developing countries (United Nations Population Fund, 1991).

A major advantage of sterilization is that it is highly effective. It is estimated that both female and male sterilization is over 99% effective in preventing pregnancy (Willis, 1985). In addition, sterilization is safe and economical. Although sterilization operations are potentially reversible, they are intended to be permanent, which may or may not be an advantage.

CONSIDERATION: In a study by Henshaw and Singh (1986), 8.6 million couples who chose sterilization (tubal ligation or vasectomy) for contraceptive reasons were asked the following questions: 1) "If it were possible for you to have a(nother) baby, would you, yourself, like to have one?" and 2) "As things look to you just now, if the operation could be safely reversed, that is, changed back, would you want to have it reversed?" Twenty-six percent of the female partners of these couples said they would like to have a child or additional children. Thirty-nine percent of these women—about 10% of the total—indicated that they and their partners (if married) would want their operation reversed. While this suggests that up to 10% of people who choose sterilization may regret their decision, the researchers suggest that,

> If people were discouraged from being sterilized, it may well be that more couples would later regret not having been sterilized than now regret that they have had the operation. (Henshaw & Singh, 1986, p. 240)

Nevertheless, before individuals decide to be sterilized they might consider how they would feel if:

- One or more of their children die.
- They divorce and their ex-spouse has primary physical custody of the children.
- A new partner wants a child.
- Their financial situation improves significantly.
- They want more children when their children leave home.

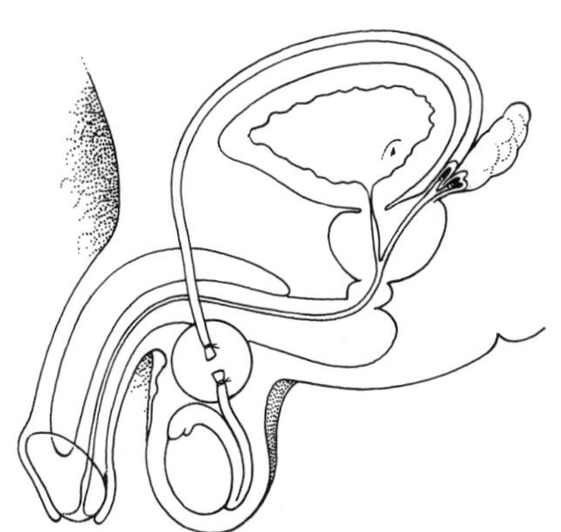

FIGURE 20.9 Vasectomy

Some states have specific requirements that must be met in order for an individual to undergo voluntary sterilization. Examples of such requirements include a minimum age (18 or 21), a waiting period between the time of informed consent and the sterilization, and second-opinion medical consultation. Some states require a married person to obtain the consent of his or her spouse in order to be sterilized.

The sterilization operation for men, called a **vasectomy**, (see Figure 20.9) is simpler, safer, and less expensive than female surgical contraception. For these reasons, vasectomy is the medically preferred procedure. The cost of a vasectomy ranges between $75 and $500; the cost of female sterilization ranges between $75 and $1,300, depending on the technique used and the place in which the procedure is performed (Belcastro, 1986).

Prior to 1975, more vasectomies than **tubectomies** (the female sterilization operation) were performed in the United States. Throughout the 1980s, tubectomies have become more frequent with a ratio of two tubectomies to every vasectomy (Hatcher et al., 1990, p. 387). Next, we briefly describe sterilization procedures for women and men.

NATIONAL DATA: In 1988, 27.5% of U.S. women aged 15 to 44 who use contraception relied on female sterilization and 11.7% relied on male sterilization as their method of birth control (for a total of 39.2%) (Mosher, 1990).

Female sterilization A woman may be sterilized by removal of her ovaries (**oophorectomy**) or uterus (**hysterectomy**). These operations are not normally undertaken for the sole purpose of sterilization because the ovaries produce important hormones, as well as eggs, and because both procedures carry the risks of major surgery. Because a hysterectomy involves greater health risks compared to other sterilization procedures, it should not be performed for contraceptive purposes alone. Rather, a hysterectomy should only be performed in the case of a gynecologic disease or condition that warrants removal of the uterus.

The usual procedures of female sterilization are the **salpingectomy**, or tubal ligation (see Figure 20.10), and a variant of it called the **laparoscopy.** Salpingec-

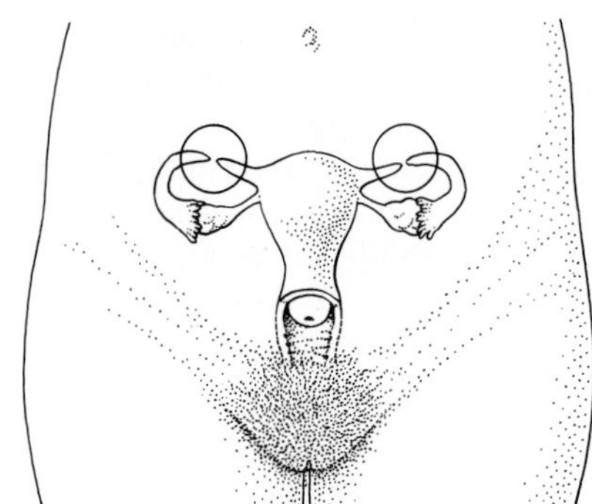

FIGURE 20.10 Tubal ligation

tomy, also known as "tying the tubes," is often performed under a general anesthetic while the woman is in the hospital just after she has delivered a baby. An incision is made in the lower abdomen, just above the pubic line, and the Fallopian tubes are tied, clamped, or cauterized (burned). The operation takes about 30 minutes. A less expensive and quicker (about 15 minutes) form of salpingectomy, which is performed on an outpatient basis, is the laparoscopy. Often using local anesthesia, the surgeon inserts a small, lighted viewing instrument (laparoscope) through the woman's abdominal wall just below the navel through which the uterus and the Fallopian tubes can be seen. The surgeon then makes another small incision in the lower abdomen and inserts a special pair of forceps that carry electricity to cauterize the tubes. The laparoscope and forceps are then withdrawn, the small wounds are closed with a single stitch, and small bandages are placed over the closed incisions. (Laparoscopy is also known as "the Band-Aid operation.") As an alternative to reaching the Fallopian tubes through an opening below the navel, the surgeon may make a small incision in the back of the vaginal barrel (vaginal tubal ligation).

These procedures for female sterilization are highly effective, but sometimes there are complications. In rare cases, a blood vessel in the abdomen is torn open during the sterilization operation and bleeds into the abdominal cavity. When this happens, another operation is necessary to find the bleeding vessel and tie it closed. Occasionally, the small or large intestine is injured, which may cause nausea, vomiting, and loss of appetite. In some cases, female sterilization may result in medical complications that lead to death. However, risks associated with female sterilization are less than risks associated with childbirth. Reported fatality rates in the United States for female surgical contraception are about three deaths per 100,000. In contrast, the maternal mortality rates are 14 deaths per 100,000 live births (Hatcher et al., 1990, p. 391).

Some women experience negative psychological reactions to sterilization, including poor self-concept, depression, and sexual dysfunction. Such negative reactions may be the result of associating sterility with lack of femininity. More negative psychological reactions have been observed following hysterectomy than tubal sterilization (Williams, 1987, p. 279).

NATIONAL DATA: About 300,000 men have vasectomies every year (Keen, 1988).

Male Sterilization The most frequent form of male sterilization is vasectomy, which is usually performed in the physician's office under a local anesthetic. Vasectomy involves the physician making two small incisions, one on each side of the scrotum, so that a small portion of each vas deferens (the sperm-carrying ducts) can be cut out and tied closed. Sperm are still produced in the testicles, but since there is no tube to the penis, they remain in the epididymis and eventually dissolve. The procedure takes about 15 minutes; the man can leave the physician's office within a short time.

In 1974, a "no-scalpel" procedure was developed in China. To reach the vas, a small puncture (rather than incision) is made in the scrotum with a specially modified surgical clamp with sharpened points. The procedure, which is the standard vasectomy in China, is almost bloodless, and no sutures are needed to close the small wound (Hatcher et al., 1990, p. 411).

After undergoing a vasectomy, sperm do not disappear from the ejaculate immediately; some sperm remain in the vas deferens above the severed portion. Therefore, another method of contraception should be used until the man has had about 20 ejaculations. He is then asked to bring a sample of his ejaculate to the physician's office so that it can be examined under a microscope for a sperm count.

TABLE 20.1 Percentage of Female Contraceptive Users Aged 15 to 44 Using Various Methods of Birth Control, 1982–1988

Method	1982 %	1988 %
Sterilization	34.1	39.2
Female	23.2	27.5*
Male	10.9	11.7
Pill	28.0	30.7
IUD	7.0	2.0**
Diaphragm	8.1	5.7
Condom	12.0	14.6*
Foam	2.4	1.1
Periodic abstinence	3.9	2.3
Withdrawal	2.0	2.2
Other (douch, sponge, jelly or cream alone, and other methods)	2.5	2.1

*Change from 1982 to 1988 is significant at 0.05 level.
**Change from 1982 to 1988 is significant at 0.01 level.

Source: Adapted from Mosher, W. D. (1990). Contraceptive practice in the United States, 1982–1988. *Family Planning Perspectives, 22,* 200. Used by permission.

First-year contraceptive failures associated with vasectomies (not including pregnancies resulting from unprotected intercourse before the reproductive tract was cleared of sperm) are reported in about 0.1% of cases (Hatcher et al., 1990, pp. 412–414). These failures result from spontaneous recanalization of the vas or division or occlusion of the wrong structure during surgery. In rare cases, the man may have more than two tubes, of which the physician was not aware.

A vasectomy does not affect a man's desire for sex, ability to have an erection, orgasm, amount of ejaculate (sperm comprise only a minute portion of the seminal fluid), or health. However, some men may feel emasculated because they no longer have the ability to procreate (Belcastro, 1986, p. 69).

In Table 20.1, we list the percentage of female contraceptive users aged 15 to 44 who reported using various methods of birth control for the years 1982 and 1988. You may notice that female sterilization and condom use increased significantly from 1982 to 1988, whereas IUD use decreased significantly.

Selecting and using a method of contraception is, in part, a psychological issue. The research perspective to follow reviews various psychological influences in contraceptive use.

RESEARCH PERSPECTIVE

Psychological Influences in Contraceptive Use

Given the high rate of unintended pregnancy among young people in this country, researchers have attempted to identify barriers to effective contraceptive use. Among high school and collegiate women, contraceptive risk taking has been linked to a negative emotional response to sexuality and negative sexual self-perception. In this Perspective, we will focus on the constructs of sex guilt, self-esteem, erotophobia-erotophilia, sexual self-concept, and love attitudes, and will discuss their effects on contraceptive use.

Continued

Continued

Sex Guilt

Sexually active women scoring high in sex guilt are more likely than low scorers to report not using any birth control method or using ineffective methods (Gerrard, 1987 a & b). In comparing sex guilt and contraceptive use of college women in 1973 and 1978 to that in 1983–84, Gerrard (1987b) documented shifting patterns, apparently a function of the sexual norms of the times. When sexual activity increased in the late 1970s but sex guilt did not decrease, the students revealed less effective contraceptive use. Perhaps women with high sex guilt felt socially compelled to engage in sexual activity, even though they did not approve of doing so. Then, in the 1980s, when there was an increase in sex guilt (sufficient to suppress sexual behavior) and a decline in sexual activity, effective contraceptive use increased.

Erotophobia-Erotophilia

As you may remember from Chapter 9, erotophobia refers to primarily negative emotional responses to a broad range of sexual topics; erotophilia refers to positive emotional responses. When you took the Sexual Opinion Survey in Chapter 9, did you score in the erotophobic or erotophilic direction? Fisher et al. reported that scores on the Mosher Sex Guilt Scale and the Sexual Opinion Survey are correlated ($r = 0.60$). Fisher et al. (1983) presented research support for seven hypotheses predicting relationships between erotophobia-erotophilia and contraceptive behavior. Following are their hypotheses and examples of studies investigating these ideas.

1. Erotophobic (versus erotophilic) people are less likely to have accurate knowledge about conception and contraception. Scores on the first examination for 40 students in a human sexuality course were compared to the students' responses to the Sexual Opinion Survey. Even controlling for overall grade point average, erotophobic students did not score as well as erotophilic students on the exam (71.16% average versus 78.90%), possibly reflecting difficulty in learning the sexual material.

However, a study by Gerrard, Kurylo, and Reis (1991) found that the knowledge deficits of erotophobic students may not simply be due to an inability to learn sexuality information. Additional factors are their active avoidance of contraceptive information and their level of self-esteem. Based on the notion that people with high self-esteem are more likely to trust their own judgment and to resist information they find threatening, Gerrard et al. hypothesized that erotophobics with high self-esteem would find it difficult to learn information on contraception and AIDS.

They found that erotophobic and erotophilic female under-graduate students were similar in their number of sexual partners, intercourse frequency, and effectiveness of reported method of contraception. In fact, when effects of self-esteem were sorted out, there was no significant difference in the groups' retention of contraceptive and AIDS information. But self-esteem did make a difference. The high self-esteem students, even the erotophilics, showed little improvement in knowledge over the semester; high self-esteem erotophobic students showed even less improvement. These students may be avoiding the information by "tuning out" threatening course content.

2. Erotophobic individuals are more likely to underestimate the probability that they will have sexual intercourse in the near future (Fisher et al., 1983). In a study of undergraduate men, respondents completed the Sexual Opinion Survey and reported whether or not they intended to have sexual intercourse in the coming month. A month later, they completed a follow-up assessment, in which they reported if intercourse had occurred and if they had used contraception. Not only were erotophobic men less likely to anticipate intercourse, but their expectations wereunderestimates. Of the erotophobic men who reported they did *not* intend to have intercourse, 17% did have it in the intervening month. As the intercourse was

Continued

Continued

unanticipated, it was also often unprotected. On the other hand, the expectations of the erotophilic men, who are more likely to overestimate their probability of intercourse, are probably more likely to be contraceptively prepared.

3. Erotophobic individuals are less likely to participate in the public behaviors necessary to acquire contraceptives.

Attitudes related to the acquisition of contraceptives were investigated by Fisher, Fisher, and Byrne (1977). Undergraduate male volunteers reported to a drugstore to participate in a research project on "male purchasing behavior." The volunteers were told they would participate in a lottery to determine which "male related" product they would purchase: condoms, acne cream, or medication for "jock itch." The lottery was rigged, and all participants received instructions to purchase a three-pack of lubricated condoms from the pharmacist on duty (who had been informed about the study). Following the condom purchase, the participants filled out a questionnaire in which they reported their emotional reaction to buying the condoms and their evaluation of condoms, the pharmacist, and the drugstore. Then the participants were debriefed (the mild deception and the purpose of the study were explained).

As the investigators expected, the more negatively the men evaluated their purchase experience, the more negative was their evaluation of condoms and their reliability, the pharmacist, and even the drugstore in which the purchase took place. The investigators interpreted these results as consistent with the idea that individuals may evaluate a contraceptive method based on how it feels to obtain that method. Accordingly, negative evaluation of contraceptive purchasing could interfere with the likelihood of further purchases.

4. Erotophobic individuals are less likely to communicate with their sexual partners about contraception. While Fisher et al. (1983) did not report any research directly testing this hypothesis, they reviewed a study that investigated the role of erotophobia-erotophilia in communication about sex in general. After reading a brief prepared speech with a sexual message in front of a camera, erotophobic students reported more negative emotional response to the task and anticipated that others would judge them and their performance negatively. The researchers (Fisher, Miller, Byrne, & White, 1980) observed that students often stumbled over pronunciation of sexual terms and noted that vocabulary deficiencies and reluctance to communicate about sex would complicate talking with one's partner about birth control.

5. Erotophobic individuals are less likely to be consistent in their contraceptive use. As discussed earlier in the section on sex guilt, people's feelings about sex may be so negative that they avoid it, or the feelings may be just negative enough to preclude actively planning and preparing for it. Fisher et al. (1983) summarized data showing that among college women, consistent contraceptors are fairly erotophilic, inconsistent contraceptors fairly erotophobic, and sexually inactive women the most erotophobic. This relationship has been documented with men as well, with erotophobic men less likely to report they or their partners had used a contraceptive during the previous month (as reported by Przybyla, cited in Fisher et al. (1983) and in the previously described study in the section on anticipation of intercourse).

6. Erotophobic individuals have more negative attitudes toward birth control. Highly erotophobic college women are more likely than highly erotophilic women to believe that using contraception would lead to major side effects, have a negative effect on their sexual morals, is unnatural and unreliable, and would give guilt feelings, decrease sexual pleasure, and make sex less romantic (Fisher et al., 1983). Erotophobic men also were more likely to believe that contraceptive use results in feeling guilty and in less sexual pleasure and were less likely to believe that using it is "good" or "right."

7. Emotional factors such as erotophobia-erotophilia and one's beliefs and expectancies each independently influence contraceptive behavior and may also

Continued

Continued

have a complementary influence. Therefore, educational interventions to enhance contraceptive use must focus on the emotional and the informational aspects.

Sexual Self-Concept

Sexual self-concept is defined as "an individual's evaluation of his or her own sexual thoughts, feelings and actions" (Winter, 1988). Sexual self-concept scores of male and female undergraduate students were correlated with frequency of contraceptive use and use at most recent intercourse (Winter, 1988). Contrary to results in other studies, results from the Sexual Opinion Survey showed that erotophobia-erotophilia was not correlated with the contraceptive behaviors in this study.

Winter also examined the relationship between sexual self-concept and choice of contraceptive method. She found that students with the highest sexual self-concept (most positive sexual self-concept) scores were more likely than other students to have used a prescription method at most recent intercourse. The next highest scores were among the nonprescription (condom or sponge) users, followed by the withdrawal and no-method group. Sexual self-concept scores increased with age. Adler and Hendrick (1991) also confirmed that for women and men contraceptive behavior was related to general self-esteem and sexual self-esteem.

Implications of the relationship between sexual self-concept and contraceptive practices further substantiate the impact of psychological variables on contraceptive behaviors. As Winter (1988) noted, sexuality education curricula that merely dispense information are insufficient; social and psychological issues surrounding sexuality must also be addressed. Evaluation of contraception educational programs should measure whether programs influence psychological results, as well as the level of knowledge.

Love Styles

Finally, love attitudes (based on Lee's typology described in Chapter 14, Love and Sexuality) have been shown to correlate with contraceptive behavior. Among women, Eros (romantic, passionate love style) was positively correlated with reliable contraception. Ludus (the game-playing style) lovers tended to be poor contraceptors (Adler & Hendricks, 1991). Among men only the Eros style was related to contraceptive behavior; it had a positive association. Adler and Hendricks noted the complexity of the problem of unreliable contraceptive behavior. They observed that relationship and individual factors must be considered, as well as current changes in gender roles and sexual norms.

References

Adler, N. L. & Hendrick, S. S. (1991). Relationships between contraceptive behavior and love attitudes, sex attitudes, and self-esteem. *Journal of Counseling & Development, 70,* 302–308.

Fisher, W. A., Byrne, D., & White, L. A. (1983). Emotional barriers to contraception. In D. Byrne & W. A. Fisher (Eds.), *Adolescents, sex and contraception* (pp. 207–239). Hillsdale, NJ: Lawrence Erlbaum.

Fisher, W. A., Fisher, J. D., & Byrne, D. (1977). Consumer reactions to contraceptive purchasing. *Personality and Social Psychology Bulletin, 3,* 293–296.

Fisher, W. A., Miller, C. T., Byrne, D., & White, L. A. (1980). Talking dirty: Responses to communicating a sexual message as a function of situational and personality factors. *Basic and Applied Social Psychology, 1,* 115–126.

Gerrard, M. (1987a). Emotional and cognitive barriers to effective contraception: Are males and females really different? In K. Kelley (Ed.), *Females, males, and sexuality: Theories and research* (pp. 213–242). Albany: State University of New York Press.

Gerrard, M. (1987b). Sex, sex guilt, and contraceptive use revisited: The 1980s. *Journal of Personality and Social Psychology, 52,* 975–980.

Continued

Continued

Gerrard, M., Kurylo, M., & Reis, T. (1991). Self-esteem, erotophobia, and retention of contraceptive and AIDS information in the classroom. *Journal of Applied Social Psychology, 21,* 368–379.

Winter, L. (1988). The role of sexual self-concept in the use of contraceptives. *Family Planning Perspectives, 20,* 123–127.

People don't plan to fail, they fail to plan.
Anonymous

In Table 20.2, we present data on the percentage of women aged 15 to 44 who became pregnant during the first year of using a particular method of birth control. These rates are referred to as first-year contraceptive failure rates. In their analysis of the 1988 NSFG data, Jones and Forrest (1992) examined failure rates to determine the effect of user characteristics. They determined that since failure rates vary among women of differing age, marital status and poverty status, the failures are due more to patterns of irregular and improper use than inherent method limitations. They found that membership in the following categories, with some qualifications, was associated with more successful contraceptive use:

- increasing age (once women are in their mid-twenties)
- married women (except for the youngest married women)
- whites, followed by Hispanics, then blacks
- family income above 200% of the poverty level
- fundamentalist Protestants, followed by Catholics, then women in other categories (among low income women).

In interpreting the failure rate data Jones and Forrest (1992, p. 18) concluded,

> The high levels of failure with currently available methods also indicate the urgent need for contraceptive research and development that will bring to the U.S. market methods that are not only effective but easier to use effectively . . . More contraceptive options are required for women in . . . stages of their lives, when a short-term method is more appropriate and when protection against both pregnancy and sexually transmitted diseases is necessary.

TABLE 20.2 First Year Contraceptive Failure Rates among Women Aged 15 to 44

Method	% Pregnant within One Year
No method	85.0 %
Spermicides	21.6 %
Sponge	16.0 %
Coitus interruptus (withdrawal)	14.7 %
Periodic abstinence	13.8 %
Diaphragm or cap	12.0 %
Condom	9.8 %
Pill	3.8 %
IUD	2.5 %
Tubal Sterilization	0.5 %
Injectables	0.4 %
Vasectomy	0.2 %
Implants	0.05%

Source: Adapted from Kost, K., Forrest, J. D., & Harlap, S. (1991). Comparing the health risks and benefits of contraceptive choices. *Family Planning Perspectives, 23,* 54–61. Used by permission.

CONSIDERATION: Some people argue that women bear the burden of contraception. For example, Sapiro (1990) stated that "in the sexual division of labor, contraception is still women's responsibility . . . [and] will probably remain primarily women's responsibility for the foreseeable future" (p. 318). However, looking at Table 20.1 presented earlier, you will note that, in 1988, over 30% of contraceptive using women aged 15 to 44 relied on male participation in contraception (male sterilization, condom, periodic abstinence, and withdrawal). Further evidence supporting men's willingness to participate in contraception is provided by a study that found that 91% of undergraduate men and women reported that it was their independent responsibility to ensure that contraception was used when they had intercourse (Sheehan, Ostwald, & Rothenberger, 1986).

Birth Control Technology And Availability: An International View

Although there appears to be a wide range of contraceptives available to Americans, many of these methods are not reliably effective in preventing pregnancy and/or have other drawbacks. Regarding contraceptives in the United States, it has been suggested that

> U.S. women have been deprived of needed choices; there is not a wide enough choice of safe, effective and acceptable reversible contraceptive methods available in the United States. . . . The range of contraceptive choices for U.S. women is narrower than for Europeans or Canadians, who variously enjoy access to postcoital contraceptives, new progestogens, a wider range of IUDs and, in several countries, injectable contraceptives. (Potts, 1988, p. 294)

Not only do U.S. women have fewer birth control choices than women in other industrialized nations, they must also pay more to obtain contraceptives than do women in those countries. In a study of 19 Western democratic countries, most of the countries provided contraceptives free or at very low cost to their citizens (Rosoff, 1988).

Many methods of birth control that have not been available in the United States are available in other countries. Some examples include the following (Prendergast, 1990):

1. Depo-Provera. Used by over 4 million women in 90 countries, **Depo-Provera** is an injectable steroid that lasts three months and has a failure rate of one pregnancy per 100 women per year. Depo-Provera was approved by an FDA advisory panel in summer 1992 and subsequently received full approval.
2. Noristerat. Used by 800,000 women (many of whom live in Mexico and China), Noristerat is an injectable steroid (norethisterone enanthate) that lasts one to two months and has a failure rate of two pregnancies per 100 women per year.
3. Multiload IUD. Used extensively in Europe.
4. Filshie Clip. The silicone rubber device is used to block the Fallopian tubes and is more easily reversed than conventional methods of sterilization.
5. RU-486. RU-486, which has been approved in France, China, and West Germany, prevents implantation of a fertilized zygote. This method is controversial because it is sometimes considered to be a form of abortion. Because of this controversy, RU-486 is not expected to be available in the United States in the near future.

The most common methods of contraception used internationally are sterilization, followed by IUDs, oral contraceptives, and condoms (Donaldson & Keely, 1988; Maudlin & Segal, 1992). Despite the wide variety of contraceptives that have been developed internationally, people in many countries do not have access to contraceptives. For example, in Poland (a predominantly Catholic country), the number of abortions performed in 1982 exceeded the number of births. Although this fact has been attributed to economic hardship, "some experts also blame the paucity of options existing in the country, making abortion the only reasonable method of contraception available" (Hatcher et al., 1990, p. 576). While IUDs and diaphragms are available in Poland, they are difficult to obtain and cost up to one-third of an average worker's monthly salary. In other developing countries, contraceptives are not affordable. One report suggests that less than half the population in many developing countries has access to affordable contraception ("Birth control," 1991). For example, an IUD would cost an average woman in Chad nearly three-fourths of a year's income. In Kenya, female sterilization could cost 89% of a person's average annual income.

The reproductive health of women who do not want to become pregnant is most threatened if they rely on chance rather than on a contraceptive method.

Kathryn Kost
Jacqueline Darroch Forrest
Susan Harlap

Early in 1992 Japan's Ministry of Health and Welfare was expected to approve the manufacture and import of oral contraceptives. Lack of the ministry's approval has effectively banned the pill in Japan, except for the prescription of high dose pills for dysmennorhea (Yamauchi, 1991). However, the approval was denied due to fear that widespread use of the pill and corresponding decreases in condom use would promote the spread of HIV infection.

CONSIDERATION: One innovative program in Australia was started by a pizza delivery service that also delivers condoms after 10 P.M. In Japan (where most reproductive-age couples rely on condoms), door-to-door saleswomen sell condoms to women in their homes (Hatcher et al., 1990).

Efforts are being made to make contraceptives available in countries throughout the world. Since the 1960s, the U.S. government has supported family planning programs in Third World countries. However, in 1984, the U.S. Agency for International Development withdrew support from any family planning organization (including the International Planned Parenthood Federation) that had any connection with abortion services (Rosoff, 1988).

Donaldson and Keely (1988) reported that over the past 25 years, total fertility rates of developing countries have fallen by an average of about one-third. This decline in population is partly due to increased prevalence of contraception. However, the United Nations Population Fund (1991) estimates that only 48% of couples in developing countries use contraceptives; in developed countries, the corresponding figure is 71%. Due to population growth, in order to simply maintain these percentages, 100 million more couples will need to be using contraception by the year 2000. Because most of the growth in population occurs in developing countries, more than 90% of the increase in numbers of couples using contraception must be achieved there. While the total number of couples practicing family planning is increasing worldwide, the international resources available to provide contraceptives are declining (Donaldson & Keely, 1988). This problem is not confined to poor countries. When inflation is taken into account, governmental expenditures for contraceptive services in the United States have fallen by one-third since 1980 (Gold & Daley, 1991).

THE FUTURE OF BIRTH CONTROL TECHNOLOGY

Despite the variety of available contraceptive methods, the search for better methods continues. Examples of new methods of birth control that are being researched include (Prendergast, 1990; Hatcher et al., 1990):

1. Vaginal ring. This silicone rubber ring the size of a diaphragm is placed in the woman's vagina. It is designed to slowly release the hormone levonorgestrel over a period of three months, which suppresses ovulation and thickens the cervical mucus (thus preventing sperm from entering the uterus). The vaginal ring is already available in some countries.
2. Biodegradable implants. Long-acting, slow-release pellets are inserted under the skin of the arm or hip. These implants release progestins that inhibit conception for one to one and a half years. If the woman changes her mind after insertion of the implants, they can be removed only within the first few months after insertion. Otherwise, they will dissolve over time. Biodegradable implants may be available by the mid-1990s.
3. Vaccines. Vaccines that would inhibit sperm, egg, and zygote are being considered. This method is not expected to be available until 2025.
4. CADCAD (Cervically Anchored Device that is Contraceptive and Anti-Disease). CADCAD is a one-inch-long cylindrical implant that releases inorganic salts into the cervix. The device is experimental, contains antichlamydia properties, and has been used in lower animals only.
5. Transdermal patches. Transdermal patches, which release hormonal contraceptives, are designed to be worn on the woman's body and replaced by the user as needed. In one system, three patches, each lasting seven days, are worn consecutively for three weeks followed by a week without a patch.
6. Ultrasound. Ultrasound has been shown to suppress spermatogenesis in dogs, cats, monkeys, and humans, suggesting the potential for ultrasound to become a method of male contraception.

> Most people tend to choose or reject birth control methods not to cast a vote for or against a cause, but to meet their personal needs in terms of what they believe to be right at the time.
>
> *Philip A. Belcastro*

In the United States, research and development of new contraceptive technologies are likely to be slow due to lack of funding. Potts (1988) noted that "many potentially useful new methods [of contraception] will not be developed in this century unless the amount of money invested in contraceptive research and development is substantially increased" (p. 288). Factors that have contributed to the scarcity of funds for contraceptive research in this country include public apathy, financial interests of companies that produce currently available contraceptives, and controversies over the moral acceptability of some forms of birth control (such as postcoital methods). However, if Americans are sincerely distressed by teenage pregnancies, unwanted children, and abortion, "a quantum leap in investment in contraceptive services and research is essential" (Potts, 1988, p. 295).

In concluding this chapter, we emphasize that while planning children and birth control are individual choices, complex social issues are involved. Elissa Rashkin suggested that,

> The ultimate solution to the question of reproductive choice is the construction of a supportive social environment in which women can choose according to their desires, uninhibited by coercive population policies, lack of social services, poverty, misinformation and other constraints. Reproductive freedom is not a question of private decision making alone, but a social need—and as such, it can only be met through the transformation of society. (Undated, p. 21)

CHOICES

One choice that is being made more frequently today than in the past is the choice to have a child without a spouse. After discussing this issue, we conclude with a scale (Contraceptive Comfort and Confidence Scale; Hatcher et al., 1990) that is designed to help you choose a method of contraception that will suit your individual preferences and needs.

Choose to Have a Child without a Partner? The Biological Clock Issue

Compared to previous decades, a higher proportion of single women today are having children. In 1950, 4% of all births involved unmarried women; in 1970, the figure was almost 11%; in 1980, it was 18%; and in 1985, it was 22% (Sapiro, 1990, p. 312). In 1987, 24.5% of live births in the United States were to unmarried women (*Statistical Abstract of the United States, 1990,* Table 90.) There are large differences between black and white women: in 1987, 16.7% of all births to white women involved unmarried women, and 62.2% of all births to black women involved unmarried women (*Statistical Abstract of the United States, 1990,* Table 90). Most of the children born to these unmarried mothers were unplanned and were born when the mother was between the ages of 15 and 24. "On the other hand, many single women are having children by choice" (Sapiro, 1990, p. 313). While some single mothers by choice are in their teens, an increasing number of single women over 30 are choosing to have children.

> For some of these women the reason for their choice is age. As they move into and through their thirties they worry that their biological aging will take away the choice to have a child. These women face important moral dilemmas: Is it right to marry a man just because one wants a child? Is this fair to the man? .... Is it fair to the woman? (Sapiro, 1990, p. 313)

In a Roper poll (1985), four in 10 women said that it is all right for adults to have children without getting married. Many women who choose to be a single parent are either tired of waiting for "Mr. Right" or have no interest in finding him. "Most are women who have achieved a measure of economic self-sufficiency but have delayed childbearing to the point where they hear their biological clocks approaching midnight" (Smolowe, 1990, p. 76). One woman said:

> I could imagine going through life without a man, but I couldn't imagine going through life without a child. My biological clock started sounding like a time bomb. (Quoted in Smolowe, 1990, p. 76)

Jean Renvoize (1985) interviewed 30 unmarried women who made a conscious choice to have a baby with the intent of rearing their child alone. Of these women, the researcher said:

> I expected to find a group of tough-minded, militant women somewhat on the defensive; instead I found mostly happy, fulfilled, strong, but gentle individuals who gave out warmth and a readiness to share with others. There were women who had made their choice after much deliberation, mostly at a mature age, and who knew in advance that nothing in life comes free. (p. 5)

Once a single woman has decided to have a child, she faces a choice of methods, including adoption, intercourse with a selected partner, insemination by a selected donor, or insemination by an unknown donor. Each of these methods may present certain problems. Adoption may involve a lengthy process of bureaucratic redtape and long waits. Adoption also means the woman has no biological ties to the child and does not experience pregnancy and childbirth, which she may view as advantages or disadvantages. If the father is known, there may be future legal conflicts over custody or access to the child. If the father is unknown, the woman may have less information about his background (although some sperm banks provide detailed medical and personal histories of donors). When the father is an unknown donor, many mothers wonder what to say to the child who asks who her or his father is.

Perhaps the greatest challenge for single parents is to satisfy—alone—the emotional needs of their children. The single parent who is tired from working all day and who has no one else with whom to share parenting at night may be less able to meet the emotional needs of a child. (It is recognized that many coupled mothers work outside the home and

Continued

Continued

receive no or limited parenting help from their partner). When single mothers are compared with mothers living with partners, single mothers report more stress and more behavior problems with single children (Webster-Stratton, 1989).

An organization for women who want children and who may or may not marry is Single Mothers By Choice (1642 Gracie Square Station, New York, New York 10028; 212–988–0993). The organization has more than 1,000 members and provides support and "thinkers' groups" for unmarried women who are contemplating whether or not to have a child. Most women attending these groups decide not to have children after they have considered the various issues.

Choose to Use Which Method of Contraception?

The following series of questions, which are adapted from the Contraceptive Comfort and Confidence Scale (Hatcher et al., 1990), is designed to help you assess whether the method of contraception that you are using or may be considering using in the future is or will be effective for you.

Most individuals will have a few "yes" answers. "Yes" answers predict potential problems. If you have more than a few "yes" responses, you may want to talk to your physician, counselor, partner, or friend. Talking it over can help you decide whether to use this method or how to use it so it will really be effective for you. In general, the more "yes" answers you have, the less likely you are to use this method consistently and correctly.

In choosing a method of contraception, you might want to keep in mind that if you want a highly effective method of contraception *and* a method that is highly effective in preventing transmission of STDs, you may have to use *two* methods (Cates & Stone, 1992). Hence, any method of contraception (except abstinence, of course) should be combined with condom use for maximum protection against STDs.

Contraceptive Comfort and Confidence Scale

Method of birth control you are currently using or are considering using:
Answer YES or NO to the following questions.

_______ 1. Have you had problems using this method before?

_______ 2. Are you afraid of using this method?

_______ 3. Would you really rather not use this method?

_______ 4. Will you have trouble remembering to use this method?

_______ 5. Have you ever become pregnant using this method? (Or, has your partner ever become pregnant using this method?)

_______ 6. Will you have trouble using this method correctly?

_______ 7. Do you still have unanswered questions about this method?

_______ 8. Does this method make menstrual periods longer or more painful?

_______ 9. Does this method cost more than you can afford?

_______ 10. Could this method cause you or your partner to have serious complications?

_______ 11. Are you opposed to this method because of religious beliefs?

_______ 12. Is your partner opposed to this method?

_______ 13. Are you using this method without your partner's knowledge?

_______ 14. Will using this method embarrass your partner?

_______ 15. Will using this method embarrass you?

_______ 16. Will you enjoy intercourse less because of this method?

_______ 17. Will your partner enjoy intercourse less because of this method?

_______ 18. If this method interrupts lovemaking, will you avoid using it?

_______ 19. Has a nurse or doctor ever told you (or your partner) NOT to use this method?

_______ 20. Is there anything about your personality that could lead you to use this method incorrectly?

_______ 21. Does this method leave you at risk of being exposed to HIV or other sexually transmissible infections?

Total number of YES answers: _______

Source: Adapted from Hatcher, R. A., Stewart, F., Trussell, J., Kowal, D., Guest, F., Stewart, G. K., & Cates, W. (1990). *Contraceptive technology: 1990–1992* (15th ed., rev.) (p. 150). New York: Irvington.

SUMMARY

1. About 3.3 million unplanned pregnancies occur in the United States each year. About 10% to 12% of pregnant U.S. women did not want to become pregnant. Almost a third of unintentional pregnancies involve teenagers.
2. Family planning benefits parents and children in that it may reduce maternal and infant deaths, allow parents to pace the financial demands of parenting, and reduce abortions, unwanted children, and relationship conflicts associated with unplanned pregnancy.
3. Family planning benefits society in helping to limit population growth. If the population is not controlled, the world faces shortages in food and health, educational and housing services, increased pollution, and depletion of environmental resources.
4. Most Americans want and expect to have children: 95% of college undergraduates and over 90% of U.S. women want children. Social influences that encourage Americans to want to have children include family and friends, religion, and government.
5. Motivations for wanting children include viewing them as sources of love and companionship, as a bond for one's marital relationship, as a mechanism for adult status and identity, and as a means to recapture youth and relive the positive experiences of childhood.
6. Difficulties and stresses associated with parenthood include financial costs, increased role demands, life-style changes, worry and grief, and dealing with negative behaviors on the part of the child(ren). Children may have either positive or negative effects on the relationship between the parents.
7. In the United States, having an only child has become more common and socially acceptable in recent years. However, the most preferred family size in the United States is two children. In planning family size, women and men may want to consider the possibility of future divorce, remarriage, and widowhood.
8. In timing the birth of children, important factors to consider include the ages of the mother and father (and related factors, such as career aspirations and economic stability) and number of years in a stable relationship.
9. Methods of contraception and efforts to control population have been traced back to the paleolithic era (10,000 B.C.). Historically, methods of birth and population control have included ingesting plant drugs, inserting substances into the vagina (e.g., elephant or crocodile dung, honey, wool tampons), infanticide, abstinence, withdrawal of penis before ejaculation, and homosexual and nonprocreative heterosexual sex. Due to opposition to birth control in early U.S. history, unmarried Americans did not have access to contraceptive devices until 1972.
10. Most U.S. women ages 15 to 44 use some form of birth control. Methods of birth control either 1) prevent sperm from fertilizing an egg, 2) prevent the fertilized egg from implanting in the uterus, or 3) terminate implantation. Each method of contraception discussed in the chapter has advantages and disadvantages related to effectiveness in preventing pregnancy, reversibility, health risks and side effects, noncontraceptive health benefits (including prevention of STDs), ease of use, and cost and availability. Latex condoms are the only method of contraception that provide a high degree of protection against STDs.
11. Many methods of contraception that are available in other countries are not available in the United States. In many developing countries, contraception is not affordable.
12. New methods of contraception are being developed to increase options in the future.

KEY TERMS

pronatalism
coitus obstructus
oral contraceptives
Norplant
condom
female condom
intrauterine device
diaphragm
cervical cap
spermicide
nonoxynol-9
douching
vaginal sponge
coitus absentia
abstention
periodic abstinence
coitus interruptus
withdrawal
postcoital contraception
sterilization
vasectomy
tubectomies
oophorectomy
hysterectomy
salpingectomy
laparoscopy
Depo-Provera

REFERENCES

Affonso, D. D., & Mayberry, L. J. (1989). Common stressors reported by a group of childbearing American women. In P. N. Stern (Ed.), *Pregnancy and parenting* (pp. 41–55). New York: Hemisphere.

Belcastro, P. A. (1986). *The birth-control book.* Boston: Jones and Bartlett.

Birth control a luxury in much of the world. (1991, July 1). *Asheville Citizen-Times,* Asheville, NC, p. 4B.

Blank, R. H. 1990. *Regulating reproduction.* New York: Columbia University Press.

Bloom, D. E., & Bennett, N. G. (1986). Childless couples. *American Demographics, 8,* 22–25, 54–55.

Boyer, D. (1991, Summer). Preliminary data summary: Victimization and other risk factors for child maltreatment among school age parents. *The Network,* 2.

Brailey, L. J. (1989). Stress experienced by mothers of young children. In P. N. Stern (Ed.), *Pregnancy and parenting* (pp. 157–168). New York: Hemisphere.

Bromwich, P., & Parsons, T. (1990). *Contraception: The facts.* Oxford: Oxford University Press.

Campbell, F. L., Townes, B. D., & Beach, L. R. (1982). Motivational bases of childbearing decisions. In G. L. Fox (Ed.), *The childbearing decision* (pp. 145–159). Beverly Hills, CA: Sage.

Cates, W., Jr., & Stone, K. M. (1992). Family planning, sexually transmitted diseases and contraceptive choice: A literature update–Part I. *Family Planning Perspectives, 24,* 75–82.

Cohen, J. B. (1985). *Parenthood after 30? A guide to personal choice.* Lexington, MA: Lexington Books.

Cowan, P. A. & Cowan, C. P. (1988). Changes in marriage during the transition to parenthood: Must we blame the baby? In G. Y. Michaels & W. A. Goldberg (Eds.), *The transition to parenthood: Current theory and research* (pp. 114–154). New York: Cambridge University Press.

Crispell, D. (1989). Three's a crowd. *American Demographics, 11,* 34–38.

Croxatto, H. B. (1992). IUD mechanisms of action. In A new look at IUDs–Advancing contraceptive choices: Abstracts of oral papers. *Contraception: An International Journal, 45,* 273–298.

Cutler, B. (1990). Rock-a-buy baby. *American Demographics, 12,* 21–34.

Daniels, P., & Weingarten, K. (1982). *Sooner or later: The timing of parenthood in adult lives.* New York: Norton.

Donaldson, P. J., & Keely, C. B. (1988). Population and family planning: an international perspective. *Family Planning Perspectives, 20,* 307–320.

Dorman, M., & Klein, D. (1984). *How to stay 2 when baby makes 3.* New York: Prometheus Books.

Dreyfous, L. (1991, October 13). In lean times, more couples opt for having only one child. *The Daily Reflector,* Greenville, NC, p. 2G.

Falbo, T., & Polit-O'Harra, D. F. (1985). Only children: What do we know about them? *Pediatric Nursing, 11,* 356–360.

Forrest, J. D. (1992). Acceptability of IUDs in the United States. In A new look at IUDs—Advancing contraceptive choices: Abstracts of oral papers. *Contraception: An International Journal, 45,* 273–298.

Gallup Organization. (1985, March 1). Attitudes toward contraception. Unpublished report to the American College of Obstetricians and Gynecologists, Princeton, NJ.

Gold, R. B., & Daley, D. (1991). Public funding of contraceptive, sterilization and abortion services, fiscal year 1990. *Family Planning Perspectives, 23,* 204–211.

Goldberg, W. A., & Michaels, G. Y. (1988). Conclusion. The transition to parenthood: Synthesis and future directions. In G. Y. Michaels & W. A. Goldberg (Eds.), *The transition to parenthood: Current theory and research,* (pp. 342–360). New York: Cambridge University Press.

Greenberg, J. S., Bruess, C. E., & Sands, D. W. (1986). *Sexuality: insights and issues.* Dubuque, IA: William C. Brown.

Gregersen, E., & Gregersen, B. (1990). The female condom: A pilot study of the acceptability of a new female barrier method. *Acta Obstetricia et Gynecologica Scandinavica, 69,* 73.

Harriman, L. C. (1986). Marital adjustment as related to personal and marital changes accompanying parenthood. *Family Relations, 35,* 233–239.

Hatcher, R. A., Stewart, F., Trussell, J., Kowal, D., Guest, F., Stewart, G. K., & Cates, W. (1990). *Contraceptive technology 1990–1992* (15th ed., rev.). New York: Irvington.

Henshaw, S. K., & Singh, S. (1986). Sterilization regret among U.S. couples. *Family Planning Perspectives, 18,* 238–240.

Hoffman, L. W., Thornton, A., & Manis, J. D. (1978). The value of children to parents in the United States. *Journal of Population, 1,* 91–131.

Jones, E. F. & Forrest, J. D. (1992). Contraceptive failure rates based on the 1988 NSFG. *Family Planning Perspectives, 24,* 12–19.

Keen, H. (1988, May 2). A decline in vasectomies. *Maclean's,* p. 10.

Kenney, J. W., & Tash, D. T. (1992). Lesbian childbearing couples' dilemmas and decisions. *Health Care Women International, 13,* 209–212.

Kestelman, P., & Trussell, J. (1991). Efficacy of the simultaneous use of condoms and spermicides. *Family Planning Perspectives, 23,* 226–232.

Knox, D., & Wilson, K. (1978). The differences between having one and two children. *Family Coordinator, 27,* 23–25.

Koop, C. E. (1989). A measured response: Koop on abortion. *Family Planning Perspectives, 21,* 31–33.

Kost, K., Forrest, J. D., & Harlap, S. (1991). Comparing the health risks and benefits of contraceptive choices. *Family Planning Perspectives, 23,* 54–61.

LeMasters, E. E., & DeFrain, J. (1989). *Parents in contemporary America.* Belmont, CA: Wadsworth.

MacDermid, S. M., Huston, T. L., & McHale, S. M. (1990). Changes in marriage associated with the transition to parenthood: Individual differences as a function of sex-role attitudes and changes in the division of household labor. *Journal of Marriage and the Family, 52,* 475–486.

Marini, M. M. (1980). Effects of the number and spacing of children on marital and parental satisfaction. *Demography, 17,* 225–242.

Marks, S. R. (1989). Toward a systems theory of marital quality. *Journal of Marriage and the Family, 51,* 15–26.

Maudlin, W. P., & Segal, S. J. (1992). IUD use throughout the world: Past, present and future. In A new look at IUDs—Advancing contraceptive choices: Abstracts of oral papers. *Contraception: An International Journal, 45,* 273–298.

Mercer, R. T. (1986). *First-time motherhood: Experiences from teens to forties.* New York: Springer Publishing Co.

Michaels, G. Y. (1988). Motivational factors in the decision and timing of pregnancy. In G. Y. Michaels & W. A. Goldberg (Eds.), *The transition to parenthood: Current theory and research,* (pp. 23–61). New York: Cambridge University Press.

Mindel, C. H., Habenstein, R. W., & Wright, R., Jr. (Eds.), (1988). *Ethnic families in America: Patterns and variations* (3rd ed.). New York: Elsevier.

Mosher, W. D. (1990). Contraceptive practice in the United States, 1982–1988. *Family Planning Perspective, 22,* 198–205.

National Center for Health Statistics. (1991). *Advance report of final natality statistics, 1989.* (Monthly Vital Statistics Report, vol. 40 no. 8, suppl.), Hyattsville, MD: U.S. Public Health Service.

Neal, A. G., Groat, H. T., & Wicks, J. W. (1989). Attitudes about having children: A study of 600 couples in the early years of marriage. *Journal of Marriage and the Family, 51,* 313–328.

Newman, S. (1990). *Parenting an only child.* New York: Doubleday.

Nullis, C. (1992, January 23). Experts welcoming female condom. *Daily Reflector,* Greenville, NC, p. C1.

Ory, H. W. (1983). Mortality associated with fertility and fertility control: 1983. *Family Planning Perspectives, 15,* 57.

Painter, K. (1991, April 23). Birth control is a medical plus in the long run. *USA Today,* p. 8D.

Petitti, D. B. (1992). Reconsidering the IUD. *Family Planning Perspectives, 24,* 33–35.

Pies, C. (1987). Considering parenthood: Psychosocial issues for gay men and lesbians choosing alternative fertilization. In F. W. Bozett (Ed.), *Gay and lesbian parents* (pp. 165–174). New York: Praeger.

Planned Parenthood Federation of America. (1991). *Norplant: The promise of new choices or the threat of new control.* Annual report. New York: Author.

Perry, S., & Dawson, J. (1985). *Nightmare: Women and the Dalkon Shield.* New York: Macmillan.

Potts, M. (1988). Birth control methods in the United States. *Family Planning Perspectives, 20,* 288–297.

Prendergast, A. (1990, October). Beyond the pill. *American Health,* pp. 37–44.

Rashkin, E. (Undated). Reproductive choice in Cuba and El Salvador: A comparative study. Women's International Resource Exchange (WIRE), NYC, NY.

Rempel, J. (1985). Childless elderly. *Journal of Marriage and the Family, 47,* 343–348.

Renvoize, J. (1985). *Going solo: Single mothers by choice.* London: Routledge and Kegan Paul.

Riddle, J.M., & Estes, J.W. (1992). Oral contraceptives in ancient and medieval times. *American Scientist, 80,* 226–233.

Rivera, R. R. (1987). Legal issues in gay and lesbian parenting. In F. W. Bozett (Ed.), *Gay and lesbian parents* (pp. 199–227). New York: Praeger.

Roper Organization. (1985). *The 1985 Virginia Slims American women's opinion poll.* New York: Author.

Rosoff, J. I. (1988). The politics of birth control. *Family Planning Perspectives, 20,* 312–320.

Rubinson, L., & De Rubertis, L. (1991). Trends in sexual attitudes and behaviors of a college population over a 15-year period. *Journal of Sex Education and Therapy, 17,* 32–40.

Sadik, N. (1992). Public policy and private decisions: World population and world health in the 21st century. *Journal of Public Health Policy, 13,* 133–139.

Sapiro, V. (1990). *Women in American society* (2nd ed.). Mountain View, CA: Mayfield.

Seashore, M. R. (1980). Counseling prospective parents about possible genetic disorders in offspring. *Medical Aspects of Human Sexuality, 14,* 97–98.

Seccombe, K. (1991). Assessing the costs and benefits of children: Gender comparisons among childfree husbands and wives. *Journal of Marriage and the Family, 53,* 191–202.

Sheehan, M. K., Ostwald, S. K., & Rothenberger, J. (1986). Perceptions of sexual responsibility: Do young men and women agree? *Pediatric Nursing, 12,* 17–21.

Shoupe, D., & Mishell, D. (1989). Norplant: Subdermal implant system for long-term contraception. *American Journal of Obstetrics and Gynecology, 160,* 1286–92.

Smolowe, J. (1990, Fall). Last call for motherhood. *Time* (Special issue). p. 76.

Sonenstein, F. L., Pleck, J. H., Ku, R. C. (1989). Sexual activity, condom use, and AIDS awareness among adolescent males. *Family Planning Perspectives, 21,* 152–158.

Statistical abstract of the United States: 1992 (112th ed.) (1992). Washington, DC: U.S. Bureau of the Census.

Tannahill, R. (1982). *Sex in history.* New York: Stein and Day.

Thomas, P. (1988, March 14). Contraceptives: Break due after decade of drought. *Medical World News,* pp. 49–68.

Travis, C. B. (1988). *Women and health psychology: Biomedical issues.* Hillsdale, NJ: Lawrence Erlbaum Associates.

Trussell, J., Warner, D. L., & Hatcher, R. A. (1992). Condom slippage and breakage rates. *Family Planning Perspectives, 24,* 20–23.

Union County applauded for plan to offer Norplant to poor women. (1991, June 22). *News and Observer,* Raleigh, NC, p. 6B.

United Nations Population Fund. (1991). *Population policies and programmes: Lessons learned from two decades of experience.* N. Sadik (Ed.). New York: New York University Press.

Urzua, R. (1992, January). The demographic dimension. *UNESCO Courier,* p. 14.

Vorhauer, B. W., Rose, B. F., McClure, D. A., & North, B. (1984). *A review of the safety and effectiveness of the Today vaginal contraceptive sponge.* Irvine, CA: VLI Corporation.

Webster-Stratton, C. (1989). The relationship of marital support, conflict, and divorce to parent perceptions, behaviors, and childhood conduct problems. *Journal of Marriage and the Family, 51,* 417–430.

Weston, K. (1991). *Families we choose: Lesbians, gays, kinship.* New York: Columbia University Press.

Wildemeersch, D. A. (1992). New IUDs. In A new look at IUDs—Advancing contraceptive choices: Abstracts of oral papers. *Contraception: An International Journal, 45,* 273–298.

Williams, J. H. (1987). *Psychology of women: Behavior in a biosocial context* (3rd ed.). New York: W. W. Norton.

Williams, L. B. (1991). Determinants of unintended childbearing among never-married women in the United States: 1973–1988. *Family Planning Perspectives, 23,* 212–221.

Willis, J. (1985, May). Comparing contraceptives. *FDA Consumer.* pp. 28–35.

Witwer, M. (1989). Oral contraceptive use linked to chlamydial, gonococcal infections. *Family Planning Perspectives, 21,* 190.

Wolinsky, H. (1988, June). A woman's condom? *American Health Magazine,* p. 10.

Yamauchi M. (1991). Japan to lift ban on oral contraception. *British Medical Journal, 303,* 1157.

CHAPTER TWENTY-ONE

Pregnancy and Childbirth

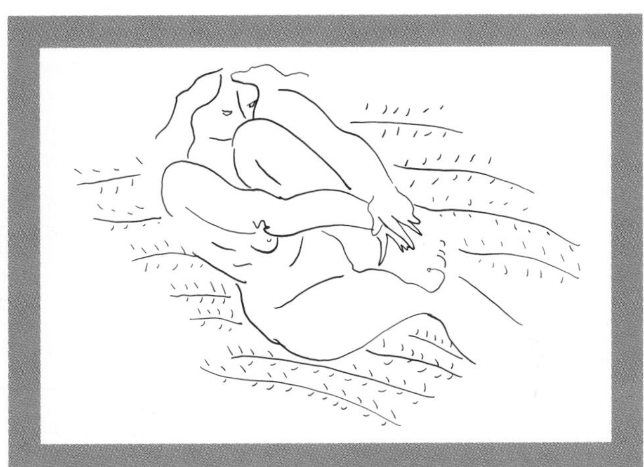

Chapter Outline

Fertilization and Conception
- Infertility
- Causes of Infertility
- Psychological Reactions to Infertility

Reproductive Technology
- Hormone Therapy
- Artificial Insemination
- Artificial Insemination of a Surrogate Mother
- Ovum Transfer
- In Vitro Fertilization
- Other Reproductive Technologies
- **Self-Assessment:** Acceptance of Adoption and Five Alternative Fertilization Techniques
- **Public Policy Perspective:** Reproductive Technology: Liberating or Enslaving?

Pregnancy and Labor
- Pregnancy Testing
- Physical Changes during Pregnancy
- Prenatal Care and Prenatal Testing
- Psychological Changes during Pregnancy
- Sex during Pregnancy
- Labor

Childbirth Preparation
- Dick-Read Method
- Lamaze Method
- Bradley Method
- LeBoyer Birth Experience

Cesarean Childbirth

The Transition to Parenthood
- The Transition to Motherhood
- The Transition to Fatherhood
- Sex after Childbirth

Choices
- Choose Home or Hospital Birth?
- Choose to Breast-feed or Bottle-feed the New Infant?
- Choices Resulting from New Reproductive Technologies

Is It True?*

1. The terms "fertilization" and "conception" have the same meaning.

2. Physicians who regularly perform artificial inseminations routinely test the sperm from donors for genetic defects and HIV status.

3. Most cesarean sections are performed on Fridays, suggesting that the social life of the physician is an important factor influencing the decision to perform a cesarean section.

4. Courts have not recognized the rights of surrogate mothers to their biological offspring once they sign a contract with a couple.

5. Fresh sperm is the sperm of choice in artificial insemination by a donor.

* 1 = F, 2 = F, 3 = T, 4 = F, 5 = F

The process of pregnancy and birth is an obvious reflection of the sexuality of the new parents.

Nancy Engel

The photograph of a seminude and pregnant Demi Moore on the cover of *Vanity Fair* magazine in 1991 emphasized the blend of sexuality and pregnancy. Such a photograph has never before been on the front cover of a national magazine. Increasingly, pregnancy and childbirth are being regarded as another aspect of one's sexuality.

In this chapter, we will address many of the choices and issues individuals and couples face in regard to pregnancy and childbirth. We begin with a discussion of fertilization and infertility and the decisions individuals and couples may face in regard to pregnancy.

Fertilization and Conception

Fertilization takes place when a woman's egg, or ovum, unites with a man's sperm (see Figure 21.1). This may occur through sexual intercourse, artificial insemination, or more recently, the method of in vitro fertilization (discussed later).

At orgasm, the man ejaculates a thick white substance called semen, which contains about 300 million sperm. Once the semen is deposited in or near the vagina, the sperm begin to travel up the vagina, through the opening of the cervix, up the uterus, and into the Fallopian tubes. If the woman has ovulated (released a mature egg from an ovary into a Fallopian tube) within eight hours, or if she ovulates during the two or three days the sperm typically remain alive, a sperm may penetrate

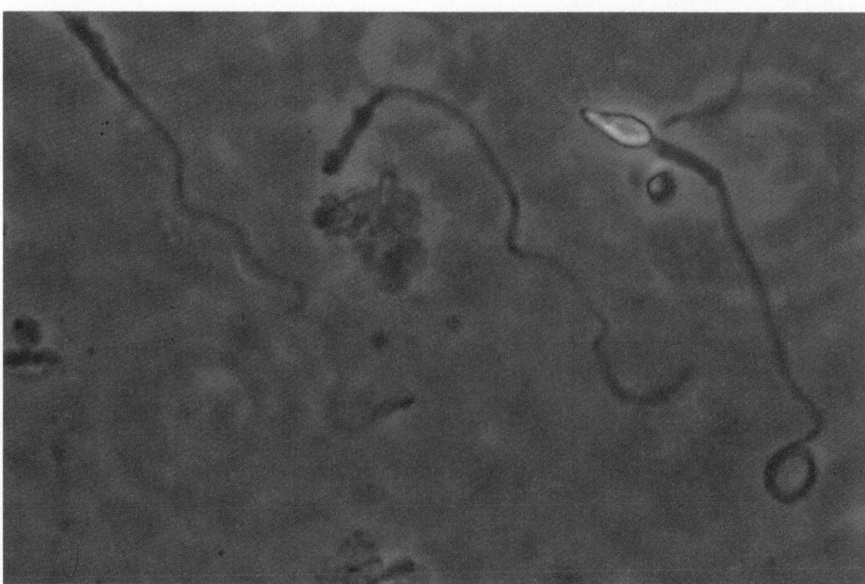

If the women ovulates during the two or three days after intercourse, the sperm will typically remain alive to fertilize the egg.

FIGURE 21.1 Process of Fertilization

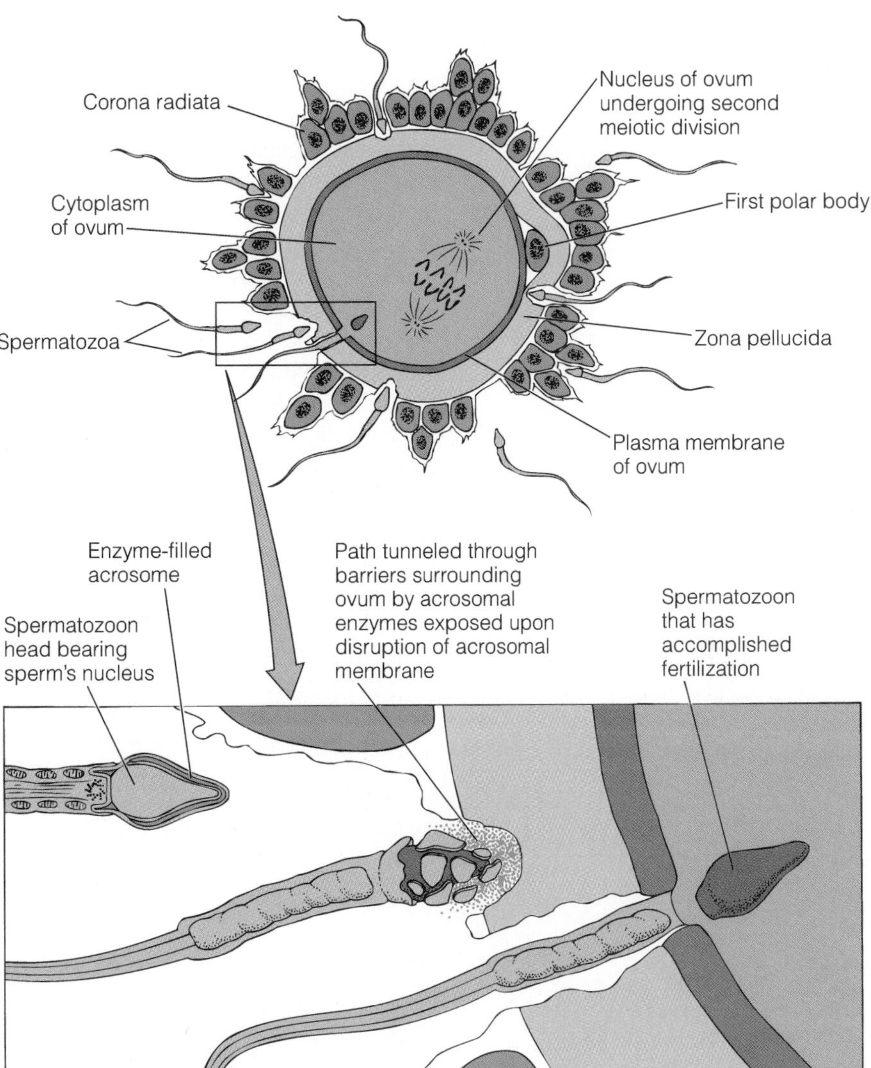

and fertilize the egg. According to the World Health Organization up to 50% of all fertilized ova do not progress beyond the first three weeks of development (Brent & Beckman, 1992).

CONSIDERATION: Although popular usage does not differentiate between the terms "fertilization" and "conception," fertilization refers to the union of the egg and sperm while **conception** refers to the fertilized egg that survives through implantation on the uterine wall. Hence, not all fertilizations result in conception. Pregnancy refers to the state of having conceived with emphasis on the developing fetus.

Since a woman is fertile for only about 48 hours each month, when is the best time to have intercourse to maximize the chance of pregnancy? In general, 24 hours before ovulation is the best time. There are several ways to predict ovulation. Many women have breast tenderness, and some experience a "pinging" sensation in their abdomen at the time of ovulation.

A woman may also detect ovulation by recording her basal body temperature and examining her cervical mucus. After menstruation, the vagina in most women is without noticeable discharge because the mucus is thick. As the time of ovulation-nears, the mucus thins to the consistency of egg white, which may be experienced by the woman as increased vaginal discharge. If pregnancy is the goal, intercourse should occur during this time. In essence, the "technology" of the periodic abstinence method to avoid pregnancy (discussed in Chapter 20) can be used to maximize the potential for pregnancy.

The position during intercourse may also be important for fertilization. In order to maximize the change of fertilization, during intercourse, the woman should be on her back and a pillow should be placed under her buttocks after receiving the sperm so a pool of semen will collect near her cervix. She should remain in this position for about 30 minutes to allow the sperm to reach the Fallopian tubes.

Infertility

Infertility is defined as the inability to achieve a pregnancy after at least one year of regular sexual relations without birth control, or the inability to carry a pregnancy to live birth. The World Health Organization has provided a more detailed definition of infertility (Derwinski-Robinson, 1990):

NATIONAL DATA: Infertility affects between 15% and 20% of married couples in the United States (Higgins, 1990).

1. Primary infertility—The woman has never conceived even though she wants to and has had regular sexual relations for the past 12 months.
2. Secondary infertility—The woman has previously conceived but is currently unable to do so even though she wants to and has had regular sexual relations for the past 12 months.
3. Pregnancy wastage—The woman has been able to conceive but has been unable to produce a live birth.

The infertility epidemic among middle-class career women over thirty was a political program—and for infertility specialists, a marketing tool—not a medical problem.

Susan Faludi

CONSIDERATION: Faludi (1991) noted that women in 1982 were frightened by an article appearing in the New England Journal of Medicine that said that women between the ages of 31 and 35 had a 40% chance of being infertile. The article was based on the research of Daniel Schwartz and M. J. Mayauz, who studied 2,193 French women at 11 artificial-insemination centers. What was misleading was that women who did not get pregnant in 12 months were defined as infertile (the earlier definition of infertility used to be five years). Indeed with time, most women do get pregnant. "Time is the greatest, and certainly the cheapest, cure for infertility. In a British longitudinal survey of more than 17,000 women, 91 percent of the women eventually became pregnant after 39 months" (p. 28).

Causes of Infertility

Forty percent of infertility problems are attributed to the woman, 40% to the man, and 20% to both of them (Derwinski-Robinson, 1990). Some of the more common causes of infertility in men include low sperm production, poor semen motility, effects of sexually transmissible diseases (such as chlamydia, gonorrhea, and syphilis), and interference with the passage of sperm through the genital ducts due to an enlarged prostate. The causes of infertility in women include blocked Fallopian tubes, endocrine imbalances that prevent ovulation, dysfunctional ovaries, chemically hostile cervical mucus that may kill sperm, and effects of sexually transmissible diseases.

Psychological Reactions to Infertility

Not being able to get pregnant is a psychological crisis, a grief experience, and an event that involves various new choices. Regarding infertility as a crisis event, one partner recalled:

> As I look back, I realize that neither of us was willing to apply the term "infertile" to us, even though several doctors had. We coped by changing doctors . . . and by keeping our desperation to ourselves. (Shapiro, 1988, p. 43)

Regarding the grief aspect of infertility, another infertile partner commented:

> Yet this is a different kind of grief. A death has finality to it, but infertility can go on indefinitely. It is like having a chronic illness; there is the continuing reminder of loss coupled with continued hope for a cure. Each month there is a new hope, the fantasy of being pregnant, and the conviction that this time it just has to work. (Lasker & Borg, 1987, p. 20)

Infertility is truly a bio-psycho-social condition.

Constance Shapiro

Higgins (1990) reported changes couples experience when confronted with infertility. For example, their sexual relations may no longer be spontaneous but become scheduled and regimented. Of their altered sex life, one respondent said:

> Making love requires such an effort. I just don't feel like it anymore. We have sex on schedule, and I'm relieved when my wife finishes ovulating so we don't have to subject ourselves to one more futile effort at making a baby. (Shapiro, 1988, p. 44)

The infertile couple may also avoid friends who have children, and they are often faced with a number of new choices (Shapiro, 1988):

1. Whom to tell? When employers question infertile individuals about missed days of work because they had to be away to take infertility tests, do these workers tell their employer the real reason for the absence? And do they tell friends and relatives about their plight? Shapiro (1988) noted that "countless infertile people who do decide to mention their infertility are surprised to learn that friends and relatives have had the same problem" (p. 115).
2. What to tell? "Infertile people are afraid that their infertility may turn other people off, bore them, or cause them to feel pity" (p. 115). Some feel cautious about discussing the alternatives they are pursuing (e.g., engaging a surrogate, artificial insemination) for fear of disapproval or unwanted questions.
3. Whether to pursue treatment? Once a diagnosis of infertility is made, the couple can choose to drop the issue or enter medical treatment to reverse the infertility. A decision to pursue treatment should involve obtaining information about the potential side effects of any recommended medication, the risks of surgery, the sequence of treatment, and how long treatment will go on. "The couple should ask their physician to outline an anticipated schedule for the next twelve to eighteen months, so that they are aware of the treatment plan and time frame involved" (p. 117).
4. Which alternatives to pursue? Assuming that the couple are not able to have a child the traditional way (using their own egg and sperm united through sexual intercourse), they may choose from an array of alternatives to achieve the goal of having a child. These alternatives are discussed in the following section.

Reproductive Technology

A number of technological innovations are available to assist women and couples in becoming pregnant. These include hormonal therapy, artificial insemination, ovum transfer, in vitro fertilization, gamete intra-fallopian transfer, zygote intra-fallopian transfer, and other procedures.

Hormone Therapy

Drug therapies are often used to treat hormonal imbalances, induce ovulation, and correct problems in the luteal phase of the menstrual cycle. Frequently used drugs include clomiphene citrate (trade name Clomid), HCG (a hormone extracted from human placenta), and HMG (trade name Pergonal, which is extracted from the urine of menopausal women) (Boston Women's Health Book Collective, 1984). These drugs stimulate the ovary to ripen and release an egg. Although they are fairly effective in stimulating ovulation, complications may include hyperstimulation of the ovary, which can result in damage to the ovary if it is not detected (Ovarian Hyperstimulation Syndrome, 1991).

Hormone therapy also increases the likelihood of ovulating multiple eggs, resulting in multiple births. The increase of triplets and higher-order multiple births over the last decade in the U.S. is largely attributed to the rise in use of ovulation-inducing drugs for treating infertility (Kiely, Kleinman, & Kiely, 1992). Infants of higher order multiple births are at greater risk of having low birth weight, and experience higher infant mortality rates. Mortality rates have improved for these babies, with the mortality rates in the mid-1980s only half of those of the 1960s, but these very low birthweight survivors may need extensive neonatal medical and social services (Kiely et al, 1992). Garel and Blondel (1992) interviewed twelve mothers one year following their deliveries of triplets in a public hospital in Paris. The mothers reported strained marriages, social isolation, and difficulty giving adequate attention to three children at the same time. Eight of the mothers reported psychological difficulties, and three had been treated for depression. The researchers recommended that families with triplets should receive increased attention, counseling, and support through specialized clinics, clubs or home visits. The mothers stated that prior to a much-wanted pregnancy parents hardly anticipate the risks and hardship of having multiple children.

NATIONAL DATA: Citing data from the National Center for Health Statistics, Centers for Disease Control, Kiely et al. (1992) noted that between 1982 and 1989 the rate of higher-order multiple births among U.S. women increased from 40 to 78 per 100,000 live births.

In one U.S. study 50% of the triplet pregnancies were attributed to use of ovulation-stimulating drugs, and 9% were attributed to invitro fertilization and gamete intrafallopian transfer (Kiely et al., 1992). Increases of higher-order multiple births have occurred in other industrialized countries as well, including Italy, Japan, England and Wales, and West Germany. In the study of the twelve French women (Garel & Blondel, 1992) two of the pregnancies had been initiated after ovarian stimulation, nine after in vitro fertilization or gamete intra-Fallopian transfer, and one was spontaneous.

Artificial Insemination

When the sperm of the male partner is low in count or motility, the sperm from several ejaculations may be pooled and placed directly into the cervix. This procedure is known as **artificial insemination** by the husband (AIH). This method is generally accepted in our culture. Out of more than 700 university students, 76% said artificial insemination of the wife with the husband's sperm was acceptable (Dunn, Ryan, & O'Brien, 1988).

NATIONAL DATA: About 172,000 U.S. women are artificially inseminated annually (Office of Technology Assessment, 1988).

When sperm from someone other than a male partner is used to fertilize a woman, the technique is referred to as artificial insemination by donor (AID). There is less acceptance for AID than for AIH. Out of more than 700 university students, only 20% said artificial insemination of a married woman by donor was acceptable (Dunn et al., 1988). Couples who have a child from donor sperm typically choose to keep this fact a secret from their child and friends (Foreman, 1990).

CONSIDERATION: Due to concerns about HIV infection, the American Fertility Society has issued a set of guidelines for donor insemination clinics and physicians. These include:

1. The donor's sperm should be screened for genetic abnormalities and sexually transmissible diseases.
2. All semen should be quarantined for 180 days and retested for HIV.
3. Fresh semen should never be used.
4. The donor should be under age 50 in order to diminish hazards related to aging (Foreman, 1990).

In reality, only about half of the physicians who regularly perform artificial inseminations test sperm donors for genetic defects or HIV status. Only 27% to 28% require donors to be tested for syphilis or gonorrhea (Office of Technology Assessment, 1988). The most blatant misuse of donor sperm was that of Cecil Jacobson, a fertility physician, age 55, who used his own sperm (without the knowledge of his patients) to father up to 75 children (Stone, 1992). (He was sentenced to five years in prison and ordered to pay over $100,000 in damages).

Sometimes the male partner's sperm is mixed with a donor's sperm, so that the couple has the psychological benefit of knowing that the male partner may be the biological father. One situation in which the male partner's sperm is not mixed with the donor's sperm is when the male partner is the carrier of a genetic disease, such as Tay-Sachs disease.

There are about 85 sperm banks in the United States, including the Repository for Germinal Choice. This controversial sperm bank in Escondido, California, specializes in providing sperm from men of known intellectual achievement. Among their donors have been three Nobel prize winners in science. No donor to the sperm bank has an IQ under 140. Critics charge that such a sperm bank resembles Hitler's attempts to build a "master race."

NATIONAL DATA: In the United States, about 65,000 infants are conceived each year through the use of artificial insemination (Office of Technology Assessment, 1988). Ten to twenty thousand of these result from sperm from a donor. The process has a national success rate of 57% (Andrews, 1984a, p. 160).

In the procedure of artificial insemination, a physician deposits the sperm through a syringe in the woman's cervix and places a cervical cap over her cervix, which remains in place for 24 hours. On the average, it takes about three inseminations before fertilization occurs.

Before artificial insemination using a donor's sperm is carried out, the parents-to-be agree that any child produced by this procedure will be their own and their legitimate heir. The potential legal problems with artificial insemination by donor have not been worked out. Donovan (1986) noted:

> A child conceived through artificial insemination using the donor's sperm is still in legal limbo in 22 states. The other 28 states have enacted laws specifying that a child conceived by means of artificial insemination that is carried out with the consent of the husband is the legal offspring of the couple. Fifteen of these states also specifically provide that a man who furnishes sperm for the artificial insemination of someone other than his wife is not the child's legal father. (p. 57–58)

Where laws are not explicit, a couple could charge a physician who participated in an artificial insemination with a donor's sperm with negligence if the child were born with a severe defect. Or, if the spouses decided to divorce, the wife could seek full custody rights since her husband is not the biological father.

Artificial Insemination of a Surrogate Mother

Sometimes artificial insemination does not help a woman to get pregnant (e.g., her Fallopian tubes may be blocked or her cervical mucus may be hostile to sperm). The couple who still want a child and who have decided against adoption may consider parenthood through a **surrogate mother.** There are two types of surrogate mothers. One is the contracted surrogate mother who supplies the egg, is impregnated with the male partner's sperm, carries the child to term, and gives the baby to the man and his partner. A second type is the surrogate mother who carries to term the baby to whom she is not genetically related. As with AID, the motivation of the prospective parents is to have a child that is genetically related to at least one of them. For the surrogate mother, the primary motivation is to help involuntary childless couples achieve their aspirations of parenthood and to make money (the surrogate mother is usually paid about $10,000). The total cost of the surrogacy arrangement (surrogate's fee, prenatal care, hospital fee, legal fees, matchmaker fee for bringing couples and surrogate together, counseling fee) is between $25,000 and $30,000 (Lasker & Borg, 1987). One firm in southern California specializing in surrogacy charges $50,000 to $60,000 (*Whose Baby is It?* 1991).

CONSIDERATION: The concept of surrogate pregnancy is not new. The Bible reports that Abraham and his wife, Sarah, could not conceive a child. Their solution was for Abraham to have intercourse with Sarah's Egyptian maid, Hagar, who bore a child for them. Modern-day surrogacy in the family is illustrated by Arlette Schweitzer, 42, of Aberdeen, South Dakota, who served as a surrogate mother for her daughter Christa, who was born without a uterus. Arlette gave birth to her own grandchildren-twins (Elmer-Dewitt, 1991).

There is limited acceptance among university students for surrogate motherhood. Out of more than 700 university students, only 15% said that having a baby by means of a surrogate mother was acceptable (Dunn et al., 1988).

Legally, there are few guidelines for involuntary childless couples who engage a surrogate mother for procreative services. The surrogate can change her mind and decide to keep the child, as did a New Jersey surrogate mother in 1987. In what became known as the "Baby M Case," Mary Beth Whitehead decided she wanted to keep her baby, even though she had signed a contract to give up the baby to William Stern and his wife, Elizabeth, for $10,000. She turned down the fee and fled the state with the baby, who was found by private investigators and returned to the Sterns. A judge upheld the surrogacy contract, severed Whitehead's parental rights and presided over Elizabeth Stern's adoption of Baby M. A year later, the Supreme Court of New Jersey ruled surrogacy for hire was illegal because it resembled baby selling and reestablished Whitehead's parental rights (it gave her visitation rights). However, the court ruled that Richard Stern was the primary custodial parent.

> It (surrogacy) is not all right because motherhood is different from babysitting. Giving up a baby is a life-long traumatic experience for women.
>
> *Laura Woliver*

In another case in 1991, surrogate mother Elvie Jordon changed her mind when she discovered that the couple she gave her baby to were getting divorced. Jordon filed suit to get custody of her 17-month-old Marissa, who was living with Bob Moschetta (the biological father and ex-husband of Cindy Moschetta). A California superior court justice ruled that Elvie Jordon and Bob Moschetta (the biological mother and father) would share joint legal and physical custody of Marissa (Cindy Moschetta was found to have no legal rights and was given no visitation privileges).

CONSIDERATION: Surrogates who change their mind and want to keep their baby are rare. Out of 500 surrogate mothers, only four have sought custody (Sharpe, 1987).

Ovum Transfer

One alternative for the infertile couple is **ovum transfer.** The sperm of the male partner is placed by a physician in a surrogate woman. After about five days, her uterus is flushed out (endometrial lavage), and the contents are analyzed under a microscope to identify the presence of a fertilized ovum, which is inserted into the uterus of the otherwise infertile partner. Although the embryo can also be frozen and implanted at a later time, fresh embryos are more likely to result in successful implantation (24% if fresh versus 8% if frozen) (Levran et al., 1990).

Infertile couples who opt for ovum transfer, also called embryo transfer, do so because the baby will be biologically related to at least one of them (the father) and the partner will have the experience of pregnancy and childbirth. As noted earlier, the surrogate woman participates out of her desire to help an infertile couple or to make money. Out of more than 700 university students, 26% said that having a baby via ovum transfer was acceptable (Dunn et al., 1988).

In Vitro Fertilization

About 2 million couples cannot have a baby because the woman's Fallopian tubes are blocked or damaged, preventing the passage of the eggs to the uterus. In some cases, blocked tubes can be opened via laser-beam surgery or by inflating a tiny balloon within the clogged passage. When these procedures are not successful (or when the woman decides to avoid invasive tests and exploratory surgery), **in vitro** (meaning "in glass") **fertilization,** also known as test-tube fertilization, is an alternative.

Using a **laparoscope** (a narrow, telescope-like instrument inserted through an incision just below the woman's navel to view the tubes and ovaries), the physician is able to see a mature egg as it is released from the woman's ovary. The time of release can be predicted accurately within two hours. When the egg emerges, the physician uses an aspirator to remove the egg, placing it in a small tube containing a stabilizing fluid. The egg is taken to the laboratory, put in a culture or Petri dish, kept at a certain temperature-acidity level, and surrounded by sperm from the woman's partner (or donor). After one of these sperm fertilizes the egg, the egg divides and is implanted by the physician in the wall of the woman's uterus. Usually, several fertilized eggs are implanted in the hope that one will survive.

NATIONAL DATA: The average cost for in vitro fertilization until conception is between $4,000 and $7,000 (*Consumer Protection,* 1989).

Occasionally, some fertilized eggs are frozen and implanted at a later time, if necessary. This procedure is known as **cryopreservation.** A separated or divorced couple may disagree over who owns the frozen embryos. Such was the case of Mary Sue Davis and Junior Davis, who took their disagreement to court. The court awarded the embryos to Mary Sue Davis (Fitzgerald, 1989).

Student acceptance of in vitro or test-tube fertilization is much greater than student acceptance of surrogate motherhood. Out of more than 700 university students, 55% said that having a baby via in vitro or test-tube fertilization was acceptable (Dunn et al., 1988).

NATIONAL DATA: Between 6% and 15% of couples who use in vitro fertilization subsequently give birth to a baby (*Consumer Protection,* 1989).

Louise Brown of Oldham, England, was the first baby to be born by in vitro fertilization. Since her birth in 1978, over 225 clinics in the United States have emerged to duplicate this procedure, resulting in about 10,000 live births.

Self Assessment

Acceptance of Adoption and Five Alternative Fertilization Techniques

The purpose of this survey is to obtain your opinion about the methods used to treat infertility. Medical and social sciences have developed several ways to enable infertile couples to have children. Using the scale below, please indicate the degree to which you would find the following acceptable for married couples.

Circle the corresponding number in the space provided that best represents the degree of YOUR acceptance of each method of treatment for infertility: Extremely unacceptable to me = 5; Unacceptable to me = 4; Undecided = 3; Acceptable to me = 2; Extremely acceptable to me = 1.

1. Artificial insemination *with husband* (placing sperm in the woman's body by a medical technique, rather than through sexual intercourse, in which *sperm* from the *husband* is used to fertilize the wife's egg in her body)	1	2	3	4	5
2. Artificial insemination *with donor* (placing sperm in the woman's body by a medical technique, rather than through sexual intercourse, in which *donor sperm* from a man other than her husband is used to fertilize the wife's egg in her body)	1	2	3	4	5
3. In vitro fertilization (egg is surgically removed from woman's body and fertilized with husband's sperm in a lab dish in a laboratory, then placed back in the wife's uterus)	1	2	3	4	5
4. Surrogate (substitute) motherhood (wife is unable to conceive so another woman is fertilized with husband's sperm by artificial insemination. The surrogate carries the child to term and then gives it to the wife and her husband immediately at birth)	1	2	3	4	5
5. Embryo transfer (the wife is unable to produce an egg to be fertilized but is able to carry a child during pregnancy. Another woman's egg is fertilized with the husband's sperm by artificial insemination. The fertilized egg is then removed and transferred to the uterus of the wife, who carries and delivers the baby at term)	1	2	3	4	5
6. Adoption (the couple adopts a child born to another mother and father)	1	2	3	4	5

Source: Survey items were obtained from Patricia Dunn, East Carolina University, Department of Health, Physical Education, Recreation and Safety, Greenville, NC 27858. Used by permission.

Scoring In designing the survey, the authors did not compute a total score for students' attitudes. They presented mean acceptance levels for each method.

Interpreting Your Score Undergraduate students in health courses at two southeastern universities completed the survey. In the university with a predominantly black student population, all sections of personal health classes were asked to participate ($n=182$). In the other university, with a predominantly white student population, students enrolled in half of the sections of the personal health course were randomly selected to participate ($n=573$). Attitudes of black students from the predominantly white university were not statistically different from those of the predominantly black university. There were so few white students from the predominantly black university and so few students at either school who were neither white nor black that their data were not included in the analyses. Mean levels of acceptance of adoption and the various technologies are reported in this chapter. In Table 1 (from Dunn, Ryan, & O'Brien, 1988), the data for white and black respondents are summarized, including analyses of differences by race. Overall, black students were less accepting of the infertility options surveyed. Analyses of differences by sex revealed a statistically significant difference only for adoption, with women more accepting of adoption. Religious preference was related to a difference in acceptability of artificial insemination by donor. Catholics and Protestants were less accepting of this option than students who indicated a religious preference of "other" or "none."

As you completed this survey, you may have noticed that the wording of the items calls for your opinion of married couples' (husband and wife) use of these technologies. It would be interesting to assess attitudes toward their use by single people or

Continued

Self-Assessment—*Continued*

TABLE 1 Percent Distribution for Level of Acceptability of Methods Dealing with Infertility by Race

Method	*Race*	Level of acceptance[a] *VA*	*A*	*U*	*UA*	*VUA*	χ^{2b}
Adoption	Black	44.9	33.4	11.0	3.2	7.3	18.0 $p < .002$
	White	58.1	31.7	4.9	1.6	3.5	
AI-Husband	Black	23.9	42.9	15.7	10.3	7.2	29.5 $p < .002$
	White	42.2	38.2	11.9	4.6	2.9	
In Vitro fertilization	Black	8.6	42.1	23.9	12.8	12.4	14.7 $p < .002$
	White	18.5	38.4	28.8	8.3	5.8	
AI-Donor	Black	2.0	12.4	19.0	33.6	32.7	18.0 $p < .002$
	White	4.5	18.5	28.8	24.4	23.5	
Surrogate mother	Black	2.0	11.4	22.8	26.9	36.7	8.1 $p > .002$
	White	2.0	14.1	29.6	29.4	24.6	
Embryo transfer	Black	2.8	17.5	34.2	24.0	21.2	6.7 $p > .002.$
	White	3.0	25.3	33.6	23.0	14.8	

[a]VA = *Very Acceptable;* A = *Acceptable;* U = *Undecided;* UA = *Unacceptable;* VUA = *Very Unacceptable.*
[b]approximation for the Kruskal-Wallis Test, here with one degree of freedom.

Source: Published by permission of the *Journal of Sex Research,* a publication of the Society for the Scientific Study of Sex.

unmarried couples. This study was published in 1988. Do you think the acceptability of the use of these technologies by married or by unmarried people would be different now, in the 1990s?

Reliability The survey measure was pilot-tested with 30 students not included in this study. Following revisions for clarification, the measure was assessed for test-retest reliability with 19 students from a health class not included in the study. A test-retest reliability coefficient of 0.77 was obtained.

Reference

Dunn, P. C., Ryan, I. J., & O'Brien, K. (1988). College students' acceptance of adoption and five alternative fertilization techniques. *Journal of Sex Research, 24,* 282–287.

Other Reproductive Technologies

A major problem with in vitro fertilization is that only about 15% to 20% of the fertilized eggs will implant on the uterine wall. To improve this implant percentage (to between 40% and 50%), physicians place the egg and sperm directly into the Fallopian tube where they meet and fertilize, then the fertilized egg travels down into the uterus and implants. Since the term for sperm and egg together is "gamete," the procedure is called **gamete intra-Fallopian transfer**, or GIFT. This procedure, as well as in vitro fertilization, is not without psychological costs to the couple:

> The emotional response to the GIFT procedure is likely to be similar to that of patients undergoing in vitro fertilization, given the parallels in the procedures. The experience of hormone therapy for the female, careful monitoring by laboratory tests, ultrasound scans, and pelvic exams, and the expectation that the male partner will produce a

semen sample a few hours before the procedure—all contribute to the stress of the couple. (Shapiro, 1988, p. 18)

Zygote intra-Fallopian transfer (ZIFT) involves fertilizing the egg in a lab dish and placing the zygote or embryo directly into the Fallopian tube. ZIFT has a success rate similar to gamete intra-Fallopian transfer.

Some infertility cases are the result of sperm that lack motility. In those cases, a physician may inject sperm directly into the egg by means of **microinjection.**

Eggs most likely to implant on the uterine wall are those whose shells have been poked open. To enhance implantation, physicians isolate an egg and drill a tiny hole in its protective shell. This procedure is known as **partial zona drilling** (PZD).

CONSIDERATION: Infertile couples seeking to get pregnant through one of the almost 250 in vitro fertilization (IVF) clinics should make informed choices by asking questions. What is the center's pregnancy rate and how is pregnancy defined? The rate should include only pregnancies verified by ultrasound, not so-called chemical pregnancies. What is the pregnancy and birth rates for other women with similar diagnosis? About 15% of high tech attempts lead to birth. How many cycles are attempted per patient?

The Society for Assisted Reproductive Technology in Birmingham, Alabama is a watchdog group which recognizes only clinics that attempt 40 IVF (in vitro fertilization) procedures a year and produce three live deliveries. The organization publishes an annual list of clinics' results.

To assess your own acceptance of various alternative fertilization techniques, see the self assessment for this chapter. Also, in view of the array of reproductive technologies available, we present the following Public Policy Perspective on their effects on our choices.

PUBLIC POLICY PERSPECTIVE

Reproductive Technology: Liberating or Enslaving?

A recent article in a popular magazine discussed women aged 40 and older bearing children. The headline proclaimed, "More and more, it's happening—thanks to new fertility techniques and women's determination" (Henry, 1992, p. 16). New reproductive technologies increase men and women's choices for controlling their lives—or do they? Many feminist critics have expressed skepticism about new reproductive technologies, suggesting that when women look this "gift horse" in the mouth, they will see that it comes at great cost (Woliver, 1989a). In this Perspective, we will review criticisms based on three arguments: gender role stereotypes and pronatalism limit one's "choice" to desire children; participants in the new technologies are often exploited, and there is great potential for further exploitation; and the development and growth of these industries uphold an unjust social and economic status quo.

"Choice" to Desire Children

Some proponents of the reproductive technologies defend their development by pointing out that women want them, even demand them. One woman described her efforts to have a baby that involved five years, nine specialists, and "every test known to woman" (Henry, 1992, p. 17). Through the gamete intra-Fallopian transfer procedure, she did have a baby, but he lived only a few hours before dying as a result of a damaged heart. She was finally able to have twins, who were two years old at the time she was interviewed. What gives women the drive to repeatedly

Continued

Continued

endure these painful, emotionally challenging, and expensive procedures? Is it biologically determined? Gena Corea (1986, p. 172) quoted an Australian "test-tube baby team leader" who explained that women in his program "are desperate to have a baby for various reasons, but behind it all is an innate wish to procreate."

Corea (1986, p. 172) proposed that "women's free choice is conditioned" by the demands of a patriarchal society that pressures women into producing children for their mates. Furthermore, Corea suggested that women are socialized to impose a definition of themselves as "nonentities" (p. 173) if they are not mothers. Davis (1989, p. 422) referred to "women who are influenced by narrow gender role definitions to experience infertility as an unbearable defect." Andrews (1989) questioned whether women who undertake in vitro fertilization (IVF) do so because of intense social pressures to be mothers and the lack of options for alternative roles. These comments are not to make light of the distress and pain felt by infertile women but to suggest why they suffer (Corea, 1986).

Pressure to conform to prescribed gender roles is not limited to women. Lasker and Borg (1989) investigated the issue of secrecy and the new reproductive technologies. Through interviews with men and women trying alternative methods of conception and professionals who performed the procedures, Lasker and Borg found that artificial insemination by donor (AID) is done with more secrecy than the other methods. Those who had used IVF were likely to tell other people and the child as well. In striking contrast, those who used AID tended not to disclose their use of this reproductive technology. Lasker and Borg concluded that the difference was motivated by the desire to cover up the husband's infertility. They hypothesized that lack of fertility is often confused with lack of virility. Also, they observed that AID disrupts the assumption of a man's dominance in the relationship; his wife has more power in bringing about the birth and in her biological tie to the offspring. The man's social dominance is also challenged; he may see his importance and control as diminished.

Exploitation of Women

One way in which women may be exploited through the use of new reproductive technologies is by their exposure to uncomfortable, physically dangerous, and experimental procedures. AID is considered safe, with possible risks of the transmission of STDs and hereditary disorders (Moghissi, 1989). Physical and emotional risks to women who donate ova include infection, the hazards of experimental drugs, ectopic pregnancy, and the possible impairment of their own fertility (Corea, 1986). Embryo donation may also be risky. In 1984, in one of the attempts at uterine lavage (flushing the embryo out of the uterus), the embryo could not be washed out, leaving the donor pregnant. It is also possible that during the lavage, the embryo may be flushed up the oviduct, resulting in an ectopic pregnancy. One obstetrician-gynecologist told Corea that if he flushed a donor's uterus and got nothing, he would have to tell her, "Golly, lady, I can't find the egg. You might have an ectopic. Come back in two weeks and we'll do an ultrasound to see if there's an ectopic in your tube" (p. 88). Ectopic pregnancy is also a risk to the recipient when the embryo is transferred into her uterus.

Success rates, in terms of pregnancies carried to term, are very low for some of the technologies. The vast majority of the thousands of women who hoped to get a baby through IVF programs have been disappointed, according to Corea.

Surrogacy is often included in discussion of reproductive technologies, because although it does not require new technology, policy issues are often intertwined with more technologically developed alternatives. Controversies regarding surrogacy were reviewed by Woliver (1990), who analyzed the Baby M case and concluded that the

Continued

Continued

mother's experience was discounted. "Whitehead's gestation, birth and genetic connection to her baby were belittled, while the sanctity of contract and the privileges of paternity were upheld" (p. 188). Andrews (1989, p. 361) observed, "The very use of the term 'surrogate' is troubling, since it seemed to be an attempt to disguise the fact that the contracting woman was actually the genetic and gestational mother."

Some critics fear exploitation of women who are vulnerable because they are poor. Chavkin, Rothman, and Rapp (1989) expressed doubt that adequate protection could ever be provided.

> Ten thousand dollars' payment for nine months work, 24 hours a day, entailing substantial physical and emotional transformations and risks comes out to about $1.50 hourly wages: a figure that would only tempt someone for whom work has always been a dead end, as it is for so many working-class women. (p. 406)

Possible abuses of these technologies must be foreseen and prevented, according to Dickstein (1990, p. 138). She identified the following possible abuses of IVF: "multiple births in families unwilling or unable to parent the offspring appropriately; the use of women's eggs and their men's sperm implanted in poor women living in third world countries to 'save the bother of pregnancy'; IVF technology to breed offspring having otherwise impossible combinations of superior physical and intellectual prowess."

A limited role for governmental regulation at the state level has been proposed by Annas (1989). Such regulation could help ensure that adults receive quality services and give informed consent. To protect the interests of future children, he recommended that detailed records of the genetic parents be kept and the information be available to the child at age 18.

Distraction from Needed Reforms

A frequently repeated criticism of the new reproductive technologies is that they offer a medical solution that distracts from solving the social and political problems that contribute to infertility. Are women "choosing" to have children later and later in life to conform to male career timetables? "What is displaced is change of the systems that pressure women to delay motherhood" (Woliver, 1989b, p. 51). Woliver argued that we are distracted from addressing the problems that cause birth defects, such as poor nutrition, environmental toxins, and unsafe working conditions.

The use of reproductive technologies can be extremely expensive, limiting their availability to the middle-class or wealthy. Andrews (1989) detailed some of the costs. Insemination, which takes 2.5 to 9.5 months for conception (two to three inseminations per month) costs from $500 to $2,850. As of 1987, the cost of IVF was $2,000 to $5,000 per attempt, with only a 30% success rate per attempt, at best. A woman who finds her own donor and inseminates herself may pay up to $2,000 for medical and genetic screening of the donor. The costs of surrogacy are approximately $25,000 ($10,000 to the surrogate, $10,000 to the attorney or facilitator, and $5,000 for medical expenses). These are sure to be underestimates of current costs, and few insurance companies cover them. Andrews observed that in some countries with national health-care systems, AID and sometimes IVF are offered. If we decide in the United States that these technologies should be widely available, then difficult decisions must be made about the priorities among health-care needs and how infertility prevention and treatment fit into the picture.

Continued

Continued

Revolutionary reproductive techniques may be used "to perpetuate only the most traditional of family arrangements" (Introduction, 1989, p. 7). Aside from economic rationing of these services, other kinds of screening of potential users is done. Some clinic directors have screened out unmarried couples, single mothers, lesbians, and physically disabled women. The single women in donor insemination programs described by Rosenthal (1990, p. 118) were typically women in their late 30s who "wanted healthy, genetically sound children before their 'biological clock' ran out." They were varied in their sexual orientations and traditionality or feminism. They sought donor programs so they could avoid custody battles and sexual encounters that exploited men just to obtain a pregnancy.

Are the new reproductive technologies truly increasing women's control over their lives? Woliver (1989b, p. 53) concluded that instead of opening new choices for women, the technologies divert "women's power over their bodies and babies" to the medical system and deflect efforts to reform the social causes of reproductive risks.

References

Andrews, L. B. (1989). Position paper: Alternative modes of reproduction. In S. Cohen & N. Taub (Eds.), *Reproductive laws for the 1990's* (pp. 361–403). Clifton, NJ: Humana Press.

Annas, G. J. (1989). Commentary: Regulating the new reproductive technologies. In S. Cohen & Taub (Eds.), *Reproductive laws for the 1990's* (pp. 411–419). Clifton, NJ: Humana Press.

Chavkin, W., Rothman, B. K., & Rapp, R. (1989). Position paper: Alternative modes of reproduction: Other views and questions. In S. Cohen & N. Taub (Eds.), *Reproductive laws for the 1990's* (pp. 405–409). Clifton, NJ: Humana Press.

Corea, G. (1986). *The mother machine.* New York: Harper and Row.

Davis, P. C. (1989). Alternative modes of reproduction: The locus and determinants of choice. In S. Cohen & N. Taub (Eds.). Reproductive laws for the 1990s (pp. 421–431). Clifton, NJ: Humana Press.

Dickstein, L. J. (1990). Effects of the new reproductive technologies on individuals and relationships. In N. L. Stotland (Ed.), *Psychiatric aspects of reproductive technology* (pp. 123–139). Washington, DC: American Psychiatric Press.

Henry, S. (1992, January 19). What it takes to bear a child at forty—and older. *Parade,* pp. 16–17.

Introduction, Working Group for the Project on Reproductive Laws for the 1990s. (1989). In S. Cohen & N. Taub (Eds.), *Reproductive laws for the 1990s* (pp. 3–10). Clifton, NJ: Humana Press.

Lasker, J. N., & Borg, S. (1989). Secrecy and the new reproductive technologies. In L. M. Whiteford & M. L. Poland (Eds.), *New approaches to human reproduction* (pp. 133–144). Boulder, CO: Westview Press.

Moghissi, K. S. (1989). The technology of AID and surrogacy. In L. M. Whiteford & M. L. Poland (Eds.), *New approaches to human reproduction* (pp. 117–132). Boulder, CO: Westview Press.

Rosenthal, M. B. (1990). Single women requesting artificial insemination by donor. In N. L. Stotland (Ed.), *Psychiatric aspects of reproductive technology* (pp. 113–121). Washington, DC: American Psychiatric Press.

Woliver, L. R. (1989a). The deflective power of reproductive technologies: The impact on women. *Women and Politics, 9,* 17–47.

Woliver, L. R. (1989b). New reproductive technologies: Challenges to women's control of gestation and birth. In R. H. Blank & M. K. Mills (Eds.), *Biomedical technology and public policy* (pp. 43–56). New York: Greenwood Press.

Woliver, L. R. (1990). Reproductive technologies and surrogacy: Policy concerns for women. *Politics and the Life Sciences, 8,* 185–193.

Pregnancy and Labor

Motherhood is both a biomedical and psychosocial experience and begins not with childbirth but with fertilization and conception. Immediately after the egg is fertilized by the sperm in the Fallopian tube, the egg begins to divide and is pushed by hairlike cilia down the Fallopian tube into the uterus, where it attaches itself to the inner wall. Furnished with a rich supply of blood and nutrients, the developing organism is called an **embryo** for the first three months and a **fetus** thereafter (see Figure 21.2).

Detecting pregnancy as early as possible is important. Not only does doing so enable the woman to begin prenatal precautions and medical care during the most vulnerable stage of fetal development, it allows those women with an unintended pregnancy time to consider if they want to have an abortion, which may then be performed when it is safest (early in pregnancy). Finally, early diagnosis may permit early detection of an **ectopic pregnancy.** Such a pregnancy involves the baby developing outside the uterus, such as in the cervix, abdominal area, or ovary (see Figure 21.3). However, most ectopic pregnancies occur in the Fallopian tube. An ectopic pregnancy is potentially dangerous, and signs of such a pregnancy should be taken seriously. These include sudden intense pain in the lower abdomen, irregular bleeding, or dizziness that persists more than a few seconds.

NATIONAL DATA: About 70,000 ectopic pregnancies, or 1% of all pregnancies, occur each year (Siller & Azziz, 1991).

New treatments for ectopic pregnancy include microsurgery incisions that allow the physician to remove the embryo while leaving the reproductive system intact. In some cases, methotrezate may be prescribed to destroy the pregnancy-related tissue.

Pregnancy Testing

Signs of pregnancy may include a missed period, morning sickness, enlarged and tender breasts, more frequent urination, and excessive fatigue. However, pregnancy is best confirmed by laboratory tests and a physical examination.

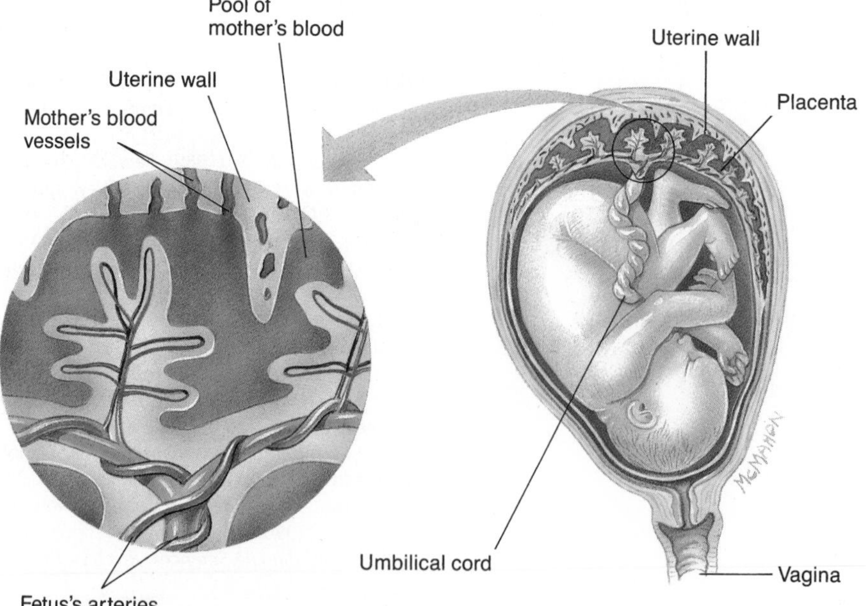

FIGURE 21.2 The Developing Embryo

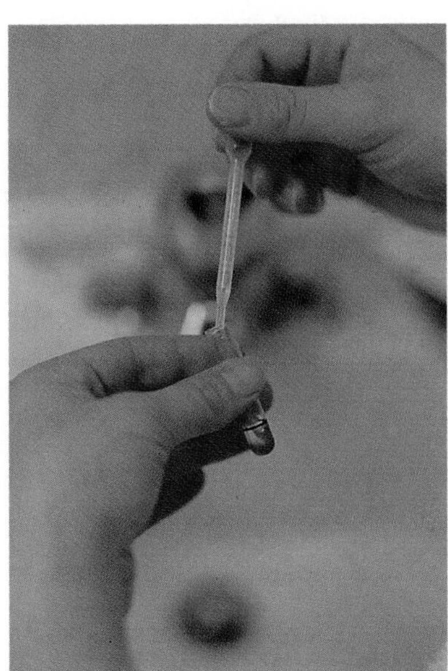

Most commercially available pregnancy tests are based on detecting the presence of a hormone called human chorionic gonadotropin (HCG).

Several laboratory tests of pregnancy have a high degree of accuracy. All of them depend upon the presence of a hormone produced by the developing embryo, human chorionic gonadotropin (HCG), which appears in the pregnant woman's urine. One procedure, formally known as the lutex agglutination inhibition immunologic slide test, detects HCG in about two and a half hours and can reveal if the woman is pregnant within 14 days after the first missed menstrual period. All commercially available pregnancy tests use the lutex agglutination principle and are reasonably reliable in providing information about the existence of a pregnancy. The most common error in the home pregnancy tests is that the woman takes the test too early in pregnancy and concludes that she is not pregnant (false negative) when, in fact, she is.

HCG also appears in the bloodstream of the pregnant woman. A radioimmunoassay test, a laboratory examination of the blood, can suggest if the woman is pregnant within eight days of conception. A new test, radioreceptorassay, also analyzes the blood and is 100% accurate on the first day after the first missed period. Pregnancy tests in which urine of the presumed pregnant woman is injected into a mouse, rabbit, or frog have been replaced by these tests (Green, 1977).

If the laboratory test indicates pregnancy, the physician usually conducts a pelvic examination to find out if the woman's uterus has enlarged or changed color. These changes take place around the sixth week of pregnancy. Confirmation of the pregnancy is dependent on hearing and counting the fetal heart pulsations (to differentiate them from the mother's heartbeat). This occurs between the sixteenth and twentieth weeks of pregnancy.

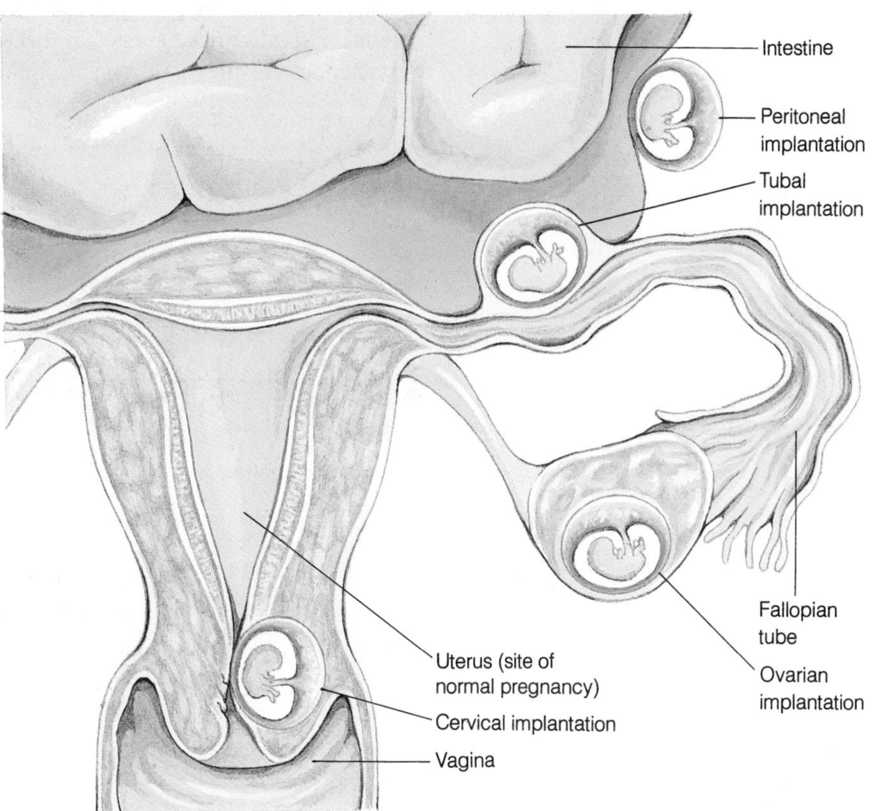

FIGURE 21.3 Ectopic Pregnancies.

Physical Changes during Pregnancy

The usual course of a typical 266-day pregnancy is divided into trimesters, or three-month periods, during which the woman may experience some discomforts due to physical changes (see Table 21.1). Women vary in the degree to which they experience these changes. "Some women experience few or none of the related symptoms, whereas others experience many and may find such changes uncomfortable" (Engel, 1990, p. 184).

Prenatal Care and Prenatal Testing

NATIONAL DATA: Almost one-fourth of the pregnant women in the United States do not receive prenatal care during the first trimester (U.S. General Accounting Office, 1987).

Ensuring a healthy baby depends on adequate nutrition, moderate weight gain, exercise and avoidance of such substances as alcohol, nicotine, cocaine, and other drugs that are harmful to the fetus. Some women do not receive prenatal care, which results in an increased risk for having a premature infant.

Ideally, women should attend to their nutrition before becoming pregnant. Not only should they eat the proper types and quantity of foods but they also should avoid foods high in sugar and fat. Ideally, underweight women should gain weight and overweight women should lose weight before becoming pregnant. Once the woman becomes pregnant she should gain about 20% of her prepregnancy weight during pregnancy (Travis, 1988). A woman who weighs about 130 pounds when she becomes pregnant should gain about 26 pounds, depending on her height. If the mother does not gain enough weight, she may give birth to an underweight baby. A low-birth weight baby is defined as one that weighs less than five and a half pounds. Birth weight is the single most potent indicator of the infant's future health status. Low birth weight is associated with a higher incidence of disease and early mortality.

Exercise is contraindicated for women who have certain risk factors (e.g. anemia, hypertension, pain of any kind, fetal distress, heart palpitations, vaginal or uterine bleeding, and other risk factors). In the absence of risk factors, however, exercise is recommended for pregnant women. Nakahata (1988) concluded that

> A review of research studies to date indicates that exercise performed for a moderate duration at a submaximal heart rate level does not compromise the healthy pregnant woman and her fetus and appears to have some beneficial effects. (p. 349)

TABLE 21.1 Side Effects of Pregnancy

	1st Trimester Week 0–14	2nd Trimester Week 15–26	3rd Trimester Week 27–40
Nausea	*		
Vomiting	*		
Frequent urination	*		*
Leg cramps	*		
Vaginal discharge	*	*	*
Fatigue	*	*	*
Constipation	*	*	*
Swelling		*	*
Varicose veins		*	*
Backache		*	*
Heartburn		*	
Shortness of breath		*	

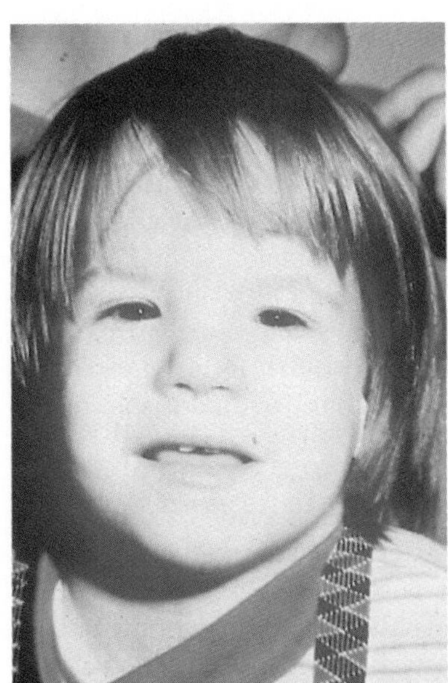

Fetal alcohol syndrome may result from drinking alcohol during pregnancy. Its effects include not only facial deformity but usually retardation.

NATIONAL DATA: Only 4% of mothers giving birth reported that they consumed alcohol during their pregnancy. Because of substantial underreporting, it is estimated that 20% or more of women drink alcohol during their pregnancy (National Center for Health Statistics, 1992b).

NATIONAL DATA: Twenty percent of mothers who gave birth reported that they had smoked during their pregnancy (National Center for Health Statistics, 1992b).

Reasons women may choose to exercise during pregnancy include the hope of an early return to a prepregnancy body shape and size, the possibility of a more comfortable labor and birth, and the sense of well-being that exercise promotes (Nakahata, 1988). Women who choose to exercise should consult with their physician to rule out contraindications. Specific guidelines for exercise during pregnancy may be obtained through a physician, childbirth educator, and/or published literature (e.g. *Exercise in Pregnancy,* Artal & Wiswell, 1986).

Pregnant women should eliminate their alcohol intake to avoid **fetal alcohol syndrome** (FAS), which refers to the negative consequences for the fetus and infant of the mother who drinks alcohol at the level of a social drinker. A heavy drinker is defined as "anyone who regularly has one drink a day (say, a glass of wine before dinner) and additionally may have two or three drinks in an occasional evening (perhaps at a party or dining out)" (Travis, 1988, p. 119). A social drinker would drink even less. Negative consequences for the developing infant include increased risk of low birth weight, growth retardation, facial malformations, and intellectual retardation. Avoiding alcohol intake during the early weeks of pregnancy is particularly critical; however, alcohol consumed in the later months may impede organ growth. "Professional advice to pregnant women is consistent: If you're pregnant, don't drink" (Travis, 1988, p. 121). And, since you usually do not know if you are pregnant for one to two months after fertilization, don't drink alcohol if you are not using a reliable method of contraception.

Smoking cigarettes during pregnancy is also associated with harm to the developing fetus. Negative consequences include lower-birth weight babies, small-for-date babies, premature babies, spontaneous abortions, lower Apgar scores (Apgar measures infant vitality), and higher fetal or infant deaths. Women who smoked during the first two trimesters of pregnancy were observed to have three times the risk of nonsmokers for placenta previa, a condition in which the placenta obstructs the cervical opening at birth. Fortunately, women who had smoked, but quit prior to the pregnancy had no increased risk compared to those who had never smoked (Williams et al., 1991). In addition, when 223 children with cancer were compared with 196 controls, children whose mothers smoked during pregnancy had a 90% higher risk of acute lymphocytic leukemia. If the fathers smoked, there was a 40% increased risk of the children contracting leukemia and a 60% increased risk of lymphoma and brain cancer (John, Savitz, & Sandler, 1991). While most studies have been conducted on active smoking by the mother, avoiding passive, secondary, or environmental smoke may also be in the best interest of the developing fetus.

Concerned about the health of their babies, some pregnant women avoid not only alcohol and nicotine but also caffeine and such over-the-counter drugs as aspirin and antihistamines and such prescription drugs as amphetamines and tranquilizers. While there is no conclusive evidence that caffeine has a serious detrimental effect on the developing baby, a physician should be consulted in regard to continuing medications before and during pregnancy. "Ideally, consumption of nonprescription drugs should stop completely *prior* to conception" (Chez, 1991, p. 56).

Illegal drugs (also nonprescription drugs), such as marijuana and cocaine, should also be avoided. Cocaine has been associated with preterm labor and delivery, lower-birth weight babies, limb defects, lower IQ, and oversensitivity to stimulation. These "crack" or "cocaine" babies may enter the world disadvantaged; however, since their mothers may have used various substances, it is difficult to isolate the specific effects of cocaine from malnutrition and lack of prenatal care (Brent & Beckman, 1992).

Prenatal care may also involve prenatal (antenatal) testing. Such tests may involve ultrasound, amniocentesis, chorionic villus sampling, florescent insitu hybridization, and preimplantation testing. **Ultrasound** involves sound waves being intermittently beamed at the fetus, producing a detailed image on a video screen. It is a noninvasive test which immediately provides pictures of the maternal and fetal outlines and inner organs. Although its long-term effects are still being studied, it appears to be one of the safest procedures for the amount of information it provides (Boston Women's Health Book Collective, 1984). Ultrasound allows the physician to determine the length of gestation (i.e. the age of the fetus) and assess the presence of structural abnormalities. While ultrasound may reveal the fetus' genital area (depending on the position of the fetus), it is not considered a reliable test to determine the sex of the fetus.

The other prenatal tests are used to identify fetuses with chromosomal and biochemical defects. These procedures are usually offered to women who have had a child with a birth defect, or some other risk factor (e.g., advanced maternal age, now defined at around 35 years of age). Their purpose is to detect defects early enough that if the test is positive, the woman can either be prepared for the birth of a child with health problems, or decide to terminate the pregnancy. Their availability has provided many people the confidence to initiate a pregnancy despite familial history of serious genetic disease or prior birth of affected children (Boston Women's Health Book Collective, 1984).

Amniocentesis (which is best performed in the sixteenth or seventeenth week of pregnancy) involves inserting a slender needle through the abdomen into the amniotic sac and taking about one ounce of fluid (see Figure 21.4). Fetal cells, which

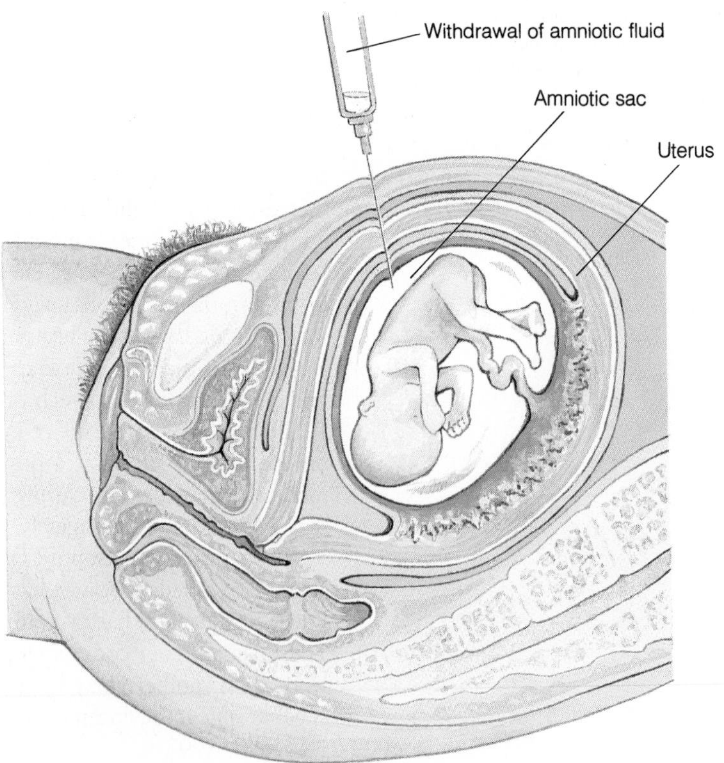

FIGURE 21.4 Amniocentesis.
Amniotic fluid is withdrawn. Fetal cells are analyzed for the fetus' sex, age, and indications of chromosomal abnormalities.

NATIONAL DATA: Thirty-two of every 1,000 live births involve amniocentesis earlier in pregnancy (National Center for Health Statistics, 1992b).

are present in this amniotic fluid, are sent to the laboratory, where they are cultured (permitted to multiply in a special medium) and then analyzed for defects.

Amniocentesis involves some risk. In rare cases (about 0.5% of the time, or one in 200 cases), the fetus may be damaged by the needle, even though an ultrasound scan has been used to identify its position. Congenital orthopedic defects, such as clubfoot, and premature birth have been associated with amniocentesis. Also, if no specific abnormality is detected (as is the case 97.5% of the time), this does not guarantee that the baby will be normal and healthy. Cleft palate, cleft lip, and most heart defects are not detected by amniocentesis. In addition to amniocentesis, a blood test that measures alpha-fetoprotein, popularly known as the AFP test, may be used to assess neural tube defects (anencephaly and spina bifida). AFP is usually conducted between the sixteenth and eighteenth weeks of pregnancy.

Unfortunately, after the amniocentesis procedure at 16 to 17 weeks of gestation, an additional three or four weeks is required for cell tissue culture and karyotyping. By this time the woman may be 20 to 22 weeks pregnant; the pregnancy is publicly visible, and she has probably felt fetal movement. Having already made the emotional transition from the "state of being pregnant" to "going to have a baby," the woman and her partner would likely find it quite traumatic to face a diagnosis of a severe fetal abnormality this late in pregnancy (Evans & Johnson, 1992). To terminate a pregnancy that had progressed to 20 or 22 weeks, a saline or prostaglandin (induced miscarriage) abortion procedure is frequently used, which involves the delivery of the fetus. A dilation and evacuation (D and E) method could be used in which the cervix is dilated and a physician uses forceps, a curette and vacuum suction to remove the uterine lining, and fetal and placental tissue. While the D and E procedure is safer and less upsetting for the woman, it is more expensive and is not widely available, as many physicians are not trained or willing to terminate a second-trimester fetus by performing a D and E (Boston Women's Health Book Collective, 1984).

In response to these problems, attempts have been made to move prenatal diagnosis into the first trimester of pregnancy. The major advantage of **chorionic villus sampling** (CVS) is that it can be done much earlier than amniocentesis, with the results available more quickly. Villi are the thread-like edges of the chorion, or membrane, surrounding the fetus. A small sample of the chorion can be obtained by passing a thin catheter, using ultrasound guidance, through the cervix and into the placenta (see figure 21.5). Sometimes, due to the placement of the placenta, the villi must be extracted through the abdomen, as in amniocentesis. The villi can then be analyzed directly or cultured and the chromosomes studied (Johnson & Miller, 1992). In addition to diagnosis of Down's Syndrome and other chromosomal disorders, CVS has been shown to reliably diagnose Tay-Sachs disease, cystic fibrosis, sickle cell anemia, and Duchenne muscular dystrophy (Evans & Johnson, 1992).

Considerable experience and coordination are needed to perform the procedure effectively and safely. The primary risk of the procedure is loss of the pregnancy, although there have been some reports of limb reduction deformities (Turner, 1992). Many clinics cite a slightly higher risk of pregnancy interruption for CVS than for amniocentesis. Evans and Johnson are on the staff of the Division of Reproductive Genetics at Hutzel Hospital/Wayne State University, one of the largest prenatal diagnosis programs in the U.S. In their opinion, "CVS has in the early 1990s reached equal parity with amniocentesis in terms of its general safety and efficacy and has allowed for a shift in prenatal diagnosis to become the mainstay of the first trimester" (Evans & Johnson, 1992, p. 176).

FIGURE 21.5 Chorionic Villi Sampling

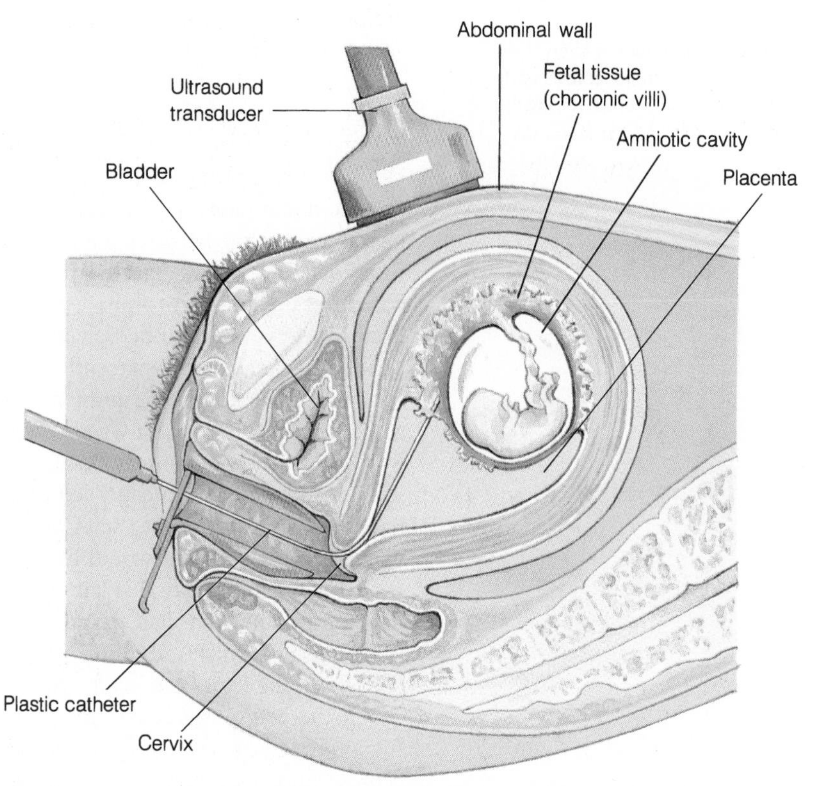

> **CONSIDERATION:** Evans and Johnson (1992) commented on their criteria for accepting women for counseling and prenatal diagnosis. They consider age 30 and above as advanced maternal age and allow women to enter their program as long as they understand the risks and benefits of the diagnostic procedures, and are not seeking prenatal diagnosis merely for sex selection. They noted that many couples, especially professional and upper socioeconomic patients, are seeking services as part of a "fewer but better babies" philosophy (p. 177).

When prenatal testing reveals a fetal abnormality the choice to terminate the pregnancy may be extremely difficult. "The factor of choice is a tremendous emotional burden for women who choose to abort" (Rice, 1992, p. 279). Rice cautioned that men's feelings of shock, hurt, and disappointment may be overlooked. A partner may feel helpless, and yet responsible. He may feel he is not entitled to his grief, and try to discount his pain. Siblings may also feel a loss. The family members may need help in honestly expressing themselves.

A new enhancement to both amniocentesis and chorionic villus sampling is a procedure known as FISH (florescent insitu hybridization). This procedure provides information within two days on the presence of chromosomal abnormalities predictive of birth defects. The method is still undergoing clinical trials and is expected to be available in 1993 (Roberts, 1991).

Also undergoing clinical trials is a preimplantation testing procedure that involves fertilizing a woman's egg in a petri dish and allowing the fertilized egg to develop about two days until it is about eight cells large. At that time, the researcher removes one of the cells and tests it for the presence of the fatal Tay-Sachs gene. Only those cells that did not have the gene would be implanted in the woman's uterus (Gordon, 1992, p. A-1).

Psychological Changes during Pregnancy

Affonso and Mayberry (1989) assessed the stresses of 221 women during and after pregnancy (81 in the first trimester, 80 in the third trimester, and 60 in the postpartum period). Stress related to physical issues was the most frequently reported problem. "The total group identified fatigue, disturbed sleep, feeling physically restricted, and nausea or vomiting as the most common physical distresses" (p. 46). The second most frequently experienced stressor was associated "with 'weight gain' and feelings of being 'fat,' 'unattractive,' and 'distorted.' " (Affonso & Mayberry, 1989, p. 48).

The third most frequently reported concern during pregnancy was for the "baby's welfare and dealing with changes relative to household arrangement and restrictions in physical activities, especially as the woman nears childbirth" (Affonso & Mayberry, 1989, p. 49). Some of the women reported that they were plagued by such frequent thoughts as "Something might happen to my baby," "Am I doing the right thing to protect my baby?" and "I shouldn't have done this because now I'm worried about how it affected my baby" (p. 49).

As women near the end of the pregnancy, fears of pain, complications, the threat of a cesarean are high-intensity stressors. And once pregnancy begins, some women feel trapped. They feel that they have begun a course of action from which they cannot easily withdraw (Engel, 1990). Various techniques of childbirth preparation (Dick-Read, Lamaze, Bradley), discussed later in this chapter, are designed to help the woman work through various concerns during pregnancy and to give her needed emotional support.

Pregnancy is also a time that the man is experiencing his own set of feelings. Shapiro (1987) interviewed 227 expectant and recent fathers and noted several concerns:

1. Queasiness. Respondents in Shapiro's study reported that their greatest fear before birth was coping with the actual birth process. They were queasy about being in the midst of blood and bodily fluids and felt they would faint or get sick. Most did neither.
2. Worry over increased responsibility. Over 80% reported feeling that they were now the sole support for three people. Many took second jobs or worked longer hours.
3. Uncertain paternity. Half of the men feared that the child their partner was carrying was not their own. "For most of them, such fears were based less on any real concern that the wife had been unfaithful than on a general insecurity brought on by being part of something as monumental as the creation of life" (p. 39).
4. Fear of the loss of spouse and/or child. Some men feared that both the wife and baby might die during childbirth and that they would be alone. They also feared that the baby would be brain-damaged or defective in some way.
5. Fear of being replaced. The words of one respondent reflect a common feeling among expectant fathers—that of being replaced:

   > The one thing that really scares me is that the best of our lives together will be gone as soon as the baby is born . . . in some ways, I'm feeling displaced . . . ." (p. 42)

   Some of the men had affairs late in their wife's pregnancy. These men perceived their wives to be more focused on and bonded with the impending baby than themselves. Since they missed the attention they had had from their wife prior to the pregnancy, they sought to replace that attention with that of other women.

In an effort to prevent the man from feeling left out and to increase his emotional bonding with the impending baby, the Empathy Belly was developed (see Exhibit 21.2). It has also been used to help teenagers have a more realistic, as opposed to a romanticized, view of pregnancy.

Sex during Pregnancy

Sexual desire, behavior, and satisfaction may change during pregnancy. Eighty-one married couples provided information the thirteenth and fourteenth weeks of pregnancy and again within one week after the birth of the baby. In regard to sexual desire, 40% of the women reported diminished sexual desire during the first and second trimesters. Seventy-four percent reported decreased sexual desire during the third trimester. Of their husbands, 9% and 17% reported decreased sexual desire the first and second trimesters, respectively, and 64% during the third trimester (Bogren, 1991).

Some pregnant women and their partners experience an increase in sexual desire during pregnancy. Changes in sexual desire may be related to the woman's changing physical appearance during pregnancy.

> Some women may perceive themselves as fat, ugly, and generally unattractive during their pregnancy. Others may find their enlarging breasts, rounding abdomens, and fuller shapes more womanly, appealing, and sexually desirable. Negative or positive feelings toward these changes in body image may influence a woman's sexual desire. (Wilkerson & Bing, 1988, p. 379)

EXHIBIT 21.2 The Empathy Belly

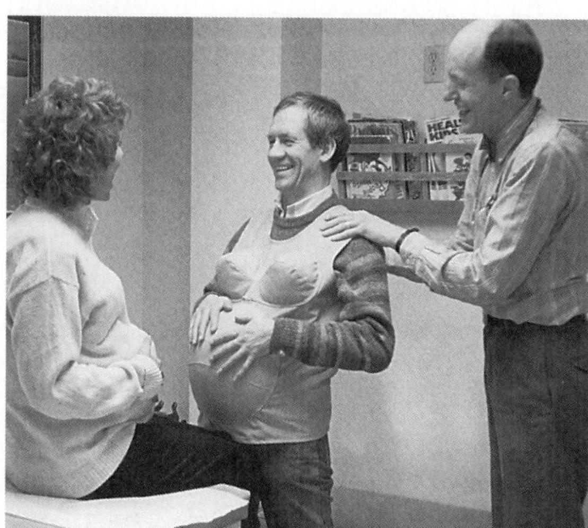

The Empathy Belly provides males with a way to experience 20 of the typical symptoms and effects of pregnancy.

Linda Ware, a childbirth educator, developed "The Empathy Belly" for men who want to increase their understanding, appreciation, and support for their partners, (the device is also used in the education of teens to deromanticize teenage pregnancy). The Empathy Belly is a 33-pound garment that enables the wearer (who will look pregnant) to experience more than 20 of the typical symptoms and effects of pregnancy, including:

- pregnant profile of enlarged breasts and protruding belly
- change in physical and personal self-image
- continuous pressure on the abdomen and internal organs
- increase in body temperature, pulse and blood pressure
- shift in one's center of gravity; low backache
- mild "fetal" kicking and stroking movements
- shallow breathing capacity and shortness of breath
- pressure on the bladder, with increased sense of urgency and frequency of urination
- increased fatigue, slowed pace, and restricted activity
- change in sexual self-image and abilities

Source: The Empathy Belly is distributed by Birthways Inc., 14804 N.E. 75th St. Redmond, WA 98052, at (800)882-3559.

In regard to sexual frequency, 41% of the women reported decreased sexual frequency during the first trimester, 40% during the second trimester, and 90% during the third trimester. The percentages of husbands reporting decreased frequencies for the first, second, and third trimester were 30%, 40%, and 83%, respectively (Bogren, 1991).

Some couples do not have intercourse during pregnancy because the health-care provider tells them not to do so. In a study of 52 pregnant women, 17% reported being told to abstain totally from intercourse during pregnancy (Gauna-Trujillo & Higgins, 1989).

CONSIDERATION: Are there any conditions under which a pregnant woman should choose to forgo intercourse and orgasmic activity? Yes. Women who are experiencing vaginal bleeding or abdominal pain, those whose amniotic membrane has ruptured, and those whose cervix has begun to efface and/or dilate after 24 weeks should abstain from sexual intercourse (Engel, 1990). Those with a history of premature delivery and a history of miscarriage are also encouraged to avoid intercourse during pregnancy (Gauna-Trujillo & Higgins, 1989). Mutual and solitary masturbation, as well as oral-genital expressions, might still be enjoyed, but the arousal of the woman should be kept at a low level. Also, care should be taken by the partner engaging in cunnilingus not to blow air into the vulva area. Some cases have been documented of pregnant women dying as a result of air emboli from air blown into the vagina (Aronson & Nelson, 1972).

When intercourse does occur, the side-by-side position is the most frequently used position. Eighty-two percent of the respondents in the Israeli study mentioned above reported using this position during the third trimester (Hart et al., 1991).

In regard to sexual satisfaction, 35% of the women in the Bogren (1991) study reported decreased sexual satisfaction during the first trimester, 30% during the second trimester, and 55% during the third trimester. The percentages reporting decreased sexual satisfaction for the first, second, and third trimesters for the husbands were 22%, 26%, and 76%, respectively (Bogren, 1991).

However, some couples experience increased sexual satisfaction during pregnancy. For both partners, freedom from worry about contraception may add to relaxation and enjoyment of sexual activities. In addition,

> Increased vascularity and engorgement of the breasts, labia, and vagina enhance sexual response during pregnancy . . . . Women often experience heightened sexual tension, more intense orgasms, and more enjoyment of sexual activities (Wilkerson & Bing, 1988, p. 381).

Even if the desire for intercourse has decreased, "there is still a great need for close physical contact. Hugging, holding, caressing, and cuddling may be extremely satisfying forms of sexual expression . . ." (Wilkerson & Bing, 1988, p. 381). Lastly, some women "progress through their pregnancy with increased feelings of sensuality, and often gain a new awareness of their bodies" (p. 381).

Labor

The beginning of labor signals the end of pregnancy. Labor occurs in three stages, and although there are great variations, it lasts an average of 13 hours for the woman having her first baby (she is referred to as a **primigravida**) and about eight hours if the woman has given birth before **(multigravida).** Figure 21.6 illustrates the birth process. It is not known what causes the onset of labor, which is marked by uterine

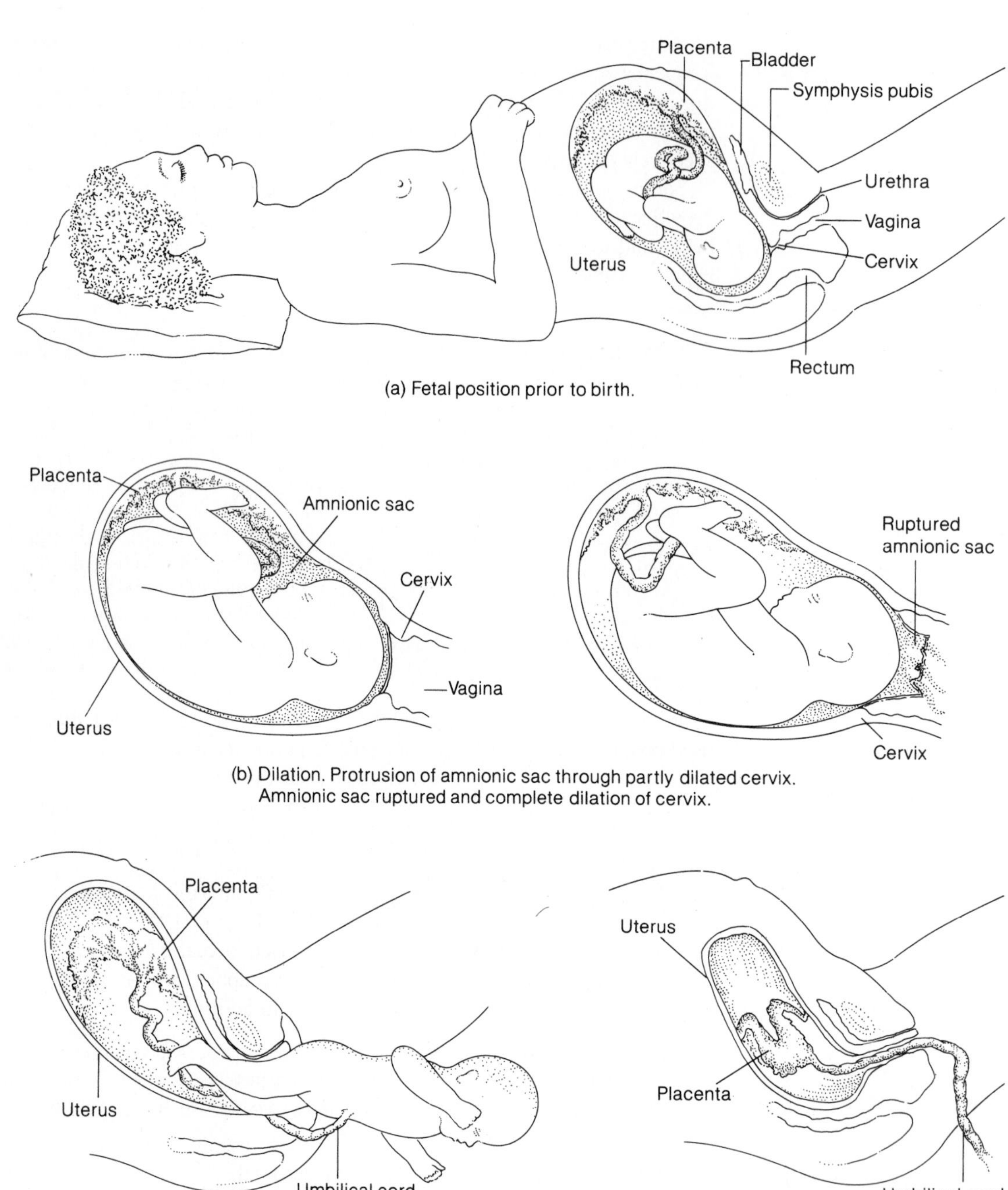

FIGURE 21.6 Stages of Labor

contractions. But there are distinctions between the contractions of true and preparatory (also known as Braxton-Hicks contractions) labor. Table 21.2 illustrates the respective differences.

First Stage of Labor Labor begins with regular uterine contractions, at 15- to 20-minute intervals, that last from 10 to 30 seconds. The first stage of labor lasts for

TABLE 21.2 Contractions Characteristic of True and Preparatory Labor

True Labor	Preparatory Labor
Occur at regular intervals	Occur at irregular intervals
Intervals gradually shorten	Intervals remain long
Intensity gradually increases	Intensity remains the same
Discomfort in back and abdomen	Discomfort chiefly in lower abdomen
Cervix dilates	Cervix does not dilate
Not affected by sedation	Usually relieved by sedation

about nine hours if it is the first baby and about five hours in subsequent deliveries. During this first stage, the woman often has cramps and backache. The membranes of the amniotic sac may rupture, spilling the amniotic fluid.

Throughout the first stage, the uterine contractions become stronger, lasting for 30 to 45 seconds, and more frequent (every three to five minutes). These contractions result in effacement and dilation of the cervix. With **effacement,** the cervix flattens out and gets longer; with **dilation,** the cervical opening through which the baby will pass gets larger. At the end of the first stage, the cervix is dilated three and a half to four inches; contractions occur every one to two minutes and last up to a minute.

During the first stage, the baby is getting into position to be born. The fetal heart rate is monitored continually by stethoscope or ultrasound, and the woman's temperature and blood pressure are checked. She may experience leg cramps, nausea, or irritability during this first stage of labor.

Second Stage of Labor Also known as the expulsive stage of labor, the second stage begins when the cervix is completely dilated and ends when the baby is born. It lasts about 50 minutes if it is the woman's first baby, 20 minutes for subsequent births. Uterine contractions may last one and a half minutes and be one to two minutes apart. These contractions move the baby further into the vaginal birth canal. The woman may help this process by pushing movements. The head of the baby emerges first, followed by the shoulders and trunk. While most babies are born head first, some are born breech. In a **breech birth,** the baby's feet or buttocks come out the vagina first. Breech deliveries are much more complicated.

To ease the birth, the physician may perform an episiotomy, which involves cutting in one of two places the perineum, the area between the vagina and the anus, to make a larger opening for the baby and to prevent uncontrolled tearing (see Figure 21.7).

Immediately after the baby is born, its nostrils are cleared of mucus using a small suction bulb. The umbilical cord is then clamped twice—about one and two inches from the infant's abdomen—and cut between the clamps. The baby is cleaned of placental matter, put in a temperature-controlled bassinet, or held by the parents.

Third Stage of Labor After the baby is born, the placenta, or afterbirth, is delivered. Usually within five minutes after the birth of the baby, the placenta separates itself from the uterine wall and is expelled from the vagina. If it does not disengage easily and by itself, the birth attendant will manually remove it. If an episiotomy was made the physician will repair it by stitching up the incision after the placenta is delivered.

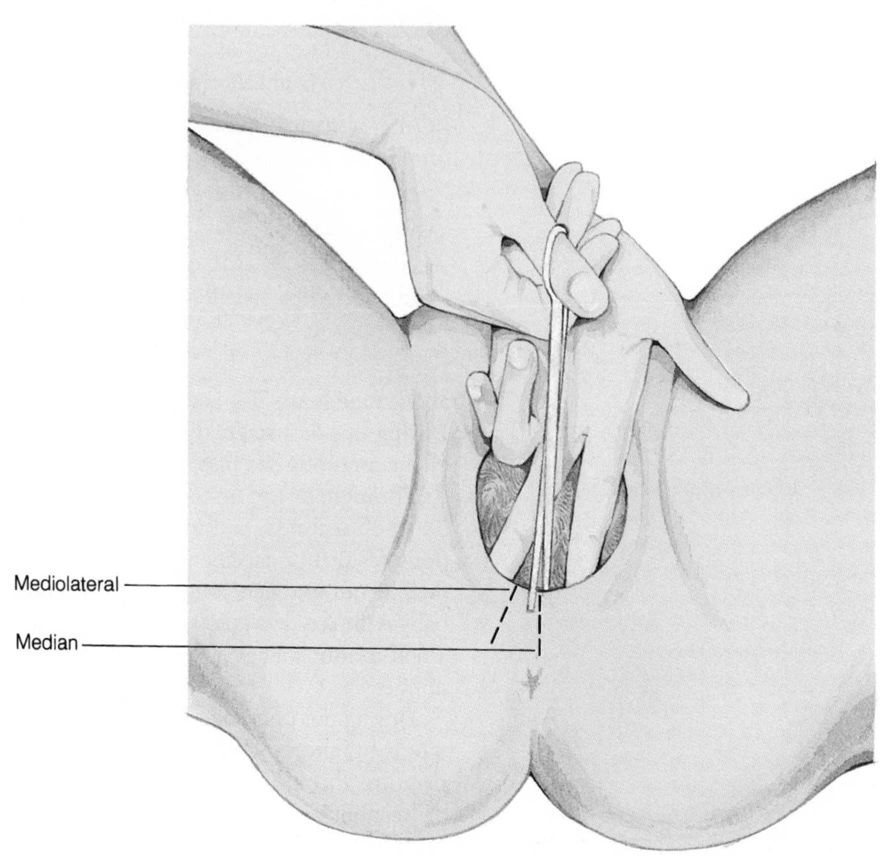

FIGURE 21.7 **Alternative episiotomy cites.**

The time from one to four hours after delivery is regarded by some physicians as a fourth stage of labor. During this time, the mother's uterus relaxes and returns to a more normal state. Bleeding of the cervix, which results from the detachment of the placenta from the uterine wall, stops.

NATIONAL DATA: Six infants out of 1,000 live births died in 1989 within 28 days of birth; eight women died in 1989 per 100,000 live births due to complications of pregnancy and childbirth (National Center for Health Statistics, 1992a).

In the U.S. childbirth is relatively safe for both the infant and the mother. However, despite our advanced technology, the U.S. has a high rate of infant and maternal mortality compared to other industrialized nations. Our teen pregnancy rate, a risk factor for low birthweight (which causes infant mortality and disabilities), is higher than all other industrialized societies (Lazarus, 1988). Women living at or below the poverty level are particularly vulnerable to poor obstetrical outcomes (Michaelson, 1988).

CONSIDERATION: Obstetric literature in the U.S. has focused mainly on technological innovations and pathology, while ethnicity and socioeconomic factors affecting reproduction have been largely ignored (Lazarus, 1988). Based on her study of Puerto Rican and white poor women, Lazarus cited the "accoutrements of poverty—unemployment, lack of support, poor education, lack of continuity of care in public clinics with long waits and the resultant stress created" as significant factors in reproductive problems (p. 41).

Michaelson (1988) listed stressful life events, common in the lives of poor women, which make pregnancy more difficult. "These included being pregnant while unmarried, the baby's father not wanting the child, having to take care of present children without the assistance of a spouse or others, and having too little money to live on" (p. 17).

Childbirth Preparation

At the turn of the century, only about 5% of U.S. babies were born in a hospital or medical setting. Because there were few physicians and fewer hospitals, a midwife was usually summoned to the pregnant woman's home to assist the laboring mother-to-be with her delivery. Home births gradually became less common, due to the high infant mortality rate, the developing political strength of the medical profession, and the development of hospital facilities to handle difficult deliveries. Today, more than 95% of all births in the United States take place in a hospital (see the Choices section on hospital versus home births at the end of this chapter).

However, considerable controversy has emerged over whether physicians exercise too much control over the birthing process. For example, traditionally, when the woman began to experience uterine contractions that were regular and intense, she was encouraged to check into the hospital, be "prepped" (her vaginal area was cleaned, her pubic hair shaved, and she was given an enema), and complete labor in a special room near the delivery room. Her husband or partner was usually not allowed to remain with her during labor and delivery. The woman was confined to bed instead of being allowed to walk about during labor. The prescribed birthing position, the lithotomy position, had the woman lying on her back on the delivery table, her legs in the air or in stirrups, and her buttocks at the table's edge. In response to the feeling of being "medically managed," expectant parents began to question physician-controlled births and emphasized that hospital childbirth procedures were too impersonal, autocratic, and rigid. They also felt that various childbirth interventions were used "primarily for the convenience of hospital staff and not for maximum safety" (Travis, 1988, p. 31).

> For example, induction of labor allows physicians to lead a more predictable social life. However, induction of labor is usually associated with more strenuous contractions during labor, making it more difficult for women to forgo analgesics and possibly precipitating fetal distress. The lithotomy position commonly promoted during labor and required during delivery also is associated with increased risk for fetal distress and stress to the perineum, making episiotomy a standard procedure . . . . It has been suggested that instead of making childbirth more safe, these methods have been promoted as a means of convincing women that childbirth must be supervised by a physician. (p. 31)

However, use of these "birth rituals" has been criticized as encapsulating birth under the technological model (Davis-Floyd, 1988). Due to consumer demand, practices such as routinely excluding the father or support person from labor and delivery, perineal shave, enema, episiotomy, and long separation of the newborn infant from the parent(s) have been dropped from standard orders by many physicians.

Out of the frustration with physician-managed births emerged the natural childbirth movement in the United States in the 1940s.

> Natural childbirth advocates stated that the psychological component of birth had a positive value, and the woman's subjective experiences deserved consideration. The challenge of the natural childbirth movement was that a woman's wishes and her

> psychological side should be given positive value. Birth should be viewed as both a psychological and physiological experience with the physician sharing control over the process with the woman. (Triolo, 1987, p. 488)

Various childbirth preparation and birthing methods emerged as a result of this movement, including Dick-Read, Lamaze, Bradley, and LeBoyer. In general, childbirth preparation courses focus on education about the anatomy and physiology of pregnancy, labor, and delivery, on breathing techniques and physical conditioning, and on methods of decreasing pain. Many childbirth preparation courses also focus on how to care for new infant, e.g. how to feed, hold, and bathe the infant.

Duncan and Markman (1988) reported that estimates of the percentage of U.S. women who participate in a childbirth preparation course prior to a hospital delivery range from 50% to 80%. Some hospitals require participation in a childbirth preparation course for partners who wish to accompany the mother during labor and delivery.

Dick-Read Method

Grantly Dick-Read (1959) introduced his concept of prepared childbirth in *Childbirth without Fear.* He believed it was a woman's fear of childbirth transmitted from mother to daughter over the generations that produced the physical pain during delivery and that the pain could be avoided by removing the fear of the unknown through education and by teaching the woman to relax. His method emphasized classes that focused on basic information about the birth event, breathing and relaxation exercises, and social support from a partner.

> Though originally scoffed at by his own colleagues, Dick-Read's writings and philosophy changed the course of childbirth history and heralded the onset of contemporary childbearing practices. (Triolo, 1987, p. 488)

Lamaze Method

The second method of childbirth to emphasize pain control came to be known as "the Lamaze method," after the French obstetrician Fernand Lamaze. Also called "natural childbirth" or "prepared childbirth," the method is based on the principles of Pavlovian conditioning, which emphasize the development of new conditioned reflexes (relaxation instead of pain) (Wideman & Singer, 1984).

Unlike the Dick-Read method, the Lamaze method involves the woman and her partner (or other support person) taking six to eight classes during the last trimester of pregnancy, usually with several other couples. The goal of these sessions is to reduce the anxiety and pain of childbirth by viewing it as a natural process, by educating the couple about labor and delivery, and by giving them specific instructions to aid in the birth of their baby.

There are several aspects of the Lamaze method:

1. Education about childbirth (information). The Lamaze instructor provides information about the anatomy and physiology of pregnancy and explains the stages of labor and delivery. The woman and her partner, or "coach," learn what is to happen at each stage of labor and delivery.
2. Timed breathing exercises (respiration techniques). Specific breathing exercises are recommended for each stage of labor to minimize the pain of the contractions. The purpose of the breathing exercises is to refocus the laboring woman's attention and keep the pressure of the diaphragm off the uterus. Lamaze breathing techniques also help to maintain a balanced level of carbon dioxide and oxygen throughout labor and delivery. These exercises are practiced between sessions, so that the couple will know when and how to use them when labor actually begins.

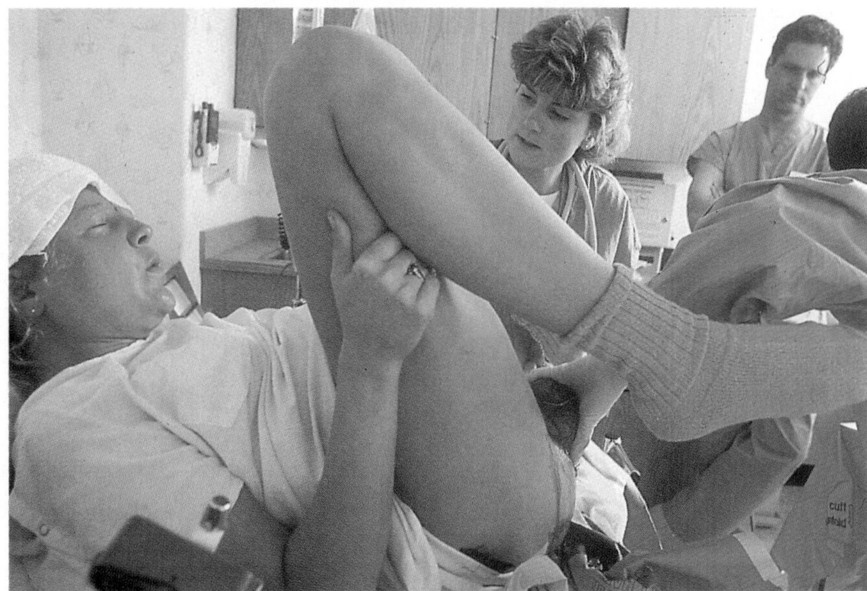

Childbirth is often a strenuous experience for which preparation can be helpful.

3. Pain control exercises (conditioned relaxation). The woman is taught to selectively tense and relax various muscle groups of her body (for example, her arm muscles). She then learns how to tense these muscle groups while relaxing the rest of her body, so that during labor she can relax the rest of her body while her uterus is contracting involuntarily. In addition, the words of her coach serve as a conditioned stimulus for relaxation. The goal of such conditioned relaxation is to reduce pain.
4. Visual focusing techniques. The woman is encouraged to look at a specific spot on the wall as a diversion from attending to the physiological events of childbirth so as to minimize any feelings of pain.
5. Social support via a coach. A major advantage of the Lamaze method is the active involvement of a coach (often the husband or close partner) throughout the birthing. The role of the coach is to prompt the woman to start and stop the various breathing exercises, give her psychological support throughout labor, let her know what stage of the birthing process she is in, and respond to her request for such items as ice and blankets. The coach attends the classes with the woman, practices outside of class with her, and may photograph or videotape the birth.

The Lamaze method of prepared childbirth has been studied extensively. Most of the women who elect this method of childbirth are young, white, and upper-middle class. Self-report data on the Lamaze method of delivery are positive. In contrast to women who did not deliver their baby through a prepared method, women who delivered their baby via the Lamaze method report greater relaxation, less anxiety, less pain, and more positive feelings about their baby. Lamaze users also are less likely to report using pharmacologic agents during delivery, and when they do use medication, they require lower doses (Wideman & Singer, 1984).

Wideman and Singer (1984) qualified their discussion on outcome research:

> Each of the five explicit components of psychoprophylactic training—information, controlled respiration techniques, conditioned relaxation, visual focusing techniques, and social support—has been proven effective in reducing anxiety, fear, and discomfort in situ-

ations other than childbirth. It is, however, unclear whether the mechanisms involved in producing the positive effects can be credited to Lamaze delivery. (p. 1368)

CONSIDERATION: Researchers have found that there is more to a "good birth experience" than the reduction of pain. Low pain levels do not necessarily mean that women enjoy childbirth; pain and enjoyment can coexist. Gennaro (1988, p. 55) summarized research which focused on a "mastery model of childbirth." Women who were active participants in their birth experiences and who felt able to influence what happened to them were more satisfied with their birth experience than women who expected to manage solely through their physicians and drugs. Taking Lamaze classes results in participants seeing themselves as agents of control.

Bradley Method

Another method of childbirth was developed by Denver obstetrician Robert Bradley. Also known as "husband-coached childbirth," the Bradley method focuses on the couple—their marital communication, sexual relationship, and parental roles—as well as on relaxation exercises and proper nutrition during pregnancy. An important aspect of the Bradley method is the couple's relationship with their physician. They are encouraged to make informed choices in regard to where they would like the birthing to occur (hospital or home) and whether the woman will breast- or bottle-feed her infant. The Bradley method also emphasizes a couple's freedom to choose the type of birth experience that is desired. If their physician is reluctant to cooperate, the couple are encouraged to seek another physician.

LeBoyer Birth Experience

The LeBoyer method of childbirth is named after its French founder, Frederick LeBoyer, who has delivered more than 10,000 babies using his method. The goal of a LeBoyer birth experience is to make the infant's transition to the outer world as untraumatic as possible. The delivery room into which the baby is born is quiet and dimly lit. After emerging from its mother, the baby is placed on the mother's abdomen, where she gently strokes and rubs her child. The umbilical cord is cut only after it stops throbbing in the belief that this will help the newborn's respiratory system adjust to its new environment.

After a few moments, the baby is immersed in water that is the approximate temperature of the amniotic sac that has housed the baby for the past nine months. The infant is allowed to relax and enjoy the bath. Then the baby is wrapped in layers of cotton and wool and placed next to the mother. Placing babies on their back is avoided because it is felt the spine should not be stressed this soon after birth.

While all of these methods emphasize drug-free deliveries, some women who intend to avoid medication during childbirth experience enough pain that they request pain medication during their labor. Triolo (1987) noted that there are considerable individual differences inherent in each woman's pain threshold, her locus of control, her ability to manage stress, and her private fears. A woman should not view herself as a "failure" if she feels the need for medication or chooses to use medications during childbirth.

We will conclude this section by describing a study in which 36 women were interviewed before and after giving birth. Seven of the women described their childbirth experience as blissful—"joy," "excitement," "a wonderful free feeling." All of these women had their husband present for the delivery. The women who reported the most childbirth pain also described more menstrual discomfort. Those who took childbirth preparation courses reported more positive feelings about childbirth. The researcher concluded,

> Our prescription for childbirth would read: "For positive emotions, take the course. For pain reduction, have a good menstrual history and take the course. For rapture, have your husband present." (Tanzer, quoted in Gennaro, 1988 p. 55)

Cesarean Childbirth

NATIONAL DATA: Twenty-three percent of births in the United States in 1989 were by cesarean section (National Center for Health Statistics, 1992b).

We have been discussing the methods of childbirth preparation assuming that the baby will be born by way of the vaginal canal. But a surprising number are born by **cesarean section,** in which an incision is made in the woman's abdomen and uterus and the baby is manually removed. During this procedure, the woman is put to sleep with general anesthesia or given a spinal injection, which enables her to remain awake and aware of the delivery.

CONSIDERATION: Although the Roman Emperor Caesar was delivered by a manner similar to today's cesarean (also spelled caesarean) section, the term refers to a law that was passed during Caesar's reign. This law made it mandatory for dying women in the advanced stages of pregnancy to have their babies removed by surgical means.

Cesarean deliveries are most often performed when there would be risk to the mother or baby in a normal delivery. For example, cesarean sections are often indicated when the fetus is positioned abnormally, the head is too large for the mother's pelvis, labor is not progressing properly, there is fetal distress, or the

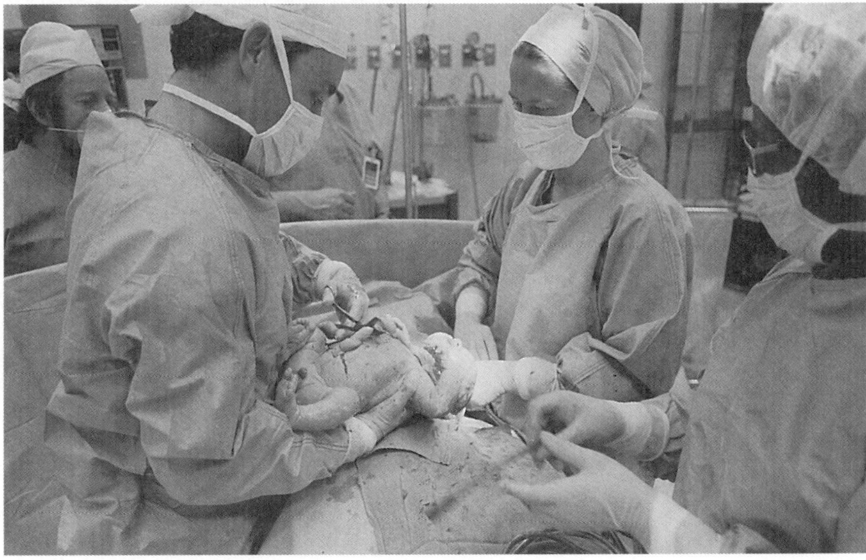

Cesarean deliveries are made when there is risk to the mother or baby in a normal delivery.

woman has an active STD or diabetes or develops toxemia during pregnancy. Travis (1988) identified additional reasons for cesarean sections, including convenience for the physicians, demand for perfect delivery outcomes and the threat of malpractice, decreased use of forceps, and increase in first pregnancy among older women.

Although cesareans are major surgery, the risk of death to the mother is low—about seven deaths per 10,000 births (Travis, 1988). When death occurs, it is usually the result of a preexisting condition, such as severe toxemia or heart disease—not a result of the surgery itself. The cesarean section, or C-section, is regarded as one of the safest of all abdominal surgeries and holds the record for the fewest postoperative problems.

CONSIDERATION: There has been considerable criticism of physicians who routinely perform cesarean surgery when it is not medically indicated. C-sections, both primary and repeat, are more likely to occur on Fridays. The difference between Friday and Sunday births for C-sections was 50% (National Center for Health Statistics, 1992b). The implication is that C-sections are being performed in reference to the physician's social life, rather than the best interests of the mother and baby.

Some women who give birth through cesarean section experience negative psychological consequences. Travis (1988) noted that

> Mothers often feel a sense of failure because their role in delivery was peripheral rather than central. Additionally there may be feelings of anger or frustration directed toward the physician, husband, or infant. (p. 156)

Behavioral consequences of cesarean section may also be negative. Travis (1988) found that, compared to women who delivered vaginally, women who delivered by cesarean section tend to discuss motherhood (one year after the birth) in more negative terms. Women who had a C-section were also found to delay longer in responding to their infant's crying (p. 156).

CONSIDERATION: Until recently, a woman who had a C-section had to have all subsequent births by C-section, and physicians were accused of creating a market for cesarean surgery. But due to advances in surgical techniques, the American College of Obstetricians and Gynecologists reversed its 75-year-old policy and said that some women who have a cesarean delivery for their first child can have subsequent vaginal deliveries. These are referred to as VBACs (vaginal births after cesarean delivery). In 1989, of 100 births to women with previous cesarean delivery, 18.9 were vaginal births (National Center for Health Statistics, 1992b).

Not all physicians are willing to perform a vaginal delivery if the woman has had a cesarean. However, VBACs are slowly increasing. Organizations that can help locate a supportive physician include the Cesarean Prevention Movement (P.O. Box 152, Syracuse, NY 13210) and Informed Homebirth/Informed Birth and Parenting (P.O. Box 3675, Ann Arbor, MI 48106).

Despite some concessions made to assertive middle- and upper-class consumers who have demanded more "natural" births, there has been little reduction of the medicalization of birth in this country. According to Davis-Floyd (1988, p. 171)

> . . . a basic pattern of consistent high technological intervention remains: most hospitals now *require* at least periodic electronic monitoring of all laboring women; analgesics, pitocin, and epidurals are widely administered; and one in five [the rate is higher now] will be delivered "from above"—by cesarean section. Thus, while some of the medicalization of birth drops away, the use of the most powerful signifiers of the woman's dependence on science and technology intensifies.

Choices regarding childbearing practices are even more limited for women of low socioeconomic status. Poor prenatal care, poor nutrition and other poverty-related factors cause many low income women to be categorized as having high risk pregnancies and therefore inappropriate for many birthing options, if they are even knowledgeable about possible alternatives. Michaelson (1988, p. 19) noted that "middle-class concerns over power and control in birthing have little impact upon the overall powerlessness of poor women to control the circumstances of their lives."

The Transition to Parenthood

Although the transition to parenthood typically refers to the period of time from the beginning of a pregnancy through the first months of having a child, "there is no requirement that the transition to parenthood be limited to the period after conception. The expectations and events that precede conception . . . will affect the transition experience" (Goldberg, 1988, p. 1).

Goldberg and Michaels (1988) synthesized the body of research on the transition to parenthood and identified several factors and interventions that influence this transition (see Table 21.1). These factors and interventions "explain why some individuals and relationships adapt smoothly to the transition to parenthood whereas others face numerous difficulties that may even reach crisis proportions" (p. 351).

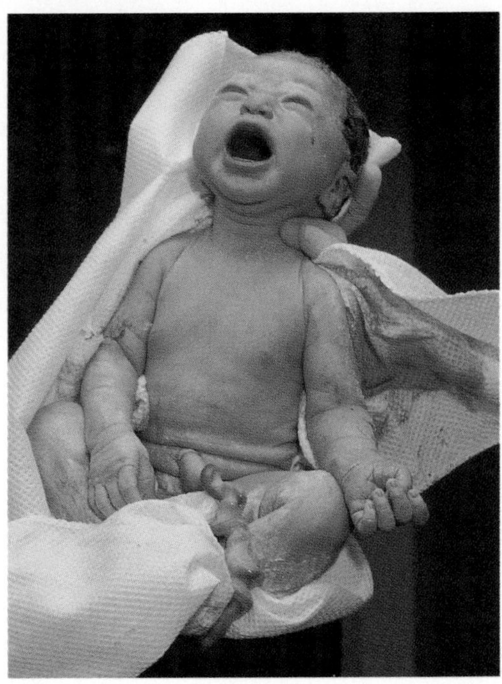

Newborns let their needs be known soon after arrival.

TABLE 21.1 Factors and Interventions Influencing the Transition to Parenthood

	Pre-conception	Pregnancy	Postnatal
Factors associated with a smooth transition to parenthood	Well-functioning marriage Adequate social support network Good relationship with own parents Adequate socioeconomic status History of psychological health History of physical health Strong motivation to become a parent Social climate supportive of children and families	Supportive spousal relationship Adequate social support network (emotional, tangible, and cognitive support from family and friends) Adequate socioeconomic status Adequate prenatal care Good relationship with obstetrician Psychological health (low anxiety, low depression, high self-esteem, good self-concept, high autonomy, high affiliation) Medically and psychologically satisfactory birth experience	Well-functioning marriage; satisfaction with division of labor Psychological health Satisfaction with work and family roles Positive change and growth in self-concept Successful adaptation to parenthood (synchronous parent-infant interaction, development of secure attachment, sensitivity to child's developmental needs) Closer intergenerational ties Well-functioning social support network Adequate socioeconomic status Adequate well-baby care
Factors associated with a difficult transition to parenthood	History of psychiatric problems Low motivation to become a parent Psychological conflicts over femininity, masculinity History of physical health problems Economic hardship Marital distress Stress and deficits in support from family, friends, and community	Maternal anxiety and depression Psychological problems Economic problems Teenager; teenage head of household Advanced maternal or parental age Maternal or fetal medical complications during pregnancy Birth problems (maternal medical complications; birth of an ill, premature, or handicapped infant) Marital distress; lack of spousal support Stress and deficits in social support network	Poor adjustment to parenthood Reactivation of unresolved psychological needs Role conflict, strain, overload Extended postpartum depression Negative change in self-concept Guilt, ambivalence, grief, and mourning if infant ill, premature, or handicapped Separation from infant due to maternal or infant health problems Financial problems Marital distress Stress and deficits in social support network
Interventions (strategies to assist prospective and active parents at each phase of the transition to parenthood)	Learn decision-making skills to assist decisions about whether and when to have a baby Learn to use social support network effectively Couple (marital) therapy to resolve conflicts; work on communication skills	Childbirth preparation to impart educational information, promote spousal support, alleviate maternal experience of pain and need for medication during labor Preparation for parenthood—anticipatory guidance (what to expect from baby, changes to expect in lifestyle, marital and employment roles) Communication skills for couples Prenatal care Medical, educational, and social-psychological care for pregnant teenagers Government subsidies for economically disadvantaged women (e.g., the WIC Program)	Informal support programs, e.g., drop-in center, peer support group, resource and referral Formal support programs, e.g., parent education, home visitors, counseling, group therapy Learn special caregiving for ill or handicapped infant Pediatric well-baby care Good-quality childcare Emotional, tangible, and cognitive support from family and friends

Source: Adapted from Goldberg, W. A. & Michaels, G. Y. (1988). Conclusion. The transition to parenthood: Synthesis and future directions Table 1 (pp. 352–353). In G. Y. Michaels & W. A. Goldberg (Eds.), *The transition to parenthood: Current theory and research* (pp. 342–360). New York: Cambridge University Press. Used by permission.

CONSIDERATION: Goldberg (1988) noted that,

> The transition to parenthood is important not only because it represents a milestone in the new parent's development, but because it marks the beginning of the new child's development. The new parent's capacity to make a successful adjustment at this time may set a future course of effective, competent parenting, whereas serious difficulties in adjustment may lead to, or exacerbate, marital discord and promote difficulties in providing for the child's needs. (p. 2)

The factors and interventions that influence the transition to parenthood generally apply to both parents. Next, we focus on experiences associated with the transition to parenthood for women and men.

The Transition to Motherhood

In general, the birth of a baby results in a more profound change for the mother than for the father (Wilkie & Ames, 1986). What is the nature of these changes, and how do women adjust to their new role as mothers?

Reaction to Childbirth Although childbirth and the labor preceding it are sometimes thought of as a painful ordeal, some women describe the birthing experience as "fantastic," "joyful," and "unsurpassed." A strong emotional bond between the mother and her baby usually develops early, so that mother and infant resist separation. Sociobiologists suggest that there is a biological basis for the attachment between a mother and her offspring. The mother alone carries the fetus in her body for nine months, lactates to provide milk, and produces oxytocin—a hormone excreted by the pituitary gland during the expulsive stage of labor that has been associated with the onset of maternal behavior in lower animals.

Not all mothers feel joyous after childbirth. Emotional bonding may be temporarily impeded by a mild depression, characterized by irritability, crying, loss of appetite, and difficulty in sleeping. From 50% to 70% of all new mothers experience "maternity blues"—transitory symptoms of depression 24 to 48 hours after the baby is born. About 10% experience **postpartum depression**—a more severe reaction than "maternity blues" (Kraus & Redman, 1986).

Postpartum depression is believed to be a result of the numerous physiological and psychological changes occurring during pregnancy, labor, and delivery. Although the woman may become depressed in the hospital, she more often experiences these feelings within the first month after returning home with her baby. Most women recover within a short time; some (about 5%) seek therapy to speed their recovery.

CONSIDERATION: To minimize "maternity blues" and postpartum depression, it is important to recognize that having misgivings about the new infant is normal and appropriate. In addition, the woman who has negative feelings about her new role as mother should solicit help with the baby so that she can continue to keep up her social contacts.

Depression among mothers is not limited to the immediate post-partum phase. A recently conducted study (Kemper & Babonis, 1992) of mothers of patients in pediatric clinics concluded that depression is common among mothers of young children. Life stresses and financial pressures seem to play a role, as the 19% of mothers who were depressed were more likely than the others to be single, nonwhite, have less education and income, and have a positive screening test results for drugs.

A mother is not a person to lean on, but a person to make leaning unnecessary.
Dorothy Canfield Fisher

Choosing Priorities For some women, motherhood is the ultimate fulfillment; for others, the ultimate frustration. Most women report mixed emotions during their mothering experience. Whatever a woman's attitude before the birth of her baby, she is not likely to take her role lightly. From the time she knows she is pregnant (or about to become an adoptive mother), no woman's life is ever the same (McKim, 1987).

Motherhood usually brings with it changes in a woman's (we will consider fatherhood in the next section) daily routine, an increased feeling of responsibility, worry, and often a need to balance the demands of job or career and family. For the traditional woman who does not work outside the home, adding the role of mother may be relatively easy. She may have the time and resources (with her partner's economic support) to cope with her infant's demands. Indeed, for some women, being at home with their baby is a dream come true. But more and more women are working outside the home and dropping out of the labor force only long enough to have their children. Women in single parent families and dual–earner families "assume not only work responsibilities outside the home, but also the larger part of domestic and parenting responsibilities inside the home" (Hall, 1992, p. 38). Even with her partner's support, the employed woman must find ways to fit the demands of motherhood into her busy schedule. The term "role overload" is used to characterize this often difficult situation. When forced to choose between her job and family responsibilities (the baby-sitter does not show up, the child is sick or hurt, or the like), the employed woman and mother (unlike the man and father) generally responds to the latter role first. (Grant, Simpson, Rong, & Peters-Golden, 1990; LaRossa, 1988; Mischel & Fuhr, 1988).

NATIONAL DATA: Sixty percent of all mothers (husband present) with preschool children are employed outside the home (*Statistical Abstract of the United States: 1992,* Table 621).

Michaelson (1988) noted that today's increase in role options for women has not demythologized the maternal role. The new mother may be faced with the "supermom" myth.

> Supermoms love the baby automatically, and, despite physical discomfort, they provide optimum care, stimulation, and love to the infant while maintaining a superior relationship with husband and other family members. In a society that romanticizes motherhood in this way, the woman who resents her infant's demands, who wishes only to sleep for more than two hours at a time, and who feels hostile when she cannot cope with the multiple demands of her family feels guilty (Michaelson, 1988, p. 259).

Women who make the smoothest adjustment to the birth of a new child tend to be those who have sufficient social support so they are not overwhelmed by the experience, and who do not try to be selfless and perfect. One midwife who had just had a baby herself observed,

> People need to be told what the realities are. When you have a new baby, life does not just go on like it did before. You're not going to get the house cleaned as often, or you might have pancakes for dinner three nights in a row (Massenda, quoted in Michaelson, 1988, p. 254).

The Transition to Fatherhood

Historically the father's role has been to protect and provide for his family. This role has expanded for many of today's fathers who participate more actively in childbirth and childrearing (Ewy & Youmans, 1988). Following are highlights of issues salient in fathers' early parenting experiences.

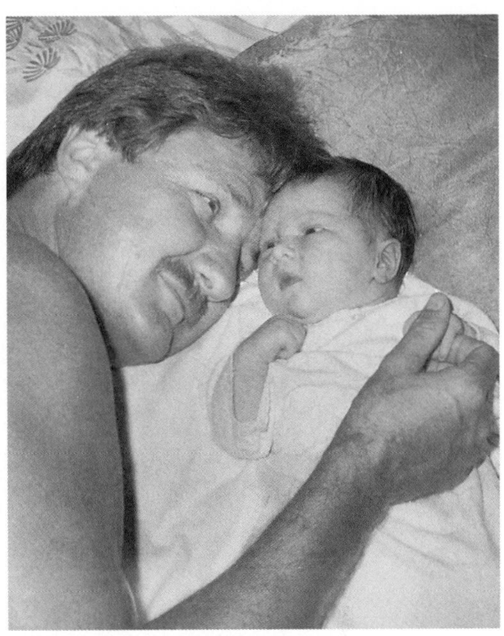

Although the new image of parenthood involves fathers taking care of their offspring, in reality, most childcare is performed by mothers. However, most fathers do emotionally bond with their children.

Interactions of Fathers and Newborns Since fathers are now more frequently involved in labor and delivery some researchers have investigated this early involvement with their children. One study (Briesemeister & Haines, 1988) recorded 30 parents' interactions with their infants in the first full hour the parents and infants were together after birth. The researchers concluded that having early contact with their babies sets up opportunities for the fathers to experience success in communicating with and taking care of their infants.

Other researchers have discovered that fathers who are involved in infant caretaking experience the same stresses as those described earlier for mothers—depression symptoms, such as irritability, sleep disturbance, and fatigue (Ewy & Youmans, 1988). Although the new image of fatherhood in our society suggests that fathers are actively involved in the caregiving role, the reality is that the bulk of caregiving is usually performed by the mother. In regard to who is actually accountable for the child's welfare and care, mothers appear to carry 90% of the load (LaRossa, 1988). Fathers who do become actively involved in the care of their children are often middle-class professionals, such as educators, artists, physicians, and social workers (LaRossa, 1988). McAdoo (1985/1986) suggested that black fathers are more nurturing, warm, and loving toward their infants and children than white fathers.

CONSIDERATION: Television is helping to provide a positive model for nurturing fathers. In a study of family-oriented television programs shown on the three networks between 7 and 9 P.M., the researchers concluded, "Clearly, males are being portrayed as active, nurturant parents" (Dail & Way, 1985, p. 497).

Increased Sense of Financial Responsibility Given our society's social script for fathers, the birth of a child sometimes "arouses anxieties in men about their capacity to provide" (Fedele, Golding, Grossman, & Pollack, 1988, p. 97). While "some fathers, fearing responsibility, run from it, leaving their families to fend for themselves without emotional or financial support" (Greenberg, 1986, p. 71), "many begin to put in more hours at work in order to bring home more money or to be a better father-provider" (Fedele et al., 1988, p. 97). One young father said after the birth of his daughter:

> I used to work a couple of days and make enough money to get by, and I could take a day off if I wanted to. Now . . . I feel more obligated to my family, and what I want to do is work. I want to get ahead and give my family things that I never had . . . (quoted in Greenberg, 1986, p. 71)

I love being a Dad. My only problem is that, when I'm working so much, I don't get to see as much of the parenting process as I'd like.

Tom Selleck

Fathers may feel conflict between the pressure to work long hours to provide financially for their families and the desire to spend more time with their families. One father said:

> When I'm working longer hours, I'm not home as often and I can't be with my child as much . . . . If I could stay home all day, keep up with my bills, and still keep my family going and be able to live a comfortable life, I would enjoy staying home with my child . . . But in this society you can't; you've got to base your life around your ability to earn in the world and hope for the best (quoted in Greenberg, 1986, p. 73).

We have to somehow get men right now involved in raising children from infancy on. Then the boys will see that men can be nurturing and it's not sissy to be empathetic.

June Stephenson

Cowan & Cowan (1988) noted that "although some new fathers increase their involvement in their jobs as a way of playing a more central family role, their wives may experience this as a retreat from involvement with the baby and the whole family enterprise" (p. 136).

Jealousy of the Baby Another common experience faced by men making the transition to fatherhood is jealousy of the baby. One new father said:

> My wife and I were really close. We would spend a lot of time together. We would walk together, hold each other, play cards, fish, or we would stay home and watch TV, lie on the couch together. Now whatever spare time we have together, the baby is there—and it's going to be that way for a long time. I couldn't accept that that's the way it has to be (quoted in Greenberg, 1986, p. 88).

Resolving this jealousy may require that the couple get help with childcare so that they can spend more recreational and leisure time together. In addition, fathers may increase their involvement in child care-giving so that child-centered activities become activities shared by the couple.

We have been discussing the adjustment of parents to babies who are healthy and normal. But about 1% or more of all births are of babies with heart malformations, urogenital anomalies, cleft lip or palate, and various musculoskeletal anomalies (National Center for Health Statistics, 1992b), which may exacerbate the adjustment. Even babies who have a difficult temperament (defined as infants who cry a great deal and have irregular sleep patterns) make adjustment on the part of the parents more difficult (Belsky & Rovine, 1990).

Sex after Childbirth

Just as the partners adjust to their new roles as parents, they also resume their roles as lovers. Traditional medical advice has been that, after giving birth, women should

The more accepting we become of breast-feeding, the less uptight we will be about our bodies and our sexuality.

Esther Davidowitz

wait six weeks before resuming intercourse. The justification for waiting six weeks is to allow time for healing without the risk of infection and to allow the physician time to prescribe medication if indicated. Some couples ignore the advice and resume intercourse within two weeks, apparently without adverse effects (Engel, 1990). However, in a study of 52 women, 90% had resumed intercourse at eight weeks after delivery. Most (42%) became active at six weeks (Gauna-Trujillo & Higgins, 1989). More recently couples are told they may have intercourse after all vaginal bleeding has stopped, discharge is no longer pink-tinged, and the episiotomy is healed (Wilkerson & Bing, 1988).

When couples do resume intercourse after childbirth, they initially report less sexual desire and intercourse frequency compared to prepregnancy levels. Fischman, Rankin, Soeken, and Lenz (1986) observed that decreases in frequency were related to the woman's physical discomfort, decline in physical strength, fatigue from taking care of the baby, and dissatisfaction with her bodily appearance.

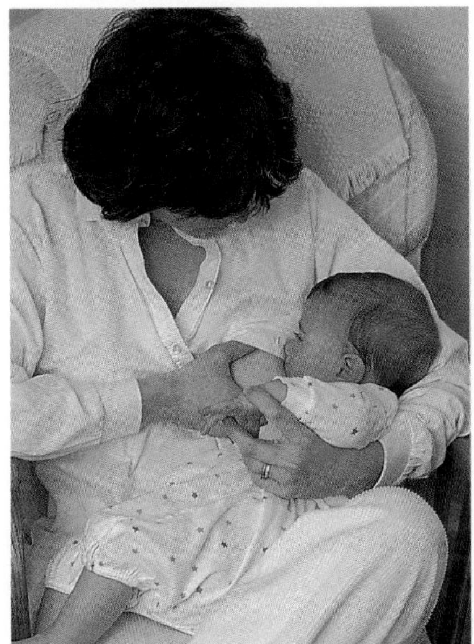

Over half of U.S. mothers breastfeed their infants.

When the mother has chosen to nurse her baby, sexual interaction may be affected by the couple's attitudes toward the mother's breasts and breastmilk. Some breast-feeding women and/or their partners feel that the nursing woman's breasts are exclusively for the baby's nourishment. Or, nursing women and/or their partners may view oral or manual breast stimulation as undesirable because of resulting milk let down (flow of milk from the breasts) is messy. While some partners may enjoy the experience of breast milk in their mouths, others may find the experience unpleasant. Problems may arise when the partners differ in their attitudes and expectations regarding breast stimulation. For example, the woman who would like her partner to orally stimulate her breasts may feel rejected if her partner wants to avoid the experience of tasting breast milk. Similarly, the partner who wants to stimulate the woman's breasts may feel rejected if the woman wants her partner to "leave my breasts alone—they're for the baby now."

CHOICES

As this chapter demonstrates, pregnancy and childbirth involve making a number of choices, including how to prepare for childbirth and how to view the entry of a baby into one's life and relationship. Other important choices include whether to have the birth in a hospital, in one's home, or in a birthing center; whether to breast- or bottle-feed one's infant; and what reproductive technologies may be used to achieve what goals. The latter set of choices have implications not only for parents but also for their children and society.

Choose Home or Hospital Birth?

Travis (1988) suggested that the choice of whether to give birth at home or in a hospital is related to one's perspective on childbirth:

> Should childbirth be viewed as a natural process, usually resulting in spontaneous delivery of healthy alert infants to healthy attentive mothers? Or is it more appropriate to perceive the process as a medical event with relatively high risk of disease or death to both women and infants? (p. 150)

The American College of Obstetricians and Gynecologists views childbirth as a medical event that should take place in a hospital. Part of the reason why the medical profession does not advocate home births is the fear of being sued if something goes wrong during a home birth.

Although over 95% of all U.S. births do occur in the hospital, some expectant parents are concerned that traditional childbirth procedures are too impersonal, costly, and potentially dangerous. Those who opt for home birth are primarily concerned about avoiding separation from the new infant, maintaining control over who can be present at the delivery, and avoiding what they view as unnecessary medical management (Sacks & Donnerfeld, 1984).

The nurse-midwife is most often asked to assist in home births. Some nurse-midwives are certified members of the American College of Nurse-Midwives and have successfully completed a master's degree in nurse-midwifery offered at various universities, including Georgetown, Emory, St. Louis, and Columbia. Two organizations—Association for Childbirth at Home (ACAH) and Home Oriented Maternity Experience (HOME)—help couples prepare for home births.

What is the relative safety of home versus hospital births? A study designed to answer this question revealed that except in special cases (such as when the mother has hypertension or diabetes), home births involve no extra risks than births in hospitals. However, the researchers warned that in cases of delayed labor, breech births or fetal distress, a hospital is the safer environment (Holmes, 1988).

Rather than choose between having their baby in a hospital or at home, some prefer a birthing center, which is more likely to be available in larger metropolitan areas. Birthing centers provide special rooms for the woman to experience labor, and the staff is more likely to consist of certified nurse-midwives than obstetricians. National data suggest that low-risk mothers who choose to have their babies in birthing centers are no more likely to have poor birth outcomes or to require a cesarean section than are low-risk women who give birth in the hospital (Rooks et al., 1989). When complications do arise, birth centers transfer the mother and baby to the hospital.

Choose to Breast-feed or Bottle-feed the New Infant?

According to Davidowitz (1992), from 1984 to 1989, the number of U.S. women who breast-fed their infants dropped from 60 to 52 percent. Some women who breast-feed do so for economic reasons—to avoid the cost of infant formula and baby food. Other reasons women breast-feed are that they feel it provides better nutrition and increased immunity against infections, enhances the bond between them and their baby, and decreases the baby's ear infections and dental malocclusions. In addition, some women breast-feed because they find it convenient and do not have schedules or other responsibilities that conflict with breastfeeding (Dix, 1991).

For some women, breast-feeding provides physical pleasure and even sexual arousal. Niles Newton, a prominent researcher in the area of breast-feeding and sexuality explained that breast-feeding and sexual response are physiologically similar (cited in Davidowitz, 1992). Both breast-feeding and sexual arousal stimulate the release of the hormone oxytocin which results in uterine contractions, erect nipples, and increased body temperature.

Continued

Continued

Advocates of breast-feeding also argue that "breast-feeding strengthens self-reliance by reducing dependence on external situations and products . . . . It is ecologically sound. Unlike infant formula and bottle feeding, which utilize nonrenewable resources, breastfeeding only requires investing in the health of the mother" (Van Esterick, 1989, p. 210). The United Nations Population Fund (1991) encouraged breast-feeding as a child-spacing technique in developing countries." Efforts to prevent erosion of current breast-feeding habits will also be important to avoid increases in fertility" (p. 147). While breast-feeding is not recommended as a contraceptive technique, it does inhibit the release of the egg in the woman, thus offering some protection against pregnancy.

Worldwide the average age for weaning breast-fed children is 4.2 years. In the United States, most women who breast-feed wean their child by the age of six months. U.S. Surgeon General Antonia Novello recommended that mothers nurse for at least one year, ideally two (Davidowitz, 1992).

La Leche League International, an organization that emphasizes the value of breast-feeding for infants and mothers, has chapters throughout the world.

In support of breast-feeding, Yoshioka, Iseki, and Fujita (1983) compared the stools of 13 healthy newborn infants (six were breast-fed; seven were bottle-fed) and concluded that the breast-fed babies had fewer neonatal diseases due to their enhanced immune systems. Alternatively, breast-feeding may transmit nicotine, pollutants, bacteria, and viruses to the baby. Research has demonstrated that HIV infection can be transmitted from infants to mothers during the postnatal period by means of colostrum and breast milk of the infected mother (Van de Perre et al., 1991).

U.S. women in favor of bottle-feeding their babies emphasize the advantages of doing so—the convenience for employed women, the involvement of the father and/or other family members, and the option of bottle-feeding the baby breast milk. Other reasons why women choose to bottle feed their infants include negative attitudes toward breast feeding, previous negative experience with breast-feeding, and health or medical reasons (Dix, 1991). Examples of negative experiences associated with breast-feeding include having sore nipples, milk not letting down (i.e. milk does not flow out) and running out of milk (Mercer, 1986).

Negative attitudes toward breastfeeding stem from the association of female breasts with sexuality. Indeed, in most states it is illegal for a woman to expose her bare breasts in public. However, courts are upholding the right to breastfeed in public. Davidowitz (1992) cited the following cases:

- A mother sued the town of Williston Park, N.Y., after it threatened to cancel her membership to the public swimming pool because she nursed her two-and-a-half-month-old baby by the pool. She won the right to nurse as well as $7,500 in damages.
- A Dubuque, Iowa mother filed a complaint with the city Human Rights Commission after the manager of a restaurant asked her to either stop nursing her baby or leave. The restaurant was ordered to permit breast-feeding on its premises.

Van Esterick (1989) suggested that negative attitudes toward breastfeeding benefit companies that make and sell infant formula.

> The embarrassment women may feel at the possible exposure of part of a breast when breastfeeding and their fear that breast- feeding will deform breasts or make them sag unattractively are the result of interpreting breasts primarilyas sex objects. These interpretations undermine a woman's sense of worth and devalue her productive potential, making it easier to sell her commercial solutions in the form of breastmilk substitutes. (p. 74)

Some mothers who bottle-feed their babies feel that they are made to feel guilty and inadequate because they do not fit the cultural image that the "perfect" way to feed a baby is through breast-feeding. Fisher (1983) suggested:

> It is then a matter of individual choice of the method that is best suited to the needs of mother, infant, and family. Every mother should be supported by her peers as well as medical professionals and respected for her choice. (p. 436)

Choices Resulting from New Reproductive Technologies

The various ways in which physicians can manipulate the fertilization and birth process (in vitro fertilization, surrogacy, ovum transfers, prenatal testing) have created a new range of choices in regard to pregnancy. Examples of such choices include the following two examples.

Example one. A young woman who wants to delay pregnancy and childrearing until after she has established herself professionally in a career may have her "healthy eggs" in her youth extracted, frozen, and later artificially inseminated when she is in her 40s or 50s. Doing so would reduce some of the risks for birth defects associated with women who elect to have children during middle age. Alternatively, a middle-aged woman may want to use a younger woman's egg that has been artificially inseminated with her partner's sperm.

What are the disadvantages of delaying pregnancy through the use of reproductive technologies? Risk to the fetus and to the mother are the predominant problems. While some risks to the fetus can be avoided by using a "young egg" ("old eggs" are much more likely to be defective), a middle-aged pregnant woman is much more likely to be diabetic and overweight and to have high blood pressure, which will also affect the fetus negatively. In addition, what are the implications for the child whose two elderly parents may die before he or she graduates from high school? Joni Mitchell decided to have a baby at age 52 and was implanted with a fertilized egg from a young woman (her husband was the sperm donor). She said of the implications for her age and its effect on her child, "If I can raise him or her until age 30, then he should be able to make it on his own" (quoted in Gorman, 1991,

Continued

Continued

p. 62). She also noted that her own mother had nine children and was currently 86.

Example two. Couples who have genetic histories including sickle-cell anemia or cystic fibrosis may have such defects tested for in several embryos and implant only those without the defects. But if embryos are destroyed because of a genetic defect, can sex of the embryo be used as a basis for discarding the embryo?

One attorney noted that the various choices resulting from new reproductive technologies make it possible for a child to have up to five parents: an egg donor, a sperm donor, a surrogate who gestates the fetus, and the couple who rear the child (Andrews, 1984b).

Miller (1983) used the term **progenesis** to refer to "the process whereby individuals and couples select for or against specific characteristics in a specific offspring on the basis of their own specific needs and values" (p. 1204). For example, individuals who want to avoid having a child with sickle-cell anemia would not marry someone carrying the gene. Similarly, those who wanted a girl or boy would time intercourse to increase the chance of the desired sex. As to criticism that such choices may be racist or sexist, Miller argued:

> There is no doubt that progenesis raises many important and complex issues both for individuals and for society as a whole. I cannot even begin to consider these in any detail. My primary goal is threefold: First, I would like to suggest that progenesis represents a very natural extension of the evolutionary trend in reproduction from chance to choice. Second, I wish to point out that it has been going on for some time and will probably only increase in scope and frequency as our technological capacity improves. Third, I want to emphasize how important it is that we all begin to examine, understand, and evaluate this activity as it emerges from its culture closet and gradually becomes sanctioned throughout society. (p. 1204)

Confronted by new options related to childbearing, many interview respondents have expressed the burdens of individual choice. Choosing among technologies available for birthing and prenatal diagnosis may be complicated and agonizing. There may be conflict over which technologies to use, and in the case of prenatal diagnosis, how to act on the information obtained.

If motherhood (or parenthood) is now a choice rather than an inevitability, and if one chooses to have fewer children in order to pursue other options in life,

> then each child born must be "worth it" with regard to those other options. Technology is the resource that promises to produce the "perfect child," and thus when physicians describe childbirth choices in terms of infant safety and long-term child development, the decision as to what kind of birth to have becomes more complicated. (Michaelson, 1988, p. 28)

Rothman (1988) interviewed 62 women who elected to have amniocentesis for prenatal diagnosis and 64 who refused it. Most of the women felt pressure to have the test. Contemporary notions of mature, responsible behavior push obtaining information and making a conscious choice—"there's no solid ground for not wanting to know" (p. 101). People feel that if there is a technology available for obtaining information, it should be used. Even with the problems inherent in these technologies—the degree to which the pregnancy has progressed, the possibility of miscarriage or damage to a fetus, the agony of how to act on the information—the pressure is still strong. In speaking of being encouraged to have amniocentesis one woman said, "What bothered me was the assumption that it was normal, denying it would be a difficult thing" (Rothman, 1988, p. 102). Rothman noted that in the next decade, as technology advances and risk to the fetus decreases, the moral issues involved in obtaining the information from prenatal testing will be salient, and the majority of women who experience pregnancy will face these issues.

In her interviews with people confronted with "positive" prenatal diagnoses (presence of a disability), Rapp (1988) noted that the medical language which is used privatizes problems; it reinforces women seeing themselves as individual patients, "rather than as a member of a larger group of women confronting a new technological possibility or coping with grief" (p. 108). She cautioned against a woman becoming "an agent of quality control on the reproductive production line" (p. 115) in the guise of expanding her choices.

Summary

1. Pregnancy begins with fertilization of a woman's egg (the ovum unites with a man's sperm) and conception (the fertilized egg implants on the uterine wall).
2. Infertility, the inability to achieve a pregnancy after at least one year of regular sexual relations without birth control, affects 15% to 20% of U.S. married

couples. Common causes of male infertility include low sperm production and poor semen motility. Causes of female infertility include blocked Fallopian tubes and impaired ovulation. The effects of some sexually transmissible diseases may result in infertility for men and women.

3. Reproductive technologies include hormone therapy, artificial insemination, artificial insemination of a surrogate mother, in vitro fertilization, ovum transfer, and other procedures described in the chapter. While reproductive technology offers more choices regarding childbearing, it has been criticized as a medical industry that exploits women physically, socially, emotionally, and economically.
4. Early signs of pregnancy include lack of menstruation; nausea and vomiting ("morning sickness"); enlarged and tender breasts; more frequent urination, and fatigue. Pregnancy is best confirmed by laboratory tests and a physical examination.

   In addition to the early signs of pregnancy, some women experience other physical changes during pregnancy, including the following: leg cramps, constipation, backache, varicose veins, swelling, heartburn, increased vaginal discharge, and shortness of breath.
5. Prenatal care helps to ensure a healthy baby and mother. Pregnant women should receive adequate nutrition and avoid substances that are or may be harmful to the fetus (e.g. alcohol, nicotine, cocaine, etc.). Moderate exercise may be beneficial during pregnancy when exercise is not contraindicated by the presence of risk factors. Prescription and nonprescription medications should only be taken with the approval of a competent physician.
6. Prenatal care may involve prenatal testing (also known as antenatal testing). Types of prenatal tests include ultrasound, amniocentesis, chorionic villus sampling, florescent insitu hybridization and preimplantation testing. Ultrasound is performed to determine the gestational age of the fetus and detect structural abnormalities in the fetus; it is not a reliable test for determining the sex of a fetus. The other prenatal tests described in the chapter may be performed with high risk pregnant women (advanced age or previous child with birth defect) to determine chromosomal and biochemical defects in the fetus. If defects are detected early enough, the woman can either be prepared for the birth of a child with health problems or decide to terminate the pregnancy.
7. Psychological changes during pregnancy include stress, concern over body image, worry over increased responsibility and changes in lifestyle, worry over the health of the baby and the mother, and fear of pain during childbirth.
8. Pregnancy may result in increased communication and intimacy as well as increased conflict for couples. Many women and some men report decreased sexual desire during pregnancy—especially during the third trimester. However, sexual desire and pleasure are enhanced for many couples during pregnancy.
9. During the first and second stages of labor, increasingly longer uterine contractions occur at increasingly shorter intervals. Effacement and dilation of the cervix occurs during the first stage of labor. The baby is born during the second stage and the placenta is expelled through the vagina during the third stage.
10. Various childbirth preparation methods have emerged. These methods focus on education about the anatomy and physiology of pregnancy, labor, and delivery; breathing techniques and physical conditioning; decreasing pain, and infant care (bathing, feeding, etc.).

11. Some women do not have vaginal deliveries, but rather have a cesarean section in which an incision is made in the woman's abdomen and uterus and the baby is manually removed. While some cesarean sections are medically indicated, others may be performed for the convenience of physician.
12. A variety of factors and interventions prior to conception, during pregnancy, and postnatally influence the transition men and women make to parenthood. During this transition, some women may experience depression and role strain. Men may feel a sense of increased financial responsibility and jealousy of the baby. Frequency of sexual activity often decreases after childbirth.
13. Three choices childbearing women may make are a) whether to have the baby in a hospital or at home b) whether or not to breast-feed (and if so, for how long), and 3) whether to undergo antenatal testing (and if so, what to do if the tests indicate a defect in the fetus).

KEY TERMS

fertilization
in vitro fertilization
conception
infertility
artificial insemination
surrogate mother
laparoscope
cryopreservation
gamete intra-Fallopian transfer
zygote intra-Fallopian transfer
microinjection
partial zona drilling
ovum transfer
ectopic pregnancy
leukorrhea
fetal alcohol syndrome
amniocentesis
chorionic villus sampling
ultrasound
embryo
fetus
primagravida
multigravida
effacement
dilation
breech birth
cesarean section
postpartum depression
progenesis

REFERENCES

Affonso, D. D., & Mayberry, L. J. (1989). Common stressors reported by a group of childbearing American women. In P. N. Stern (Ed.), *Pregnancy and parenting* (pp. 41–55). New York: Hemisphere.

American College of Obstetrics and Gynecology. (1988). *Report of a 1987 survey of ACOG's membership*. Washington, DC: Author.

Andrews, L. B. (1984a). *New conceptions: A consumer's guide to the newest infertility treatments*. New York: St. Martin's Press.

Andrews, L. B. (1984b). The stork market: The law of the new reproductive technologies. *American Bar Association Journal, 70,* 56.

Aronson, M. E., & Nelson, P. K. (1972). Fatal air embolism in pregnancy resulting from an unusual sex act. *Obstetrics and Gynecology, 30,* 127–130.

Artal, R. & Wiswell, R. A. (1986). *Exercise in pregnancy*. Baltimore: Williams & Wilkins.

Belsky, J., & Rovine, M. (1990). Patterns of marital change across the transition to parenthood: Pregnancy to three years postpartum. *Journal of Marriage and the Family, 52,* 5–19.

Bogren, L. Y. (1991). Changes in sexuality in women and men during pregnancy. *Archives of Sexual Behavior, 20,* 35–45.

Boston Women's Health Book Collective (1984). *The new our bodies, ourselves*. New York: Simon & Schuster.

Brent R. L. & Beckman, D. A. (1992). Principles of teratology. In M. I. Evans (Ed.). *Reproductive risks and prenatal diagnosis* (pp. 43–68). Norwalk, CT: Appleton & Lange.

Briesemeister, L. H. & Haines, B. A. (1988). The interactions of fathers and newborns. In K. L. Michaelson (Ed.). *Childbirth in America: Anthropological perspectives.* (pp. 228–238). South Hadley, MA: Bergin & Garvey.

Chez, R. A. (1991). Identifying maternal/fetal risks before pregnancy. *Medical Aspects of Human Sexuality, 25,* 54–58.

Cowan, P. A., & Cowan, C. P. (1988). Changes in marriage during the transition to parenthood: Must we blame the baby? In G. Y. Michaels & W. A. Goldberg (Eds.), *The transition to parenthood: Current theory and research* (pp. 114–154). New York: Cambridge University Press.

Dail, P. W., & Way, W. L. (1985). What do parents observe about parenting from prime-time television? *Family Relations, 34,* 491–499.

Davidowitz, E. (1992). The breast-feeding taboo. *Redbook,* July, 92–95, 114.

Davis-Floyd, R. E. (1988). Birth as an American rite of passage. In K. L. Michaelson (Ed.). *Childbirth in America: Anthropological perspectives* (pp. 153–177). South Hadley, MA: Bergin & Garvey Pub.

Derwinski-Robinson, B. (1990). Infertility and sexuality. In C. I. Fogel & D. Lauver (Eds.), *Sexual health promotion* (pp. 291–304). Philadelphia: W. B. Saunders.

Dick-Read, G. (1959). *Childbirth without fear: The original approach to natural childbirth* (2nd rev. ed.). New York: Harper.

Dix, D. N. (1991). Why women decide not to breastfeed. *Birth, 18,* 222–225.

Donovan, P. (1986). New reproductive technologies: Some legal dilemmas. *Family Planning Perspectives, 18,* 57–60.

Duncan, S. W. & Markman, H. J. (1988). Intervention programs for the transition to parenthood: Current status from a prevention perspective. In G. Y. Michaels & W. A. Goldberg (Eds.), *The transition to parenthood: Current theory and research* (pp. 270–310). New York: Cambridge University Press.

Dunn, P. C., Ryan, I. J., & O'Brien, K. (1988). College students' level of acceptability of the new medical science of conception and problems of infertility. *Journal of Sex Research, 24,* 282–287.

Engel, N. S. (1990). The maternity cycle and sexuality. In C. I. Fogel & D. Lauver (Eds.), *Sexual health promotion* (pp. 179–205). Philadelphia: W. B. Saunders.

Evans, M. I. & Johnson, M. P. (1992). Chorionic villus sampling. In M. I. Evans (Ed.). *Reproductive risks and prenatal diagnosis* (pp. 175–184). Norwalk, CT: Appleton & Lange.

Ewy, D. H. & Youmans, J. M. (1988). The early parenting experience. In F. H. Nichols & S. S. Humenick (Eds.). *Childbirth education: Practice, research, and theory* (pp. 69–93). Philadelphia: W. B. Saunders.

Faludi, S. (1991). *Backlash: The undeclared war against American women.* New York: Crown.

Fedele, N. M., Golding, E. R., Grossman, F. K. & Pollack, W. S. (1988). Psychological issues in adjustment to first parenthood. In G. Y. Michaels & W. A. Goldberg (Eds.), *The transition to parenthood: Current theory and research* (pp. 85–113). New York: Cambridge University Press.

Fischman , S. H., Rankin, E. A., Soeken, K. L., & Lenz, E. R. (1986). Changes in sexual relationships in postpartum couples. *Journal of Obstetrics and Gynecological Nursing, 15,* 58–63.

Fisher, P. J. (1983). Breast or bottle: A personal choice. *Pediatrics, 72,* 434–436.

Fitzgerald, M. (1989, August 9). Couples fawn over frozen embryos, expert says. *USA Today,* p. 3A.

Foreman, S. (1990, March 26). Risk is small in hiding the identity of donor. *USA Today,* p. 7A.

Garel, M. & Blondel, B. (1992). Assessment at 1 year of the psychological consequences of having triplets. *Human Reproduction, 7,* 729–732.

Gauna-Trujillo, B., & Higgins, P. G. (1989). Sexual intercourse and pregnancy. In P. N. Stern (Ed.), *Pregnancy and parenting* (pp. 31–40). New York: Hemisphere.

Gennaro, S. (1988). The childbirth experience. In F. H. Nichols & S. S. Humenick (Eds.). *Childbirth education: Practice, research, and theory* (pp. 52–68). Philadelphia, W. B. Saunders.

Goldberg, W. A. (1988). Introduction. Perspectives on the transition to parenthood. In G. Y. Michaels & W. A. Goldberg (Eds.), *The transition to parenthood: Current theory and research* (pp. 1–20). New York: Cambridge University Press.

Goldberg, W. A. & Michaels, G. Y. (1988). Conclusion. The transition to parenthood: Synthesis and future directions. In G. Y. Michaels & W. A. Goldberg (Eds.), *The transition to parenthood: Current theory and research* (pp. 342–360). New York: Cambridge University Press.

Gordon, D. (1992, April 12). Gene test of embryos may spot defects. *Virginia Pilot and The Ledger Star,* Norfolk, VA. p. A-1.

Gorman, C. (1991, September 30). How old is too old? *Time,* p. 62.

Grant, L., Simpson, L. A., Rong, Z. L., & Peters-Golden, H. (1990). Gender, parenthood, and work hours of physicians. *Journal of Marriage and the Family, 52,* 39–49.

Green, T. H. (1977). *Gynecology: Essentials of clinical practice.* Boston: Little, Brown.

Greenberg, M. (1986). *The birth of a father.* New York: Continuum Publishing Co.

Hall, C. M. (1992). *Women and empowerment.* Washington, D.C.: Hemisphere Publishing Co.

Higgins, B. S. (1990). Couple infertility: From the perspective of the close-relationship model. *Family Relations, 39,* 81–86.

Holmes, P. (1988). Squeeze on alternatives to hospital births. *New Statesman, 116,* 6.

John, E. M., Savitz, D., & Sandler, D. P. (1991). Prenatal exposure to parents' smoking and childhood cancer. *American Journal of Epidemiology, 133,* 123.

Johnson, M. P. & Miller, O. J. (1992). Cytogenetics. In M. I. Evans (Ed.) *Reproductive risks and prenatal diagnosis* (pp. 237–249). Norwalk, CT: Appleton & Lange.

Kemper, K. J. & Babonis, T. R. (1992). Screening for maternal depression in pediatric clinics. *American Journal of Diseases of Children, 146,* 876–878.

Kiely, J. L., Kleinman, J. C., & Kiely, M. (1992). Triplets and higher-order multiple births: Time trends and infant mortality. *American Journal of Diseases in Children, 146,* 862–868.

Kraus, M. A., & Redman, E. S. (1986). Postpartum depression: An interactional view. *Journal of Marital and Family Therapy, 12,* 63–74.

LaRossa, R. (1988). Fatherhood and social change. *Family Relations, 37,* 451–457.

Lasker, J. N., & Borg, S. (1987). *In search of parenthood.* Boston: Beacon Press.

Lazarus, E. S. (1988). Poor women, poor outcomes: Social class and reproductive health. In K. L. Michaelson (Ed.) *Childbirth in Amer-*

ica: Anthropological Perspectives (pp. 39–54). South Hadley, MA: Bergin & Garvey.

Levran, D., Dor, J., Rudak, E., Nebel, L., Ben-Shlomo, I., Ben-Rafael, Z., & Mashiach, S. (1990). Pregnancy potential of human oocytes—The effect of cryopreservation. *New England Journal of Medicine, 323,* 1153–1156.

McAdoo, J. L. (1985/1986). A black perspective on the father's role in child development. R. A. Lewis & M. B. Sussman (Eds.). *Marriage and Family Review, 9,* 117–133.

McKim, M. K., (1987). Transition to what? *Family Relations, 36,* 22–25.

Mercer, R. T. (1986). *First-time Motherhood: Experiences from teens to forties.* New York: Springer Publishing Co.

Michaelson, K. L. (1988). Childbirth in America: A brief history and contemporary issues. In K. L. Michaelson (Ed.). *Childbirth in America: Anthropological perspectives* (pp. 1–32). South Hadley, MA: Bergin & Garvey.

Miller, W. B. (1983). Chance, choice, and the future of reproduction. *American Psychologist, 38,* 1198–1205.

Mischel, H. N., & Fuhr, R. (1988). Maternal employment: Its psychological effects on children and their families. In S. M. Dornbusch and M. H. Strober (Eds.), *Feminism, children and the new families* (pp. 194–195). New York: Guilford Press.

Nakahata, A. K. (1988). Exercise. In F. H. Nichols & S. S. Humenick (Eds.), *Childbirth education: Practice, research, and theory* (pp. 344–361). Philadelphia: W. B. Saunders Co.

National Center for Health Statistics. (1992a). *Advance report of final mortality statistics, 1989.* (Monthly Vital Statistics Report, vol. 40, no. 8, supp. 2). Hyattsville, MD: U.S. Public Health Service.

National Center for Health Statistics. (1992b). *Advance report of new data from the 1989 birth certificate.* (Monthly Vital Statistics Report, vol. 40, no. 12, suppl.). Hyattsville, MD: U.S. Public Health Service.

Office of Technology Assessment. (1988). *Artificial insemination: Practice in the United States, summary of a 1987 survey—Background paper.* Washington, DC: U.S. Government Printing Office.

Ovarian hyperstimulation syndrome. (1991). [Editorial]. *The Lancet, 338,* p. 1111.

Rapp, R. (1988). The power of "positive" diagnosis: Medical and maternal discourses on amniocentesis. In K. L. Michaelson (Ed.). *Childbirth in America: Anthropological perspectives* (pp. 103–116). South Hadley, MA: Bergin & Garvey.

Rice, N. (1992). Psychological reaction to prenatal diagnosis and loss. In M. I. Evans (Ed.). *Reproductive risks and prenatal diagnosis* (pp. 277–282). Norwalk, CT: Appleton & Lange.

Roberts, L. (1991, October 18). FISHing cuts the angst in amniocentesis. *Science,* pp. 378–379.

Rooks, J. P., Weatherby, N. L., Ernst, E. K., Stapleton, S., Rosen, D., & Rosenfield, A. (1989). Outcomes of care in birth centers. *New England Journal of Medicine, 321,* 1804–1811.

Rothman, B. K. (1988). The decision to have or not to have amniocentesis for prenatal diagnosis. In K. L. Michaelson (Ed.). *Childbirth in America: Anthropological perspectives* (pp. 90–102). South Hadley, MA: Bergin & Garvey.

Rothman, B. K. (1989). *Recreating motherhood: Ideology and technology in a patriarchal society.* New York: W. W. Norton.

Ryan, K. J. (1988). Giving birth in America, 1988. *Family Planning Perspectives, 20,* 298–301.

Sacks, S. R., & Donnerfeld, P. B. (1984). Parental choice of alternative birth environments and attitudes toward childrearing philosophy. *Journal of Marriage and the Family, 46,* 469–475.

Shapiro, J. L. (1987, January). The expectant father. *Psychology Today,* pp. 36–42.

Shapiro, C. H. (1988). *Infertility and pregnancy loss.* San Francisco: Jossey-Bass.

Sharpe, R. (1987, February 17). Baby M case good advertising. *USA Today,* p. 1A.

Siller, B., & Azziz, R. (1991). New ways of managing ectopic pregnancy. *Medical Aspects of Human Sexuality, 25,* 30–39.

Statistical abstract of the United States, 1992. (112th ed.) (1992). Washington, DC: U.S. Bureau of the Census.

Stone, A. (1992, February 10). Virginia 'babymaker' on trial. *USA Today,* p. 3A.

Travis, C. B. (1988). *Women and health psychology: Biomedical issues.* Hillside, NJ: Lawrence Erlbaum Associates.

Triolo, P. K. (1987). Prepared childbirth. *Clinical Obstetrics and Gynecology, 30,* 487–493.

Turner, R. (1992). First-trimester chorionic villus sampling may raise risk of spontaneous abortion and limb abnormality. *Family Planning Perspectives, 24,* 45–46.

United Nations Population Fund. (1991). Population policies and programmes: Lessons learned from two decades of experience. Edited by N. Sadik. New York: New York University Press.

U.S. General Accounting Office. (1987). *Prenatal care: Medicaid recipients and uninsured women obtain insufficient care* (GAO/HRD-87-137). Washington, DC: U.S. General Accounting Office.

Valentine, D. P. (1982). The experience of pregnancy: A developmental process. *Family Relations, 31,* 243–248.

Van DePerre, P., Simonon, A., Msellati, P., Hitimana, D., Vaira, D., Buzubagira, A., Van Goethem, C., Stevens, A., Karita, E., Sondag-Thull, D., Dabis, F., & LePage, P. (1991). Post natal transmission of human immunodeficiency virus type 1 from Mother to infant. *New England Journal of Medicine, 325,* 593–598.

Van Esterick, P. (1989). *Beyond the breast-bottle controversy.* New Brunswick, New Jersey: Rutgers University Press.

Whose baby is it? [Videocassette and transcript of broadcast of CBS Television's "48 Hours."] Denver: Journal Graphics.

Wideman, M. V., & Singer, J. E. (1984). The role of psychological mechanisms in preparation for childbirth. *American Psychologist, 39,* 1357–1371.

Wilcox, A. J., Weinberg, C. R., O'Connor, J. F., Baird, D. D., Schlattereer, J. P., Canfield, R. E., Armstrong, E. G., & Nisula, R. C. (1988). Incidence of early loss of pregnancy. *New England Journal of Medicine, 319,* 189–194.

Wilkie, C. F., & Ames, E. W. (1986). The relationship of infant crying to parental stress in the transition to parenthood. *Journal of Marriage and the Family, 48,* 545–550.

Williams, M. A., Mittendorf, R., Lieberman, E., Monson, R. R., Schoenbaum, S. C., & Genest, D. R. (1991). Cigarette smoking during pregnancy in relation to placenta previa. *American Journal of Obstetrics and Gynecology, 165,* 28–32.

Wilkerson, N. N. & Bing, E. (1988). Sexuality. In F. H. Nichols & S. S. Humenick (Eds.), *Childbirth education: Practice, research, and theory* (pp. 376–393). Philadelphia: W. B. Saunders Company.

Woliver, L. R. (1989). The deflective power of reproductive technologies: The impact on women. *Women and Politics, 9,* 17–47.

Yoshioka, H., Iseki, K., & Fujita, K. (1983). Development and differences of intestinal flora in the neonatal period in breast-fed and bottle-fed infants. *Pediatrics, 72,* 317–320.

CHAPTER TWENTY-TWO

Abortion and other Pregnancy Outcomes

Chapter Outline

Attitudes Toward Abortion
- **Self-Assessment:** Abortion Attitude Scale
- Attitudes of the General Public
- Attitudes of College Students
- Abortion Advocacy Groups: Prolife and Prochoice

Ethical Issues and Abortion
- When Does Personhood Begin?
- Is Abortion Immoral?

Methods of Induced Abortion
- Suction Curettage and Dilation and Suction
- Dilation and Evacuation
- Saline Abortion
- How Safe Are Surgical and Saline Abortions?
- Prostaglandins
- RU-486
- Menstrual Extraction

A Cross-Cultural View of Abortion
- Abortion in Preliterate Societies
- International Trends in Abortion

Abortion in the United States
- Incidence of Abortion
- Who Gets an Abortion and Why?
- **Theoretical Perspective:** Gilligan's Study of Abortion Decision Making
- Availability of Abortion Services

Abortion Legislation in the United States
- Historical Background of Abortion Legislation
- *Roe v. Wade* and Rulings Since 1973

Psychological Effects of Abortion

Other Pregnancy Outcomes
- Miscarriage and Stillbirth
- Perinatal Death
- Adoption
- Parenting the Baby

Choices
- Multifetal Pregnancies: Choose Selective Termination?
- Choose Whether to Have an Abortion? Some Guidelines

Is It True?*

1. Most abortions occur within the first 12 weeks of pregnancy.

2. The abortion rate in the United States is one of the lowest in the world.

3. In the United States, fewer maternal deaths are associated with childbirth than with legal abortions.

4. According to the World Health Organization, 200,000 women die each year as a result of illegal abortions.

5. U.S. citizens are equally divided on the abortion issue; about half are antiabortion and about half are prochoice.

* 1 = T, 2 = F, 3 = F, 4 = T, 5 = F

Abortion, for many women, is more than an experience of suffering beyond anything most men will ever know; it is an act of mercy, and an act of self-defense.

Alice Walker

NATIONAL DATA: Over a third (36.9%) of the pregnancies among individuals aged 15 to 44 in the United States are unplanned. Of these, about 10% are unwanted (Jones, Forrest, Henshaw, Silverman, & Torres, 1988).

Abortion is a complex issue for individuals, especially women, whose lives are most affected by pregnancy and childbearing. Abortion is also a complex issue for societies, which must respond to the pressures of conflicting attitudes toward abortion and the reality of a high rate of unintended and unwanted pregnancy.

An **abortion** refers to the removal of an embryo or fetus from the woman's uterus before it can survive on its own. There are two major categories of abortions. An **induced abortion** is the deliberate termination of a pregnancy through chemical or surgical means. A **spontaneous abortion**, commonly referred to as a miscarriage, is the unintended termination of a pregnancy. In this text, we use the term "abortion" to refer to induced abortion.

The question that society must answer is this: Shall family limitation be achieved through birth control or abortion? Shall normal, safe, effective contraceptives be employed, or shall we continue to force women to the abnormal, often dangerous surgical operation? Contraceptives or Abortion—which shall it be?

Margaret Sanger

In this chapter, we discuss abortion and other pregnancy outcomes, including keeping the baby, placing the baby for adoption, and experiencing miscarriage or the death of one's newborn infant. Our discussion focuses on the personal, social, legal, and ethical issues surrounding abortion in the United States.

Attitudes Toward Abortion

Few issues in human sexuality are as controversial as abortion. Attitudes toward abortion range from fierce opposition to abortion under any circumstance (including rape and endangerment of the woman's life) to staunch support for legal and affordable access to abortion on request. In the next section, we look at attitudes toward abortion among the general U.S. public, college students, and advocacy groups ("prolife" and "prochoice" groups). Before you read further, you may want to complete the Self-Assessment: Abortion Attitude Scale.

Attitudes of the General Public

The Research Perspective in Chapter 2 ("Abortion Attitudes Reflect Relativism") describes survey research on attitudes toward abortion. In one national telephone survey, 74% of respondents agreed with the following statement ("Majority in Poll," 1989):

> I personally believe that abortion is morally wrong, but I also feel that whether or not to have an abortion is a decision that has to be made by every woman for herself.

What most Americans want to do with abortion is to permit it but discourage it also.

Roger Rosenblatt

Other survey research described in the Research Perspective in Chapter 2 suggests that 1) the percentage of adults in the United States who believe that abortion is acceptable and should be legal has increased slightly from 1988 to 1990, and 2) the attitudes of most adults toward abortion vary according to the circumstances under which the abortion occurs. For example, abortion is more likely to be viewed as an acceptable option if the mother's health is endangered by continuing the pregnancy, if a severe birth defect exists, or if the pregnancy is the result of rape or incest.

Self Assessment

Abortion Attitude Scale

Directions This is not a test. There are no wrong or right answers to any of the statements, so just answer as honestly as you can. The statements ask you to tell how you feel about legal abortion (the voluntary removal of a human fetus from the mother during the first three months of pregnancy by a qualified medical person). Tell how you feel about each statement by circling one of the choices beside each sentence. Here is a practice statement:

SA A SIA SID D SD Abortion should be legalized.

(SA = Strongly agree; A = Agree; SIA = Slightly agree; SID = Slightly disagree; D = Disagree; SD = Strongly disagree)

Please respond to each statement and circle only one response. No one else will see your responses without your permission.

	SA	A	S1A	S1D	D	SD
1. The Supreme Court should strike down legal abortions in the United States.	5	4	3	2	1	0
2. Abortion is a good way of solving an unwanted pregnancy.	5	4	3	2	1	0
3. A mother should feel obligated to bear a child she has conceived.	5	4	3	2	1	0
4. Abortion is wrong no matter what the circumstances are.	5	4	3	2	1	0
5. A fetus is not a person until it can live outside its mother's body.	5	4	3	2	1	0
6. The decision to have an abortion should be the pregnant mother's.	5	4	3	2	1	0
7. Every conceived child has the right to be born.	5	4	3	2	1	0
8. A pregnant female not wanting to have a child should be encouraged to have an abortion.	5	4	3	2	1	0
9. Abortion should be considered killing a person.	5	4	3	2	1	0
10. People should not look down on those who choose to have abortions.	5	4	3	2	1	0
11. Abortion should be an available alternative for unmarried, pregnant teenagers.	5	4	3	2	1	0
12. Persons should not have the power over the life or death of a fetus.	5	4	3	2	1	0
13. Unwanted children should not be brought into the world.	5	4	3	2	1	0
14. A fetus should be considered a person at the moment of conception.	5	4	3	2	1	0

Scoring and Interpretation As is apparent in its name, this scale was developed to measure attitudes toward abortion. It was developed by Sloan (1983) for use with high school and college students. To compute your score, first reverse the point scale for Items 1, 3, 4, 7, 9, 12, and 14. Total the point responses for all items. Sloan provided the following categories for interpreting the results:

70–56 Strong proabortion
55–44 Moderate proabortion
43–27 Unsure
26–16 Moderate prolife
15–0 Strong prolife

Reliability and Validity The Abortion Attitude Scale was administered to high school and college students, Right to Life group members, and abortion service personnel. Sloan (1983) reported a high total test estimate of reliability (0.92). Construct validity was supported in that Right to Life members' mean scores were 16.2; abortion service personnel mean scores were 55.6, and other groups' scores fell between these values.

Reference

Sloan, L. A. (1983) Abortion attitude scale. *Health Education, 14,* (3), 41–42. Used by permission.

According to a 1992 USA Today/CNN/Gallup public opinion poll, 34% of respondents reported that abortion should be legal under any circumstances, 48% said abortion should be legal under certain circumstances, and 13% said that abortion should be illegal in all circumstances; 5% said they didn't know (Sanchez, 1992). In 1975, the percentages were 21, 54, and 22, respectively (reported in Muldoon, 1991). These data suggest that since 1975, attitudes have shifted toward favoring the legality of abortion.

Attitudes of College Students

Among college students, the majority view abortion as acceptable and support legal access to abortion (Hollis & Morris, 1992; Wright & Rogers, 1987). These researchers found that college students who either had an abortion or were responsible for a pregnancy that had been terminated were more likely to support the legal availability of abortion. One study of approximately 700 college students enrolled in a human sexuality class found that the percentage of students who favored abortion on demand decreased from 87% in 1972 to 62% in 1991 (Rubinson & De Rubertis, 1991).

In a study of 704 unmarried college students (Ryan & Dunn, 1988), abortion was the second most frequent option students said they would choose if faced with an unintended, nonmarital pregnancy (see Table 22.1). The most preferred option was for the pregnant woman to get married and continue the pregnancy.

Advocates and Advocacy Groups: Prolife and Prochoice

A dichotomization of attitudes toward abortion is reflected in two opposing groups of abortion activists. Individuals and groups who oppose abortion are commonly referred to as "prolife," or "antiabortion." Prolife groups advocate restrictive policies or a complete ban on abortion. Prolife advocates essentially believe that (Callahan & Callahan, 1984):

For prochoice women to achieve their goals, they must argue that motherhood is not a primary, inevitable or natural role for women. For prolife women to achieve their goals, they must argue that it is.
Kristin Luker

- The unborn fetus has a right to live and that right should be protected.
- Abortion is a violent and immoral solution to unintended pregnancy, which is a natural part of life.
- The community should be obligated to provide support for pregnant women so that they may continue their pregnancies.
- The life of an unborn fetus is sacred and should be protected even at the cost of individual difficulties.

Persons most likely to be prolife are over 44, female, and the mother of three or more children, have a high school education or less, are affiliated with a religion, have an

I am not pro-abortion—but I am passionately pro-choice.
George F. Regas

Women are to be respected as moral agents. They can be trusted to make decisions that support the well being of their families, children and society and enhance their own integrity and health.
Catholics for a Free Choice Official Statement

TABLE 22.1 How Over 700 College Students Would Deal with an Unintended, Nonmarital Pregnancy

Option	Percent Selecting
Get married and continue the pregnancy	37.5%
Have an abortion	30.5%
Keep and rear the child as a single parent	13.9%
Give the child to adoptive parents	12.7%
Keep the child and let the grandparents rear the child	5.4%

Source: Ryan, I. J., & Dunn, P. C. (1988). Association of race, sex, religion, family size, and desired number of children on college students' preferred methods of dealing with unplanned pregnancy. *Family Practice Research Journal, 7,* 153–161. Used by permission.

Both prochoice and prolife advocacy groups feel very strongly about their respective positions.

annual family income of $30,000 or less, and are married to a small business owner or lower-income white-collar worker (Luker, 1984; Granberg, 1991).

Prochoice advocates support the legal availability of abortion for all women. They essentially believe that (Callahan & Callahan, 1984):

- Freedom of choice is a central human value.
- The individual conscience is sovereign, particularly in cases of moral doubt.
- Those who must personally bear the burden of their moral choices ought to have the right to make those choices.
- Procreation choices must be free from governmental control.

Persons most likely to be prochoice are under age 44, female, and the mother of one or two children, have an annual family income of over $50,000, are employed, have some college or postcollege training, and are married to a professional (Luker, 1984).

CONSIDERATION: "It is difficult to label the opposing groups in the abortion controversy" (Koop, 1989, p. 31). Some prochoice advocates object to the use of the term "prolife" to refer to their opponents because it implies that prochoice advocates do not value life. Prochoice advocates argue that they too value the quality of life for both women and children. They argue that restricting or banning legal abortion lessens the quality of life for women by forcing them to either bear unwanted children or to obtain an illegal, and perhaps unsafe, abortion. The quality of life for children born unwanted is also a concern of prochoice advocates.

Some prochoice advocates also object to the label "proabortion" because "some who are prochoice are personally opposed to abortion" (Koop, 1989, 31). Prochoice advocates do not like abortion; they often combine their efforts to make and keep abortion available with efforts to reduce abortion by promoting planned parenthood and the use of effective contraception.

Contrary to common notion, not all religious groups oppose the legal availability of abortion. For example, Catholics for a Free Choice (CFFC) supports the right to legal abortion and promotes family planning to reduce the incidence of abortion and to increase women's choice in childbearing and child rearing. Similarly, the Religious Coalition for Abortion Rights (RCAR) is comprised of 35 mainline Protestant, Jewish, and other faith groups who believe that

> Every woman must have the *right* to consider all options when she faces a problem pregnancy and *freedom* to allow her to come to a decision that's in harmony with her own moral and religious values—*without government intrusion.* (Religious Coalition for Abortion Rights, 1992, p. 1)

The Catholic position [on abortion] is not so cohesive, not so monolithic as is often presented. It is my conviction that the church will come to a more nuanced position in this area. . . .
Sister Mary Theresa Glynn

Just as not all religious groups oppose the legal availability of abortion, not all self-identified feminists are prochoice. Exhibit 22.1 describes a feminist organization called Feminists for Life of America, that opposes abortion.

Truly liberated women reject abortion because they reject the male world view that accepts violence as a legitimate solution to conflict.
Feminists for Life of America Official Statement

CONSIDERATION: The dichotomization of the abortion issue into prolife versus prochoice overlooks a third segment of the population that has mixed views on abortion. In a study of teenagers' attitudes toward abortion, "most of the participants agreed that it was possible to be antiabortion and prochoice at the same time, but felt that the issue was never discussed that way by the press" (Stone & Waszak, 1992, p. 56).

EXHIBIT 22.1 Opposition to Abortion: A Feminist View

Feminists have been a major driving force behind the prochoice movement (Staggenborg, 1991). However, a minority segment of feminists are not prochoice but rather are prolife. In 1972, an organization for prolife feminists called Feminists for Life of America was formed. As of May 1992, this organization reported a membership of nearly 4,000 (Feminists for Life of America, 1992).

Feminists for Life of America emphasizes that "feminism is part of a larger philosophy that values all life . . . abortion is incompatible with this feminist vision" (quoted in Muldoon, 1991, p. 146). Feminists for Life of America also believes that abortion allows men to escape responsibility for their own sexual behavior. Furthermore, this organization contends that abortion benefits employers (who are primarily men) because it reduces the concessions that employers must make to pregnant women and mothers. Finally, Feminists for Life of America stated that

> Feminists who demand the right to abortion concede the notion that a pregnant woman is inferior to a non-pregnant one. They admit that pregnancy and motherhood are incompatible to being a fully functioning adult, and that an unencumbered, unattached male is the model for success. By settling for abortion instead of working for the social changes that would make it possible to combine children and career, pro-abortion feminists have agreed to participate in a man's world under a man's terms. They have betrayed the majority of working women—who want to have children (Quoted in Muldoon, 1991, p. 147).

Ethical Issues and Abortion

It is better to debate a question without settling it than to settle a question without debating it.

Joseph Joubert (1754–1824)

Many controversies regarding abortion center around ethical issues. Two primary ethical concerns involve the questions "When does personhood begin?" and "Is abortion immoral?"

When Does Personhood Begin?

Although some religions encourage baptism and "proper" disposal of the early products of conception, most secular practitioners and institutions treat the fetus as a surgical specimen.

Jack Stack

A fetus is no more a human being than an acorn is an oak tree.

Caroline Lund and Cindy Jaquith

The child in the womb . . . is an actual person, just like the rest of us.

Stephen Schwarz

Much of the controversy surrounding abortion stems from the debate over the question "When does personhood begin?" Scientists, philosophers, physicians, and theologians have proposed various answers to this question, including personhood begins at conception, at the first sign of brain activity, or at viability (the point in the fetus' development when it can survive outside the woman's uterus). When the U.S. Supreme Court issued its *Roe v. Wade* decision in 1973, viability was generally considered to be around 28 weeks; today, it is around 24 weeks (Rhoden, 1985). Only about one tenth of 1% of all abortions are performed after 24 weeks of gestation (Henshaw, Binkin, Blaine, & Smith, 1985).

Some arguments concerning the question "When does personhood begin?" follow:

- As for potential human beings, an acorn is not an oak tree! With cloning, every nucleated cell in your body is a potential person. This being the case, brushing one's teeth should be a crime on a par with murder, since one destroys countless epithelial "potential people" with every scrape across the gums. (Zindler, 1991, p. 30)
- It is false that the being in the womb is merely a potential person. It is not a potential person, but an actual person, a fully real person, the same person it will later be. . . . Just as the small born baby is not a potential person but an actual person, so too is the pre-born baby, who is simply a baby at an earlier phase of development. (Schwarz, 1991, p. 34)
- Considering the fetus a person is a dead-end path and is in fact a distraction from the real issue at the heart of the abortion crisis: should women be forced by the state

to be mothers, or should they be free to choose motherhood for themselves? Women, not fetuses, are the people we need to pay attention to. (Bettencourt, 1991, p. 42)

A conclusive answer to the question whether a fetus is a person is unattainable.
Jane English

- Conservatives maintain that human life begins at conception and that therefore abortion must be wrong because it is murder. But not all killings of humans are murders. Most notably, self-defense may justify even the killing of an innocent person.

  Liberals, on the other hand, are just as mistaken in their argument that since a fetus does not become a person until birth, a woman may do whatever she pleases in and to her own body. . . . If a fetus is not a person, that does not imply that you can do to it anything you wish. Animals, for example, are not persons, yet to kill or torture them for no reason is considered wrong. (English, 1991, p. 44)
- According to Peter Wenz (1992), beliefs about the personhood of fetuses younger than 21 weeks are fundamentally religious in nature. Therefore, any governmental restrictions on abortion that are based on the view that a fetus younger than 21 weeks is a person represents a breech of religious freedom. Some view beliefs about the personhood of a fetus at any stage in development as a religious matter. The Religious Coalition for Abortion Rights (1992) stated that "any law passed to restrict abortion would impose a religious view held by some citizens and, in effect, prevent all other citizens from freely practicing their own religions" (p. 2).

Is Abortion Immoral?

No one has the right to choose to put an innocent human being to death.
John O'Connor

Many people involved in the abortion debate are concerned with the issue of whether abortion is moral. Some people believe that abortion is the killing of an unborn child and is never morally justified. Others feel that abortion is wrong but may be justified under certain conditions, such as when the woman's life is in danger.

Some abortion rights activists argue that morality is irrelevant to the abortion issue and that abortion is simply a necessary and important right that all women should be allowed to exercise. These individuals may believe that banning or restricting abortion, rather than abortion itself, is immoral.

For some individuals, the concept of morality is related to the religious concept of sin. For these individuals, abortion is immoral if it is considered a sin. In Exhibit

EXHIBIT 22.2 Abortion is not (Necessarily) a Sin: A Catholic View

The official Canon Law of the Catholic Church states that anyone who commits the "sin" of abortion automatically excommunicates herself from the church. However, members of Catholics for a Free Choice (CFFC), a prochoice organization established in 1973, disagree with the notion that abortion is necessarily sinful in all circumstances.

> To commit the sin of abortion you have to think that an abortion in your case, with all the circumstances of your life and your pregnancy, is a sin against God. You then have to decide that you are going to do it anyway, thus going against your conscience. . . . If you carefully examine your conscience and then decide that an abortion is the most moral act you can do at this time, you are not committing a sin. (Catholics for a Free Choice, 1992, p. 1)

Thus, CFFC suggests that the Catholic woman who has a "moral" abortion is not excommunicated and does not need to tell about her abortion in confession. If a woman feels that her abortion was obtained against her conscience and that it was a "sin," CFFC suggests that the woman may "seek reconciliation with the church by speaking to a priest in the sacrament of Reconciliation [confession] (p. 1)."

In sum, CFFC views abortion as a moral decision that each woman must make for herself. Furthermore, "conscience is the final arbiter of any abortion decision" (CFFC, 1992, p. 1).

Source: Catholics for a Free Choice. (1992). *You are not alone: Information for Catholic women about the abortion decision.* Washington, DC: Author. Used by permission.

The decision to have an abortion is made responsibly, in the context of a morally lived life, by a free and responsible moral agent.

Mary Gordon

22.2, we describe the view held by the organization Catholics for a Free Choice that suggests that abortion is not necessarily a sin.

Methods of Induced Abortion

Prior to the availability of modern surgical techniques, abortion in the late eighteenth and early nineteenth centuries was performed by flushing the uterus with caustic substances (gunpowder, quinine, oil of juniper) or by inserting sticks of silver nitrate into the cervix (Potts, Diggory, & Peel, 1977). Next, we look at modern methods of abortion and their safety.

Suction Curettage and Dilation and Suction

Pregnancy may be terminated during the first six to eight weeks through a procedure called **suction curettage**, also referred to as vacuum aspiration abortion (Keenan, 1990). In this procedure, cervical dilation is usually not required. After the administration of a local anesthetic, a hollow plastic rod attached to a suction aspirator is inserted into the woman's uterus through the cervix (see Figure 22.1). The device draws the fetal tissue and surrounding matter out of the uterus into a container. Following the suction procedure, the uterine cavity is explored with a small metal curette to ensure that all the tissue has been extracted.

Suction curettage can be performed on an outpatient basis in a clinic or physician's office and takes about 10 to 20 minutes. In 1989, the cost of suction curettage in an abortion clinic, a physician's office, and in the hospital (outpatient service) was \$245, \$360, and \$1,539, respectively (Henshaw, 1991).

Dilation and suction (D & S) is a method of abortion used during the first 12 weeks of pregnancy (Keenan, 1990). This method is essentially the same as suction currettage, except that the cervix is dilated before the suction procedure. Cervical dilation may be achieved through inserting laminaria into the cervix the day before

FIGURE 22.1 Suction Curettage and Dilation and Currettage

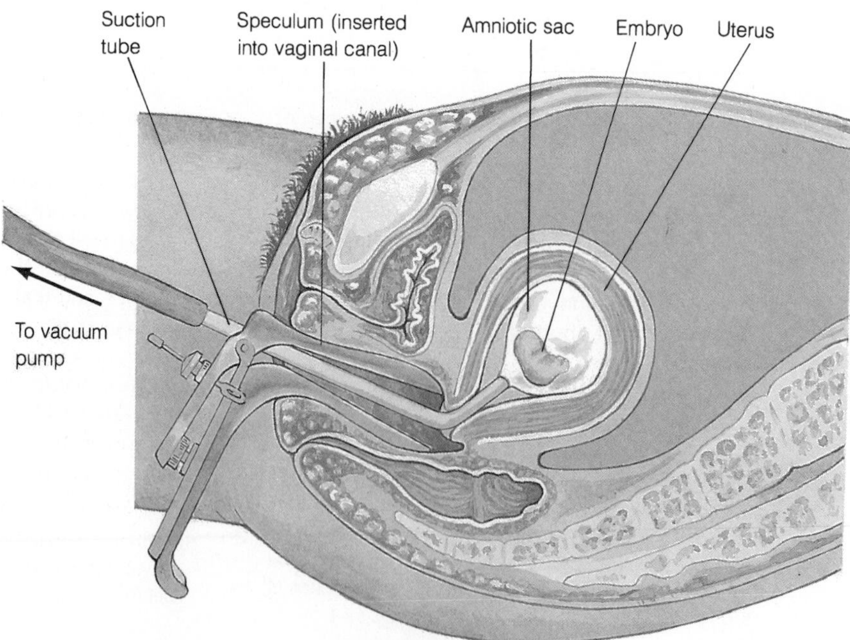

the abortion is performed. **Laminaria** are dried, sterile rods of compressed seaweed stems that, when inserted into the cervix, absorb moisture and increase in diameter, thereby dilating the cervix. Cervical dilation may also be achieved by using a metal device designed to dilate the cervix just prior to the abortion. The dilation and suction method of abortion also involves using a metal surgical instrument to scrape any remaining fetal tissue and placenta from the walls of the uterus. (This method is also referred to as dilation and currettage, or D & C). A general anesthetic is sometimes administered.

Dilation and Evacuation

In the second trimester of pregnancy (13 to 24 weeks' gestation), the surgical method of abortion is called **dilation and evacuation** (D & E). This procedure is similar to D & S, except that greater dilation of the cervical opening is required and a larger suction device is used because of the increased volume of tissue (Keenan, 1990). Extraction instruments called ringed forceps are also used to remove the fetal tissue. General anesthesia may be used because of the increased complexity and time associated with this more involved surgical procedure.

While the D & E procedure may be performed as late as 24 weeks gestation, the majority take place earlier in the second trimester. This procedure does not permit post-abortion examination of an intact fetus, which may provide useful information for future reproductive counseling. Another problem is that the operator performing the procedure must handle the stressful situation of removing fetal parts (Diukman & Goldberg, 1992).

Prior to 16 weeks, surgical methods of abortion are regarded as safer than using instillation techniques (injection of substances such as saline or prostaglandins which induce labor and delivery). After 16 weeks maternal mortality does not differ between the two types of techniques, but the D & E procedure is associated with a lower risk of complications. It is relatively quick and less stressful than the midtrimester instillation techniques, but some couples request instillation because of the destructive process of the D & E. Diukman and Goldberg (1992) presented data from 1984–1985 showing that at 21 weeks or more of gestation, about half of abortions were performed surgically, about one-third by saline instillation, and 5% by prostaglandin instillation.

Saline Abortion

NATIONAL DATA: Less than 1% (0.7%) of all abortions are performed using the saline injection method (Kochanek, 1991).

A **saline abortion**, generally performed between 16 and 24 weeks' gestation, involves injecting a solution of saline into the amniotic sac, causing rapid death of the fetus (Keenan, 1990). This procedure involves inserting a long needle containing a concentrated salt solution through the abdominal and uterine walls into the amniotic cavity. From six to 48 hours later, the uterus contracts until the dead fetus is pushed out. Saline abortions are performed under local anesthesia.

CONSIDERATION: A concern regarding second-trimester abortions involves the ethical issue of aborting a fetus that is more developed and that may possibly survive the abortion. At 24 weeks (the end of the second trimester and beginning of third trimester), the fetus is potentially viable. That is, at 24 weeks, the fetus has a chance of surviving outside the womb. A fetus aborted at the end of the second trimester (or during the third trimester) may continue to breathe, have a heart rate, or show other signs of voluntary muscle movement, and is thus considered a live birth. Data on abortions that result in live births are incomplete because "physicians and hospitals may be hesitant to announce this untoward outcome" (Grimes, 1984, p. 264).

How Safe Are Surgical and Saline Abortions?

Legal abortions performed by competent professionals are statistically safer than childbirth, using an IUD, or taking oral contraceptives (Sloane, 1990). Physical complications can occur and include perforation (an instrument punctures the uterine wall), hemorrhage (heavy blood flow), or infection. According to the Alan Guttmacher Institute, abortion, especially in the first trimester, is a relatively safe procedure (*Facts in Brief,* 1992):

- Less than 1% of all abortion patients experience a major complication.
- The risk of death associated with childbirth is about 11 times as high as that associated with abortion.
- The risk of death associated with abortion increases with the length of pregnancy, from one death for every 500,000 abortions at eight weeks or less to one per 30,000 at 16 to 20 weeks and one per 8,000 at 21 or more weeks (*Facts in Brief,* 1992). The primary causes of late-abortion-related deaths are infection (30.4%), amniotic fluid embolism (21.7%), and hemorrhage (15.2%) (Grimes, 1984).
- Most abortions (89%) are performed during the first trimester, or first 12 weeks of pregnancy (*Facts in Brief,* 1992). Complications associated with abortions performed in the first trimester are infrequent. In a study of 170,000 first-trimester abortions, there were no deaths; 0.71 per 1,000 abortions required subsequent hospitalization for major complications (suspected perforation, hemorrhage, incomplete abortion, infection, or ectopic pregnancy); 8.46 per 1,000 involved minor complications (Hakim-Elahi, Tovell, & Burnhill, 1990).
- There is no evidence of problems with later childbearing among women who have an early abortions through vacuum aspiration procedures (the most common procedure used) (*Facts in Brief,* 1992; Hogue, Cates, & Tietze, 1983). However, pregnancies following induced abortion by means of dilation and evacuation are more likely to result in subsequent premature delivery and low-birth weight babies (Atrash & Hogue, 1990).
- Most women who obtain an abortion have no lost work days or return to work in three to four days (Bitsch, Jacobsen, Prien-Larsen, & Frelund, 1990; Keenan, 1990).

Prostaglandins

Prostaglandins are hormonelike substances that cause the uterus to contract. When introduced into the vagina as a suppository or injected into the amniotic sac, prostaglandins induce labor, and the fetus is aborted. Prostaglandins may induce abortion early in pregnancy or as late as the twenty-fourth week of gestation (Keenan, 1990).

The most frequent side effects are gastrointestinal disturbances, such as nausea, vomiting, diarrhea, and uterine pain (Bygdeman & Van Look, 1989). More serious complications of prostaglandins are incomplete abortion or missed abortion, infection, and bleeding. When performed in the later weeks of pregnancy, the delivery of a living but nonviable fetus is possible, which creates ethical concerns for the care of the fetus (Keenan, 1990). To avoid this possibility, prostaglandins may be combined with the saline method.

In a follow-up study of Swedish women who had an induced abortion by prostaglandins or by vacuum aspiration, most women preferred prostaglandins (Rosen, 1990). The major advantage was that prostaglandins could be self-administered, whereas vacuum aspiration would require the involvement of medical personnel.

RU-486

As noted in Chapter 20, Planning Children and Birth Control, Mifepristone (**RU-486**) is a synthetic steroid that effectively terminates pregnancies within the first nine weeks of gestation. Also referred to as a "morning-after pill" although taken for two to four days, RU-486 is considered to be a method of abortion, as well as a form of postcoital contraception. By blocking the normal action of progesterone in the uterus, RU-486 prevents the implantation of a fertilized egg and induces menstruation if implantation has already occurred. RU-486 is most effective when used within seven weeks of the last menstrual period and when accompanied 48 hours after ingestion by a dose of prostaglandin (either suppository or injection) (Klitsch, 1991). When taken with prostaglandin up to eight weeks after conception, RU-486 is 95% to 96% effective in inducing abortion (Kovacs, 1990; Klitsch, 1991). (Without administration of low doses of prostaglandins, RU-486 is only 80% effective; Spitz, Shoupe, Sitruk-Ware, & Mishell, 1989). Hence, some pregnancies continue even if RU-486 is used on day zero to induce a first-trimester abortion (Somell, Olund, Carlstrom, & Kindahl, 1990). When RU-486 fails, a suction abortion or D & C is required. If pregnancy continues after RU-486 is administered, the effect on the growing fetus is unknown. However, there are at least three known cases where a woman took RU-486 without prostaglandin and went on to have a baby that appeared normal (Norsigian, 1990).

Abortion is distasteful, but it is an essential recourse.

Etienne-Emile Baulier

RU-486 has been used in France by over 80,000 women and is also available in Great Britain and China, but as of 1992, it is not available in the United States. Advocates of RU-486 point to the fact that worldwide, 200,000 women die annually because of botched illegal abortions and that RU-486 would actually save lives (Baulieu & Rosenblum, 1991). In essence, women can take RU-486 and induce an abortion themselves. Use of vacuum aspiration, although an effective and safe procedure, requires skilled personnel. In the absence of RU-486 or trained medical personnel, women may feel they have no choice but to seek an abortion from someone without adequate medical training (Van Look & Bygdeman, 1989). In addition, RU-486 does not involve surgical invasion and the trauma associated with surgical abortion procedures.

Menstrual Extraction

Some people refer to the vacuum aspiration abortion as a menstrual extraction, but currently this term is used for another procedure. **Menstrual extraction** is an experimental procedure which involves using a flexible plastic instrument to remove the uterine lining at about the time one's menstrual period is due (Boston Women's Health Book Collective, 1984). It was developed in the early 1970's by women's self-help groups, such as those at the Feminist Women's Health Center in Los Angeles.

> Menstrual extraction is done most commonly to eliminate the general nuisance of menstrual flow and to relieve menstrual pain, including such symptoms as cramps and lower back ache. It can also be used to reduce the need for abortion (Punnett, 1990, pp. 101–102).

It was originally proposed to be done, not by a woman on herself, but by lay women, in small advanced self-help groups. Rather than being in the passive patient role, the woman is actively in control of the process.

Some women see menstrual extraction as a contraceptive technique or a backup method. "The extraction is also probably one in a series of regular monthly extractions and would have been done whether or not there was a chance of pregnancy" (Punnett, 1990, p. 103). Any woman participating in the procedure should be aware there are no long-term data on the procedure's side effects. Punnett suggested that menstrual extraction represents one possible option for addressing limited abortion access, especially if further limitations occur.

Punnett (1990) differentiated menstrual extraction from menstrual regulation, which she described as promoted by the medical establishment instead of the women's self-help movement. Menstrual regulation is used internationally as a very early abortion method and as a population control technique.

A Cross-Cultural View of Abortion

Abortion is like poverty: no one likes it, but it will always be with us.

Roger Short

Abortion "is an option to which people at all times and places have resorted, with or without religious consent, legal approval, or medical supervision" (Tribe, 1990, p. 52). In this section, we look at abortion in other times and places so as to understand the wide range of cultural responses to the abortion issue.

Abortion in Preliterate Societies

Underlying every era and instance in which the [abortion] issue arises is the same fear and wonder that people are capable of creating and uncreating themselves.

Roger Rosenblatt

On one end of the continuum is the Kafir tribe in Central Asia in which an abortion is strictly the choice of the woman. In this preliterate society, there is no taboo or restriction in regard to abortion, and the woman is free to exercise her decision to terminate her pregnancy. One reason for the Kafir's approval of abortion is that childbirth in the tribe is associated with high rates of maternal mortality. Since birthing children may threaten the life of significant numbers of adult women in the community, women may be encouraged to abort. Such encouragement is particularly strong in the case of women who are viewed as too young, too sick, too old, or too small to bear children.

Abortion may also be encouraged by a tribe or society for a number of other reasons, including practicality, economics, lineage, and honor. Abortion is practical for women in migratory societies. They must control their pregnancies since they are limited in the number of children they can nurse and transport. Economic motivations become apparent when resources (e.g., food) are scarce—the number of children born to a group must be controlled. Abortion for reasons of lineage or honor are encouraged when a woman becomes impregnated in an adulterous relationship; to protect the lineage and honor of her family, she may have an abortion.

While the Kafirs have an open policy on abortion, their policy is an exception throughout the world. "Whether or not abortion is justified in some situations, it appears generally in most cultures to be considered a 'wrong' " (Tribe, 1990, p. 53).

International Trends in Abortion

The legal status of abortion today is considerably different from 50 years ago, when abortion was virtually outlawed in every nation (Henshaw, 1986). As of 1986, 76% of the world's population lived in countries where induced abortion was legally permitted: about 39% had access to abortion on request; about 24% for socioeconomic reasons, such as inadequate income, housing, or unwed status; and 13% on broader health grounds. The remaining 24% of the world's population lived in countries where abortion was either prohibited or permitted only on grounds of saving the life of the mother (United Nations Population Fund, 1991).

Today, approximately 33 million legal abortions are performed in the world annually. Estimates of total number of abortions (legal and illegal) range from 40 million to 60 million per year. It is calculated that 20% to 30% of pregnancies that occur worldwide end in induced abortion (United Nations Population Fund, 1991).

While there are wide variations in abortion availability across different countries, several international trends have been described (Sachdev, 1988):

1. Following the enactment of liberal abortion laws, many countries reported first an increase in the number and rate of abortions and then a tapering off or moderate decline. The downward shift reflected the increase in use of modern contraceptive methods. However, in the 1970s, abortion rates increased following reports questioning the safety of the birth control pill, which led many women taking the pill to revert to less effective methods of birth control.
2. The proportion of married women seeking abortion is steadily decreasing due to the high percentage of married women who undergo sterilization after attaining their desired family size.

3. No government that has enacted permissive abortion laws has advocated continued use of abortion as a primary method of birth control.
4. All countries have laws that regulate abortion procedures. Most countries require that the procedure be carried out in a hospital or other approved medical facility.
5. In most countries, there is inequality of access to legal abortion. Many women are unable to afford an abortion or are forced to travel a considerable distance to obtain one. When access to legal abortion is limited, many women resort to illegal abortion.

Past experience suggests that when women are sufficiently desperate, they will terminate their pregnancies by any means available.

Richard Lacayo

CONSIDERATION: In societies with restrictive abortion laws, many women seek illegal abortions that are performed by unskilled personnel with resulting high death rates, hemorrhages, genital tract trauma, and related ill health and sterility (Ladipo, 1989). In Third World countries, an estimated 200,000 women, or one woman every three minutes, die from illegal abortions (Fried, 1990b). In these countries, illegal abortion is the leading cause of maternal mortality.

The risks of uterine bleeding or perforation of the uterus are especially high when women try to abort themselves with such instruments as knitting needles. "That is why the wire coat hanger has come to symbolize the hazards of illegal abortions" (Katchadourian, 1990).

6. Abortion continues to be a divisive and political issue in many countries. Consequently, many governments are under increasing pressure to restrict or ban abortion. "Despite fierce controversy, women in all societies continue to practice abortion, legal or illegally, as a solution to their problem pregnancies" (Sachdev, 1988, p. 12).

Abortion in the United States

How many abortions occur in the United States? Who gets abortions and why? What is the availability of abortion services in the United States? These questions are answered in the following sections.

Incidence of Abortion

Each year in the United States, nearly three out of 10 women aged 15 to 44 have an abortion; 43% have had at least one previous abortion, and 49% have had a previous birth (*Facts in Brief*, 1992). Table 22.2 lists the abortion rate and the abortion ratio in the United States for selected years. **Abortion rate** refers to the number of abortions per 1,000 women aged 15 to 44; **abortion ratio** refers to the number of abortions per 100 pregnancies (excluding miscarriages).

NATIONAL DATA: In 1988, there were 1.6 million abortions performed in the United States (*Statistical Abstract of the United States: 1992*, Table 101). Most (90%) induced abortions occur within the first 12 weeks of pregnancy (Kočhanek, 1991).

CONSIDERATION: Compared to other developed countries, the United States has one of the highest abortion rates and abortion ratios (*Facts in Brief*, 1992; Jones et al., 1988). This is believed to be due to 1) the inadequate sex education socialization of children in the United States in regard to the importance of contraception and 2) the lack of societal support for making contraception available to sexually active teenagers (Westoff, 1988).

TABLE 22.2 Abortion rates and ratios in the United States for Selected Years

	Rate (# of abortions per 1,000 women aged 15–44)	Ratio (# of abortions per 100 pregnancies)
1973	16.3	19.2
1975	21.7	26.5
1980	29.3	30.0
1985	28.0	29.8
1988	27.3	28.6

Sources: Tietze, C., Darroch Forrest, J., & Henshaw, S. K. (1988). United States of America. In P. Sachdev (Ed.), *International handbook on abortion* (pp. 473–494). New York: Greenwood. S. Henshaw. (1992). Abortion trends in 1987 and 1988: Age and race. *Family Planning Perspectives, 24,* 85–86, 96. (Data reported to Alan Guttmacher Institute).

Who Gets an Abortion and Why?

Women of all ages, races, socioeconomic statuses, marital statuses, and religions may obtain an abortion. However, certain characteristics are associated with getting an abortion:

Even in 1958, I did not confuse my capacity to breed with my capacity to mother.

Letty Cottin Pogrebin

1. Unmarried. Unmarried women are five times more likely than married women to have an abortion (*Facts in Brief*, 1992). Seventy-nine percent of women who decide to get an abortion are not married at the time of the decision; 21% are married (Kochanek, 1991).

CONSIDERATION: The willingness of unmarried teenagers to have a child outside of marriage is increasing. In 1970, 30% of births outside of marriage were to women under age 20. By 1987, 67% of births outside of marriage were to women 19 and younger (Miller & Moore, 1991, p. 315). Black unmarried teenagers are also more willing than white unmarried teenagers to keep their babies (Kochanek, 1991).

NATIONAL DATA: It is estimated that nearly one out of 10 college females has had an abortion (Leatherman, 1989).

2. Young. The majority (58.3%) of women who had legal abortions in 1988 were under 25 years old. About 25% of women who had legal abortions in 1988 were between 15 and 19 years old. Only 20% were age 30 and older (Henshaw, 1992) (see Table 22.3).
3. Poor. Poor women are three times more likely than women who are not poor to have an abortion. Nevertheless, 11% of abortions are obtained by women whose household incomes are $50,000 or more (*Facts in Brief*, 1992).
4. Prochildren. About 70% of women having abortions say they intend to have children in the future (*Facts in Brief*, 1992).
5. Minority. Proportionately, minority women (nonwhite) are more likely to have an abortion than white women. In 1988, minority women obtained 36% of all legal abortions in the United States. Their abortion rate of 57 per 1,000 women was 2.7 times that of white women, whose rate was 21 abortions per 1,000 women (Henshaw, 1992).

NATIONAL DATA: The abortion rate (rate of abortions per 1,000 women) for white women declined from 24.3 in 1980 to 21.2 in 1988. In the same years, the abortion rate for black and other minority women increased from 56.8 in 1980 to 57.3 in 1988 (Henshaw, 1992).

TABLE 22.3 Percentage Distribution of Legal Abortions by Age, 1988

Age	Percentage of Legal Abortions in 1988
Under 20	25.6
Under 15	0.9
15–19	24.7
15–17	10.0
18–19	14.7
20–24	32.7
25–29	21.8
30–34	12.4
35–39	6.0
Over 40	1.5

Source: Adapted from Henshaw, S. K., (1992). Abortion trends in 1987 and 1988: Age and Race. *Family Planning Perspectives, 24,* 85–86, 96. Used by permission.

CONSIDERATION: Fifty-three percent of black women and 40% of white women who get abortions have had a previous abortion (Kochanek, 1991). The higher abortion rate among blacks is related to the much higher pregnancy rate among blacks than whites, which may be primarily due to the lack of access to effective forms of contraception. However, about half of the women having abortions became pregnant even though they were using some form of contraception, either because they used the method inconsistently or incorrectly or because the method failed (Fried, 1990c).

6. Religious affiliation. Women who report no religious affiliation have a higher rate of abortion than women who report some affiliation. Catholic women are about as likely to obtain an abortion as all women nationally; Protestants and Jews are less likely (*Facts in Brief,* 1992).
7. Other characteristics. In addition to the above characteristics, individuals who use illicit drugs, who have partners who encourage abortion, and who have parents, siblings, and/or friends who encourage them to get an abortion (Miller & Moore, 1991) are more likely to opt for an abortion. Similarly, having intercourse at an earlier age, having a steady partner, and having had a previous partner have also been associated with an abortion (Wielandt & Hansen, 1989).

Women have abortions for a variety of reasons. About three-fourths of U.S. women who have an abortion say that having a baby would interfere with work, school, or other responsibilities. About two-thirds say that they cannot afford to have a child. Half say they do not want to be a single parent or that they have problems in their relationship with their husband or partner (*Facts in Brief,* 1992).

CONSIDERATION: Women who choose to get an abortion often do so for more than one reason. Rossi and Sitaraman (1988) noted that most women cite an average of four reasons. These reasons are more likely to be personal, social, and economic than related to concerns over the woman's or the baby's health.

Some women obtain an abortion if they become pregnant as the result of rape or incest. In the United States, about 16,000 abortions each year are obtained because the woman became pregnant as the result of rape or incest. Lastly, about 1% of women having abortions have been advised that their fetus has a defect, and an additional 12% fear that the fetus may have been harmed by drugs, medications, or other conditions (*Facts in Brief*, 1992).

In the following Theoretical Perspective, we discuss Gilligan's study of abortion.

THEORETICAL PERSPECTIVE

Gilligan's Study of Abortion Decision Making

Carol Gilligan, a psychologist at Harvard University, conducted a study (1982) on how women think about and resolve abortion decisions. The study was based on interviews with 29 women referred by abortion and pregnancy counseling services. The women ranged in age from 15 to 33 and were varied in ethnic background and social class. The explanations offered by the women for the pregnancies spanned a range of circumstances, but there were some common threads. The adolescents often did not use contraception because they did not think they could get pregnant. Some women did not anticipate having sexual intercourse, so they were not prepared with birth control methods. Some of the pregnancies occurred as the women were in the process of ending the relationship with their partner. Contraceptive failure precipitated some pregnancies, and others were the result of a joint decision to allow pregnancy but later reconsidered.

Since the focus of the study was on the relationship between women's judgment and action, rather than on abortion per se, Gilligan did not attempt to obtain a sample representative of all women considering abortion. The counselors probably tended to refer women for the interviews who were in the greatest conflict over the decision. Four of the 29 women elected to have the baby, two miscarried, 21 had abortions, and two were undecided at the time of the interview and could not be reached for follow-up.

The women were interviewed twice, during the first trimester of pregnancy and then at the end of the following year. In the initial interview, the focus was on the abortion decision, the options they were considering, the pros and cons of each alternative, what conflicts they felt, and the relationships that would be affected.

Gilligan found that the women's responses reflected a different sense of self and a different approach to relational conflicts from those reported in previous theories of self and moral development—the theories of Freud, Erikson, Piaget and Kohlberg. She found that where the traditional voice presumes separation and tends to discuss moral issues in terms of rights and rules, women's voices emphasized a connected sense of self and approached decisions in terms of responsiveness and responsibilities in relationships. While authors such as Mednick (1989) have critiqued the notion of different voices in moral development, others (Crow, Fok, Hartman, & Payne, 1991) have documented gender-related differences in value systems and decision making. Gilligan identified three positions in women's psychological development, each reflecting a different sense of self in relation to others or a different moral perspective.

Survival

The first perspective focuses on a pragmatic concern for self-survival. Examples are the comments of two of the 18-year-olds. When asked what she thought about the pregnancy, one said, "I really didn't think anything except that I didn't want it. [Why was that?] I didn't want it, I wasn't ready for it, and next year will be my last year

Continued

Continued

and I want to go to school'' (Gilligan, 1982, p. 75). Another saw having a baby as ''the perfect chance to get married and move away from home,'' although she did acknowledge that having a baby would restrict her freedom ''to do a lot of things'' (p. 75).

In the transition from the first perspective toward the second, the idea of moving from selfishness to responsibility was voiced. The women's thinking reflected recognition that being responsible for caring for and protecting a child requires first being able to care for oneself, which is not selfish, given the connection between self and child. A 17-year-old responded,

> I was looking at it from my own sort of selfish needs, because I was lonely. . . . But I wasn't looking at the realistic side, at the responsibility I would have to take on. I came to this decision that I was going to have an abortion because I realized how much responsibility goes with having a child. . . . And I decided that I have to take on responsibility for myself and I have to work out a lot of things. (pp. 76–77)

Goodness

When the shift to responsibility is made, one's self-worth is defined in terms of the conventions of feminine goodness: ''the ability to care for and protect others'' (Gilligan, 1988, p. 79). Conflict develops over the issue of causing hurt. One woman lamented, ''I think what confuses me is it is a choice of either hurting myself or hurting other people around me'' (p. 80). The conventional feminine solution to such conflict is that self-sacrifice is the ''right'' resolution. Denise was a 25-year-old woman who had an abortion she did not want, out of concern for her lover and his wife and children.

> I just wanted the child, and I really don't believe in abortions. . . . But I felt a responsibility, my responsibility if anything ever happened to [his wife]. He made me feel that I had to make a choice and there was only one choice to make and that was to have an abortion and I could always have children another time, and he made me feel if I didn't have it that it would drive us apart. (p. 81)

Instead of making a decision based on how goodness or relationship appears in the eyes of others, the transition to the next phase involves determining the ''truth'' of relationships: that relationships involve both others and self. Janet, a 24-year-old Catholic married woman, found herself pregnant again just two months after the birth of her first child. Based on her religious views, she believes abortion is wrong, but she said she must consider her life, her son's, and her husband's. After speaking with her priest and weighing her beliefs, she concluded she could not be ''so morally strict as to hurt three other people with a decision just because of my moral beliefs'' (Gilligan, 1988, pp. 83–84).

Care

In the third perspective, the focus is on what relationships mean and what constitutes care—an inclusion of both self and others. Sarah, a 25-year-old woman, had an abortion when she discovered she was pregnant after her lover left her. Pregnant again, she used the second crisis as ''sort of a learning, a teeing-off point, which makes it useful in a way'' (Gilligan, 1988, p. 94). She considered what she might gain from having the baby: the adoring love of the child, more of a home life, and admiration for being a struggling single mother. Negative points included: hurrying the demise of the relationship with her partner, loss of a good job, anticipated hatred from her parents, loss of independence, needing a lot of help. The most difficult

Continued

Continued

thing about the abortion option would be facing the guilt. Sarah reluctantly felt the benefits of having the abortion outweighed the other choices.

> I would not have to go through the realization that for the next twenty-five years of my life I would be punishing myself for being foolish enough to get pregnant again and forcing myself to bring up a kid just because I did this. . . . I would not be doing myself or the child or the world any kind of favor having this child. I don't need to pay off my imaginary debts to the world through this child, and I don't think that it is right to bring a child into the world and use it for that purpose. (p. 92)

Gilligan concluded that the abortion study reveals a distinctive sense of self and a different approach to moral decisions: one based on relationships and responsibilities rather than rights and rules. It involves growing past both self-interest and self-sacrifice toward responsible caring in which the relationships–responsibilities to all those affected by an abortion are considered. Perhaps this approach could be used to reframe current discussion on abortion, which is often framed in terms of "rights" of women, men, and fetuses.

References

Crow, S. M., Fok, L. Y., Hartman, S. J., & Payne, D. M. (1991). Gender and values: What is the impact on decision making? *Sex Roles, 25,* 255–268.

Gilligan, C. (1982). *In a different voice.* Cambridge: Harvard University Press.

Mednick, M. T. (1989). On the politics of psychological constructs: Stop the bandwagon, I want to get off. *American Psychologist, 44,* 1118–1123.

Availability of Abortion Services

Abortion in the United States is available in a variety of settings—a hospital, physician's office, or various types of "abortion" clinics. About two-thirds of all abortions in the United States are performed in abortion clinics (Henshaw, 1991).

NATIONAL DATA: As of May, 1992, there were about 2,500 places in the U.S. that provide abortions, down from 2,908 in 1982 (Lacayo, 1992).

Abortion clinics are not easily accessible for about 10% of pregnant women who must travel more than 100 miles; 18% must travel 50 to 100 miles to a specialized abortion clinic (Henshaw, 1991). As of May 1992, 1) abortion was not available in 83% of the counties in the United States, 2) a single clinic served 24 counties in northern Minnesota, and 3) one doctor provided abortions in the entire state of South Dakota (Lacayo, 1992).

> You have religious leaders saying that doctors who perform [abortion] should go to hell. You have anti-abortion groups that harass medical staff. What professionals would continue to do a service that subjected them to this kind of abuse?
>
> *Dr. Curtis Boyd*
> *A recipient of death threats for running a clinic that provides abortions*

Even when a woman has access to abortion services, she may face a financial burden in paying for the abortion. The average cost of a first-trimester abortion in a clinic is $251 (Lacayo, 1992). In contrast, an abortion of 10 weeks' gestation in a hospital costs an average of $1,757. (Henshaw, 1991, p. 246). Only 12 states routinely provide Medicaid financing for abortion (Lacayo, 1992).

For women who are economically disadvantaged, the cost of the abortion may be compounded by travel expenses to get to an abortion clinic. Furthermore, some states require a waiting period (24 hours or more) from the time women appear at the clinic to the time the abortion is performed. Thus, there is the additional expense of overnight accommodations. For some women who decide to obtain an abortion, "by the time they get the money together, they have advanced into the second trimester, when the cost is higher" (Lacayo, 1992, p. 28).

> Abortion is least available to those who are least able to support the emotional and financial costs of pregnancy.
>
> *Hyman Rodman*
> *Betty Sarvis*
> *Joy Walker Bonar*

CONSIDERATION: Almost one-half of women who have an abortion after 15 weeks of pregnancy are delayed because of problems, usually financial, in arranging an abortion (*Facts in Brief, 1992*).

About two-thirds of all abortions in the United States are performed in abortion clinics.

Abortion Legislation in the United States

One of the most controversial political issues in our society is abortion legislation. After a brief look at the historical background of abortion legislation, we discuss the landmark *Roe v. Wade* case, as well as more recent legislative actions regarding abortion in the United States.

Historical Background of Abortion Legislation

In the early post-Revolution United States, abortion was neither prohibited nor uncommon. During this time, the states were governed by English common law, which accepted the view that abortion was permitted until "quickening," the time when movement of the fetus was perceived by the pregnant woman (usually the fourth or fifth month of pregnancy) (Tribe, 1990). According to common law, even when an abortion was performed after "quickening," the woman involved was immune from prosecution.

CONSIDERATION: Before quickening occurred, it could not be confirmed that a woman was pregnant. Hence, many women did not view themselves as pregnant but as "irregular," in that they were missing their periods. They came to doctors, not to abort a fetus (for they could not be sure that they were pregnant), but rather because they wanted to restore the menses and become "regular" again (Petchesky, 1990, pp. 53–54).

The legal control of abortion by statute began in 1821. Because thousands of women had died by taking medically prescribed poisons to induce abortions, Connecticut passed a law prohibiting the use of poisons to induce postquickening abortions. This statute existed primarily to protect the lives of women. The view that a woman had the right to end an unwanted, early pregnancy still predominated (Tribe, 1990). The first statute dealing with the abortion of an unquickened fetus was a New York 1828 law that viewed abortion of an unquickened fetus as a misdemeanor crime and abortion of a quickened fetus as second-degree manslaughter, unless the abortion was necessary to preserve the woman's life (Sapiro, 1990). By 1840, only eight states had enacted any kind of statutory restriction on abortion (Tribe, 1990).

In the mid-nineteenth century, the American Medical Association led the campaign to criminalize abortion (Petchesky, 1990). The medical profession advocated restrictive abortion laws as a result of economic as well as moral concerns. "Regular" physicians (those who had received formal medical school training) were in economic competition with midwives, who not only assisted in births but also in abortion. Doctors discredited midwives by labeling them "quacks" and "purveyors of wickedness" in an effort to legitimize the medical profession and monopolize the market in health care and childbirth.

Moral concerns in the medical community over abortion resulted, in part, from advances in the scientific understanding of human development. The science-based view of human development as a continuous process, rather than as a sudden event, led physicians to question the relevance of the distinction between quick and non-quick fetuses (Tribe, 1990).

Another factor that influenced the movement toward restrictive abortion legislation was the concern over the increasing number of married, white, middle-class Protestant women who were having abortions in the mid-nineteenth century. At the same time, immigrant and Catholic birthrates climbed. Medical professionals warned that "respectable" women (white, middle-class Protestants) would be "outbred" by ignorant, lower-class aliens (Petchesky, 1990, p. 82). Incidentally, middle-class Protestant women comprised a major segment of the clientele for physicians.

The medical profession opposed contraception, as well as abortion. "Both contraception and abortion were associated by a male, upper-middle-class, WASP medical profession with obscenity, lewdness, sex, and worst of all, rebellious women" (Petchesky, 1990, p. 82). Thus, abortion and contraception were viewed as threats to traditional gender roles and conservative sexual values. Physicians condemned women who had abortions as "selfish" and criticized them for abandoning maternal and childcare duties. Opposition to contraception and abortion was further supported by the argument that

> Female chastity is necessary to protect the family and its descent . . . female chastity must be enforced with severe social and legal sanctions, among which fear of pregnancy functioned effectively and naturally. (Gordon, 1977, p. 261)

By 1900, abortion was illegal in all U.S. jurisdictions. In most states, the sole legal ground on which abortion could be performed was if continuation of the pregnancy threatened the life of the woman. Women who decided to terminate an unwanted pregnancy for personal, social, or economic reasons were forced to seek more dangerous illegal abortions. In spite of the criminalization of abortion during this era, it is estimated that as many as one in three pregnancies was terminated by induced abortion (Rubin, 1987).

Roe v. Wade and Rulings Since 1973

Although physicians were primarily responsible for laws regarding abortion before the twentieth century, "feminists and family planning advocates led the twentieth-century movement to legalize abortion" (Staggenborg, 1991, p. 3). Next, we look at the landmark *Roe v. Wade* decision and other rulings on abortion since 1973.

Roe v. Wade In 1973, the U.S. Supreme Court ruled in the famous *Roe v. Wade* case that any restriction on abortions during the first trimester of pregnancy was unconstitutional. During the first three months of pregnancy, the decision to have an abortion was between the pregnant woman and her physician. In the second trimester (fourth through sixth month of pregnancy), the state may regulate the abortion procedure (e.g., require that the abortion be performed in a hospital) so as to protect the woman's health. During the last trimester, the state has an interest in protecting the viable fetus, so the state may restrict or prohibit abortion (Fried, 1990a). In effect, the Supreme Court ruled that the fetus is a potential life and not a "person" until the third trimester. The *Roe v. Wade* decision was based on the right to privacy; government intrusion into the doctor-patient relationship and into a woman's reproductive decisions were seen as violations of that right.

Rulings Since 1973 Since the landmark *Roe v. Wade* decision, the Supreme Court has made a series of rulings regarding abortion, some of which are described below (Fried, 1990a):

1. 1976—*Planned Parenthood of Central Missouri v. Danforth.* The Court overturned a law requiring a married woman to obtain her husband's consent for an abortion. This ruling stated that a woman's right to choose abortion is not subject to the veto of her spouse. The Court also stated that all minors, no matter how mature or under what circumstances, could not be required to obtain at least one parent's consent in order to have an abortion.
2. 1979—*Bellotti v. Baird.* The Court reconsidered the issue of requiring minors to obtain parental consent for abortion. It upheld a Massachusetts law requiring minors to notify both parents or obtain their consent for an abortion. The Court held that parental consent or notification does not infringe on a minor's rights if the minor can bypass the parents by obtaining a "judicial bypass." A minor may seek this judicial bypass from a judge, who will determine if the minor is "mature" enough to make the abortion decision herself and whether abortion is in the minor's best interest. Reasons why some minors choose to seek a court bypass include fear of parental disapproval, the father is absent from the home, and the desire to avoid contributing to stress in the family (Blum, Resnick, & Stark, 1990).
3. 1980—*Harris v. McRae* and *Williams v. Zbaraz.* The Court upheld the right of Congress and state legislatures to refuse to use public tax monies to pay for medically necessary abortions for poor women.
4. 1983—*Akron Center for Reproductive Health v. City of Akron.* The court invalidated a variety of restrictions on abortion, including state-imposed waiting periods and "informed consent" requiring that women seeking abortions be told that a fetus is a "human life," its precise gestational age, and that abortion is a major surgical procedure. The Supreme Court also declared unconstitutional regulations requiring that 1) all abortions for women more than three months' pregnant be performed in hospitals, rather than clinics; 2) physicians tell women seeking abortions about possible alternatives, abortion risks, and that the fetus is a human life; 3) there be at least a 24-hour waiting period between the time a woman signs a consent form and the abortion is performed; and 4) all pregnant, unwed girls under 15 must obtain a parent's consent or have a judge's approval before having an abortion.
5. 1989—*Webster v. Reproductive Health Services.* The Court upheld various restrictions on abortion in Missouri. The Court declared that a state may prohibit

"public facilities" and "public employees" from being used to perform or assist with abortions not necessary to save the life of the pregnant woman.

6. 1990—*Hodgson v. Minnesota* and *Ohio v. Akron Center for Reproductive Health.* In the Minnesota case, the Court declared that a state could require a pregnant minor to inform both her parents before having an abortion, so long as the law provides the option of a judicial bypass. In the Ohio case, the court ruled that the state may require a minor to notify one parent, while allowing the judicial-bypass alternative. The Court did not rule on whether judicial bypass must be offered as an alternative when notice to only one parent is required. The Court also upheld the constitutionality of requiring waiting periods before the abortion can be performed.

CONSIDERATION: Parental notification laws have been fiercely opposed by some critics on the grounds that they increase the likelihood that a pregnant minor will seek an illegal (and often unsafe) abortion to avoid disclosing the pregnancy to her parent(s). Such was the case for Becky Bell, a 17-year-old from Indianapolis, who obtained an illegal abortion in 1988 and died from an abortion-related infection. According to her friends, Becky was unwilling to hurt her parents with news of her pregnancy, so she obtained an illegal abortion. Becky's mother said of the incident, "She died because of a law I didn't know existed" (Sharpe, 1990, p. 80).

7. 1991—*Rust v. Sullivan.* In May 1991, the Supreme Court, by a vote of 5 to 4, ruled that federally funded family planning clinics (there are about 4,000) are prohibited from giving a woman any information about abortion ("Court Upholds," 1991). Such a policy was consistent with the Reagan administration's goal of using Title X family planning programs to restrict abortion. This prohibition (labeled by prochoice advocates as the "gag rule") will have the greatest effect on low-income women. When these pregnant women ask specifically for abortion information, they are to be told that the family planning clinic "does not consider abortion an appropriate method of family planning" (Marcus, 1991, p. 2).

   Speaking on behalf of the prohibition, Chief Justice William H. Rehnquist noted that the government has a right to "selectively fund a program to encourage certain activities it believes to be in the public interest" (Marcus, 1991, p. 1). Douglas Johnson, legislative director of the National Right to Life Committee, hailed the decision as a "landmark ruling."

   Speaking against the new ruling, Justice Harry A. Blackmun said that the decision to withhold information abandons "with disastrous results" the principle that a woman has the freedom to choose whether she will continue her pregnancy to term (Marcus, 1991, p. 1). Rachael Pine of the American Civil Liberties Union noted that "this opinion is close to giving the government the blank check it sought."

The court turned somersaults to avoid overturning *Roe v. Wade* in an election year.

Deborah Levy

8. 1992—*Planned Parenthood of Southeastern Pennsylvania v. Casey.* The Supreme Court upheld by a vote of 5 to 4 the right of a woman to obtain an abortion but affirmed the right of Pennsylvania to restrict the conditions under which an abortion may be granted. Restrictions that were upheld include a 24-hour waiting period, parental consent for minors, informed consent, and detailed physician reports to the government on each abortion performed. Struck down was the requirement that the husband must be notified before a wife obtains an abortion (Mauro, 1992).

9. Pending—*Bray v. Alexandria Women's Health Clinic*. In the summer of 1992 the U.S. Supreme Court rescheduled oral arguments for the next Court session. In this case the Court is considering whether federal civil rights law protects women's access to abortion clinics from interventions by groups such as Operation Rescue, which blockades clinics. The Bush Administration filed a brief in this case arguing that Operation Rescue's tactics do not violate women's civil rights, while Kate Michelman, NARAL President, referred to the tactics as terrorism (From All Quarters, 1992).

The future of abortion legislation is unknown. Legislation under consideration at the time of this writing includes a U.S. Congressional bill called the Freedom of Choice Act, which would legislate the principles of the Supreme Court's Roe v. Wade ruling and confirm legality of abortion in all states. The Freedom of Access to Clinic Entrances Bill proposes to prohibit abortion protest groups from blockading health clinics (From All Quarters, 1992). Legislation regulating abortion is also on the agenda in many state legislatures. "During the 1991 legislative term, 293 bills were introduced in 47 legislatures: 181 bills would have restricted abortion rights, while 81 bills sought to protect abortion rights" (Haffner, 1992, p. 2).

> I have personally taken care of women with red rubber catheters hanging out of their uterus and a temperature of 107 degrees. Once a physician has watched that happening, he or she will never be willing to watch the laws go back.
>
> *Dr. David Grimes*
> *University of Southern California School of Medicine*

Although the conservative Supreme Court of 1992 may overturn *Roe v. Wade,* Rossi and Sitaraman (1988) suggested that "the antiabortion movement has succeeded only in imposing a temporary brake on a long-term historical trend toward increased public acceptance of abortion in early pregnancy as . . . a private matter in which the state should not interfere" (p. 273). Referring to the abortion debate, Rosenblatt (1992) said that "we have been at war for the past twenty-five years, and the war we have waged on this issue is greater than that of any other nation in history" (p. 98). Indeed, the United States may have to learn to live with conflicting attitudes, values, and beliefs its citizens have about abortion.

Psychological Effects of Abortion

Regarding the research on the experience of abortion, on January 9, 1989, at the request of President Ronald Reagan, U.S. Surgeon General C. Everett Koop presented a report on the effects of abortion. Based on a review of the scientific literature and consultations with scientific and medical experts, Koop (1989) concluded that

> Data do not support the premise that abortion does or does not cause or contribute to psychological problems. (p. 31)

Hence, Koop suggested that the data on the psychological effects of abortion are inconclusive.

The American Psychological Association (APA) challenged Koop's claim that data on the psychological effects of abortion are inconclusive. Rather, the APA emphasized that the data show that when psychological effects occur, "they are mild and temporary" (Wilmoth, 1989, p. 7).

Rogers, Stoms, and Phifer (1989) examined 76 research articles on the psychological effects of abortion that were published between 1966 and 1988. They found that the reported incidence of negative psychological outcomes resulting from abortion "vary substantially across studies" (p. 370). Their analysis suggests that research-based conclusions on the effects of abortion vary because of different research methods used in the various studies. For example, different criteria are used to establish negative outcomes of having an abortion, and different methods of assessment are used to measure these criteria.

CONSIDERATION: Rogers et al. (1989) suggested that because abortion outcome studies vary in their conclusions, "both advocates and opponents of abortion can prove their points by judiciously referencing only articles supporting their political agenda" (p. 370).

The analysis of abortion outcome research conducted by Rogers et al. also suggests that many abortion outcome studies have numerous methodological limitations in the design of the research and how it is reported in the literature. Rogers et al. described 20 such limitations, including small sample sizes, low or unknown reliability and validity of assessment instruments, incomplete information (data and/or methods were reported incompletely), recall distortion (the study used data subject to memory failure or distortion, such as that obtained by asking a woman one year following an abortion if she recalled being depressed the first few days after the abortion), sterilization (the abortion was accompanied by concomitant sterilization, rendering it impossible to attribute any outcome to the abortion alone), and unclear criteria (the dependent variable was undefined or poorly defined, e.g., "worse mental state" was reported without describing how "worse mental state" was defined).

CONSIDERATION: Another methodological flaw in abortion outcome research prior to 1973 was that "evidence regarding the emotional effects of aborting a pregnancy was confounded with the emotional effects of breaking the law" (Rodman, Sarvis, & Bonar, 1987, p. 72). In addition, prior to 1973, some women who wanted a legal abortion could obtain one only on mental health grounds. Thus, the legal restriction on abortion encouraged women "to feign psychiatric symptoms, to mouth suicidal ideas, and to present themselves generally as emotionally disordered when in fact they are not" (Pfeiffer, 1970; quoted in Rodman et al., 1987, p. 74). Lastly, negative attitudes of physicians and other medical personnel may contribute to adverse reactions experienced by women after having an abortion. Marder (1970) gave several examples of abortion patients being harassed by "nurses, interns, and residents, as well as medical students, [who] demonstrated anger and resentment toward a patient by voicing an old theme: 'You've had your fun and now you want us to take care of it for you' " (quoted in Rodman et al., 1987, p. 74).

Methodologically sound studies of the psychological effects of abortion were reviewed by Adler et al., (1990). Adler and her colleagues concluded that U.S. women who obtained legal nonrestrictive abortions experienced the greatest degree of distress *before* the abortion, during the time the decision-making process was occurring. Other findings by Adler and her colleagues include:

- There is a low incidence (5% to 10%) of women who report severe negative reactions to abortion. Most describe their feelings as those of relief and happiness.
- Positive reactions (relief) outweigh negative reactions (guilt).
- Psychological profiles on the Minnesota Multiphasic Personality Inventory of women who have abortions and those who give birth to their babies are very similar.

CONSIDERATION: Those women who tend to have negative psychological effects from having an abortion were very ambivalent about the decision to abort, had values that conflicted with abortion, tended to wait until after the first trimester to abort, and had little support from family, friends, and partner for the abortion decision (Adler et al., 1990). Women pressured into the operation either by relatives or because their pregnancy has medical complications also may be more likely to experience negative reactions after having an abortion (Romans-Clarkson, 1989). Conversely, women in the Adler et al. study who had little negative reaction were not ambivalent about their decision to terminate the pregnancy, did so early in the first trimester, held no antiabortion values, had social support for their decisions, and expected a positive outcome from their decision (Adler et al., 1990).

Adding to the body of research that suggests that depression and anxiety decrease after abortion is a study by Urquhart and Templeton (1991) at the University of Aberdeen, Scotland. Ninety-one abortion patients were assessed two days before the abortion and one week and four weeks after the abortion. The woman's emotional state was assessed using the Edinburgh Postnatal Depression Scale. Scores could range from zero to 39, with a score of over 15 considered to indicate feelings of anxiety and depression. Of the women having a nonsurgical abortion (mifepristone and a prostaglandin), 61% had a score of over 15 before the abortion, 15% had scores that high one week after the abortion, and 10% had scores that high four weeks after the abortion. Among the women who had a surgical abortion, the proportions with scores greater than 15 fell from 68% to 26% and 6% over the course of the three tests (Urquhart & Templeton, 1991).

CONSIDERATION: Rodman et al. (1987) noted that

> Women seeking abortion are often angry at themselves for getting pregnant, at their sexual partners for getting them pregnant, at a biological situation that makes women pay a heavy price for sexual pleasure without effective contraception, at parents or partners or a society that coerces them into making an abortion decision about which they are ambivalent. (p. 76)

In another study, 63 women who had an abortion reported mild, transient, short-term negative effects and generally benign long-term effects (Lemkau, 1991). Few regretted their decision.

Zabin, Hirsch, and Emerson (1989) compared black teenagers who had an abortion with those who carried their babies to term to assess the effects two years later. Those who opted for abortion were more likely to have graduated from high school, to be better off financially, and to not have had a subsequent pregnancy. In addition, they were no more likely to have psychological problems than those who chose to have their babies. The researchers summarized their findings: "Thus, two years after their abortions, the young women who had chosen to terminate an unwanted pregnancy were doing as well as (and usually better than) those who had had a baby" (Zabin et al., 1989, p. 248).

Most research on the psychological effects of abortion has looked only at the women experiencing the abortion. Relatively few studies have looked at the effects on the woman's male partner and on their relationship. However, a study based on questionnaire responses from 1,000 men accompanying women undergoing abortions at clinics suggests that men may experience anxiety, anger, and guilt (Shostak & McLouth, 1984).

Other Pregnancy Outcomes

As noted in the beginning of this chapter, pregnancy may not only be terminated intentionally (induced abortion) but also unintentionally (spontaneous abortion). Next, we discuss spontaneous abortion, also referred to as miscarriage or stillbirth, and perinatal death (the death of an infant near the time of birth). Finally, we note alternatives to induced abortion: placing the baby for adoption and keeping the baby.

Miscarriage and Stillbirth

A miscarriage is a loss experienced at a personal and intrapsychic level to a much greater degree than is recognized by family and friends, or even by herself at a conscious level.

Jack Stack

NATIONAL DATA: Between 10% and 20% of all known pregnancies end in a miscarriage (Friedman & Gath, 1989; Stack, 1984).

A **miscarriage** is the unintended death of an embryo or fetus up until the twentieth week of pregnancy. Three-fourths of miscarriages occur before the 12th week of pregnancy; they are called early miscarriages (Lietar, 1986). While the causes of a particular miscarriage are generally unknown, it is believed that most miscarriages are caused by severe abnormalities in the developing zygote, embryo, or fetus (Huisjes, 1990). Late miscarriages, from week 13 to week 20 of pregnancy, are often due to problems with uterine structure, the cervix, or implantation (Lietar, 1986).

CONSIDERATION: Until recently, there was little recognition that the woman (and her partner) would experience profound grief in response to the loss of a fetus. "Caregivers, family, and friends often encourage denial and intellectualization with phrases such as, 'You didn't get to know it,' . . . 'It would have been deformed anyway.' They rarely encourage the woman to cry, to talk about her loss, and to assume the role of a bereaved person" (Stack, 1984, p. 165).

In fact, the woman may be deeply distressed. In a study of 65 women who had miscarried anywhere from two to 21 weeks after conception, a sense of sadness was universal; 30% of the women reported feelings of frustration, disappointment, or anger (Cole, 1987). In another study of 67 women who were interviewed four weeks after they had miscarried, almost half (48%) were "psychiatric cases" (as measured by the Present State Examination) (Friedman & Gath, 1989). They were depressed and grieving over their loss.

Of the 67 women, 24 (35%) were in denial as they reported feelings of still being pregnant and had to keep reminding themselves that they no longer were. Some women believed there had been a mistake in diagnosis and that they were still pregnant or had been carrying twins and lost only one of them. These thoughts of continuing pregnancy were comforting, rather than distressing (Friedman & Gath, 1989).

Those women who reported more distress were not married and had no children (Friedman & Gath, 1989). Other researchers have found that women who had sought the pregnancy intensely, who had no signs that there was trouble, and who had put their careers on hold experienced more distress over their miscarriage. As might be expected, experiencing a miscarriage further along in pregnancy is associated with greater distress than is a miscarriage shortly after conception (Herz, 1984).

Aside from depression, many women feel guilt, a sense of failure, anger, and jealousy following a miscarriage (Witzel & Chartier, 1989). Their guilt results in blaming themselves for the miscarriage; some feel that they are being punished for something they have done in the past—frequent, casual anonymous premarital sex; an abortion; an extramarital affair. Others feel that they have failed not only as a woman or mother but also in living up to the expectations of their husband, parents, and other children (women who have a miscarriage are often inappropriately urged to "try again" rather than to focus on their grief). Others are angry at the insensitivity of their friends who show little empathy for their feelings of sadness and emptiness at the loss of "their baby" (p. 18). Many report feeling extreme jealousy when hearing other women talk of their pregnancies and seeing other women with their infants.

Coping may take decades. Shulamit Reinharz (1988) said of her miscarriage:

> My sense of loss which resulted from losing the "baby" remains even after more than a decade. Having given birth to two children in the ensuing years has not reduced my feeling of loss, because children are not interchangeable (p. 84). . . . My friends and relatives tried to help me forget. Some told me about their own miscarriages. My husband focused his anger at the doctor. Together we tried to grieve for someone we had never known, but we had no ceremonies or rituals for doing so. (p. 100)

CONSIDERATION: The woman's relationship with her partner is usually not damaged by a miscarriage. Of 63 women with partners who had miscarriages, 31 reported an improved relationship with their partner since the miscarriage; 23 reported the relationship was unchanged. Nine said that it got worse (Friedman & Gath, 1989).

When interpersonal strain does occur, it may be caused by the different ways that men and women react to the miscarriage. Men tend to be action-oriented, to seek distraction in movies or vacations, while women tend to relive the miscarriage over and over. "In this dynamic, the wife may perceive her husband's suggestions to go out as unhelpful or uncaring, while the husband may see his wife's desire to talk about the event as obsessive. The two withdraw from each other, and other unresolved strains in the marriage may surface" (Cole, 1987, p. 65).

Perinatal Death

Even more devastating than a miscarriage is a **perinatal death**, which is the death of an infant near the time of birth. A **fetal death** occurs when an infant is born dead. **Early infant death** refers to the death of an infant within seven days of birth.

NATIONAL DATA: In the United States, about 18,000 fetal deaths (28 weeks or more gestation) and 21,000 early infant deaths occur annually (*Statistical Abstract of the United States: 1992,* Table 110).

Like a miscarriage, perinatal deaths result in the parents experiencing shock, denial, anger, and intense grief. Healthcare and mental health service providers, clergy, and funeral directors are changing attitudes toward perinatal death, with increased attention to bereavement and parents' emotional experiences (Hutchins, 1986) and less discounting of grief and minimizing of loss (Nichols, 1986). A mother who experienced the stillbirth of her daughter said,

> Who would believe that a stillborn baby could generate so much grief and sadness and leave such a trail of sorrow? She was like a shooting star—gone before I was sure she was there, but indelibly imprinted in my memory and leaving a sense of wonder and deep emotion. (Esposito, 1987, p. 333)

A number of suggestions have been provided for caregivers to help families cope with death of a baby before or soon after it is born (Hutchins, 1986; Nichols, 1986; Woods, 1987a&b). Among these are giving parents the options of deciding whether to induce or wait for spontaneous labor if the baby died in utero; seeing, touching, and holding the baby; naming the baby; obtaining photographs and momentos; planning a baptism, funeral, or memorial service; and making contact with others who have had similar experiences. Compassionate intervention can help families handle the loss, not only of the child, but of what the child represented to them.

Adoption

Compared to other outcomes of unintended pregnancy, little research has been done on placing children for adoption. That is probably because this option is so rarely chosen. Although before 1973, 9% of children born to unmarried women were relinquished for adoption, this number decreased to 4% for 1973–1981, and to 2% during 1982–1988 (Bachrach, Stolley & London, 1992). Most of the studies done on the process and consequences of placing a child for adoption have been conducted on small samples of adoption agencies or maternity homes.

Kalmuss, Namerow, and Cushman (1991) studied three groups of pregnant women living in maternity residences who were confronted with the decision to put their baby up for adoption, keep their baby, or have an abortion. Seventeen percent of the 430 women reported that they intended to place their baby with adoptive parents upon first learning that they were pregnant.

The maternity home residents most likely to place their baby with adoptive parents were white (92%), unmarried, between the ages of 15 and 19, from more

Pregnant teenagers are more likely to place their baby for adoption if they are from an economically advantaged and educated home.

economically advantaged backgrounds, and intending to go to college. Other research has also found that pregnant teenagers are more likely to place their baby for adoption if they are from an economically advantaged and educated home (Cooksey, 1990).

The conditions favoring the decision to place one's baby in an adoptive home in contrast to parenting one's own baby included being able to meet and choose the adoptive parents and being assured of being able to receive yearly updates about the baby (Kalmuss et al., 1991). Those who chose to put their baby up for adoption were also encouraged by their fathers, mothers, and boyfriends to do so.

In addition, those who chose the adoption alternative felt that they would enhance their chance of having a job and a better standard of living and improve their relationship with their mother by doing so. They also predicted a better life through adoption for their baby. Researchers have found that adopted children have fared better in material terms than children who have remained with their unmarried mothers (Bachrach, 1986).

Bachrach et al. (1992) examined data regarding relinquishment of premarital births from the 1982 and 1988 cycles of the National Survey of Family Growth. Based on probability samples of the U.S. population, over 16,400 women were surveyed, but there were only 124 reports of children placed for adoption. While past data have demonstrated a greater prevalence of relinquishment by white women than black women, these data from the 1980s show almost no difference between blacks and whites. Higher levels of maternal education and increasing maternal age were associated with adoption placement. This may be due to older mothers receiving less family support, or to the maturity involved in considering the mother's and the child's best interests. The researchers found that boys were less than half as likely to be placed for adoption as girls. Perhaps this is due to unmarried mothers' knowledge that couples seeking to adopt prefer girls, or the mothers may be more likely to keep their sons for the link they provide to the child's father or because of the "continuation of the family name" (Bachrach et al., 1992, p. 31).

The researchers noted that a great deal is known about attitudes toward abortion, but, "virtually nothing is known about attitudes and beliefs concerning adoption, and about how those attitudes respond to changes in adoption practice—moving from closed adoption records toward open records, for example" (Bachrach et al., 1992, p. 32). They called for research about the decision-making process of adoption placement and the factors which shape it.

Parenting the Baby

Young women in maternity residences who decide to keep and parent their babies resulting from unintended pregnancies are more likely to be black, economically deprived, educationally deprived, and receiving public assistance (Kalmuss et al., 1991, p. 18). African-American families have traditionally been more accepting of premarital pregnancies and have absorbed the baby into the kinship system. White families have more often stigmatized premaritally pregnant teenagers and their children.

While many unplanned children are well-cared for by their parents, unplanned children may be at risk for abuse. One study found that a child from a family with two unplanned births is 2.8 times more likely to be abused than a child from a family with no unplanned births; a child from a family with three unplanned births is 4.6 times more likely to be abused (Zuravin, 1991).

In *Born Unwanted: Developmental Effects of Denied Abortion,* editors reviewed studies that looked at the longitudinal development of children born to women who gave birth involuntarily following denial of request for legal abortion or when abortion was not a legally available option (David, Dytrych, Matejcek, & Schuller, 1988). The editors concluded that an unwanted pregnancy reflects and foreshadows "a family atmosphere which in many instances is not conducive to healthy childrearing and likely to impact negatively on the child's subsequent psychosocial development " (Matejcek, David, Dytrych, & Schuller, 1988, p. 111). Given these findings, the editors suggested that "everything possible should be done to reduce the incidence of not only unwanted pregnancies but also of children born involuntarily" (p. 125).

As we end this chapter, we wish to identify common ground between polarized views of whether abortion should remain a legal choice for U.S. women. Mario Cuomo, Governor of New York, offered some general principles. "First, we should try to teach young men and women their responsibility in creating and caring for human life" (Cuomo, 1992, p. 17A). Responsible sex education, including contraceptive information are important. An investment in simpler and safer contraceptive technology must be made. And, for women who might choose abortion out of economic necessity, we must create a society where concern for life includes providing adequate food, housing, and education for all children. "To allow the current differences on this subject to postpone humane and constructive action to reduce the need for abortion and improve the lot of our children would be foolish" (Cuomo, 1992, p. 17A).

Likewise, Jasper Wyman, head of the "pro-life" Christian Civic League, advocates an agenda to eliminate the root causes of abortion. Wyman describes himself as both "pro-life" and "pro-choices." He recommends a legislative program that supports birth control and also includes "job protection for pregnant women, speedier adoption laws, prenatal care, increased welfare, sex education, [and] teen parenting programs." He predicts, "In our lifetime we'll see abortion greatly reduced but only when we have a humane society that provides choices" (Goodman, 1992, p. 13A).

Pro–life, pro–choices. You can be both.
Ellen Goodman

CHOICES

In this section, we look at a medical procedure called **selective termination** that involves terminating the lives of fetuses in order to protect the lives of other fetuses. Then we offer some guidelines that may be helpful to women who are considering whether or not to have an abortion.

Multifetal Pregnancies: Choose Selective Termination?

Women with multifetal pregnancies (a common outcome of the use of fertility drugs; see Chapter 21) may have a medical procedure performed called "transabdominal first-trimester selective termination." This procedure has been performed on women who were pregnant with from three to as many as nine fetuses (Evans et al., 1990; Lynch, Berkowitz, Chitkara, & Alvarez, 1990).

Selective termination may be viewed as a form of abortion, in that it involves the intentional termination of fetal life. Thus, those who oppose abortion may also oppose selective termination. However, there is potential harm to the woman who has a multifetal pregnancy. In addition, by not undergoing selective termination, the multifetal pregnant woman takes the risk that all of the fetuses will be miscarried. Theoretically, selective termination sacrifices the lives of some fetuses so that other fetuses may have a better chance of surviving.

However, while the selective termination procedure has a high likelihood of success (Evans et al., 1990), there is some risk of total pregnancy loss. That is, undergoing this procedure may result in losing all of the fetuses, not only those that are "selectively terminated." In a study of 85 women who underwent first-trimester "transabdominal multifetal pregnancy reduction," 45 women delivered viable infants and eight women lost all of the fetuses (32 pregnancies were ongoing at the time the research report was written) (Lynch et al., 1990).

Evans et al. (1990) suggested that selective termination in multifetal pregnancies is a complex issue.

> We have tried to balance the arguments about the direct harms of performing selective termination and the obstetric risks of not performing selective termination. We believe that selective termination should not be considered a "social" procedure. Our data do not yet make clear whether one, two, or three is the optimal number of embryos to leave. Therefore, on the basis of both current obstetric risk factors and ethical reasoning we will continue to support our protocol of optimally leaving twins. (p. 1568)

Choose Whether to Have an Abortion? Some Guidelines

Abortion continues to be a complex decision. Of 74 women who waited until the sixteenth week of gestation (or later) to get an abortion, 78% said that they did so because of the difficulty of making a decision (Torres & Forrest, 1988). Women who are faced with the question of whether or not to have an abortion may benefit by considering the following guidelines:

1. Consider all the alternatives available to you, realizing that no alternative may be all good or all bad. As you consider each alternative, think about both the short-term and long-term consequences of each course of action.
2. Obtain information about each alternative course of action. Inform yourself about the medical and financial aspects of abortion and childbearing.
3. Talk with trusted family members, friends, or unbiased counselors. Consider talking with the man who participated in the pregnancy. If possible, also talk with women who have had abortions, as well as women who have kept and reared their baby or placed their baby for adoption. If you feel that someone is pressuring you in your decision making, look for help elsewhere.
4. Consider your own personal and moral commitments in life. Understand your own feelings, values, and beliefs concerning the fetus, and weigh those against the circumstances surrounding your pregnancy.

Summary

1. Survey research suggests that most adults and college students believe that abortion should be legal.
2. Individuals and groups who are opposed to abortion are known as "prolife" (or antiabortion); individuals and groups who support the right to legal abortion are known as "prochoice" (or proabortion). Many people have mixed feelings regarding abortion; they may be personally opposed to abortion yet may support the right for every woman to make an abortion decision for herself.
3. Two ethical questions regarding abortion are "When does personhood begin?" and "Is abortion immoral?" There are a variety of opinions on these issues.
4. Methods of abortion include a) suction curettage, which is performed during the first six to eight weeks of pregnancy and involves using a vacuum aspiration device and a metal scraping instrument; b) dilation and suction, which is performed during the first 12 weeks of pregnancy and is similar to suction curettage, except the cervix is dilated before the procedure; c) dilation and evacuation, which is performed between the thirteenth and twenty-fourth weeks of pregnancy and is similar to dilation and suction, except greater cervical dilation and a larger suction device are required; d) saline abortion, which is performed between the sixteenth and twenty-fourth weeks of pregnancy and involves injecting a saline solution into the amniotic sac, causing fetal death; e) injection or suppository of prostaglandins, performed early in pregnancy or as late as 24 weeks, which causes contraction of the uterus and expulsion of fetus; f) RU-486, a synthetic hormone taken in pill form (followed by prostaglandin) within the first nine weeks of pregnancy; and g) menstrual extraction, an experimental procedure in which a flexible plastic instrument is used to remove the uterine lining at about the time a woman's menstrual period is due.
5. Legal abortions are generally considered safe procedures, especially during the first trimester, when 89% of abortions are performed. Possible complications include perforation of the uterus, hemorrhage, or infection. Less than 1% of abortion patients experience a major complication.
6. As of 1986, 76% of the world's population lived in countries where induced abortion was legally permitted; 24% of the world's population lived in countries where abortion was either prohibited or permitted only on grounds of saving the life of the mother. All countries have laws regulating abortion procedures. No government that has permissive abortion laws has advocated continued use of abortion as a primary method of birth control.
7. Each year in the United States, nearly three out of 10 women aged 15 to 44 have an abortion. An estimated one out of 10 college women has had an abortion. Compared to other developed countries, the United States has one of the highest abortion rates.
8. U.S. women who obtain an abortion tend to be unmarried, young, poor, and in a racial minority. Reasons women have an abortion include a) having a baby would interfere with work, school, or other responsibilities, b) the woman cannot financially afford to have a child, c) the woman does not want to be a single parent, and/or d) the woman is having problems in her relationship with her partner. Also, some women choose an abortion if their pregnancy is the result of rape or incest. Lastly, some women abort if the fetus has a defect or they fear the fetus has been harmed by drugs, medications, or other conditions.

9. Many women in the United States do not have easy access to abortion services and/or cannot afford to pay for an abortion.
10. Since the 1973 *Roe v. Wade* Supreme Court decision that allowed women the constitutional right to have an abortion in the first trimester of pregnancy, the Court has issued a series of rulings on abortion. Some of these have upheld abortion rights, while others have restricted them. The future of abortion legislation is unknown.
11. Research on the psychological effects of having an abortion varies considerably, which in part reflects the use of different research criteria to establish negative outcomes of having an abortion and different methods of assessment to measure these criteria. The chapter describes numerous methodological limitations of abortion-outcome research. A review of sound research on the psychological effects of abortion suggests that the greatest psychological distress occurs before the abortion, during the time of the decision-making process. While most abortion-outcome research focuses on effects on the woman, some research suggests that the male partners of women having an abortion may also suffer anxiety, guilt, and anger.
12. Women and their partners who experience unintentional pregnancy loss or spontaneous abortion (also known as miscarriage or stillbirth) or perinatal death (the death of an infant at or near the time of birth) experience intense grief.
13. Women who experience an unintentional and/or unwanted pregnancy may choose to place the baby for adoption or keep the baby, instead of having an abortion.

KEY TERMS

abortion
induced abortion
spontaneous abortion
suction curettage
dilation and suction
laminaria
dilation and evacuation
saline abortion
prostaglandins
RU-486
abortion rate
abortion ratio
perinatal death
miscarriage
stillbirth
fetal death
early infant death
selective termination

REFERENCES

Adler, N. E., David, H. P., Major, B. N., Roth, S. H., Russo, N. F., & Wyatt, G. E. (1990). Psychological responses after abortion. *Science, 248,* 41–44.

Atrash, H. K. & Hogue, C. J. (1990). The effect of pregnancy termination on future reproduction. *Baillieres Clinical Obstetrics and Gynaecology, 4,* 391–405.

Bachrach, C. A. (1986). Adoption plans, adopted children, and adoptive mothers. *Journal of Marriage and the Family, 48,* 246.

Bachrach, C. A., Stolley, K. S. & London, K. A. (1992). Relinquishment of premarital births: Evidence from national survey data. *Family Planning Perspectives, 24,* 27–35.

Baulieu, E., with Rosenblum, M. (1991). *The abortion pill.* New York: Simon & Schuster.

Bettencourt, M. (1991). The fetus is not a person. In C. P. Cozic & S. L. Tipp (Eds.), *Abortion: Opposing viewpoints* (pp. 37–42). San Diego: Greenhaven Press.

Bitsch, M., Jacobsen, A. B., Prien-Larsen, J. C., & Frelund, C. (1990). IUD (Nova-t) insertion following induced abortion. *Contraception, 42,* 315–322.

Blum, R. W., Resnick, M. D., & Stark, T. (1990). Factors associated with the use of court bypass by minors to obtain abortions. *Family Planning Perspectives, 22,* 158–160.

Boston Women's Health Book Collective (1984). *The new our bodies, ourselves.* New York: Simon & Schuster.

Bygdeman, M., & Van Look, P. F. (1989). The use of prostaglandins and antiprogestins for pregnancy termination. *International Journal of Gynaecology and Obstetrics, 29,* 5–12.

Callahan, S., & Callahan, D. (1984). Abortion: Understanding differences. *Family Planning Perspectives, 16,* 219–221.

Catholics for a Free Choice. (1992). *You are not alone: Information for Catholic women about the abortion decision.* Washington, DC: Author.

Cole, D. (1987). It might have been: Mourning the unborn. *Psychology Today, 21* (7), 64–65.

Cooksey, E. C. (1990). Factors in the resolution of adolescent premarital pregnancies. *Demography, 27,* 207.

Court upholds Title X ban on abortion information. (1991). *Family Planning Perspectives, 23,* 178–181.

Cuomo, M. M. (1992, August 7). Reducing casualties in abortion war. *The News & Observer,* Raleigh, NC, p. 17A.

David, H. P., Dytrych, Z., Matejcek, Z., & Schuller, V. (Eds.). (1988). *Born unwanted: Developmental effects of denied abortion.* (New York: Springer.

Diukman, R. & Goldberg, J. D. (1992). Termination of pregnancy. In M. I. Evans (Ed.), *Reproductive risks and prenatal diagnosis* (pp. 299–309). Norwalk, CT: Appleton & Lange.

English, J. (1991). It is impossible to know whether the fetus is a person. In C. P. Cozic & S. L. Tipp (Eds.), *Abortion: Opposing viewpoints* (p. 46). San Diego: Greenhaven Press.

Esposito, J. L. (1987). A mother's stillbirth experience. In J. R. Woods & J. L. Esposito (Eds.). *Pregnancy loss: Medical therapeutics and practical considerations* (pp. 307–333). Baltimore: Williams & Wilkins.

Evans, M. E., May, M., Drugan, A., Fletcher, J. C., Johnson, M. P., & Sokol, R. J. (1990). Selective termination: Clinical experience and residual risks. *American Journal of Obstetrics and Gynecology, 162,* 11568–11572.

Facts in brief: Abortion in the United States. (1992). New York: Alan Guttmacher Institute.

Feminists for Life of America. (1992). Personal telephone communication.

Fried, M. G. (1990a). Key United States Supreme Court abortion and privacy cases. In M. G. Fried (Ed.), *From abortion to reproductive freedom: Transforming a movement* (pp. 45–48). Boston: South End Press.

Fried, M. G. (1990b). Abortion and sterilization in the Third World. In M. G. Fried (Ed.), *From abortion to reproductive freedom: Transforming a movement* (pp. 63–64). Boston: South End Press.

Fried, M. G. (1990c). Who has abortions in the United States? In M. G. Fried (Ed.). *From abortion to reproductive freedom: Transforming a movement* (pp. 129–130). Boston: South End Press.

Friedman,T., & Gath, D. (1989). The psychiatric consequences of spontaneous abortion. *British Journal of Psychiatry, 155,* 810–813.

From all quarters. (1992, Summer). *NARAL News,* p. 2.

Goodman, E. (1992, Sept. 19). A crusader for life—AND choices. *The News and Observer,* Raleigh, N.C., p. 13A.

Gordon, L. (1977). *Woman's body, woman's right: A social history of birth control in America.* Baltimore: Penguin.

Granberg, D. (1991). Conformity to religious norms regarding abortion. *Sociological Quarterly, 32,* 267–275.

Grimes, D. A. (1984). Second-trimester abortions in the United States. *Family Planning Perspectives, 16,* 260–266.

Haffner, D. W. (1992). Report card on the states: Sexual rights in America. *SIECUS Report,* 20 *(3),* 1–7.

Hakim-Elahi, E., Tovell, H. M., & Burnhill, M. S. (1990). Complications of first-trimester abortions: A report of 170,000 cases. *Obstetrics and Gynecology, 76,* 129–135.

Henshaw, S. K. (1986). Induced abortion: A worldwide perspective. *Family Planning Perspectives, 18,* 250–254.

Henshaw, S. K. (1991). The accessibility of abortion services in the United States. *Family Planning Perspectives, 23,* 246–252.

Henshaw, S. K. (1992). Abortion trends in 1987 and 1988: Age and race. *Family Planning Perspectives, 24,* 85–86, 96.

Henshaw, S. K., Binkin, N. J., Blaine, E., & Smith, J. C. (1985). A portrait of American women who obtain abortions. *Family Planning Perspectives, 17,* 90.

Herz, E. (1984). Psychological repercussions of pregnancy loss. *Psychiatric Annals, 14,* 454–457.

Hogue, C. J. R., Cates, W., Jr., & Tietze, C. (1983). Impact of vacuum aspiration abortion on future childbearing: A review. *Family Planning Perspectives, 15,* 119–126.

Hollis, H. M., & Morris, T. M. (1992). Attitudes toward abortion in female undergraduates. *College Student Journal, 26,* 70–74.

Huisjes, H. J. (1990). Introduction: Spontaneous abortion—the concept. In H. J. Huisjes & T. Lind (Eds.), *Early pregnancy failure* (pp. 1–4). New York: Churchill Livingstone.

Hutchins, S. H. (1986). Stillbirth. In T. A. Rando (Ed.). *Parental loss of a child* (pp. 129–144). Champaign, IL: Research Press.

Jones, E. F., Forrest, J. D., Henshaw, S. K., Silverman, J., & Torres, A. (1988). Unintended pregnancy, contraceptive practice and family planning services in developed countries. *Family Planning Perspectives, 20,* 53–67.

Kalmuss, D., Namerow, P. B. & Cushman, L. F. (1991). Adoption versus parenting among young pregnant women. *Family Planning Perspectives, 23,* 17–23.

Katchadourian, H. A. (1990). *Biological aspects of human sexuality.* Fourth Ed. Fort Worth: Holt, Rinehart & Winston.

Keenan, C. (1990). Multidimensional aspects of caring for the abortion patient. In C. I. Fogel & D. Lauver (Eds.), *Sexual health promotion* (pp. 268–290). Philadelphia: W. B. Saunders.

Klitsch, M. (1991). Antiprogestins and the abortion controversy: A progress report. *Family Planning Perspectives, 23,* 275–282.

Kochanek, K. D. (1991). *Induced terminations of pregnancy: Reporting states, 1988. (Monthly Vital Statistics Report,* Vol. 39). Hyattsville, MD: U.S. Public Health Service.

Koop, C. E. (1989). A measured response: Koop on abortion. *Family Planning Perspectives, 21,* 31–32.

Kovacs, L. (1990). Future direction of abortion technology. *Baillieres Clinical Obstetrics and Gynaecology, 4,* 407–414.

Lacayo, R. (1992, May 4). Abortion—the future is already here. *Time,* pp. 27–32.

Ladipo, O. A. (1989). Preventing and managing complications of induced abortion in Third World countries. *International Journal of Gynecology and Obstetrics, 3,* (Suppl.), 21–28.

Leatherman, C. (1989, May 31). Nearly 1 in 10 female college students has had an abortion, Gallup survey finds; Polling officials are surprised. *Chronicle of Higher Education,* p. 23A.

Lemkau, J. P. (1991). Post-abortion adjustment of health care professionals in training. *American Journal of Orthopsychiatry, 61,* 92–102.

Lietar, E. F. (1986). Miscarriage. In T. E. Rando (Ed.). *Parental loss of a child.* Champaign, IL: Research Press.

Luker, K. (1984). The war between the women. *Family Planning Perspectives, 16,* 105–110.

Lynch, L., Berkowitz, R. L., Chitkara, U., & Alvarez, M. (1990). First-trimester transabdominal multifetal pregnancy reduction: A report of 85 cases. *Obstetrics and Gynecology, and Reproductive Science, 75,* 735–738.

Majority in poll backs abortion right. (1989, March 19). *The News and Observer,* Raleigh, NC, p. 1.

Marcus, R. (1991, May 24). Court upholds ban on abortion advice. *News and Observer,* Raleigh, NC, pp. 1–2.

Marder, L. (1970). Psychiatric experience with a liberalized therapeutic abortion law. *American Journal of Psychiatry, 126,* 1230–1236.

Matejcek, Z., David, H. P., Dytrych, Z., & Schuller, V. (1988). Questions and answers: Discussion and suggestions. In H. P. David, Z. Dytrych, Z. Matejcek, & V. Schuller (Eds.), *Born unwanted: Developmental effects of denied abortion.* (pp. 111–127). New York: Springer.

Mauro, T. (1992, June 30). High court reins in 'Roe'. *USA Today* pp. A1.

Miller, B. C., & Moore, K. A. (1991). Adolescent sexual behavior, pregnancy, and parenting: Research through the 1980s. In A. Booth (Ed.), *Contemporary families* (pp. 307–326). Minneapolis: National Council on Family Relations.

Muldoon, M. (1991). *The abortion debate in the United States and Canada: A source book.* New York: Garland.

Nichols, J. A. (1986). Newborn death. In T. A. Rando (Ed.). *Parental loss of a child* (pp. 145–157). Champaign, IL: Research Press.

Norsigian, J. (1990). RU-486. In M. G. Fried (Ed.), *From abortion to reproductive freedom: Transforming a movement* (pp. 197–203). Boston: South End Press.

Petchesky, R. P. (1990). *Abortion and woman's choice: The state, sexuality, and reproductive freedom* (rev. ed.) (Northeastern Series in Feminist Theory). Boston: Northeastern University Press.

Potts, M., Diggory, P., & Peel, J. (1977). *Abortion.* New York: Cambridge University Press.

Punnett, L. (1990). The politics of menstrual extraction. In M. G. Fried (Ed.) *From abortion to reproductive freedom: Transforming a movement* (pp. 101–111). Boston: South End Press.

Reinharz, S. (1988). What's missing in miscarriage? *Journal of Community Psychology, 16,* 84–103.

Religious Coalition for Abortion Rights. (1992). *No woman is required to build the world by destroying herself.* [Public information brochure] Washington, DC: Author.

Rhoden, N. K. (1985). Late abortion and technological advances in fetal viability—some legal considerations. *Family Planning Perspectives, 17,* 160–161.

Rodman, H., Sarvis, B., & Bonar, J. W. (1987). *The abortion question.* New York: Columbia University Press.

Rogers, J. L., Stoms, G. B., Phifer, J. L. (1989). Psychological impact of abortion: Methodological and outcomes summary of empirical research between 1966 and 1988. *Health Care for Women International, 10,* 347–376.

Romans-Clarkson, S. E. (1989). Psychological sequelae of induced abortion. *Australian and New Zealand Journal of Psychiatry, 23,* 555–565.

Rosen, A. S. (1990). Acceptability of abortion methods. *Baillieres Clinical Obstetrics and Gynaecology, 4,* 375–390.

Rosenblatt, R. (1992). *Life itself: Abortion in the American mind.* New York: Random House.

Rossi, A. S., & Sitaraman, B. (1988). Abortion in context: Historical trends and future changes. *Family Planning Perspectives, 20,* 273–281.

Rubin, E. (1987). *Abortion, politics, and the courts: Roe v. Wade and its aftermath* (2nd ed.). Westport, CT: Greenwood Press.

Rubinson, L., & De Rubertis, L. (1991). Trends in sexual attitudes and behaviors of a college population over a 15-year period. *Journal of Sex Education and Therapy, 17,* 32–41.

Ryan, I. J. & Dunn, P. C. (1988). Association of race, sex, religion, family size, and desired number of children on college students' preferred methods of dealing with unplanned pregnancy. *Family Practice Research Journal, 7,* 153–161.

Sachdev, P. (1988). Abortion trends: An international review. In P. Sachdev (Ed.), *International handbook on abortion* (pp. 1–21). New York: Greenwood Press.

Salmon, D. K. (1991, May). Coping with miscarriage. *Parents,* pp. 106–108.

Sanchez, S. (1992, June 30). Poll: Abortion restrictions favored. *USA TODAY,* p. 1A.

Sapiro, V. (1990). *Women in American society.* (2nd ed.). Mountain View, CA: Mayfield.

Schwarz, S. (1991). The fetus is a person. In C. P. Cozic & S. L. Tipp (Eds.), *Abortion: Opposing viewpoints* (pp. 31–36). San Diego: Greenhaven Press.

Sharpe, R. (1990, July/August). She died because of a law. *Ms.,* pp. 80–81.

Shostak, A. B., & McLouth, G. (1984). *Men and abortion: Losses, lessons, and love.* New York: Praeger.

Sloane, B. C. (1990). *Partners in health.* Atlanta, GA: Printed Matter.

Somell, C., Olund, A., Carlstrom, K., & Kindahl, H. (1990). Reproductive hormones during termination of early pregnancy with mifepristone. *Gynecologica and Obstetric Investigation, 30,* 224–227.

Spitz, I. M., Shoupe, D., Sitruk-Ware, R., & Mishell, D. R., Jr. (1989). Response to the antiprogestagen RU486 (mifepristone) during early pregnancy and the menstrual cycle in women. *Journal of Reproduction and Fertility, 37* (Suppl.), 253–260.

Stack, J. M. (1984). The psychodynamics of spontaneous abortion. *American Journal of Orthopsychiatry, 54,* 162–167.

Staggenborg, S. (1991). *The pro-choice movement.* New York: Oxford University Press.

Statistical abstract of the United States: 1992 (112th ed.) (1992). Washington, DC: U.S. Bureau of the Census.

Stone, R., & Waszak, C. (1992). Adolescent knowledge and attitudes about abortion. *Family Planning Perspectives, 24,* 52–57.

Torres, A., & Forrest, J. D. (1988). Why do women have abortions? *Family Planning Perspectives, 20,* 169–176.

Tribe, L. H. (1990). *The clash of absolutes.* New York: W. W. Norton.

United Nations Population Fund. (1991). *Population policies and programmes: Lessons learned from two decades of experience.* Nafis Sadik (Ed.), New York: New York University Press.

Urquhart, D. R., & Templeton, A. A. (1991). Psychiatric morbidity and acceptability following medical and surgical methods of induced abortion. *British Journal of Obstetrics and Gynecology, 98,* 396–399.

Van Look, P. F., & Bygdeman, M. (1989). Medical approaches to termination of early pregnancy. *Bulletin of the World Health Organization, 67,* 567–575.

Wenz, P. S. (1992). *Abortion rights as religious freedom.* Philadelphia: Temple University Press.

Westoff, C. F. (1988). Unintended pregnancy in America and abroad. *Family Planning Perspectives, 20,* 254–261.

Wielandt, H., & Hansen, U. M. (1989). Sexual behavior, contraception and unintended pregnancy among young females. *Acta Obstetricia et Gynecologica Scandinavia, 68,* 255.

Wilmoth, G. (1989, Winter). APA challenges Koop's abortion report. *Advancing the Public Interest,* p. 7.

Witzel, P. A., & Chartier, B. M. (1989). The unrecognized psychological impact of miscarriage. *Canada's Mental Health, 37,* 17–20.

Woods, J. R. (1987a). Stillbirth. In J. Woods & J. Esposito (Eds.), *Pregnancy loss: Medical therapeutics and practical considerations* (pp. 51–74). Baltimore: Williams & Wilkins.

Woods, J. R. (1987b). Death of a newborn: Merging parental expectations and medical reality. In J. R. Woods & J. L. Espotito (Eds.) *Pregnancy loss: Medical therapeutics and practical considerations* (pp. 75–106). Baltimore: Williams & Wilkins.

Wright, L. S., & Rogers, R. R. (1987). Variables related to prochoice attitudes among undergraduates. *Adolescence, 22,* 517–524.

Zabin, L. S., Hirsch, M. B., & Emerson, M. R. (1989). When urban adolescents choose abortion: Effects on education, psychological status and subsequent pregnancy. *Family Planning Perspectives, 21,* 248–255.

Zindler, F. R. (1991). Human life does not begin at conception. In C. P. Cozic & S. L. Tipp (Eds.), *Abortion: Opposing viewpoints* (pp. 23–30). San Diego: Greenhaven Press.

Zuravin, S. J. (1991). Unplanned childbearing and family size: Their relationship to child neglect and abuse. *Family Planning Perspectives, 23,* 155–161.

CHAPTER TWENTY-THREE

Sex Education

Chapter Outline

Sex Education

- Components of an Ideal Sex Education Program
- **Self-Assessment:** Miller-Fisk Sexual Knowledge Questionnaire (SKQ)
- Goals of Sex Education
- Extent of Sex Education
- Special Audiences for Sex Education

Sources of Sex Education

- Parents
- Friends
- School Teachers
- Family Planning Clinic Personnel
- Religion
- Media
- Pornography

Effects of Sex Education

- Effect on Knowledge
- Effects on Sexual Behaviors
- Effects on Attitudes
- Effects on Contraceptive Usage
- Effect on Teenage Pregnancy
- **Research Perspective:** The Fourth Generation of Sex Education Curricula

Choices

- Choose to Allow Children to Sleep in Their Parents' Bed or to Expose Children to Parental Nudity?
- Choose to Have Parents Participate in Sex Education Programs?
- What Should the Schools Teach about Sex?

Is It True?*

1. Adolescents who have taken sexuality courses usually begin having sexual intercourse at an earlier age than adolescents who have not had sexuality education courses.

2. Research suggests that parents are the major source of sex information for their children.

3. Most public school teachers feel confident that they are good sex educators and don't want to be bothered with sex education workshops that they are required to take.

4. Sex education programs that combine content with access to birth control through school-based clinics are associated with reduced teen pregnancies in those schools.

5. The federal government, not the individual states, is responsible for identifying the nature and extent of sex education in the nation's public schools.

* 1 = F, 2 = F, 3 = F, 4 = T, 5 = F

Less than ten percent of American school children are exposed to anything approaching meaningful sex education.

Sol Gordon

The United States is anxious and ambivalent about what it teaches its youth about sexuality. Although hot sexuality permeates entertainment media (MTV, R-rated films), there is limited content in reference to responsible sexuality. However, the public disclosures of Magic Johnson and Arthur Ashe of their having HIV coupled with the alarming incidence of HIV infection and other sexually transmissible diseases in our population have resulted in an intense concern about how our society provides for the sex education of its youth. The effect has been to take sex education out of the closet and to make it a national priority. In a survey of 207 sexually active teenagers, 87% said that they were afraid of getting AIDS, and 96% said that it was important to learn about AIDS in school (McGill, Smith, & Johnson, 1989).

NATIONAL DATA: Over 16,000 deaths occur annually in the United States due to HIV infection. It is the fourth leading cause of death among individuals aged 25 to 44 (National Center for Health Statistics, 1992). Although the incidence of AIDS among teenagers is still low, it is doubling every 14 months (Gibbs, 1991).

In addition to HIV infection, the alarming incidence of teenage pregnancies has increased concern about sex education. Some teenagers are particularly at risk for unintended pregnancy. Sixty percent of 212 adolescents who had come under the jurisdiction of the juvenile justice system reported that they "never or seldom" used birth control. Only 16% reported that they used birth control the first time they had intercourse (Melchert & Burnett, 1990).

NATIONAL DATA: Over 12% of all U.S. births are to teenagers, representing almost half a million babies every year. Almost 25% of these babies were born to adolescents who already had one or more children. The sharpest increase in teen births has been occurring among adolescents aged 15 to 17 (Center for Population Options, 1991).

In response to HIV infections and teenage pregnancy rates, then-Surgeon General C. Everett Koop (1986) publicly advocated that sex education, including AIDS education, be directed toward preadolescents and adolescents since they were particularly vulnerable to new sexual explorations. In this chapter, we examine what sex education is, who provides it, what its effects are, and what choices we have in reference to it. We begin by defining sex education.

SEX EDUCATION

Sex education is a global term that describes the transmission of information and skills in an effort to integrate sexuality into one's life in a way that is productive for one's self and others. Sex education, also referred to as sexuality education, is a lifelong process of acquiring information about forming attitudes toward identity, relationships, and intimacy (SIECUS, 1992). The sex education movement began around 1900 and was characterized by lectures on the dangers of sex and the need for control (these lectures were given to groups of boys only). In the 1940s, sex education was more focused on healthy sexual adjustment in the family and on the prevention of venereal disease (Strouse & Fabes, 1985).

At its best, sexuality education is about social change—about helping to create a world where all people have the information and the rights to make responsible sexual choices.

Debra W. Haffner

In the 1960s, the "youth revolution" refocused the scope and purpose of sex education away from a "prevention of sexual degeneracy model" to that of providing factual information, nonjudgmental discussion, and values clarification. "The purpose [of sex education] has been, and continues to be: to promote healthy sexual relationships, encourage responsible decision making and reduce the incidence of unintended teenage pregnancies and sexually transmitted diseases (STDs)" (Strouse & Fabes, 1985, p. 251). The assumption of such a model is that if young people get the facts about the consequences of sexual actions, they will change their behavior accordingly. As we will discuss later, this may be a false assumption.

Sex education has more recently become focused on avoiding HIV infection with an emphasis on condom use. However, this level of specificity neglects the broader issues involved in one's choices about life-styles, relationships, and responsibilities (Martin, 1990). Next, we look at the various components of ideal sex education programs.

Components of an Ideal Sex Education Program

It is rare that any sex education program provides all of the following. However, such an ideal program would include:

The information that educators provide, or fail to provide, in helping young people make choices, could mean the difference between life and death.
Elizabeth Calamidas

1. Anatomy and physiology of human sexuality. Some sex education programs teach the various parts of sexual anatomy and how these parts function during sexual response.
2. The anatomy and physiology of reproduction, pregnancy, and childbirth. One of the basic elements of sex education is to teach students about "the birds and the bees": the processes of fertilization and conception, embryonic development, and childbirth.
3. Prevention of unwanted pregnancy. Teaching adolescents how to avoid unwanted pregnancy may involve teaching the value of abstinence. But for sexually active adolescents, preventing unwanted pregnancy requires an understanding of methods of contraception—what the various methods are, how to obtain them, and how to use them correctly.
4. Unwanted pregnancy options. Some sex education programs incorporate content on unwanted pregnancy options: having the child and rearing it as a single parent, getting married and having the child, placing the child for adoption, and getting an abortion.

CONSIDERATION: Teenage pregnancy is associated with dropping out of school. In addition to teaching adolescents how to avoid teenage pregnancy, sex education programs may promote ways for pregnant teenagers to stay in school.

Isn't the real "C" word for sex education commitment, not condoms?
Sharon Sheehan

5. Values clarification and sexual decision making. Sex education programs often incorporate values clarification exercises that help students identify their own values regarding such issues as premarital sex, sex with or without love, and extradyadic sex. Students may be encouraged to implement their values through responsible decision making and consideration of alternative courses of actions and their consequences.
6. Communication. Incorporating communication skills training into sex education programs helps students become comfortable using sexual terms and discussing sexual concerns. Communication skills training may focus on teaching students how to be assertive and resist peer pressure and how to negotiate sexual involvement, including how to say no to a sexual proposition. It is also important for students to learn how to discuss contraception and sexually transmissible diseases with their current or prospective partner(s). Modeling and role-playing exercises are particularly useful in developing such communication skills.
7. Drug education. Sex education programs should include material on how drugs and alcohol affect sexual decision making. For example, drug use is associated with more anonymous sex partners, failure to use contraception and practice "safer sex," and becoming involved in nonconsenting sex. In addition, the effects of drugs on sexual functioning and on the development and health of unborn and breastfed children should be emphasized.

8. Resources. Individuals should be made aware of where they can go to obtain contraception and counseling for sexual concerns and to feel comfortable investigating these resources, should they become pregnant.
9. Sex abuse prevention. Children should be taught the concepts of body ownership, acceptable touching, good versus bad secrets, saying no, and telling adults when they have had an uncomfortable sexual interaction with others. Teenagers should be made aware of date rape—what it is, how to avoid it, what the legal consequences are for the perpetrator, and how the victim of date rape might proceed in reporting the event. Sex education may also address how victims of various types of sexual abuse may psychologically cope with and get help for having had such experiences.
10. Gay and lesbian issues. Some sex education programs attempt to dispel myths and negative stereotypes about homosexuality and reduce prejudice and discrimination against gay individuals. For young gay and lesbian students, such content in sex education programs may help them accept their sexual orientation and develop comfort in "coming out" to others (if they choose to do so). In addition, myths and negative stereotypes about homosexuality contribute to homophobia, which interferes with HIV infection education. Reducing homophobia increases the openness to information and prevention of HIV infection.
11. Gender and sexual identity. The impact of gender roles and gender role nonconformity should be included. Sears (1992) suggested that a sexuality curriculum should examine the social and cultural construction of gender, and address issues such as how being male or female defines one's sexual options.
12. Promotion of self-esteem and aspirations. Postponing pregnancy is related to young people's life goals and aspirations. The overall academic and extracurricular programs offered by the schools are critical in helping young people develop hope and direction. "The ability of the school and family to build a teenager's sense of self and of the future will probably have a far greater impact on the likelihood of teen pregnancy than any special programs of short duration designed expressly around that goal" (Kenney, 1987, p. 731).
13. Evaluation component. In order to assess the effectiveness of a sex education program, it should include pre- and postevaluations on knowledge, attitudes, and behaviors of the students exposed to the program. Blatt (1989) noted that program administrators need to assess accomplishments in a more rigorous way than simply collecting endorsements—"The students all said that they *loved* the course!" (p. 269). Four program evaluation activities described by Blatt include: setting objectives, designing systematic methods for evaluation that permit unambiguous interpretation, measuring the process and accomplishments of the program, and determining if the results were significant.

Sexuality education can help bridge the gap between the personal and political by exploring the ideological bases for gender and sexual identities.

James T. Sears

An example of a measure that is sometimes used to assess sexual knowledge is the Miller-Fisk Sexual Knowledge Questionnaire. It is reproduced in the Self-Assessment in this chapter.

CONSIDERATION: Although the preceding represents an ideal sex education program, the content of such programs vary according to the characteristics of the students for whom they are intended. Such characteristics include developmental age, socioeconomic status, ethnicity, race, and geographic location (urban versus rural). Content of sex education also depends on who is teaching it (e.g., psychologist, biologist, sociologist, health educator).

Goals of Sex Education

Sex education programs have different goals, depending on who is sponsoring them and where they are conducted. Religious organizations, for example, might identify abstinence as a goal, while some public schools might emphasize responsible decision making. As an example of responsible decision making, Sylvia Schecter (1986) reported on the goals of a "family life education" program implemented throughout the New York City school system from kindergarten through high school:

> These goals are simple—they are the basic 3 r's—respect, responsibility, and reasoned decision. Respect for oneself, one's family and religious values, and one's friends. Responsibility toward oneself, and others. Reasoned decisions—in a society filled with sexually stimulating and often conflicting messages. (p. 57)

Simply teaching them to say no to sex or drugs is not enough. It needs to be linked with other teachings, other learnings, and other life skill opportunities.
Michael Carrera

Other public school sex education programs may emphasize abstinence. In their nationwide study of public school teachers, Forrest and Silverman (1989) noted that "encouraging abstinence is one of the most commonly cited goals of sex education teachers" (p. 69).

"Save Sex" is the message our young people can live with.
Beverly LaHaye

CONSIDERATION: An area of general agreement among parents and teachers is their support for the value of sexual abstinence. Ninety percent of teachers in a national survey reported that they teach abstinence as the best alternative for preventing pregnancy (Alan Guttmacher Institute, 1989, p. 9). Sol Gordon (1986) agreed that teenagers are "too young and too vulnerable" for sexual intercourse and recommends abstinence. However, he suggested that schools be realistic and provide a net for teenagers who choose to be sexually active. Similar to the "don't drink, but if you do drink, don't drive" approach to alcohol, he suggests don't have premarital intercourse, but if you do, use a reliable contraceptive.

CONSIDERATION: Carol Cassell (*former AASECT President*) (1987) noted that it is unrealistic to expect a sex education program to prevent teen pregnancy. She suggested the analogy that having such an expectation is the same as believing that teaching history will prevent war.

Regardless of the reasons, based upon the measured rates of adolescent pregnancies, abortions, and STDs, one is left with the inescapable conclusion that sex education in the United States has fallen far short of achieving its intended goal.
Jeremiah Strouse
Richard Fabes

While such social problems as adolescent pregnancy and HIV transmission should be addressed, Cassell and Wilson (1989) observed that it is a mistake to promote sexuality education by promising to reduce problems. They suggested that the best and most appropriate reasons for sexuality education programs are the following:

- to help prepare people for upcoming stages of development
- to increase comfort with the topic of sexuality
- to increase the attitude that sexuality is a normal and positive part of human existence
- to provide responsible answers to questions and concerns that arise in an age when the media bombards us with sexual messages
- to increase skills that will enable people to live happy, safe, and responsible lives as sexual beings. (Cassell & Wilson, 1989, p. xxiv)

Sex education occurs not only in churches and public schools but also in family planning clinics and public health departments. The U.S. government affects sex education content by requiring those agencies that receive federal funds to promote abstinence as the sexual value for adolescents. In 1990, Congress passed Title X of the Health Services Act and the Adolescent Family Life Act mandating such content.

NATIONAL DATA: About 4.7 million U.S. teenagers are affected by Title X projects (Bullis, 1991).

Self Assessment

A 24-Item Version of the Miller-Fisk Sexual Knowledge Questionnaire (SKQ)

Instructions For each item, select the answer you think is correct and then place an X in front of that option.

1. The single most important factor in achieving pregnancy is:
   a. time of exposure in the cycle
   b. female's desire or wish to become pregnant
   c. frequency of intercourse
   d. female's overall state of health
2. Which of the following is the most dependable (effective) method of contraception or birth control:
   a. condom (male prophylactic)
   b. diaphragm plus jelly or cream
   c. rhythm
   d. pill
3. Following release from the ovary the human ovum (egg) is capable of being fertilized for:
   a. 6 to 12 hours
   b. 24 hours
   c. 48 hours
   d. 4 to 6 days
4. A good index of a female's relative fertility (ability to achieve pregnancy) is:
   a. her overall health
   b. the regularity of her periods
   c. the level of intensity of her sex drive
   d. her ability to achieve orgasm
5. Which of the following methods of contraception is most effective:
   a. condom (male prophylactic)
   b. rhythm
   c. diaphragm plus jelly or cream
   d. intrauterine device (loop or bow)
6. The normal female most often ovulates (gives off egg):
   a. 2 weeks before the onset of menstruation
   b. just prior to menstruation
   c. immediately following menstruation
   d. at unpredictable times throughout the cycle
7. Infertility (inability to achieve pregnancy) is:
   a. familial or inherited
   b. a male problem in one-third of cases
   c. a female problem in 90% of the cases
   d. easily diagnosed after six months of marriage
8. Which of the following is the poorest or least dependable method of contraception:
   a. condom (male prophylactic)
   b. diaphragm
   c. post-intercourse douching
   d. rhythm
9. A normal human ovum (egg) is approximately the same size as:
   a. a pinhead
   b. a small pearl
   c. a dime
   d. none of the above
10. Fertilization (union of sperm and egg) normally occurs in which of the following anatomical locations:
    a. the uterus (womb)
    b. the cervix (mouth of womb)
    c. the tube
    d. the vagina
11. Menopause is a time of:
    a. diminished sexual desire
    b. absolute infertility
    c. rapid aging
    d. altered reproductive and menstrual functioning
12. The rhythm method of contraception is:
    a. always effective
    b. avoidance of intercourse during unsafe (or fertile) times
    c. a technique of intercourse
    d. none of the above
13. Pregnancy would be impossible in early adolescence when menstruation has not yet even begun or is not at all regularly scheduled.
    a. true
    b. false
14. Menstrual blood is similar to a body "poison" or toxin that must be eliminated in order for a woman to remain healthy.
    a. true
    b. false
15. A woman who begins to menstruate on the first Wednesday of every month is "as regular as a clock."
    a. true
    b. false
16. In order to have a normal period there must be a moderate to heavy flow in terms of amount of blood and/or duration of flow.
    a. true
    b. false

Continued

Self-Assessment—*Continued*

17. The loss of one ovary through disease or surgery diminishes a woman's fertility (ability to conceive) little if at all.
a. true
b. false

18. Anatomical differences (i.e., size, shape, capacity, etc.) of the genital organs has a great bearing on sexual compatibility or satisfaction.
a. true
b. false

19. Unplanned or undesired pregnancies have a greater likelihood of miscarrying than do planned pregnancies.
a. true
b. false

20. Failure to have an orgasm on the part of the female eliminates or substantially reduces the likelihood of becoming pregnant.
a. true
b. false

21. Withdrawal is an effective means of contraception (birth control).
a. true
b. false

22. Birth control pills directly increase the sex drive (desire) in most women.
a. true
b. false

23. Sperm retain their ability to fertilize (cause pregnancy) for one to two days following ejaculation (release).
a. true
b. false

24. Most women are more fertile during one particular season of the year than another.
a. true
b. false

Scoring The correct response to each item follows. Your total score is computed by summing the number of correct responses.

1. a.	2. d	3. c	4. b	5. d	6. a	7. b	8. c
9. a	10. c	11. d	12. b	13. b	14. b	15. b	16. b
17. a	18. b	19. b	20. b	21. b	22. b	23. a	24. b

Reliability and validity Analysis of the scores of 209 male and 146 female college students in introductory psychology classes at the University of California at Berkeley revealed odd-even reliability coefficients of 0.67 for the total sample (0.70 for the men, 0.62 for the women) (Gough, 1974). Gough (1988) concluded that sexual knowledge is specific, as it is only moderately related to intellectual aptitude and academic performance. In a sample of 69 college sophomores, he found that SKQ scores correlated 0.12 with high school grades, 0.07 with two-year college grades, 0.18 with the Scholastic Aptitude Test (SAT) verbal score, and 0.22 with SAT quantitative score.

Interpreting your score Gough (1974) found a small difference between the scores of men and women students, favoring the women. The men in the introductory psychology classes obtained a mean SKQ score of 15.51 (SD = 3.77), and the women had a mean of 16.55 (SD = 3.47).

More recently, Werner (1988) studied the relationship of SKQ scores with personality functioning and adjustment. In a study of 200 couples whose names were randomly selected from telephone directories from the San Francisco Bay area, a similar pattern was found, with men scoring a mean value of 16.22 (SD = 3.18) and women a mean of 18.00 (SD = 3.05).

References

Gough, H. G. (1974). A 24-item version of the Miller-Fisk sexual knowledge questionnaire. *Journal of Psychology, 87,* 183–192. Used by permission.

Gough, H. G. (1988). A 24-item version of the Miller-Fisk sexual knowledge questionnaire. In C. M. Davis, W. L. Yarber, & S. L. Davis (Eds.), *Sexuality-related measures: A compendium* (pp. 199–200). Lake Mills, IA: Graphic.

Werner, P. D. (1988). Personality correlates of reproductive knowledge. *Journal of Sex Research, 25,* 219–234.

Source: Used by permission of Harrison G. Gough, Professor of Psychology, Emeritus, University of California–Berkeley.

Extent of Sex Education

Almost all of the states either require or encourage the teaching of sex education in the public schools, and nearly nine in 10 large school districts across the United States support sex education instruction (Kenney, Guardado, & Brown, 1989). Despite the high percentage of schools that teach sex education, only 10% of the respondents in the Forrest and Silverman (1989) study whose schools provide sex education say that it is offered as a separate course. Sex education is usually taught as part of another subject, and it is often taught in more than one subject. The most common course that covers sex education is health education. Other courses that include sex education content are home economics, biology or another science, and physical education.

NATIONAL DATA: In the study by Forrest and Silverman (1989), 93% of the public school teachers surveyed reported that sex education or AIDS education is offered in their school at one or more grade levels. Seventy-seven percent reported that both sex education and AIDS education are provided.

It is also important to keep in mind that each state, rather than the federal government, is responsible for sex education in the public school system. As a result, school systems that offer sex education are highly variable in terms of what they offer. There is considerable variation among the states in grade level, length, and frequency of classroom offerings, as well as approach (Welbourne-Moglia & Moglia, 1989). Table 23.1 reflects state laws regarding sexuality education.

Special Audiences for Sex Education

Individuals with special needs are sometimes provided with specific sex education programs. Such special audiences include intellectually disabled children and adults, and various racial and ethnic groups.

Persons Who Are Intellectually Disabled In the past, sex education for the intellectually impaired, or mentally retarded, focused on hygiene, morality, and prohibitions. More recently, sex education programs in schools, institutions, community service agencies, and homes "help mentally retarded adolescents and adults explore and enjoy this aspect of their humanity appropriately and responsibly" (Patton, Payne, & Beirne-Smith, 1986). Such programs cover the following areas (Patton et al., 1986; Koch, 1992).

1. Issues related to anatomy: Health care, body processes and changes, conception, pregnancy;
2. Means of expression: Masturbation, heterosexuality, homosexuality;
3. Sexual responsibility: Birth control, sexually transmissible diseases, parenthood;
4. Interpersonal relationships: Appropriate behaviors with strangers, friends, boyfriends and girlfriends;
5. Body ownership: The idea that one's body belongs to one's self and the concept of getting, giving, or not giving permission to touch or be touched in various situations.
6. Values, morals, and laws; and
7. Decision-making skills.

Persons with intellectual disability are particularly vulnerable to sex abuse and exploitation. One sex education program for this group uses a "circles concept" whereby students are shown a large set of concentric circles and informed of appropriate touching behavior within each of the six circles. For example, some people (parents) are allowed to hug (those in the second circle), while others are only allowed to shake hands (a new acquaintance) (Walker-Hirsch & Champagne, 1991).

Another program developed by Haseltine and Miltenberger (1990) taught self-protection skills to eight adults with mild retardation. A small-group format across nine 24- to 30-minute sessions used instruction, modeling, rehearsal, feedback, and praise to teach these adults how to discriminate and safely respond to abduction and sexual abuse situations. A six-month follow-up revealed that all but one of the participants learned to express the self-protection skills taught in the program.

Racial and Ethnic Groups Other special audiences are comprised of various ethnic groups. Bowen and Michael-Johnson (1990) noted the importance of sex

TABLE 23.1 Legal Status of Sex Education and HIV and AIDS Education

	MANDATES[1]		RECOMMENDATIONS[2]	
	Sexuality Education	*HIV/AIDS Education*	*Sexuality Education*	*HIV/AIDS Education*
Alabama		•	•	
Alaska			•	•
Arizona		•	•	
Arkansas	•	•		
California		•	•	
Colorado			•	•
Connecticut		•	•	
Delaware	•	•		
District of Columbia	•	•		
Florida	•	•		
Georgia	•	•		
Hawaii			•	•
Idaho		•	•	
Illinois		•	•	
Indiana		•	•	
Iowa	•	•		
Kansas	•	•		
Kentucky			•	•
Louisiana			•	•
Maine			•	•
Maryland	•	•		
Massachusetts				•
Michigan		•	•	
Minnesota		•	•	
Mississippi				•
Missouri			•	•
Montana			•	•
Nebraska			•	•
Nevada	•	•		
New Hampshire		•	•	
New Jersey	•	•		
New Mexico	•	•		
New York		•	•	
North Carolina		•	•	
North Dakota			•	•
Ohio			•	
Oklahoma		•	•	
Oregon		•	•	
Pennsylvania		•	•	
Rhode Island	•	•		
South Carolina	•	•		
South Dakota		•		
Tennessee			•	
Texas			•	•
Utah	•	•		
Vermont	•	•		
Virginia	•	•		
Washington		•	•	
West Virginia	•	•		
Wisconsin			•	•
Wyoming				
TOTAL	17	34	30	14

[1]A state **mandate** is a requirement that all school districts provide sexuality education and/or HIV/AIDS education to their students, usually in the form of family life education programs or comprehensive health education. Mandates are usually accompanied by suggested curricula to be implemented at the local level.

[2]**Recommendations** refer to any provisions by state legislatures or state departments of education, which support sexuality education and/or HIV/AIDS education, but do not require it. While curricula may be suggested, it is left up to the local districts to design and implement such programs.

Source: Haffner, D. W. (1992). 1992 Report card on the states: Sexual rights in America. *SIECUS Report, 20* (3), 1–7. Table appears on p. 3. Used by permission.

educators being aware of the cultural attitudes and beliefs of African-American adolescents in the development of AIDS prevention campaigns for this group. Individuals from lower socioeconomic backgrounds are less likely to use condoms because they are not available in their communities or are poorly promoted (Hansen, Hahn, & Wolkenstein, 1990). Because some ethnic groups are overrepresented in the lower socioeconomic class, the importance of condom use must be promoted in sex education programs for these groups. As we noted in Chapter 18, some Hispanic communities view "the use of condoms as both immoral and contrary to the principles of machismo" (Adler et al., 1991). Sex education programs in these communities face a challenge in changing this negative cultural outlook on condom use.

Attempts to influence Hispanic women to use birth control have had to be sensitive to their values for motherhood, tradition of male dominance, and norms for appropriate sexual expression. Ortiz and Casas (1990) found that Mexican-American women who were willing to use birth control devices were only marginally acculturated into traditional Mexican values.

Sex educators among the Quechua-speaking Indians in a Peruvian community observed that these people had a cultural norm that dictated that sexual matters are not to be discussed between women and men (Maynard-Tucker, 1989). This cultural norm interfered with the goals of sex education.

CONSIDERATION: The dissemination of sex education to a wide audience requires using the language of the consumer. For example, the National AIDS Clearing House (1–800–458–5231) answers phone calls with a recording that is in both English and Spanish. In addition, there are English-, Spanish-, and French-speaking telephone representatives available.

There are 21 million Spanish-speaking Americans, comprising 7% of the U.S. population. Yet only half of 25 brands of condoms provide instructions in Spanish. Manufacturers might consider the Spanish-speaking population in their development of condom literature (Richwald, 1989). In addition, instructions printed on condom packages should take into consideration the reading level of the consumer. A study of the readability of condom instructions included in 25 condom brands sold in the U.S. revealed that all required a 10th-grade reading level, and most required reading at the level of a high school graduate to fully comprehend the instructions (Richwald, Wamsley, Coulson, & Morisky, 1988).

Sources of Sex Education

Duncan and Nicholson (1991) distributed a questionnaire assessing sources of sexual information to 206 women and 182 men enrolled in general education courses at a southeastern state university. For both sexes, the ranking of the various sources of sex information from most to least important was as follows: friends, books, mass media, parents, teachers.

Parents

Parents have traditionally been inadequate sources of sex education for their children (Reis & Seidl, 1989). Gordon (1986, p. 22) reported that less than 15% of over 8,000 students reported that they received a "meaningful sex education" from their parents. The obstacles that parents face as sex educators for their children include (Jaccard & Dittus, 1991; Valentich & Gripton, 1989):

1. Parents fear that telling their children about sex will promote premature sexual activity.
2. Parents feel insecure about their own level of sexual knowledge and do not know what words to use when talking about sex to their children.

Parents who have open communication with their children are more likely to have children who delay having first intercourse and who use contraception once they become sexually involved.

3. Parents sometimes feel anxious about breaking the incest taboo by presenting themselves as sexual persons (and thereby acknowledging the possibility of sexual arousal between family members).
4. Parents fear disapproval of friends and relatives for not reaffirming traditional sexual values. An example of a sexual value that some parents feel obligated to uphold is referred to by Valentich and Gripton (1989) as the "normative space myth." This myth suggests that sexual activity occurs only under very limited conditions—"through genital stimulation, during sexual intercourse, between legally married heterosexual partners under the age of 50 using the missionary position initiated by the male preferably for procreation ending in orgasm for the male and perhaps for the female" (p. 94). The reality, that sex includes nongenital caressing, masturbation, oral sex, premarital sex, homosexual sex, elderly sex, and so on, may generate greater discomfort for the parent.
5. Parents feel that their teenage child will learn about sex and birth control from other sources, so the parent doesn't need to talk about it.

Because of these obstacles, most parents avoid talking with their children about sex. When "parents" do talk about sex, the parent is more often the mother, and she is most likely to talk about the menstrual cycle, how pregnancy occurs, and birth control methods (Dawson, 1986). Beyond such instruction, the "rest of the teaching could be summed up in one word: 'DON'T' " (Gordon, 1986, p. 22).

CONSIDERATION: What parents don't say about sex they often model behaviorally. Single and divorced parents may become involved in a series of dating and/or sexual relationships that reflect the implicit value of sex outside of marriage. Strouse and Fabes (1985) suggested that "divorced and single parents need to be more discrete about their adult sexual liaisons" (p. 260).

Continued

Continued

However, Lewis and Janda (1988) suggested that "it seems that the attitudes toward sex that parents convey to their children may be more important to their subsequent sexual adjustment than any particular family practice" (p. 359). This conclusion was based on data provided by 77 male and 133 female undergraduates in regard to their comfort level in talking with their father and mother about sex.

Whereas many parents provide virtually no sex education for their children, other parents (as reported by adolescents) provide a context of open communication with their children. In this context, adolescents report greater discussion of an array of sexual topics with parents (Baldwin & Baranoski, 1990). In addition, Fisher (1987) observed that when parents are open about sex with their children, the children are more likely to adopt the attitudes and values of the parents. In addition, researchers have found that parents who talk to their teenagers about sex are more likely to have children who delay having first intercourse and to use contraception once they become sexually involved (Akpom, Akpom, & Davis, 1976; Lewis, 1973).

One study of 179 black women concluded that mothers are the most important source of sexual socialization of teenagers (particularly in black families) and that family planning educators and practitioners should focus on the information about sexual matters that mothers are disseminating to their adolescent children (Tucker, 1990).

Nolin and Petersen (1992) found striking gender differences in parent-child communication about sexuality. Eighty-four mother-father-adolescent triads participated by completing questionnaires, and some joined in focus group discussions. Parental communication with daughters covered more topics, especially factual and moral topics. Substantial differences were found between mothers and fathers as communicators, with mothers more likely to discuss birth control, adolescent pregnancy, and sexual morality issues. "Therefore, sons were less likely than daughters to learn about sexuality in the context of a family relationship, less likely to discuss sexual topics with the same sex parent, and perhaps less likely to learn family norms for appropriate sexual behavior" (p. 69). The adolescents in the focus groups reported that in their dating relationships it is the boys who hold the balance of power in making sexual decisions. Nolen and Petersen noted that since boys have little communication with fathers, and limited discussion with mothers regarding sexuality, they may be especially susceptible to the influence of their peers. These family communication patterns may be the result of, and function to perpetuate, a sexual double standard.

Some parents elect to become involved in a sex education program designed to promote communication with their adolescents about various sexual topics. One study compared parents who participated in four two-hour sessions designed to promote parent-adolescent communication with a control group. A postcourse follow-up questionnaire revealed that parents in the training group discussed an average of 11 topics with their adolescents, in contrast to the parents in the control group, who discussed about three topics (Huston, Martin, & Foulds, 1990).

Still another sex education program for parents focuses on teaching them to develop comfort in using sexual terms and skills in talking with their children about sex (Bundy & White, 1990). Reports from parents who participated in this program indicated improvement in their talking with their children about sex. Other sex education courses focusing on adolescent-parent communication have been successful in increasing such communication between adolescents and their parents (Green & Sollie, 1989). The Choices section at the end of this chapter discusses further how parents can be effective sex educators for their children.

Friends

Teenagers learn much more powerful messages about sexuality in the halls, locker rooms, and playing fields than they do in their health classes.

Debra W. Haffner

Since friends are a major source of sex education for adolescent youth (Strouse & Fabes, 1985), attempts have been made by sex educators to involve student peers in sex education programs. One such program was used at the Henry W. Grady Memorial Hospital in Atlanta in which older teenagers helped younger students resist peer and social pressure. Follow-up based on telephone interviews with 536 students revealed that those who had not had intercourse at the time of the sex education program were more likely to continue to be abstinent through the end of the ninth grade than were similar students who did not participate in the program.

Strouse, Krajewski, and Gilin (1990) used undergraduate students as peer discussion facilitators in human sexuality classes at Central Michigan University. Data from 417 students enrolled in four sections revealed that 42% listed the "discussion groups" as the best feature of the course (p. 233).

One variation of peer sex education involves adolescents talking to other adolescents who have been pregnant and/or who have had a sexually transmissible disease. Campbell and Campbell (1990) emphasized that because adolescents have a short-term perspective, peers may be particularly important.

> It seems reasonable to adults that one should place high value on future health consequences of one's behavior. To the adolescent, long-term consequences of current actions may be too remote and abstract to effectively guide current behavior. (p. 187)

School Teachers

Because sexual decision-making skills are largely based upon personal values and feelings about certain issues, just teaching the facts is not enough.

Jeremiah Strouse
Laurice Krajewski
Shannon Gilin

NATIONAL DATA: About 50,000 public school teachers in the United States reported providing sex education in grades seven through 12 in 1987–1988 (Forrest & Silverman, 1989). Their teaching specialties were physical education (31%), health education (26%), home economics (23%), and biology (17%); 3% were school nurse (Glazer, 1989).

As noted earlier, when public school teachers were asked what message they most wanted to give their students, they noted the importance of responsibility regarding sexual relationships and parenthood, the importance of abstinence, and the ways of resisting pressures to become sexually active. The teachers also stressed the importance of AIDS education (Forrest & Silverman, 1989).

Teachers tend to favor providing students with information about where they can obtain effective contraception. Ninety-seven percent of the teachers in the Forrest and Silverman (1989) study said that sex education classes should make students aware of where they can obtain a method of contraception. However, due to some schools wanting to avoid the perception that they are encouraging teenagers to have sex, only 48% reported that this is done in their school.

Teachers often do not feel adequate to teach sex education (Jackson, 1989). Out of 32 supervisors of high school health education classes in the 50 school districts in southern New Jersey, none indicated that the teachers "responsible for teaching the units on AIDS and STD education are specialists in sex education" (Calamidas, 1990, p. 57).

In the Forrest and Silverman study (1989), 89% of the teachers who taught sex education reported that they had undergone training that specifically prepared them to teach sex education. However, the primary identity of these teachers was as a teacher of a subject other than sex education. Almost none of the teachers in this study was certified as a sex educator by the American Association of Sex Educators, Counselors, and Therapists or the National Council on Family Relations.

Although children in the elementary and middle grades receive some exposure to sex education, adolescent junior high school youth represent the primary target of sex education.

Teachers at the elementary school level feel unprepared and need specific instruction to prepare them for AIDS and HIV education. A study of 47 sixth-grade sex education teachers revealed that they gave correct answers to an average of 70% of the questions on a sex knowledge inventory (Gingiss & Hamilton, 1989). Sex education teachers in grades seven through 12 also lack complete and accurate knowledge regarding sexuality concerns.

About 10% of the teachers in the Forrest and Silverman (1989) study indicated that they have personal difficulties teaching sex education: "They feel that they have been inadequately trained, or they experience conflicts with their personal values, or they find it difficult to be objective about what they are teaching" (p. 71). These difficulties may be overcome by additional training. A study of 59 middle-school teachers showed that an inservice training course on sex education increased their knowledge about human sexuality and their level of comfort in teaching the subject (Levenson-Gingiss & Hamilton, 1989).

CONSIDERATION: The lack of training of teachers in sex education is severe. Dr. Mary Krueger (1991) of the Department of Health Education at Emory University in Atlanta noted that there are "no accredited undergraduate degree programs in sexuality education at any American university, and only two accredited graduate programs" (p. 1). She emphasized the need to "lobby for compulsory teacher training provisions as attachments to all sexuality education mandated legislation" (p. 3).

Insufficient training is not the only obstacle facing sex education teachers in public schools. The most common problem in teaching sex education reported by teachers in the Forrest and Silverman (1989) study was pressure or lack of support from parents, the community, or the school administration. Another problem reported by these teachers was the lack of adequate teaching materials. Twenty-five percent of the teachers reported that "one of their biggest problems is with the students themselves, who do not feel free to talk about or are embarrassed by sex education topics" (Forrest & Silverman, 1989, p. 70).

Sexuality courses are popular at the college level. Polyson, Lash, and Evans (1986) surveyed 1980–83 catalogs for 225 randomly selected colleges and universities. They found that 41% of the colleges offered at least one human sexuality course. Psychology departments were most likely to offer the courses; 44% were in psychology departments, 20% in sociology departments, 14% in health and physical education. Additionally, 7% were offered in nursing departments, 6% in home economics, 5% in biology, and 3% in other departments. The larger colleges and universities were more likely to offer the courses, with no difference between religiously affiliated institutions and nonaffiliated.

Family Planning Clinic Personnel

Sex education specific to contraception and STDs is also provided by family planning clinics. Such clinics may be part of a state health department or independent agencies. Planned Parenthood of Toronto is an example of the latter, which provides information on anatomy, physiology, methods of birth control, sexually transmissible diseases, and general health concerns. Todres (1990) compared the effectiveness of lay volunteers and public health personnel and found that individuals who came to the clinic learned equal amounts of knowledge independent of the source.

Religion

While religious denominations vary in what they teach about sex, the Catholic Church has traditionally condemned premarital sex, the use of condoms, and other uses of birth control. However, ". . . in Seattle, it appears that administrators of many Catholic and other private religious schools are attempting a much more delicate balance—emphasizing abstinence while giving youngsters who are sexually active the facts about condoms and safe sex practices" (Ostrom, 1987, p. 6).

Advocates of religion-based sex education programs believe that such programs are important for providing comprehensive discussion of sexual issues, with emphasis on a values framework. Powell and Jorgensen (1985) described a short–term church-based program which was documented (using a pre-posttest control group design) as resulting in increases in sex information and clarity of personal sexual values. The long-term effects of a church-based program to promote sexuality communication between adolescents, their parents, and peers were measured by Green and Sollie (1989). They found an increase in 14 to 15 year-old adolescents' self-disclosure to their mothers and fathers and foster parents. Allen-Meares (1989) proposed that the black church should take a leadership role in developing educational programs that include sexual development from childhood through adolescence.

Curricula have been developed to present human sexuality as a divine gift to be celebrated and to offer religious guidance for its expression. For example, R. Kenneth Ostermiller (1991), a United Church of Christ minister, has prepared a booklet for parents to help them talk about sexuality with a child under the age of 12. A bibliography of religious publications on sexuality and sex education is available from SIECUS.

The division between religious and educational instruction about sex is not always clear. *Sex Respect: The Option of True Sexual Freedom* (Mast, 1986) is a religiously oriented sex education manual designed for use in the public school system. This manual encourages middle and high school-age students to avoid all sexual activity (including necking and petting) until marriage as a means of preventing unplanned teenage pregnancy and sexually transmissible diseases. Educators Trudell and Whatley (1991) criticized this approach on several grounds:

1. Although marketed as a "public health manual," the orientation is religious.
2. The approach uses guilt to promote premarital chastity.
3. Abortion is not presented as an alternative for a premarital pregnancy.
4. The approach is presented as one that "works." Yet there is insufficient documentation of this claim.

Media

Young people are exposed to an array of messages about sexuality through the media. These include popular music, television, and magazines.

Popular Music Sexual themes permeate popular music. Some examples follow:

Girl you make me feel so good,
I just wanna, I just wanna get you.
Don't say anything at all,
Just lay back, enjoy the ride.
Ooh, I want to sex you up. by Color Me Badd
Push it, push it real good. by Salt-N-Pepa
You can do me in the morning,
You can do me in the night,
You can do me when you wanna do me,
Anytime is alright. by Bell Biv Devoe

> The media could do much to improve the sex education of teenagers and adults by balancing descriptions of pleasures of sexual activity against the need for neither party to be exploited and the problems of planning effective contraception.
> *Royal College of Obstetricians and Gynaecologists*

Researchers St. Lawrence and Joyner (1991) looked at the effects of sexually violent rock music on men's acceptance of violence against women. Based on an experimental study of 75 male undergraduate students at a southern university, the researchers reported that "exposure to heavy-metal rock music increased males' sex-role stereotyping irrespective of its lyrical content" (p. 59).

Aware of the potential for popular music to reach sexually active teenagers, two popular songs with cautionary messages about young love were produced by a commercial recording company and played as background music on a telephone hotline staffed by experienced counselors (Silayan-Go, 1990). The musical approach was begun out of fear of the alarming increase in premarital pregnancies among Filipino teenagers.

> It is bad enough that people are dying of AIDS, but no one should die of ignorance.
> *Elizabeth Taylor*

Television Television is a major source of values and information for young people. With few exceptions, television portrays sexuality as "distorted, recreation-oriented, exploitive, casual activity, without dealing with the consequences" (Strouse & Fabes, 1985, p. 255). Television is "full of antisexual messages of rape, violence and infidelity" (Gordon, 1986, p. 24). For example, Lowry and Towles (1989) studied the content of afternoon soap operas and observed that, since 1979, there has been a substantial increase in sex between unmarried persons. In addition, the soap operas nurture the norm of promiscuous sex with few consequences (Lowry & Towles, 1989). Music videos (such as shown on MTV) also provide a continuous theme of sexuality.

Television commercials often have sexual messages. The Center for Science in the Public Interest gives annual awards for the most "unfair, misleading and irresponsible" ads. In 1991, one of these awards went to Old Milwaukee beer for its "Swedish bikini team" spots, which visually associated sexual conquest with drinking.

That "sex sells" is known throughout the advertising industry.

CONSIDERATION: More recently, the television industry has begun to use its powerful medium to encourage more responsible sexual choices. For example, the theme of a 1991 episode of *"Beverly Hills, 90210"* emphasized that forcing sexual activity with a dating partner is wrong. In addition, each year the Center for Population Options sponsors the Nancy Susan Reynolds Awards to honor television programs for outstanding portrayals of sexuality, family planning, and reproductive health. In 1990, there were 64 entries ("CPO Honors," 1991).

Magazines Magazines are an important source of information about sexuality. They regularly feature articles about sexuality and sexual relationships. Examples of recent magazines and lead articles include *Cosmopolitan* ("Women Who Say Yes to Sex But No to Love"), *Mademoiselle* ("The Best Friends in Life Are Gay Men"), *Glamour* ("Sex and Health"), and *Redbook* ("Too Tired for Sex").

Magazines also provide information about sexually transmissible diseases. In a study of 608 undergraduate psychology students attending the University of North Carolina at Wilmington or the University of Georgia, 58% reported that their primary source of information about genital herpes was from magazines (Bruce & Bullins, 1989). In December 1991, *Newsweek* reported that it had published 11 cover stories on AIDS (Adler et al., 1991).

Pornography

A frequently unacknowledged source of sex information is pornography. In the study by Duncan and Nicholson (1991), women ranked pornography seventh out of seven sources; men ranked pornography sixth out of seven sources (ahead of church). However, when asked whether pornography contributed to their knowledge of 10 sexual topics, 38% of the women and 54% of the men reported that pornography had contributed to their knowledge of oral-anal sex. Other topics about which they learned more information from pornography were masturbation, anatomy, and foreplay. Negative messages about sexuality are also conveyed in pornographic material; these are discussed in Chapter 19.

Effects of Sex Education

Does sex education result in increased premarital pregnancies, abortions, HIV infections, and other STDs? Does sex education result in fewer premarital pregnancies and lower HIV and STD infection rates? Or does sex education have no effects on the sexual behavior of youth? Next, we look at some research on the effects of sex education on knowledge, behavior, attitudes, contraceptive usage, and premarital pregnancy.

Effect on Knowledge

Sex education programs usually increase the knowledge that participants have about human sexuality (Stiff, 1990; Isberner, 1990; Kirby, 1989). Some evidence suggests that the knowledge may be retained for up to two years. Researchers in a rural South Carolina school found that a 12-unit reproductive health course in the ninth grade not only increased knowledge but that this knowledge was sustained at a two-year follow-up (Thomas et al., 1985).

Not all individuals exposed to a sex education course learn or retain the information. Gerrard, Kurylo, and Reis (1991) found that not only do some students actively avoid exposure to sex information (cut classes) but they also "tune out" information that may arouse too much fear or anxiety. In a study of undergraduate psychology students, those who had high self-esteem and who were erotophobic were much less likely to retain contraceptive and AIDS information presented in class than low-self esteem and erotophilic students, who both learned and retained the sexual material. The researchers concluded that those with high-self esteem do not want to expose themselves to any information that may threaten their positive self-concept (e.g., they are at risk for getting an STD or AIDS). Students who were erotophobic felt the need to "tune out" content that created anxiety. Low-self esteem individuals were not threatened by sexual information and had no anxiety in reference to it. Hence, they were comfortable learning and retaining the information.

Effects on Sexual Behaviors

Studies differ in regard to the effects of sex education on subsequent sexual behavior.

Sex Education Is Not Associated with Behavior Change Several studies fail to show any link between exposure to sex education content and subsequent behavior change. In a review of various studies, Stout and Rivara (1989) and Kirby (1989) observed that there is little or no effect from school-based sex education on sexual activity. Gray and Saracino (1989) also found that there is no relationship between increased knowledge and changes in sexual behavior. Their study was based on information provided by 459 undergraduates in regard to their perceptions of AIDS risk and sexual behavior. Similarly, Dawson's (1986) national study on teenage women revealed "no consistent relationship between exposure to contraceptive education and subsequent initiation of intercourse" (p. 169).

Marsiglio and Mott (1986) analyzed data on over 6,000 women and men and concluded that sex education has little, if any, impact on the timing of first intercourse. Variables that do seem related to first intercourse at an early age include infrequent church attendance, having parents with less than 12 years of education, and being black.

CONSIDERATION: Based on information provided by 208 adolescents in both public and private (Catholic) high schools, Cullari and Mikus (1990) identified curiosity, need for love, and peer pressure as the primary motivations for having intercourse and fear of pregnancy and STDs and AIDS as primary reasons for avoiding such activity. One of the reasons sex education courses may not result in behavior change is that these motivations are difficult to counter. Satisfying sexual curiosity, meeting students' need for love (or teaching them that sex does not equal love), and developing skills to cope with peer pressure are very difficult goals for sex education programs to achieve. In addition, Gordon (1990) noted that effective sex education must include enhancing self-esteem, reducing drug use, and preventing students from dropping out of school. These are also very difficult goals to achieve.

Another reason that sex education may not affect teenagers' decisions about sex and birth control is that it may come too late. Marsiglio and Mott (1986) reported that of those who begin sex by age 18, no more than half have had a course, and no more than two-fifths have had instruction on birth control.

Exhibit 23.1 reveals why 866 French and English students attending seven Montreal colleges continued to engage in high-risk sexual behavior in spite of their knowledge about AIDS.

EXHIBIT 23.1 Why AIDS Risk-Taking Behavior Continues

Based on completed questionnaires and interviews of 866 undergraduates, Maticka-Tyndale (1991) concluded, "Interviewees generally did not perceive themselves as susceptible to infection with HIV, even when their personal sexual activities exposed them to a large degree of risk, and when they demonstrated knowledge of this risk in response to questions about HIV transmission" (p. 61). Reasons students continued such high-risk behavior included:

1. Denial. Students felt that the risk of contracting the AIDS virus was low and that they would not contract it. They also believed that "AIDS is hard to get."
2. Partner selection. "The most popular prophylactic for these young adults was the selection of noninfected sexual partners" (Maticka-Tyndale, 1991, p. 62). Students believed that they could identify an infected partner and that they were safe from HIV transmission due to their careful choice of sexual partners.
3. No direct exposure to AIDS victims. Most of the students did not know someone who had AIDS or who had been tested for HIV. This lack of direct exposure to persons with HIV or AIDS contributes to the assumption that only people in other social circles get infected with the AIDS virus.
4. Condoms are viewed as contraceptives. No student who used, or whose partner used, oral contraceptives also used condoms. When the pill was being used, there was no perceived need to use a condom.

CONSIDERATION: Glazer (1989) argued that even if exposure to sex education courses isn't immediately associated with behavior changes, sex education is still worthwhile. Advocates note that "it often takes a long time, possibly several generations, to influence people's behavior in any kind of public-health campaign, whether it be smoking habits, nutrition or birth control" (p. 42)

Sex Education Is Associated with Behavior Change In contrast to those studies showing no effect of sex education programs on subsequent sexual behaviors, other studies demonstrate that there are behavioral changes. For example, Davidson and Darling (1988) compared masturbation behavior of female college students who were exposed to sex education lectures on masturbation in a marriage and family class with those who had no similar exposure. Based on a two-year follow-up, the researchers found that those women who were exposed to sex education lectures on masturbation increased their masturbatory behavior more than did the women in the control group.

Some research suggests that young people who are exposed to sex education are more likely to postpone sexual involvement. Howard and McCabe (1990) reported that eighth-grade students who had been involved in a sex education program led by older teenagers were more likely to continue abstinence than similar eighth-grade students who had not been involved in the program.

In another controlled study of 1,444 males and females aged 13 to 19 who were exposed to sex education programs, the males who had never had intercourse were more likely to remain abstinent for the 12 months following the program. No such effect was observed for the females (Eisen, Zellman, & McAlister, 1990).

Two researchers (Warzak & Page, 1990) provided some evidence for the effectiveness of "refusal skills training" in a group of sexually active handicapped female adolescents. Various scenarios were role-played within the framework of rationale, modeling, rehearsal, feedback, and reinforcement. A one-year follow-up showed decreased sexual activity by each participant.

A study of 1,444 male and female 13-19-year-olds who had sex education instruction, revealed that such instruction was associated with increased use of contraception.

A team of researchers (Cohen, Dent, & MacKinnon, 1991) also demonstrated that behavioral change followed a condom skills education program. Ninety-seven individuals who came to a public health sexually transmissible disease clinic in Los Angeles attended a condom skills education program at the clinic. These individuals were compared with 95 others who also came to the clinic for treatment of STDs but did not attend the condom skills education program. Most were black (70%), single (90%), and heterosexual (97%) (Cohen et al., 1991, p. 141).

The condom skills program consisted of a health educator providing information about condoms in a group setting. The lecture portion emphasized three points: 1) use condoms made of latex, 2) use condoms that are lubricated with the spermicide nonoxynol-9, and 3) use condoms with a reservoir tip or space left at the end. A poster was provided that displayed different types of unwrapped condoms full length and the accompanying package to provide easy identification. To demonstrate how the condom was put on (see Figure 23.1), the health educator used her hand as a "proxy phallus and stretched the condom in all directions to show that 'one size fits all' " (Cohen et al., 1991, p. 140).

> A properly used condom will give the user at least 0.03 mm of protection, and that could be the difference between life and death.
>
> *William Darrow*

One year after the demonstration, the groups who did and did not attend the condom skills education program were compared. Ten percent of those who attended the program were reinfected and returned to the clinic for treatment, in contrast to 20 percent of those who did not attend the program.

A comprehensive approach to AIDS and sex education was shown to effect a modest, but significant decrease in recent sexual activity, along with an increase in condom use, among teenage men (Ku, Sonenstein & Pleck, 1992). The young men who had had AIDS education reported fewer partners and less frequent intercourse within the previous year. Consistent with results of other studies,

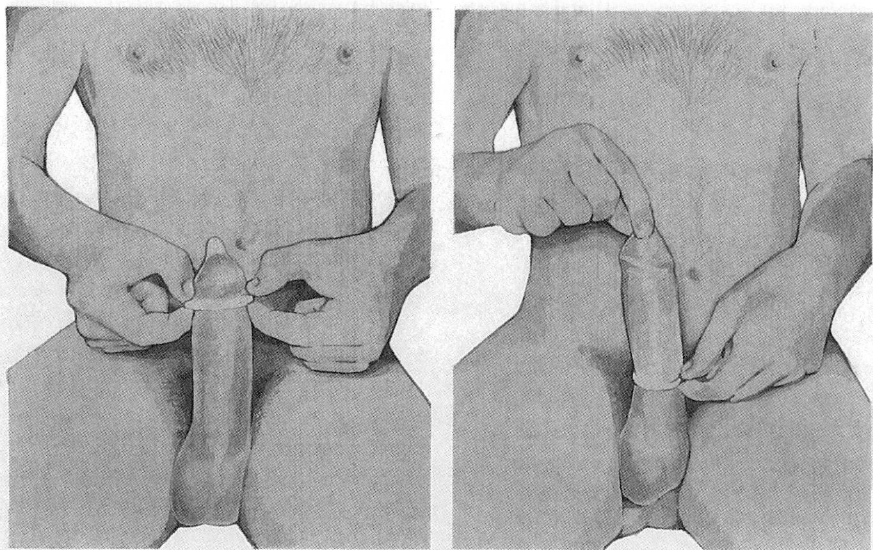

FIGURE 23.1 Using a condom
Roll the rim of the condom to the base of the penis before inserting the penis into the vagina, leaving a reservoir at the tip to accommodate ejaculated sperm. After ejaculation, immediately withdraw the penis, holding the condom near the base of the penis to prevent semen from seeping out.

instruction in the skills involved in resisting sexual intercourse were more helpful in reducing sexual activity than AIDS education or birth control instruction alone.

Decision-making behavior may also be affected by exposure to sex education. Alemi, Cherry, and Meffert (1989) developed a computer game to simulate various sexual decision-making scenarios. They have suggested that playing this computer game improves decision-making skills.

Effects on Attitudes

Weis, Rabinowitz, and Ruckstuhl (1992) assessed the attitudes of 48 male and 124 female college students before and after they took a human sexuality course. Examples of attitude topics included acceptance of intercourse under conditions of affection, love, and engagement and approval of masturbation, homosexuality, and abortion. Results indicated that sexual attitudes became more permissive during the period of the course. Permissive attitude changes were particularly noted among individuals who "were members of social groups with restricted sexual norms (females, younger age, residence with parents)" (p. 56).

Davidson and Darling (1988) found that university women who had been exposed to information about masturbation in a marriage and family class were much more likely to be approving and accepting of masturbation. When compared with women at the same university who had not taken the marriage and family course, the women in the experimental group were more likely to approve of masturbation among their female and male acquaintances, to view masturbation in marriage as not indicative of poor sexual adjustment, and to regard masturbation as a healthy practice.

In an earlier study, Gunderson and McCary (1980) found that students who had taken a course in human sexuality became more tolerant of sexual practices that differed from their own and became less tolerant of the sexual double standard. In addition, taking a course in human sexuality was not shown to result in students rejecting traditional values of sex with love, monogamy, and fidelity.

Effects on Contraceptive Usage

Researchers disagree on whether sex education programs increase the consistent use of effective contraception. In a review of five studies, Stout and Rivara (1989) observed that there is little or no effect from school-based sex education on the use of contraception. Taylor (1989) also found that male adolescents who were exposed to brief or moderately in-depth contraceptive education did not alter their contraceptive behavior. Similarly, Zelnik and Kim (1982) found that students who had taken a sex education course were no more likely to use condoms or other contraceptives than students who had not taken such a course.

CONSIDERATION: Most adults know that they should use their seat belts while driving, exercise regularly, and avoid smoking cigarettes. Despite this knowledge, many adults continue to drive without a seat belt, live the life of a "couch potato," and smoke cigarettes. Similarly, teenagers know that they should use an effective contraceptive if they have intercourse, yet this knowledge often does not affect contraceptive behavior (Helge, 1990).

NATIONAL DATA: Seventy-three percent of the teenagers in a national study who had had a sex education course used an effective contraceptive, in contrast to 64% who had not had a sex education course (Marsiglio & Mott, 1986).

Boys should be educated about their role in family responsibilities including family planning and childrearing. They should learn to respect people including girls and women, and to be responsible for their actions.

Nafis Sadik

The results of some studies suggest that sex education increases contraceptive usage among teenagers. A study of 1,444 male and female 13- to 19-year-olds who had sex education instruction increased their use of an effective contraceptive, and this usage was maintained at a one-year follow-up (Eisen et al., 1990). This finding held true independent of the type of sex education program in which the adolescent had been involved. A previous national study found that teenagers who have taken a sex education course are significantly more likely to use effective contraceptive methods (e.g., pill, condom, diaphragm, IUD) than are teenagers who have never taken a sex education course (Marsiglio & Mott, 1986).

In another national study of teenage females (ages 15 to 19), those who were sexually active and who had had formal sex education were more likely to use contraception than the sexually active teenage females who had not had formal instruction in sex education (Dawson, 1986).

Effect on Teenage Pregnancy

U.S. taxpayers spent over $21 billion in federal monies in 1989 to support families begun by teenage mothers. "Clearly, the cost of unintended teen pregnancy is too great in dollars and much too great in compromised lives" (Senderowitz, 1991, p. 2).

In Arkansas, we're going to put the father's social security numbers on birth certificates. Any time he works, he's going to have to pay a percentage of his salary to his children.

Joycelyn Elders

While sex education programs are regarded as one means of preventing unintended teen pregnancies, in a review of five studies, Stout and Rivara (1989) observed that there is little or no effect from school-based sex education on teenage pregnancy. Marsiglio and Mott (1986) analyzed national data on teenagers and reached the same conclusion: ". . . it is clear that attendance at a sex education course in no way increases a young woman's probability of becoming pregnant" (p. 160).

CONSIDERATION: We should not be surprised at the limited effects of formal sex education on sexual knowledge, attitudes, and behavior. Formal sex education programs are only one source of sex education that must compete with peers, media, and parents as other influences on sexual knowledge, attitudes, and behaviors. To expect that a time-limited course in sex education will override these other socialization forces may be unrealistic. However, sex education programs coupled with access to birth control in the school system does result in fewer teen pregnancies in those schools (Zabin, Hirsch, Smith, Streett, & Hardy, 1986; Kirby, 1984).

In the following Research Perspective we review the types of sexuality education curricula which have been developed in the United States in the last two decades. Some of the recent curricula have yielded promising results!

RESEARCH PERSPECTIVE

The Fourth Generation of Sex Education Curricula

Over the last 15 years, virtually hundreds of sex education curricula have been presented in junior and senior high schools, with the goal of reducing the high rate of adolescent pregnancies. Kirby, Barth, Leland and Fetro (1991) suggested that, although varied in their approaches, these programs can be loosely grouped into four generations. The emphases of these four generations of curricula are reviewed in this Perspective, and two programs of the fourth generation are profiled.

First Generation: Reproductive Knowledge

The first generation of sex education programs focused on the dissemination of reproductive knowledge, emphasizing the risks and consequences of pregnancy. Kirby et al. observed that the underlying premise in this focus was that if adolescents knew more about sexual intercourse, pregnancy risks and consequences, and birth control, then they would choose not to have unprotected intercourse. While many sex education programs can demonstrate increases in knowledge, that is often insufficient in bringing about changes in behavior. Thus, the emphasis on reproductive knowledge, referred to by Sol Gordon (1983, p. 393), a prominent sexuality educator, as "the relentless pursuit of the fallopian tubes," expanded to include other sexuality concerns.

Second Generation: Decision-Making and Communication Skills

The second generation of curricula still imparted reproductive information but added attention to values clarification, communication skills, and general decision-making skills. The underlying premise in this focus is that if adolescents had clearer values and stronger decision-making skills, they would be less likely to engage in risk-taking behavior. With improved communication skills, adolescents could more effectively communicate their sexual decisions to their partner. According to Kirby et al. (1991), research on the effects of these programs has yielded mixed results but, in general, has shown no dramatic reduction in risk-taking behavior or teenage pregnancy, although contraceptive use may have been slightly increased.

Third Generation: Abstinence Programs

In reaction to the "value-free" second-generation programs, the third generation of sex education curricula emphasized a "Just Say No" theme. These programs teach the value that sexual intercourse is only acceptable within one's marriage. Many of these programs do not include a discussion of contraception to try to avoid the possibility of communicating an endorsement of teenage sexual activity. Programs such as Teen Aid and Sex Respect show short-term attitude change toward less acceptance of premarital intercourse, but long-term effects did not persist or were not measured. Kirby et al. reported that no data have been presented to confirm that abstinence programs delay intercourse or prevent pregnancy.

Fourth Generation: Theoretical and Research-Based Models

The fourth generation of sex education curricula combines aspects of the prior efforts. These programs do not employ the smorgasbord approach, in which choices and information are laid out so that young people might freely choose among them

Continued.

Continued

The implicit and expressed values are that (a) young people are better off delaying sexual intercourse until they are older, and (b) when one does begin having intercourse, an effective method of contraception should be used. Furthermore, these programs are based upon theoretical approaches shown to be effective in influencing other health behaviors, and more rigorous evaluation is used to document effectiveness. An example of a fourth-generation sex education program is the Postponing Sexual Involvement program, described in the Research Perspective in Chapter 12.

Reducing the Risk Another fourth-generation program is Reducing the Risk (RTR). Kirby et al. described the program and published an evaluation of the effects for 586 program participants in 123 California high schools. RTR establishes and reinforces the norm that young people should avoid unprotected intercourse, either by abstaining from sex or by using contraception. The theoretical approaches upon which this program is based include: social learning theory, social inoculation theory, and cognitive behavior theory. Social learning theory emphasizes observational learning. Therefore, a modeling component is included in RTR. Teachers and classroom peers model behaviors (such as avoiding unwanted intercourse), and students rehearse those behaviors through role-playing.

To help develop a resistance to social pressure, social inoculation involves discussing social pressures to have sex, identifying "lines" that are used to talk a person into having sex, and developing strategies and skills to resist the pressures. Students repeatedly role-play, first with much scripting, then with less assistance, discussions about abstinence and birth control.

Cognitive behavior theory includes elements from the previous two models. As applied in RTR, cognitive behavior components include activities to (a) personalize information about sexuality, birth control, and reproduction; (b) practice assertive communication and decision-making skills, and (c) rehearse the application of these skills and knowledge in challenging situations. The situations include obtaining contraceptive information from stores and clinics and other ways to reduce unsafe behavior.

RTR can be used in conjunction with a more comprehensive sexuality education curriculum. It lasts 15 class periods and is taught by classroom teachers. It is also designed to spark parent-child discussion and includes an assignment that requires students to find out their parents' views on abstinence and birth control.

In evaluating the educational and behavioral outcomes of RTR, the researchers found that in comparison to control students, those who participated in RTR showed a significant increase in contraceptive knowledge. Eighteen months after the program, there was a 24% reduction in initiation of intercourse in the RTR students. Contrary to the fears of some critics of the program, there was no evidence of increased intercourse as a result of RTR. Among students not already sexually active prior to the program, there was a reduction of unprotected intercourse when they did begin sexual activity. These results are very similar to the results for the Postponing Sexual Involvement program, and together, they suggest that it may be easier to help students delay sexual intercourse than to increase contraceptive use. The results confirmed that programs such as RTR are helpful components in a comprehensive sexuality education program.

The School/Community Program Kirby et al. (1991) acknowledged that more complete solutions to reducing teenage pregnancy include the school, parents, and the community. Another program that fits in the category of fourth-generation

Continued

Continued

sexuality programs and includes a strong school-family-community link is the School/Community Program for Sexual Risk Reduction Among Teens (Vincent,Clearie, & Schluchter, 1987). The program was implemented in a South Carolina county that ranked in the top 20% of the state's counties for estimated pregnancies among girls 14 to 17 years old. The program was based on a public health model and employed multiple strategies: knowledge regarding human reproduction, physiology, and contraception; self-esteem enhancement; improving decision-making and communication skills; and aligning student's personal values with those of the family, church, and community.

The goal of the School/Community Program was to decrease unintended teen pregnancy. Trained teachers from kindergarten through grade 12 taught the program in what is called an integrated curriculum approach. In other words, there is not a separate "sex education" class, but sexuality information was woven into the lessons in biology, science, social studies, and other relevant areas. In addition, clergy, church leaders, and parents were recruited to attend training sessions.

Examination of pregnancy rates for girls aged 14 to 17 in the western portion of the county in which the intervention was implemented showed striking results. Compared to the eastern portion of the county and to similar counties, there was a sustained decline in estimated pregnancy rate two to three years after the School/Community Program was implemented. Vincent et al. encouraged other researchers to replicate the project elsewhere and determine whether similar results can be realized. Given the successes of Postponing Sexual Involvement, Reducing the Risk, and the School/Community Program, the fourth-generation curricula seem to offer promising models for addressing the significant problems of adolescents' exposure to risks from early sexual involvement.

References

Gordon, S. (1983). The politics of prevention and sex education. In G. W. Albee, S. Gordon, & H. Leitenberg, (Eds.), *Promoting sexual responsibility and preventing sexual problems* (pp. 389–401). Hanover, NH: University Press of New England.

Kirby, D., Barth, R. P., Leland, N., & Fetro, J. V. (1991). Reducing the risk: Impact of a new curriculum on sexual risk-taking. *Family Planning Perspectives, 23,* 253–263.

Vincent, M. L., Clearie, A. F., & Schluchter, M. D. (1987). Reducing adolescent pregnancy through school and community-based education. *Journal of the American Medical Association, 257,* 3382–3386.

CHOICES

Both parents and society at large are confronted with choices in regard to the sex education of children. In this section, we look at the questions of whether parents should allow their children to sleep in the same bed with them and whether parents should be naked in the presence of their children. We also look at whether sex education in the public schools should be compulsory and what constitutes appropriate sex education content.

Choose to Allow Children to Sleep in Their Parents' Bed or to Expose Children to Parental Nudity?

In a presentation by William Masters and Virginia Johnson we once heard the statement that parents conduct sex education "by aura." Masters and Johnson were referring to the idea mentioned earlier in this chapter that parents do most of their teaching through the atmosphere they create in their home. Parents are often concerned about how family practices related to sexuality will affect their children. They worry about how to create an atmosphere that is intimate and loving, but not sexually charged or inappropriately stimulating. Two questions related to this conflict are whether to allow children to sleep in their parents' bed or to see their parents nude.

To provide data on the question, Lewis and Janda (1988) asked 77 male and 133 female undergraduates to identify the frequency with which they slept in their parents' bed when they were between zero and five years old and between six and 11 years and to provide information about their current level of sexual adjustment. For male students in this study, sleeping in the bed with their parents was related to increased self-esteem, feeling less guilty and anxious about sex, having an increased frequency of sex, and viewing sex with a sense of openness and freedom. For women in this study, sleeping in the family bed was related to feeling comfortable about physical contact and affection and an increased tendency to feel an openness and freedom about sex.

Lewis and Janda (1988) concluded that sleeping in the parental bed can be characterized as being associated with the absence of sexual adjustment problems. "A representative comment for both men and women was, 'It always gave me a feeling of security to know that if I had a bad dream, I could crawl into bed with my mom and dad' " (p. 359). However, negative consequences of regularly sleeping in the family bed may be never learning to sleep alone and being ridiculed as not being independent enough from one's family.

Lewis and Janda (1988) looked at the relationship between being exposed to parental nudity and subsequent sexual development of the children. The researchers based their study on self-report data of a sample of undergraduates who were asked to identify the degree to which they were exposed to parental nudity. For men, exposure to parental nudity was associated with comfort in physical contact and affection, positive self-esteem, and a tendency to engage in casual sexual relationships. For females, parental nudity was associated with increased comfort in physical contact and affection, sex frequency, and tendency to engage in casual sexual relationships. Summarizing their findings, Lewis and Janda (1988) stated:

> Some may interpret these data as supporting their position on the harmful effects of parental nudity, since increased sexual activity may be seen as problematic. However, increased sexual activity in the absence of guilt, anxiety, sexual dysfunction, and other adjustment problems also lends itself to the interpretation we favor, namely, that increased exposure to nudity in the family fosters an atmosphere of acceptance of sexuality, one's body, and increased comfort in this arena. (p. 357)

Choose to Have Parents Participate in Sex Education Programs?

One choice that parents may make is to participate in a sex education program. These programs, which may be of-

Continued

Continued

fered at mental health centers, community colleges, churches, and other community organizations, are designed to help parents overcome their reservations about talking with their children about sex and to provide them with skills and knowledge to do so. Cooperation between parents and the school may increase the effectiveness of both in influencing responsible sexual behavior in youth. Specific areas that should be addressed in parent sex education programs include the following (Valentich & Gripton, 1989; Jaccard & Dittus, 1991):

1. Acknowledging that children are sexual persons. While parents often assume that their children are asexual, they might acknowledge that their children are curious about sex and are in the process of developing their sexual identity. Parents may also be advised about the tendency for parents to underestimate the sexual activity of teens. In the Jaccard and Dittus (1991) study, 13.6% of the teenagers reported having engaged in sexual intercourse, while parental estimates yielded a figure of 5.1% (p. 85).
2. Becoming knowledgeable about sexuality (sexual development, STDs, pregnancy, contraception, masturbation, etc.). Parents can respond to the curiosity of their children by initiating conversations about sex, encouraging them to ask questions, and showing a positive interest in their sexual development.
3. Learning to talk about sex through group discussion and behavior rehearsal. Parents may observe a group leader model talking with a child or teenager about sex. The parents may then practice on each other while getting feedback and reinforcement from the group leader. Or, parents may practice discussing sex with teenagers they do not know who participate in the program. Parents get feedback from both the teenagers with whom they practice and the group leader.
4. The importance of promoting responsible sexual behavior for both boys and girls (Jaccard and Dittus noted that parents in their study reflected a double standard in that they emphasized sexual responsibility more for teenage girls than for teenage boys).
5. Helping parents structure the "right time and place" to talk with their teen.
6. Exploring various themes about premarital sexual intercourse (e.g., the danger of diseases, issues of responsibility, risk of pregnancy, emotional impact of sexual relations, love versus lust).
7. Encouraging parents, where appropriate, to make specific recommendations about birth control methods that the teen should consider using. While some parents may encourage their teenagers to use contraceptives if they are sexually active, Jaccard and Dittus (1991) noted that

   > Psychological research has shown that persuasive messages addressing various problem areas are more effective when they contain specific behavioral recommendations about what the individual should do. General discussions of birth control on the part of parents without such recommendations may be less effective in promoting responsible use of contraception by teenagers. (p. 81)

8. Initiating talk with children. Watching together a video on sexuality from the local library, asking children what kids are saying about STDs or AIDS at school, or simply providing children with a list of topics and discussing the topics with them are ways parents can begin talking about sex.
9. Helping parents to develop honest and constructive communication patterns and good overall relations with their teenager. In this regard, Jaccard and Dittus (1991) suggested that

   > The foundations for effective parent-teen communication are established over the course of childhood. . . . Waiting until the teen years to offer the parent an education program requires that one deal with a lifetime of experiences that have already formed the basis for communication patterns. (p. 100)

What Should the Schools Teach about Sex?

While there is general agreement that some form of sex education is appropriate, differences exist over content and explicitness. A current debate is whether sex education should be focused on avoiding HIV infection and other sexually transmissible diseases or on avoiding teenage pregnancy.

> The emphasis on disease prevention is historically consistent with the roots of formal sex education in America, which grew out of concern over the spread of such sexually transmitted diseases as gonorrhea at the turn of the century. In addition, schools appear to be much more comfortable instructing students in the dangers of AIDS than in discussing such topics as the prevention of pregnancy. (Glazer, 1989, p. 342)

Sol Gordon (1986) noted that teenagers are often not asked what sex education they want. But from 50,000 sex questions he has received from teenagers, he observed, "Young people want to know about homosexuality, penis size, masturbation, female orgasm, and the answers to such questions as how can I tell if I'm really in love, what constitutes sexual desire, when are you most likely to get pregnant, and various questions about oral and anal sex" (p. 24). In a study of 75 boys and 88 girls from three high schools in rural New York, 57% reported that they wanted to "learn more about contraceptives and venereal disease prevention" (McCormick, Folcik, & Izzo, 1985, p. 581).

Disagreement also arises over explicitness. Antonio (1990) observed that sex education classes today are too explicit and that some parents regard such classes as a "form of sexual molestation" (p. 72). He gave examples of school children who were required to put condoms on cucumbers, hold life-size models of erect penises, and say words like "vagina" and "penis" in front of the classroom. Some view these exercises as "traumatizing" the students and feel they should be stopped.

Some sex educators contend that these exercises provide valuable experiences to students about condom use and their bodies and how to become comfortable talking about sex. They contend that knowing how to put a condom on may prevent those who become sexually active from becoming pregnant or con-

Continued

Continued

tracting an STD or AIDS. Knowing about the genitalia of men and women and feeling comfortable using the appropriate terminology to discuss them is healthy.

School administrators are also aware of the importance of parental support for sex education. In Florida, over half of the school districts invite parents to review the curriculum (59%) and observe classes during the year (56%) (Reinzo, 1989).

Another disagreement over content of public school sex education concerns whether homosexuality should be presented as a viable life-style alternative. Some parents feel that such a suggestion is inappropriate.

Similarly, dispensing condoms in schools without parental consent, without a fee, and without counseling is controversial. Chancellor Joseph Fernandez of the New York City Board of Education recommended distributing condoms to the city's 120 public high schools. In response, enraged parents, politicians, and clergy gathered on the steps of city hall with placards that read "Dump King Condom Fernandez" (Tifft, 1991, p. 66).

Opponents of school programs or **school-based clinics** that provide students with contraceptives argue that such programs encourage sexual activity among students. However, an evaluation of six school-based clinics indicated that the clinics neither hastened the onset of sexual activity nor increased its frequency (Kirby, Waszak, & Ziegler, 1991). In fact, when there were differences between the clinic and comparison schools most often the data revealed less sexual activity among students attending schools in which the clinics were located. The researchers were disappointed to find that the clinics did not reduce the school-wide pregnancy rate in the two years studied. They concluded that merely making contraceptives available does not significantly increase use. To increase the effectiveness of school-based clinics Kirby et al. recommended the following:

1. Place high priority on prevention of pregnancy and HIV transmission.
2. Develop more outreach programs in the schools.
3. Develop programs to delay and decrease sexual activity.
4. Identify and reach out to sexually active students.
5. Dispense contraceptives at the clinic.
6. Emphasize the use of condoms and men's responsibility.

Controversies over sex education in the United States are likely to continue, despite the fact that, although the United States is one of the most advanced industrialized nations in the world, its teenage pregnancy rate is almost twice that of France, England, and Canada, three times that of Sweden, and seven times that of the Netherlands. Teenagers in these countries are as sexually active as U.S. teenagers but have easier access to sex education and contraception. Indeed, in Sweden, there is compulsory sex education for all children in Swedish schools beginning at age eight (Goldman & Goldman, 1982). Swedish sex education teachers emphasize avoiding sexual exploitation and casual sex and stress the importance of sexual fidelity and a single (as opposed to double) sexual standard (Boethias, 1985; Glazer, 1989).

Cassell and Wilson (1989) identified challenges facing sexuality educators. These include: obtaining funds for education programs that are not "problem" focused, determining the effects of the AIDS epidemic on young people's developing sexuality and how best to do AIDS education, determining whether promoting abstinence is the best goal for adolescents and whether petting and masturbation should be suggested as alternatives to coitus, and developing ways to reach out to aging citizens. "Today there are more quality sexuality education programs than ever before, paving the way for the important work that still remains to be done" (Cassell & Wilson, 1989, p. xxv).

Summary

1. Increases in HIV infection and STDs as well as teenage pregnancy rates have resulted in sex education becoming a national priority.
2. Philosophies of sex education have, historically, focused on morals and facts. However, a current emphasis is on HIV prevention.
3. Sex education involves anatomy and physiology (of sexual response, reproduction, and childbirth), values clarification, communication skills, sexual decision making, prevention of unwanted pregnancy, exploration of unwanted pregnancy options, drug education, sex abuse prevention, learning about contraception and sexual counseling resources, exploration of gay and lesbian issues, examination of gender roles and their impact, and the promotion of self–esteem and aspirations.

4. All sex education programs should have an evaluation component.
5. The individual states, not the federal government, are responsible for the sex education of their citizens. As a result, sex education in the public school system is highly variable.
6. Open parent-child communication about sexual issues is associated with delayed first intercourse and the use of contraceptives and/or condoms when it occurs.
7. Some sex education programs in the public school system that are combined with access to birth control through school-based clinics are associated with decreases in sexual activity in those schools.
8. People exposed to sex education programs do not necessarily alter their risk-taking behavior because of denial—the belief that the chance that they personally will contract HIV or other STDs is low.

KEY TERMS

sex education
school-based clinics
AASECT
SIECUS

REFERENCES

Adler, J., Wright, L., McCormick, J., Annin, P., Cohen, A., Talbot, M., Hager, M., & Yoffe, E. (1991, December 9). Safer sex. *Newsweek,* pp. 52–56.

Akpom, C. A., Akpom, K. L., & Davis, M. (1976). Prior sexual behavior of teenagers attending rap sessions for the first time. *Family Planning Perspectives, 8,* 203–206.

Alan Guttmacher Institute. (1989). *Risk and responsibility: Teaching sex education in American schools today.* New York: Author.

Allen-Meares, P. (1989). Adolescent sexuality and premature parenthood: Role of the black church in prevention. *Journal of Social Work and Human Sexuality, 8,* 133–142.

Baldwin, S. E., & Baranoski, M. V. (1990). Family interactions and sex education in the home. *Adolescence, 25,* 573–582.

Blatt, J. (1989). How to talk about evaluation of sex education programs without blushing or stammering. In C. Cassell & P. M. Wilson (Eds.) *Sexuality education: A resource book* (pp. xix–xxvi). New York: Garland.

Boethius, C. G. (1985). Sex education in Swedish schools: The facts and the fiction. *Family Planning Perspectives, 17,* 276–279.

Bowen, S. P., & Michael-Johnson, P. (1990). A rhetorical perspective for HIV education with black urban adolescents. *Communication Research, 17,* 848–866.

Bruce, K. E. M., & Bullins, C. G. (1989). Students' attitudes and knowledge about genital herpes. *Journal of Sex Education and Therapy, 15,* 257–270.

Bullis, R. K. (1991). "Gag rules" and chastity clauses: Legal and ethical consequences of Title X and the AFLA for professionals in human sexuality. *Journal of Sex Education and Therapy, 17,* 91–102.

Bundy, M. L., & White, P. N. (1990). Parents as sexuality educators: A parent training program. *Journal of Counseling and Development, 68,* 321–323.

Calamidas, E. G. (1990). AIDS and STD education: What's really happening in our schools? *Journal of Sex Education and Therapy, 16,* 54–63.

Campbell, T. A., & Campbell, D. E. (1990). Considering the adolescent's point of view: A marketing model for sex education. *Journal of Sex Education and Therapy, 16,* 185–193.

Cassell, C. (1987). *Straight from the heart: How to talk to your teenagers about love and sex.* New York: Fireside Books.

Cassell, C. & Wilson, P. M. (1989). Introduction. In C. Cassell & P. M. Wilson (Eds.), *Sexuality education: A resource book* (pp. xix–xxvi). New York: Garland.

Center for Population Options. (1991). Cost of teen pregnancy assistance is soaring. *Options, 6,* 1.

Centers for Disease Control. (1989). *AIDS and human immunodeficiency virus infection in the United States, 1988 update* (Mortality and Morbidity Weekly Report, Vol. 38, Supp. S-4). Hyattsville, MD: U.S. Public Health Service.

Cohen, D., Dent, C., & MacKinnon, D. (1991). Condom skills education and sexually transmitted disease reinfection. *Journal of Sex Research, 28,* 139–144.

CPO Honors 1990 Nancy Susan Reynolds Award Winners. (1991). *Options, 4,* 6.

Cullari, S., & Mikus, S. (1990). Correlates of adolescent behavior. *Psychological Reports, 66,* 1179–1184.

Davidson, J. K., Sr., & Darling, C. A. (1988). Changing autoerotic attitudes and practices among college females: A two-year follow-up study. *Adolescence, 23,* 773–792.

Dawson, D. A. (1986). The effects of sex education on adolescent behavior. *Family Planning Perspectives, 18,* 162–170.

Duncan, D. F., & Nicholson, T. (1991). Pornography as a source of sex information for students at a southeastern state university. *Psychological Reports, 68,* 802.

Eisen, M., Zellman, G. L., & McAlister, A. L. (1990). Evaluating the impact of a theory-based sexuality and contraceptive education program. *Family Planning Perspectives, 22,* 261–271.

Fisher, T. D. (1987). Parent-child communication about sex and young adolescents' sexual knowledge and attitudes. *Adolescence, 21,* 517–527.

Forrest, J. D., & Silverman, J. (1989). What public school teachers teach about preventing pregnancy, AIDS and sexually transmitted diseases. *Family Planning Perspectives, 21,* 65–72.

Gerrard, M., Kurylo, M., & Reis, T. (1991). Self-esteem, erotophobia, and retention of contraceptive and AIDS information in the classroom. *Journal of Applied Social Psychology, 21,* 368–379.

Gibbs, N. (1991, September 2). Teens: The rising risk of AIDS. *Time,* pp. 60–61.

Gillman, R., & Whitlock, K. (1989). Sexuality: A neglected component of child sexual abuse education and training. *Child Welfare, 68,* 317–329.

Glazer, S. (1989). Sex education: How well does it work? *Editorial Research Reports, 1,* 338–350.

Goldman, R., & Goldman, J. (1982). *Children's sexual thinking.* London: Routledge & Kegan Paul.

Gordon, S. (1986, October). What kids need to know. *Psychology Today,* pp. 22–26.

Gordon, S. (1990). Sexuality education in the 1990s. *Health Education, 21,* 4–5.

Gray, L. A., & Saracino, M. (1989). AIDS on campus: A preliminary study of college students' knowlege and behaviors. *Journal of Counseling and Development, 68,* 199–202.

Green, S. K., & Sollie, D. L. (1989). Long-term effects of a church based sex education program on adolescent communication. *Family Relations, 38,* 152–156.

Gunderson, M. P., & McCary, J. L. (1980). Effects of sex education on sex information and sexual guilt, attitudes and behaviors. *Family Relations, 29,* 375–379.

Haffner, D. W. (1991). Help SIECUS protect sexual rights. *SIECUS Report,* 19, 10–12.

Haffner, D. W. (1992). 1992 Report card on the states: sexual rights in America. *SIECUS Report, 20* (3), 1–7.

Hansen, W. B., Hahn, G. L., & Wolkenstein, B. H. (1990). Perceived personal immunity: Beliefs about susceptibility to AIDS. *Journal of Sex Research, 27,* 622–628.

Haseltine, B., & Miltenburger, R. B. (1990). Teaching self-protection skills to persons with mental problems. *American Journal of Mental Retardation, 95,* 188–197.

Helge, D. (1990). Needs of rural schools regarding HIV education. *Rural Special Education Quarterly, 10,* 21–29.

Howard, M., & McCabe, J. R. (1990). Helping teenagers postpone sexual involvement. *Family Planning Perspectives, 22,* 21–26.

Huston, R. L., Martin, L. J., & Foulds, D. M. (1990). Effect of a program to facilitate parent-child communication about sex. *Clinical Pediatrics, 29,* 626–633.

Isberner, F. R. (1990). Sex education in rural churches. *Human Services in the Rural Environment, 13,* 6–12.

Jaccard, J., & Dittus, P. (1991). *Parent-teen communication: Toward the prevention of unintended pregnancy.* New York: Springer-Verlag.

Jackson, D. (1989). Sex education in Halton secondary schools. *Health Visitor, 62,* 219–221.

Kenney, A. M., Guardado, S., & Brown, L. (1989). Sex education and AIDS education in the schools: What states and large school districts are doing. *Family Planning Perspectives, 21,* 56–64.

Kenney, A. M. (1987). Teen pregnancy: An issue for schools. *Phi Delta Kappan, 68,* 728–736.

Kirby, D. (1984). *Sexuality education: An evaluation of programs and their effects, an executive summary.* Bethesda, MD: Mathtech.

Kirby, D. (1989). Research on effectiveness of sex education programs. *Theory into practice, 28,* 165–171.

Kirby, D., Waszak, C., & Ziegler, J. (1991). Six school-based clinics: Their reproductive health services and impact on sexual behavior. *Family Planning Perspectives, 23,* 6–16.

Koch, P. B. (1992). Integrating cognitive, affective, and behavioral approaches into learning experiences for sexuality education. In J. T. Sears (Ed.), *Sexuality and the curriculum: The politics and practices of sexuality education* (pp. 253–266). New York: Teachers College Press.

Koop, C. E. (1986). Surgeon General's report on acquired immune deficiency syndrome. Washington, DC: US Department of Health and Human Services.

Krueger, M. M. (1991). The omnipresent need: Professional training for sexuality education teachers. *SIECUS Report, 19,* 1–5.

Ku, L. C., Sonenstein, F. L., & Pleck, J. H. (1992). The association of AIDS education and sex education with sexual behavior and condom use among teenage men. *Family Planning Perspectives, 24,* 100–106.

LaHaye, B. (1991, November 19). Abstinence education, not condoms or safe sex, is what children need. *USA Today,* p. 12A.

Levenson-Gingiss, P., & Hamilton, R. (1989). Evaluation of training effects on teacher attitudes and concerns prior to implementing a human sexuality education program. *Journal of School Health, 59,* 156–160.

Lewis, R. A. (1973). Parents and peers: Socialization agents in the coital behavior of young adults. *Journal of Sex Research, 9,* 156–170.

Lewis, R. J., & Janda, L. H. (1988). The relationship between adult sexual adjustment and childhood experiences regarding exposure to nudity, sleeping in the parental bed, and parental attitudes toward sexuality. *Archives of Sexual Behavior, 17,* 349–362.

Lowry, D. T., & Towles, D. E. (1989). Soap opera portrayals of sex, contraception, and sexually transmitted diseases. *Journal of Communication, 39,* 76–83.

Marsiglio, W., & Mott, F. L. (1986). The impact of sex education on sexual activity, contraceptive use and premarital pregnancy among American teenagers. *Family Planning Perspectives, 18,* 151–162.

Martin, J. (1990). Youths and the galaxy of questions raised by AIDS. Which themes to address? *Hygiene, 9,* 22–24.

Mast, C. K. (1986). *Sex respect: The option of true sexual freedom.* Golf, IL: Project Respect.

Maticka-Tyndale, E. (1991). Sexual scripts and AIDS prevention: Variations in adherence to safer-sex guidelines by heterosexual adolescents. *Journal of Sex Research, 28,* 45–66.

Maynard-Tucker, G. (1989). Knowledge of reproductive physiology and modern contraceptives in rural Peru. *Studies in Family Planning, 20,* 215–224.

McCormick, N., Folcik, J., & Izzo, A. (1985). Sex-education needs and interests of high school students in rural New York County. *Adolescence, 20,* 581–592.

McGill, L., Smith, P. B., & Johnson, T. C. (1989). AIDS: Knowledge, attitudes and risk characteristics of teens. *Journal of Sex Education and Therapy, 15,* 30–35.

Melchert, T., & Burnett, K. F. (1990). Attitudes, knowledge, and sexual behavior of high-risk adolescents: Implications for counseling and sexuality education. *Journal of Counseling and Development, 68,* 293–298.

National Center for Health Statistics. (1992). *Advance Report of Final Mortality Statistics, 1988* (Monthly Vital Statistics Report, vol. 39, no. 7, supp.). Hyattsville, MD: U.S. Public Health Service.

Nolin, M. J. & Petersen, K. K. (1992). Gender differences in parent-child communication about sexuality: An exploratory study. *Journal of Adolescent Research, 7,* 59–79.

Ortiz, S., & Casas, J. M. (1990). Birth control and low-income Mexican-American women: The impact of three values. *Hispanic Journal of Behavioral Sciences, 12,* 83–92.

Ostermiller, R. K. (1991). *Talking with your child about sexuality.* Cleveland: Pilgrim Press.

Ostrom, C. M. (1987, June 7). AIDS and teens: Getting smart. *Seattle Times/Post-Intelligencer,* pp. A1.

Patton, J. R., Payne, J. S., & Beirne-Smith, M. (1986). *Mental retardation* (2nd ed.). Columbus, OH: Charles E. Merrill.

Polyson, J., Lash, S., & Evans, K. (1986). Human sexuality courses: Where and how many? *Teaching of Psychology, 13,* 221–222.

Powell, L. H., & Jorgensen, S. R. (1985). Evaluation of a church-based sexuality education program for adolescents. *Family Relations, 34,* 475–482.

Reis, J., & Seidl, A. (1989). School administrators, parents, and sex education: A resolvable paradox? *Adolescence, 24,* 639–645.

Richwald, G. A. (1989). Are condom instructions in Spanish readable? Implications for AIDS prevention. *Hispanic Journal of Behavioral Sciences, 11,* 70–82.

Richwald, G. A., Wamsley, M. A., Coulson, A. H., & Morisky, D. E. (1988). Are condom instructions readable? Results of a readability study. *Public Health Reports, 103,* 355–359.

St. Lawrence, J. S., & Joyner, D. J. (1991). The effects of sexually violent rock music on males' acceptance of violence against women. *Psychology of Women Quarterly, 15,* 49–63.

Schecter, S. (1986). The New York City School system's family life education program. *Journal of Community Health, 11,* 54–57.

Sears, J. T. (1992). The impact of culture and ideology on the construction of gender and sexual identities: Developing a critically based sexuality curriculum. In J. T. Sears (Ed.), *Sexuality and the curriculum: The politics and practices of sexuality education* (pp. 139–156). New York: Teachers College Press.

Senderowitz, J. (1991). The need for healthy options. *Options, 4,* 2.

SIECUS Fact Sheet #2 On Comprehensive Sexuality Education (1992, February/March). *SIECUS Report, 20,* p. 22.

Silayan-Go, A. (1990). Entertainment for health. *World Health Forum, 11,* 297–301.

Stiff, J. (1990). Learning about AIDS and HIV transmission in college-age students. *Communication Research, 17,* 743–758.

Stout, J. W., & Rivara, F. P. (1989). Schools and sex education: Does it work? *Pediatrics, 83,* 375–379.

Strouse, J., & Fabes, R. A. (1985). Formal versus informal sources of sex education: Competing forces in the sexual socialization of adolescents. *Adolescence, 20,* 251–262.

Strouse, J. S., Krajewski, L. A., & Gilin, S. M. (1990). Utilizing undergraduate students as peer discussion facilitators in human sexuality classes. *Journal of Sex Education and Therapy, 16,* 227–235.

Taylor, M. E. (1989). Effects of contraceptive education on adolescent male contraceptive behavior and attitudes. *Health Education, 20,* 12–17.

Thomas, L. L., Long, S. E., Whitten, K., Hamilton, B., Fraser, J., & Askins, R. V. (1985). High school students' long-term retention of sex education information. *Journal of School Health, 55,* 274–278.

Tifft, S. (1991, January 21). Better safe than sorry. *Time,* p. 60.

Todres, R. (1990). Effectiveness of counseling in the transmission of family planning and sexuality knowledge. *Journal of Sex Education and Therapy, 16,* 279–285.

Tucker, S. K. (1990). Adolescent patterns of communication about the menstrual cycle, sex, and contraception. *Journal of Pediatric Nursing, 5,* 393–400.

Trudell, B., & Whatley, M. (1991). Sex respect: A problematic public school sexuality curriculum. *Journal of Sex Education and Therapy, 17,* 125–140.

Valentich, M., & Gripton, J. (1989). Teaching children about AIDS. *Journal of Sex Education and Therapy, 15,* 92–102.

Walker-Hirsch, L., & Champagne, M. P. (1991). Circles revisited: ten years later. *Sexuality and Disability, 9,* 143–159.

Warzak, W. J., & Page, T. J. (1990). Teaching refusal skills to sexually active adolescents. *Journal of Behavior Therapy and Experimental Psychiatry, 21,* 133–139.

Weis, D. L., Rabinowitz, B., & Ruckstuhl, M. F. (1992). Individual changes in sexual attitudes and behavior within college-level human sexuality courses. *Journal of Sex Research, 29,* 43–59.

Wurtele, S. K., Melzer, A. M., & Kast, L. C. (1992). Preschoolers' knowledge of and ability to learn genital terminology. *Journal of Sex Education and Therapy, 18,* 115–122.

Zabin, L. S., Hirsch, M. D., Smith, E. A., Streett, R., & Hardy, J. B. (1986). Evaluation of a pregnancy prevention program for urban teenagers. *Family Planning Perspectives, 18,* 119–126.

Zelnik, M., & Kim, Y. J. (1982). Sex education and its association with teenage sexual activity, pregnancy, and contraceptive use. *Family Planning Perspectives, 14,* 117–126.

Glossary

A

Abortion the removal of an embryo or fetus from the woman's uterus before it can survive on its own.

Abortion rate the number of abortions per 1,000 women aged 15 to 44.

Abortion ratio the number of abortions per 100 pregnancies (excluding miscarriages).

Absolutism a belief system that is based on the unconditional power and authority of science, law, tradition, or religion.

Abstention *see coitus abstentia.*

Abstinence Refraining from sexual intercourse.

Acquaintance rape nonconsensual sex between adults who know each other.

Adolescence the time from age 12 to age 22 involving physical, social, and cognitive changes.

Adrenal (uh-DREE-nuhl) glands endocrine glands located on each kidney. These glands produce small amounts of estrogen, progesterone, and androgen.

Adultery (uh-DUL-tuh-ree) sexual intercourse by a married person with someone other than that person's spouse.

Affair sexual involvement outside a committed intimate relationship without the consent of the partner.

Agape (Ah-GAH-pay) unselfish love that is concerned only with the welfare of the beloved.

AIDS acquired immune deficiency syndrome, the last stage of HIV infection in which the immune system of a person's body is so weakened so that it becomes vulnerable to disease and infection, which ultimately results in death.

Alpha bias the body of theory and research that exaggerates differences between men and women.

Amenorrhea (ay-mehn-uh-REE-uh) the absence of menstruation for three or more months when the woman is not pregnant, not breast-feeding, or past menopause.

Amniocentesis (am-nee-oh-sehn-TEE-suhs) the procedure whereby cells from the developing fetus are extracted by a needle from the amniotic sac and tested for genetic disorders.

Anabolic steroids hormones that resemble testosterone and have the effect of accelerating tissue growth.

Anal stage according to Freud, the second psychosexual stage in which sexual pleasure is derived from the anus and activities of elimination.

Anaphrodisiacs (an-AF-roh-DIHZ-ee-aks) those substances thought to decrease sexual desire.

Anatomy the study of body structure.

Androgen (AN-droh-juhn) the general class of male sex hormones. Testosterone is one example of an androgen.

Androgen-insensitivity syndrome *see testicular feminization syndrome.*

Androgenital syndrome the condition in which the external genitals of a genetically female (xx) individual appear to be male, but the internal organs are those of a female.

Androgyny (an-DRAH-juh-nee) a blend of traits that are stereotypically associated with masculinity and femininity.

Anus the opening of the rectum located between the buttocks.

Aphrodisiacs (AF-roh-DIHZ-ee-aks) substances that are thought to stimulate sexual desire.

ARC AIDS-related complex. A series of symptoms characteristic of persons with AIDS. Persons with ARC eventually develop AIDS, which results in swollen lymph nodes, persistent fever, diarrhea, night sweats, weight loss, fatigue, and so on.

Areola (eh-ree-OH-lah) the darkened area around the nipple.

Artificial insemination the introduction of sperm into a woman's vagina or cervix by means of a syringe, rather than a penis. The sperm may be from a partner, a husband (artificial insemination by husband—AIH), or a donar (artificial insemination by donor—AID).

Asceticism (uh-SEHT-uh-sihzm) the doctrine that self-denial and avoidance of sensual pleasure is required for spiritual life.

Asexual (ay-SEHK-shoo-uhl) a person who has no interest in sex and does not engage in any form of sexual activity.

Asexual reproduction one organism has the capacity to reproduce without involvement of another organism.

AASECT American Association of Sex Educators, Counselors, and Therapists.

Autoerotic asphyxia syndrome an unusual, potentially lethal form of male masturbation. The man uses a noose on his neck to cut off his air supply while masturbating.

Autoeroticism sexual self-pleasuring, commonly referred to as masturbation.

Autonepiophilia a paraphilia that involves deriving sexual arousal or gratification from wearing wet diapers.

Aversion (uh-VER-zhun) therapy a type of behavior therapy in which the person learns to associate the inappropriate behavior with a painful consequence. The goal is to decrease the desire to engage in the inappropriate behavior.

B

B-love unneeding or unselfish love.

Bartholin's (BAR-toh-lihnz) glands two small glands just inside the vaginal opening that secrete a small amount of fluid during sexual arousal.

Bestiality (behs-chee-AL-uh-tee) sexual activity between a human being and an animal.

Beta bias the body of theory and research that minimizes differences between women and men and stresses their similarities.

Biased sample a sample that is not representative of the population from which it is taken.

Biosexology the study of the biological aspects of sexuality.

Bisexuality (bigh-SEHK-shooAL-ih-tee) cognitive, emotional, and sexual attractions to members of both sexes.

Blended orgasms orgasms characterized by vulval contractions and deep terminative enjoyment.

Body image attitudes toward one's own body and perceptions of how one looks to others.

Brachioprotic (BRAY-kee-oh-PROH-tihc) eroticism an aspect of gay male sexual behavior whereby one man inserts his hand and forearm in the anus of a partner; also called "fisting."

Bradley method of childbirth also known as husband-coached childbirth, this method emphasizes marital communication, the couple's sexual relationship, and parental roles.

Brainstorming a solution generating technique that involves suggesting as many alternatives as possible, without evaluating them until all ideas have been suggested.

Breech birth birth in which the feet or buttocks of the baby emerge first.

Bulbocavernosus (buhl-boh-kav-er-NOH-suhs) muscle the ring of sphincter muscles surrounding the opening to the vagina.

C

Candidiasis (kan-dih-DIGH-uh-sihs) an inflammatory infection of the vaginal tissues caused by a yeast-like fungus.

Case study research the study in detail of one individual or situation, rather than numerous individuals or situations.

Castration (kas-TRAY-shun) the surgical removal of the testes (orchiectomy) or ovaries (ovariectomy) or inactivation of their function by radiation, drugs, or disease.

Causal analysis data analysis designed to ascertain if one variable (e.g., abortion) is the cause of another variable (infertility).

Celibate (SEHL-ih-buht) a person who does not engage in sexual behavior with other people. Celibacy may be voluntary (as with priests) or involuntary (as with a hospitalized person).

Central arousal the brain, central nervous system, and cognitions involved in transmitting and processing sexual stimuli.

Cervical (SER-vih-kuhl) cap a birth control device consisting of a small rubber or plastic cap that fits snugly over the cervix to prevent sperm from entering the uterus.

Cervical mucus a thin, watery lubricative secretion produced by the cervix that aids sperm migration from the vagina to the egg in the Fallopian tubes.

Cervix (SER-vihks) the narrow portion of the uterus that projects into the vagina.

Cesarean (suh-ZAIR-ee-uhn) the delivery of a baby by cutting open the woman's abdomen and uterus, rather than delivery through the vaginal canal.

Chancre (SHAN-ker) a small sore that appears on the genitals and indicates the presence of a viral infection.

Chancroid (SHAN-kroyd) a soft chancre that is transmitted through sexual contact with either the chancroid ulcer or discharge from infected local lymph glands.

Chicken porn slang term for child pornography.

Childhood the time from age one to age 12 involving physical, cognitive, and social development.

Chlamydia known as the silent disease, a sexually transmitted disease caused by a bacterium that may be successfully treated with antibiotics.

Chorionic villus sampling (CVS) a prenatal test that involves placing a tube through the vagina into the uterus. Chorionic tissue, which surrounds the embryo, is removed and analyzed for genetic defects, such as Down's syndrome.

Chromosomes (KROH-moh-sohmz) thin, threadlike structures carrying genes, which are located within the nucleus of every cell.

Chronic obstructive pulmonary disease also known as COPD, a collective term for diseases that affect the air flow into the body (e.g. asthma, bronchitis, and emphysema).

Circumcision (ser-kuhm-SIHZ-uhn) the surgical removal of the foreskin of the penis of a man or the clitoral hood of a woman.

Classical conditioning the process of learning whereby a stimulus that is originally not linked with a reflex or response comes to be so linked.

Climacteric (kligh-MAK-tuh-rihk) the aging process of the reproductive system in females, occurring between ages 45 and 60, which involves hormonal changes in the ovaries, pituitary gland, and hypothalamus. The term may also refer to the aging process of the male reproductive system.

Clitoral circumcision the surgical removal of the clitoral hood.

Clitoral orgasm an orgasm resulting from stimulation of the clitoris. Freud viewed such an orgasm as a sign of immaturity and/or fixation in early psychosexual development.

Clitoridectomy (klit-uhr-ih-DEK-toh-mee) surgical removal of the glans and shaft of the clitoris and the labia minora.

Clitoris (KLIHT-uh-ruhs) a small, erectile structure embedded in the tissues of the vulva at the junction of the minor labia. Its primary function is pleasure.

Closed-ended question a question that can be answered with one word, such as yes or no, and thus does not provide the person asking the question with much detail.

Cohabitation (coh-hab-uh-TAY-shun) two people living together and sharing a common bed without being legally married.

Coitus (KO-ih-tuhs) sexual intercourse.

Coitus abstentia also referred to as abstinence, refraining from penile-vaginal intercourse.

Coitus interruptus the withdrawal of the penis from the woman's vagina before ejaculation.

Coitus obstructus an ancient Chinese technique for diverting seminal fluid (it was thought) from the penis into the bladder.

Comarital sex a form of extradyadic sexual involvement in which the partners of one couple have sexual relations with the partners of another couple.

Combination pill an oral contraceptive containing estrogen and progesterone which act to prevent ovulation and implantation.

Coming out the process whereby homosexuals or bisexuals acknowledge their sexual orientation to themselves and others.

Communication the process of exchanging information between two or more individuals. To be effective, the exchange must be timely, accurate, and precise.

Companionate love intimacy and commitment without passion.

Conception (kahn-SEP-shun) the implantation of a fertilized egg on the wall of the uterus.

Concubine female nonmarital sexual mate.

Condom (KAHN-duhm) also referred to as a "rubber," "safe," and "prophylactic," a thin sheath, usually made of synthetic material, that is rolled over and down the erect penis before intercourse to provide a barrier to the sperm entering the vagina. Also used to prevent transmission of STDs during vaginal, anal, and oral sex.

Condom skills program a sex education program in which individuals learn how to buy, talk about, and put on condoms in the context of helping to ensure a safer sex experience.

Conflict theories sociological theories that view society as comprised of different parts competing for power and resources.

Conjoint therapy a therapeutic context in which the therapist sees both partners at the same time.

Consummate love intimacy, passion, and commitment combined.

Contraception (kahn-truh-SEP-shun) using artificial means to prevent sperm from fertilizing an egg or to prevent the fertilized egg from implanting on the uterine wall.

Control group in a research study, the group that is not exposed to the experimental treatment.

Convenience sampling a sampling procedure that involves selecting members of a sample to whom the researcher has convenient access.

Conversion therapy a controversial form of therapy for ego-dystonic gay individuals who want to become heterosexual.

Comarital sex a form of extradyadic sexual involvement in which the partners of one pair-bonded relationship have sexual relations with the partners of another relationship.

Corona (kohr-OH-nuh) the raised rim above the body of the penis that begins the glans of the penis.

Corpora cavernosa (KOR-por-uh kav-er-NO-suh) twin cylinders of spongy tissue in the penis that become engorged with blood, resulting in an erection. Also present in the clitoris.

Corpora spongiosum (KOR-por-uh spun-jee-OH-suhm) a cylinder of spongy tissue in the penis that becomes engorged with blood during an erection.

Corpus luteum (KOR-puhs LOO-tee-uhm) a yellow structure that forms on the surface of the ovary at the site of ovulation. It produces the progesterone characteristic of the second half of the menstrual cycle and is necessary to prepare the uterine lining for implantation by the fertilized egg.

Correlation the relationship between two or more variables.

Covert sensitization a behavior therapy technique whereby the person learns to associate negative feelings with the inappropriate behavior by thinking of negative associations.

Cowper's (KOW-perz) glands also known as bulbourethal glands; two pea-sized glands located below the prostrate that act to neutralize the natural acidic environment of the uretha. The small amount of clear, sticky fluid that is visible at the urethral opening prior to ejaculation is from these glands.

Cross-sectional research research that involves collecting data at one point in time in contrast to collecting data across time.

Crura (CROO-ruh) two structures linking the top of the shaft of the clitoris to the pubic bone. Similar structures also link the penis to the pubic bone.

Cryopreservation a procedure whereby fertilized eggs are frozen for possible implantation at a later time.

Cultural relativism understanding another culture by taking into account its own standards.

Cunnilingus (kuhn-ee-LIHN-guhs) the stimulation of the vulva area by the partner's mouth.

Cystitis (sihs-TIGH-tuhs) inflammation and infection of the bladder.

D

Date rape nonconsensual sex between people who are dating.

Dental dam a flat latex device to cover a woman's vaginal area, preventing direct contact between her genital area and her partner's mouth.

Dependent variable in research, the variable that the researcher wants to explain.

Depo-Provera (DEPH-oh-proh-VAIR-uh) also known as medroxyprogesterone acetate or MPA; a synthetic progestinic hormone that is used as a method of contraception. In sufficient doses, it protects the woman against conceiving for three months following an injection. The hormone has also been associated with decreased sexual interest and is sometimes used in the treatment of sex offenders.

DES (Diethylstilbestrol)(digh-EHTH-yl-stihl-BEHS-trohl) known as the morning-after pill, it contains high levels of estrogen to prevent implantation of the fertilized egg on the uterine wall.

Descriptive analysis a type of data analysis that involves describing the quantitative and/or qualitative aspects of the phenomenon being observed, in contrast to conducting statistical tests.

Detane commercial ointment placed on the glans of the penis to delay ejaculation. Such ointments are ineffective.

Determinism the view that human behavior is caused by past and present factors in our heredity and environment.

Diaphragm (DIGH-uh-fram) a circular rubber dome two to four inches in diameter that covers the cervix and prevents sperm from entering the uterus.

Dick-Read childbirth method a method of natural childbirth.

Dilation (digh-luh-TAY-shun) a widening of the cervical opening. Prior to delivery, the cervix dilates from three and a half to four inches.

Dilation and curretage *see Dilation and suction.*

Dilation and evacuation also known as a D & E, a method of abortion used in the second trimester of pregnancy (13 to 24 weeks' gestation). Similar to D & S except greater dilation of the cervical opening is required and a larger suction device is used because of the increased volume of tissue.

Dilation and suction known as D & S, a method of abortion used during the first 12 weeks of pregnancy involving dilating the cervix and suctioning the embryo and placenta from the walls of the uterus. This method also involves using a metal surgical instrument to scrape any remaining fetal tissue and placenta from the walls of the uterus (this method is also referred to as dilation and curretage, or D & C).

Dildo (DIHL-doh) an item used as a penis substitute.

Dimorphism (digh-MOR-fihzm) the condition of a species having two different forms, e.g. female and male.

D-love selfish love that seeks gratification, rather than growth.

Domestic partnerships legal relationships that allow the partners to have some of the same benefits that legally married spouses have (e.g., health and insurance benefits).

Double standard the condition in which one behavior standard is applied to men and another to women.

Douching (DOOSH-ihng) the process of rinsing and cleaning the vaginal canal.

Down's syndrome a genetic defect resulting in a baby who is physically and mentally deficient and has a shorter life span.

Duct system canals or tubular passages.

Dysmenorrhea (dihs-mehn-uh-REE-uh) painful menstruation.

Dyspareunia (DIHS-puh-ROO-nee-uh) recurrent or persistent genital pain experienced by either a woman or a man before, during, or after sexual intercourse.

E

Early ejaculation also known as "premature ejaculation" or "rapid ejaculation," persistent or recurrent ejaculation with minimal sexual stimulation or before, upon, or shortly after penetration and before the person wishes it.

Early infant death infant death within seven days of birth.

Ectopic (ehk-TAHP-ihk) pregnancy a pregnancy in which implantation takes place outside the uterine cavity, usually in one of the Fallopian tubes.

Effacement a flattening and extension of the cervix.

Ego in psychoanalytic terms, the part of the person's personality that regulates the desires of the id.

Ego–dystonic homosexuality the condition in which a gay individual feels persistent and marked distress over his or her sexual orientation (as classified in the American Psychiatric Association's DSM-III).

Ejaculation (ih-jak-yoo-LAY-shun) the expulsion of semen from the penis. See also **female ejaculation.**

Ejaculatory duct the short canal at the end of the vas deferens that empties into the urethra.

Ejaculatory incompetence also referred to as retarded ejaculation, absence of ejaculation, ejaculatory impotence, and inhibited ejaculation; the inability to ejaculate inside a woman's vagina.

Electra (ih-LEHK-truh) complex according to Freudian theory, the young girl (at about age four) recognizes she has no penis, wishes she did (penis envy), and blames her mother for its absence.

Embryo (EHM-bree-oh) the human organism from about two weeks after fertilization until the end of the eighth week.

Empty love commitment without passion or intimacy.

Endocrine (EHN-doh-krihn) system a system of ductless glands producing hormones, including the pituitary, parathyroid, thyroid, and adrenal glands and the testes and ovaries.

Endocrinologist (ehn-doh-krihn-AHL-uh-jihst) a physician who specializes in the diagnosis and treatment of diseases of the hormone systems.

Endometriosis (ehn-doh-MEE-tree-OH-sihs) a condition where endometrium, the tissue that normally lines the uterine cavity, grows on other surfaces, such as the Fallopian tubes and ovaries.

Endometrium (ehn-doh-MEE-tree-uhm) the inner layer of the uterine wall where the fertilized egg implants.

Epididymis (ehp-uh-DIHD-uh-mis) tubes running from the testes to the vas deferens.

Episiotomy (ih-pee-zee-AHT-uh-mee) an incision of the vaginal opening sometimes made during childbirth to make it easier for the baby to be born without tearing the vagina.

Erectile dysfunction also known as impotence, a man's inability to create and maintain an erection sufficient for intercourse.

Eros romantic, passionate love.

Erotica literature, art, photographs and film intended to arouse sexual desire.

Erotocentrism the belief that one's sexual behavior and attitudes are superior to all others and that one's own sexuality is the standard by which all others should be judged.

Erotophilia the quality of deriving great joy, pleasure, and comfort in sexual thoughts and behaviors.

Erotophobia the fear or intense dislike of sex.

Essentialist view a theoretical view of sexuality that emphasizes that sexuality is basically a biological drive or instinct and the female nature and male nature are fundamentally different.

Estrogen (EHS-truh-jehn) a hormone produced primarily by the ovaries to stimulate the development of cervical mucus and ovulation and to help prepare the uterine lining for possible implantation after fertilization. Estrogen also stimulates the development of female secondary characteristics, such as breasts.

Estrogen replacement therapy (ERT) a treatment sometimes recommended for women in the climacteric who experience severe symptoms. ERT reduces or completely alleviates hot flashes. Some evidence suggests that ERT may increase the risk of uterine cancer.

Ethics moral codes that guide decisions and behaviors.

Ethnocentrism judging other cultures according to the standards of one's own culture.

Ethnography the description of cultures or subcultures.

Ethnology the comparison of two or more cultures or subcultures.

Eunuch (YOO-nuhk) a person who has been castrated.

Excitement phase the first of four stages of the sexual response cycle described by Masters and Johnson. Vaginal lubrication and penile erection are the primary responses during this phase.

Exhibitionism an intense, recurrent sexual urge of at least six months' duration, often accompanied by sexually arousing fantasies, to expose one's genitals to a stranger.

Experiment a research method that involves manipulating the independent variable to determine its effect on the dependent variable.

Experimental group the research group that is exposed to the experimental treatment.

Extinction the termination of the reinforcement of a behavior, which results in the behavior eventually stopping.

Extradyadic sexual behavior sexual involvement with someone other than one's spouse or primary partner.

Extrafamilial child sexual abuse unwanted sexual experiences with persons unrelated by blood or marriage ranging from petting to rape before the victim is age 14. Also includes completed or attempted rape from ages 14 to 17.

F

Fallopian (fuh-LOH-pee-uhn) tubes tubes leading from each ovary to the uterus; also known as oviducts (egg tubes).

False labor irregular contractions of the undilated uterus that mimic true labor.

Family planning clinics clinics in which birth control information and services are available.

Fatuous love passion and commitment without intimacy.

Fellatio (fuh-LAH-shee-oh) stimulation of the penis by the partner's mouth.

Female condom a large, lubricated polyurethane sheath that fits inside the woman's vagina to help protect her from pregnancy and sexually transmissible diseases.

Female ejaculation the emission of a fluid described as looking like "watered-down fatfree milk" from the Skene's glans just inside the urethral opening; occurs in about 10% of women. Other researchers say the fluid is primarily urine.

Female genital mutilation a term referring to various operations performed on female genitalia for cultural reasons. Includes the removal of the clitoral hood (*sunna* or "female circumcision"), clitoridectomy, and infibulation.

Female pseudohermaphrodites genetically female individuals who have gonads matching the female sex chromosomes but whose external genitalia resemble those of a male.

Female sexual arousal dysfunction also known as impaired sexual arousal, persistent or recurrent partial or complete failure to attain or maintain the lubrication-swelling response of sexual excitement until completion of sexual activity or the lack of a subjective sense of sexual excitement.

Fertilization (fuhr-tih-lih-ZAY-shun) the union of a sperm and an egg resulting in a zygote and the development of an embryo.

Fetal alcohol syndrome refers to the negative consequences for the fetus and infant of a mother who drinks alcohol at the level of a social drinker or more heavily while she is pregnant.

Fetal death occurs when an infant is born dead.

Fetishism (FEHT-ihsh-iszm) a pattern for at least six months' duration of deriving sexual arousal or sexual gratification from actual or fantasized inanimate objects.

Fetus the developing human organism from the third month of conception until delivery.

Fimbriae (FIHM-bree-ee) hairlike fibers in the Fallopian tube that pick up the egg from the ovary as it is released.

Follicle (FAHL-ih-kuhl) the structure in the ovary that has nurtured the ripening egg and from which the egg is released.

Follicle-stimulating hormone (FSH) a hormone produced and released by the pituitary gland. In the female, it stimulates estrogen production and the development of follicles in the ovary. In males, FSH stimulates sperm production.

Follicular phase *see preovulatory phase.*

Formicophilia a rare paraphilia in which sexuoerotic arousal and orgasm are dependent on the sensation produced by small creatures, such as snails, frogs, ants or other insects, creeping, crawling, and nibbling on the body, especially the genitalia, perianal area, or nipples.

Free will the capacity to choose for oneself.

Frenulum (FREHN-yoo-luhm) a thin strip of skin that connects the glans of the penis with the shaft of the penis.

Frotteurism (fro-TUR-izm) recurring, intense sexual urges for at least six months' duration, accompanied by arousing fantasies, to touch or rub against a nonconsenting person.

Fundus (FUHN-duhs) the broad, rounded part of the uterus.

G

G spot abbreviation for Grafenberg spot; an alleged sensitive area on the front wall of the vagina about one or two inches into the opening. Not all women report the existence of a G spot. Scientists also do not agree on its existence.

Gamete (GAM-eet) mature reproductive cells; sperm in men and eggs in women.

Gamete intra-Fallopian transfer also known as GIFT, a procedure whereby the egg and sperm are placed directly into the Fallopian tube by a physician.

Gang rape a rape that involves more than one perpetrator.

Gender the social and psychological characteristics associated with being female and male.

Gender dysphoria the condition in which one's gender identity does not match one's biological sex.

Gender identity the psychological state of viewing oneself as a girl or boy (or woman or man).

Gender role the set of social norms that dictate what is socially regarded as appropriate female and male behavior.

Gender role ideology a belief system that specifies what is regarded as the proper role relationships between women and men.

Gender role transcendence abandoning gender schema so that personality traits, social and occupational roles, and other aspects of our life become divorced from gender categories.

Gender schema a network of associations with the concepts of female and male (or feminity and masculinity) that organizes and guides perception.

Gene (jeen) that part of a chromosome that transmits a particular heredity characteristic (e.g., left-handedness).

Genital apposition a form of petting in which the partners rub their genitals together while lying close together with or without their clothes on and without having intercourse.

Genital herpes also known as herpes simplex type 2; a sexually transmissible viral infection. The virus may also be transmitted during birth to the newborn infant.

Genital stage according to Freud, the final stage of psychosexual development in which sexual pleasure shifts from self-pleasure through masturbation to interpersonal sexual pleasure.

Genital warts sexually transmitted lesions that may appear in the cervix, vulva, urethra, or rectum.

Gestation (jehs-TAY-shun) the time from conception to delivery.

Gigolo (JIHG-uh-loh) a male prostitute who services women.

Glans (glanz) the head of the penis or clitoris.

Gonads (GOH-nadz) the testes in the male and ovaries in the female, which produce sperm and eggs, respectively.

Gonorrhea (gahn-uh-REE-uh) also known as "the clap," "the whites," and "morning drop"; a bacterial infection that is sexually transmitted.

Granuloma inguinale (gran-yuh-LOH-muh ihn-gwih-NAH-lee) a sexually transmitted disease that may be successfully treated with antibiotics; it is prevalent in Vietnam, Indonesia, Africa, Southern New Guinea, and Southern India.

Group sex sexual encounters involving three or more individuals.

H

Hebephilia similar to pedophilia, except the object of sexual urge is an adolescent.

Hedonism (HEE-duh-nihzm) the value system emphasizing the pursuit of pleasure and the avoidance of pain.

Hepatitis B virus (HBV) a virus often acquired through sexual contact or blood transfusions and causes liver disease.

Hermaphroditism (her-MAF-ruh-dight-ihzm) a condition in which an individual (usually genetically female) has both ovarian and testicular tissue. In some cases, the individual has one ovary and one testicle.

Herpes simplex virus type 1 (HSV-1) a viral infection that may cause blistering, typically of the lips and mouth; it may also infect the genitals.

Herpes simplex virus type 2 (HSV-2) a viral infection that may cause blistering, typically of the genitals; it may also infect the lips, mouth, and eyes.

Heteroeroticism *see Heterosexuality.*

Heterosexuality also referred to as heteroeroticism, a predominant cognitive, emotional, and sexual attraction to those of the other sex.

Heterosexism an ideology that denies, denigrates, and stigmatizes any nonheterosexual behavior, identity, or relationship.

HIV *see human immunodeficiency virus.*

Homoeroticism *see Homosexuality.*

Homophobia negative attitudes and reactions toward homosexuals and bisexuals.

Homosexuality also referred to as homoeroticism, a predominate cognitive, emotional, and sexual attraction to those of the same sex.

Hooded clitoris also known as clitoral foreskin adhesions; the condition in which the foreskin of the clitoris covers the glans of the clitoris.

Hormones (HOR-mohns) chemical substances produced by the gonads and various endocrine glands that enter the bloodstream and influence physiological functioning.

Hormone replacement therapy *see estrogen replacement therapy.*

Human chorionic gonadotropin (koh-ree-AHN-ihk goh-nad-uh-TROH-pihn) referred to as HCG; a hormone produced by the human placenta, which can be detected in the pregnant woman's urine.

Human immunodeficiency virus (HIV) a virus which attacks the immune system and may lead to AIDS.

Human papilloma virus (HPV) a sexually transmissible viral disease that may produce genital warts or condyloma.

Human sexuality a broad concept including such issues as values, relationships, behaviors, cognitions, emotions, and variability.

Hustler a male prostitute who serves other males seeking homosexual relations.

Hymen (HIGH-muhn) the thin membrane that may cover the vaginal opening.

Hyperventilation excessive rapid and deep breathing.

Hypoactive sexual desire low interest in sexual fantasies or sexual activities; also referred to as inhibited sexual desire and low sexual desire.

Hypothalamus (high-poh-THAL-uh-muhs) the region of the brain just above the pituitary gland that controls the hormone production of the pituitary gland and produces releasing factors (RF) for hormones produced by the pituitary gland.

Hypothesis a prediction about how one variable is related to another.

Hysterectomy (hihs-tuh-REHK-tuh-mee) surgical removal of the uterus and cervix.

Hysterotomy (hihs-tuh-RAH-tuh-mee) a method of abortion in which the fetus is removed by means of a cesarean section.

I

Id in psychoanalytic terms, that part of the person's personality that refers to instinctive biological drives, such as the need for sex, food, and water.

Identification in reference to gender-role learning, identification occurs when the child takes on the demeanor, behaviors, and personality of the same-sex parent.

Impotence *see erectile dysfunction.*

Incest (IHN-sehst) sexual relations between relatives, such as father-daughter, mother-son, and brother-sister. Sexual relations may include intercourse, oral sex, and genital manipulation.

Incest taboo Strong social norms against sexual relations between members of the same family (other than spouses); considered a near–universal taboo.

Independent variable in research, the variable that is expected to affect or explain change in the dependent variable.

Induced abortion the deliberate termination of a pregnancy through chemical or surgical means.

Infatuation a passion or attraction not based on reason.

Infertility the inability of a heterosexual couple to conceive a pregnancy after one year of regular, unprotected intercourse.

Infibulation a form of female genital mutilation that involves stitching together the two sides of the vulva to allow only a small opening for the passage of urine and menstrual blood.

Infundibulum (ihn-fuhn-DIHB-yuh-lum) the funnel-shaped end of the Fallopian tube leading to the ovary.

Inhibited female orgasm also known as anorgasmia and orgasmic dysfunction; the persistent or recurrent delay in or absence of orgasm following normal sexual excitement during sexual activity that is judged to be adequate in focus, intensity, and duration.

Inhibited male orgasm persistent or recurrent delay in or absence of orgasm in a male following normal sexual excitement during sexual activity that is judged to be adequate in focus, intensity, and duration; also known as retarded ejaculation and inhibited ejaculation.

Inhibited sexual desire also known as sexual apathy; the condition in which the person lacks sexual desire.

Intellectual disability commonly referred to as mental retardation, subaverage general intellectual functioning existing concurrently with deficits in adaptive behavior, and manifested during the developmental period.

Intersexed infants infants with ambiguous genitals.

Intrafamilial child sexual abuse exploitive or attempted sexual contact or between relatives before the victim is 18 years old.

Intrauterine (ihn-truh-YOOT-uh-rihn) device also known as the IUD; a small object placed in the uterus to prevent the fertilized egg from implanting on the uterine wall or to dislodge the fertilized egg if it has already implanted.

Introitus (ihn-TROH-ih-tuhs) the opening to the vagina.

In vitro fertilization involves removing the woman's ovum and placing it in a lab dish, fertilizing it with a partner's or donor's sperm, and inserting the fertilized egg into the woman's uterus.

Isthmus (IS-muhs) the narrow end of the Fallopian tubes leading to the uterus.

K

Kegel exercises repeated contractions of the pubococcygeal muscles designed to strengthen them. Researchers disagree on the benefits of such exercises.

Klinefelter's (KLIHN-fehl-terz) syndrome a sex chromosome pattern of XXY or XXXY. The result is a male child with abnormal testicular development, infertility, low libido, and sometimes mental retardation.

Klismaphilia (klihz-muh-FIHL-ee-uh) sexual arousal and gratification from an enema.

L

Labia majora (LAY-bee-uh muh-JOR-uh) outer lips of the vulva.

Labia minora (LAY-bee-uh muh-NOR-uh) inner lips of the vulva.

Lamaze (lah-MAHZ) childbirth a method of childbirth whereby the couple take a series of classes to educate them about childbirth and to prepare them for the experience.

Laminaria dried, sterile rods of compressed seaweed stems that, when inserted into the cervix, absorb moisture and increase in diameter; used to dilate the cervix in some abortion procedures.

Laparoscope a narrow, telescope-like medical instrument. One use involves inserting the instrument through an incision just below the woman's navel to view the Fallopian tubes and ovaries.

Laparoscopy (lap-uh-RAHS-koh-pee) a tubal ligation performed with the use of a laparoscope.

Late luteal phase dysphoric disorder (LLPDD) a proposed diagnostic category in the *Diagnostic and Statistical Manual of Mental Disorders* (3rd ed., rev. 1987) that refers to a group of negative symptoms that occur late in the luteal phase of a woman's menstrual cycle.

Latency stage according to Freud, the fourth stage in a person's psychosexual development characterized by repression of sexual urges.

Legalism adherence to a strict set of laws or code of conduct as a guide to decision making.

Lesbian a female homosexual. *See homosexual.*

Lesbian–feminism lesbianism that is based on the ideological belief that heterosexuality is a political institution that perpetuates male supremacy and is detrimental to women's freedom.

Leukorrhea a whitish mucal vaginal discharge occurring during the first trimester of pregnancy and continuing until delivery.

Liberal feminism a theoretical view that emphasizes that biological differences between women and men are minimal and gender inequality is socially created.

Libertarianism *see free will.*

Libido (lih-BEE-doh) Freud's term for sexual drive.

Liking intimacy without passion or commitment.

Locus of control the degree to which an individual views outcomes (events and rewards) as happening because of her or his own ability (internal control) or because of chance, fate, or powerful others (external control).

Longitudinal research research that involves collecting data across time, often on the same individuals, as opposed to collecting data only at one time.

Lovemap a term developed by John Money to describe a mental representation, or template, which develops within the first few years of life and depicts an individuals idealized lover and idealized program of sexuoerotic activity.

Lumpectomy removal of only the malignant mass from the breast.

Luteal (LOOT-ee-uhl) phase the last 14 days of the ovulatory cycle in which the corpus luteum is formed and the uterus is prepared to nourish a fertilized egg.

Luteinizing (LOOT-ee-ihn-eye-zihng) hormone also known as LH; it is produced and released by the pituitary gland and is responsible for ovulation and the maintenance of the corpus luteum for progesterone production. In the male, it stimulates testosterone production and the production of sperm cells.

Lymphogranuloma venereum (lihm-foh-gran-yuh-LOH-muh vuh-NIHR-ee-uhm) (LG) a sexually transmissible disease that may be successfully treated with antibiotics; it is prevalent in South America, the West Indies, Africa, and Southeast Asia.

M

Male genital mutilation a term referring to various operations performed on male genitals for cultural reasons. Includes surgical removal of the foreskin (circumcision), penile supraincision and penile subincision.

Male menopause time during middle age when the male begins to respond to lowered testosterone production.

Male pseudohermaphrodites genetically male individuals who have testes embedded in the abdomen and whose external genitalia resemble those of a female.

Mammography (muh-MAH-gruh-fee) an X–ray of the breast that is used to detect growths that may be cancerous.

Mania possessive, dependent love.

Manual stimulation sexual activity in which the genitals of one partner are caressed and stimulated by the hands of the other.

Mastalgia (mas-TAHL-juh) the painful swelling of the breasts.

Mastectomy (mas-TEHK-toh-mee) the surgical removal of the cancerous tissue and the surrounding tissue of the breast.

Masturbation (mas-tuhr-BAY-shun) stimulating one's own genitals for pleasure.

Meatus (mee-AY-tuhs) the opening at the top of the penis through which urine and semen are expelled.

Menarche (muh-NAHR-kee) the first menstrual period in a woman's life.

Menopause (MEHN-oh-pawz) the cessation of the menstrual cycle. Physiologic menopause is when the event occurs naturally (around age 50); surgical menopause occurs when the ovaries and/or uterus are removed surgically.

Menorrhagia (mehn-uh-RAJ-ee) excessive or prolonged menstruation.

Menses (MEHN-seez) another term for menstruation.

Menstrual extraction an experimental procedure that involves using a flexible plastic instrument to remove the uterine lining at about the time one's menstrual period is due. Menstrual extraction is done to relieve menstrual discomfort and to terminate early pregnancies. (Some people refer to the vacuum aspiration or suction currettage method of abortion as menstrual extraction.)

Menstruation (mehn-stroo-WAY-shun) the cyclic shedding of the uterine lining, resulting in vaginal bleeding about two weeks after an egg is released from any ovary and is not fertilized.

Microinjection the procedure whereby the physician injects sperm directly into the egg.

Middle age commonly thought of as the years between 40 and 60. Also defined as the time from when the last child leaves home until retirement.

Minipill an oral contraceptive containing low doses of progesterone and no estrogen.

Miscarriage the unintended death of an embryo or fetus up until the twentieth week of pregnancy.

Mittleschmerz (MIHT-tuhl-shmehrtz) pain felt by some women at midcycle during ovulation.

Modeling learning through observation.

Modified radical mastectomy the removal of the breast and lymph nodes but not the underlying muscles.

Mons veneris (mahns vuh-NAIR-ihs) the soft cushion of fatty tissue overlaying the pubic bone.

Morning sickness often a sign of early pregnancy; symptoms involve feeling nauseous and vomiting in the morning.

Mullerian (myoo-LEER-ee-uhn) ducts the duct system in the female embryo that later develops into the Fallopian tubes, uterus, and vagina in the adult female.

Multicultural feminism a theoretical view that emphasizes the diversity among women of different classes and races.

Multigravida (muhl-tee-GRAV-ihd-uh) the condition of having given birth before.

Multiple orgasm the ability to have several orgasms in succession with no refractory period and no break in stimulation. Both women and men are capable of multiple orgasms.

Mutual masturbation masturbation as a couple activity in which each person stimulates himself or herself.

Myometrium (migh-uh-MEE-tree-uhm) strong uterine muscles that contract and aid in delivery during childbirth.

N

Natural childbirth the term used to describe various methods of childbirth (LeBoyer, Lamaze, and Dick-Read) emphasizing preparation of the couple for delivery.

Necrophilia (nek-ruh-FIHL-ee-uh) deriving sexual arousal or gratification from a dead person.

Negative reinforcement increasing the frequency of a behavior by associating it with the removal of a stimulus.

Nocturnal emission male ejaculation during sleep while having an erotic dream; also known as a "wet dream."

Nocturnal orgasm female vaginal vascular engorgement during sleep while having an erotic dream.

Nocturnal penile tumescence erection during sleep.

Nonbattering marital rape rape within marriage in response to a long-standing conflict or disagreement about sex.

Nongonococcal urethritis (nahn-gahn-uh-KAHK-uhl yoor-ee-THRIGHT-uhs) (NGU) an inflammation of the urethra that results from microorganisms other than the gonococcus germ.

Nonlove the absence of passion, commitment, and intimacy.

Nonoxynol-9 the active agent in most spermicides; it provides some protection against organisms that cause sexually transmissible diseases.

Nonprobability sampling a sampling procedure in which there is no way to know the probability that any given member of the population has been included.

Nonprocreative sex sexual activity that can not result in producing children.

Nonspecific vaginitis (vaj-uh-NIGHT-uhs) the classification used when all the symptoms of vaginitis are present but no cause can be found. Antibiotics are used as treatment.

Nonterminative orgasms brief, clitoral orgasms that are not deeply satisfying.

Norplant long-acting reversible hormonal contraceptive implanted under the skin in a woman's upper arm.

O

Obsessive marital rape rape in which the husband rapes his wife in an obsessive, ritualistic, bizzare way.

Oedipal (ED-uh-puhl) complex according to Freudian theory, the male child views his father as a rival for his mother's attention, fears his father wants to castrate him, and wants to kill his father.

Oligomenorrhea (ahl-ee-goh-mehn-uh-REE-uh) unpredictable, irregular menstrual periods.

Oophorectomy the removal of the ovaries.

Open-ended question a question that encourages a person to provide an answer that contains a lot of information.

Operant learning theory a learning theory that emphasizes that behavior is a function of the consequences that follow the behavior. Reinforcement increases or maintains the frequency of behavior; punishment decreases it.

Oral contraceptives birth control pills containing hormones that prevent pregnancy by inhibiting the release of mature eggs from the ovaries.

Oral stage according to Freud, the first of four psychosexual stages in which pleasure is derived through stimulation of the lips and mouth (e.g. sucking, licking, chewing).

Orchiectomy surgical removal of one or both testicles.

Orgasm (OR-gaz-uhm) the climax of sexual excitement often experienced as a release of tension involving intense pleasure. Orgasm involves a number of physiological changes (such as vasocongestion and myotonia).

Orgasmic platform the narrowing of the outer third of the vagina that occurs after a woman reaches a high level of sexual arousal.

Ovary the primary female sex gland, which produces ova (eggs) and hormones, such as estrogen, progesterone, and androgen. There are two ovaries, one on each side of the uterus.

Ovulation (ahv-yoo-LAY-shun) the release of a mature egg from a follicle in an ovary.

Ovum the female reproductive cell; egg.

Ovum transfer sperm is placed into a surrogate woman. When the egg is fertilized, her uterus is flushed out, and the zygote is implanted into the otherwise infertile partner.

P

Pap smear the procedure in which surface cells are scraped from the vaginal walls and cervix to detect the presence of cancer.

Paraphilia (pair-uh-FIHL-ee-uh) overdependence on a culturally unacceptable or unusual stimulus for sexual arousal and satisfaction.

Partial mastectomy also known as lumpectomy; removal of the cancerous lump from the breast.

Partial zona drilling referred to as PZD, the procedure involves drilling tiny holes in the protective shell of the egg to increase the chance of it being fertilized.

Participant observation the collection of data while being involved in the phenomenon being studied.

Participation bias the fact that participants in a research study may differ from those who choose not to participate in a study.

Pedophilia (peh-doh-FIHL-ee-uh) recurrent, intense, sexual urges and sexually arousing fantasies for at least six months involving sexual activity with a prepubescent child.

Pelvic examination an external and internal visual and manual examination whereby the physician evaluates the health of a woman's reproductive organs.

Penile prosthesis (prahs-THEE-sihz) a penile implant. Two types are (1) semi-rigid rods implanted in the penis and (2) inflatable cylinders surgically placed inside the penis and attached to a pumping device placed in the man's scrotum. Used in cases in which the erectile dysfunction is physiologically based.

Penile subincision a form of male genital mutilation that involves slitting the ventral side of the penis into the urethra.

Penile supraincision a form of male genital mutilation that involves making a longitudinal slit through the dorsal of the foreskin.

Penis (PEE-nihs) the male sexual organ used for sexual intercourse and urination.

Performance anxiety anxiety that results from having excessive concern about the adequacy of one's own sexual performance.

Perimetrium (pair-uh-MEE-tree-uhm) the external cover of the uterus.

Perinatal death the death of an infant near the time of birth.

Perineum (pair-uh-NEE-uhm) the sensitive area of skin between the vaginal opening and the anus.

Periodic abstinence refraining from sexual intercourse each month during the time when the woman is thought to be fertile.

Peripheral arousal changes in heart rate, blood pressure, breath rate, skin color, skin temperature, and pupillary dilation that accompany sexual arousal.

Petting any interpersonal physical stimulation that does not include intercourse.

Phallic stage according to Freud, the third psychosexual stage in which sexual pleasure is derived primarily from self-stimulation of the genitals.

Phenylethylamine (feh-nihl-EHTH-uhl-ah-meen) a chemical, similar to amphetamine, that is associated with falling in love.

Pheromones (FEHR-uh-monz) odorous substances or smells that act as chemical messengers among many animals and serve as a foe repellant, boundary marker, child–parent bonding agent, or mating attractant.

Philanthropia (Fil-an-TARO-pee-uh) love of humankind.

Phileo (FIL-ee-o) love that is based on friendship.

Physiology the study of body functions.

PID Pelvic inflammatory disease; an infection and inflammation of the uterus and Fallopian tubes.

Pimp a man who manages the business affairs of a prostitute in exchange for money and/or sex. Pimps may provide care and assistance for their prostitutes; however, pimps may also treat prostitutes in a brutal, exploitive fashion.

Pituitary (pih-TOO-uh-tair-ee) gland known as the "master gland," the pituitary gland is located at the base of the brain and secretes several hormones that stimulate the production of other hormones (such as testosterone, estrogen, and progesterone) important in sexual and reproductive functioning.

Plateau phase the second of four stages of the sexual response cycle described by Masters and Johnson. This phase occurs after reaching a high level of sexual arousal. In women, the outer third of the vagina tightens and the clitoris withdraws behind the clitoral hood. In men, the diameter of the penis may increase slightly and the size of the testicles may increase considerably. Both women and men experience muscle contractions and spasms, heavy breathing, and increased heart rate and blood pressure.

Polyandry the practice of having more than one husband.

Polygamy the practice of having more than one spouse.

Polygyny the practice of having more than one wife.

Population in research, all of the cases in which the researcher is interested.

Pornography any material designed to arouse or excite a person sexually; often includes a form of aggression.

Positive reinforcement increasing or maintaining the frequency of behavior through the administration of a stimulus after the behavior has occurred.

POSSLQ term used by the U.S. Census Bureau to identify cohabitants. The acronyn stands for "persons of the opposite sex sharing living quarters."

Postcoital contraception various types of "morning-after pills" that may be used after unprotected intercourse during the woman's fertile time of the month.

Postpartum depression a severe depressive reaction to the birth on one's baby.

Postovulatory phase the third stage of the menstrual cycle in which the corpus luteum of the ovary secretes hormones (estrogen and progesterone) that prepare the uterus for a fertilized egg to implant.

Pragma (PRAG-muh) logical, pragmatic love.

Predatory rape also known as classic rape; rape in which the offender does not know the victim.

Premarital intercourse sexual intercourse before marriage.

Premature ejaculation *see early ejaculation.*

Premenstrual syndrome (PMS) the physical and psychological problems some women experience from the time of ovulation to the beginning of, and sometimes during, menstruation.

Preovulatory phase the stage of the menstrual cycle that begins with the release of follicle-stimulating hormone (FSH) from the pituitary, which stimulates the growth of a follicle in the ovary.

Priapism a condition in which a male has a painful erection that will not subside.

Primary sex characteristics biological characteristics, such as genitalia, gonads, chromosomes, and hormones, that differentiate females from males.

Primary sexual dysfunction a dysfunction that the person has always experienced.

Primigravida (pre-mih-GRAV-ih-duh) a woman who is pregnant for the first time.

Probability sampling a sampling procedure that allows the researcher to specify the probability that any given member in the population will be included in the sample.

Process of communication the way in which the content is delivered, received, and responded to.

Prochoice the political and/or philosophical position that supports the right of a woman to choose to have an abortion.

Procreation creating or producing offspring.

Progenesis the process whereby individuals and couples select for or against specific characteristics in a specific offspring on the basis of their own specific preferences and values.

Progesterone (proh-JEHS-tuh-rohn) a hormone produced and released by the corpus luteum of the ovary during the second half of the ovulatory cycle. It is necessary for the preparation of the lining of the uterus for the implantation of the fertilized egg. Progesterone is also produced by the placenta during pregnancy.

Progestin synthetic progesterone.

Prolife an antiabortion political and/or philosophical position that supports the right of a fetus to live.

Proliferative (proh-LIHF-er-uh-tihv) phase *see preovulatory phase.*

Pronatalism (proh-NAYT-uhl-ihzm) a social bias that having children is good; social influences that encourage procreation.

Pronatalistic a social bias in favor of having children.

Prophylactic (proh-fuh-LAK-tihk) condom.

Prostaglandins (prahs-tuh-GLAN-dihnz) hormone-like substances that cause the uterus to contract. When introduced into the vagina as a suppository or injected into the amniotic sac, prostaglandins induce labor, and the fetus is aborted.

Prostate (PRAHS-tayt) the gland that surrounds the male urethra as it exits from the bladder and contributes secretions to the seminal fluid.

Prostatectomy (prahs-tuh-TEK-tuh-mee) the surgical removal of the prostate gland.

Prostatic urethra (prah-STAT-ik yoo-REE-thruh) that portion of the urethra that passes through the prostate.

Prosthesis (prahs-THEE-sihs) an artificial substitute for a missing part.

Prostitution the exchange of sexual services for money.

Pseudohermaphroditism (soo-doh-her-MAF-ruh-dight-ihzm) a condition in which an individual has the gonads matching the sex chromosomes but the external genitals resembling those of the other sex.

Psychoanalysis a type of therapy developed by Sigmund Freud that assumes that many problems are the result of improper psychosexual development and can be solved by exploring one's unconscious impulses, anxieties, and internal conflicts.

Psychosexology the study of how psychological processes both influence and are influenced by sexual development and behavior.

Puberty (PYOO-ber-tee) the age at which the testes of the male and the ovaries of the female begin to function and the person becomes capable of reproduction, usually around age 12 or 13. At this time, secondary sex characteristics also appear.

Pubic lice also known as "the crabs"; blood suckers that attach themselves to the base of coarse hair.

Pubococcygeal (pyoo-boh-kahk-SIH-jee-uhl) muscles muscles surrounding the outer third of the vaginal barrel.

Pudendum (pyoo-DEHN-duhm) another term for vulva.

Punishment a decrease in a behavior as a result of adding a stimulus (positive punishment) or removing a stimulus (negative punishment).

Q

Qualitative research research that focuses on the subjective aspects of human experience and the meanings and interpretations that humans ascribe to their world.

Quantitative research research that focuses on numerical quantification of human and social phenomena and statistical analysis of relationships among variables.

R

Radical feminism a theoretical view that emphasizes essential differences between females and males.

Radical mastectomy (mas-TEHK-toh-mee) the removal of the entire breast, all underlying tissue, and lymph nodes.

Radical prostatectomy the removal of the prostate.

Random sample a sample in which every member in the population being studied has an equal chance of being selected.

Rape forced sexual relations against a person's will; may include intercourse, oral sex, anal sex, and insertion of an object into the person's vagina or anus.

Rape trauma syndrome the acute, long-term reorganization process that results from forcible rape or attempted forcible rape.

Realistic love also known as conjugal love; love based on information and interaction with the partner over a number of years. The opposite end of the continuum from romantic love.

Reflective listening a communication technique that involves paraphrasing or restating what the person you are listening to has communicated to you (either verbally or nonverbally).

Refractory (ree-FRAK-tuh-ree) period the period following orgasm during which the person cannot be sexually aroused.

Reinforcement increasing or maintaining a behavior by adding a stimulus (positive reinforcement) or removing a stimulus (negative reinforcement).

Relativism a value system that emphasizes making decisions in the context of a particular situation.

Reliability the consistency of a measuring tool or technique.

Representative sample a sample that accurately reflects the population from which it is selected and allows the researcher to make inferences from the sample to the population.

Resolution phase the last of four stages of the sexual response cycle described by Masters and Johnson. During this stage, the body returns to its preexcitement-orgasm condition.

Reversion therapy a controversial form of therapy for ego-dystonic gay individuals who have previously lived a heterosexual life–style and who want to become heterosexual again.

Rhythm also known as the rhythm method; a procedure whereby the woman avoids intercourse at times she feels she is most likely to get pregnant. This time is determined by carefully monitoring her menstrual cycle.

Rimming manual or oral stimulation of the anus and surrounding area.

Romantic love intense emotional feelings for another person that are based on self-constructed illusions about that person. Romantic love may involve drastic mood swings, palpitations of the heart, and intrusive thinking about the partner.

RU-486 a synthetic steroid that effectively terminates pregnancies within the first nine weeks of gestation. Also referred to as a "morning-after pill," RU-486 is considered to be a method of abortion, as well as a form of postcoital contraception.

S

Saline abortion generally performed between 16 and 24 weeks' gestation, the procedure involves injecting a solution of saline into the amniotic sac, causing rapid death of the fetus.

Salpingectomy (sal-pihn-GEHK-toh-mee) also known as tubal ligation or "tying the tubes"; a sterilization procedure in which a section of the woman's Fallopian tubes are cut out and the ends are tied, clamped, or cauterized so that eggs cannot pass down the Fallopian tubes to be fertilized.

Sample a portion of the total population that is studied and from which generalizations are made to the larger population.

Satiation repeated exposure to a stimulus resulting in the loss of its ability to reinforce.

Satyriasis (Sat-uh-RIGH-uh-sihs) an extremely high need in a male for continuous sexual stimulation.

Scabies (SKAY-beez) condition in which a parasite penetrates the skin and lays eggs. The larvae make tunnels in the skin, causing intense itching.

Scrotum (SCROH-tuhm) the pouch beneath the penis containing the testes.

Secondary dysfunction dysfunction that the person is currently experiencing after a period of satisfactory sexual functioning.

Secondary sex characteristics physical changes that occur during puberty, which include the development of larger breasts in females, different patterns of facial and body hair in females and males, and a deeper voice in males.

SEICUS Sex Education and Information Council of the United States; an organization dedicated to improving sex education.

selective termination the removal of one or more embryos or fetuses from multiple pregnancy.

Self-disclosure the process of communicating personal information to another person.

Self-fulfilling prophecy behaving to make the expectations come true. A person who is expected to engage in a particular behavior (be faithful, be unfaithful) will tend to behave consistently with those expectations.

Semen (SEE-muhn) also known as seminal fluid; a thick mixture emitted from the penis during intense sexual arousal, which contains sperm from the testes and fluids from the prostate, seminal vesicles, and Cowper's glands.

Semen conservation doctrine the belief that good health depends on conserving vital fluids (i.e. semen) of the body.

Semen's technique a technique developed by James Semens for treating early ejaculation. The man signals his partner to stop stimulation when he feels the urge to ejaculate and signals again when the feeling of impending ejaculation dissipates.

Seminal vesicles (SEHM-uh-nuhl VEHS-ih-kuhlz) twin glands on either side of the male prostate that secrete fluid into the vas deferens to enhance sperm motility.

Seminiferous tubules (sehm-uh-NIF-er-uhs TOOB-yoolz) structures in the testes that produce the sperm.

Sensate focus a series of exercises developed by Masters and Johnson that involve sensual touching without the goal of orgasm and are intended to remove performance anxiety. May be used to treat sexual dysfunctions or enhance a sexual relationship.

Sex education formal and informal learning about the biological, sociological, psychological, and interpersonal aspects of human sexuality aids in the integration of sexuality into one's life in a way that is productive for one's self and others.

Sex flush the vasocongestive skin response to increasing sexual tensions.

Sex guilt a tendency toward self-punishment for violating one's personal sexual standards.

Sexism an attitude, action, or institutional structure that subordinates or discriminates against an individual or group because of their sex.

Sexology the study of the sexual life of the individual from the viewpoint of medicine and the social sciences.

Sex steroids a group name for compounds, including sex hormones, with estrogenic and androgenic properties.

Sexual addiction the condition in which sexual thoughts and/or behavior negatively affect one's health, relationships, and/or work.

Sexual apathy *see inhibited sexual desire.*

Sexual aversion persistent or recurrent aversion to and avoidance of genital contact with a sexual partner.

Sexual celibacy no sexual behavior with another but with one's self, or no sexual behavior either with others or with one's self.

Sexual coercion the use of force (actual or threatened) to get a person to engage in sexual acts against the person's will.

Sexual dysfunction an impairment or difficulty that affects sexual functioning or that produces sexual pain.

Sexual fantasy a dynamic intrapsychic process that involves imagined sexual content and is sexually arousing.

Sexual fulfillment the state of being satisfied with one's sex life and sexual relationships.

Sexual harassment unwanted sexually oriented behavior in a work or academic setting.

Sexual identity a multidimensional concept encompassing biological sex, gender identity, gender role, sexual orientation, erotic fantasies, patterns of arousal and sexual response, and self-concept.

Sexual intercourse the insertion of the male penis into the female vagina.

Sexual jealousy any aversive emotional reaction that occurs as the result of a partner's extradyadic relationship that is real, imagined, or considered likely to occur.

Sexual masochism recurrent, intense, sexual urges and sexually arousing fantasies of at least six months' duration in which sexual arousal or gratification is obtained through enacting scripts that involve experiencing suffering and pain.

Sexual orientation the combination of one's sexual behavior, thoughts, fantasies, emotions, attractions, and self-concept in regard to members of the same sex, the other sex, or both.

Sexual response Physiological and psychological reactions to sexual stimuli.

Sex roles a term that is often confused with and used interchangeably with the term "gender roles." However, while gender roles are socially defined and can be enacted by either sex, sex roles are defined by biological constraints and can be enacted by members of only one sex (e.g. childbearer, sperm donor).

Sexual sadism recurrent, intense, sexual urges and sexually arousing fantasies of a least six months' duration involving acts that hurt or humiliate the sexual partner.

Sexual self-concept an individual's evaluation of his or her own sexual feelings and actions.

Sexual values moral guidelines for sexual behavior.

Sexually open marriage *see swinging.*

Sexually transmissible diseases (STDs) diseases that may be transmitted, and often are, through sociosexual contact; formerly known as venereal or social diseases.

Shaping rewarding small approximations to the desired goal.

SIECUS Sex Information and Education Council of the United States.

Simultaneous orgasm two partners engaging in sexual activity and reaching orgasm at the same time.

Situation ethics decision making on the basis of the context of a particular situation, not on the basis of a prescribed set of laws or codes of action. Also known as relativism.

Situational dysfunction a sexual dysfunction that occurs in one context or setting and not in another.

Smegma (SMEHG-muh) foul-smelling secretions beneath the clitoral hood and the foreskin of the uncircumcised penis.

Social constructionist view a theoretical view that emphasizes that sexuality, sexual meanings, sexual identities, and gender relations are socially defined and controlled.

Social learning theory a theory that emphasizes that learning occurs through observation and imitation.

Social scripts shared interpretations and expected behaviors of a social situation.

Socialist feminism a theoretical view that suggests that sexism and discrimination against women are the result of how societies are structured economically and reproductively.

Sociosexology the study of how social and cultural forces both influence and are influenced by sexual attitudes, beliefs, and behaviors.

Sodomy sexual activity that involves the mouth or anus of one person in contact with the genitals of another person. Sometimes refers to anal intercourse between two men.

Sonogram (SAH-nuh-gram) a live video image of the fetus resulting from an ultrasound scan that is used in prenatal testing.

Spectatoring excessive self-awareness during sexual relations that interferes with sexual response.

Spermatozoa (sper-maht-uh-ZO-uh) mature sperm cells.

Spermicide a contraceptive chemical that kills sperm.

Spermicidal (sper-muh-SIGHD-uhl) foam a birth control substance containing chemicals lethal to sperm. When applied around the cervix, sperm are killed before entering the uterus.

Spermicidal gel a sperm-killing substance that is applied to the diaphragm before it is inserted.

Sponge a soft, pliable, contraceptive device containing spermacides that is inserted into the vagina before intercourse to prevent sperm from entering the uterus.

Spontaneous abortion commonly referred to as a "miscarriage," the unintended termination of a pregnancy.

Spirochete (SPIGH-roh-keet) bacteria that cause syphilis.

Squeeze technique a procedure sometimes used in the treatment of early ejaculation. The procedure involves squeezing the penis below the coronal ridge before the male feels ejaculation is inevitable so he will lose his urge to ejaculate.

Sterilization a surgical procedure designed to permanently prevent the capacity of either sex to reproduce.

Stillbirth a fetal death after twenty weeks of gestation.

Storge (STOR-gay) friendship, companionate love.

Stroke cerebral malfunctions that are also referred to as cerebrovascular accidents.

Structural-functional theories sociological theories that view society as made up of interconnected parts that operate together to achieve social stability.

Stuffing technique a procedure whereby the partners literally stuff the penis in the vagina. Used by elderly men who have soft erections and by spinal cord-injured males.

Suction curettage an abortion procedure used to terminate pregnancy during the first 6–8 weeks. Also referred to as menstrual extraction (ME) or vacuum aspiration abortion. Involves inserting a hollow plastic rod attached to a suction aspirator into the woman's uterus through the cervix and drawing the fetal tissue and surrounding matter out of the uterus into a container. Following the suction procedure, the uterine cavity is explored with a small metal curette to ensure all tissue has been extracted.

Superego in psychoanalytic terms, that part of the person's personality that guides the person to do what is morally right and good. The person's conscience.

Surrogate partner therapy a form of sex therapy in which a surrogate partner, also known as a sex therapy practitioner, provides sexual experiences with the client that are recommended by the therapist so that the client learns new ways of relating sexually in a controlled environment. Sexual surrogates may be either women or men and may have either women or men as clients.

Surrogate mother a woman who voluntarily agrees to be artificially inseminated, carry a baby to term, and give up the legal right to the baby at birth to a couple or individual desiring such baby.

Survey research a method of research that involves collecting data by interviewing people or giving them a questionnaire.

Swinging *see comarital sex.*

Symbolic interaction theories sociological theories that suggest that human behavior is based on definitions and meanings that are learned through interaction with others.

Syphilis (SIHF-uh-lihs) a sexually transmissible disease caused by spirochete entering the mucous membranes that line various body openings.

Systematic desensitization a procedure whereby the person learns to become more relaxed and at ease when in the presence of the stimulus that previously caused anxiety.

Systems theory a sociological theory that emphasizes the role of interpersonal and relationship aspects of behavior.

T

Telephonicophilia a variation of exhibitionism in which the individual is aroused by and derives satisfaction from using obscene language on the telephone with a stranger.

Terminative orgasms orgasms described as longer more satisfying orgasms that result from contractions in the vagina and uterus.

Testes (TEHS-teez) also known as testicles; the male gonads located inside the scrotum that produce sperm and male hormones (androgen and testosterone).

Testicular (tehs-TIHK-yoo-ler) feminization syndrome (TFS) a condition in which a genetic male (XY) has the external genitals of a female but the internal organs (testes embedded in abdomen) of a male. TFS is also known as androgen-insensitivity syndrome.

Testosterone (teh-STAHS-tuh-rohn) the principal androgen or male sex hormone produced by the testes, which is responsible for the development of male secondary sex characteristics and influences the sex drive in both males and females. Testosterone is also produced by the adrenal cortex and the ovaries.

Test-tube fertilization also known as in vitro fertilization; a procedure in which an egg is removed from a ripe follicle and fertilized by a sperm cell in a culture dish. The fertilized egg is allowed to divide for about two days and then inserted into the woman's uterus, where it implants.

Total dysfunction sexual dysfunction that occurs in all contexts.

Toucheurism recurring, intense sexual urges, of at least six months' duration, to use one's hands to touch a non-consenting person.

Toxic shock syndrome a condition in which the bacteria staphylococcus aureus produce a poison that is released into the bloodstream. Larger, more absorbent tampons are thought to produce a favorable environment for the growth of such bacteria.

Transsexuals (trans-SEHK-shoo-uhl) individuals who have the genetic and anatomical characteristics of one sex but the self-concept of the other sex (i.e. transsexuals experience gender dysphoria). Some transsexuals undergo sex reassignment surgery to alter their genitals to match their self-concept.

Transvestic fetishism recurrent, intense, sexual urges and sexually arousing fantasies of at least six months' duration involving cross-dressing.

Tranvestites individuals (usually male) who dress in the clothing of the other sex as a means of achieving sexual arousal.

Trichomoniasis (trihk-oh-moh-NIGH-uh-sihs) a vaginal infection that results in vulvar burning and itching; usually, but not always, sexually transmitted.

Tubectomy a female sterilization procedure involving tying the Fallopian tubes of a woman to prevent the egg from implanting on the uterine wall.

Tumescence engorgement of body parts or organs, caused by vasocongestion.

Turner's syndrome a condition in which a female has only one sex chromosome (XO), rather than two (XX). The result is abnormal development of the ovaries, failure to menstruate, and infertility.

U

Ultrasound scan a procedure whereby sound waves are used to project an image on a video screen; used in prenatal testing.

Urethra (yoo-REE-thruh) in females, a short tube connecting the bladder to the urethral opening; in males, the tube connecting the bladder to the end of the penis, where urine is expelled.

Urethral (yoo-REE-thruhl opening) the opening to the female urethra located below the clitoris and above the vaginal opening.

Urethritis (yoor-ih-THRIGHT-uhs) inflammation of the urethra and bladder in males.

Uterine orgasms orgasms caused by deep intravaginal stimulation and characterized by a deep sense of satisfaction.

Uterus (YOOT-uh-ruhs) a pear-shaped organ in which the fertilized egg implants and develops into a fetus.

V

Vacuum curettage (kyoor-uh-TAHJ) an abortion method whereby a hollow plastic rod is inserted into the woman's uterus to suck out the embryo and the placenta.

Vagina (vuh-JIGH-nuh) an elastic canal from the cervix to the vulva. A passageway for menstrual flow and for the fetus at birth.

Vaginal opening *see introitus.*

Vaginal orgasm an orgasm that results from intercourse or vaginal stimulation without direct clitoral stimulation.

Vaginal sponge *see sponge.*

Vaginismus (vaj-uh-NIHZ-muhs) recurrent or persistent involuntary, spasmodic contraction of the vaginal muscles making penetration during sexual intercourse difficult or impossible.

Vaginitis (vaj-uh-NIGHT-uhs) infection of the vagina.

Validity the degree to which a research instrument measures what it intends to measure.

Variable any measurable event, characteristic, or property that varies or is subject to change.

Vas deferens (vas DEF-uh-renz) ducts in the male that carry sperm from the epididymis to the ejaculatory duct.

Vasectomy (vas-EHK-toh-mee) a minor surgical procedure whereby the vas deferens are cut so as to prevent sperm from entering the penis; the primary method of male sterilization.

Vasocongestion (vays-oh-kahn-JEHS-chuhn) congestion of the blood vessels; a primary physiologic response to sexual stimulation that involves increased blood flow to the genital area.

Vestibular bulbs muscles beneath the bulbocavernosus muscles on both sides of the vaginal opening that help to grip the penis.

Vestibule the area between the labia minora that includes the urethral and vaginal openings.

Voyeurism (VOY-yer-ihzm) recurrent, intense urges of at least six months' duration to look at unsuspecting people who are naked, undressing, or engaging in sexual behavior.

Vulva (VUHL-vuh) the external genital region of the female.

Vulval orgasms orgasms similar to clitoral or nonterminative orgasms that are characterized by spastic contractions of the outer third of the vagina.

W

Win-win solution a solution in which both people involved in a conflict feel satisfied with the agreement or resolution.

Withdrawal an ineffective method of contraception that involves the man withdrawing his penis from the woman's vagina before he ejaculates. Also known as coitus interruptus.

Wolffian (WUHL-fee-uhn) ducts the duct system in the male embryo that later develops into the epididymis, vas deferens, ejaculatory ducts and urethra in the adult male.

X

X chromosome the sex chromosome that produces a female.

Y

Y chromosome the sex chromosome that produces a male.

Z

Zoophilia (zoo-FIL-ee-uh) intense, recurrent sexual urges and sexual fantasies involving sexual contact with animals.

Zygote (ZIGH-goht) a fertilized egg resulting from the union of a sperm and an egg. Represents the first cell in the development of a human being.

Zygote intra-Fallopian transfer (ZIFI) a procedure whereby the egg is fertilized in a lab dish and the zygote or embryo is placed directly into the Fallopian tube.

Appendices

APPENDIX A Sexual Choices Autobiography Outline

Your instructor may ask you to write a sexual autobiography as part of the human sexuality course in which you are enrolled. Check with your instructor to ascertain if you may complete a sexual autobiography, how much (if any) credit it is worth, and the degree to which your autobiography will be regarded as private and confidential with no one other than your instructor reading it.

The outline to follow emphasizes the theme of choices in regard to your sexual development. Use the outline to develop your paper. You may feel that some topics are too personal and you may want to omit writing about them.

I. Choices: Free will versus determinism

Based on the discussion provided in Chapter 1, what is your view of the degree to which the sexual choices you make are "free" or "determined"? Give examples.

II. Sexual Beginnings

- **A.** What is your earliest memory of sex and sexuality? Provide details.
- **B.** What did you learn about sex from your parents, peers, and teachers (both academic and religious)?
- **C.** What sexual experience with others did you have, in what context, with what frequency, as a child?
- **D.** To what degree are your sexual values absolutist, legalistic, or relative?
- **E.** How physically healthy are you?

III. Masturbation

- **A.** How did you learn about masturbation, at what age did you first experience it, and what was the context of your first experience (alone or with others)?
- **B.** How did you feel about masturbation when you first began? How do you feel about it now?
- **C.** With whom have you talked about masturbation—parents, peers, lovers? What has been the context of these discussions?
- **D.** Have you experienced what you define to be an orgasm by means of masturbation?

IV. Intercourse

- **A.** How did you learn that people had intercourse? Provide details.
- **B.** How old were you the first time you had intercourse, what was the relationship with your partner, how did you feel about the experience, and how did it affect the relationship with your partner?
- **C.** To what degree are you comfortable being the initiator of a sexual encounter leading to intercourse?

V. Intrapsychic Factors

- **A.** What sexual behaviors have you engaged in that have created the most guilt?
- **B.** What level of emotional involvement have you had with your sexual partner(s)? How do you feel about this level?
- **C.** What sexual fantasies do you have? To what degree are they a part of your masturbatory and intercourse experiences? To what degree have you shared your sexual fantasies with a partner?
- **D.** What is your sexual self-concept?
- **E.** How has your sexual self-concept changed since adolescence?
- **F.** What is your self-concept and body image? How have these changed since adolescence?
- **G.** What is the level of your libido?
- **H.** What influences your libido?

VI. Communication

- **A.** How comfortable do you feel talking about sex?
- **B.** How comfortable do you feel telling your partner what you like and don't like sexually?
- **C.** How have your sexual partners responded to your communication or lack of it in reference to your sexual interaction?
- **D.** How comfortable do you feel talking about heterosexuality, homosexuality, oral sex, and anal sex?

VII. Sexual Abuse

- **A.** To what degree have you been pressured or forced to participate in sexual activity against your will?
- **B.** How did you react to this experience at the time?
- **C.** What is your feeling now about the experience?
- **D.** To what degree have you pressured or forced others to participate in sexual experiences against their will?

VIII. Safer Sex

- **A.** What is the most "risky choice" you have made in regard to your sexual behavior?
- **B.** What is the "safest choice" you have made in regard to your sexual behavior?
- **C.** How comfortable are you buying condoms?
- **D.** How comfortable are you discussing the need to use a condom with a potential sex partner?

IX. Reproductive Choices

- **A.** What is your preferred form of contraception?
- **B.** How comfortable do you feel discussing the need for contraception with a potential sex partner?
- **C.** How many children (if any) do you want, and at what intervals?
- **D.** How important is it to you that your partner want the same number of children as do you?
- **E.** How do you feel about sterilization and abortion?
- **F.** How do you feel about the use of reproductive technologies?

APPENDIX B Resources and Organizations

Abortion

Prochoice:

National Abortion Rights Action League
1101 14th St. N. W., Suite 500
Washington, DC 20005

Religious Coalition for Abortion Rights
100 Maryland Ave., N.E.
Washington, DC 20002-5625

Prolife:

National Right to Life Committee
419 7th St., N.W.
Washington, DC 20045

Feminists for Life of America
811 E. 47th St.
Kansas City, MO 64110

Breast Implants

FDA Breast Implant Information
800-532-4440
Hearing Impaired 800-688-6167

Contraception

Association for Voluntary Sterilization, Inc.
122 E. 42nd St.
New York, NY 10168

National Clearinghouse for Family Planning Information
P. O. Box 10716
Rockville, MD 20850

Planned Parenthood Federation of America
810 Seventh Ave.
New York, NY 10019

Gender Equality

National Organization for Changing Men
P. O. Box 451
Watseka, IL 60970

National Organization for Women
1000 16th St., N. W., Suite 700
Washington, DC 20036

Infertility and Reproductive Technology

American Fertility Society, Dept. P
2140 11th Ave., So., Suite 200
Birmingham, AL 35205-2800

Resolve
5 Water St.
Arlington, MA 02174
617-643-2424
(provides phone counseling and referral for persons experiencing infertility)

Pregnancy and Childbirth

American Society for Psychoprophylaxis in Obstetrics (ASPO/Lamaze)
1840 Wilson Blvd., Suite 204
Arlington, VA 22201

La Leche League International
9616 Minneapolis Ave., Box 1209
Franklin, IL 60131-8209

Sexual Abuse

Incest Survivors Anonymous
P.O. Box 5613
Long Beach, CA 90805-0613

Feminist Alliance Against Rape
P.O. Box 21033
Washington, DC 20009

C. Henry Kempe National Center for the Prevention and Treatment of Child Abuse and Neglect
1205 Oneida St.
Denver, CO 80220

National Center for the Prevention and Control of Rape
5000 Fishers Lane, Room 6C-12
Rockville, MD 20857

National Clearinghouse on Marital and Date Rape
2325 Oak St.
Berkeley, CA 94708

The Safer Society Program
Prison Research Education/Action Project
Shoreham Depot Road
Orwell, VT 05760

Victims of Clergy Abuse Linkup (VOCAL)
P. O. Box 1268
Wheeling, IL 60090

Victims of Incest Can Emerge Survivors (VOICES)
P.O. Box 148309
Chicago, IL 60614
312-327-1500

Women Against Pornography
358 W. 47th St.
New York, NY 10010

Working Women's Institute
593 Park Ave.
New York, NY 10021

Sexual Addiction

Sexaholics Anonymous
P. O. Box 300
Simi Valley, CA 93060

Sexuality Credentialing, Education, and Research

The Alan Guttmacher Institute
111 Fifth Ave.
New York, NY 10003

American Association of Sex Educators, Counselors, and Therapists (AASECT)
11 Dupont Circle, N.W., Suite 220
Washington, DC 20036

Harry Benjamin Gender Dysphoria Association, Inc.
900 Welch Road, Suite 402
Palo Alto, CA 94304

Kinsey Institute for Sex Research
Room 416, Morrison Hall
Indiana University
Bloomington, IN 47401

Masters and Johnson Institute
24 S. Kings Highway
St. Louis, MO 63108

Sex Information and Education Council of the United States (SIECUS)
New York University
32 Washington Plaza
New York, NY 10003

Society for the Scientific Study of Sex
P.O. Box 208
Mt. Vernon, IA 52314

Sexual Orientation

International Gay and Lesbian Human Rights Commission (IGLHRC)
2978 Folsom St.
San Francisco, CA 94110

International Lesbian and Gay Association (ILGA)
141 Cloudesley Rd.
London, N1, England

National Coalition for Black Lesbians and Gays
19641 West Seven Mile Road
Detroit, MI 48219

National Federation of Parents and Friends of Gays (NF-PFOG)
8020 Eastern Ave., N.W.
Washington, DC 20012

National Gay and Lesbian Task Force
1734 14th St., N.W.
Washington, DC 20009-4309

National Gay and Lesbian Crisis Line
800-221-7044

Parents and Friends of Lesbians and Gays (PFLAG)
P.O. Box 27605
Washington, DC 20038

Sexually Transmissible Diseases

American Foundation for AIDS Research (AMFAR)
Suite T-3601
1515 Broadway
New York, NY 10036

American Social Health Association
(Herpes Resource Center and HPV Support Program)
P.O. Box 13827
Research Triangle Park, NC 27709

Centers for Disease Control
National Center for Infectious Diseases
Atlanta, GA 30333

Multicultural Inquiry and Research on AIDS (MIRA)
6025 Third St.
San Francisco, CA 94124

National AIDS Hotline
800-342-AIDS
Spanish Speaking 800-344-7432
Hearing Impaired 800-243-7889

National Association for People with AIDS (NAPWA)
1413 K St., N.W., 10th Floor
Washington, DC 20005-3405

National Herpes Hotline
919-361-8488 Monday–Friday 9 A.M.to 7 P.M. Eastern

National STD Hotline
800-227-8922 Monday–Friday 8 A.M. to 11 P.M. Eastern

INDEX

A

Abortion
  adolescent, and parental consent, 12–13
  attitudes toward, 832–36
    as reflected in relativism, 46–49
  availability of services, 848
  characteristics of women getting, 844–46
  costs of, 848
  as crime, 69, 849–50
  decision making in, 796, 802, 824, 846–48, 860, 861
  of defective fetus, 801
  definition of, 832
  ethical issues in, 836–38
  as immoral, 837–38
  incidence of, 843–44
  induced, 832
  international trends in, 842–43
  IUD as form of, 756
  legislation on, 849–50
  methods of
    dilation and evacuation, 801, 839
    dilation and suction, 838–39, 841
    menstrual extraction, 841
    prostaglandins, 801, 840
    RU-486, 764, 772, 840–41
    saline, 801, 839, 840
    suction curettage, 838, 840
  in preliterate societies, 842
  postcoital contraception as, 764
  psychological effects of, 853–56
  spontaneous, 832
  Supreme Court rulings on, 850–53
  time limits on, 70
  of unplanned pregnancies, 735
Abortion Attitude Scale, 833
Abortion rate, 843, 844
Abortion ratio, 843
Absolutism, on sexual values, 42–44
Abstention, 760–61
Abstinence, 748, 871
  Acceptance of Adoption and Five Alternative Fertilization Techniques, 790–91
Accidental death, and masturbation, 339
Acer, David, 671
Achonodroplasis, 746
Acquaintance rape, 682–83, 701
  Acquired immunodeficiency syndrome (AIDS). *See* AIDS; HIV infection
Acrotomophilia, 621, 636
Active self-determinism, 5
Acyclovir, for genital herpes, 652
Adolescence
  beginning and end of, 446
  and competence in making sexual choices, 11–14
  national surveys of, 151
  peer influence in, 291–92
  pregnancy in, 734
    and abortion, 844
    effects of sex education on, 871, 888–89
    and low birthrate, 808
  sexuality in, 446–54
    physical changes in, 447–48
    psychological changes in, 449
    sexual behaviors in, 449–53
  stages of, 446–47
Adolescent Family Life Act (1990), 871
Adoption, 858–59
Adrenocorticotrophin (ACTH), 514
Adult circumcision, 213
Adultery, 69
  and Jewish heritage, 50
  laws on, 68
Affairs, 369. *See also* Extradyadic sexuality
AFT test, 801
Agape, 503, 505
Age
  as factor in sexual dysfunction, 538–40
  in value of woman, 299
Aging Sexual Knowledge and Attitudes Scale, 460–63
AIDS (Acquired Immune Deficiency Syndrome), 32, 641, 659. *See also* HIV infection
  and circumcision, 214
  education on, 663, 667, 868, 879, 880, 886
  and extradyadic sex, 389
  and gay lifestyle, 428, 429, 430
  and HIV clinical trials, 128–29
  knowledge and attitudes about, 644–46
  reasons for continuation of risk-taking behavior, 670, 885
  and safe sex, 42, 180, 429
  and workplace, 70
AIDS/HIV Treatment Directory, 649
AIDS-related complex (ARC), 641
Akron Center for Reproductive Health v. *City of Akron,* 851
Alcohol
  as cause of sexual dysfunction, 534, 546–47
  consumption of, during pregnancy, 799
  and date rape, 683
  impact of, on sexual response, 248–52
  and rape prevention, 699
  social psychology of, and sexual effects, 250–52
  treating abuse of, 632
Aleut male, extramarital sex for, 89
Alpha bias, in gender theories, 288–89
Alternatives to Fear (ATF), 702
Alzheimer's disease, 580, 581
Ambivalence, 7
Amenorrhea, 204
American Association of Sex Educators, Counselors, and Therapists (AASECT), 562, 565, 879
American Baptist Church, on sexual values, 61
American Fertility Society, guidelines for donor insemination, 787
American Law Institute, 412
Amniocentesis, 800–1, 824
Amphetamines
  as cause of sexual dysfunction, 534
  effects of, on sexual response, 254
Amyl nitrate, effects of, on sexual response, 254–55

Anabolic steroid
impact of, on sexual response, 248
side effects of, 248
Anal intercourse, 383
condom use for, 384, 433, 643, 753
as form of petting, 383–84
among homosexuals, 406, 432–33
in rape, 685
as unnatural act, 81
Anal stage of development, 161
Anal stimulation, 337, 383
Anatomy, 190. *See also* Sexual anatomy and physiology and human sexuality, 16
Androgen, 244, 281
Androgen-insensitivity syndrome, 276–77
Androgenital syndrome, 276
Androgen replacement therapy, 281
Androgyny, 305–7
and sexual relationships, 307
Anger rape, 687
Annular hymen, 193
Anorexia nervosa, 320
Anorgasmia, 550–53
Antabuse, 250, 632
Antenatal testing. *See* Prenatal testing
Antianxiety drugs, impact of, on sexual response, 247
Antidepressant drugs, impact of, on sexual response, 247
Antigay violence, 407–9
Antihypertensive medications, impact of, on sexual response, 247
Antilibidimal drugs, for intellectual disabilities, 588
Anus, 807
Anxiety
as cause of sexual dysfunction, 536–37, 546
impact of, on sexual arousal, 233
Apert syndrome, 746
Apgar scores, 799
Aphrodisiac, 246
Apotomnophilia, 621
Areola, 209–10
Arousal
genital, 228
physiological and subjective aspects of, 228
subjective, 228
Arousal myths, 230, 233
Arousal-phase dysfunctions, 544–45
female sexual arousal dysfunction, 545
causes and contributing factors of, 545
treatment for, 545
male erectile dysfunction, 545–50
causes and contributing factors of, 546–47
treatment for, 547–50
Arthritis, 599
Artificial insemination, 33, 786–87
by donor (AID), 786, 793, 795
in homosexual relationships, 740–41
by husband (AIH), 786
Asceticism, 43–44
Asexuality, 321
Asexual reproduction, 160
Ashe, Arthur, 642, 868
Asian cultures, sexual values in, 53–55
Asphyxiophilia, 621
Assertiveness training, for rape, 693
Association for Childbirth at Home (ACAH), 822
Association of Gay Psychologists, 425
Astrology, 5
Athletes, anabolic steroid use among, 248
Attitudes, effects of sex education on, 887
Attitudes Toward Timing of Parenthood Scale (ATOP), 744–45
Attitude Toward Feminism Scale, 176–77
Audiotapes, in sex therapy, 563
Autoepiophilia, 621
Autoerotic asphyxia syndrome, 339
Autoeroticism. *See* Masturbation
Autonepiophilia, 616, 636
Aversive conditioning, for decreasing deviant sexual arousal, 628–30
Azidothymidine (AZT), 649–50

B

"Baby M Case," 788, 793
Band-Aid operation, 766
Bandura, Albert, 166–67
Barbiturates
as cause of sexual dysfunction, 534
effects of, on sexual response, 253
Bartholin's glands, 192
Basal body temperature (BBT) method, 762, 784
Batak males, homosexuality in, 91
Battering marital rape, 685
Bean-Bayog, Margaret, 566
Beck, Aaron, 167
Behavior, and human sexuality, 18–19
Bellotti v. *Baird,* 851
Bem Sex Role Inventory, 284–85, 306, 367, 535
Bergalis, Kimberly, 671
Bestiality, and Jewish heritage, 50
Beta bias, in gender theories, 288–89
Beverly Hills 90210, media reports on, 27
Bias
gender, 80
participation, 126
researcher, 146
self-presentation, 146
Biased sample, 125
Billings method of periodic abstinence, 762
Biochemical associations of love, 514–16
Biochemical defects, identifying fetuses with, 800
Biodegradable implants, 774
Biological clock issue, 775–76
Biological factors
in sexual dysfunctions, 533–34
in sexual orientation, 414–16
Biological theories
evolutionary theories, 159–60
of paraphilia, 623–24
physiological theories, 158–59
of rape, 686
Biopsy, 218–19
Biosexology, 115
Bipolar disorder, 589
Birth control. *See also* Family planning
calendar method, 761–62
choices in, 775–76
effect of, on sexuality, 27–28
effects of sex education on, 887–88, 894
failure rates, 771
future of technology in, 774
history of, 746–48
methods of
abstinence, 748, 871
cervical cap, 758
coitus absentia, 760–61
coitus interruptus, 748, 763–64
condom, 27, 32, 33, 664–67, 747, 753–55, 773, 875–76, 886–87
diaphragm, 757–58
female condom, 755
intrauterine device (IUD), 755–57, 773
male hormonal contraceptives, 753
Norplant, 751, 752

oral contraceptives, 748–51, 773
periodic abstinence, 761–63
postcoital contraception, 764
spermicides, 753, 757, 758–59
sterilization, 10, 764–67, 773
vaginal sponge, 759–60
psychological influences in, 767–71
and sex education, 869
and sexual values, 59
technology and availability of, 772–73
withdrawal, 217
as woman's responsibility, 772
Birth control pills, 748–51
Birthing centers, 822
Bisexuality, 399–400, 433, 643
in marriage, 366
Black churches, and sexual values, 61–62
Black Muslims, and sexual values, 62
Blacks, comparison of sexuality of, with whites, 96
Blended orgasms, 235
Blood transfusions, in transmission of HIV, 641
B-love, 504, 517
Body image, 582
as aspect of self-concept, 318–19
and eating disorders, 320
as liability, 18
and mate selection, 18
negative impact of media on, 27
and self-concept, 17
and sexual harassment, 18
and value of women, 299
Bondage, 619
Bondage and discipline (B and D), 618
Bottle feeding, 822–23
Bowers v. *Hardwick,* 407
Brachioprotic eroticism, 433
Bradley method of childbirth, 812
Brain, importance of, in sexual response, 225
Brainstorming, 496
Braxton-Hicks contractions, 806
Bray v. *Alexandria Women's Health Clinic,* 853
Breast cancer, 210, 590–91
diagnosis of, 218–19
Breast feeding, 821, 822–23
Breast implant, 218
Breasts, female, 209–10
Breast self-examination, 220
attitudes toward, 596–98
Breast stimulation, 337, 379, 821
Breech birth, 807
Brief encounters, 369
Brown, Louise, 789
Buddhism and sexual values, 54–55
Buddhist conception, of love, 503
Buddhist Tibetans, and polyandry, 100
Bulbocavernosus muscles, 193
Bulbourethal glands, 217
Bulimia nervosa, 320
Bundling, 53

C

Calendar method of birth control, 761–62
Calvin, John, 52
Canada, mate selection in, 100
Cancer
breast, 210, 590–91
diagnosis of, 218–19
cervical, 199, 219, 591, 594, 653
endometrial, 469, 594
penile, 599
prostate, 217, 219, 594, 596
testicular, 220, 596
uterine, 199, 219, 591, 594
vulvar, 653
Candidiasis, 661–62
Cardiovascular disease, 600–1
Card sort technique, in assessing sexual interest in sex offenders, 627
Case studies, 132–33
Castration anxiety, 57
Catholic Church
on abortion, 835, 837, 838
on absolutism, 42
on homosexual behavior, 403
on masturbation, 325
and sexual celibacy, 323–24
and sexual values, 60, 61
Catholics for a Free Choice (CFFC), 835, 837, 838
Causation, 140
Cayapa Indians, and incest, 90
Celibacy, 321, 323–24, 325
in marriage, 366
Cell tissue culture, 801
Centers for Disease Control (CDC), 640, 643
Center for Science in the Public Interest, 882
Central arousal, 225–26
Cerebral palsy, 578, 586
Cerebrovascular accidents, 584
Cervical cancer, 199, 219, 591, 594, 653
Cervical cap, 758
Cervical ectropion, 751
Cervically anchored device that is contraceptive and anti-disease, 774
Cervical mucus, 749, 784
Cervical mucus method, 762–63, 784
Cervix, 198
Cesarean Prevention Movement, 814
Cesarean section, 813–15
Chancre, 657
Chancroid, 660–61
Chemotherapy, 219
Chicken porn. *See* Child pornography
Childbirth. *See also* Pregnancy
cesarean, 813–15
choices in, 822–24
at home versus hospital, 822
labor, 805–9
Bradley method, 812
Dick-Read method, 810
first stage of, 806–7
induction of, 809
Lamaze method, 810–12
LeBoyer birth experience, 812–13
second stage of, 807
third stage of, 807
mother's reaction to, 817–18
preparation for, 809–10
safety of, 808
sex after, 820–21
Childbirth Without Fear (Dick-Read), 810
Child-free alternative, 741
Childhelp USA, 709
Childhood, sexuality in, 445–46
Child molestation, 69
Child pornography, 721–22
functions of, 722
Children. *See also* Pedophilia
coming out to, 423–24
costs of, 738–39
exposure to parental nudity, 892
factors to consider in timing of, 743, 746
impact of divorce on, 29
and marital intercourse, 455
motivations for having, 737–38
negative behaviors of, 739
optimum number of, 741–42
sex abuse of. *See* Sexual abuse
social influences on deciding to have, 736–37
Child sexual abuse accommodation syndrome, 708

China
mate selection in, 102
sexual values in, 53–54
Chlamydia, 655–56, 659
as cause of infertility, 784
and use of oral contraceptives, 751
Chloasma, 750
Chorionic villus sampling (CVS), 801
Christian Civic League, 860
Christian heritage, and sexual values, 50–52
Chromosomal abnormalities, 275
identifying fetuses with, 800
Klinefelter's syndrome as, 275–76
and timing of children, 743, 746
Turner's syndrome as, 276
Chromosomes, 272
Chronic obstructive pulmonary disease (COPD), 602
Circles concept, 874
Circumcision, 98, 212–14
adult, 213
female, 97–98
newborn, 213
City of God (St. Augustine), 51
Clarke Sexual History Questionnaire, in assessing sexual interest in sex offenders, 628
Classical conditioning theory, 165–66
Classic rape, 682
Climacteric, 458
Clinical interview, in assessing sexual interest in sex offenders, 627
Clinical trials, 127
for AIDS and HIV, 128–29
Clinton, Bill, 40
Clinton, Hillary, 40
Clitoral orgasm, 235
Clitoral stimulation, 381–83
via penis, 383
Clitoridectomy, 97–98
Clitoris, 192–93
Clomid, 786
Clomiphene citrate, 786
Closed-ended questions, 490–91
Cocaine
effects of, on sexual response, 254
use of, in pregnancy, 797
Coercion, versus informed consent, 479–82
Coercive sex, 69
Cognitions, and human sexuality, 19
Cognitive/affective theories, 167–68
Cognitive behavior theory
and sex education curricula, 890
Cognitive control, choices in, 603
Cognitive-developmental theory, on gender role acquisition, 285–86
Cognitive factors, in sexual dysfunction, 538
Cognitive restructuring, for sex offender, 697
Cognitive therapy
for rape, 693
for sex therapy, 560–61
Cohabitating rape, 685
Cohabitation
definition of, 29, 360–62
incidence of, 360–62
measuring quality of relationship in, 366, 367
as preparation for marriage, 361
Presbyterian Church on, 61
and sexuality, 29, 361–63
types of, 360–62
Coitus. *See* Sexual intercourse
Coitus absentia, 760–61
Coitus interruptus, 748, 763
Coitus obstructus, 747
College campus
bar scene on, 356–58
gay and lesbian life on, 409–11
rape prevention on, 700–2
College students
attitudes of, on abortion, 834
availability of birth control for, 27–28
knowledge of, on sexuality, 24–25
masturbation among, 19
sexual behavior among, 18–19, 23
Colposcope, 653
Comanche, extramarital sex for, 89
Comarital sex, 370
Combination pill, 749
Coming of Age in Samoa (Mead), 80
Coming out, 420
to friends and employers, 424–25
to heterosexual partner or spouse and children, 423–24
to one's parents and siblings, 421–23
to one's self, 420–21
Committee for Children, 711
Communication
asking open-ended questions, 490–91
choices in, 498
components of effective, 478–79, 482–83
content in, 483–84
deception in, 479, 480–81
definition of, 478
informed consent versus coercion, 479–82
"I" statements in, 492–93
maintaining eye contact in, 490
parent-child, 876–79
process in, 484
reflective listening in, 491–92
in relationships, 484–85, 490
resolving interpersonal conflict in, 493–97
sexual interaction as, 497
Communication skills training, in sex education programs, 869
Companionate love, 506
Comstock, Anthony, 748
Comstock Act, 27, 748
Conception, 783
differentiation between fertilization and, 783
Concerned Women for America, 68
Concubine, 102
Conditioned stimulus, 165
Condoms, 753–55, 773
for anal intercourse, 384, 433, 643, 753
availability of, 27
female, 33, 755
first use of, 747
in gay relationships, 429, 432–33
prostitute use of, 717
and safe sex, 32, 664–67, 670
school clinic dispensation of, 666–67, 894
in sex education classes, 875–76, 886–87
Condom skills program, 886
Condyloma, 653, 655
Conflict-habituated relationship, 364
Conflict theory, on premenstrual syndrome, 171–73
Congenital defects, 739, 801
Conjoint therapy, 567
for rape, 693
Conjugal love, 506, 507
Consummate love, 506
Contact tracing, 647
Contraception. *See* Birth control
Contraceptive comfort and confidence scale, 775, 776
Content, in communication, 483
Contraceptives. *See* Birth control
Control group, 126
Convenience sampling, 125
Conversion therapy, 436
Coolidge effect, 371

Copper T IUD, 755–56
Coprophilia, 621
Corona, 211
Corpora cavernosa, 211
Corpus cavernosum, 225
Corpus luteum, 203, 204
Corpus spongiosum, 211
Correlation, 139–40
Courtship disorder, 622, 624–25, 631
Covert sensitization, for decreasing deviant sexual arousal, 630
Co-workers, sexual involvements with, 374–77
Cowper's glands, 217
COYOTE (Call Off Your Old Tired Ethics), 714–15
Cribriform hymen, 193
Crisis counseling, for rape, 692
Criterion validity, 142
Cross-cultural research in human sexuality, 79–80
  age at first intercourse, 84
  extramarital sex, 89–90
  frequency, 84
  gender roles, 92–95, 285
  homosexual sex, 91–92, 405
  incest, 90–91
  mate selection, 100–103
  menstruation, 91
  positions, 84
  premarital sex, 88–89
  on sex guilt, 66
  sexual intercourse, 84, 88
Cross dressing, 616–18
Cross-Gender Fetishism Scale, 617
Cross-sectional research, 118
Crotamiton (Eurax), 662
Crura, 192, 211
Cryopreservation, 789
Cryotherapy, 219
Cryptorchidism, 214
Cultural contexts, permissive and restrictive, 95–97
Cultural forces, influence of, on sexual choices, 15–16
Cultural relativism, 106–8
  versus ethnocentrism, 83–84
Culture
  and sexual guilt, 66
  and sexual values, 73
Culture-specific sex practices
  female genital mutilation, 97–98
  male genital mutilation, 98–99
  polygamy, 99–100
Cunnilingus, 382–83
Curvilinear correlation, 139
Cystic fibrosis, diagnosis of, in fetus, 801
Cystic infection, 192
Cystitis, 194, 384

D

Dahomey, and incest, 90
Dalkon Shield, 755, 756–57
Danazol, for endometriosis, 602
Darwin, Charles, 159
Date rape, 682–83, 870
  media reports on, 27
Dating
  and college bar scene, 356–58
  among divorced and widowed, 358–60
  functions of, 354–55
  sexual expectations in, 355–56
Daughters of Bilitis (DOB), 411-12
Davenport, C. B., 57–58
Davis, Junior, 789
Davis, Mary Sue, 789
Day-care, 30
  sex abuse in, 444, 608, 723
ddC for HIV infection, 650
Deception, in communication, 479, 480–81
Decriminalization of prostitution, 724
Deep kissing, 378
Defense mechanisms, in coping with identity confusion, 419
Delancey Street, 722
Dental dam, 664
Dependent variable, 123
Depo-Provera, 772
  for paraphiliac sex offender, 629
Depotestosterone, 278
Depression
  as cause of sexual dysfunction, 537
  postpartum, 817
  reactive, 581
  and sexual desire, 589
Derogatis Sexual Functioning Inventory, 67
DES (diethylstibestrol), 764
Desensitization, in resolving jealousy, 524
Description, in sex research, 138
Desire-phase dysfunctions, 540–41
  hypoactive sexual desire, 541–43
    causes and contributing factors, 542
    treatment of, 542–43
  sexual aversion, 543–44
    causes and contributing factors, 544
    treatment of, 544
Destructive phrase, 202
Determinism, 4–6
  alternative views on, 5
Detumescence, 242
Devitalized relationship, 364
Diabetes mellitus, 601–2
Diagnostic and Statistical Manual of Mental Disorders
  on paraphilia, 608, 611, 621
  on phobias, 401
  on posttraumatic stress disorder, 690
  on premenstrual disorder, 207–8
  on rape, 622
  on sexual addiction, 540
  on sexual orientation, 436
Dial-a-porn services, 69
Diaphragm, 757–58
Diaries, 134
Dick-Read childbirth method, 810
Dideoxyinosine (DDI), for HIV infection, 650
Diethylstibestrol (DES), 764
Digital examination, 595
Digital rectal exam (DRE), 219
Dilation, 807
Dilation and curretage, 839. *See also* Dilation and suction
Dilation and evacuation (D and E) method, 801, 839
Dilation and suction, 838–39, 841
  Disabilities. *See also* Intellectual disabilities; Neurological
disabilities
  myths about, 578–79
Disciples of Christ, acceptance of homosexuality by, 403
Discrimination, 166
  against homosexuals, 406–7
Disease, myths about, 578–79
Disulfiram (Antabuse), 250, 632
Divorced
  and child care, 359, 742
  dating among, 358–60
  sexuality among, 28–29, 456–57
D-love, 504
Domestic partnerships, 413
Donahue, Phil, 27
Donor semen, 642
Donor sperm, 786–87
Double blinding, 128
Double standard, 59
  cross-culturally, 89
  definition of, 24
  existence of, 24, 356
  perpetuation of, 268

Douching, 758, 759
Down's syndrome, 801
  diagnosis of, in fetus, 801
Dream analysis, in sex therapy, 558
Drug addiction, and risk of prostitution, 715–16
Drug education, in sex education programs, 869
Drugs
  and date rape, 683
  for decreasing deviant sexual arousal, 628
  for erectile dysfunction, 549
  and first intercourse, 451
  for intellectual disabilities, 588
  intravenous, in transmission of HIV, 434, 641, 667
  in pregnancy, 799
  in sex therapy, 563
  and sexual response, 247–55
Dual sex team, 568
Duchenne muscular dystrophy, diagnosis of, in fetus, 801
Duct system, 215–16
Ductus deferens, 215
Duff, Richard, 671
Dysmenorrhea, 204
Dyspareunia, 556–57, 760
  causes and contributing factors in, 557
  treatment for, 557

E

Early ejaculation, 554–56
  causes and contributing factors of, 555
  treatment for, 555–56
Early infant death, 857
East Bay, homosexuality in, 91
Eating disorders, and body image, 320
Economic values, and Puritan view, 52
Ectopic pregnancy, 199, 756, 793, 796
Education. *See also* Sex education
  AIDS, 663, 667, 868, 879, 880, 886
  drug, 869
  level of, and masturbation, 335
  role of, in gender role acquisition, 293–93
Educational factors, in sexual dysfunction, 538
Education Amendments Act (1972), Title IX, 293, 297
Edwards, Jonathan, 53
Edward VIII, 44
Effacement, 807
Egalitarian marriage, 364
Egalitarian relationships
  choices in, 309–10
  value of, 566
Ego, 160–61
Ego-dystonic homosexuality, 436
Ego-idea theory of love, 513
Eisenstadt v. *Baird,* 748
Ejaculation, first, 448
Ejaculatory disturbances, in diabetic men, 601
Ejaculatory duct, 216–17
Ejaculatory orgasm, 236–37
Elderly
  and sexual celibacy, 325
  sexual choices among, 469–70
  sexuality in, 334–35, 464–68
Electra complex, 57, 161, 163, 283
Electro-ejaculation, 584
Electrocoagulation, 219
Electrovibration, 584
ELISA (enzyme-linked immunosorbent assay), 646–47
Ellis, Albert, 167
Ellis, Havelock, 57, 59, 114–15
Ellis's and Beach's two-stage models, 242–43
Embryo, 796
Embryo transfer, 789
Emotions, and human sexuality, 20
Empathy belly, 804
Employers, coming out to, 424–25
Empty love, 506
Endocrine system, 226, 227
Endometrial cancer, 469, 594
Endometrial lavage, 789, 793
Endometriosis, 204–5, 602
Endometrium, 198, 203, 204
Ephebophilia, 621
Ephebosexual behavior, 614
Epididymis, 215, 220
Episcopal Church, on sexual values, 42, 61
Episcopalians United, and absolutism, 42
Episcopal Synod of America, and absolutism, 42
Episiotomy, 807
Erectaid System, 550
Erectile dysfunction, 365, 545–50
  and arthritis, 599
  and cardiovascular disease, 600
  causes and contributing factors of, 546–47
  and diabetes, 601
  in elderly, 470
  intrapsychic factors in, 536
  treatment of, 547–50
Erection, 228
Erikson, E. H., 162
Eros, 503, 504, 505
Erotica, 717–18
  breasts as, 379
  and sexual response, 255–56, 258
Erotic stimulus pathway (ESP) model, 243–44
Erotocentrism, 84
Erotophilia, 321, 768–70
Erotophobia, 321, 768–70
Erotophonophilia, 621
Essentialist view, 180
Estinyl, 278
Estradiol-17B, 204
Estrogen, 244, 275, 458–59, 749
Estrogen deficiency
  in determining sexual response patterns, 182
  in female sexual arousal dysfunction, 545
Estrogen replacement therapy (ERT), 219, 459
  choice of, 469
Ethical issues
  and abortion, 836–38, 839, 840
  and sexuality research, 134–37
Ethnic groups, as audience for sex education, 874–76
Ethnocentrism, 106
  versus cultural relativism, 83–84
Ethnography, 78–79
Ethnology, 78–79
Eugenics, definition of, 114
Eunuchs for the Kingdom of Heaven (Ranke-Heinemann), 61
Evangelical Lutheran Church in America, on sexual values, 61
Evolutionary theory
  of love, 511
  of rape, 686
Excitement phase, 465
  in men in later years, 466
  in sexual response, 227–33
  in women in later years, 465
Exercise
  choices in, 603
  during pregnancy, 798–99
Exhibitionism, 69, 609–12, 612
  psychoanalytic perspective of, 622–23
Experimental groups, 126
Experiments, 126–27

Exposure, for increasing nondeviant sexual arousal, 631
Extinction, 165
Extradyadic sex, 15, 30, 367, 369
choices involving, 389–91
for lesbians, 431
motivations and reasons for, 371–73
types of involvements in, 369–71
at workplace, 374–77
Extrafamilial abuse, 706–7
Extrafamilial child sexual abuse, 702–3
Extramarital intercourse
cross-cultural variations in, 89–90
and sexual values, 40
Eye contact, maintaining, 490

F

Face-to-face interviews, 127, 129–30
Face validity, 142
Fallopian tubes, 199, 782
blockage of, 789
False labor, 806
Family
developing new definition of, 412
gay and lesbian couples as, 413, 427, 429
Family bed, 892
Family leave, 30
Family planning. *See also* Birth control
decision-making in, 735–43, 746
and detection of ovulation, 783–84
and incidence of unplanned pregnancy, 734
personal and social benefits of, 735
Family planning clinic personnel, as source of sex education, 880
Family therapy, in developing positive gay self-concept, 426
Fatalism, 5
Father
age of, in timing of children, 746
feelings of, during wife's pregnancy, 803–4
interaction with newborn, 818–20
Father-daughter incest, 704–5
Fatherhood, transition to, 818–20
Fatigue, 581
as cause of sexual dysfunction, 534
Fatuous love, 506
Faulty cognitions, changing, 632
Fear, as cause of sexual dysfunction, 537
Fecal blood test, 219
Fellatio, 380–81, 432
in child pornography, 721
in rape, 685
Female circumcision, 97
Female condom, 755
Female ejaculate, 236
Female genital mutilation, 97–98
Female pseudohermaphrodites, 276
Females
alternative sexual responses in, 239
bond with children, 300
changes in number of, in workplace, 29–30
concern over body image, 17
condoms for, 33
consequences of traditional socialization, 296–301
effect of erotica on, 256
exploitation of, in reproductive technology, 792–95
gay relationships in, 430–32
gender role of, 267–68
impact of birth control on, 28
life expectancy of, 300
masturbation techniques for, 336–38
media portrayal of, 27
menopause in, 457–59
in middle age, 457–59
orgasm in, 235–37
physiological sexual changes in later years, 465
and rape, 26
self-concept of, 298–99
sex guilt in, 15
sex preferences among, 23
sexual fantasies of, 19, 344–45
sterilization in, 765–66
value of, 299
Female sexual arousal dysfunction
causes and contributing factors of, 545
treatment for, 545
Feminine hygiene sprays, 196
Feminist perspective, 175, 178
of abortion, 835, 836
on eating disorders, 320
essentialist view in, 180
liberal feminism, 178
multicultural feminism, 179
of paraphilia, 623
radical feminism, 178–79
of rape, 687
on sexology, 120–21
social constructionist view on, 180–82
socialist feminism, 179
Feminists for Life of America, 835, 836
Feminist-vegetarian theory, 273
Feminization of love, 509–10
Fertilization, 782–83
differentiation between conception and, 783
process of, 783
Fetal alcohol syndrome (FAS), 799
Fetal death, 857
Fetal tissue transplants, as moral dilemma, 47–48
Fetishism, 610, 614–16
Fetus, 796
as person, 836–37
as patient, 70
Fibro-dysplasis ossificans progressiva, 746
Fijians, extramarital sex for, 89
Films, in sex therapy, 563
Filshie clip, 772
Fimbria, 199
FISH (florescent insitu hybridization), 802
Fisting, 433
Flexigard Intrauterine Copper Contraceptive (ICC), 757
Flooding
for rape, 692
in resolving jealousy, 524
Florescent insitu hybridization (FISH), 802
Flowers, Gennifer, 40
Follicle-stimulating hormone (FSH), 199, 749
Forcible rape, 678
Formicophilia, 621, 632, 636
treatment of, 633
Fragmentation, 160
Fraternity houses, gang rape at, 170
Free association in sex therapy, 558
Freedom of Access to Clinic Entrances Bill, 853
Freedom of Choice Act, 853
Free will, 4
alternative views on, 5
Free Will-Determinism Scale, 6, 8–9
French kissing, 378
Frenulum, 211
Frequencies, 138
Freud, Anna, 162
Freud, Sigmund, 56–57, 58, 78, 115, 160–63, 283, 331, 512–13
Freudian theory, of child sexual abuse, 703
Friends
coming out to, 424–25
as source of sex education, 879

Frottage, 68–69, 612
Frotteurism, 610, 611, 612
Fructose, 216
Fundus, 198
Fungus, 661–62

G

Gamete intra-fallopian transfer (GIFT), 791
Gamma benzene hexachloride, 662
Gang rape, 684
  at fraternity houses, 170
Gay and Lesbian Community Action Council, 412
Gays. *See* Homosexuality
Gay bashing, 407–9
Gayellow Pages, 427
Gay liberation movement, 411–13
  and sexual values, 59–60
Gay pride, 59
Gay subculture, 426–27
Gender, definition of, 266–67
Gender bias, in cross cultural sex research, 80
Gender differences, in sexual fantasies, 344–45
Gender discrimination, 285
Gender dysphoria, 277–78
Gender identity, definition of, 267
Gender role(s)
  agents of socialization in
    education, 292–93
    media, 294–96
    parents, 290–91
    peers, 291–92
    religion, 293–94
  biological beginnings of, 272–80
  challenges to traditional, 59–60
  cognitive-developmental theory on, 285–86
  consequences of traditional female socialization, 296–301
  consequences of traditional male socialization, 301–4
  cross-cultural variations in, 92–95
  definition of, 267–68
  expectations, as cause of sexual dysfunction, 534–36
  gender schema theory on, 286–87
  identification theory on, 283–84
  impact of divorce on, 29
  influence on sexual choices, 15
  in the Middle East, 92–93
  in sex education classes, 870
  social learning theory on, 284–85
  sociobiological theory on, 280–82
  in Sweden, 93
  terminology for, 266–68, 271
  in Western Samoa, 92
Gender role ideology, 271
Gender role transcendence, 308
Gender schema, 286
  and gender role acquisition, 286–87
Gender stereotyping, 292–93
Gender theories, alpha bias and beta bias in, 288–89
Generalization, 166
General sexual dysfunction, 545
Genital apposition, 383
Genital arousal, 228
Genital herpes, 650–53, 659
  psychological reactions to, 654
Genital mutilation
  female, 97–98
  male, 98–99
Genital responses, 226
Genital stage of development, 161–62
Genital warts, 653, 655, 659
Gerontophilia, 621
GIFT (gamete intra-fallopian transfer), 791
Gigolos, 717
Gilbert Islands, and premarital sex, 88–89
Ginkgo biloba extract, 549
Glans, 211
Gonorrhea, 656–57, 659
  as cause of infertility, 784
  and use of oral contraceptives, 751
Grafenberg, Ernest, 196–97
Grafenberg Spot, 196–97
Granuloma inguinale (GI), 660
Group sex, 371
  for sexual dysfunctions, 567–68
Group therapy
  for rape, 693
  for sex offender, 697
G spot. *See* Grafenberg spot
Guilt. *See* Sexual guilt
Gynecomastia, side effects of, 248

H

Habitation, 352
Halcion, 15
Harris v. *McRae,* 851
Havasupai Indians, and incest, 90
HCG, 786
Health, and love, 520–21
Health belief model, 597
Health care workers, testing for HIV, 671
Health Services Act (1990), 871
Heart disease, 521
Hebephilia, 614
Hedonism, and sexual values, 45
Hepatitis B, 661
Heredity, as explanation for sexual orientation, 414–15
Hermaphroditism, 276
Heroin, 254
Herpes Resource Center (HELP), 654
Herpes simplex virus type 1 (HSV-1), 651
Herpes simplex virus type 2 (HSV-2), 650
Heteroeroticism, 397
Heterosexism, 401–6
Heterosexual-Homosexual Rating Scale, 397–98, 399
Heterosexuality
  definition of, 397–98
  prevalence of, 398–99
Heterosexual partner, coming out to, 423–24
Heterosexuals, HIV infection in, 643
Heterosexual women, choices for, 309
Hidatsa, extramarital sex for, 89
Hijras of India, cross-cultural perspective of, 93–95
Hill, Anita F., 374, 712, 713
Hill Maria Gond, and menstruation, 91
Hirschfeld, Magnus, 57, 114–15
Historical research, 133
Hitler, Adolf, 737
Hivid, for HIV infection, 650
HIV infection. *See also* AIDS
  allocation of government funds to research on, 671
  and artificial insemination, 787
  categories of, 640–41
  choices in being tested for, 670–71
  and drug use, 15
  in heterosexuals, 643
  in homosexuals, 642–43
  knowledge and attitudes about, 644–46
  media attention on, 27
  prevalence of, and AIDS, 643–44
  prevention models for, 667–69
  in sex education classes, 871, 869
  and sexuality, 32–33
  symptoms of, 640–41
  and testing of health care workers, 67

tests for, 646–47, 649
transmission of, and high-risk behaviors, 641–42
treatment for, 649–50
and use of condoms, 753, 754
HMG, 786
Hodgson v. *Minnesota,* 12, 852
Home Oriented Maternity Experience (HOME), 822
Homoeroticism, 397
Homophobia, 401–6, 708
Homosexuality, 397. *See also entries beginning with* Gay; Lesbian
and antigay violence, 407–9
on college campuses, 409–11
coming out, 420
to friends and employers, 424–25
to heterosexual partner or spouse and children, 423–24
to one's parents and siblings, 421–23
to one's self, 420–21
cross-cultural perspective on, 21–22, 91–92
definition of, 397–98
developing positive gay self-concept, 426
ego-dystonic, 436
gay female relationships, 430–32
gay male relationships, 427–30
and hypoactive sexual desire, 541
and Jewish heritage, 50
among nonhuman primates, 104
and parenting concerns, 740–41
Presbyterian Church on, 61
prevalence of, 398–99
in public opinion on, 413
role of the gay subculture, 426–27
in sex education classes, 870
sexual behavior of gays, 432–33
sexually transmissible diseases in, 433–34
social constructionist views of, 181
Troiden's four-stage process
commitment, 420
identity assumption, 420
identity confusion, 418–19
and sensitization, 418
as unnatural acts, 81
Homosexual relationship, and extradyadic sex, 373
Homosexuals
discrimination against, 406–7, 424–25
HIV infection in, 642–43
measuring quality of relationship in, 366–67
prejudice against, 401–6
Homosexual sodomy, 407
Honesty, and sexual values, 71
Honeymoon cystitis, 194
Hooded clitoris, 192
Hormonal abnormalities, 276
androgen-insensitivity syndrome as, 276–77
androgenital syndrome as, 276
female pseudohermaphrodites as, 276
hermaphroditism as, 276
intersexed infants as, 277
male pseudohermaphrodites as, 277
pseudohermaphroditism as, 276
testicular feminization syndrome as, 276
Hormonal theories of human sexuality, 158–59
Hormone-in-urine method, 763
Hormones, 273–75
definition of, 244
as explanation for sexual orientation, 415–16
and sexual response, 244–46
Hormone therapy, 786
choices on, 469
for paraphiliac sex offenders, 629
for transsexualism, 278
Horney, Karen, 162
How Much Do You Know About Sexuality Scale, 539–40
Human chorionic gonadotropin (HCG), 797
Human immunodeficiency virus (HIV) infection. *See* AIDS; HIV infection
Human papilloma virus (HPV), 653, 655
Human sexuality. *See* Sexuality; Theoretical views of human sexuality
Human Sexual Response Cycle Model, 227–30, 233–42
Hungary, homosexuality in, 91–92
Husband-coached childbirth, 812
Hustlers, 717
Hymen, 193–94
Hypertension, 600
Hypoactive sexual desire, 541–43
causes and contributing factors of, 542
treatment of, 542–43
Hypothalamus, 275
Hypothesis, 123
Hysterectomy, 198, 219, 458, 594, 765

I

Iatrogenic factors, 328
Id, 160–61
Ideal marriage (van de Velde), 57
Identification theory, on gender role acquisition, 283–84
Identity assumption, 420
Identity confusion, 418–19
Immu Vir, for genital herpes, 653
Impaired sexual arousal, 545
Imperforate hymen, 193
Implantation, 748
Implosion
for rape, 692
in resolving jealousy, 524
Incest
cross-cultural variations in, 90–91
and decision to have abortion, 846
father-daughter, 704–5
mother-son, 705–6
sibling, 706
Incest taboo, 90–91, 877
Independent variable, 123
Index of Attitudes Toward Homosexuals (IAH), 404–5
Index of Sexual Satisfaction (ISS), 368
India, sexual values in, 54–55
Induced abortion, 832. *See also* Abortion
Infant
breast versus bottle feeding of, 822–23
circumcision in, 213
interaction with father, 819
sexual abuse of, 444
sexuality in, 444–45
Infanticide, 746–47
Infatuation, 506, 508
Infertility
causes of, 784
definition of, 784
effect of, on sexual relations, 785
psychological reactions, 785
Infibulation, 97–98
Informed consent, 135–36
versus coercion, 479–82
Informed Homebirth/Informed Birth and Parenting, 814
Infundibulum, 199
Inhibited ejaculation, 553
Inhibited female orgasm, 550
causes and contributing factors of, 551
treatment for, 551–53

Inhibited male orgasm, 553–54
  causes and contributing factors of, 553–54
  treatment for, 554
Inis Beag, sexual attitudes in, 96–97
Injection therapy, for erectile dysfunction, 549
Institute of Sexology, 114
Integrated planning, and sexual dysfunction, 562
Intellectual disabilities
  as audience for sex education, 874
  effectiveness of refusal skills training for, 885
  and sexuality, 587–89
Intensive therapy, 559
Intercourse. *See* Sexual intercourse
International Professional Surrogates Association (IPSA), 562
Interpersonal conflict, 493
  addressing recurring disturbing issues, 493
  finding out other person's point of view, 494
  focusing on what you want, 494
  generating solutions to, 494–97
Interpersonal noncoital sexual behavior, 377
  breast stimulation, 379
  clitoral stimulation, 381–83
  kissing, 378–79
  penile stimulation, 379–81
  touching, 377–78
Intersexed infants, 277
Intimacy, in relationship, 484–85, 490
Intrafamilial child sexual abuse, 703
Intrapsychic factors, in sexual dysfunctions, 536–37
Intrauterine device (IUD), 755–57, 773
Introitus, 193
Intromission and ejaculatory mechanism (IEM), 243
In vitro fertilization, 789
  abuses of, 794
Involuntary sexual celibacy, 325
Islam, and sexual values, 55
Israel, mate selection in, 101
"I" statements, 492–93

J

Jackson, Janet, 27
Jealousy
  causes of, 521–22
  consequences of, 522–24
  definition of, 521
  reactive, 522
  techniques for resolving, 524
Jehovah's Witnesses, and sexual values, 62
Jennifer Fever, 373
Jesus, teachings of, 50
Jews
  acceptance of homosexuality by, 403, 405
  circumcision as religious rite for, 213
  on masturbation, 325
  and sexual values, 49–50
Johnson, Magic, 640, 868
Jordon, Elvie, 788
Jordon, Marissa, 788

K

Kamasutra, 54
Kaplan, Helen, three-stage model of, 243
Kaposi's sarcoma (KS), 641
Karma, 54
Karyotyping, 801
Kathoey, 405
Kegel exercises, 193, 198
Kenuzi Nubians, premarital sex for, 89
Kerrey, Bob, 40
Kiddie porn. *See* Child pornography
Kimam, and menstruation, 91
Kinsey, Alfred, 59
Kinsey Institute
  Report on sexual knowledge, 148–49
  on sexual behavior, 147–48
  on sexual values, 148
Kissing, 378–79
  in adolescence, 449–50
  origin of mouth, 378
Klinefelter's syndrome, 275–76
Klismaphilia, 621
Knowledge, effects of sex education on, 883–84
Krafft-Ebing, R. von, 58
Kwell, 662

L

Labia, 191–92
Labia majora, 191
Labia minora, 192
Labor, 805–9. *See also* Childbirth
  first stage of, 806–7
  fourth stage of, 808
  induction of, 809
  second stage of, 807
  third stage of, 807
Lamaze, Fernand, 810
Lamaze method of childbirth, 810–12
Laminaria, 839
Landers, Ann, 27
Language, sexist, 271–72, 294
Laparoscopy, 765–66, 789
Late luteal phase dysphoric disorder (LLPDD), 207–8
Latency stage of development, 161
Later years. *See* Elderly
Laws
  on abortion, 849–50
  and discrimination against homosexuals, 407
  and sex, 68–70
Learning theories, 163, 185
  classical conditioning theory, 165–66
  of love, 511–12
  operant learning theory, 163
  of paraphilia, 623
  punishment, 163
  reinforcement, 163
  social learning theory, 166
Leboyer birth experience of childbirth, 812–13
Lesbian. *See* Homosexuality
Lesbian-feminism, 413–14
Leydig cells, 215
Liberal feminism, 178
Libertarianism, 4. *See also* Free will
Libido, 162
Liking, 505
Listening, reflective, 491–92
Locus of control, 335
Longitudinal research, 118–19
Love
  ancient views of, 502–3
  B, 504
  biochemical associations of, 514–16
  Buddhist conception of, 503
  companionate, 506
  conjugal, 506, 507
  consummate, 506
  D, 504
  ego-ideal theory of, 513
  empty, 506
  evolutionary theory of, 511
  fatuous, 506
  feminization of, 509–10
  Greek and Hebrew conceptions of, 503–4
  and health, 520–21
  infatuation, 508
  learning theory of, 511–12
  making choices about, 525

modern views of, 504–6
as motivation for having children, 737
ontological theory of, 513–14
organizing theories of, 516–17
psychosexual theory of, 512–13
realistic, 506–7
romantic, 506–7
simultaneous, 519
styles of, 504
triangular theory of, 505
unfulfilled, 519
Love Attitudes Scale, 504–5, 506–7, 508–9
Lovemap, paraphilia as vandalized, 624
Love relationships. *See* Relationships
Low-birth weight baby, 798, 808
Lozano, Paul, 566
Ludus, 504, 505
Lumpectomy, 591
Luteal phase, 202
Luteinizing hormone (LH), 202
Lutex agglutination inhibition immunologic slide test, 797
Luther, Martin, 52
Lymphadenopathy syndrome (LAS), 641
Lymphogranuloma venereum (LGV), 660

M

Madonna, 27
Magazines, as source of sex education, 883
Male gender role socialization, and child sexual abuse, 613, 703
Male genital mutilation, 98–99
Male prostitutes, 717
Male pseudohermaphrodites, 277
Males
alternative sexual responses in, 239–41
consequences of traditional socialization, 301–4
effect of erotica on, 256
gay relationships for, 427–30
gender role of, 267–68
hormonal contraceptives for, 753
life expectancy of, 302
masturbation techniques for, 338–39
menopause in, 459, 464
in middle age, 459, 464
orgasm in, 237–38
physiological sexual changes in later years in, 466
rape of, 680–81
sex preferences among, 23
sexual fantasies of, 19, 344–45
sterilization in, 766–67
Malinowski, Bronislaw, 78
Mammography, 218–19, 591
Mangaians, sexual attitudes in, 96
Mania, 504, 505
Manic-depression, 589
Manual stimulation, 382
Marfan syndrome, 746
Marijuana
as cause of sexual dysfunction, 534
effects of, on sexual response, 253
use of, in pregnancy, 797
Marital rape, 172, 366, 678, 684–86
Marital sexuality, 55
Marquesans, and premarital sex, 88–89
Marriage
cohabitation as preparation for, 361
effect of children on, 740
erection difficulties in husbands, 365
frequency of intercourse in, 365
level of enjoyment of sex, 365
measuring quality in, 367
motivations for, 362–63
orgasm in wives, 365
satisfaction of women in, 299
sexuality in, 365–66, 455–56
types of relationships in, 364
Marshallese, extramarital sex for, 89
Masochism, sexual, 618–20
Massage, 378
Mastectomy, 591
Masters and Johnson's research on sexual response, 150, 227–30, 233–42
Masturbation
and accidental death, 339
benefits of, 331–33
choices in, 346, 347
among college students, 19
definition of, 325
disadvantages of, 333
effects of, on relationships, 340
female techniques in, 336–38
for increasing nondeviant sexual arousal, 631
in infancy, 445
for inhibited female orgasm, 552–53
and Jewish heritage, 50
male techniques, 338–39
and medicine, 327–28
and parents, 331
and psychotherapy, 331
and religion, 325–27
research on, among spouses, 339–40
as sex therapy, 566
and sexual dysfunction, 543
and sexual fantasies, 338, 340–41
and sexual guilt, 319, 340
social and psychological correlates of, 333–35
some not-so-helpful "advice" from "experts" on, 328–30
as unnatural acts, 81
in widowed, 468
Masturbatory satiation, for decreasing deviant sexual arousal, 630
Maternity leave, 30
Mate selection
cross-cultural view of, 100–103
and dating, 355
physical appearance, 18
sociobiological explanation for, 282
value theory of, 41
McConnel v. *Anderson,* 412
Mead, Margaret, 92
Means, 138
Meatus, 211
Media
in gender role acquisition, 294–96
sex in, 27
sexual research in, 122–23, 151
as source of sex education, 881–83
Median, 138
Medications. *See* Drugs
Medicine, and masturbation, 327–28
Meese Commission Report on pornography, 68, 720–21
Mellaril, for paraphiliac sex offender, 629
Men. *See* Males
Menarche, 200
Meningitis, 657
Menopause, 457–59
cross-cultural view of, 459
male, 459, 464
stages of, 458
Menorrhagia, 204
Men's movement, 304
and sexuality, 32
Menstrual Attitude Questionnaire (MAQ), 201–2
Menstrual cycle, 761–62
Menstrual extraction, 841
Menstrual phrase, 203
Menstruation, 199–200
attitudes toward, 200–2
cross-cultural variations in, 91
phases of, 202–4
problems of, 204–8
Methadone, 254

Methotrezate, for ectopic pregnancy, 796
Metronidazole, 661, 662
Microinjection, 792
Middle age
  definition of, 457
  men in, 459, 464
  women in, 457–59
Middle East, gender roles in, 92–93
Middle pain, 204
Mifepristone. *See* RU-486
Military's ban on homosexuals, 425
Miller-Fisk Sexual Knowledge Questionnaire (SKQ), 870, 872–73
Minipill, 749
Miscarriage, 756, 856–57
Miscegenation, 58
Mittelschmerz, 204, 762
Modeling, impact of, on development of gender-role behavior, 284–85
Modified radical mastectomy, 591
Monilia, 661–62
Monogamy, 456
  and nonhuman primate sexual behavior, 104–5
Mons pubis, 191
Mons veneris, 191
Moore, Demi, 782
Moral development, 286
  influence of, on sexual decision-making, 67–68
Moral maturity, Presbyterian Church on, 61
Mormons, and practice of polygyny, 99–100
Morning-after pill, 764, 840–41
Morphine, 254
Moschetta, Bob, 788
Moschetta, Cindy, 788
Mosher Guilt Inventory, Sex-Guilt Subscale Revised, 63, 64–65
Moslems
  circumcision as religious rite for, 213
  female circumcision of, 98
  on gender roles, 92–93
  on homosexuality, 406
Mother, age of, in timing of children, 743, 745
  and handling of incest, 705
Mother-child transmission of HIV, 642
Motherhood, transition to, 817–18
Mother-son incest, 705–6
Mullerian duct-inhibiting substance, 274
Mullerian ducts, 273, 274
Multicultural feminism, 179
Multidimensional Sexuality Scale (MSS), 399–400
Multifetal pregnancies, 786, 861
Multigravida, 805
Multiload IUD, 772
Multiorgasmic women, 239
Multiphasic sex inventory, in assessing sexual interest in sex offenders, 627–28
Multiple births, 786
Multiple male orgasm, 240
Multiple sclerosis, 584–85
Music, as source of sex education, 881–82
Muslim cultures. *See* Moslems
Myometrium, 198
Myths
  arousal, 230, 233
  normative space, 877
  sexual, 22–26

N

Narratophilia, 621
National Committee for Sexual Civil Liberties, 412
National Council on Family Relations, 879
National Crime Survey (NCS), 680
National Gay and Lesbian Task Force (NGLTF), 411, 412
National Organization for Women (NOW), 31
National Right to Life Committee, 852
Natural childbirth, 810
Natural childbirth movement, 809–10
Necrophilia, 621
Negative correlation, 139
Negative punishment, 164–65
Negative reinforcement, 164
  and paraphilia, 623
Nepiophilia, 621
Neurological disabilities, 582
  cerebral palsy as, 586
  choices in sexuality in, 603
  multiple sclerosis as, 584–85
  spinal cord injury as, 583–84
  stroke as, 584
  traumatic brain injury as, 585–86
Never-married adults, sexuality among, 454–55
Newborn. *See* Infant
Nigeria, mate selection in, 101–2
Nipple, 209
Nocturnal emissions, 238
Nocturnal orgasm, 238
Nocturnal penile tumescence (NPT), 547
Nonbattering marital rape, 685
Nondeviant sexual arousal
  decreasing, 628–30
  increasing, 631
Nongonococcal urethritis (NGU), 660
Nonlove, 505
Nonmonogamy, and relationships, 353–54
Nonoxynol-9, 664, 758
Nonparticipant observation research, 132
Nonprobability sampling method, 125
Nonprocreative sex, 748
Nonspecific vaginitis, 662
Nonterminative orgasms, 235
Nontraditional occupational roles, 310
Nonverbal behavior, 483–84
Noristerat, 772
Normative space myth, 877
Normophilic lovenap, 624
Norplant, 10, 751, 752
Nuku Hiva Islanders, and premarital sex, 88–89
Nurse-midwife, 822

O

Obscene phone calls, 69, 612
Obscenity, legal definition of, 718–19
Obsessive marital rape, 685
Occupational discrimination, against homosexuals, 406–7, 424–25
Occupation, and gender role, 296–98, 301–2, 310
Oedipal complex, 57, 161, 163, 283, 622–23
Off-diagonal behaviors, 609
Ohio v. *Akron Center for Reproductive Health,* 852
Olfactophilia, 621
Oligomenorrhea, 204
Onanism, 327
Ontological theory of love, 513–14
Oophorectomy, 458, 765
Open-ended questions, 490–91
Open marriages, 369–70
Operant conditioning, and paraphilia, 623
Operant learning theory, 163
Operation Rescue, 853
Opportunistic infections, 641
  treatment for, 649–50
Oral contraceptives, 748–51, 773
  complications associated with, 750

Oral drug treatment, for erectile dysfunction, 549
Oral sex, 81, 662
Oral stage of development, 161
Oral stimulation. *See* Cunnilingus; Fellatio
Orchiectomy, 596, 598–99
Organ transplant, in transmission of HIV, 642
Orgasm, 782
- blended, 235
- clitoral, 235
- ejaculatory, 236–37
- female, 235–37
- male, 237–38, 240
- nonterminative, 235
- sexual myths on, 23
- in spinal cord-injury cases, 583
- terminative, 235
- uterine, 235
- vaginal, 235
- vulval, 235
- in wives, 365

Orgasmic dysfunction, 550–53
Orgasmic platform, 234
Orgasm phase, 235–38, 465
- in men in later years, 466
- in women in later years, 465
- of the sexual response cycle, 257–58

Orgasm-phase dysfunctions
- causes and contributing factors, 551
- early ejaculation, 554–56
  - causes and contributing factors of, 555
  - treatment for, 555–56
- inhibited female orgasm, 550
  - causes and contributing factors of, 551
  - treatment for, 551–53
- inhibited male orgasm, 553–54
  - causes and contributing factors of, 553–54
  - treatment for, 554

Orgastic dysfunction, 550–53
Origin of Species (Darwin), 159
Ovarian hyperstimulation syndrome, 786
Ovaries, 199
Oviducts, 199
Ovral, 764
Ovulation, 782–83
- hormone therapy for, 786
- pain during, 762
- predicting, 783–84

Ovulation method, 762
Ovulatory phrase, 202
Ovum, 199, 202
Ovum transfer, 789
Oxytocin, 817

P

Pain, 580–81
- sexual dysfunctions involving, 556–57

Pap smear, 199, 219, 594–95
Paraphilia, 608–9
- choices regarding, 636
- as courtship disorder, 624
- definition of, 608
- biological theory on, 623–24
- feminist perspective on, 623
- learning theory on, 623
- legal versus illegal, 621–22
- psychoanalytic perspective of, 622–23
- rape as, 622
- treatment of coercive, 625–628
  - changing faulty cognitions, 632
  - decreasing deviant sexual arousal, 628–30
  - increasing nondeviant sexual arousal, 631
  - resolving sexual dysfunctions, 632
  - teaching social skills, 631–32
  - treating alcohol abuse, 632
- types of, 609, 621
  - exhibitionism, 609–12
  - fetishism, 614–16
  - frotteurism, 612
  - pedophilia, 612–14
  - sexual masochism, 618–20
  - sexual sadism, 618
  - transvestic fetishism, 616–18
  - voyeurism, 614
- as vandalized lovemap, 624

Paraphiliac sex offenders
- hormone therapy for, 629
- tranquilizers for, 629

Parental consent, and adolescent abortion, 12–13
Parents, 815
- acceptance of gay lifestyle by, 429, 435–36
- coming out to, 421–23
- and decisionmaking, 859–60
- difficulties and stresses associated with, 738–41
- in gender role acquisition, 290–91
- in homosexual relationship, 407
- and masturbation, 331
- motivations in becoming, 737–38
- as source of sex education, 876–79, 892–93
- transition to fatherhood, 818–20
  - financial responsibility, 820
  - interactions of fathers and newborns, 819
  - jealousy of the baby, 820
- transition to motherhood, 817–18

Parous introitus, 193
Partialism, 621
Partial mastectomy, 591
Partial zona drilling (PZD), 792
Participant observation research, 132
Participation bias, 126
Partner identification, 647
Passive-congenial relationship, 364
Passive self-determinism, 5
Paternity leave, 30
Pause technique, 556
Pavlov, I., 165
PC muscle, 193
Peak symptom, 762
Pedophilia, 610, 611, 612–14
- and child pornography, 722
- feminist perspective of, 623

Peeping, 614
Peers, role of, in gender role acquisition, 291–92
Peggy Lee Syndrome, 451
Pelvic examination, 199, 219, 594–95
Pelvic inflammatory disease (PID), 656, 751, 756, 757, 759
Pelvic steal syndrome, 547
Penectomy, 599
Penile amputation, 599
Penile cancer, 599
Penile erection, 230
Penile implants, 33, 470, 548–49
Penile plethysmograph, 625–27
Penile prosthesis implant, 583
Penile sheath, 747
Penile stimulation, 379–81
- in gay relationships, 432

Penile subincision, 99
Penile supraincision, 98
Penis, 211–13
- clitoral stimulation via, 383

Penis envy, 57, 283, 558
Pentamidine for HIV infection, 650
Performance anxiety, 536
Pergonal, 786
Perimenopause, 458
Perimetrium, 198
Perinatal death, 857–58
Perineum, 191–92, 807

Periodic abstinence, 761–63, 784
basal body temperature (BBT) method, 762
calendar method, 761–62
cervical mucus method, 762–63
hormone-in-urine method, 763
Peripheral arousal, 226–27
Personal attributes questionnaire, 306
Personality
development of, in psychoanalytic theory, 161–63
structure of, in psychoanalytic theory, 160–61
Personhood, beginning of, 836–37
Petting, effects of, 384
Peyronie's disease, 557
Phallic stage, 161
Phenylethylamine (PEA), 514–15
Pheromone, 230
Philanthropia, 503
Philebus (Plato), 45
Phileo, 503
Phobia, 401
sexual, 543–44
Photoplethysmograph, 230
Physical appearance. *See* Body image
Physiological measures, in assessing sexual interest in sex offenders, 625–26
Physiological theories, 158–59
Physiology, 190. *See also* Sexual anatomy and physiology and human sexuality, 16
Pictophilia, 621
Pi Kappa Phi, campaign of, against date rape, 170
Pimp, 716
Pituitary gland, 199, 275, 447, 817
Placebo, 128–29
Placenta, 807, 808
Planned Parenthood, 748
Planned Parenthood of Central Missouri v. *Danforth,* 851
Planned Parenthood of Southeastern Pennsylvania v. *Casey,* 852
Plasma free testosterone, 245
Plateau phase, 465
in men in later years, 466
in sexual response, 234
in women in later years, 465
PLISSIT Model approach, 559
Pneumocystis carinii pneumonia (PCP), 641
treatment of, 650
Pokomo, polygyny in, 99
Poland, mate selection in, 100–1
Polyandry, 100
Polygamy, 99–100
Polygraph testing, in assessing sexual interest in sex offenders, 627
Polygyny, 99–100
Population, definition of, 124
Pornography, 69, 717–18
child, 721–22
fellatio in, 381
as source of sex education, 883
studies of, and U.S. government policy recommendations, 719–20
Positive correlation, 139
Positive punishment, 164
Positive reinforcement, 164
POSSLQ (Persons of Opposite Sex Sharing Living Quarters), 29
Postcoital methods of contraception, 33, 764
Postmarital intercourse, 468
Postmodern approach to sex therapy, 561–62
Postovulatory phase, 202
Postpartum depression, 817
Posttraumatic stress disorder, 690–91
Poten Test, 547
Power of attorney, in homosexual relationships, 429
Power rape, 687
Pragma, 504
Prayer Book Society, and absolutism, 42
Predatory rape, 682
Pregnancy, 783. *See also* Childbirth; Reproductive technology
choices in, 822–24
conception in, 783
ectopic, 199, 756, 793, 796
fertilization in, 782–83
and fetal alcohol syndrome, 799
and illegal drugs, 799
incidence of unplanned, 734
and infertility, 784–85
and labor, 796
multifetal, 861
and ovulation, 783
physical changes in, 798
prenatal care in, 798–800
psychological changes in, 803–4
sex in, 804–5
and smoking, 799
teenage, 734, 844, 871, 888–89
testing for, 796–97
tubal, 756
Pregnancy wastage, 784
Prejudice, against homosexuals, 401–6
Preliterate societies, abortion in, 842
Premarital intercourse, 40
acceptability of, 20, 25–26, 46
cross-cultural variations in, 88–89
penalty for, in colonial era, 82–83
and sexual values, 40
Premature ejaculation. *See* Early ejaculation
Premenstrual syndrome (PMS), 173, 205–6
conflict theory on, 173
and DSM-III-R controversy, 207–8
structure-function theory on, 173
symbolic interaction theory, 173
Prenatal testing, 70, 800–803, 824
AFP test, 801
amniocentesis, 800–801
cell tissue culture, 801
chorionic villus sampling, 801
FISH, 802
karyotyping, 801
ultrasound, 800
Prenatal care, 798–800
Preovulatory phrase, 202
Prepared childbirth, 810
Prepuce, 192, 212
Presbyterian Church
on sexual orientation, 403
on sexual responsibility, 16
on sexual values, 60–61
Prescription drugs, impact of, on sexual response, 247–48
Pretend, in resolving jealousy, 524
Prevalence, in sexual behavior, 80–81
Priapism, 549
Primary dysfunction, 533
Primary infertility, 784
Primates, sexuality in nonhuman, 103–4
Primigravida, 805
Prince, 27
Privacy
and sex research, 130
versus social morality, 68
Probability sampling, 125–26
Process in communication, 483–84
Prochoice advocates, beliefs of, 835
Proctoscope, 219
Progenesis, 824
Progestasert, 755–56
Progesterone, 204, 244, 281, 749
Progestin, 749
PROJECT 10, 426
Prolife advocates, beliefs of, 834, 860

Proliferative phrase, 202
Promiscuous person, 25
Pronatalism, 736, 737
Prophylactic. *See* Condom
Prostaglandins, 216, 801, 840
Prostate cancer, 217, 219, 594, 596
Prostatectomy, radical, 596
Prostate gland, 216–17
Prostate rectal exam, 219
Prostatitis, 217
Prostitutes
  customers of, 716–17
  male, 717
Prostitution, 69, 714–17
  choices in legalizing and decriminalizing, 724
Prudishness, 55
Pseudohermaphroditism, 276
Psychoanalytic theory, 160–63
  on paraphilias, 622–23
  on personality structure, 160–61
  on sex therapy, 558–59
  on sexual orientation, 417–18
Psychobiological factors, in sexual health, 580–81
Psychogenic amnesia, 690
Psychological disturbances, in sexuality, 589–90
Psychological theories
  classical conditioning theory, 165–66
  learning theories, 163
  psychoanalytic theory, 160–63
  social learning theory, 166–67
Psychopathological theory, of rape, 686–87
Psychosexology, 117
Psychosexual development, 57
Psychosexual theory of love, 512–13
Psychosocial factors, in sexual health, 581–82
Psychotherapy
  and masturbation, 331
  for transsexualism, 278
Psychotropic medications, impact of, on sexual response, 247
Puberty, 447
Pubic hair, 191, 447
Pubic lice, 662
Pubococcygeus muscle, 198
Pudendum, 190
Punishment, 163
  negative, 164–65
  positive, 164
Puritans, and sexual values, 52–53

Q

Quakers, acceptance of homosexuality, 403
Qualitative descriptions, 138
Qualitative research, 119
Quantitative descriptions, 138
Quantitative research, 119
Questionnaires, 130–31
Quickening, 849

R

Racially mixed marriages, 57–58
Radical feminism, 178–79
Radical mastectomy, 591
Radical prostatectomy, 596
Radioimmunoassay test, 797
Radioreceptorassay, 797
Randomization, 126, 128, 146
Range, 138
Ranke-Heinemann, Uta, 61
Rape
  acquaintance, 682–83, 701
  anger, 687
  biological theory of, 686
  classic, 682
  as crime, 68, 69
  date, 682, 683, 870
  and decision to have abortion, 846
  evolutionary theory of, 686
  feminist theory of, 687
  forcible, 678
  gang, 170, 684
  impact of, 689–91
  marital, 172, 366, 678, 684–86
  as paraphilia, 622
  patterns of, 682–86
  power, 687
  predatory, 682
  prevalence and incidence of, 679–81
  prevention of, 698–702
  psychopathological theory of, 686–87
  and risk of prostitution, 715
  sadistic, 687
  in sexual fantasies, 344
  social learning theory of, 687–89
  statutory, 678
  theories of, 686–89
  and women, 26
Rape crisis centers, 690
Rape Empathy Scale, 694–96
Rape perpetrator, treatment for, 693, 696–98
Rape Prevention Education Project, 701
Rape survivor, treatment for, 691–93
Rape trauma syndrome, 690
Raphael, Sally Jesse, 27
Rapid ejaculation. *See* Early ejaculation
Raptophilia, 621
Rational emotive therapy (RET), 167
Reactive jealousy, 522
Realistic love, 506
Reality principle, 161
Reasoned Action, theory of, 596–98, 669
Reducing the Risk program, 890
Reed, David, erotic stimulus pathway (ESP) model, 243–44
Reflective listening, 491–92
Refractory period, 240
Refusal skills training, 885
Reinforcement, 163
  negative, 164
  positive, 164
Relationship contracts, in gay relationships, 429
Relationships
  and androgyny, 307
  communication and intimacy in, 484–85, 490
  comparisons of types of partners, 366–67
  conditions for development of, 518–19
  definition of, 521
  dilemmas of, 519–20
  effect of infertility on, 785
  effect of masturbation on, 340
  as factor, in sexual dysfunction, 537–38
  and human sexuality, 20–21
  and nonmonogamy, 353–54
  and sex frequency, 352–53, 365
  sexual jealousy in, 521–24
  social construction of sexuality in, 352–54
Relativism
  reflection of, in abortion attitudes, 46–49
  and sexual values, 44
Reliability, 141, 146
Religion
  influence of, on decision to have children, 736
  influence of, on sexual choices, 15
  influence of, on sexual values, 67
  and masturbation, 325–27, 335
  in the 1990s, 60–62
  opposition to birth control, 748
  and Puritan view, 52

role of, in gender role acquisition, 293–94
and sexual dysfunction, 534
and sexual guilt, 319
as source of sex education, 881
Religious Coalition for Abortion Rights (RCAR), 835, 837
Religious groups, on homosexual behavior, 403
Religious Orientation Scale, 67
Remarriage and sexual abuse, 29
Repository for Germinal Choice, 787
Representative sample, 124–25
Reproduction
asexual, 160
sexual, 160
Reproductive choice
alternative methods of, 70
interference with, 70
Reproductive hazards in the workplace, 70
Reproductive issues, and the law, 70
Reproductive technology, 785
artificial insemination, 786–87
of surrogate mother, 788, 793–94
choices resulting from new, 823–24
exploitation of participants, 792–95
gamete intra-fallopian transfer, 791
hormone therapy, 786
microinjection, 792
ovum transfer, 789
partial zona drilling (PZD), 792
in vitro fertilization, 789
abuses of, 794
zygote intra-fallopian transfer, 792
Researcher bias, 146
Research population, 124
Resolution phase, 238–39, 465
in men in later years, 466
in women in later years, 465
Retarded ejaculation, 553–54
Reversion therapy, 436
Revised Sexual Opinion Survey, 322–23
Rhythm. *See* Calendar method of birth control
Rimming, 383
Rivera, Geraldo, 27, 444
Roberts, Julia, 319
Roe v. *Wade,* 836, 850–51, 853
Role function, 582
Roman Catholic Church. *See* Catholic Church
Romantic love, 506
RU-486, 764, 772, 840–41
Rubber. *See* Condom
Rubin's assessment of the sexual and gender revolutions, 150
Rust v. *Sullivan,* 852

S

Sadism, sexual, 618, 623
Sadistic rape, 687
Sadomasochism (S and M), 619
Safe. *See* Condom
Safe sex, 42, 180
St. Augustine, 51, 53
St. Paul, 50–51
St. Thomas Aquinas, 51, 53
Saline abortion, 801, 839
Salpingectomy, 765–66
Salpingitis, 657
Sambia, homosexuality in, 91
Samoa, gender roles in Western, 92
Sample, 146
biased, 125
definition of, 124
representative, 124–25
Sanger, Margaret, 748
Satiation, 455–56
Scabies, 662
Schizophrenia, 590
School-based clinics, 894
School/Community Program for Risk Reduction among Teens, 890–91
Scientific sexual ideologies, and sexual values, 56–59
Scrotum, 214
Secondary dysfunction, 533
Secondary infertility, 784
Secondary sex characteristics, 447
development of, 275
Secretory phase, 202
Selective termination, 861
Self-abuse. *See* Masturbation
Self-assessment
Abortion Attitude Scale, 833
Acceptance of Adoption and Five Alternative Fertilization Techniques, 790–91
Aging Sexual Knowledge and Attitudes Scale, 460–63
Attitudes Toward Timing of Parenthood Scale, 744–45
Attitude Toward Feminism Scale, 176–77
Cross-Gender Fetishism Scale, 617
Free Will-Determinism Scale, 8–9
How Much Do You Know About Sexuality, 539–40
Index of Sexual Satisfaction, 368
Love Attitudes Scale, 508–9
Menstrual Attitude Questionnaire, 201–2
Miller-Fisk Sexual Knowledge Questionnaire, 870, 872–73
Mosher Guilt Inventory, Sex-Guilt Subscale Revised, 64–65
Rape Empathy Scale, 694–96
Revised Sexual Opinion Survey, 322–23
Sex Anxiety Inventory and Its Development, 143–45
Sex Knowledge and Attitude Test, 85–87
Sexual Arousability Inventory, 231–32
Sexual Double Standard Scale, 269–70
Sexual Self-Disclosure Scale, 486–89
STD Attitude Scale, 648–49
Torabi-Seffrin Cancer Attitude Scale, 592–93
Self-concept, 318, 581–82
developing positive gay, 426
development of, 354
positive, in developing love relationship, 518
Self-determinism, 5
Self-disclosure, 519
Self-efficacy, 597
Self-esteem, low, as cause of sexual dysfunction, 537
Self-examinations, 219–20
Self-identity function, and sexual values, 40–41
Self-presentation bias, 146
Self-report data, validity measures of, 142, 145–46
Self-report measures, in assessing sexual interest in sex offenders, 626–27
Self-report offender surveys, 681
Semen, 782
donor, in transmission of HIV, 642
Semen-conservation doctrine, 327
Seminal fluid, 217
Seminal vesicles, 216
Sensate focus, 543, 544, 548, 552, 554, 557, 559
Sensitization, 418
Septate hymen, 193
Seventh-Day Adventists, and sexual values, 62
Sex
definition of, 266
in the media, 27

Sex abuse prevention, in sex education classes, 870
Sex Addicts Anonymous groups, 634
Sex and Love Addicts Anonymous, 634
Sex and Repression (Malinowski), 78
Sex Anxiety Inventory and Its Development, 143–45
Sex chromosomes, 272
Sex differences, critiques of research on, 287
Sex education
  and abortion rate, 843, 860
  choices in, 892–94
  components of ideal program, 869–70
  content of classes, 893–94
  definition of, 868
  effects of, 883
    on attitudes, 887
    on contraceptive usage, 887–88
    on knowledge, 883–84
    sexual behaviors, 884–87
    teenage pregnancy, 888–89
  extent of, 873–74
  fourth generation of curricula, 889–91
  goals of, 871
  parent participation in program for, 892–93
  and postponing sexual involvement, 453–54
  refocus of scope and purpose of, 868–69
  sources of
    family planning clinic personnel, 880
    friends, 879
    media, 881–83
    parents, 876–79
    pornography, 883
    religion, 881
    school teachers, 879–80
  special audiences for, 874–76
  and use of empathy belly, 804
Sex guilt, 62–63, 66, 319, 768
  as cause of sexual dysfunction, 534, 537, 546
  and culture, 66
  and masturbation, 340
  Mosher inventory on, 64–65
  and use of birth control, 768
  in women, 15
Sexism, 298. *See also* Gender role(s)
Sexist language, 271–72, 294
Sex knowledge and attitude test, 85–87
Sex offenders
  assessment of sexual interest in, 625–28
  masturbation in reconditioning treatments for, 333
Sexology
  cross-sectional research in, 118
  definition of, 114
  feminist approaches to, 120–21
  interdisciplinary nature of, 115
    biosexology, 115
    psychosexology, 117
    sociosexology, 117–18
  longitudinal research in, 118–19
  qualitative research in, 119
  quantitative research in, 119
  roots of, 114–15
Sex reassignment surgery, 278, 279–80
Sex research
  belief in conclusions of, 146
  choices in, 152–53
  data analysis
    causation, 140
    correlation, 139–40
    description, 138
    reliability, 141
    validity, 141–42
  ethical considerations in, with human participants, 134–37
  initial procedures and methods
    formulating hypothesis and defining variables, 123–24
    formulating research question, 121–22
    reviewing literature, 122–23
    selecting sample, 124–26
  methods of data collection
    case studies, 132–33
    clinical trials, 128–29
    diaries, 134
    experiments, 126–27
    historical research, 133
Sex roles. *See also* Gender role(s)
  definition of, 267
Sex studies, 146–47
  at Kinsey Institute
    on sexual behavior, 147–48
    on sexual knowledge, 148–49
    on sexual values, 148
  magazine surveys, 151
  Masters and Johnson's research on sexual response, 150
  national surveys of adolescents, 151
  Rubin's assessment of the sexual and gender revolutions, 150
Sex therapist
  sexual involvement between client and, 565–66
  training requirements for, 565
Sex therapy
  alternative aids used in, 563
  choices in, 567–68
  cognitive therapy approach on, 560–61
  effectiveness of, 563–65
  Helen Kaplan's approach on, 561
  LoPiccolo's postmodern approach on, 561–62
  Master and Johnson's, 559
  PLISSIT model approach on, 559
  psychoanalytic approach on, 558–59
  for rape, 693
  surrogate partner therapy in, 562
  usefulness of, 26
  values in, 566
Sexual abuse, 68, 69, 702–3
  as cause of sexual dysfunction, 537
  in childhood, 446, 703–4
  in daycare, 444, 608, 723
  impact of, 707–8
  incidence and prevalence of extrafamilial and intrafamilial, 703
  in infancy, 444
  and male gender role socialization, 613, 703
  patterns of, 704–7
  prevention of, 710–11
  and remarriage, 29
  and risk of prostitution, 715
  theories of, 703–4
  treatment of, 708–10
  of unplanned children, 859–60
Sexual abusers
  choices in prosecuting, 723
  treatment of, 708–10
Sexual acts, criminal classification of, 69
Sexual addiction, 633
  characteristics of, 633–34
  effectiveness of treatment programs, 635
  social constructionist views of, 181
  treatment of, 634–35
Sexual aids, 580
Sexual anatomy and physiology
  female breasts, 209–10
  female external anatomy, 190
    clitoris, 192–93
    labia, 191–92
    mons veneris, 191

urethral opening, 194
vaginal opening, 193
female internal anatomy
Fallopian tubes, 199
ovaries, 199
pubococcygeus muscle, 198
uterus, 198–99
vagina, 194, 196–98
male external anatomy, 211
duct system, 215–16
penis, 211–13
prostate gland, 216–17
scrotum, 214
seminal vesicles, 216
testes, 214–15
menstruation, 199–200
attitudes toward, 200–2
phases of the menstrual cycle, 202–4
problems of the menstrual cycle, 204–8
Sexual appetite or drive, in sexual desire, 224
Sexual arousability inventory (SAI), 231–32
Sexual arousal, measures of, 230
Sexual arousal mechanism (SAM), 243
Sexual aversion, 543–44
causes and contributing factors in, 544
treatment for, 544
Sexual behavior
causes of, 4
defining normal, 80–84
effects of sex education on, 884–87
of gays, 432–33
morally correct, 81
natural, 81
patterns in, 562
prevalence in, 80–81
Sexual celibacy, 321, 323–24, 325
Sexual choices
competence of adolescents in making, 11–14
continual, 6
continuous, 8–9
and decisionmaking, 6–7
dichotomous, 8
either/or, 8
importance of making, 4
influence of drug use on, 15–16
influence of gender role socialization on, 304
influence of social context and cultural forces on, 15
nature of, 6–14
as revocable, 9–10
tradeoffs in, 7
Sexual coercion, 678–79
impact of, on rape and sexual assault, 689–91
patterns of rape, 682–86
prevalence and incidence of rape, 679–81
prevention of rape, 698–702
theories of rape, 686–89
treatment for rape perpetrator, 693, 696–98
treatment for rape survivor, 691–93
Sexual contact, in transmission of HIV, 641
Sexual desire, definition of, 224
Sexual Double Standard Scale, 269–70
Sexual dysfunction, 569
aging factors, 538–40
arousal-phase dysfunctions, 544–45
causes and contributing factors, 546–47
female sexual arousal dysfunction, 545
male erectile dysfunction, 545–50
treatment for, 547–50
biological factors in, 533–34
classification of, 533
definition of, 532
desire-phase dysfunctions, 540–41
causes and contributing factors, 542
hypoactive sexual desire, 541–43
sexual aversion, 543–44
treatment of, 542–43
educational and cognitive factors in, 538
intrapsychic factors in, 536–37
orgasm-phase dysfunctions, 550
causes and contributing factors, 551
early ejaculation, 554–56
inhibited female orgasm, 550
inhibited male orgasm, 553–54
treatment for, 551–53
prevention of male, by challenging sexual myths
and gender role stereotypes, 534–36
relationship factors in, 537–38
resolving, 632
sexual pain dysfunctions, 556
dyspareunia, 556–57
vaginismus, 557–58
sociocultural factors in, 534
Sexual fantasies, 19, 340–41
choices concerning, 346–47
content of, 342–44
definition of, 341
functions of, 341–42
gender differences in, 344–45
and masturbation, 338, 340–41, 543
rape in, 344
Sexual fetishes, 165
Sexual harassment, 27, 30
choices in, 723–24
consequences of, 713
definition of, 712
and physical appearance, 18
prevalence and incidence of, 712
prevention of, 714
responses to, 713
theories of, 712–13
Sexual health
psychobiological factors in
depression, 581
fatigue, 581
pain, 580–81
psychosocial factors
body image, 582
role function, 582
self-concept, 581–82
Sexual identity, 268
Sexual interaction, as communication, 497
Sexual intercourse. *See also* Extramarital intercourse; Premarital intercourse
after childbirth, 820–21
cross-cultural variations in, 84, 88
choosing, with new partner, 71–72
enjoyment of, in marital relationships, 365
extramarital, and sexual values, 40
first, 84, 88, 450–51, 452
frequency of, 84, 365, 352–53
and the law, 68–70
to maximize chance of pregnancy, 783
positions, 84
and fertilization, 784
man-on-top position, 385
rear-entry position, 386–87
side-by-side position, 386, 805
sitting position, 387
standing position, 387–88
variations, 388
woman-on-top position, 385
during pregnancy, 804–5
sexual myths on, 23
and spinal cord injury, 583
Sexual involvement
with co-workers, 374–77
postponing, 453–54

Sexuality. *See also* Theoretical views of human sexuality
in adolescence, 446–54
new sexual behaviors in, 449–53
physical changes in, 447–48
psychological changes in, 449
and cohabitation, 361–63
college students' knowledge of, 24–25
commercial uses and abuses of, 714–22
comparison of, in black and white individuals, 96
cross-cultural research in, 78–80
problems in, 79–80
cross-cultural variations in
age at first intercourse, 84
choices in, 106–8
extramarital sex, 89–90
frequency, 84
gender roles, 92–95
homosexual sex, 91–92
incest, 90–91
menstruation, 91
positions, 84
premarital sex, 88–89
sexual intercourse, 84, 88
and dating, 354–60
among divorced, 456–57
elements of, 16–22
anatomy, 16
behavior, 18–19
cognitions, 19
and emotions, 20
physiology, 16
relationships, 20–21
sexual self-concept, 17–18
values in, 19–20
variability in, 21–22
intrapersonal aspects of, 318
body image, 318–19
erotophilia, 321
erotophobia, 321
self-concept, 318
sexual guilt, 319
involuntary, 325
knowledge about, 23
in later years, 464–68
legal definition of obscenity, 718–19
in marital relationship, 365–66
among married, 455–56
myths about, 578–79
among never-married adults, 454–55
in nonhuman primates, 103–4
pimp connection, 716
social changes and their effects on, 26–33
social construction of, 352–54
voluntary, 323–24
among widowed, 468
Sexual jealousy. *See* Jealousy
Sexual Life of Savages in North-western Melanesia (Malinowski), 78
Sexually open marriages, 369–70
Sexually transmissible diseases, 27, 433–34, 759
acquired immunodeficiency syndrome, 659
candidiasis, 661–62
as cause of infertility, 784
chancroid, 660–61
chlamydia, 655–56, 659
choices involving, 670–71
economic costs associated with, 663
genital herpes, 650–53, 659
genital warts, 659
gonorrhea, 656–57, 659
granuloma inguinale, 660
hepatitis B, 661
human immunodeficiency virus infection, 640–50
human papilloma virus, 653, 655
lymphogranuloma venereum, 660
nongonococcal urethritis, 660
nonspecific vaginitis, 662
prevention of, 662–69
pubic lice, 662
scabies, 662
syphilis, 657–58, 659
trichomoniasis, 661
and use of condoms, 753, 754
vaginitis, 661–62
Sexual masochism, 610, 618–20
Sexual myths, 22–26
Sexual offense, 481
Sexual orientation, 396–97
biological explanations for heredity, 414–15
bisexuality, 399–400
choices in regard to, 435–36
conflict concerning one's, 537
distinguishing features of one's, 397–98
and gay liberation movement, 411–13
heterosexuality
definition of, 397–98
prevalence of, 398–99
homosexuality
definition of, 397–98
discrimination against, 406–7
prejudice against, 401–6
prevalence of, 398–99
lesbian-feminism, 413–14
psychoanalytic explanations, 417–18
seeking therapy over, 436
social learning explanations, 416–17
social-psychological explanations, 416–17
Sexual pain dysfunctions
dyspareunia, 556–57
causes and contributing factors of, 557
treatment for, 557
vaginismus, 557–58
causes and contributing factors of, 558
treatment for, 558
Sexual panic disorder. *See* Sexual aversion
Sexual phobia. *See* Sexual aversion
Sexual relationships. *See* Relationships
Sexual reproduction, 160
Sexual response
central arousal, 225–26
choices in, 257–58
David Reed's erotic stimulus pathway (ESP) model of, 243–44
and drugs, 247–55
Ellis's and Beach's two-stage models of, 242–43
and erotica, 255–56, 258
genital responses, 226
Helen Kaplan's three-stage model of, 243
hormones and, 244–46
Masters and Johnson's four-stage model of, 227
critiques, 241–42
excitement phase, 227–33
male and female differences in, 239–41
orgasm phase, 235–38, 257–58
plateau phase, 234
resolution phase, 238–39
peripheral arousal, 226–27
sexual appetite or drive in, 224
Sexual responsibility, Presbyterian Church on, 16
Sexual sadism, 610, 618
feminist perspective of, 623
Sexual self-concept, 17–18, 318, 770
Sexual Self-Disclosure Scale, 486–89
Sexual trauma, 689
Sexual values
and absolutism, 42–44
in Asian cultures, 53–55
and birth control, 59

changes in, 45–46
choices in, 71–72
and culture, 73
definition of, 40
functions of, 40–41
and hedonism, 45
historical roots of, 46, 49–59
influence of, on sexual emotions, attitudes and behaviors, 62–63, 66
influences affecting, in U.S. society, 59–62
and relativism, 44
Shingles, 641
Sibling incest, 706
Siblings
acceptance of gay lifestyle by, 429
coming out to, 421–23
Sickle cell anemia, diagnosis of, in fetus, 801
Side-by-side position, 805
Simpson, Wallis, 44
Simultaneous loves, 519
Singlehood, 298
Single women, and deciding to have child, 746, 775–76
Situational dysfunction, 533
Situation ethics, 44
Sixty-nine, 383
Skene's glands, 194
Skinner, B. F., 163
Smegma, 214
Smoking, during pregnancy, 799
Snap Gauge Band, 547
Social changes, effects of, on sexuality, 26–33
Social constructionist view, 180–82
Social context, influence of, on sexual choices, 15
Social inoculation, and sex education curricula, 890
Socialist feminism, 179
Socialization
consequences of traditional female, 296–301
consequences of traditional male, 301–4
in gender role acquisition
education, 292–93
media, 294–96
parents, 290–91
peers, 291–92
religion, 293–94
Social learning theory, 166–67
on alcohol and sexuality, 249
on child sexual abuse, 703
on gender role acquisition, 284–85
on rape, 687–89
and sex education curricula, 890
on sexual orientation, 416–17
Social morality versus private rights, 68
Social-psychological explanations, for sexual orientation, 417
Social scripts, 169–71
Social skill training, 631–32
Social values, and Puritan view, 52
Society for Assisted Reproductive Technology, 792
Society for the Scientific Study of Sex, 115
Sociobiological theory, 280–82
Sociocultural factors, in sexual dysfunction, 534
Sociological theories, 168
conflict theories, 171–72
structural-functional theories, 171
symbolic interaction theories, 168–69, 171
systems theories, 172, 174
Sociosexology, 117–18
Sodomy, homosexual, 407
Sodomy laws, 68
Somnophilia, 621
Soul kissing, 378
Soviet Union, homosexuals in the former, 92
Spectatoring, 536–37, 551, 553
Sperm, 782
donor, 786–87
Spermatogenesis, 248, 774
Sperm banks, 787
Spermicides, 664, 753, 757, 758–59
Spinal cord injury, 583–84
Spirochetes, 657, 658
Sponge, vaginal, 759–60
Spontaneous abortion, 832
Spouses
coming out to, 423–24
masturbation among, 339–40
Spurious correlation, 139
Squeeze technique, 168, 555–56
Statutory rape, 678
STD Attitude Scale, 648–49
Sterilization, 764–67, 773
female, 765–66
male, 766–67
permanency of, 10
Stern, Elizabeth, 788
Stern, William, 788
Stillbirth, 856–57
Stone, Hannah, 748
Stop-start technique, 556
Storge, 504
Stress inoculation training, for rape, 692–93
Stroke, 584
Structural-functional theories, 171
on premenstrual syndrome, 173
Stuffing technique, 470, 583
Subdermal contraceptive implants, 33
Subjective arousal, 228
Suction curettage, 838
Suicide, and coming out, 420
Suku of southwest Zaire, extramarital sex for, 89
Summa Theologica (Aquinas), 51–52
Sunna, 97
Superego, 161
Surgeon General's Workshop on Pornography and Public Health, 721
Surrogacy, 788, 793–94
Surrogate partner therapy, 562
for person with severe cerebral palsy, 586
Surveys, 127, 129–32
Sweden, gender roles in, 93
Swinging, 370
Symbolic interaction theories, 168–69, 171
on premenstrual syndrome, 173
Syphilis, 657–58, 659
as cause of infertility, 784
and use of condoms, 747
Systematic desensitization
for increasing nondeviant sexual arousal, 631
for rape, 692
Systems theories, 172, 174
on sexual dysfunctions, 561–62

T

Tarrying, 53
Tay-Sachs disease, diagnosis of, in fetus, 801
Teachers, as source of sex education, 879–80
Technology, and human sexuality, 33
Teenagers. *See* Adolescence
Telephonicophilia, 612, 621
Television, as source of sex education, 882
Terminative orgasms, 235
Testes, 214–15, 273–74
Testicular cancer, 220, 596

Testicular feminization syndrome (TFS), 276
Testicular self-exam, 220
Testicular self-examination, 596
  attitudes toward, 596–98
Testosterone, 244, 274, 275, 459
  plasma free, 245
Testosterone enanthate, 753
Test-retest method, 141
Test-tube fertilization, 33, 789
Theoretical views of human sexuality, 158
  biological theories
    evolutionary theories, 159–60
    physiological theories, 158–59
  choices in, 185–86
  cognitive/affective theories, 167–68
  essentialist, 180
  feminist theories, 175, 178
    liberal feminism, 178
    multicultural feminism, 179
    radical feminism, 178–79
    socialist feminism, 179
  integrated approach, 181–84
  psychological theories
    classical conditioning theory, 165–66
    learning theories, 163, 185
    psychoanalytic theory, 160–63
    social learning theory, 166–67
    social constructionist, 180–81
  sociological theories, 168
    conflict theories, 171–72
    structural-functional theories, 171
    symbolic interaction theories, 168–69, 171
    systems theories, 172, 174
Thermistor clip, 230
Thermography, 218
Thigh pressure, 337
Thomas, Clarence, 374, 712, 713
Tissue transplant, in transmission of HIV, 642
T-lymphocytes, 640
Tobacco, effect of, on sexual response, 254–58
Tongue kissing, 378
Topless dancing, 69
Torabi-Seffrin Cancer Attitude Scale, 592–93
Total dysfunction, 533
Total relationship, 364
Touch and ask rule, 491
Toucheurism, 612
Touching, 377–78
Toxic shock syndrome (TSS), 205, 757, 760
Traditional marriage, 364
Tranquilizers, for paraphilic sex offenders, 629
Transabdominal first-trimester selective termination, 861
Transcendence, gender role, 308
Transdermal patches, 774
Transrectal ultrasound, 219
Transsexualism, 267, 277–78
  therapy for, 278–80
Transvestic fetishism, 610, 616–18
Transvestism, and Jewish heritage, 50
Transvestites, 278
Transvestites (Hirschfeld), 57
Traumatic brain injury, 585–86
Triangulation, 119
Trichomoniasis, 661
Troiden's four-stage process
  in developing gay identity, 418–20
    commitment, 420
    identity assumption, 420
    identity confusion, 418–19
    sensitization, 418
Tubal pregnancy, 756
Tubectomies, 765
Tumescence, 230, 242
Turner's syndrome, 276
Twin research on sexual orientation, 415

U

Ultrasound
  in birth control, 774
  in prenatal testing, 800
  transrectal, 219
Unconditioned stimulus, 165
Unfulfilled love, 519
Unipolar depression, 589
Unitarians
  acceptance of homosexuality by, 403
  and sexual values, 60
United Methodist Church, on sexual values, 61
United States, mate selection in, 100
U.S. Commission on Obscenity and Pornography, 152, 719–20
United States v. *One Package,* 748
Urethra, 194
Urethral opening, 193, 194, 211
Urethritis, 215–16, 557
Urinary tract infection, 757, 759
Urophilia, 621
Uterine cancer, 199, 219, 591, 594
Uterine orgasms, 235
Uterus, 198–99

V

Vaccines, in birth control, 774
Vacuum aspiration abortion, 838, 840, 841
Vacuum device, for erectile dysfunction, 549–50
Vagina, 194, 196–98
Vaginal births after cesarean delivery, 814
Vaginal condom, 755
Vaginal infrared probe, 230
Vaginal insertion, 337
Vaginal opening, 193
Vaginal orgasm, 235
Vaginal ring, 774
Vaginal spermicides, 664, 753, 757, 758–59
Vaginal sponge, 759–60
Vaginismus, 198, 557–58
  causes and contributing factors, 558
  treatment for, 558
Vaginitis, 661–62
  in diabetes, 602
  nonspecific, 662
VAL-I.D. PCR (polymerase chain reaction), 647
Validity, 141–42, 146
Valium, 15
Values
  and human sexuality, 19–20
  in sex therapy, 566
Values clarification, in sex education programs, 869
Value theory of mate selection, 41
Van Buren, Abigail, 27
Vandalized lovemap, 622, 624
Van de Velde, Theodore Hendrik, 57
Van Leeuwenhoeck, Antony, 57
Variability, and human sexuality, 21–22
Variable, 123
Vas deferens, 215, 766
Vasectomy, 765, 766–67
Vasocongestion, 228–29
  vaginal, 230
Vestibule, 193
Vibrator, 337, 346
Victimization surveys, 680–81
Victimless crimes, 611
Victorians, sexual values of, 55–56
Videx, for HIV infection, 650
Virginity, 194
Vital relationship, 364

Voluntary sexual celibacy, 323–24
Voyeurism, 69, 610, 612, 614
Vulva, 190
Vulval orgasms, 235
Vulvar cancer, 653

W

Water massage, 337
Webster v. *Reproductive Health Services*, 851–52
Weight gain, effect of, on self-image in adolescence, 448
Western blot test, 647
Wet dream, 238
  first, 448
Whitehead, Mary Beth, 788, 794
Whites, comparison of sexuality of, with blacks, 96
Widowed
  and child care, 742
  dating among, 358–60
  sexuality among, 468, 469–70
Williams, Robin, 444
Williams v. *Zbaraz*, 851
Wills, in homosexual relationship, 429
Winfrey, Oprah, 27
Winger, Debra, 40
Win-win solutions, 496
Withdrawal, 763–64
Wolffian ducts, 273, 274
Wolof man (of Gambia), 89
Womb veil, 748
Women. *See* Females
Women's movement, 304–5
  and sexuality, 30–32
Women's Rights Convention, 33
Workplace
  sexual involvements at, 374–77
Workplace changes, and sexuality, 29–30
World Congress of Gay and Lesbian Jewish Organizations, 405

X

Xandria Collection Gold Edition Catalogue, 580
X chromosome, 272

Y

Y chromosome, 272, 273–74
Yolngu, polygyny in, 99
Yoruba, polygyny in, 99
"You" statements, 493

Z

Zoophilia, 621
Zovirax, for genital herpes, 652
Zygote, 272
Zygote intra-fallopian transfer (ZIFT), 792

PHOTOS, Continued
161 UPI/Bettmann **163** The Bettmann Archive **164** UPI/Bettmann **166** ©Bob Kramer/Stock Boston **169** ©Henry Bagish/Anthro-Photo **178** ©Harry Gustafson **225** ©VEGA/Photo Researchers **236** ©Jeane-Claude LeJuene/Stock Boston **242** The Bettmann Archive **245** ©Barbara Alper/Stock Boston **254** ©Frank Siteman/Stock Boston **278** ©John Barrett/Globe Photos **290** ©Jeffrey W. Myers/Stock Boston **295** ©Mark Allan/Alpha/Globe Photos **296** ©Addison Geary/Stock Boston **301** ©Spencer Grant/Stock Boston **303** ©Michael Dwyer/Stock Boston **305** ©Richard Pasley/Stock Boston **308** ©Bob Daemmrich/Stock Boston **319** ©George Zimbel/Monkmeyer Press **326** ©Bob Daemmrich/Stock Boston **328** The Museum of Questionable Medical Devices, Minneapolis/St. Paul **337** (a) Photo used with permission of Hitachi Corp.; (b) Photo used with permission of D.A.V.E., Inc; (c) Photo used with permission of Vibratex, Inc. **343** ©Jerry Howard/Stock Boston **354** ©Owen Franken/Stock Boston **363** ©Peter Menzel/Stock Boston **372** The Bettmann Archive **379** ©Willie L. Hill, Jr./Stock Boston **402** ©Barbara Alper/Stock Boston **406** ©David Austin/Stock Boston **428** authors' files: used with permission **430** ©Elena Olivo/Brooklyn Image Group **433** ©Hazel Hankin/Stock Boston **445** ©Rob Crandall/Stock Boston **447** ©Gabor Demjen/Stock Boston; ©Eva Demjen/Stock Boston **450** ©Larry Ghiorsi/Brooklyn Image Group **451** ©Gale Zucker/Stock Boston **464** ©Rick Smolan/Stock Boston **467** ©J. Berndt/Stock Boston **479** ©Frank Siteman/Stock Boston **484** ©Christopher Brown/Stock Boston **490** ©Curtis Willocks/Brooklyn Image Group **494** ©Bob Daemmrich/Stock Boston **503** ©Historical Picture Services **507** ©Patrick Ward/Stock Boston **512** ©Frank Siteman/Stock Boston **514** ©Historical Picture Services **521** ©David R. Austen/Stock Boston **538** ©Susan Rosenberg/Photo Researchers **542** ©Frank Siteman/Stock Boston **560** ©Bob Daemmrich/Stock Boston **579** ©Spencer Grant/Stock Boston **585** ©John Barnett/Globe Photos **591** ©M. Marshall, M.D./Custom Medical Stock **597** ©Amethyst/Custom Medical Stock **600** ©Bill Horsmann/Stock Boston **611** ©Jeane-Claude LeJuene/Stock Boston **612** ©Bachmann/Stock Boston **615** ©Hazel Hankin/Stock Boston **616** ©Cathy Cheney/Stock Boston **619** ©Charles Kennard/Stock Boston **642** ©Laurence Migdale/Stock Boston **646** ©Stacy Pick/Stock Boston **651** Centers for Disease Control **652** Centers for Disease Control **653** Centers for Disease Control **656** Centers for Disease Control **657** Centers for Disease Control **658** Centers for Disease Control **684** ©Bob Daemmrich/Stock Boston **688** ©Ann McQueen/Stock Boston **692** ©Billy E. Barnes/Stock Boston **697** ©Bob Daemmrich/Stock Boston **711** ©Lionel J-M Delevinge/Stock Boston **714** ©Barbara Alper/Stock Boston **716** ©Dorothy Littell/Stock Boston **719** ©Neal Boenzi/NYT Pictures **736** ©Michael Hayman/Stock Boston **743** ©Stephen R. Swinburne/Stock Boston **748** UPI/Bettmann **750** ©Willie Hill, Jr./Stock Boston **782** ©R. Rawlins/Custom Medical Stock **797** ©L. Steinmark/Custom Medical Stock **799** ©Streissgath, A.P.; Clarren, S.K.; Jones, K.L. (1985, July) National History of the Fetal Alcohol Syndrome: A ten-year follow-up of eleven patients. *Lauret II, 89-92* **811** ©Custom Medical Stock **813** ©Jim Harrison/Stock Boston **815** ©Keith/Custom Medical Stock **819** Authors files **821** ©Peter Southwick/Stock Boston **835** ©Curtis Willocks/Brooklyn Image Group **849** ©Gale Zucker/Stock Boston **858** ©Gale Zucker/Stock Boston **877** ©Richard Sobol/Stock Boston **880** ©Elizabeth Crews/Stock Boston **882** ©Bob Daemmrich/Stock Boston **886** ©Will and Deni McIntyre/Photo Researchers **892** ©Jeffry W. Myers/Stock Boston

PART OPENER CREDITS
Part I *Pablo Picasso.* The Love of Jupiter and Semele, *plate opposite page 70 from* Les Metamorphoses d'Ovid, *published Lausanne, Albert Skira, Editeur, 1931. Etching (executed 1930), printed in black, page: 12 13/16 × 10 1/4". Collection, The Museum of Modern Art, New York. The Louis E. Stern Collection. © 1992 ARS, New York/SPADEM, Paris.* **Part II** Pablo Picasso, Spanish, 1881–1973 *The Lovers,* canvas, 1923, 51¼ × 38¼ in; National Gallery of Art, Washington, Chester Dale Collection. © 1992 ARS, New York/SPADEM, Paris. All rights reserved. **Part III** Otto Müller, *The Gypsy Lovers. © 1992 Bridgeman/Art Resource, New York.* **Part IV** © The Great Storm/The Image Bank **Part V** © Cathleen Toelke **Part VI** Pablo Picasso, Spanish, 1881–1973, *Mother and Child,* oil on canvas, 1921, 143.5 × 162.6 cm; Gift of Maymar Corporation, Mrs. Maurice L. Rothschild, Mr. and Mrs. Chauncey McCormick; Mary and Leigh Block Charitable Fund; Ada Turnbull Hertle Endowment; through prior gift of Mr. and Mrs. Edwin E. Hokin, 1954. 270 © 1992 The Art Institute of Chicago; ARS, New York/SPADEM, Paris. All rights reserved.